WITHDRAWN

Child Psychopathology

Jeffrey J. Haugaard, PhD
University at Albany
State University of New York

**McGraw-Hill
Higher Education**

Boston   Burr Ridge, IL   Dubuque, IA   New York   San Francisco   St. Louis
Bangkok   Bogotá   Caracas   Kuala Lumpur   Lisbon   London   Madrid   Mexico City
Milan   Montreal   New Delhi   Santiago   Seoul   Singapore   Sydney   Taipei   Toronto

The McGraw·Hill Companies

McGraw-Hill
Higher Education

CHILD PSYCHOPATHOLOGY

Published by McGraw-Hill, an imprint of The McGraw-Hill Companies, Inc., 1221 Avenue of the Americas, New York, NY 10020. Copyright © 2008. All rights reserved. No part of this publication may be reproduced or distributed in any form or by any means, or stored in a database or retrieval system, without the prior written consent of The McGraw-Hill Companies, Inc., including, but not limited to, in any network or other electronic storage or transmission, or broadcast for distance learning.

This book is printed on acid-free paper.

1 2 3 4 5 6 7 8 9 0 DOC/DOC 0 9 8 7

ISBN: 978-0-07-340550-6
MHID: 0-07-340550-7

Editor in Chief: *Michael Ryan*
Publisher: *Beth Mejia*
Executive Editor: *Suzanna Ellison*
Executive Marketing Manager: *James Headley*
Supplement Editor: *Emily Pecora*
Production Editor: *Karol Jurado*
Production Service: *Jean Dal Porto*
Manuscript Editor: *Meg McDonald*
Designer: *Andrei Pasternak*
Illustrator: *Dartmouth Publishing, Inc.*
Production Supervisor: *Dennis Fitzgerald*
Media Project Manager: *Ron Nelms, Jr.*
Composition: *10/12 Sabon by Aptara, Inc.*
Printing: *45# New Era Matte, R.R. Donnelley & Sons*
Cover image: © *Image Source/PunchStock*

Credits: **P1.1,** © ImageState/PunchStock; **P1.2,** © PhotoLink/Photodisc/Getty Images; **P1.3,** © Elyse Lewin/Brand X Pictures; **P2.1,** © image100/PunchStock; **P3.1,** © Creatas; **P3.2,** © RubberBall Productions/Getty Images; **P3.3,** © Kim Steele/Getty Images; **P4.1,** © Stockbyte/PunchStock; **P4.2,** © Royalty-Free/Jack Hollingsworth/Corbis; **P5.1,** © Mel Curtis/Getty Images; **P5.2,** © BananaStock/PunchStock; **P5.3,** © Scott T. Baxter/Getty Images; **P6.1,** © BananaStock; **P6.2,** © Royalty-Free/Ole Graf/zefa/Corbis; **P6.3,** © BananaStock/PunchStock; **P7.1,** © Royalty-Free/Ole Graf/zefa/Corbis; **P7.2,** © BananaStock/PunchStock; **P7.3,** © Digital Vision/PunchStock; **P7.4,** © BananaStock/PunchStock; **P8.1,** © Royalty-Free/Ole Graf/zefa/Corbis; **P8.2,** © Mel Curtis/Getty Images; **P9.1,** © Geostock/Getty Images; **P9.2,** © Royalty-Free/Brooklyn Production/Corbis; **P9.3,** © BananaStock/PunchStock; **P10.1,** © Royalty-Free/Ole Graf/zefa/Corbis; **P10.2,** © Royalty-Free/Corbis; **P10.3,** © Brand X Pictures/PunchStock; **P11.1,** © Digital Vision/PunchStock; **P11.2,** © S. Pearce/PhotoLink/Getty Images; **P11.3,** © Digital Vision/PunchStock; **P12.1,** © David Toase/Getty Images; **P12.2,** © Ingram Publishing/Fotosearch; **P12.3,** © Royalty-Free/Ole Graf/zefa/Corbis; **P14.1,** © The McGraw-Hill Companies, Inc./Leroy Webster, photographer; **P14.2,** © Emma Lee/Life File/Getty Images; **P14.3,** © Brand X Pictures/PunchStock; **P14.4,** © Mel Curtis/Getty Images; **P14.4,** © Royalty-Free/image 100/Corbis; **P14.5,** © Royalty-Free/Corbis; **P15.1,** © Royalty-Free/Corbis; **P15.2,** © Royalty-Free/Corbis

Library of Congress Cataloging-in-Publication Data

Haugaard, Jeffrey J., 1951–
    Child psychopathology / Jeffrey Haugaard—1st ed.
        p. cm.
    ISBN-13: 978-0-07-340550-6 (alk. paper)   ISBN-10: 0-07-340550-7 (alk. paper)
    1. Child psychopathology. I. Title.
    [DNLM: 1. Child Behavior Disorders. 2. Mental Disorders. 3. Child.   WS 350.6 H371c2007]
RJ499.H3953 2007
618.92′89—dc22   2007010575

The Internet addresses listed in the text were accurate at the time of publication. The inclusion of a Web site does not indicate an endorsement by the authors or McGraw-Hill, and McGraw-Hill does not guarantee the accuracy of the information presented at these sites.

www.mhhe.com

For the friends and family who have enriched and guided my life for decades:

Cindy Hazan and Rick Canfield
Quan Pham Howard
Laurie and Edward Mulvey
Nancy and Todd Tomlitz

Brief Contents

CHAPTER 1   *Introduction 1*

CHAPTER 2   *Research Methods and Ethical Issues 19*

CHAPTER 3   *Basic Psychological Theories 64*

CHAPTER 4   *Quantitative Behavioral Genetics 102*

CHAPTER 5   *Classification, Diagnosis, and Assessment 122*

CHAPTER 6   *Conduct Disorder and Oppositional Defiant Disorder 151*

CHAPTER 7   *Attention-Deficit/Hyperactivity Disorder 206*

CHAPTER 8   *Bipolar Disorder 257*

CHAPTER 9   *Depressive Disorders 288*

CHAPTER 10   *Anxiety Disorders 344*

CHAPTER 11   *Mental Retardation 396*

CHAPTER 12   *Autism and Other Pervasive Developmental Disorders 453*

CHAPTER 13   *Childhood-Onset Schizophrenia 508*

CHAPTER 14   *Disorders Associated with Trauma or Maltreatment 544*

CHAPTER 15   *Disorders Related to Physical Health and Functioning 616*

Contents

CHAPTER 1   *Introduction 1*

Who Should Know about Child
    Psychopathology? 3

Basic Principles 5

*Disorders Develop through a Complex Set
    of Influences Unique to Each Child 5*

Disorders Can Occur Together 9

*Behaviors and Disorders Lie along a
    Continuum 10*

*Understanding Disorders and the
    Children Who Experience Them
    Involves the Use of Values 10*

*Our Ultimate Focus Is on Children, Not
    Disorders 11*

The Field of Developmental
    Psychopathology 12

*Concepts in Developmental
    Psychopathology 14*

*Using the Concepts of Risk and
    Protective Factors in Preventive and
    Therapeutic Interventions 17*

CHAPTER 2   *Research Methods and
                Ethical Issues 19*

Research Methods 20

Introduction 21

Methods 23

Participants 23

Measures 26

Procedures 30

Results 40

Discussion 42

Ethical Issues 43

Case Study: Handling Parental
    Expectations 44

Case Study: A Proposed Trial of a New
    Medication 46

Development of Laws and Ethical
    Guidelines for Research and
    Therapy 48

Principles for the Ethical Treatment
    of People Involved in Research
    or Therapy 49

Autonomy 49

Beneficence and Nonmaleficence 53

Confidentiality 56

Institutional Review Boards 60

CHAPTER 3   *Basic Psychological
                Theories 64*

Psychodynamic Theories 65

Fundamental Ideas 65

The Therapeutic Process 70

*Applicability to Child
    Psychopathology 71*

Behavioral Theories 72

Fundamental Ideas 73

The Therapeutic Process 75

*Applicability to Child
    Psychopathology 79*

Cognitive Theories 80

Fundamental Ideas 80

The Therapeutic Process 84

*Applicability to Child
    Psychopathology 85*

Attachment Theory 86
  Fundamental Ideas 86
  The Therapeutic Process 90
  Applicability to Child
    Psychopathology 91
Family Systems Theories 92
  Fundamental Ideas 93
  The Therapeutic Process 96
  Applicability to Child
    Psychopathology 97
Common Features of the Theories 98
  Which Theory Is Best? 99

CHAPTER 4   Quantitative Behavioral
            Genetics 102

History 103
Basic Research Strategy 105
Common Research Strategies in
    Quantitative Behavioral
    Genetics 107
  Family Studies 108
  Twin Studies 108
  Adoption Studies 110
Quantifying the Influences on
    Development 111
  Heritability 112
  Shared Environmental Influences 114
  Nonshared Environmental Influences 115
Gene and Environment
    Relationships 117
  Genotype–Environment Interactions 117
  Genotype–Environment Correlations 118

CHAPTER 5   Classification, Diagnosis,
            and Assessment 122

Disorders 123
Why Have a Classification System and
    Diagnose Disorders? 124
  Potential Advantages 125

Potential Disadvantages 126
  Emphasizing Advantages and
    Minimizing Disadvantages 127
Basic Issues in Classification 128
  Classification Systems 128
  Categorical or Dimensional
    Classification 129
  Disorders Not Otherwise Specified 131
  Reliability and Validity 131
The DSM Classification System 132
  The Multiaxial System 133
  Diagnostic Criteria Provided for
    Future Study 136
Clinical Assessment 137
  Clinical Interviews 139
  Behavioral Assessment 143
  Psychological Tests 145
  Neuroimaging 147

CHAPTER 6   Conduct Disorder and
            Oppositional Defiant
            Disorder 151

Case Study: Early-Onset Conduct
    Problems 153
Case Study: Adolescent-Onset
    Conduct Problems 154
History 156
  Diagnostic Criteria in the DSM 157
Diagnosis and Assessment 158
  Diagnostic Criteria 158
  Controversial and Unresolved Issues 161
  Determining that an Individual Child
    Has a Conduct Disorder 165
Characteristics and Experiences of
    Children with Oppositional
    Defiant Disorder and Conduct
    Disorder 169
  Intelligence and Cognitive Issues 169
  Personality Issues 170
  Peer and Family Issues 171
  Other Forms of Psychopathology 172

Subtypes of Children with Conduct
Disorder 173
  Age of Onset 174
  Patterns of Behaviors 175
  Motivation for Behavior 177
Prevalence 178
Course 179
  Early Onset, with Continuing
  Problems 179
  Early Onset, with Discontinuation of
  Problems in Late Childhood or
  Adolescence 180
  Few Early Problems, Increased Problems
  during Adolescence 181
Families of Children with Conduct
Disorder 182
Etiology of Conduct Problems 184
  Early-Onset Conduct Problems:
  Initial Development 184
  Early-Onset Conduct Problems:
  Ongoing Development 190
  Early-Onset, Limited Duration Conduct
  Problems 194
  Adolescent-Onset Conduct Problems 196
Preventive and Therapeutic
Interventions 198
  Attending to Cultural Issues 198
  Prevention 199
  Early Intervention 200
  Interventions during the School-Age
  Years and Adolescence 202

CHAPTER 7   Attention-Deficit/
             Hyperactivity
             Disorder 206

Case Study: A Dramatic Influence of
Medication 207
Case Study: Conflict over Taking
Medication 209
History 211
Diagnosis and Assessment 212
  Diagnostic Criteria 212

Controversial and Unresolved Issues 214
Determining that an Individual Child
Has ADHD 217
Characteristics and Experiences of
Children with Attention-Deficit/
Hyperactivity Disorder 219
  Core Features of ADHD 220
  Associated Features 223
Prevalence 226
Course 227
  Symptom Onset 227
  Ongoing Development 228
Families of Children with ADHD 229
  Observations of Parent–Child
  Interactions 230
Etiology 232
  Theoretical Perspectives on the Central
  Deficit in ADHD 233
  Possible Sources of Neurological
  Problems in ADHD 237
  Family and Other Environmental
  Influences on the Development of
  ADHD 240
  A Developmental Model 241
Prevention 243
Therapeutic Interventions 243
  Medication 244
  Parenting Interventions 248
  Educational Interventions with
  Children 248
  Psychosocial Interventions with
  Children 250
  Combined Treatments 250
  Issues Still to Be Addressed in
  Treatment for ADHD 253

CHAPTER 8   Bipolar Disorder 257

Case Study: Three Women, One Girl, and
Two Cases of Bipolar Disorder 258
Case Study: A Treatment-Resistant
Case of Bipolar Disorder 260
History 262

Diagnosis and Assessment 262

Diagnostic Criteria 262

Determining that an Individual Child Has a Bipolar Disorder 266

The Existence of Bipolar Disorders in Prepubertal Children 268

Characteristics and Experiences of Children with Bipolar Disorders 272

Core Features 272

Associated Characteristics 276

Prevalence 278

Course 278

Families of Children with Bipolar Disorders 279

Etiology 280

Neurological Studies 281

Genetic Influences 281

Environmental Stress 282

A Diathesis–Stress Model 282

Prevention 283

Therapeutic Interventions 284

Medication 284

Psychosocial Interventions 285

CHAPTER 9   Depressive Disorders 288

Case Study: "Hidden" Depression in an Early Adolescent 289

Case Study: A Gradual Decline into Depression 291

History 293

Diagnosis and Assessment 294

Diagnostic Criteria 294

Controversial and Unresolved Issues 298

Determining that an Individual Child Has a Depressive Disorder 301

Characteristics and Experiences of Children with Depressive Disorders 304

Core Features 304

Associated Features 305

Prevalence 306

Course 308

Onset and Course of Depressive Disorders 308

Onset and Course of Depressive Symptoms 309

Sex Differences in Depression Beginning in Adolescence 313

Suicide 315

Defining Terms 315

Prevalence 316

Characteristics and Experiences of Children Who Are Suicidal 317

The Development of Suicidal Thinking and Behavior 317

Attempting Suicide 319

Families of Children with Depressive Disorders 320

Etiology of Depression 320

Biologically Based Theories 321

Theories Based on Affect Regulation 324

Cognitive Theories 325

Influences of Life Stress 329

Interpersonal Theories 330

Two Developmental Models 331

Prevention 334

Therapeutic Interventions 337

Medication 337

Psychosocial Interventions with Children 338

Therapeutic Interventions with Families 340

CHAPTER 10   Anxiety Disorders 344

Case Study: A Child with Separation Anxiety 345

Case Study: A Sudden Fear of Dogs 347

History 349

Basic Issues in Childhood Anxiety 350

Many Meanings of Anxiety 351

Do Children Experience Specific Anxiety Disorders or High Levels of Anxiety? 351

Cultural Influences on Anxiety 351

Anxiety Disorders 352

Separation Anxiety Disorder 352

Specific Phobia 355

Social Phobia or Social Anxiety Disorder 358

Obsessive–Compulsive Disorder 362

Generalized Anxiety Disorder 366

Panic Disorder 369

Adjustment Disorder with Anxiety 373

Anxiety Disorder Not Otherwise Specified 373

Etiology of Anxiety Disorders 373

Genetically Based Vulnerability to Anxiety 375

A Brief Foray into Thinking about Risk Taking 378

The Influence of Experience on the Development of Anxiety 380

Maintaining and Intensifying Anxiety 384

Prevention 387

Therapeutic Interventions 389

Systematic Desensitization 389

Cognitive–Behavioral Psychotherapy 390

Family Interventions 392

Medication 393

CHAPTER 11 Mental Retardation 396

Case Study: The Early Life of a Girl with Mild Mental Retardation 397

Case Study: A Young Boy's Influence on His Family 399

Intelligence and Intelligence Testing 400

Intelligence as One Trait or Many Traits 401

Culture and Intelligence 404

Measuring Intelligence 405

History 409

Diagnosis and Assessment 411

Diagnostic Criteria 412

Determining that an Individual Child Has Mental Retardation 412

Characteristics and Experiences of Children with Mental Retardation 415

Cognitive Abilities 415

Prevalence 420

Sex and Race Differences 420

Families of Children with Mental Retardation 421

Parents 422

Siblings 423

Etiology 425

Two Groups of Children Who Have Mental Retardation 425

Mental Retardation of Known Organic Cause 427

Mental Retardation with No Discernible Pathologic Basis 436

Prevention 439

Mental Retardation of Known Organic Cause 439

Mental Retardation of No Discernible Pathological Basis 440

Educational Interventions 441

Early Intervention 441

Elementary and High School Education 442

Transition to Adulthood 443

Other Therapeutic Interventions 444

Psychopathology and Other Problem Behaviors 444

Self-Injurious Behavior 446

Family Training and Support 448

CHAPTER 12 Autism and Other Pervasive Developmental Disorders 453

Case Study: Experiences of a High-Functioning Person with Autism 454

History 456

Diagnosis and Assessment 459

Diagnostic Criteria 459

A Controversial and Unresolved Issue: Autism Spectrum Disorder 459

Determining that an Individual Child Has a Pervasive Developmental Disorder 463

Characteristics and Experiences of Children with Autistic Disorder or Asperger's Disorder 464

Autistic Disorder: Core Features 464

Autistic Disorder: Associated Features 471

Asperger's Disorder 472

Prevalence 475

Course 477

Initial Onset of Symptoms 477

Development during Childhood and Adolescence 478

Long-Term Prognosis 478

Families of Children with a Pervasive Developmental Disorder 479

Etiology 481

Theoretical Perspectives on the Fundamental Deficits in ASD 481

Neurological Bases for the Symptoms of ASD 486

Causes of the Yet-to-Be-Understood Neurological Impairments 488

Rett's Disorder 492

Characteristics and Experiences of Children with Rett's Disorder 493

Prevalence and Developmental Course 493

Etiology 494

Childhood Disintegrative Disorder 495

Characteristics and Experiences of Children with Childhood Disintegrative Disorder 495

Prevalence and Developmental Course 496

Etiology 496

Therapeutic Interventions 497

Early Interventions 498

Interventions during the School-Age Years 500

Medication 502

Facilitated Communication 503

Interventions for Families 504

CHAPTER 13   Childhood-Onset Schizophrenia 508

Case Study: A Child with Many Risk Factors for Schizophrenia 509

Case Study: Childhood-Onset Schizophrenia from "Out of the Blue" 511

History 512

Diagnosis and Assessment 514

Diagnostic Criteria 514

Controversial Issue: Continuity between Childhood-Onset Schizophrenia and Adult-Onset Schizophrenia 516

Cultural Issues When Diagnosing Childhood-Onset Schizophrenia 517

Characteristics and Experiences of Children with Schizophrenia 518

Positive Symptoms 518

Negative Symptoms 520

Cycle of Symptoms 521

Prevalence 523

Course 523

Premorbid Functioning 523

Initial Onset of Symptoms 524

Long-Term Course 525

Families of Children with Schizophrenia 526

Etiology 526

Neurobiological Dysfunctions in Schizophrenia 527

Possible Causes of Neurobiological Dysfunction 529

The Role of Stressful or Dysfunctional Family Environments 531

Three Theories about the Development of Schizophrenia 533

The Development of Schizophrenia during Childhood 535

Prevention 537

Markers of Vulnerability 537

Possible Preventive Interventions 538

Therapeutic Interventions 538

Antipsychotic Medications 539

Psychological Interventions 540

CHAPTER 14   Disorders Associated with Trauma or Maltreatment 544

POSTTRAUMATIC STRESS DISORDER AND ACUTE STRESS DISORDER 545

Case Study: Living through a Tornado 545

History 547

Diagnosis and Assessment 548

Diagnostic Criteria 548

Controversial and Unresolved Issue: Different Diagnostic Criteria for Preschool Children 552

Determining that an Individual Child Has Acute Stress Disorder or PTSD 552

Characteristics and Experiences of Children with PTSD 554

Core Features 554

Associated Features 556

Prevalence 558

Characteristics Distinguishing Children Who Do and Do Not Develop PTSD 559

Course 561

Initial Onset of Symptoms 561

Recovery from Symptoms 561

Families of Children with PTSD 562

Etiology 563

Influences of Trauma on Brain Development and Functioning 563

Cognitive Models of the Etiology of PTSD 568

Prevention 570

Therapeutic Interventions 572

Interventions for the Child with PTSD 572

Interventions for Family Members 574

DISSOCIATIVE DISORDERS 575

Case Study: A Sexually Abused Boy 576

History 577

Toward Understanding Dissociative Disorders: Common Dissociative Experiences 579

Normal Dissociation in Children 579

Diagnosis and Assessment 580

Diagnostic Criteria 580

Controversial Issue: Does Dissociative Identity Disorder Exist? 583

Determining that an Individual Child Has a Dissociative Disorder 585

Characteristics and Experiences of Children with Dissociative Disorders 587

Core Features 587

Associated Features 588

Prevalence and Course 589

Etiology 589

Development of Chronic Dissociation 590

Development of Alternate Personality Identities 592

Preventive and Therapeutic Interventions 594

Prevention 594

Therapeutic Interventions with the Child 594

Interventions with Family Members and Other Caregivers 596

REACTIVE ATTACHMENT DISORDER 597

Case Study: Researchers' Interactions with a Young Child 598

History 599

Diagnosis and Assessment 600

Diagnostic Criteria 600

Controversial and Unresolved Issues 601

Determining that an Individual Child Has
Reactive Attachment Disorder 602

Characteristics and Experiences of
Children with Reactive
Attachment Disorder 603

Core Features 604

Associated Features 605

Prevalence and Course 605

Etiology 607

Studies of Children Raised in Deprived
Institutions 609

Preventive and Therapeutic
Interventions 611

Prevention 611

Therapeutic Interventions for Children
and Families 612

CHAPTER 15   Disorders Related to
Physical Health and
Functioning 616

SOMATOFORM DISORDERS AND
SOMATIZATION PROBLEMS 617

Case Study: The Function of a Child's
Injury in Her Family 618

Diagnosis and Assessment of
Somatoform Disorders 620

Diagnostic Criteria for the Somatoform
Disorders 620

Determining that an Individual Child
Has a Somatoform Disorder 622

Somatization Problems 624

Characteristics and Experiences of
Children with Somatization
Problems and Their Families 624

Prevalence and Course 626

Etiology 627

Therapeutic Interventions for the
Child and Family 631

Medical Interventions 631

Behavioral Interventions 632

Cognitive Interventions 633

Interventions for Parents and
Families 633

CHILDHOOD OBESITY 634

Case Study: A Girl's Ongoing Struggle
with Weight 635

Defining and Measuring Obesity 637

Prevalence and Course 638

Consequences of Childhood
Obesity 640

Physical Health 640

Psychological and Social
Consequences 641

Etiology 642

Genetic Influences 644

Parental Obesity, Activity Levels,
and Diet 644

A Model for the Development of
Childhood Obesity 645

Prevention 647

Therapeutic Interventions 648

ANOREXIA NERVOSA AND BULIMIA
NERVOSA 651

Prevalence of Body Dissatisfaction
and Dieting among School-Age
Children 652

Development of Body Dissatisfaction
and Dieting 653

Diagnostic Criteria for Anorexia
Nervosa and Bulimia Nervosa 655

Prevalence and Course of Anorexia
Nervosa and Bulimia Nervosa 657

Development of Anorexia Nervosa and
Bulimia Nervosa 658

Prevention 663

Individual and Family
Treatment 664

ELIMINATION DISORDERS 667

Case Study: Primary Enuresis 668

Enuresis 669

Diagnostic Criteria 669

*Characteristics and Experiences of
   Children with Enuresis 671*

Prevalence and Course 674

Families of Children with Enuresis 675

Etiology 676

Prevention 679

Therapeutic Interventions 679

Encopresis 684

Diagnostic Criteria 684

*Characteristics and Experiences of
   Children with Encopresis 686*

Prevalence and Course 687

Etiology 688

Prevention 689

Therapeutic Interventions 690

References R-1

Name Index I-1

Subject Index I-14

Preface

The field of child psychopathology is vibrant and exciting, in part because of all that has been learned recently about many of the disorders that are considered forms of child psychopathology. Researchers have expanded our knowledge about these disorders dramatically over the past few decades and are poised to continue this process during the next decade. Therapists have created a wide range of preventive and therapeutic interventions, many of which have a strong research base, and continue to revise these interventions as more research accumulates about them. Students who envision themselves as therapists, researchers, teachers, social workers, nurses, physicians, or others who work extensively with children should feel a sense of excitement about being involved in a field where so much has been learned over the past few decades.

Conversely, the field of child psychopathology is also made vibrant and exciting by all that we do not know. There are many disorders about which we know only a little; and even for those about which much is known, fundamental questions continue to be the focus of debate and research. This field is characterized by the excitement of a growing discipline, and today's students will have an important role in this continuing growth.

Finally, the field of child psychopathology is vibrant and exciting because it focuses on individual children and their families, with all the variation that personal, family, community, and cultural issues bring to the experiences of these children and their families. At its best, it is a very humane field. It is at its best when researchers, therapists, and others understand and appreciate the uniqueness of each child and of each child's family—and work to use that understanding to benefit the child and family. Doing this introduces a complexity that those in few other fields can appreciate, as well as rewards that those in few other fields can achieve.

I have written this text to give students an appreciation for the vibrancy and excitement associated with the field of child psychopathology and to help them appreciate the complexity of the field. All students who will one day work with children or families can gain a basic foundation for understanding child psychopathology from this text, and this understanding will benefit them and the children and families with whom they will work. Students whose careers will focus in the mental health, physical health, or social work fields will find extensive information about childhood disorders, their prevention, and their treatment. All readers will gain an appreciation for the complexity of the field and the need to base interventions on research and on a humane attitude toward each child and family.

❧ Focusing on the Development of Disorders and on Interventions

Two primary goals of most people working in the field of child psychopathology are to prevent the development of disorders and to treat disorders effectively when they develop. Even most researchers who do not provide preventive or therapeutic interventions have the ultimate goal of understanding a disorder more thoroughly so that it can be prevented or treated more effectively. However, effective prevention or treatment is possible only when the processes through which the various disorders develop are understood. Because understanding how disorders develop is so fundamental to this field, one of my main goals while writing this text has been to help students understand what is currently known about these development processes. Rather than merely providing the many research-based facts that have been learned about each disorder, I have written each chapter in a way that synthesizes these facts and then integrates them with current theories to help students clearly understand current conceptualizations about how these disorders develop in individual children. When students finish the chapter about a disorder, they will understand the influences on the development of the disorder and how these influences combine and interact with other aspects of a child's life to shape the child and his or her family.

Another primary focus has been to describe the various forms of preventive and therapeutic interventions that are currently used with each disorder. I clearly describe current interventions, along with the theories and research that support them. In addition, when there is a research base to do so, I focus on issues related to culture or gender that can influence which interventions may be most effective with a child. I use two strategies in the prevention and intervention sections of most chapters. The first is to make clear connections between the interventions and our current understanding of how a disorder develops. For example, I describe how the use of medication and psychosocial interventions with children who have attention-deficit/hyperactivity disorder are linked to what we know about the brain functioning and the social functioning of these children. The second strategy is to highlight the ways in which a child's family should be involved in preventive and therapeutic interventions. The important role that a child's family—broadly defined—plays in the life of a child is emphasized in each chapter.

❧ Understanding the Complexity of Child Psychopathology

A theme that runs throughout this text is that there are many pathways through which psychopathology can develop in a child. We cannot say, for example, "This is how somatization develops in children," or "This is how autism develops." Rather, we must always say, "These are the ways in which somatization or autism develops in children," or to be more accurate, "These are the ways in which we currently believe somatization or autism develops in children."

As a result, my discussion of the development of psychopathology is always multifaceted. First I describe the variety of individual (genetic, biological, cognitive, emotional), family, community, and cultural issues that can influence the development of a disorder. This helps students broaden their thinking about the development of disorders. Next, using the concepts of developmental psychopathology, I provide models for understanding how these influences combine and interact over time to increase the risk that some children will experience a disorder. For example, I help students understand how a genetically based temperament that makes an infant more reactive to unfamiliar situations can influence the parenting that she receives during her preschool years—and consequently the cognitive and emotional reactions that she may experience in certain situations while in elementary school. I frequently remind students of a central tenet of the text: The issues that influence the development of a disorder vary among individual children, as do the relative strengths of those issues. For example, community and parenting issues influence the development of conduct disorder in some boys, whereas genetic and parenting issues influence the development of conduct disorder in others. Within this second group, genes will be the primary influence for some boys and parenting will be the primary influence for others. This approach is designed to expand students' thinking about child psychopathology and discourage them from thinking simplistically about any of the disorders discussed in this text.

❧ What Is Known, Unknown, and Controversial

An important feature of this text is that I include, to the extent that current research allows, a discussion of what is known about each disorder, important issues that remain unknown, and controversies that continue to exist. For example, rather than just describing the role that intelligence tests play in the assessment of mental retardation, I discuss controversies about what intelligence is and whether it can be measured in the same way in children from different cultures. Rather than simply describing the prevalence and course of depression in children, I discuss the ongoing debate about whether distinct depressive disorders exist in young children or whether these disorders are better conceptualized as part of an overall angst that many children experience. Similarly, I address the current debates about whether several distinct pervasive developmental disorders exist or whether disorders such as autism and Asperger's disorder should best be conceptualized as components of a broader autism spectrum.

❧ Comprehensive Introductory Material

All professionals in the field of child psychopathology recognize that knowledge of many basic issues is essential for understanding foundational theories and research. I introduce each of these issues in the first four chapters of this text. For example, I review the concepts of **developmental psychopathology** to provide a foundation for much of the information provided in the rest of the text. **Research methods** are discussed in sufficient detail to allow an instructor to assign students to critique research articles using the information in this text. A significant discussion of **ethical issues** is included because students should be familiar with the ethics of this field from their first contact with it. I include a chapter about **basic psychological theories** to provide background for understanding much of the information that appears in the sections about the development, prevention, and treatment of each disorder. Finally, I include a full chapter about the basic concepts of **quantitative behavioral genetics**. As we understand more clearly the role that genes play in the development of disorders, it is essential that students understand the research paradigms from which we gain the information about the genetic influences on disorders.

⋈ Common and Uncommon Disorders

Research over the past two decades has shown that some children have disorders that were once considered only disorders of adulthood, such as schizophrenia and bipolar disorder. In addition, researchers and therapists have been learning more about rare disorders in children, such as reactive attachment disorder or somatization disorder. Although the prevalence of these disorders is much lower than the prevalence of disorders such as attention-deficit/hyperactivity disorder and conduct disorder, it is important for students to be familiar with them. Familiarity will allow students to begin to understand some of the issues that distinguish the rarer disorders from the more common disorders (such as the differences in the quality of the irritability found among children with bipolar disorder and conduct disorder), as well as how prevention and therapeutic interventions for the rarer disorders may differ from prevention and therapeutic interventions for the more common disorders.

Meaningful coverage is given to the less common disorders, and some of these disorders are given their own chapter. Although the relative lack of research on some of these less common disorders shortens my discussion of them, they all receive coverage that is thorough enough to provide even advanced students with an appropriate grasp of key points.

Content to Enhance Learning

This text includes several features to enhance and broaden students' learning:

- Each chapter begins with a **Chapter Plan** to show students what will follow and how sections of each chapter relate to each other.
- Most chapters include **Case Studies** that illustrate important issues discussed in each chapter. These case studies portray sufficient information about the children and families to allow class discussions of how the disorders may have developed in the children and why specific interventions may have been useful for preventing the disorders in the children or treating them effectively.
- Topics for discussion follow each case study in a section called **Some Issues Worth Noting.**
- **Key Concepts** are highlighted frequently to help students monitor whether they have understood the main points of each section.

- A **Chapter Glossary** appears at the end of each chapter as a study aid for students.
- In **"Notes from the Author"** I highlight intriguing facts from each chapter or draw on my own experiences as a clinician, researcher, and teacher to illustrate important points.
- Where appropriate, I highlight important research methods issues by relating them to research results discussed in the chapters in **"Illustrating an Important Research Issue"** boxes. This helps students understand important methods issues by relating them to specific examples.

✦ Acknowledgments

Many students helped me throughout the process of writing this text through discussions and by carefully finding and recording thousands of research articles and chapters. Thanks very much to Sarah Agudo, Hannah Hirschland, Jesse Hutchinson, Arielle Kurtzweil, Anika March, Allison Santopolo, and Lindsay Wick.

Reviewers

Margaret Appel, *Ohio University*
Connie Callahan, *Eastern Kentucky University*
Kristin Christodulu, *University at Albany, SUNY*
Sally During, *University of Calgary*
Tanya Eckert, *Syracuse University*
Jon B. Ellis, *East Tennessee State University*
Robert Emery, *University of Virginia*
C. D. Fernald, *University of North Carolina–Charlotte*
Renee Galliher, *Utah State University*
Deborah Harris O'Brien, *Trinity University*
Erin Ingoldsby, *University of Utah*
Christopher Kearney, *University of Nevada–Las Vegas*
Steven Landau, *Illinois State University–Normal*
Mark A. Laumakis, *San Diego State University*
Susan McCammon, *East Carolina University*
Rich Milich, *University of Kentucky*
Kimberly Renk, *University of Central Florida*
Shulamit Ritblatt, *San Diego State University*
Julia Rucklidge, *University of Canterbury*
Brandon Schultz, *James Madison University*
Mary Schwendener-Holt, *Earlham College*
Debra Schwiesow, *Creighton University*
Wendy K. Silverman, *Florida International University*
Timothy Snyder, *Lander University*
Ric G. Steele, *University of Kansas*
Susan Waldman, *San Francisco State University*
Andrea Zevenbergen, *SUNY–Fredonia*

Introduction

Child psychopathology is a complex and exciting field.

Hello and welcome. You are probably beginning your exploration of child psychopathology as you read this introductory chapter. I, on the other hand, am ending this phase of my exploration of child psychopathology because this is, perhaps paradoxically, the last chapter I am writing in this text. I have worked on this text for many months, plowing through chapter after chapter, rewriting, and returning to completed chapters to insert new research. For me, this has been a long and educational process, and I now know much more about child psycho-pathology than before I started writing this text. By the time you finish reading it, I hope you can say the same.

One issue that became clear to me as I wrote this text is that many, many children experience one or more forms of child psychopathology. Recently several researchers reviewed a wide range of studies of the prevalence of various forms of child psychopathology conducted during the previous decade (Costello, Egger, & Angold, 2005). Their results are shown in Figure 1.1. The bar next to each category represents the range of prevalence estimates found in the studies (showing that our knowledge about psychopathology prevalence is incomplete, as discussed in the next paragraph). The mark on each line represents the median prevalence estimate from the studies (half the studies show a higher prevalence, and half show a lower prevalence). As can be seen, the median estimate is that about one-quarter of all children surveyed had experienced at least one form of psychopathology. That is a huge number of children. Clearly child psychopathology is an issue related to the lives of many children, their friends and families, and others with whom they interact.

A second issue that became clear to me as I wrote this text is that we still have much to learn about child psychopathology. Research during the past few decades has dramatically increased the number of facts we know about many disorders and the children who have them. However, we are still in the process of understanding what these facts mean. For example, we know that the performance of many girls with attention-deficit/hyperactivity disorder (ADHD) on neurocognitive tests declines as they get older and that the performance of many boys tends to improve, but we know little about why this occurs (Gaub & Carlson, 1997). Similarly, we know that the biological functioning of most children with major depressive disorder differs from the biological functioning of most adults with major depressive disorder, but we know little about why this is so (Armitage et al., 2002). In addition, although we have learned much about the many influences on the development of disorders, such as the influences of genes, family and neighborhood environments, and children's experiences, we continue to struggle to understand the mechanisms through which these factors influence the disorders. The first professor for whom I was a teaching assistant when I was in graduate school put it succinctly when he wrote this on the board during his first lecture: Know? No!

Our expanding but still small knowledge about childhood disorders means that the field of child psychopathology is a vibrant and growing field that should attract those of you who are interested in creating new knowledge and using that knowledge to help children and families. It is not a field for people who need to know all that there is to know about something: Few issues in child psychopathology are settled. It is instead a field for people with imagination and a willingness to struggle along using what is known while contributing to our expanding knowledge.

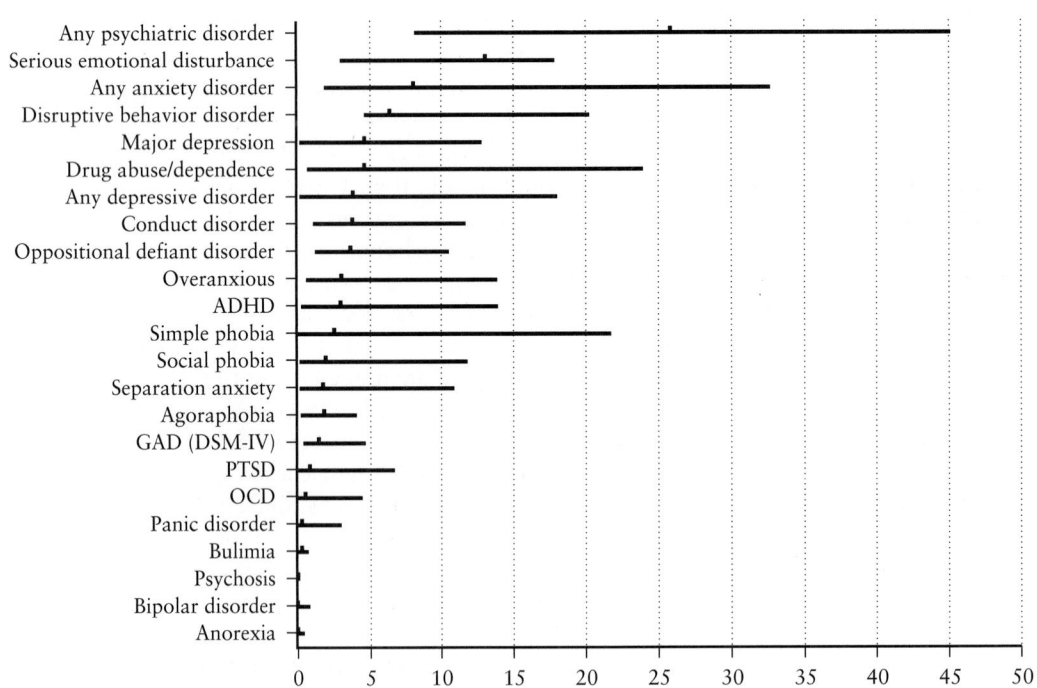

FIGURE 1.1   *Summary of Results of Prevalence Studies since 1993: Highest, Lowest, and Median Estimates for Ages 5–17*

Chapter Plan

This chapter and several following chapters contain introductory material that will be important for you to know as you begin exploring the field of child psychopathology. In the first part of this chapter, we explore the variety of professionals who can benefit from knowledge about child psychopathology and note that this knowledge can be useful to all parents, whatever their professions. We then review several basic principles that are found throughout this text. At the end of this chapter we explore the field of developmental psychopathology by noting how the perspective of specialists in developmental psychopathology may differ from the perspectives of those in clinical child psychology or psychiatry, and we explore fundamental principles of developmental psychopathology.

Who Should Know about Child Psychopathology?

Professionals working in many fields need current, accurate knowledge about child psychopathology. Obviously clinical or counseling psychologists, psychiatrists, clinical social workers, and other psychotherapists and counselors need thorough knowledge about this subject. Physicians, nurses, and other medical professionals also need to know about child psychopathology. Many parents who become concerned about their children's behaviors or emotional problems turn to their pediatricians, family physicians, or community medical clinics for help. Consequently physicians, nurses, and others must be able to recognize the presence of a behavioral or emotional disorder[1] and refer parents and children to mental health professionals when appropriate. In addition, many medical professionals are asked to prescribe medication to children with behavioral or emotional disorders, such as antidepressant medication for children who are depressed or stimulant medication for children with ADHD. So a clear understanding of the potential benefits and unwanted side effects of prescribing medication for these children is essential.

Educators need to know about child psychopathology. Through their close work with children, they can be the first to recognize that a child is experiencing a behavioral or emotional disorder and refer the child for treatment before the symptoms of the disorder become severe. Educators may also be able to recognize the early signs that a disorder is developing. We know that early signs exist for many disorders. For example, many school-age children who are depressed exhibited sad and withdrawn behavior when in preschool (Mesman & Koot, 2000a). Educators who are alert to these early signs may be able to refer a child to a mental health professional for intervention that will reduce the likelihood of the disorder developing.

---

[1]As discussed in more detail in the chapter about classification, diagnosis, and assessment, in this text the term *behavioral or emotional disorder* will be used as a label for disorders that others might refer to as *mental disorders, psychiatric disorders,* or *psychological disorders.*

Those working in faith-based organizations, community organizations such as the Boys' and Girls' Clubs, and youth sports also need to know about child psychopathology. They may be the first people to whom parents turn when they are concerned about their children's problems. Like teachers, their close work with children may allow them to identify children experiencing disorders so they can be referred for appropriate treatment.

Law enforcement officials and workers in the juvenile justice system who know about child psychopathology may be able to recognize a disorder in a child who comes to their attention. Similarly, lawyers and other legal professionals working with children and families may be able to recognize a disorder in a child they represent and use the legal system to obtain needed treatment for the child or the child's family. For example, depression is at the foundation of the acting-out behaviors of some troubled children (Essau, 2003). To the extent that these children can be identified and their depression treated effectively, they may be able to end their acting-out behavior before it becomes a significant problem for them and their community.

Public policy professionals need to be aware of issues related to child psychopathology if, as a society, we are to devote sufficient resources to understanding the causes of behavioral and emotional disorders, how to prevent them, and how to treat them effectively. For too long we have focused much more energy on adult disorders than childhood disorders. Further, the cost to our society of childhood disorders is high. It is estimated that about 20% of children in the United States will experience significant mental health problems, and that only about a quarter of them will receive any type of treatment (U.S. Public Health Service, 2001). Knowing about the prevalence and consequences of childhood disorders can encourage people in the public and private sectors to insist that more research be done on childhood disorders and on effective preventive and intervention strategies for them. To the extent that our society is concerned about the lives of children, much more must be done.

Finally, whatever their professions, parents should know about child psychopathology. Being able to recognize the possible signs of a behavioral or emotional disorder in their own children, in children in their extended families, or in their neighbors' children may let a child receive needed help while a disorder is beginning to develop, resulting in a better life for the child and all concerned.

Key Concepts

- Professionals in many fields can benefit from an understanding of child psychopathology, whether they are providing therapeutic services to children or are in positions to refer children for therapeutic services.
- A better understanding of the prevalence and consequences of childhood behavioral and emotional disorders could encourage a more concerted public and private effort to understand these disorders and help the children who experience them.

Basic Principles

Several basic principles are woven into all the chapters in this text. Thinking about them as you begin your exploration of child psychopathology will help you recognize them as you come across them.

Disorders Develop through a Complex Set of Influences Unique to Each Child

The influences on the development of almost all the disorders discussed in this text form a complex web. In addition, each child who develops a disorder is unique and has a unique set of life experiences. Because this complex web of influences interacts with the unique qualities and experiences of each child as a disorder develops, simple answers to questions about the development of disorders in children are always wrong. Simplistic answers about the development of some disorders abound: Eating disorders are the result of cultural pressure for girls to be thin; severe child abuse causes reactive attachment disorder; conduct problems are caused by inadequate parenting. Although each of these statements may partly describe the development of a disorder in some children, none of them fully explains the development of a disorder in any child.

To understand the development of disorders in children we must be willing to struggle with the complexity of influences on these disorders. We will explore this complexity in this section.

- First we will see that many different issues can influence the development of the disorders we will explore in this text—such as genes, cognitive styles, the parenting a child receives, the neighborhood in which a child is raised, and the culture that surrounds the child.
- Next we will explore how each issue can influence the development of a disorder in some children but not in others. For example, genes and the parenting a child receives may influence the development of depression in some children but have little influence on the development of depression in others.
- Finally, we will note that the relative strengths of the issues influencing the development of a disorder vary between children. For example, genes may have a strong influence and parenting a minor influence on the development of depression in some children, whereas parenting will have a strong influence and genes a minor influence on the development of depression in others.

Development Is Influenced by Many Issues

Many types of issues influence a child's development. Consequently, to understand the development of a child, we must consider the potential influences of each of these issues.

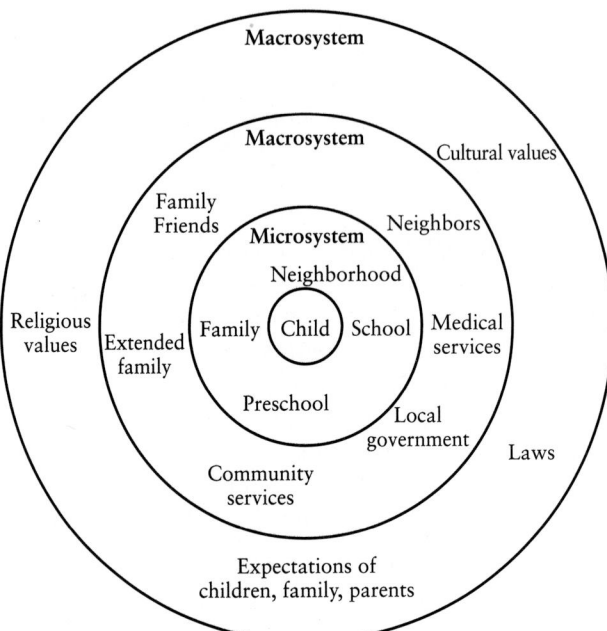

FIGURE 1.2 *Bronfenbrenner's Model of Child Development*

In the late 1970s Urie Bronfenbrenner proposed a model of the many influences on a child's development. This model has become so accepted today that it can be difficult to understand how important a contribution it was at the time and how much it expanded the thinking of psychologists (Bronfenbrenner, 1979). As you can see in Figure 1.2, the child and the child's individual characteristics are at the center of the model. The child's characteristics include genetically inherited strengths and vulnerabilities, temperament, cognitive style, and physical health. The *microsystem* includes the people and institutions that the child encounters regularly. The child's family is the most important component of the microsystem early in his or her life. As the child develops, other people and institutions become part of the microsystem—such as the child's preschool and the teachers and other students in it, the child's faith-based community and the people in it, and the child's neighborhood and the adults and other children in it. The *mesosystem* connects components of the microsystem. For example, if a child's parents have significant substance abuse problems, their limited employment opportunities may require that they live in a neighborhood that has high levels of crime and violence, and the child may attend a school that provides fewer educational opportunities than schools in more affluent neighborhoods. Thus the parents' characteristics are connected to the neighborhood in which the child is raised.

The *exosystem* includes people and institutions that are further removed from the child's immediate day-to-day experiences: members of the child's extended family, community and medical services available to the child and his or her family, and the mass media. Finally, the *macrosystem* includes cultural, religious, and national values, attitudes, and beliefs. Values about the ways in which good parents should care for their children or about the importance of girls being thin or quiet are examples of influences from the macrosystem.

Because influences on childhood disorders can come from each of these levels, we must consider the potential influences from each level when conceptualizing how a disorder develops in a child. For example, consider a child with a somatoform disorder, which is diagnosed when a child has physical symptoms (such as chronic stomach pains) that are not fully explained by a medical condition (APA, 2000). It may be important to consider the child's genetic predisposition to physical symptoms and any significant illnesses the child has experienced, the responses of the child's parents and teachers to his or her physical symptoms (microsystem), the availability of medical services in the child's community (exosystem), and the influences of beliefs about physical and psychological symptoms in the child's culture (macrosystem). Keeping this complex web of influences in mind when thinking about the development of a child's somatoform disorder is essential because effective interventions for the child must address all the influences on the disorder's development.

Influences Combine in Many Ways That Differ between Children

To complicate matters further, the myriad issues that can influence the development of a disorder combine in different ways to influence the development of the disorder in individual children. For example, consider the issues that can contribute to high levels of anxiety in children. As we will discuss in the chapter about anxiety disorders, these include the child's genetically based temperament, the parenting the child experiences, the level of violence or other problems in the child's neighborhood, and the child's experiences in school and other institutions. However, not all these issues influence the development of high levels of anxiety in every child. Instead some issues influence high levels of anxiety in some children but have little influence on the development of high levels of anxiety in other children. For example, some children have temperaments characterized by high levels of fear in unfamiliar situations, and this may be at the foundation of their anxiety. Other highly anxious children may not have this fearful temperament but are raised by highly anxious parents whose overprotectiveness teaches the child that the world is a dangerous place.

Although a group of children may have similar levels of anxiety, the issues that influence the anxiety of individuals in that group may differ. Therefore, knowing the many issues that can influence a disorder is only part of the information that psychologists and others working with individual children need. They must also understand which issues influenced the development of a disorder in that child. This is because effective interventions for an individual child must be based on this understanding. For example, an effective intervention for one anxious child may require helping the parents

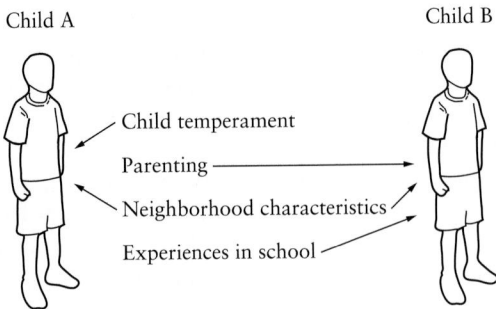

FIGURE 1.3 *Differing Influences on High Anxiety*

understand and work effectively with his fearful temperament. An effective intervention for another anxious child may require helping her parents overcome their own anxiety so they do not pass it along to her through their parenting (see Figure 1.3).

The Relative Influence of Many Issues Can Vary from Child to Child

To complicate matters even further, the relative importance of the issues influencing the development of disorders can vary between children. For example, consider two children whose high levels of anxiety have been influenced by their temperament, the parenting they have experienced, and their experiences in school. As you can see in Figure 1.4, the influence of temperament is high for one child, with the influences of parenting and school experiences being relatively low; on the other hand, the influence of parenting is high for the other child, with the influences of temperament and school experiences being low. Knowing the relative importance of these influences would be essential to a therapist working with these two children. Interventions to cope with a fearful temperament will be more important for one child, whereas interventions to change the child's parenting will be more important with the other.

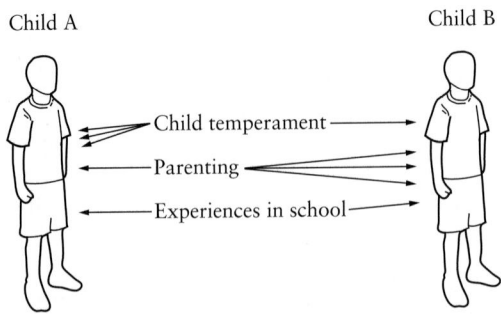

FIGURE 1.4 *Varying Levels of the Influences on High Anxiety*

Influences Interact with and Affect Each Other

To complicate matters still further, the various influences on a child's development do not occur independently. As an illustration, consider a child with highly aggressive behavior. One influence on this behavior can be a genetically influenced temperament that inclines him to enjoy rough-and-tumble play. This interest will influence his choice of friends, many of whom will also be interested in rough-and-tumble play. It is likely that these friends will reinforce his aggressive behavior. As discussed in more detail in the chapter about quantitative behavioral genetics, this is referred to as a *genotype–environment correlation:* His genes and his environment both influence his aggressive behavior, and his environment is influenced in part by his genes (Plomin, DeFries, McClearn, & McGuffin, 2001). So considering the wide range of influences on a child's development can be insufficient: It is frequently important to consider how those influences interact to fully understand their influence on a child.

Disorders Can Occur Together

A text such as this describes each disorder in a separate chapter or a separate section. This can suggest that children experience only one disorder at a time. As we will see throughout this text, however, this is not true. Many children experience two or more disorders. When this occurs, the disorders are called *comorbid*. Understanding an individual child requires understanding all the disorders the child is experiencing.

Some children develop two or more disorders independently. For example, an adolescent may have an eating disorder and a specific phobia about spiders that developed for unrelated reasons. Perhaps the fear of spiders developed during middle childhood because of two frightening experiences involving spiders, whereas the eating disorder developed when the adolescent entered high school for reasons unrelated to anxiety about spiders.

More often, however, disorders occur together because they are related in some way:

- In some cases, one or more issues influence the development of two disorders. For example, children with Prader–Willi syndrome commonly experience both mental retardation and obesity. It is believed that the abnormalities on the 15th chromosome that cause Prader–Willi syndrome affect the child's cognitive abilities and also the child's appetite (Dimitropoulos et al., 2000).

- In other cases, the presence of one disorder influences the development of a second disorder. For example, girls with major depressive disorder are more likely than other girls to develop an eating disorder during adolescence (Kovacs, Obrosky, & Sherrill, 2003). Depression appears to influence their eating patterns and consequently their likelihood of developing an eating disorder. Similarly, many children with conduct disorder develop a depressive disorder later in childhood or adolescence; it is hypothesized that the consequences of their conduct-disordered behaviors influence the development of their depression (Kovacs, Paulauskas, Gatsonis, & Richards, 1988).

As we will discuss throughout this text, effective therapeutic and preventive interventions must be based on an understanding of how a disorder has developed in an individual child. Consequently, understanding any relationships between comorbid disorders will always be important when we design interventions. For example, if one disorder has influenced the development of a second disorder, an intervention focused on the second disorder is likely to fail because an important influence on that disorder (the first disorder) has not been treated.

Behaviors and Disorders Lie along a Continuum

The behaviors and emotions that are the symptoms of each disorder discussed in this text can be thought of as lying along a continuum. Consider depression, for example. Mild forms of a depressed mood might cause a child to feel sad for a few days and have reduced energy for schoolwork or social activities. Moderate forms might generate more pronounced feelings of sadness and periodic withdrawal from school and social activities. More severe forms of depression might include ongoing strong feelings of sadness, a sense of hopelessness that the sadness will never end, and minimal involvement in school, social, or family activities. Extreme forms could involve such strong feelings of sadness and hopelessness that a child cannot get out of bed.

Because symptoms of disorders lie along a continuum, there is a point along that continuum where the symptoms become severe enough that a disorder can be diagnosed. This issue is discussed more fully in the chapter about classification, diagnosis, and assessment; but two points are worth noting here. First, many children experience mild symptoms of a disorder. They may experience periodic sadness, occasional physical symptoms with no apparent medical cause, and moderate levels of anxiety in new social situations. Children with these common experiences are not considered to be experiencing a disorder. Second, you should not be alarmed when you see some of your behaviors or emotions described in this text—all of us experience behaviors or emotions that can be considered mild forms of the symptoms of a disorder. Recognizing these behaviors or emotions in yourself may be of value because this may help you understand the experiences of children with more severe forms of the symptoms. Experiencing feelings of sadness, helplessness, and despair after breaking up with a boyfriend or girlfriend, for example, may give you a glimpse into the lives of children with major depressive disorder, who experience strong feelings of sadness almost every day.

Understanding Disorders and the Children Who Experience Them Involves the Use of Values

Values influence the way we think about childhood disorders and how they develop, as well as the importance we assign to reducing or eliminating them. Values also influence the meanings we ascribe to the behaviors of children, parents, and other adults; whether we conclude that these behaviors are appropriate or inappropriate; and consequently how we respond to them. For example, some researchers assert that school-age boys are more aggressive than school-age girls because social values are more tolerant of aggression in boys than girls, so parents, teachers, and other adults focus more attention on reducing aggression in girls than boys (Coie & Dodge, 1998).

Recognizing the role that values play in our thinking helps us accurately assess the extent to which our thinking is influenced by our values rather than by some objective understanding of the way the universe functions. For example, recognizing the role of values in our thinking reduces the chance that we will label a child's behavior as a symptom of a disorder simply because it does not conform to our views of appropriate behaviors for children. We can use our values to conclude that a behavior is a problem, and possibly that it should be reduced or eliminated; but it is important to understand that this conclusion is based partly on our values.

Many types of values can influence how we think about children's behaviors. Some values come from the cultural contexts in which we live. Most people in our culture, for example, believe that all people should be afforded the same basic rights. This is one reason that we consider the sexual abuse of children to be wrong: An adult should not be able to damage a child in pursuit of sex because doing so says that the adult is fundamentally more important than the child. Other values may be based on racial, ethnic, national, or religious heritage. Some childhood behaviors might be considered problematic in many Asian–American families but not in most European–American families. A behavior considered wrong by fundamentalist Christians might not be considered wrong by Hindus.

Values can also come from smaller contexts, such as neighborhoods or families. For example, physical aggression in response to a verbal challenge might be viewed differently in large urban neighborhoods than in the suburbs surrounding the same urban areas, and these differences might cross races and religions. The values of individual families in a neighborhood may differ: Some families think physical aggression in response to a verbal challenge is wrong, whereas other families disagree.

Our Ultimate Focus Is on Children, Not Disorders

Although our focus in this text is on childhood disorders, it is essential to keep in mind that our ultimate focus is on the children with these disorders. As we try to understand the development of schizophrenia in a child, for example, we must remember that we are discussing a child who is troubled and in pain. While we work to understand how a disorder develops, often using data gathered through scientific methods, we must not forget our humanity or lose sight of the children who are struggling with the disorder, the members of their families, and many others who know them and care about them.

Our ultimate focus is on children and their families.

Key Concepts

- Many issues influence the development of child psychopathology. They form a complex web of influences that is unique for each child.
- Issues often combine to influence the development of psychopathology in a child.
- The relative influence of issues varies from child to child.
- Many children experience more than one disorder. In some cases, two or more disorders develop independently; but more frequently one disorder influences the development of an additional disorder.
- The behaviors and emotions that are the symptoms of each disorder lie along a continuum.
- Values influence how we define and think about child psychopathology.
- It is important to remember that our ultimate focus is on children experiencing disorders, their families, and those who interact with them in their communities.

The Field of Developmental Psychopathology

The field of developmental psychopathology began to emerge in the 1970s as several researchers began to think about psychopathology in children and adults in new ways (Cicchetti, 1984). The perspective taken by these researchers was broader than the perspectives of many researchers in the fields of clinical child psychology or psychiatry. Whereas those in clinical child psychology or psychiatry focused primarily on children who had been diagnosed with one or more disorders, those in developmental psychopathology were also interested in understanding the connections between normal and disordered behaviors and the development of children who showed early signs of psychopathology but never developed a disorder (Sroufe & Rutter, 1984). In addition, developmental psychopathologists focused on how disorders developed in children over time, including the characteristics and experiences of the children and their environments that seemed to push some toward developing a disorder and pull others away from developing the same disorder.

For example, consider several preschool-age girls who are badly abused by their parents and whose abuse influences them to believe that relationships are based on aggression and power. In elementary school, some of these girls may become aggressive and bully other children, and some may become meek and withdraw from other children. In high school, some of the aggressive girls may join gangs in which they can express their aggression and dominance over others. Other aggressive girls may join athletic teams, and one might even be the first girl on her school's wrestling team and be seen in her school as a crusader for women's rights. Some of the withdrawn girls may enter a series of relationships with boys in which they are victimized. Others may find work in a nursery school for abused children, where their quiet nature makes them effective teachers for frightened children. Developmental psychopathologists are interested in understanding how their characteristics and experiences pushed some of these girls in one direction and others of them elsewhere, and how these characteristics and experiences interacted with their physical, cognitive, emotional, and social development to produce the types of behaviors they exhibited during childhood and adolescence (Achenbach, 1990).

As shown in Figure 1.5, Achenbach (1990) suggests that theories from many different paradigms can be used by people in the developmental psychopathology field to understand the development or absence of psychopathology in children. (Many of these paradigms and theories are discussed in the following chapters covering basic psychological theories and quantitative

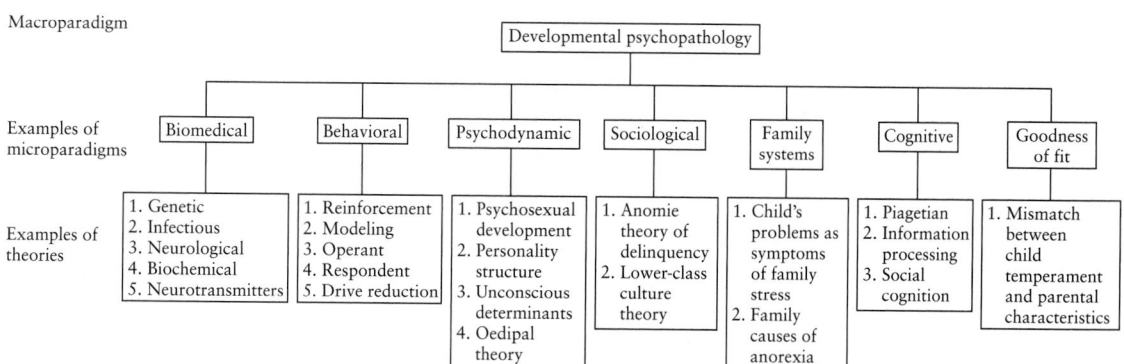

FIGURE 1.5   *Schematic Overview of Developmental Psychopathology in Relation to Other Conceptual Levels*

behavioral genetics.) For example, when contemplating the adolescent behaviors of the girls just mentioned, developmental psychopathologists might consider the following:

- The genetically influenced tendencies toward impulsivity that pushed some girls toward aggression and the genetically influenced tendencies toward anxious and fearful behavior that pushed others toward withdrawal.
- The different patterns of reinforcement the girls experienced for various behaviors.
- The girls' unconscious issues and how these issues influenced them at different stages in their cognitive and emotional development.
- The extent to which the girls' behaviors played important roles in the functioning of their families.
- How the girls' temperaments matched the styles of their parents.

Combining the information from Achenbach's model with the information from Bronfenbrenner's model (Figure 1.2) paints the complex web of influences on children's lives that those in the field of developmental psychopathology consider. An important goal in developmental psychopathology is to assess how these influences operate in the lives of children throughout their development.

Concepts in Developmental Psychopathology

Several concepts emerged from the work of early developmental psychopathologists based on their interest in (1) exploring the influences on normal and abnormal development and (2) distinguishing the characteristics and experiences of children from similar circumstances who developed disorders and who did not. In this section we review two of these concepts that have been the most influential in understanding child psychopathology. Both focus on the complex web of issues that can influence an individual child's behavior.

Multifinality and Equifinality

Multifinality is the term describing the concept that similar experiences can result in different outcomes (Wilden, 1980). For instance, the abuse experienced by the girls in the previous example influenced all their lives, but the outcomes of the abuse differed. As another example, consider three brothers who are close in age and have parents who are very concerned about their sons' academic achievement. The parents monitor their sons' academic performance, provide enriching activities such as trips to museums, and provide extra homework each night. By the time they are in high school, one son may have thrived on the parents' attention and be at the head of his class academically and socially; another may have become highly anxious about his academic performance but still receives excellent grades; and the third may have become so angry with his parents that he frequently refuses to do his homework or study for tests and so is barely making passing grades.

Of course many different characteristics and experiences of children influence their different outcomes despite their common experiences. Some of these characteristics or experiences may be present before their common experiences. Returning to the example of the three brothers, one brother may have a genetically influenced level of intelligence that is below that of his brothers and so may experience ongoing frustration with his parents' insistence on high academic performance. Other characteristics or experiences may occur after or during the common experiences. For example, the first- and second-grade teachers of one brother might have put considerable academic pressure on him, whereas the teachers of the other brothers were more relaxed.

Overall, then, multifinality prevents us from starting with one experience and predicting the future outcome for a child. Instead each experience can lead to many possible outcomes, depending on the myriad other characteristics and experiences that are part of the child's life (Cicchetti, 2002).

Equifinality is the term used for the concept that different characteristics and experiences can lead to the same outcome (Wilden, 1980). For example, as we will explore in the chapter about anxiety disorders, several characteristics and experiences can lead to high levels of anxiety. Some children have a genetically influenced level of fearfulness that can generate high levels of anxiety; other children are raised in families where anxious behavior is reinforced; and others live in neighborhoods where frequent violence causes high levels of anxiety. Consequently, equifinality prevents us from observing a common outcome for a group of children and then believing that we can look back in time to discover the common characteristics or experiences that created the outcome. Instead we must explore for the many different characteristics and experiences that may have led to the outcome.

Risk Factors and Protective Factors

A hallmark of the field of developmental psychopathology is the focus on risk factors and protective factors. **Risk factors** are characteristics or experiences of a child or the child's environment that increase the child's likelihood of experiencing a negative outcome such as school failure or developing a disorder. **Protective factors** are characteristics or experiences that reduce the child's likelihood of experiencing a negative outcome.

The concept of risk and protective factors came from pioneering research by Norman Garmezy and his colleagues. Their initial research in the 1950s focused on children of parents who had schizophrenia, investigating the characteristics and experiences of these children that were associated with an increased or decreased likelihood of their developing a disorder or other significant problem during their childhood or adolescence (Garmezy & Rodnick, 1959). This led to a broader inquiry, Project Competence, that investigated children's characteristics and experiences associated with positive developmental outcomes, particularly in children living in circumstances (such as poverty) with a higher likelihood of poor developmental outcomes

Poverty is a risk factor for many forms of child psychopathology.

(Garmezy, 1985; Garmezy & Rutter, 1983). Project Competence provided some of the first systematic information about the role of protective factors in children's lives (Rutter, 1981).

Ongoing research through Project Competence and other programs has identified a variety of characteristics and experiences at the individual, family, and community levels that are associated with a greater likelihood of poor and good developmental outcomes (Masten & Coatsworth, 1998). Most of these characteristics and experiences can be seen as lying along a continuum, with the characteristic or experience being a risk factor if it is toward one end and a protective factor if it is toward the other (Masten & Powell, 2003). For example, individual-level protective factors include good intellectual functioning, a sociable and outgoing style of interacting with others, appropriate levels of self-esteem and self-confidence, one or more talents, and a sense of faith. Protective factors at the family level include a close relationship with caring parents, family income that is adequate to meet basic needs, connections to a supportive extended family, and parents with high levels of warmth, structure, and expectations. Community-level protective factors include relationships with caring adults outside the family (such as teachers or coaches), involvement with social organizations (like Boys' and Girls' Clubs), and attending good schools (Yates, Egeland, & Sroufe, 2003). Risk factors include characteristics such as poor intellectual functioning, low self-esteem, distant relationships with parents, living in poverty, few relationships with caring adults outside the family, and attending dysfunctional schools.

A consistent finding of risk factor research is that the number of risk factors a child experiences, rather than any particular risk factor, is the best predictor of negative developmental outcomes (Masten & Powell, 2003). In studies of aggression, for example, children who experience three or four risk factors are much more likely to have problematic levels of aggression than are children experiencing one risk factor (Loeber & Hay, 1997). Studies of protective factors show the same pattern: Children experiencing several protective factors are much less likely to experience a negative outcome than are children with one protective factor.

Finally, we do not know enough about risk and protective factors to balance the factors experienced by a specific child and accurately predict outcomes. Studies of risk and protective factors have used groups of children and so can say that, within a group of children, those with more risk factors and fewer protective factors are more likely to experience negative developmental outcomes. However, this knowledge does not let us predict the outcome of each child in the group. For example, some children experiencing several risk factors and few protective factors will have good developmental outcomes. The percentage of children with several risk factors and few protective factors who experience good developmental outcomes will be lower than the percentage of children with few risk factors and several protective factors; but some who are less likely to have good developmental outcomes will nevertheless do well. So we must be careful not to assume the future of an individual child based on knowledge of the risk and protective factors that he or she has experienced.

Using the Concepts of Risk and Protective Factors in Preventive and Therapeutic Interventions

Knowing about risk and protective factors is useful for designing preventive and therapeutic interventions. For example, many community-based programs created to foster children's positive development employ the concept of protective factors. Boys' and Girls' Clubs, 4-H Clubs, and other youth organizations foster positive development by providing caring adults with whom children can associate, developing children's skills, and enhancing children's social interactions. The usefulness of understanding protective factors in preventing specific disorders can also be seen in programs designed for children or their parents. For example, preventive interventions designed to foster good parenting skills have successfully reduced the frequency of children's attachment problems and conduct problems (Olds, 1989; Toth et al., 2002).

Many therapeutic interventions are also based on knowledge of risk and protective factors. For example, as we will see throughout this text, therapeutic interventions for many disorders include social skills training for children. Poor social skills are often not directly related to the development of the disorders for which the children are receiving therapy. However, our knowledge that good social skills are protective factors for children, and thus can enhance their functioning and help them avoid a relapse of their disorder, encourages the inclusion of social skills training in their therapy.

Key Concepts

- The field of developmental psychopathology focuses on understanding the connections between normal and disordered behaviors, how certain experiences or characteristics of children interact with their development to cause disorders and other problems, and how disorders develop over time.
- Developmental psychopathology employs many theories from clinical and developmental psychology to understand the development of disordered and nondisordered behavior.
- *Multifinality* refers to the concept that many outcomes can be influenced by a common experience.
- *Equifinality* refers to the concept that many experiences can influence a common outcome.
- Risk factors are characteristics or experiences of a child or the child's environment that increase the child's likelihood of experiencing a negative developmental outcome.
- Protective factors are characteristics or experiences of a child or the child's environment that increase the child's likelihood of experiencing a positive developmental outcome or that reduce the child's likelihood of experiencing a negative outcome.
- The value of understanding risk and protective factors can be seen in the frequency with which they are involved in preventive or therapeutic interventions.

CHAPTER GLOSSARY

Equifinality refers to the concept that a common outcome can be influenced by many different experiences.

Multifinality refers to the concept that a common experience can result in many different outcomes.

Protective factors are characteristics or experiences of a child or the child's environment that increase the child's likelihood of experiencing a positive developmental outcome.

Risk factors are characteristics or experiences of a child or the child's environment that increase the child's likelihood of experiencing a negative developmental outcome.

Research Methods and Ethical Issues

Many ethical issues must be considered during research with children.

All psychologists and other mental health practitioners need to understand two foundations of work with children and families: research methods and ethical issues. Research forms the scientific foundation for work with children and families, and ethical principles guide research and clinical interventions.

Chapter Plan

We start this chapter by exploring some basic research methods and issues. I will take a somewhat unique approach and organize our exploration as research articles are usually organized. We begin by exploring the information provided in the introduction to a research article and the reasons why researchers provide this information before they discuss the methods and results of their studies. We then explore the most important section of any research article: the methods section. We examine issues related to the sample used in the study and the population the sample represents, basic characteristics of measures that can be used in a study, and the variety of research designs that can be employed. We then explore the results section and focus on the meaning of the probability statistic. Finally we explore the interpretation of the results that appears in the discussion section. In the second part of this chapter we explore a variety of ethical issues. After two case examples, we explore three basic ethical principles: autonomy, beneficence and nonmaleficence, and confidentiality. We review each basic principle and focus on how it relates specifically to therapy and research involving children. Finally we review the function of institutional review boards—committees at many institutions charged with ensuring that research conducted there meets ethical and legal standards.

Research Methods

Some social science students approach courses in research methods and statistics with anxiety and a sense that they will learn little useful material. This is sad because research forms the foundation of our knowledge in the social sciences and in child psychopathology in particular; and knowing how research is conducted and how data are analyzed is essential for understanding the foundation of our science. Further, as we discuss in this chapter, the quality of individual studies varies. Those who examine research to understand the prevalence, consequences, or etiology of behavioral or emotional disorders must be able to identify good research to correctly understand these disorders. In addition, those who use research to create and implement therapeutic interventions for children and families must be able to distinguish good research from poor research because interventions based on poor research may be ineffective or harmful. Thus knowledge about research methods and statistics is essential for those working with children and families, even for those who do not conduct research themselves.

People who do not understand research methods and statistics also miss learning that the research process is fascinating and intellectually challenging. Most researchers enjoy having a whole day to explore the data from their studies. The results from one analysis can raise interesting questions, and it is a joy to have the time to explore these other questions as they arise. Too often other obligations get in the way of researchers having enough time to *play* with their data, squeezing out all the interesting bits of information.

Notes from the Author: Initial Responses to Research Methods and Statistics

I must admit that both as an undergraduate and then as a graduate student, I faced my first courses in statistics and research methods with trepidation. However, my trepidation was greatly reduced when I took additional courses in these areas because I used the basic knowledge from my first courses to address more complex and interesting questions. I also remember apprehension when I met my first therapy client and, now that I think of it, when I drove for the first time, began my first college course, and presented my research at a conference for the first time. There seems to be a pattern here. Unfortunately many students never take more than one statistics or research methods course, so they never experience the lessened anxiety and greater interest that come with advanced courses.

Research is challenging partly because researchers must make many difficult decisions about how to maximize the value of their research given the constraints they inevitably face. Who should be included in the research? There is seldom enough money to gather a sample that is as large and diverse as a researcher might like. What measures should be included? Research participants have limited patience and energy and are unwilling to complete every measure a researcher might want to administer. Deciding which statistical analyses to use can also be challenging because new statistical procedures are introduced regularly. Potential benefits and limitations are associated with each decision a researcher must make as a project is designed and implemented, and even the most experienced researchers find these challenges intellectually stimulating.

Not all the intricacies of research methods can be explored in this chapter; doing so would take an entire textbook. However, we will discuss many basic issues to provide a foundation for understanding the research presented in subsequent chapters.

Introduction

In the introduction to a research article, the researchers describe theories and previously completed studies that are relevant to the issues addressed by their research. There are two basic reasons for doing this.

The first reason is that describing theory and earlier research lets a researcher place the current study in historical context. Research in all sciences is an iterative, circular process (see Figure 2.1). Initially a theory or hypothesis can be created through observations, earlier research, or logical thought. For example, researchers studying depression in children might observe that children with depression have little contact with their peers during school hours. They might hypothesize that the other children push them away from activities because their depressed mood is bothersome. Studies can then be created to test the theory or hypothesis, or components of it. The studies' findings may cause revision of the theory or hypothesis to account for the findings. For example, the researchers may find that acting-out children are actively rejected by their peers, but children who are depressed are ignored by their peers. They may revise their hypothesis to state that children with depression are neglected by their peers rather than rejected by them. The revised theory or hypothesis can be tested through other studies and possibly revised again. Providing historical context lets the researchers describe where in this iterative process the current research appears.

A second reason for discussing theory and previous research in the introduction is that our knowledge about childhood behavioral or emotional disorders is based on a body of research. Knowledge in our field is not created by one or two massive studies that investigate all the relevant characteristics of a disorder and the children who have that disorder. Rather, it

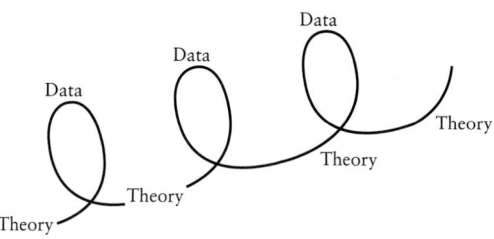

FIGURE 2.1 *The Iterative Process of Research*

is built gradually by amassing a body of research that includes many studies, each of which investigates a specific question using a sample of children with specific characteristics. For example, among researchers investigating conduct disorder, some will focus on its prevalence. One researcher might conduct studies that focus on prevalence differences between boys and girls, and another might examine prevalence differences among boys of different ages. Others will look into the etiology of conduct disorder, with some examining genetic influences, some family influences, and some peer influences. Even among those investigating family influences, some researchers might spotlight the influence of harsh parenting practices, some the role of parental stress, and some the physical spaces in which families live.

The introduction allows the researchers to describe how their study fits into the developing body of research about a disorder and how their study might enhance what is currently known. For example, a researcher might note that studies exploring interactions between children with ADHD and their parents have focused on mother–son interactions and that this study is designed to broaden our knowledge by focusing on father–son interactions (or perhaps mother–daughter or father–daughter interactions).

The introduction also gives researchers a chance to describe the limitations of previous studies and how the researchers' study avoids these limitations. For example, a researcher studying the etiology of phobias in children may note that previous studies included only children receiving treatment for a phobia. The researcher could then describe how this study includes both children who are receiving treatment and those who are not, thus painting a more comprehensive picture of the etiology of phobias.

Notes6 from the Author: Good and Bad Research

Almost all of us were educated in a system in which, from our earliest years, we read information in textbooks, tried to remember that information, and then were tested on it. The basic assumption was that what we read in our textbooks was true and thus should be remembered. These years of schooling have encouraged us to assume that when we read something *academic* we should remember it because it is true. However, this assumption can be incorrect. It is possible to find research published in some social science journals or book chapters that is so badly conducted that it is not clear whether its information is useful. To be a smart consumer of social science research, you must rid yourself of the belief that if you read something in a journal or a book it must be true. It *may* be true, but it may not be.

If it is not possible to automatically conclude that the findings of every published study provide useful information, then you are responsible for evaluating the usefulness of findings you read. The only way to assess the quality of a study is to read and analyze its methods section. As discussed in the following paragraphs, the methods section should contain detailed information about the sample, measures, and procedures used in the study. Only by analyzing the methods used in a study can you draw conclusions about the usefulness of its results.

Unfortunately, many people read the introduction to a research article and then skip to the results and discussion sections (or, even worse, skip directly to the discussion section). The danger of doing this is that a study may have been conducted in a way that dramatically reduces its usefulness. Those who skip the methods section will not know this, and thus they may absorb inaccurate and misleading information. Finally, I note with amazement that some journals print the methods section in a smaller font than the rest of a research article. This is silly because it may suggest that the methods section is the least important part of the research article. I believe publishers should print the methods section in a larger font to emphasize it.

Key Concepts

- The introduction to a research article includes theories and previous studies related to the study described in the article.
- The research process is a circular, iterative process. Theories or hypotheses are created and tested through research. They may be altered based on the research results. The altered theories or hypotheses are then tested through subsequent research.
- Through the accumulation of a body of research, knowledge about a childhood disorder is created. Researchers describe the current body of research in the introduction and how their research enhances what is currently known.

Methods

Participants
Population and Sample

Most statistics used in social science data analysis are **inferential statistics.** The goal of inferential statistics is to infer something about a **population** from a **sample** of that population that a researcher has included in a study. The population is the entire group a researcher is interested in investigating, and the researcher selects a sample from that population to include in the research.

Researchers select population samples because they usually do not have enough time or resources to include the whole population in their research. However, they are rarely interested in understanding the characteristics of only the sample. Rather, they want to use the results from their sample to understand something about the population that the sample represents. For example, say I was interested in learning whether there is a difference in intelligence between male and female undergraduates at Cornell. Because it is unlikely that I would have the time or funding to give IQ tests to all 13,000 Cornell undergraduates (the population), I could test 100 male undergraduates and 100 female undergraduates (the sample). I would then use inferential statistics to estimate the likelihood that any IQ differences in my sample (the 200 undergraduates) represent differences in the population (the 13,000 undergraduates at Cornell).

When assessing the meaning of study results, it is important to determine what population the study sample is meant to represent. Researchers often want to apply their research results to a large population. For example, consider a researcher who has assessed the effectiveness of a specific family therapy intervention provided to 50 families in Albuquerque, New Mexico, with adolescents who have conduct disorder. She is likely to want her research results to inform clinicians about this intervention with conduct-disordered adolescents across the United States, not just those living in Albuquerque. Similarly, researchers investigating the development of conduct disorder in a large sample of children in New Zealand probably want their research to lead to a further understanding of the development of conduct disorder in children overall, not just children in New Zealand.

The potential problem here, however, is that if any characteristics of a sample are related to the issue being investigated and are specific to the sample, it may be inappropriate to generalize the sample results to a larger population. For example, if characteristics of some families in Albuquerque make them more amenable to family therapy (perhaps Albuquerque families have higher levels of cohesion than families across the United States), then the results from the Albuquerque study of family therapy may not apply to families elsewhere. Similarly, if cultural issues specific to New Zealand influence the development of conduct problems (such as attitudes about the appropriateness of aggression in boys), results from the New Zealand study may not apply to the development of conduct problems in children in other countries.

To apply the research results obtained from a sample to a population, we must be sure the sample is *representative* of that population; that is, the characteristics and experiences of the sample that are related to the issue being investigated must be similar to the characteristics and experiences of the population. Not every characteristic or experience of the population must be present in the sample. However, all the population's characteristics and experiences that are theoretically or empirically related to the issue addressed by the research should be represented in the sample. For example, perhaps I want to examine the types and levels of aggression in elementary school girls in the United States by studying 2,000 elementary school girls from many different regions in New York State. It is obvious that my sample does not represent some characteristics of the population of U.S. elementary school girls (all of the girls come from one region of the country). However, if I can argue convincingly that the characteristics and experiences related to aggression in girls throughout the United States are represented in my sample (such as family income, type of neighborhood, and experiences of abuse), and that any unique characteristics of my sample (the region of the country in which the girls live) are not related to aggression, then I can assert that the results from my sample can be used to understand aggression in elementary school girls across the United States. Others may disagree and argue that some characteristics related to aggression are not represented in my sample. Honest disagreements about the representativeness of a sample can occur. These disagreements may be resolved through future research.

Random Selection   The best way to gather a representative sample from a population is to select that sample randomly from the population. **Random selection** occurs when each person in the population has an equal chance of being included in a sample. When the population is large, such as all children in the United States, this can be impossible because it is not feasible to create a sample in which every child in the United States has an equal chance of participating. However, several strategies can be used to approximate random selection of children from the United States. For example, several large, well-funded studies have used the strategy of randomly selecting U.S. schools and including a random sample of all children from those schools in their research. The National Longitudinal Study of Adolescent Health, for example, organized the 26,666 U.S. high schools into 80 groups based on several characteristics (such as region, school size, and percentage of children who were European–American or African–American) and then randomly chose one high school from each group and one junior/middle school that fed students into that high school. They then administered questionnaires to all students in the selected schools.

Random selection can also be difficult when the population being studied is more circumscribed. One impediment to gathering a random sample is that those in a study must participate voluntarily (and if children are in the sample, their parents must give them permission to participate). To the extent that people who choose to participate have different characteristics or experiences than those who do not choose to participate, the sample is not randomly selected. For example, if I were to study the family environments of children with anxiety disorders, I might select a sample from all the children showing high levels of anxiety in several schools. However, if few parents in families with high conflict are willing to have their children participate in the study because they are concerned about my observing their family conflict, and many parents in families with low conflict are willing to have their children participate in the study, the group of families from which I can select my sample may overrepresent families with low conflict levels and underrepresent families with high conflict levels. Consequently, even if I randomly select a sample from among the families willing to participate, my sample will not be representative of all families from those schools that have anxious children.

When study participants are not randomly selected from the population they are meant to represent, hypotheses need to be formed about how the sample differs from the population. These hypotheses are then used when interpreting the study results. If, for example, I believe that my study of family environments of anxious children included more children from low-conflict families, I need to interpret my results in that light. Perhaps I would conclude that my results represent the high end rather than the broad range of family functioning among children with anxiety disorders.

Response Rate   An important measure of the extent to which a sample is likely to represent a population is the **response rate**—that is, the percentage of the people who *could have* participated in the study who *did* participate. A low response rate raises concerns about sample representativeness because the small percentage choosing to participate may have characteristics or experiences that (1) influence their decision to participate in the study and (2) distinguish them from those who do not participate in ways that relate to issues addressed by the study.

For example, if I were interested in the prevalence of suicidal ideation (thinking seriously about suicide) among college students, I might distribute a questionnaire asking about suicidal ideation to 300 students in one of my courses. If only 30% of the students returned the questionnaire, I would be concerned that some characteristic related to suicidal ideation distinguished those who did and did not return the questionnaire. Perhaps those who had experienced suicidal ideation were more likely to return the questionnaire because it was an important topic to them. This would result in a prevalence estimate higher than the true prevalence among the 300 students because those who had not experienced suicidal ideation would be less likely to return the questionnaire. Alternately, perhaps experiencing suicidal ideation is so traumatic that those with that experience are less likely to return such a questionnaire because they do not want to recount their traumatic experiences. This would result in an artificially low prevalence estimate. However, if 90% of the students returned the questionnaire, I would be more confident that the prevalence estimate from the returned questionnaires represented the actual prevalence among the 300 students (although I would still worry about the responses from the 10% who did not participate).

Offering an incentive to complete a questionnaire or participate in other types of studies often increases response rates. For example, giving one point of extra credit has typically resulted in a response rate increase from about 30% to about 80% in courses where I have distributed questionnaires. Other researchers provide cash incentives to participate or enter all those who participate into a drawing for various prizes. However, as discussed later in this chapter, incentives cannot be so large that some potential participants feel coerced into participating. I cannot, for example, offer to raise everyone's grade one full letter for participating in a study, even though this might dramatically increase the response rate, because this very large incentive could coerce some students into participating even if they prefer not to do so. (This particular incentive might also skew the sample representativeness by encouraging participation by struggling students while having no effect on students who usually get top grades.)

Measures

The measures in a research study are the instruments used to gather information from participants. Structured and unstructured interviews, direct observations, neurological examinations, self-reports, reports by others, and tests are all types of measures commonly used in social science research. Each type of measure has potential benefits and liabilities, and these are discussed throughout this text—primarily in the section of each chapter about the process of determining whether a child meets the diagnostic criteria for a disorder. Consequently we will not explore the potential benefits and liabilities of different types of measures here. Rather we will focus on two basic characteristics of all measures: reliability and validity. To be of any value, measures must be both reliable and valid. As we will see, several types of reliability and validity exist.

Reliability

Reliability refers to the degree to which a measure produces consistent results. A reliable measure produces stable scores that are influenced to only a small degree by error. Different types of reliability are important, depending on the type of measure being used.

> **Error:** *Error* has a somewhat unique meaning in research. Rather than meaning that the researcher has done something wrong, *error* refers to any variability of scores that is not directly related to the issue being measured. For example, consider error in the measurement of intelligence. Intelligence tests include a wide array of questions that range from very easy to very difficult. The more questions a child answers correctly, the higher the child's IQ score will be (see the chapter about mental retardation for more information about intelligence tests). During an intelligence test, most children will guess the answers to several questions. Some children will guess more items correctly than will other children. So children's *success at guessing* has some influence on their IQ scores. Because the variation in IQ scores due to success at guessing is caused by something other than intelligence (the issue being measured), the variation caused by success at guessing is considered error.

The type of reliability that is usually the most important for tests is **test–retest reliability:** a measure of the extent to which a person receives the same scores on a test when taking it more than once during a short period (such as a week). Test–retest reliability is usually measured by the correlation of a person's scores from two administrations of the test. Because the characteristics measured by most tests (such as intelligence or self-esteem) do not change much over a short period, a useful test should have high test–retest reliability. Scores of tests that vary by a meaningful amount over a short period are likely to contain a significant amount of error (in other words, something other than the issue being measured is influencing the test scores).

As a straightforward example of this, consider measuring the height of a sample of children (Mitchell & Jolley, 2001). To test your measuring device (perhaps a tape measure), you measured a child at noon each day for three days in a row in exactly the same conditions. If you found that this child's height was 48 inches one day, 47 inches the next day, and 49 inches the third day, you would likely become concerned about the reliability of your measuring device because you know that a child's height does not increase or decrease by inches over the period of a day. You would know that the different heights you obtained were probably due to error produced by your measuring device, and you would probably say, "Get rid of this tape measure—it is no good." The same conclusion could be reached if you measured intelligence in a sample of children once a month for three months using the same test in the same conditions. If you found that the scores of may children differed guide a bit from month to month, you would become concerned about the amount of error associated with the test. You might want to get rid of that measuring device also.

A reliable test is not expected to produce exactly the same score every time for every person: Error produced by issues other than the measuring device is likely to influence some scores. For example, if a child taking an intelligence test for the second time is not feeling well or did not get enough sleep the night before, his scores on the test may be lower than they were during the first administration. However, a reliable test should produce similar scores for most people taking a test twice during a short period.

One form of reliability that is commonly assessed with interviews and direct observations is **interrater reliability,** which refers to the extent to which two individuals agree on their assessment of something. If two people are rating the amount of conflict during interactions between mothers and sons, for example, they should provide the same conflict rating if they both observe the same mother–son interaction. If they provide different ratings (perhaps one rates the conflict as high and the other as moderate), then the ratings' variability would be due to something related to the observers rather than to the amount of conflict in the interaction. Consequently, the variability would be due to error. To increase interrater reliability, specific rules or guidelines for rating observations are given to raters, who are trained to use these guidelines to produce the same ratings (that is, error is minimized).

Validity

There are several meanings to the term **validity** in research, but generally it refers to whether a measure truly measures what it claims to. **Construct validity** is the extent to which a measure truly measures the construct it claims to measure. Does the Beck Depression Inventory truly measure depression, or does it measure some other characteristic (like crabbiness or nervousness)? Does the State–Trait Anxiety Scale truly measure state anxiety and trait anxiety, or does it measure something else (such as sadness or embarrassment)?

> **Constructs:** A **construct** (pronounced with the accent on the first syllable) is a psychological characteristic that we have constructed/ created (we con struct´ a con´ struct). A construct does not exist in the same way that a walnut, a house, or you and I exist. Rather, people have decided that it exists and have named it. Most characteristics that psychologists find interesting are constructs, such as intelligence, self-esteem, motivation, depression, and anxiety. Constructs cannot be measured directly, and in this way they differ from characteristics such as height or weight. Because we cannot measure constructs directly, we create tests to measure them; so there are tests for intelligence, self-esteem, depression, and so forth.

Mitchell and Jolley (2001) describe several steps to establish the construct validity of a measure. First a visual inspection of the measure assesses whether it adequately covers all the components of the construct it is designed to measure. This is referred to as **content validity.** For example, a scale measuring ADHD should include items that assess all the symptoms included in the diagnostic criteria for ADHD.

Next the measure is given to a large sample of people (or many samples), and their scores on the measure are used to assess several characteristics of the measure. First **internal consistency** is assessed. This is the extent to which all the items in the measure, or all the items in each subscale of the measure, assess the same construct. A statistic can be computed to measure internal consistency, which is basically the mean of the correlations of each item with the other items in the measure or subscale. Individual items that do not correlate highly enough with the other items can be identified and dropped from the measure.

Once a measure has satisfactory internal consistency, the next step is to assess its **convergent validity,** which is the extent to which the measure produces scores similar to those of other valid indicators of the construct. A test's convergent validity is frequently assessed by correlating scores from the test with scores from other tests that are valid measures of the construct. For example, to assess the convergent validity of a new test for depression, I might give it and the Beck Depression Inventory (a valid test of depressive symptoms) to a sample of undergraduates and calculate the correlation of each person's scores on the two tests. If the correlation is high, I can argue that the new test for depression has convergent validity. Convergent validity for a test can also be assessed by correlating test scores with other indicators of a construct. For example, I could assess how well scores on the new test for depression correlate with clinicians' assessments of the severity of depressive symptoms.

Finally, **discriminant validity** is assessed; this is a measure's ability to distinguish between the construct being measured and other constructs. For example, a measure of depression should correlate more strongly with another measure of depression than it does with a measure of anxiety. To have discriminant validity, a measure does not have to be unrelated to other constructs—some constructs are likely to occur together in many people, so we would expect to find positive correlations between measures of these constructs. However, we should find higher positive correlations between constructs that frequently occur together than we would find for constructs that seldom occur together. For example, we should find higher positive correlations between tests of depression and tests of anxiety than between tests of depression and tests of self-esteem.

To the extent that a new measure adequately assesses a construct (content validity), has good internal consistency, produces scores that correlate highly with valid measures of the same construct (convergent validity), and discriminates between the construct being measured and other constructs, we can argue that the new measure has good construct validity.

**Notes from the Author: Lack of Clarity about
Construct Validity**

Many tests used in social science research have well-established reliability and validity. However, not all do; so the conclusions drawn from research using these tests must be viewed with caution. An example of the problems associated with using a test without construct validity comes from two studies of the racial/ethnic identity of transracially/transethnically adopted children. Both studies used the Twenty Statements Test, which has a child give 20 short answers to the question "Who am I?" McRoy, Zurcher, Lauderdale, and Anderson (1982) found that black children adopted by white families (their descriptive terms) gave answers that referred to their race more frequently than black children adopted by black families. They interpreted this finding as meaning that the transracially adopted children had more conflict about their racial identity. Andujo (1988) found that Mexican–American children adopted by white families referred to themselves as Mexican–American less frequently than Mexican–American children adopted by Mexican–American families. She interpreted this finding as meaning that the transethnically adopted children had a poorer general acceptance of their ethnicity. Essentially these researchers asserted that their results indicated poorer racial/ethnic identity in children raised in transracial/transethnic families, but they based their arguments on opposite results from the Twenty Statements Test.

The problem in interpreting the results of either study is that the validity of the Twenty Statements Test for measuring the construct of racial/ethnic identity has not been established. If a child includes a response that mentions her race/ethnicity, does this mean that she has stronger or weaker racial/ethnic identity? It simply is not clear. Thus the validity of the Twenty Statements Test for measuring the construct of racial/ethnic identity is not obvious, and interpretations of the findings from research based on the Twenty Statements Test are suspect.

Procedures

Almost all social science research involves comparisons. These comparisons can take place on many levels: A child's behavior after taking a medication can be compared to her behavior beforehand; the IQs of children living in a commune can be compared to norms for children their ages; the number of aggressive behaviors displayed by boys can be compared to the number displayed by girls; or the dieting behavior of a group of girls can be compared each year as they progress through adolescence. Without comparison, it is difficult or impossible to know what an observation of a child's behavior means. For example, if I know that a sample of 7-year-old maltreated girls wet their beds on average once a month, this knowledge is not particularly useful unless I know how often older maltreated girls wet their beds or how often 7-year-old girls who have not been maltreated wet their beds. Many research designs create the types of comparisons that are useful in the social sciences.

In this section we first review some basic distinctions between these research designs and then focus on several specific research designs.

Basic Distinctions in Research Designs

Experimental Designs   An important strategy in many types of research is to isolate the influence a variable has on some outcome so that variable's amount of influence on the outcome can be assessed. Experimental designs are particularly useful for isolating the influence of a specific variable. For example, a researcher may be interested in whether a medication decreases children's symptoms of obsessive–compulsive disorder. An experimental design can isolate the influence of the medication on the symptoms of obsessive–compulsive disorder from the influence of other variables (such as child temperament, number of siblings in the child's family, or quality of the child's day care). Consequently the specific influence of the medication can be assessed. In experimental designs, the **independent variable** is the variable manipulated in the study (in our example, the medication), and the **dependent variable** is the variable that the independent variable is hypothesized to influence (obsessive–compulsive symptoms in our example).

The hallmark of an **experimental design** is that the research participants are **randomly assigned** to one of two or more groups, each of which receives a different level of the independent variable. For example, in a study of the influence of medication on obsessive–compulsive disorder, one group might receive a high dose of the medication, one group a low dose, and one group no medication. Random assignment occurs when each participant has an equal chance of being assigned to any group. To randomly assign 60 children to the three groups used in this study, for example, I might place 20 yellow, 20 green, and 20 red slips of paper in a box and randomly draw one slip for each child, thus assigning that child to one of the three groups.

Random assignment is the best way to equally distribute among groups all the characteristics and experiences of research participants that might influence the dependent variable. In this way, the other characteristics and experiences are *controlled*—that is, they are equalized among the groups. Thus when differences in the level of the dependent variable are observed, they can be attributed to the independent variable because it is the only factor that has varied systematically among the groups.

Correlational Designs   Although experimental designs offer the most assurance that variables other than the independent variable have been controlled, experimental designs are difficult to use for investigations of many issues of interest to researchers in the area of child psychopathology. For example, it is obvious that children cannot be randomly assigned to a group that receives harsh parenting and another group that does not receive harsh parenting to assess the influence of this factor on conduct-disordered behavior. Similarly, children cannot be randomly assigned to anxious or nonanxious parents to assess the influence of parental anxiety on children's anxiety.

Because of these challenges, much research in the area of child psychopathology is **correlational research,** which involves exploring for characteristics that are associated; the correlation statistics are used to determine the strength of the associations. For example, I could measure the intensity of anxiety in a sample of parents and their children and compute a correlation statistic describing the strength of the association between parental and child anxiety for the sample. Similarly, I could measure the frequency of harsh parenting that each child in a sample has experienced and the level of the child's conduct-disordered behavior, and calculate their correlation.

Several different correlation statistics can be calculated, depending on the type of data gathered. However, all correlation statistics range from -1 to $+1$. Positive correlations indicate that the association between two variables goes in the same direction. For example, height and weight are often positively correlated: Greater heights are usually associated with greater weights. Negative correlations indicate that the association between two variables goes in the opposite direction. For example, the correlation between symptoms of ADHD and academic achievement is usually negative: Greater levels of ADHD symptoms are usually associated with lower academic achievement levels.

To the degree that two characteristics are correlated, I can hypothesize about the influence of one characteristic on the other. If there is a strong positive correlation between frequent harsh parenting and conduct-disordered behavior, for example, I can hypothesize that harsh parenting influences conduct-disordered behavior.

The principal shortcoming of correlational research is that it cannot confirm hypotheses about the direction of influence between two variables. "Correlation does not equal causation" is the mantra of many researchers and statistics professors. If I find a strong positive correlation between harsh parenting and conduct-disordered behavior, I cannot conclude that harsh parenting causes conduct-disordered behavior. Correlational designs do not allow assessment of what is causing something else; they simply show whether things are associated. For example, perhaps I found a correlation of .45 between harsh parenting and conduct-disordered behavior in a sample of children. I would find this same correlation if any of the following were true:

- Harsh parenting influenced the development of conduct-disordered behaviors in children.
- A child's conduct-disordered behaviors influenced the development of harsh parenting.
- One or more other issues influenced both harsh parenting and conduct-disordered behaviors—such as neighborhood violence or a genetic tendency toward impulsivity in the parents and child.

It is tempting to speculate about cause and effect from the results of correlational research. However, this must be done with caution because conclusions about cause and effect cannot be based solely on studies using correlational designs.

Retrospective and Prospective Designs **Retrospective designs** ask people to recall events from their past. In some research, retrospective designs may assess the timing of the onset of a disorder's symptoms. For example, parents may be asked to recall when a child's first significant symptoms of depression began, or a child may be asked to recall when his frequent headaches began. Retrospective studies can also explore associations between past experiences or between past experiences and current symptoms. For example, undergraduates may be asked to describe childhood abuse or neglect experiences and complete tests of their current self-esteem and depression. The researcher could then explore associations between the intensity of the participants' early maltreatment and their current self-esteem and depression.

Retrospective studies have a strong advantage of being relatively easy to design and implement because information about many years of a person's life can be gathered through an interview or questionnaire. The principal disadvantage of retrospective studies is uncertainty about whether participants are recalling events accurately. In some cases, it may simply be difficult to recall something accurately, such as whether a 10-year-old's autistic symptoms began at 12 or 18 months of age. We also know that the biases of people's perceptions and memories can significantly influence the accuracy of their retrospective reports. As we will see in several following chapters, for example, children with conduct disorder often have a biased perception of the world in that they see hostility where most children do not. Similarly, children with anxiety disorders often perceive danger and threat where other children do not. Thus data about childhood experiences provided by adults with criminal histories or high levels of anxiety may reflect the biases of their childhood memories and perceptions as well as their actual experiences. As a result, the accuracy of retrospective reports is often unclear, which can raise questions about the usefulness of the data gathered.

Prospective designs follow a group of people forward in time and assess certain characteristics and experiences through periodic interviews, observations, or behavioral reports. An obvious advantage of prospective designs is that behaviors, cognitions, or emotions can be assessed while they are happening (such as periodic observations of parent–child interactions). Even when prospective studies ask about recent events ("How frequently have you experienced headaches in the past two weeks?"), the period a child or parent is asked to recall is shorter, so memories are likely to be more accurate.

However, prospective studies can take years to complete and often are expensive. For example, a researcher may be able to complete a retrospective study of the association between early childhood attachment and symptoms of adolescent depression in several months, whereas a researcher using a prospective design will have to wait 15 years or so to complete a similar study. In addition, knowing that they will be questioned by a researcher periodically may change the "natural" course of children's behavior, so the information from a prospective study may not accurately reflect the experiences of children not involved in a study. For example, pretend you are in a prospective study of romantic relationships and are asked, with your partner present, how often you express your love for him or her during interviews occurring every four months. Would knowing that you will be asked about this periodically influence how often you express your love?

Specific Research Designs

Single-Case Designs   **Single-case designs** compare one person's behaviors or characteristics at different points in time. Typically these designs are used to test the effectiveness of an intervention. For example, a boy diagnosed with pica (eating nonnutritive substances) might be given a behavioral intervention to reduce his pica behaviors. The frequency of his pica behaviors could be monitored before the intervention, right after the intervention, and then periodically for several weeks. Comparing the frequency of his pica behaviors before and after the intervention would assess its effectiveness. Similar studies could be done with medication. For example, a child diagnosed with ADHD could be given the stimulant medication Ritalin on some days and a **placebo** (an inert substance) on other days; comparing his behaviors across these days could show whether the Ritalin was influencing his behavior.

Between-Group Designs   **Between-group designs** compare behaviors or characteristics of people in two or more groups. The goal of between-group designs is to judge whether the characteristic that distinguishes the groups is associated with the issue being assessed. For example, the frequency of aggressive behavior could be compared between 6-year-old boys and 6-year-old girls. To the extent that an association exists, it can be hypothesized that sex, the characteristic that distinguishes these groups, influences the frequency of aggressive behavior.

To evaluate any association between a characteristic that distinguishes groups and the issue being assessed, it is important to minimize any other characteristics that distinguish the groups. If the groups differ in more than characteristic, we cannot hypothesize which characteristic may be influencing the issue being assessed. For example, if in the study of aggression in 6-year-olds the girls had a higher level of intelligence than the boys, it would not be possible to know whether sex or level of intelligence was associated with aggression level.

It is often difficult or impossible in between-group designs to form groups that are identical except for one characteristic. However, the influences of other characteristics can be controlled statistically if they have been measured. This requires that all other characteristics that distinguish the groups be measured. For this reason, researchers often measure many characteristics that may distinguish the groups so that if any of them do, their influence can be controlled during the statistical analysis. However, it can be difficult to know if all the characteristics that distinguish the groups have been measured, which can limit confidence in the conclusions from studies using between-group designs.

Between-Group Designs in Intervention Research   The effectiveness of preventive or therapeutic interventions is often assessed using between-group designs. Typically one group of children receives an intervention and another group does not, and their functioning is compared after the intervention. When the effectiveness of an intervention is being assessed, the groups are often divided into experimental groups (those receiving the intervention) and a comparison or control group (those not receiving the intervention). In many studies these groups are formed through random assignment.

An important ethical consideration in between-group studies of interventions is what to do with those in the control group. If it is hypothesized that the intervention will be useful to those receiving it, it may be unethical to withhold this potentially useful intervention from those in the control group. Many researchers overcome this potential ethical problem by using a **wait-list control group**. Those in a wait-list control group are eligible to receive the same intervention as those in the experimental group but at a later time. Once the data collection period is over, the intervention is offered to those in the wait-list control group if it has been effective. Another strategy is to use a **community-care control group**. In this strategy, the experimental group is given a specific intervention, and those in the community-care control group are told to pursue whatever treatment they would normally pursue in their communities. Thus those in the community-care control group are not denied any intervention; they are simply denied the specific intervention that those in the experimental group receive.

A potential problem with using between-group designs to assess the effectiveness of an intervention is that it can be difficult to determine whether the specific intervention caused differences observed between the groups or whether simply being involved in any form of intervention caused these differences. For example, if eight weeks of cognitive–behavioral therapy are given to a sample of children with major depressive disorder, and three months after the intervention they are less depressed than children in the wait-list control group, it is not possible to know if the specific nature of the cognitive–behavioral therapy reduced the depression or whether simply meeting with a caring adult for eight weeks caused this improvement.

An attention control group can help determine whether the nature of an intervention caused any differences observed between experimental and control groups. Those in an **attention control group** receive the same amount of contact with a professional as those in an experimental group, but this contact is designed to not include any characteristics of the intervention being assessed. For example, children in an attention control group might meet with a research team member who helps them with their schoolwork, plays with them, or works with them on art projects for the same amount of time that children in the experimental group are meeting with a therapist. If children in the experimental group have fewer symptoms than those in the attention control group at the end of the study, it can be argued with more confidence that the specific characteristics of the intervention reduced the symptoms.

Cross-Sectional and Longitudinal Designs   Because the field of developmental psychopathology is particularly concerned with the development of disorders over time, two research designs that allow comparisons at different ages are often used: cross-sectional designs and longitudinal designs. **Cross-sectional designs** explore characteristics or behaviors among groups of children of different ages. For example, the frequency of anxiety symptoms could be assessed in groups of 6-, 9-, and 12-year-old children to determine whether the frequency of anxiety symptoms is associated with age. Cross-sectional designs are popular because they can be completed in a relatively short period and consequently are often less expensive. However, as with between-group designs, care must be taken to ensure that any characteristics or experiences, other than their age, that distinguish the children in the groups are controlled through sample selection or measured and controlled through statistical analysis.

Longitudinal designs follow a group of children (called a **cohort**) over time, with information gathered from the group at different ages. For example, rather than measuring the frequency of anxiety symptoms in 6-, 9-, and 12-year-old children using a cross-sectional design, the frequency of anxiety symptoms in a cohort of children could be measured at ages 6, 9, and 12. Longitudinal designs have an advantage over cross-sectional designs in that unmeasured characteristics or experiences that might distinguish groups of children of different ages are not present because the same children are followed throughout the study. However, longitudinal studies take years to complete, so they require patience and plentiful funding.

Another problem with longitudinal studies is that some participants almost always drop out during the study—because they move and cannot be located, because they choose not to continue, or for other reasons. It can be difficult to know if participants with certain characteristics or experiences were more likely to drop out of the study, which can influence the results. For example, if children with higher levels of anxiety are more likely to drop out of a longitudinal study of the frequency of anxiety symptoms, anxiety symptoms for the older ages will be less frequent than they would have been if the highly anxious children had not withdrawn from the study. This can create a misleading picture of the frequency of anxiety symptoms at different ages. In addition, longitudinal designs can include **cohort effects,** which are effects due to the specific time in which a group of children lives. For example, children in New York City entering school in 2001 may have had many different experiences following the destruction of the World Trade Center towers than children entering school before 2001; so results from a longitudinal study of their anxiety symptoms may provide misleading information about the general development of anxiety symptoms in children. Finally, the process of being studied on an ongoing basis may influence the development of children, which can affect the results of longitudinal studies.

Internal Validity and External Validity

Internal validity and external validity are important concepts in studies involving interventions designed to change the behaviors of the participants in the study—for example, whether playing soft music reduces negative interactions between a mother and child, whether providing cognitive–behavioral therapy reduces children's anxiety symptoms, or whether administering Ritalin reduces hyperactive behaviors in children diagnosed with ADHD. Most commonly these studies involve a pretest–posttest design. That is, some assessment of the behavior of interest is made (the pretest); the treatment is provided; and then the behavior is assessed again (the posttest).

Internal Validity   **Internal validity** is the extent to which a study can demonstrate that the intervention, rather than some other issues, produced any observed differences between pretest and posttest assessments. For example, did the soft music turned on halfway through the observation of a mother and her child reduce the negative interactions between them? Or was this caused by some other factor, such as their increasing comfort with observation as time went on? Similarly, did the cognitive–behavioral therapy reduce anxiety symptoms? Or did the children simply "grow out of" their anxiety over time?

In a classic book, Campbell and Stanley (1963) described eight fundamental threats to internal validity. Each threat describes a possible influence on the difference between pretest and posttest assessments other than the intervention being evaluated:

- *History:* Aspects of the participants' environment other than the treatment may have changed. For example, if children have moved to a new grade between the pretest and posttest, their new teachers and classmates may influence their behaviors.
- *Testing:* Changes may be due to participants taking tests or completing other measures as part of the study. For example, having parents complete a report about their interactions with a child may alert them to the number of negative interactions they have, which may change their behavior between the pretest and posttest assessments.
- *Instrumentation:* Different methods may be used to gather data at various points in the study. For example, a new version of an intelligence test used later in a study may affect test scores.
- *Regression effects:* Children with extreme scores on a measure during the pretest are likely to have less extreme scores when the measures are administered again (this is known as *regression to the mean*), which may affect their scores on the posttest.

- *Mortality:* Differences observed may be due to some participants dropping out of the study. For example, in a longitudinal study of conduct problems, some children's families may move away, and the results of the study will be influenced by the end of their participation.
- *Maturation:* Normal growth and development can influence the results of a study. For example, most children become less aggressive as they enter school, so a reduction in aggression between ages 4 and 6 may be due to maturation rather than intervention.
- *Selection:* Children in the treatment and comparison groups may have been selected using different criteria. For example, children receiving treatment might have had more severe symptoms.
- *Selection by maturation interaction:* Differences observed in the study may be due to differences in selection of the groups that predisposed the groups to grow apart. For example, because girls are more likely than boys to experience reductions in aggression as they enter school, a selection process that places more girls than boys in either the treatment or no-treatment group can influence the results of a study.

It is usually impossible to eliminate all threats to internal validity. For example, by their nature, children mature neurologically, cognitively, emotionally, and socially from a pretest to a posttest, even if the time between the tests is short. The goal for most researchers, then, is to reduce threats to internal validity as much as possible. To the extent that they can do this, they can state with more confidence that the intervention influenced any differences in pretest and posttest assessments. However, if there are clear, strong threats to internal validity, any conclusions about the influence of the intervention are suspect.

External Validity   **External validity** refers to the extent to which results from one study can be generalized to other people, in other places, or at other times. For example, if my study found that cognitive–behavioral therapy was effective in reducing depressive symptoms in fifth- and sixth-grade boys and girls with moderate levels of depressive symptoms from an urban school district, could I argue that cognitive–behavioral therapy would also be effective with younger children, children from rural schools, or children with severe depression? To the extent that I can argue logically that the characteristics that might influence how other groups of children would respond to cognitive–behavioral therapy are similar to those of the children in my study, I can argue that my results can be generalized to the other groups. However, if the characteristics of the children in these other groups are likely to cause them to respond differently to cognitive–behavioral therapy, I may not be able to argue that my results can be generalized to them.

A useful strategy for establishing external validity is to replicate a study with different groups of subjects. If I conducted other studies using the same cognitive–behavioral therapy with younger children and children from a rural school district, and I found results similar to those of my first study, I would have more evidence that the results from my research program could be generalized to many children. However, if I were to find different results in each of my studies, then it would be less likely that the results from any of the studies could be generalized to other children. Similarly, if several researchers found that the same cognitive–behavioral therapy was effective with children who had different characteristics, then we could use the body of research about the effectiveness of the cognitive–behavioral therapy to generalize the findings to other children.

Key Concepts

- A sample is drawn from a population it is meant to represent. Inferential statistics assess the extent to which differences observed in a sample are likely to represent differences in the population.
- Random sampling is a strategy for increasing the likelihood that a sample represents the population from which is it drawn.
- The response rate is the percentage of people who participate in a study who could have participated. A high response rate increases the likelihood that an appropriately drawn sample will represent the population from which it is drawn.
- The reliability of a measure refers to its consistency. High test–retest reliability is an important characteristic of a test; high interrater reliability is an important characteristic of observations.
- Construct validity is the extent to which a measure assesses the construct that it claims to assess. Important components of construct validity include content validity, internal consistency, convergent validity, and discriminant validity.
- Experimental designs randomly assign participants to different levels of an independent variable.
- Correlational designs assess the association between two or more characteristics or experiences of the participants. Correlational designs can be used to hypothesize about the influence of one variable on another but cannot be used to confirm an influence.
- Retrospective designs ask children to recall events from their past; prospective designs periodically assess a group of children over time.
- Single-case designs compare behaviors or characteristics of a child at different points in time. They are typically used to assess the effectiveness of an intervention.
- Between-group designs compare behaviors or characteristics of children in two or more groups.
- Cross-sectional studies assess characteristics or behaviors among groups of children of different ages.
- Longitudinal studies follow a group of children over time, with information gathered at different ages.

- Internal validity is the extent to which an intervention (rather than extraneous influences) produced any observed differences between pretest and posttest assessments.
- External validity is the extent to which the results from one study can be generalized to other people, in other places, or at other times.

Results

The results section describes the statistical analyses that were conducted and the results of those analyses. A *statistic* is a numerical representation of some characteristic of a sample (from the Latin *staticus,* referring to affairs of the state). *Descriptive statistics* describe characteristics of the sample. The mean, standard deviation, median, mode, and range are all descriptive statistics. For example, descriptive statistics about the mean, standard deviation, and range of the age of the participants in a study, and the levels of symptoms they are experiencing, could be included in the results section. *Inferential statistics,* as already noted, assess the extent to which information about a population can be inferred from the sample used in the study. Descriptive and inferential statistics are often presented together. If I were investigating differences in the frequency of bipolar disorder symptoms between school-age girls and school-age boys, for example, I would present the descriptive statistics for the frequency of symptoms in the two groups; then I would present the results from an inferential statistic (perhaps a *t*-test) assessing the probability that I could infer that any differences in my sample represent differences in the population from which my sample was drawn.

This chapter does not focus on statistics, so we will not explore the variety of inferential statistics that could be included in a results section. However, one issue is worth examining: the meaning of the p value, or probability, that is reported in many inferential statistics. The usefulness of the p value has been debated for years. Some statisticians think it provides useful information; others think it is poorly understood and provides little useful information (Hagen, 1997).

As just noted, the p represents the probability that differences observed in a sample represent differences in the population from which the sample was drawn. A finding of $p = .05$ means there is a 5% chance that differences observed in a sample *do not* represent differences in the population—so there is a 95% chance that differences in the sample *do* represent those in the population. The generally accepted convention in psychology and many other social sciences is that a p value of .05 or smaller is considered *statistically significant.*

A common misperception about p is that it indicates the size or meaningfulness of any differences observed in a sample, and that as the size of p decreases, the size or meaningfulness of the observed differences increases. For example, those with this misperception might believe that a difference between two groups that is statistically significant at the $p = .001$ level is larger than a difference that is statistically significant at the $p = .05$ level. This is incorrect. The p only provides information about our ability to infer to a population the results from our sample; it does not tell us anything about the size or meaningfulness of that difference (McCall, 1970).

To demonstrate what p represents, it is instructive to examine the formula for a common inferential statistic, the Student t-test (or as it is more commonly called, the t-test). The formula for comparing the means of some characteristic between two independent groups is noted in the margin. The larger the t, the smaller the p associated with it will be. Note that the numerator is the difference between the means of the two groups. Because a larger number in the numerator will produce a larger t (with the other numbers remaining constant), larger differences in the means of the two groups will produce a smaller p. The denominator consists of two numbers: the standard deviation of the scores in the sample and n, the number in the sample. As can be seen, as the standard deviation increases, the denominator will increase, reducing the size of the t (given that the other numbers remain constant). This indicates that when there is more variability of the characteristic being examined, the size of p will increase. The n is also in the denominator, but it is a divisor. Consequently as n gets larger, the denominator gets smaller, which increases the size of the t when the numerator is held constant. Thus the larger the sample, the smaller the p will be when the mean difference and standard deviation are held constant.

$$t = \frac{\bar{X}_1 - \bar{X}_2}{\sqrt{\dfrac{S_1^2}{N_1} + \dfrac{S_2^2}{N_2}}}$$

So a larger mean difference between the groups, a smaller standard deviation, or a larger sample can all increase the t and decrease the p. To show that a smaller p does not necessarily mean a greater difference between groups, consider the following example: If I had a sample of 20 boys and 20 girls with bipolar disorder, measured the severity of their symptoms on a 6-point scale, and found that the boys had a mean of 4.2 and the girls had a mean of 4.4, with a standard deviation in both groups of 0.8, a t-test might produce a p that was greater than .05, so the differences between the groups would not be considered statistically significant. If, however, I dramatically increased the size of my sample to 200 boys and 200 girls and found exactly the same means and standard deviation, the results of the t-test would produce a p that was smaller than .05, so the differences between the groups would be considered statistically significant. Because the only difference between these two t-tests is the size of my sample, this example clearly shows that a lower p does not indicate a greater or more meaningful difference between groups.

Key Concepts

- Descriptive statistics describe characteristics of a sample.
- Inferential statistics assess the extent to which information about a population can be inferred from a sample.
- The probability statistic, which is reported from inferential statistical tests, describes the probability that differences observed in a sample represent differences occurring in the population from which the sample was drawn. It does not describe the size or meaningfulness of any observed differences.

Discussion

The discussion section typically contains two components: the researcher's interpretation of the results and a discussion of how the results fit into the current body of research on the topic being investigated. When reading a discussion section, it is essential to keep in mind that the process of gathering and reporting data from a study (reported in the methods and results sections) differs from the process of interpreting the data (reported in the discussion section). For example, consider the studies presented in the chapter about weight and eating disorders that shows that African–American, Hispanic–American, and Native–American children are at greater risk for obesity than are European–American or Asian–American children (Kim & Oberzanek, 2002; Salbe, Weyer, Lindsay, Ravussin, & Tataranni, 2002b; Vander Wal, 2004). The data clearly show that children from some racial and ethnic groups are more likely to be obese. However, interpreting the data is not so straightforward. One interpretation might be that genetic differences between the groups influence who is more likely to be obese; another might be that children from low-income families might be more likely to be obese; and a third might be that parental altitudes about weight might differ between the groups. The data do not provide the interpretation; the researcher must do this. One researcher's interpretation of the data may vary from another researcher's interpretation of the same data.

Because our ways of thinking about issues are influenced, in part, by our cultural values, we should consider these influences when interpreting data (Vargas & Koss-Chioino, 1992). A researcher from one cultural group might interpret the data about group differences in obesity differently than a researcher from another cultural group. Care must be taken by those conducting research and by those reading it that any cultural influences in data interpretation be acknowledged so that cultural expectations and beliefs of one culture are not imposed on the data. As in all aspects of research or interventions with children and families, the influence of culture must be appreciated.

To put the results of a study into the broader context of the body of research on the topic, a researcher will often return to the descriptions of other studies presented in the introduction and describe how the researcher's study supports or refutes the earlier results. When results differ from those of earlier studies, the researcher may hypothesize about variations in the sample or the procedures that may have influenced these differences.

Key Concepts

- There are two components of the discussion section: the interpretation of the data by the researcher and the researcher's beliefs about how the results from his or her study fit into the larger body of research on the topic being investigated.

Ethical Issues

Children, adolescents, and adults have contact with psychologists and other mental health professionals in two primary ways: as therapy clients and as participants in research. Some of you reading this text have been in therapy, and many of you have participated in psychological research at your college or university. The conduct of therapy and of research with children and adults is regulated by laws, administrative regulations, and ethical standards (Koocher & Keith-Spiegel, 1990), which are the focus of this section.

Laws are enacted by legislative bodies. All U.S. states have laws regulating contact between therapists and their clients, such as prohibiting sexual contact between therapists and clients and regulating the confidentiality of interactions between therapists and clients (Koocher & Keith-Spiegel, 1990). Therapists who do not follow these laws can be prosecuted. Administrative agencies can issue regulations governing the actions of institutions and individuals. For example, the U.S. Department of Health and Human Services has created many regulations governing the treatment of research participants and enforces them with any university or other institution that receives federal funding. Institutions that do not follow these guidelines, or that do not ensure that all their employees follow them, can have federal funding withheld, which often amounts to a substantial financial penalty. As another example, the agency that licenses psychologists in New York enforces a variety of regulations, such as keeping records of therapy sessions. Failure to follow these regulations can result in revocation of a person's license to practice psychotherapy.

Many professional organizations have ethical guidelines that members of those organizations are expected to follow. The American Psychological Association (APA), for example, has a long, detailed set of ethical standards that psychologists must follow when providing therapy, conducting research, or teaching. The APA states that its **Ethics Code** "provides a common set of principles and standards upon which psychologists build their professional and scientific work" (APA, 2002, p. 1061). Fewer sanctions are available to professional organizations for those who break ethical standards, the most severe generally being expulsion from the professional organization (Koocher & Keith-Spiegel, 1990).

In a general sense, **ethics** is defined as the system of morals of a person or group (*morals* refers to distinguishing between right and wrong); the term *ethical behavior* refers to behavior that conforms to moral or professional standards of conduct. *Ethical standards* are laws, rules, or guidelines designed to ensure ethical behavior.

Ethical standards are determined by the values of groups or individuals. Consequently, as we explore current ethical standards, keep in mind that they reflect current views of which behaviors are right and wrong held by those with the power or influence to write or enforce the standards. Behavior viewed as ethical in one group, nation, or culture may be viewed as unethical in others. As an example, consider how women or children are treated today in various cultures and nations. Similarly, behavior considered ethical at one time may be considered unethical at another. For example, when I was in junior high school in the mid-1960s, "paddling" misbehaving students was legal and was viewed by many as ethical and appropriate; now many states prohibit corporal punishment in schools.

It is also important to remember that ethical standards may not reflect the beliefs of everyone in a group, nation, or culture. Consider, for example, current debates about abortion, same-sex marriages, and owning handguns. Ethical standards and the behaviors they proscribe should not be seen as necessarily representing a consensus of the group from which they come.

Although it can be challenging to determine the appropriate ethical behaviors in some situations involving adults in research or therapy, situations involving children can be even more challenging. We will explore several of these difficult ethical issues in this chapter, beginning with two vignettes that describe the ethical issues faced by a therapist and a researcher.

Case Study: Handling Parental Expectations

Dr. Chavez is a clinical psychologist who specializes in working with school-age children. A mother brings her sixth-grade daughter, Karen, for a consultation. Karen's mother describes her as a girl who has always excelled in school. The mother has encouraged Karen's academic brilliance and states that, as a single mother, she understands the value of a good education for a girl who may someday have to raise children on her own. Karen consistently receives A or A− grades in all her subjects and has received the highest grades in her class for three years. However, at the beginning of this academic year, a girl transferred into Karen's class who consistently receives slightly higher grades than Karen. Karen has been upset by her new status as second-best student in her class. Because of this, in her mother's opinion, Karen's grades have suffered, and she now receives an occasional B+ on exams. The mother would like Dr. Chavez to work with Karen so that her grades will improve and she can be restored to her position as the best student in her class. Further, the mother states that because she is so concerned about Karen, she would like to meet regularly with Dr. Chavez to discuss what is occurring in therapy.

Dr. Chavez states that although she has concerns about the mother's request to know the content of Karen's therapy sessions, she is willing to assess Karen's situation, which will require a few meetings with Karen, conversations with Karen's teachers, and possibly some testing of Karen. Dr. Chavez says she will discuss her conclusions about the assessment with Karen and her mother, and they can decide whether to proceed with therapy. Karen and her mother agree.

Dr. Chavez meets with Karen three times. The first time she discusses Karen's perceptions of her academic performance and her mother's expectations, and gathers information about Karen's relationships with her peers, teachers, and mother. Karen states that she would like to have the best grades in her class, but achieving this goal is less important for her than it is for her mother. Karen is primarily concerned about the high level of anxiety she feels about her schoolwork and the loneliness she often experiences because she has few friends. During the next two sessions, Dr. Chavez administers an intelligence test and several achievement tests to assess Karen's performance in math and language. She also meets three of Karen's teachers.

Based on the information she gathers, Dr. Chavez reaches several initial conclusions:

- Karen's overall intelligence is above average but not in the superior range. Her school grades and academic achievement are higher than might be expected of a girl with her intelligence; it appears that her performance is achieved by working much harder at her schoolwork than other children.
- Karen has one or two friends at school and she mostly keeps to herself. She is not disliked by the other children, but she has little contact with them because she is often doing homework in the library while the other children are playing.
- Karen often becomes upset when she is unable to understand math problems or when she gets answers wrong on tests in other subjects. Her response to these situations is to withdraw from others and concentrate even harder on her schoolwork.
- Karen would like to be the best student in her grade, but she feels that being the second-best student is acceptable. However, she worries about displeasing her mother and knows that her mother wants her to be the top student.
- Karen is willing to come to therapy with Dr. Chavez but is not sure how therapy will help her with her grades; she is worried that she might say something in therapy that will upset her mother.

Dr. Chavez believes that the primary problems faced by Karen are stress caused by her attempts at high achievement and anxiety caused by this stress. She worries that Karen's levels of stress and anxiety are likely to increase if she tries to regain her position as best student in her class. She is concerned about Karen's lack of peer relationships and believes that this is likely to become more of a problem for Karen as she becomes an adolescent. She believes that therapy would help reduce Karen's anxiety and increase her social skills, and Dr. Chavez knows that she has been helpful to other children with these problems. However, she sees little value in increasing Karen's academic performance. Dr. Chavez believes that individual therapy with Karen will be helpful and that some sessions with Karen and her mother together would be beneficial. She also believes that it would be best not to reveal to her mother what is discussed in Karen's individual sessions because doing so may inhibit Karen from discussing her mother's expectations. However, Dr. Chavez does not want to preclude Karen's coming to therapy by alienating her mother.

Dr. Chavez meets with Karen and her mother and presents her findings about Karen's intelligence, academic achievement, and peer relations. She says she believes Karen's academic performance is probably being hurt by her anxiety and that an important focus of therapy would be reducing this anxiety. Dr. Chavez avoids discussing whether Karen should strive to be the best student in her class and whether the mother's expectations are too high, believing that it would be best for these issues to come out in therapy. Dr. Chavez suggests that she meet with Karen every other week and with Karen and her mother together every other week. Dr. Chavez states that she will describe the general issues raised during Karen's individual sessions to her mother, but she will not describe the specific things Karen says during therapy. Dr. Chavez's plan is to avoid telling the mother about any issues Karen raises that Dr. Chavez believes would upset the mother.

What Do You Think?

What do you think of Dr. Chavez's plan? She has formulated it based on her expertise and experience as a child psychologist and on her expectations about what would be best for Karen. She describes accurately the type of therapy that she foresees will be helpful to Karen, and includes her mother in the process, but is careful not to say things she thinks may upset Karen's mother and reduce the likelihood that she will agree to bring Karen for therapy. Can you think of ethical dilemmas that may arise during Karen's therapy? (For example, Karen's mother may ask to see Dr. Chavez's notes about Karen's therapy sessions.)

Once you have thought about Dr. Chavez's plan, consider whether your views would change under these conditions:

- Karen states clearly to Dr. Chavez that her goal is to be the top student in her class and that she wants Dr. Chavez to help her become the top student.
- Karen is a 17-year-old high school junior rather than a sixth-grader.
- The child in question is not Karen but is a boy.
- The results of Karen's intelligence tests show that she is in the superior range and suggest that her academic performance is somewhat lower than might be expected from a child with her level of intelligence.

Thinking about how you might respond differently to these variations may help you understand what principles you use when you think about this case. Principles of this type are the foundation upon which ethical standards are often built. As we explore the variety of ethical standards that affect therapy and research with children, see whether your beliefs about Dr. Chavez's interactions with Karen and her mother change.

Case Study: A Proposed Trial of a New Medication

Dr. Baxter has been working for many years on a new medication to treat attention-deficit/hyperactivity disorder (ADHD). After careful testing with animals and closely monitored trials with a few children who had not responded to other types of medication, he is prepared to initiate a study with a medium-sized group of children. He believes that the results of his early work show that the new medication has the potential to be just as effective as current medications but with fewer side effects. He also believes that it may be effective with children for whom currently available medications are ineffective.

Dr. Baxter proposes the following study to the institutional review board at his medical school: Through a school that specializes in working with children with behavioral and educational problems, he will approach the parents of 50

10- to 13-year-old students who are already on medication for problems with ADHD. He will describe to these parents how, during the study, he will randomly assign 25 students to a group that will receive the new medication and 25 to a group that will receive a placebo. All the students in the experiment will be required to stop taking their current medications for two weeks and then will start either the new medication or the placebo. None of the study participants will know who is receiving the medication and who is receiving the placebo. Teachers and parents will be asked to rate the children's behaviors daily for one month. At the end of the month, it will be revealed who was taking the medication and who was taking the placebo. Based on the results of the study, the children may then either return to taking their old medications, stop taking any medication, or begin taking the new medication if it proves effective and is approved for continued use. Dr. Baxter will meet with each student and his or her parents to describe the process of the study, the potential value of the new drug, and the potential side effects. He acknowledges, however, that because the new medication has been used with only a few children, side effects of which he is not aware may occur in some children. Parents who are willing to give their children permission to participate in the study will sign a form indicating this. The children will then be asked to sign a form indicating their assent.

Dr. Baxter also proposes that he be allowed to involve 20 students from the same school who have some attention problems but do not have ADHD. He would randomly divide these children into two groups of 10 and follow the procedures just described. Dr. Baxter argues that although these children do not have ADHD, the new medication might effectively reduce their attention problems. If this occurred, the medication might help children with less severe forms of attention problems.

Dr. Baxter has received two grants from a drug company to conduct this research. Therefore, he will pay each family $750 for their participation.

What Do You Think?

If you were a member of the institutional review board, would you approve Dr. Baxter's proposed research? If not, what are your specific concerns about this project? Would your decision about approving this project change under these conditions?

- The study involved 5- to 6-year-old children who, because of their age, would not be required to sign a form giving their assent.
- The medication that Dr. Baxter was developing was designed to replace medications currently given to reduce severe self-injurious behavior.
- There was reason to believe that the new medication would be much more effective than currently available medications, but there was also a chance of serious side effects occurring with one or two children.
- The study was proposed to take place at an institution for abandoned children, so no parental permission could be obtained and the $750 fees would be paid directly to the school.

What reasons can you give for any different responses that you might have to these alternative conditions? As with the previous vignette, analyzing the reasons for any different responses might provide insight into the principles you used to make your decisions.

Development of Laws and Ethical Guidelines for Research and Therapy

Unfortunately, in the past, children have been involved in research and therapy that most would now find repugnant (Meaux & Bell, 2001), as shown by these examples:

- In the 1800s several studies involved infecting institutionalized children with a variety of diseases, including leprosy, syphilis, gonorrhea, and tuberculosis, to determine whether some children were immune from the diseases and whether certain treatments would be effective.
- In 1896 a study was published in which 29 healthy children were each given a spinal tap to see if this could be done safely. Although the spinal taps were completed safely, considerable concern was raised about the study because there was no benefit to any of these children.
- From the 1950s through the 1970s, researchers at the Willowbrook State School infected children who were mentally retarded with hepatitis to study its natural course. They claimed that there was a high likelihood that the children would have contracted the disease in the institution anyway. Although the parents of the children consented to their children's participation in the research, the waiting time for admission to the facility for children whose parents consented was much shorter than the waiting time for those whose parents did not.

The movement toward developing specific ethical principles for involving humans in research was propelled by the Nuremberg Trials after World War II, during which many Nazi researchers were condemned to death for their use of concentration camp inmates in experiments (Glantz, 1996; Meaux & Bell, 2001). The guidelines that came from these efforts required the informed, uncoerced, and voluntary consent of all research participants. Although these guidelines had some influence on research, it was not until 1974 that the U.S. Department of Health, Education, and Welfare created specific regulations to protect research subjects. These regulations have been revised several times, and now the U.S. Department of Health and Human Services provides and enforces regulations that must be used in research by any institution that receives financial support from the U.S. government. The content of many of these regulations is described next.

Many professional organizations have also created ethical principles that those in their organizations are expected to follow. For example, the American Psychological Association has a set of ethical guidelines that govern psychologists' roles as researchers, teachers, and clinicians. The most recent version of these ethical standards was approved in 2002.

Key Concepts

- An initial impetus for the development of laws, regulations, and ethical principles was the Nuremberg Trials.

- In 1974 the U.S. Department of Health, Education, and Welfare created specific regulations to protect research participants.
- The American Psychological Association has a set of ethical principles for psychologists that have been revised several times, the most recent revision occurring in 2002.

Principles for the Ethical Treatment of People Involved in Research or Therapy

Several overriding principles form the foundation for the ethical treatment of those involved in research and therapy (APA, 2002; King & Churchill, 2000; Koocher & Keith-Spiegel, 1990; Marsh, 1997). These include autonomy, beneficence, nonmaleficence, and confidentiality. In this section we explore these principles and how they influence all research and therapy. We also discuss a variety of complexities in applying these principles to children.

Autonomy

Autonomy refers to an individual's right to self determination—to act as he or she sees fit if these actions do not infringe on the rights of others. The principle of autonomy requires that individuals decide whether to participate in research or therapy and that this decision be made voluntarily and without coercion. Further, it requires that individuals be allowed to end their participation in research or therapy without penalty or coercion.

Basic Issues
Informed Consent   The most important concept relating to the principle of autonomy is informed consent (Melton & Ehrenreich, 1992). A person (or that person's representative) must give informed consent before participating in research or therapy. **Informed consent** requires that three conditions be met: The person must have sufficient information to understand all the consequences of the decision to participate; he or she must be competent to make the decision (that is, he or she must have the cognitive ability to make a reasoned judgment); and he or she must make the decision voluntarily (Henkelman & Everall, 2001; Melton & Ehrenreich, 1992).

The *informed* part of informed consent requires that a person be given enough information about the potential benefits and drawbacks of participating in therapy or research so that he or she can make a reasoned decision (Rae & Fournier, 1999). For example, potential research participants must be told about what will occur during their participation and about its potential benefits and negative consequences.

The second requirement of informed consent is that a person have the cognitive ability to understand the information given to him or her and then weigh the potential benefits and liabilities of participation while deciding whether to participate. The legal **presumption** is that adults without significant intellectual problems have the required cognitive abilities to consent.

Children, on the other hand, are generally presumed not to have the cognitive abilities to consent, so their parents are usually required to give them permission to participate (Melton & Ehrenreich, 1992). The age at which most children develop the ability to give informed consent has not been determined, but research on people's cognitive abilities suggests that most adolescents aged 15 years and older have abilities to consent that are similar to adults' and that many younger children also have these abilities (Arnold et al., 1996; Kaser-Boyd, Adelman, & Taylor, 1985). Despite the cognitive abilities of many adolescents, permission of parents is usually required for those under the age of 18.

The final component of informed consent is voluntariness. A voluntary decision requires that a person not experience coercion to decide one way or another (Arnold et al., 1996; Weise, Smith, Maschke, & Copeland, 2002). For example, I could not tell my students that only those who complete a questionnaire will be able to receive an A in my course because doing so will coerce some students into completing the questionnaire. In addition, researchers cannot offer such a powerful incentive or reward that people who would normally choose not to participate feel pressure to do so. I cannot, for example, offer to raise the grade of anyone who participates in a study by two letter grades because, even though people who choose not to participate are not punished, the reward I am offering is so great that some may feel pressure to participate.

Inducements to participate in research can be offered, but they must only compensate a person for his or her time or effort. I can, for example, offer a point or two of extra credit for participation in my study because this inducement can be seen as fair compensation for the student's time (if a student were to study for one of my exams for an extra amount of time equal to the time spent participating in the research, it is likely that he or she would receive a point or two more on the exam), and the inducement is not so large that those who would not normally participate would feel pressure to do so.

Similarly, I cannot say things in therapy to a child or parent that are not solidly based in fact and that would coerce the child into therapy. For example, I cannot state that if the child does not receive therapy his condition will continue to worsen to the point where he may need to be hospitalized (Rae & Fournier, 1999; Yanagida, 1998).

Special Issues Related to Children
In most aspects of their lives, children have much less autonomy than do adults. In many situations, parents have more control over what happens to a child than the child has. Parents' influence on what their child can, cannot, and must do often complicate research and therapy with a child.

Research   A two-step process is required for older children and adolescents to participate in research, rather than the one-step informed consent given by adults (Glantz, 1996). First a parent must give *permission* for the child to participate; then the child must **assent** (or agree) to participate. The parents and the child must all be given enough information about the study, in age-appropriate language, so that they can provide *informed* permission or assent (Henkelman & Everall, 2001). Infants and young children are not required to give their assent, so parental permission is all that is required with these children (Meaux & Bell, 2001). The age at which assent must be obtained from a child is left up to the institutional review board (IRB) that approves a particular research project (Meaux & Bell, 2001).

Baylis, Downie, and Kenny (1999) reported on a Canadian conference that explored several intriguing issues related to children's assent to participate in research. Central to these issues was whether children should be able to refuse to participate in research if their parents have given permission for them to participate. They raised the interesting question of whether a child who is not considered competent to decide to participate in research should be considered competent to decide *not* to participate. Should a 9-year-old with obsessive–compulsive disorder, for example, be able to refuse to participate in a study of a new medication that might relieve her symptoms if her parents have given their permission for her to participate? All conference participants believed that children should be actively involved in the process of deciding whether they should participate in research, at a level appropriate with their abilities. Disagreement existed about whether a child's dissent about participation should prohibit the child from being involved. Some people argued that the dissent should be used as one piece of information by the parents as they decide whether the child should participate, whereas others believed that the child's dissent should end any chance of the child's participation. Clearly this remains a controversial issue.

Parental permission for a child to participate in research is not required under two circumstances (Santelli & Rogers, 2002). The first is when an IRB finds that getting parental permission might pose risks to the children in the research. For example, it might not be necessary to obtain parents' permission for adolescents to participate in a research project assessing the effectiveness of a support group for gay or lesbian high school students if it is believed that contacting parents about their children's sexual orientation and their participation in the group might put the children at risk for psychological or physical harm. The second exception involves research that an IRB finds involves only minimal risk, that will not adversely affect the rights of the children, and that could not be done if parental permission were required. For example, researchers planning to interview sixth-grade children about a new social studies curriculum could obtain a waiver of parental permission based on the minimal risk of the interview and their argument that most parents might not bother returning a permission form, which would mean that they could not get useful results from the few students who could participate.

Of course, both the permission of the parent and the assent of the child must be voluntary. It can be difficult to judge the voluntariness of a child's assent because most children are socialized to accede to the wishes of adults (Meaux & Bell, 2001). Thus children, especially young ones, may not understand that they can decline to participate in research. Consequently, it is necessary for those doing research with young children to make it as clear as possible to them that they can choose whether to participate.

As already noted, incentives to participate in research cannot be so large that they coerce people to participate. In many studies in which children are interviewed briefly or participate in tasks that are not onerous, they might be given something like a small toy to thank them for their participation (Lewis, 2002). Researchers must also be cautious about what they give to participants in schools or other group settings where some children do not have parental permission to participate: It would be unethical to upset the children who do not participate by not giving them the toy. Some researchers handle this potential problem by providing all the children in a classroom with the same "thank you" reward, regardless of their participation (Lewis, 2002).

Therapy   Except in a few circumstances, parents must give permission before their children can receive psychotherapy or medications for psychological problems. In some states, adolescents can consent to receiving psychological or medical services related to pregnancy, sexually transmitted diseases, and drug and alcohol use without parental permission (Melton & Ehrenreich, 1992). These exceptions have been made because of the assumptions that some adolescents facing these issues might choose not to receive help for them if getting help required that their parents be notified of their condition, and that this would negatively affect their health or the health of others.

However, unlike participation in research, children and adolescents do not need to assent to participate in therapy, and they cannot refuse therapy that their parents have given them permission to receive (Rae & Fournier, 1999). This may impinge on children's freedom less during outpatient therapy than inpatient therapy. All therapists who work with children or families experience situations in which children are brought to therapy against their wishes. Most therapists work to gain the cooperation of the child because they know that successful therapy with a reluctant child client is difficult to achieve. Of more consequence, however, is that parents can "voluntarily" commit their minor children to inpatient hospitalization (Melton & Ehrenreich, 1992). Adults who enter a hospital voluntarily can leave the hospital whenever they want. However, children who are admitted by their parents cannot leave the hospital unless their parents approve (Melton & Ehrenreich, 1992). Consequently, many cases of voluntary commitment by parents represent involuntary commitment from the perspective of the children.

In a landmark case, the U.S. Supreme Court ruled that children could be admitted to a psychiatric hospital at the request of their parents with no judicial review of their hospitalization (*Parham v. J. R.*, 442 U.S. 584, 1979). The Court stated that parents were responsible for, and acted in the best interests of, their children, and that a review of the child's condition by the admitting officer of a hospital served the same function as a judicial review. The benefits of this approach can be seen in some circumstances. For example, adolescents with significant substance abuse or eating problems may not agree to hospitalization even when it is needed to ensure their physical health or save their lives. However, concern can also be raised about parents having children admitted to a hospital under circumstances that are less severe, such as when a child is acting out at home or refusing to obey the parents' wishes. Although hospitals might not admit some of these children, concern exists that some admitting officers may give greater weight to the financial needs of the hospital than the needs of the child when making admissions decisions (Koocher & Keith-Spiegel, 1990).

Beneficence and Nonmaleficence

The principle of **beneficence** refers to the expectation that research and therapy will provide some benefit to those who participate in them. **Nonmaleficence** refers to the expectation that no harm will be done to a participant in research or therapy or that any harm will be minimized. Beneficence requires some sort of action to create a benefit, whereas nonmaleficence can be accomplished either actively (for example, by making sure sterile conditions exist when drawing blood from someone) or passively (for example, by not asking questions that will upset people completing a questionnaire) (King & Churchill, 2000).

Basic Issues

The principle of beneficence can be most easily understood in relation to therapy: It is expected that a person will benefit from attending therapy (Koocher & Keith-Spiegel, 1990). Therapists are expected to know which therapeutic techniques are useful for clients with various problems and to use those techniques effectively. Although it is understood that not everyone will benefit from attending therapy, the therapist is expected to pursue a strategy that has a clear likelihood of benefiting the client.

Beneficence is more complicated in the research context (King & Churchill, 2000). Most research is designed to create knowledge that will be helpful to many; however, in most studies, some or all of the participants will receive no direct benefit (Koocher & Keith-Spiegel, 1990). Consequently, the potential benefit to others, rather than a specific benefit to the research participants, fulfills the requirement of beneficence. For example, half of a group of depressed children in a study of a new antidepressant drug may be given a placebo, and it is assumed that they will not benefit directly from their study participation. However, the knowledge generated by this research may benefit many children with depression in the future, possibly including them (Vitiello & Jensen, 1997). Similarly, it is usually assumed that no children completing questionnaires about their peer relationships and their mental health will receive any benefit from doing so. However, the knowledge gained from the study may provide important information to those developing programs to improve the mental health of students.

Because many participants are unlikely to benefit directly from research participation, the focus often shifts to nonmaleficence: doing little or no harm to research participants. A key concept related to nonmaleficence is minimal risk. Whenever possible, researchers are expected to provide an environment in which the participants will experience minimal risk.

Minimal risk is defined as the probability that the harm and discomfort anticipated in the research are no greater than those ordinarily encountered in daily life or during the performance of routine physical or psychological examinations or tests (OHSR Information Sheet #10, 1993). As you can see, minimal risk does not equal no risk (Vitiello & Jensen, 1997). For example, drawing blood can be painful and involves some risk of infection; but because drawing blood is part of routine physical examinations, it is considered a minimal risk. Similarly, completing questionnaires about peer relationships might be embarrassing for some children; but because embarrassment is considered a normal part of children's lives, completing these questionnaires is considered to involve minimal risk (Koocher & Keith-Spiegel, 1990).

By its nature, some research involves more than minimal risk. For example, trials of a new medication often involve more than minimal risk because of potential side effects of the medication. Clear justification must be provided for research that involves more than minimal risk; efforts must be made to keep this risk as low as possible; and there must be an obvious likelihood that the potential benefits of the research outweigh the risks to the participants (Porter, 1996; Vitiello & Jensen, 1997).

Special Issues Related to Children

Therapy   As just described, an expectation exists that beneficence will occur in therapy. An important issue in therapy with children, however, is who will receive the benefit. Sometimes the benefits to the child and family are clear: If therapy reduces the symptoms of a depressed or anxious child, both the child and family can benefit. However, consider one of the vignettes earlier in this chapter. If the therapist decides to work to improve Karen's academic performance, who benefits? It could be argued that Karen would receive little or no benefit (and perhaps may be harmed, if her anxiety increases) and that the beneficiary would be her mother.

Another example of a situation in which the recipient of the benefit may be unclear is cases of children who have a **gender identity disorder** (such as a boy who identifies more as a girl than a boy). In whose benefit is it for a therapist to work to reduce gender identity issues in a child? Because children with gender identity disorders can be ostracized by peers, it may benefit the child for the therapist to work to change the child's sense of gender identity (Rekers, Bentler, Rosen, & Lovaas, 1977). However, what if the child is generally content with his or her gender identity, despite any negative consequences, and the parents are unhappy? It may be easy to answer that the therapist should focus on the child's desires and not work to change his or her gender identity. But what if the child is 6 years old? Usually people in our culture are reluctant to let 6-year-olds make decisions that could have broad influences on their lives. Should the therapist accede to the wishes of a 6-year-old and ignore the wishes of that child's parents? There are no easy answers to these types of dilemmas, and reasonable people can argue convincingly on both sides.

The strategy for many therapists when the potential benefits for the child and parents appear to differ is to work with the parents and child to get them to agree on goals that they all believe are beneficial, and then work to accomplish those goals (Rae & Fournier, 1999). But what if the parents' and child's goals remain at odds with each other? How can the therapist choose goals? A key issue is whether the therapist sees the parents or the child as the client. Therapists are ethically obligated to act in their clients' best interests (APA, 2002); so identifying the client may guide the therapist toward the goals to pursue (Koocher & Keith-Spiegel, 1990). However, identifying the client does not automatically dictate which goals to pursue. What if a therapist views an 8-year-old as her client but believes that the child's goals for therapy are not in the child's best interest? Competent therapists will ponder these situations carefully. A solution for many therapists will be to decide what is in the client's best interest and then tell the parents and the child about his or her decision (Koocher & Keith-Spiegel, 1990; Rae & Fournier, 1999). The parents may then decide (possibly in consultation with the child) to continue working with the therapist using the goals that the therapist believes are appropriate, or seek another therapist who might be more willing to act as the parents and child prefer.

Research   The principle of minimizing risk to research participants applies to both children and adults. However, there is concern that parents may sometimes be enticed to allow their children to participate in research that has inappropriately high levels of risk. For example, in the example of the Willowbrook State School described earlier, parents were enticed to allow their children to participate in the research by the enhanced likelihood that their children would be admitted to the school sooner. Money or other incentives may also entice some parents to allow their children to participate in risky research, and these incentives many be particularly persuasive with parents who are struggling financially (Weise et al., 2002).

To reduce the likelihood of children participating in inappropriately risky research, the U.S. government has created standards for children's inclusion in research. These standards cannot be overridden by parental permission. As shown in Table 2.1, all children can participate in research with minimal risk if they assent and receive parental permission. Children can participate in research involving levels of risk that are slightly above minimal if it is likely that they will benefit directly from the research. For example, children with schizophrenia could participate in a study of a new medication if there is evidence to suggest that the drug is likely to benefit them, even if there is more than a minimal risk of negative side effects (Vitiello, Jensen, & Hoagwood, 1999).

It is also permissible to put research participants at a minor increase over minimal risk if they have a disorder or condition about which important information could be learned, even if they do not receive any direct benefit from the research. For example, it would be permissible to randomly assign children with ADHD to either a group that received a new drug or a group that received a placebo. Those receiving the placebo would get no direct benefit from the research; but because this research might benefit all children

TABLE 2.1

Elements to Consider in Evaluating the Ethics of Research in Children (Minors)

Type of Research	Critical Elements
A. Research has potential benefit to the research subject.	• *Risk–benefit ratio* must be favorable to the research subject.
B. Research has no potential benefit to the research subject.	• No greater than *minimal risk* is allowed.
C. Research has no potential benefit to the research subject, but knowledge can be gained that is relevant to the subject's disorder or condition.	• No more than a *minor increase over minimal risk* is allowed. • In the research, subjects are exposed to experiences reasonably commensurate with those inherent in their actual or expected medical, dental, psychological, social, or educational situations. • Research is likely to yield *knowledge that is of vital importance* for the understanding or amelioration of the research subject's disorder or condition.
D. Research is not otherwise approvable under the above criteria.	• The Secretary of Health and Human Services, in consultation with a panel of appropriate experts, has determined that the proposed research presents a reasonable opportunity to further the understanding, prevention, or alleviation of a serious problem affecting the health and welfare of children.

Source: Code of Federal Regulation: Title 45, Part 46: Protection of Human Subjects, DHHS 1991. Also available on the Web site of the Office for the Protection from Research Risks at *www.nih.gov:80/grants/oprr/ humansubjects/45cfr46.htm.*

with ADHD, they can receive the placebo if doing so creates no more than a minor increase over minimal risk. This is allowed because of the possibility that a new treatment for ADHD could be developed that might eventually benefit the children in the placebo control group.

Confidentiality
Basic Issues
Confidentiality is an issue that is most commonly associated with therapy. With few exceptions, laws and ethical guidelines require that conversations between a client and therapist remain confidential—that is, they must not be revealed to anyone else by the therapist without the client's permission (the

client can reveal what is discussed in therapy to whomever he or she wants). This is seen as a cornerstone of therapy. Without confidentiality, people might not be forthcoming during therapy sessions, and consequently the value of therapy would be diminished substantially (Rae & Fournier, 1999).

Some exceptions to confidentiality exist. In some states, therapists are required to warn those whom a client has threatened to kill or harm (Melton & Ehrenreich, 1992). In addition, in some states, therapists are expected or allowed to inform others if a client presents a substantial risk of harm to himself or herself. For example, if an adolescent talks about attempts to commit suicide in therapy, the therapist may be allowed or required to contact parents to warn them about the adolescent's behavior so they can help protect the adolescent from suicide. All states require that therapists and many other professionals report reasonable suspicions of child maltreatment. Thus a therapist is required to make a report if a child discloses being the victim of physical or sexual abuse during a therapy session (Kotch, 2000).

Confidentiality is also an important issue in research. Researchers are expected to limit access to the responses of individual participants to people who must have this information. This can be accomplished in several ways. For example, completed questionnaires might be identified with numbers, with only the project director having access to a list that connects the numbers with participant names. Videotapes or audiotapes of research activities that could allow identification of individuals and their responses must be kept carefully secured, with only those needing to see the videotapes having access to them (Hibbs & Krener, 1996).

Although confidentiality is important in all research, it is particularly vital when the issue being investigated involves illegal activities (like drug use) or activities about which the participants might not want others to know (such as sexual behavior). Researchers engaged in sensitive research can apply to the National Institutes of Health to receive a **certificate of confidentiality.** This certificate, created by the federal Public Health Service Act, exempts researchers from having to reveal individual responses if ordered to do so by a court or administrative agency (Kotch, 2000). The certificate would exempt the researchers, for example, from revealing the responses of an adolescent who responded to a survey about her sexual behaviors, even if a parent obtained a court order to see her responses. This procedure is designed to give research participants confidence that they can answer questions about their behaviors honestly without worrying about their answers being revealed to others. This should result in more accurate responses from many participants, thus increasing the accuracy and value of the research.

Special Issues Related to Children

Therapy   Children do not have the same level of confidentiality during therapy sessions as adults. In most states, parents are authorized to access their children's therapy records and obtain information about their children's therapy from the therapist (Melton & Ehrenreich, 1992). This authorization is granted to parents because they are responsible for their children and are allowed to know what is occurring in their lives. However, knowing that their parents can learn about issues discussed in therapy may inhibit some children, especially adolescents, from being forthright in therapy and discussing issues that they know are important but do not want revealed to their parents (Koocher & Keith-Spiegel, 1990).

This situation can create a dilemma for therapists: They may believe that it will help their child clients to discuss important issues with them without having those issues revealed to a parent; on the other hand, the therapists know that parents have the right to know about issues addressed in therapy if they ask about them specifically. Many therapists cope with this dilemma by describing to the parents and children how they would like to handle the issue of confidentiality. Some therapists working with adolescents, for example, tell parents that they will provide therapy only with the understanding that issues discussed during therapy will not be revealed to the parents, even though there is no legal basis for this type of arrangement (Rae & Fournier, 1999). Many parents and children are willing to abide by this arrangement.

As with adults, some legal restrictions to confidentiality apply to work with children. Incidents of child abuse or neglect must be reported to appropriate state officials, and concerns about suicidal or homicidal behavior must often be reported to parents or other legal guardians of a child (Kotch, 2000; Melton & Ehrenreich, 1992). Because parents have an interest in maintaining the safety of their children, it may be appropriate to break confidentiality to report other dangerous behaviors to parents, such as substantial drug use or unsafe sexual practices (Melton & Ehrenreich, 1992; Rae & Fournier, 1999). However, legal and ethical guidelines are less clear about revealing dangerous behaviors that do not reach the level of seriousness of suicidal or homicidal behavior.

Research   The parents of some children involved in research may want to learn the information a researcher gathers from their children. For example, parents might want to know their children's IQ scores or the levels of their anxiety or depression. Researchers are often reluctant to reveal this information. In part this is due to the procedures used in many research projects. For example, if I were interested in an association between IQ and memory in young children, I might give one or two subtests from an intelligence test to estimate a child's IQ. I would worry that the scores the child receives on these subtests might not accurately reflect his or her intelligence, and telling the parents the child's scores might give them an incorrect view of the child's intelligence and adversely affect their behavior toward the child.

Most researchers handle the potential problem of revealing this type of information by stating on the parent's permission form that they will not reveal the responses of individual children (Koocher & Keith-Spiegel, 1990). Children of parents who do not agree with this condition are simply not included in the research. This provides a basis for a researcher's refusal to provide information about individual children. Whether a parent could legally force a researcher to reveal individual information, even after signing a permission form saying that individual responses will not be revealed, has not been settled in the courts.

Confidentiality can become more complicated when children reveal information about themselves or their families that suggests potential danger. Consider, for example, research about adolescents' suicidal ideation. How do researchers respond if the scores on an adolescent's questionnaire suggest that he or she may be seriously considering suicide? What if the issue involves less danger than suicide—say if a questionnaire suggests that a child is highly anxious? Even if the researcher has stated that individual responses will not be released to parents, the ethical principles of beneficence and nonmaleficence suggest that researchers may need to contact parents if it is in the best interests of a child to do so. Koocher and Keith-Spiegel (1990) suggest that researchers obtain additional information about a child whose research responses raise concerns, which could include asking a school counselor whether the child is receiving services or whether the problem has already been reported to parents. The researchers might also have a child therapist talk with the child to learn whether concern about the child's mental health is warranted. This additional information can help researchers decide whether to contact the child's parents.

Key Concepts

- Autonomy, an individual's right to self-determination, requires that individuals decide voluntarily whether to participate in research or therapy.
- Informed consent is an important component of the principle of autonomy. To give informed consent, a person must (1) have sufficient information to understand the consequences of his or her decision, (2) be competent to make the decision, and (3) make the decision voluntarily.
- Children under the age of 18 cannot legally consent to participate in most research or therapy; they usually must have parental permission to participate.
- It is usually expected that older children and adolescents will give their assent before participating in research. Assent is not required, however, before a child enters therapy.
- Incentives to participate in research must not be coercive, particularly when those incentives are given to parents.
- Beneficence is the expectation that research or therapy will provide some benefit to those who participate; nonmaleficence is the expectation that no harm will be done to a participant or that any harm will be minimized.
- Minimal risk is risk that is no greater than that ordinarily encountered in daily life or during the performance of routine physical or psychological examinations or tests.
- Children can participate in research with minimal risk. They can participate in research involving risk that is slightly above minimal if they are likely to benefit directly from the research. They can participate in research with no more than a minor increase over minimal risk if

they have a disorder or condition about which important information could be learned, even if they do not receive any direct benefit from the research.

- Confidentiality requires that information provided by a therapy client or research participant not be revealed to others without the person's permission.
- Exceptions to confidentiality in therapy involve situations in which a person is at risk for harming himself or herself or others, or when the therapist has a reasonable suspicion that child maltreatment has occurred.
- Parents have access to their children's therapy records and have a right to obtain information about their children's therapy.
- Parents may have a right to see information collected from their children during research, although this remains unsettled by the courts.

Institutional Review Boards

As we have seen in discussions throughout this chapter, although several principles exist to guide the ethical treatment of those involved in research or therapy, decisions about specific issues arising in individual research projects can be controversial. For example, it may be unclear whether a research project poses more than minimal risk for a child or whether parental permission for a child to participate can be waived; also in question may be the extent to which information gathered from a child can or should be shared with parents.

Before 1974 decisions about how to interact with participants were made by individual researchers. Individual researchers, however, have a significant interest in completing research projects, and this self-interest made it difficult for some researchers to protect the interests of research participants. This created cases in which research participants were treated in ways that many considered inappropriate.

In response to such problems, the U.S. government established regulations creating **institutional review boards (IRBs)** at all institutions conducting research, shifting the responsibilities of ensuring the safety of research participants to these IRBs (Beh, 2002). Each IRB is comprised mostly of scientists who are familiar with the type of research reviewed by the IRB, and each IRB must also have at least one nonscientific member and one member who is not associated with that institution. Some institutions that care for children or adults who may participate in research (such as residential treatment centers for delinquent children or hospitals for children with chronic illnesses) also have IRBs to protect the safety of their residents.

Members of an IRB read the procedures for a proposed project and then, within the guidelines set by various laws and administrative regulations, decide whether the procedures comply with ethical and legal expectations. Studies that comply can proceed; those that do not cannot. The primary advantage of IRBs is that decisions about the safety of participants in a specific study are made by experts not associated with that study. These experts may have a more realistic view of the risks and benefits to research participants than those who would like to carry out the study.

Criticisms of IRBs often focus on the many studies they must approve and the resulting lack of time they can devote to approving studies and monitoring them to ensure that the approved procedures are being followed (Beh, 2002). Concern has also been raised that because the majority of IRB members are scientists, they may have pro-research biases that could encourage them to approve questionable research procedures. The deaths of some participants in medical studies during the past few years have prompted questions about the effectiveness of some institutions' IRBs (Beh, 2002), and a recent court decision resulting from a study of the effects of lead in low-income housing on children's blood lead levels chastised an IRB for approving the study inappropriately (*Grimes v. Kennedy Krieger Institute*, 782 A.2d 807, 2001).

Key Concepts

- Beginning in 1974, responsibility for the well-being of research participants was switched from those conducting research projects to their institutions' IRBs.
- IRBs are comprised primarily of scientists but must also include a nonscientist from the institution and a community member with no links to the institution.
- The IRB reviews each proposed research project, and projects cannot take place without IRB approval.

CHAPTER GLOSSARY

Assent generally means agreement. In research it usually refers to a child's active agreement to participate in a study.

Those in an **attention comparison group** receive the same amount of contact with a professional as those in an experimental group, but the contact is designed so that components of the intervention that is being assessed are not present.

Autonomy is the general principle referring to a person's right to self-determination and the right to be free of undue influence when choosing actions.

Beneficence is the general principle of doing good for others or benefiting others.

Between-group designs compare behaviors or characteristics of people in independent groups.

A **certificate of confidentiality** obtained from the U.S. government gives researchers a legal safeguard so that they cannot be compelled to reveal individual responses given during research.

A **cohort** is a group of people involved in a longitudinal study.

A **cohort effect** is an influence on the characteristics or behaviors of a cohort due to the specific time in which the cohort lives.

Those in a **community-care control group** do not receive the intervention being investigated in a study and are told to pursue whatever services they would normally pursue in their communities.

Confidentiality is the expectation that interactions between people will not be revealed to others.

A **construct** is a characteristic that cannot be directly measured, such as intelligence or self-esteem.

Construct validity is the extent to which a measure assesses the construct it claims to assess.

Content validity refers to whether a measure assesses all the components of a construct that it is designed to measure.

Convergent validity is the extent to which scores on a measure agree with scores from other indicators of the construct being assessed.

Correlational research explores for characteristics that are associated, and the correlation statistic is used to determine the strength of the association.

Cross-sectional designs explore for age effects by studying groups of people of different ages.

A **dependent variable** is a variable that the independent variable is expected to influence.

Discriminant validity refers to a measure's ability to distinguish between the construct it is designed to measure and other constructs.

Ethics refers to the system of moral beliefs of a person or group.

An **ethics code** is a set of principles and behavioral standards focused on distinguishing moral or appropriate behavior from immoral or inappropriate behavior.

Experimental designs randomly assign participants to groups, each of which will get a different level of the independent variable being investigated by the study.

External validity refers to the extent to which the results from one study can be generalized to other people, in other places, or at other times.

Gender identity disorder is a disorder described in the DSM-IV-TR in which a person experiences persistent dissatisfaction with his or her biologically determined sex and has a persistent desire to be the opposite sex or insists that he or she is of the opposite sex.

In an experiment, an **independent variable** is a variable that is being manipulated by the researchers.

Inferential statistics are used to assess the probability that the results from a sample can be generalized to the population from which the sample was drawn.

Informed consent occurs when a person agrees, without coercion, to participate in some activity after being fully informed about what the activity entails and its potential benefits and liabilities. The person must have the cognitive ability to understand the information provided and weigh the potential benefits and costs of participation.

An **institutional review board** is designated by an institution to review proposed research and ensure the safety of research participants.

Internal consistency refers to the extent to which all the items in a measure, or in a subscale of a measure, assess the same construct.

Internal validity refers to the extent to which a study can demonstrate that an intervention being assessed, rather than other issues, produced any observed differences between pretest and posttest assessments.

Interrater reliability refers to agreement between individuals on their assessment of something.

Longitudinal designs explore for age effects by studying one group of children over time.

Minimal risk is a term used in research, indicating that the risk of participation is no greater than one would encounter in daily life or during routine physical or psychological examinations or tests.

Nonmaleficence is a general principle directing that no harm should be done or that any necessary harm should be minimized.

A **placebo** is an inert substance or treatment given as part of research to learn if another substance or treatment is effective.

The **population** is the entire group that a researcher is interested in investigating.

A **presumption** is an assumption about the truth, based on reasoning but without any proof. For example, it is presumed that an adult is competent to give informed consent.

Prospective designs follow a group of people forward in time, assessing certain characteristics and experiences at various times during the study.

Random assignment is used in experimental designs and occurs when all participants have an equal chance of being assigned to any of the groups in a study.

Random selection involves randomly choosing members of a sample from the population the sample is meant to represent. Each population member has an equal chance of being included in the sample.

Reliability refers to the consistency of a measure.

Response rate is the percentage of the people who could have participated in the study who did participate.

Retrospective designs ask people to recall events from their past.

A **sample** is drawn from a population and is meant to be representative of that population.

Single-case designs compare behaviors or characteristics of an individual at different points in time, usually to test the effectiveness of an intervention.

Test–retest reliability is a measure of the similarity of a person's scores on a test when the test is taken more than once over a short period.

Validity refers to whether a measure truly measures what it claims to measure.

Those in a **wait-list comparison group** do not receive an intervention during the experimental stage of a study, but they are eligible to receive the intervention when the experimental stage ends.

Basic Psychological Theories

Several psychological theories attempt to explain how we became who we are.

This chapter explores five psychologically based theories that can help us understand the development of child psychopathology. I call these *psychologically based* because they focus on issues related to the thoughts and feelings of children.

Psychologically based theories are useful for understanding the development of some—but not all—forms of child psychopathology. We know that some disorders, such as mental retardation, autism, and childhood-onset schizophrenia, are caused primarily by biologically based problems with brain functioning. However, even with these disorders, psychologically based theories can illuminate issues that may affect the degree of impairment a child with one of them experiences. For example, behavioral theories can help us understand the development of self-injurious behavior in some children with severe mental retardation, and family systems theories can show us why some children with childhood-onset schizophrenia experience higher levels of impairment than others.

The goal of this chapter is to describe some key principles of these theories that relate to child psychopathology, thus providing context for the following chapters' discussions of the development and treatment of disorders. By necessity, the descriptions of the theories must be brief, although references are included for those interested in additional information. For example, I describe Freud's hypothesis that humans have a life instinct and a death instinct, but I do not provide Freud's detailed justification for this hypothesis. By necessity, I also focus on aspects of the theories that are of particular relevance to the discussions in the remainder of this text. For example, although I discuss the importance of the unconscious in Freud's theory, I do not describe the Oedipus conflict. This is because I believe that knowing about the possibility of unconscious motivations helps us understand many issues related to child psychopathology, but an understanding of the Oedipus conflict does not.

Chapter Plan

We will review five psychological theories, describing some key concepts of each. We will also review the therapeutic process supported by each theory and the contributions of each theory to understanding child psychopathology. After reviewing the five theories, we will explore some features they have in common. Finally, I will give my answer to the question, "Which theory is best?"

Psychodynamic Theories

Psychodynamic theories focus on how a child's instinctual mind interacts with his or her social environment and the important people in it to produce many characteristics and behaviors. A child's mind is viewed as a dynamic and active force. It has certain characteristics, many of which are innate, that drive the child to act in certain ways. In addition, components of the mind interact with each other; the results of these interactions influence how a child thinks, feels, and behaves.

In this section we explore the psychodynamic theories of two men who have significantly influenced how we think about human development: Sigmund Freud and Carl Rogers. Although many of their views of human nature are fundamentally different, their theories have many basic similarities.

Fundamental Ideas
Conflicts between Human Instincts and Societal Expectations
Freud and Rogers both believed that the human mind emerges at birth with certain **instincts** (Ziegler, 2002). All humans have them; we never lose them; and they influence our behaviors throughout our lives. They are part of what makes us human. These instincts have energy, and they drive our behavior in predictable ways. This is an essential concept. Our instincts push us to think, feel, and behave in certain ways rather than simply reacting to the world around us. Just as we drive a nail into wood, a car down the highway, or our parents crazy, our instincts drive us.

Conflicts develop when our instinctual drives contact the society around us, which is often intolerant of our instincts and demands that we conform our behavior to societal expectations (Ziegler, 2002). Beginning early in our lives, we realize that we cannot simply follow the impulses of our instinctual drives. Instead we must regularly restrain them so that we do not act in ways that anger those on whom we depend (our parents early in our lives, but also teachers, romantic partners, drill sergeants, employers, and others as we go through life). So there is ongoing tension between the drives of our instincts and the demands of the society around us. Who we are as children and later as adults is largely determined by how we handle this tension. To the extent that our instincts and the expectations of society can coexist, we are content. To the extent that they cannot, we are anxious, frustrated, angry, or unhappy.

Freud's Views　Freud postulated two instincts: a life instinct and a death instinct (Arlow, 1989). The energy from these instincts strives to be expressed in our lives through drives. The sexual drive is the primary drive associated with the life instinct (drives toward eating, staying warm, and the other conditions needed to sustain life also exist, although Freud paid less attention to them); the aggressive drive is the primary drive associated with the death instinct. Consequently, humans have considerable mental energy focused on sex and aggression—energy that strives for expression in a variety of ways. Why are movies and songs containing sexual and aggressive themes so popular in our society? They reflect the sexual and aggressive energy of all humans. Why do wars, murder, rape, and torture have such prominent places in human history? At our most fundamental level, humans are driven by sexual and aggressive energy.

An essential aspect of appreciating Freud's theory is understanding his definition of *sex*. Freud defined *sex* much more broadly than the definitions most people use today. For Freud, *sex* meant any activity that resulted in physical pleasure. Thus a child's sexual energy is released when someone rubs his back or cuddles with him. Sex does not need to involve the genitalia. Viewed in this way, discussions of children's sexual drive make more sense.

These instinctual energies originate in the **id**—the primitive, fundamental part of our mind. The newborn's personality is all id, and the newborn's behavior is focused solely on satisfying his or her drives. However, even early in life, an infant begins to experience the world as a place where his or her drives cannot always be satisfied immediately: A parent may not immediately feed a hungry infant or may leave an infant to cry in her crib during nap time. In addition, trying to satisfy a drive's demand may create problems. For example, a parent might become angry with a crying infant or spank a toddler who acts aggressively. As a consequence, the **ego,** another component of the child's mind, begins to develop. The ego's primary goal early in a child's life is to modulate the demands of the id so that the child can live in the world successfully. In infancy and early childhood, the ego is quite weak and has little control over the id. However, with proper socialization, the ego gradually gains strength and can exert control over the id's demands as the child matures (Arlow, 1989).

The ego develops a variety of strategies for controlling the id's drives. In some situations, the ego can block the instinctual energies of the id. A good example of this is when a young child stops herself from hitting another child who has just taken something from her. However, just blocking energy does not make it disappear. Rather, it remains and builds, and it must be released at some point. As the ego matures, it develops the ability to redirect energy from instinctual drives, allowing for its release in more socially acceptable ways. For example, the energy from the aggressive drive can be released through participation in sports or by drawing pictures of monsters destroying a town (Arlow, 1989).

An important tool of the ego is **repression.** Thoughts, feelings, and conflicts that are too troubling for the conscious mind of a child (for example, fury at a parent or fear that a parent will kill the child) can be repressed

A young child's instincts frequently conflict with societal expectations.

into the unconscious by the ego. This frees the child's conscious mind of the feelings or conflicts. However, as we will explore in the next section, these repressed feelings, thoughts, and conflicts continue to influence the child's life, even though they are not available to his or her conscious mind.

The **superego,** the third component of the mind, begins to develop in childhood. The superego represents the expectations and rules of society, initially represented by the expectations and rules of parents. The superego develops as a child takes parental and societal values into himself or herself. That is, the values of parents and society become internalized as the child's own values (Freud called this process *introjection*). The child with a superego no longer has to have a parent nearby to prevent him from doing something wrong; he prevents himself from wrongdoing because his own values prohibit it. The superego enforces its values through guilt: A child who acts against his or her own values feels the painful experience of guilt and so is less likely to act against those values in the future (Arlow, 1989).

As the superego develops, the ego must contend with the instinctual energy of the id and the values of the superego, working out a strategy to satisfy both. Problems develop when the ego does not develop sufficient strength to do this, which results in some children's characters being dominated by their id and other children's characters being dominated by their superego. If the id dominates a child's life, his or her sexual and aggressive energies are often unchecked and are likely to be expressed in socially inappropriate ways. If the superego dominates, a child is frequently guilt-ridden. In short, how a child learns to negotiate conflicts between his or her instinctual drives and the requirements of society influence how content the child is.

Rogers's Views   Rogers has been described as having a much more optimistic view of human nature than Freud. He viewed the primary human instinct as the **actualizing tendency:** an innate drive to develop ourselves fully. Our actualizing tendency drives us toward flexibility rather than rigidity, openness rather than defensiveness, and freedom rather than control (Nye, 1986; Thorne, 1992). The developing infant instinctually knows what is good for himself or herself. Rogers called this **organismic valuing.** If a child is given the appropriate environment in which to develop, he or she will pursue a path to **self-actualization**—the full realization of what it is to be human. The appropriate environment for the child's development is one in which significant people (parents initially, and then other adults) consistently give the child **unconditional positive regard.** That is, parents and others must be willing to value the whole child fully and give the child consistent support (Raskin & Rogers, 1989; Rogers, 1992).

Some have interpreted Rogers's notion of unconditional positive regard as requiring that parents and other adults let children behave any way they want (Thorne, 1992). This is not accurate. Rogers would say, for example, that parents should not allow an angry child to hit her brother. However, the parents should accept the child's anger as an important part of who she is and should express their love and positive regard for her even when she is angry. Behaviors do need to be controlled, especially in younger children; but a child deserves unconditional positive regard even when she is acting in ways that parents dislike (Raskin & Rogers, 1989).

Another instinctual drive of the developing infant (and later the child, adolescent, and adult) is to seek love from others (Raskin & Rogers, 1989). Conflicts arise for the child when those from whom the child seeks love provide that love only when the child behaves in certain ways. For example, if parents withhold love from a child when she is angry, the child learns that parts of herself are bad and unacceptable. This causes the child to experience conflict between her instinctual actualizing tendency and the need to restrict who she is to keep the love of important adults. Because their need for love is so strong, most children experiencing this conflict begin to abandon organismic valuing and value themselves based on the rigid evaluations of others (I am lovable when I am like this, I am not lovable when I am like that). This sows the seeds of confusion and self-doubt, and they begin to exchange their instincts toward flexibility and openness for a personal style of rigidity and pleasing others (Ziegler, 2002). To do this successfully, they must begin to split the unlovable parts of themselves from the lovable parts. In essence, they lose touch with all of who they are, becoming what others want them to be. This leads to anxiety, depression, and a sense of being unworthy.

Importance of the Unconscious

Psychodynamic theorists view the mind as having several levels. Of particular importance is the **unconscious**—the part of the mind that is never open to conscious thought or inspection. The unconscious played a major role in Freud's theory of human development; and although Rogers focused on it less, it was an important component of his theory also (Ziegler, 2002).

The unconscious is, by definition, a part of our mind that we can never access directly. It is not as if we could access it if we tried hard enough, such as when we search our minds for the name of someone we met last month. Rather, the mind is constructed so that unconscious material is never directly available. Consequently, the unconscious is a good place for feelings, thoughts, desires, and parts of ourselves that are too painful or dangerous to have in consciousness. Freud suggested that many dangerous desires of the id were repressed into the unconscious by the ego. (The repression process is unconscious, carried out by that part of the ego that is unconscious, so we are not even aware that something is being repressed.) Rogers believed that children repress into their unconscious the parts of themselves that are unacceptable to their parents or other significant people in their lives (Arlow, 1989).

You might think that once something is placed in the unconscious, it is out of the way for good—out of sight, out of mind. With the unconscious, however, this is only half true: The repressed material is out of sight, but it is not out of mind. It is not available to the conscious mind, but it is still in the mind and continues to influence how we think, feel, and behave.

Freud believed that it was possible to gain an indirect understanding of some unconscious material through analysis of a person's dreams because unconscious material can be expressed in dreams. Unconscious material could also be inferred through analysis of a person's repetitive problem behaviors or psychiatric symptoms. For example, a person's fury at his parents for not meeting all his needs, which was repressed as a young child, might be revealed in his chronic lateness for meals with his family or by his repeated and inappropriate expressions of anger toward his employer (another authority figure). For Rogers, the parts of a person that had been split off and put into the unconscious could be inferred through the person's anxieties or through behaviors that he or she regularly engaged in but wished did not occur. For example, if I am consistently and irrationally furious at other drivers (such as those going 29 mph in a 30 mph zone), this may result from energy emitted by the angry part of me that I repressed as a young child (Arlow, 1989; Kahn, 2002).

An important part of Freud's theory, the **repetition compulsion**, is related to unconscious forces. Freud noticed that many of his patients repeated the same problematic behaviors again and again despite their anguish over them. You may have noticed the same thing about a friend or even about yourself. Freud was intrigued by this apparent compulsion to engage in behaviors that create outcomes we dislike. Although he never developed a clear explanation for the repetition compulsion, it was clear that it had roots in unconscious material that drove us to behave in certain ways (Kahn, 2002). Because this unconscious material does not disappear, we continue to behave in the same ways.

Importance of Early Experience

Although this may be clear from the discussion so far, it is worth emphasizing that psychodynamic theories view early experience as critical in a person's life. Young children must struggle with conflicts between their instincts and the expectations of parents and society. The ways in which they resolve their initial struggles will influence how they deal with the next struggle they face, and how they cope with that struggle will influence how they cope with subsequent struggles. Consequently, early experiences can have dramatic influences by setting into motion patterns of behaving and thinking that can stay with a child throughout his or her life.

Particularly important to Freud's theory was the concept of **transference** (Kahn, 2002). Repressed feelings and conflicts from early in a child's life can emerge and attach themselves to other important people in the child's (and then the adult's) life. For example, repressed feelings toward a parent can emerge and influence how a child experiences his teachers and consequently how he acts toward them. These same feelings can transfer themselves to dating partners in high school and to a spouse during adulthood. In essence, the ways in which we relate to many important people in our lives are influenced strongly by unconscious material associated with those who were important to us in early childhood.

The Therapeutic Process

Although the strategies of the therapies proposed by Freud and Rogers differ dramatically, both are based on the belief that problematic behaviors and symptoms are influenced by unconscious material. Consequently, the therapeutic process should help a person (1) understand this unconscious material and the influence it is having on his or her life and (2) express it in ways that cause the person less anguish.

The fundamental goal of Freud's psychoanalysis was to "make the unconscious conscious," and the long and laborious process of psychoanalysis was designed to uncover and understand unconscious material. During psychoanalysis, the therapist interprets information provided by the patient. Dreams are often interpreted, as are the patient's behaviors toward the psychoanalyst (that is, transference) and the patient's *free associations* (saying whatever comes to mind during therapy). Although the patient can never gain direct access to the unconscious material, as he or she gradually comes to appreciate the unconscious material through interpretation by the therapist, he or she gains more control over it. Understanding the power of the unconscious material allows the patient to recognize it when it arises and use cognitive and other strategies to counteract it. For example, an adolescent who seems to create negative relationships with all his teachers may learn that unconscious anger at his parents is driving his behavior toward other authority figures. This understanding does not diminish the unconscious anger, but it lets the adolescent modify his behavior toward his teachers. When he finds himself preparing to say something negative to a teacher, for instance, he can say to himself, "This is just my unconscious anger trying to express itself"; this understanding helps him avoid making the negative comment (Kahn, 2002).

The goal of Rogers's *person-centered therapy* is to allow the person to *reclaim* the parts of himself or herself that were previously split into the unconscious (Thorne, 1992). This is accomplished by the therapist's creating a therapeutic environment in which a person consistently experiences unconditional positive regard. As a person talks about anxiety, anger, hatred of her family, feelings of worthlessness, attraction to a teacher, or other issues, the therapist maintains an accepting attitude toward all the feelings she expresses and always maintains unconditional positive regard for her as a person. The therapist may encourage her not to engage in some behaviors and to engage in others, but never expresses dismay or disapproval of her or her feelings. As she experiences consistent unconditional positive regard in the therapeutic setting, possibly for the first time in her life, she gradually recaptures a sense of organismic valuing. Because she does not have to act in certain rigid ways to gain approval from the therapist, she can begin to explore and appreciate all the different parts of herself: She can resume her journey toward self-actualization (Rogers, 1992).

As the person recaptures her sense of organismic valuing, she can reclaim the parts of herself that had been split off and ignored. This dramatically reduces the influence of these split-off parts on her behavior. For example, to the extent that she can reclaim the angry part of herself and appreciate it and use it for growth, it will not impose itself on her life through irrational anger at her family.

Applicability to Child Psychopathology

Psychodynamic theories about the development of child psychopathology are not as widely accepted these days as they once were, largely because it is difficult to measure unconscious influences on behavior; consequently it is difficult to do research on psychodynamic processes. In addition, our developing knowledge of many disorders with a primarily biological basis, such as bipolar disorder, schizophrenia, and enuresis, has helped us understand that they are not caused by psychodynamic forces as was previously thought.

Despite their relative lack of current popularity, considering psychodynamic explanations for some disorders or problem behaviors can enhance our ability to understand their development. For example, a child's aggressive behavior might be partly influenced by unconscious anger toward a parent. In addition, understanding transference can help us comprehend seemingly illogical and inappropriate behavior of a child toward peers or adults. For example, knowing about transference can help us understand the angry and aggressive behaviors toward parents and teachers of a child adopted into a loving home at age 8.

Because unconscious forces play such an important role in psychodynamic theories, those looking for proof that these theories are correct are always frustrated in their search. The proof, if it exists, is hidden in our unconscious. Despite the difficulty of knowing whether psychodynamic theories are correct, they offer us an informative way to think about our development.

Key Concepts

- The human mind emerges at birth with certain instincts, and a variety of conflicts develop when our instinctual drives contact the demands of society.

- Freud postulated two instincts—a life instinct and a death instinct. The sexual drive is the primary drive associated with the life instinct, and the aggressive drive is the primary drive associated with the death instinct.
- The ego attempts to balance the instinctual demands of the id with the introjected societal demands of the superego.
- Rogers viewed the primary human instinct as the actualizing tendency: an innate drive to develop ourselves fully. Another instinct is the need for the love of others. Conflicts arise when those from whom a child seeks love provide it only when the child acts in certain ways.
- The mind has several levels, and the unconscious mind, or that part of the mind that is never open to inspection, is particularly important. Material in the unconscious exerts a continuing influence on a person, even though the person is unaware of it.
- Early experience is particularly important in a person's life.
- Although Freud's and Rogers's therapeutic strategies differ significantly, both are designed to help a person understand unconscious material, integrate it into his or her life, and express it in ways that cause the person less anguish.
- Psychodynamic theories broaden our perspective on child psychopathology by suggesting that some causes of problem behavior may be unconscious.

Behavioral Theories

Behavioral theories differ fundamentally from psychodynamic theories in many ways. Rather than focusing on the interplay of unseen dynamic forces of the mind, they focus on observable behaviors; rather than arguing that a person's unconscious has important influences on his or her behaviors, they state that forces in the environment and outside the person have the primary influence.

Two founding theorists of the behavioral movement were John Watson and Ivan Pavlov (Wilson, 1989). Watson was an influential American psychologist who wrote passionately in the early 1900s against the prevailing psychoanalytic theories of the time, asserting that psychoanalysis was "based largely on religion, introspective psychology and Voodooism" (Watson, 1924). Watson rejected theories that relied on unseen mental forces, claiming that they were unscientific. Rather, he argued, environmental influences determined who a person became, and understanding human behavior required the scientific study of these environmental forces.

Pavlov was a Russian physiologist who established the foundation for understanding what has since been called **classical conditioning** (Wilson, 1989). In his famous experiment with dogs, Pavlov showed that some behaviors are reflexively elicited by the environment (placing meat powder on a dog's tongue reflexively elicits salivation) and that when another stimulus is paired repeatedly with the stimulus that reflexively elicits the behavior (in Pavlov's case, the sound of a bell), the second environmental stimulus can soon elicit the response by itself (the bell elicits salivation by itself).

In this section we explore briefly the behavioral theories of two psychologists: B. F. Skinner, an American who developed a detailed theory of human behavior based on operant conditioning, and Joseph Wolpe, a South African who used Pavlov's theories to create therapeutic strategies for eliminating many problem behaviors. Skinner's theory focuses on how human behaviors are shaped by the responses to those behaviors. The behavior occurs and then is shaped by environmental response. Wolpe's therapeutic strategies are based on classical conditioning, in which a person's behaviors are elicited by environmental stimuli. Something in the environment occurs, and it elicits a behavior. As with the two theories presented in the previous section, despite the differences between these two theories, they share many concepts.

Fundamental Ideas
Focus on Behavior

As you might assume, behaviorists focus on behaviors (Wilson, 1989). Behaviors, they believe, are shaped by their antecedents (things occurring before the behavior) or consequences (things occurring after the behavior) or both, rather than by unseen mental processes. Thus as they try to understand a child's behavior, behaviorists focus not on processes inside the child's mind but on observable stimuli that elicit the child's behavior or on observable responses to the child's behavior.

Focus on the Present

When analyzing a particular behavior, behaviorists focus primarily on the present. Although they might have some interest in how a behavior developed earlier in a child's life to provide some context for understanding it, the primary focus is on how that behavior is being maintained by current antecedents and consequences. Although behaviorists understand that it is through past environmental influences that behaviors have developed, their primary goal is to understand how behaviors are maintained currently so that they can be changed in the present (Wilson, 1989).

Behaviors Are Shaped by the Environment

Behaviorists believe that our behaviors are shaped by the environment. As first shown by Pavlov's experiments with dogs, some behaviors are elicited by environmental stimuli that have been connected to other stimuli that reflexively elicit the behaviors. In a later experiment, Watson showed that fear behaviors could be elicited from a toddler by the presence of a rabbit after the presence of the rabbit had been paired repeatedly with a loud sound, which reflexively elicits fear in a young child (Wilson, 1989). The behaviors elicited by the sound of a bell or the sight of a rabbit occur because the dog, child, or other organism has learned that there is a connection between the two stimuli. A dog learns, for example, that when a bell rings meat powder will soon be available, so it salivates when a bell rings. Similarly, a child learns that when a rabbit is present a loud sound will soon occur, so he responds with fear behaviors when he sees a rabbit.

In the **operant conditioning** paradigm described by Skinner, a person or other animal in a novel situation emits a variety of behaviors somewhat randomly (Skinner, 1953). Some of these behaviors are strengthened by responses from the environment (*reinforcement*), whereas others are weakened by responses from the environment (*punishment*). For example, as infants emerge into the world, they begin "operating" on the environment by behaving, and their behaviors are shaped by responses from their environment. If an infant cries when she is hungry and is fed, the feeding (which relieves the hunger) reinforces the behavior of crying when hungry, and the baby is more likely to cry when hungry in the future. If, however, the child is still crying when hungry at age 4 years, the frown or rebuke from her mother will punish her crying behaviors, and she will be less likely to cry when hungry. A behavior can be **extinguished** if it occurs many times with no reinforcement. A teacher ignoring the misbehavior of a student probably hopes to extinguish the behavior by not responding to it.

Two types of reinforcement can occur. *Positive reinforcement* occurs when something valued by a child follows a behavior, such as receiving an extra-large dessert after eating vegetables or receiving a parent's smile after getting all the words correct on a spelling test. *Negative reinforcement* occurs when something noxious to the child is removed following a behavior, such as if a parent stops nagging a child after the child eats his vegetables or if a bully stops hitting a child after the child gives the bully her lunch money. Positive and negative reinforcement both make it more likely that the behavior that has been reinforced will occur again under similar circumstances. (Because of the word *negative*, some people equate negative reinforcement with punishment. However, negative reinforcement increases the likelihood of a behavior, whereas punishment decreases the likelihood of a behavior.)

As a child develops, the reinforcements or punishments the child experiences following his or her gradually expanding repertoire of behaviors determine which of these behaviors occur more or less frequently (Skinner, 1953). For example, a child who receives praise (reinforcement) whenever she tries a new activity will be more likely to try new activities in the future; a child who is chastised or made fun of (punishment) when she tries a new activity and fails will be less likely to try new activities in the future. Through this process, a developing child amasses a set of behaviors that become seen as the child's personality: The child's behaviors are who the child is (Nye, 1979).

Although behaviorists see the environment as shaping individuals' behaviors, they do not see humans as automatons, blindly responding to the environment. People have self-control, and in many situations, each of us has clearly chosen to behave in particular ways: going out to a party or staying home and studying, going home to visit parents over a holiday or going somewhere with friends, having or not having sex. Behaviorists argue, however, that the choices we make are shaped by the environment rather than by unseen forces such as "inner strength" or "a sense of responsibility" (Nye, 1986). We decide how to behave, but the basis for these decisions comes from years of environmental influence.

Notes from the Author: Swimming at College

Cornell University, where I worked during the years I was writing this text, is unique in several ways. The university has a decentralized system of education, and almost all graduation requirements are specified by individual colleges at Cornell, not by the university. As far as I know, the university specifies only two graduation requirements: A student must earn 120 semester credits and must be able to swim. The swimming requirement can be met by passing a swimming test or by taking two swimming classes. For some students passing the swimming requirement is the most frightening part of their education. Some students who walk bravely into advanced engineering or chemistry courses are gripped with fear when they have to enter the deep end of a swimming pool. (My understanding is that the swimming requirement was started because some Cornell alumni died in rivers or lakes during World War I because they could not swim. In response, the university administration adopted the requirement that everyone must be able to swim before graduating; exceptions are granted to students who cannot swim for religious or medical reasons.)

A wonderful instructor at Cornell, Al Gannert, works individually with frightened students for hours to help them overcome their fear of swimming by gradually introducing them to swimming in deep water. Many students who were never able to swim have been helped by him. His work with these students is based on the concept of reciprocal inhibition—a therapeutic strategy developed by Wolpe that is discussed in the next section.

The Therapeutic Process

As you might expect, because the environment is viewed by behaviorists as shaping individuals' behavior, facilitating environmental change is at the foundation of behavioral therapy. Occasionally behavioral therapists may work with children individually or in small groups. More often, however, behavioral therapists work with a child and the adults who are in regular contact with the child to create an environment that will shape the child's behaviors in new ways. The behavioral therapist is seen as a collaborator, helping the child, parents, teachers, and others understand the reasons for a child's behavior and how it can be changed.

Operant Conditioning

Behavioral therapy based on Skinner's operant conditioning paradigm requires careful analysis of the environments in which problem behavior occurs. This process, called **applied behavioral analysis** (Wilson, 1989), involves careful assessment of the antecedents and consequences of problem and nonproblem behaviors, either through direct observations of a child's behaviors or from detailed reports from parents, teachers, or others who know the child well. Information from the assessment is analyzed by the therapist, who then describes to the child and important adults how the child's behaviors are being shaped. Then, working collaboratively with all involved, the therapist helps create a plan through which problem behaviors can be extinguished or punished and more appropriate behaviors can be reinforced. Detailed instructions are given to the child and adults regarding the creation of a new set of antecedents and consequences to the child's problem and socially appropriate behaviors. The therapist monitors the accuracy with which the plan is implemented, providing corrective instruction if the plan is not implemented correctly. The child's behavior is monitored, and changes to the plan are made as appropriate (Nye, 1979).

For example, consider a child who acts out in class. Analysis of the child's behavior might reveal that the teacher has the child stay after school in detention with her when he misbehaves. From conversations with the teacher, it becomes clear that the frequency of the detentions has increased during the school year, as has the child's acting out in class. The therapist might conclude that the detentions are not punishment, as the teacher believes they are, but are actually positive reinforcements for the child's acting out because this behavior has increased. Talking with the child might reveal that detention stopped him from having to face bullies on the playground after school or gave him the opportunity to be close to a teacher on whom he had developed a crush. The therapist might then consult with the teacher about ways to change the consequences of the child's acting out and thus to change the child's behavior. For example, the therapist might suggest that the child be allowed to remain in the classroom after school only when he behaves during the school day.

If the therapist is correct that staying with the teacher after school is positive reinforcement, then altering the requirements for earning this reinforcement should change the child's behavior. If, however, the child's acting-out behavior does not decrease after the teacher institutes her new requirements for his staying after school, the therapist's analysis may be incorrect. Further analysis will need to be conducted and a new plan developed and monitored. Note that this entire process is done in collaboration with the child, teacher, and possibly the parents. Most often behavioral therapy is not a process done *to* a child—it is done *with* the child (Nye, 1979).

Classical Conditioning

Based on the principles of classical conditioning, Joseph Wolpe developed a therapeutic process called *systematic desensitization* (Wolpe, 1958). It is used primarily to treat phobias, which are persistent, irrational fears (such as fears of heights, spiders, or enclosed spaces). Systematic desensitization uses a technique called **reciprocal inhibition**, which pairs a response that inhibits anxiety (typically relaxation) with the source of the phobia. If the stimulus associated with the phobia can be paired with relaxation frequently enough, the connection between the stimulus and the fear it once evoked will be broken. For example, if the swimming instructor at Cornell can gently encourage frightened students to be in a swimming pool in a relaxed state, the connection between the swimming pool and the students' fear will gradually be weakened.

In Wolpe's system a client first describes the source of the fear or anxiety. A list is created in collaboration with the client that specifies, in ascending order, situations that evoke the fear or anxiety. For example, the list for a child who is anxious speaking in front of the class might look like Table 3.1. The therapist spends a session or two teaching the child how to relax and encourages the child to practice relaxing at home. During the next therapy session, the therapist tells the child that she is going to ask the child to relax and then to imagine each situation on the list, starting with the least anxiety-provoking one. The child is instructed to lift a finger if she feels anxious while imagining the scene. The therapist again helps the child relax and asks her to imagine the least anxiety-provoking situation. If the child raises her finger again, the therapist tells her to stop imagining the situation. After relaxing, the child imagines the least anxiety-provoking situation again. If the child can imagine that situation while still feeling relaxed, the therapist asks her to imagine the next situation on the list. If the child signals that anxiety is occurring, the therapist goes back to the previous item on the list, where she can be relaxed. During several sessions, the therapist and child may be able to get through the entire list, with the child always feeling relaxed while imagining each situation before moving to the next item on the list. Following this, the therapist and child might engage in some behaviors on the list, rather than just imagining them. Again, the goal is to have the child feel relaxed in a situation that previously evoked anxiety. In this way, connections between the situations and relaxation are established, which weakens the connections between the situations and anxiety.

TABLE 3.1

Events That Can Cause Anxiety:

1. The teacher handing out oral report assignments.
2. Thinking about having to learn the material for an oral report.
3. Looking up the material for an oral report.
4. Writing note cards for the oral report.
5. Thinking about having to give the oral report.
6. Trying to remember the cards for the oral report.
7. Practicing the oral report with my mother.
8. Getting out of bed the day I have to give the oral report.
9. Walking to school the day I have to give the oral report.
10. Saying the pledge of allegiance the day I have to give the oral report.

•••

17. Sitting in my desk right before I have to give the oral report.
18. Hearing the teacher call my name.
19. Walking to the front of the class.
20. Standing in front of everyone.
21. Starting to give my oral report.

Systematic desensitization has been used effectively to reduce anxiety.

Recent technological advances have allowed some therapists to use virtual reality during reciprocal inhibition. A client may observe the source of his or her fear on a screen in a virtual reality laboratory. For example, observing a spider as the client looks around a room in virtual reality can be more powerful than simply imagining a spider but less anxiety-provoking that having to be in a room with a spider (Winerman, 2005).

Of course, because operant and classical conditioning paradigms can work together to create problem behavior, more than one type of behavioral intervention might be combined during an intervention. For example, the therapist working with the girl who is anxious about public speaking might create a behavioral plan in which parents or teachers provide positive reinforcement each time she speaks in front of the class.

Notes from the Author: Experiment with Systematic Desensitization

You can be your own therapist and try systematic desensitization to change your own fears. When I was a graduate student, I developed a strong fear of lightning after being in a house that was hit by lightning. My fear became problematic because I often could not sleep when thunderstorms were in my area. I decided to try systematic desensitization to reduce my fear of lightning. I found a long hallway in the psychology building with a window that looked in the direction from which many thunderstorms came. I could stand in the hallway and listen to the thunder and see the lightning. However, I felt safe because the building was very large and I was on a lower floor. I started by standing in the hallway far enough away from the window so that I did not feel any fear when observing the lightning. Each time there was a thunderstorm, I went into the hall, stood far from the window, and relaxed. I then moved toward the window a step at a time. If I began to feel fearful, I stepped back until I felt relaxed. Once I was relaxed, I tried moving forward again, always moving back if I felt fearful. Within a few months I could stand by the window and watch the beauty of thunderstorms. They still make me nervous, and I quickly go inside if one is near; but now I feel safe inside, and hearing thunder and seeing lightning are not nearly as frightening as before.

You can do the same thing. Are you terribly afraid of snakes? Go to the nearest zoo and stand as far away from the snakes in their cages as necessary for you to feel relaxed. Gradually move toward the cages, always stepping back when you start to feel fear.

Applicability to Child Psychopathology

Behavioral theories have broadened our thinking about the development of behavioral or emotional disorders by showing that they can develop in response to environmental conditions. They have helped us see that troubling behavior occurs not because of something that is wrong with the child (perhaps requiring that the child be isolated or treated like a second-class person) but because of the environmental conditions in which the child has developed. For example, a child's aggression can be conceptualized as the result of reinforcement of aggressive behavior (such as being praised by older siblings for being tough) and lack of reinforcement of nonaggressive behavior (being ignored by other children except when being aggressive); a child's anxiety about school can be seen as resulting from the pairing of school attendance and naturally occurring fear (such as fear of being assaulted while walking to school) and from reinforcement of anxious behavior (being allowed to stay home when anxious).

Behavioral theorists and therapists have also helped us understand that well-meaning adults can create environments in which children learn problem behaviors, despite the best intentions of the adults. The example of the teacher and the child in detention is an instance of this: The teacher intended to create an environment in which the child's acting-out behavior would decrease, but instead she created one in which the behavior increased.

Key Concepts

- When explaining behaviors, behaviorists focus on their current antecedents and consequences rather than on unseen mental processes or how the behaviors might have developed initially.
- Behaviors are shaped by the environment. The classical conditioning paradigm suggests that some behaviors are elicited by environmental stimuli; the operant conditioning paradigm suggests that a person engages in a variety of behaviors with some being strengthened and others being weakened through responses from the environment.

- Humans are not automatons. People choose their behaviors, but these choices are shaped by the environment rather than by unseen forces such as a sense of responsibility.
- Behavioral therapy based on operant conditioning requires careful analysis of the reinforcements and punishments for a behavior and changes to those reinforcements and punishments.
- Reciprocal inhibition, a therapy based on classical conditioning, pairs relaxation with a stimulus that evokes anxiety, thereby weakening the connection between the stimulus and the anxiety.
- Behavioral theories have been influential in helping us understand that the development and exacerbation of many disorders are influenced by learning.

Cognitive Theories

Cognitive theories focus on how our thoughts influence our emotions and behaviors. Behaviors are seen as resulting mainly from thoughts and belief systems rather than emerging from unconscious drives or being shaped by the environment. In this section we focus on the cognitive theories of two psychologists, Aaron Beck and Albert Ellis, and the cognitive therapies based on these theories. Although the theories of both men have many fundamental similarities, they differ in some important ways.

Fundamental Ideas

Belief Systems

All of us have many beliefs about ourselves (for example, I am generally competent; I am not very good-looking), our lives (I have a good life; I must struggle to get everything), and our world (most people are supportive and helpful; people are generally out to get only what is good for them). Many of our beliefs are organized into systems called **schemata**: fundamental beliefs and assumptions about how we and the world function (Robins & Hayes, 1993). These schemata develop and evolve over a person's lifetime based on his or her experiences and observations. As a child grows, for example, she develops schemata about herself based on how she functions in the world and how others treat her; and she develops schemata about neighborhoods, friends, adults, teachers, school, and other components of her life based on her experiences with them. For example, consider a child raised in a family where she receives considerable support and encouragement whenever she undertakes a new activity (like riding her tricycle, playing the piano, or finger painting) whether or not she is initially successful. She is likely to develop schemata that reflect these experiences: The world is an exciting place, she is competent, and people are supportive and encouraging. Consider another child whose initial efforts at a new activity are derided if they are not completely successful and whose mistakes are consistently emphasized. This child is likely to develop schemata that reflect his experience: The world is a frustrating place, he is incompetent, and people are critical and unsupportive.

Schemata develop because they help us organize our experiences so we can make sense of them and our world more easily (Robins & Hayes, 1993). For example, schemata help us respond to new experiences by linking them to categories of beliefs about ourselves and our world. When we encounter a new situation, we do not have to struggle to develop a whole new strategy for reacting to it; rather, we can classify it with our schemata and respond with strategies that we have used in similar situations in the past. The girl just mentioned, for example, will probably take on new academic, athletic, or social challenges with confidence. The boy, on the other hand, is likely to shrink from challenges and either avoid them or approach them with pessimism.

Notes from the Author: Your "Professor" Schemata

You probably have schemata about what professors are like and how to interact with them. If you go to the office of a professor you have never met before, your initial behavior is likely to be influenced by the professor schemata you have developed through your experiences with professors. You may act differentially, barge in and act assertively (or aggressively), or stand quietly and see how the professor responds to your presence. However you act, your initial decisions about how to act are made easier by your schemata: You do not need to start from scratch in deciding how to behave around a professor every time you meet one. Can you think of schemata you have about others in your environment (athletes, fraternity and sorority members, engineers, clerks at K-Mart)? How do your schemata influence your interactions with them?

Despite their value, schemata can also create problems because they bias our perceptions of people and the world (Beck & Weishaar, 1989). Our perceptions of others and their behaviors are often strongly influenced by how we expect them to act, and these expectations are based on our schemata. Our subsequent behaviors are then influenced by our perceptions. Beck (1999) provides the following thought-provoking example for considering how our schemata can influence our behaviors:

Suppose you see a flying object in the distance. As it comes closer, you decide that it is probably a bird. If you are not particularly interested in birds, your attention wanders to other things. . . . Now imagine that your country is at war. . . . Your attention is riveted to the distant flying object. If you think it may be an enemy aircraft, your psychological and physiological systems are totally mobilized. . . . Also, as you move about off duty, you will be poised to recognize enemy agents who might be mingling in the crowd. . . . You will focus on small details such as a man's slight foreign accent, his ignorance of certain sports figures in your country, or his secret, suspicious-looking meetings with other strangers. (pp. 71–72)

As another example of the influence of schemata, consider a child who has a schema that adults are hostile and dangerous, developed through several years of being surrounded by adults with these characteristics. This child is likely to perceive a new teacher as hostile and dangerous. Thus on the first day of school, when the teacher says, "All right, everyone get in line," the child may experience this as the teacher "yelling" at him; when the teacher says to the whole class, "It's time to stop playing and go back to the classroom," the child may perceive this as the teacher stopping the game because he is having so much fun playing. Beck calls these biased perceptions *cognitive distortions* and asserts that they have important influences on our behaviors. This child, for example, may act in hostile ways toward a teacher who he believes is being hostile to him. To an outside observer, the child's hostility seems unwarranted and out of place. To the child, however, his actions are logical given his perception that the teacher is being hostile.

Ellis also describes the importance of belief systems in our lives. He says we have a biologically based capacity to form rational and irrational beliefs and to hold doggedly to these beliefs once they form (Ellis, 1989). We do not develop schemata merely because they help us organize our experiences; we develop them because we are predisposed to do so.

Cognitions Influence Emotions and Behaviors

When most of us consider the connections between our emotions and our thoughts, we tend to believe that our emotions drive our thinking: If we are feeling sad we will think about sad things; if we are feeling anxious we will think about things and people that make us anxious. Consequently, when we are feeling sad or anxious, we try to change our emotions so we will stop having so many negative thoughts. Cognitive theorists, however, believe just the opposite: Our thoughts drive our emotions. I feel sad because I am thinking depressive thoughts; I feel anxious because I am thinking anxious thoughts. Thus changing how we think will change our emotions. If we stop thinking about so many depressing things, we will feel less depressed; if we stop thinking about everything that can go wrong next week, we will stop feeling anxious.

Ellis proposed a clear link between thoughts, emotions, and behaviors, using what he called the *ABC model of behavior* (Ellis, 1989). An event activates (A) one or more beliefs (B), and these beliefs lead to emotional and behavioral consequences (C). For example, consider a child who has to give an oral report in front of her class. Preparing to give the oral report (A) activates certain beliefs (B): "I am always terrible when I give oral reports" or "The other kids are going to laugh and make fun of me." These beliefs lead to emotional consequences (C), such as anxiety, and to behavioral consequences such as moping in her room rather than preparing for her oral report—which is likely to result in her doing poorly on the oral report, which will reinforce her beliefs.

Ellis focused on our tendencies to form irrational beliefs. As just noted, he believed these tendencies were innate in humans and that the social systems in which many of us are raised exacerbate these innate tendencies toward irrationality. One tendency Ellis highlighted is our tendency to *catastrophize:*

to inflate dramatically the actual or anticipated negative consequences of some event. Catastrophizing can generate strong negative emotions and inappropriate behaviors. These emotions and behaviors can create additional beliefs and even stronger emotions and more problematic behaviors, as Ellis describes in this amusing (but accurate for many of us) paragraph:

> Thus, if you originally start with something like (A): "I did poorly on my job today." (B): "Isn't that horrible!" you will wind up with (C): feelings of anxiety, worthlessness, and depression. You may now start over with (A^2): "I feel anxious and depressed and worthless!" (B^2): "Isn't that horrible!" Now you end up with (C^2): even greater feelings of anxiety, worthlessness, and depression. . . . You now have two consequences or symptoms for the price of one, and you often go around and around, in a vicious cycle of (a) condemning yourself for doing poorly at some task, (b) feeling guilty or depressed because of this self-condemnation, (c) condemning yourself for your feelings of guilt and depression, (d) condemning yourself for condemning yourself, (e) condemning yourself for seeing that you condemn yourself and for still not stopping condemning yourself, (f) condemning yourself for going for psychotherapeutic help and still not getting better, (g) condemning yourself for being more disturbed than other individuals, (h) concluding that you are indubitably hopelessly disturbed and that nothing can be done about it; and so on, in an endless spiral. (Ellis, 1989, p. 207)

As you can see in Ellis's description, our irrational thoughts can get out of control, with severe consequences for our feelings and behaviors.

Another type of damaging irrational beliefs is based on "musts." "I *must* be happy all the time," "I *must* get an A on every assignment," and "I *must* be liked by everyone who knows me" are examples of what Ellis calls **must-urbation** (Ellis, 1993). These musts are always problematic. If we *must* be happy all the time, the sadness or anxiety we all experience periodically is *terrible* rather than just uncomfortable. If we *must* be liked by everyone, the social slights we all experience feel *awful* and *devastating* rather than just irritating.

Finally, Ellis asserts that the habit of viewing negative experiences as indicators of personal worth can produce intensely negative consequences. For example, a girl can believe that *she* is a failure because she is not in the top reading group or because she failed to make the first string on her softball team; or a boy can believe that *he* is a social outcast because a girl he likes will not go to a school dance with him. Being sad in the face of a failure or setback is appropriate, but it is irrational to base self-evaluations on the outcomes of individual experiences. "They can say, '*It* is good that I succeed and am loved' or '*It* is bad when I fail and get rejected.' But they had better not say '*I* am good for succeeding' and '*I* am bad for getting rejected'" (Ellis, 1993, p. 4).

Beck also provides a model for understanding how our thoughts influence our emotions and behaviors. He suggests that dysfunctional schemata produce **automatic thoughts** that arise spontaneously, are fleeting, and often go unrecognized by the person having them (Robins & Hayes, 1993). These thoughts can dramatically affect a person's perceptions of events and can also influence his or her emotions and behaviors. For example, consider a child walking into a school dance with a schema that she is unattractive and a social outcast. She may have the automatic thought "No one is going to ask me to dance," which quickly produces feelings of anxiety and sadness and may cause her to spend most of the dance standing off to the side of the room. If she notices someone smiling at her, her schema is likely to influence how she perceives the smile and interprets it. She may think, "He is smiling because no one has asked me to dance" or "He is just pitying me." Her thoughts may cause her to look away or walk to another part of the room rather than smile back. Her behaviors, of course, will contribute to the fact that no one asks her to dance, which will reinforce her schema. Consider another example: Many students experience math anxiety, which is usually associated with a schema about not being able to learn math. A student with this schema may experience automatic thoughts such as "I always fail at math" or "I never understand math" when enrolling for a course, preparing to take an exam, or taking an exam. These thoughts and emotions may produce lack of effort on homework ("Why even try?") and heightened anxiety during tests, which are likely to cause poor performance and rein-force the schema from which the automatic thoughts sprang.

The Therapeutic Process

Cognitive therapy has been described as "collaborative empiricism" (Beck, 1967). The primary goal of the early stage of cognitive therapy is to help clients recognize irrational or automatic thoughts, note the circumstances under which they occur, and observe the changes in mood and behavior that they cause (Beck & Weishaar, 1989). Once the cognitions have been identified, the therapist and client work together to determine whether they are accurate (rational) or whether other beliefs might be more appropriate. The therapist does not try to force the client to think differently but gently challenges the client to consider whether other cognitions might be more appropriate.

For example, consider a 12-year-old who is depressed. Early conversations with a therapist might reveal that she is often lonely and believes that peers and adults avoid her because they do not like her. Her therapist might encourage her to pay attention to her thoughts when she is around other children and to pay particular attention to her thoughts when she is feeling lonely or depressed. She might discover that when she sees other children playing together she thinks, "No one will ever play with me" and "Everyone hates me." Her therapist might help her understand the connection between her thoughts, feelings, and behaviors by asking her how she felt and what she did after she had these thoughts. This might help the girl recognize that her feelings of sadness and her decision to sit by herself at the edge of the playground are the consequences of her negative thoughts. This can be an important realization for the girl: It helps her understand that she has some control over her feelings and behaviors and can change how she feels and acts by changing her cognitions. She can learn that she is not just a helpless victim of life; rather, her thinking (which she can control) is influencing what happens to her.

The therapist might then begin to gently challenge the girl's beliefs. He might ask her, for example, whether she believed the other children would not play with her because they had repelled her attempt to join the game or because she just assumed they would not. He could ask whether there were times when she and another child had worked successfully together on a class project. He might ask whether other children are friendly with the girl when she attends church or summer camp. Such questioning can help the child begin to understand that her schema about no one liking her is not always accurate.

Long-term cognitive therapy focuses on a child's schemata, "musts," or other basic cognitions that are the source of automatic thoughts or irrational beliefs (Beck, 1993). For example, the girl who thought no one would dance with her may have a schema of "I am an unlikable person" or may have a series of "musts" such as "Everyone must like me." The therapist and child work to uncover and describe these fundamental beliefs, hypothesize about how they developed, and assess whether they are accurate.

For several decades Ellis has advocated a therapeutic style he developed called rational emotive therapy (RET), which "attempts to show clients that they had better give up perfectionism if they want to lead a happier, less anxiety-ridden existence" (Ellis, 1989, p. 213). RET focuses on helping clients identify irrational beliefs and how they influence their lives, and on helping them identify their own "shoulds, oughts, and musts . . . and how to accept reality, even when it is pretty grim" (p. 213). RET often involves assignments outside therapy to help clients understand that failure might be uncomfortable but is not catastrophic. Clients are also encouraged to reward themselves after attempting new activities (whether successful or not) and to enjoy life whenever possible.

Applicability to Child Psychopathology

Cognitive therapy has become widely used with children experiencing many problems and disorders. It has also received the most research attention and has been shown to be effective with a wide range of problems such as depression, anxiety, and conduct problems (three of the most common forms of childhood psychopathology); it is used successfully to treat children who have experienced many types of traumas, such as sexual abuse (Kendall, 1993; Saywitz, Mannarino, Berliner, & Cohen, 2000).

Cognitive theory has helped those working with troubled children to understand more clearly how dysfunctional cognitions can influence children's lives. Thus cognitive theories provide therapists and others working with children an appreciation of another important influence in the development of child psychopathology: the children's cognitions. By identifying this influence, cognitive therapists give us another strategy for helping children overcome many of the problems they face.

Key Concepts

- Schemata are belief systems that develop during a person's life and assist in the organization of a person's experiences and the responses that he or she makes in novel situations.
- Schemata can bias a person's perception of others or of events. These biased perceptions influence how a person responds to others or to events.
- Cognitive theorists argue that our thoughts are at the foundation of our emotions and our behaviors.
- Ellis's ABC model suggests that an event activates (A) one or more beliefs (B) that then lead to emotional and behavioral consequences (C).
- *Catastrophizing* refers to irrational thinking that dramatically inflates the anticipated negative consequences of an event.
- *Must-urbation* refers to people's tendency to have many "musts" in their lives that create strong negative beliefs when they are not met.
- *Automatic thoughts* are fleeting and arise spontaneously during certain events. They can influence how a person responds to events emotionally and behaviorally.
- Cognitive therapy involves examination of a person's thoughts, connection of thoughts to emotions and behaviors, and changing of irrational or problematic thoughts.
- Cognitive therapy is effective with children having a wide range of problems; it has illuminated the strong influence thoughts have in all of our lives.

Attachment Theory

In 1950 John Bowlby, a British psychiatrist, was invited by the World Health Organization to report on the mental health of the many London children who had been made homeless by the war. The report asserted that disruptions in relationships with primary caregivers, especially during the first three years of life, put children at greatly increased risk for mental illness and behavior problems (Bowlby, 1951). Although the report was well received and influential in shaping social policy and caseworker training, it was deficient in one important respect: It failed to explain why or how such experiences could produce these harmful effects. The report motivated a search for answers that spanned many years. The outcome of this work was a new theory of child development, *attachment theory;* Bowlby eventually published three volumes in which the basic tenets and supporting evidence for attachment theory were described (Bowlby, 1969, 1973, 1980).

Fundamental Ideas

The foundation of attachment theory comes from evolutionary thinking. Humans, like other primates, face the challenge of having children who are born in such an extreme state of immaturity that they cannot survive without adult protection and care for many years. Over many generations in early human history, certain behaviors of infants and their mothers developed that promoted the safety of the infant and increased the chance of the infant surviving into childhood. Through the process of natural selection, these complementary behaviors became part of all humans.

Bowlby called these complementary behaviors between an infant and mother an **attachment behavioral system;** this system promotes the survival of an infant by encouraging physical proximity between a mother and child. For example, when an infant is frightened, hungry, cold, or uncomfortable, he or she cries. This sound not only alerts the mother to the infant's distress, but it also bothers the mother. Consequently she is likely to hold, feed, or warm the infant. This usually stops the crying, which is a relief to the mother, and causes smiling, cooing, or other behaviors from the infant that the mother finds pleasing. This behavioral dance between the infant and the mother promotes the survival of the infant by keeping the mother close to the infant and attentive to the infant's needs. Interestingly, from the behavioral perspective, the mother's comforting behaviors are being positively reinforced (by the baby's smiling) and negatively reinforced (by the cessation of the baby's crying); and the baby's crying behaviors are being positively reinforced (by the comfort received from the mother).

The attachment behavioral system can be easily observed in young children as well as in infants. For example, consider a 2-year-old playing at a neighborhood playground. She plays near her mother and may make occasional forays farther from her mother to explore playground equipment. She is content as long as she feels close to her mother, and she makes frequent reassuring checks on her mother's whereabouts. If she encounters something or someone alarmingly unfamiliar, she will immediately retreat to her mother for comfort or cry or engage in other behaviors that bring her mother to her. In Bowlby's view, the attachment behavioral system ensures that a young child can explore and learn about his or her environment in a safe way.

Development of Attachment

Unlike the imprinting in birds and other animals that promotes physical proximity between an infant and parent, an attachment bond between a human infant and parent takes considerable time to develop. The attachment bond develops similarly for infants and parents living in a wide range of environments, and this similarity is a strong indication that the attachment behavioral system is a universal human characteristic. For example, much research has shown that attachment develops in about the same way across all human cultures and that it develops in similar ways whether infants are raised in nuclear families or reared in larger social groups, and whether they spend almost all their time with a parent or spend much of their time in day care (Colin, 1996; Kagan, 1982).

During the first two months of life, infants do not care who responds to their cries as long as someone does. Between the ages of three to six months, they begin to be more selective. When they are upset, they direct their bids for comfort to one or two primary caregivers. Between six and eight months, they become very particular about who takes care of them, especially when they are upset. For most infants, this is their mother. It often comes as an unpleasant surprise to fathers and other family members when an infant no longer seems comfortable around them and suddenly starts to cry whenever his or her mother leaves. This change occurs around the time the infant learns to crawl: Just when an infant has developed the ability to wander away from his or her mother, the infant has established the kind of attachment that makes him or her keep track of the mother's whereabouts and resist separations from her. At this point, the child is fully attached to his or her primary caregiver. All normal human infants, given the opportunity to form an attachment to a primary caregiver, will do so by their first birthday.

The Importance of Attachment

Beyond the obvious benefits of having someone to protect them and satisfy their basic needs for food and protection (which almost anyone could do), the relationships that infants form with their primary caregivers have other important functions. Specifically, infants rely on their attachment figures to regulate their emotional and physiological arousal. When an infant experiences emotional and physiological arousal, such as when frightened, he or she has only minimal ability to reduce the arousal and return to a more neutral or positive state. Therefore a parent or attachment figure must be available to help the infant with this by holding and warming the infant, singing or talking in a comforting voice, or feeding the infant. Without a consistently available primary caregiver, an infant will experience extended periods of anxiety, fear, and other negative emotions and will fail to experience a sense of "felt security" that a trusted person is consistently available to him or her (Sroufe & Waters, 1977).

Infants and toddlers who experience extended periods of anxiety and other negative emotions because a primary caregiver is unavailable are less likely to engage in growth-promoting activities like play and exploration. In addition, unavailability of a consistent primary caregiver can result in dys-regulation of several physiological systems. This dysregulation can disturb sleeping and eating behavior and harm the cardiac, neuroendocrine, and immune systems. Thus when the attachment relationship is either severed or not working well, the costs to the developing child can be wide-ranging and long-lasting.

Patterns of Attachment

Bowlby's initial investigations involved homeless children who had been separated from their primary caregivers. One of his collaborators, Mary Ainsworth, an American psychologist, and her colleagues (Ainsworth, Blehar, Waters, & Wall, 1978) established the presence of different patterns of attachment and the detrimental effects of some of them. The different patterns were revealed through a laboratory procedure designed by Ainsworth called the **Strange Situation.** In the Strange Situation, a child (usually around the age of 18 months) and mother play together in a laboratory setting. A stranger enters the room and is seated. After a minute or so, the mother leaves the room. This creates a stressful situation for the child. Within a short time the mother returns. The key issue is how the child responds to her return.

When a primary caregiver consistently responds appropriately to an infant's attachment behaviors, the infant develops a **secure attachment** to the primary caregiver. The infant has learned that his or her needs will be met by the primary caregiver and acts as if they will by seeking the primary caregiver when needs arise. In the Strange Situation, securely attached children respond to the mother's return by going directly to her, holding onto her, and often asking to be picked up.

If a primary caregiver does not consistently respond to an infant's attachment behaviors, the infant is likely to form an *insecure attachment* to the primary caregiver. Two types of insecure attachments can be formed: anxious/resistant attachment and avoidant attachment.

If the primary caregiver is inconsistent in responding to an infant's attachment behaviors—sometimes responding appropriately and other times responding in an angry or indifferent way—the infant is likely to develop an anxious/resistant attachment. The **anxious/resistant attachment** pattern is characterized by excessive clinging (indicating anxiety) mixed with angry resistance to the parent's attempts to comfort the child. For example, in the Strange Situation, a child with an anxious/resistant attachment may approach the mother when she returns and whine and seem anxious, but then may appear angry with her and refuse to be touched or picked up.

If a caregiver consistently ignores an infant's attachment behaviors, the infant is likely to develop an **avoidant attachment,** which is characterized by active avoidance of the caregiver. Avoidance is most evident in situations where comfort-seeking would be expected, such as when the infant is distressed. For example, an infant with an avoidant attachment may not cry or go to her primary caregiver after falling down, and she may engage in self-soothing behaviors. In the Strange Situation, children with an avoidant attachment often act as if the mother has not returned to the room when she does—possibly looking in her direction but then continuing to play by themselves.

Both insecure patterns of attachment represent strategies by which children deal with emotional challenges in ways that are appropriate given the environments in which they are being raised. Anxious/resistant infants have learned that if they fuss hard enough and long enough, eventually they may get the response they are seeking. Consequently, they anxiously seek out their primary caregivers; but they are so accustomed to being in a state of high anxiety and anger by the time the primary caregivers finally respond that they approach the caregivers with anxiety and anger. In contrast, avoidant infants have learned that their needs for comfort are not likely to be met, and may even be met by a punitive response from their primary caregivers.

So their typical response is to withdraw. Neither pattern is optimal, and both have short-term and long-term negative consequences; but each represents an adaptive solution to a type of inadequate care.

Many studies have shown that in average, nonclinical American samples, about 60% of infants exhibit secure patterns of attachment, whereas about 25% are classified as avoidant and 15% as anxious/resistant (Campos, Barrett, Lamb, Goldsmith, & Stenberg, 1983).

Internal Working Model

An important prediction of attachment theory is that early attachments shape future relationship behaviors. As just noted, through repeated interactions with caregivers, infants learn what to expect from them and adjust their behavior accordingly. These expectations form the basis of what Bowlby called the **internal working model** of attachment relationships. A child's internal working model of attachments influences the child's expectations about how others will act in subsequent relationships. These expectations influence the developing child's (and later the adolescent's and adult's) behaviors in relationships. These behaviors are likely to evoke behaviors from others that frequently reinforce the child's internal working model (Sroufe, 1983).

For example, avoidant attachment in school-age children is associated with hostility and aggressiveness toward peers. These behaviors often result in social rejection—a situation similar to what the avoidantly attached infant experienced with her primary caregiver. Anxious/resistant attachment in school-age children is associated with frequent seeking of approval from others. These behaviors can result in other children ignoring the child because the frequent approval seeking may bother them, as well as occasional approval, which parallels the child's early experience (Matas, Arend, & Sroufe, 1978).

The Therapeutic Process

Although no particular therapeutic style has developed from attachment theory, the theory does provide guidance for therapeutic work that may benefit children and their families (Steele, 2003). The goal of most therapy that addresses problems with attachment is to improve the attachment between an infant, preschool child, or school-age child and his or her primary caregivers. As the attachment improves, many negative short-term and long-term consequences to a child of an insecure attachment may recede or end.

Much therapeutic work in this area is done with mothers and their infants, and it often involves mothers whose characteristics or circumstances suggest that they may be at risk for parenting their infants in a way that will result in an insecure attachment. For example, a program in the Netherlands brought together a group of mothers who were at risk for providing poor care to their infants (Van den Boom, 1994). The mothers and their infants participated in three training sessions that provided instruction in sensitive caregiving. The result was improved mother–child relationships (Van den Boom, 1995).

Other therapeutic work focuses on supporting parents or other caregivers (such as foster or adoptive parents, teachers, coaches, and others) as they try to develop and maintain a caring relationship with a child who is insecurely attached. There is compelling evidence that such a child can benefit from a single warm and stable relationship, and it does not seem to matter whether this person is a parent, teacher, family friend, or community volunteer (Main, Kaplan, & Cassidy, 1985). What matters is that the individual is consistently available to and supportive of the child when that child is with the adult. This can be challenging for the adult, however, because the child's behaviors may repeatedly pull for the type of ineffective parenting the child experienced as an infant. For example, a child with an anxious/resistant attachment may repeatedly seek comfort from an adult and then reject it. Consequently, many adults working with children who have attachment problems need ongoing support to help them maintain appropriate behaviors.

Applicability to Child Psychopathology

Because the attachment relationship between an infant and his or her primary caregiver has so many implications for the infant's physical and psychological development, attachment theory is useful for understanding many problems that may develop in an infant or child. Early problems with emotional regulation can have a long-term influence on the developing child, including problems with anxiety, depression, anger, and impulsivity. The internal working model of relationships that develops from the initial attachment relationship can also influence the degree to which parents, teachers, and other adults in a person's life can influence his or her moods and behaviors.

Key Concepts
- All infants are prepared at birth to attach to a primary caregiver, and they do so given an appropriate parent–child relationship.
- Attachment develops over the first year of an infant's life and is in place by the time the infant can move away from a primary caregiver.
- Attachment has important implications for a developing infant's ability to regulate emotion.
- Three styles of attachment have been identified in most children: secure attachment and two forms of insecure attachment—anxious/resistant attachment and avoidant attachment.
- Children develop an internal working model of relationships based on their attachment to a primary caregiver. A child's internal working model influences the child's behaviors in future relationships.
- Therapies based on attachment theory attempt to repair a child's attachment by improving parenting behaviors or giving a developing child a person who can provide consistent and warm caregiving.

Family Systems Theories

Family systems theory and family therapy differ in many fundamental ways from the other theories and therapies described in this chapter (Nichols & Schwartz, 1998). Rather than hypothesizing that human behavior is influenced primarily by cognitions, inner drives, or environmental influences, the focus of family systems theory is on how the functioning of a family prods individuals in the family to develop specific patterns of behaviors. These patterns are then maintained because they serve an important function for the family, even though they may be detrimental to the individuals.

The early development of family systems theory was influenced by two programs of research (Nichols & Schwartz, 1998). The first was work with small groups of unrelated adults. Several decades ago, Kurt Lewin, interested in how small groups functioned, spent time observing them (Lewin, 1951). He began to perceive the groups as more than just a collection of individuals. He saw them as an entity, a psychologically cohesive whole, that was more than simply the sum of the individuals in the group. It became clear, for example, that it was possible to talk about a "personality" of a group that was something other than just the collected personalities of the group's individuals. Discoveries such as this led family systems theorists to focus on the "personality" of a family rather than focusing only on the personalities of individual family members.

Lewin's work with groups also showed that changes in individual group members' behaviors and attitudes occurred more easily through changes in group behaviors and attitudes than through therapeutic work with the individuals. This discovery led to the T-group movement, and later the encounter group movement, which focused on individual growth through intense interactions among members of small groups (Nichols & Schwartz, 1998). Individual growth occurred through the growth of the group as the group's beliefs and behaviors were "unfrozen" and then "refrozen" in new ways. This same strategy is used in most family therapy today: pushing the family out of its accustomed way of behaving and prompting it to act in healthier ways.

The second research program that influenced the early development of family systems theory focused on the etiology of schizophrenia in the 1950s. At that time people were mystified by schizophrenia, and its causes were not understood. In addition, antipsychotic medications for treating schizophrenia were not in wide use, so those with schizophrenia often lived with parents or in an institution where attempts were made to help them cope with their psychotic symptoms. During this time, some researchers and therapists began to notice an interesting pattern in some families that had a young adult member who was hospitalized for schizophrenia: When the family member was preparing to leave the hospital and return home, problems at home often escalated to the point where the patient became so disturbed by them that he or she had to remain in the hospital (Jackson & Weakland, 1959). Although these families wanted their family members to improve and often appeared eager to have their family members return home, forces that no one understood seemed to drive the families to engage in behaviors that ensured that the family members with schizophrenia continued to be highly disturbed. This prompted the researchers to wonder if having members with schizophrenia had become such an important part of these families that they functioned in ways to maintain the disturbed behavior of the members with schizophrenia. They hypothesized that the behaviors of individuals in a family could be influenced substantially by the needs of a family system.

Fundamental Ideas

Many styles of family therapy have been created over the past few decades, based on differing hypotheses about the development of problems in individuals and families. Despite the differences in the hypotheses and the therapeutic styles they support, most family systems theories share several key concepts.

The Family as the Unit of Analysis

A fundamental issue differentiating family systems theory from other theories is that family systems theory considers the family, rather than the individual, as the best unit of analysis for understanding behavior. When most of us try to understand human behavior and development, we focus on the individual as the unit of analysis. We may explore an individual's history, thoughts, emotions, goals, motivations, genetic inheritance, or temperament because we believe that understanding these individual characteristics will lead us to understand the individual's behaviors. Family therapists, on the other hand, focus on the family as the unit of analysis, exploring its history, thought patterns, emotional expression, goals, and motivation because they believe that understanding these family characteristics will lead to the best understanding of individual family members' behaviors (Nichols & Schwartz, 1998).

Using the family as the unit of analysis can be a difficult concept to understand because most of us automatically use individuals' characteristics as units of analysis. How can we analyze the characteristics and behaviors of a family? To conceptualize this, pretend you are nearsighted and are standing at one end of a large lecture hall, with a family grouped closely at the other end. If you have your glasses on, you are likely to view individuals as the unit of analysis because you can see the individuals clearly. You may notice that one person is shouting, another is throwing something across the room, and another is dancing. However, if you remove your glasses, you can no longer see individuals; you see an amorphous shape at the other end of the room. You can perceive this shape making noise, tossing things about, and moving around. As you observe what is happening at the other end of the lecture hall, you now have to see the family as the unit of analysis: This blob of a family, not individual family members, is performing the behavior. In many ways this is how family therapists work: seeing families behaving rather than individuals. Family therapists understand that families can be influenced by individuals but try to focus on the functioning of the family unit rather than on its individual members.

Behavior Occurring in a Family Context

Family systems theorists and family therapists hypothesize that an individual child's behavior can be influenced dramatically by the needs and expectations of the family unit (Minuchin, 1974). They believe that understanding the needs, expectations, rules, and behavior patterns of the family is essential for understanding a child's behavior, and the family must change before a child's behaviors can change. The family is not to blame for a child's behaviors, nor are individuals in the family (such as the parents) to blame; rather, the child's behaviors developed as part of the behaviors of the family, so the family's behavior must change if the child's behavior is to change.

When considering the problem behavior of a family member, family therapists often ask, "What is the function of this behavior in this family?" In essence, they are trying to determine what role the behavior plays in the family. Consider, for example, a family in which a 5-year-old experiences high levels of anxiety that often require him to stay home from school. A family therapist might notice that the mother of the 5-year-old, who has stayed home and cared for him throughout his preschool years, has not returned to her job as planned because of the need to care for the child when he stays home from school. The therapist could conceptualize the child's anxiety as serving the function of maintaining the mother–child relationship by giving the family a reason for the mother to remain at home. Note that the mother in this case would not be considered responsible for somehow manipulating her son to stay home from school to meet her needs. Rather, the son's behaviors would be conceptualized as serving an important function for the entire family unit by allowing a set of family behaviors to continue unchanged.

As another example, consider a 13-year-old girl who starts acting out and stops doing her homework when she enters middle school. A family therapist might notice that this behavior has encouraged more frequent contact between the girl's parents, who had been drifting apart emotionally and who had become progressively less able to work together raising their children. The therapist could conceptualize the girl's behavior as serving an important function for the family unit by keeping her parents connected.

In both of these cases, there may be other important influences on the children's behaviors. For example, biological issues could influence the boy's anxiety, and neighborhood issues could influence the girl's acting out. Family therapists might look at these other possible influences but would carefully explore the function that a child's behavior serves in his or her family, thus adding another dimension of analysis to understanding the child's behavior.

Homeostasis

Families, like all groups, are conservative in nature: They do not want to change (Minuchin, 1974). Family therapists refer to the force that encourages families to stay the same as **homeostasis**. All families are homeostatic. It is not that someone in the family says, "We are not going to change." Rather, the tendency of all groups, including families, is to continue functioning in the same way once a pattern of functioning has been established. Some level of homeostasis is important in all families (Minuchin & Fishman, 1981). Homeostasis allows members of a family to know that how the family functions is not going to change continually. This gives all family members a sense of security.

The function of some individuals' behaviors is to maintain family homeostasis, and the family system can pressure individuals to behave in ways that maintain the homeostasis of the family system. The example in the previous section of the boy with anxiety is an illustration of this: His behavior allowed the functioning of the family to remain constant. As another example, Nichols and Schwartz (1998) described an interesting case in which a man complained about his wife's frigidity. She attended therapy and her frigidity diminished, whereupon he suddenly became impotent. The couple's sex life remained the same: The powerful force of homeostasis influenced the man's behavior.

However, another strong force on families pushes them to change: the development of individual family members, particularly children (Nichols & Schwartz, 1998). Throughout the life of a family, it must adapt to changes caused by its members' development. For example, when a first child is born, the family patterns of behaviors must change so the parents can provide needed care to the baby. As the child eventually enters adolescence, many family behavior patterns must change to accommodate the adolescent's increased autonomy and the changing relationships between the adolescent and the parents. When this child leaves home for college or work, more family system changes must occur to adjust to the child no longer being consistently present in the home.

Successful families can balance the forces of homeostasis with those requiring change and adaptation (Minuchin & Fishman, 1981). When the need for homeostasis is too strong, individuals within the family may develop behaviors that, although problematic for them, maintain the homeostatic functioning of the family. For example, a new college student may develop depression or become pregnant, requiring her to return home and returning the structure of the family to what it was before she left for college.

Circular, Rather than Linear, Causation of Problems

Most theorizing about the development of psychological disorders or other problems is linear: Some series of biological or environmental events or relationships causes a problem to develop. Each of the other theories discussed in this chapter tends to be linear. Conflicts between instinctual drives and social expectations, behavioral antecedents and consequences, or irrational beliefs cause problematic emotions and behaviors. Family therapists, on the other hand, see things in a more circular way. For example, consider a family in which a 12-year-old son, Jeremy, acts out in school and where Jeremy often feels too distant from his father. It is not that Jeremy acts out at school because his father is too distant (linear reasoning—father's behavior influences Jeremy's behavior). Rather, Jeremy acts out at school because his father is too distant *and* his father is too distant because Jeremy acts out at school (circular reasoning—father's behavior influences Jeremy's behavior and Jeremy's behavior simultaneously influences father's behavior). Problems and conflicts that develop between parents are often understood in the same way. Consider a family in which the mother is angry that she is always the disciplinarian and that the father is too easygoing with the children. It is not that father is too permissive because mother is too demanding (linear reasoning). Rather, father is too permissive because mother is too demanding *and* mother is too demanding because father is too permissive (circular reasoning) (Nichols & Schwartz, 1998).

The circularity of influences on behaviors helps maintain them. Jeremy might act out less if his father would pay more attention to him, but his father does not pay more attention to him because of Jeremy's acting out. So Jeremy continues to act out and father remains distant. Similarly, the father in the second family cannot become more demanding because the mother is already too demanding, and the mother cannot become more easygoing because the father is already too easygoing. Consequently, the mother remains too demanding and the father remains too easygoing.

Seeing problems this way saves family therapists from having to find a specific cause for a behavior (which often means finding whom to "blame" for a problem). Instead family therapists can focus on changing the interacting pattern of behaviors (Minuchin & Fishman, 1981). For example, a family therapist might "prescribe" a week in which Jeremy and his father spend at least one hour each day doing something they both enjoy, with discussions of school and of Jeremy's behavior prohibited. Similarly, a therapist might prescribe a week during which the mother is prohibited from disciplining the children and is required to spend at least two evenings away from the home, and the father must be in charge of all discipline and cannot be criticized or overruled by his wife. In both cases, everyone participates in the solution to the problem. No single person is identified as a culprit who must change.

The Therapeutic Process

Many different family therapy styles and strategies have developed over the years. Fundamentally, however, they all work to (1) identify the problematic aspects of family functioning that are being supported by problem behaviors of individual family members and then (2) change patterns of family functioning so individual problem behaviors are no longer needed by the family system (Nichols & Schwartz, 1998).

Most often, family therapy is initiated when a parent calls a therapist because of a problem a child in the family is exhibiting. A family therapist will ask that all members of the family attend therapy so the therapist can better understand the child and his problem. While giving attention to the problem that brings the family into therapy, the therapist will also spend the first few therapy sessions gathering information about relationships between family members, how the family functions, and other events or issues that are important to the family. This information is gathered by observing family interactions during therapy sessions and by asking family members for additional information. For example, a therapist might observe that the parents in a family with an acting-out 8-year-old are distant from each other and interact, often in an angry way, only when discussing the son's behavior. In another family, a therapist might observe that expressions of love between a mother and stepfather are often interrupted by a 13-year-old insulting her younger sister.

The therapist uses this information about the family to form hypotheses about the family's functioning and how it may be problematic. Using these hypotheses, the therapist designs strategies to change the functioning of the family. These strategies might include encouraging different relationships within a family or different strategies for solving family conflicts. In some cases, the behavior that brings the family to therapy receives little direct attention during therapy sessions; in other cases it may be the primary focus. Some therapists become integral parts of the family system and tussle with the family to create needed change. Other therapists are more remote and analytical and struggle not to get involved in the ongoing family issues.

For example, the therapist for the family with the acting-out 8-year-old just described might hypothesize that the acting out helps keep the parents connected to each other. She might work on developing a closer relationship between the parents, focusing their energy on each other and away from their child. The child's acting out may receive little or no attention during therapy sessions. If the therapist is correct about the function of the child's behavior in the family, as the parents' relationship becomes healthier, the child's acting out will decrease or disappear because it no longer has a function within the family system. The therapist for the stepfamily, hypothesizing that the frequent hostility between the siblings serves the function of keeping the stepparent distant from the family, might work to develop a better relationship between the stepparent and the children. Alternatively, the therapist might encourage the stepparent to be more distant, hypothesizing that the stepparent's attempts to be too close to the children are fueling the hostility between the siblings.

Applicability to Child Psychopathology

Family systems theory provides important insights into child psychopathology by showing that forces influencing the development of psychopathology do not always lie within an individual child. Thus family systems theory helps broaden our understanding of the wide range of influences on the development of child psychopathology. Family systems theory also reminds us of the importance of exploring the family context in which psychopathology develops.

Key Concepts

- Family systems theories focus on how individuals' behaviors are influenced by the functions they serve within a family.
- The family, rather than the individual, is the basic unit of analysis in family systems theories.
- Homeostasis is the force that encourages families and other systems to stay the same. All families experience homeostasis.
- The changing needs of family members as they develop require that the family system change and adapt, which runs counter to the force

of homeostasis. Successful families can balance the need to adapt and the desire to stay the same.

- Family theorists employ circular rather than linear reasoning when analyzing problem behavior.
- The therapeutic process, which usually involves the whole family, involves changing family behaviors so that problematic individual behaviors can change.
- Family systems theories provide insight into how problem behaviors are influenced by the contexts in which they occur, rather than only by issues within an individual.

Common Features of the Theories

We can find some similarities among the five theories discussed in this chapter if we look hard enough. For example, each suggests that there are forces driving children and adults to feel and act in ways that make them unhappy and that they wish they could change. Whether these forces are unconscious impulses, dysfunctional schemata, influences from the environment, internal working models of attachments, or pressures from a family system, each theory suggests that our feelings and behaviors are not completely under our control. Another similarity of these theories is that they suggest that experiences during childhood have long-lasting influences on behavior. The impulses we repress into our unconscious, the irrational thoughts we develop through interactions with our parents, the patterns of behavior shaped during our early years, our internal working models of relationships, and the roles we take in our families when we are young can all influence us throughout our lifetimes. Another similarity among the theories is the extent to which feelings, thoughts, and events that are outside our memories can influence our behaviors. We are often unaware of the impulses or schemata that drive our behavior and how the environment, our early attachments, and our family structures have shaped our behavior. In this sense, the old saying "What you don't know can't hurt you" is not true. These theories all suggest that what we do not know about ourselves often significantly influences us.

I have a plaque in my office with a saying that I read now and again. It says, "To interfere with the life of things means to harm both them and oneself. He who imposes himself has the small manifest might; he who does not impose himself has the great secret might. . . . The perfected man does not interfere in the life of beings, he does not impose himself on them, but he helps all beings to their freedom." In many ways the therapeutic strategies that have emerged from each theory discussed in this chapter strive to "help people to their freedom"—that is, to unburden them from dysfunctional thoughts, feelings, or influences from the environment. Most therapies do this through a therapist helping a person uncover influences on his or her behavior of which he or she may be unaware. Doing this lets a child or adult realign his or her life; live more consciously than unconsciously; and have more direct control over thoughts, feelings, and relationships. So at their foundation, each of these therapies strives for the same goal: providing support and guidance as a child or adult works to create a new, more conscious, and self-directed life.

Which Theory Is Best?

One of our cultural values is that it is possible and desirable to rank things or people and that it is important to determine which of these things or people is "the best." For example, we seem to need a "national champion" in every sport. This emphasis on ranking things and people can be problematic. We seem unable to see things or people as different without having to decide which of them is better. Are men better than women? Is your college better than mine? Is cognitive therapy better than family systems therapy? (My belief, by the way, is that the answer to all these questions is no.)

A significant amount of research has been completed to determine whether one type of psychologically based therapy is better than the others. Some research suggests that certain forms of therapy are more effective with certain people and with various problems. For example, cognitive–behavioral therapy has been found to be better than supportive–psychodynamic therapy for several childhood problems, including depression and conduct disorders (Kendall, 1993). Family therapy has been shown to be more effective than individual therapy with adolescent substance abusers (Waldron, 1997). What strikes me about these studies, however, is that even the "better" therapies are not more effective with every client. This might be due partly to clients' lack of motivation (perhaps no form of therapy will work with unmotivated clients) and could be partly due to differences in therapists' skills. However, the explanation that I prefer is that all therapies work with *some* children, adults, and families—and that all therapies do *not* work with other children, adults, and families. Perhaps some therapies work more frequently than others in certain circumstances, so their use ought to be considered in those circumstances; but many therapies, delivered by competent therapists who believe in them, are helpful to many people.

Good therapists can combine theories as appropriate. If I am doing family therapy with a family that has a child with attention-deficit/hyperactivity disorder, I might focus on the extent to which family dynamics exacerbate the child's symptoms; on changing the parents' patterns of reinforcing the child's behavior so that they pay less attention to his hyperactive behaviors and more attention to his prosocial behaviors; and on the influence of the child's cognitions on his compliance with taking medication. When I combine theoretical approaches in this manner, I believe that I am correctly comprehending the complexity of the child, his family, and the circumstances in which they live.

Personally, I find each theory fascinating and am intrigued with how they help me understand my own behavior, the behavior of my friends and family, and the behaviors of the children, adolescents, and families I see in therapy. This may seem odd: Important concepts of each theory contradict tenets of other theories. However, my experiences over the years have led me to find truth in all these theories and realize that they all have limitations. Further, I have found that understanding each theory has given me a richer sense of the complexity of human development.

CHAPTER GLOSSARY

Actualizing tendency is the term used by Rogers to describe the innate drive of humans to develop fully and to be flexible, open, and free.

Anxious/resistant attachment is a form of insecure attachment that develops when an infant learns that a primary caregiver responds inconsistently to his or her needs. It is characterized by excessive clinging mixed with angry resistance to attempts at comforting.

Applied behavioral analysis is a process of analyzing the antecedents and consequences of a behavior.

An **attachment behavioral system** is a complementary set of behaviors between an infant and a primary caregiver that promotes proximity and an emotional bond between them.

Automatic thoughts are spontaneous, fleeting thoughts produced by dysfunctional schemata that can influence a person's behavior even though they may go unnoticed.

Avoidant attachment occurs when a primary caregiver consistently rebuffs an infant's attachment behaviors. It is characterized by active avoidance of the caregiver by the infant.

Classical conditioning is a form of learning caused by pairing a neutral stimulus with a stimulus that reflexively elicits a response. After a series of pairings, the neutral stimulus will elicit the response by itself.

Ego is the English translation of the term used by Freud to describe a part of the mind, mostly conscious but partly unconscious, that directs a person's life in a way that satisfies the demands of the id, the superego, and the external world.

A behavior is **extinguished** if, after not being reinforced, it ceases to occur.

Homeostasis is a force that influences a family or other system to remain the same.

Id is the English translation of the term used by Freud to describe the primitive structure of the mind that is present at birth and that contains the basic human instincts.

An **instinct** is an innate tendency to emit a specific behavior in a particular circumstance.

An **internal working model** of attachments develops from an infant's attachment to his or her primary caregiver and influences how a person approaches future relationships and acts during them.

Must-urbation is Ellis's humorous term for a person's use of many "musts" in his or her life.

Operant conditioning is a form of learning in which behaviors are shaped by their consequences—either reinforcement that increases the frequency of the behavior or punishment that decreases its frequency.

Organismic valuing is a term used by Rogers to describe our innate knowledge about what is best for us and what will lead us toward self-actualization.

Reciprocal inhibition is a style of therapy initially designed by Wolpe that pairs relaxation with a stimulus that causes anxiety or fear. After many pairings, the stimulus evokes less fear or anxiety.

Repetition compulsion is the term used by Freud to describe a pattern of repeated distressing or dangerous behavior influenced by unconscious forces.

Repression is a defense mechanism of the ego that banishes unacceptable thoughts, desires, and fears into the unconscious.

A **schema** (plural *schemata*) is a fundamental belief system about how we and the world function.

A **secure attachment** occurs when an infant learns that his or her needs are met consistently by a primary caregiver.

Self-actualization is the goal of Rogers's actualizing tendency: to be a fully developed person.

The **Strange Situation** is a procedure used to determine the type of attachment between an infant and primary caregiver.

Superego is the English translation of the term used by Freud to describe the part of the mind that is the judge and censor of a person's life. It is partly conscious and partly unconscious and develops as societal and parental values are taken in by a child and become part of who the child is.

Transference is an important part of Freud's theory that involves the redirection of feelings that evolved during early relationships (such as with a mother) to later relationships (such as a spouse).

Unconditional positive regard is a term used by Rogers to describe constant positive regard for another person (although not constant approval of all the person's actions).

The **unconscious** is the part of the mind that is unavailable to a person's consciousness. The unconscious contains a variety of thoughts, desires, and fears that influence a person's life, despite the person not being aware that they are present.

Quantitative Behavioral Genetics

The study of monozygotic twins has provided important information in the field of quantitative behavioral genetics.

Quantitative behavioral genetics is the study of the sources of differences in the abilities, characteristics, or behaviors of individuals (Plomin, DeFries, McClearn, & McGuffin, 2001; Reiss, Neiderhiser, Hetherington, & Plomin, 2000). For example, quantitative behavioral genetics research has explored why individual children have different levels of intelligence, anxiety, or conduct problems.

Researchers in the field of quantitative behavioral genetics do not focus solely on the genetic sources of individual differences. Instead they work to quantify the influences that genes and environments have on individual differences. For much of the 20th century, the debate about the influences of genes and environments was called the **nature–nurture controversy,** and it focused primarily on whether either nature (genes) or nurture (environment) influenced individuals' development. This either–or debate swung from one pole to the other during most of the early 20th century. However, the simplistic debate ended during the last few decades of the 20th century as it became clear that both genes and the environment influence individual differences in a variety of complex ways (Rutter, 2005). The more recent focus has been on quantifying the relative influence of genes and the environment on a wide range of individual characteristics and behaviors, and on identifying specific genes or groups of genes that influence these characteristics or behaviors; the field concerned with identifying specific genes is often called **molecular behavioral genetics** (Plomin et al., 2001). In this chapter we focus on the research strategies used in the field of quantitative behavioral genetics. Information about specific genes that influence some disorders is included in the chapters about those disorders in this text.

A review of some basic terms in quantitative behavioral genetics is useful as we begin this chapter. A **gene** (from the Greek *genes,* meaning "born") is a section of deoxyribonucleic acid (DNA) that directs protein production within a cell. It is the basic unit of inheritance. Most genes are identical across all members of a species—so they do not contribute to individual differences. However, many genes vary slightly among individuals in a species. These are called **alleles** (from the Greek *allel,* "one another"). Because they vary across individuals, alleles can be an important source of individual differences. All of a person's genes and alleles are considered the person's **genome.** The collection of all a person's alleles is the person's **genotype.** A person's genotype represents the genetic source of individual differences.

A fundamental goal of quantitative behavioral genetics research is to assess the influence of a person's genotype on his or her **phenotype** (from the Greek *phainein,* "to show," and *typos,* a "mark"). A phenotype is an observed characteristic or behavior of an individual, such as height, intelligence, or level of depression. Quantitative behavioral genetics tries to quantify the influences of genotype and environment on the individual differences of a phenotype.

Chapter Plan

We first explore some history of the field of quantitative behavioral genetics and note that it has often been controversial. We next examine the basic research strategy used in quantitative behavioral genetics and note that its focus on the covariation of a characteristic between pairs of individuals is fundamentally different from the research strategies used in most social sciences. After understanding this basic research strategy, we see how it is used in the three types of research commonly used in quantitative behavioral genetics: family studies, twin studies, and adoption studies. We then explore the three primary influences on human characteristics and behaviors described by quantitative behavioral genetics—heritability, shared environment, and nonshared environment—and see how environmental and genetic influences can combine through interactions and correlations.

History

Most people in the quantitative behavioral genetics field credit Francis Galton with initiating research into the genetic influences on behavior during the second half of the 1800s. Galton was inspired by Charles Darwin's writing about evolution; knowing that evolution depended on heredity, he became interested in the heritability of human behaviors. He was particularly interested in the genetic influences on the characteristic of eminence (Plomin, 1990). His research strategy involved determining the number of eminent people ("notables") who had lived between 1453 and 1853 (he found 605) and then assessing how many of their relatives were also notables. He found that 102 relatives of notable people were also notable, and he used this association between being notable and having notable relatives to argue that the qualities necessary for eminence were inherited (these qualities included intelligence, good health, love of mental work, strong purpose, and ambition) (Rothstein, 1999). Galton also conducted the first family, twin, and adoption studies, and he developed the statistical techniques of correlation and regression, both of which are essential in the study of quantitative behavioral genetics. Although his research strategy would not be considered credible today, many scientists in the 1800s and 1900s were strongly influenced by his thinking (Plomin, 1990).

Galton was an early advocate of *eugenics* (from the Greek *eu,* "well or good," and *genein,* "to produce"), which is concerned with bettering the human species through selective breeding—either by encouraging "better" people to have more children or by discouraging or prohibiting "unfit" people from having children. Although eugenics is now considered wrong by most people in Western society, it was embraced by many prominent leaders in the first part of the 1900s, including all the U.S. presidents from Theodore Roosevelt to Herbert Hoover and many members of the U.S. Congress and Supreme Court (Rothstein, 1999).

Despite the popularity of eugenics, the field of behavioral genetics had little influence on psychology during the first half of the 1900s. The two dominant theories during this time, behavioral theory and psychoanalytic theory, emphasized the role of the environment in human development (Rowe & Jacobson, 1999). In addition, Bowlby's attachment theory emphasized the importance of early experience on many aspects of a child's development. Consequently, the primary focus of psychology was understanding environmental influences on individuals' characteristics and behaviors. In addition, the use of genetics as a justification for genocide by the Nazis was the coup de grâce ending the use of genetic research during and after World War II (Rowe & Jacobson, 1999; Rutter, Moffitt, & Caspi, 2006).

Behavioral genetics began to exert more influence in psychology during the 1960s, primarily because of research programs showing strong genetic influences on cognitive abilities and schizophrenia (Plomin, 1990). Interest in the field increased, and new strategies for investigating genetic influences on a variety of human characteristics began to emerge. Much of this work was brought to an abrupt halt by the publication in 1969 of an article arguing that a great deal of the difference observed on IQ tests between African–Americans and European–Americans was due to genetic differences between the races (Jensen, 1969). This paper caused a firestorm of controversy and chased many away from the field of behavioral genetics (Plomin, 1990).

Despite these setbacks, researchers in the field of quantitative behavioral genetics continued to refine their methods and the statistics used to analyze the results from their studies. Research in the 1970s began to show conclusively that genes influenced a variety of human characteristics and behaviors, and this research fueled an expanded interest in the field (Rutter et al., 2006).

In addition, in 1979 many in the United States were fascinated with the story of Jim Springer and Jim Lewis: identical twins who had been separated at birth, living in adoptive families in adjoining states and reunited as adults. The similarities of many of their characteristics and behaviors were amazing, although they had never met before age 40. Both preferred the same brands of beer and cigarettes. Both had been married to and divorced from women named Linda and then had married women named Betty. One named his first son James Alan, and the other named his first son James Allen. They had histories of similar physical diseases and school achievements; both had high blood pressure and high levels of anxiety; and both had become volunteer sheriff's deputies (Clark & Grunstein, 2000). They became part of the Minnesota Study of Twins Reared Apart; the results of this research program, first published in the early 1990s, showed that identical twins raised apart in adoptive families had many characteristics as similar as those of identical twins raised together in their birth families. This research program provided new impetus for examining the influence of genes on many human characteristics. It and similar programs have helped maintain a strong interest in quantitative behavioral genetics ever since (see, for example, Bouchard, 1994; Bouchard, Lykken, McGue, Segal, & Tellegen, 1990).

Key Concepts

- Francis Galton was the first researcher to systematically explore the heritability of human characteristics and behaviors; he focused on the concept of eminence.
- Galton and many other eminent people of his time were involved in the eugenics movement, which sought to better the human race by influencing the birthrates of "fit" and "unfit" people.
- Behavioral genetics research had little sway in psychology for most of the 20th century because the dominant theories focused on the influence of early environments on human behavior.
- Studies of cognitive abilities and schizophrenia in the 1960s showed the influence of genes, but efforts to quantify genetic influences were derailed by the publication of a paper arguing that genes were responsible for differences in the cognitive abilities of African–Americans and European–Americans.
- Research has continued to document that genes have an important influence on human characteristics and behaviors.

Basic Research Strategy

Most social science research during the past several decades has paid attention to groups of people, exploring differences in the mean levels of characteristics between the groups (Plomin et al., 2001). For example, researchers have examined differences in the respective mean levels of anxiety symptoms, conduct problems, and eating disorders between groups of (1) children who have been sexually abused and children who have not been sexually abused, (2) children living in affluent neighborhoods and children living in low-income neighborhoods, and (3) girls and boys. The goal of these studies is to identify characteristics or experiences that are associated with an issue of interest. For example, is the experience of being sexually abused associated with having an anxiety disorder? Is neighborhood income associated with intelligence levels?

As shown in Figure 4.1, the basic strategy of these studies is to compare the mean level of an issue of interest between two groups. If one group has a higher mean level of some issue than another group, a reasonable hypothesis can be formed that the characteristic or experience that distinguishes the groups influences that issue. For example, if a group of children living in an affluent environment has a higher mean level of self-esteem than a similar group of children living in a low-income environment, we can hypothesize that the characteristics that distinguish affluent from low-income environments influence self-esteem. Similarly, if the mean level of posttraumatic stress

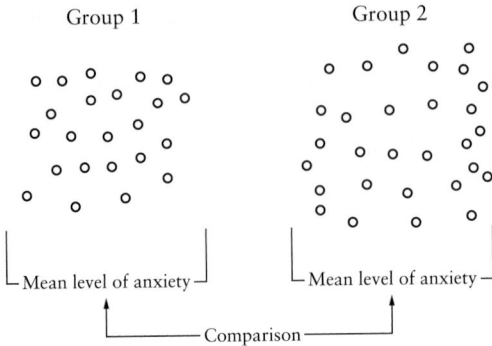

Group 1   Group 2

Mean level of anxiety   Mean level of anxiety

Comparison

If the mean of one group is higher
than the other, the characteristic
distinguishing the groups may be
related to anxiety.

FIGURE 4.1   *Comparing a Characteristic between Groups*

disorder symptoms is higher in a group of girls who have experienced a traumatic event than in a group of boys who have experienced a similar traumatic event, we can hypothesize that one or more of the characteristics that distinguish girls from boys influence the development of posttraumatic stress disorder symptoms.

The fundamental research strategy in quantitative behavioral genetics differs from the strategy of comparing group means. As shown in Figure 4.2, it involves calculation of the **covariation**[1] of a phenotype between pairs of individuals who have some genetic or environmental relationship to each other. The covariation calculated for a sample of pairs of individuals with one level of relatedness is then compared with the covariation calculated for a sample of pairs with a different level of relatedness. To the extent that the covariation between the samples differs, we can argue that the characteristic distinguishing the relationships between the two samples influences the phenotype.

For example, to assess genetic and environmental influences on impulsivity, we could calculate and compare the covariation of impulsivity among a sample of pairs of siblings with the covariation of impulsivity among a sample of pairs of cousins. If there were a higher covariation of impulsivity in the sample of sibling pairs, a genetic influence on impulsivity would be suggested because siblings are more closely related genetically than are cousins. Alternatively, if there were little or no difference in the covariations

---

[1]*Covariation* is a measure of the extent to which a phenotype varies systematically in pairs of people. That is, is there a pattern to the variability of a phenotype in pairs of people, or does the phenotype vary randomly? High covariation indicates that a characteristic varies systematically in a sample of pairs. For example, in 50 pairs of twins, when one twin has high anxiety, the other twin is likely to have high anxiety; when one twin has low anxiety, the other twin is likely to have low anxiety. Of course this systematic variation will not be found in every twin pair; but to the extent that it is found frequently, the covariation will be high. Low covariation indicates that a characteristic does not vary systematically in the pairs: In a sample of twins, if one twin has high anxiety, the other is just as likely to have high anxiety, moderate anxiety, or low anxiety.

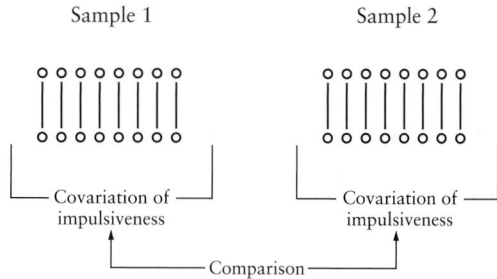

FIGURE 4.2   *Comparing Covariation of a Characteristic between Pairs of Individuals*

between the sibling pairs and the cousin pairs, this would suggest that genes have little influence on impulsivity because the pairs vary in their genetic relatedness but do not vary in their covariation of impulsivity.

As another example, we could compare the covariation of impulsivity in a sample of sibling pairs raised in the same home with the covariation of impulsivity in a sample of sibling pairs raised in separate adoptive homes. If we found a higher covariation of impulsivity in the sample of sibling pairs raised in the same home, an influence of the environment would be suggested because siblings raised in the same home have more environmental relatedness than siblings raised in different homes. Alternately, if there were little or no difference in the covariations among the pairs of siblings raised together and the pairs of siblings raised apart, this would suggest that environment has little influence on impulsivity because the pairs vary in their environmental relatedness but do not vary in their covariation of impulsivity.

Thus the basic research strategy in quantitative behavioral genetics differs fundamentally from the basic research strategy used in most other social science studies. Rather than focusing on differences in mean levels of characteristics between groups of unrelated individuals, it focuses on covariations of characteristics within samples of pairs of individuals who have some relationship to each other.

Common Research Strategies in Quantitative Behavioral Genetics

The three most common research strategies in quantitative behavioral genetics are family studies, twin studies, and adoption studies. Each type of study is useful because it allows examination of the covariation of a phenotype between pairs of individuals who have varying degrees of genetic or environmental relatedness.

Family Studies

Family studies contrast the covariation of a phenotype among members of nuclear or extended families; for example, they might contrast the covariation of depressive symptoms between father–son pairs and uncle–nephew pairs. Because of the mechanism of genetic inheritance, the genetic relatedness of family members can be quantified. For example, on average children share 50% of the same genes with each parent and with their siblings. They also share an average of 25% of the same genes with uncles, aunts, and grandparents and an average of 12.5% of the same genes with first cousins (Gottesman, 1991).

Comparing the extent by which a phenotype varies among pairs of relatives with different genetic relatedness can suggest the genetic influence on the phenotype. For example, Gottesman (1991) assessed the frequency with which pairs of relatives were concordant for the presence of schizophrenia (*concordance* is explained in our imminent discussion of heritability). By combining the results from many studies, he found that among adults with schizophrenia, about 13% of their children, 5% of their grandchildren, and 2% of their cousins also had schizophrenia (compared with a rate of schizophrenia in the general population of about 1%). The higher concordance rates among those with greater genetic relatedness supported the hypothesis that genes play an important role in the development of schizophrenia.

The primary limitation of family studies is that although they can support hypotheses about genetic influences, they cannot quantify the influence of a genotype on a phenotype because family members share genes and environments. Parents obviously share both genes and environments with their children who live with them. Uncles and nieces may also share some of the same environment because the niece's grandparents influenced the upbringing of her uncle and one of her parents, and this upbringing may cause environmental similarities in the relatives' homes. Consequently, most family studies cannot disentangle the unique influences of genes and the environment on the development of a phenotype.

Twin Studies

Contrasting MZ and DZ Twins

The most frequently used strategy in **twin studies** is to compare the covariation of a phenotype between pairs of **monozygotic (MZ)** twins and **dizygotic (DZ)** twins. If the covariation is higher among MZ twins than DZ twins, genes are implicated in the phenotype because of the greater genetic relatedness of MZ twins.

The term *monozygotic* refers to the fact that MZ twins develop from the same zygote (a zygote is a fertilized egg). For reasons not yet known, some zygotes split during the first few weeks after egg fertilization. Because no cell specialization takes place soon after an egg is fertilized, the mass of cells in a zygote can split and produce two or more complete individuals (Clark & Grunstein, 2000; Plomin et al., 2001). MZ twins originate from one zygote, so their genes are identical. DZ twins result when two eggs are fertilized by two sperm. Therefore the genetic similarity of DZ twins is about

50%, which is the same as the genetic similarity among all siblings who are not MZ twins.

However, conclusions from comparison of MZ and DZ twins are based on the assumption that the environments experienced by the MZ twin pairs are no more similar than the environments experienced by DZ twin pairs. If the environments experienced by MZ twins were more similar than the environments experienced by DZ twins, a higher covariation among MZ twins would have to be attributed to greater similarity in both their genes and their environments. There has been significant controversy about the environmental similarities experienced by MZ and DZ twins and consequently whether twin studies overestimate the genetic influences on phenotypes (Maccoby, 2000).

Although it is true that MZ twins are more likely to dress similarly, have friends in common, and have more contact with each other in adulthood than DZ twins, many studies suggest that the overall environments experienced by MZ twins are not that much more similar than the environments experienced by DZ twins (Plomin et al., 2001). In addition, the environmental characteristics that are more similar for MZ twins do not appear to significantly influence the phenotypes commonly investigated in quantitative behavioral genetics studies, such as cognitive ability or personality style (DiLalla, 2002). However, even if the environments of MZ twins are somewhat more similar than the environments of DZ twins, this difference may have some influence on their development; and if this influence is assumed to be zero, the estimates of the genetic influence on a phenotype will be inflated (Maccoby, 2000).

A potential source of difficulty in twin studies arises when phenotypes are measured by reports from parents or teachers. As described in several following chapters, reports from parents and teachers tend to show a greater difference in the covariation between MZ twins and DZ twins than reports from the twins themselves (Maccoby, 2000; Rowe & Jacobson, 1999). Thus reports from parents or teachers generate a higher estimate of the influence of genes on a phenotype than reports from the twins. For example, in studies of depression, the genetic influence on depression is estimated at 50–60% when parents' reports are used and 20–30% when reports from the twins are used (Rice, Harold, & Thapar, 2002).

This pattern appears to occur because parents and teachers view MZ twins as more similar than do the MZ twins themselves. The greater physical similarity of MZ twins may tempt parents and teachers to generalize a behavior in either twin to "the twins." This would artificially increase the covariation of a phenotype between MZ twins and cause overestimation of the genetic influence on a phenotype.

Contrasting Twins Raised Together and Apart

Another useful strategy in twin studies is comparing the covariation of a phenotype among pairs of twins who were either raised together in their birth families or separated at birth and raised in different adoptive families. If the covariation among those raised in the same home is higher than that of those raised in different homes, we can argue that environment influenced the phenotype because the twins' genetic relatedness is the same while the environment experienced by those raised in the same home is more related than the environments of those raised in different homes. However, if the covariations between pairs raised in the same home and pairs raised in different homes are about the same, we can argue that environment had little influence on the phenotype, so genes must have had an important influence on the phenotype. For example, several studies have shown that the covariation of cognitive abilities of twins raised in adoptive families is about the same as that of twins raised in their birth homes—supporting the hypothesis that genes play an important role in cognitive ability (Bouchard et al., 1990).

Adoption Studies

Studying children who have been adopted soon after birth allows many comparisons and estimates of the influences of genotype and environment on a phenotype (Rowe & Jacobson, 1999). For example, the covariation of a phenotype can be compared between pairs of (1) adopted children and their "genetic" birth parents and (2) adopted children and their "environmental" adoptive parents. Covariation between adopted children and their birth parents is likely due to genetic influences because the children and parents share genes but not environment, whereas covariation between children and their adoptive parents is likely due to environment because they share environment but not genes.

Comparisons of the covariation of a phenotype can also be made between pairs of (1) adoptive parents and their birth children and (2) adoptive parents and their adopted children. Similarly, in families with more than one birth child and an adopted child, comparisons can be made between birth sibling pairs and birth sibling and adopted sibling pairs. Higher covariations between birth relatives than between adoptive relatives implicate genes in the development of the phenotype.

Several issues can complicate adoption studies. First, birth mothers provide the prenatal environment for their children as well as some of their children's genes. Consequently, it is difficult to distinguish the influence of prenatal environment from the influence of genes in studies involving adopted children and their birth mothers (DiLalla, 2002). For example, the health of mother and child may be influenced if the mother smokes while she is pregnant, and it can be challenging to determine whether covariation in their health problems is due to the genes or the prenatal smoking environment they shared.

A second issue is that children may be selectively placed in adoptive homes that resemble the homes of their birth mothers. This practice was especially prevalent during the first six or seven decades of the 1900s, when adoption agencies tried to match adoptive home characteristics to those of birth parents' homes—even to the point of placing children in an adoptive home where the parents were of the same religion as the birth mother (Goodman, Emery, & Haugaard, 1998). Adoption studies assume that the environments of the child's birth family and adoptive family are not related, so any covariation between adopted children and their birth parents can be attributed to genetic influences. However, if the environments in the adoptive and birth homes are related because of selective placement, any covariation between adopted children and their birth parents may be due to genetic influences and to the influences of the related home environments. If all this covariation of a phenotype is attributed to genetic influences, the estimate of the genetic influences will be inflated (Plomin et al., 2001).

Key Concepts

- Quantitative behavioral genetics studies focus on differences in the covariation of a phenotype between two groups of pairs of individuals with varying degrees of genetic or environmental relatedness.
- Family studies explore the covariation of a phenotype between pairs of relatives with varying degrees of genetic relatedness.
- A limitation of family studies is that they cannot quantify the relative influence of genes and environment because family members often share both genes and environment.
- Most twin studies compare the covariation of a phenotype between MZ twins and DZ twins. Another type of twin study compares the covariation of a phenotype between twins raised together in the same family and twins raised apart in adoptive families.
- Limitations of twin studies include the possibility that MZ twins have a more similar environment than DZ twins and that parents or teachers are more likely to generalize the behavior of one twin to "the twins" in MZ pairs than in DZ pairs.
- Adoption studies compare the covariation of a phenotype between birth relative pairs (such as a child and birth mother) and adoptive relative pairs (such as a child and adoptive mother).
- Limitations of adoption studies include the possibility that prenatal environmental influences may be attributed to genetic influences and that selective placement of adopted children may cause significant similarities in the environments of their birth and adoptive homes.

Quantifying the Influences on Development

Early studies in quantitative behavioral genetics estimated the influences of genes and the environment on a phenotype. This early research showed that the influence of the environment could be divided into two categories: shared environmental influences and nonshared environmental influences. As a result, quantitative behavioral genetics has more recently focused on three influences on individual differences:

- Heritability (genetic influences).
- Shared environment (environmental influences that make pairs of people similar).

- Nonshared environment (environmental influences that make pairs of people dissimilar).

The basic procedure for estimating these three influences is to first assess the influence of genes on a phenotype. Then all the other influence is considered environmental. The next step is to calculate the influence of shared environment on the phenotype. The remaining influence is attributed to non-shared environment (and in some studies to error of measurement, a topic discussed at the end of this section).

Heritability

Heritability is a statistic that describes the genetic contribution to the variability of a phenotype observed in a population at a particular age and at a specific point in time (Plomin et al., 2001). Three important points from this sentence must be noted. First, heritability estimates describe the genetic contribution to the phenotype of the population as a whole, not any individual. Individuals and groups within a population are likely to vary in the extent to which their genotypes and environments have influenced the phenotype being investigated. For example, the influence of genes on nonverbal intelligence is much lower for children born very prematurely than it is for other children (Marlow, Wolke, Bracewell, & Samara, 2005). Thus the results from quantitative behavioral genetics studies cannot be used to estimate the degree to which a phenotype of a specific child or a particular group of children has been influenced by genes or environment.

Second, heritability estimates provide information about the genetic influence on a phenotype at a specific age, not for that phenotype across the life span (Reiss & Neiderhiser, 2000). Several studies have shown that the heritability for some characteristics and behaviors changes at different ages. For example, studies of adolescent alcohol consumption have shown a higher genetic influence on the drinking of 18-year-olds than when those same adolescents were 16 (Rose, Dick, Viken, Pulkkinen, & Kaprio, 2001).

Finally, heritability estimates provide information about genetic influence at a specific point in time. If the environment changes significantly from one year to the next, or from one decade to the next, the influence of genes on behaviors measured during different points in time can change (Rutter et al., 2006). For example, if the environment significantly restricts behaviors, genetic influence on those behaviors can drop dramatically. The influence of genes on the age of first intercourse, for instance, was much lower in men and women born between 1922 and 1952, when there were many more social restrictions on adolescent sexuality (32% in women, 0% in men), than for those born after 1952 (49% for women, 72% for men) (Dunne et al., 1997).

Heritability can be estimated in two ways: using concordance rates and calculating correlations. **Concordance** is used to estimate the heritability of characteristics or behaviors represented by dichotomous variables (*dichotomous* comes from the Greek *dicha*, "in two"). Most frequently, concordance is used in assessing the genetic influence on the presence of a disorder. To calculate concordance, a sample of pairs of people with some genetic relatedness is gathered in which one member of each pair has the disorder being investigated. The concordance rate is the percentage of pairs in which both have the disorder; these pairs are considered *concordant* for the disorder. For example, consider a study of 100 pairs of siblings in which one of the siblings has schizophrenia. If an assessment of all the siblings showed that both siblings in 10 of the pairs had schizophrenia (that is, 10 of the pairs were concordant for schizophrenia), there would be a 10% concordance rate for schizophrenia in that sample (Plomin, 1990).

In twin studies, two types of concordance rates can be calculated: pairwise concordance and probandwise concordance (Plomin, 1990). *Pairwise concordance* is the percentage of pairs that are concordant for the disorder being investigated (as described in the previous paragraph). *Probandwise concordance* is the percentage of people in the sample that have the disorder. For example, consider a study of 10 twin pairs in which one twin is diagnosed with mental retardation. If 5 of the pairs are concordant for mental retardation, the pairwise concordance would be 50%. However, among the 20 individuals in the sample, 15 have mental retardation (one member of each pair and five of their twins). Consequently, 75% of the sample has mental retardation, so there is a 75% probandwise concordance. In twin studies of concordance, the probandwise concordance rate is often preferred because it can be compared with concordance rates from other family groups.

The second strategy for estimating heritability, **correlation,** is used in studies of phenotypes that are continuous, such as height, level of self-esteem, or number of depressive symptoms. Different mathematical formulas estimate heritability using correlations, depending on the type of study being conducted (such as twin or adoption). However, all the formulas take into account the percentage of genes shared among those being studied and the similarity of their environments.

Methods of calculating heritability from correlations have been discussed by Plomin (1990) in several straightforward examples, using height as the phenotype of interest. For example, in studies of MZ twin pairs raised apart in adoptive families, the correlation of their height directly measures the genetic influence on height because they have identical genotypes and are assumed to have no shared environment. Studies of the height of MZ twin pairs raised apart show that their height is correlated about .90, indicating that 90% of the influence on their height is due to their genotype. A similar study with DZ twin pairs would require that the correlation observed in their heights be doubled to assess the heritability of their height because they share only 50% of the same genes. True to form, most studies of height in DZ twin pairs raised apart show a correlation of about .45, which, when doubled, provides the same heritability estimates as do studies using MZ twin pairs. Adoption studies or studies comparing MZ and DZ twin pairs require subtracting the correlation of those with less genetic similarity from the correlation of those with more genetic similarity. For example, the correlation of the heights from adopted sibling pairs is subtracted from the correlation of the heights from birth sibling pairs (and then doubled because the siblings share only 50% of the same genes) to obtain an estimate of the heritability of height (again, studies show a heritability of 90% using this method).

Shared Environmental Influences

In the definition employed by those in the quantitative behavioral genetics field, **shared environmental influences** are those that make pairs of individuals more similar (Plomin et al., 2001). Almost all shared environmental influences are believed to occur within families.

Shared environment has only a minor influence on most phenotypes. This is surprising to most people because we tend to assume that, for example, siblings raised in the same family share a great deal of the same environment and that this shared environment significantly influences many of their characteristics. Many people have expressed concern about the relatively small influence of shared environment found in most quantitative behavioral genetics studies because they believe that the small influence of shared environments suggests that family life has little influence on children's development. They point to findings from other types of studies showing that family life has an important influence on child development (Maccoby, 2000).

A clear understanding of what constitutes shared environment helps us understand how family life can have important influences on children's development even if there is little influence of shared environment on most phenotypes. Four characteristics are required for an influence to be considered a shared environmental influence, and these characteristics reduce dramatically the number of influences from family life that are considered shared environmental influences (Rowe & Jacobson, 1999):

1. Environmental influences that are nearly universal within a population are not considered shared environmental influences. For example, almost all second-generation U.S. families speak English as their primary language, so English being spoken by all family members is not viewed as a shared environmental influence.

2. A shared environmental influence must be experienced by all children in a family. For example, an automobile accident involving two members of a four-person family would not be considered a shared environmental influence. Although all family members might be affected by the accident, the effect is likely to differ for those in the accident and those not in it, so this is not a shared environmental influence.

3. A shared environmental influence must directly affect the phenotype being investigated. Rowe and Jacobson (1999) use an example of household exposure to radon gas to illustrate this point. If cognitive abilities are the phenotype being investigated, the common experience of living in a house with high levels of radon gas would not be considered a shared environmental influence because there is no evidence that exposure to radon influences cognitive abilities. However, exposure to radon gas would be considered a shared

environmental influence if the development of cancer was the phenotype being investigated because radon is carcinogenic.

4. A shared environmental influence must influence all the children in the family in the same direction. For example, consider an assessment of the influence of parental divorce on children's academic performance. Parental divorce meets the first three characteristics of a shared environmental influence: It does not occur universally in the population, it is experienced by all the children in the family, and it has been correlated with academic performance. However, if parental divorce decreases academic performance in some children (possibly because their emotional reaction to the divorce distracts them from their studies) while increasing academic performance in other children (possibly because they cope with the divorce by spending more time concentrating on their studies), the parental divorce would not be a shared environmental influence. The *event* is shared by all children in the family, but the *influence* of the event on the phenotype is not shared by the children.

These four characteristics of shared environmental influences help us understand how family life can have an important influence on children without being a shared environmental influence. For example, harsh parenting practices have been associated with higher levels of conduct problems in children (Loeber & Farrington, 2000). However, if one child in a family is singled out for harsh parenting, this would not be a shared environmental influence. Similarly, the onset of depression in a mother may significantly affect the development of a 3-year-old who is at home with the mother all day long but may have little influence on her 17-year-old brother who spends most of his time at school or with his friends. So in this case having a depressed parent would not be considered a shared environmental influence.

One common strategy for estimating shared environment is to examine a phenotype's correlations among siblings in an adoptive family. Because birth children and adopted children in a family share no genes, their similarities must be caused by shared environment. Studies of cognitive abilities in school-age adopted siblings, for example, show a correlation of about .25 (Plomin et al., 2001). This suggests that about 25% of school-age children's cognitive abilities are due to shared environmental influences. Interestingly, research with adolescent adopted siblings shows almost no correlation in their cognitive abilities—suggesting that although shared environment has some influence on cognitive abilities in school-age children, this influence disappears by adolescence.

Nonshared Environmental Influences

Nonshared environmental influences make pairs of individuals dissimilar (Rowe & Jacobson, 1999). The sources of nonshared environmental influences are wide-ranging; they include problems during embryonic development, problems during birth, early childhood diseases or injuries, different treatment by parents, different friends, and differences in schooling. The list of nonshared environmental influences is almost unlimited.

Error of Measurement

In many quantitative behavioral genetics studies, the influence of nonshared environment can be inflated by error of measurement (Rutter, Silberg, Connor, & Simonoff, 1999). This occurs because, as already noted, after the influences of genotype and shared environment on a phenotype have been calculated, all other influences are considered to be due to nonshared environment. **Error of measurement** is not included in the estimates of heritability or shared environment, so it is included as nonshared environment if not assessed separately.

As discussed elsewhere in this text, *error* in social science research refers to any influence on a measurement that is not due to the characteristic being measured. For example, when measuring the circumference of a person's waist, some people may pull a measuring tape more snugly than others pull it. The "snugness of pull" is error because it has an influence on waist measurement that is not due to waist circumference. Similarly, because luck in guessing answers on an intelligence test can influence the results of the test, and because "luck in guessing" is not the characteristic being measured by an intelligence test, the variability in scores of intelligence tests due to guessing is considered error.

Almost all measurements in the social sciences have some error. Extensive analyses of some measures have generated estimates of their error of measurement. For example, all well-known intelligence tests provide estimates of their error of measurement. However, estimates of error have been calculated for only a minority of measures, so the error associated with most measures is unknown.

A careful reading of some quantitative behavioral genetics studies will show that error of measurement has been assessed and is reported separately from nonshared environment. For example, in a figure in this text's chapter about mental retardation, the genetic influence on intelligence is estimated to be about 50%, the environmental influences about 40%, and error about 10% (Plomin et al., 2001). However, in research on many phenotypes, the influence of error is not considered separately from that of nonshared environment (often because the error associated with the measurement of the phenotype is not known)—thereby inflating, to some unknown degree, the estimate of the influence of nonshared environment.

Key Concepts

- Heritability is a measure of the genetic contribution to variability of a phenotype observed in a population, at a given age, and at a particular point in time. It can be estimated in two ways: concordance and correlation.
- Shared environmental influences make pairs of individuals more similar. Events experienced by a pair of individuals are considered

shared environmental influences only if they have a specific influence on a phenotype and if the direction of their influence is the same for both members of the pair.

- Nonshared environmental influences make pairs of individuals dissimilar. Many influences are considered nonshared environmental influences. In some cases, error of measurement may inflate the estimate of the contribution of nonshared environmental influences.

Gene and Environment Relationships

One intriguing result from several quantitative behavioral genetics studies performed during the 1970s and 1980s was that studies designed to isolate the environmental influences on a phenotype consistently showed a mixture of genetic and environmental influences (Kendler & Eaves, 1986). This seemed odd. Theorizing about this conundrum led to the conclusion that the contributions to a phenotype from a person's genotype and environment were not always distinct. Rather, there was often a relationship between a person's genotype and his or her environment (Plomin et al., 2001). These relationships were conceptualized as *genotype–environment interactions* and *genotype–environment correlations* (Rowe & Jacobson, 1999).

Many studies have now made it clear that genotype–environment relationships add to the phenotypic variability observed between individuals. However, the influences of these relationships have been difficult to quantify in the same way that heritability, shared environment, and nonshared environment have been quantified because the relative contributions of genotype and environment to these relationships have been difficult to isolate (DiLalla, 2002). Consequently, most investigations of genotype–environment relationships have focused on describing when and how they occur rather than on quantifying their influence (Plomin et al., 2001; Rutter et al., 2006).

Genotype–Environment Interactions

Genotype–environment interactions occur when a phenotype changes dramatically in the presence of a specific combination of a genetic and an environmental influence (Rowe & Jacobson, 1999). The disorder phenylketonuria (PKU) is a good example of a genotype–environment interaction. As described in more detail in the chapter about mental retardation, PKU is a disorder involving a mutation of the phenylalanine hydroxylase (PAH) gene. This results in a person being unable to properly metabolize phenylalanine (a substance present in milk, cheese, eggs, and many other food proteins), which causes severe cognitive deficits (DiLella & Woo, 1987). Thus, for PKU to occur, there must be both a genetic influence (the mutated PAH gene) and an environmental influence (the dietary presence of phenylalanine). PKU does not occur if the PAH gene is present but no phenylalanine is present in a child's diet; nor does it occur if phenylalanine is present in a child's diet but there is no mutation of the PAH gene. Consequently, a specific combination of genetic and environmental influences causes a child to have PKU; in other words, PKU develops through a genotype–environment interaction.

The development of PKU illustrates how phenotypes influenced largely by genes can also be influenced by the environment. Some have raised concern about our increasing knowledge of the influence of genes because this knowledge suggests that certain phenotypes cannot be changed by environmental conditions—that a person is somehow "hardwired" by his or her genes to be a certain way (Clark & Grunstein, 2000). This may result in few attempts to create environments in which these phenotypes are less likely to occur. The example of PKU, however, shows that our phenotypes are not hardwired by our genes and that environmental changes can significantly influence disorders or behaviors that have a substantial genetic influence.

Genotype–Environment Correlations

Genotype–environment correlations, which are much more common than genotype–environment interactions, occur when a person's genotype influences his or her environment (and consequently the influences of that environment) (Rutter et al., 2006). For example, consider academic achievement. Children's educational environment has an important influence on their academic achievement: Children in schools with low student–teacher ratios, computers, and modern equipment are more likely to have high academic achievement than children in schools with high student–teacher ratios, no computers, and outdated textbooks. But children are not assigned to schools randomly in our country. Rather, children of affluent parents are more likely to attend well-to-do schools, whereas children of less affluent parents are more likely to attend troubled schools. Because parents who have higher intelligence are more likely to be affluent than are parents with lower intelligence, the children of more intelligent parents are more likely to attend good schools than are children of less intelligent parents. Thus there is a relationship between a child's school environment and the child's genes: The parental genes have a genetic influence on a child's intelligence and also influence the environment in which the child is educated (with this environment also influencing the child's intelligence). This is a genotype–environment correlation.

As another example, consider athletic ability. A girl with a genotype that results in strong athletic ability is more likely to play athletic games as a young child and be involved in athletic teams as a school-age child and adolescent. On the other hand, a girl with a genotype that results in poor athletic ability is less likely to be involved in these activities. As the girl with the genotype that enhances her athletic ability practices these skills, her athletic ability increases. In this way, her environment has an important influence on her athletic ability. However, the athletic environment in which she develops is related to her genotype because her genotype influenced her involvement in an athletic environment. Consequently, a genotype–environment correlation exists.

Three types of genotype–environment correlations can occur. **Passive** genotype–environment correlations occur when a child inherits both the genes and an environment that influence a phenotype. For example, consider musical ability (Plomin et al., 2001). The child of parents who are musically gifted is likely to both inherit genes related to musical ability and live in an environment where music is played and enjoyed. This is a passive genotype–environment correlation because, without any action by the child, he experiences both the genes and an environment that are conducive to developing musical ability. **Evocative** genotype–environment correlations occur when a child's genetic propensity evokes behaviors from others in his or her environment that enhance that propensity. For example, a child with musical ability may be encouraged by his teachers to participate in the school orchestra or chorus, and participation in these activities will increase his musical ability. In this case the child's genetically influenced musical ability evokes encouragement from teachers for him to participate in a musical environment, so an evocative genotype–environment correlation exists. **Active** genotype–environment correlations occur when a child actively seeks environments that enhance his or her genetic propensities. For example, a child with genetically influenced musical ability may seek friends with similar abilities or look for opportunities to join community musical groups, thereby creating an environment in which his genetically based musical talents flourish.

A parent with musical talent may contribute genes to a child that enhance the child's musical talent and also create an environment that enhances the child's musical talent.

Key Concepts

- Genotype–environment interactions occur when the combination of a genotype and a specific environment dramatically influences a phenotype.
- Genotype–environment correlations occur when a person's environment is influenced by his or her genotype. Three types of genotype–environment correlations have been identified: passive, evocative, and active.

CHAPTER GLOSSARY

Active genotype–environment correlations occur when a child seeks environments that enhance his or her genetic propensities.

Adoption studies involve children who have been adopted soon after birth, allowing comparisons of covariations between them and their "genetic" and "environmental" relatives.

An **allele** is a gene that varies slightly among individuals in a species.

Concordance is used in estimating the heritability of a dichotomous variable, such as the presence or absence of a disorder.

Correlation is used in estimating the heritability of a continuous variable, such as height, level of self-esteem, or number of depressive symptoms.

Covariation, as used in quantitative behavioral genetics, is a measure of the extent to which a phenotype varies systematically in pairs of people.

Dizygotic (DZ) twins result when two eggs are fertilized by two sperm. DZ twins share about 50% of the same genes.

Error of measurement refers to any influence on a measurement that is not due to the characteristic being measured. Error of measurement can appear as a nonshared environmental influence in some studies.

Evocative genotype–environment correlations occur when a child's genetic propensity evokes behaviors from others in his or her environment that enhance the genetic propensity.

Family studies contrast the covariation of a phenotype among pairs of nuclear or extended family members who have different levels of genetic relatedness.

A **gene** is a section of DNA that directs protein production within a cell. It is the basic unit of inheritance.

A person's **genome** is the collection of all his or her genes and alleles.

A person's **genotype** is the collection of all his or her alleles.

Genotype–environment correlations occur when a person's genotype influences his or her environment and consequently the influence that the environment has on his or her phenotype.

Genotype–environment interactions occur if a phenotype changes dramatically when a combination of a genetic and environmental influence occurs.

Heritability is a measure of the genetic contribution to a phenotype observed in a population at a particular point in time.

Molecular behavioral genetics is the study of the influence of a specific gene or genes on a phenotype.

Monozygotic (MZ) twins develop from the same zygote that has split during the first few days or weeks following the fertilization of an egg. They are genetically identical.

The **nature–nurture controversy** is a longstanding debate about whether a person's environment or genes are the primary influence on his or her development.

Nonshared environmental influences make pairs of individuals dissimilar.

Passive genotype–environment correlations occur when a child inherits both the genes and an environment that is conducive to his or her genetically based skills.

A **phenotype** is an observed characteristic or behavior of an individual, such as height, intelligence, or level of anxiety.

Shared environmental influences make pairs of individuals more similar. Almost all shared environmental influences are believed to occur within families.

Twin studies commonly compare the covariation of a phenotype between pairs of MZ and DZ twins. Less frequently they compare twins reared in their birth families and twins reared apart in adoptive families.

Classification, Diagnosis, and Assessment

It is important to consider cultural issues during every assessment.

Most of this text is devoted to exploring many of the behavioral or emotional disorders that can be diagnosed in children and adolescents, as well as the characteristics and experiences of children who are diagnosed with them. Before we begin this exploration, it is important to review what disorders are and how they are diagnosed. Without this basic knowledge, we can misunderstand what it means for a child to be diagnosed with a disorder.

The system used most frequently in the United States to classify and diagnose disorders is contained in the ***Diagnostic and Statistical Manual of Mental Disorders*** (the commonly used acronym is *DSM*), published by the American Psychiatric Association. The DSM includes all the conditions that the American Psychiatric Association believes are disorders, classifies these disorders into groups (such as mood disorders and anxiety disorders), and specifies the criteria that must be met for a disorder to be diagnosed.

It is important to note that the DSM does not diagnose or classify *people* (APA, 2000). Rather, the DSM classifies *disorders* and provides the criteria that must be met for a disorder to be diagnosed. The distinction between classifying and diagnosing people or disorders is an important one—it is not simply an issue of wording or semantics. If people were diagnosed or classified, it could suggest that the whole of the person could be summed up with one or two diagnoses. For example, the parlance in many clinical settings a few decades ago referred to some children as "depressives" and other children as "mental retardates." These phrases suggest that depression or mental retardation is what the child is. We know that this is not true, so it is important to avoid language suggesting that it is. By classifying and diagnosing disorders, the DSM makes it clear that a disorder is only one characteristic of a child or adult and that we must consider many other characteristics to understand the full experience of a child or adult.

As we will see in this chapter and throughout this text, the classification system of the DSM is not static. It has evolved over time in response to our steadily increasing knowledge about disorders, and it will continue to evolve as we learn more. For example, the disorder we now call *attention-deficit/hyperactivity disorder (ADHD)* has had a different name, and has included different diagnostic criteria, in each edition of the DSM. This shows that what we "know" about ADHD has changed several times, and some researchers suggest that what we "know" about ADHD now is not completely accurate (Barkley, 2003; Milich, Balentine, & Lynam, 2001). Consequently, it is important to understand that how we characterize and classify disorders today is based not on The Truth, but rather on our current state of knowledge—what we believe to be the truth now but know may not be the truth in the future.

Chapter Plan

We start this chapter by defining what a disorder is. This is an essential first step before examining how disorders are classified and diagnosed. Next we explore the fundamental issue of whether specific disorders should exist and examine the potential advantages and disadvantages of defining specific disorders and diagnosing them in children. Following the discussion of these two basic issues, we examine classification systems in general and then the DSM classification system. Finally, we explore the variety of ways that information about a child can be gathered by a clinician as he or she assesses whether the child meets the diagnostic criteria for one or more disorders.

Disorders

Before we explore how disorders are classified and diagnosed, we should define what a disorder is. Although the disorders discussed in this text are included in the *Diagnostic and Statistical Manual of Mental Disorders,* the term *mental disorder* is used rarely in the current edition of the DSM. The name of the manual has not changed since it was first published, but the term *mental disorder* has fallen from common use. In part this is because the term suggests a sharp distinction between mental disorders and physical disorders. This distinction was once considered clear. However, it is now recognized that many mental disorders have a physical cause and that the intensity of many physical disorders can be significantly influenced by psychological issues (Campo & Garber, 1998; Kirmayer & Young, 1998). Thus it is no longer seen as appropriate to consider disorders as either mental or physical.

In addition, the term *mental disorder* has a pejorative sound: It suggests there is something wrong with a person's mind. As we will see in this text, disorders develop in many children because of their experiences, and it is unlikely that there is anything disordered about their minds. To avoid the potentially inaccurate and negative connotations that accompany the term *mental disorder,* many people now prefer the term *behavioral or emotional disorder.* This longer term is more accurate and descriptive because all the disorders are characterized by emotions or behaviors that are distressing to a child or impair a child's functioning. Further, it suggests that the child's emotions or behaviors are disordered, rather than the child's mind.

The DSM (APA, 2000, p. xxxi) defines a **disorder** as

> A clinically significant behavioral or psychological syndrome or pattern that occurs in an individual and that is associated with present distress (e.g., a painful symptom) or disability (i.e., impairment in one or more important areas of functioning) or with a significantly increased risk of suffering death, pain, disability, or an important loss of freedom. In addition, this syndrome or pattern must not be merely an expectable and culturally sanctioned response to a particular event. . . . Neither deviant behavior (e.g., political, religious, or sexual) nor conflicts that are primarily between the individual and society are behavioral or emotional disorders.

Several points in this definition are worth noting. First, the symptoms of a disorder occur in a syndrome (from the Greek *syn,* "together," and *dromos,* "course"). A **syndrome** is a set of symptoms that frequently occur together and follow a similar course. So each disorder in the DSM consists of a set of symptoms that are likely to occur together over time. Second, these symptoms must create distress or disability for a child or be associated with the possibility of a negative future outcome. Many disorders are associated with distress for children; for example, children with separation anxiety disorder are distressed when they must leave their parents, and children with major depressive disorder are distressed by the profound sadness they feel. However, not all disorders are associated with distress. A child with conduct disorder, for example, may not be distressed by his behaviors even if they bother others. But conduct disorder can inhibit a child's educational achievement (a disability) or can result in a child being arrested and incarcerated (an important loss of freedom), so it is considered a disorder even if a child is not distressed by the behaviors associated with this disorder.

Cautions appear in many places in the DSM that behaviors or emotions that are culturally sanctioned are not symptoms of a disorder. For example, having visions as part of a culturally sanctioned religious ceremony would not be considered symptoms if the visions are viewed as a positive part of the ceremony by the culture's members. Similarly, a child's quiet and withdrawn behaviors would not be considered symptoms if the values of the child's culture are that it is proper for a child to be quiet and withdrawn. As we will discuss in many upcoming chapters, understanding and appreciating the role of culture in the development of children's emotions and behaviors is important whenever we diagnose a disorder or work in a therapeutic environment with a child or family.

Finally, behaviors that result from conflicts between an individual and society are not symptoms of a disorder. Protests against laws or government actions, for example, are not symptoms of a disorder, even if the protests cause significant loss of freedom (such as being put in prison).

Why Have a Classification System and Diagnose Disorders?

Another important issue to address is whether psychologists and other mental health professionals should diagnose disorders in children at all (Scotti & Morris, 2000). Why not simply assess the problems a child is having and work to eliminate those problems without developing a classification system for disorders and determining which of the diagnoses in the classification system should be given to a specific child? If these processes are not useful, going through them may simply waste time. Potentially even more troubling is that giving a diagnosis to a child may create problems for the child and thus may be harmful. As we explore in this section, there are potential advantages and disadvantages to diagnosing behavioral or emotional disorders in children.

Potential Advantages

A principal advantage of a classification system that includes specific diagnostic criteria for disorders is that it promotes research. This research may improve understanding of the disorder and lead to interventions that are successful in preventing or treating the disorder. A classification system with specific diagnostic criteria promotes research in two primary ways. First, it allows a researcher to systematically gather a sample of research participants who are all experiencing the same syndrome of symptoms, and it helps the researcher exclude from the sample people experiencing other symptoms. This lets the researcher investigate one distinct disorder and avoid the problems that can occur if people with several disorders are included in a study. An example of this benefit comes from the study of severe disorders in children. Until the 1970s, children with what we now call *autism* and children with what we now call *childhood-onset schizophrenia* were included in a broad diagnostic category of *childhood schizophrenia*. Studying these children was difficult because their symptoms were so different. It was not until the work of Kolvin and his colleagues that children with childhood-onset schizophrenia were seen as having a disorder distinct from autism (Kolvin, 1971). After that distinction was made and the diagnostic criteria for both disorders were established, children with either autism or early-onset schizophrenia could be studied separately. This dramatically increased our knowledge about both disorders.

Another way in which a classification system promotes research is that it permits many researchers to contribute to a body of research for a specific disorder. Clear and specific diagnostic criteria allow different researchers to gather and study samples of children or adults who all meet the same diagnostic criteria. For example, the effectiveness of a medication to treat children who have obsessive–compulsive disorder can be assessed by several researchers, each working with a distinct sample of children, if the children in each sample meet the same diagnostic criteria. Similar findings from all the researchers can provide strong evidence about the effectiveness of the medication. Differences in their findings (perhaps more children in a sample of 12- to 15-year-olds respond to the medication than do children in a sample of 7- to 10-year-olds) can indicate which children are more likely to respond to the medication. However, studies can be combined in this way only if the children in each study meet the same diagnostic criteria for obsessive–compulsive disorder.

A second potential advantage of a widely used classification system is that it promotes communication between professionals working with a child or the child's family. For example, a school psychologist who learns that a child has received a diagnosis of separation anxiety disorder from a clinical psychologist in the community knows about the syndrome of symptoms that the child is experiencing. Of course knowing that a child has received a diagnosis does not provide information about the intensity of the child's symptoms or about the child's many other characteristics, so knowing that a child has a diagnosis provides only some information about the child. However, this information can help other professionals work with the child.

A third potential advantage is that knowing that a child has a specifically defined disorder helps clinicians plan an effective intervention for the child and family. For example, research has shown that the stimulant medication Ritalin can reduce symptoms of ADHD but that it does not reduce the symptoms of bipolar disorder and may exacerbate bipolar symptoms. Consequently, knowing whether a child meets the diagnostic criteria for ADHD or for bipolar disorder helps a clinician determine whether stimulant medication or another form of treatment is likely to be effective with the child.

Potential Disadvantages

A significant potential disadvantage to diagnosing disorders in children is that a diagnosis may stigmatize a child. For example, knowing that a child has been diagnosed with conduct disorder may influence a teacher's beliefs about the child even before the teacher meets him. These beliefs may influence how the teacher interacts with the child and consequently the relationship that develops between them. Similarly, if a teacher knows a child has been diagnosed with mental retardation, he or she may have inappropriately low expectations for the child's academic achievement, which may discourage the child's academic progress. Peers may also stigmatize a child if they know that he or she has been given a diagnosis—such as by shunning a child who has been diagnosed with ADHD because they believe the child is "crazy."

A second potential disadvantage is that a diagnosis may narrow the view that others have of a child to the characteristics associated with the disorder. For example, people who know a child has major depressive disorder may come to see the child as simply being depressed, forgetting that the child is gifted musically or athletically or that the child can relate well to younger troubled children. Similarly, a child's view of himself or herself may be narrowed by a diagnosis, causing the child to focus solely on the characteristics associated with the disorder. This can inhibit the child from pursuing activities that use his or her strengths, thus making it more difficult for the child to recover from or cope with the disorder.

Another potential disadvantage of diagnosing disorders in children is that because the diagnosis is given to an individual child, it may encourage beliefs that the child is responsible for having the disorder. Consider a 6-year-old boy from an aggressive family and neighborhood who has been given the diagnosis of conduct disorder. The diagnosis may encourage others to believe the child is responsible for the symptoms that have led to the diagnosis (after all, *he* is the one with the diagnosis) and may discourage them from seeing the child's behavior as a reflection of the environment in which he was raised. In other words, they may blame the child for the disorder and thus interact differently with him than they would if they saw the child as the victim of a dysfunctional family and neighborhood.

Finally, a generally accepted classification system for diagnosing disorders can limit the thinking of current and future researchers and clinicians. For example, as you learn about how disorders are classified, you may come to see the current system as reflecting The Truth about behavioral or emotional disorders. This may discourage you from thinking creatively about better ways to conceptualize and classify disorders.

Emphasizing Advantages and Minimizing Disadvantages

Knowing the potential advantages and disadvantages of diagnosing behavioral or emotional disorders in children can help people maximize the advantages and minimize the disadvantages. By understanding the advantages of clearly defined disorders in a widely used classification system, researchers can gather groups of children with specific disorders to study, and clinicians can use this research-based knowledge to develop effective treatment plans. Understanding the potential disadvantages of diagnosing disorders in children can encourage clinicians, physicians, teachers, and others to avoid stigmatizing a child diagnosed with a disorder. Similarly, knowing that a diagnosis may limit how they view a child may encourage specific efforts to view the child as a complex person. Finally, knowing that a generally accepted classification system can reduce creative thinking can encourage students and professionals to question the appropriateness of the current classification system and suggest alternative ways of conceptualizing disorders.

Key Concepts

- In the DSM, a disorder is a psychological or behavioral syndrome that produces distress, impairment, or an increased risk of significant negative outcomes.
- Potential advantages of a classification system of clearly defined behavioral or emotional disorders include promotion of research, accumulation of a body of research, enhanced communication between professionals, and effective therapeutic interventions.
- Potential disadvantages include stigmatizing a child, limiting the view of a child, blaming a child for a disorder, and reducing creativity in the field.

Basic Issues in Classification

Classification Systems

A **classification system** is used to divide a group into categories. The group being divided could be objects such as rocks or fruit, historical eras, or behavioral or emotional disorders. Because any group can be divided in several ways, the rules used to classify the group components must be specified. Categories resulting from the use of one rule may differ fundamentally from categories created with a different rule. For example, at least two rules could be used to classify the objects in Figure 5.1 (size, shape), and each rule would result in categories that have different components.

As another example of the use of rules in classification, consider how various forms of child abuse could be classified. The strategy used by most people working in the child maltreatment field is to classify abuse into three categories: sexual abuse, physical abuse, and emotional abuse. The rule creating these categories is "classify by the behavior of the perpetrator of the abuse" (sexual contact, nonsexual physical contact, verbal interaction). This rule for categorizing abuse is so commonly used that most people do not even consider that other rules could be used (Haugaard, 2006). However, other possibilities exist. For example, the rule could be "classify by the intensity of the child's physical or psychological pain." Using this rule, one category might include slapping a child in the face, fondling a child's legs, and calling a child insulting names. Another category might include beating up a child, having intercourse with a child, and intensely humiliating a child.

Classification rules can have important influences on how we deal with people or objects. For example, the classification of abuse as physical, sexual, and emotional has resulted in different interventions being developed for children experiencing each of these categories of abuse. Several strategies for helping sexually abused children have been developed, for example, and many of these are distinct from the strategies developed for assisting children who have been physically or emotionally abused (Haugaard, 2006). If abuse were to be categorized by the intensity of a child's pain, an entirely different set of interventions might have been developed, based on that intensity.

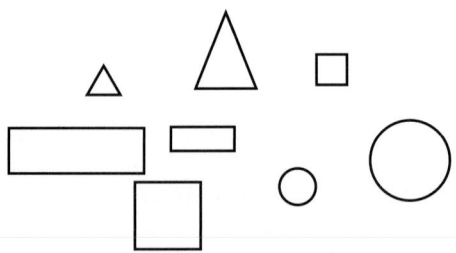

FIGURE 5.1 *Categorizing Shapes*

Categorical or Dimensional Classification

Two basic strategies for classification are the categorical and dimensional approaches. The **categorical approach** is a *qualitative* approach: The groups created using the categorical approach are seen as qualitatively different from each other. Pregnancy is a good example of categorical classification. A woman is either pregnant or not pregnant (she cannot be "somewhat" pregnant), and she is in a qualitatively different category when pregnant than when not pregnant.

Alternatively, the **dimensional approach** is a quantitative approach based on a continuous dimension. Rather than creating qualitatively different groups, categorization using a dimensional approach results in people, objects, or characteristics appearing along a continuum. Intelligence is a good example of classification using a dimensional approach. Intelligence is not something that a person either has or does not have; rather it is something that everyone has to a greater or lesser degree. Consequently, a psychologist classifies intelligence as present to a greater or lesser degree in individuals.

The DSM uses a categorical, dichotomous approach to classify behavioral or emotional disorders (APA, 2000). A variety of criteria are stated for a disorder, and if a person exhibits those criteria the disorder is said to exist in that person. For example, autistic disorder is either present or not present in a child (*dichotomous* comes from the Greek *dicha*, "in two").

However, as we will discuss repeatedly in this text, most behavioral or emotional disorders can be conceptualized using the dimensional approach. For example, anxiety, conduct problems, and weight problems can all be categorized using a dimensional approach. To illustrate this, draw three lines to represent the continua of anxiety, weight problems, and conduct problems, and plot where you and five of your friends are on each continuum. You may find that you clump together on one or more of these continua (for example, you and your friends may have few conduct problems). However, even if you clump together, you may be able to distinguish which of you has slightly more or less of the problem represented by that continuum. On another continuum you and your friends may be quite different. For example, some may have significant weight problems while others do not.

Making Categories from Dimensions

Because the DSM uses a categorical approach for classification, but most behavioral or emotional problems can be classified using a dimensional approach, an important issue is how the DSM authors create categories from dimensions. For example, if conduct problems can be thought of as lying along a dimension, how is it decided where along this dimension conduct problems become severe enough to be considered as being in the category of conduct disorder?

One way of conceptualizing this process is that a line is drawn somewhere along the continuum representing a problem behavior or emotion, and it is declared that those on one side of the line have a disorder and those on the other side of the line do not (Egger & Angold, 2006). A clear example of this is mental retardation. One diagnostic criterion for mental retardation is that a child's IQ must be two standard deviations below the mean of children that age. Children slightly above this cutoff are not considered to have mental retardation, and those slightly below this cutoff are considered to have mental retardation (if they meet the other diagnostic criteria). As another example, consider conduct disorder. To be diagnosed with conduct disorder, a child must engage in 3 or more conduct-disordered behaviors from a list of 15 behaviors. A child who engages in 2 of these behaviors cannot be given the diagnosis of conduct disorder, even if he or she engages in these behaviors repeatedly.

The place along the continuum that divides those with a disorder from those who do not have it is drawn so that those with the disorder experience clinically significant distress or disability—a defining characteristic of a disorder (Egger & Angold, 2006). The decision about where to divide the continuum is often informed by research, and where the continuum is divided can change as research accumulates suggesting which children are at risk for experiencing significant distress or disability. For example, in the 1960s the diagnostic criteria for mental retardation required an IQ one standard deviation below the mean; this was changed to two standard deviations below the mean in 1973 (Grossman, 1973). Similarly, more symptoms were required for the diagnosis of conduct disorder in the DSM-III-R (APA, 1987) than in the DSM-III (APA, 1980).

Because children diagnosed with a disorder experience significant distress or disability, their experiences can be thought of as qualitatively different from those of many other children. For example, if Figure 5.2 represents the dimension of anxiety experienced by children separated from their parents, those on the continuum labeled C experience significant distress each time they are separated from their parents, whereas those on the continuum labeled A experience little or no distress. Consequently, those whose anxiety is at the level represented by C have qualitatively different experiences from those whose anxiety is represented by A.

However, it is also clear that the experiences of children with a disorder do not differ qualitatively from those of all children who do not have the disorder. For example, those whose anxiety is represented by C do not have qualitatively different experiences from those whose anxiety is represented by B, whose anxiety is also strong but not quite strong enough for it to be considered a disorder. From the dimensional perspective, children in areas B and C have anxiety experiences that are similar. But from the categorical

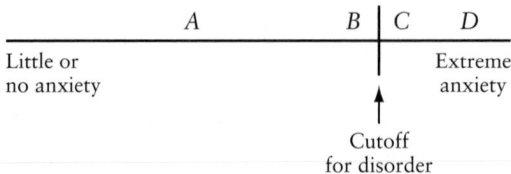

FIGURE 5.2   *The Continuum of Anxiety*

perspective, some are considered to have a disorder while others are considered not to have a disorder—a qualitative difference.

A significant drawback of this categorical approach is that it can insidiously invade our thinking to the point where we consider the experiences of children who have been diagnosed with a disorder as qualitatively different from the experiences of all children who do not have that disorder. This is not accurate. As just illustrated in Figure 5.2, many children with a disorder may have symptoms that are similar to, but somewhat more intense than, the symptoms experienced by some children who do not have the disorder.

Another drawback to the categorical approach is that all children who have been diagnosed with a disorder may be viewed as belonging to one homogeneous group. This is also not accurate. For example, a child with anxiety represented by C may have difficulty separating from parents to attend preschool, and may feel marked distress when at school, but can attend school most days. A child whose anxiety is represented by D may have such severe anxiety around separation that she is unable to attend preschool. Similar patterns can be seen in all other disorders. For instance, some researchers and clinicians classify children who meet the diagnostic criteria for autism as either "high functioning" or "low functioning" (Tanguay, 2000).

Disorders Not Otherwise Specified

One strategy the DSM uses to address the difficulties of creating categories from dimensions is to include a **not otherwise specified** disorder in each category of disorders. These disorders can be diagnosed when a child meets most of the diagnostic criteria for a disorder in that category, but not all of them (APA, 2000). For example, a child whose anxiety is represented by B in Figure 5.2 might receive a diagnosis of *anxiety disorder not otherwise specified* if his anxiety had a clinically significant influence on his life but was not quite severe enough to meet the diagnostic criteria for separation anxiety disorder.

Reliability and Validity

Two characteristics for evaluating the usefulness of any classification system are reliability and validity. *Reliability* refers to consistency. It is used in a variety of ways in the social sciences, and several of these are described in the chapter about research methods. The most common use of reliability in classification systems is **interrater reliability,** which refers to the degree of agreement between people classifying something (Sattler, 2001).

A reliable classification system for behavioral or emotional disorders results in multiple competent clinicians providing the same diagnosis for a child when they are given the same information about the child. If competent clinicians disagree about the diagnosis, perhaps the classification system has not provided enough specificity or clarity about the disorders to allow clinicians to distinguish between them. If a classification system for behavioral or emotional disorders does not have high reliability, a particular child might receive the diagnosis of one disorder by one clinician, the diagnosis of another disorder by a second clinician, and no diagnosis from a third clinician. In such a situation, none of the potential advantages of a classification system could be realized (such as using a diagnosis to plan effective interventions), thereby dramatically reducing the value of the classification system.

Validity also has a variety of meanings in the social sciences. When used to describe a classification system, **validity** refers to the system's usefulness. In essence, the validity of a classification system for behavioral or emotional disorders refers to the extent to which giving a diagnosis to a child provides useful information about the child. **Concurrent validity** refers to validity in the present. For example, does knowing that a child has major depressive disorder rather than separation anxiety disorder give a clinician, parent, teacher, or others useful information about this child as they work with the child to overcome his difficulties? **Predictive validity** refers to the extent to which a diagnosis helps predict how a child might be in the future. Does knowing that a child has childhood-onset schizophrenia rather than autism help those working with her plan for her future?

Key Concepts

- A classification system is used to divide a group into categories. Any group can be divided in more than one way, so the rules used to divide the group must be specified.
- The categorical approach to classifying behavioral or emotional disorders is a dichotomous approach: specifying whether a disorder is present or not.
- The dimensional approach is a continuous approach that represents the intensity of a child's symptoms along a continuum.
- Because the DSM uses a categorical approach for symptoms that frequently lie along a continuum, some children who are diagnosed with a disorder may experience symptoms that are only somewhat more severe than those of children who are not diagnosed with that disorder.
- Most categories in the DSM include a *not otherwise specified* diagnosis that can be given to children whose symptoms are significant but who do not meet all the diagnostic criteria for another disorder in that category.
- *Reliability* of a classification system for behavioral or emotional disorders refers to the degree to which clinicians provide the same diagnosis for a child when given the same information about the child.
- *Validity* of a classification system for behavioral or emotional disorders refers to the degree to which providing a diagnosis for a child gives useful information about the child.

The DSM Classification System

The *Diagnostic and Statistical Manual of Mental Disorders* was first published by the American Psychiatric Association in 1952. Since then it has gone through several revisions. It will continue to be revised based on developing knowledge about the disorders it describes and classifies. The second edition of the DSM (DSM-II) was published in 1968. Although the first two editions of the DSM provided categories and descriptions of disorders, neither contained specific diagnostic criteria for them. Therefore they provided only minimal diagnostic guidance for clinicians and researchers (APA, 1980). The DSM-III, published in 1980, was a major revision of the previous editions and represented a significant step forward in the diagnosis of behavioral or emotional disorders. Several important features that first appeared in the DSM-III have been included in subsequent editions:

- Each disorder is defined by a specific set of diagnostic criteria. Both inclusion criteria and exclusion criteria are included. *Inclusion criteria* must be met for a disorder to be diagnosed. For example, a child must engage in at least six of nine listed behaviors associated with either inattention or impulsivity/hyperactivity to meet the diagnostic criteria for ADHD. *Exclusion criteria* prohibit a diagnosis from being made. For example, if a manic episode is brought on by medications, a diagnosis of bipolar disorder cannot be made.
- The diagnostic criteria for each disorder are *descriptive,* and no attempt is made to explain how or why the disorder develops.
- The disorders and their diagnostic criteria are *atheoretical.* The first DSM used language to describe many disorders that was based on psychoanalytic or psychodynamic theory. Language suggesting that one or another theory is best at explaining disorders was eliminated in the DSM-III.
- A multiaxial system is used, allowing several types of information about a person receiving a diagnosis to be given.

The DSM-III-R (for *revised*), published in 1987, contained changes in the diagnostic criteria for many disorders. Many of these changes were impelled by research since the publication of the DSM-III showing that some previous criteria were difficult to apply in clinical and research settings or were not as strongly associated with a disorder as previously thought. The DSM-IV was published in 1994, again with refinements and changes to the diagnostic criteria for some disorders. In 2000 the DSM-IV-TR (for *text revision*) was published. It did not contain diagnostic criteria changes but did update information about the disorders. This edition of the DSM is currently in use.

The Multiaxial System

The multiaxial system in the DSM-IV-TR (see Table 5.1) is designed to provide several types of information about a child who is experiencing a behavioral or emotional disorder. Five axes are used in this system. The disorders contained in the DSM are listed on either Axis I or Axis II, with personality disorders and mental retardation listed on Axis II and all other disorders listed on Axis I.

More than one disorder can be listed on either Axis I or Axis II. When more than one disorder is listed, they are considered **comorbid** disorders: two or more disorders that occur together. Comorbid disorders are common. For

TABLE 5.1

Multiaxial System of the DSM-IV-TR

Axis I	Clinical disorders
Axis II	Mental retardation; personality disorders
Axis III	General medical conditions
Axis IV	Psychosocial and environmental problems
Axis V	Global assessment of functioning

Source: DSM-IV-TR (APA, 2000).

example, 60–90% of children with bipolar disorder also have ADHD (Spencer et al., 2001), and 40–70% of children with ADHD also have conduct disorder or oppositional defiant disorder (Banaschewski et al., 2003). Consequently, many children receive more than one diagnosis on either Axis I or Axis II. If appropriate, either axis can be left blank. Axis II is left blank for most children because most of those with a disorder listed on Axis I do not have either mental retardation or a personality disorder.

Axis III is used for noting any medical conditions that may influence the disorders listed on Axis I or II or that may need to be considered when interventions are being planned. For example, children with a severe or chronic medical condition, such as cystic fibrosis, diabetes, or cancer, may experience a depressive or anxiety disorder related to their medical condition. Thus including the medical condition on Axis III gives useful information to those assisting the child or the child's family. Axis III is left blank if no relevant medical condition is present.

Axis IV and Axis V provide information about a child's life and functioning. Psychosocial or environmental problems that may affect the onset, course, or treatment of a disorder are listed on Axis IV. Several categories of problems are provided in the DSM-IV-TR, including problems in a child's primary support group (such as recent parental divorce), problems related to the social environment (like being the target of discrimination), educational problems (with teachers, perhaps), and economic problems (such as a parent losing a job). The specific problems a child is experiencing are written on Axis IV. A clinician's **global assessment of functioning** for a child is entered on Axis V. As shown in Table 5.2, the DSM uses a scale from 1 to 100, with 1 indicating the most problematic functioning and 100 indicating superior functioning in all areas of life. Thus Axis V gives a broad overview of the functioning of a child at a given point in time.

Limitations of the Current Multiaxial System

The current multiaxial system used in the DSM has some limitations that are particularly meaningful with children. First, there is no axis for including information about a child's family. Some of this information can be mentioned on Axis IV if the child's family is particularly problematic. However,

TABLE 5.2

Global Assessment of Functioning (GAF) Scale

Consider psychological, social, and occupational functioning on a hypothetical continuum of mental health–illness. Do not include impairment in functioning due to physical (or environmental) limitations.

Code   (Note: Use intermediate codes when appropriate, e.g., 45, 68, 72.)

100 | 91	Superior functioning in a wide range of activities, life's problems never seem to get out of hand, is sought out by others because of his or her many positive qualities. No symptoms.
90 | 81	Absent or minimal symptoms (e.g., mild anxiety before an exam), good functioning in all areas, interested and involved in a wide range of activities, socially effective, generally satisfied with life, no more than everyday problems or concerns (e.g., an occasional argument with family members).
80 | 71	If symptoms are present, they are transient and expectable reactions to psychosocial stressors (e.g., difficulty concentrating after family argument); no more than slight impairment in social, occupational, or school functioning (e.g., temporarily falling behind in schoolwork).
70 | 61	Some mild symptoms (e.g., depressed mood and mild insomnia) OR some difficulty in social, occupational, or school functioning (e.g., occasional truancy, or theft within the household), but generally functioning pretty well, has some meaningful interpersonal relationships.
60 | 51	Moderate symptoms (e.g., flat affect and circumstantial speech, occasional panic attacks) OR moderate difficulty in social, occupational, or school functioning (e.g., few friends, conflicts with peers or coworkers).
50 | 41	Serious symptoms (e.g., suicidal ideation, severe obsessional rituals, frequent shoplifting) OR any serious impairment in social, occupational, or school functioning (e.g., no friends, unable to keep a job).
40 | 31	Some impairment in reality testing or communication (e.g., speech is at times illogical, obscure, or irrelevant) OR major impairment in several areas, such as work or school, family relations, judgment, thinking, or mood (e.g., depressed man avoids friends, neglects family, and is unable to work; child frequently beats up younger children, is defiant at home, and is failing at school).
30 | 21	Behavior is considerably influenced by delusions or hallucinations OR serious impairment in communication or judgment (e.g., sometimes incoherent, acts grossly inappropriately, suicidal preoccupation) OR inability to function in almost all areas (e.g., stays in bed all day; no job, home, or friends).

(continued)

TABLE 5.2

Global Assessment of Functioning (GAF) Scale (*Continued*)

20 | 11	**Some danger of hurting self or others** (e.g., suicide attempts without clear expectation of death; frequently violent; manic excitement) **OR occasionally fails to maintain minimal personal hygiene** (e.g., smears feces) **OR gross impairment in communication** (e.g., largely incoherent or mute).
10 | 1	**Persistent danger of severely hurting self or others** (e.g., recurrent violence) **OR persistent inability to maintain minimal personal hygiene OR serious suicidal act with clear expectation of death.**
0	Inadequate information.

The rating of overall psychological functioning on a scale of 0–100 was operationalized by Luborsky in the Health–Sickness Rating Scale (Luborsky L: "Clinicians' Judgments of Mental Health." *Archives of General Psychiatry* 7:407–417, 1962). Spitzer and colleagues developed a revision of the Health–Sickness Rating Scale called the Global Assessment Scale (GAS) (Endicott J, Spitzer RL, Fleiss JL, Cohen J: "The Global Assessment Scale: A Procedure for Measuring Overall Severity of Psychiatric Disturbance." *Archives of General Psychiatry* 33:766–771, 1976). A modified version of the GAS was included in DSM-III-R as the Global Assessment of Functioning (GAF) Scale.

there is little opportunity to note other family issues that may be valuable for clinicians to consider (such as a primary caregiver being a grandparent or the child's parents being in the military).

A second limitation is that there is no process for noting strengths of the child, the family, or the child's environment. With the possible exception of Axis V, information on the axes is problem-focused. This limitation may restrict others' perceptions of the child to only the problems that the child is experiencing, creating a more negative perception of the child than is appropriate. In addition, the strengths of the child or the child's environment, which should be used to advantage during therapeutic interventions, may be ignored. For example, knowing that a child with a depressive disorder has many positive peer relationships, is an excellent soccer player, or has parents who are concerned and supportive may help a clinician plan interventions that capitalize on these strengths.

Diagnostic Criteria Provided for Future Study

The DSM-IV-TR contains a section of disorders that may be included in future editions of the DSM and their proposed diagnostic criteria. These disorders cannot be diagnosed currently. However, the proposed diagnostic criteria are supplied to encourage research that may inform the editors of future DSM editions about the usefulness of including the disorders. Fifteen disorders are included in this section, as well as possible changes to some diagnostic criteria for schizophrenia and dysthymia. Some of the disorders related to children are *minor depressive disorder* (a disorder of the same length as major depression but with milder symptoms), *mixed anxiety–depressive disorder* (a disorder involving a period of at least one month with significant symptoms of depression and anxiety), and *binge-eating disorder* (recurrent episodes of binge eating without the purging behaviors that occur in bulimia nervosa).

Key Concepts

- Six versions of the DSM have appeared, the most recent in 2000 (DSM-IV-TR).
- The DSM uses a multiaxial system with five axes. All behavioral or emotional disorders are listed on Axis I, except mental retardation and the personality disorders, which are listed on Axis II. Axis III describes relevant medical conditions; Axis IV is for listing psychosocial or environmental problems; and a global assessment of a child's functioning is noted on Axis V.
- The current multiaxial system provides minimal information about a child's family and about the strengths of a child or the child's family and environment.
- Fifteen disorders and their proposed diagnostic criteria are described for possible inclusion in future DSM editions.

Clinical Assessment

Clinical assessment is the process that a psychologist or other mental health professional goes through to gather information about a child and the child's world and then determine (1) whether it is appropriate to diagnose one or more behavioral or emotional disorders and (2) what type of clinical intervention, if any, is appropriate for the child and his or her family. Information gathered during a clinical assessment should be wide-ranging and should include characteristics and experiences of the child as well as characteristics of the child's family and environment. In many ways this information relates to each of the many levels of influence on a child's development described in the introductory chapter (Bronfenbrenner, 1979):

- *Biological factors* such as any abnormalities or problems with brain structure or functioning, genes or chromosomes, hormone or neurotransmitter levels, and central or peripheral nervous systems.
- *Psychological factors* such as personality or temperament style, cognitive style, intelligence, social skills with peers and adults, and emotional or behavioral problems.
- *Family factors* such as relationships between family members, involvement of extended family members in the child's nuclear family, personal characteristics of nuclear family members and extended family members, and significant issues in the family history.
- *Social factors* such as the quality of the neighborhood in which the child lives, the quality of the school the child attends, and significant issues that may have occurred or are occurring in the child's immediate social environment.
- *Cultural factors* such as cultural values and expectations, and relationships between members of the child's culture and other cultural groups.

The information gathered about each of these issues should include the following:

- *Specific problems or dysfunctions:* For example, problems or dysfunctions could include functioning of the child's thyroid gland, a cognitive style that is prone to anxiety, poor social skills with peers, a family in which the parents have violent arguments, a school environment characterized by aggression, or living in a cultural group considered inferior by other cultural groups.
- *Specific strengths:* Examples of strengths include good physical functioning and athletic ability, an agreeable temperament, an above-average level of intelligence, the supportive and positive involvement of grandparents in the child's nuclear family, a creative and supportive after-school program that the child attends daily, and cultural values that support families and encourage parents to be actively involved in their children's lives.

After gathering a wide range of information, the psychologist tries to absorb it and then applies his or her knowledge of child development, family life, cultural influences, and other issues to create a thorough description of the child in his or her world. By mingling information about the child and the psychologist's knowledge about individual, family, and cultural issues, decisions are made about whether a child is experiencing any behavioral or emotional disorders and whether interventions for the child or the child's family are needed.

Notes from the Author: The Value of Assessment

I must admit that I developed a rather negative attitude toward clinical assessment while in graduate school. Assessments were procedures that graduate students *had* to do, and few of us were eager to interrupt our courses, research, and therapy training to do them. In addition, it seemed to me that we were always looking for problems that might exist, and therefore our assessments were occasionally more negative than they should have been. My thinking and interest in clinical assessment changed, however, during my internship at the Children's Psychiatric Hospital at the University of New Mexico Medical Center because of two instructors who taught the assessment course. One instructor performed clinical assessments as a primary part of his clinical practice. He spoke eloquently about the intellectual challenge of conducting a good clinical assessment, describing how a good clinical assessment could help create successful interventions for a child and the child's family. The second instructor noted that the assessments done for children at the psychiatric hospital were of greatest value if they uncovered the strengths of the child and the child's family that could ground therapeutic interventions. She pointed out that all of the children had significant problems—they were, after all, patients in a psychiatric hospital. She also noted that most of them had been evaluated by psychiatrists or psychologists several times before being admitted to the hospital, so their problems were usually well known. My internship experiences showed me that clinical assessments are intellectually challenging for the psychologist performing them, can help the child being assessed, and should be an important source of information about strengths of the child and his or her family.

Information gathered during a clinical assessment can come from many people and through several different procedures. Gathering information from multiple people with varied procedures is essential for a good assessment because, as we discuss in this section and in many subsequent chapters, strengths and limitations are associated with the information from each of these sources. By gathering information from many people in numerous ways, the limitations of each source can be counterbalanced by the strengths of others. Because the quality and usefulness of the information gathered from different people vary depending on the problems a child is experiencing, these factors are discussed in the subsequent chapters about the various disorders. In this chapter we focus on the strengths and limitations of the different procedures that can be used during a clinical assessment.

Clinical Interviews

Clinical interviews are the most widely used method for gathering information about a child and family during an assessment (Sattler, 1998). They involve a clinician talking with a child and possibly members of the child's family about the child, the child's family, and the child's environment. Some clinicians prefer to conduct the entire clinical interview with all members of a family present. Others prefer to talk with all members of a family for part of the interview, then the child alone, and then the parents alone. Other combinations are also possible, depending on the child's and family's circumstances (for instance, talking with siblings or grandparents may be an important component of some clinical interviews).

Clinical interviews let a child and members of the child's family describe the child's life, the problems the child is experiencing, and the strengths of the child and the family. In addition, they allow the child and family members to express their concerns in their own way and in their own words. If the clinician demonstrates interest in their perspectives, this can help establish positive and respectful rapport between the child, family, and clinician.

Some clinical interviews are unstructured. Without following any particular script, the clinician uses his or her skill, experience, and knowledge of child development to ask questions that help the child or parent describe the child's problems and strengths in a way that helps the clinician understand the child's functioning and that of his or her family. The clinician may start by asking some general questions; the answers may lead to more detailed questions.

A clinician may also use a structured interview. Structured interviews contain a list of specific questions that the clinician asks. As with unstructured interviews, answers to general questions may prompt more specific questions. For example, if a child states that she has been on a diet during the past month, a series of questions may follow about her eating habits and whether she engages in any binge eating or purging.

Observing how a child engages in tasks during a clinical interview can provide important information about the child.

The structured nature of the interview helps ensure that the clinician obtains information about all relevant issues. Several structured interviews have been developed to assess symptoms of the most common childhood behavioral or emotional disorders. For example, the Diagnostic Interview Schedule for Children (Shaffer, Fisher, Lucas, Dulcan, & Schwab-Stone, 2000) and the Children's Interview for Psychiatric Syndromes (Weller, Weller, Fristad, Rooney, & Schecter, 2000) are structured interviews given to a child or parent that include specific questions about most DSM diagnoses.

Developmental History

An essential part of any clinical interview, whether structured or unstructured, is a **developmental history** of the child and family. A developmental history gives the clinician a context within which the child's past and current functioning can be understood, and it may suggest potential problems that need to be explored in more depth. Components of a developmental history include the following:

- *The mother's pregnancy and the child's birth:* Difficulties during pregnancy or birth may suggest the presence of neurological problems in the child, and the mother's behaviors during pregnancy (such as smoking or consuming alcohol or other drugs) may also suggest the possibility of some neurological problems.
- *Attaining developmental milestones:* Did the child meet physical and cognitive developmental milestones in a normal time frame? Delayed attainment of developmental milestones may suggest the possibility of neurological problems, learning disabilities, or a problematic home environment.
- *Medical history:* Has the child experienced any significant medical problems or hospitalizations?
- *Family characteristics and history:* What is the structure of the family? Has it changed in any meaningful way during the child's life (such as parental divorce)? Has the family experienced significant stressors (such as immigration or a parent losing a job)? Where is the child in the sibling order?
- *Child's educational history:* What type of schooling has the child received? Has the child been evaluated for or received special education services? How has the child related to teachers and other students? Have any significant issues occurred during the child's schooling (perhaps the death of a teacher or student)?
- *Neighborhood characteristics and history:* In what type of neighborhood does the family reside? What types of relationships do the child and family have with neighbors? Have there been significant changes in the composition of the neighborhood, or have significant problems occurred in the immediate neighborhood or in the larger community (such as the abduction of a child from a local playground)?

Behavioral Observations

An important component of every clinical interview is the impressions that the clinician forms while observing the behaviors of the child, parents, and other family members during the interview. Observations of the child's and parents' behaviors can provide clues about problems that may be particularly relevant or about the parent–child relationship. For example, a child may be more animated when talking about her day at school and more morose when talking about her evening at home; a child may look to a parent when answering questions; or a parent may interrupt the child when the child is describing his home life but let the child speak when the child is describing his school day. Interactions between a parent and child can also be observed. For example, if the clinician asks the parents to leave the room so she can talk with the child alone, what do the parents say to the child? "You be sure and behave," or "If you get nervous you can come out and find me," or "I'll see you in a few minutes when you're done."

Limitations of Clinical Interviews

There are several limitations to clinical interviews, which occur primarily in two areas: missing information and problems with interpretation. Missing information can occur for several reasons. A clinician may fail to ask about issues that are important to the child or parent, and the child or parent may not volunteer this information. In addition, young children in particular may not know that some of their behaviors, emotions, or experiences are unusual or may not think they are important enough to mention (for example, a young child who thinks about suicide may assume that all children do this and therefore may not see it as an important issue to mention). Structured interviews can reduce this problem, although even structured interviews are not designed to ask about all concerns that may be relevant to a child or family. Another cause of missing information is that the child or parent may be reluctant to acknowledge certain behaviors, emotions, or experiences and thus fail to describe them when asked.

A clinician's interpretation of the information gathered during a clinical interview can lead to inaccurate assessment of a child or family. All the information that a clinician gathers during an interview is filtered through his or her perceptions, expectations, and biases. A clinician may overemphasize the importance of responses to some questions and underemphasize the importance of other responses. This may cause inaccurate understanding of the child's overall functioning. In addition, all the observations of the child's and parents' behaviors must be interpreted by the clinician. For example, a clinician must interpret what it means when a child looks to a parent before answering certain questions or when a child appears reluctant to answer certain questions. A clinician may misinterpret some behaviors, which can lead to inaccurate beliefs about the child or family. For example, if a child seems reluctant to describe a problem incident that occurred in the family, the clinician might interpret this as indicating that the child is particularly upset by the incident, when in fact the child simply has little knowledge of it. The possibility of a clinician misinterpreting information from a clinical interview increases when the clinician is from a different cultural group than the child and family: The clinician may apply his or her own cultural values when interpreting a behavior that has a different meaning in the child's or parents' culture.

Finally, problems, concerns, or symptoms might be suggested by a clinician during a clinical interview. For example, if a clinician says, "I'm sure that you were very upset when your father died; can you tell me how you coped with that whole experience?" this statement may suggest to a child that he should have been upset when his father died even if he was not. The child may alter what he says about his reaction to his father's death to comply with the clinician's suggestion that he should have been upset. Similarly, a clinician could ask, "Did you get angry when your mother spent so much time at the hospital when your sister was sick?" This may suggest to a child that she should have felt angry. The clinician's suggestion may change how the child describes her reactions to her mother's absence and possibly how she feels about her mother's absence.

Behavioral Assessment

Behavioral assessments provide specific information about the types and intensities of children's prosocial and problematic behaviors. Some behavioral assessments gather information about a wide range of behaviors; others focus on one or two specific behaviors (such as aggression or interactions with peers). Some behavioral assessments involve reports of a child's behaviors from a child, parent, teacher, or others. Other behavioral assessments involve direct observation of a child by a clinician (Francis & Chorpita, 2004).

One useful strategy for understanding a child's behavior is a **functional behavioral assessment,** which is used to identify the antecedents and consequences of specific behaviors (Beck, 2000). Identifying these antecedents and consequences can improve understanding of the influences on a behavior and, when the behavior is troublesome, lead to an effective intervention. For example, consider a second grader who is occasionally disruptive in class. A functional behavioral analysis may detect that his outbursts are usually preceded by failure on an academic task and that his teacher often sends him to stand in the hallway after an outburst (which removes him from the frustrating academic situation). The child, and his parents and teachers, may not recognize that this pattern is occurring, and thus they may not understand the influence of academic frustration on initiating an outburst or that the outbursts are being positively reinforced by removal from class. Once this pattern is understood, changes in antecedents and consequences can be initiated to reduce his outbursts. For example, he may be encouraged to stop and relax for a few seconds when frustrated with an academic task, and his teacher may provide a reward when he can handle his frustration without creating a disturbance in the classroom.

Behavior Rating Scales

Behavior rating scales provide a quantitative analysis of a child's behaviors. The Child Behavior Checklist (CBCL) (Achenbach & Edelbrock, 1981) is a commonly used behavior rating scale. It asks the person doing the rating to describe the frequency with which a child engages in a wide range of behaviors. These behaviors can then be grouped into categories, such as withdrawn behavior, somatic complaints, and aggressive behavior; and the frequency with which the child engages in each category of behaviors can be quantified and compared with norms for children of the same age. Norms for behaviors are obtained by gathering information about their frequency from large and diverse samples of children and computing the means and standard deviations of these frequencies. The ability to compare the frequency of one child's behaviors to norms for children of the same age is a particular strength of behavior rating scales.

Behavior Observations

Behavior can also be assessed through direct observation of a child (Dishion & Granic, 2004). Some **behavior observations** are informal. For example, an observer might sit in the back of a child's classroom and observe the child's behavior or may observe the child on the playground. Because of his or her

Observing a child at school can provide important information about the child's behaviors.

training, an observer may be able to identify problem behaviors and their antecedents and consequences.

Structured behavior observations can also occur, in which an observer looks for and records the frequency of one or more specific behaviors. Structured observations can take place in naturalistic settings, such as a classroom, or they can take place in a laboratory setting. For example, a child might be brought to a laboratory playroom and encouraged to play with the toys available; the observer might note how frequently the child moves from one toy to another or how many times she engages in aggression.

Structured behavior observations can occur with more than one person. For example, four children might be told that they have a half-hour to play with the toys in a laboratory playroom. The behaviors of each child, and how the children interact with each other, can be recorded. Interactions between a child and parent can also be observed (Danforth, Barkley, & Stokes, 1991; DuPaul, McGoey, Eckert, & VanBrakle, 2001). For example, a parent and child might be brought to a laboratory playroom, with the parent instructed to have the child engage in free play for 10 minutes, complete a specific task during the next 10 minutes, and then put the toys away. The behaviors of the parent and the child can then be observed—for example, what the parent does when the child is playing, how the parent moves the child from free play to the specific task, and how the child responds to the parent's instructions.

Some behavior observation procedures are designed to assess family functioning. For example, the Family Interaction Coding System was designed by Patterson and his colleagues to assess interactions between family members in their homes (Jones, Reid, & Patterson, 1975). An observer visits a home and records the interactions among all members of a family, who are instructed to stay in two rooms during the observation.

Limitations of Behavioral Assessments

Behavior rating scales require honest answers. If a child is reluctant to state how often he or she engages in certain behaviors, or if a parent or teacher is angry with a child and so exaggerates the frequency of problem behaviors, the rating scales will provide inaccurate information.

An important limitation of behavior observations is that they are expensive and time-consuming. Observers must be trained and then monitored so that they provide accurate and reliable ratings of the behaviors they observe. In naturalistic settings, an observer must then concentrate on a child (or in some cases, a small number of children) for one or two hours to gather sufficient behavioral information.

Another limitation is that behavior observations usually occur only over a short period. If a child's behavior is not typical during that time, the clinician may form an inaccurate picture of the child's behaviors. For example, if a child is coming down with a cold on the day he is observed, he may be less active in the classroom than is typical. In addition, if children or parents know they are being observed, they may avoid behaviors that they believe would be viewed as socially inappropriate, even if they engage in these behaviors frequently when not being observed. For example, during a laboratory observation, a parent may not yell at a child even if this occurs frequently at home. This can also contribute to an inaccurate assessment of their behaviors. Finally, some behaviors of concern, such as aggression or self-injurious behavior, may occur rarely and thus not be observed during an observation period.

Psychological Tests

A **psychological test** is a task or set of tasks designed to provide information about a specific aspect of a child's functioning. The administration of many tests is **standardized:** that is, the tests include specific instructions on how they should be administered, and they are administered in the same way to all children. This increases the likelihood that differences in children's scores on the test reflect differences in their functioning, rather than differences in how the test was administered.

Most psychological tests come with a set of *norms,* which are obtained by giving the test to many children and computing the mean and standard deviation of their scores. If the test is given to a large and diverse enough group of children during the process of creating norms, norms can be established by age, sex, cultural group, or other characteristics. For example, many psychological tests provide separate norms for boys and girls at each age. The value of norms is that the score of an individual child can be compared with the scores obtained from many children with similar characteristics, which can provide important information about the child's functioning. For example, if a girl's score on a test of anxiety shows that she is two standard deviations above the mean for girls her age, the results of the test suggest that she is more anxious than about 98% of other girls her age. The ability of a clinician or researcher to compare an individual child's test results to a set of norms is a particular strength of many psychological tests.

Psychological tests are often divided into three categories: objective tests, projective tests, and neuropsychological tests.

Objective Tests

Objective tests provide specific questions that a child answers; the answers are assigned numerical values that can be summed to give information about the child. For example, the Children's Depression Inventory is a 27-item scale designed to be completed by children and adolescents from ages 7 to 17 years. High scores on the test indicate that a child is experiencing many symptoms of depression. Intelligence tests are objective tests that are frequently given to children. They are described in the chapter about mental retardation.

Many objective tests are designed to be completed by a parent or other adult who knows a child well, particularly when the child being assessed is young. Parents may complete objective tests about their children's self-esteem, anxiety, depression, eating problems, or other characteristics.

Some objective tests are designed to assess family environments. For example, the Family Environment Scale (Moos, 1974) contains a series of questions about the family; it is completed by each member of the family separately. Scores from the Family Environment Scale can be used to evaluate family characteristics such as cohesion, conflict, and organization and to note whether family members have similar or different perceptions of these characteristics.

Projective Tests

During **projective tests** a child is given an ambiguous stimulus and asked to describe it or tell a story about it. The best-known projective test is the Rorschach Inkblot Test. Children are shown a series of 10 inkblots and asked to describe what they see. Another well-known projective test is the Thematic Apperception Test, during which children are given a series of pictures and asked to tell a story using the picture.

The theory behind projective tests is that in the face of an ambiguous stimulus, the child must project part of himself or herself onto the stimulus, thus revealing part of his or her inner psychological life. For example, when shown an inkblot, a child must give one of nearly an infinite number of potential responses. Why does the child choose a particular response? When given a picture of a girl sitting on a woman's lap, why do some children tell a story in which the child is being scolded for misbehaving and other children tell a story about a child giving good news to her mother? Theory says that the child will use something from his or her psychological self to provide the answer, allowing a glimpse of that psychological self.

Although projective tests are used frequently by clinicians, they remain controversial (Verma, 2000; Wood, Lilienfeld, Garb, & Nezworski, 2000). Some assert that projective tests provide useful information about a child that cannot be gained through objective tests, behavior observations, or interviews, and thus they are valuable components of an assessment. Others argue that the relative lack of reliability and validity of projective tests reduces their usefulness, and that the information gathered by a projective test can often be gathered in a more systematic way using procedures with higher reliability and validity.

Neuropsychological Tests

Neuropsychological tests involve asking a child to perform verbal or physical tasks that have been associated with specific deficits in brain functioning (Sattler, 1998). The connections between the tasks and brain function have usually been demonstrated by studies showing that people with known injuries to particular areas of their brains have problems completing the tasks. For example, studies of people with injuries to their brains in areas associated with fine motor control show that they have difficulty putting small metal pegs into rows of holes quickly. Consequently, a task such as this can be given to a child; if he or she performs the task much more slowly than most children, it can be hypothesized that he or she may be experiencing some difficulties of brain functioning in the area associated with fine motor control. Several neuropsychological tests are described in the chapter about ADHD.

Limitations of Psychological Tests

The primary limitation of objective tests is that a child, parent, or other person can purposely give inaccurate answers. For example, a child who wants to appear less depressed than she is can give answers on a test of depressive symptoms that minimize her depressive symptoms. Similarly, a parent or teacher who wants to emphasize a child's depressive symptoms can give answers that accentuate those symptoms.

Significant concerns about the reliability and validity of projective tests exist. Most projective tests do not provide norms, primarily because so many responses to each ambiguous stimulus are possible. A clinician must often interpret the responses given during a projective test (such as the meaning of a story that a child tells while taking the Thematic Apperception Test). If the interpretation is inaccurate, an incorrect assessment of a child's feelings or thoughts may occur.

Neuroimaging

Significant advances in our ability to observe and measure the brain, and to assess the functioning of various areas in the brain, have occurred during the past few decades. Although these techniques are seldom used in clinical practice because of their expense, they are used with greater frequency in clinical research to assess the role of brain functioning in various behavioral or emotional disorders (Daniel, Zigun, & Weinberger, 1994).

Computerized tomographic scanning (CT scanning) and **magnetic resonance imaging** (MRI) are two procedures for static brain imaging. Both provide images of specific brain structures that can be used to assess the size of those structures. CT scans use X-rays; MRI images are produced by radio signals passed through a strong magnet field. MRI images usually produce a finer-grained analysis of brain structures than do CT scans.

Recent advances in neuroimaging now allow dynamic brain imaging, which shows the brain as it functions. **Positron emission tomography** (PET) scans assess glucose metabolism in various parts of the brain during a specific task, thus identifying which brain areas are functioning during that task. **Functional magnetic resonance imaging** (fMRI) techniques assess blood flow in various parts of the brain during a task, which also provides information about the brain areas being used during that task. Both procedures can identify differences in brain functioning in children with certain disorders. For example, fMRI studies have shown that individuals with autism process visual perceptions of faces in the part of the brain that those without autism use to process visual perceptions of objects (Dawson et al., 2002; Schultz et al., 2000).

Limitations of Neuroimaging

Although neuroimaging can reveal differences in brain structure or functioning, it cannot assess why those differences are occurring or why they may be associated with the development of behavioral or emotional disorders. In addition, because of their expense and the equipment involved, they are available to only a few researchers and are seldom involved in clinical practice.

Key Concepts

- The information gathered during a clinical assessment is far-ranging, including the functioning of the child, the child's family, and the child's environment.
- Information about a child's strengths and problems, as well as the strengths and problems of the child's environment, should be gathered during a clinical assessment.
- A clinical interview is an important component of most clinical assessments. Clinical interviews can be structured or unstructured. Clinical interviews let a child and parent describe their lives in their own words. Limitations involve missing information and possibly inaccurate clinician interpretation.
- A developmental history is an essential component of a clinical interview.
- Behavioral assessments can involve behavior rating scales completed by a child or a parent, teacher, or other adult who knows the child well. Direct observations of a child or a child's interactions with others can also be part of a behavioral assessment.

- A functional behavioral assessment is used to determine the antecedents and consequences of a child's problem behaviors.
- Inaccurate or incomplete information from a behavior rating scale and behavior that is not typical during a behavior observation can limit the information gathered through behavioral assessments.
- Psychological tests are administered the same way to all children and provide information about a specific aspect of a child's functioning.
- Objective tests, projective tests, and neuropsychological tests are types of psychological tests.
- Neuroimaging techniques can provide static brain images (CT scans, MRI) or assess brain functioning (PET, fMRI).

CHAPTER GLOSSARY

Behavioral assessments provide specific information about the types and intensities of children's prosocial and problematic behaviors.

Behavior observations involve a trained observer recording a child's general behavior or the frequency of specific behaviors. A child may be observed alone, with other children, with a parent, or with others.

Behavior rating scales provide a quantitative analysis of a child's behaviors that can be compared with norms for children of that age, sex, or other characteristic.

The **categorical approach** to classification of behavioral or emotional disorders is usually a dichotomous approach in which a disorder is classified as present or not present.

A **classification system** is used to divide a group into categories.

A **clinical assessment** involves gathering information about a child and the child's world and then determining whether a diagnosis is appropriate and what type of clinical intervention, if any, is appropriate.

A **clinical interview** usually involves a discussion between a clinician and a child and/or the child's parents. Structured clinical interviews ask a specific set of questions of a child or parent.

Comorbid disorders are two or more disorders that occur together.

Computerized tomographic (CT) **scanning** can provide static pictures of brain structure.

Concurrent validity, when used with a classification system for behavioral or emotional disorders, refers to usefulness for providing a diagnosis to a child in the present time.

A **developmental history** provides information about the physical and psychological development of a child and the family and environment in which a child has lived.

The *Diagnostic and Statistical Manual of Mental Disorders* (DSM) is published by the American Psychiatric Association and is the system used most frequently in the United States to classify and diagnose behavioral or emotional disorders.

The **dimensional approach** to classification is based on a continuous dimension rather than on discrete categories.

A **disorder** is defined in the DSM as a clinically significant behavioral or psychological syndrome associated with present distress or disability, or with a significantly increased risk of death, pain, disability, or an important loss of freedom.

A **functional behavioral assessment** is used to identify the antecedents and consequences of specific behaviors.

Functional magnetic resonance imaging (fMRI) techniques assess blood flow in various parts of the brain during a task, which provides information about the brain areas used during that task.

Global assessment of functioning is noted on Axis V of the DSM multiaxial system and indicates the overall level of a child's functioning, rated from 1 to 100.

Interrater reliability refers to the degree of agreement between people classifying something.

Magnetic resonance imaging (MRI) is a static brain imaging technique used to assess brain structure.

Neuropsychological tests are verbal or physical tasks that have been associated with specific neurological deficits.

A disorder **not otherwise specified** can be diagnosed in each category of disorders in the DSM when a child meets most but not all of the diagnostic criteria for a disorder in that category.

Objective psychological tests provide specific questions that a child or parent answers, with numerical values assigned to each answer that can be summed to provide information about the child by comparing them with norms for children of the same age, sex, or other characteristic.

Positron emission tomography (PET) scans provide an image of brain functioning during specific tasks by assessing glucose metabolism.

Predictive validity, when used with a classification system for behavioral or emotional disorders, refers to the extent to which a diagnosis helps predict how a child might be in the future.

Projective psychological tests involve giving a child an ambiguous stimulus and asking the child to describe it or tell a story about it.

Psychological tests involve one or more tasks, administered the same way to all children, that provide information about a specific aspect of a child's functioning.

A **standardized** psychological test is a test designed to be administered in the same way each time it is given.

A **syndrome** is a set of symptoms that frequently occur together and follow a similar course.

When used to describe a classification system, **validity** refers to the usefulness of the system.

Conduct Disorder and Oppositional Defiant Disorder

Some children appear to enjoy acting in a defiant way.

In this chapter we focus on two disorders that are characterized primarily by behaviors that disrupt the lives of children and those around them: *conduct disorder,* which involves a persistent pattern of behaviors that violate the rights of others, and *oppositional defiant disorder,* which involves a persistent pattern of hostile and defiant behaviors. Of all the forms of child psychopathology, disruptive behavior disorders create the most concern in our society. Although many disorders significantly influence the lives of children and their families, children with most disorders go unnoticed by many people in their communities. The struggles of most children who are depressed or anxious, for example, are not known by those outside their immediate families. However, many children[1] with disruptive behavior disorders are highly visible in their communities because their behaviors directly affect community institutions and other individuals (Hill, 2002). The costs of disruptive behavior disorders to society can be high. Monetary costs include incarcerating delinquent children, repairing vandalism, and replacing items stolen from stores. Social costs include diminished educational environments in classrooms, increased fear and anxiety in neighborhoods, and the loss of the positive contributions to society that could be made by delinquent children (Frick & Ellis, 1999).

Of particular concern to society are the relatively few children whose disruptive behaviors occur in many settings and persist throughout their lives: "biting and hitting at age 4, shoplifting and truancy at age 10, selling drugs and stealing cars at age 16, robbery and rape at age 22,

---

[1]It is worth a reminder at this point that throughout this text I use the term *children* to include those in childhood and adolescence (this saves me from repeating "children and adolescents" each time I refer to this group). When I need to refer to specific age groups, such as preschool children, school-age children, or adolescents, I do so.

and fraud and child abuse at age 30 . . . (they) lie at home, steal from shops, cheat at school, fight in bars, and embezzle at work" (Moffitt, 1993). The behaviors of these children are particularly difficult to change, and many adults working with them in schools or communities may give up trying to change their behaviors and simply wait for them to be arrested and jailed.

Delinquent and disruptive behaviors have been studied for generations by those in many disciplines, including psychology, sociology, anthropology, medicine, education, and law. Despite all this study, we are still perplexed by the number of children with significant disruptive behaviors, and we have yet to understand clearly the development of disruptive behaviors in these children's lives (Caspi & Moffitt, 1995). However, we continue to make progress toward understanding the complex web of influences on the development of disruptive behaviors. This progress has been enhanced by our increasing understanding that children with disruptive behaviors do not form one homogeneous group. Rather, they can be divided into several groups based on the age at which they start their disruptive behaviors, the types of their behaviors, and the motivations for their behaviors (Hill, 2002). It has become clearer that children in each group follow different developmental pathways and that, consequently, different interventions may be needed to reduce their troubling behaviors. Studying each group of children separately may help us understand the development of their disruptive behavior more clearly, which may enhance our ability to intervene effectively with all children who have a disruptive behavior disorder.

We have made far less progress in understanding girls with disruptive behavior disorders than we have in understanding boys with disruptive behavior disorders (Keenan, Loeber, & Green, 1999; Silverthorn & Frick, 1999). For many years it was thought that only a few girls had significant disruptive behaviors, so they were seldom the focus of research. However, over the past decade or so we have learned that the number of girls with disruptive behaviors has been underestimated (Maccoby, 2004). Fortunately the growing research interest in the development of disruptive behaviors in girls has begun to increase our knowledge about them and their experiences.

Chapter Plan

After two vignettes, we look briefly at the history of concerns about children with disruptive behaviors. Next we explore the diagnostic criteria for conduct disorder and oppositional defiant disorder and several controversial issues about these criteria, and we discuss the characteristics and experiences of children who have been diagnosed with the disorders. Because there is some controversy about how to divide the heterogeneous group of children with disruptive behaviors into more homogeneous groups for research and intervention, we will address this issue before examining what is known about the prevalence of conduct disorder and oppositional defiant disorder. We then explore the developmental course of three groups of children with disruptive behavior disorders: those with an early onset of disruptive behaviors that continue through their lives, those with an early onset of disruptive behaviors that end during late childhood or adolescence, and those with an adolescent onset of disruptive behavior. We also discuss the etiology of disruptive behavior disorders for the children in these three groups. Finally we examine three types of interventions: prevention programs to stop the initial development of disruptive behaviors, early intervention programs to stop young children with signs of disruptive behaviors from developing chronic and severe problems, and therapeutic interventions for children and adolescents who have disruptive behavior disorders and their families.

Case Study: Early-Onset Conduct Problems

Darren was the youngest of six siblings born into a family that owned a dairy farm. His father worked long hours along with a hired hand, tending and milking their moderately sized herd and maintaining their 25 acres of alfalfa. His mother handled the farm's business accounting and correspondence from an office in their home. All the children worked a few hours a day on the farm, but during the school year they had little time to help because the 45-minute bus ride to school and from school, as well as the school day, kept them away from home most of the day.

Darren's mother had several complications during her pregnancy with Darren, and he was born about one month prematurely. She described her pregnancy as difficult, in part because of the high level of activity Darren had in the womb—much more than her other children. Darren was a fussy and energetic infant, and he continued to wake through the night and cry long past the age at which his siblings had done this. After he began to crawl and then toddle around the house, someone had to watch him frequently because he would get into places where he should not and break things. Darren's mother often assigned one of his older siblings to watch him, but they found this bothersome, partly because of Darren's activity level and partly because it took them from other activities. Darren's mother worried that his siblings were having too many negative interactions with Darren; however, she was often unable to watch him because of her work.

When Darren was 3, the wholesale price of milk dropped sharply. The hired hand had to be let go, and Darren's mother began working with her husband on the farm in addition to maintaining the business. She had much less time with her children and made Darren's siblings watch him for most of the day. Darren's activity level was still very high, which frustrated his siblings. They alternated between punishing him by hitting him and just letting him do what he wanted when he misbehaved. All of this was unknown to Darren's parents, who knew that Darren was a handful but not about all the trouble his siblings were having controlling his behavior.

When Darren started school, his teachers reported that he was often aggressive with them and the other children in the class when he did not get his way. Darren's parents met with his teachers several times, but they had little time to attend to his educational problems because of their long farm hours. Darren's behavior at home continued to be challenging; his parents told his older siblings that they would just have to figure out a way to handle him. They found this increasingly difficult and would resort to hitting Darren when he misbehaved or locking him in his room.

Darren's interactions with his teachers and the other students in his class continued to be problematic. The other children did not like his aggressiveness and often refused to let him play with them. Darren usually responded by trying to force his way into the other children's activities. This made them more angry, and he gradually had fewer and fewer interactions with them. By the end of the first grade, Darren mostly played by himself, but would occasionally play with older children who were also aggressive. He got into several fights with the older children, but he seemed to enjoy the fights, even when he was bruised or cut. His parents were unsure how to handle these situations, and they told Darren he could not play with the older children; but he continued to anyway.

By the time he was in the fifth grade, Darren was behind the other students in his class academically and was known by them and by his teachers as a bully and a problem. He was often out of his seat during class and seemed unable to attend to his class work more than a few minutes at a time. He often initiated fights when he thought the other children were treating him poorly, and he was suspended from school twice. His parents tried to take a more active role with Darren at home and at school, but they seemed unable to change his aggressive behaviors.

As he entered middle school, Darren was known as one of the more troubled children in his grade. He argued with teachers and peers and exasperated his parents and siblings. He and several other students began vandalizing their school, although they were careful enough not to get caught. He had little contact with other students, preferring to spend most of his time with three other boys who were also aggressive and doing poorly in school. There seemed to be little that anyone at school or at home could do to change Darren's problem behaviors.

Some Issues Worth Noting

- The symptoms of ADHD that appeared early in Darren's life.
- The fact that ineffective parenting is not always done by parents—in Darren's life it was often done by his siblings.
- The influence that the modeling of aggression by those in parenting roles can have on the development of aggression in children.
- The role that issues related to family finances, which are often out of the control of parents, can have on family stress, roles of parents and siblings in families, and the behaviors of all family members.

Case Study: Adolescent-Onset Conduct Problems

Joleen's mother, Lauren, became pregnant with her when she was 16. Although Lauren's mother encouraged her to have an abortion, Lauren was determined to continue with her pregnancy because two of her friends were also pregnant and planned to give birth. After Joleen was born, Lauren and Joleen continued to live at home with Lauren's mother, and Lauren continued to attend high school, although her attendance became more sporadic. It was unclear who Joleen's father was; and whoever he was, he had no involvement with Joleen after she was born.

Lauren and her mother lived in a low-income housing complex in a major city. When Joleen was born, Lauren's mother was working full-time as a clerk in a local grocery store. She reduced her hours so she could help raise Joleen because Lauren and her mother were both determined to give Joleen a good upbringing. Lauren worked 10 hours a week in the same store as her mother to help maintain the family income, although, with the reduction in her mother's hours, their already precarious family income became even more problematic. However, by scrimping wherever they could, and with loans from relatives when they were needed, they paid their bills each month. Between Lauren and her mother, they provided care to Joleen for most of the day, although one of Lauren's aunts watched Joleen several hours each day when Lauren's mother was at work and Lauren was at school.

Joleen was described by her grandmother as a beautiful but difficult infant. She cried often and was hard to calm when upset. She could be calmed if Lauren or her mother held Joleen and rocked her gently, although this often took quite a while. Once Joleen learned to crawl, she moved around their apartment constantly. Keeping her in her playpen was difficult, and once Joleen started to walk, it was even more difficult to keep her safe because Joleen was seemingly in constant motion. Lauren and her mother were always patient with Joleen. However, keeping track of her was exhausting; both Lauren and her mother were often tired at work or at school.

When Joleen was 3, her mother had just managed to graduate from high school. Her grandmother returned to work full-time, and Lauren found a job for 20 hours each week. They enrolled Joleen in an Early Head Start program, and either Lauren or her mother tried to attend with Joleen most days. In the Head Start program, Joleen was very active. She occasionally got into short fights with the other children and sometimes got angry when frustrated and threw toys in the playroom. Her teachers, mother, and grandmother worked hard to get Joleen to express her anger and frustration verbally rather than physically, and Joleen's fighting gradually decreased although it never stopped entirely. When she entered kindergarten, the same pattern of angry and frustrated behaviors reemerged, which her teacher found troubling. However, again with focused work by Lauren and her mother, Joleen was able to control her anger and frustration.

Joleen had a generally positive experience during grade school. Although she got in trouble occasionally for fighting and other aggressive behavior, she was liked by most of her peers and teachers. Her grandmother insisted that Joleen spend more and more time in their apartment as she got older because of the violence and illegal activities that plagued their neighborhood. Lauren and her mother tried to create an "island of calm" for Joleen in their apartment. However, they continued to worry about Joleen being exposed to the drug use and violence that they often observed in their neighborhood.

When Joleen entered high school, her mother and grandmother became increasingly concerned that she was associating with "hoodlums" (as her grandmother called them). Joleen seemed particularly attracted to boys who were in gangs. Despite increasing restrictions from her mother and grandmother, Joleen spent more time with friends who were involved in illegal activities. This caused great concern and heartbreak for her mother and grandmother. They alternated between pleading with her to associate with other friends, restricting her behavior, and trying to get her involved in activities through their church and neighborhood youth center. However, Joleen seemed to drift gradually to peers who were in trouble with the police, finding that their lifestyle was much more exciting than that of those whom she met at church or at the neighborhood center.

When she was 15, Joleen was arrested twice for shoplifting. In both cases she and three other girls had worked together to shoplift from a department store in a nearby suburb. The arrests horrified Joleen's mother and grandmother; but they seemed increasingly unable to enforce rules with Joleen, who became increasingly bold in telling her mother and grandmother that they could no longer control her life. When she was still 15, Joleen and several other girls got in a fight with girls from another neighborhood, and Joleen was stabbed in the arm. While she was in the hospital being treated for her wound, a general exam revealed that Joleen was pregnant. Although her mother and grandmother pleaded with her to consider an abortion, Joleen said that she planned to carry through with her pregnancy so she could have a baby just as her mother had 15 years earlier.

Some Issues Worth Noting

- The similarities in the difficulties that rural and urban parents face when their financial situation becomes precarious.
- The role that good parenting played in helping Joleen overcome her early emotional and behavioral problems.
- The weakening of parental influence as Joleen became older and the consequent change in Joleen's behaviors.
- The heartbreak that many parents in problematic neighborhoods experience as they see their children or grandchildren become more involved in delinquent or dangerous behaviors, despite years of efforts to parent their children well.

History

Society has been concerned about delinquent behavior in children and adolescents for centuries. For example, there are reports from the Middle Ages of groups of French adolescents committing crimes and fighting with rival groups, and of English adolescents who formed gangs such as the Mims, Hectors, and Dead Boys (Fagan, 1996). Significant concern was raised about adolescent gangs in New York and other large cities in the 1700s and 1800s as organized gangs such as the Bowery Boys, Roach Guards, and Plug-Uglies began to multiply. Psychologists have focused on delinquency and conduct problems in children and adolescents for years. For example, in an early text on adolescent development, the American psychologist G. Stanley Hall wrote that "the proportion of juvenile delinquents seems to be everywhere increasing and crime is more and more precocious" (Hall, 1904, p. 325).

Early work distinguishing different types of delinquent children was done in the 1940s, when Hewitt and Jenkins (cited in Hinshaw & Lee, 2003) used statistical techniques to show that delinquent children could be divided into two groups—those who were undersocialized and those who were socialized. **Undersocialized** children primarily engaged in aggressive behaviors carried out alone, whereas **socialized** children primarily engaged in nonaggressive group behaviors such as vandalism or theft. As we will see throughout this chapter, this distinction has been shown over the years to provide a useful way of grouping children engaged in disruptive behaviors.

Diagnostic Criteria in the DSM

The changing diagnostic criteria for the disruptive behavior disorders over the editions of the DSM provide an interesting example of how research informs conceptualizations of childhood disorders. Specific diagnostic criteria for conduct disorder first appeared in the DSM-III (APA, 1980). Four specific diagnoses were included, based on two dimensions of behavior. The first dimension came from the work of Hewitt and Jenkins: undersocialized and socialized. The second dimension focused on whether the conduct problems involved aggression or were primarily nonaggressive. This resulted in four diagnostic groups: undersocialized aggressive, undersocialized nonaggressive, socialized aggressive, and socialized nonaggressive. The undersocialized groups were characterized by children who had few social bonds, felt little empathy for others, and were likely to inform on peers if it was to their advantage. The socialized groups typically included children who engaged in conduct-disordered behaviors in groups (Frick & Ellis, 1999).

The DSM-III also introduced *oppositional disorder* for children who showed a pattern of oppositional and negative behaviors that had a compulsive nature to them. This disorder was created to identify young children who were at an early stage of developing conduct problems (Hinshaw & Lee, 2003).

Several changes to conduct disorder appeared in the DSM-III-R (APA, 1987), primarily because researchers had difficulty reliably distinguishing the undersocialized from the socialized groups. The diagnostic criteria were changed to include three subgroups: *group type,* in which most conduct problems occurred as part of a group; *solitary–aggressive type,* characterized by aggression primarily carried out alone; and *undifferentiated type,* including those who met the criteria for conduct disorder but did not fall into either of the other types. In addition, the criteria for the diagnosis were made more stringent, requiring more conduct-disordered behaviors and requiring that they occur for at least six months. This resulted in fewer children meeting the diagnostic criteria for conduct disorder (Lahey, Loeber, Stouthamer Loeber, & Christ, 1990).

The DSM-III-R also changed the name of oppositional disorder to *oppositional defiant disorder,* increased the number of behaviors that must be present for the diagnosis to be made, and required that they occur for at least six months. As with conduct disorder, the revised criteria for oppositional defiant disorder in the DSM-III-R reduced the number of children receiving the diagnosis (Lahey et al., 1990).

The ways of classifying children with conduct disorder changed dramatically in the DSM-IV. Rather than distinguishing subgroups by whether their conduct problems occurred in a group, subgroups were based on the age at which significant conduct problems began. This change was based on research showing that the age of onset of conduct problems was a better predictor of their severity and longevity than whether they occurred in groups (Laird, Jordan, Dodge, Pettit, & Bates, 2001). The diagnostic criteria for oppositional defiant disorder in DSM-IV remained similar to those in the DSM-III-R.

Key Concepts

- Concern has been raised for centuries about delinquent behavior among children and adolescents.
- The DSM-III included four forms of conduct disorder based on whether a child was socialized or undersocialized and whether the child's behaviors were primarily aggressive or nonaggressive. Oppositional disorder was also included and was seen as a precursor to conduct disorder.
- The DSM-III-R included three conduct disorder diagnoses, based on whether the conduct-disordered behaviors were carried out in a group or alone, and included more stringent diagnostic criteria.
- The DSM-IV included two conduct-disordered diagnoses, based on the age at which significant conduct problems first appeared.

Diagnosis and Assessment

Diagnostic Criteria
Conduct Disorder

As shown in Table 6.1, the diagnostic criteria for conduct disorder require a pattern of behavior that is persistent and repetitive. Consequently, children who occasionally steal, lie, or get into fights do not qualify for a diagnosis of conduct disorder. As can also be seen, some behaviors—such as bullying, fighting, or lying—must occur "often" to be considered a symptom of conduct disorder, presumably because many children engage in these behaviors occasionally. Other behaviors, such as physical cruelty, forcing someone to engage in sex, or breaking into someone's house, can be considered a symptom of conduct disorder if they occur even once because few children engage in these behaviors, and they represent a significant violation of others' rights.

As noted earlier, there are two types of conduct disorder: **childhood onset** when significant symptoms are present before age 10 and **adolescent onset** when significant symptoms are not present until after age 10. In addition, the severity of a child's conduct problems is specified, depending on the number of problem behaviors and the frequency with which they occur. However, distinctions based on severity are seldom seen in clinical or research literature, and their usefulness is unclear (Loeber, Burke, Lahey, Winters, & Zera, 2000).

As with other disorders, a child's conduct-disordered behaviors must create clinically significant impairments in his or her life for a diagnosis of conduct disorder to be made. Some children with conduct problems do not believe their behaviors are impairing their lives, and they may revel in their

TABLE 6.1

Diagnostic Criteria for Conduct Disorder

A. A repetitive and persistent pattern of behavior in which the basic rights of others or major age-appropriate societal norms or rules are violated, as manifested by the presence of three (or more) of the following criteria in the past 12 months, with at least one criterion present in the past 6 months:

Aggression to people and animals

(1) Often bullies, threatens, or intimidates others.

(2) Often initiates physical fights.

(3) Has used a weapon that can cause serious physical harm to others (e.g., a bat, brick, broken bottle, knife, gun).

(4) Has been physically cruel to people.

(5) Has been physically cruel to animals.

(6) Has stolen while confronting a victim (e.g., mugging, purse snatching, extortion, armed robbery).

(7) Has forced someone into sexual activity.

Destruction of property

(8) Has deliberately engaged in fire setting with the intention of causing serious damage.

(9) Has deliberately destroyed others' property (other than by fire setting).

Deceitfulness or theft

(10) Has broken into someone else's house, building, or car.

(11) Often lies to obtain goods or favors or to avoid obligations (i.e., "cons" others).

(12) Has stolen items of nontrivial value without confronting a victim (e.g., shoplifting, but without breaking and entering; forgery).

Serious violations of rules

(13) Often stays out at night despite parental prohibitions, beginning before age 13 years.

(14) Has run away from home overnight at least twice while living in parental or parental surrogate home (or once without returning for a lengthy period).

(15) Is often truant from school, beginning before age 13 years.

B.   The disturbance in behavior causes clinically significant impairment in social, academic, or occupational functioning.

C.   If the individual is age 18 years or older, criteria are not met for Antisocial Personality Disorder.

Code based on age at onset:

312.81 Conduct Disorder, Childhood-Onset Type: onset of at least one criterion characteristic of Conduct Disorder prior to age 10 years

312.82 Conduct Disorder, Adolescent-Onset Type: absence of any criteria characteristic of Conduct Disorder prior to age 10 years

312.89 Conduct Disorder, Unspecified Onset: age at onset is not known

Specify severity:

Mild: few if any conduct problems in excess of those required to make the diagnosis **and** conduct problems cause only minor harm to others

Moderate: number of conduct problems and effect on others intermediate between "mild" and "severe"

Severe: many conduct problems in excess of those required to make the diagnosis **or** conduct problems cause considerable harm to others problematic behavior (which distinguishes them from most children with other disorders, such as anxiety or depressive disorders, who are aware of the impairments caused by their disorders and wish they would end). However, if a child's behaviors have a significant negative influence on his or her educational achievement, ability to avoid incarceration, or relationships with others, or if they increase a child's chance for physical injury, they are considered to have a clinically significant influence on his or her life, even if not recognized as such by the child.

To address the issue of behaviors that develop in some children because of the circumstances in which they live, the DSM-IV-TR includes the following statement, indicating that conduct-disordered behaviors should not be considered symptoms of conduct disorder in every case. The statement does not condone the behaviors or suggest that they should not be changed, but it does indicate that conduct problems are symptoms of conduct disorder in some cases but an understandable response to life circumstances in others:

> Concerns have been raised that the Conduct Disorder diagnosis may at times be misapplied to individuals in settings where patterns of undesirable behavior are sometimes viewed as protective (e.g., threatening, impoverished, high-crime). Consistent with the DSM-IV definition of mental disorder, the Conduct Disorder diagnosis should be applied only when the behavior in question is symptomatic of an underlying dysfunction within the individual and not simply a reaction to the immediate social context. Moreover, immigrant youth from war-ravaged countries who have a history of aggressive behaviors that may have been necessary for their survival in that context would not necessarily warrant a diagnosis of Conduct Disorder. It may be helpful for the clinician to consider the social and economic context in which the undesirable behaviors have occurred. (APA, 2000, pp. 96–97)

Oppositional Defiant Disorder

As shown in Table 6.2, oppositional defiant disorder is characterized by a pattern of disobedient, hostile, uncooperative behaviors that create a clinically significant impairment in a child's life. Each behavior must occur often to be a symptom of oppositional defiant disorder; periodic problems with disobedience or hostility are not considered symptoms of oppositional defiant disorder.

As with all the disorders discussed in this text, a child's behaviors must be considered within the context of the typical behaviors for a child that age (APA, 2000). For example, defiant behaviors are more common in preschool children than school-age children, so a higher frequency or intensity of defiant behaviors would be necessary for a preschool child to be diagnosed with oppositional defiant disorder (Coie & Dodge, 1998). Other characteristics of the child must also be considered when deciding whether a diagnosis of oppositional defiant disorder is appropriate. For example, a 14-year-old child who is diagnosed with mental retardation and who has a mental age of 6 would not be given a diagnosis of oppositional defiant disorder if her oppositional behaviors were similar to those of 6-year-olds.

TABLE 6.2

Diagnostic Criteria for 313.81 Oppositional Defiant Disorder

A. A pattern of negativistic, hostile, and defiant behavior lasting at least six months, during which four (or more) of the following are present:

(1) Often loses temper.

(2) Often argues with adults.

(3) Often actively defies or refuses to comply with adults' requests or rules.

(4) Often deliberately annoys people.

(5) Often blames others for his or her mistakes or misbehavior.

(6) Is often touchy or easily annoyed by others.

(7) Is often angry and resentful.

(8) Is often spiteful or vindictive.

Note: Consider a criterion met only if the behavior occurs more frequently than is typically observed in individuals of comparable age and developmental level.

B. The disturbance in behavior causes clinically significant impairment in social, academic, or occupational functioning.

C. The behaviors do not occur exclusively during the course of a Psychotic or Mood Disorder.

D. Criteria are not met for Conduct Disorder, and, if the individual is age 18 years or older, criteria are not met for Antisocial Personality Disorder.

Disruptive Behavior Disorder Not Otherwise Specified

Finally, the diagnosis of *disruptive behavior disorder not otherwise specified* can be given if a child exhibits clinically significant disruptive behaviors that do not meet the criteria for either oppositional defiant disorder or conduct disorder. For example, a child might engage in two of the behaviors that are symptoms of conduct disorder and two that are symptoms of oppositional defiant disorder frequently enough that they create a significant impairment in his life. There is a general lack of discussion of this diagnosis in the literature, however, suggesting that it is used infrequently.

Controversial and Unresolved Issues

Is Oppositional Defiant Disorder a Viable Diagnosis?

Debate has occurred for decades about whether oppositional defiant disorder should be considered a disorder. One concern with oppositional defiant disorder is that it is unclear whether its symptoms indicate an underlying disorder because most young children and adolescents engage in oppositional or defiant behaviors (Coie & Dodge, 1998). The characteristic that distinguishes symptoms of oppositional defiant disorder from normal oppositional and defiant behaviors is their frequency, and it can be difficult to determine when the frequency of the behaviors has reached the point indicating a symptom. This determination may be even more difficult with children from a variety of cultural, neighborhood, and family backgrounds: A level of an oppositional or defiant behavior that is considered frequent in some cultures, neighborhoods, or families might not be considered frequent in others (Helms & Cook, 1999; Timimi, 2005).

A second concern with the diagnosis of oppositional defiant disorder is whether making the diagnosis accomplishes anything. The diagnosis can be helpful if it identifies children at an early stage of developing conduct problems, as it was originally intended, and if this leads to interventions that decrease conduct-disordered and oppositional behaviors (Campbell, Shaw, & Gilliom, 2000). However, the diagnosis might harm young children if it stigmatizes them and changes the behaviors of parents, teachers, and other adults toward them in a way that increases the intensity of their oppositionality or defiance. As we become better able to determine which children with oppositional or defiant behaviors are more likely to engage in increasing problems, we may be able to determine more accurately when the diagnosis of oppositional defiant disorder is useful.

Are Oppositional Defiant Disorder and Conduct Disorder Distinct?

Another controversial issue is whether oppositional defiant disorder is an early form of conduct disorder or a disorder distinct from conduct disorder (Rowe, Maughan, Pickles, Costello, & Angold, 2002). Some evidence suggests that the disorders are distinct. First, the symptoms of the two disorders are clearly different. In addition, about two-thirds of young children who meet the diagnostic criteria for oppositional defiant disorder do not develop conduct disorder (Greene & Doyle, 1999). If oppositional defiant disorder were an early form of conduct disorder, one would expect that a higher percentage of those with oppositional defiant disorder would develop conduct disorder. Finally, although conduct disorder is more prevalent in school-age boys than school-age girls, the prevalence of oppositional defiant disorder is about the same for boys and girls (Rowe et al., 2002). If oppositional defiant disorder and conduct disorder were the same disorder, one might expect a similar pattern of sex differences in their prevalence.

Other evidence suggests that oppositional defiant disorder may be an early manifestation of conduct disorder. The average age of the onset of oppositional defiant disorder is about three years earlier than the average age of the onset of conduct disorder, and most children diagnosed with conduct disorder met the diagnostic criteria for oppositional defiant disorder earlier in their lives (Hinshaw & Lee, 2003). Further, oppositional defiant disorder and conduct disorder share many individual, family, and community risk factors, suggesting that they may have a common etiology (these risk factors are discussed in the section about etiology) (Lahey, Loeber, Quay, Frick, & Grimm, 1997).

Thus the distinction between oppositional defiant disorder and conduct disorder remains confusing. Although many researchers have concluded that oppositional defiant disorder is distinct from conduct disorder (Loeber, Burke, Lahey, Winters, & Zera, 2000), it might be best to consider the issue as still needing additional research.

Are Girls Being Underdiagnosed with Conduct Disorder?

The relative prevalence of conduct problems in boys and girls changes during childhood and adolescence. Few differences exist in the amounts and types of aggression initiated by boys or girls before age 3 years; and when aggressive and nonaggressive behavioral problems are considered together, few differences between boys and girls are found before age 6 (Coie & Dodge, 1998; Keenan & Shaw, 1997). During the school-age years, however, about four times as many boys as girls are diagnosed with conduct disorder. This gap narrows considerably during adolescence to about 1.5 times as many males as females. Although male adolescents continue to show higher levels of aggression than females, about equal percentages of male and female adolescents engage in nonaggressive conduct problems such as stealing and vandalism (McGee, Feehan, Williams, & Anderson, 1992; Moffitt & Caspi, 2001; Silverthorn & Frick, 1999).

At issue is whether the changes in the prevalence rates across childhood and adolescence represent true differences in conduct problems between boys and girls during different developmental stages, or whether they reflect an underestimation of conduct problems in school-age girls (Maccoby, 2004). This is not simply an important issue for prevalence researchers: If girls with conduct problems are not being identified during their elementary school years, they may not receive preventive or therapeutic interventions and so may develop a pattern of conduct problems that is more difficult to change as they grow older.

Some research suggests that the changes in prevalence rates over time accurately reflect boys' and girls' behavior. Parents and social institutions are usually less accepting of conduct problems in school-age girls than boys and exert more pressure on girls to behave "correctly," resulting in their having fewer conduct problems (Coie & Dodge, 1998). The influence of this social pressure is supported by the observation that conduct problems decrease for girls after age 5 while staying the same or increasing for boys (Silverthorn & Frick, 1999). During adolescence, when there is less direct adult control of the behaviors of boys and girls, girls whose conduct problems had been inhibited by social pressure may begin to engage in more of them. So perhaps school-age girls do engage in fewer conduct problems than school-age boys, and this may occur because social pressures are more effective at keeping conduct problems in check for school-age girls.

However, other research suggests that the observed differences between school-age boys and girls may not accurately reflect their levels of conduct problems. One possibility is that school-age girls are better than school-age boys at concealing their conduct-disordered behaviors. In one study showing this, Pepler and Craig (1995) studied bullying by boys and girls on school playgrounds and found that (1) girls reported that they engaged in less bullying than boys, (2) playground observers reported less bullying by girls than by boys, but (3) observations of bullying made surreptitiously with wireless microphones found no differences in the amounts of bullying done by girls and boys. In addition, girls are more likely to engage in covert conduct problems such as shoplifting, while boys are more likely to engage in overt conduct problems such as aggression and vandalism. So adults may notice the conduct problems of boys more easily even if they occur with the same frequency as conduct problems of girls (Delligatti, Akin Little, & Little, 2003).

It may also be true that because the diagnostic criteria for conduct disorder and oppositional defiant disorder were developed almost entirely from studies of boys, the criteria may not be sensitive to conduct problems found more frequently among girls (Delligatti et al., 2003; Zoccolillo, Tremblay, & Vitaro, 1996). Perhaps if conduct-disordered behaviors that were more specific to girls were included in the diagnostic criteria for conduct disorder, similar numbers of boys and girls would be identified as having conduct problems.

As an example of a conduct problem that is more frequent among girls than boys and is not included in the diagnostic criteria for conduct disorder, Crick and her colleagues have written extensively about **relational aggression** among school-age and adolescent girls. Relational aggression is almost always verbal; it involves purposely excluding girls from activities, spreading gossip, and turning some girls against others (Crick, Ostrov, Appleyard, Jansen, & Casas, 2004). At issue is whether acts of relational aggression should be considered symptoms of conduct disorder. Some think they should. For example, one might consider relational aggression as a nonphysical counterpart to the conduct disorder symptom of "often bullies, threatens, or intimidates others." Similarly, it might be considered the psychological counterpart to "has been physically cruel to people." Others, however, assert that relational aggression differs from the type of physical aggression considered a symptom of conduct disorder, saying that if being "mean" to other children is a symptom of conduct disorder, then a much larger percentage of both boys and girls would qualify for a diagnosis of conduct disorder (Zahn-Waxler, 1993).

At this time, not enough evidence exists to determine whether conduct disorder is being underdiagnosed in school-age girls. Useful information about this issue could be provided by research on the development of school-age girls who would receive a diagnosis of conduct disorder if behaviors such as relational aggression were considered a symptom of conduct disorder; such research would investigate whether they follow the same developmental pathways as boys who are currently given a diagnosis of conduct disorder, such as an increase in problem frequency during early and middle adolescence and a reduction in problem frequency at the end of adolescence. We must wait for the results of future research before conclusions about the underdiagnosis of conduct disorder in girls can be made.

Some researchers argue that relational aggression could be considered a symptom of conduct disorder.

Determining that an Individual Child Has a Conduct Disorder

As with the other disorders described in this text, a clinician determines that a child meets the diagnostic criteria for conduct disorder or oppositional defiant disorder after gathering information about the child's behaviors. This process can be difficult, however, because some children keep their conduct-disordered behavior secret from parents, teachers, or others who might report their behavior. Alternatively, parents or teachers who are angry with an acting-out child may exaggerate the frequency or severity of his or her problem behaviors. Thus using multiple methods to gather information from several sources is often important when diagnosing conduct disorder or oppositional defiant disorder (Loney & Lima, 2003).

Multiple Methods

As described more fully in the chapter about assessment and diagnosis, several methods can be used to assess the level of children's disruptive behavior, and each has strengths and limitations (Loeber, Burke, Lahey, Winters, & Zera, 2000). The most common method is an unstructured interview, during which a clinician talks with a child, parent, or teacher about the child's behaviors (Loney & Lima, 2003). The lack of structure in the interview allows exploration of a wide range of issues but can result in a clinician inadvertently failing to ask about some of the child's disruptive behaviors. Structured interviews can also be used, such as the Diagnostic Interview Schedule for Children (DISC). They provide detailed lists of questions to ask a child, parent, or teacher, decreasing the likelihood that important issues will be missed. However, they can be costly in time and money to administer.

Observation of a child in school or observations of parent–child interactions in the home or clinician's office can supply useful information about the antecedents and consequences of the child's behaviors. For example, a classroom observation might show that a child becomes aggressive after being picked on by other children or after raising his hand and not being called on by the teacher. This information might not be available if a teacher is simply asked to rate the frequency of the child's behavior problems. But observations are costly, and many behaviors associated with conduct disorder occur infrequently and out of the sight of adults and thus are unlikely to be observed.

Finally, self-report measures completed by the child, parent, or teacher can afford information about the type and frequency of disruptive behaviors, allowing comparison of the child's behaviors to norms for children of the same age. Some measures, such as the Child Behavior Checklist, have separate forms for the child, parent, and teacher, permitting comparison of their reports. Unfortunately self-report measures may not identify some conduct problems if a child is unwilling to acknowledge them and parents or teachers are unaware of them. In addition, they give no information about the contexts in which the behaviors occur or about the antecedents and consequences of the behaviors.

Multiple Informants

Not only is it useful to employ different methods when gathering information about a child's disruptive behaviors; gathering information from different informants—most often the child, parents, and teacher—can be useful (Loeber, Burke, Lahey, Winters, & Zera, 2000). Multiple informants can describe the child's behaviors in several contexts, thus painting a richer picture of the child's behaviors.

Interestingly, the relative usefulness of each source of information about a child's behavior varies depending on the child's age and type of behavior being reported. Children are poor informants about their oppositional or defiant behaviors—particularly if they are younger than 10. When reports from children are compared with those of their parents or teachers, it is usually found that the children underreport oppositional and defiant behaviors and seldom report behaviors that have not been reported by parents or teachers (Loeber, Green, Lahey, & Stouthamer Loeber, 1991). Consequently, reports from a child will usually not add helpful information to that provided by teachers or parents; and if considered alone, they may underestimate the child's oppositional and defiant behaviors. Conversely, many children supply more information about their conduct-disordered behaviors than is provided by their parents and teachers. In particular, children are better informants than adults about covert problems like vandalism and theft (Loeber, Burke, Lahey, Winters, & Zera, 2000). The information in Table 6.3, taken from a large study of conduct problems among Canadian adolescents, shows not only how frequently several behaviors occurred but how much more

TABLE 6.3

Conduct Problems among Some Canadian Adolescents

DSM-III-R Disorder Symptom Item Used in Questionnaire	Percentage with a Positive Response				
	Parent		Teacher		Youth
	6–11	12–16	6–11	12–16	12–16
Conduct disorder					
(1), (12) • Steals	N/A	N/A	6.3	4.1	N/A
• Steals at home	8.5	9.2	N/A	N/A	9.2
• Steals outside the home	4.3	6.1	N/A	N/A	7.2
(2) • Runs away from home	0.7	2.4	N/A	N/A	4.8
(3) • Lying or cheating	36.5	32.7	14.8	12.8	42.6
(4) • Sets fires	1.3	1.8	0.1	0.4	5.0
(5) • Truancy, skips school	1.1	14.3	2.8	11.9	20.0
(6) • Has broken into someone else's house, building, or car	0.2	1.1	N/A	N/A	2.5
(7) • Vandalism	1.7	2.2	3.3	5.0	7.5
(8) • Cruel to animals	2.9	2.8	0.6	1.3	6.1
(9) • N/A					
(10) • Uses weapons when fighting	5.3	2.5	2.1	1.6	8.4
(11) • Physically attacks people	8.6	6.9	12.0	7.1	11.0
(13) • Cruelty, bullying, or meanness to others	33.6	31.1	27.9	19.0	53.3
Oppositional disorder					
(1) • Temper tantrums or hot temper	41.2	41.3	17.1	16.1	53.9
(2) • Argues a lot with adults	49.8	53.1	16.3	19.7	55.8
(3) • Defiant, talks back to adults (staff)	47.8	48.8	13.8	17.0	63.2
(4) • Does things that annoy others	55.9	54.0	31.8	27.6	62.1
(5) • Blames others for own mistakes	60.9	48.3	29.7	25.4	37.6
(6) • Easily annoyed by others	52.4	55.7	29.8	26.9	73.7
(7) • Angry and resentful	31.5	34.4	22.4	23.7	31.2
(8) • Gets back at people	19.6	23.2	18.9	14.9	55.4
(9) • Swearing or obscene language	21.1	38.5	11.3	16.2	69.8

frequently they occurred in the adolescents' reports than in the reports from their parents or teachers (Boyle, Offord, Racine, & Sanford, 1993).

Comparing Reports from Multiple Informants   Although reports from multiple informants can draw a full picture of a child's behavior, a clinician may have to reconcile reports from various informants showing different levels of disruptive behaviors. It appears that the most common strategy is to consider the reports containing the highest frequency of disruptive behaviors as the most accurate. For example, if a child describes few disruptive behaviors at school and a teacher describes many, most clinicians will suspect that many are occurring. Similarly, if a child describes more aggression than is reported by parents or teachers, the assumption is that the child's version is the most accurate. The belief seems to be that parents, teachers, and children have little motivation to overreport disruptive behaviors, although no empirical evidence supports this belief. This strategy is likely to maximize the number of children who are diagnosed with conduct disorder or oppositional defiant disorder, which may be a reason why so many children receive one of these diagnoses.

Considering Cultural, Neighborhood, and Family Issues
We need to weigh several issues when considering the disruptive behaviors of children, particularly their aggressive behaviors. Some cultural values may be more supportive of aggression in children, particularly boys and especially in situations where a boy is challenged verbally or physically (Morales, 1992; Timimi, 2005). Similarly, children living in violent neighborhoods or families may learn that aggression is necessary to protect themselves, family members, or friends. Consequently, it is important to understand the wide range of potential influences on aggressive and other disruptive behaviors, and to consider these influences when determining the types of interventions that may be best for a child exhibiting disruptive behaviors.

Key Concepts
- A diagnosis of conduct disorder requires a persistent pattern of behaviors that violate the rights of others.
- Two types of conduct disorder are included in the DSM-IV-TR: childhood onset (significant symptoms before age 10) and adolescent onset (significant symptoms at age 10 or later).
- Oppositional defiant disorder is characterized by a persistent pattern of disobedient, hostile, and uncooperative behaviors.
- Concern has been raised for years whether oppositional defiant disorder is a viable diagnosis.
- Whether oppositional defiant disorder is distinct from conduct disorder continues to be debated, although many now believe that it is a distinct disorder.
- Whether school-age girls are underdiagnosed with conduct disorder remains controversial.

- Determining whether an individual child meets the diagnostic criteria for conduct disorder or oppositional defiant disorder usually involves reports about the child's behaviors from several sources. These sources are of varying value, depending on the age of the child and the type of disorder.
- Considering cultural, neighborhood, and family values is essential when determining the influences on a child's aggressive or other disruptive behaviors.

Characteristics and Experiences of Children with Oppositional Defiant Disorder and Conduct Disorder

The core features of oppositional defiant disorder and conduct disorder are described well by their diagnostic criteria, so they will not be repeated in this section. However, we will explore other characteristics of children with these disorders and note how these characteristics influence, and are influenced by, the core features of the disorders.

Intelligence and Cognitive Issues
Intelligence

Children with significant conduct problems have, on average, lower IQ levels than other children (Lynam, Moffitt, & Stouthamer Loeber, 1993). There is some controversy about whether this is true for both girls and boys. Some studies have found that boys with conduct problems have deficits in IQ and that girls do not (Sonuga-Barke, Lamparelli, Stevenson, & Thompson, 1994), whereas other research has shown a pattern of lower IQ for both boys and girls (Moffitt & Caspi, 2001).

The reasons for the association between conduct problems and lower IQ remain unclear and are probably varied. Lower intelligence can increase the risk for some children developing conduct disorder. For example, children with lower intelligence may be less able to resist encouragement from siblings or peers to engage in delinquent behavior (Alvarez & Ollendick, 2003). Alternatively, some children with conduct problems may learn less in school because of their behavior problems, and their lack of learning may reduce their scores on intelligence tests.

Social Cognition

Children with conduct problems show several problems with **social cognition**— that is, the way they think about social situations. Many of them have biased ways of perceiving others' actions: They frequently interpret many behaviors of peers and adults as hostile, even those that most other children would perceive as neutral or positive (Crick & Dodge, 1994; Waldman, 1996). For example, if a child with conduct problems is bumped by a peer while standing in line, she is more likely than other children to think that this was done on purpose and that it was done to bother or challenge her. In addition, children with conduct problems are less likely than other children to change their initial belief about the hostility of another person's behavior if the other person makes some conciliatory gesture, such as smiling or saying "sorry." In part this is because children with conduct problems are less likely to notice conciliatory gestures, and in part it is because they are more likely to interpret such gestures as also being hostile (Dodge & Frame, 1982).

Many children with conduct problems engage in aggression with those who they inaccurately believe are being hostile toward them (Fontaine, Salzer Burks, & Dodge, 2002). This aggression often elicits aggression from their peers and punishment from teachers, parents, or other adults. These elicited responses then reinforce the children's perceptions about the hostile intentions of others by giving them even more examples of how others are hostile. A frequent result is increased aggression toward others.

Finally, children with conduct problems underestimate the impact of their verbal or physical aggression on others. They often appear to believe that others are not hurt or bothered by their aggression, even if there are clear indications that this is not true, such as another child crying. Further, they overestimate the rewards or benefits that they are likely to achieve by being aggressive. For example, they may believe other children look up to them when they bully another child (Alvarez & Ollendick, 2003). Both beliefs are likely to increase the likelihood that a child will act aggressively in a variety of social situations.

Personality Issues

Three personality issues have been a focus of research with children who have conduct problems: impulsivity, self-esteem, and a callous–unemotional interpersonal style.

Many children with conduct problems are more impulsive than other children. As noted elsewhere in this chapter, many children with conduct disorder are also diagnosed with ADHD, which may be the source of this impulsivity (Christian, Frick, Hill, & Tyler, 1997; Moffitt, 1993). They think less about the potential consequences of their actions before they act, which may get them in trouble more often than other children. (It may also mean that when they say, "I didn't mean to do it," they are telling the truth: They had not thought through the situation to the point where the consequences were clear to them.)

For many years it was believed that children with conduct problems had low self-esteem and that their acting out reflected this. Further, it was assumed that the self-esteem of a child with conduct disorder was lowered by being frequently chastised and punished (Loeber & Hay, 1997). However, recent research has suggested that many children with conduct problems have inappropriately high levels of self-esteem. Many have higher levels of self-esteem than other children, and their views of themselves are more positive than the views that others have of them (Baumeister, Smart, & Boden, 1996; Edens, Cavell, & Hughes, 1999). The current hypothesis about the association between high self-esteem and conduct problems is that children with inappropriately high self-esteem are more likely to consider normal treatment by others as insulting because they have such a positive view of themselves. They are then likely to respond to these perceived insults with verbal or physical aggression.

Frick and his colleagues (Christian, Frick, Hill, & Tyler, 1997; Frick & Ellis, 1999) have explored the existence of a **callous–unemotional personality trait** in children with conduct problems. Using clinical samples of boys with conduct problems, they found that about 10% had a personality style characterized by (1) low levels of guilt, sympathy for others, and need for social approval and (2) high levels of selfishness and adventure seeking. These boys were less distressed than other children by negative reactions from others or by the punishments they received. In addition, they focused primarily on the rewards or potential rewards of their behaviors and paid little attention to adverse consequences. Frick expressed particular concern about the long-term outcomes for this small group of children, arguing that their lack of guilt and distress over others' pain, and their focus on rewards and lack of focus on punishments, puts them at risk for developing an antisocial personality disorder and engaging in a wide range of delinquent and criminal behaviors throughout their lives.

Peer and Family Issues

Children with conduct problems experience problematic relationships in their families and with many of their peers. Two consistent findings about the peer relationships of children with conduct problems are (1) they are often rejected by their peers during their school-age years and (2) they associate primarily with other conduct-disordered peers during adolescence (Espelage, Holt, & Henkel, 2003; Hinshaw & Lee, 2003). Laird, Jordan, Dodge, Pettit, and Bates (2001) have suggested a model to account for both these findings:

- Early conduct problems, particularly aggression, cause rejection by other children because most children do not like being the targets of aggression or observing other children being hurt (Coie & Dodge, 1998).
- Peer rejection intensifies conduct problems because rejected children have fewer opportunities to learn prosocial behaviors (Kupersmidt, Coie, & Dodge, 1990) and are more likely to associate with other rejected children, who reinforce each other's conduct problems.
- Aggressive children therefore associate primarily with other aggressive children as they enter adolescence, when mutual reinforcement can further increase the frequency and intensity of their antisocial behavior.

Relationships between parents and children with conduct disorder or oppositional defiant disorder have been investigated less frequently than the children's peer relationships. In one recent study, Luby and colleagues (2006) observed pairs of preschool children with disruptive behavior disorders and their mothers. Compared to the interactions of preschoolers with no behavior problems and their mothers, the children with disruptive behaviors were noncompliant more often, were less enthusiastic, and avoided their mothers more.

Other Forms of Psychopathology

As also discussed in the chapter about ADHD, there is a high comorbidity between conduct disorder and ADHD, particularly with the predominantly hyperactive–impulsive type of ADHD. Estimates from various studies suggest that about 40–60% of children with conduct disorder also have ADHD (Banaschewski et al., 2003). Children with ADHD and conduct disorder have a particularly problematic development. The onset of conduct problems is earlier in children with both ADHD and conduct disorder, and children with both ADHD and conduct disorder are more likely to have chronic behavior problems than those with conduct disorder alone (Hinshaw, Lahey, & Hart, 1993). Perhaps the impulsive and hyperactive behaviors of children with ADHD and conduct disorder increase the likelihood of frequent, impulsive conduct problems, generating more problematic relationships and an earlier and more chronic course of conduct problems.

Mood disorders (depressive disorders and bipolar disorders) also occur in many children with conduct disorder (Essau, 2003). Controversy exists about whether conduct disorder usually develops before or after a depressive disorder—an issue that is important because it may suggest whether conduct disorder increases a child's risk for developing a mood disorder or whether a mood disorder increases risk for developing conduct disorder. Some studies report that conduct disorder begins two to three years before the onset of depression in most children with both disorders, suggesting that conduct disorder leads to the development of mood disorders (Biederman, Faraone, Mick, & Lelon, 1995). However, a longitudinal study found that depression developed first in about 50% of children with comorbid depression and conduct disorder, whereas about 25% developed conduct disorder before the depression (Kovacs, Paulauskas, Gatsonis, & Richards, 1988). Consequently, it appears that both patterns occur. In some children, the unpleasant social consequences of conduct disorder may cause their withdrawal and increase their risk for developing depressive symptoms. Other children may act out in response to depressive feelings, and this acting out may escalate to a conduct disorder for some. Finally, a third pattern is worth noting: The characteristics of some children and the environments in which they are raised may place them at risk for both conduct disorder and depression, with other issues influencing whether a conduct disorder or mood disorder develops first in individual children.

Key Concepts

- On average, children diagnosed with conduct disorder have lower levels of intelligence than other children.

- Differences in social cognition are often found in children with conduct disorder. They perceive more social interactions as having a hostile component; they are less likely to change their initial beliefs about the hostile intent of others; and they underestimate the impact of their aggression or other conduct problems on others.
- Children with conduct problems are more likely than other children to be impulsive and to have a more positive view of themselves than others have of them.
- A personality trait labeled *callous–unemotional* has been identified in some children with conduct problems. These children have decreased feelings of guilt and concern for others, as well as increased selfishness and adventure seeking.
- Many children with conduct problems, particularly those who are aggressive, are rejected by peers who do not have conduct problems.
- Many children diagnosed with conduct disorder have comorbid ADHD, and some of them have a comorbid depressive or anxiety disorder.

Subtypes of Children with Conduct Disorder

As noted earlier, children who meet the diagnostic criteria for conduct disorder form a heterogeneous group. If we were to examine a large sample of 14-year-olds who meet the diagnostic criteria for conduct disorder, we would find that some of them had been engaged in conduct problems for many years, whereas others would have begun just a year or two earlier; some would fight and bully other children while others would engage primarily in vandalism or shoplifting; and some of those who were aggressive would use aggression primarily to gain material goods, whereas others would focus mostly on being cruel for no material gain. As discussed in several chapters in this text, many problems can occur when we try to do research or interventions with heterogeneous groups of children. For example, if some issues influence the development of conduct-disordered behavior in one subgroup of children, it may be impossible to identify these issues when studying the whole group of children with conduct problems because their lack of influence on others may obscure their influence on the subgroup. The same is true for designing interventions. If a specific intervention is effective with one subgroup and another intervention is effective with another subgroup, they both may be ineffective with the entire group because each intervention has little effect on some children in the entire group (see Figure 6.1).

Several groups of researchers have suggested criteria for grouping children with conduct disorder: the age of onset of their symptoms, the types of behaviors they engage in, and the motivations for their behaviors. (Similar efforts to divide children with oppositional defiant disorder into subgroups have not occurred, so we will focus on conduct disorder.) Because these criteria have not been integrated into one that is used most frequently, we will explore each separately.

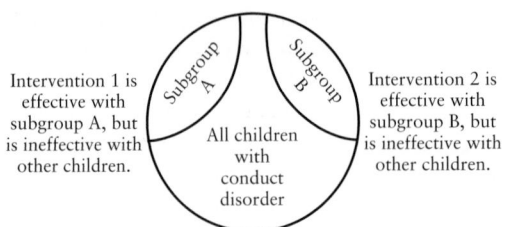

FIGURE 6.1   *Problems Assessing Therapy Outcomes in Heterogeneous Groups*

Age of Onset

The most common criterion for dividing children with conduct disorder into subgroups is the age of the onset of their conduct problems—the criterion used in the DSM-IV-TR. Moffitt (1993), for example, distinguished between children who engage in life-course-persistent and adolescent-limited antisocial behaviors. Those in the **life-course-persistent** group begin their conduct problems early in life and exhibit them throughout their lives, whereas those in the **adolescent-limited** group begin their conduct problems in adolescence and usually stop them as they enter adulthood. Patterson and his colleagues also describe the usefulness of distinguishing between early starters and late starters when describing children with conduct problems, with the *early starters* beginning noticeable behavior problems during their preschool years and the *late starters* not showing problems until their school-age years (Patterson, 1982). Similarly, Aguilar, Sroufe, Egeland and Carlson (2000) describe two pathways to antisocial behavior: the **early-onset/persistent pathway,** in which children's antisocial behavior begins early in life and persists through adolescence and into adulthood, and the **adolescent-onset pathway** in which significant problems do not begin until adolescence.

Several characteristics distinguish children in these two groups. One obvious difference is the course of the disorder, with one group having a chronic course of conduct problems beginning early in life, whereas the other group has a more time-limited course of conduct problems during late childhood or adolescence (Hill, 2002). Moffitt (1993) found several neurological differences between children with the life-course-persistent pattern and children with no conduct problems, but did not find these differences between adolescents with adolescent-limited conduct problems and adolescents with no conduct problems. This suggests that neurological characteristics distinguish those with early and late onset of conduct problems. Family characteristics also distinguish the groups. Children with early-onset conduct problems are more likely than other children to come from dysfunctional families, but adolescents with late-onset conduct problems are no more likely than other adolescents to come from dysfunctional families (Aguilar et al., 2000; Moffitt, 1993; Patterson, Forgatch, Yoerger, & Stoolmiller, 1998). Finally, there is a more pronounced genetic influence on the development of early-onset conduct problems than on conduct problems that begin later in life (Moffitt, 1993).

Patterns of Behaviors

Several ways of grouping children with conduct problems have been based on the types of conduct problems they display. For example, Loeber and his colleagues have suggested three groups: an **overt group** that engages in behaviors involving personal confrontation, a **covert group** that engages in acts against property rather than people, and a **defiant group** that has many conflicts with authority (Loeber & Stouthamer Loeber, 1998). As illustrated in Figure 6.2, many children engage in some less severe behaviors associated with each group, and some children progress to acts that are more serious.

Two groups of researchers have used statistical techniques to determine groups of conduct-disordered behaviors that commonly occur together. One project analyzed the behaviors of about 8,000 children and found that the overt–covert dimension provided the most useful division of their behaviors (Achenbach, Conners, Quay, & Verhulst, 1989). The overt group of behaviors included some symptoms of oppositional defiant disorder, such as being argumentative and defiant, and some symptoms of conduct disorder, such as bullying and fighting. Their common feature was that they all involved personal confrontation with others. The covert group included children who

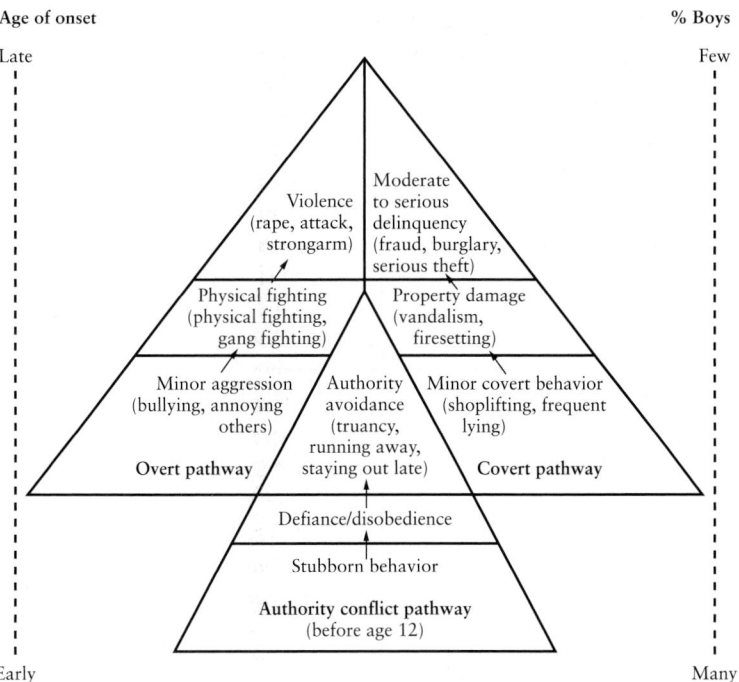

FIGURE 6.2 *Three Pathways to Boys' Problem Behavior and Delinquency*

primarily engaged in behaviors that did not involve direct confrontation with others, such as vandalism, stealing, and setting fires. The second group of researchers analyzed the results from 60 factor analyses of conduct problems that included the behaviors of more than 28,000 children (Frick et al., 1993). Similar to Achenbach and colleagues, they found a covert–overt dimension. However, they also found that a destructive–nondestructive dimension was useful in grouping the children's behaviors. Their groupings are shown in Table 6.4.

Several characteristics distinguish children with primarily overt and primarily covert conduct problems. Anger is frequently experienced by children involved in overt confrontations with others, but it is usually not experienced by those engaging in covert behaviors (Loeber & Stouthamer Loeber, 1998). Also, many children engaged in overt problems show specific biases in their cognitions—often viewing the behaviors of others as intentionally harmful—and these cognitions have not been found among most children who engage primarily in covert behaviors (Coie & Dodge, 1998). Family issues also distinguish the overt and covert groups, with greater family adversity and parental conflict associated with overt but not covert behaviors (Coie & Dodge, 1998). Finally, genetic influences are

TABLE 6.4

Four Clusters of Conduct Problems Based on a Meta-Analysis of Factor Analytic Studies[a]

Destructive

Property Violations	Aggression
Cruel to animals	Assaults others
Lies	Blames others for mistakes
Sets fires	Bullies others
Steals	Cruel to others
Vandalism	Physical fights
	Spiteful/vindictive

Covert Status Offenses	Oppositional Overt
Breaks rules	Angry–Resentful
Runs away from home	Annoys others
Swears	Argues with adults
Truancy	Defies adults' requests
	Stubborn
	Temper tantrums
	Touchy/easily annoyed

Nondestructive

[a]The symptom clusters were based on the meta-analysis by Frick et al. (1993).

more strongly associated with covert behaviors than overt behaviors (Frick & Ellis, 1999).

Motivation for Behavior

A final way of grouping children with conduct problems focuses on those with aggressive behaviors and is based on a long history of research showing two primary motivations for aggression in humans and other animals. Research with nonhuman animals has shown that their aggression can be divided into two broad categories: predatory and affective. *Predatory aggression* is proactive, offensive, and involves little arousal, such as a cat stalking and pouncing on a mouse. *Affective aggression* is reactive, defensive, and involves high levels of arousal, such as the furious attack by the same cat when a dog backs it into a corner (Vitiello & Stoff, 1997).

Human aggression has commonly been classified into these same two categories, although different labels have been used. Predatory aggression is often called **instrumental aggression,** although it has also been called *covert, proactive, offensive,* or *controlled aggression.* It is characterized by planning and low levels of arousal and is focused on achieving some goal such as taking another child's money or stealing a purse. Affective aggression is often called **reactive aggression** in humans, although it has also been called *hostile, overt, defensive,* or *impulsive aggression* (Shaw & Campo Bowen, 1995). It is typically accompanied by fear or anger and high levels of arousal. It is often unplanned and impulsive and, as the name implies, occurs in reaction to some act or perceived act by another person. Because of the high levels of arousal that accompany it, reactive aggression can escalate quickly to levels never intended by the aggressor (Vitiello & Stoff, 1997).

Many of the same differences found between children engaging in overt and covert behavior problems are also found between children primarily engaging in instrumental and reactive aggression. As one would expect, children who engage in reactive aggression are more likely to show high levels of anger in their lives and are more likely to have cognitive biases that cause them to frequently see aggression intentionally aimed at them (Coie & Dodge, 1998). In addition, children engaged in reactive aggression are more likely to come from families in which they experienced frequent physical punishment or physical abuse. They also have poorer peer relationships than those engaged in instrumental aggression (Hill, 2002).

Key Concepts

- Various criteria have been suggested for dividing the heterogeneous group of children with conduct problems into more homogeneous groups.
- The most common way to create subgroups is based on the age of the onset of conduct problems, with an early-onset group who show problems from their preschool years and a group with few conduct problems until late childhood or adolescence.

- Another strategy is to base subgroups on whether the conduct-disordered behaviors are primarily overt or covert.
- Subgroups of aggressive children have been based on whether they engage primarily in instrumental or reactive aggression.

Prevalence

Prevalence estimates for conduct disorder and oppositional defiant disorder from large community samples of children range widely, so the prevalence of these disorders remains unclear. Most prevalence estimates for conduct disorder range from 1% to 10% (Essau, 2003; Hinshaw & Lee, 2003). Prevalence estimates for boys range from 4% to 10%, whereas those for girls range from 1% to 5%—showing, as we noted earlier, that boys are more likely than girls to meet the diagnostic criteria for conduct disorder.

As also noted earlier, studies of the prevalence of conduct disorder based on age show different patterns for boys and girls. Few differences between boys and girls appear until age 5 (Keenan & Shaw, 1997). Many more boys than girls are diagnosed with conduct disorder during their school-age years (Delligatti et al., 2003; Messer, Goodman, Rowe, Meltzer, & Maughan, 2006). Beginning in adolescence, there is a significant increase in the number of girls with symptoms of conduct disorder—principally in nonaggressive conduct problems such as theft and vandalism—with a smaller increase among boys (Silverthorn & Frick, 1999). Consequently, the difference in prevalence for boys and girls narrows during adolescence.

Prevalence estimates for oppositional defiant disorder range from 1% to 5% for school-age children. Sex differences for oppositional defiant disorder are less clear than for conduct disorder. Some studies show two to three times as many boys as girls with oppositional defiant disorder; others show little difference between boys and girls (Rowe et al., 2002). The prevalence of oppositional defiant disorder is higher during the preschool years (about 7% of preschoolers in one study [Egger & Angold, 2006]), decreases during the school-age years, and then increases during early and middle adolescence (Loeber, Burke, Lahey, Winters, & Zera, 2000). This pattern is found for both boys and girls.

There is some indication that the prevalence of conduct disorder is increasing among children and that this is not due to children with conduct problems being reported to clinicians or researchers more frequently (Costello, Foley, & Angold, 2006). For example, researchers in England recently examined the frequency of a wide variety of conduct problems in English adolescents. They took advantage of the fact that parents of large samples of 15- to 16-year-olds had been asked to complete similar questionnaires about the conduct problems shown by their children in 1974, 1986, and 1999. When they compared the data from these three groups of adolescents, they found that the frequency of conduct problems had increased during each time period, and that these increases were true for males and females and for adolescents from families across the economic spectrum (Collishaw, Maughan, Goodman, & Pickles, 2004).

Key Concepts

- Prevalence estimates for conduct disorder range from 4% to 10% for boys and 1% to 5% for girls.
- Prevalence estimates for oppositional defiant disorder range from 1% to 5%. Sex differences in the prevalence of oppositional defiant disorder are less clear than for conduct disorder.
- During the school-age years, about four times as many boys as girls receive the diagnosis of conduct disorder, with the difference narrowing during adolescence.
- Patterns of oppositional defiant disorder are similar for boys and girls, with a higher prevalence during the preschool and adolescent years than during the school-age years.

Course

Research programs that have followed groups of children with conduct problems longitudinally have identified three basic developmental patterns: (1) early onset of high levels of conduct problems during the preschool years with this level staying the same or increasing through childhood and adolescence; (2) early onset of conduct problems with a decline in these problems in late childhood and adolescence; and (3) late onset of conduct problems, typically during adolescence. In this section we explore the developmental course of these three groups, and later we will explore the etiology of each of these patterns of disordered behaviors.

As we find for all the disorders discussed in this text, common developmental patterns never describe the development of disorders for all children. Some children follow a different developmental path for conduct problems—perhaps developing them for the first time in middle childhood because of specific influences (such as moving into a troubled neighborhood during the fifth grade). Consequently, it is important to remember that these three paths describe the development of conduct problems in most but not all children.

Early Onset, with Continuing Problems

A small percentage of children—possibly about 5% of boys and about a tenth as many girls—engage in what Moffitt and her colleagues have called the *life-course-persistent* pathway of conduct problems (Moffitt, 1993). Although it is developmentally appropriate for toddlers to be defiant and to lash out at others, these behaviors decline dramatically in most children around age 3 or 4 (Campbell et al., 2000). However, the defiance and aggression of the small percentage of children on the life-course-persistent pathway do not diminish at age 3 or 4; rather, these behaviors often increase during their early childhood. These toddlers and young children display conduct problems that are severe and frequent and that occur in multiple settings and with multiple people (Campbell et al., 2000).

Upon entry to school, the behaviors of children on the life-course-persistent pathway often cause conflicted relationships with their teachers and active rejection by other children. In addition, their classroom behaviors often impede their learning, so they begin to fall behind others in academic skills. Consequently, they are often outside the mainstream of the social and academic worlds of elementary school, and their conduct problems frequently increase during these years (Laird et al., 2001; Moffitt, 1993).

In adolescence, most of these children are behind their peers academically and socially, and they associate primarily with antisocial peers (Laird et al., 2001). The frequency and variety of their conduct problems may increase, and they are likely to have early involvement with the legal system (Patterson et al., 1998). Most of those who are arrested early in their adolescence experience more frequent arrests as they progress through their adolescence.

Those who continue their antisocial behavior into early adulthood face a bleak future, including "drug and alcohol addiction, unsatisfactory employment, unpaid debts, homelessness, drunk driving, violent assault, multiple and unstable relationships, spouse battery, [and] abandoned, neglected or abused children" (Caspi & Moffitt, 1995, p. 497). Females are likely to experience early and frequent pregnancies and are likely to have disrupted relationships with their children, including placement of their children in foster care (Fergusson & Woodward, 2000).

Early Onset, with Discontinuation of Problems in Late Childhood or Adolescence

Less is known about this group of children than about those with the life-course-persistent pattern of conduct problems. Many researchers in the 1980s and 1990s believed that few children with early conduct problems experienced a reduction in those problems during late childhood or adolescence (Moffitt, Caspi, Harrington, & Milne, 2002). However, longitudinal studies have identified a significant number of children who follow this path (Laird et al., 2001; Moffitt et al., 2002). For example, Laird and colleagues (2001) found that 40% of a group of children with early-onset conduct problems had reduced their conduct problems considerably by adolescence.

Moffitt, Caspi, Silva, and Stanton (1996) also found that some children with significant early conduct problems experienced reduced problems in adolescence. They initially labeled these children "recoveries" in that they appeared to have recovered from their conduct problems. However, their long-term follow-up assessment at age 26 showed that most of those who had "recovered" were withdrawn from others, depressed, and anxious. In addition, many were unemployed or underemployed, and only a few had established positive relationships (Moffitt et al., 2002). On a more optimistic note, about 15% showed no problematic symptoms or behaviors and may have recovered from their early conduct problems. Moffitt and colleagues (2002) hypothesized that most of the children in this group had such poor peer relationships during their school-age years and adolescence that eventually they were rejected even by other conduct-disordered children. This resulted in withdrawal, depression, and anxiety. Their conduct problems were reduced by their withdrawal because the conduct problems of most adolescents are done in groups. Ladd and Burgess (1999) provide some support for this hypothesis. They found that children who were rejected by most or all of their peers, including others with conduct problems, were more likely to withdraw from social interactions altogether, be victimized by peers, have frequent conflicts with teachers and parents, and have a fundamental sense of loneliness and dissatisfaction with their life.

Few Early Problems, Increased Problems during Adolescence

Many adolescents with conduct problems do not exhibit such problems during their school-age years. This group has been described as having *adolescent-limited* conduct problems (Moffitt, 1993) or *adolescent-onset* conduct problems (Aguilar et al., 2000). Despite their late start, the conduct problems of these adolescents, both males and females, are as frequent and severe during adolescence as the problems of those whose conduct problems began in childhood (Moffitt et al., 2002).

Most children in the adolescent-onset group end their conduct-disordered problems as they approach or enter early adulthood; thus most of those following this pathway experience a few years of significant conduct problems with infrequent problems before and after (Aguilar et al., 2000; Loeber & Stouthamer Loeber, 1998; Patterson et al., 1998). However, not all with an adolescent onset of conduct problems reduce their antisocial behaviors when they reach young adulthood. In their long-term follow-up of males with adolescent-onset conduct problems, Moffitt and colleagues (2002) found that many continued antisocial behavior during their young adulthood, although their antisocial behaviors were not as frequent or severe as the antisocial behaviors of those who had followed the life-course-persistent path.

Considerable debate during the past few years has focused on the developmental course of girls who begin conduct problems during their adolescence. Based on their review of many clinical studies, Silverthorn and Frick (1999) contend that the characteristics and experiences of most girls in the adolescent-onset group are similar to those of most boys in the life-course-persistent group. They assert that many girls who are at risk for early-onset conduct problems are discouraged from following that path by their socialization. In adolescence, when girls are more influenced by peers and can escape socialization pressures from adults, the influence of the risk factors kept at bay by the girls' socialization increases, resulting in the onset of conduct problems.

Moffitt and Caspi (Moffitt & Caspi, 2001) disagree with Silverthorn and Frick's analysis and use data from their community study to show that the characteristics and experiences of girls following the adolescent-limited pathway are similar to those of boys following the adolescent-limited pathway, and are different from those of the small percentage of girls following the life-course-persistent pathway. They argue that the influences on life-course-persistent or adolescent-limited conduct problems are the same for girls and boys and that their community-based sample provides better data for addressing this issue than the clinical samples used by Silverthorn and Frick.

At this point, it may be best to recognize that our knowledge about the development of adolescent-onset conduct problems in girls is incomplete. Because most research has focused on those following the life-course-persistent pathway, and also because most research has focused on boys, we know little about girls following the adolescent-onset pathway. A more substantial research focus on these girls in the future will tell us more about their development.

Key Concepts

- Some children with early-onset conduct problems exhibit these problems throughout their lives. They are often out of the mainstream of the academic and social worlds from early in life. They tend to fall further behind in academic achievement as they get older and associate increasingly with other conduct-disordered children.
- Other children with early-onset conduct problems have a significant reduction in conduct problems during their late school-age years and early adolescence, although some may withdraw and experience depression or anxiety.
- Some children have few early conduct problems but develop conduct problems during adolescence. Most end their conduct problems as they become adults. Debate continues about whether girls in this group are similar to boys in the early-onset group or boys in the adolescent-onset group.

Families of Children with Conduct Disorder

As we emphasize in many chapters in this text, it is important to recognize that children with conduct and other disorders come from families with a wide range of characteristics. Consequently, it is not possible to describe *the* type of family from which children with conduct disorder come. However, we know that compared with other families, families who have a child with conduct disorder are more likely than other families to be characterized by high stress, problematic parenting, and dysfunctional family functioning. As we will see in the section about etiology, each of these characteristics can play a role in the development of conduct problems.

Many families with a child who has conduct disorder experience one or more circumstances that cause high levels of stress for the parents. High stress can reduce the quality of parenting because parents can be too tired, depressed, or distracted to provide the type of consistent parenting needed by children, particularly children who are also living in stressful environments (Campbell et al., 2000). For example, children with conduct problems are more likely to be raised in families living in poverty or in high-crime neighborhoods. They are also more likely to live in single-parent families, particularly families with teenage mothers who receive little support from their families (Jaffee, Caspi, Moffitt, Belsky, & Silva, 2001). Children with conduct disorder are also more likely to come from large families (Campbell et al., 2000). In part this is because there is an association between large family size and living in poverty. In addition, parents in large families often have less time to supervise their children because of spending more time outside the home working; and when they are home, they have less time to focus on the needs of each child.

As we will also discuss in the next section, an important source of stress in families is the behavior of a child with conduct problems (Aguilar et al., 2000). Confrontations between a parent and a child with conduct problems can be loud and rancorous and can create considerable tension within the family. Parents may have less time to focus on other siblings in the family and may spend little time celebrating the accomplishments of family members, which can make the environment in the family tense, negative, and hostile. Siblings may be angry with the child with a conduct disorder for "causing" the family problems; and they may ignore or reject the child, which can increase stress among the siblings. In some two-parent families, the parents may disagree considerably about how to handle a child's conduct problems, which can create harsh feelings between the parents and impede their ability to work together.

Girls who are incarcerated because of delinquency are likely to come from families in which they have been chronically abused (Rosenbaum, 1989; Widom, 1989). As noted in several chapters in this text, we are becoming more aware of the extent to which physical and sexual abuse harms many children.

Boys and girls with conduct disorder are more likely than other children to have parents with criminal histories or who engage in significant antisocial behavior (Silverthorn & Frick, 1999). Not only may the children see problematic behaviors modeled by their parents (aggression toward each other, planning illegal activities with friends); parents with significant antisocial problems are less likely to spend time with their children than are other parents and are less likely to expect their children to conform to social norms.

Key Concepts

- Many families of children with conduct disorder experience high levels of stress, such as living in poverty or in violent neighborhoods.
- An important source of stress in these families comes from the rancorous interactions that often occur between children with conduct problems and their parents and siblings.
- Child abuse and harsh physical punishment are more common in these families than in others.
- Parental criminal behavior is also more common in these families than others.

Etiology of Conduct Problems

In this section we explore the complex issue of the etiology of conduct disorders. Most research in this area does not distinguish between the development of oppositional defiant disorder and conduct disorder. Consequently, we will focus on the etiology of conduct problems generally. As noted earlier, most research in this area has focused on boys, and controversy exists about whether the influences on the development of conduct problems in boys and girls are similar (Moffitt & Caspi, 2001; Silverthorn & Frick, 1999). Therefore the information in this section may be mostly applicable to boys, although the development of conduct problems in girls will be addressed whenever sufficient research is available to provide useful information about it.

Because of the research showing the different developmental course followed by those with early-onset conduct problems and those with problems that first appear in adolescence, and because the DSM-IV-TR distinguishes these two groups, we will discuss these two groups separately. Within the early-onset group, we will also consider those who stop significant conduct-disordered behavior in late childhood or adolescence and those whose conduct-disordered behavior continues into adulthood. However, much more is known about those with early-onset, chronic problems.

Early-Onset Conduct Problems: Initial Development

An essential part of understanding the initial development of early-onset conduct problems is knowing that aggression and other conduct problems are normal in young children. Most children, for example, have considerable conflict with their parents and other caregivers during the "terrible twos," and the frequency of physical aggression is highest around the ages of 2 and 3 years in most children. Aggression and other conduct problems then decline steadily through the preschool and school-age years in most children as parents, teachers, and others socialize the children to be less aggressive (Loeber & Stouthamer Loeber, 1998). Consequently, frequent aggression and other conduct problems during the preschool years reflect a failure of toddlers' normal aggression and conduct problems to diminish over time—rather than an onset of aggression and other conduct problems during the preschool years. So as we explore the initial development of early-onset conduct problems, we will focus on issues that cause children not to be socialized away from conduct problems during their preschool years.

The basic model for the initial development of early-onset conduct problems involves two components: a genetically influenced child temperament and parenting behaviors (Campbell et al., 2000). Although only one component may influence the development of conduct problems in some young children (for example, parenting behaviors may create conduct problems in some children who do not have a temperament that predisposes them to develop conduct problems), both components are involved in the development of conduct problems in most children. The parenting behaviors that

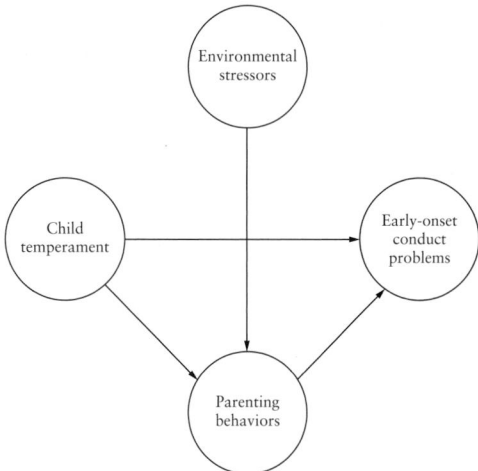

FIGURE 6.3   *Influences on Early-Onset Conduct Problems*

influence conduct problems are often influenced by a child's temperament and the context in which the parents and child live. Consequently, we will also explore these influences on parenting behaviors (see Figure 6.3).

Notes from the Author: Are 2-Year-Olds Really the Most Aggressive?

Many people are surprised to learn that aggression is at its highest around ages 2 and 3; most think adolescence is the time of greatest aggression, especially for boys. But think about family gatherings where young children are present. Two-year-olds often hit others, either when frustrated or apparently just to see how others will respond. How often have you seen a 15-year-old do this at a family gathering? It is usually much less frequent. The aggression of 2-year-olds is usually much less bothersome, partly because it is expected and partly because their aggression seldom does much damage (they cannot hit that hard). Older children hit harder and know where and when to hit to cause more pain, so they can inflict greater injuries. However, for pure frequency of aggression, the award goes to the younger children.

Genetic Influences on Child Temperament

Discussion of the genetic influence on conduct problems has been controversial. This controversy has occurred because research into the genetic influences on conduct problems has been misinterpreted and used improperly by some who want to argue that certain racial or ethnic groups in our society are genetically inferior or genetically programmed to engage in aggression, theft, or other conduct problems. A correct understanding of the genetic influence on conduct problems, however, shows that the research should not be interpreted in this way. As Hinshaw and Lee (2003) point out clearly, studies of genetic heritability estimate the extent to which genes influence a behavior across a population being studied. Even when genetic influences are found, this does not preclude the strong role of environmental influences in the development of a problem for an individual child. Further, no studies of the genetic influence on conduct problems have concluded that there are one or more "aggressive" or "criminal" genes (Rutter, Moffitt, & Caspi, 2006). Therefore, arguing that an individual is aggressive or criminal because of his or her genes, or that a group of people is more aggressive or criminal because of their genes, can be done only if the genetic research is misinterpreted.

A significant body of research shows that genes influence certain temperament styles, such as negativity and impulsivity, and that these temperament styles increase the risk that a child will develop early-onset conduct problems. In this section we first explore research on the strength of the genetic influence on conduct problems and then examine how genes influence conduct problems through their influence on temperament.

Several twin studies have shown a significant influence of genes on children having a diagnosis of conduct disorder or oppositional defiant disorder, as well as on the numbers of antisocial acts committed by them. However, heritability estimates have varied considerably between studies—from 25% to 69% (Eaves et al., 1997; Meyer et al., 2000) with a weighted mean among the studies of 37% (Slutske, Cronk, & Nabors Oberg, 2003). Some variability between the studies is due to who provided the information about the child's behavior. Higher heritability estimates occur when parents report children's behaviors than when twins report their own behavior. (This pattern has also been found in estimating the heritability of depression and anxiety, as discussed in those chapters.) However, even studies in which children rate their own behaviors show significant rates of heritability.

Genetic influences are much stronger on early-onset conduct problems than on adolescent-onset conduct problems (Burt, Krueger, McGue, & Iacono, 2001). Studies that have explored heritability separately for boys and girls have found similar rates, suggesting that genes have a comparable influence on the development of conduct problems in boys and girls (Rhee & Waldman, 2002).

Most researchers believe genes influence the development of early-onset conduct problems through their effect on a child's temperament. **Temperament** consists of relatively consistent, basic characteristics of a person. These characteristics influence the person's activity, reactivity, emotionality, and sociability. Most elements of a person's temperament are present early in life and are believed to be influenced primarily by genes (Goldsmith et al., 1987).

Many children who develop early-onset conduct problems exhibit a temperament characterized by irritability, impulsiveness, and resistance to having their behavior managed. They are difficult to calm when upset, frequently act without thinking, and often resist following instructions from parents and other caregivers. Although all children show these characteristics at times, children with this temperament show them consistently (Loeber & Hay, 1997; Loeber & Stouthamer Loeber, 1998).

Children with this temperament are more likely to exhibit frequent conduct problems because of their tendency to act impulsively when facing a situation they find displeasing. For example, they may be impulsively aggressive toward children or adults who anger them. In addition, because they resist instructions from their parents and others, it is more difficult to socialize them away from the normal aggression toddlers exhibit. Consequently, children with this temperament are more likely to enter their preschool and school-age years without having experienced a reduction in aggression and other conduct problems.

Parenting Influences

Not all children with an impulsive or difficult temperament have early-onset conduct problems. Most of those that do have parents with a parenting style that is ineffective for socializing children with this temperament. Two studies illustrate the connections between children's temperament and parenting behaviors in the development of conduct problems. One study found that among a group of toddlers who had a temperament characterized as "resistant to control," those whose parents provided few restrictions on their behaviors were more likely to have conduct problems during their school-age years than those whose parents provided more restrictions (Bates, Pettit, Dodge, & Ridge, 1998). In a study with complementary findings, among a group of boys whose mothers provided a low level of discipline, those who had frequent temper tantrums as toddlers had higher levels of conduct problems during their school-age years than those who had infrequent temper tantrums as toddlers (Stoolmiller, 2001). Together these studies suggest that the combination of a child who is hard to manage and a parent who provides little discipline is associated with the development of conduct problems. The studies also suggest that effective parenting can reduce the likelihood that children with difficult temperaments will develop conduct problems—an issue to which we will return in the section about therapeutic interventions (Lahey, Waldman, & McBurnett, 1999).

Gerald Patterson and his colleagues (e.g., Patterson, 1982; Patterson, Reid, & Dision, 1992) have created and tested a well-known model for understanding a process through which children's behaviors, and parents' responses to them, can have a powerful influence on the development of conduct problems. (The model was developed through studies of boys but seems relevant for girls also.) This process typically begins when the child is a toddler, when it is developmentally appropriate for children to resist parents' instructions. If the parent makes a demand ("You need to pick up your toys") and the child resists the demand with verbal or physical aggression (yelling "no" or throwing a toy), and the parent then withdraws without requiring that the child meet the parent's demand ("All right, leave your room looking like a mess"), the parent has negatively reinforced the child's verbal or physical aggression (see Figure 6.4). Consequently, the child is more likely to react aggressively to a parent's demand in the future. To the extent that this pattern is repeated, it can steadily increase the child's aggressive behaviors.

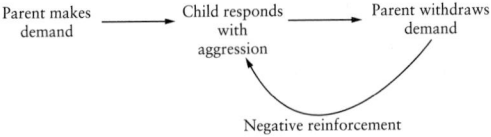

FIGURE 6.4 *Negative Reinforcement of Aggression*

During such interactions with the child, the parent may make the demand several times before withdrawing and may argue with the child for a time. However, if the parent eventually withdraws in the face of the child's verbal or physical aggression, the child's aggression has been **negatively reinforced**. In addition, as the child learns that verbal or physical aggression will eventually make the parent withdraw demands, the child learns to persist in aggression when demands are made. As you can imagine, this can easily lead to long, tumultuous interactions between parent and child; interactions between parents and children in these families are often characterized by negativity.

Notes from the Author: When Do Parents Mean What They Say?

Many children become adept at learning when a parent's demands require action and when they do not. In the previous example, a child may learn that the third demand from a parent does not carry any weight because the third demand is often followed by the parent withdrawing. My favorite example of this comes from a study I once did with families adopting school-age children. While we were observing a family having a meal together, one child misbehaved consistently. Exasperated, his mother finally said, "This is your final, final, final, final warning: The next time you do that you'll have to go to your room." I suppose the mother saw the final, final, final, final warning as having more weight than the final, final, final warning. However, the child had learned otherwise from past experiences and within 10 minutes was misbehaving again. He was never told to go to his room. (Apparently, that would have required a final, final, final, final, final warning.)

Contextual and Child Temperament Influences on Ineffective Parenting

How is it, you might ask, that parents develop an ineffective style of interacting with their children that influences the initial development of early-onset conduct problems? Part of the influence may be from the parents' genes. A child with a genetically influenced difficult temperament may have a parent with a similar temperament. When a parent and child with these temperaments interact, they may experience frequent conflict and negativity. Another possible influence is that the parent may not have learned effective parenting strategies because he or she was raised in a family in which ineffective parenting strategies were used (Brook, Whiteman, & Zheng, 2002). Two other important influences on parenting are the environmental context of parenting and the temperamental characteristics of the child. We explore these latter two influences in this section.

Contextual Influences   As noted earlier in this chapter, many children with conduct problems are raised in stressful environments, such as low-income or violent neighborhoods. These influences, however, are not believed to directly affect the conduct problems of a young child (that is, neighborhood families' lack of money does not cause a child to develop conduct problems). Rather, these contextual issues are believed to affect parents' abilities to rear children effectively (Aguilar et al., 2000; Linares et al., 2001).

Parents living in poverty or in violent neighborhoods are often less available to their children. For example, they may need to work long hours to provide for their families. Consequently, their children may be left alone, in the care of neighbors, or in poor-quality child care more often. Thus their children may receive less effective supervision (Aguilar et al., 2000; Lahey, Gordon, Loeber, Stouthamer Loeber, & Farrington, 1999). In addition, parents in these neighborhoods are likely to be more stressed and so may have less patience with their children's normal misbehavior. This may cause them to ignore their children's misbehavior or use harsh discipline more frequently than parents who are less stressed. They may be too tired to provide consistent supervision for their children or feel demoralized from being surrounded by violence, graffiti, garbage, and schools with chronic problems; this can undermine their ability to provide the consistent parenting that all children need, and that children growing up in chaotic neighborhoods may need even more than others. Finally, some parents may use alcohol or other drugs to cope with stress or unhappiness, which can reduced their parenting effectiveness.

The Influence of Children's Temperament on Parenting   A potent influence on parenting is the behaviors of their children, and these behaviors can be influenced by a child's temperament—which, as we have already discussed, is influenced primarily by a child's genes. As a parent struggles to interact with a child who is impulsive and difficult to manage, the parent is more likely to react either in a hostile way or by withdrawing from a child, either of which represents ineffective parenting. In this way the child's behaviors evoke problematic parenting.

The effect of children's genetically influenced temperament on the behaviors of their parents has been shown by two studies of children adopted as infants or young children (Ge, Conger, & Elder, 1996; O'Connor, Deater Deckard, Fulker, Rutter, & Plomin, 1998). The researchers in both studies measured the children's birth mothers' antisocial behaviors before their children were born and the parenting behaviors of the adoptive parents when their adopted children were school-age. Results from both studies showed that the adoptive parents of children whose birth mothers had higher ratings of antisocial behavior used less effective parenting practices to handle their

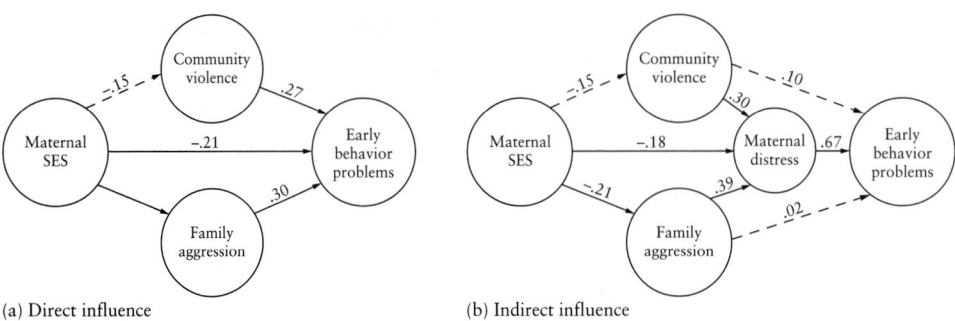

FIGURE 6.5   *Direct and Indirect Influence of Violence on Behavior Problems*

children's misbehavior than did the adoptive parents of children whose birth mothers had engaged in little or no antisocial behavior. The researchers argued that birth mothers with more antisocial behaviors were more likely to have a difficult temperament, and this temperament was likely to be inherited by their children. The children's temperament then influenced the parenting styles of their adoptive parents. Children with temperaments that made them more difficult to parent were more likely to evoke ineffective parenting behaviors from their adoptive parents.

Summary

Taken together, the studies reviewed in this section show that child temperament and parenting style have important influences on the initial development of early-onset conduct problems. Some children have a genetically influenced temperament that makes them more irritable and less likely to respond to parents' expectations and directions. If their parents use an ineffective parenting style, the developmentally inappropriate conduct problems they exhibit as toddlers are unlikely to decrease (as occurs with most children) and are likely to increase.

The studies also showed that ineffective parenting styles are influenced by children's temperament and by the context in which the parents and children live. Thus children with difficult temperaments are more likely to evoke parenting styles that increase the likelihood of their developing conduct problems, especially if the parents are experiencing high levels of environmental stress. What we learn from these studies, then, is that children's temperament has a direct influence on their increasing misbehavior and an indirect influence on their increasing misbehavior by influencing the parenting they receive.

Early-Onset Conduct Problems: Ongoing Development

Several issues can increase the frequency and intensity of a child's early-onset conduct problems during his or her school-age years (Loeber & Stouthamer Loeber, 1998). Some of these influences are the same ones that led to the

ILLUSTRATING AN IMPORTANT RESEARCH ISSUE: DISTINGUISHING DIRECT FROM INDIRECT INFLUENCES ON BEHAVIOR

As we see throughout this chapter, there are many influences on children's conduct-disordered behavior. Some influences are direct in that they influence a child's behavior without any intervening person or event. For example, if three girls praise one of their friends for shoplifting, that praise directly influences the friend's behavior if the positive reinforcement, by itself, has an influence. Other influences are indirect. An indirect influence occurs when one issue influences a second issue, and that second issue directly influences a child's behavior. For example, consider family income. Low family income is associated with increased conduct problems in children. However, the fact that a child's family has little or no money in the bank does not directly influence his behavior; rather, having little money may force a family to live in a neighborhood where the child is exposed to street crime and drugs, and these factors may directly influence his conduct problems. So low family income has an indirect influence on his conduct problems.

Determining whether an influence is direct or indirect has important implications for prevention and intervention programs. If, as in our example, family income has an indirect influence on a child's conduct problems, simply increasing the family income (such as by giving the parents $10,000) will not influence the child's behaviors if nothing else is done because the child will still live in the same neighborhood that is having a direct influence on his behavior. However, helping the family move to a safer neighborhood may influence the child's behavior even if the family income remains the same.

A good example of the assessment of direct and indirect influences can be seen in a study of the influences of neighborhood violence and family aggression on the conduct problems of young children (Linares et al., 2001). The researchers used a statistical technique called *structural equation modeling* to explore the correlations between several variables and early behavior problems in children. In particular, they explored whether community and domestic violence directly influenced children's behavior problems or whether the violence had an indirect influence through its affect on maternal distress (with maternal distress having a direct influence). The strategy for doing this includes two steps. The first step involves looking for direct effects of the variables on children's conduct problems—in this case the influence of maternal socioeconomic status (SES), community violence, and family aggression. The results from this step are shown in Figure 6.5(a). The path coefficients show how each variable is associated with behavior problems: The positive path coefficients show a positive correlation (as community violence increases, child behavior problems increase), and the negative coefficient shows a negative correlation (as maternal SES decreases, child behavior problems increase).

The next step involves adding the variable representing maternal distress to the model and reanalyzing it. As shown in Figure 6.5(b), this second analysis found a strong association between maternal distress and child behavior problems. However, when maternal distress was added to the model, the path coefficients from community violence and family aggression to child behavior problems were reduced to the point that they were no longer statistically significant. This drop in their path coefficients demonstrates that community violence and family aggression do not influence early behavior problems directly but have an indirect influence through their influence on maternal distress, which does directly influence children's conduct problems.

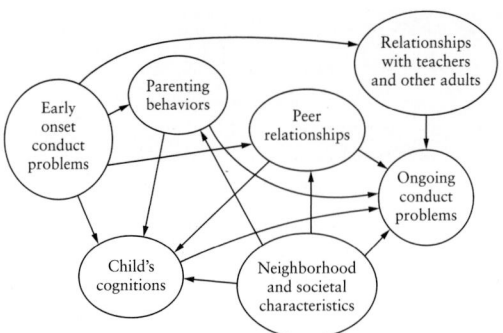

FIGURE 6.6   *A Multitude of Influences*

onset of conduct problems, such as the parenting the child receives. Additional influences emerge during childhood, such as the child's developing cognitive style, problematic interactions with peers, and the consequences of earlier conduct problems. We explore these additional influences in this section (see Figure 6.6).

Cognitive Influences

As discussed in several chapters in this text, a child's cognitions can have an important influence on his or her behavior. Among children with conduct problems, the cognitions of children who are aggressive during social interactions have been studied most often. Many studies have shown that they have schemata that the world is a hostile place, that most people are hostile toward them, and that the best strategy for dealing with this hostility is through aggression (recall from the chapter about basic psychological theories that schemata are fundamental belief systems about how we and the world function) (Crick & Dodge, 1994; Waldman, 1996).

Our knowledge of the experiences of young children who later develop conduct problems provides clues about how their hostile schemata might develop initially by showing that many of them develop in environments characterized by hostility. Many of these children experience frequent physical punishment by their parents. Thus they are likely to live in a home environment in which hostility is regularly present (Deater Deckard, Dodge, Bates, & Pettit, 1998). In addition, being physically abused dramatically increases a child's risk for developing conduct problems and can influence a child's beliefs about the hostile and painful nature of personal interactions (Aguilar et al., 2000). Similarly, children who live in violent families or neighborhoods are more likely to have conduct problems than other children. The aggression they observe in these environments is likely to influence their view of the world as a hostile place and the need to act aggressively for self-protection (Campbell et al., 2000). Finally, the comments of parents or other important adults about the hostility of the world, or of particular groups of people in the world, may strongly influence the developing schemata of young children.

Once a hostile schema begins to develop in a child, the schema biases the child's perceptions and memories. Aggressive children are more likely to focus on and remember social interactions that involve hostility and are less likely to focus on and remember interactions that are not hostile (Crick & Dodge, 1994). In addition, aggressive children often interpret ambiguous social interactions as involving intentional harm or hostility. For example, if one child knocks another child over during a soccer game, aggressive children are more likely than others to believe that this was done intentionally.

As you might imagine, the biased perceptions and memories of aggressive children reinforce their schemata about the world as a hostile place because they can point to many social interactions that involve hostility. Their strengthened schemata bias their perceptions further, resulting in more memories of hostile acts and even stronger beliefs that the world is a hostile place. Consequently, they are likely to believe that many of the interactions they have with others involve hostile behavior—including interactions that other children would not view as hostile. Thus they are primed to act aggressively in many social interactions.

Besides perceiving hostility more frequently, children with conduct problems have fewer nonaggressive behaviors in their repertoire of possible social behaviors than do other children (Moffitt, 1993). One strategy researchers use to investigate this issue is to ask children to name all the possible responses that they could make to a provocative social interaction. ("What are all the things you could do if one of your classmates cuts in line in front of you?") Investigations with children from preschool to adolescence have shown that aggressive children can name fewer possible responses to these provocative situations than can other children, and the responses they name are more likely to involve aggression (Coie & Dodge, 1998).

Finally, aggressive children are more likely to choose an aggressive response from their repertoire of possible responses. For example, Fontaine, Salzer Burkes, and Dodge (2002) asked a group of ninth graders to respond to a variety of videotaped vignettes (like the following) in which a potentially provocative interaction was initiated by an adult or a peer:

> Students and teacher are appropriately seated in a classroom. Students are busy doing schoolwork while the teacher is writing quietly at his desk. A student (the protagonist) gets up from his seat to sharpen his pencil and starts to walk across the classroom toward the pencil sharpener. The teacher sharply asks the student what he is doing out of his seat. (p. 111)

When asked how they would respond to this situation, those who had higher levels of conduct problems were more likely to give an aggressive potential response than those who did not have conduct problems. In addition, when the conduct-disordered adolescents later observed an aggressive response given by the protagonist in the vignette, they were more likely than nonaggressive adolescents to rate the aggressive response as likely to achieve an important goal for the protagonist.

Taken together, investigations of the cognitions of aggressive children show that they differ from those of other children in many ways that are likely to increase the likelihood of aggression in social interactions. They are more likely to perceive hostility from others and to believe that this hostility reflects a generally hostile world. They have fewer responses to social interactions that they perceive as hostile, and most of their responses involve aggression. Finally, they are more likely to choose an aggressive response because they believe in the usefulness of aggression in social situations.

Peer Influences

As noted earlier in this chapter, children with conduct problems, particularly those who are aggressive, are likely to be rejected by peers who do not have conduct problems and accepted by peers who also have conduct problems (Coie & Dodge, 1998). Thus they are less likely to be in social situations in which they can learn and be reinforced for prosocial behaviors, and more likely to be in social situations where they can learn and be reinforced for conduct-disordered behaviors. This peer reinforcement for conduct problems is likely to become increasingly important during late childhood and adolescence, when peer influences on a range of behaviors increase and influences from adults decrease.

Consequences of Early Conduct Problems

Several consequences of their behavior can limit the opportunities of children and adolescents with conduct problems and ensnare them in an ongoing pattern of conduct problems (Moffitt, 1993). As their academic achievement lags behind that of their peers, children and adolescents with conduct problems may come to see themselves as having few options to do well in school and achieve a good job once they leave school. Their reputations may increase the hostility they experience from others and decrease their opportunities for part-time jobs, dating, and engaging in athletic, cultural, or other prosocial activities. Involvement with the police may prevent them from getting part-time jobs while they are in school or full-time jobs after leaving school (Patterson et al., 1998). All these consequences may result in the belief that they have little hope of succeeding in life by pursuing prosocial activities and that their only chance for success is through antisocial activities, intensifying their conduct problems.

Early-Onset, Limited Duration Conduct Problems

As noted earlier, not all children with early-onset conduct problems continue having those problems throughout their childhood (Laird et al., 2001). A significant amount of research has shown that no specific personal or family risk factors consistently predict whether a child will end conduct problems or continue them through adolescence. What has been found, however, is that the number of risk factors a child experiences is associated with whether he or she will continue conduct problems (Aguilar et al., 2000; Campbell et al., 2000; Deater Deckard et al., 1998; Laird et al., 2001; Shaw, Owens, Vondra, & Keenan, 1996).

Loeber and Farrington (2000) compiled a list of the risk factors associated with delinquency and other conduct problems in children and adolescents (see Table 6.5). Research shows that children with fewer of these risk factors are more likely to stop engaging in conduct problems during their late childhood or adolescence. This information should be particularly encouraging to those concerned about early intervention programs for young children with conduct problems. It suggests that intervening to strengthen parents' effectiveness, improve the quality of schools, decrease neighborhood crime, or improve children's social relationships can all increase the likelihood that children will reduce their conduct-disordered behaviors.

Laird and colleagues (2001) found that peer relationships had an important influence on reducing conduct problems in many children they studied. Meaningful relationships with untroubled peers allowed some children with conduct problems to (1) avoid primary associations with other conduct-disordered

TABLE 6.5

Childhood Risk Factors for Child Delinquency and Later Serious and Violent Juvenile Offending

Child factors
Difficult temperament
Hyperactivity (but only when co-occurring with conduct disorder)
Impulsivity
Substance use
Aggression
Early-onset disruptive behavior
Withdrawn behavior
Low intelligence
Lead toxicity

Family factors
Parental antisocial or delinquent behavior
Parental substance abuse

Parents' poor child-rearing practices
Poor supervision
Physical punishment
Poor communication
Poor parent–child relations
Parental neglect
Maternal depression
Mother's smoking during pregnancy
Teenage motherhood
Parental disagreement about child discipline
Single parenthood

Large family
High turnover of caretakers
Low SES of family
Unemployed parent
Poorly educated mother
Family members' carelessness in allowing children access to weapons, especially guns

School factors
Poor academic performance
Old for grade
Weak bonding to school
Low educational aspirations
Low school motivation
Poorly organized and functioning schools

Peer factors
Associations with deviant/delinquent siblings/peers
Rejection by peers

Neighborhood factors
Neighborhood disadvantage and poverty
Disorganized neighborhoods
Availability of weapons
Media portrayal of violence

children, which (2) reduced their conduct-disordered behavior in childhood, which (3) lessened the likelihood of them associating with deviant peers during adolescence, which (4) decreased their antisocial behaviors during adolescence. Why some children with early conduct problems develop positive peer relationships and others do not remains unclear.

Adolescent-Onset Conduct Problems

Most theorists agree that conduct problems that begin during adolescence are principally due to environmental influences. Most of those who begin conduct-disordered behavior during adolescence do not experience the same individual, family, or social risk factors experienced by children whose conduct problems begin early (Burt et al., 2001; Caspi & Moffitt, 1995). Instead most cases of adolescent-onset conduct problems develop either because of changes in the risk and protective factors that occur as children become adolescents or because of the allure of conduct-disordered behavior.

Changes in Risk and Protective Influences

Adolescents who have been at some risk for developing conduct problems because of personal or environmental characteristics, and who are protected from developing conduct problems by other personal or environmental characteristics, may become conduct disordered if the relative strengths of those risk and protective influences change (Loeber & Stouthamer Loeber, 1998). In many cases the strengths of the risk and protective factors change as an adolescent moves away from the protective influence of his or her family and into a world in which peers have more influence.

For example, a child being raised in a violent and crime-ridden environment, and who attends a school with many children who have conduct problems, may be protected from the risks associated with that environment by a strong and positive family. However, as the child enters adolescence and experiences less influence from his prosocial parents and more influence from antisocial peers, the changing balance of those influences may encourage the development of antisocial behavior. Consider also a child being raised in an area that is high in poverty and low in opportunity. The influence of his family, teachers, and members of his faith-based community may help him work to become accomplished in school so he can go to college or get a good job after high school. However, if he becomes increasingly aware of the significant social barriers to his becoming successful in mainstream society, he may become disillusioned and begin to seek out alternative, and possibly illegal, strategies for becoming successful.

The Allure of Conduct Problems

Moffitt and her colleagues suggest that another path that can lead to adolescent-onset conduct problems has foundations in adolescents' attempts to separate from their parents and show their independence from adults (Caspi & Moffitt, 1995; Moffitt, 1993). They argue that although adolescents are physically mature, our culture does not allow them to engage in most adult activities. Thus many early and mid-adolescents are frustrated in their attempts to achieve the type of independence to which they believe their physical and cognitive maturity entitles them.

As they observe other adolescents, they notice that those who have engaged in conduct-disordered behavior for years are more adultlike than their peers: They often have more possessions, drink and use illegal drugs, have sex and seem more comfortable with their sexual partners, and live a life that seems based on their own rules. Consequently, many adolescents become drawn to these peers, even though they had avoided them as children; and they may begin to emulate them to feel more adultlike. "Every curfew broken, car stolen, joint smoked, and baby conceived is a statement of independence" (Caspi & Moffitt, 1995).

A higher percentage of those with adolescent-onset conduct problems than those with early-onset conduct problems end those problems as they enter adulthood (Caspi & Moffitt, 1995). It appears that an important influence on this pattern is that most of those with adolescent-onset conduct problems have developed positive peer and adult relationships during their childhood and early adolescence, have better academic achievement, and have successfully participated in a variety of socially acceptable activities (Moffitt, 1993). Thus they have a foundation of prosocial behaviors and relationships to which they can return when the tasks of young adulthood loom. This allows most of them to resume a more socially acceptable lifestyle when it is in their best interest to do so.

Key Concepts

- The primary influences on the initial development of early-onset conduct problems are a genetically influenced difficult temperament in a child and a parenting style that is ineffective for socializing the child.
- Children identified as having impulsive, negative, and difficult-to-manage temperaments are more likely than other children to develop conduct problems. These temperaments are believed to be primarily influenced by the child's genes.
- One problematic style of parenting involves the parents providing negative reinforcement for the child's aggressive behaviors, which increases the frequency of the behaviors.
- A highly stressful environment can sap parents' energy for parenting their children effectively, thus increasing the likelihood that their children will develop conduct problems. One source of this stress is the difficulty of parenting a child with an impulsive, negative, and difficult-to-manage temperament.
- A child's developing cognitive style can intensify conduct problems.
- Because they are often rejected by other children, many children with conduct problems associate with each other and provide mutual reinforcement for conduct-disordered behaviors.
- Most of those with adolescent-onset conduct problems do not experience the same risk factors as those with early-onset problems.

- Some adolescents develop conduct problems when the relative strengths of their risk and protective factors change as they are influenced less by parents and more by peers.
- Others engage in conduct problems because they provide an indication of their freedom.

Preventive and Therapeutic Interventions

Preventive and therapeutic interventions for conduct problems have typically been provided to (1) parents of children who are at risk for developing early-onset conduct problems or who have already shown signs of early conduct problems or (2) the children themselves. Some interventions are obviously preventive, such as those for mothers living in circumstances that place them at risk for having a child with early-onset conduct problems. Other interventions are clearly therapeutic, such as cognitive–behavioral therapy (CBT) for school-age children or adolescents who have been diagnosed with a conduct disorder. Other interventions are less easily classified as preventive or therapeutic because they have characteristics of both. These interventions are usually provided to parents of preschool or kindergarten children who show problems with aggression, or to the children themselves, with the intent of reducing current problems and preventing the development of chronic conduct problems. These programs may best be thought of as early intervention programs. We will explore each of these types of interventions separately.

These interventions are grounded in our research-based understanding of the development of conduct-disordered behaviors. For example, preventive and early intervention programs use our knowledge of the role that ineffective parenting can play in the development of conduct problems. Other therapeutic interventions focus on changing children's cognitions or their peer relationships, based on our knowledge of the role that cognitions and peer relationships can play in intensifying conduct problems. Together, then, these interventions demonstrate how our knowledge of the development of a disorder informs our efforts to change the lives of children who have the disorder.

Attending to Cultural Issues

Considering cultural issues is always important when intervening with children and families. It is important that a clinician recognize his or her own cultural expectations about children's and parents' behaviors and not force children and families from other cultures to accept them (Vargas & Koss-Chioino, 1992). Doing so can reduce the effectiveness of interventions by requiring that children or families ignore their own cultural values. In addition, interventions that are not culturally sensitive can pit families against those in their cultural groups, or children against their parents, if they try to follow guidance that runs counter to their cultural expectations. For example, an intervention to change the parenting style of parents in a family from one culture because that parenting style is associated with conduct problems in children from families in the more dominant culture may cause the parents anguish as they must choose between adhering to their cultural values and following the expectations of a therapist. Of equal importance, because of cultural values, the parenting style that adheres to the minority cultural values may work more effectively in the families in that culture than do parenting styles that work more effectively in the more dominant culture (Helms & Cook, 1999). Culturally sensitive interventions not only honor the expectations and values of different cultural groups—they also are much more likely to be effective.

Prevention

Prevention programs focus on strengthening parents' abilities to rear their children effectively (Webster Stratton & Taylor, 2001). Most programs target parents who have characteristics, or who live in environments, that place them at risk for providing poor parenting—such as single or teenage mothers, couples or single parents living in poverty, or those with few sources of family or neighborhood support. Some of these programs engage the parents while the mothers are pregnant or soon after a child is born; others engage parents within the first few years of their children's lives—possibly through referrals from social service agencies.

Therapists involved in prevention programs may work with parents individually or in groups to provide knowledge about child development and to help them learn and practice techniques for effective parenting. Many prevention efforts also focus on helping parents cope with stresses related to their financial or social situations: helping them contact social service agencies that might provide them better housing, helping one or both parents find jobs, or finding appropriate day care (Dadds & Fraser, 2003).

One of the best examples of primary prevention comes from a longitudinal study by David Olds and his colleagues in upstate New York (Olds, 1989). About 400 young, single, pregnant women were randomly assigned to (1) the normal community care available to all women in their area, (2) community care plus periodic visits from a specially trained public health nurse during their pregnancies, or (3) community care plus periodic public health nurse visits during their pregnancies and for the first two years of their children's lives.

Fewer of the mothers receiving nurse visits gave birth to low–birth weight babies or had premature deliveries, both of which are signs of the mothers receiving better prenatal care. The researchers then followed the mothers and children for 15 years, monitoring family and child issues. Results from the mothers showed that those who had received public health nurse visits for two years after the births of their children differed from those in the other two groups in several ways. They had fewer problems with drugs and alcohol, fewer arrests, fewer reports for child abuse or neglect, and fewer subsequent births, and they had received welfare payments for fewer months (Olds et al., 1998). Results in the children showed similar patterns. Those whose mothers had received visits for two years after their birth had been arrested fewer times, had run away fewer times, consumed less alcohol, and had fewer sexual partners than the children in the other groups (Olds et al., 1998). Similar programs have also shown success in reducing the frequency of delinquency and other conduct problems (Dadds & Fraser, 2003).

Two issues from the Olds study are worth particular note. First, there were few long-term differences between the groups receiving public health nurse visits only during the mother's pregnancy and those receiving no visits. This suggests the value of having professionals available to help mothers with their earliest attempts at parenting. Second, an intervention that stopped 2 years into the child's life continued to show positive effects 13 years later. This demonstrates the long-term effectiveness of helping parents who are at risk for poor parenting get off to a good start with their children.

Early Intervention
Parenting Programs

One focus of early intervention programs is helping parents of children who show early signs of aggression or other conduct problems parent their children more effectively, thus reducing their child's conduct problems or preventing the problems from becoming chronic (Reyno & McGrath, 2006). One strategy, *parent management training*, is based on the work of Patterson and his colleagues discussed earlier (Patterson et al., 1992). The two primary goals of parent management training are to change parenting practices that may inadvertently foster children's aggression and to improve parents' monitoring of their children's behaviors inside and outside the home. To change the pattern of negative reinforcement of aggressive behaviors that are commonly found in these homes, parents learn to identify and observe their children's behaviors in an objective and unemotional manner, use positive reinforcement for prosocial behaviors (like praising a child when he does what he is asked to do), and employ appropriate punishment in response to problem behaviors (such as using "time out" if a child acts aggressively toward siblings). Parents are also taught strategies to monitor their children's behaviors when the children are away from home. For example, they are encouraged to be in close contact with their children's teachers, know where their children are playing after school, and have the children check with them periodically when away from home. This type of consistent monitoring not only reduces the likelihood of a child engaging in problem behaviors; it also encourages closeness between a child and parent and involves the parent in the child's activities throughout the day.

Evaluations of several parent management training programs have shown that they are effective (Kazdin, 2005). For example, Webster-Stratton and Hammond (1990) found that, compared with a wait-list group, children whose parents were involved in a 10-week parent management training program exhibited fewer conduct problems one month after the training ended and at a one-year follow-up. However, parent training is less effective for lower-income families than it is for middle- and upper-income families. Perhaps the lower-income families experience more stress and so are struggling more; or parent training programs may not address issues of particular importance to lower-income families or may be presented in ways that are not as effectively learned by parents in lower-income families (Reyno & McGrath, 2006).

Two additions to parent management training have been shown to enhance its benefits. A study that included both parent management training and social skills training for conduct-disordered 4- to 7-year-old children found that the combined treatments produced greater behavioral improvement than parent management training alone (Webster-Stratton & Hammond, 1997). The social skills of the children who received social skills training improved more than those of the children whose families received only parent management training, and their enhanced social skills resulted in better peer relationships and better relationships with parents and teachers. Thus this study showed that an intervention that reduces problem behaviors of children and increases their prosocial behaviors is better than a program that just reduces their problem behaviors—a pattern also seen in interventions with children who have ADHD, as described in that chapter.

A second strategy that improved the effectiveness of parent management training was the inclusion of specific efforts to help parents cope with stress. Not only did these efforts help reduce the stress experienced by parents; they also helped to form a closer alliance between the parents and the therapist, which kept the parents engaged in the therapy process for a longer period (Kazdin & Whitley, 2003; Prinz & Miller, 1994). Thus attending to the needs of parents creates a more effective therapeutic intervention for their children (which corresponds to the knowledge, discussed earlier, of the extent to which a stressful environment harms parents' ability to rear their children effectively).

Child-Focused Programs

Another early intervention strategy teaches children who show early signs of aggression or other conduct problems how to interact more successfully with peers, teachers, and parents. Some interventions involve small groups of children identified as having early conduct problems (Webster-Stratton & Hammond, 1997); others include small groups of children, some of whom have conduct problems and some of whom do not (Prinz, Blechman, & Dumas, 1994). The groups focus on helping children develop better social skills with peers and helping them achieve goals during social interactions in a nonaggressive way. For example, children may be taught how to enter games or solve interpersonal conflicts without using aggression. Thus this type of intervention helps children who are at risk of being rejected by their peers learn skills to avoid this rejection, which reduces their risk for intensifying conduct problems.

Evaluations of these interventions have been mixed. Prinz and colleagues (1994) found an overall reduction of aggression in the children involved in their intervention; however, many children continued to display problematic levels of aggression. Webster-Stratton and Hammond (1997) also found only marginal improvements in the children in their intervention. These results suggest that early intervention programs focused solely on children do not produce significant changes in their behaviors (Taylor, Eddy, & Biglan, 1999). Rather, as noted in the previous section, they are most effective when used with interventions for parents. This can be interpreted as suggesting that attempts to change children's behaviors are only marginally successful if changes in their home environments do not occur.

Interventions during the School-Age Years and Adolescence
Social Skills Training for School-Age Children

Most interventions during the school-age years are similar to the child-focused early intervention programs just described. These interventions are most effective for children who engage in reactive rather than instrumental aggression because they focus on changing the cognitive biases and high levels of anger that are often associated with reactive aggression. They are also more likely to be effective with children who engage in overt conduct problems than those who engage primarily in covert problems.

One well-researched intervention is *social problem-solving skills training*, developed by Alan Kazdin and his colleagues. This intervention encourages aggressive children to think more methodically about difficult social situations and then choose socially appropriate responses to them (Kazdin, Siegel, & Bass, 1992). In a series of sessions with specially trained therapists, children first learn to pay close attention to social cues by looking at others while they talk and thinking about what they are saying. Second, the children are encouraged to consider how they think and feel during difficult social situations. This phase provides an opportunity to discuss the children's cognitive styles, including any cognitive biases such as viewing behaviors of others as hostile, and the feelings aroused by their cognitions. The therapist then encourages the children to consider alternative interpretations of social scenarios. For example, a child might be asked to consider a situation in which he gets knocked over by another child while playing basketball: what his initial thoughts and feelings might be ("He did it to make everyone laugh at me") and what alternative explanations might be appropriate ("He was dribbling too fast and couldn't stop before hitting me"). Children are then taught a full range of prosocial responses to social problems and ways to calm down when angry so they have more opportunity to use a prosocial response. Finally, children learn to stop before acting, consider the possible consequences of their actions, and reconsider responses in light of those consequences.

As with the early intervention programs for young children, evaluations of Kazdin's program and similar programs show mixed results

(Kazdin et al., 1992; Southam-Gerow, 2003). Children involved in the intervention show reduced levels of aggression and other conduct problems when compared with children in wait-list comparison groups. However, the behavior of many children who have completed the program remains in the problematic range. Children with more severe behavioral problems, who come from families with more conflict and parental psychopathology, and who are living in troubled neighborhoods are more likely to continue to show significant conduct-disordered behavior after an intervention (Kazdin, 2005). Perhaps expecting these children to change their behaviors dramatically if their home, school, and neighborhood environments change little is expecting too much. In addition, by the time aggressive children reach their school-age years, their behaviors and their reputations among other children may be fairly strongly fixed—making it difficult for them to change.

Interventions for Adolescents and Their Families

Most interventions with conduct-disordered adolescents focus on them and their families. One of the most widely known interventions is *multisystemic therapy*, an intense therapy usually used with adolescents who have significant records of delinquency and aggression (Henggeler & Borduin, 1990). Specially trained therapists are assigned to an adolescent and his or her family and supply frequent services at several levels, such as (1) helping parents and extended family members provide more effective parenting, (2) decreasing the adolescent's involvement with delinquent peers, (3) increasing the adolescent's success in school, and (4) teaching the adolescent better social skills and anger management skills. Therapists are assigned a few adolescents and their families and are available to the families 24 hours a day, seven days a week. Initial contact with the family, adolescent, or school may be daily, or even several times a day, although contact eventually drops to once or twice a week within a few months.

Therapists use a variety of techniques to influence families and adolescents. Family therapy may be used with an entire family to help them work together more effectively to influence their adolescent's behaviors. Marriage therapy may be used to strengthen a marriage and cognitive–behavioral therapy may be used with the adolescent. The goal of the therapist is to be flexible in choosing treatment strategies: assessing the specific needs of a family and adolescent and then applying empirically supported treatment techniques to those needs (Borduin, Schaeffer, & Ronis, 2003).

Several studies have shown the effectiveness of multisystemic therapy. Compared with delinquent adolescents receiving the usual services in their community, adolescents receiving multisystemic therapy have shown lower rates of alcohol and other drug use, fewer arrests for drug use, and increased school attendance (Henggeler, Pickrel, & Brondino, 1999). In addition, the number of subsequent arrests and the number of days incarcerated for delinquent adolescents receiving multisystemic therapy have been about half those of delinquent adolescents receiving regular community services; this pattern holds even in long-term follow-ups of about a dozen years (Borduin et al., 2003). Many adolescents receiving multisystemic therapy continue to engage in delinquent behavior. However, their delinquent behavior is usually less severe than the delinquent behavior of adolescents not receiving the intervention. Given the long history of significant delinquent behavior of the adolescents that are typically involved in multisystemic therapy, perhaps this indicates success.

Notes from the Author: Measuring Success

An important goal for anyone intervening with children, adolescents, or families is to determine the indications of a successful intervention. Those evaluating multisystemic therapy have considered a reduction in the number of arrests a sign of success, possibly because of the characteristics of the adolescents with whom they work. Therapists working with adolescents with less history of delinquent behavior might not consider a reduction in arrests a sign of success; they might consider any arrest a sign of failure.

Most of you reading this text will have been primarily successful in the tasks of childhood, adolescence, and young adulthood. When you work with children and families, or read about the work of others, it is important not to assume that the measures of success that you (or your parents) have applied to yourself should be applied to others. What are appropriate signs of success for children with moderate mental retardation or girls with a long history of anorexia nervosa? What are the signs of success of an intervention designed for teenage mothers trying to raise a child with no family support? There are no easy answers to these questions, and each of them requires careful thought and attention to the needs and interests of the children and their families. We must be careful not to accept levels of success that are too low; but we must also be careful not to aim for levels of success that are not achievable.

Key Concepts

- Most prevention programs focus on parents who are more likely to have a child who is at risk for conduct problems, such as visiting nurse programs for women who are pregnant or who have recently given birth.
- Some early intervention programs teach parents of young children with conduct problems how to parent their children more effectively.
- Other early intervention programs teach social skills to young children who are aggressive or have other conduct problems.
- Social skills training for school-age children or adolescents has been used to reduce their aggression and increase their ability to interact effectively with peers, thereby avoiding being rejected by them. However, these programs have only been moderately effective.
- Interventions for delinquent adolescents, such as multisystemic therapy, influence many aspects of the adolescents' lives, including family and social environments.

CHAPTER GLOSSARY

The **adolescent-limited** pathway for conduct problems, originally described by Moffitt (1993), involves conduct problems that begin and end during adolescence, with only minor conduct problems in childhood.

Adolescent-onset conduct disorder is diagnosed with the DSM-IV-TR when significant symptoms are not present until age 10 or after.

The **adolescent-onset pathway**, described by Aguilar and colleagues (2000), involves conduct problems that begin in adolescence (there is less of a sense that they also end in adolescence, which is suggested by Moffitt's *adolescent-limited* pathway).

A **callous–unemotional personality trait** has been identified in some children with conduct disorder. The trait is characterized by decreased guilt, sympathy for others, and need for social approval and by increased selfishness and adventure seeking.

Childhood-onset conduct disorder is diagnosed with the DSM-IV-TR when significant symptoms are present before age 10.

The **early-onset/persistent pathway** for conduct problems, described by Aguilar and colleagues (2000), is similar to the life-course-persistent pathway described by Moffitt (1993). It involves an early onset of conduct problems that continue through adolescence.

Instrumental aggression is characterized by planning and low levels of arousal and is generally focused on achieving some goal.

The **life-course-persistent** pathway for conduct problems, originally described by Moffitt (1993), involves conduct problems that begin early in life and persist through adulthood.

Negative reinforcement occurs when the removal of a noxious stimulus after a behavior increases the likelihood that the behavior will occur in the future.

One strategy for distinguishing groups of children with conduct problems is to divide them into an **overt group** that engages in behaviors involving personal confrontation, a **covert group** that engages in acts against property, and a **defiant group** that has conflicts with authority.

Reactive aggression is typically accompanied by fear or anger and high levels of arousal, is often unplanned and impulsive, and usually occurs in reaction to some act by another person.

Relational aggression involves purposely excluding others from activities, spreading gossip, and turning some children against others. It is found most commonly among school-age and adolescent girls.

Social cognition refers to how people think about social situations.

Socialized delinquent children engage in primarily nonaggressive group behaviors such as vandalism or theft. This was one of the early categories of delinquent children.

Temperament consists of relatively consistent, basic characteristics of a person.

Undersocialized delinquent children engage in primarily aggressive behaviors carried out alone. This was one of the early categories of delinquent children.

Attention-Deficit/Hyperactivity Disorder

Many families with a child who has ADHD experience heightened stress and anger.

Attention-deficit/hyperactivity disorder (ADHD) is a noteworthy childhood disorder for several reasons. It is one of the most common childhood disorders, with estimates of its prevalence ranging up to 14% (Scahill & Schwab-Stone, 2000). It is also the childhood disorder that has received the most research attention, with hundreds of studies of its prevalence, development, and treatment being completed in just the past two decades (Wolraich, 1999). Finally, it remains one of the most controversial childhood disorders. Debates continue about whether ADHD is a disorder or simply a label for children who are more active and disruptive; what the core features of the disorder are; what causes the disorder; and whether the widespread use of medications with children who are diagnosed with ADHD is appropriate (Connor, 2002).

As we will see in this chapter, children diagnosed with ADHD struggle in many ways. Their problems with attention and their overactivity influence their academic performance, making them less successful in school than they would be without the disorder. Teachers often find their classroom behavior disruptive and may dread having to deal them. Many of their peers are bothered by their overactivity and may avoid or actively reject them. Their parents may become frustrated with their ongoing behavior problems, and their relationships with parents and other family members are often strained.

Although ADHD was once thought to be exclusively a disorder of childhood, we now know that it continues into adolescence and adulthood for many who have it as children (Mannuzza & Klein, 2000). Some adults now take medications such as **methylphenidate (MPH)** to reduce problems with attention and hyperactivity, and you or one of your friends may be taking such medications (the most common brand name of MPH is Ritalin). Some adults who take medication have been doing so for decades, whereas others have started more recently, having just discovered that they have been struggling with ADHD throughout much of their lives.

Chapter Plan

After two case studies, we start this chapter by reviewing the history of ADHD and noting that beliefs about several fundamental characteristics of ADHD have changed over the years. We then examine the diagnostic criteria for ADHD and the characteristics and experiences of children who have been diagnosed with it. After reviewing the research on the prevalence and developmental course of ADHD, we widen our focus to discuss the families of children with ADHD and how the symptoms of ADHD can influence parent–child relationships and family functioning. We then shift our focus to the etiology of ADHD. Unfortunately a clear picture of the causes of ADHD has yet to emerge, but we will explore what is currently known about them. Once we have developed a sense of how ADHD develops, we can explore strategies to prevent ADHD and to treat it when it arises.

Case Study: A Dramatic Influence of Medication

Jimmy was adopted by his parents at age 7. Jimmy had been removed from his birth family at age 3 because of chronic neglect, and he had lived in four different foster homes before he was adopted. His foster parents had all found him too disruptive and had asked for his removal from their homes because of the influence he was having on their families and their other foster children.

His new adoptive parents were particularly concerned about his hyperactivity, conduct problems, and high levels of anxiety. His mother described him as a child who was a classic example of someone with an "emotional problem." She said that once he began to experience an emotion he could not bring it under control. His emotions often escalated to the point where their energy seemed to be "coming out through his pores." For example, when he began to feel angry or anxious, the intensity of these emotions grew to the point where he acted aggressively toward other children and adults, broke things, and could not sit still. Only when he sat on one of his parents' laps for an extended period, often rocking himself, did his emotional arousal eventually run its course.

When Jimmy was not anxious or angry, he was enjoyable to be with. He was warm toward his parents and extended family and had a sense of humor. Based on his ability to be friendly when not emotionally aroused, his parents worked with him extensively on ways to control his anxiety and anger. They believed that once he was better able to control his emotions, his positive qualities would show through more consistently. However, their efforts had only a small influence on his emotions and his behavior. He remained very sensitive to perceived criticism from others, particularly from other children; and his anxiety and anger flared in the face of minor problems, such as spilling a glass of milk at the dinner table.

Jimmy was nearly fearless in many situations. He created ramps for jumping his bicycle off high places, rode his skateboard down steep hills, and fought with older and bigger children with little apparent concern for his safety. His parents found that they often had to keep a close eye on him to prevent him from injuring himself.

His parents, who were dedicated to Jimmy and determined to help him overcome his emotional struggles, were strong advocates for him in the school system, where he was enrolled in a special education class for children with behavioral disabilities. They also encouraged him to participate in many community activities. They built on Jimmy's interests, such as skateboarding and karate, enrolling him in classes and giving him many opportunities to practice emerging skills with them and on his own. Eventually they also saw a therapist as a family. However, the first two therapists seemed ineffective, and their work with them was short-lived.

When Jimmy was 10, his parents reluctantly agreed with their third therapist, Dr. Flores, to give him Ritalin. Dr. Flores believed that Jimmy's hyperactive behaviors were probably due to one or more biologically based problems. He pointed out to Jimmy's parents that their behavioral interventions had changed Jimmy's behavior little, and he argued that this supported his belief that Jimmy's hyperactivity had a biological basis. He hypothesized that Jimmy's prenatal environment had been unhealthful and that it may have caused neurological problems that were influencing Jimmy's behavior. Dr. Flores also pointed out that Jimmy's bursts of anxiety or anger often followed some situation that had been created by his hyperactive behavior and suggested that reducing his hyperactivity would result in fewer problems with anxiety or anger.

The influence of the medication on Jimmy's hyperactive behavior was immediate and dramatic. For example, he ate dinner without spilling his milk and began using the table manners his parents had been teaching him for years. He engaged in fewer risky behaviors, which allowed his parents to stop monitoring his behavior so closely. He began to ask his parents before trying a new activity, and they were able to decide together how to engage in it safely. If his parents prohibited him from trying a new activity, he was better able to tolerate his frustration. In school, he sat at his desk for longer periods and completed more of his schoolwork. Although he continued to have problems with other children, the number of problems declined.

The medication did interrupt Jimmy's sleep. He found it difficult to fall asleep and often woke up early and moved around the house. His parents found this bothersome, but when they tried stopping the medication Jimmy's problems at home and at school escalated, so they decided to keep him on the medication. To handle Jimmy's early rising, they made videotapes of television shows he liked and let him watch them in his room from 5:00 to 6:00 each morning.

Overall, Jimmy and his parents were pleased with the effects of his medication. Jimmy reported that the medication kept him from getting so anxious and angry and made it easier for him to behave and stay out of trouble. He pointed with pride to what he could accomplish while on medication, and he believed that the medication allowed the "real" him to emerge.

Jimmy's parents remained concerned about the potential for long-term negative consequences to his health of taking Ritalin. They also found it difficult to accept that the medication seemed to have a greater influence on Jimmy's behavior than had their efforts as parents. Dr. Flores acknowledged their concerns. He pointed out that biologically based problems often require biologically based solutions, and he said they would continue to monitor Jimmy for any adverse health consequences from the medication. He also noted that it was while taking medication that Jimmy was able to behave in the ways they had been trying to teach him, suggesting that the combination of the medication and their dedication as parents had improved Jimmy's behavior so dramatically.

Jimmy continued to experience many social problems and still struggled to avoid being overwhelmed by anxiety and anger. He continued to present his parents and teachers with many challenges, and the medication did not eliminate the emotional problems that had their foundation in his early life. However, his parents and Jimmy were pleased with the role that the medication played in his life.

Some Issues Worth Noting

- The possible mixture of biological and early home environment effects in the development of Jimmy's ADHD.
- The difficulty the adoptive parents had with medication.
- The suddenness of Jimmy's behavioral changes.
- The lack of influence of the medication on important parts of Jimmy's life.

Case Study: Conflict over Taking Medication

Amy was the second child in a family of high achievers. Her parents were both successful attorneys and had active lives. They were often away from home for many hours each day; and aside from their jobs, both were involved in several community activities. Amy's father was active in their local chapter of the NAACP, and her mother was on the board of directors of their local Boys' and Girls' Clubs. Both sang in their church choir. When at home, they were often involved in several activities at the same time. Each year they hired a college student visiting the United States from an African country to help with child care. The parents believed that having the opportunity to interact with people from several countries would benefit Amy and her brother, who was 5 years older, and would help them learn about several African cultures.

Amy had been a more difficult infant and toddler than her brother, which dismayed her parents. She was more active than her brother and was more irritable. Her parents could not take their eyes off her when she was a toddler because she would run off into other areas of the house and occasionally break things while she was exploring them. Consequently, they had the succession of college students spend more time specifically watching Amy.

Amy was enrolled in a preschool at age 4. She was anxious about attending school but was comforted by her brother, who told her he had gone to the same school and had enjoyed it. He gave her suggestions about what to do and which types of toys to play with. Despite her brother's encouragement, Amy had difficulty adjusting to preschool. She found it difficult to sit still during reading and music times, and she often got up and looked around the room until a teacher insisted that she return to the activity. She had difficulty during nap time, often trying to talk with the children near her rather than sleep. This resulted in her being moved to an area of the room by herself for naps. She also had difficulty during free play periods. She wanted to play with other children, but she often barged into their activities. This made many of the other children avoid her. She got upset when the other children rebuffed her attempts to play with them and occasionally hit one of them when she was angry.

Her preschool teachers suggested that Amy's parents consult with their pediatrician about her behavior problems; the pediatrician suggested the possibility of Amy taking Ritalin to help her control her activity. Her parents were concerned about this but said that they were willing to give Amy Ritalin if they could be sure that it was helping her. The pediatrician said that would be easy: She would give them

10 numbered envelopes with three pills in each. Half the envelopes would contain Ritalin and half would contain a placebo, and only the pediatrician would know which was which. The parents would start with envelope number 1 and would give Amy a pill at 8:00 in the morning and 4:00 in the afternoon; the nurse at the preschool would give her a pill at noon. The parents would monitor Amy's behavior at home and would ask the preschool teachers to do the same during the day. At the end of the 10-day trial, everyone would report Amy's daily behavior to the pediatrician. If her behavior was better on the days when she took Ritalin, they could conclude that it was helping with her behavior.

At the end of the 10-day trial, Amy's behavior at school and at home was clearly better when she was taking Ritalin, although she seemed somewhat groggy when taking it. The pediatrician said she would prescribe a lower dose of Ritalin, which would probably lessen Amy's grogginess. The parents agreed, and Amy began taking Ritalin each day.

Amy was glad that she was in less trouble at school while taking medication, but she hated having to go to the nurse each day for a pill at noon. The other children believed that she went to the nurse to take a pill because she was "crazy," and they made fun of her. Amy occasionally refused to take her medication, and the nurse required that Amy stay with her until she complied. When Amy's behavior at school became more problematic, it was discovered that she had developed a trick of appearing to take her medication but actually hiding it in her cheek and then spitting it out. In response, the nurse began watching Amy swallow the medication and then looked in her mouth and under her tongue to make sure she had swallowed it. This made Amy even angrier about having to go to the nurse, and taking the medication seemed to develop into a battle of wills between the nurse and Amy.

Amy complained repeatedly to her parents about having to take her medication and about how the nurse treated her. Her parents consulted with the nurse about ways to reduce the tension around Amy taking her medication; but no matter what they tried, Amy remained defiant. Her parents began viewing the issue of Amy taking her medication as a battle between them and Amy, and they continued to require that she take it because they did not want to back down on such an important issue.

When Amy entered kindergarten, her parents consulted with the school nurse about giving Amy her medication each day. Although the medication continued to help Amy focus on her schoolwork and avoid problems with the other children in her class, it continued to be an area of conflict between her and her parents. However, her parents believed that the value of Amy taking her medication outweighed the problems it created in their relationship.

Some Issues Worth Noting

- Possible connections between the parents' high level of activity and Amy's hyperactivity.
- The difficulties that Amy's hyperactivity presented in school settings and during peer interactions.
- The extent to which the medication became a central issue in Amy's life.
- The growing possibility that taking the medication will harm the relationship between Amy and her parents.
- Whether Amy's early behaviors are developmentally appropriate or indications of ADHD.

History

Although ADHD has been recognized as a childhood problem for many years, beliefs about the core features of ADHD and its causes have changed frequently. The first written description of the disorder was in a children's book that featured Fidgity Phil and Harry Who Looks in the Air, written by the German psychiatrist Heinrich Hoffman in the mid-1800s. As you can guess from their names, these characters exhibited many behaviors that are now viewed as core features of ADHD (Wolraich, 1999).

The first significant medical interest in ADHD is usually traced to a series of lectures given by George Still in 1902 at the Royal College of Physicians (Stubbe, 2000; Wolraich, 1999). Still urged his colleagues to take an interest in a disorder that was characterized by restlessness, inattentiveness, and overarousal that he had observed in many children who were in institutional care. He argued that the disorder inhibited children from internalizing rules for appropriate behavior, which resulted in defects in "moral control" (Still, 1902, p.1008). By *moral control,* Still meant that the children could maintain appropriate behavior but chose not to (Rafalovich, 2001).

Beliefs about the causes of the restless and hyperactive behaviors described by Still changed around the time of World War I, based on observations of children and adults who experienced *encephalitis lethargica* after recovering from the flu (Rafalovich, 2001) (encephalitis is a swelling of the brain that can cause significant cognitive and physical problems). The behaviors of many who recovered from *encephalitis lethargica* included restlessness, inattention, impulsivity, and hyperactivity (Kennedy, 1924). The fact that these behaviors were exhibited by children who had recovered from a physical disease led to the hypothesis that the behaviors had a neurological basis—a hypothesis that, as we will see later in this chapter, has received considerable support from recent research.

Although hyperactivity in children continued to interest clinicians for many years, it was not until 1968 that it became a diagnosis in DSM II (APA, 1968). It was labeled **hyperkinetic impulse disorder,** showing that the core feature of the disorder was excessive, impulsive activity. Based largely on the research of Virginia Douglas and her colleagues in the 1970s, hypotheses about the core feature of ADHD changed from a focus on hyperactivity to a focus on problems with attention (Stubbe, 2000). Consequently, in the DSM-III (APA, 1980) the disorder was renamed **attention deficit disorder** (ADD), indicating that the core feature of the disorder was difficulty regulating attention and arousal. Children were diagnosed as having one of two subtypes: ADD or ADD with hyperactivity, depending on whether they had high levels of motor activity.

However, reviews of research when the next edition of the DSM was being compiled resulted in the conclusion that not enough evidence existed to support two distinct subtypes of ADD. Consequently, in the DSM-III-R the name of the disorder was changed to **attention-deficit hyperactivity disorder,** and the symptoms of the disorder were listed in one category—requiring that any eight symptoms of hyperactivity or inattentiveness be present for the disorder to be diagnosed (APA, 1987). No subtypes were included. Thus the core feature of the disorder was conceptualized as a combination of inattention and hyperactivity.

Further research (Lahey et al., 1988) determined that two clusters of ADHD symptoms existed: inattention and hyperactivity/impulsivity. Consequently, the DSM-IV (APA, 1994) labeled the disorder **attention-deficit/ hyperactivity disorder** (note the addition of the slash between *deficit* and *hyperactivity*) and recognized that the core features can be inattentiveness, hyperactivity/impulsivity, or both. Three subtypes were included: *predominantly inattentive type, predominantly hyperactive–impulsive type,* and *combined type* (Tannock, 1998).

Key Concepts

- The history of ADHD has been characterized by changes in beliefs about the fundamental characteristics of the disorder.
- The earliest conceptualizations of ADHD viewed it as a lack of moral control by children.
- Subsequent studies of children who had recovered from *encephalitis lethargica* suggested that hyperactive behavior was the result of a neurological problem.
- In the DSM, ADHD was first characterized as a disorder primarily of behavior, then of attention, then of a combination of behavior and attention, and now as either behavior or attention.

Diagnosis and Assessment

Diagnostic Criteria

As can be seen in Table 7.1, the diagnostic criteria for ADHD in the DSM-IV-TR include symptoms of (1) inattention, (2) hyperactivity/impulsivity, or both. A child who meets the criteria for both (1) and (2) can receive the diagnosis of **ADHD—combined type;** a child who meets the criteria for only (1) can receive the diagnosis of **ADHD—predominantly inattentive type;** and a child who meets the criteria for only (2) can receive the diagnosis of **ADHD—predominantly hyperactive–impulsive type.**

Several aspects of the diagnostic criteria for ADHD are worth noting. First, as can be seen in the descriptions of (1) and (2) and in criterion D, the child's behaviors must be both maladaptive and inconsistent with his or her developmental level. Consequently, a child who is very active, yet whose activity level does not create problems, would not meet the diagnostic criteria for ADHD. This is consistent with all disorders in the DSM: A person's behaviors must result in impaired functioning for a disorder to be diagnosed. Similarly, a child's developmental level must be considered when deciding whether his or her behaviors meet the diagnostic criteria for ADHD. For

T A B L E   7 . 1

Attention-Deficit/Hyperactivity Disorder

A. Either (1) or (2):

(1) Six (or more) of the following symptoms of **inattention** have persisted for at least six months to a degree that is maladaptive and inconsistent with developmental level:

Inattention

   (a) Often fails to give close attention to details or makes careless mistakes in schoolwork, work, or other activities.

   (b) Often has difficulty sustaining attention in tasks or play activities.

   (c) Often does not seem to listen when spoken to directly.

   (d) Often does not follow through on instructions and fails to finish schoolwork, chores, or duties in the workplace (not due to oppositional behavior or failure to understand instructions).

   (e) Often has difficulty organizing tasks and activities.

   (f) Often avoids, dislikes, or is reluctant to engage in tasks that require sustained mental effort (such as schoolwork or homework).

   (g) Often loses things necessary for tasks or activities (e.g., toys, school assignments, pencils, books, or tools).

   (h) Is often easily distracted by extraneous stimuli.

   (i) Is often forgetful in daily activities.

(2) Six (or more) of the following symptoms of **hyperactivity–impulsivity** have persisted for at least six months to a degree that is maladaptive and inconsistent with developmental level:

Hyperactivity

   (a) Often fidgets with hands or feet or squirms in seat.

   (b) Often leaves seat in classroom or in other situations in which remaining seated is expected.

   (c) Often runs about or climbs excessively in situations in which it is inappropriate (in adolescents or adults, may be limited to subjective feelings of restlessness).

   (d) Often has difficulty playing or engaging in leisure activities quietly.

   (e) Is often "on the go" or often acts as if "driven by a motor."

   (f) Often talks excessively.

Impulsivity

   (g) Often blurts out answers before questions have been completed.

   (h) Often has difficulty awaiting turn.

   (i) Often interrupts or intrudes on others (e.g., butts into conversations or games).

B. Some hyperactive–impulsive or inattentive symptoms that caused impairment were present before age 7 years.

C. Some impairment from the symptoms is present in two or more settings (e.g., at school [or work] and at home).

(continued)

TABLE 7.1

Attention-Deficit/Hyperactivity Disorder (*Continued*)

D. There must be clear evidence of clinically significant impairment in social, educational or occupational functioning.

E. The symptoms do not occur exclusively during the course of a Pervasive Developmental Disorder, Schizophrenia, or other Psychotic Disorder and are not better accounted for by another mental disorder (e.g., Mood Disorder, Anxiety Disorder, Dissociative Disorder, or a Personality Disorder).

Code based on type:

314.01   Attention-Deficit/Hyperactivity Disorder, Combined Type: if both Criteria A1 and A2 are met for the past six months

314.00   Attention-Deficit/Hyperactivity Disorder, Predominantly Inattentive Type: if Criterion A1 is met but Criterion A2 is not met for the past six months

314.01   Attention-Deficit/Hyperactivity Disorder, Predominantly Hyperactive–Impulsive Type: if Criterion A2 is met but Criterion A1 is not met for the past six months

Coding note: For individuals (especially adolescents and adults) who currently have symptoms that no longer meet full criteria, "In Partial Remission" should be specified.

example, because most 5-year-old children cannot focus on a task as long as most 10-year-olds, an attention level that might be a symptom of ADHD for a 10-year-old might not be a symptom for a 5-year-old. It is also worth noting that each behavior listed in (1) and (2) includes the term *often*. A child who occasionally exhibits some of the behaviors—perhaps when under stress or when overly excited—would not meet the diagnostic criteria for ADHD (although how frequently a behavior must occur for it to be present *often* is not specified).

Criterion C requires that the maladaptive behavior be present in more than one setting. This is a change from earlier versions of the DSM, which allowed a diagnosis of ADHD if significant symptoms occurred in only one setting (such as at school). This criterion may be included because it is likely that the behavior of a child with problems in only one setting is being influenced primarily by characteristics of the setting rather than by a disorder experienced by the child.

Controversial and Unresolved Issues

Controversies exist about several basic characteristics of ADHD. As described in the previous section, the diagnostic criteria for ADHD have changed in each edition of the DSM. As we see in this section, controversies about the current diagnostic criteria may mean that they will change in future editions.

Age of Onset

Criterion B requires that some symptoms causing impairment be present before age 7. No clear explanation for this specific age criterion exists. There is some evidence that it may be inappropriate: Some children with ADHD symptoms do not show impairments before age 7 (Barkley, 2003). For example, in a study of 380 children diagnosed with ADHD, their parents and teachers were interviewed regarding the earliest age at which their ADHD symptoms created an impairment (Applegate et al., 1997). Whereas 98% of those with the predominantly hyperactive–impulsive type had experienced impairment before the age of 7, only 82% of those with the combined type and 57% of those with the predominantly inattentive type had experienced impairment before the age of 7. Technically, then, 18% of those with the combined type and 43% of those with the predominantly inattentive type should not have received the diagnosis of ADHD (the researchers noted that the clinicians who gave the diagnoses appeared to have ignored the age criterion). This research suggests that the age-of-onset criterion may need to be changed or eliminated.

Distinguishing the Predominantly Inattentive Type from the Other Types

Several researchers have argued that the predominantly inattentive type of ADHD is distinct enough from the other two types to be considered a separate disorder (Barkley, 2003; Milich, Balentine, & Lynam, 2001). Support for this argument comes mainly from research showing that children with the predominantly inattentive type have characteristics that are distinct from children with the other types. For example, those with the predominantly inattentive type are more likely to be described as "sluggish," "hypoactive," and "lost in space," whereas those with the other types are described as "hyperactive," "distractible," and "disinhibited" (Milich et al., 2001, p. 480). As just described, there is some evidence that the age of onset of the symptoms of ADHD is different for the subtypes. In addition, those with the combined and predominantly hyperactive–impulsive subtypes are more likely to have comorbid conduct problems and to be rejected by their peers, whereas those with the predominantly inattentive type are more likely to experience anxiety and depression and to be neglected by their peers (Maedgen & Carlson, 2000). Finally, those with the predominantly inattentive type are less likely to respond to medication that those with the other types (DuPaul, Barkley, & McMurray, 1991).

As discussed in the chapter about classification and diagnosis, determining whether one set of characteristics differs sufficiently from another set to support establishing separate disorders is both a science and an art. It remains to be seen whether those who create future editions of the DSM will decide that the predominantly inattentive type is distinct enough from the others to be considered a separate disorder. However this is resolved in the future, important differences among the three types exist.

Comorbidity with Conduct Disorder and Oppositional Defiant Disorder

Another ongoing controversy is whether children who have ADHD and either conduct disorder or oppositional defiant disorder should be considered as having a disorder that is distinct from those who meet only the diagnostic criteria for ADHD. This is an important issue because of the large percentage of children with ADHD who also meet the diagnostic criteria for conduct disorder or oppositional defiant disorder. Across various studies, about 40–70% of children with ADHD have either conduct disorder or oppositional defiant disorder, and about 40–60% of children with conduct disorder or oppositional defiant disorder also have ADHD (Banaschewski et al., 2003).

All editions of the DSM have considered ADHD, conduct disorder, and oppositional defiant disorder as distinct disorders. However, the system for classifying diseases used primarily in Europe and Great Britain, the World Health Organization's *International Classification of Diseases,* **10th edition (ICD-10)** (1992), has one diagnosis of *hyperkinetic disorder* (symptoms of ADHD only) and a separate diagnosis of *hyperkinetic conduct disorder* (symptoms of both ADHD and conduct disorder/oppositional defiant disorder).

Banaschewski and colleagues (2003) suggest three possibilities for understanding the relationship (if any) between ADHD and conduct disorder/oppositional defiant disorder:

- ADHD-only and ADHD with conduct disorder/oppositional defiant disorder are manifestations of the same underlying disorder; environmental differences determine which children show just ADHD symptoms, which show just conduct disorder/oppositional defiant disorder symptoms, and which show both groups of symptoms.
- Three distinct disorders exist: ADHD, conduct disorder, and oppositional defiant disorder. Their high comorbidity is partly due to ADHD increasing a child's risk of developing conduct disorder or oppositional defiant disorder. (ADHD develops before conduct disorder or oppositional defiant disorder in most cases, suggesting that conduct disorder and oppositional defiant disorder are not risk factors for ADHD.)
- Four distinct disorders exist: ADHD with conduct disorder/oppositional defiant disorder, ADHD-only, conduct disorder, and oppositional defiant disorder.

Research showing distinct characteristics of children with ADHD and children with conduct disorder or oppositional defiant disorder suggests that the first possibility is probably not correct (Newcorn & Halperin, 2000). For example, many children with ADHD have a history of developmental problems and cognitive impairments; many children with conduct disorder/oppositional defiant disorder have a history of family adversity and criminality; and many children with both ADHD and conduct disorder/oppositional defiant disorder have a history including all four of these characteristics. Finally, children who have ADHD with conduct disorder/oppositional defiant disorder often present a more severe clinical picture and have poorer long-term outcomes than children with ADHD-only (Banaschewski et al., 2003).

Some recent evidence suggests that the third possibility just listed may be better than the second. Banaschewski and colleagues (2003) used the continuous performance test (discussed later in this chapter) to compare children with the combined type of ADHD-only to (1) children who had both ADHD and conduct disorder/oppositional defiant disorder and (2) children with none of these disorders. They measured brain functioning through **event-related potentials,** which measure electrical activity in the brain during a task. They found that children with ADHD-only showed more delayed response times than those in the other groups. If ADHD, conduct disorder, and oppositional defiant disorder were distinct disorders, we would not expect to find that those with ADHD-only had slower response times than those with ADHD and conduct disorder/oppositional defiant disorder because both groups have ADHD. This suggested to the researchers that ADHD-only is a disorder distinct from ADHD with conduct disorder/oppositional defiant disorder. Although firm conclusions cannot be drawn from this one study, it does suggest that the ICD-10 diagnostic criteria may be better than the DSM-IV-TR diagnostic criteria—a hypothesis that will need to be addressed through future research.

Determining that an Individual Child Has ADHD

Determining which children meet the diagnostic criteria for ADHD can be a complicated process. As with many childhood disorders, no biological indications of ADHD exist, requiring that the determination be based on judgments about a child's behavior (Scahill & Schwab-Stone, 2000). Because judgments about the developmental appropriateness of a child's behavior and about the impairment a child experiences from the behavior must be made, one professional might decide that a particular child meets the criteria for ADHD and another professional might decide that the same child does not meet the criteria. At this stage in our knowledge about ADHD, this level of diagnostic ambiguity is unavoidable.

The information available to a clinician who is assessing a child who may have ADHD can come from several sources, and information from each of them has strengths and limitations. Direct observations can be made by a trained professional in the child's classroom or home. An advantage of this approach is the clinician's knowledge of behavioral norms and his or her ability to apply these norms while observing the child in the child's natural environment. However, direct observations are expensive and can focus on a child's behavior only for an hour or two in one or two settings. Consequently, clinicians often rely heavily or exclusively on reports of a child's behavior from parents or teachers, who may be asked to describe the child's behavior or to complete one or more behavioral rating scales (some items from a behavioral rating scale, the Connor's Rating Scale, are included in Table 7.2).

Asking parents to report on the behavior of their children has several potential advantages. Parents usually know their children and their developmental histories better than others (Wolraich, 1999). In addition, many parents have

TABLE 7.2

Items from the ADHD Subscale of the Connor's Rating Scale*

Excitable, impulsive
Restless in the "squirmy" sense
Destructive
Fails to finish things
Distractibility or attention span a problem
Mood changes quickly and drastically
Easily frustrated in efforts
Disturbs other children

*All items are rated on a four-point scale, from "not at all" to "very much."

direct knowledge of their children's behaviors in several settings. A potential problem with parent reports is that most parents have limited experience with children, so they may not know whether their children's behavior is developmentally appropriate. A parent with inappropriate expectations of the ability of a 6-year-old to sit still for long periods, for example, may report that the activity level of her child is too high.

Gathering information from teachers also has potential advantages. Teachers have more experience with children and so may be better than a parent at determining whether a child's behavior is developmentally appropriate. In addition, teachers interact with children in a more structured environment than parents, and many children with ADHD have particular problems in structured settings. However, teachers may also have inappropriate expectations for the children in their class and may be more likely to report inappropriately high levels of activity for a child who is a source of aggravation.

Because of the advantages and disadvantages of the various ways of gathering information about a child's behaviors, it is often recommended that information from several sources be considered by the clinician making the diagnosis. However, this recommendation is often not followed, and many diagnoses are made based on the reports of parents alone (Wolraich, 1999).

Determining whether preschool children meet the criteria for a diagnosis of ADHD can be particularly complicated (Connor, 2002). The ability to maintain attention and suppress activity develops at an earlier age for some children and a later age for others; so it can be ambiguous whether a preschool child's inability to control activity and attention levels reflects a lag in his or her development or the presence of ADHD. In addition, many preschool children experience transient problems with attention or activity that resolve on their own (Shepard, Carter, & Cohen, 2000). Thus it can be unclear whether a child's problems with attention and activity are transient or indicate the presence of ADHD. Because of these complications, the diagnosis of ADHD in young children must be made carefully and tentatively. Unfortunately this is often not what occurs, and many young children receive the diagnosis of ADHD and are put on medication earlier in life than is appropriate (Wolraich, 1999).

Two studies show that issues other than children's behaviors may influence whether they receive a diagnosis of ADHD. Mann and colleagues (1992) asked experienced clinicians from several countries to rate videotapes of children's behavior and found differences in the percentages of the children who were rated as hyperactive based on the nationalities of the raters. Stevens (1981) had school psychologists, parents, and teachers watch videotapes of children from several ethnic groups and read "biographies" of the children. The biographies varied systematically so that each child was described as coming from a low-income family to some raters and a middle-income family to others, with all other characteristics of the child and family remaining the same. When they were described as coming from a low-income family, children were more likely to be rated as hyperactive than when the same children were described as coming from a middle-income family. These studies raise concern that cultural expectations, beliefs, and biases of raters may cause some children to be diagnosed with ADHD inappropriately.

Key Concepts

- The diagnostic criteria for ADHD are divided into two groups: those involving problems with hyperactivity–impulsivity and those involving problems with attention.
- Impairments from the symptoms of ADHD must be present before the age of 7. This criterion is controversial because some children showing impairments do not exhibit them before that age.
- Many children with ADHD also meet the diagnostic criteria for conduct disorder or oppositional defiant disorder, and some evidence suggests that ADHD with conduct disorder/oppositional defiant disorder is distinct from ADHD alone.
- Some evidence suggests that the predominantly inattentive type is a disorder distinct from the predominantly hyperactive–impulsive and combined types.
- ADHD is diagnosed through reports about a child's behavior. These reports commonly come from parents and may also come from teachers, from the child, or from direct observations of the child's behavior.
- Determining whether preschool children meet the diagnostic criteria for ADHD is often more complicated than for older children.

Characteristics and Experiences of Children with Attention-Deficit/Hyperactivity Disorder

Children with ADHD have a variety of characteristics and experiences that differ from those of other children. Before exploring these, we should note two issues that complicate the process of drawing conclusions about them. First, many studies of children with ADHD have included those who have

ADHD and conduct disorder or oppositional defiant disorder. Consequently, identifying the characteristics specifically associated with ADHD may be difficult. Second, some studies do not distinguish between the characteristics of children with the various types of ADHD, which can make it difficult to know whether certain characteristics are common among all children with ADHD or only those with a particular type. Notably, children with the predominantly inattentive type are often not distinguished from those with the other two types, even though, as just discussed, there is some evidence that their characteristics are often distinct (Hodgens, Cole, & Boldizar, 2000; Maedgen & Carlson, 2000).

Core Features of ADHD
Hyperactivity–Impulsivity

Many behaviors of children with ADHD have both a hyperactive and an impulsive component, so hyperactivity and impulsivity are often considered as one dimension of their behavior; for example, a child who rushes to the teacher's desk to ask a question unrelated to a test she is taking is engaging in excess activity (getting out of her seat) that is impulsive (asking the question as soon as it comes to mind). Children with ADHD have problems with hyperactivity–impulsivity in many settings, and their parents and teachers often describe them as running with their "motor" at full speed (APA, 2000). For example, they may be frequently out of their seats in school, out of their seats several times during dinner, and pacing around outside the dugout rather than waiting for their turn at bat during a Little League game. If they are seated, they may be tapping pencils, slapping their legs, or looking around the room to see what others are doing.

Such hyperactivity–impulsivity often influences their social interactions. They often find it hard to play a game to its conclusion, may interrupt when others are talking, and have difficulty waiting their turn. They may act impulsively on their emotions, such as hitting someone when angry or running from the classroom when upset.

Although some of their hyperactive–impulsive behaviors can be relatively benign, such as blurting out answers in school, others can be more dangerous, such as skateboarding down a steep street. As a result, children with ADHD sustain more physical injuries than other children and have more emergency room visits (Barkley, 2003). Similarly, adolescents and young adults with ADHD are more likely to be in automobile accidents, to receive citations for speeding, and to have their drivers' licenses suspended than are other adolescents and young adults (Woodward, Fergusson, & Horwood, 2000).

A variety of situational factors influence the levels of hyperactivity and impulsivity in children with ADHD (APA, 2000). They experience more problems during tasks involving persistence than those that can be finished quickly (for example, completing homework is more of a problem than taking out the garbage); and they are more active in situations where they are under scrutiny than when they are on their own or with one or two familiar people (they may create more problems in a restaurant than they do eating lunch at home with a parent). They have more difficulty controlling their behavior in situations requiring consistent restraint than they do in situations allowing more freedom of behavior (they are less able to control themselves in the classroom than at recess). In summary, they appear to have more difficulty in situations where they are expected to be quiet and behave, and fewer problems when they have more freedom to choose what to do.

Inattention

Many children with ADHD have difficulty attending to what is going on about them or to tasks they are required to complete (Van der Meere, Shalev, Burger, & Gross-Tsur, 1995). Although hyperactivity can contribute to some children's difficulty with attention, children with ADHD often have difficulty attending even when they are not being physically active.

Children with ADHD may act impulsively in ways that endanger their health.

Research by cognitive psychologists has shown that there are several components to attention (Van der Meere et al., 1995). Most children with ADHD appear to have primary difficulty with one of these components—sustained attention:

- **Orientation and reorientation:** During many tasks a person must orient to relevant stimuli and reorient to relevant stimuli after attention has been drawn away from them. Laboratory studies have found no differences in these abilities between children with ADHD and other children.
- **Capacity:** Each of us can attend to and maintain in our working memory only a limited amount of information. Children with ADHD can maintain the same amount of material in their working memory as other children.
- **Focused attention** (or the opposite, **distractibility**): Focused attention is a person's ability to maintain attention on relevant material despite experiencing distractions from irrelevant stimuli (for example, maintaining your focus on reading this text despite the noise going on around you in the library). Although it was once assumed that children with ADHD were more distractible than other children, a variety of laboratory studies have shown that they are not. In addition, children with ADHD who are taking the medication MPH are no less distractible than children with ADHD who are not taking medication. This also suggests that children with ADHD do not have problems with distractibility: The medication that treats ADHD successfully should significantly influence their distractibility if it were an important component of their attention problems.
- **Sustained attention:** Sustained attention is a person's ability to maintain attention on a task over time, even though the person might want to switch attention to something else (by this point in the day, for example, you might want to switch your attention from the task of reading this textbook to something more enjoyable). Sustained attention is the component of attention with which most children who have ADHD struggle. However, as Van der Meere and colleagues (1995) point out, the issue of sustained attention is even more complex. Laboratory studies have shown that when relevant stimuli are presented frequently during a task, children with ADHD can sustain their attention as well as other children their age. However, if the relevant stimuli are presented infrequently, children with ADHD show a significant deficit in sustained attention. Thus they may be able to sustain attention as well as other children when playing soccer as a forward or defender (relevant stimuli occur frequently) but not as a goalie (relevant stimuli are less frequent). Similarly, they may be able to sustain attention when they are working with one other child on multiplication flashcards (every other flashcard is relevant for them) but not if all students in the room are participating (only every 20th flashcard is relevant for them).

Associated Features
Peer Relationships

A consistent finding of research with children who have ADHD is that many of them have significant problems with peer relationships. Guevremont and Dumas (1994), for example, found that about 50% of children with ADHD had significant peer problems—about twice the percentage of other children.

A characteristic that strongly influences the peer relationships of many children with ADHD is aggression. On average, children with ADHD are more aggressive than other children, and those with the combined and predominantly hyperactive–impulsive types are most likely to be aggressive (Hodgens et al., 2000; Maedgen & Carlson, 2000; Stormont, 2001). Most children do not like aggressive peers and avoid them or actively reject them (Coie & Dodge, 1983). In addition, children with ADHD are more likely than other children to be aggressive for no apparent reason or to engage in instrumental aggression, and this type of aggression is particularly distasteful to other children (Stormont, 2001). Consequently, children with ADHD who are aggressive are often shunned by their peers.

Why are children with ADHD more aggressive? Most children have a negative reaction to boisterous and trouble-making behaviors, but many children with ADHD enjoy those behaviors in themselves and others and so are more likely to engage in them (Nixon, 2001). In addition, they tend to have fewer potential responses to social situations than other children and are more likely to choose an aggressive response in a variety of social situations (Bloomquist, August, Cohen, & Doyle, 1997; Stormont, 2001).

It is not only aggression that leads to poor peer relationships for many children with ADHD. They are also more disruptive in class and in social situations than other children, which contributes to their rejection by others, even when they are not being aggressive (Nixon, 2001; Taylor, Chadwick, Heptinstall, & Danckaerts, 1996). In addition, when children with ADHD join activities with other children they are more likely to engage in behaviors that call attention to themselves (talking loudly, interrupting other children), that try to change the focus of the group activity (trying to insert new rules into an activity), or that encourage others to engage in prohibited activities (insisting that they play in a prohibited area) (Whalen & Kenker, 1985). These types of intrusions are unwelcome and bothersome to most children.

Another possible reason for their difficult peer relationships is that many children with ADHD view their interactions with peers more positively than their peers view them (Diener & Milich, 1997). They often believe that their social interactions are going well while other children find them troubling. Consequently, children with ADHD often have little motivation to try to improve their social interactions.

The few studies that have focused on children with the predominantly inattentive type of ADHD have found that they are more socially withdrawn than other children. Although this usually does not result in other children actively rejecting or disliking them, it does curtail their social interactions with others so they have fewer friends (Hodgens et al., 2000; Maedgen & Carlson, 2000).

Academic Achievement

As a group, children with all types of ADHD achieve less in academic settings than other children: They score lower on standardized tests, receive worse grades, and are more likely to be retained (Carlson & Mann, 2000). Several issues can influence their poor academic performance. Many children with ADHD are behind their peers academically even in preschool, so they begin elementary school with inferior academic skills (Barkley, 2003). Their difficulty with attention and their excess activity may result in their falling farther behind as they continue their schooling. The conflicted relationships that many children with ADHD have with their teachers may further influence their academic performance: They may find school frustrating and bothersome, and their teachers may spend less time helping them with their academic work (Stormont, 2001).

Another contributor to lower academic achievement is that many children with ADHD have lower scores on intelligence tests than their classroom peers and lower scores than their siblings who do not have ADHD (averaging 7–10 points) (Stormont, 2001). Because the scores received on most intelligence tests are partly based on acquired knowledge, some differences in intelligence may be a result of children with ADHD having learned less than other children. However, the neurological issues that influence the development of ADHD may also influence children's intelligence (Barkley, 2003).

Children with the predominantly inattentive type of ADHD have difficulty sustaining their attention, particularly on tasks they find boring.

Consequently, perhaps the lower academic performance of children with ADHD is due partly to a somewhat lower level of intelligence.

Notes from the Author: The Energy Needed to *Not* Behave

Most of us find it easy to obey the parental admonition to "behave yourself" (with occasional lapses that we often regret later). This can make it difficult for us to understand that behaving properly can be a difficult, energy-consuming task for some children. During graduate school, one of my clinical placements was in a family practice clinic at the University of Virginia Medical Center. One case I observed was with a family of two parents and two brothers who had been adopted when they were 3 and 4 years old. The older boy, who was 13 when I was observing the family, was diagnosed with ADHD. His parents did not want him placed on medication and had worked with him over the years to help him control his hyperactive and impulsive behaviors. He was a polite, pleasant, cheerful boy who clearly loved his family and was loved by them. However, he had great difficulty sitting still, even for the one-hour therapy session.

During one therapy session, I was interested to hear that he often had a nap after school. It seemed odd that a boy who was so active could sleep in the middle of the afternoon. The reason for the naps became apparent, however, as he described how exhausted he was at the end of the school day. He was exhausted because of the effort that he expended trying to behave. The effort that you or I might expend constantly getting out of our seats and dashing around a classroom was equivalent to what he expended trying to keep himself in his chair and focused on his schoolwork. It took huge amounts of energy for him *not* to move. Hearing him describe how exhausting it was to behave gave me a new appreciation of the challenges faced by many children with ADHD.

Motor Skills

Many children with ADHD have problems with physical coordination and with gross motor and fine motor skills (Barkley, 2003). They have more difficulty with balance, with coordinated large muscle movements, and with fine motor skills such as writing. Thus children with ADHD may be less successful in playground games or in sports, which may influence their peer relationships; and they may have difficulty writing or speaking clearly, which may influence their academic performance.

Other Forms of Psychopathology

As described earlier, a high comorbidity exists between ADHD and conduct disorder/oppositional defiant disorder. In addition, children with ADHD are about three times more likely to experience an anxiety disorder and five times more likely to experience a depressive disorder than other children (Angold, Colstello, & Erkanli, 1999). It is not clear whether problems with anxiety and depression develop in response to the issues that children with ADHD face (perhaps a child with ADHD becomes depressed because of his poor relationships with peers and adults) or whether these disorders develop for other reasons. Families of children with ADHD are more likely to have members with depression or anxiety disorders, suggesting that there may be some genetically based increased liability for anxiety and depression in children with ADHD (Biederman, Mick, & Farone, 1998). This liability by itself, or with the stressors that children with ADHD experience, may lead to a higher likelihood of them developing an anxiety or depressive disorder.

Key Concepts

- Hyperactive children often find it difficult to sit still and may engage in a variety of impulsive behaviors. They have more difficulty maintaining acceptable behavior in situations requiring extended control and when they are under others' scrutiny.
- Attention problems in children with ADHD are primarily due to problems with sustained attention.
- Many children with ADHD experience significant problems in peer relationships. Many children with the predominantly inattentive type are withdrawn and may be neglected by their peers. Many children with the other types are aggressive and are often actively rejected by other children.
- Children with ADHD have poorer academic achievement than other children, which may be partly due to a lower level of intelligence.
- Some children with ADHD have difficulties with gross motor skills, coordination and balance, and fine motor skills.
- Many children with ADHD also experience a mood disorder, anxiety disorder, or conduct disorder.

Prevalence

As noted in the introduction to this chapter, ADHD is one of the most frequently diagnosed childhood disorders. To estimate the prevalence of ADHD, Scahill and Schwab-Stone (2000) reviewed 13 studies that assessed the prevalence of ADHD in school-age children. The prevalence rates varied widely across the studies, from 2% to 14%, and it was unclear why so much variation existed. Scahill and Schwab-Stone concluded that the best estimate for the prevalence of ADHD is between 5% and 10% for school-age children. A few researchers have examined the prevalence of ADHD among preschool children and have found rates of between 3% and 6%, suggesting that fewer preschool than school-age children have ADHD (Egger & Angold, 2006).

Recent studies from several countries also show a wide range of prevalence estimates for ADHD: 4% of Dutch 6- to 8-year-olds, 5% of Chinese

6- to 11-year-olds, 6% of Brazilian 12- to 14-year-olds, 15% of Colombian 4- to 17-year-olds, 15% of children from the United Arab Emirates, and 20% of Ukrainian 10- to 12-year-olds (Barkley, 2003). The differences are probably due to a variety of factors, such as different sources of information about the children's behaviors (observations, parent reports) and different cultural beliefs about the level of inattention or hyperactivity required for a child to be experiencing an impairment. These studies show, however, that the types of behaviors that are symptoms of ADHD are present in children from many cultures.

Boys are more likely than girls to be diagnosed with ADHD. In community samples, the ratio of boys to girls is about 3:1 (Gaub & Carlson, 1997). One study suggested that there are sex differences by type of ADHD, with the ratio of boys to girls being about 2:1 for the predominantly inattentive type and 5:1 for the predominantly hyperactive–impulsive type (Baumgaertel, Wolraich, & Deitrich, 1995). When samples of children referred to counseling clinics are examined, a much higher ratio of boys to girls with ADHD is found—between 6:1 and 9:1 in various studies (Gaub & Carlson, 1997). A comparison of the ratios from community and clinical samples suggests that boys with ADHD are more likely than girls to be referred for counseling services. Perhaps the behaviors of boys with ADHD are more noticeable and troubling to adults, increasing the chance of their being referred for counseling.

Course

Symptom Onset

The first symptoms of ADHD appear during the preschool years for most children, and they are usually related to hyperactivity rather than inattention. In many children, symptoms appear 2½ years or so before they become serious enough to constitute an impairment (Jensen, Martin, & Cantwell, 1997a). Thus many children show symptoms of hyperactivity years before the symptoms become severe enough to warrant a diagnosis of ADHD.

Children with the predominantly hyperactive–impulsive type of ADHD show clinically significant symptoms at an earlier age than those with the other two types (Barkley, 2003). Applegate and colleagues (1997), for example, found that the average ages of children when their symptoms became severe enough to be considered an impairment were 4.2 years for the predominantly hyperactive–impulsive type, 4.9 years for the combined type, and 6.1 years for the predominantly inattentive type. However, it is unclear whether these age differences are caused by true differences in the ages of symptom onset or whether they reflect which behaviors adults are more likely to notice in children of various ages. A child who is hyperactive may be more noticeable early in life because most adults expect children to be able to sit still in certain situations even at a young age. Problems with attention may not be noticed until a child enters kindergarten or first grade, when tasks requiring attention become more common. Despite these issues, it is clear that the symptoms of ADHD appear early in the lives of most children who eventually receive a diagnosis of ADHD.

Ongoing Development

Once the symptoms of ADHD emerge in early childhood, they are usually chronic unless some type of intervention occurs. In addition, many children who exhibit problems with hyperactivity–impulsivity early in their lives begin to show problems with attention as they enter school. As already noted, many also begin to show symptoms of oppositional defiant disorder and conduct disorder. Thus many children with early symptoms of ADHD experience a worsening of these symptoms and of their overall functioning during their early school-age years (Barkley, 2003).

Although more boys than girls are diagnosed with ADHD, girls are more likely than boys to experience increasing levels of problems during their school-age years. For example, the percentage of girls with ADHD who become rejected by their peers increases during the school-age years, while the percentage of boys stays about the same. In addition, many girls do more poorly on neurocognitive tasks as they proceed through their school-age years, while boys tend to improve (Gaub & Carlson, 1997). The changes in peer relationships may be influenced by societal expectations that girls are quieter and less active than boys. Consequently, girls who are overactive and possibly aggressive may be more troublesome to their peers than boys. The reasons for the changes in neurocognitive functioning remain unclear.

It was once thought that ADHD ended for most children when they entered adolescence (the hypothesis then was that the biological changes associated with puberty caused the disorder to end). However, it is now clear that ADHD continues into adolescence for many children (Gingerich, Turnock, Litfin, & Rosen, 1998). Children whose ADHD symptoms appear at an earlier age are more likely to continue to experience ADHD into adolescence (Jensen, Mrazek, & Knapp, 1997b). Perhaps ADHD that starts earlier in life is more severe than ADHD that starts later (a pattern seen in other disorders such as schizophrenia and bipolar disorder), which may influence why earlier-onset ADHD is more likely to persist. Children who have ADHD with conduct disorder/oppositional defiant disorder are more likely to experience continuing problems into adolescence (Jensen et al., 1997b). Perhaps these children have fewer opportunities to learn to cope with their ADHD symptoms because they have alienated parents, teachers, or peers who might help them. Alternately, as discussed previously, ADHD with conduct disorder/oppositional defiant disorder may be a distinct or more chronic disorder than ADHD alone.

Only a few studies have followed children diagnosed with ADHD into adulthood (Barkley, Fischer, Smallish, & Fletcher, 2006; Hechtman, 1996; Mannuzza & Klein, 2000). They found that although most adults who had ADHD as children were leading successful lives, on average they completed fewer years of schooling, were more likely to have not graduated from high school, had lower-status occupations, were more likely to be fired from a job, had more difficulties at home, and reported lower levels of self-esteem than other adults. Consequently, it appears that the consequences of ADHD significantly influence the entire lives of some people.

Key Concepts

- The prevalence of ADHD is currently thought to be between 5% and 10% of school-age children.
- ADHD appears in cultures throughout the world, and boys are more likely than girls to have ADHD.
- Initial symptoms of ADHD appear in many children about 2½ years before impairments significant enough to warrant a diagnosis of ADHD occur.
- Impairments with hyperactivity–impulsivity appear earlier (around age 4) than do impairments with inattention (around age 6).
- Many girls with ADHD experience increasing impairment during their school-age years while the impairment for most boys remains about the same.
- Symptoms of ADHD continue into adolescence for many children. Children experiencing an earlier onset of symptoms or comorbid conduct disorder/oppositional defiant disorder are more likely to continue to experience ADHD into adolescence.
- Most adults who had ADHD as children are successful, but they often have lower academic achievement and lower-paying jobs than do those who did not have ADHD.

Families of Children with ADHD

As one can imagine from the description of the characteristics and experiences of children with ADHD, many of them present ongoing challenges to their parents and siblings. Families with a child who has ADHD experience more stress and conflict than other families, and parents experience more daily hassles such as attending meetings with their child's teacher and breaking up conflicts between siblings (Hankin, 2001; Johnston & Mash, 2001).

Some differences in parent reports of stress can be seen when subgroups of children with ADHD are considered separately. Families with a child diagnosed with ADHD alone experience less stress and conflict than do families with a child who has ADHD and conduct disorder/oppositional defiant disorder; and families of children with the combined type experience more stress and conflict than do families with a child who has the predominantly inattentive type (Paternite, Loney, & Roberts, 1996). These differences may be influenced by the aggression and lack of compliance that are more common among children with ADHD and conduct disorder/oppositional defiant disorder and among those with the combined and predominantly hyperactive–impulsive types (Danforth, Barkley, & Stokes, 1991).

Possibly because of this stress and conflict, many parents of children with ADHD view their competence as parents more negatively than do other parents. In addition, they are more likely to view their children's misbehavior as a stable characteristic over which they have little control (Johnson, 2000; Johnston, Reynolds, Freeman, & Geller, 1998). The combination of their sensed lack of competence and their belief that they have little control over their children's behavior can cause parents to spend less time with their children and less time helping them develop good social skills. This can result in poorer behavior in the children and a corresponding increase in the sense of frustration and lack of competence in the parents, creating a gradually widening gulf between the parents and children.

Observations of Parent–Child Interactions

A large body of research has accumulated over the past few decades on the interactions between parents and their children with ADHD, based on observational studies of parent–child dyads at home or in a laboratory. During these studies, the parent and child are typically seated in a room alone and asked to engage in a structured task (like building something together), an unstructured task (such as free play for the child), and one or more other activities. The results of these studies consistently show that children with ADHD are less compliant with parental instructions than other children; they comply for shorter periods when they do comply; and they engage in more negative behaviors (Danforth et al., 1991; DuPaul et al., 2001). As one might expect, they are less compliant during structured tasks than unstructured tasks. In addition, children with ADHD and conduct disorder/oppositional defiant disorder are less compliant and engage in more negative behaviors than do children with ADHD alone (Johnston & Mash, 2001).

The most common behavior pattern of the parents of children with ADHD during these observations is to focus negative attention on their children when they misbehave and to give them little attention when they behave (Danforth et al., 1991; DuPaul et al., 2001). Overall, it appears as if the parents believe that they must actively control their children when they are behaving badly and that they can "take a break" when their children are behaving well. A potential problem with this style, however, is that it can create a pattern of interactions that are almost always negative.

Given the negative quality of their interactions, one might expect that children with ADHD would be less engaged with their parents. However, this is not what most studies find. Rather, children with ADHD spend less time working independently, even during unstructured tasks, and spend more time near their parents, asking questions, making comments, and trying to engage their parents (Danforth et al., 1991). However, as just noted, this engagement is often negative.

Notes from the Author: Changing Parents' Attention from the Negative to the Positive

In most of my therapy cases with a child who has behavior problems, I work with the parents and child to develop a behavior chart—usually posted on the refrigerator—designed to track and reward appropriate behavior by the child. For example, a child might receive a check each morning, afternoon, and evening that he does not talk back to his parents, and he might be able to stay up a half hour later on a weekend night whenever he accumulates 10 checks.

There are many potential benefits to this intervention. The child's behavior often changes in a positive way; the child realizes he or she can control his or her behavior; and the parents realize they can influence the behaviors of their child. However, I believe the most important benefit is that the intervention changes the focus of the parents' interactions with the child from consistently negative interactions to more positive interactions. On good days, the parent will put several checks on the list—reminding the parent that the child is behaving and reminding the child that the parent is noticing his or her good behavior. As noted in this section, it is easy for parents of children with behavior problems to slip into a pattern of responding harshly when the child misbehaves and ignoring the child when he behaves. An important goal of therapy with many of these families is to interrupt this pattern by helping the parents provide more praise for good behavior and less correction for poor behavior. This often increases the child's positive behaviors and improves the relationship between the child and parents.

Evidence suggests that the negative parenting style of parents who have a child with ADHD is influenced by their child's behaviors rather than the child's behaviors being influenced by the parenting style. For example, several studies compared child and maternal behaviors during laboratory tasks when the children were receiving medication for ADHD and when they were not (Barkley & Cunningham, 1979; Humphries, Kinsborne, & Swanson, 1978). When children were taking medication, they complied more with parental requests, engaged in fewer negative behaviors, and worked independently for longer periods. At the same time, the mothers gave fewer directions, praised their children's accomplishments more, and spent more time observing their children than interacting negatively with them. Because the impetus for the behavior change in these studies was the medication given to the child, it appears that the child's changed behavior influenced the mother's change in behavior.

The overall picture, then, of many families who have a child with ADHD is one in which the child's behaviors increase parental stress and reduce the parents' sense of competence, which in turn can influence the parents' negative affect and parenting style, which can increase the child's problem behaviors. A cycle of difficulty is created in which all family members may feel a sense of frustration and bewilderment (see Figure 7.1).

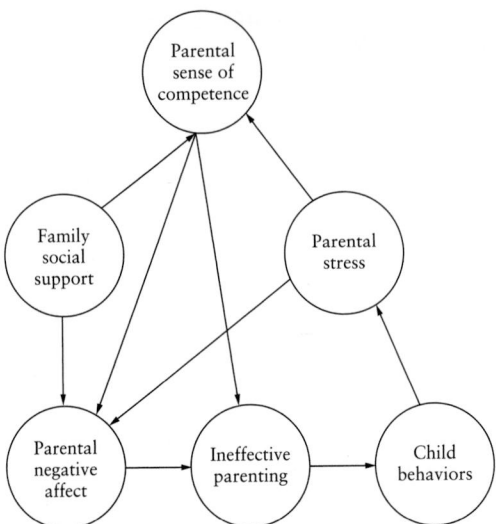

FIGURE 7.1   *Reciprocal Influences of Child and Parent Behaviors*

Key Concepts

- Families with a child who has ADHD report more conflict and more parenting problems than other families, particularly if the child is also experiencing conduct disorder or oppositional defiant disorder.
- Children with ADHD are less compliant with parental instructions and engage in more negative behaviors than other children, particularly in structured situations.
- Laboratory studies show that many parents of children with ADHD develop a negative style of interacting with their children that includes overinvolvement and criticism, and they provide few positive comments when their children are complying or completing tasks properly.

Etiology

Most researchers today agree that ADHD is usually caused by a combination of a neurological problem in the child and a family or social environment that accentuates the neurological problem (Campbell, 2000). The neurological problem is often influenced by a child's genes, but it may be influenced by a child's prenatal environment or by experiences after birth. Family or social issues are often related to family adversity (such as poverty or marital dysfunction) or to a mismatch between parenting styles and children's responses to them.

Neurological problems or problematic parenting may create almost all or all the influence on the development of ADHD in some children. For example, some children may have sufficiently severe neurological problems that even the most effective parenting will not reduce the child's symptoms below a level that creates an impairment for a child. Alternatively, the family and social environment in which some children live may cause significant hyperactivity or inattention even if the children do not have any neurological problems. However, it appears that a combination of neurological and environmental issues usually influences the development of ADHD.

To date, no clear picture of the specific causes of ADHD has emerged. As with most disorders discussed in this text, it is likely that several causes of ADHD exist, and each of these may influence ADHD in some children but not others (Campbell, 2000). Thus we will not be exploring for *the* cause of ADHD in this section but rather will focus on a list of potential causes. In addition, most research on the etiology of ADHD has focused on children with the predominantly hyperactive–impulsive type. Consequently, we know more about the etiology of this type and little about the etiology of the predominantly inattentive type (Barkley, 2003).

This will be our strategy in this section. First we will ask what central deficit is at the foundation of ADHD. That is, what fundamental problem results in children with ADHD being less able to meet the demands placed on them by school, family, and peers? As we will see, several central deficits have been proposed, and each has some empirical support. Next we will explore the research trying to discover the causes of the proposed central deficits. We will start by looking at potential causes of the neurological problems associated with ADHD—initially by exploring the genetic influence on them and then by examining other influences, such as those associated with pregnancy or birth complications. We will also explore how a child's family and social environment may influence the development of ADHD. Finally, following the advice of Campbell (2000), we will use a developmental model to explore the unfolding of ADHD in children.

Theoretical Perspectives on the Central Deficit in ADHD

Most currently preferred theories explaining the combined and predominantly hyperactive–impulsive types of ADHD focus on deficiencies in behavioral inhibition, primarily in the inhibition of prepotent motor responses (Nigg, 2001). In this section we explore three of these theories. Two theories focus on deficiencies in behavioral inhibition as the primary deficit of ADHD. One theory focuses on the role that the executive functions of the brain play in behavioral inhibition and the other on the influence of the behavioral inhibition system. The third theory suggests that problems with arousal regulation are at the foundation of problems with behavioral inhibition and thus are more fundamental.

Prepotent means something that is superior or stronger than something else. A prepotent response is one that, at a given time, has more power or salience than other responses. A prepotent motor response involves movement. For example, as you are reading this text in your room, you may have had the thought, "I wonder if Bill is still having a party Saturday?" At that point, your thought about the party had a superior position to your thoughts about ADHD, and the motor response of going down the hallway to talk with Bill may have had a superior position to continuing to move your eyes across the pages of this text. If you did not motor down the hallway to talk with Bill, you inhibited that prepotent motor response. Children with the predominantly hyperactive–impulsive and combined types of ADHD have difficulty inhibiting prepotent motor responses. Results from studies using neuropsychological tests suggest that one or more neurological deficits influence this difficulty (Nigg, 2001; Pennington & Ozonoff, 1996).

Behavioral Inhibition as the Central Deficit in ADHD

In this section we focus on two theories suggesting that behavioral inhibition is the central deficit in ADHD. Each of them suggests that problems with behavioral inhibition come from a different source.

Executive Functions   The theory of Russell Barkley (2003) states that deficits in behavioral inhibition are associated with the function of the brain labeled **executive function.** Executive functions are considered the higher functions of the brain. They are involved in planning and implementing goal-directed behaviors by considering options, forming plans, working toward the goal, and inhibiting behaviors that interfere with the attainment of the goal. For example, your executive functions were involved when you decided not to walk to Bill's room to ask about the party because of your goal of receiving a good grade in the class for which you are reading this text. Barkley argues that the executive functions of children with ADHD do not operate effectively, resulting in them having more difficulty maintaining behavior toward achieving future goals, as well as engaging in more behaviors related to an immediate interest or impulse.

Executive functions appear to take place primarily in the **prefrontal cortex,** the part of the cortex that is the farthest in front of the brain. This conclusion is supported by case studies of children who have experienced lesions to the prefrontal cortex and who then begin to show behavioral problems related to executive functions (Pennington & Ozonoff, 1996). It is also supported by **functional studies** of the brain that allow examination of brain functioning during a task. For example, a study using **functional magnetic resonance imaging** (fMRI) showed that children making the fewest errors of commission on the go/no-go test had greater activation in the orbitoprefrontal cortex (Casey et al., 1997). In addition, **electroencephalograph** (EEG) studies have shown greater activation in the prefrontal cortex during the no-go trials than the go trials of the go/no-go test, suggesting that the prefrontal cortex is particularly involved in behavioral inhibition (Young et al., 2000).

Barkley's theory is supported by research showing that the prefrontal cortex of children with ADHD functions less effectively than other children's. For example, several studies of cerebral blood flow have shown that children with ADHD have lower levels of blood flow to the prefrontal cortex and to the pathways between the prefrontal cortex and the limbic system (Barkley, 2003). In addition, an fMRI study using the go/no-go test showed increased

NEUROPSYCHOLOGICAL TESTS OF COGNITIVE ABILITY

Neuropsychological tests are designed to assess the extent to which specific brain functions influence behavior. A neuropsychological test involves a task shown to be related to one or more brain functions. The connection between the task and a brain function has usually been demonstrated by studies showing that people with known injuries to a particular area of their brains have problems completing the task. The goal of many cognitive neuropsychological tests is to isolate a particular cognitive deficit that a person may have. This can be difficult because most tasks involve more than one type of cognitive function. Over the years, however, several neuropsychological tests have been created that relate primarily to one type of cognitive function (Tannock, 1998).

Several neuropsychological tests can assess a child's ability to inhibit behavior. Because children's ability to inhibit behavior is a focus of research on ADHD, these tests have been used frequently to assess issues related to behavioral inhibition in children with ADHD. Three commonly used tests are reviewed here (these descriptions come from Nigg, 2001):

- **Continuous performance test:** Several versions of this test exist, all using the same theme. A child sits in front of a computer screen on which individual letters appear at a prearranged frequency. The child is told to watch the screen and to respond by pressing a button each time a particular letter appears that was immediately preceded by another particular letter (for example, when an X appears that was immediately preceded by an A). The button is not to be pushed at any other time. The target sequence appears infrequently, with other letters appearing the rest of the time. This test usually continues for

a long time—perhaps 15 minutes for a young child and longer for older children and adults—requiring a lengthy period of vigilance with infrequent responses. Errors of commission (pressing the button inappropriately) may indicate a lack of behavioral inhibition. Errors of omission (not pressing the button in response to the target sequence) may indicate a lack of sustained attention.

- **Go/no-go test:** A child is seated in front of a computer screen and is told that either an A or a B will appear on the screen. Whenever the A appears, the child is to push a button. Whenever a B appears, the child is not to make any response. An A appears on the screen with much greater frequency than a B, causing the child to experience a prepotent response of pushing the button. Errors of commission (pushing the button on the rare occasion when the B appears) suggest a lack of behavioral inhibition.

- **Stop signal test:** A child is seated in front of a computer screen and is told to push a button on one side of the computer whenever an A appears on the screen and to push a button on the other side of the computer whenever a B appears on the screen. The child is told to push the button "as quickly as possible" after the letter appears. However, the child is told that when he or she hears a tone, he or she is not to push the appropriate button. An A or B then appears randomly with equal frequency. Occasionally the tone is heard right after a letter appears (just as the child is starting to respond). Errors of commission suggest a lack of behavioral inhibition.

activation of the prefrontal cortex in children with ADHD when they were taking MPH (Vaidaya, Austin, & Kirkorian, 1998). Because MPH reduces the symptoms of ADHD, this study suggests that increased activation in the prefrontal cortex may be related to decreased hyperactive–impulsive behaviors.

Together these studies suggest that executive functions occur in the prefrontal cortex, that poor functioning of the prefrontal cortex is related to problems with behavioral inhibition, and that children with ADHD show reduced functioning in the prefrontal cortex. Arguably, then, the deficits in behavioral inhibition that many children with ADHD exhibit may be related to less efficient functioning of their prefrontal cortex.

Behavioral Inhibition System   The theory proposed by Herbert Quay (1997) uses the concept of the *behavioral inhibition system* originally described by Gray (1987). Gray suggested that three independent but interrelated brain systems control behavior:

- A fight–flight system that responds to unexpected pain or punishment and produces fight or flight.
- A **behavioral activation system** that responds to stimuli that an organism has learned indicate the presence of reward or relief from punishment and pushes the organism to act to gain rewards or avoid punishment.
- The **behavioral inhibition system** (BIS) that responds to stimuli that an organism has learned indicate the presence of punishment or nonreward. An active BIS produces cessation of behavior, increased overall arousal, and attention focus on relevant stimuli.

Consider a student who regularly makes amusing comments during class. Each time she does this, she expects to be rewarded by receiving a laugh from her peers, so her behavioral activation system is involved. However, if she notices that the teacher is in a bad mood and so does not make amusing comments because she expects that she will be punished for them, her behavior is being influenced by her BIS.

Quay (1997) suggests that children with ADHD have deficiencies in the functioning of their BIS. This results in their failing to notice signals from the environment that they will experience punishment or nonreward if they behave in a certain way, which increases the chance that they will behave that way.

The primary laboratory task used to demonstrate deficiencies of the BIS is the stop signal test, which requires a balance between the behavioral activation system (push the button in response to the letter) and the BIS (stop the process of pushing the button because the tone just sounded). Children with ADHD are more likely than other children to push the button after the tone sounds; this may occur because their BIS is deficient and does not effectively counterbalance the behavioral activation system (Schachar, Tannock, Marriott, & Logan, 1995). Interestingly, children with ADHD and high levels of anxiety are better at inhibiting responses on the stop signal test (Pliszka, Borcherding, Spratley, & Leon, 1997). One would expect that those with higher levels of anxiety would have a more active BIS, so finding that children with higher anxiety are better at the stop signal test suggests that their more active BIS helps them inhibit their responses. In addition, children with ADHD make fewer errors on the stop signal test when they are taking MPH than when they are not, suggesting that MPH influences the BIS.

Optimum Arousal as the Central Deficit in ADHD

Van der Meere and colleagues (1995), Sergeant and Van der Meere (1990), and others have argued that the deficits in behavioral inhibition seen in children with ADHD result from deficits in state arousal, which they believe is the central deficit in ADHD. (*State* arousal refers to a child's arousal at a specific time and is distinguished from *trait* arousal, which refers to the child's general level of arousal across a variety of situations.) They argue that the level of arousal in children with ADHD is frequently too low for them to effectively inhibit behavior when they should do so. They cite several laboratory findings to support their hypothesis. First, as discussed in an earlier section, most children with ADHD show deficits in sustained attention, as shown by studies using the continuous performance test. Van der Meere and Sergeant argue, however, that if children with ADHD have particular problems sustaining their attention, one would expect a declining performance throughout the continuous performance test. That is, one would expect a child to do worse on the task after 12 minutes than he or she does after 3 minutes. However, most of the data about children with ADHD do not find such declining performance throughout the continuous performance task. Therefore, they argue, the issue affecting their functioning on the continuous performance test is not sustained attention.

Results from several variations of the continuous performance task with children who have ADHD suggest that the issue influencing their performance is their level of arousal (Van der Meere, 1996). First, when the stimuli on the test are presented slowly, the performance of children with ADHD does decline over time (which is different from the lack of decline over time, just noted, that occurs when the stimuli are presented quickly). Second, the performance of children with ADHD who are taking an appropriate dose of MPH does not differ from the performance of other children (Van der Meere et al., 1995). Finally, the performance of children with ADHD improves when an experimenter is sitting next to them during the continuous performance test (Van der Meere, 1996). All these results suggest that when something increases the arousal of a child with ADHD (fast pace of stimuli presentation, medication, presence of the experimenter), the child performs better. This suggests that the child can perform well when his or her arousal level is at an appropriate level and does poorly when it is not as high. Consequently, it can be argued that the fundamental deficit is a low level of state arousal.

Possible Sources of Neurological Problems in ADHD

In the previous section we explored three possible fundamental deficits related to ADHD. In this section we explore research focused on the possible neurological bases for these deficits. Several potential sources of these neurological deficits have been investigated. It is likely that there are several sources of these neurological problems, so we must be careful not to dismiss those that do not appear to influence the behaviors of many children. However, we must be equally careful not to overemphasize the importance of a source that appears to influence only a few children.

Genetic Influences on Neurological Functioning

A growing body of research suggests an important genetic influence on the etiology of ADHD, with genes probably influencing brain functioning through the monoamine group of neurotransmitters (dopamine, norepinephrine, and serotonin). Family, twin, and adoption studies all confirm a genetic influence on ADHD.

Several studies have shown that ADHD aggregates in families (*aggregate* is from the Latin *gregare,* "to herd"). That is, some families have several members with ADHD and others have none, rather than people with ADHD being equally distributed across families (Hechtman, 1996). For example, one study found that first-degree relatives of children with ADHD were more likely to have ADHD than were first-degree relatives of children with other psychiatric disorders or first-degree relatives of children with no disorder (25%, 5%, and 4%, respectively) (Biederman, Farone, Keinan, Knee, & Tsuang, 1990).

Twin studies have found higher concordance rates of ADHD among MZ twins than DZ twins and have found higher correlations between MZ than DZ twins on measures of activity and attentiveness. For example, one study found a 79% concordance rate for ADHD among 37 MZ twin pairs and a 32% concordance rate among 37 DZ twin pairs (Gillis, Gilger, Pennington, & DeFries, 1992). A study by Sherman, Iacono, and McGue (1997) found correlations of .78 for MZ twins and .57 for DZ twins on a measure of inattention and correlations of .69 for MZ twins and .42 for DZ twins on a measure of hyperactivity–impulsivity. This suggested that about 39% of the variability in the twins' scores for inattention and about 69% of their variability on hyperactivity–impulsivity were due to genetic influences.

Adoption studies also support a genetic influence on ADHD. For example, one study examined the adoptive parents and siblings of 25 children who had been adopted by their first birthday and were later diagnosed with ADHD, the parents and siblings of 101 nonadopted children who had been diagnosed with ADHD, and the parents and siblings of 50 nonadopted children with no disorder (Sprich, Biederman, Crawford, Mundy, & Faraone, 2000). As shown in Figure 7.2, a much higher percentage

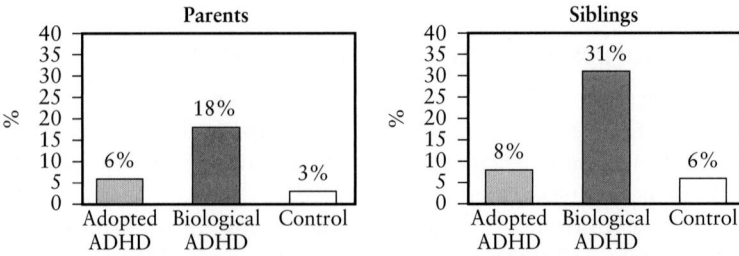

FIGURE 7.2   *ADHD among Parents and Siblings of Adopted and Nonadopted Children with ADHD*

of parents and siblings of nonadopted children with ADHD also had the disorder than did relatives of the other children. For example, 18% of the biological parents of children with ADHD also had ADHD, whereas only 6% of the adoptive parents of children with ADHD also had ADHD. In addition, the adoptive parents and siblings of children with ADHD had ADHD at about the same rates as did the parents and siblings of non-adopted children who did not have ADHD. If genes had little influence on ADHD, one would expect to find similar rates of ADHD among the birth relatives and adoptive relatives of children with ADHD; but this is not what was found.

Pathways of Genetic Influences It is likely that several genes influence ADHD (Cook, 1999), and the search for them has recently begun as procedures for investigating the influence of specific genes have been developed. The primary focus has been on genes associated with dopamine. This focus has been encouraged by two lines of research—one showing that most medications that treat the symptoms of ADHD increase dopamine transmission, and the second showing that, in studies of mice, when certain genes associated with dopamine transmission are "knocked out" of their genetic sequence, the result is high levels of hyperactivity in the mice (Mercugliano, 1995; Swanson, Castellanos, Murias, LaHoste, & Kennedy, 1998).

The first gene examined was the dopamine transporter gene (DAT) because MPH appears to have its principal effect by blocking the **reuptake** of dopamine (the transporter mechanism is responsible for reuptake). Initial studies found a particular repeat sequence in the DAT gene more frequently in a group of children with ADHD than in other children (Thapar, 1999). Another series of studies has focused on the dopamine D4 receptor gene, one of the genes that influence the receptor sites of dopamine neurons; a particular repeat sequence in the D4 gene is associated with an increased risk of ADHD in some children (Thapar, 1999).

Two patterns of research results show the complex nature of the influence of dopamine genes on ADHD (Cook, 1999). First, there is some indication that children with the repeat sequences associated with ADHD in the DAT gene do not have the repeat sequences associated with ADHD in the D4 gene, and vice versa. This suggests that each gene may independently influence ADHD. Second, some studies have not found associations between the DAT and D4 genes and ADHD. This suggests that the DAT and D4 genes are associated with ADHD in some children but not others. Much more work is needed before a clearer picture of the effects of these and other genes on ADHD can emerge.

Birth and Pregnancy Complications

Some studies have found small but statistically significant associations between pregnancy or birth complications and higher rates of ADHD—such as fetal distress during pregnancy, long duration of labor, or problems during delivery. However, other studies have not found these associations. Consequently, the influence of these complications on ADHD is not clear, and they may influence a few cases but not many (Barkley, 2003). Issues such as low birth weight and maternal smoking or drinking during pregnancy (which are themselves related to low birth weight) do have a small but consistent association with rates of ADHD (Sykes et al., 1997). It appears that these issues are more likely to influence the development of ADHD in children who are genetically at higher risk for ADHD.

Toxins and Food Ingredients

As described in more detail in the chapter about mental retardation, lead has been present in the environment for many years. Although it is no longer expelled into the environment at the levels it once was, residual amounts are still present, particularly in urban areas. There is some evidence that low levels of lead in a child's blood can cause neurological deficits that increase his or her risk for developing ADHD (Mendola, Selevan, Gutter, & Rice, 2002). Unfortunately research has not yet clearly distinguished between the direct influence of lead on ADHD and the extent to which other influences associated with lead exposure, such as living in a low-income urban neighborhood, may cause ADHD. So the specific influence of lead remains unclear.

In a somewhat historical note, it is worth mentioning that considerable attention was given in the 1970s and 1980s to the possibility that food additives and sugar were causing ADHD (Feingold, 1975). The Feingold Diet, which included only foods without sugar and food additives, was used by many families with children who had ADHD. Despite the popularity of the diet, several controlled studies eventually showed that sugar and food additives influenced hyperactivity in only a few children—probably those with some type of allergy to them (Barkley, 2003).

Family and Other Environmental Influences on the Development of ADHD

Few studies have focused on the specific role of the family environment in the development of ADHD. In one longitudinal study that did focus on family environment, Carlson and colleagues (1995) followed the development of 191 firstborn children in low-income families. They measured a variety of child, mother, and environmental characteristics at birth and at 3½, 6, 8, and 11 years through parent self-report measures and direct observations of child behaviors and mother–child interactions. At 3½ years they observed the children in a structured play task and rated them on "distractibility," which they defined as "amount of time flitting from one object to another versus playing with an object or staying on task, and overactivity (fidgetiness and restlessness)" (p. 40). (Thus their category of distractibility is probably more closely related to sustained attention and hyperactivity than distractibility, using the terms described by Van der Meere.) They found that higher levels of maternal anxiety and aggression, higher amounts of intrusive caregiving by the mother, and lower levels of social support for the mother predicted higher levels of distractibility at age 3½. At ages 6, 8, and 11, early maternal characteristics, caregiving style, and social support continued to influence levels of hyperactivity. This study suggested that intrusive and overstimulating caregiving by an anxious or aggressive mother can have an early and enduring influence on the development of hyperactivity for some children.

Our knowledge about the families of children with ADHD and the children's relationships with teachers, peers, and others also provides information about how family and social environments can influence a child's hyperactivity or attention problems. For example, as discussed earlier, parents of children with ADHD may interact with their children in primarily negative ways when the children are misbehaving and have few interactions when the children are behaving properly (DuPaul et al., 2001). This pattern of interactions may increase a child's hyperactive and problem behaviors because only when the child is acting this way does he or she receive parental attention. Similarly, if a child with ADHD is rejected by his or her peers because of aggression or other behavior problems, he or she may begin to associate primarily with other rejected and aggressive children who may reinforce the child's aggression and other behavior problems (Guevremont & Dumas, 1994). (This pattern of behavior is described in more detail in the chapter about conduct disorders.) In addition, if the interactions between a child with ADHD and teachers are primarily negative and punitive, the child may have little incentive to control his or her hyperactive behavior and may begin to misbehave purposely to express anger or sadness about the interactions with teachers (Stormont, 2001). Taken together, the negative interactions that a child with ADHD has with parents, teachers, peers, and others can accentuate a child's tendencies toward hyperactive and impulsive behaviors—increasing them until they become the primary ways in which the child interacts with others.

A Developmental Model

As noted earlier, the preferred model for understanding the development of the predominantly hyperactive–impulsive and combined types of ADHD in most children involves some neurological problem, usually influenced by a child's genes, that pushes the child's behavior to be more active. The responses of parents and other caregivers to a young child's behaviors may accentuate these problems, and the responses of teachers and other important adults in a child's life may do the same as he or she develops. Although (as is true for all the disorders discussed in this text) ADHD can develop in a variety of ways, we explore one model in this section.

To the extent that a child's ADHD is influenced by his or her genes, the potential genetic influence is present at birth. Research has not described the early years of children who are later diagnosed with ADHD, so we do not know whether the genes that influence a child's behaviors begin their influence in infancy or whether they become influential during the preschool years. Once these genes start to influence a child's behavior, these infants or young children may have difficulty regulating their own levels of activity. Their executive functions may be influenced, making it more difficult for them to respond appropriately to their environment. Underactivation of their BIS or problems with their executive functions may make it hard for them to inhibit behaviors when it is appropriate to do so. The result may be young children who are excessively active, irritable, and difficult to parent.

How these young children's problems with self-regulation are handled by parents and other caregivers can influence their eventual severity. For example, if a parent of a child who has difficulty with self-regulation works quietly with her when she begins racing around the house, helping her calm herself and helping her develop strategies to cope with her overactivity, the child's problems with self-regulation may lessen. If the parent continues to work with the child, she will keep developing skills to regulate her behavior, resulting in lower levels of activity, impulsivity, and irritability that do not develop into an impairment, although they may cause occasional problems in her life.

However, if the parent is uninterested or unavailable to the child (because of stress, overwork, or emotional problems), or if the parent does not have the skills needed to parent a highly active child, the child will have few opportunities to learn self-regulation. If the child continues to be difficult to parent, a pattern of negativity between the child and parent may develop (Danforth et al., 1991; DuPaul et al., 2001). This may be particularly likely if the parent has little support or guidance when dealing with a difficult child. This pattern of negativity can interfere in the relationship between the parent and child, further reducing the influence that the parent can have on her socialization. Because any neurological problems will continue to influence the child's activity or impulsivity, her behavior may become increasingly problematic.

As a child with relatively poor ability to regulate her activity and attention enters school, she will face a variety of challenges, especially in kindergarten or first grade when she is expected to remain seated and focused for longer periods (Stormont, 2001). She may begin to fall behind academically and socially; and unless better control over her activity levels and attention can be established, she will be at risk for falling steadily behind. Thus by the middle of her school-age years, this child may lag academically and socially and may have primarily negative relationships with her parents, teachers, and peers.

A similar pattern may continue into adolescence and adulthood. Some children will develop little control over their activity and impulsivity, continuing to have problems in academic and social settings. Others will develop more control, either on their own or with the help of others, resulting in an improved academic and social life.

Key Concepts

- It is likely that there are several causes of ADHD, with each of them influencing the development of ADHD in some children but not others.

- Three theories about the etiology of ADHD focus on deficits in behavioral inhibition. One suggests that the central deficit is related to problems in executive functioning; one focuses on the BIS; and the third suggests that the central deficit is related to underarousal.
- Genes significantly influence the development of ADHD in most cases. It is likely that many genes have an influence, although the genes that have received the most research attention are the dopamine transporter gene and the D4 dopamine receptor gene.
- Birth or pregnancy complications may influence neurological functioning and consequently the development of ADHD in a few children. Low birth weight appears to have an influence in a few cases.
- Food additives or toxins such as lead may influence the development of ADHD in a few cases.
- Neurologically based risk for the development of ADHD may be increased in children who live in families in which the parents are overly involved with their children emotionally, especially where this involvement is characterized by negativity.

Prevention

Interestingly, almost nothing appears in the literature about the prevention of ADHD, and no evaluations of interventions to prevent ADHD have been described. Is the prevention of ADHD possible? It may be.

We can identify children who are at higher risk for developing ADHD. Recall that studies of the genetic influences on ADHD have shown that it aggregates in families. In addition, children who exhibit problems with hyperactivity early in life may be at higher risk than others. Interventions for children from families with other members experiencing hyperactivity or children showing early signs of hyperactivity might prevent the development of ADHD in some of them.

As we explore in the next section, several therapeutic interventions have been developed for the families of children with ADHD to improve parenting, enhance family functioning, and promote positive parent–child relationships. These same interventions might be used with families that have a child who is at higher risk for developing ADHD or who is showing early symptoms of ADHD. They might help the parents assist their child with self-regulation and might help them avoid the type of negative parenting that can exacerbate the child's problem behaviors.

Therapeutic Interventions

Therapeutic interventions for children with ADHD fall into three categories: medication for the child, parent training or family therapy for the child's family, and psychosocial interventions for the child. In this section we explore these interventions and then examine the effectiveness of interventions that have combined two or three of them.

As we discuss these therapeutic interventions, in particular the more controversial aspects of stimulant medication for children with ADHD, keep in mind the variability in the intensity of ADHD symptoms in children and the range of impairments they cause. Interventions that are effective with children who have milder symptoms may not succeed with children who have more severe symptoms. Similarly, interventions that are effective for children who come from families where they receive considerable support and guidance may not be effective for children who come from families with uninvolved parents. Consequently, as we explore the effectiveness of various interventions, we must be careful not to fall into the trap of looking for an answer to the simplistic question of which intervention is best. Rather, we should be open to the possibility that several types of interventions may be effective, depending on the child with whom and the circumstances in which they are used.

Medication

Most children who have been diagnosed with ADHD take some type of medication to reduce their symptoms (Breggin, 1999; Wolraich, 1999). The most commonly prescribed medication is the stimulant methylphenidate (MPH; the most common brand name of MPH is Ritalin); other stimulants such as dextroamphetamine and permoline have been prescribed as well (American Academy of Child and Adolescent Psychiatry, 2000). Antidepressants such as desipramine and imipramine have been prescribed with positive effects in a few cases (American Academy of Child and Adolescent Psychiatry, 2000; Cooperative Group MTA, 1999).

MPH has received the most research attention of the medications used for ADHD (Castellanos, 1997; Swanson et al., 1998). In many ways, it seems illogical that a stimulant medication could help children whose behavior already involves higher levels of activity than most children. Early conceptualizations of the reasons for the effectiveness of MPH were that it had a "paradoxical effect" on the neurology of prepubertal children. It was believed to reduce their levels of neurological activity, although the reasons for this reduction were not clear. Research over the past few decades, however, has shown that MPH and other stimulants do not have a paradoxical effect on children's neurology, but they do stimulate parts of the brain. The areas that they stimulate allow children to regulate their behavior more effectively, thus helping them reduce their levels of activity or increase their attention.

We now know that MPH acts primarily through its influence on the dopamine system. Activity in some parts of the dopamine system is increased by MPH blocking the reuptake of dopamine. This appears to facilitate executive functioning by helping the frontal cortex screen out extraneous stimuli and focus on relevant stimuli. Interestingly, MPH also appears to reduce the activity of other parts of the dopamine system, primarily those that regulate activity level, by inhibiting dompaminergic neurotransmission. This may reduce a child's level of activity.

Prevalence of the Use of Medications

The use of medication for ADHD has increased steadily over the past several decades, and concerns about the overmedication of children have been raised periodically (Breggin, 1999; Wolraich, 1999). For example, a widely publicized report in 1970 claiming that 5–10% of the children in the Omaha, Nebraska, school district were taking medication for ADHD raised questions about its use and decreased the frequency with which it was given across the United States. However, despite periodic decreases, the use of MPH doubled every four to seven years during the 1970s and 1980s (Safer, Zito, & M. Fine, 1996).

The percentage of children taking stimulant medication for ADHD jumped dramatically during the 1990s. The size of this increase has been shown in several dramatic ways. The U.S. Drug Enforcement Agency, for example, reported that the amount of MPH produced annually in the United States increased eightfold between 1990 (1,768 kg) and 1998 (14,442 kg) (Breggin, 1999). A study of all students in the Baltimore County Public Schools in Maryland showed that the percentage of 5- to 14-year-old children taking MPH nearly doubled between 1991 and 1995 (Safer et al., 1996). Another study focused on 2- to 4-year-old children in two regional Medicaid programs and a regional HMO (Zito et al., 2000). Between 1991 and 1995, the percentage of 2- to 4-year-old children taking MPH increased two to three times. Children who received care through Medicaid were about twice as likely to be given MPH as those who received care through an HMO,

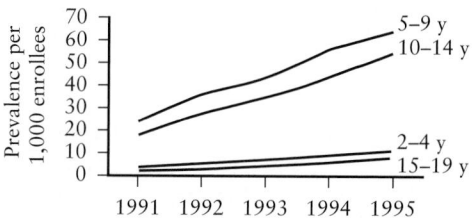

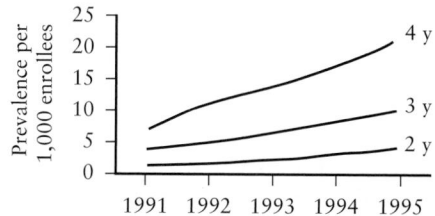

*Note: Top graph shows usage in ages 2–19; bottom graph expands this graph showing usage by those aged 2–4.

Source: Zito, Safer, dos Reis, Gardner, Boles, & Lynch, 2000.

FIGURE 7.3   *Use of Methylphenidate by Children in a Midwestern State Medicaid Program*

suggesting that children from low-income families are more likely to receive medication than those from more affluent families. Figure 7.3 shows the increase between 1991 and 1995 for four age groups in one of the Medicaid programs. Interestingly, the greatest increase was among 15- to 19-year-olds (311%). The highest rate of children receiving MPH was in the 5- to 9-year-old group, with about 6% receiving MPH in 1995.

Effectiveness of Medication for ADHD

Many placebo-controlled studies have shown that the symptoms of ADHD are reduced substantially in preschool and school-age children taking stimulant medication (American Academy of Child and Adolescent Psychiatry, 2000; Connor, 2002; Farmer, Compton, Burns, & Robertson, 2002; Short, Manos, Findling, & Schubel, 2004). Most children taking MPH experience reduced activity levels, complete school assignments more frequently, and engage in fewer problem behaviors.

As previously noted, the negative and controlling behaviors of parents who have children with ADHD are also reduced when their children take medication, and positive parent–child interactions often increase (Barkley & Cunningham, 1979; Humphries et al., 1978). Interactions with teachers are often more positive when children with ADHD are taking medication, and the peer social status of children with ADHD improves when they are taking medication, probably because of a reduction in their aggression or other socially aversive behaviors (Whalen, Henker, & Dotemoto, 1980). Consequently, another encouraging outcome of stimulant medication is more positive family and social interactions.

Medication is effective more often with children diagnosed with the combined and predominantly hyperactive–impulsive types of ADHD than the predominantly inattentive type (Carlson & Mann, 2000). DuPaul, Barkley, and McMurray (1991) reported that only 5% of children with hyperactivity did not respond to medication, whereas 24% of those with primarily inattentive symptoms did not respond. However, children with hyperactivity often need higher medication doses for effective response than do children who primarily have problems with inattention.

Several caveats to the generally positive outcomes of children taking medication should be noted. First, medication reduces the symptoms of ADHD but does not affect the underlying disorder (much as aspirin reduces fever and body aches but does not affect the disease causing these symptoms). Consequently, when a child stops taking medication for ADHD, his or her symptoms usually return. As a result, medication must often be taken for many years (American Academy of Child and Adolescent Psychiatry, 2000). Second, although children's short-term behaviors and academic performance improve when they take medication, most studies show that there is no improvement in long-term academic performance and peer relationships (Pelham & Fabiano, 2000). This is a curious finding; the reasons for it are not well understood. One reason may be that although medication reduces ADHD symptoms, it does not increase academic skills or prosocial behavior

(Pfiffner, Calzada, & McBurnett, 2000). A child who has experienced the negative consequences of ADHD for several years may lag behind his or her peers in academic and interpersonal skills. Although the medication may put a child in a better position to improve these skills, they often do not improve without additional focused interventions.

Caution is warranted when stimulant medication is given to children under the age of 4 years (Barkley, 1990). There is some indication that it is less effective with young children, and it might interfere with the normal development of the prefrontal cortex. In addition, as noted in the next section, young children typically experience more side effects than older children from medication.

Side Effects of Medication

All psychotropic medications, such as stimulants, have the potential to produce unwanted side effects in some children. Common physical side effects of stimulant medication are loss of appetite, feeling sad or drowsy, and having stomachaches and headaches (Connor, 2002). These side effects are usually mild and often disappear over time or when a lower dose of medication is given (American Academy of Child and Adolescent Psychiatry, 2000). However, severe side effects occur in a few cases, so regular monitoring by a physician is important. Higher doses of MPH produce more side effects than do lower doses, and more side effects are reported for preschool children than for school-age children (Connor, 2002).

Two placebo-controlled studies have examined side effects of MPH in preschool children (Firestone, Musten, Pisterman, Mercer, & Bennett, 1998; Short et al., 2004), and a third study has explored side effects in school-age children (Barkley, 1990). Firestone and colleagues found that although almost all parents reported side effects while their children were taking MPH, parents of children who were taking a placebo also reported a high frequency of side effects (97% of the parents of preschoolers and 72% of the parents of school-age children). Similarly, Short and colleagues found that many parents identified side effects such as irritability during the weeks that their children were taking a placebo. The high percentage of children experiencing side effects on a placebo may be a result of parents paying more attention to the children's behaviors when they were in the study or children reporting more problems because of the psychological consequences of taking a medication.

Concern has also been raised about the psychological consequences of children taking medication, such as lower self-esteem or feeling less in control of their behaviors. The results of research in this area are mixed. Although most children do not experience negative psychological consequences from taking medication, some do (Pelham, Hoza, Kipp, & Gnagy, 1997). Many children view medication as helpful and may even experience increased self-esteem as their behavior becomes less problematic. Some, however, are embarrassed about taking medication and attribute behavioral improvements to the medication rather than to their own efforts and abilities (Breggin, 1999). It appears that the reactions of adults and peers, and the support they receive from parents and other adults, influence how children view taking medication for ADHD.

It is important to note that no long-term studies of the physical consequences of taking MPH or other medications for ADHD have been completed (Wolraich, 1999). Consequently, we have no information about the possible physical or psychological consequences of taking MPH for many years, as many children and adolescents are now doing.

Parenting Interventions

Studies of parenting interventions have focused primarily on parents of preschool children who exhibit aggression or other behavior problems associated with ADHD. Typically these interventions teach parents operant conditioning behavioral techniques that they can then use to influence their children's behaviors. For example, parents learn to use time-outs when a child misbehaves, give clear instructions on how a child should act, and provide positive reinforcement when a child behaves appropriately (Dubey, O'Leary, & Kaufman, 1983; Pisterman et al., 1989). Overall, evaluations of these interventions have shown that parenting effectiveness improves, children's problematic behaviors decrease, and better relationships develop between the children and parents (Danforth et al., 1991).

Some research, however, has shown limits to the effectiveness of parenting interventions (Barkley et al., 2000; Shelton et al., 2000). One study, for example, evaluated the effectiveness of training for parents and teachers of kindergarten children who had ADHD. Although the behavior of the children whose parents and teachers received the intervention was more improved at the end of the school year than the behavior of similar children in a no-treatment classroom, no differences in behaviors were found at the one-year and two-year follow-up assessments. Thus interventions for parents and teachers seem to share a characteristic of medication treatment: Once the treatment is withdrawn, problem behaviors reassert themselves. It may be that, just as with medication, ongoing efforts with parents and teachers of children with ADHD are required for the children's behavior to maintain improvement (Hinshaw, Klein, & Abikoff, 2002).

Educational Interventions with Children

Beginning in 1991, children with ADHD could qualify for special education services that are available to children with disabilities (Beirne-Smith, Ittenbach, & Patton, 2002). To qualify for special education services, an assessment of a child must find that the ADHD has a significant influence on his or her educational performance and that special education services are necessary to address the influence of the ADHD. If a parent, teacher, counselor, or other educational professional requests an assessment of a child to ascertain whether the child qualifies for special education services, a legally mandated process is put into place that includes assessments of the

ILLUSTRATING AN IMPORTANT RESEARCH ISSUE: THE VALUE OF PLACEBOS

Most social science research involves comparisons. One useful comparison can be between those receiving a medication for some disorder and those receiving a **placebo** (an inert substance designed to appear similar to the medication; the word *placebo* comes from Middle English for "I shall please," showing that placebos were used by physicians to give a medication to a patient who did not need one but insisted on being given one). Placebo control groups let researchers estimate how much of the effect of taking a medication can be attributed to the specific characteristics of the medication and how much is due simply to the fact that the participants are taking a pill that may benefit them. If a placebo control group has a response similar to those receiving the medication, it is likely that the characteristics of the medication are having little effect.

As an example of the value of placebo control groups, consider the fact that almost all the preschool children taking MPH in a study just described experienced one or more side effects (Firestone et al., 1998). Egad! you might say—stop giving preschool children MPH. However, when you learn that 97% of the children taking a placebo experienced side effects, you might think differently about the safety of MPH. Without the comparison to those on a placebo, the information about side effects of those taking MPH is misleading. Consider also a study of the influence of sugar on hyperactive behavior (Hoover & Milich, 1994). Mothers and their children, whom the mothers believed were sensitive to sugar, completed several tasks together. The researchers told some mothers that their children would receive a drink with sugar in it before the task and told the others that their children would receive a drink with artificial sweetener. In reality, all children received a drink with artificial sweetener (that is, they all received a placebo). Mothers who believed that their children had received a drink with sugar rated their behavior as more hyperactive than did the mothers who believed that their children had received a drink with artificial sweetener, and they were more critical and hovering during the tasks. It appeared that the mothers' expectations about how their children would act after consuming sugar, rather than the sugar itself, influenced the mothers' perceptions and behaviors.

child and the child's environment. (This process is described in more detail in the chapter about mental retardation.)

If a child with ADHD qualifies for special education services, he or she may receive one or more of a variety of services available to all children with disabling conditions, such as these:

- Assistance from a special education teacher while the child is in his or her regular class.
- Resource room assistance, where the child spends part of each day receiving special education services in a separate room and rejoins his or her class for the remainder of the day.
- Placement in a special education class for the entire school day.
- Placement in a special school for children with learning disabilities (Beirne-Smith et al., 2002).

Federal law requires that all children with disabilities receive educational services in the *least restrictive environment* in which they can be successfully given; so many children with ADHD are likely to receive services in their regular classes or through resource rooms. Much more information about special education services is provided in the educational interventions section of the chapter about mental retardation.

Psychosocial Interventions with Children

Several types of individual and group therapy have been used with children who have ADHD. Play therapy or other types of psychodynamic or supportive therapies have not been effective in addressing the core symptoms of ADHD in most children (Stubbe, 2000). Similarly, cognitive therapy that helps children monitor their thoughts, improve their problem-solving skills, and take others' perspectives has not been effective in most cases (Pfiffner et al., 2000).

Social skills training has been more successful in changing the behavior of children with ADHD. These programs work with children in groups to enhance their social skills through instruction, role playing and practice, and reinforcement for positive social engagements (Pfiffner et al., 2000). Because the goal of these programs is to enhance prosocial behaviors, they are often used in conjunction with other interventions that reduce the core symptoms of ADHD, such as medication. As an example of such a program, Pfiffner and McBurnett (1997) worked with groups of elementary school children during eight 90-minute sessions to help them develop skills such as good sportsmanship, accepting consequences of their behaviors, ignoring mild provocation from peers, and dealing with feelings. Children in the intervention group showed improved social skills at school and at home compared to a wait-list control group, and the improved skills carried over into the next school year with new teachers.

Intensive interventions during summer camps have also been used successfully with children who have ADHD and comorbid conduct problems (Pelham & Fabiano, 2000). A typical program includes eight weeks of summer camp, with children sleeping in cabins under close supervision by trained counselors and engaging in a variety of academic and camp activities. During the camp, several medications at different doses may be tried to determine which has the most positive influence on a child. The camp also provides a place for children to learn and practice social skills with peers and adults. Evaluations of the program developed by Pelham and his colleagues showed that the children enjoyed the experience and felt that it helped them, that counselors rated most of the children's behavior as significantly improved by the end of the session, and that parents noticed significant positive changes in their children's behaviors and in their relationships with them.

Combined Treatments

Several research projects have evaluated the effectiveness of two or more interventions given separately or in combination. These studies are particularly

Comprehensive interventions with children who have ADHD may involve helping them to catch up with their peers academically.

helpful for understanding the relative effectiveness of several interventions because they allow comparison of the effectiveness of each intervention given alone and in combination with another intervention.

One study (Abikoff & Hechtman, described in Hinshaw, Klein, & Abikoff [2002], included 102 7- to 9-year-olds who had responded well to MPH treatment. They were divided into three groups. One continued MPH medication and had no contact with members of the project staff; one continued MPH and had extensive child, parent, and teacher psychosocial interventions; and the third continued MPH and interacted regularly with project staff but did not receive the extensive interventions of the second group. All groups responded well to treatment, and no additional benefit could be noted for those who received the combination of psychosocial interventions and MPH. Children in the combined medication and psychosocial intervention group had their medication withdrawn at one point to assess whether the psychosocial intervention could replace the medication. However, all children were returned to MPH within two weeks because their behavior had deteriorated.

A second similar study used behavior therapy as the psychosocial treatment. It found that children in the combined MPH and behavior therapy group performed significantly better at posttest on measures of behavior than those who remained on MPH but did not participate in the behavioral therapy (Klein & Abikoff, 1997). As with the previous study, when children in the combined medication and behavioral intervention group were taken off MPH, their behavior deteriorated and they were returned to medication.

The largest study of combined treatments for ADHD was sponsored by the National Institute of Mental Health (Cooperative Group MTA, 1999). It involved 579 children between the ages of 7 and 10, all of whom met the diagnostic criteria for the combined type of ADHD (40% had comorbid oppositional defiant disorder, 14% had comorbid conduct disorder, and 33% had a comorbid anxiety disorder). The interventions were delivered at six sites across the United States and Canada. The children were randomly assigned to one of four groups:

- Closely monitored administration of MPH.
- An extensive behavioral intervention that included parent training, teacher consultation, family therapy, and an intensive summer camp program for the children.
- A combined treatment that included medication and behavioral interventions.
- A **community-care control group** that did not receive any specific services through the study but continued to engage in whatever interventions they would normally pursue in their community (67% received MPH or other medication through their physicians, and others received various forms of psychosocial intervention—so this group was not a no-treatment control group).

Assessments of the core features of ADHD at the end of the study showed the following results:

- MPH was superior to the community-care control and behavioral treatments on most parent and teacher ratings.
- The combined treatment was not superior to MPH alone on most of these ratings.
- The behavioral intervention was not superior to the community-care control condition (but recall that most of those in the community-care control condition received some intervention).

However, a different pattern emerged from assessments of other characteristics of the children (conduct problems, oppositionality, anxiety, depression, and social skills) and from assessments of parent–child relationships:

- The influences of MPH alone and behavioral interventions alone were similar on most parent and teacher ratings.
- Neither MPH alone nor behavioral interventions alone were superior to the community-care control condition on most measures.
- The combined treatment was not superior to either MPH alone or the behavioral interventions alone on most measures.
- The combined treatment was superior to the community-care control condition on most measures.

Additional analyses showed that when measures of the core features of ADHD were combined with measures of oppositional defiant disorder and conduct disorder, the combined treatment produced a greater reduction in symptoms than either MPH alone or behavioral interventions alone. Further, 68% of the children in the combined intervention group, 56% in the MPH-alone group, and 34% in the behavioral intervention–alone group were not experiencing clinically significant symptoms or behavior problems at the end of the study (Swanson et al., 2001).

What do these combined treatment studies tell us? Hinshaw, Klein, and Abikoff (2002), Pelham and Fabiano (2000), and others assert that the pattern of results shows that combining medication and behavioral interventions produce better outcomes for children with ADHD than medication alone. They contend that the best way to evaluate the effectiveness of the treatments is through their influence on the full pattern of symptoms exhibited by children (the core symptoms of ADHD and the behavioral symptoms of conduct disorder and oppositional defiant disorder), and that combined treatment is superior to either treatment alone in overall influence on children's behaviors. A potential reason for this greater overall improvement can be found in the earlier discussion of the value of behavioral treatments: They help children develop more positive behaviors rather than simply reduce their inattentiveness and hyperactivity–impulsivity.

Issues Still to Be Addressed in Treatment for ADHD

Ongoing work is needed to explore the value of various interventions for ADHD. As we end this section, two areas that have received little attention are worth noting. First, few studies have explored the effectiveness of interventions for children who have the predominantly inattentive type of ADHD. As noted earlier, MPH is effective in treating these children but helps them less than children who have the other two types (DuPaul et al., 1991). However, the effectiveness of other interventions has not been assessed specifically with these children. The reasons for this lack of attention are not clear.

Second, research on the treatment of children with the combined and the predominantly hyperactive–impulsive types of ADHD is not yet fine-grained enough to assess the relative effectiveness of the various available interventions for children with different levels of severity of ADHD symptoms or for children who live in different types of families and neighborhoods. As noted at the beginning of this chapter, the range of the severity of symptoms exhibited by children with ADHD is large. Perhaps children with more severe symptoms might respond to some treatments but not others, and children with less severe symptoms might respond to different treatments. Similarly, children in families in which the parents can implement a behavioral intervention may benefit from that type of intervention more than children whose parents cannot do this consistently.

Key Concepts

- The use of medication for children with ADHD has increased dramatically during the past several decades, particularly during the 1990s.
- MPH and other medications reduce the core symptoms of ADHD. Children with the combined and predominantly hyperactive–impulsive types are more likely than children with the predominantly inattentive type to respond positively to MPH.
- Many children experience side effects when taking medication for ADHD, but these are often temporary and can usually be eliminated by reducing the dose.
- Interventions for parents often focus on helping them manage the behaviors of their children more effectively.
- Since 1991, children with ADHD have been able to qualify for special education services.
- Successful psychosocial interventions for children with ADHD focus on helping them develop more positive social skills. Intensive interventions during summer camps have also resulted in improvements.
- Studies that compare treatment types generally show that MPH is more successful than behavioral interventions at reducing the core symptoms of ADHD, and that the combination of the two is no more effective than MPH alone. However, combined treatments are often more effective than MPH alone for other problems related to ADHD, such as parent–child relationships, conduct problems, and deficits in social skills.

CHAPTER GLOSSARY

Attention deficit disorder was the name used in the DSM-III for the disorder most closely related to ADHD. **Attention-deficit hyperactivity disorder** was the name used in the DSM-III-R. **Attention-deficit/hyperactivity disorder** is the name used in the DSM-IV.

The **behavioral activation system** is a theoretical system in the brain that responds to

stimuli that an organism has learned indicate the presence of reward or relief from punishment and that motivates the organism to act.

The **behavioral inhibition system** (BIS) is a theoretical system in the brain that responds to stimuli that an organism has learned indicate the presence of punishment or nonreward and that motivates the organism to stop acting, increase arousal, and focus attention on relevant stimuli.

Capacity, when related to attention, involves how much information a person can maintain in working memory at one time.

Combined type is the subtype of ADHD in which children display symptoms of inattention and hyperactivity–impulsivity.

A **community-care control group** is used in some intervention studies. Its members receive no specific services during the study and are asked to use whatever services they would normally use in their communities.

The **continuous performance test** is a neuropsychological test that measures a person's ability to focus on and respond properly to stimuli appearing infrequently on a computer screen.

Distractibility refers to the extent to which a person is distracted from relevant stimuli by irrelevant stimuli.

An **electroencephalograph** is an instrument used to record, on graphs, electrical activity occurring in the brain.

Encephalitis lethargica was a disorder diagnosed in the early 1900s. Many of those who recovered from *encephalitis lethargica* showed symptoms of restlessness, inattention, impulsivity, and hyperactivity.

Event-related potentials are responses observed on an electroencephalograph that indicate brain activity is being activated.

Executive functions are brain functions involved in maintaining an appropriate strategy for attaining a goal; they include creating strategic plans, putting those plans into action, and inhibiting responses that interfere with attaining the goal.

Focused attention refers to a person's ability to maintain attention on relevant material despite experiencing distractions.

Functional magnetic resonance imaging (fMRI) is a noninvasive procedure that measures blood oxygenation in the brain during cognitive or perception tasks, showing which areas of the brain are being used with the task.

Functional studies of the brain allow examination of brain functioning during a task.

The **go/no-go test** is a neuropsychological test designed to assess behavioral inhibition.

Hyperkinetic impulse disorder was the name of the disorder most closely related to ADHD used in the DSM-II.

International Classification of Diseases, **10th edition (ICD-10)** is the categorization system for physical and mental disorders used primarily in Europe and Great Britain.

Methylphenidate (MPH) is a stimulant medication that is most commonly used to treat ADHD.

Neuropsychological tests are procedures to assess the extent to which specific brain functions influence behavior.

Orientation and reorientation, when related to attention, involve the extent to which a person can orient to relevant stimuli and reorient to the appropriate stimuli after attention has been drawn away.

A **placebo** is an inert substance designed to appear similar to a medication.

Predominantly hyperactive–impulsive type is the type of ADHD in which children exhibit significant symptoms of hyperactivity and/or impulsivity, but not inattention.

Predominantly inattentive type is the type of ADHD in which children exhibit significant symptoms of inattention, but not hyperactivity–impulsivity.

The **prefrontal cortex** is the part of the cortex farthest forward in the brain. It is involved in executive functions.

Prepotent is something that is superior to or stronger than something else.

Reuptake is the process of reabsorbing a neurotransmitter from the synaptic cleft into the terminal button of the presynaptic neuron (the neuron secreting the neurotransmitter).

The **stop signal test** is a neuropsychological test that assesses behavioral inhibition.

Sustained attention refers to the extent to which a person can maintain attention on something over time.

Bipolar Disorders

Sadness and irritability are characteristics of many children with bipolar disorders.

The bipolar disorders are characterized by dramatic mood swings that usually occur in cycles. Each cycle usually involves a period of exhilaration and agitation called **mania** (from the Greek *mania*, "madness"), followed by a period of depression, and then a period of more normal mood. Most adults with bipolar disorder experience two or three of these cycles in a year, with the periods of mania and depression each lasting several weeks or months. However, a few adults and most children with bipolar disorder experience a rapid cycling of moods. They may experience a complete cycle each day or even three to four cycles in a day (National Institute of Mental Health, 2001).

All of us experience swings in mood—we feel better for a few days or weeks and then not so good for a few days or weeks—often with no clear reason for the changes. Our mood swings often influence our behavior. We may have less interest in going places and doing things when feeling "down" and more energy for projects and more excitement about life when feeling "up." These experiences can give us a sense of the cycle of mood changes that children with bipolar disorder experience. However, their mood swings are more extreme, resulting in behaviors that are more intense and debilitating. For example, they may engage in dangerous behaviors that put their health and life at risk when in a manic state and may have too little energy to go to school or engage with friends or family when depressed. Many children with a bipolar disorder experience multiple hospitalizations to help control their symptoms, and as adolescents they are at higher risk for developing substance abuse problems and committing suicide (Emslie & Mayes, 2001).

Like **schizophrenia**, the onset of bipolar disorder is most common in late adolescence and early adulthood. However, it has become clear over the past few decades that some cases begin in childhood and that, also like schizophrenia, these cases are usually more severe and chronic than those that emerge in late adolescence or adulthood (American Academy of Child and Adolescent Psychiatry, 2000; Geller, Zimerman, Williams et al., 2002b). Consequently, there has been greater research interest in bipolar disorders in children over the past decade or so, although our knowledge about them remains sparse.

The bipolar disorders provide an interesting bridge between externalizing disorders (such as conduct disorder and ADHD) and internalizing disorders (such as depression and anxiety disorders) in children. Bipolar disorders are included in the *mood disorder* category of the DSM-IV-TR because their primary feature is a disturbance of mood (APA, 2000). However, these moods fuel behaviors that are similar to those exhibited by children with externalizing disorders (Biederman, Faraone, Chu, & Wozniak, 1999; Biederman, Mick, Faraone et al., 2002). Consequently, this chapter appears between the chapters about externalizing disorders and those about internalizing disorders. Perhaps our growing knowledge of the bipolar disorders will illuminate the connections between the internalizing and externalizing disorders in children.

Chapter Plan

After vignettes describing the experiences of two children with bipolar disorder, we explore the short history of research and clinical interest in childhood bipolar disorder. After reviewing the diagnostic criteria for the bipolar disorders, we spend an extended time exploring two questions that are currently unresolved: whether bipolar disorders truly exist in prepubertal children and, if they exist, whether they are the same disorders seen in adults. We then discuss the characteristics and experiences of children with bipolar disorders and the small amount of research on the disorders' prevalence and course. We review information about the etiology of bipolar disorders, noting the influences of neurological problems and stress in their development. Finally we examine the interventions currently used with children who have a bipolar disorder and their families.

Case Study: Three Women, One Girl, and Two Cases of Bipolar Disorder

About halfway through the school year, May's third-grade teacher, Ms. Chan, had become increasingly concerned about May's behavior in class and on the playground. May had been in fights with several students and had become loud and rude in class. Over the past month, Ms. Chan had sent May to the principal's office several times because of her disruptive behavior in class. Among other things, she had begun to tell other students how they should complete their work rather than doing her own work, which disturbed the class several times each week. Ms. Chan wondered if some disturbing events were occurring in May's life and so had asked her mother to come for a conference, the second that year.

As she waited for May's mother on the afternoon of the conference, Ms. Chan reflected that May had always been an energetic child. She was often out of her seat and engaged in two or three activities, seemingly at the same time. She also reflected on May's ongoing difficulties with the other students. She often interrupted their games, joked with them when they wanted to be left alone, and bothered them in a variety of ways. As a result, by the third month of school most of the other children avoided May. She often spent recesses and lunch hours with Ms. Chan while she was correcting papers in the classroom. Ms. Chan enjoyed May and found her smile and her outgoing nature captivating, so she did not mind that May preferred to spend much of her free time in the classroom.

Ms. Chan also recalled the first conference she had with May's mother. During the second month of the school year, Ms. Chan had asked May's mother to come for a conference to discuss May's behavior. Ms. Chan was concerned that May showed many of the symptoms of ADHD, and she wanted to encourage May's mother to take her to a psychologist for an assessment. May's mother and aunt came to the conference. Ms. Chan was amazed at the withdrawn and quiet behavior of her mother—behavior that was the opposite of May's. May's aunt did most of the talking with Ms. Chan during the conference, and they agreed to take May for an assessment. However, they never told Ms. Chan about the outcome of the assessment.

When May's mother and aunt appeared for the second conference, Ms. Chan was startled by the changes in May's mother. She was dressed flamboyantly, with a low-cut blouse, a multicolored long skirt, and a dozen or so necklaces. She immediately asked Ms. Chan what she thought of the skirt, saying that because the conference was so important for May, she had been up all night sewing it. She talked loudly and quickly, telling Ms. Chan what a wonderful teacher she was, how lucky May was to have her as a teacher, and how gifted May was. She said that she wanted to help May in any way she could and was delighted that Ms. Chan had taken an active interest in May's well-being. However, when Ms. Chan began to describe her concerns, May's mother had trouble sitting still. She looked around the classroom at the students' work, exclaiming periodically about the creativity of the various pieces of art displayed throughout the classroom. May's aunt sat quietly throughout most of the meeting, although she asked several questions about May's behavior and took notes. After about a half hour, May's aunt said they would seek the help of a psychologist, and she and May's mother left. Ms. Chan marveled at the energy she felt in the room during the meeting, although she felt drained by the experience.

May's aunt called to talk with Ms. Chan at the end of the next school day. She apologized for her sister's behavior. She said that she, her sister, and May lived together, and that she had moved in with her sister when May was 2 years old. Before this, her sister had been leaving May with her for several weeks at a time and was exhausted and depressed when she returned to get May. May seemed bewildered by her mother's disappearances, and the aunt felt that she provided the only stability in the household.

Ms. Chan consulted with the school psychologist, who said that both May and her mother might be experiencing the symptoms of a bipolar disorder. She explained that while May's behavior was similar to that of children with ADHD or conduct disorder, it was also characteristic of children with a bipolar disorder. She noted that the significant changes in May's mother's behavior between the two conferences suggested that she might have a bipolar disorder. Ms. Chan contacted May's aunt and convinced her to make an appointment with a child psychiatrist who consulted at their school once a month. Ms. Chan suggested that she present the possibility of an appointment with the psychiatrist to May's mother as something that was important to do for May, and said the three of them should attend the appointment together.

After several appointments with the psychiatrist, May's mother agreed to begin taking medication for the bipolar disorder the psychiatrist had diagnosed. After several months, she reported that it helped her avoid the severe depressions she experienced occasionally, and she agreed to let the psychiatrist prescribe the same medication for May. Within a month of taking the medication, May's loud, boisterous, and angry behaviors had subsided dramatically. Ms. Chan and May then had several appointments with the school psychologist, who helped teach May how to interact more effectively with the other children in the class. The three of them also agreed on a system of reinforcements that involved May being able to spend an hour after school with Ms. Chan when her behavior met certain goals. By the end of the year, Ms. Chan noticed that May had developed better relationships with several students in the class and seemed much less dependent on Ms. Chan for social interactions.

Some Issues Worth Noting

- The connections between May's behaviors and her mother's behaviors, suggesting the role of genes in bipolar disorder.
- How May's exuberance interfered with her ability in the classroom and with her social relationships.
- The positive relationship that May had with her teacher, despite May's behavioral problems.
- How successful treatment with medication for May's mother paved the way for the same intervention with May.

Case Study: A Treatment-Resistant Case of Bipolar Disorder

Mr. Garfield, one of the sixth-grade teachers at Grover Elementary School, was dismayed when he returned from the summer to find that Rudy had been assigned to his class. He knew Rudy had a reputation of being a problem student and did not look forward to the challenges he would present. In conversations with Rudy's fourth- and fifth-grade teachers, Mr. Garfield learned about Rudy's loud and unpredictable behaviors. He also learned that Rudy's parents were difficult and that conferences with them were often characterized by anger and their claims that the teachers were not doing their job well. Rudy's parents had refused to have him evaluated for special education services when he was in the fourth grade, and his fourth-grade teacher had suspected that they had been drinking before the two meetings she had with them. Finally, Mr. Garfield learned that Rudy's older brother, who also had a reputation as a problem student at Grover Elementary, had committed suicide at the age of 17.

Mr. Garfield was determined to work closely with Rudy to help him succeed that year. However, despite Mr. Garfield's efforts, Rudy was often disruptive in class and had to be sent out of the classroom several times during the first month. During the second month of school, Rudy got into a fight with a fifth-grade boy and beat him so badly that the boy had to be taken to the hospital. Students who were in the area when the fight began said they did not notice any provocative behavior from the fifth-grade boy, and it seemed to them that Rudy began the fight for no reason. Rudy claimed he knew that the boy and several of his friends were planning to beat Rudy up after school, and he was just defending himself by fighting with the boy before he and his friends could attack Rudy.

Because of the fight, Rudy was taken into custody by the police and placed in the local juvenile detention facility. While he was there, a psychology doctoral student completed an assessment of him. The assessment concluded that Rudy was probably experiencing a bipolar disorder and recommended that he be placed in a psychiatric hospital for further evaluation and possible treatment. The family court judge agreed to this placement despite strong objections from Rudy's parents, who claimed they would see to it that he behaved if the judge would release Rudy to them.

Rudy's behavior in the psychiatric hospital was problematic. He was belligerent, angry, and physically aggressive with staff members and other children. This anger would flare most frequently when the rules were not relaxed to give him the special treatment he believed he deserved. He often talked about suicide, requiring that the staff take special precautions to protect him from attempting suicide.

Based on an assessment of Rudy's behaviors, the child psychiatrist working with Rudy began treatment with lithium, a medication that is often successful in stabilizing the moods of a person with bipolar disorder. After about six weeks, little improvement had been noted in Rudy's behaviors; so his medication was changed to a mild antipsychotic medication. This medication had some influence on Rudy's angry behaviors but also made him sedated and sluggish. However, it was decided to keep him on this medication because of the reduction in his anger and aggression. The hope was that the sedation would ease as he continued to take the medication.

Meanwhile, Rudy's therapists worked to help him develop control over his behavior; as he gained more control, he was reinforced with increased privileges. Despite his improved behavior, Rudy continued to experience ongoing problems. In particular, his anger and aggression flared several times each week. Family therapy was attempted but was generally viewed as unsuccessful. Rudy's parents frequently missed appointments and, when they did attend a therapy session, spent much of it expressing anger at Rudy and his therapists. Rudy was noticeably upset by these sessions, and his behavior usually became more aggressive for several days after them.

After four months in the hospital, Rudy's behaviors had improved somewhat, and a combination of three medications had some influence on his moods and aggressive behaviors. However, it was determined that it would not be in Rudy's best interest to return to his family because of his strained relationship with his parents and concern that they would not insist that Rudy continue to take his medication. Consequently, he was placed in a residential treatment facility by the family court. Rudy's behavior continued to flare occasionally in the residential facility but was usually under control. He continued taking his medications, although he often complained about them. Rudy had little contact with his parents, who seemed not to have much interest in his life. At age 15, Rudy was moved to a group foster home. He began vocational training as a carpenter and took classes to help him live independently; the goal was to prepare him for life on his own when he left the group foster home at age 18.

Some Issues Worth Noting

- The degree to which Rudy's behaviors could inappropriately be considered simply delinquent behaviors.
- The extent to which Rudy's parents' behaviors, possibly influenced by their own disorders, interfered with his ability to receive effective interventions.
- The fact that medical treatment, often effective in cases of adult bipolar disorder, was not effective in treating Rudy's bipolar disorder.
- The fact that interventions designed to help Rudy cope with his ongoing disorder, rather than treat the disorder itself, appeared to be the most effective plan for him.

History

Although occasional case reports of a child with manic symptoms have appeared in clinical literature for decades, and although some clinicians reported manic symptoms in children in the 1960s and 1970s, the prevailing view before the 1980s was that very few, if any, prepubertal children experienced a bipolar disorder (Findling et al., 2001; Weckerly, 2002; Weller, Weller, & Fristad, 1995). This view was part of an overall sense among clinicians and researchers until the 1970s that mood disorders did not exist in children. When problems with mood were identified in some children, they were usually considered exacerbations of their normal moodiness.

Based on case studies and some early research, the DSM-III included depressive and bipolar disorders among those that could be diagnosed in children (APA, 1980). Using the diagnostic criteria from the DSM-III, researchers began to identify increasing numbers of children with symptoms of a bipolar disorder. Further, they asserted that bipolar disorders were being underdiagnosed in children and early adolescents because the symptoms of bipolar disorders in children differed from those of bipolar disorders in adults (Akiskal, Downs, & Jordan, 1985; Garber, 1984).

This initial research encouraged clinicians and researchers to consider a wider range of behaviors as symptoms of a bipolar disorder in children, which resulted in increasing numbers of children being given the diagnosis of a bipolar disorder in the 1990s. Interestingly, concern is now being raised that bipolar disorders are being overdiagnosed in children (Hammen & Rudolph, 2003). Children with significant behavior problems who experience mood fluctuations are said to be receiving a diagnosis of a bipolar disorder even if they do not meet all the criteria for the diagnosis. (At a recent meeting I attended with a group of clinicians from several residential treatment centers, many agreed that it seemed as if almost every child entering their centers had a diagnosis of bipolar disorder.)

Underdiagnosis of bipolar disorders is a problem because children who might benefit from treatment do not get it. Overdiagnosis is also a problem because children incorrectly diagnosed with bipolar disorder will be given inappropriate treatment and may not be given treatment from which they would benefit. Perhaps we will see a leveling out of the frequency with which bipolar disorder is diagnosed over the next decade, resulting in an appropriate level that is somewhere between what it was in the 1970s and what it is today.

Diagnosis and Assessment

Diagnostic Criteria

Four disorders comprise the bipolar disorders in the DSM-IV-TR: *bipolar I disorder, bipolar II disorder, cyclothymia,* and *bipolar disorder not otherwise specified* (BPDNOS) (APA, 2000). The first three disorders differ from each other in the severity or duration of their symptoms, and BPDNOS is a diagnosis for children with significant bipolar symptoms that do not meet all the diagnostic criteria for any of the first three disorders.

The diagnoses of bipolar I disorder and bipolar II disorder require the presence of a manic episode, a hypomanic episode, or a mixed episode; so we will discuss the diagnostic criteria for these episodes first. As described in Table 8.1, a **manic episode** is a period of highly elevated mood that lasts at least one week and features symptoms indicating disturbances in emotion (such as grandiosity), behavior (such as excessive talking), and biological functioning (such as a decreased need for sleep). Symptoms caused by drug use, including medications for depression or other disorders, are not considered in deciding whether a child is experiencing a manic episode (a diagnosis of **substance-induced mood disorder** can be given to a child with symptoms related to medications or other drugs).

A **hypomanic episode** has the features of a manic episode but is less severe. As you can see by comparing Tables 8.1 and 8.2, the symptoms in

---

TABLE 8.1

Criteria for Manic Episode

A. A distinct period of abnormally and persistently elevated, expansive, or irritable mood, lasting at least one week (or any duration if hospitalization is necessary).

B. During the period of mood disturbance, three (or more) of the following symptoms have persisted (four if the mood is only irritable) and have been present to a significant degree:
   (1) Inflated self-esteem or grandiosity.
   (2) Decreased need for sleep (e.g., feels rested after only three hours of sleep).
   (3) More talkative than usual or pressure to keep talking.
   (4) Flight of ideas or subjective experience that thoughts are racing.
   (5) Distractibility (i.e., attention too easily drawn to unimportant or irrelevant external stimuli).
   (6) Increase in goal-directed activity (either socially, at work or school, or sexually) or psychomotor agitation.
   (7) Excessive involvement in pleasurable activities that have a high potential for painful consequences (e.g., engaging in unrestrained buying sprees, sexual indiscretions, or foolish business investments).

C. The symptoms do not meet criteria for a Mixed Episode.

D. The mood disturbance is sufficiently severe to cause marked impairment in occupational functioning or in usual social activities or relationships with others, or to necessitate hospitalizations to prevent harm to self or others; or there are psychotic features.

E. The symptoms are not due to the direct physiological effects of a substance (e.g., a drug of abuse, a medication, or other treatment) or a general medical condition (e.g., hyperthyroidism).

Note: Manic-like episodes that are clearly caused by somatic antidepressant treatment (e.g., medication, electroconvulsive therapy, light therapy) should not count toward a diagnosis of Bipolar I Disorder.

TABLE 8.2

Criteria for Hypomanic Episode

A. A distinct period of persistently elevated, expansive, or irritable mood, lasting throughout at least four days, that is clearly different from the usual nondepressed mood.

B. During the period of mood disturbance, three (or more) of the following symptoms have persisted (four if the mood is only irritable) and have been present to a significant degree:
   (1) Inflated self-esteem or grandiosity.
   (2) Decreased need for sleep (e.g., feels rested after only three hours of sleep)
   (3) More talkative than usual or pressure to keep talking.
   (4) Flight of ideas or subjective experience that thoughts are racing.
   (5) Distractibility (i.e., attention too easily drawn to unimportant or irrelevant external stimuli).
   (6) Increase in goal-directed activity (either socially, at work or school, or sexually) or psychomotor agitation.
   (7) Excessive involvement in pleasurable activities that have a high potential for painful consequences (e.g., the person engages in unrestrained buying sprees, sexual indiscretions, or foolish business investments).

C. The episode is associated with an unequivocal change in functioning that is uncharacteristic of the person when not symptomatic.

D. The disturbance in mood and the change in functioning are observable by others.

E. The episode is not severe enough to cause marked impairment in social or occupational functioning, or to necessitate hospitalization, and there are no psychotic features.

F. The symptoms are not due to the direct physiological effects of a substance (e.g., a drug of abuse, a medication, or other treatment) or a general medical condition (e.g., hyperthyroidism).

Note: Hypomanic-like episodes that are clearly caused by somatic antidepressant treatment (e.g., medication, electroconvulsive therapy, light therapy) should not count toward a diagnosis of Bipolar II Disorder.

criterion B are the same for a manic and a hypomanic episode. However, the symptoms must be present for only four days and they must cause a distinct change in a child's behavior but not a significant impairment in a child's life. For example, a child experiencing a hypomanic episode may suddenly begin staying up late into the night working on three new projects yet have sufficient energy and focus to continue his schoolwork. His decreased need for sleep and sudden excess activity suggest manic symptoms, but his behaviors are not impairing his life.

As described in Table 8.3, a **mixed episode** is one in which the symptoms of a manic episode and the symptoms of major depression occur together for at least one week. Some children experiencing a mixed episode have rapid cycling of manic and depressive moods (such as feeling euphoric

TABLE 8.3

Criteria for Mixed Episode

A. The criteria are met both for a Manic Episode and for a Major Depressive Episode (except for duration) nearly every day during at least a one-week period.

B. The mood disturbance is sufficiently severe to cause marked impairment in occupational functioning or in usual social activities or relationships with others, or to necessitate hospitalization to prevent harm to self or others; or there are psychotic features.

C. The symptoms are not due to the direct physiological effects of a substance (e.g., a drug of abuse, a medication, or other treatment) or a general medical condition (e.g., hyperthyroidism).

Note: Mixed-like episodes that are clearly caused by somatic antidepressant treatment (e.g., medication, electroconvulsive therapy, light therapy) should not count toward a diagnosis of Bipolar I Disorder.

in the morning and evening and depressed in the afternoon and night). Others experience manic and depressive symptoms together (perhaps engaging in high levels of risky activity while feeling depressed and considering suicide).

Several variants of bipolar I disorder are listed in the DSM-IV-TR. As illustrated in Figure 8.1, bipolar I disorder is most commonly diagnosed when a manic or mixed episode alternates with a **major depressive episode** (see the chapter about depressive disorders for a description of a major depressive episode). Most adults with bipolar I disorder also experience periods of normal mood interspersed with manic and depressed periods, although this is not a diagnostic requirement. Bipolar I disorder can also be diagnosed if a child has experienced a manic episode but has never experienced a major depressive episode, although this type of bipolar I disorder occurs infrequently (APA, 2000).

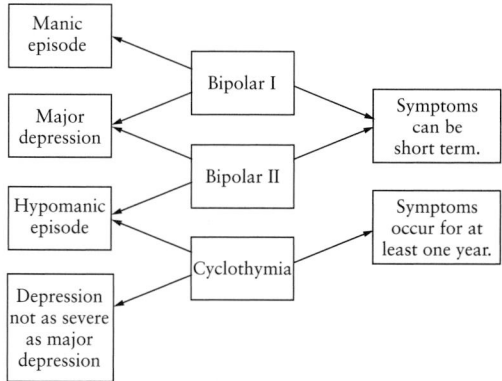

FIGURE 8.1   *Distinguishing Bipolar I, Bipolar II, and Cyclothymia*

Bipolar II disorder is diagnosed when a hypomanic episode alternates with a major depressive episode (again with a possible period of a normal mood). Thus bipolar II disorder can be considered less severe than most variants of bipolar I disorder because it involves hypomanic rather than manic episodes. More children are diagnosed with bipolar II disorder than bipolar I disorder because most children's elevated mood does not continue for the week required for a manic episode (American Academy of Child and Adolescent Psychiatry, 1997).

Cyclothymia disorder is also a disorder involving the cycling of moods. The moods in cyclothymia are less intense that those in bipolar I or bipolar II disorders. They involve alternating hypomanic episodes and depressive symptoms that are not severe enough to constitute a major depressive episode. However, a diagnosis of cyclothymia requires that children and adolescents experience these cycling moods for at least one year (two years for adults). Cyclothymia (and its close relative, dysthymia, in the category of depressive disorders) is therefore diagnosed when a child experiences long-term symptoms of a less severe cycling mood.

BPDNOS is a diagnosis that can be given when a child exhibits many symptoms of a bipolar disorder but not all the symptoms required for the diagnosis of one of the other bipolar disorders. For example, a child might experience most of the symptoms of bipolar II disorder but never have manic symptoms lasting for four to six days. Similarly, a child might experience periodic hypomanic episodes with no significant depressive symptoms. As we will see in an upcoming section, children are more likely than adults to be diagnosed with BPDNOS because their manic symptoms often do not meet the duration required for bipolar I disorder or bipolar II disorder.

Determining that an Individual Child Has a Bipolar Disorder

Determining that an individual child has a bipolar disorder is done in the same way as with most disorders: gathering information about the child's behaviors through direct observations, conversations with the child, and conversations with the child's parents or teachers—and then determining whether the child's behaviors meet the diagnostic criteria for a bipolar disorder. Several structured interviews are available to help a psychologist or other mental health professional in this process (Carlson, 1998).

However, the process of gathering information about possible symptoms of a bipolar disorder in children is more complicated than gathering this information about adults. In some cases it can be difficult to distinguish bipolar symptoms from the common unstable moods of children (Bowring & Kovacs, 1992). Whereas the mood swings of children with bipolar I disorder or bipolar II disorder are usually intense enough to make a diagnosis fairly straightforward, it is more difficult to distinguish the symptoms of cyclothymia disorder or BPDNOS from the normal mood swings of children. How much more intense the mood swings need to be for them to be considered symptoms of cyclothymia disorder or BPDNOS is not clear, so this is open to interpretation by the clinician making the diagnosis (Geller, Zimerman, Williams et al., 2002b).

Another complicating issue is that most children with a bipolar disorder experience other, more common childhood disorders, such as ADHD or conduct disorder (Evans et al., 2005). Because the symptoms of the more common disorders are almost always present before the symptoms of a bipolar disorder, it can be difficult to determine whether a child's symptoms represent a worsening of an earlier disorder or the onset of a comorbid bipolar disorder (Carlson, 1998). For example, do a child's heightened symptoms of overactivity indicate an exacerbation of his ADHD or the occurrence of a hypomanic episode?

Finally, the magnitude of a child's manic symptoms can be limited by the constraints to most children's behaviors, making the symptoms less noticeable (Bowring & Kovacs, 1992). For example, it may be obvious when an adult is experiencing a manic episode because she may spend large amounts of money, start five remodeling projects at home, and suddenly take a trip across the country. Children obviously cannot do these things, so their manic behaviors may be less evident.

Key Concepts

- A manic episode is a discrete period of highly elevated mood that lasts at least one week.
- A hypomanic episode is a discrete period of elevated mood that lasts for at least four days and that does not significantly impair functioning.
- A mixed episode is a period in which symptoms of a manic episode occur with symptoms of a major depressive episode.
- Bipolar I disorder is diagnosed when a manic or a mixed episode has occurred or is occurring.
- Bipolar II disorder is diagnosed when a hypomanic episode alternates with a major depressive episode.
- Cyclothymia disorder in children involves at least one year of alternating periods of hypomanic symptoms and depressive symptoms that are not severe enough to be a major depressive episode.
- BPDNOS is diagnosed in the presence of clinically significant bipolar symptoms that do not meet all the diagnostic criteria for another bipolar disorder.
- The determination of whether a child meets the diagnostic criteria for a bipolar disorder is made through observations of the child's behaviors or reports from parents, teachers, or others who know the child well.
- In some cases it can be difficult to distinguish symptoms of a bipolar disorder in children from the normal mood swings of children and from behaviors associated with more common disorders such as ADHD and conduct disorder.

The Existence of Bipolar Disorders in Prepubertal Children

Despite the increasing number of children being given the diagnosis of a bipolar disorder, controversy continues to exist about the bipolar disorders in prepubertal children. This controversy focuses on two questions: whether bipolar disorders occur at all in prepubertal children and, if they occur, whether they are the same disorders as those that start during late adolescence or adulthood. A considerable amount of recent research has addressed these questions. Consequently, we will take some time in this chapter to explore them and to see how researchers try to comprehend the nature of disorders in children and adults.

Sachs and Lafer (1998) suggest four possible answers to the questions about the occurrence of bipolar disorders in prepubertal children:

- Bipolar disorders do not occur in children: The behaviors considered symptoms of bipolar disorders are better conceptualized either as behaviors that are at the far end of the continuum of appropriate childhood behaviors or as developmentally appropriate responses to high levels of transient stress.
- Bipolar disorders do not occur in children: The behaviors considered symptoms of bipolar disorders are better conceptualized as manifestations of other childhood disorders such as ADHD or conduct disorder.
- Bipolar disorders do occur in children: They are different disorders from those that begin during late adolescence or early adulthood.
- Bipolar disorders do occur in children: They are the same disorders as those that begin during late adolescence or early adulthood.

In this section we review the research that addresses each of these possibilities. To organize the research, we will use a model suggested by Cantwell (1996) that outlines strategies for determining whether a disorder exists and whether a disorder is distinct from other disorders. The strategy involves comparing characteristics of two groups of people.

When we try to decide if a disorder exists, we compare groups with the hypothesized disorder and with no apparent disorder (see Figure 8.2).

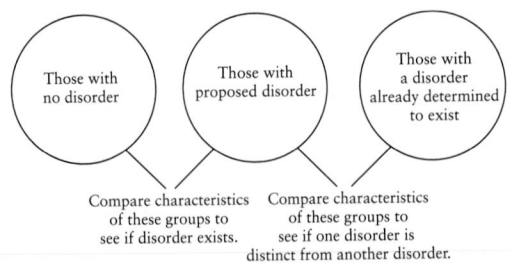

FIGURE 8.2 *Comparing Groups to Determine if a Disorder Exists*

The characteristics compared include those listed next. There is support for the existence of the disorder if those with the hypothesized disorder share these characteristics and if there are differences in these characteristics between those with the hypothesized disorder and those with no disorder.

When we try to decide whether one disorder is distinct from another, we compare groups with each disorder according to the same types of characteristics. There is support for the two disorders being distinct if the characteristics of those with one of the disorders are distinct from the characteristics of those with the other disorder. Here are some characteristics that can be used in these comparisons:

- Demographic characteristics, such as sex, age, family income level, or ethnicity.
- Neurological characteristics, such as brain morphology or neurotransmitter functioning.
- Family characteristics.
- Genetics.
- The clinical presentation of the disorder—both the core features of the disorder and characteristics associated with the disorder.
- The natural course of the disorder.
- Response to intervention.

Do Bipolar Disorders Occur in Children?

The first two possibilities suggested by Sachs and Lafer are that bipolar disorders do not occur in children. To address their first possibility (behaviors that some consider to be the symptoms of a bipolar disorder are within the range of developmentally appropriate childhood behaviors), researchers explore whether the characteristics of children who are diagnosed with a bipolar disorder differ from the characteristics of children with no disorder. To address the second possibility (behaviors that some consider to be the symptoms of a bipolar disorder are exacerbations of other disorders), researchers compare the characteristics of children diagnosed with a bipolar disorder and the characteristics of those diagnosed with other disorders.

Does Bipolar Disorder Represent Developmentally Appropriate Behavior?   By definition, children diagnosed with a bipolar disorder share a set of characteristics: the symptoms of a bipolar disorder. This provides partial support for the first requirement in Figure 8.2—a set of similar characteristics. Of more interest is whether the second requirement is met: Do the characteristics of children diagnosed with a bipolar disorder differ from those of children with no disorder? Several studies suggest that they do. For example, children with a bipolar disorder have more white matter in their brains than do other children (neurological characteristics; Lyoo, Lee, Jung, Noam, & Renshaw, 2002). In addition, genetic studies have shown a much higher prevalence of mood disorders in the families of children diagnosed with a bipolar disorder than in the families of children with no disorder (genetics and family characteristics; Wozniak, Biederman, Monuteaux, Richards, & Faraone, 2002). Thus there are some differences in the characteristics of children with a bipolar disorder and children with no disorder.

The argument that the behaviors of children with bipolar disorder are simply extreme examples of normal childhood behaviors is not persuasive: As discussed throughout this text, almost all childhood disorders represent extremes of behaviors that are common in children. Mental retardation, for example, is diagnosed in children who have less intelligence than most children; children with social phobia experience much higher levels of anxiety in social situations than most children. A disorder can be diagnosed if extreme levels of a normal childhood behavior impair a child's life.

Does Bipolar Disorder Represent Manifestations of Other Disorders?   Concern about this issue has been raised by research showing the high comorbidity between bipolar disorders and two common disorders in children: ADHD and conduct disorder. Among children diagnosed with a bipolar disorder, 60–90% also have ADHD and 45–70% also have conduct disorder (Spencer et al., 2001). Because the bipolar disorders share several diagnostic criteria with conduct disorder and ADHD, perhaps children with a bipolar disorder simply have severe cases of conduct disorder or ADHD. Most research in this area has focused on distinguishing bipolar disorders and ADHD.

Biederman and his colleagues explored this possibility by using the **subtraction/proportion method** to rediagnose children who met the criteria for both a bipolar disorder and ADHD (Biederman et al., 2002). This method involves (1) creating revised diagnostic criteria for both disorders by excluding the symptoms they share and reducing the number of symptoms that must be present for each disorder by the proportion excluded, and then (2) reassessing whether children who had been diagnosed with both disorders continue to meet the revised diagnostic criteria for both disorders. These researchers identified three overlapping symptoms of ADHD and bipolar disorders and so excluded these symptoms to create revised diagnostic criteria for each disorder. They then reassessed a group of children who had been given the diagnosis of a bipolar disorder and ADHD and found that 69% of the children met the revised diagnostic criteria for bipolar disorder and that 93% of the children met the revised diagnostic criteria for ADHD. From these data they concluded that the high comorbidity between ADHD and bipolar disorder was not due to overlapping symptoms. This finding strengthened the argument that the children had both ADHD and bipolar disorder, rather than an extreme form of ADHD.

The argument that ADHD and bipolar disorder are distinct is also reinforced by studies showing differences in the characteristics of children with the disorders. For example, children with bipolar disorder have much higher rates of some behaviors such as daredevil acts, hypersexuality, elated mood, and grandiosity (differences in clinical presentation; Geller, Zimerman, Williams et al., 2002a). In addition, stimulant medications that successfully treat ADHD have little or no effect on the symptoms of bipolar disorder (differences in response to intervention; Biederman et al., 2002).

Is Childhood-Onset Bipolar Disorder a Different Disorder than Adult-Onset Bipolar Disorder?

We have just looked at evidence that bipolar disorder exists in children and is distinct from ADHD; but whether it is the same as bipolar disorder in adults is still an open question. Some evidence suggests that it is the same disorder. For example, children and adults share some core symptoms of bipolar disorder. In addition, the strength of the genetic influence on the development of bipolar disorder in children and adults appears similar (Findling et al., 2001; Kessler, Avenevoli, & Merikangas, 2001). As already noted, medical interventions that work well with adults who have a bipolar disorder also work well with many children diagnosed with a bipolar disorder (Weckerly, 2002).

However, other evidence suggests the disorders may be distinct. Some clinical features differ. Most children with a bipolar disorder do not show symptoms of grandiosity or elation and do show symptoms of severe irritability, whereas most adults with a bipolar disorder exhibit the opposite pattern. In addition, as already discussed, the cycle of symptoms between adults and children is often different, with most adults showing distinct periods of mania and depression whereas most children experience rapid cycling of symptoms (National Institute of Mental Health, 2001). Finally, a smaller percentage of children than adults with a bipolar disorder respond favorably to medication (Weller, Danielyan, & Weller, 2002).

The different characteristics of children and adults diagnosed with bipolar disorder raise three possibilities:

- The disorder with a childhood onset is different from the disorder with an adult onset.
- Bipolar disorders are the same in children and adults, with different symptoms in childhood because the symptoms are related to developmental differences between children and adults (Bowring & Kovacs, 1992).
- Bipolar disorders that are most common in children are the same disorders that occur in about 10–20% of adults (characterized by rapid cycling or mixed symptoms), and bipolar disorders seen in a minority of children are the same disorders as those seen in most adults. In other words, two disorders exist in both children and adults, one with rapid cycling of symptoms and one with slower cycling.

Research to date does not resolve this issue; however, longitudinal studies that are now under way may resolve it in the future. The goal is to follow groups of children displaying various patterns of bipolar symptoms through their adolescence and into adulthood, monitoring changes in their symptoms and neurological functioning over time. Through these studies, researchers hope to determine more clearly whether children (1) are experiencing the early symptoms of bipolar disorder seen in adults (their symptoms would change into symptoms common in adult-onset bipolar disorder as they mature); (2) are experiencing a distinct type of a bipolar disorder (their symptoms would remain similar over time and distinct from those with an adult-onset bipolar disorder); or (3) are experiencing symptoms that will lead to another disorder (their symptoms would change to resemble the diagnostic criteria of another disorder, such as a depressive disorder) (Leibenluft, Charney, Towbin, Bhangoo, & Pine, 2003). We will need to wait another decade before the children enrolled in these studies reach adulthood so we can see which developmental paths they take.

Key Concepts

- Differences between children with a bipolar disorder and those with no disorder suggest that the symptoms of bipolar disorders are not extreme forms of normal childhood functioning.
- Evidence suggests that bipolar disorders are not extreme forms of ADHD.
- Some evidence suggests that childhood-onset bipolar disorders are the same as adult-onset bipolar disorders; however, other evidence suggests that they are distinct disorders. Ongoing research may help show whether the two disorders are the same or distinct.

Characteristics and Experiences of Children with Bipolar Disorders

Core Features

As we have already noted several times, the symptoms of bipolar disorders alternate between periods of mania and periods of depression (Geller, Zimerman, Williams et al., 2002b). In this section we focus on manic symptoms; the depressive symptoms are described in detail in the chapter about depressive disorders. Weckerly (2002) provides an interesting look at the variety of manic behaviors of children with a bipolar disorder, contrasting them with the types of behaviors that are more common in older adolescents and adults (see Table 8.4).

A common misperception about periods of mania is that they are times when a child feels very happy and joyful. Although children often describe a heightened sense of excitement and a greater sense of feeling alive during manic episodes, these episodes do not just involve positive feelings. A child is often driven by his or her mood during a manic episode. Projects *must* be started, furniture *must* be rearranged, food *must* be consumed, people *must* be dealt with. They are not merely encouraged to start projects or make new friends by their joy and optimism—they feel driven to do these things (APA, 2000).

Although this sense of elation can be experienced in a positive way by children with a bipolar disorder, it can be so intense that it causes problems (Hammen & Rudolph, 2003). An adolescent may feel so elated

TABLE 8.4

Developmental Expressions of Manic and Depressive Symptoms

Symptom	Adult Presentation	Preadolescent Presentation
Grandiosity	Adult claims to be next "Don Juan"; adult announces about to write the world's greatest novel; adult is overly solicitous and/or patronizing with waiter.	Child tells school personnel that he's president's son; child insists that N Sync (rock group) is coming to birthday party; child indiscriminately engages strangers.
Decreased sleep	Adult reports several nights in a row without sleep or with little sleep, usually without feelings of fatigue; adult reports little sleep is due to working on a project.	Child has great difficulty settling down to sleep, wakes up frequently in the middle of the night, engages in activity in the middle of the night; child walks out of the house in the middle of the night.
Pressured speech	Adult is hard to interrupt.	Child "proselytizes," is difficult to interrupt, perseverates on topic.
Racing thoughts	Adult jumps from one thought to another without logical train of thinking.	Child talks nonstop; child is very hard to redirect.
Distractibility	Adult cannot stick to topic of conversation, comments on dress, extraneous events.	Child unable to engage in usual activities; child moves from one activity to another.
Increased goal-directed activity	Adult begins spontaneous house renovations (without previous plans); adult writes letters to congressional representatives; adult joins many new social clubs.	Child wants to rearrange room at 10 p.m.; child sorts and resorts baseball cards.
Excessive involvement in reckless activities/hypersexuality	Adult goes gambling, on drinking or drug binges, on spending sprees; adult acts on hypersexual feelings without taking precautions.	Child tries to jump off roof; child begins self-stimulating without feeling self-conscious; child "propositions" adult; child removes clothing in a public place.
Irritability and/or tantrums	Adult gets in fight at bar; adult throws plate at wall because of noise.	Child threatens parent with a knife; child tries to smother sibling with a pillow; child kicks holes in walls.
Change in appetite	Adult loses appetite during depressive episode.	Child shows wide variation in appetite from hardly eating to "gorging" or "stuffing" food.
Feelings of worthlessness	Adult has feelings of being a failure; adult feels there is nothing to live for.	Child insists parents never wished child's birth; child expresses feelings of not belonging.
Recurrent thoughts of death/suicidal ideation	Adult fears death, has thoughts about sudden death; adult expresses wish to die.	Child talks about death; child makes explicit threats to harm self; child talks about wanting to be dead; child threatens to hang self with a belt.

(continued)

TABLE 8.4

Developmental Expressions of Manic and Depressive Symptoms (*continued*)

Symptom	Adult Presentation	Preadolescent Presentation
Psychotic symptoms	Adult sees spirit; adult sees image in the mirror change to other; adult hears voices of deceased relatives.	Child believes classmates want to trick child; child sees snake coming out of the wall; child hears voices directing child to do "bad things"; child reports seeing wall turn red.

that he fails to consider all the consequences of his actions, which can lead to dangerous behaviors such as taking his parent's car for a joyride or engaging in unsafe sexual behaviors. A child may giggle, laugh, and sing during her social studies class, resulting in punishment from the teacher and rejection by the other students.

In addition, for those who experience a clear cycle of manic and depressive moods, each manic period involves the knowledge that it will eventually end and be followed by a period of severe depression. Some adults with bipolar disorder describe trying to prolong their manic periods to put off the inevitable periods of depression—which some can do for a short period but no one can do permanently (Jamison, 1995).

Irritability

The most notable characteristic of children with a bipolar disorder is chronic irritability that is often expressed through anger and aggression (Biederman et al., 1996). A child may yell or scream at caregivers or peers even when they have not acted in ways that would make most children angry. He or she may lash out and say angry things or may become physically aggressive. As noted in the chapter about depression, many children express their depressed mood through irritability; consequently, irritability is likely to occur during periods of depression as well as during periods of mania. During depressed periods, a child may be morose and withdrawn—angrily refusing to talk with others while remaining alone and sulking.

Irritability is often accompanied by "affective storms" of prolonged and intense temper outbursts that may include impulsive aggression or threatening behavior toward others (Biederman et al., 1996). These storms are usually beyond the child's control and are often the primary reasons for hospitalizing children with a bipolar disorder (Wozniak & Biederman, 1996). Therapists who have treated these children in psychiatric hospitals have described them as "completely wild" or "explosive" (Wozniak et al., 1995).

Grandiosity

Although grandiosity is not as common among children as it is among adults with a bipolar disorder, some children do experience grandiosity. **Grandiosity** can be thought of as inappropriately high self-esteem or "feelings of being superbly healthy, exceptionally intelligent, or extraordinarily talented" (Colman, 2001, p. 314). Whereas a child with high self-esteem may feel confident in her ability to do arithmetic, a child who is experiencing grandiosity may insist that the teacher allow her to teach the class arithmetic because she knows how to do it much better than the teacher (Geller, Zimerman, Williams et al., 2002b). Similarly, whereas a child may derive a sense of high self-esteem from his ability as a softball player, a child who is feeling grandiose may insist that he organize the softball game during recess and may stop the game frequently to provide coaching tips to other children. It is not hard to imagine the exasperation other children would experience with him.

In some cases, grandiosity can take on psychotic features (Geller, Zimerman, Williams et al., 2002b). For example, a child may believe she has a special relationship with God because God speaks with her regularly, and she may want to tell the other children in her class about how God wants them to behave.

Hyperactivity

Children with a bipolar disorder are very active during their manic periods (APA, 2000). As noted previously, there is a driven quality to much of their activity. They may be involved in many projects at the same time and insist that others allow them to engage in these projects. They may find it impossible to sit still and may move about even more than a child with ADHD. It may be exhausting just to watch them, and others are often amazed at how much energy they have.

Despite their high level of activity, children often do not accomplish much during manic periods. Thinking during a manic phase is often characterized by racing thoughts that are quickly replaced by others. Consequently, children are often unable to focus their thinking long enough to accomplish goals and finish projects (Geller, Zimerman, Williams et al., 2000). In addition, their driven behaviors often result in hurrying through one project to get to another, or simply losing interest in a half-completed project and setting it aside.

A notable characteristic of manic periods is a significant decrease in the need for sleep (Geller, Zimerman, Williams et al., 2000). After only a few hours of sleep at night, children experiencing mania are awake and engaged in their next activity. This pattern can continue for several days or weeks, often causing exhaustion when a manic period ends. As can be imagined, a child's lack of sleeping can be problematic for other members of his or her family, who must cope with a child who is awake and frantically doing things throughout much of the night.

Dangerous Behaviors

During manic phases, children may engage in pleasurable activities that can have severe outcomes. For example, they may ride their skateboards down steep hills or play "chicken" with cars while riding their bicycles. Hypersexuality has been observed in many children during manic phases. A child may touch others inappropriately, remove his or her clothing when around others, or encourage others to be sexual. Hypersexual behavior can become even more intense after puberty, including sexual behavior with peers, older adolescents, and adults (Geller, Zimerman, Williams et al., 2000).

Associated Characteristics
Peer Relationships

Geller, Bolhofner, Craney, and colleagues (2000) compared the peer relationships of children with a bipolar disorder, children with ADHD, and children with no disorder through structured interviews given to the children and their mothers. Most children with a bipolar disorder had more problematic peer relationships than children with ADHD or no disorder (which is significant because, as discussed in the chapter about ADHD, most children with ADHD have difficulties with peer relationships).

It is not hard to imagine the reasons for the peer difficulties that many children with a bipolar disorder experience. Their manic moods may bother others, particularly when they involve physical or verbal aggression. Their irritable, depressive moods often result in their withdrawing from other children and other children withdrawing from them. In addition, the rapid or periodic changes in their moods are likely to be confusing and bothersome to other children.

Other Problem Behaviors and Disorders

Most children with a bipolar disorder also have another disorder. As already noted, 60–90% of them also have ADHD and 45–70% also have conduct disorder (Spencer et al., 2001). In addition, about half of children with a bipolar disorder experience two or more anxiety disorders (Wozniak et al., 2002). It is clear, then, that most children with a bipolar disorder experience a wide range of symptoms.

Children and adolescents with a bipolar disorder are also at higher risk for other serious problems, and the presence of these problems shows how disturbing bipolar symptoms can be. They are much more likely than others to develop a substance abuse disorder during their adolescence (Biederman, Mick, Faraone et al., 2000). This may be related to the adolescents' attempts to relieve their manic or depressive symptoms by using drugs in some cases, and in others may relate to the dangerous and pleasurable behaviors associated with manic periods. Adolescents with a bipolar disorder are much more likely than other adolescents to attempt suicide (44% compared with 1.2% in one study; Lewinsohn, Klein, & Seeley, 1995). In addition, they are about nine times more likely to complete suicide than adolescents with no disorder and about four times more likely to complete suicide than adolescents with a depression disorder (James & Javaloyes, 2001).

Key Concepts

- The elation present during manic periods is often intense and results in a child being driven by his or her moods.

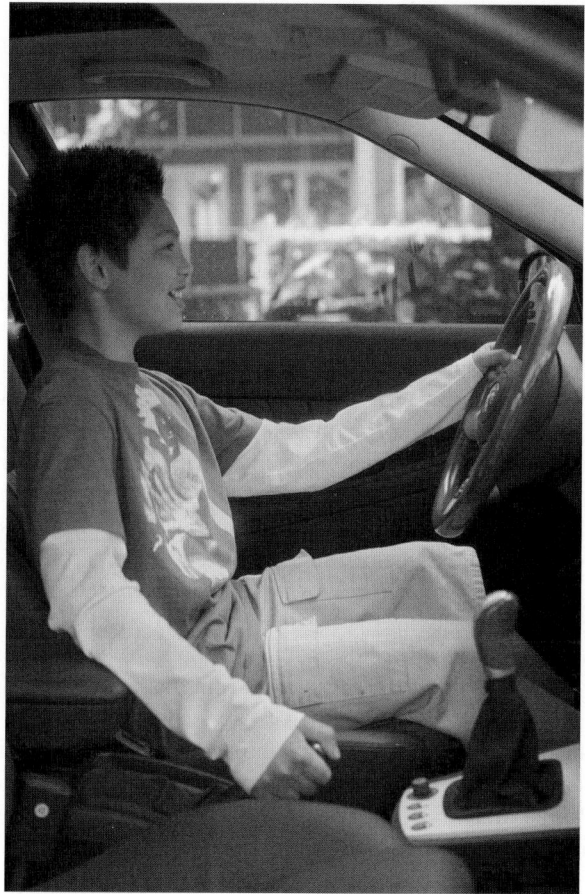

Children with a bipolar disorder may engage in many dangerous behaviors.

- The most common symptom during manic periods for children is extreme irritability that is often accompanied by anger, aggression, and affective storms.
- Although grandiosity is less frequent among children than adults, when it does occur it resembles inappropriate levels of high self-esteem. In some cases, grandiosity can have a psychotic component.
- Children with a bipolar disorder experience hyperactivity during manic periods, characterized by racing thoughts, overactivity, and a decreased need for sleep.
- Pleasurable activities that can be dangerous often occur during manic periods.
- Children with a bipolar disorder often experience problematic peer relationships brought on by their manic and depressive symptoms.
- ADHD, conduct disorder, and anxiety disorders are often comorbid with a bipolar disorder in children. Adolescents with a bipolar

disorder are at higher risk for developing a substance abuse problem and for attempting or completing suicide.

Prevalence

Not much information exists about the prevalence of the bipolar disorders in children and adolescents because the large research projects that have been used to estimate the prevalence of psychological disorders in children have not asked about manic or bipolar symptoms (Evans et al., 2005). However, a few studies have provided some useful prevalence information. For example, a study in Denmark identified about 1% of children and adolescents under the age of 15 as having a bipolar disorder (Thomsen, Moller, Dehlholm, & Brask, 1992); and a study of mood disorders among Oregon high school students found a lifetime prevalence of about 1% for the bipolar disorders, with most of those being bipolar II disorder or cyclothymia (Lewinsohn et al., 1995). Because the prevalence of bipolar disorders increases during middle and late adolescence, and because both studies included mid-adolescents and Lewinsohn and colleagues included late adolescents, it seems reasonable to conclude that the prevalence of the bipolar disorders in school-age children and young adolescents is less than 1% and that the prevalence of bipolar I disorder (the most severe of the bipolar disorders) is quite a bit below 1%.

During adolescence, about equal numbers of males and females are diagnosed with a bipolar disorder. However, more boys than girls are diagnosed with bipolar disorder before puberty (American Academy of Child and Adolescent Psychiatry, 1997). The reasons for more boys being diagnosed with a bipolar disorder remain unclear.

Course

Unfortunately, little is known about the course of bipolar disorder in children. Some recent research has begun to describe the short-term course of bipolar disorders in children, but much remains to be learned about that also.

The age of the onset of childhood bipolar disorders is difficult to estimate because studies of this issue have relied on retrospective accounts of symptom onset from parents or children. Not only may it be difficult for them to remember accurately when symptoms first appeared; it is probably even more difficult for them to recall when the symptoms became severe enough to meet the diagnostic criteria of a bipolar disorder. For example, a child may have exhibited some symptoms of elevated mood at 6 years of age, with those symptoms becoming severe enough for a diagnosis of a bipolar disorder at 10 years. Parents asked about initial symptoms may state that they occurred at 6 years. Consequently, these retrospective reports may underestimate the age of symptom onset.

Keeping this caveat in mind, a study of a community sample of 14- to 18-year-olds with the symptoms of a bipolar disorder found that the average

age of symptom onset was about 12 years (Lewinsohn et al., 1995). Two studies of children and adolescents referred for therapeutic services for a bipolar disorder found a younger age of onset, which may reflect that children with more severe symptoms are referred for services at a younger age. One study of 7- to 16-year-olds found that the onset of bipolar disorder symptoms was 7.3 years (Geller, Craney, Bolhofner et al., 2002), which is similar to the findings from a study of 5- to 17-year-olds with bipolar I disorder that showed an onset of 6.7 years (Findling et al., 2001).

The short-term course of bipolar disorder is severe and chronic for most children. For example, among children with a bipolar disorder who were enrolled in a two-year treatment program, 35% never experienced a period without significant symptoms, and almost two-thirds of those who did experience a reduction of symptoms at some point had those symptoms return later (Geller, Zimerman, Williams et al., 2002b). An important finding from this study for those providing therapeutic services was that 42% of the children from families characterized by high mother–child warmth had symptoms return after they had been reduced, whereas 100% of the children from families characterized by low mother–child warmth had symptoms return.

Little is known about the long-term course of childhood-onset bipolar disorders. The small amount of information available suggests that the disorders are often chronic. It is estimated that about 90% of children with a bipolar disorder will continue to have the disorder into adulthood (Kessler et al., 2001).

Key Concepts

- The prevalence of the bipolar disorders is about 1% among children and adolescents, with a lower prevalence during childhood and a higher prevalence in adolescence.
- Before puberty, it appears that more boys than girls have a bipolar disorder.
- Determining the age of onset of bipolar disorder can be difficult because it is often unclear whether early symptoms are severe enough to meet diagnostic criteria.
- Among adolescents with a bipolar disorder, the average age of onset is about 12 years.
- Among children diagnosed with a bipolar disorder, the average age of onset is about 7 years.
- The short-term course of the bipolar disorders in most children is chronic, and some research suggests that most children will continue to experience a bipolar disorder into adulthood.

Families of Children with Bipolar Disorders

The small amount of available research suggests that families of children with bipolar disorder experience more disruptions, poorer marital relationships, and poorer mother–child relationships than other families. Because (as discussed in the next section) genes play an important role in the development of bipolar disorder, one would expect that one or both parents of many children with a bipolar disorder would also have a mood disorder or significant mood problems. One study of children with bipolar I disorder found that this was true: 81% of them had at least one parent with a mood disorder, and 28% of the mothers and 43% of the fathers had a bipolar disorder (Findling et al., 2001). Given the impairments experienced by adults with mood disorders, and particularly with bipolar disorders, one can hypothesize that the family lives of many children with bipolar disorders may be problematic.

Several differences in interpersonal relationships have been found between families with a child who has a bipolar disorder and other families. One study found that marital relationships in families that had a child with a bipolar disorder were more often characterized by frequent irritability (33% versus 8% for families with children with no disorders), frequent complaining (45% and 12%), and frequent tension (29% and 5%; Geller, Craney, Bolhofner et al., 2000). Further, mother–child relationships were more often characterized by frequent hostility (79% and 2%) and frequent tension (68% and 0%).

Key Concepts

- Children with a bipolar disorder are more likely than other children to have at least one parent with a mood disorder, which can disrupt the parenting in their families.
- The relationships in families with a child with a bipolar disorder are tense and conflicted more often than in other families.

Etiology

In this section we focus on what we know about the etiology of bipolar disorders in children. As evidenced by the relative brevity of this section compared to corresponding sections in other chapters in this text, we know less about the etiology of bipolar disorders in children than about the etiologies of most other disorders. Our lack of knowledge is partly due to the short time that childhood-onset bipolar disorder has been a focus of research. However, researchers focused on adult-onset bipolar disorder also have not made significant strides in understanding its etiology (Hammen & Rudolph, 2003). Overall, the causes of bipolar disorder remain a mystery.

Current hypothesizing about the etiology of bipolar disorder focuses on neurological issues. The severe and chronic nature of bipolar disorders, the strong genetic influence on them, and studies with animals showing the influence of brain development on behaviors that resemble the symptoms of bipolar disorders all suggest that neurological problems are at their foundation (Pillai et al., 2002; Post, Leverich, Xing, & Weiss, 2001). However, as we will see, few specific differences in the neurological functioning of children with a bipolar disorder and other children have been identified.

First we will discuss the research that has focused on the neurological functioning of children with a bipolar disorder. Then we will examine the potential role of genes and early environmental stress on neurological functioning and consequently on the development of bipolar disorder. Finally we will explore a model for understanding the development of bipolar disorder.

Neurological Studies

Only a few issues related to the neurological functioning of children with bipolar disorder have been studied. The primary focus has been on the white matter densities in their brains—a focus encouraged by findings that adults with a bipolar disorder have higher densities of white matter in their brains. (**White matter** consists primarily of axons connecting the neurons of the cerebral cortex to other parts of the brain. It has a whitish color because of the myelin surrounding the axons—hence its name; Carlson, 1986.) Two studies have found higher densities of white matter in the brains of children with bipolar disorder, particularly in the frontal cortex, when compared with children who have no disorder or who have schizophrenia (Lyoo et al., 2002; Pillai et al., 2002). Interestingly, Lyoo and colleagues (2002) also found higher densities of white matter in children with depression, conduct disorder, and ADHD, compared with children with no disorder. This may be noteworthy because of the mood and behavioral similarities between children with a bipolar disorder and these other disorders.

Unfortunately, the meaning of the increased white matter in the brains of children with a bipolar disorder is not known at this time. One hypothesis is that it may reduce gray matter, which may influence bipolar symptoms. Another hypothesis is that it may indicate another disease process in the brain that is creating bipolar symptoms. However, investigations into this issue are continuing (Pillai et al., 2002).

Genetic Influences

It is currently believed that genes have an important influence on the development of the bipolar disorders in children through their influence on neurological development. This belief is based partly on the clear genetic influence on bipolar disorders in adults. For example, twin studies of adults suggest that about 80% of the influence on the development of bipolar disorders is genetic—much higher than the approximately 50% genetic influence on the development of depressive disorders (Bertelsen, Harvald, & Hauge, 1977). In addition, studies of the families of children with bipolar disorder have shown a high frequency of mood disorders, and of bipolar disorders in particular, in their parents (Findling et al., 2001; Kessler et al., 2001).

The mechanisms by which genes influence the development of bipolar disorder are not well understood. One group of researchers suggests an intriguing possibility that may explain why bipolar disorder occurs in children more rarely than adults and why it is more virulent when it does (Post et al., 2001). They note that in Huntington's disease, the number of trinucleotide repeats in a region of DNA influences the disorder. Below 40 repeats, no disease is present; between 50 and 70 repeats, the disease appears in adulthood; and more than 80 repeats often cause an early onset of a more virulent form of Huntington's disease. They suggest that the same process may occur in the bipolar disorders: A genetic problem resulting in more repeats in one or more genes may influence the disorder. Those with a high number of repeats may have a more serious disorder that starts during childhood and is more chronic. Future research will be needed to determine whether this hypothesis has empirical support.

Environmental Stress

Although no clear links between environmental stress and the initial development of bipolar disorder have been made for either children or adults, Post and colleagues (2001) provide an interesting discussion of experiments with rats that may point to early deprivation as a stressor influencing bipolar disorder. A series of studies has shown that when rat pups experience the stressful experience of being repeatedly separated from their mothers for three hours each day, they show signs of agitation and anxiety that last through their lifetimes with behaviors that resemble the symptoms of bipolar disorders. In addition, as adults the deprived rats self-administer higher levels of alcohol and cocaine—another behavior that occurs more frequently in adolescents and adults with a bipolar disorder (Francis, Caldji, Champagen, Plotsky, & Meaney, 1999). In another series of studies in which rat pups were stressed by being removed from their mothers for one 24-hour period, researchers found that the *brain-derived neurotrophic factor* was reduced by 30–40% in the hippocampus of the pups, and programmed cell death in the hippocampus doubled (Zhang, Xing, Levine, Post, & Smith, 1997). This is particularly interesting given the role that the hippocampus plays in the regulation of emotion and the central role that emotional disturbance has in bipolar disorders.

Although studies of the development of deprived rats' brains cannot be used to understand the development of human brains directly, the rat studies raise the question of whether deprivation early in life may influence the development of bipolar disorders by affecting early neurological development. Although all of this is speculation at this time, it does point researchers in important directions for their future work.

A Diathesis–Stress Model

The **diathesis–stress model** has been used to understand the etiology of several disorders. A **diathesis** is a genetically influenced predisposition to a disorder. As noted previously, there is strong evidence of a genetic influence on the development of bipolar disorders through their influence on neurological development. Thus these genetically influenced neurological differences may provide the diathesis for the onset of a bipolar disorder. The stress influencing the development of bipolar disorders may come from early deprivation.

Various combinations of genetically based neurological susceptibility and stress may result in the onset of a bipolar disorder. Children with more intense susceptibility may develop a bipolar disorder when they experience moderate levels of stress. Children with moderate susceptibility may not develop a bipolar disorder after experiencing moderate levels of stress, but they may develop one if they experience high levels of stress. Ongoing research will be needed to assess whether this model is appropriate.

Post and colleagues (2001) also speculate about why childhood-onset bipolar disorders are more severe and chronic than adult-onset bipolar disorders. There is some evidence that each manic or depressive episode sensitizes the brain to the episodes, which increases the likelihood that another episode will occur. This process may be particularly strong in the developing brain of a child. If early manic episodes are not recognized as such, a child may experience several manic episodes before the disorder is diagnosed and treated. By the time the disorder is recognized, the child's brain may be sufficiently sensitized to result in a more serious and chronic disorder.

Key Concepts

- Little is currently known about the etiology of bipolar disorder in children.
- Two studies have found increased densities of white matter in the brains of children with bipolar disorder. Although the relevance of this is unclear, similar patterns have been found in the brains of children with conduct disorder and ADHD, both of which have symptoms similar to those of bipolar disorder.
- A strong genetic influence exists in the etiology of bipolar disorders in adults, and a similar influence appears to influence the development of bipolar disorders in children.
- Early deprivation may play a role in the development of bipolar disorder, possibly by influencing neurological development.

Prevention

Almost nothing is known about the prevention of bipolar disorders in children. In part this is because we know so little about the early signs of risk that a child may develop a bipolar disorder, so it is difficult to gather samples of children to include in prevention research. However, even if these risk factors were known, little information exists to guide the development of specific preventive strategies (Evans et al., 2005).

The single known risk factor is that children with at least one parent with a mood disorder are at increased risk for a bipolar disorder, especially if a parent has a bipolar disorder (James & Javaloyes, 2001). Families with a parent who has a bipolar disorder could be encouraged to monitor their children for the onset of bipolar symptoms and take their children to a mental health professional if these symptoms appear. This strategy could help children with an emerging bipolar disorder receive services quickly. If the hypothesis (Post et al., 2001) about the sensitization that episodes of bipolar disorder create in the brains of children is true, these efforts might reduce the chance that an emerging bipolar disorder becomes chronic and severe. However, strategies for this type of prevention program have not been developed.

Therapeutic Interventions

A range of medical and psychosocial interventions is needed by children experiencing a bipolar disorder and their families. Treatment for the core symptoms of bipolar disorder is accomplished primarily through medication. However, psychosocial interventions are also essential to help the child and family cope with the child's symptoms.

As just noted in the section about prevention, early intervention in cases of bipolar disorder is important. Not only is it possible that episodes of mania sensitize the brain and make additional episodes more likely (Post et al., 2001); they can be very detrimental to a child's interpersonal relationships. The irritable, aggressive, and elated behaviors associated with mania can be startling and aggravating to parents, teachers, and peers. To the extent that a child engages in these for months or years before a bipolar disorder is diagnosed and treatment begins, he or she may develop a reputation as a troubled and odd child. This may impede his or her ability to create healthy family and peer relationships once treatment begins.

Hospitalization may be required for some children whose manic or depressive moods make it impossible for parents to manage the child's symptoms or provide the supervision necessary to keep the child safe (American Academy of Child and Adolescent Psychiatry, 1997). During hospitalization, trials with various medications can occur to determine which are best at controlling the child's symptoms. In addition, the child and his or her parents can be helped to develop strategies for assisting and supporting the child after he or she leaves the hospital.

Medication

Medication is the foundation of treatment for most children with bipolar disorder because this is the only way to successfully control their manic and depressive symptoms (American Academy of Child and Adolescent Psychiatry, 1997). **Lithium carbonate** (often called simply *lithium*) is the medication most commonly used, although **divalproex sodium** (Depakote) and **carbamazepine** (Tegretol) have also been used (Evans et al., 2005).

All of these medications reduce the intensity of the high and low moods that those with a bipolar disorder experience. As a result, the behaviors associated with those moods also diminish. Although there is less research on the effectiveness of the medications with children than with adults, several recent studies have shown that they are effective with some children. A placebo-controlled study of lithium, for example, found that adolescents treated with lithium had better overall functioning at the end of a six-week trial than did those on a placebo (Geller et al., 1998). A comparison of the effectiveness of three medications showed that 34% of children with bipolar I or bipolar II disorder responded favorably to carbamazepine, 42% responded favorably to lithium, and 46% responded favorably to divalproex sodium (Kowatch et al., 2000).

The percentage of children and young adolescents who respond to each of these medications is lower than the percentage of older adolescents and adults who respond (Weller et al., 2002). As seen in the previous paragraph, only a minority of children respond to any medication. Interestingly, the percentage of children who respond to medication is about the same as the percentage of the minority of adults with rapid cycling of symptoms who respond. Consequently, it appears that it is this type of bipolar disorder that is less responsive to medication, rather than there being some characteristic of children that makes them less responsive.

Most children and adolescents who take medication for bipolar symptoms experience unwanted side effects. Although most are only bothersome, some can be fatal if not identified quickly (American Academy of Child and Adolescent Psychiatry, 1997). Common side effects include nausea, diarrhea, enuresis, tremors, fatigue, and sedation (Weller et al., 2002). A few children experience heart or kidney problems, which can be very serious if not identified quickly (American Academy of Child and Adolescent Psychiatry, 1997).

An important treatment issue is the amount of time that children who have responded to a medication should continue taking it once their moods have been stabilized (American Academy of Child and Adolescent Psychiatry, 1997; James & Javaloyes, 2001). Most psychiatrists recommend maintaining children who have responded to a medication on lower levels of the medication once they are functioning well to reduce the likelihood of a relapse. The single published study of the effectiveness of maintaining children on medication showed a much higher rate of recurring symptoms among children who stopped taking lithium (92%) than among those who continued to take a low dose (38%) (Strober et al., 1995). However, concern has been raised about the consequences of long-term medication use on physical development; and the medications' side effects may make children reluctant to take them once their moods have stabilized (Weller et al., 1995).

Psychosocial Interventions

Psychosocial interventions are an important component of the services for a child with a bipolar disorder and his or her family. In cases where medications have successfully reduced the symptoms of a bipolar disorder, psychosocial interventions can help prevent the return of symptoms, help the family function better, and help the child develop skills to interact more positively with peers, teachers, and others. When medication has not reduced a child's symptoms, psychosocial interventions can help the child and family cope as effectively as possible with his or her moods and behaviors (American Academy of Child and Adolescent Psychiatry, 1997).

Parents need information about bipolar disorder so they can understand the apparently wild behaviors of their children. Helping them understand the possible neurological basis of these behaviors can reduce the chance that they will blame their children for a lack of behavioral control or themselves for a failure to teach their children to behave properly. In addition, group or individual psychotherapy can provide a supportive environment where parents can express their frustration and struggles and receive suggestions for coping with neighbors, teachers, and others who react negatively to them and their children. One small study found that multifamily psychoeducational groups, in which the parents from several families met to discuss their situations and receive information from the therapists, were seen by the families as helpful (Fristad, Goldberg Arnold, & Gavazzi, 2002).

Helping parents develop strategies for ensuring their children's compliance with medication can be an important part of reducing the chance of symptom recurrence. In addition, maintaining a warm, supportive home environment despite the children's moods and behaviors is important: As noted earlier, children who have warm relationships with their mothers are less likely to experience symptom recurrence than those who have distant relationships (Geller, Zimerman, Williams et al., 2002b).

A child with bipolar disorder may have developed problematic relationships with parents, teachers, and peers, especially if the disorder was not properly diagnosed for several years after it developed. A therapist may need to help the child develop social skills to allow him or her to be more successful in school and with peers on the playground and in the neighborhood (American Academy of Child and Adolescent Psychiatry, 1997). A therapist may also need to consult with a child's teacher about the disorder, giving the teacher a better understanding of the child's behaviors and how they might be handled effectively in the classroom.

Finally, family interventions may focus on identifying other members of the family who may be experiencing a mood disorder. Providing appropriate interventions for other family members may be an important benefit of identifying one child in the family as experiencing a bipolar disorder.

Key Concepts

- It may be possible to identify children at risk for developing a bipolar disorder and provide them with early intervention that can reduce the chance of their developing bipolar disorder or limit its severity.
- Medication is the foundation of therapy for children with a bipolar disorder. Medication helps stabilize moods and reduce the behaviors associated with these moods.
- Side effects of medications for bipolar disorders are common. Although most are bothersome, some can be life-threatening.
- It is unclear how long children should remain on medication after their moods have stabilized.
- Psychosocial interventions often focus on giving parents information about bipolar disorder and helping them cope with the behaviors exhibited by their children.
- Psychosocial interventions can help children develop better social skills that will help them overcome problems with peers and family members that may have developed during their disorders.
- Identification of other family members with bipolar disorder or another mood disorder is important.

Chapter Glossary

Carbamazepine is an antimanic medication that can be used to treat bipolar disorder.

The **diathesis–stress model,** used to understand the etiology of several disorders, postulates that a **diathesis** (a genetically influenced predisposition to a disorder) combines with stress to influence the development of a disorder.

Divalproex sodium is another antimanic medication that can be used to treat bipolar disorder.

Grandiosity is characterized by feelings of self-esteem that are inappropriately high, or by feelings of being superbly healthy, exceptionally intelligent, or extraordinarily talented.

A **hypomanic episode** has the features of a manic episode but can be shorter and involves milder symptoms.

Lithium carbonate (often simply called *lithium*) is the medication most commonly given to adults and children with bipolar disorder.

A **major depressive episode** is characterized by a period of at least two weeks in which there is a significantly depressed mood or a loss of interest and pleasure in most aspects of life.

Mania is characterized by high levels of exhilaration and agitation.

A **manic episode** is a discrete period of elevated mood that lasts at least one week.

A **mixed episode** is one in which symptoms of a manic episode occur with symptoms of a major depressive episode for at least one week.

Schizophrenia is a severe, chronic neurological disorder characterized by psychotic symptoms such as hallucinations, delusions, disorganized thinking, and grossly disturbed behaviors.

Substance-induced mood disorder is a diagnosis made when a mood disorder is caused by illegal drugs or legal medications.

The **subtraction/proportion method** is a procedure for assessing whether a child has comorbid disorders when the disorders have overlapping symptoms. The symptoms in common are excluded, and a determination is made about whether the child can continue to receive both diagnoses without considering the overlapping symptoms.

White matter includes parts of the brain that consist primarily of axons connecting the neurons of the cerebral cortex to other parts of the brain.

Depressive Disorders

Some children with depressive disorders can feel sad almost all of the time.

Depression has a powerful influence on the lives of many children. Children who are depressed are often withdrawn from others and so may learn few social skills; they may have little energy for schoolwork and so may fall behind academically; and their troubled emotions can strain relationships with parents, teachers, and other adults. Even moderate levels of depression that do not reach the intensity required for a diagnosis of a depressive disorder can impede the development of children (McGrath & Repetti, 2002). Moreover, because the behavior of children who are depressed is usually not disruptive, their symptoms can go unnoticed for years. They may sit quietly in the back of their classrooms, play by themselves during recess, and watch television for hours at home. Consequently, many children who are depressed do not receive needed attention from counselors and therapists.

Despite the potential influence of depression in the lives of children, far more attention has been paid to adults with depressive disorders than children with depressive disorders. For example, about 200 placebo-controlled studies of treatment for depression in adults were published between 1981 and 1999, while only 12 similar studies were published on the treatment of children with depression (Kaufman, Martin, King, & Charney, 2001). Because of this lack of attention, we have limited knowledge about depressive disorders in children; and as we will see throughout this chapter, many basic questions about them remain unanswered.

Exploring the topic of depression in children or adults is complicated by the fact that the term *depression* is used in many ways by researchers in their research and by others in their conversations (Cantwell & Baker, 1991; Nurcombe, 1994). It is used to describe transient sad feelings (I was depressed when I got my grades), prevailing moods (she always seems depressed), and specific mood disorders (he has major depressive disorder). As a result, confusion can occur when the term is used but its meaning is not clarified. For example, it is not clear whether the statement "Twenty percent of high school students are depressed" means that 20% are feeling sad at any particular moment, have a few symptoms of depression, or have a depressive disorder. Therefore it is important to be clear about the meaning of the term *depression* when it is used in conversation or to describe research results.

Chapter Plan

After two vignettes begin this chapter, we explore the history of theories about childhood depression. We then focus on the diagnostic criteria for four depressive disorders and several controversies about them, including whether childhood depression is the same disorder as depression that begins in adulthood. We will also see that there are several challenges to determining whether a child has a depressive disorder. The characteristics and experiences of children who are depressed are reviewed, and we explore the prevalence and course of depressive disorders and depressive symptoms. We discuss two topics related to depression: why depression is more prevalent among females during and after adolescence and the development of suicidal thinking or behaviors in some children and adolescents. The characteristics of many families that raise children who are depressed are then explored. In our focus on the etiology of depression in children, we first review five theories about the development of depression and then integrate these theories into two models of the development of depression. Finally, we examine efforts to prevent depression in children and therapeutic strategies to treat depression if it develops.

Case Study: "Hidden" Depression in an Early Adolescent

Donald was raised in a family in which both of his parents had experienced bouts of depression for many years. When his mother was depressed, she was withdrawn and had little to do with him. However, when she was not depressed, she nurtured him and provided for his needs. When Donald's father was depressed, he was angry and abusive to Donald and his mother. His abusive behavior usually occurred after he had been drinking, which he did frequently when feeling depressed. If Donald's mother was not depressed during these times, she protected Donald from his father's abuse; but when she was depressed, Donald was occasionally beaten by his father.

When Donald was 7, his mother was killed in an automobile accident. He continued to live with his father. However, without the presence of his mother he received much less nurturing and was abused more frequently by his father. When he was 8, child protective services removed Donald from his father's home following an investigation initiated when a specialist who was checking the hearing of the students in Donald's class noticed marks on the back of his head and suspected that his ears had been damaged. Donald was placed in the home of his aunt, who was a single mother and had a son about two months younger than Donald. His father moved from the area and had no contact with Donald; at age 10 Donald was adopted by his aunt.

After his adoption, Donald's behavior at home and at school was often characterized by anger and aggression. He was repeatedly in trouble at school for fighting. He liked his adoptive brother but would occasionally get angry and fight with him. After one particularly tragic incident, one of the brother's testicles had to be surgically removed after Donald kicked it.

Donald's adoptive mother struggled to provide a nurturing home for Donald. To help with his anger and aggression, she arranged for Donald to see a child psychologist, and the family attended family therapy with another therapist. Despite her concern for Donald, she could not help but feel angry and frustrated with him, particularly after he injured her other son.

Donald's therapist worked hard to help him develop better control over his anger, using a variety of cognitive–behavioral therapy techniques. He worked with the family therapist to help Donald's adoptive mother reinforce Donald's attempts to contain his anger and aggression. Because of his consistent problem with concentration in school, Donald was referred to a child psychiatrist who suggested a trial of Ritalin (a medication commonly given to children with attention-deficit/hyperactivity disorder) to see if it would increase his concentration and allow him to be more successful in school. However, little change was seen in his school behavior while he was taking Ritalin, so it was stopped after one month.

Donald's therapist found this case particularly frustrating because therapeutic strategies that help many angry, acting-out children were ineffective with Donald. He decided to refer Donald for a thorough psychological evaluation to see if the psychologist completing the evaluation could provide guidance for developing a better therapeutic strategy. The psychologist completing the evaluation spent several sessions with Donald and talked with his adoptive mother and his teachers. He also administered several psychological tests. He noticed that on two projective tests, the Rorschach Inkblot Test and the Thematic Apperception Test, Donald provided many responses commonly given by children who are depressed; and on a behavior rating scale, Donald's adoptive mother noted a high frequency of a few depressive symptoms (such as high irritability). Based on his assessment, the psychologist reported his suspicion that Donald might be experiencing a depressive disorder.

Based on the assessment, the child psychiatrist who had initially prescribed Ritalin for Donald suggested a trial of an antidepressant medication, to which Donald and his adoptive mother agreed. Within several weeks Donald's aggression had almost disappeared. Donald, his adoptive mother, and his teachers were amazed and delighted. Donald reported that he occasionally became angry but that the skills he had learned from his therapist allowed him to control his anger and avoid becoming aggressive.

Psychotherapy with Donald then entered a new phase. Donald reported strong feelings of guilt for how he had treated those around him, particularly his adoptive mother and brother. His therapist and Donald worked hard to understand his previous behavior, with the goal of avoiding heightened feelings of depression associated with Donald's guilt. Although Donald did feel depressed for a while and seemed withdrawn from his family, these feelings passed after a few months and Donald began to form a more positive relationship with his family.

Some Issues Worth Noting

- A possible genetic link between Donald's depression and his parents' depression.
- The principal observable symptoms of Donald's depression being irritability and anger, not sadness.

- The extent to which the lack of success of initial therapeutic efforts led to a reevaluation of Donald's diagnosis.
- The need for Donald's therapist to shift therapeutic attention once Donald's depression was relieved.

Case Study: A Gradual Decline into Depression

Magda arrived in the United States from Mexico with her parents when she was 2 years old. After several years of trying, her parents had obtained a U.S. visa allowing them to work, and they moved to a small town in northern California where Magda's uncle had been living for several years. Magda's parents both worked, and she spent most of her days with her aunt and her three cousins. It was felt by all that it was important for Magda and her parents to learn to speak English, so both Spanish and English were spoken in their home interchangeably. By the time she entered kindergarten, Magda spoke English well but with an accent that reflected how it was spoken in her home.

Magda was shy at school, which was similar to how she acted at home. Her accent and the fact that she was rather plump made her the target of occasional teasing by several students, but Magda ignored them and did not show any outward signs of being upset.

During her first few years in school, Magda was an average student. Her performance worried her parents, however, because they wanted her to excel at school as her cousins did. They often worked with Magda for several hours in the evening on her homework, which caused high levels of frustration some evenings. However, despite their efforts, Magda remained an average student, earning Bs and Cs on most of her work.

As she became more comfortable at school, Magda developed friendships with several children but remained withdrawn from others. She preferred sitting in the back of her classroom and played quietly with one or two other children at recess. She seldom played games such as foursquare and kickball with the other children, so she had poor skills in these games. As a result, she was often the last picked when teams were formed for games during physical education classes.

In the fourth grade, two girls who had known Magda since they began school together began to tease her frequently about her body size and her accent (which was hardly noticeable by that time), although always out of the hearing of teachers or other adults. They also claimed that she was not an American but a Mexican, which they said with a sneer. Whereas before these girls had teased Magda for a while and then stopped when she did not respond, they were now more unrelenting. Magda seldom responded to them, but she became sad and angry. When she told her mother about the teasing, her mother said that all children had to endure teasing and that Magda would have to learn to live with it. The teasing became worse the next year when, after the World Trade Center collapse on 9/11/01, the two girls began to claim that Magda and her family were probably terrorists. Other children began laughing at Magda about this, and her two friends at the time stopped playing with her after being told by the two girls that they would not be real Americans if they played with a terrorist.

Magda's behavior became more withdrawn. Her teacher was concerned and spoke with the school psychologist. The school psychologist asked about Magda's academic performance, and the teacher said that it had improved a bit over the past few months. The school psychologist suggested that a cultural value typically found in families from Mexico was that girls should be quiet and demure. She suggested that Magda was reaching an age at which she would be expected to be quieter, and because her academic performance was improving, Magda's withdrawal was probably a reflection of cultural values rather than a sign for concern.

Based on the psychologist's recommendation, Magda's teacher did not pursue the issue further. Magda continued to be withdrawn and, by the end of the school year, seemed very remote. She seldom looked directly at the teacher, a behavior that the teacher assumed also reflected cultural values. When she began the fifth grade, Magda remained withdrawn, and her schoolwork was of much lower quality. However, she had a new teacher, who assumed that the quality of Magda's work was what it had always been. Her new teacher was less engaged with all of the children in the class than her fourth-grade teacher had been, so Magda had few interactions with her. At home, Magda was withdrawn from her family and seldom participated in family activities that she once enjoyed. However, her parents had heard from several of their friends that girls Magda's age often go through "phases" when they are unhappy; so they believed that if they waited a while, Magda would become happier and more involved in family activities.

Partway through the fifth grade, Magda began to write stories and create art that had death as themes. Her teacher found the stories and pictures disturbing. As her teacher described Magda's stories to several colleagues before a faculty meeting, she was overheard by the school psychologist, who remembered her conversations with Magda's fourth-grade teacher. She became concerned and decided to talk directly with Magda. Although Magda was reluctant to talk with the school psychologist, she eventually described how the other children had been teasing her and how much this upset her. The school psychologist then arranged to meet with Magda's parents. Although she was reluctant to appear ignorant in front of Magda's parents, the school psychologist decided to ask them about her assumption that cultural values were being reflected in Magda's quiet and withdrawn nature. Her parents were a bit confused about the meaning of the term *cultural values,* but they said that it was important for Magda to be respectful to everyone, especially adults. However, they did not expect her to be quiet, and in fact they were worried that Magda had developed into a girl who was not outgoing enough to succeed in the United States.

Based on this new information, the school psychologist recommended that Magda and her parents begin psychotherapy together. The school principal spoke with several of the girls who had been teasing Magda, and her teachers monitored these students' interactions with Magda.

Magda's parents were reluctant to attend therapy, and they expressed their reluctance to the school psychologist. In response, the school psychologist consulted with a Mexican–American colleague, who recommended a Mexican–American therapist who had worked effectively with many children and families. The school psychologist helped Magda's parents contact the therapist, and an appointment was made. Magda and her parents felt comfortable with this therapist and were willing to attend therapy regularly and follow the therapist's guidance. In addition to their discussions about Magda, Magda's parents talked with the therapist about their difficulties adjusting to life in the United States; the therapist was able to help with several of their concerns. Based on her therapy and the changes in her school environment, Magda's depression gradually lifted.

Some Issues Worth Noting

- The difficulty of determining the potential influence of cultural values on Magda's behaviors and the value that cultural "experts" (in this case, Magda's parents) played in helping others make this determination.
- The value of a counselor or school psychologist who can monitor children's behaviors across several grade levels, noting differences that teachers who have a child in a classroom for one year might not notice.
- The extent to which local, national, or international events can influence the lives of individual children who are far removed from the event itself.
- The fact that having a therapist in their cultural group helped Magda's parents enter therapy.

History

Beliefs about whether children experience depressive disorders have vacillated over the years. Little mention of child or adolescent depression was made in medical texts before the 1800s. In the middle 1800s some physicians began to include depression as a childhood disorder (which they called **melancholia** from the Greek *melas,* "black," and *chole,* "bile," reflecting ancient hypotheses that depression was caused by an excess of black bile in a person's system). Explanations for melancholia at this time included heredity, epilepsy and other seizure disorders, anxiety, bereavement, excessive study, religious excitement, and parental brutality (Parry-Jones, 1995). (Interestingly, current research suggests that many of these explanations were accurate.)

In the early and middle 1900s, several researchers focused on depression in infants. Rene Spitz (1945) observed the behavior of infants being raised in large institutions where they received proper nourishment but had little human contact. He coined the term **anaclitic depression** to describe the severe withdrawal of these infants, who lay quietly for hours in their cribs and seldom responded to human contact when it occurred. John Bowlby's (1969) work on attachment theory was influenced by his observations of infants raised in similar environments. At the same time, however, **psychoanalytic theory** influenced many people to believe that children and early adolescents could not experience true depression (Munroe, 1955). It was believed that only those with a mature superego could experience depression and that it was not until later adolescence that the superego matured. As a result, the withdrawal in the infants observed by Spitz and Bowlby was considered a disorder separate from depression experienced by adults, and the depressed mood seen in many children and adolescents was viewed as a transitory, normal part of childhood (Evans et al., 2005).

Beginning in the 1960s, observations that many children and adolescents who had depressive symptoms also engaged in disruptive behaviors led to the concept of **masked depression** (Glaser, 1968; Toolan, 1962). It was hypothesized that children and adolescents did experience depression but that the underlying disorder was masked by the observable symptoms of hyperactivity, conduct problems, and learning disabilities.

A steadily increasing body of research beginning in the late 1970s showed that the depressive symptoms experienced by many children and adolescents were similar to those experienced by adults (Kaufman et al., 2001). In addition, many adults who were depressed recalled that their depression started during childhood or adolescence. Consequently, the theories that children did not experience depressive disorders or that they occurred only in masked form began to lose support, and many researchers and clinicians began to view childhood depression and adult depression as the same disorder.

So we have seen an interesting pattern of thinking about depression in children: First it did not exist as a clinically significant problem; then it existed but was different from adult depression; and now it exists and is the same as depression seen in adults. This pattern continues to evolve: Some researchers have begun to question again whether childhood depression is the same as depression in adults, as described in a following section (Kaufman et al., 2001).

Key Concepts

- Early medical texts included little or nothing about childhood depression.
- In the mid-1900s, Spitz and Bowlby studied severely withdrawn behavior in infants living in institutions, labeled by Spitz as anaclitic depression.
- Through the 1960s, it was assumed by many that children were not capable of experiencing a depressive disorder.
- In the 1960s, the concept of masked depression suggested that children did experience depression but that it appeared in masked form as acting-out behaviors.
- Research beginning in the late 1970s led to the conclusion that children could experience the same depressive disorders as adults.

Diagnosis and Assessment

The depressive disorders are included in the **mood disorders** category of the DSM-IV-TR, along with the **bipolar disorders** (this text describes the bipolar disorders in a separate chapter). As with all the mood disorders, the primary feature of the depressive disorders is a disturbed mood; but as we will see throughout this chapter, this mood disturbance can influence many aspects of a child's life.

Diagnostic Criteria

The four disorders described in this chapter—*major depressive disorder, dysthymic disorder, adjustment disorder with depressed mood,* and *depressive disorder not otherwise specified*—vary in two ways: the intensity of the depressive symptoms and the length of time that the symptoms are present.

Major depressive disorder involves symptoms that are the most intense but that may be present for a relatively short period. For major depressive disorder to be diagnosed, a child must experience one or more *major depressive episodes* (APA, 2000). The diagnostic criteria for a major depressive episode are shown in Table 9.1. As you can see, the symptoms must be present for a minimum of two weeks (compared with dysthymic disorder, for which they must be present for one year). The symptoms must also be intense and occur most of the time. Children and adolescents must meet the same criteria as adults for a major depressive episode with one exception: An irritable mood may substitute for a depressed mood. Thus children and adolescents who have major depression may be crabby, angry, and frequently frustrated rather than sad.

If a child or adult has a **mixed episode,** which involves symptoms of depression and mania appearing simultaneously, a diagnosis of bipolar disorder is made rather than major depressive disorder. In addition, if the depressed mood is caused primarily by legal or illegal drug use, a *substance use disorder* is diagnosed. Deciding whether a substance use disorder or a depressive disorder is the appropriate diagnosis when depression and drug use occur together can be difficult because those experiencing a depressive disorder may use alcohol or an illegal drug to cope with their symptoms. This diagnostic difficulty is more likely to be present with adolescents than children.

Dysthymic disorder or *dysthymia* is a longer-lasting but less intense depressive disorder (see Table 9.2). For example, the depressed mood must be present *for more days than not*, compared with *nearly every day* for a major depressive episode; and feelings of low self-esteem are a symptom of dysthymia, whereas feelings of worthlessness are a symptom of a major depressive episode. Symptoms must be present for one year for children and adolescents (two years for adults), which is much longer than the two-week period for major depressive disorder. As with a major depressive episode, children and adolescents may exhibit an irritable mood rather than a sad mood.

Adjustment disorder with depressed mood (ADDM) is included not in the mood disorder category of the DSM-IV-TR but in the **adjustment disorder** category. Adjustment disorders can be diagnosed when a child or adult is having significant difficulty adjusting to a specific stressor (such as the death of a grandparent or moving to a new school) and is experiencing significant distress or impairment (APA, 2000). By definition, the symptoms of ADDM are less intense than those of a major depressive episode: The diagnosis of major depressive disorder is given if the severity of symptoms meets the criteria for both ADDM and a major depressive episode. Similarly, ADDM is of shorter duration than dysthymia: ADDM can be diagnosed only for six months following the cessation of the stressor.

T A B L E   9 . 1

Criteria for Major Depressive Episode

A.   Five (or more) of the following symptoms have been present during the same two-week period and represent a change from previous functioning; at least one of the symptoms is either (1) depressed mood or (2) loss of interest or pleasure.

Note: Do not include symptoms that are clearly due to a general medical conditions, or mood-incongruent delusions or hallucinations.

(1)   Depressed mood most of the day, nearly every day, as indicated by either subjective report (e.g., feels sad or empty) or observation made by others (e.g., appears tearful). Note: In children and adolescents, can be irritable mood.

(2)   Markedly diminished interest or pleasure in all, or almost all, activities most of the day, nearly every day (as indicated by either subjective account or observation made by others).

(3)   Significant weight loss when not dieting or weight gain (e.g., a change of more than 5% of body weight in a month), or decrease or increase in appetite nearly every day. Note: In children, consider failure to make expected weight gains.

(4)   Insomnia or hypersomnia nearly every day.

(5)   Psychomotor agitation or retardation nearly every day (observable by others, not merely subjective feelings of restlessness or being slowed down).

(6)   Fatigue or loss of energy nearly every day.

(7)   Feelings of worthlessness or excessive or inappropriate guilt (which may be delusions) nearly every day (not merely self-reproach or guilt about being sick).

(8)   Diminished ability to think or concentrate, or indecisiveness, nearly every day (either by subjective account or as observed by others).

(9)   Recurrent thought of death (not just fear of dying), recurrent suicidal ideation without a specific plan, or a suicide attempt or a specific plan for committing suicide.

B.   The symptoms do not meet criteria for a Mixed Episode.

C.   The symptoms cause clinically significant distress or impairment in social, occupational, or other important areas of functioning.

D.   The symptoms are not due to the direct physiological effects of a substance (e.g., a drug of abuse, a medication) or a general medical condition (e.g., hypothyroidism).

E.   The symptoms are not better accounted for by Bereavement; that is, after the loss of a loved one, the symptoms persist for longer than two months or are characterized by marked functional impairment, morbid preoccupation with worthlessness, suicidal ideation, psychotic symptoms, or psychomotor retardation.

TABLE 9.2

Diagnostic Criteria for 300.4 Dysthymic Disorder

A.   Depressed mood for most of the day, for more days than not, as indicated either by subjective account or observation by others, for at least two years. **Note:** In children and adolescents, mood can be irritable and duration must be at least one year.

B.   Presence, while depressed, of two (or more) of the following:
(1)   Poor appetite or overeating.
(2)   Insomnia or hypersomnia.
(3)   Low energy or fatigue.
(4)   Low self-esteem.
(5)   Poor concentration or difficulty making decisions.
(6)   Feelings of hopelessness.

C.   During the two-year period (one year for children or adolescents) of the disturbance, the person has never been without the symptoms in Criteria A and B for more than two months at a time.

D.   No Major Depressive Episode had been present during the first two years of the disturbance (one year for children and adolescents); that is, the disturbance is not better accounted for by chronic Major Depressive Disorder, or Major Depressive Disorder, In Partial Remission.
Note: There may have been a previous Major Depressive Episode provided there was a full remission (no significant signs or symptoms for two months) before development of the Dysthymic Disorder. In addition, after the initial two years (one year in children or adolescents) of Dysthymic Disorder, there may be superimposed episodes of Major Depressive Disorder, in which case both diagnoses may be given when the criteria are met for a Major Depressive Episode.

E.   There has never been a Manic Episode, a Mixed Episode, or a Hypomanic Episode, and criteria have never been met for Cyclothymic Disorder.

F.   The disturbance does not occur exclusively during the course of a chronic Psychotic Disorder, such as Schizophrenia or Delusional Disorder.

G.   The symptoms are not due to the direct physiological effects of a substance (e.g., a drug of abuse, a medication) or a general medical condition (e.g., hypothyroidism).

H.   The symptoms cause clinically significant distress or impairment in social, occupational, or other important areas of functioning.

Specify if:
  Early Onset: if onset is before age 21 years
  Late Onset: if onset is age 21 years or older
Specify (for most recent two years of Dysthymic Disorder):
  With Atypical Features

Notes from the Author: A Preference for the Diagnosis of ADDM

As described in the chapter about the classification and diagnosis of mental disorders, concern exists that providing a diagnosis for a child may have several untoward consequences, such as stigmatizing the child and influencing how parents, teachers, and others act toward the child. ADDM is considered by many clinicians to be a less severe diagnosis than major depressive disorder or dysthymia because it suggests that the child's difficulties can be traced to a stressor rather than to some characteristic of the child. Consequently, when it can be given appropriately, many clinicians prefer a diagnosis of ADDM rather than a mood disorder. If the symptoms of the mood disturbance continue longer than six months after the end of the stressor, then the diagnosis must be changed; but until then ADDM is seen by many clinicians as a diagnosis with less chance of creating a stigma for the child than a mood disorder.

Finally, *depressive disorder not otherwise specified* (DDNOS) can be diagnosed if a child has depressive episodes that create impairments and (1) last at least two weeks but do not meet all the diagnostic criteria of major depressive disorder or (2) meet all the other diagnostic criteria of major depressive disorder but last for less than two weeks. DDNOS can also be diagnosed when it is impossible for a clinician to determine whether the depressive symptoms are due to an underlying medical condition or substance use.

Controversial and Unresolved Issues
Do Distinct Depressive Disorders Exist in Children?

Controversy exists about whether childhood depression is better conceptualized as a distinct disorder of childhood or as part of a "general childhood unhappiness" that includes symptoms of depression, anxiety, and conduct problems (Angold & Costello, 2001; Nurcombe, 1994; Poznanski & Mokros, 1994). The proposition that depressive symptoms are better thought of as part of a more general childhood unhappiness is supported by several observations. First, most children and adolescents diagnosed with a depressive disorder also experience at least one **comorbid disorder.** For example, various studies have found that 25–50% of children diagnosed with a depressive disorder have a comorbid anxiety disorder and that 33–60% have a comorbid disruptive behavior disorder (Axelson & Birmaher, 2001; Kovacs & Devlin, 1998). Second, the symptoms of the depressive disorders and the comorbid disorders often wax and wane together, which one would not expect if a child were experiencing two or more distinct disorders (Angold & Costello, 2001; DuBois, Felner, Bartels, & Silverman, 1995; Wilkinson & Walford, 1998). Finally, the cognitive styles that appear to influence depression in children are also experienced by children with anxiety and conduct problems—suggesting that these cognitions may influence feelings of general unhappiness rather than just depression (Gladstone & Kaslow, 1995; Marton, Connolly, Kutcher, & Korenblum, 1993).

However, some evidence suggests that the depressive disorders and their comorbid disorders are distinct. Most studies show that the comorbid disorders develop before the depressive disorder. For example, in 65–85% of children with comorbid anxiety and depressive disorders, the anxiety disorder began first (Axelson & Birmaher, 2001). This raises the possibility that the development of a distinct depressive disorder was influenced by the comorbid disorder, perhaps because of the stress it presented.

The results from one study may help explain why some research suggests that depression is part of a general childhood unhappiness and other research suggests it is a distinct disorder. The researchers assessed symptoms of anxiety and depression in a community sample of children. They found that it was difficult to distinguish the symptoms of the two disorders in children who were experiencing less intense symptoms and that distinct constellations of depressive symptoms and anxiety symptoms could be observed in children with more intense symptoms (Gurley, Cohen, Pine, & Brook, 1996). Thus this study suggested that the answer to the question of whether depression is a distinct disorder in childhood is *sometimes*. Milder symptoms of depression may be part of general childhood unhappiness; more severe symptoms may be part of a distinct depressive disorder.

Are Child-Onset Depressive Disorders the Same as Adult-Onset Depressive Disorders?

Questions about whether child-onset depression is the same disorder as adult-onset depression have been propelled by consistent research findings showing that several aspects of the biological functioning of children with a depressive disorder differ from those of adults with a depressive disorder (Kaufman et al., 2001). For example, many adults who are depressed experience different sleep patterns than other adults, including difficulty falling asleep, delayed onset of **rapid-eye-movement (REM) sleep,** differences in REM sleep, and prolonged periods of deep sleep. Similar differences occur only rarely between children who are depressed and those who are not (Armitage et al., 2002). In addition, about half of adults with a depressive disorder secrete high levels of **cortisol** (a hormone secreted by the adrenal gland), and these hypersecretions are rare in children with a depressive disorder. Many adults who are depressed have lowered levels of immunity to physical diseases, as shown by a reduced number of lymphocytes in their blood; this pattern is also rarely found in children who are depressed. Finally, whereas tricyclic antidepressants effectively treat depression in most adults, they are seldom effective with children who are depressed (Brooks-Gunn, Auth, Petersen, & Compas, 2001).

Despite the many differences, some aspects of biological functioning are similar in children and adults who are depressed. The best known of these is the **dexamethasone suppression test.** When dexamethasone (a synthetic hormone) is injected into most adults and children, their secretion of cortisol is suppressed. However, about 60% of children, adolescents, and adults who have major depressive disorder (and a small percentage who do not) do not suppress cortisol secretion when given dexamethasone (Kaufman et al., 2001). In addition, recent studies of the effectiveness of selective serotonin reuptake inhibitors (SSRIs, of which the most common brand name is Prozac) show that they are effective with many children and adults (Emslie et al., 1997).

What could be causing this apparently confusing array of similarities and differences in the biological functioning of children and adults who are depressed? Kaufman and colleagues (2001) suggest three possibilities:

- Depression is a different disorder in children and adults, even though they share many symptoms.
- Depression is the same disorder in children and adults. Because some neurological systems involved in depression do not reach full maturity until adulthood, the functioning of the relatively immature biological systems of children who are depressed differs from that of adults who are depressed.
- Depression is the same disorder in children and adults. Each time that a child or adult experiences a major depressive episode, his or her neurological functioning becomes more severely compromised. Because adults are likely to have experienced more major depressive episodes than children, adults' neurological systems are more likely to be compromised, leading to their having more neurological abnormalities.

At this time, it is not clear which of these possibilities is most likely to be correct. Although most children who have major depressive disorder continue to have problems with depression into adulthood, no longitudinal studies have examined the biological functioning of children who are depressed into their adulthood. If child-onset and adult-onset depression were the same disorder, one would expect the biological functioning of children who are depressed to change as they get older, eventually resembling the functioning of adults with depression. However, if the disorders are different, one would not expect to see this change. Perhaps ongoing longitudinal research will begin to address this issue.

Are Major Depressive Disorder and Dysthymic Disorder Distinct in Children?

The final controversial issue we will explore is whether major depressive disorder and dysthymia in children are distinct disorders, different levels of severity of the same disorder, or different stages in the development of a disorder. Research supporting each of these possibilities exists. For example, about 80% of children diagnosed with dysthymia will experience a major depressive episode, and dysthymia is almost always present before a child has a major depressive episode (Kovacs, Akiskal, Gatsonis, & Parrone, 1994). This suggests that dysthymia is an early form of major depressive disorder: It is unlikely that such a high percentage of children would develop major depressive disorder after dysthymia if the two disorders were distinct.

Alternatively, other research has shown that the clinical course, pattern of symptoms, and level of impairment of children experiencing either dysthymia alone or major depressive disorder alone are similar, and that children experiencing both major depressive disorder and dysthymia exhibit a higher level of impairment and a longer course than those with either disorder alone (Goodman, Schwab Stone, Lahey, Shaffer, & Jensen, 2000). This suggests, on one hand, that major depressive disorder and dysthymia are the same disorder because their course and level of impairment are similar when they appear alone. On the other hand, when they occur together, they produce a more negative clinical picture, suggesting that they may be two disorders, each of which is producing a unique amount of impairment. Clearly this issue remains unresolved.

It is worth noting that most research on depression in children, including research on the effectiveness of therapeutic interventions, includes children diagnosed with major depressive disorder, dysthymia, or both disorders. This suggests that many researchers are not convinced that major depressive disorder and dysthymia are different enough to use only children with one or the other disorder in their research.

Determining that an Individual Child Has a Depressive Disorder

As with all the disorders discussed in this text, the determination that a child has a depressive disorder is made by a clinician after a careful evaluation of the child's behaviors and other symptoms. However, making this determination can be difficult because it requires that a clinician understand the subjective emotional experience of a child. Due to the complex nature of this determination, we will focus on it a bit longer in this chapter than in other chapters.

Because the primary symptoms of depression involve internal, subjective experiences, the clinician must often rely primarily on descriptions of these experiences from a child because the child is likely to know his or her feelings better than parents, teachers, or others who observe the child. To help with this, a clinician may use self-report measures, such as the Child Depression Inventory, or structured clinical interviews, such as the Schedule for Affective Disorders and Schizophrenia for School-Aged Children (K-SADS) (Hammen & Rudolph, 2003). However, there are significant limitations to what some children, particularly young children, can reveal about their emotions. They may not be able to distinguish their various moods and may not have a vocabulary to describe them (Garber & Kaminski, 2000). This may be particularly difficult for children who have experienced a depressed mood throughout much of their lives because it may be difficult for them to describe it as a specific emotion. In addition, some children may purposely keep sad or other negative moods secret because they are concerned about how others will react, so they may be unwilling to describe them when asked to do so (Garber & Kaminski, 2000).

Because of the difficulty of gathering information about their moods directly from children, clinicians often gather information from parents, teachers, or others. However, several limitations to this information also exist. As discussed later in this chapter, many children who have a depressive disorder have comorbid behavioral problems, such as oppositional defiant disorder or ADHD. The symptoms of these disorders are more readily observed than symptoms of depression, so parents, teachers, and others may focus on a child's behavioral problems, resulting in underreporting of depressive symptoms (Mesman & Koot, 2000a). In addition, as will be discussed in the section about etiology, a lack of parental involvement and interest in a child's life is a risk factor for depression. Therefore, some depressed children have parents who are not sensitive to their moods and thus are poor reporters of them. Even parents who are attuned to their children's moods may not be aware of some of their children's feelings, such as self-blame, guilt, and low self-esteem. Children may prefer not to share this information with their parents, and children who are feeling sad may be more withdrawn from their parents, increasing the difficulty the parents have understanding their children's moods (Cole et al., 2002).

One intriguing study that focused on adolescents had clinicians interview mothers and adolescents using the K-SADS. They then compared the intensity of the symptoms experienced by the adolescents after dividing them into three groups:

- The results from only the adolescent interviews were positive for depression.
- The results from only the mother interviews were positive for depression.
- The results from both the adolescent and the mother interviews were positive for depression.

The adolescents who were the most depressed were identified by both themselves and their mothers; those with moderate depression were identified only by their mothers; and those with the lowest levels of depression were identified only by themselves (Braaten et al., 2001). This suggested that adolescents can identify milder mood disturbances better than their mothers and that mothers are better able to identify moderate mood disturbances. It may be that milder mood disturbances do not create behavioral changes that are obvious to parents. Perhaps moderate symptoms of depression interfere with an adolescent's functioning to the point that the adolescent has a reduced ability to notice and report the symptoms. Regardless of the reasons, this study shows that identifying symptoms of depression can be difficult without reports from several sources.

Cultural and Family Issues

Whenever a child's behaviors and emotions are being assessed to determine if he or she might have a depressive disorder, the clinicians, researchers, or others must take any cultural or familial expectations about children's behaviors into consideration. In some cases, these cultural or familial expectations might encourage behaviors in the child that, if not recognized as influenced by these expectations, might be considered symptoms of depression. For example, if a child is expected to be quiet and reserved around adults, particularly adults in a position of authority, the child might appear sad and withdrawn to an observer unfamiliar with this expectation. Similarly, a child who is expected to be quiet and nonconfrontational may appear withdrawn and sad to a teacher who promotes an open, boisterous atmosphere in her classroom (Koss-Chioino & Vargas, 1992).

Conversations with a child's parents or with those who know the family and child well can help those assessing the child's behaviors consider cultural and family expectations. Understanding general cultural expectations can be useful; but because there is variation among families in any culture in how much they conform to cultural expectations, it is important to know the extent to which parental or family expectations influence these cultural expectations (Vargas & Koss-Chioino, 1992).

Key Concepts

- A major depressive episode occurs when a child experiences intense symptoms of depression for at least two weeks. A child who experiences a major depressive episode can be given the diagnosis of major depressive disorder.
- Dysthymia can be diagnosed when a child experiences depressive symptoms for at least one year that are less intense that those required for major depressive disorder.
- ADDM can be diagnosed when a child has a depressed mood related to a significant stressor that lasts for no more than six months following the end of the stressor.
- DDNOS can be diagnosed if a child has significant episodes of depression that do not meet all the diagnostic criteria for major depressive disorder or dysthymia.
- Some evidence suggests that depressive disorders may be distinct disorders in children; other evidence suggests that depressive symptoms may be part of a general childhood unhappiness that also includes symptoms of anxiety and behavioral problems.
- The biological functioning of most children diagnosed with a depressive disorder differs sufficiently from that of most adults with a depressive disorder that it is unclear whether depression that begins in childhood is the same as that which begins in adulthood.
- It is unclear whether major depressive disorder and dysthymia are distinct disorders or whether dysthymia is a milder or earlier form of major depressive disorder.
- Determining that an individual child has a depressive disorder is difficult because it is not possible to directly observe a child's emotions. Children may have difficulty describing their emotions, and some adults may be unaware of a child's emotions.

Characteristics and Experiences of Children with Depressive Disorders

Core Features

The two primary features of the depressive disorders in children are a sad or irritable mood (or both) and loss of interest in most activities (APA, 2000). Almost everyone reading this text has experienced strong feelings of sadness, so we know about these feelings. Children with a depressive disorder, however, experience these feelings consistently, whereas they lessen after a few hours or days for most of us. Also, the sad feelings of those of us who are not depressed often wax and wane throughout a day or week. We may feel particularly sad when we are in a class with an ex-boyfriend or ex-girlfriend, but our sadness lifts when we are in another class or are involved in another activity. However, children with a depressive disorder experience their strong feelings of sadness most of the time.

Instead of, or in addition to, feelings of sadness, some children with depressive disorders experience strong feelings of irritability. They are chronically annoyed, frustrated, angry, and exasperated. They feel irritable about themselves and their lives, about others, and about the circumstance in which they find themselves.

Another common feature of depression is a marked decline in pleasure that was once associated with people, things, and activities. A child who once enjoyed playing on the soccer team, who got pleasure out of building elaborate settings with blocks, or who looked forward to weekends with a favorite relative suddenly has no interest in them and does not find them enjoyable (APA, 2000). Further, new activities that are often exciting for children are of no interest to a child who is depressed. A term used for this lack of interest is **anhedonia** (from the Greek *an*, "without," and *hedone*, "pleasure"). We all have days when nothing interests us, but most days are like this for children who are depressed.

Most children who are depressed also experience several physical symptoms. Many experience sleep disturbance—either having difficulty falling asleep or sleeping for many hours each day (**hypersomnia**) (Birmaher et al., 1996). Children who are depressed often feel tired and have little energy, even when they sleep for many hours. Many of them experience changes in their appetite. Some eat more than usual and some eat less than usual, which often results in noticeable weight gain or loss (or failure to gain expected weight as they grow taller) (APA, 2000).

Depression also influences children's thoughts. Many children who are depressed experience a sense of personal worthlessness. Although many of us occasionally feel inadequate or are frustrated when we do poorly on some important task, children who are depressed experience an overall sense of worthlessness and can think of nothing good about themselves. Many children who are depressed find it hard to concentrate. They are often unable to focus on their schoolwork as well as others their age, and they may even find it

Irritability is a common feature of depression in young children.

difficult to engage in conversation or focus on a television program (APA, 2000). Finally, most children who are depressed have consistently negative thoughts about themselves, their world, and their future—a topic discussed at more length in the section about etiology (Kaslow, Brown, & Mee, 1994).

Associated Features

Children who are depressed are often withdrawn from others, including parents, teachers, and peers. They seldom seek others out and so have few social interactions. They tend to have few friends, if any, and spend most of their time by themselves (Kaslow et al., 1994). Their reduced social interactions give them poorer social skills than other children their age because they have fewer opportunities to observe social skills and practice them with others (Birmaher et al., 1996).

Some children who are depressed have difficult relationships with parents and other adults caused by their withdrawal. For example, during interactions with their mothers, preschool children who were depressed were less enthusiastic and had fewer positive interactions than a group of preschoolers who were not depressed (Luby et al., 2006). In situations where a parent or teacher expects a child to be energetic and involved in activities, the child's withdrawal may be seen as deliberate misbehavior. If a parent or teacher berates a child in an attempt to gain his or her participation in activities, he or she may withdraw more, creating an ongoing conflict.

Many children who are depressed experience academic difficulties. Their withdrawal often causes lack of involvement in classroom academic activities. In addition, their difficulty concentrating and their fatigue impair their ability to complete homework and work in the classroom (Kovacs & Goldston, 1991). This can result in poor academic performance, which may increase stress and feelings of depression.

Key Concepts

- Chronic feelings of sadness and/or irritability are the primary features of the depressive disorders in children.
- A marked decline in interest in activities that a child once found enjoyable is a hallmark of depression in children.
- Physical symptoms associated with depression include sleep disturbance, fatigue, and changes in appetite.
- Cognitive symptoms include a sense of worthlessness, difficulty concentrating, and a negative view of self and the world.
- Their withdrawal from others often impedes the development of social skills in children who are depressed and can harm their relationships with peers, parents, and other adults.
- Many children with depressive disorders experience academic difficulties, which are likely influenced by their withdrawal, fatigue, and poor concentration.

Prevalence

Data about the prevalence of depressive disorders in children are sparse, particularly for younger children. However, two studies that used personal interviews with children and adolescents have provided some information about the percentage meeting the diagnostic criteria for a depressive disorder. A study of 9- to 13-year-olds found that 1.6% met the criteria for at least one depressive disorder during the past three months: 0.03% for major depressive disorder, 0.13% for dysthymic disorder, and 1.45% for DDNOS (Costello et al., 1996). A second study included those aged 9 to 17. It reported that 3% met the criteria for at least one depressive disorder: 1% for major depressive disorder, 0.3% for dysthymic disorder, and 1.7% for DDNOS (Angold et al., 2002). Egger and Angold (2006) found that 2% of preschool children met the diagnostic criteria for a depressive disorder.

Besides the prevalence estimates, three points are worth noting from these studies. First, the study that included older adolescents reported a higher prevalence rate, which supports other findings that the prevalence of depression increases during adolescence. Second, more children and adolescents met the criteria for DDNOS than the other two disorders combined, which shows that many children show significant signs of depression yet do not meet the criteria for major depressive disorder or dysthymic disorder. Finally, the prevalence rate for preschool children appears to be approximately the same as for school-age children.

As one might expect, studies examining a longer time frame than three months have reported higher prevalence estimates. For example, one study focused on children through young adults and found the prevalence of any depressive disorder during the previous 12 months to be 1.8% for 11-year-olds, 4.2% for 15-year-olds, 18% for 18-year-olds, and 18.6% for 21-year-olds, highlighting the higher prevalence in younger adolescents and a sharp increase in prevalence among older adolescents and young adults (Newman et al., 1996). Another study found a 14% **lifetime prevalence** of major depressive disorder in a large sample of 15- to 18-year-olds, and that an additional 11% experienced dysthymic disorder or DDNOS (Kessler & Walters, 1998).

Other research has explored the prevalence of depressive symptoms rather than depressive disorders. For example, DuBois and colleagues (1995) found that 10% of their sample of 4th to 10th graders had moderate to severe symptoms of depression at one point in their lives, and that an additional 11% had mild to moderate symptoms. Garber and colleagues (1993) found that 12% of 7th to 12th graders had moderate to severe symptoms of depression at the time of their study and that an additional 28% showed signs of mild to moderate depression.

Sex Differences

More prepubertal boys than girls experience a depressive disorder, particularly major depression (Evans et al., 2005). However, by late adolescence, about twice as many females as males experience a depressive disorder (APA, 2000). As discussed more fully in a following section, the prevalence of depression increases steadily among females beginning around the ages of 13 or 14. The pattern for males is less clear, with some studies showing a relatively small increase for males during adolescence and other studies showing no increase from childhood (Angold & Costello, 2001; Twenge & Nolen Hoeksema, 2002).

Is the Prevalence of Depression Increasing?

Using the results from several similar studies carried out over the past 40 years, Hammen and Rudolf (2003) concluded that there has been a steadily increasing rate of depressive disorders in children born since 1960. It does not appear that the increasing rate is due solely to methodological issues; rather, some or much of the increase appears to be due to increased stress in the lives of many children because of disrupted family lives, increased academic and social pressures, and fewer sources of social support. Therefore, it does appear that the prevalence of childhood depression is increasing.

Key Concepts

- About 2% of children, 4% of mid-adolescents, and 18% of late adolescents and young adults have experienced a depressive disorder in the past year.

- About 10% of children and adolescents experience moderate to severe depressive symptoms, and about 15–30% experience mild to moderate symptoms.
- Boys are more likely than girls to experience a depressive disorder before puberty. By late adolescence, about twice as many females as males experience depression.
- The prevalence of childhood depression has increased over the past several decades.

Course

Studies of the course of depression in children can be divided into two groups. The first group explores the onset and course of depressive disorders. The second group examines changes in the frequency of depressive symptoms during childhood and adolescence.

Onset and Course of Depressive Disorders
Onset of Symptoms

It does not appear that any study of children with depressive disorders has estimated an onset age of their symptoms. It may be too difficult for researchers to gain enough specific information retrospectively from children or parents to help them determine when a child's depressive symptoms became severe enough to meet the diagnostic criteria for a depressive disorder. However, one study showed that preschool teachers' ratings of depressive symptoms at ages 4 to 5, such as "unhappy, sad, depressed," "lonely," and "feels too guilty," and their ratings of several social behaviors, such as "acts too young," "too dependent," and "clumsy," were predictive of the children's levels of depressive symptoms at ages 10 to 11 (Mesman & Koot, 2000b). This suggests that many school-age children with symptoms of depression have an early onset of symptoms, even if the symptoms are not severe enough to constitute a depressive disorder when they begin.

Duration and Recurrence of Symptoms

Major Depressive Disorder   The average length of an initial major depressive episode in children is between seven and nine months (Cicchetti & Toth, 1998). About 90% of these episodes end within two years, but some can continue for many years. Because of the long duration of a few cases, the median length of major depressive episodes may be a better indicator than the mean of the experience of most children. The median length of major depressive episodes is about two months (Hammen & Rudolph, 2003).

Most children and adolescents who recover from a major depressive disorder, in that they are free of the symptoms of a major depressive episode for a time, have one or more additional major depressive episodes later in their childhood or adolescence. Lewinsohn and colleagues (1994) found that 5% of adolescents who had recovered from a major depressive disorder had another major depressive episode within six months, 12% had one within one year, and 33% had one within four years. Rao and colleagues (1995) found that 69% of adolescents had one or more additional major depressive episodes over seven years; the median number of episodes was two, with a range from one to six. Children or adolescents who experience ongoing family conflicts, high stress, or personal losses are more likely than others to experience a relapse (Birmaher, Arbelaez, & Brent, 2002). This is probably related to the role that stress and loss play in depression—a topic covered in the section about etiology.

Adolescents with major depressive disorder have an increased risk of experiencing major depressive disorder as adults (Birmaher et al., 2002). An optimistic finding in one study, however, showed that adolescents who had experienced only one major depressive episode were no more likely than other adolescents to have major depressive disorder as adults, whereas those with two or more episodes were more likely to experience major depressive disorder as adults (Rao et al., 1995). This suggests that successful therapeutic efforts to limit the number of depressive episodes to one during adolescence can have an important influence on a person's life.

Dysthymia   The average length of the duration of dysthymia is, by definition, much longer than a major depressive episode, and is estimated to be about four years for children (Cicchetti & Toth, 1998). However, this is only a rough estimate because it is difficult to note when symptoms become severe enough for dysthymia to be diagnosed and when they eventually end. About 80% of children who are diagnosed with dysthymia will develop major depressive disorder, usually within three years of the diagnosis of dysthymia, suggesting that an intensifying of depressive symptoms occurs in many children with dysthymia (Kovacs et al., 1994).

Development of Additional Disorders

Several longitudinal studies following children with a depressive disorder into their adolescence and young adulthood have shown that they are at risk for developing other forms of psychopathology (Birmaher et al., 1996; Kovacs et al., 2003; Weissman et al., 1999):

- Adolescents, particularly males, are at higher risk for developing a substance use disorder (possibly from their attempts to use drugs to relieve their symptoms of depression).
- As many as 5–10% will commit suicide within 15 years of their initial diagnosis with a depressive disorder.
- Girls are at higher risk for developing an eating disorder during their adolescence.
- About 30% will develop bipolar disorder.

Onset and Course of Depressive Symptoms

Studies of large community samples of children and adolescents show that before age 12 or 13, the number of depressive symptoms experienced by them

ILLUSTRATING AN IMPORTANT RESEARCH ISSUE: MEAN, MEDIAN, AND MODE

As most people learn in their first statistics course, the mean, median, and mode are measures of central tendencies of distributions of data. The mean is the arithmetic average of the data points; the median is the point that divides the data points so that half are below the median and half are above; and the mode is the most frequently occurring value. When a distribution is normal or when it is symmetrical and bimodal, the mean and median are the same. However, when the distribution is skewed in one direction, the mean and median are different. Distributions that are highly skewed can have a median and mean that are quite different.

When the mean is used as the only measure of central tendency in skewed distributions, it can provide misleading information. For example, the data on the length of major depression episodes are skewed. Most cases end relatively soon, some cases take much longer to end, and a few cases continue for years. When the mean is the only measure of central tendency given, it can make it appear that the length of major depression episodes for most children is longer than it truly is. Learning that the mean length of a major depressive episode is seven to nine months causes most of us to think that many children experience episodes that last about this long. This is because most of us tend to assume that data are normally distributed. We may persist in this belief even if given clues that it is not true, such as the information that 10% of cases persist longer than two years. Learning the median can change our view. In this case, learning that the median is about two months can give us a different sense of the length of the episodes for most children. Consequently, knowing both the mean and the median often provides a better understanding of data that are not normally distributed than the mean alone.

is fairly consistent from year to year (see Figure 9.1). This does not mean that all children's depressive symptoms remain constant from year to year. Fluctuations in the symptoms of individual children occur, but at any one time about equal numbers of children experience increasing symptoms while others experience decreasing symptoms—so the average remains constant (Cole et al., 2002). However, when children make the transition into middle school or junior high school, a noticeable increase in depressive symptoms occurs, particularly for girls (Twenge & Nolen Hoeksema, 2002). The increased social, academic, and family stress that many children experience during this time appears to influence this rise in depressive symptoms (Cole et al., 2002).

Two studies provide interesting information about the differences between boys and girls during this time of increasing depressive symptoms. Heath and Camarena (2002) examined the depressive symptoms of a group of boys and girls from the sixth through the eighth grades. As shown in Table 9.3, they divided the children into those with stable depressive symptoms (high, medium, and low levels), those whose symptoms increased or decreased, and those who experienced episodic changes (symptoms increased and then returned to previous levels). They found similar percentages of boys and girls at each of the stable levels. However, boys were more likely to experience episodic changes in depressive symptoms, and girls were more likely to experience steadily increasing symptoms. These results are similar to those found by Ge and colleagues (2003), who assessed depressive

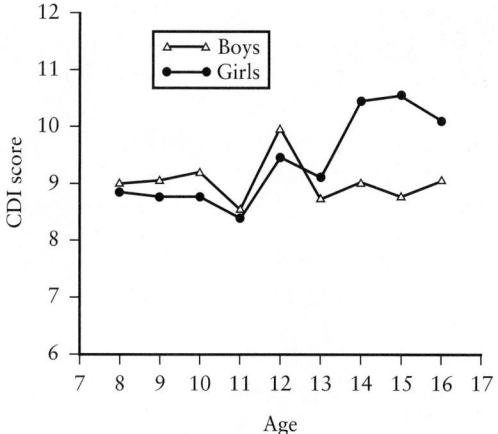

FIGURE 9.1 *Significant Differences in Depression Symptoms for Boys and Girls Emerge in Adolescence*

TABLE 9.3

Frequencies of Depressed Affect Groups by Gender

Group	Boys		Girls	
	n	Percentage	*n*	Percentage
Low stable	36	27	36	27
Medium stable	40	30	45	34
High stable	11	8	14	10
Episodic	28	21	12	9
Decreaser	12	9	5	4
Increaser	8	6	22	16

symptoms in African–American boys and girls at ages 11 and 13. They found that early-maturing girls experienced more symptoms of depression at both ages than did later-maturing girls. Early-maturing boys, on the other hand, had higher levels of depressive symptoms at age 11, but these dissipated by age 13. Thus the depressive symptoms of girls were more chronic, whereas the depressive symptoms of boys were more episodic (which may also explain the spike in depressive symptoms in boys at age 12 in Figure 9.1).

These two studies suggest that girls in early adolescence are more likely than boys of the same age to experience chronic symptoms of depression. This may partly explain the higher prevalence of depressive disorders among females in their late adolescence: Males are more likely to experience and then recover from a period of depression, whereas females are more likely to experience chronic depression once it begins. We explore this topic in more detail in the next section.

Early-maturing girls are at increased risk for depressive disorders.

Key Concepts

- It is difficult to assess when symptoms of depressive disorders begin in children, but some symptoms are noticeable during the preschool years.
- The median length of a major depressive episode for children is about eight weeks. However, some have ongoing symptoms for many months or years.
- Most children who have a major depressive episode will experience another one within several years.
- Adolescents who experience two or more major depressive episodes are likely to continue to experience depression as adults.
- Most children who meet the diagnostic criteria for dysthymic disorder will develop major depressive disorder in their childhood or adolescence.
- Children and adolescents with depressive disorders are at higher risk for other disorders and problems, such as bipolar disorder, an eating disorder, a substance use disorder, or suicide.

- Depressive symptoms in community samples of children remain fairly constant during the preschool and school-age years, with a significant increase during the transition to middle school.

Sex Differences in Depression Beginning in Adolescence

A consistent finding in the literature about depression is that many more female adolescents and adults are depressed than males, even though, as noted earlier, more prepubertal boys than girls experience a depressive disorder (Evans et al., 2005). This difference between females and males begins around age 13, becomes more dramatic between the ages of 15 and 18, and then remains relatively stable through adulthood (Ge et al., 2003).

Several hypotheses have been proposed to explain this difference. Because the change in the prevalence of depression begins at about the same time as the biological changes of puberty, one reasonable hypothesis is that the biological changes push more females to experience depression. Most studies, however, have not found an association between pubertal biological changes and depression. For example, Angold and Rutter (1992) reasoned that if hormonal changes at puberty influenced depression, one would find different levels of depression, at any given chronological age, between females who had completed the biological changes of puberty, those who were in the midst of the changes, and those who had not yet begun the changes. However, they detected no such pattern in a large group of females at various stages of pubertal development. In addition, several other studies have explored the influence of levels of hormones on depression in adolescence and adulthood, and none have found consistent correlations between hormone levels and depressive symptoms (Brooks-Gunn & Warren, 1989; Nolen-Hoeksema & Girgus, 1994). A more recent study did find that higher levels of testosterone and estrogen during puberty were associated with higher levels of depression in a group of 9- to 15-year-old females (Angold, Costello, Erkanli, & Worthman, 1999). The researchers noted that, by themselves, these hormones could not account for the onset of depression because all females eventually experience them at heightened levels during puberty; but they might interact with increased stress to produce higher levels of depression in some females.

Another line of research has focused on stress because, as discussed in the section about etiology, there is an association between high levels of stress and depression. Several studies have shown that female adolescents are more likely than males to experience high levels of stress, which may increase the females' likelihood of experiencing depression. For example, many females view their physical changes during puberty more negatively than do males, and body dissatisfaction has a stronger association with depression in females than males (Allgood-Merten, Lewinsohn, & Hops, 1990; Nolen-Hoeksema & Girgus, 1994). In addition, female adolescents experience more health problems after puberty than do males, and the level of these health problems is related to their level of depression (Williams, Colder, Richards, & Scalzo, 2002). Females are more likely than males to experience sexual abuse during their adolescence, which adds stress to their lives and may accentuate issues related to their bodies (Haugaard & Reppucci, 1988). In addition, females experience higher levels of stress than males associated with dating and romantic relationships, which often occur for the first time in adolescence (Nolen-Hoeksema & Girgus, 1994).

In addition to the increased stress they experience in early adolescence, some research suggests that females may have fewer resources or strategies for handling this stress. For example, many girls who have increased conflict with their mothers during early adolescence experience less support from their mothers, but loss of maternal support is not common among boys who experience conflict with their mothers (Jenkins, Goodness, & Buhrmester, 2002). Thus girls may feel less support from an important person in their lives when support is especially needed. In addition, females are more likely than males to cope with stressful events by ruminating about them and thinking negatively of themselves (Nolen-Hoeksema, 1987). People who ruminate about negative events are likely to experience depressive symptoms that are more severe and chronic, suggesting that this response to stressful negative events that is more common among females may intensify their depression (Lyubomirsky & Nolen-Hoeksema, 1993). Girls also engage in co-rumination more frequently than boys—sharing negative experiences with friends and talking extensively about them. Although this process deepens friendships among early adolescent females, it also leads to greater symptoms of depression (Rose, 2002).

Girls who enter puberty earlier than most of their peers are particularly susceptible to developing depression. Ge and his colleagues (2003) suggest that this pattern is likely to occur because early-maturing girls experience stress that is more sudden and lasts longer than that experienced by later-maturing girls. The sudden nature of the stress occurs because the onset of menses is an event that happens suddenly and that immediately tells an early-maturing girl that she is no longer a "part of the gang" with her friends but has entered a new phase of her life. Because early-maturing girls often associate with older females and males, they can be unprepared emotionally or socially for the activities engaged in by those who are older, particularly sexual activities. The stress associated with these activities can last for several years.

Most early-maturing males, on the other hand, do not experience sudden and sustained stress. Although they may experience increased stress, this stress is often less intense because of the more gradual onset of puberty in males. In addition, their physical changes may make them better at activities prized by other males, such as sports. They are less likely to associate with older adolescents because the natural lag in the physical maturation between males and females means that early-maturing males often experience puberty at about the same time as most of the females their age (Ge, Conger, & Elder, 2001).

Taken together, the research to date suggests that many females experience heightened levels of stress after puberty, which may be accentuated by the hormonal changes they experience. This stress may put them on a path that leads to greater short-term levels of depression. The ongoing issues they face as they continue into adolescence, such as low levels of social support and a cognitive and friendship style that includes rumination about the stressors they experience, may continue and deepen their depression. Most males do not experience the same sustained stress experienced by females, so any increase in depression that they feel around the time of puberty is episodic. The result is that by the end of adolescence, many more females than males are experiencing a depressive disorder.

Key Concepts

- Most studies have not found that depression is influenced by the biological changes that occur during puberty; however, one recent study suggested that some biological changes may interact with stress to make females more susceptible to depression.
- More females than males experience high and sustained levels of stress during their adolescence.
- The cognitive style of many female adolescents, including rumination and co-rumination, is likely to increase their feelings of depression.
- Females who enter puberty early are at increased risk for developing depression, probably because of the increased stress they experience. Early-maturing males also experience heightened levels of depression, but this is transitory for most of them.

Suicide

Suicide is a significant and growing problem with children and especially with adolescents. Because most children and adolescents who are suicidal experience depression, we discuss suicide in this chapter. (Remember that throughout this text, the term *children* is used to refer to children and adolescents; specific ages are used as appropriate.)

Defining Terms

Suicide ideation refers to serious thoughts about suicide (Lewinsohn, Rohde, & Seeley, 1996). The fleeting thoughts that many children have about suicide are generally not considered suicide ideation. Some children who experience suicide ideation will attempt suicide; most will decide not to make any attempt at all.

A **suicide attempt** is a purposeful act that a person believes can or will result in his or her death but that does not cause death (Lewinsohn et al., 1996). Some researchers have created a subgroup among suicide attempts: **medically significant suicide attempts.** Usually this refers to attempts that require medical intervention to save a person's life. Medically significant suicide attempts are usually a small percentage of all suicide attempts (Gould, Greenberg, Velting, & Shaffer, 2003).

Determining whether a child has attempted suicide can be difficult when his or her intent is unclear. For example, consider a case in which a child who has been severely depressed for several weeks steps in front of a moving bus and is badly injured. Did he step in front of the bus with the intent of killing himself, or did his depression make him less conscious of what was around him so that he stepped in front of the bus accidentally? It is possible to simply ask the child if he intended to kill himself, but he might lie and deny a suicide attempt because of shame or fear.

Completed suicides are those that result in death. In some cases it is clear that a child's death is a suicide. However, determining that a death is suicide can be difficult in other cases—even more so than after a suicide attempt because the child cannot be asked about the act. Many physicians, medical examiners, and others are hesitant to call a child's death a suicide when the cause of the death is questionable because knowing that a child has committed suicide can place an added burden on family members and others (Gould, Shaffer, & Greenberg, 2003). Consequently, the prevalence of completed suicides is often underestimated.

Prevalence

Completed suicide is rare in children and young adolescents. For example, within the 5- to 14-year-old age range, about 1 boy in every 100,000 and 1 girl in every 200,000 completes suicide (in comparison, the completed suicide rate for males of all ages is 18 per 100,000 and for females of all ages is 4.5 per 100,000; National Center for Health Statistics, 2006). Almost all completed suicides involve either suffocation (including hanging) or shooting with a firearm. A small percentage of adolescents commit suicide through poisoning (including a purposeful overdose of medication), although that percentage is small when compared with either suffocation or the use of firearms. It is noteworthy that adolescents are more likely than younger children to use firearms, probably because they have easier access to them (Gould, Greenberg et al., 2003; Vieweg et al., 2005).

Suicide attempts are much more frequent than completed suicides. Data from the 2005 Youth Risk Behavior Survey (National Center for Health Statistics, 2006) show that, among high school students, 11% of females and 6% of males made a suicide attempt in the previous 12 months, and that 2.9% of females and 1.8% of males made a medically significant suicide attempt. Evans and colleagues (2005) reviewed 60 studies of suicide attempts among adolescents and found that the mean lifetime prevalence across the studies was 9.7% and that the mean prevalence of a suicide attempt during the past year was 6.4%. Suicidal ideation is even more common, with about 30% of adolescents seriously considering suicide at some time in their lives and about 20% of adolescents seriously considering suicide in a 12-month period (Evans et al., 2005; Gould, Greenberg et al., 2003).

Characteristics and Experiences of Children Who Are Suicidal

Many researchers have explored characteristics that are associated with an increased risk for suicide attempts or completed suicide. About 60% of school-age children and young adolescents who attempt or complete suicide have been diagnosed with a behavioral or emotional disorder. Depressive disorders are the most commonly diagnosed, but conduct disorder is also frequently diagnosed, particularly with males (Gould, Greenberg et al., 2003). A consistent association between substance abuse disorders and attempted or completed suicide has been found. Although the reasons for this association are not completely clear, it may be that alcohol or other drugs are used by some depressed adolescents to help ease their depression, with some of these depressed adolescents attempting or completing suicide. Another possibility is that some drugs, such as alcohol, may reduce an adolescent's inhibitions to suicide, thereby increasing the adolescent's risk of suicide (Wu et al., 2004).

A family history of suicide is strongly associated with child suicide (Brent & Mann, 2003). Some research suggests a genetic influence on suicide attempts and completed suicide, possibly through genes' influence on the neurotransmitter serotonin. The same genes that influence suicide in a parent or other relative may also influence suicide in a child. In addition, perhaps some family environments place parents and children at risk for suicide; or observing one family member take his or her life may increase the risk that other family members will do the same (Gould, Fisher, Parides, Flory, & Shaffer, 1996).

The Development of Suicidal Thinking and Behavior

For most of our lives, almost all of us feel a strong desire to live. As we have just seen, however, some children feel ambivalent about life and consider, attempt, or complete suicide (Shneidman, 1991). Their desire to live is accompanied by a desire to die. This desire to die is only slight in most children who feel it; however, it can be quite strong in others, and irresistible in a few.

In this section we explore individual and environmental characteristics that can push some children toward suicide. As we will see, high levels of stress are often associated with initial suicidal thinking. A child's emotions, cognitions, and behaviors can then push a highly stressed child who has thought about suicide to consider it seriously or attempt it.

Influences of Stress

Initial thinking about suicide often occurs in children experiencing high levels of stress who have few resources for coping with this stress. Physical diseases, being the victim of traumatic experiences such as physical or sexual assault, and having a history of early childhood behavior problems are all stressful for a child and have been associated with increased risk for suicide (Laederach, Fischer, Bowen, & Ladame, 1999; Reinherz, Giaconia, Silverman, &

Friedman, 1995). Being raised in a family that is chaotic, unsupportive, or overly intrusive, or experiencing parental expectations that are more than a child can achieve, are also stressors associated with an increased risk for suicide (Jurich & Collins, 1996). In addition, children who are isolated from and rejected by their peers are also at risk for suicide (Garland & Zigler, 1993). Characteristics associated with alienation from peers and suicidal tendencies have included sexual identity problems, poor social skills, and academic giftedness. Adolescents who have recently ended a serious romantic relationship or who are having ongoing problems with a boyfriend or girlfriend also are at greater risk for suicide (Gould, Greenberg et al., 2003).

Emotions and Suicide

The common emotional experience of children who are suicidal is psychological pain (Shneidman, 1991). The pain can come from many sources, often feels intolerable, and can be so dominant in the lives of some children that it seems to define their emotional experience.

Most, but not all, children who are suicidal are depressed (Gould, Greenberg et al., 2003). The relationship between suicide and depression can be complex. In some cases, strong feelings of depression can be so painful that they might cause a child to be suicidal. Alternatively, being suicidal may increase depression. For example, the shame about considering suicide may increase a child's feelings of depression.

Intense, ongoing anger is also found in some suicidal adolescents (Borst & Noam, 1993; Brown, Overholser, Spirito, & Fritz, 1991). As with depression, the pain of high levels of anger, particularly anger at important people in a child's life, may push a child to consider suicide. In addition, high levels of anger may be directed at people whose actions have increased the adolescent's suicidal feelings. For example, an adolescent considering suicide because of school failure, the breakup of a relationship, or sexual abuse may feel high levels of anger toward a teacher, ex-girlfriend, or abusing parent. In addition, higher levels of aggression are associated with suicide in some adolescents (Apter & Wasserman, 2003), possibly reflecting their style of dealing with problems in an aggressive and angry way, even if the aggression and anger are aimed at themselves.

Cognitions and Suicide

The thoughts of many suicidal children are characterized by **constriction** (Gould, Greenberg et al., 2003), which refers to a narrowing of a person's view of the world. One way that cognitions can be constricted is through biased perception. As discussed later in this chapter, children who are depressed perceive their world in a biased way: They notice and remember negative events readily, classify many neutral events as negative, and fail to notice or remember most positive events. Angry/aggressive children also have biased perception in that they see more aggression aimed at them than occurs and are likely to disregard the supportive nature of some events and relationships. As they perceive their world more negatively, their depression or anger/

aggression may grow. This can bias their perceptions further, which in turn can increase their depression or anger/aggression.

Cognitions can also be constricted through **tunneling,** which occurs when a person's attention gradually becomes focused more and more on one or two issues. The thinking of many suicidal children becomes focused on the stresses and problems that are causing them pain, and they are unlikely to notice or think about other events or relationships (Leenaars & Lester, 1995). In addition, once a child begins to consider suicide seriously, much of his or her attention may be focused on suicide. Consequently, thoughts of suicide and stress may begin to gradually dominate his or her attention, eventually becoming the only important issue in his or her life.

The cognitions of suicidal children are also characterized by hopelessness, although it is not clear whether children who are suicidal have higher levels of hopelessness than children with other behavioral or emotional disorders (Gould, Shaffer et al., 2003). Hopelessness and depression are often associated, and they can reinforce each other. Together, they can encourage a negative view of a child's current life—a life dominated by the issue of suicide—and provide little sense that the future will be any different.

Behaviors and Suicide

Two clusters of behaviors that are associated with suicide are related to the emotions of depression and anger. The first cluster is a set of withdrawn and passive behaviors that are common to depression (Apter & Wasserman, 2003). Suicidal children may withdraw from activities they once enjoyed and from friends and family. They may be physically absent from school and other activities; or they may be psychologically absent if physically present.

The second cluster of behaviors consists of aggressive behaviors often associated with anger. Studies of community samples of adolescents in a psychiatric hospital found significant correlations between violent behavior and suicidal ideation; suicidal adolescents also have more contact with legal authorities than nonsuicidal adolescents and engage in more property damage and vandalism (Fergusson & Lynskey, 1995).

Attempting Suicide

Children who feel a strong pull toward death must wrestle with the decision about whether to attempt suicide. Most of these children repeatedly decide not to attempt suicide. However, some decide, at some point, to make a suicide attempt. Two explanations have been suggested for understanding these decisions (Brown et al., 1991). One is that the slow build-up of stressors finally becomes too much for a child to handle, and he or she attempts suicide. The second involves a more hasty or impulsive attempt by a child who has just experienced a significant stressor. It is not clear what percentage of children who attempt suicide have either of these experiences.

Whether awareness of a recently committed suicide encourages suicide attempts (known as **suicide contagion**) continues to be debated. Some case studies suggest that suicide contagion does occur. For example, Brent and colleagues (1989) reported on two completed suicides, seven suicide attempts, and 23 cases of strong suicidal ideation in a single high school, all of which occurred within 18 days of two earlier suicides at that school. Most of those who became suicidal after the earlier suicides had clear evidence of a psychiatric disorder before the earlier suicides. In addition, a more recent study using the National Longitudinal Study of Adolescent Health (Cerel, Roberts, & Nilsen, 2005) found a strong connection between knowing about a peer's suicide and the presence of suicidal ideation or a suicide attempt in adolescence.

Families of Children with Depressive Disorders

As discussed later in this chapter, many children with a depressive disorder are raised in families with a depressed parent. In particular, depression in a mother is strongly associated with increased risk of depression in one or more of her children (Cicchetti & Toth, 1998; Leech, Larkby, Day, & Day, 2006). Many families in which a mother is depressed are less organized and characterized by higher levels of negativity than other families, and they are more likely than other families to experience frequent marital discord, parent–child discord, and stress (Kaslow et al., 1994). Although not all children who are depressed are raised in families with a parent who has a depressive disorder, many are, and thus they experience this type of troubled family environment.

Even when a parent is not depressed, many families with a child who is depressed show higher amounts of strife than other families, including more marital discord, less cohesion, and more negativity (Kovacs & Sherrill, 2001). Further, many families with a child who is depressed are more isolated and have fewer sources of support than other families. All these characteristics are likely to increase the stress experienced by children in these families, which may contribute to their depression.

Etiology of Depression

Several theories have been put forward to explain the initial and ongoing development of depressive disorders in children, including those focused on affect regulation, cognitions, biological functioning, stress, and interpersonal relationships. Although each of these theories focuses on a different characteristic of children or of children's lives, it would be inappropriate to consider them as competing. Rather, the range of these theories reflects the range of the impairments that have been found in children with depressive disorders and the range of issues that can influence these impairments.

These theories can combine in several ways to provide a more thorough understanding of the development of depression in children:

- One theory may focus on issues of particular importance to the development of depression at one age, whereas another theory may focus on issues that are more important at a later age. For example, issues related to stress may be more influential on the development of depression at an earlier age, and cognitive style may be more influential later.

- The issues focused on by two or more theories may interact to influence the development of depression. For example, the biological functioning of some children may make them more susceptible to the type of stress that influences depression.
- The issues focused on by one theory may influence the development of issues focused on by another theory. For example, problems with affect regulation early in life may influence the onset of depression and, several years later, influence a child's interpersonal style in a way that can maintain or deepen this depression.

In addition, as we have discussed in other chapters in this text, some theories effectively explain the development of depression in some children while other theories explain it in other children. Consequently, we do not need to decide which theory is "best." Rather, by understanding all the theories, we have a better chance for understanding the development of depression in a wide range of children.

In this section we first explore the five categories of theories that are most commonly used to understand the development of depression in children. We then explore two models that illustrate how the issues relating to each theory can interact to influence the development of depression.

Biologically Based Theories
The Role of Biological Functioning in Depression

Biologically based theories of depression focus on how the functioning of a person's central nervous system (CNS) influences his or her mood (Evans et al., 2005). The importance of a person's CNS in his or her mood has been known for years. An early discovery about the role of the CNS in behavioral or emotional disorders came from observations of adults who were given the medication **reserpine** to reduce high blood pressure (Carlson, 1986). About 20% of them became severely depressed, suggesting that their biological functioning—influenced by the medication—was causing their depression.

It was later discovered that reserpine significantly reduced the actions of the **monoamine neurotransmitters** (norepinephrine, dopamine, and serotonin) in the CNS. This discovery led to the **monoamine hypothesis:** A reduction in the monoamine neurotransmitters causes depression (Brooks-Gunn et al., 2001). This hypothesis led to the development of **tricyclic antidepressant** medications, such as imipramine, that increase monoamine neurotransmission and reduce feelings of depression.

Ongoing research, however, showed that the monoamine hypothesis was too simplistic and that many neurotransmitters are involved in depression in adults (Brooks-Gunn et al., 2001). Although the exact way in which neurotransmitters create a depressed mood remains unclear, it is currently thought that complex interactions between several of them are likely to result in a depressed mood (Evans et al., 2005). Researchers are attempting to clarify these complex interactions. Whether the same interactions that influence depression in adults also influence depression in children is also a focus of ongoing research.

Another line of research has focused on the role of the **hypothalamic–pituitary–adrenal (HPA) axis** in depression because of its role in responses to stress (Hammen & Rudolph, 2003). The HPA axis is a self-regulating system that is part of the endocrine system. It has an important role in the regulation of basic functions such as hunger, sleep, mood, and sexual activity. Hormones released from the hypothalamus stimulate the release of different hormones from the pituitary gland, which stimulate the release of a third type of hormones from the adrenal glands (Sokolov & Kutcher, 2001). All can have a significant influence on physical functioning.

Several biological functions related to the HPA axis are disrupted in most adults who are depressed (Evans et al., 2005). For example, adults who are depressed have higher levels of cortisol in their systems (secreted by the adrenal glands), have abnormal cortisol regulation, and have elevated levels of **corticotrophin-releasing hormone (CRH),** which is secreted by the hypothalamus. These characteristics of adults who are depressed suggest that the HPA axis has a role in depression; however, its specific role remains unclear. As discussed earlier, it is also unclear whether the HPA axis plays a role in the development of childhood depression: Some disruptions in HPA axis functioning found in most adults who are depressed are not found in many children who are depressed.

So although differences in biological functioning appear to play a role in many cases of adult depression, their role in childhood depression remains unclear. However, they continue to be the focus of research because of the possibility that they play an important part in both childhood and adult depression.

Influences on Biological Functioning and Depression: The Role of Genes

Many studies have shown that genes influence the development of depression in adults by influencing their biological functioning, although the specific mechanisms through which genes have their influence remain unknown (Sullivan, Neale, & Kendler, 2000). However, the extent of the genetic influence on the development of childhood depression remains less clear, and some studies in this area provide conflicting conclusions.

Family studies of children with depression show that a high percentage of the children's first-degree relatives also have a mood disorder, and studies of mothers who are depressed show that a high percentage of their children also experience depression (Hammen & Rudolph, 2003). However, children of depressed mothers experience a wide range of psychological problems, including anxiety disorders and conduct disorders; so it is not clear that they have inherited a specific genetic tendency toward depression.

Twin studies with children who are depressed suggest a genetic influence on depression, but the findings remain ambiguous. No studies have been done with children diagnosed with major depressive disorder, but several studies have used questionnaires to obtain information about children's depressive symptoms (Rice, Harold, & Thapar, 2002). A relatively high estimate of genetic heritability (about 50–60%) has been obtained when correlations between parents' reports of their MZ and DZ twins' depressive symptoms are compared; however, much lower heritability estimates are obtained when the twins' self-reports are compared (about 20–30%). The reasons for these differences remain unclear, but there is a possibility that parents may generalize their beliefs about their twins' symptoms to a greater degree with MZ twins than with DZ twins because of the greater physical similarity of MZ twins (Rowe & Jacobson, 1999).

Two twin studies with children have reported intriguing results when the level of depression was considered (Rende, Plomin, Reiss, & Hetherington, 1993; Rice et al., 2002). Both found that genes had a moderate influence on depressive symptoms and that the twins' shared family environment had little influence. However, when only those twins with high levels of depression were considered (possibly similar to those with major depressive disorder), an insignificant influence of genes and a significant influence of shared family environment was found. This suggests that genes play a more important role in the development of moderate forms of childhood depression and have less influence on severe forms.

To further complicate matters, Rice and colleagues (2002) found differences in genetic influence related to the age of the participants: The genetic influence on adolescent depression was stronger than for childhood depression. Shared environmental influences conversely had a stronger influence on childhood depression than on adolescent depression. In some ways these results resemble those found in a longitudinal study in which high levels of stress in early childhood were associated with an onset of depression between the ages of 11 and 15 years but not with an onset in adulthood (Jaffee et al., 2002). These two studies raise the possibility that depression that begins in childhood or adolescence is influenced more by environmental issues than genes, and that depression with an onset in late adolescence or adulthood is influenced more by genes than environmental issues.

To complicate matters even further, two adoption studies of depressive symptoms in children and adolescents showed no significant genetic influence (Rice et al., 2002). Thus the twin and adoption studies suggest different conclusions about genetic influences on childhood depression. We must wait for additional research to achieve a clearer understanding of the role of genes in childhood depression.

Influences on Biological Functioning and Depression: The Role of the Environment

Evidence is beginning to accumulate, primarily from studies with animals other than humans, that early exposure to neglectful or abusive parenting may influence the development of an infant's HPA axis, and possibly other brain systems, which may make a child more susceptible to depression caused by stress (Heim & Nemeroff, 2001; Schore, 2001). As also discussed in the chapter about bipolar disorders, studies of rats and nonhuman primates have shown that early deprivation causes neurological changes, in particular to CRH neurons, that increase an organism's sensitivity to stress. The changes in CRH neurons may affect the functioning of serotonin neurons, which may affect mood. For example, rats exposed to repeated maternal deprivation as pups eat less sweetened solution (suggesting anhedonia) and have increased agitation and anxiety throughout their lives (Francis, Caldji, Champagen, Plotsky, & Meaney, 1999; Heim & Nemeroff, 2001).

Although it is not possible to translate research directly from rats to understanding childhood depression, the research with rats can point human research in particular directions. Some research has found disrupted CRH functioning in children who are depressed and who have been exposed to repeated child abuse, but not in depressed children who have not been abused (Kaufman et al., 1997). This suggests that early abuse may influence the development of depression in some children by affecting their early neurological development, with this development then having long-lasting influences on how they respond to stress (Heim & Nemeroff, 2001).

Theories Based on Affect Regulation

Theories based on affect regulation suggest that some experiences of infants and young children make them less able to regulate their negative moods. As a result, they experience negative moods more frequently and for longer periods, which increases their likelihood of developing a depressive disorder as children or adolescents.

Problems with affect regulation can be traced to infancy in many children. An important goal of infancy is learning to regulate the emotional arousal caused by physiological stress (such as needing to be fed or being cold). Although infants have some capabilities for self-calming during stressful times, it is primarily through the care provided by others that their arousal is modulated (being fed, being held and warmed) (Cicchetti & Toth, 1998; Sheeber, Allen, Davis, & Sorensen, 2000). Because of their dependence on others, infants whose caregivers are not sensitive to their needs often experience prolonged periods of arousal and negative affect.

Attachment theory is particularly useful for understanding the development of poor affect regulation (Bowlby, 1969, 1973, 1980). Children who have an insecure attachment are unlikely to achieve a state of *felt security*, which occurs when an infant is confident that a trusted person is consistently available to him or her (Sroufe & Waters, 1977). Without a sense of felt security, infants feel anxious frequently, which inhibits many growth-promoting activities like play and exploration and also results in the dysregulation of several physiological systems. Disruption of these systems and frequent anxiety make affect regulation difficult for the infant or toddler. In addition, the unavailability of a consistent primary caregiver means that the child has little assistance in regulating his or her affect. As a result, these infants do not develop a sense that their negative affect can be controlled; and neural pathways for experiencing these emotions may be strengthened, making it more likely that they will experience these moods frequently (Cicchetti & Toth, 1998).

Interactions between parents and young children can facilitate or impede children's ability to develop affect regulation. For example, consider a parent who picks up a toddler who has just fallen and comforts her. The warmth of the parent's body, the soothing words, and perhaps the parent's attempt to distract the child ("Oh, look at the birdie in the tree") all soothe the child and teach the child early skills for regulating negative affect (Abela, Brozina, & Haigh, 2002). In contrast, consider a toddler who falls and is left to cry: He is likely to feel a negative mood for an extended period and is unlikely to begin to learn skills for regulating his affect. Similarly, a school-age child who is upset because of being picked on, or an adolescent who is upset after breaking up with a girlfriend, may receive the type of parental help that allows him or her to better regulate and deal with emotional arousal, or may experience little help and thus fail to learn progressively more mature strategies for regulating his or her own emotions.

Children and adolescents with few age-appropriate skills for affect regulation can experience a variety of problems. Not only are they more likely to experience frequent and prolonged bouts of sadness, anxiety, and anger; they are more likely to have poor peer relationships because they will be more emotionally reactive when dealing with peers. They may be more angry or aggressive, which also affects relationships with peers, parents, teachers, and other adults (Cicchetti & Toth, 1998). This can lead to rejection by others or more frequent angry interactions with them, both of which increase the stress these children experience. They may respond to this rejection by withdrawing from others, which reduces the likelihood of having positive interactions. All these interpersonal problems are stressful for children and can contribute to the acute or chronic sadness that is at the foundation of the depressive disorders.

The research on the role of affect regulation on childhood depression has focused primarily on depressed mothers and their children. Because of their own depression, many depressed mothers are withdrawn and unavailable to their children, have more difficulty matching their moods to the moods of their children, and give their children far less help in regulating their emotional arousal (Garber, Braafladt, & Weiss, 1995). As a result, many children of depressed mothers experience difficulty with affect regulation. This is believed to influence the development of depression in these children, which can partially explain the relatively frequent depression seen in children of depressed mothers (Leech et al., 2006).

Cognitive Theories

Several cognitive theories about the development of depression have been suggested, and a significant body of research supports them (Hammen & Rudolph, 2003). In addition, cognitive therapy is an effective intervention for children and adults who are depressed, supporting the theory that cognitions play a role in depression (Lewinsohn & Clarke, 1999).

Most cognitive theorists do not claim that cognitions cause the onset of depression. Rather, they argue that certain types of negative thoughts and certain styles of thinking cause a child to experience the emotion of sadness, and that the child's negative cognitions and sadness cause the child to withdraw from others. This combination of cognitions, emotions, and behaviors can strengthen feelings of depression in a child who may be vulnerable to depression for other reasons (Beck, Rush, Shaw, & Emery, 1979). In this section we explore two cognitive theories.

Negative Views of Self, the World, and the Future

The cognitive theory of Aaron Beck (Beck, 1976) states that the experiences of some children cause them to develop patterns of negative thinking about themselves, their world, and their future. A variety of experiences may lead to these negative patterns of thinking, such as chronic abuse or neglect (which, as just discussed, may also lead to poor affect regulation), being frequently demeaned by parents or other adults, or consistently failing to meet the expectations of parents or others. A child's negative views of self can lead to low self-esteem and derogatory self-evaluations. Negative views of the world can lead to beliefs that the world is unfair and malicious. Negative views of the future can lead to a sense of hopelessness.

All children (and all the rest of us) experience these negative thoughts occasionally, and when they occur they cause us to feel sad or angry. If a child's thinking is dominated by these negative thoughts, he or she feels sad or angry much of the time—which is the emotional experience of depression. In addition, the child's frequent depressed mood causes him or her to withdraw from others. This withdrawal gives the child few opportunities for positive experiences and a great deal of time to think about his or her failures and unhappy life, which can maintain or deepen the child's experience of depression [see Figure 9.2(a)].

Not only do negative thoughts lead to increased feelings of depression; they can also bias the ways that children perceive and remember events around them. Children with consistently negative beliefs are more likely than other children to notice and remember negative events and are less likely to notice and remember positive events. For example, children who are depressed perceive their performance on tasks more negatively than do their peers, even when objective task performance measures show no difference between the children who are depressed and those who are not (Kaslow et al., 1994; Leitenberg, Yost, & Carroll Wilson, 1986). These biased perceptions and memories reinforce a child's negative views of self, world, and future because the child remembers many negative events and few positive ones. This, in turn, strengthens the child's biased perceptions. Thus a cycle of negative thoughts leading to biased perceptions leading to increased negative thinking can occur, which deepens depression.

Another cognitive style common to children who are depressed is **rumination**, which involves thinking passively and repetitively about the negative events in one's life. Children with this cognitive style show higher levels of depressive symptoms than other children, and rumination is often associated with increases in depressive symptoms over time (Abela et al., 2002). Children who engage in **co-rumination** with their friends (discussing their symptoms and failures together) display more symptoms of depression than those who do not engage in co-rumination (Rose, 2002).

Attributional Style

The attributional cognitive theory of depression was developed from the work of Martin Seligman and his colleagues (Abramson, Seligman, & Teasdale, 1978), which focused on the concept of **learned helplessness.** The concept of learned helplessness was developed from experimental and naturalistic observations showing that people and other animals can learn that they cannot stop negative events from occurring in their lives, and so they stop trying to do so. This leads to passivity, which often results in negative events occurring with increasing frequency, which reinforces the person's belief that he or she has no influence over these events. For example, a child who believes that he cannot influence whether other children tease him will stop trying to end this teasing, which can result in his becoming the target of teasing more frequently. Similarly, a girl who believes that she cannot influence how well she does on academic tasks will not study for exams, causing increasingly poor academic performance.

Attributional theory has many connections to learned helplessness. It focuses on how children and adults attribute (that is, understand) the causes of positive and negative events in their lives (Abramson et al., 1978). A wide range of studies has shown that many children who are depressed have a different attributional style than those who are not depressed.

Children who are depressed are more likely than other children to attribute negative events to internal, global, and stable factors. That is, they attribute a negative event or failure to one or more of their own characteristics (*internal attribution*), to the fact that negative experiences and failures occur throughout their lives (*global attribution*), and to the fact that negative events have always happened to them and always will (*stable attribution*) (Gladstone & Kaslow, 1995). For example, a depressed girl who is not asked to a party might attribute her lack of an invitation to beliefs that she is unattractive and unlikable, that she is a failure at everything that is important, and that none of this will change in the future. Similarly, children who are depressed are more likely than others to attribute positive events to external, specific, and unstable causes. For example, if the girl had been asked to the party, she would likely attribute this invitation as follows: The other girl's mother made her ask me; the other children will not ask me to parties because their parents will not make them ask me; so I will not be asked to any other parties no matter how well this one goes. We can imagine this girl's behaviors when she attends the party (standing by herself; rebuffing attempts by others to talk with her). It is likely that these behaviors will irritate the other children, thereby reducing her chance of being invited to other parties and reinforcing her negative attributions.

When experiencing a stressful event, the attributional style of children who are depressed leads them to feel a sense of helplessness about their ability to cope with it (this is the principal connection between attributional theory and learned helplessness). This helplessness leads to a sense of hopelessness, which leads to the emotional experience of depression (Dixon & Ahrens, 1992). Moreover, when positive events or successes occur, children with this attributional style either ignore them or consider them only fleeting and unlikely to occur again, which can reinforce their attributional style and lead to greater feelings of depression [see Figure 9.2(b)].

A variety of experiences can influence the development of a child's negative attributional style (Abramson et al., 1978). For example, consistent negative events such as being abused by a parent, being bullied by other children, or experiencing academic failure can influence the development of negative attributions. In addition, a child's parents may teach the child repeatedly about the accuracy of negative attributions—particularly if the parent

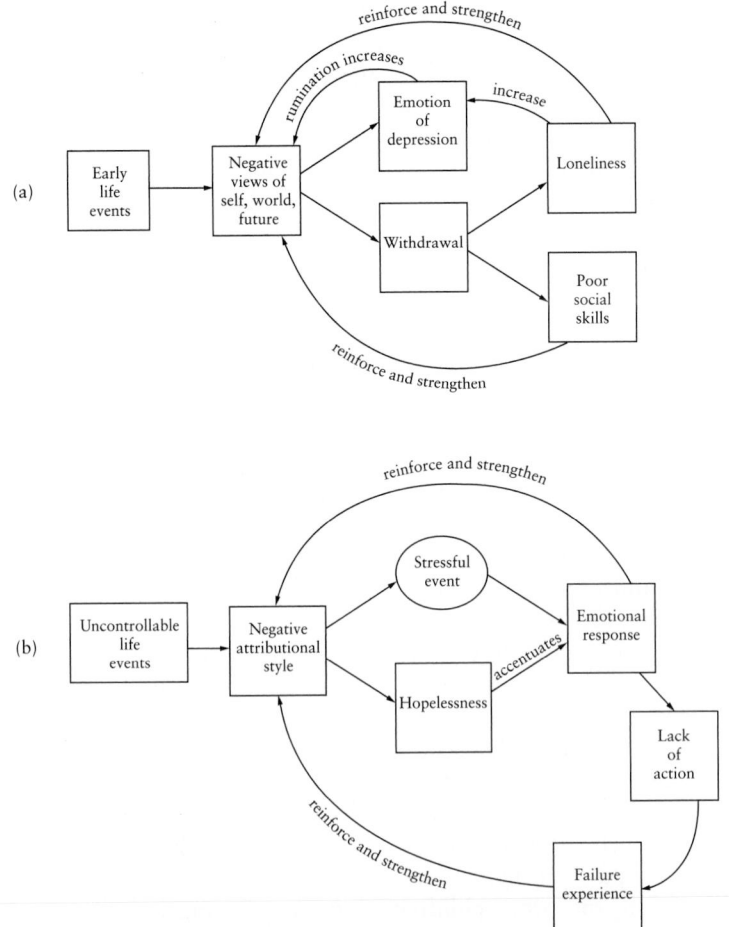

FIGURE 9.2   *Two Cognitive Processes and Depression*

is depressed—which can intensify a child's negative attributions ("Don't ever think that it will get any better, because it won't").

Influences of Life Stress

It has been clear for years that higher levels of stress are associated with depression in children, particularly stress associated with their family lives and relationships with their parents (Cicchetti & Toth, 1998). As already discussed, early adolescence—which is stressful for many children because of the physical, social, academic, and family changes occurring then—is a time when the incidence of depression increases, which reinforces the connection between stress and depression (Ge et al., 2003; Heath & Camarena, 2002; Sagrestano, Paikoff, Holmbeck, & Fendrich, 2003). In addition, children and adolescents living in situations where they experience chronic stress, such as in poverty, isolated areas, or violent neighborhoods, show more symptoms of depression than those living without chronic stress (DuRant, Getts, Cadenhead, Emans, & Woods, 1995; Fergusson & Lynskey, 1995).

Unfortunately, a clear understanding of how stress influences depression has not been developed (Hammen & Rudolph, 2003). One possibility is that stress pushes children toward depression directly, possibly by creating changes in brain functioning that produce a depressed mood (Carlson, 1986) [see Figure 9.3(a)]. An alternative possibility is suggested by the **diathesis–stress model:** Stressful events interact with a child's cognitions to create depression. Thus an adolescent who has a negative attributional style may be pushed

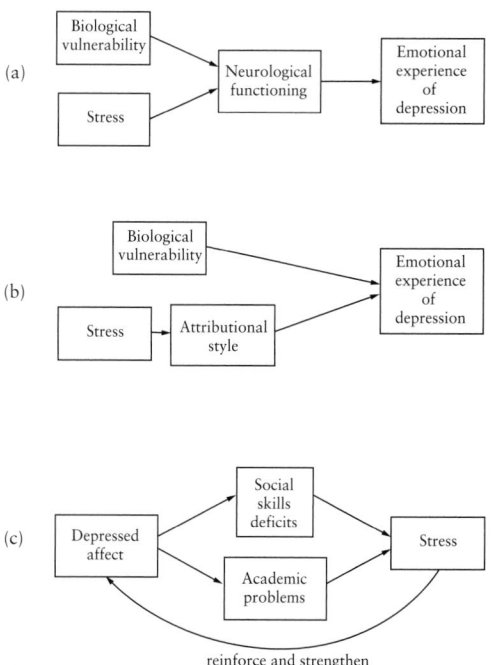

FIGURE 9.3   *Possible Influences of Stress on Depression*

toward depression by stressful events (Dixon & Ahrens, 1992). In essence, the stressful event activates the negative attributional style, and together they are perceived by the child as indicating, once again, that life is unfair, hurtful, and impossible, which creates feelings of depression [see Figure 9.3(b)].

Finally, Hammen (1992) has suggested an interesting alternative to the diathesis–stress model. She asserts that the behaviors of a child who has become depressed are likely to produce stress in the child's life. For example, the withdrawn behavior of a depressed child may cause her to be teased by peers, do poorly on academic tasks, and lose support from parents or other adults. All these consequences can create stress in her life. This stress can then interact with her cognitions to increase her depression, which in turn can increase her dysfunctional behavior and the stress caused by it. In this way, stress is both a cause and a consequence of depression [see Figure 9.3(c)].

Interpersonal Theories

Rather than providing a model for the initial development of depression, interpersonal theories focus on how the interpersonal interactions of a child or adolescent who is depressed can maintain or deepen feelings of depression. Studies of college roommates and adolescents and their mothers have shown the types of interpersonal interactions that can maintain or intensify depression.

Sheeber and colleagues (2000) studied interactions between depressed and nondepressed adolescents and their mothers. The adolescent–mother dyads were asked to discuss a topic that they agreed caused friction in their family, such as "adolescent disobeying parent"; the researchers monitored the duration of the adolescents' positive and negative moods. As the researchers expected, the adolescents who were depressed displayed a negative mood for longer periods during these interactions than the other adolescents. Interestingly, when the mothers of the adolescents who were depressed responded to the adolescents' negative mood with warmth and supportive comments, their depressed moods lasted longer. The researchers suggested that the mothers' warmth and support may have positively reinforced the adolescents' depressed moods, thereby prolonging them.

Notes from the Author: Parenting Sad Children

So what is a mother to do, you might ask? If her warmth increases her child's depressed mood, should she berate her child when he or she is depressed (which could be considered a form of punishment)? No. Operant theory suggests that the mother should positively reinforce nondepressive behaviors when they occur to increase them and thereby reduce the frequency of depressive moods. Recall from the earlier chapter about basic psychological theories that positive reinforcement of alternative behaviors is often more powerful than punishment of behaviors that a parent would like to reduce.

A second exploration of the influence of interpersonal relationships on depression comes from two studies of college students. Although these studies involved young adults, their results may also apply to the interactions of adolescents or children. In the first study, female undergraduates who were not depressed were randomly assigned to engage in a 15-minute "get acquainted" conversation with either a female undergraduate who was depressed or a female undergraduate who was not depressed (Gotlib & Robinson, 1982). Those who talked with an undergraduate who was depressed smiled less often, had fewer pleasant facial expressions, talked about more negative things, and were less supportive. This suggested that undergraduates who are depressed evoke negative interactions from their peers. These negative interactions may reinforce the undergraduates' negative cognitions or attributional style, resulting in a deepening sense of depression.

In a second study, Siegel and Alloy (1990) studied freshman roommates, all of whom had been assigned randomly to their rooms. Men who were roommates of mildly depressed men rated them more negatively than did roommates of anxious or nonanxious/nondepressed men. There were no differences in the ratings given by females to their mildly depressed, anxious, or nonanxious/nondepressed roommates. However, the mildly depressed females rated their nondepressed roommates as having a more negative effect on them than did the anxious or the nonanxious/nondepressed roommates. Consequently, both the male and female pairs of roommates in which one of them was depressed experienced more difficult times together than did the other pairs. These more negative experiences may have caused more stress for the depressed undergraduates and may have reinforced their cognitions about others and about their ability to get along with others, both of which may have maintained or deepened their sense of depression.

Two Developmental Models

To better understand how influences on depression combine in children's lives, we will explore two models: one examining the early onset of depression and one examining onset during early adolescence. In these models we will discuss factors that increase the likelihood of depression developing and factors that may protect a child from experiencing depression. As with the models presented in other chapters in this text, these are examples of how depression can develop. Many children who become depressed follow pathways that differ from those described here.

Early-Onset Depression

In this model, consider an infant being raised by one or two parents who are generally neglectful of the infant's needs. The parents may be overwhelmed by stressors in their lives or simply uninterested in their child. Perhaps one or both of them are depressed, which may account for their often feeling overwhelmed. If at least one parent is depressed, the infant may have inherited genes that predispose him to being depressed or to feeling negative moods more intensely than others. If his needs are neglected by his parents, he may experience prolonged bouts of negative moods, and these may accentuate any genetic influences on his neurological development—possibly strengthening neural pathways for experiencing anger, frustration, and sadness. As a toddler and young child, he may continue to experience prolonged negative moods and will not begin to develop the skills to mollify these moods (Cicchetti & Toth, 1998). An additional consequence of the lack of involvement by his parents is that he may learn few age-appropriate social skills.

When he enters preschool, he may have difficulty interacting with the other children and with the teachers. Although all the children in the preschool will experience anger, frustration, and sadness, he will have more difficulty controlling these moods, resulting in prolonged bouts of angry and sad feelings, and possibly in aggression and withdrawal. His behaviors may anger peers and his teachers, and they may reject him or ignore him, which is likely to increase his negative moods.

At this time a preschool teacher who understands the possible foundation of the boy's negative moods and behaviors may spend time helping him develop the skills to control them. The teacher might also refer him for therapy, and his work with a therapist may complement the efforts of the teacher. Similarly, if his parents receive services for their depression and training in how to be more effective parents, they may be able to help their son with his moods and behaviors. This may allow him to restrain his moods and develop social skills and better relationships with peers and teachers—reducing the chance that he will develop a depressive disorder. However, if there are too few teachers in the preschool, if they are more interested in maintaining order than in working with the troubled children, or if his parents receive no help, his problematic emotions and behaviors are likely to continue.

If the child is not helped to establish some control over his moods and behaviors, he is likely to continue to behave in ways that anger and frustrate others. If he is treated badly by them in return (being hit by other students, being told repeatedly that he is a "bad boy" by the teachers), he is likely to have many negative and stressful experiences in preschool and later in kindergarten and the primary grades. In addition, if he is withdrawn from others, he will have few positive interactions with them. These consistent stressful events may push him to develop beliefs about himself (he is bad), the world (it is consistently negative), and his future (it is bleak) that result in a frequent depressed mood (Nolen-Hoeksema, Seligman, & Girgus, 1992).

Because depression is often unnoticed in young children, particularly children who are withdrawn at school and who receive little attention at home, he may experience these moods and cognitions for many years—which will strengthen them and make them more difficult to counteract. However, if he develops a positive and consistent relationship with a teacher, neighbor, Big Brother from the local university, playground supervisor, or custodian at his school, this relationship may provide enough positive experiences, and enough support for his fragile self-esteem, that his cognitions about self and the world may become less negative, which may protect him from developing a depressive disorder. Similarly, if he can develop a more positive relationship with his parents, he may experience more support, develop fewer negative cognitions, and develop a better ability to regulate his emotions. However, if these events do not occur, he may continue through his elementary school years as an unhappy and angry child—making the physical transitions that he will experience at puberty, and the social and emotional transitions that he will experience as he moves from elementary school to middle school, even more difficult.

Depression with an Onset in Early Adolescence

In this model, consider a girl being raised by a single mother who is depressed, which may have resulted in the girl inheriting tendencies toward depression. This mother, however, receives considerable support from her family, which helps her to parent her daughter effectively most of the time. In addition, the daughter receives considerable nurturing directly from the mother's family. Consequently, the daughter develops the ability to regulate her affect fairly effectively. The mother and daughter experience occasional difficulties that are acutely stressful (such as the mother being arrested for shoplifting or their having to move between apartments several times). Although these troubles are infrequent, they sensitize the daughter to negative events happening in her life.

Overall, the daughter does well in preschool and elementary school. However, her transition to middle school in the sixth grade involves several meaningful stressful events. Perhaps she must attend a new school because her mother has moved again, and she knows no one there. In addition, perhaps she has entered puberty before most of the other girls and so arrives at her new school with significant breast development, which results in many other girls treating her in a hostile way and many older boys being attracted to her and encouraging her to engage in sexual activity with them (Ge et al., 2003). These stressors may push her toward feeling depressed; and if she has inherited a genetic predisposition toward depression from her parents, she may be particularly susceptible to depression in the face of these stressors. Her peer interactions may also encourage withdrawal, which may leave her more time to ruminate about her changed body and her inability to make friends in her new school.

To the extent that she can create positive friendships in her new school, or to the extent that her mother and other family members can provide support and encouragement during this difficult time, she may not develop depressive symptoms, or the symptoms may flare for a few months and then subside (Heath & Camarena, 2002). However, if she is unable to create positive friendships, or if her mother and other family members are unavailable (possibly because of a recurrence of her mother's depression and other family members having their attention diverted in other directions), her sense of depression may deepen. She may begin to believe that her life has taken a negative turn from which she cannot recover—believing that although her life as a girl was pleasant, her life as a developing woman is likely to be negative. Her cognitions may result in a growing sense of helplessness and hopelessness. If she spends time ruminating about her unhappiness, she may have less energy to focus on her schoolwork, which may suffer—reinforcing her belief that her life has taken a negative turn. As her depression deepens, she may withdraw more from peers, teachers, and her family, thereby reducing the likelihood that someone will notice her depression and provide help for it. Further, her interactions with adults and peers are likely to have a more negative tone, which may push adults and peers away from her, thus increasing her negative cognitions and her sense of rejection and loneliness.

Key Concepts

- Neurotransmitter functioning in the CNS and the functioning of the HPA axis influence depression in adults and may play a role in the development of childhood depression, although their role in childhood depression is less clear.
- Family and twin studies suggest a role of genes in the development of childhood depression, particularly in the development of moderate levels of depression and depression in school-age children. However, adoption studies have not shown this same genetic influence.
- An early environment characterized by abuse and neglect may create dysfunction in the HPA axis that may predispose children to developing depression.
- Problems with affect regulation early in life, often associated with an insecure attachment, can result in prolonged and intense negative emotions in young children, which may predispose them to developing depression.
- Beck's cognitive theory is that the experiences of some children cause them to develop negative beliefs about the self, the world, and the future, which create biases in perception and memory, which reinforce these negative beliefs. The negative beliefs can lead to the emotions and behaviors associated with depression.
- Seligman's theory of attributional style states that children who develop a style in which negative events are attributed to internal, global, and stable characteristics are more likely to develop depression.
- Acute or chronic stress has been associated with increased risk for developing depression.
- Interpersonal theories state that the interactions between a child who is depressed and others often have characteristics that intensify or prolong the child's feelings of depression.

Prevention

Depression is the target of preventive efforts more frequently than most of the other disorders discussed in this text. The interest in prevention of depression is likely due to several factors:

- The prevalence of children and adolescents experiencing significant symptoms of depression is high (DuBois et al., 1995).
- Depression can be debilitating even at intensity levels that are not sufficient to diagnose a depressive disorder (Birmaher et al., 1996).

- Some children who are at a higher risk for developing depression can be identified, such as children of depressed parents, children who have experienced significant losses, and children living in poverty (Beardslee & Gladstone, 2001).
- Several forms of psychotherapy have been shown to treat depression effectively, and the techniques of some of these therapies can be translated into prevention programs (Curry, 2001).

Some prevention programs are designed for specific groups of children, such as children of depressed parents or children who have experienced the death of a parent (Beardslee et al., 1997; Sandler et al., 1992). Other programs include children who are experiencing elevated symptoms of depression, usually shown by their high scores on measures of depression distributed to all children in a grade or school (Gillham, Reivich, Jaycox, & Seligman, 1995). Finally, some programs are presented to all children in a particular grade or school (Spence, Sheffield, & Donovan, 2003).

Most prevention programs have focused on one or more of the following (Beardslee & Gladstone, 2001):

- Changing cognitive styles associated with depression by (1) teaching about the role of cognitions in depression, (2) helping children identify cognitions that promote sad feelings, and (3) providing strategies for changing these cognitions into ones that are less likely to produce depression.
- Developing problem-solving skills to increase children's abilities to resolve stressful situations rather than reacting passively to them (such as ruminating about them).
- Increasing social skills to help children who may be withdrawn reengage with peers, parents, and others effectively.

Many prevention programs show good short-term outcomes. For example, after a prevention program was given to fifth- and sixth-grade children who showed symptoms of depression, the children had fewer negative attributions and depressive symptoms and maintained their improvements through a 12-month follow-up assessment (Gillham et al., 1995). Similarly, a program provided to all eighth-grade students in eight schools showed reduced symptoms of depression at the end of the prevention program, compared with students in eight other schools who did not receive the intervention. The reduction in symptoms was particularly strong for students who had higher levels of depressive symptoms before the intervention program (Spence et al., 2003).

However, the long-term effects of these programs have been less pronounced. The program for fifth and sixth graders showed no differences in those who received the intervention and those who did not at 30 and 36 months following the intervention (Gillham & Reivich, 1999); the program for eighth graders found no differences in depressive symptoms between the

ILLUSTRATING AN IMPORTANT RESEARCH ISSUE: REGRESSION TO THE MEAN

A well-documented phenomenon in social science research is that scores at the extreme ends of a distribution at one time move toward the mean (**regress to the mean**) over time. This can be seen clearly in the data from the Spence and colleagues (2003) study of a prevention program for depression. By examining the data from the control groups in Figure 9.4, you can see that the scores on the BDI for the children in the high-risk group declined over time, and the scores of the children in the low-risk group increased over time even though none of them received an intervention. Although the scores of those in the high-risk group were still above the scores of those in the low-risk group at the 12-month follow-up, the difference between the two groups had diminished considerably.

Assessing the effectiveness of many prevention or intervention programs requires attention to the effects of regression to the mean—particularly because many of these programs are aimed at those experiencing high levels of some problem. For example, consider an intervention to reduce anger in a group of children with high levels of anger. Because their anger at the start of the intervention is likely to regress to the mean, part of an observed reduction in their anger at the end of the intervention is likely to be caused by regression to the mean. The degree to which the reduction was influenced by the intervention or merely reflects regression to the mean can be unclear. One strategy for teasing apart these influences is to include a no-treatment control group with similar levels of anger. The extent to which the control group changes over time may indicate the influence of regression to the mean. If the group receiving the intervention changes more than the control group, the additional change may reflect the influence of the intervention.

two groups at a 12-month follow-up (see Figure 9.4; *BDI scores* are scores on the Beck Depression Inventory) (Spence et al., 2003).

These results show that programs to reduce depressive symptoms, and possibly to prevent the onset of a depressive disorder, can be effective. However, they also show that a preventive intervention loses effectiveness over time. The researchers involved in both projects suggested that "booster" programs each school year, in which the concepts of the intervention are reviewed, are probably necessary for prevention efforts to have long-term effectiveness.

Key Concepts

- Some prevention programs involve children at risk for depression or those showing early signs of depression; others are delivered to all children in a grade or school.
- Most prevention programs focus on identifying and changing problematic cognitions, developing problem-solving skills, and enhancing social skills.

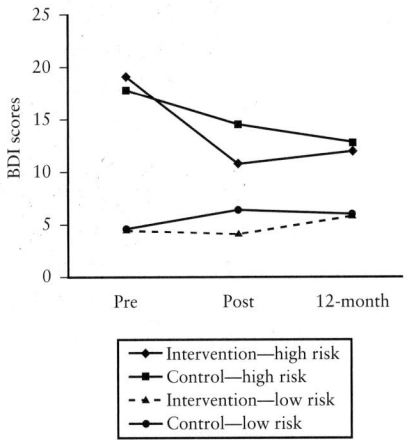

FIGURE 9.4   *Influence of a Prevention Program for Depression*

- Short-term evaluations of prevention programs show that many of them are effective; however, the long-term effect of the programs is less pronounced and "booster" sessions may be needed to maintain the value of the prevention programs.

Therapeutic Interventions

Several therapeutic interventions have been used with children experiencing major depressive disorder and dysthymia, as well as those experiencing depressive symptoms that do not reach the intensity of a depressive disorder. As described in this section, many interventions are based on our developing understanding of the etiology of depressive disorders: Medications attempt to reduce biologically based problems, and various forms of psychotherapy focus on reducing stress, reducing dysfunctional cognitions, enhancing emotional regulation, and improving interpersonal relationships.

Medication

Several different categories of antidepressant medications exist, and each has a different effect on neurotransmitter functioning in the CNS. Monoamine oxidase inhibitors (MAOIs) and tricyclic antidepressants have been used for several decades. Although these medications reduce acute depressive feelings in most adults, most evaluations of them with children and younger adolescents have shown that they are not effective (Schultz & Remschmidt, 2001). Hypothesized reasons for their lack of effectiveness with children are (1) the etiology of depression in children may differ from that in adults (as discussed earlier); (2) children may metabolize antidepressant medications more quickly, or with more variability, making it difficult to determine an effective dose for them; and (3) developmental differences in brain receptor functioning between children and adults may result in the medications, having minimal influence on the biology of children.

A new category of medications, the **selective serotonin reuptake inhibitors (SSRIs)**, developed in the 1980s, has been more effective with children. Fluoxetine (Prozac) is the most commonly prescribed SSRI; others include sertraline (Zoloft) and paroxetine (Paxil) (Findling, Feeny, Stansbrey, Delporto Bedoya, & Demeter, 2002). Only two placebo-controlled studies of the SSRIs, both using fluoxetine, have been conducted with children (Evans et al., 2005). Both studies found that children and adolescents taking fluoxetine experienced a greater reduction in depressive symptoms than those taking a placebo (Emslie et al., 2002; Emslie et al., 1997). However, the percentage of children and adolescents who responded positively to fluoxetine in these studies was not as high as the percentages seen in most studies with adults, suggesting that even this type of medication is not as effective with children as with adults.

Side Effects

Several side effects have been noted in children taking fluoxetine, although they are severe in only a few cases. Common side effects include restlessness, headaches, gastrointestinal problems, and changes in sleep patterns (Schultz & Remschmidt, 2001). Of particular concern, however, is that the SSRIs may promote impulsivity and hyperactivity and may increase the likelihood of a manic episode in some children (Biederman, Mick, Spencer, Wilens, & Faraone, 2000). There is also some indication that SSRIs may be associated with an increased risk for suicide, although the evidence for this is not completely clear (Evans et al., 2005). The reasons for the increased risk of a manic episode or suicide are unclear and are puzzling because a similar increase in risk has not been reported in adults.

Psychosocial Interventions with Children

Psychosocial interventions are often essential with children who are depressed, even when medications improve their sad or irritable mood, because the problematic cognitions and patterns of social interactions experienced by many children who are depressed are unlikely to be changed by medication. Kendall and colleagues (1992) describe four components of psychotherapy that are particularly helpful with children who are depressed. The first component is helping children recognize the various emotional states they experience. Children with depression are likely to experience many troubling moods, including sadness, anger, anxiety, and frustration (Axelson & Birmaher, 2001; Kovacs & Devlin, 1998). Helping them distinguish these emotions increases their self-understanding and gives them the language to communicate more effectively with others. (For example, rather than yelling, "I HATE this," a child can say, "This makes me very angry" or "This makes me very sad," which can help others respond more effectively to the child.)

The second component of therapy is cognitive intervention. As discussed in more detail in the chapter about basic psychological theories, cognitive interventions help children identify cognitions that may be maintaining or exacerbating their depression. During cognitive therapy, the therapist discusses with the child the ways that his or her thinking can affect his or her mood, and the accuracy of problematic cognitions is challenged gently. For example, if a child states, "No one likes me," the therapist might help the child identify situations where others have been kind to the child. The therapist can then use this as an example of a cognitive bias and encourage the child to notice and remember positive as well as negative experiences. In addition, children are helped to interrupt their problematic patterns of thinking and to substitute more accurate thoughts when appropriate. For example, rather than think, "No one likes me," the child may be encouraged to think, "I can't get any of the popular kids to like me at school, but I have friends at home." Similarly, a child who thinks, "I'm a failure," might be encouraged to think, "I can't play sports well, but I'm great at art and I'm good in math."

Many studies have assessed the effectiveness of cognitive therapy with children and adolescents; almost all have found that it helps them reduce their problematic styles of thinking and lessens feelings of depression (Kovacs & Sherrill, 2001). For example, Weiss and his colleagues (Weisz, Thurber, Sweeney, Proffitt, & LeGagnoux, 1997) reported on an eight-week program of cognitive–behavioral therapy for children with moderate symptoms of depression. The program was designed to (1) help children manage their lives more effectively and engage in pleasurable activities more often and (2) when facing an unpleasant situation over which they had no control, engage in appropriate cognitions to minimize the influence of the situation. Compared with a group that received no therapy, those who received therapy had lower scores on measures of depressive symptoms at the end of the eight-week program and then again at a nine-month follow-up assessment.

A third component is social skills training. As discussed earlier, children who are depressed often withdraw from others and have difficulties with peer relationships. Social skills training involves instruction in, and then practice of, skills for interacting effectively with peers, teachers, parents, and others. For example, a therapist might provide instruction and practice in how to join other students at a lunch table or how to interact with others at a party.

Evaluations of several social skills training programs with depressed adolescents have shown that they increase the adolescents' social interactions and reduce feelings of sadness (Curry, 2001). For example, one group of researchers provided a 12-week program to a group of adolescents with major depression that helped them develop skills to interact more effectively with peers and family members (Mufson, Weissman, Moreau, & Garfinkel, 1999). A comparison group of adolescents with similar levels of depression was monitored by a psychologist during monthly meetings but received no specific form of psychotherapy. (Adolescents in the comparison group who showed deterioration in functioning were removed from the study and given needed treatment.) At the end of the 12-week program, those in the therapy group exhibited fewer symptoms of depression and had higher scores on social adjustment than did those not receiving therapy. Thus depressive symptoms improved at the same time as social skills, even though depressive symptoms were not targeted by the therapy.

The fourth component, behavioral interventions, can reinforce participation in pleasurable activities and positive interactions with peers. For example, reinforcers can be used to encourage positive and active behaviors (joining a club at school, attending a party). Often the pleasurable aspects of these activities become reinforcing in themselves over time, and the other reinforcers can be withdrawn. Kendall and colleagues (1992) also include relaxation training as a behavioral intervention. After learning relaxation skills, children are encouraged to use them when they begin to experience negative cognitions. This can interrupt the cycle of dysfunctional cognitions, which may help a child regulate his or her affect and recover more quickly when sadness or depression is experienced.

Therapeutic Interventions with Families

Therapeutic work with the family of a child who is depressed is often important. One goal may be providing needed therapy to other members of the family. As noted several times in this chapter, children who are depressed are more likely than other children to have a parent who is depressed. Helping to relieve a parent's depression is likely to improve the emotional climate in the home and the quality of parent–child interactions—both of which are likely to reduce depression in the child. In addition, the siblings of children with depression may also be experiencing depressive symptoms or a depressive disorder, and they may also benefit from therapeutic interventions.

As also noted earlier, many families with a child who is depressed experience high levels of conflict and stress and low levels of cohesion and social support (Kovacs & Sherrill, 2001). Sometimes family problems may have influenced the onset of depression in a child; in other cases, family difficulties may be the result of having a child with depression; and both processes may occur in some families. Reducing family conflict and improving relationships among family members may reduce the stress that a child is experiencing and improve his or her negative mood. Changes in the family environment may also facilitate changes in the child's cognitions that may be a focus of therapy. (For example, reducing the likelihood that an angry parent will tell a child that he is the source of all the family's problems may enhance a therapist's efforts to have the child change a problematic attributional style.)

Finally, families in which attachment issues may be contributing to a child's depression may need interventions focused on attachment. Sensitivity training for parents of infants at risk for developing insecure attachments significantly increases the rate of secure attachment (Van den Boom, 1990) and may have similar benefits for preschool children or older children. Therapy for the primary caregiver (usually the mother) designed to work through her own troubled attachment history can also have positive effects on the parent–child relationship (Main, Kaplan, & Cassidy, 1985).

Considering Cultural and Family Issues during Therapeutic Interventions

All therapeutic interventions have to relate to, and be respectful of, the child's cultural and family history and expectations. As noted previously, behaviors that might indicate withdrawal and depression in children from some cultural groups may indicate respect and appropriate behavior in others. For example, it may be inappropriate in some cultures or families for young children, especially girls, to initiate interactions with adults in a position of authority, such as teachers, coaches, or ministers (Koss-Chioino & Vargas, 1992). Interventions for a child from a family with this belief should avoid teaching this type of behavior even though it might be a component of therapy offered to children from cultural groups where initiating interactions with adults is seen as appropriate. Being attuned to cultural or family values and expectations helps a clinician avoid pushing a child to behave in ways that the child is being told by others is inappropriate and promotes a better relationship between the clinician and the family (Seeley, 2000).

Key Concepts

- Tricyclic antidepressant medication is ineffective for reducing symptoms of depression in most children. SSRIs have been more effective but not as much as they are with adults.
- Cognitive–behavioral therapy helps children identify and change dysfunctional cognitions that are influencing their depressive moods.
- Social skills training provides instruction on interacting effectively with peers and adults.
- Behavioral interventions can be used to reinforce active participation in pleasurable activities.
- Therapeutic interventions with families can focus on reducing depression in parents and siblings, and on developing a more positive and nurturing home environment.

CHAPTER GLOSSARY

Adjustment disorders are a category in the DSM characterized by short-term disturbances in mood or behavior related to difficulty in adjusting to a specific stressor.

Anaclitic depression was a term coined by Spitz to describe the profound withdrawal of infants who received only minimal human contact while being raised in institutions.

Anhedonia is a lack of interest in pleasant or interesting activities.

Attachment theory was originally described by Bowlby and was based on an infant's innate ability to attach to a primary caregiver. The primary caregiver's responses to the infant's behaviors influence whether a secure or insecure attachment forms between the infant and the primary caregiver.

Attributional theory, based on the concept of learned helplessness, focuses on how children and adults comprehend the causes of positive and negative events in their lives.

Bipolar disorders and depressive disorders comprise the **mood disorders** category in the DSM. Bipolar disorders are usually characterized by cycles of manic and depressed moods.

Comorbid disorders occur when two or more disorders are present at the same time.

Completed suicides are those that result in death.

Constriction, as used in the study of suicide, refers to a narrowing of a person's view of the world.

Corticotrophin-releasing hormone (CRH) is a hormone secreted by the hypothalamus that influences an organism's response to stress.

Cortisol is a hormone secreted by the adrenal gland.

Co-rumination occurs when a group of friends talks repeatedly about a negative topic with each other (such as how unhappy they are).

The **dexamethasone suppression test** is believed to be a marker for depression. When dexamethasone (a synthetic hormone) is injected, secretion of cortisol is suppressed in most children and adults who are not depressed, but only in about 40% of children and adults who are depressed.

The **diathesis–stress model,** when applied to the onset of depression, suggests that some event or characteristic makes an individual more prone to depression (the diathesis) and that depression occurs when the individual experiences stress.

Hypersomnia is excessive sleeping.

The **hypothalamic–pituitary–adrenal (HPA) axis** is part of the endocrine system and has an important role in regulating hunger, sleep, mood, and sexual activity.

Learned helplessness is a condition described by Seligman in which people and other animals have learned that they cannot influence their lives and so stop trying to do so.

The **lifetime prevalence** of a disorder is the percentage of a sample or population who have experienced the disorder at any time in their lives. They do not need to be experiencing the disorder when they are surveyed.

Masked depression is a concept suggesting that depression existed in children but was masked by acting-out and other behavioral problems.

A **medically significant suicide attempt** is one that requires medical intervention to save a person's life.

Melancholia is a term used previously for depression, often indicating depression that appeared for no apparent reason.

A **mixed episode** involves symptoms of depression and mania appearing simultaneously.

The **monoamine hypothesis** suggested that a reduction in the monoamine neurotransmitters in a person's CNS caused depression

The **monoamines** are a group of CNS neurotransmitters with a similar molecular structure: norepinephrine, dopamine, and serotonin.

Psychoanalytic theory was the theory of the development of human personality and behavior initially described by Sigmund Freud.

Regression to the mean occurs when scores at the extreme ends of a distribution at one point in time move toward the mean over time.

REM sleep (rapid-eye-movement sleep) is a stage of the sleep cycle occurring about every 90 minutes and characterized by rapid eye movements and vivid dreams.

Reserpine is a medication given for high blood pressure. About 20% of adults taking reserpine experience severe depression.

Rumination involves thinking about something repeatedly—turning it over in one's mind many times.

Selective serotonin reuptake inhibitors (SSRIs) are a class of medications used in the treatment of depression and other disorders. The most common brand of the SSRIs is Prozac.

A **suicide attempt** is a purposeful act that a person believes can or will result in his or her death, but that does not cause death.

Suicide contagion refers to the issue of whether a recently committed suicide encourages suicide attempts in others.

Suicide ideation refers to serious thoughts about suicide.

Tricyclic antidepressants were one of the first groups of medications used to treat depression.

Tunneling is the term used most commonly to describe the way in which a suicidal child's attention gradually becomes focused more and more on one or two issues.

Anxiety Disorders

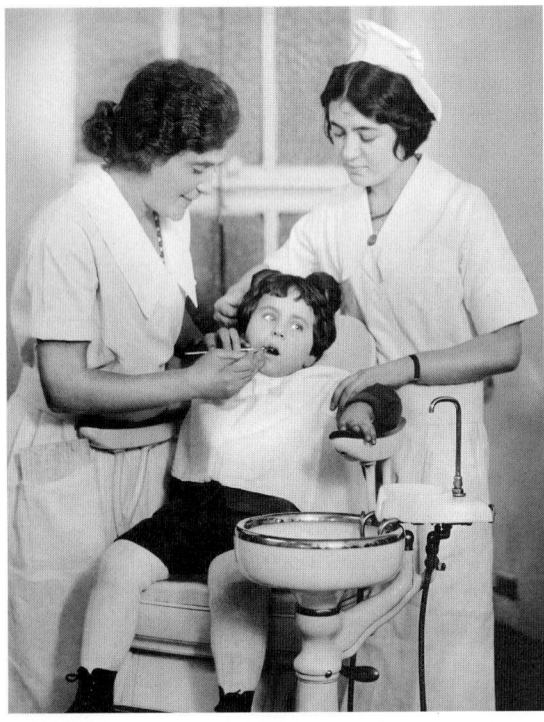

Yikes!

All of us experience anxiety (the word *anxiety* comes from the Latin *angere,* "to choke, give pain, or torment"). Although anxiety can be uncomfortable at times and agonizing at others, it also plays a valuable role in our lives by helping to keep us from situations that might be dangerous (Westermeyer & Dieperink, 2001). One could argue, for example, that it is anxiety that keeps us from going too close to the edge of a cliff, from walking alone at night in a strange city, and from going to a big party the night before an important exam. However, when anxiety becomes too intense it can stop us from engaging in necessary activities and can impair our performance in others (Albano, Chorpita, & Barlow, 2003). So the influence of anxiety can be conceptualized using the *inverted u:* Too little anxiety can be a problem because we may engage in behaviors that are harmful, and too much anxiety can stop us from engaging in behaviors that are necessary or beneficial. A middling level of anxiety seems to work best for most of us (see Figure 10.1).

As you probably remember from your own youth, worry, fear, and anxiety are a part of everyone's childhood. Most young children have one or more significant fears, such as fear of the dark, spiders, monsters, or being separated from a parent (Spence, Rapee, McDonald, & Ingram, 2001). These fears do not interfere significantly in the lives of most children, and they generally become less intense as a child gets older. However, the fears of some children build to the point where they interfere significantly in their lives. They may be unwilling to play outside, answer questions when called on at school, sleep over at a friend's home, or go into their basement. Anxiety can cause some children to fall behind academically, fail to learn social skills, and be isolated from others. Once problematic anxiety has become a feature in a child's life, it can continue to build and become increasingly troubling during adolescence and adulthood (Woodward & Fergusson, 2001).

Although anxiety has long been recognized as part of the lives of children, only within the past two or three decades have its debilitating effects on many children been recognized (this is similar to our understanding of depression in the lives of children, as discussed in the previous chapter). Consequently, childhood anxiety has been the focus of research for a relatively short time.

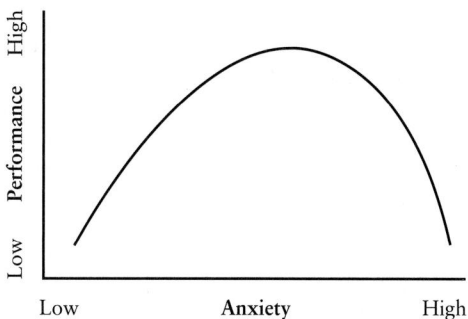

FIGURE 10.1 *The Inverted U*

We know that many children are affected by anxiety disorders. One estimate is that on any given day, between 3% and 5% of children and adolescents must cope with an anxiety disorder (Foa et al., 2005). However, we know little about its development, particularly in toddlers and preschool children (Spence et al., 2001). As a result, we often to fail to recognize high levels of anxiety in young children and fail to provide interventions that might reduce the influence of anxiety on their development (Albano et al., 2003). Fortunately many researchers are now working to understand childhood anxiety better, so our knowledge of it should grow.

In this chapter we focus on all the disorders included in the DSM-IV-TR category of anxiety disorders except posttraumatic stress disorder. Posttraumatic stress disorder will be discussed in a later chapter in the part of this text that focuses on disorders related to traumatic events.

Chapter Plan

As with other chapters in this text, we start this chapter with two vignettes and a discussion of the history of clinical and research interest in childhood anxiety. We then depart from the pattern of most chapters and explore the diagnostic criteria, prevalence and course, and characteristics of each anxiety disorder separately—because there are many differences in the disorders and the experiences of the children who are diagnosed with them. We then move to a general discussion of the etiology of anxiety disorders, exploring the genetic influences on the predisposition of some children to experience high levels of anxiety and the experiences in their families, schools, and neighborhoods that intensify the anxiety of some of these children. Finally, we use this understanding of the etiology of anxiety to examine several strategies for preventing anxiety disorders in children or providing therapeutic interventions to children with them.

Case Study: A Child with Separation Anxiety

Xavier was the only child in his family. He and his parents lived in a small apartment in subsidized housing in an inner city. His father worked as a mechanic at a local garage, and his mother stayed home and cared for him. His parents had been married when they were 32—the first marriage for both of them. Both parents were devoted to each other and to Xavier. Xavier's mother focused most of her attention on him, and they spent much of each day engaged in activities at home together. His mother was anxious when they were away from their home because of the high level of crime in their neighborhood, so they spent most of their time at home. When she shopped for groceries at the local market, she made sure to keep Xavier close to her and watched him constantly. When they traveled on the city bus, such as when they visited Xavier's pediatrician, his mother was careful to keep Xavier away from others on the bus. She and Xavier's father spent considerable time instructing Xavier on how to be quiet and inconspicuous when outside their home.

Xavier was a happy boy during his preschool years. He and his mother did many educational tasks together, and by the time he was 4, he could read short sentences and do simple addition. He also liked to create sculptures with items that he found around their apartment or that his parents purchased for him. He and his parents were proud of his many accomplishments. Although he was eligible for participation in the local Head Start program, Xavier's parents declined to enroll him, preferring that he remain at home.

Xavier was usually well behaved, and his parents seldom had to discipline him. Once, when he was 3, he wandered into a nearby apartment. His mother was frantic when she could not find him; when he finally appeared out of the other apartment in response to her calling, she was very angry with him. Later that night, he got the only spanking of his life from his father.

Xavier's mother was apprehensive when it came time to enroll him in kindergarten. However, she did, and accompanied him to his first day of school—walking with him the three blocks to the local elementary school. Xavier was bothered by the noise and apparent confusion as the children and many of their mothers gathered in the kindergarten room that first day. He stayed close to his mother until the teacher announced that it was time for the parents to leave. Several children started to cry when their mothers began to leave, including Xavier. He stayed close to his mother, and she was reluctant to leave the room. She asked the teacher if she could stay for a little while; but the teacher told her that although it was difficult for Xavier, it would be best for her to leave so he could get used to being in the classroom without her. With great reluctance, she pried Xavier's hands from around her leg and told him that he needed to be a "big boy" and stay in the classroom, and she returned home.

When Xavier's mother returned that afternoon, the teacher told her that Xavier had cried most of the day and did not participate in activities. When a teacher's aide talked with him, he said that he was worried about his mother and concerned that she might get hurt walking in the neighborhood or while in their apartment. The aide's reassurances did not quell Xavier's crying. When Xavier returned home with his mother he was much happier, and they played several games in their apartment and made dinner together. His mother felt that it was important to be particularly attentive to Xavier because of the difficult time he had experienced in school.

Although Xavier's parents told him it was important for him to attend school, and although were reassured by his teacher that his anxiety would dissipate over the first week of school, Xavier continued to have great difficulty separating from his mother in the morning. When his father decided to take some time off from work to walk Xavier to school, thinking this might make it easier for Xavier, it was hard for Xavier to leave the apartment, and he cried all the way to school. By the end of the first week, some other boys had begun to tease Xavier about being a "crybaby," but this had no influence on his behavior. Xavier also began to feel sick in the mornings before school, which eventually resulted in his staying home two or three days each week from school.

Xavier's parents disagreed about how to handle his behavior. His father wanted to take him to school each day, even if he felt sick, and punish him if he continued to cry and not participate in school activities. His mother raised the possibility of homeschooling Xavier. They consulted with Xavier's teacher, and at her suggestion visited the school psychologist as a family. The school psychologist talked with Xavier and his parents about their anxiety related to him attending school, and in particular she focused on the anxiety that his mother and father felt. She acknowledged the parents' fears about Xavier's safety but said that attending school was important for Xavier. The parents agreed that this was important, and they worried that Xavier was going to do poorly in school because of his crying.

The school psychologist said she would be happy to work out a plan to help Xavier focus on his work in school. She arranged for Xavier's teacher to keep a card on her desk for Xavier on which she would place a check each hour that he participated in class activities. Each time he got five checks, he and his mother would make a special dessert together. The psychologist advised Xavier's parents not to punish him and not to raise the possibility of homeschooling. Further, they were encouraged to continue to support Xavier and to view his anxiety as a challenge that he would have to overcome with their support. She also referred Xavier's parents to the school social worker, who had grown up in their neighborhood. She worked with Xavier's mother on strategies for staying safe in their neighborhood and for helping Xavier remain safe at home and in school while not experiencing high levels of anxiety.

Gradually Xavier had more days of being able to attend kindergarten with low anxiety. This allowed him to use his academic and artistic skills, which impressed his teacher and the other children in the class. The other children stopped teasing Xavier and often asked him to work with them during art projects. With the social worker's help, Xavier's mother became involved in several neighborhood organizations, which gave her an activity during the day and enhanced the environment in their neighborhood.

Some Issues Worth Noting

- The important role that neighborhood environment can have on the development of childhood disorders, either directly through their influence on a child or indirectly through their influence on a child's parents.
- Whether Xavier's parents' anxiety suggests that they may have a genetically influenced predisposition to anxiety that Xavier may have inherited.
- The parenting challenges that parents living in problematic neighborhoods face.

Case Study: A Sudden Fear of Dogs

Six-year-old Kim was a generally happy girl who lived with her 8-year-old brother, Alex, and their parents. One Saturday when her father had taken her and her brother to play in the neighborhood park, a fight broke out between a neighbor's dog and a stray dog that had wandered into the park. Despite their father's warning not to go near the dogs, she and her brother ran to get closer to the fight. When they got near the dogs, the dogs separated, and the neighbor's dog, which seemed disoriented, spun around and snapped at Alex's leg. The dog's teeth made three large cuts on Alex's right calf. He and Kim screamed, and the dog ran off. Their father, who had been running in their direction, scooped Alex up, took the children to their car, and drove Alex to the hospital. Alex's leg was bleeding, but not badly, and Alex was crying loudly. The father called his wife, who met them at the hospital and took Kim home. Alex arrived home an hour later with large bandages on his leg. His father said there was no permanent damage to his leg, and they could remove the bandages in a few days. By that time, Alex was excited to tell about all that happened to him in the hospital, and he was allowed to go to several friends' homes to show off his leg and tell his harrowing story.

Her parents noticed that Kim was very quiet when Alex returned home from the hospital and talked with her to reassure her that everything was fine. Despite their reassurances, Kim seemed unusually withdrawn the rest of that day. During dinner, the neighbor whose dog who had bitten Alex visited, with the dog on a leash, to apologize and to ask about Alex. Alex showed his leg to the neighbor and petted the dog, saying he knew it was not the dog's fault. Kim, however, seemed afraid of the dog and ran to her room. After the neighbor left, her parents again tried to calm her, but she cried and said she never wanted to see "that terrible dog" again.

Beginning the next day, Kim began to show a fear of dogs. She was reluctant to walk to school, saying she feared a dog might attack her. Her parents had Alex walk with her to school to provide some comfort. Kim chose not to play with her friends outside after school, again saying she was concerned about a dog biting her. Her parents assumed this was a normal reaction; so they allowed her to stay inside and, in response to her request, began driving her the short distance to her school in the morning and picking her up in the afternoon.

Kim began noticing dogs everywhere. She told her parents that many more dogs were around at home and at school than had been there the previous year. Her parents replied that they did not see many more dogs and said maybe she was just noticing them more. Kim insisted that she was not. She pointed out dogs on television programs and commented on how mean they looked. Her parents and brother often responded that they did not look mean and would point out how they were acting friendly. Kim responded that her parents and brother were wrong, and even if the dogs seemed friendly, they were not and were probably just waiting for an opportunity to bite someone or another dog.

Although her parents expected Kim's fear of dogs to dissipate, it appeared to grow stronger over the next several months. Kim was happy and content when inside her house and engaged in her usual activities, but she was anxious for an hour or so before she had to leave the house for school or another activity. She insisted that her parents drive her to school and was reluctant to go with her father grocery shopping and with her mother to the library—two activities she had enjoyed in the past. She also began to get into trouble at school because she often refused to go outside for recess.

Her parents were unsure how to handle Kim's fear. They were amazed that while Alex seemed to have recovered completely, Kim's fear of dogs had grown over the months. They wanted to reassure Kim and keep her from situations that made her anxious, but they were concerned that she would never grow out of her fears.

Some Issues Worth Noting

- The extent to which Kim's fear of dogs influenced many aspects of her life.
- The ways in which Kim's perceptions of dogs were influenced by her anxiety, and how reassurances from others had little influence on these perceptions.
- That Kim, who was not bitten, was more fearful of dogs than her brother was.

History

Two of the best-known cases of child psychopathology in the early 1900s involved anxious children. Each case was used to illustrate one of the two predominant developmental theories at that time: psychoanalysis and behaviorism.

Sigmund Freud's analysis of the case of Little Hans was a famous illustration of the ways in which unconscious thoughts and feelings could influence children's behaviors. When 5-year-old Hans was walking along the streets of Vienna with his nurse, he became very frightened of a horse on two occasions, causing him to run home and into the arms of his mother. This occurred even though he had never been hurt by a horse and had never appeared frightened of them before. Hans's father was concerned about Hans's fear (a fear of horses was a significant impairment in 1900) and consulted with Freud. Freud suggested the following conceptualization: Hans was in the middle of struggling with the Oedipal stage of his psychosexual development and consequently had considerable fear of his father. Hans had repressed this fear into his unconscious (as all young boys did, according to Freud's theory). Through the unconscious defense mechanism of **displacement,** this repressed fear was then transferred onto the horse. That is, the unconscious fear of the father was expressed as a conscious fear of a horse. The value of displacement for Hans, according to Freud, was that it allowed him to discharge the energy associated with his fear of his father in a socially acceptable way. This process of displaced anxiety was at the root of many unreasonable fears, in Freud's view (Freud, 1909/1955).

In many ways, behaviorism was a competitor of psychoanalytic theory, especially in the early and middle 1900s. John Watson, a proponent of behaviorism, wanted to show that anxiety was a learned behavior rather than one emanating from a person's unconscious. Watson used (which is probably the correct term in this situation) a toddler, Little Albert, in an experiment to induce fear of a white rat. At the beginning of the experiment, Albert showed no fear of white rats. During the learning phase of the experiment, Watson placed a white rat in front of Albert and had someone create a loud noise behind Albert. Albert naturally responded to the loud noise with fear and crying. (In the language of classical conditioning, the rat was the conditioned stimulus, and the loud noise was the unconditioned stimulus.) After several pairings of the rat and the noise, Albert showed clear signs of fear when the white rat was placed in front of him. Albert's fear also generalized to other small white animals and even to clumps of cotton (Watson & Rayner, 1920). Apparently Albert's mother found out about this experiment and removed Albert from it, so we do not know whether Albert ever recovered from his fears of rats and other white objects.

Besides occasional case studies such as those of Hans and Albert, anxiety in children received little research attention during the early half of the 1900s. The normal fears of children were the focus of some research.

One outcome of this research was the belief that childhood anxiety was part of their normal development (Laurent & Ettelson, 2001). Consequently, there was little motivation to study the prevalence or development of severe anxiety in children.

An accumulation of case studies and a few empirical studies in the 1960s and 1970s led to the understanding that intense and debilitating anxiety can occur in children. As a result, three childhood anxiety disorders were included in the DSM-III: separation anxiety disorder, avoidant disorder of childhood or adolescence, and overanxious disorder (APA, 1980). The inclusion of these disorders intensified research interest in children's anxiety. This research showed that children with the three childhood anxiety disorders could be reliably distinguished from those with normal childhood fears and that some children met the diagnostic criteria for what had been considered "adult" anxiety disorders. Consequently, the three childhood anxiety disorders remained in the DSM-III-R, and children meeting the diagnostic criteria for other anxiety disorders could be given those diagnoses (APA, 1987).

Because of the growing body of research showing that the symptoms of anxiety disorders displayed by adults and children were similar, the DSM-IV (APA, 1994) eliminated the category of childhood anxiety disorders. Separation anxiety disorder continued to be a diagnosis in the DSM-IV and was moved to the category of disorders usually beginning in infancy, childhood, or adolescence. The other two childhood anxiety disorders were subsumed into the anxiety disorder category: Most children who would have met the diagnostic criteria for avoidant disorder of childhood or adolescence met the DSM-IV diagnosis of social phobia, and most children who would have met the diagnostic criteria for overanxious disorder met the DSM-IV diagnosis of generalized anxiety disorder.

Key Concepts

- Case studies with Hans and Albert were used to illustrate the value of the psychoanalytic and learning theories for understanding the development of anxiety in children.
- Early research on anxiety in children focused on the normal development of their fears and worries.
- Later research showed that some children developed anxiety disorders that were similar to the disorders seen in adults.
- Three specific anxiety disorders of childhood were introduced in the DSM-III, although only one of those, separation anxiety disorder, remains in the DSM-IV-TR.

Basic Issues in Childhood Anxiety

Before we explore each of the anxiety disorders, we will examine several issues that provide a foundation for understanding them.

Many Meanings of Anxiety

A difficulty of discussing *anxiety* is that the term is used in several ways: as a description of periodic feelings (I am anxious whenever I talk with my girlfriend's parents), general patterns of feelings (he always seems anxious and on edge), and as clinically significant disorders (she has generalized anxiety disorder). (This is also an issue in discussing depression, as noted in the previous chapter.) Consequently, the term *anxiety* can be misleading if it is not defined carefully when it is used. Unfortunately this is not always done, which can lead to confusion (Foa et al., 2005).

Do Children Experience Specific Anxiety Disorders or High Levels of Anxiety?

One concern raised by several researchers is whether anxiety in children, particularly younger children, is best conceptualized by the categorical system of the DSM, in which they are given a diagnosis of one or more specific anxiety disorders, or by a dimensional system in which their overall symptoms of anxiety are considered together and no attempt is made to diagnose specific disorders (see the chapter about classification, diagnosis, and assessment for a fuller description of this issue) (Albano et al., 2003). The principal issue is that many children who meet the diagnostic criteria for one anxiety disorder also meet the diagnostic criteria for one or two other anxiety disorders. This suggests that many children's anxiety has not become focused enough to make distinguishing one form of anxiety from another useful for either conceptualizing their anxiety or developing effective therapeutic interventions (Last & Strauss, 1989; Rapoport et al., 2000). At this time, the categorical system for anxiety disorders in children is the most commonly used. However, ongoing research may suggest that the dimensional approach provides better information about the experiences of an anxious child.

Cultural Influences on Anxiety

Cultural expectations and practices may influence the degree to which children and adults experience anxiety and how this anxiety is expressed. Although most studies of cultural influences on anxiety have focused on adults, some findings may apply to children.

Some differences in types of anxiety have been found across racial and cultural groups in the United States. For example, higher rates of social phobia in adults have been found among African–Americans than European–Americans in two large cities, which may indicate the higher levels of anxiety that African–Americans experience as they interact with members of their own and other racial groups in social situations (Westermeyer & Dieperink, 2001). In addition, more Japanese men than men in other Asian countries experience social phobia, which may be related to the important role that evaluations by others can play in the occupational success of Japanese men.

Cultural issues may also influence how people express symptoms of anxiety. For example, children in different cultural groups may express their anxiety through physical symptoms such as stomachaches, excessive worry, or acting-out behaviors (Rogler, 1993; Westermeyer & Dieperink, 2001). Consequently, knowing how anxiety is commonly expressed in various cultures is important when we assess the degree to which children in those cultures are experiencing symptoms of anxiety.

Finally, it may be inappropriate in some cultures for children to express their anxiety, particularly to authority figures such as teachers, therapists, nurses, or physicians (Seeley, 2000). This may be particularly true for girls. Consequently, when interacting with children from different cultures, a clinician or researcher must know how to elicit information about anxiety in a way that does not require a child to violate a cultural expectation about discussing anxiety.

Key Concepts

- The term *anxiety* can refer to transient feelings, general moods, or disorders.
- It is unclear whether it is better to conceptualize childhood anxiety as a dimension or as a series of discrete disorders, especially in young children.
- Cultural expectations may influence the development of anxiety disorders and how anxiety is expressed.

Anxiety Disorders

Separation Anxiety Disorder

As noted in a previous section, of the three anxiety disorders of childhood first included in DSM-III, separation anxiety disorder is the only one still considered a childhood anxiety disorder. The basic features of separation anxiety disorder have remained the same in the various editions of the DSM: high levels of distress when separated from home or attachment figures (usually the parents, often the mother); excessive worry about parents being injured or dying; and great reluctance to engage in activities requiring physical separation from parents (APA, 2000). Although many young children are afraid of leaving their parents when they first engage in a new activity, such as attending preschool, most become less anxious each time they leave their parents for this activity. Children with separation anxiety disorder, however, experience intensifying anxiety as they are repeatedly separated from their parents (Silove & Manicavasagar, 2001).

Diagnostic Criteria

As shown in Table 10.1, the anxiety that children experience during separations can be expressed in a variety of ways, including through their emotions (such as recurrent distress), cognitions (excessive worry), behaviors (refusal to go to school), and physical symptoms (headaches or stomachaches; APA,

TABLE 10.1

Diagnostic Criteria for 309.21 Separation Anxiety Disorder

A. Developmentally inappropriate and excessive anxiety concerning separation from home or from those to whom the individual is attached, as evidenced by three (or more) of the following:
  (1) Recurrent excessive distress when separation from home or major attachment figures occurs or is anticipated.
  (2) Persistent and excessive worry about losing, or about possible harm befalling, major attachment figures.
  (3) Persistent and excessive worry that an untoward event will lead to separation from a major attachment figure (e.g., getting lost or being kidnapped).
  (4) Persistent reluctance or refusal to go to school or elsewhere because of fear of separation.
  (5) Persistently and excessively fearful or reluctant to be alone or without major attachment figures at home or without significant adults in other settings.
  (6) Persistent reluctance or refusal to go to sleep without being near a major attachment figure or to sleep away from home.
  (7) Repeated nightmares involving the theme of separation.
  (8) Repeated complaints of physical symptoms (such as headaches, stomachaches, nausea, or vomiting) when separation from major attachment figures occurs or is anticipated.
B. The duration of the disturbance is at least four weeks.
C. The onset is before age 18 years.
D. The disturbance causes clinically significant distress or impairment in social, academic (occupational), or other important areas of functioning.
E. The disturbance does not occur exclusively during the course of a Pervasive Developmental Disorder, Schizophrenia, or other Psychotic Disorder and, in adolescents and adults, is not better accounted for by Panic Disorder with Agoraphobia.
  Specify if:
    Early Onset: if onset occurs before age 6 years

2000). Many children with separation anxiety disorder show symptoms in several of these areas. The anxiety must cause clinically significant levels of distress that last for at least four weeks. This time requirement is included to distinguish children experiencing developmentally appropriate transient anxiety following separations from parents from those whose anxiety is more chronic. Finally, in keeping with separation anxiety disorder being a disorder of childhood, the symptoms must be present before the age of 18.

Characteristics and Experiences of Children with Separation Anxiety Disorder

The experiences of children with separation anxiety disorder can be conceptualized as a cycle of four stages: low anxiety and feelings of safety when near their parents, mounting anxiety as children think about upcoming separations, high anxiety when separated from parents, and diminishing anxiety when reunited with parents (Last, Hersen, Kazdin, Finkelstein, & Strauss, 1987).

As with all disorders, the intensities of separation anxiety disorder symptoms range along a continuum. Children with less severe symptoms may dawdle in the morning before school, have difficulty concentrating while at school, and return home as soon as possible in the afternoon. Children with moderate symptoms might try to stay home from school frequently, refuse to play outside with friends when they are at home, and stay close to their parents while in their house. Children with severe symptoms might refuse to attend school, experience a variety of physical symptoms whenever they anticipate being separated from their parents, and refuse to go to sleep unless in their parents' bedroom.

Separation anxiety disorder usually interferes with a child's performance in school and with his or her peer relationships (Albano et al., 2003). Academic performance can be impaired if the child is often absent from school or if his or her anxiety makes it difficult to focus on schoolwork. Some children with separation anxiety disorder may sit alone and worry during recess or lunch periods and hurry home in the afternoon. Thus they have few opportunities for peer interactions and consequently are likely to have poorly developed social skills. To the extent that their lack of social skills results in unpleasant social interactions with peers, their anxiety when being away from home may grow.

Prevalence and Developmental Course

Studies of separation anxiety disorder in large community samples of children have reported prevalence rates of 2–4% (APA, 2000; Egger & Angold, 2006; Silove & Manicavasagar, 2001). The prevalence of separation anxiety disorder is higher in preschool and early school-age children than in older children, and it is uncommon among adolescents. One study found a higher prevalence among females than males (Ehringer, Rhee, Young, Corley, & Hewitt, February 2006).

The onset of separation anxiety disorder is usually during early childhood (Last et al., 1987). The onset often follows a precipitating event involving either a difficult separation from a parent (perhaps starting preschool) or a threat to the health or life of a parent (such as a severe illness). However, many children who develop separation anxiety disorder have shown difficulties with separations throughout their lives. Consequently, in many cases the precipitating event appears to intensify a tendency that a child has exhibited for years. Although most older children or adolescents with separation anxiety disorder have experienced the disorder from early childhood, some have had a more recent onset. As with younger children, the onset usually follows a traumatic event or separation.

The course of separation anxiety disorder is chronic for most children, and without treatment, many of them experience gradually intensifying symptoms as they get older (Albano et al., 2003; Last et al., 1987). For example, a child who dawdles at home until the last minute in the primary grades may refuse to attend school a few years later. Most children experience periodic waxing and waning of symptoms rather than having symptoms of a consistent intensity. More intense symptoms usually follow periods of high stress.

Clinical reports suggest that anxiety around separations may remain an issue throughout adolescence and adulthood for some who have separation anxiety disorder, although the focus of their anxiety may change as they get older. For example, girls with separation anxiety disorder are at higher risk for developing panic disorder with agoraphobia in late adolescence or adulthood (Silove & Manicavasagar, 2001). In addition, children with separation anxiety disorder are at higher risk for developing generalized anxiety disorder and a depressive disorder as they get older (Last & Strauss, 1989).

Families of Children with Separation Anxiety Disorder

There is some evidence that parents of many children with separation anxiety disorder are overprotective (Silove & Manicavasagar, 2001). Thus the parents may be fearful when their children are separated from them, and they may express this fear to their children in overt or covert ways. The parents' fears may influence the development of anxiety in their children, and the parents may subtly reinforce their children's desire to stay with them because of their own fears and concerns.

Key Concepts

- Separation anxiety disorder is characterized by high levels of distress when separated from parents, excessive worry about parents, and unwillingness to engage in activities requiring separation from parents.
- Many children with separation anxiety disorder experience academic and peer difficulties.
- The prevalence of separation anxiety disorder is about 2–4%, with higher prevalence among younger children than older children.
- The onset is usually in early childhood and is often tied to a stressful event involving loss or separation.
- Parents of many children with separation anxiety disorder are overprotective.

Specific Phobia

Specific phobias are characterized by intense anxiety associated with particular things or events. A child may be intensely afraid of spiders, to the point where she insists that her parents check her bedroom for spiders before she enters it, but may have no more than normal fears of dogs, cats, and other animals. Similarly, a child may be intensely afraid of driving over bridges, to the point where his parents must take long detours to avoid bridges, but may have no noticeable fear of being driven other places. In earlier editions of the DSM this disorder was called simple phobia. The name was changed in DSM-IV to indicate that the phobias are specific and often not simple.

Diagnostic Criteria

As shown in Table 10.2, a specific phobia involves fear that is excessive or unreasonable and that impairs the child's functioning (APA, 2000). A child's strong fear of lions and tigers would not be considered a specific phobia, for example, if his life is not affected by the fear (his refusal to go near the lions and tigers when visiting the zoo would not be considered a meaningful

TABLE 10.2

Diagnostic Criteria for 300.29 Specific Phobia

A. Marked and persistent fear that is excessive or unreasonable, cued by the presence or anticipation of a specific object or situation (e.g., flying, heights, animals, receiving an injection, seeing blood).

B. Exposure to the phobic stimulus almost invariably provokes an immediate anxiety response, which may take the form of a situationally bound or situationally predisposed Panic Attack. **Note:** In children, the anxiety may be expressed by crying, tantrums, freezing, or clinging.

C. The person recognizes that the fear is excessive or unreasonable. **Note:** In children, this feature may be absent.

D. The phobic situation(s) is avoided or else is endured with intense anxiety or distress.

E. The avoidance, anxious anticipation, or distress in the feared situation(s) interferes significantly with the person's normal routine, occupational (or academic) functioning, or social activities or relationships, or there is marked distress about having the phobia.

F. In individuals under age 18 years, the duration is at least six months.

G. The anxiety, Panic Attacks, or phobic avoidance associated with the specific object or situation are not better accounted for by another mental disorder, such as Obsessive–Compulsive Disorder (e.g., fear of dirt in someone with an obsession about contamination), Posttraumatic Stress Disorder (e.g., avoidance of stimuli associated with a severe stressor), Separation Anxiety Disorder (e.g., avoidance of school), Social Phobia (e.g., avoidance of social situations because of fear of embarrassment), Panic Disorder with Agoraphobia, or Agoraphobia without History of Panic Disorder.

   Specify type:
   Animal Type
   Natural Environment Type (e.g., heights, storms, water)
   Blood–Injection–Injury Type
   Situational Type (e.g., airplanes, elevators, enclosed places)
   Other Type (e.g., fear of choking, vomiting, or contracting an illness; in children, fear of loud sounds or costumed characters)

impairment). In addition, the fear must impair a child's functioning for at least six months. Transient fears do not meet this criterion for a specific phobia even if they disrupt a child's life for a few weeks (for example, a child who is afraid of riding her bicycle for a few weeks after taking a bad fall).

A difference in the diagnostic criteria for adults and children is that adults must recognize that their fear is unreasonable, whereas this is not required of children. This difference exists because children may not have the experience or cognitive ability to recognize that a fear is unreasonable.

Finally, a fear related to another anxiety disorder would not be considered a specific phobia (such as a fear of swimming that is due to social phobia). As can also be seen in the diagnostic criteria, several subtypes of specific phobia can be diagnosed, depending on the focus of the fear.

Characteristics and Experiences of Children with Specific Phobias

Children with specific phobias often worry about encountering the focus of their fear and envision catastrophic outcomes of any encounter (APA, 2000). Thus they may experience high levels of anxiety even when not in contact with the focus of their fear. Their anxiety can interfere with their academic performance and social interactions. For example, a child may act awkwardly when with a group of peers if an activity may lead to having to cross a busy street, or may avoid being with friends to avoid this awkwardness. Some children may refuse to participate in activities that may bring them in contact with a feared object or event, such as refusing to participate in swimming classes because of a fear of drowning. Older children may recognize the social inappropriateness of their fears and refuse to describe their fears as the reason for their refusal to participate. As a result, their refusal may be seen as an act of defiance rather than an indication of anxiety. This may result in their being considered defiant or as having a behavior problem.

Because most children, especially young children, seldom have control over their lives, they may find themselves required to engage in activities that involve the focus of their phobias (such as going to the doctor where they may get an injection). When this occurs they may become highly aroused and cling to parents, refuse to move, or cry and scream. In particularly intense cases, they may hit others to escape the feared object or event (Albano et al., 2003). Unless this behavior is understood as the result of anxiety, a child's behavior may be conceptualized as a conduct problem, resulting in punishment rather than efforts to help the child reduce his or her fear.

Prevalence and Developmental Course

Prevalence rates for specific phobias from three large community samples of children ranged from 2% to 4% (Albano et al., 2003; Egger & Angold, 2006). The prevalence of specific phobias is higher among girls than boys. Although the reasons for this difference remain unclear, it may be due to boys experiencing greater social pressure to reduce or eliminate their fears ("Big boys aren't afraid to climb on the roof") (Muris & Merckelbach, 2001).

The developmental course of specific phobias varies among children (Muris & Merckelbach, 2001). Specific phobias develop slowly in some children, usually involving a gradual intensification of one or more normal childhood fears (Spence et al., 2001). Others develop suddenly following a frightening experience.

Specific phobias in many children end on their own even if the child does not receive treatment (Muris & Merckelbach, 2001). However, children who once had a specific phobia are more likely than others to develop other specific phobias later in childhood or adolescence—suggesting that their basic predisposition to higher levels of anxiety remains even when they are not experiencing a specific phobia.

Key Concepts

- Specific phobias are characterized by intense anxiety associated with particular things or events that often results in efforts to avoid or escape the focus of the fear.
- The fear must be unreasonable or excessive and must last for at least six months.
- Prevalence estimates range from 2% to 4%. Girls are more likely to experience a specific phobia than boys.
- Specific phobias may develop gradually or have a sudden onset following a frightening event. Many disappear on their own, although children who had a specific phobia are at greater risk for developing another specific phobia later in their lives.

Social Phobia or Social Anxiety Disorder

Social phobia is characterized by persistent fear of social situations in which a person is with unfamiliar people or believes that he or she is likely to be evaluated unfavorably by others (APA, 2000). For example, a child who has a persistent fear of speaking in front of his or her class, playing in games or sports, or going to parties may have social phobia.

Most people experience spikes of anxiety in certain social situations: meeting the parents of a boyfriend or girlfriend, taking a driving test, or speaking at a meeting. The primary difference between these spikes of anxiety and social phobia is that most of us can handle our spikes of anxiety fairly effectively. Our performance may be less effective than we would like (perhaps we say things we later regret when meeting the parents of a boyfriend or girlfriend), but we engage in the situation and our performance is generally adequate. In addition, as we engage in these situations repeatedly, we usually feel less anxious and our behavior is more effective (the third dinner with the parents usually goes better than the first). The experience of those with social phobia, in contrast, is that their performance is significantly impaired by their anxiety; they often choose to avoid situations that cause them anxiety even when doing so is problematic; and their anxiety during these situations often increases over time (Ollendick & Hirshfeld Becker, 2002).

Diagnostic Criteria

As shown in Table 10.3, the diagnostic criteria for social phobia require that high levels of fear must "almost always" accompany the anxiety-provoking social situation. Periodically experiencing intense fear in social situations does not constitute social phobia. At least one social situation that evokes fear in

---

TABLE 10.3

Diagnostic Criteria for 300.23 Social Phobia

A. A marked and persistent fear of one or more social or performance situations in which the person is exposed to unfamiliar people or to possible scrutiny by others. The individual fears that he or she will act in a way (or show anxiety symptoms) that will be humiliating or embarrassing. **Note:** In children, there must be evidence of the capacity for age-appropriate social relationships with familiar people and the anxiety must occur in peer settings, not just in interactions with adults.

B. Exposure to the feared social situation almost invariably provokes anxiety, which may take the form of a situationally bound or situationally predisposed Panic Attack. **Note:** In children, the anxiety may be expressed by crying, tantrums, freezing, or shrinking from social situations with unfamiliar people.

C. The person recognizes that the fear is excessive or unreasonable. **Note:** In children, this feature may be absent.

D. The feared social or performance situations are avoided or else are endured with intense anxiety or distress.

E. The avoidance, anxious anticipation, or distress in the feared social or performance situation(s) interferes significantly with the person's normal routine, occupational (academic) functioning, or social activities or relationships, or there is marked distress about having the phobia.

F. In individuals under age 18 years, the duration is at least six months.

G. The fear or avoidance is not due to the direct physiological effects of a substance (e.g., a drug of abuse, a medication) or a general medical condition and is not better accounted for by another mental disorder (e.g., Panic Disorder with or without Agoraphobia, Separation Anxiety Disorder, Body Dysmorphic Disorder, a Pervasive Developmental Disorder, or Schizoid Personality Disorder).

H. If a general medical condition or another mental disorder is present, the fear in Criterion A is unrelated to it; for example, the fear is not of Stuttering, trembling in Parkinson's disease, or exhibiting abnormal eating behavior in Anorexia Nervosa or Bulimia Nervosa.

Specify if:

Generalized: if the fears include most social situations (also consider the additional diagnosis of Avoidant Personality Disorder)

a child must occur in interactions with peers, probably because fears of evaluation from adults are normal in children. In addition, the anxiety must be present for at least six months in children and adolescents (but not adults) to distinguish social phobia from the significant but short-term social anxiety that many children experience.

Finally, as with all disorders, significant impairment or distress must be apparent. Children who are anxious about speaking in class or changing for physical education in front of others would not be given the diagnosis of social phobia if they can do so without excessive distress. As one might imagine, many more children have anxiety about social situations than meet the criteria for social phobia. For example, one study found that 20% of a group of children had significant anxiety about public speaking, but only about 2% experienced impairment or distress sufficient to receive a diagnosis of social phobia (APA, 2000).

The **specific type** of social phobia is diagnosed when a child experiences high levels of anxiety in only one or two settings; the **general type** is diagnosed when a child's anxiety occurs in many social settings. The general type is usually more chronic and severe, and children with the general type are more likely than those with the specific type to have comorbid depressive, conduct, or additional anxiety disorders (Ollendick & Hirshfeld Becker, 2002).

Characteristics and Experiences of Children with Social Phobia

Children with social anxiety often experience physical symptoms when anticipating or engaging in social activities—for example, stomachaches or headaches, a pounding heart, blushing, sweating, a trembling voice, or feelings of faintness (Spence et al., 2001). The behaviors of young children may include clinging to familiar adults in social situations, crying if separated from them, and refusing to attend school or participate in social activities. In this way, their behaviors can resemble those of young children with separation anxiety disorder. It is the fear of the social situation itself, rather than the separation from a parent, that distinguishes children with social phobia from those with separation anxiety disorder.

Older children and adolescents with social phobia may refuse to participate in group activities in school, refuse to participate in physical education (especially if changing clothes in front of others is required), and withdraw from contact with other students when they can. As can be imagined, they are often lonely and have few friends (La Greca & Lopez, 1998). Albano and colleagues (2003) describe a case of one adolescent with social phobia who spent every lunch hour during high school sitting in a bathroom stall.

Most children with social phobia feel inadequate, are highly self-critical, and wonder what it is about them that makes it impossible to be social (Ollendick & Hirshfeld Becker, 2002). Their highly critical self-evaluation predisposes many of them to feelings of depression, which can increase their negative self-evaluation and lead to greater withdrawal from others.

Prevalence and Developmental Course

Prevalence rates of social phobia in community samples of children and adolescents are about 1% (Albano et al., 2003). Although a common belief is that adolescents are more likely to experience social phobia than children because they are more sensitive to evaluation by their peers, the small amount of research to date does not support this belief. For example, the prevalence of social phobia at age 11 was about 1% in a large community sample of children in New Zealand, which was similar to the rate when the same group of children was assessed four years later (McGee et al., 1990). Social phobia is less common than most other anxiety disorders. For example, McGee and colleagues (1990) found rates of 6% for generalized anxiety disorder, 2% for separation anxiety disorder, and 4% for specific phobia, compared with 1% for social phobia.

Cultural values may influence the prevalence of social phobia if they emphasize the importance of correct social performance or evaluations by others. For example, Dong, Yang, and Ollendick (1994) found higher levels of fears about social evaluation in Chinese adolescents and young adults than in their Western peers.

Little information is available about the age of onset of social phobia. The DSM-IV-TR states that the onset is usually in mid-adolescence, although, as just noted, some research suggests that as many school-age children and early adolescents experience social phobia as do mid-adolescents (APA, 2000). When adolescents and adults with social phobia were asked about the onset of their anxiety, most of them remembered feeling anxious in social situations since they were children (Ollendick & Hirshfeld Becker, 2002). Gauging the age of onset from this research is difficult, however, because these adolescents and adults may recall anxiety that did not reach the intensity needed for a diagnosis of social phobia. However, research suggests that the anxiety that may eventually build into social phobia often begins early in a person's life.

The course of social phobia, if left untreated, is often chronic (APA, 2000). Because children with social phobia either avoid social situations or leave them as quickly as they can, they have few social experiences in which they do not feel highly anxious. Consequently, their anxiety is maintained and often strengthens over time.

Long-term studies of children with social phobia show that many experience other significant problems during their adolescence. For example, they are more likely to develop a substance abuse problem (possibly by taking drugs to relieve their anxiety) or depression (possibly caused by the stress caused by their anxiety) during their adolescence. High school students with social anxiety are less likely than their peers to seek a suitable college or university, and undergraduates with social anxiety are less likely to take the needed steps to be admitted to a graduate or professional school (Axelson & Birmaher, 2001; Kessler & Frank, 1997).

Parenting in Families with a Child Who Has Social Phobia

Several parenting styles have been found in families with a child who has social phobia or who is exceedingly shy. Parents in many of these families emphasize the importance of paying attention to social scrutiny and emphasize the shamefulness of behaviors such as immodesty or making a mistake in public (Buss, 1986). Consequently, their children may be particularly sensitive to evaluation by others. In addition, many adults with social phobia recall that their parents were very concerned with the opinions of others and that their families were socially isolated (Bruch & Heimberg, 1994; Bruch, Heimberg, Berger, & Collins, 1989). Perhaps the lack of an opportunity to observe others in social situations and practice social behaviors had a negative influence on the children's developing social skills. The combination of concern about social performance and a relative lack of social skills may have contributed to the children's development of social phobia.

Key Concepts

- Social phobia is characterized by a persistent fear of social situations involving unfamiliar people or evaluation by others.
- For children, at least one feared situation must involve interactions with peers, and the social anxiety must last at least six months.
- The specific type is diagnosed when excessive anxiety is limited to one or two situations; the general type is diagnosed when excessive anxiety occurs in many settings.
- The prevalence of social phobia is estimated at 1%.
- The age of onset is unclear. However, symptoms of social phobia often appear during early childhood.
- The course of social phobia is often chronic. Adolescents and young adults with social phobia are more likely than others to develop a substance abuse problem or depression.

Obsessive–Compulsive Disorder

Obsessive–compulsive disorder is characterized by a pattern of repeated thoughts (obsessions) and behaviors (compulsions) that interfere with a person's life and over which the person has little or no control (APA, 2000). Compulsive behaviors can be embarrassing and can consume hours of a child's time each day. Despite the difficulties they present, compulsions are repeated because the child feels awash with anxiety and may feel overwhelmed by obsessive thoughts if the compulsions are not repeated.

Obsessions are persistent thoughts that intrude into a child's mind and that cause the child marked anxiety (APA, 2000). Common obsessions experienced by children with obsessive–compulsive disorder involve disease or contamination (such as thoughts about germs or impure food), physical safety (thoughts about being in a fire or drowning), and morality or religious issues (concerns about sexuality or about going to heaven). Their intrusive nature distinguishes obsessions from children's normal concerns and worries. For example, a child who is concerned about germs in the bathroom at school may wash her hands carefully before she leaves but seldom think about germs otherwise. A child with obsessive thoughts about contamination, however, may think about germs throughout the day despite trying to focus on her schoolwork.

Excessive worries about real-life concerns are not considered obsessions, so it is important to know about a child's life circumstances and culture when considering whether his or her thoughts are obsessions. For example, a child from a violent family may worry repeatedly about domestic violence; a child about to engage in a culturally important religious ceremony may worry repeatedly about religious issues. Neither of these children would be considered to be experiencing obsessions.

Compulsions are repeated behaviors over which a child feels little or no control (APA, 2000). It is generally believed that compulsions develop because they help a child avoid anxiety-provoking obsessions. In some cases, a compulsion may allow a child to focus attention on the compulsive behaviors and away from anxiety-provoking obsessions. In other cases, a child may believe that engaging in a compulsive behavior will ward off an obsession in the same way that superstitious behavior is believed to ward off bad luck.

The most common compulsions are washing, checking, and ordering. Washing compulsions often relate to obsessions about disease or contamination. A child with a washing compulsion may wash her hands many times each day, taking several minutes each time and always washing her hands in exactly the same way. Checking compulsions often relate to safety concerns. A child may need to check the locks on all the doors and windows in his house before having dinner and before going to bed, and he may need to get up from dinner or out of bed several times to be sure he has checked each door and window properly. Ordering compulsions may reduce the anxiety related to a variety of obsessions because they can distract the child from them. For example, a child may need to arrange her toys in a particular way before she can leave her room in the morning, and she may need to return to her room several times before leaving for school to ensure that they are in the correct order. Another child may need to follow a specific procedure before getting into bed—for example, arranging the pillows in a certain way, touching each side of the bed three times, and then ensuring that the bed is exactly centered under a window.

Although many children, particularly young children, have specific rituals they like to follow during activities such as mealtime or bedtime, these are not considered compulsions (Albano et al., 2003). Typically these rituals fade over time; the children who engage in them do not feel obliged to complete them if it is inconvenient or embarrassing (for example, a child may like to arrange his food in a particular way before eating but does not do this if a friend is having dinner with the family); and they do not feel anxiety if the rituals are not completed. These characteristics distinguish childhood rituals from compulsions, which often become more intense and elaborate over time, must be completed even when doing so is embarrassing, and cause significant anxiety if they are not completed.

Diagnostic Criteria

As seen in Table 10.4, either obsessions or compulsions are sufficient for a diagnosis of obsessive–compulsive disorder, although obsessions and

TABLE 10.4

Diagnostic Criteria for 300.3 Obsessive–Compulsive Disorder

A. Either obsessions or compulsions:

    Obsessions as defined by (1), (2), (3), and (4):

    (1) Recurrent and persistent thoughts, impulses, or images that are experienced, at some time during the disturbance, as intrusive and inappropriate and that cause marked anxiety or distress.

    (2) The thoughts, impulses, or images are not simply excessive worries about real-life problems.

    (3) The person attempts to ignore or suppress such thoughts, impulses, or images, or to neutralize them with some other thought or action.

    (4) The person recognizes that the obsessional thoughts, impulses, or images are a product of his or her own mind (not imposed from without as in thought insertion).

    Compulsions as defined by (1) and (2):

    (1) Repetitive behaviors (e.g., hand washing, ordering, checking) or mental acts (e.g., praying, counting, repeating words silently) that the person feels driven to perform in response to an obsession, or according to rules that must be applied rigidly.

    (2) The behaviors or mental acts are aimed at preventing or reducing distress or preventing some dreaded event or situation; however, these behaviors or mental acts either are not connected in a realistic way with what they are designed to neutralize or prevent or are clearly excessive.

B. At some point during the course of the disorder, the person has recognized that the obsessions or compulsions are excessive or unreasonable. **Note:** This does not apply to children.

C. The obsessions or compulsions cause marked distress, are time-consuming (take more than one hour a day), or significantly interfere with the person's normal routine, occupational (or academic) functioning, or usual social activities or relationships.

D. If another Axis I disorder is present, the content of the obsessions or compulsions is not restricted to it (e.g., preoccupation with food in the presence of an Eating Disorder; hair pulling in the presence of Trichotillomania; concern with appearance in the presence of Body Dysmorphic Disorder; preoccupation with drugs in the presence of a Substance Use Disorder; preoccupation with having a serious illness in the presence of Hypochondriasis; preoccupation with sexual urges or fantasies in the presence of a Paraphilia; or guilty ruminations in the presence of Major Depressive Disorder).

E. The disturbance is not due to the direct physiological effects of a substance (e.g., a drug of abuse, a medication) or a general medical condition.

    Specify if:

        With Poor Insight: if, for most of the time during the current episode, the person does not recognize that the obsessions and compulsions are excessive or unreasonable compulsions occur together in most children. As with several other anxiety disorders, a child is not expected to recognize the excessive nature of the obsessions or compulsions, although adults must have this recognition.

Characteristics and Experiences of Children with Obsessive–Compulsive Disorder

Many children with obsessive–compulsive disorder are severely impaired by their disorder (Last & Strauss, 1989). Their compulsions often prevent them from participating in educational and social activities. For example, some children spend so much time with compulsive behaviors that they do not have sufficient time to complete homework or class work. Children with elaborate compulsions around bedtime may be unwilling to spend the night at a friend's home; those with washing compulsions may be unwilling to attend parties, dances, or other social activities.

To the extent that a child is unable to keep his or her compulsions secret from other children, the child may become a target of jokes and ridicule. This may have a significant negative influence on the child's peer relationships. For example, Albano and colleagues (2003) describe a case of a 12-year-old boy who had to repeat several dancelike steps before he could cross a doorway and enter a room. This became acutely embarrassing for him in middle school when he had to change classes each hour and led to his being the target of many jokes from his peers.

Prevalence and Developmental Course

The lifetime prevalence of obsessive–compulsive disorder in community samples of children is about 2% (Rapoport et al., 2000; Whitaker et al., 1990). (*Lifetime prevalence* refers to the prevalence of those who have met the diagnostic criteria at some point in their lives, although they might not have the disorder at the time they are asked about it.) Some studies have found a higher prevalence in boys, others have found a higher prevalence in girls, and others have found similar prevalence rates among boys and girls; so the issue of whether boys or girls are more likely to be diagnosed with obsessive–compulsive disorder remains unclear.

Many children with obsessive–compulsive disorder try to hide their compulsive behaviors from others. Consequently, studies relying on parents' or teachers' reports significantly underestimate the prevalence of obsessive–compulsive disorder. This was shown by one study in which children and their parents were interviewed separately about the children's anxiety disorder symptoms. Thirty-five children out of 1,285 (2.7%) were identified as having obsessive–compulsive disorder; however, only four of them (0.3%) were identified through reports from their parents. The parents of the other 31 children were unaware of their children's compulsive behaviors (Rapoport et al., 2000).

The age of onset is in early or middle childhood for most children who have obsessive–compulsive disorder. Several studies have found a younger age of onset for boys than girls. For example, Rapoport and colleagues (2000) found an onset age of about 7 for boys and about 11 for girls. The reasons for the differences in onset for boys and girls remain unclear.

The course of obsessive–compulsive disorder is often chronic (Albano et al., 2003). Some children experience obsessive–compulsive disorder symptoms for several months and then have the intensity of the symptoms decrease dramatically or have them disappear for several months—with a later intensifying of the symptoms. Other children, however, experience chronic, intense symptoms or symptoms that grow steadily over time. Specific obsessions and compulsions often change during childhood and adolescence—so the propensity to have obsessive–compulsive disorder symptoms may remain strong in some children while the focus of their obsessions and compulsions changes over time.

Key Concepts

- Obsessive–compulsive disorder is characterized by a pattern of repeated, anxiety-provoking, intrusive thoughts (obsessions) and time-consuming, ritualistic behaviors (compulsions) that interfere in a child's life.
- Common obsessions focus on disease or contamination, physical safety, and morality or religious issues; common compulsions involve washing, checking, and ordering.
- Lifetime prevalence rates among children are about 2%.
- Children are often reluctant to acknowledge having symptoms of obsessive–compulsive disorder, so the disorder may remain hidden for many years.
- The age of onset is often in middle childhood; boys appear to have an earlier onset than girls. The course is often chronic. Some children experience changes in specific obsessions or compulsions over time.

Generalized Anxiety Disorder

Generalized anxiety disorder is characterized by excessive anxiety and worry about several issues. The DSM-IV-TR describes *worry* as "apprehensive expectation"; that is, one is apprehensive about something that might happen (APA, 2000). Children with generalized anxiety disorder worry about many things, and their worrying uses a significant amount of their time and energy each day.

As noted earlier, all children worry, and some worry more than others. Interestingly, when the number of worries of children with generalized anxiety disorder was compared with the number of worries of children without any anxiety disorder, they were approximately the same. However, the intensity of the worries of children with generalized anxiety disorder was much higher (Silverman, La Greca, & Wasserstein, 1995; Weems, Silverman, & La Greca, 2000). So the higher level of intense worry, and their inability to stop worrying when they try to, distinguish children with generalized anxiety disorder from other children.

Diagnostic Criteria

As shown in Table 10.5, the principal characteristic of generalized anxiety disorder is excessive anxiety or worry about "a number of events or

TABLE 10.5

Diagnostic Criteria for 300.02 Generalized Anxiety Disorder

A. Excessive anxiety and worry (apprehensive expectation), occurring more days than not for at least six months, about a number of events or activities (such as work or school performance).

B. The person finds it difficult to control the worry.

C. The anxiety and worry are associated with three (or more) of the following six symptoms (with at least some symptoms present for more days than not for the past six months). **Note:** Only one item is required in children.

 (1) Restlessness or feeling keyed up or on edge.

 (2) Being easily fatigued.

 (3) Difficulty concentrating or mind going blank.

 (4) Irritability.

 (5) Muscle tension.

 (6) Sleep disturbance (difficulty falling or staying asleep, or restless unsatisfying sleep).

D. The focus of the anxiety and worry is not confined to features of an Axis I disorder; for example, the anxiety or worry is not about having a Panic Attack (as in Panic Disorder), being embarrassed in public (as in Social Phobia), being contaminated (as in Obsessive–Compulsive Disorder), being away from home or close relatives (as in Separation Anxiety Disorder), gaining weight (as in Anorexia Nervosa), having multiple physical complaints (as in Somatization Disorder), or having a serious illness (as in Hypochondriasis), and the anxiety and worry do not occur exclusively during Posttraumatic Stress Disorder.

E. The anxiety, worry, or physical symptoms cause clinically significant distress or impairment in social, occupational, or other important areas of functioning.

F. The disturbance is not due to the direct physiological effects of a substance (e.g., a drug of abuse, a medication) or a general medical condition (e.g., hyperthyroidism) and does not occur exclusively during a Mood Disorder, a Psychotic Disorder, or a Pervasive Developmental Disorder.

---

activities" that lasts for at least six months (APA, 2000). The specific number of events or activities is not specified. In addition, a child must have difficulty controlling the anxiety or worry associated with generalized anxiety disorder. A child who can set his or her worries aside when engaging in schoolwork or other activities is not experiencing generalized anxiety disorder.

The anxiety or worry must be out of proportion to the likelihood of the events occurring or to the consequences of the events. This requires knowledge about the context in which the child lives before deciding whether the child is exhibiting symptoms of generalized anxiety disorder. For example, a child living in Kansas who worries a lot about tornadoes may be experiencing reasonable worry, whereas the same level of worry in a child living in central California would be excessive. We must also consider cultural expectations when deciding whether a worry is excessive. Children who worry a great deal about an event that evokes anxiety in most people in their culture might not be experiencing a symptom of generalized anxiety disorder (an example might be turning a certain age), whereas a child in another culture with a similar level of anxiety about the event might be experiencing a symptom of generalized anxiety disorder.

Characteristics and Experiences of Children with Generalized Anxiety Disorder

Children with generalized anxiety disorder spend much of their time worrying. Although the content of the worry varies from child to child, research and clinical reports suggest that the range of worries is often extensive and includes issues about which they have some control as well as issues about which they have little or no control (Albano et al., 2003). Common worries of children with generalized anxiety disorder focus on their safety or the safety of their families, and on current and future performance in school, extracurricular activities, or social events. Many children with generalized anxiety disorder also worry about adult concerns, such as family finances and the safety of their home (Bell-Dolan & Brazeal, 1993).

As just noted, by definition the worries of children with generalized anxiety disorder are excessive. For example, they may believe that the likelihood of their being kidnapped or of a parent getting cancer is high even though these events are unlikely. Similarly, they may worry about a parent losing a job and the family being destitute even though the parents have significant savings. In addition, their experiences have little influence on the amount or intensity of the worries. For example, they may worry extensively about their school performance even if they frequently receive high grades on assignments and tests (Axelson & Birmaher, 2001).

Many children with generalized anxiety disorder are perfectionists. They believe they must do very well on all the tasks they attempt, and they worry that they will not. When their performance is not what they believe it should be, they are very harsh with themselves—often much harsher than their parents, teachers, or peers (Bell-Dolan & Brazeal, 1993). Consequently, they are frequently disappointed with themselves, which can lead to sadness and frustration and sometimes a comorbid depressive disorder (Axelson & Birmaher, 2001).

Although no research has focused on the peer or adult relationships of children with generalized anxiety disorder, one can hypothesize that they would be troubled. Many peers, teachers, and others may find the combination of perfectionism and excessive worry in these children to be bothersome. Because attempts to allay the child's worries are usually unsuccessful, those who try are likely to find their interactions with the child frustrating. Children with generalized anxiety disorder may become friends with peers who also worry extensively; and as we will discuss in an upcoming section, the reinforcement they give each other for worrying may maintain or exacerbate the intensity and frequency of their worries.

Prevalence and Developmental Course

The few prevalence estimates for childhood generalized anxiety disorder vary quite a bit. Two studies using community samples of children in the United States found prevalence rates of 13% (Kashani & Orvaschel, 1988) and 7% (Muris, Meesters, Merchelbach, Sermon, & Zwakhalen, 1998). The reasons for the prevalence differences between the studies are unclear, but it does appear that excessive worry is characteristic of many children.

Adolescents are more likely than school-age children to experience the symptoms of generalized anxiety disorder (Ehringer et al., February 2006; Weems et al., 2000). For example, a study of 11-year-olds in New Zealand found a prevalence of 3%, with a prevalence of 6% in the same group when they were 15 (McGee et al., 1990). However, a study of preschoolers found that 7% experienced generalized anxiety disorder (Egger & Angold, 2006). Consequently, there may be a curvilinear relationship between age and generalized anxiety disorder, with younger children and adolescents having a higher prevalence than school-age children. (A similar pattern exists for oppositional defiant disorder.

Little is known about the onset and course of generalized anxiety disorder in children. About half of adults diagnosed with generalized anxiety disorder state that they had significant worries since early childhood, suggesting that the symptoms of generalized anxiety disorder start for many in childhood, or at least that a pattern of having many worries begins then (APA, 2000). The course of the disorder seems to vary in intensity, with periods of reduced symptoms and also of more intense worry. Periods of intense worry are more likely to occur during times of stress, suggesting that stress accentuates a predisposition toward worrying in some children.

Key Concepts

- Generalized anxiety disorder is characterized by excessive and intense worry about several issues. The worries of children with generalized anxiety disorder intrude on their lives, and they have little control over them.
- Children with generalized anxiety disorder may worry about issues over which they have control (like school performance) and issues over which they have no control (like family finances).
- Prevalence estimates vary considerably from 3% to 13%.
- Little is known about the onset and course of generalized anxiety disorder. Many adults with generalized anxiety disorder report excessive worry during their childhood, suggesting that a pattern of worry, and possibly the disorder itself, may often begin during childhood.

Panic Disorder

Panic disorder involves recurrent panic attacks followed by intense concern about the meaning of the attacks and whether they will occur again (APA, 2000). Although all anxiety symptoms can be intense and uncomfortable, panic attacks are extraordinarily intense, and the physical symptoms associated with them can even make a person believe that he or she is dying. Until the past two decades, it was generally believed that panic attacks occurred only in adults. However, interviews with children in clinical and community samples have shown that a small percentage of them experience panic attacks (Albano et al., 2003).

Diagnostic Criteria

As just noted, panic disorder requires the presence of recurrent panic attacks (although how many panic attacks must occur is not specified). As shown in Table 10.6, a panic attack occurs when intense physical and cognitive symptoms occur abruptly and quickly. There are three types of panic attacks: **unexpected (uncued) panic attacks,** in which the attacks occur apparently at random and for no apparent reason; **situationally bound (cued) panic attacks,** in which an attack almost always occurs in a particular situation (such as seeing blood); and **situationally predisposed panic attacks,** in which attacks are more likely to occur in a particular situation but do not occur in that situation invariably (APA, 2000).

Children with panic disorder experience persistent concern about future attacks, and this concern often limits their behaviors (see Table 10.7). For example, a child who has experienced a panic attack during a physical education class may be so concerned about future attacks that she refuses to

---

TABLE 10.6

Criteria for Panic Attack

Note: A Panic Attack is not a codable disorder. Code the specific diagnosis in which the Panic Attack occurs (e.g., 300.21 Panic Disorder with Agoraphobia). A discrete period of intense fear or discomfort, in which four (or more) of the following symptoms developed abruptly and reached a peak within 10 minutes:

(1) Palpitations, pounding heart, or accelerated heart rate.
(2) Sweating.
(3) Trembling or shaking.
(4) Sensations of shortness of breath or smothering.
(5) Feeling of choking.
(6) Chest pain or discomfort.
(7) Nausea or abdominal distress.
(8) Feeling dizzy, unsteady, lightheaded, or faint.
(9) Derealization (feelings of unreality) or depersonalization (being detached from oneself).
(10) Fear of losing control or going crazy.
(11) Fear of dying.
(12) Paresthesias (numbness or tingling sensations).
(13) Chills or hot flashes.

TABLE 10.7

Diagnostic Criteria for
300.01 Panic Disorder without Agoraphobia

A. Both (1) and (2):
    (1) Recurrent unexpected Panic Attacks.
    (2) At least one of the attacks has been followed by one month (or more)
         of one (or more) of the following:
         (a) Persistent concern about having additional attacks.
         (b) Worry about the implications of the attack or its consequences
              (e.g., losing control, having a heart attack, "going crazy").
         (c) A significant change in behavior related to the attacks.
B. Absence of Agoraphobia.
C. The Panic Attacks are not due to the direct physiological effects of a
    substance (e.g., a drug of abuse, a medication) or a general medical
    condition (e.g., hyperthyroidism).
D. The Panic Attacks are not better accounted for by another mental disorder,
    such as Social Phobia (e.g., occurring on exposure to feared social
    situations), Specific Phobia (e.g., on exposure to a specific phobic situation),
    Obsessive–Compulsive Disorder (e.g., on exposure to dirt in someone with
    an obsession about contamination), Post-traumatic Stress Disorder (e.g., in
    response to stimuli associated with a severe stressor), or Separation Anxiety
    Disorder (e.g., in response to being away from home or close relatives).

---

attend physical education classes, despite the consequences of her refusal. Similarly, a child who has experienced a panic attack while shopping with parents may have such great concern about an attack occurring again that he refuses to return to the mall where it occurred or perhaps refuses to go into any store.

Because panic attacks can occur as a part of other anxiety disorders, panic disorder is not diagnosed if panic attacks occur only in situations associated with another anxiety disorder (APA, 2000). For example, if a child with social phobia experiences panic attacks only before speaking in front of her class, she would not be given the diagnosis of panic disorder.

Panic disorder can occur with or without **agoraphobia** (from the Greek *agora,* "marketplace"). Agoraphobia is a fear of being in a place where, if a panic attack were to occur, escape would difficult or impossible (see Table 10.8) (APA, 2000). Imagine yourself experiencing the severe symptoms of a panic attack. You would most likely want to be completely by yourself or with one supportive person, and you would want to avoid being around others who might react badly at the time of your attack or make fun of you later. A child with agoraphobia may fear being in a school assembly, riding on a bus, or being in a large shopping center—all places from which it would be difficult to escape if a panic attack began. Although it could be argued that escape from some of these situations could be easy (a child could leave

TABLE 10.8

Criteria for Agoraphobia

Note: Agoraphobia is not a codable disorder. Code the specific disorder in which the Agoraphobia occurs (e.g., 300.21 Panic Disorder with Agoraphobia or 300.22 Agoraphobia without History of Panic Disorder).

A.　Anxiety about being in places or situations from which escape might be difficult (or embarrassing) or in which help may not be available in the event of having an unexpected or situationally predisposed Panic Attack or panic-like symptoms. Agoraphobic fears typically involve characteristic clusters of situations that include being outside the home alone; being in a crowd or standing in a line; being on a bridge; and traveling in a bus, train, or automobile.

　　Note: Consider the diagnosis of Specific Phobia if the avoidance is limited to one or only a few specific situations, or Social Phobia if the avoidance is limited to social situations.

B.　The situations are avoided (e.g., travel is restricted) or else are endured with marked distress or with anxiety about having a Panic Attack or panic-like symptoms, or require the presence of a companion.

C.　The anxiety or phobic avoidance is not better accounted for by another mental disorder, such as Social Phobia (e.g., avoidance limited to social situations because of fear of embarrassment), Specific Phobia (e.g., avoidance limited to a single situation like elevators), Obsessive–Compulsive Disorder (e.g., avoidance of dirt in someone with an obsession about contamination), Posttraumatic Stress Disorder (e.g., avoidance of stimuli associated with a severe stressor), or Separation Anxiety Disorder (e.g., avoidance of leaving home or relatives).

a school assembly and go to the nurse's office), the sudden and intense nature of panic attacks means that they quickly become debilitating, so escape from any public place is often difficult.

Children who experience unexpected panic attacks or situationally bound panic attacks in many situations are more likely to develop agoraphobia than those who experience situationally bound panic attacks in only one or two situations. Over time, those with unexpected panic attacks may find themselves restricting their activities more and more. Some adults with severe forms of agoraphobia, for example, are unable to leave their homes without experiencing severe distress (APA, 2000).

Prevalence

Not much is known about the prevalence or course of panic disorder in children because it has seldom been a focus of research (Albano et al., 2003). A few prevalence studies using community samples of children have found rates between 0.5% and 1.5%, showing that it is rarer than other anxiety disorders (Whitaker et al., 1990; Wittchen, Reed, & Kessler, 1998). One study found that girls who were past puberty were more likely to experience panic attacks than those who had not begun puberty (Hayward et al., 1992).

Key Concepts

- Panic disorder involves the repeated experience of panic attacks followed by intense concern about the meaning of the attacks and whether they will recur.
- A panic attack involves intense physical and cognitive symptoms that occur abruptly.
- Panic disorder may occur with agoraphobia, which is a fear of being in a place where escape is difficult if a panic attack were to occur.
- Prevalence estimates among children range from 0.5% to 1.5%; little is known about the developmental course of panic disorder.

Adjustment Disorder with Anxiety

Adjustment disorder with anxiety is included not in the anxiety disorder category of the DSM-IV-TR but in the **adjustment disorder** category. As shown in Table 10.9, adjustment disorder with anxiety can be diagnosed when a child is having a difficult time adapting to a specific stressor and the primary symptoms involve anxiety. For example, a child whose parent was killed in a car accident and who is very anxious about other family members dying or about being in a car may be experiencing adjustment disorder with anxiety. An adjustment disorder can be diagnosed only for six months following the cessation of the stressor. If significant anxiety exists longer than six months, the diagnosis is changed to one of the anxiety disorders.

Anxiety Disorder Not Otherwise Specified

Finally, as in most categories of disorders in the DSM-IV-TR, a *not otherwise specified* diagnosis is included. This diagnosis can be given to a child who experiences significant distress or impairment from anxiety but whose symptoms do not meet all the diagnostic criteria for one of the other anxiety disorders or adjustment disorder with anxiety.

Etiology of Anxiety Disorders

As noted earlier, current theories about the development of anxiety disorders in children focus on three components. First, some children appear to have a genetic predisposition to experiencing higher levels of anxiety and having more intense fears than other children. This predisposition is evident in a temperament characterized by shyness and fear, particularly when a child is in novel situations. Second, the experiences of some of these children, particularly in the home, create a cognitive style and a pattern of behaviors that

TABLE 10.9

Diagnostic Criteria for Adjustment Disorders

A. The development of emotional or behavioral symptoms in response to an identifiable stressor(s) occurring within three months of the onset of the stressor(s).
B. These symptoms or behaviors are clinically significant as evidenced by either of the following:
    (1) Marked distress that is in excess of what would be expected from exposure to the stressor.
    (2) Significant impairment in social or occupational (academic) functioning.
C. The stress-related disturbance does not meet the criteria for another specific Axis I disorder and is not merely an exacerbation of a preexisting Axis I or Axis II disorder.
D. The symptoms do not represent Bereavement.
E. Once the stressor (or its consequences) has terminated, the symptoms do not persist for more than an additional six months.
    Specify if:
        Acute: if the disturbance lasts less than six months
        Chronic: if the disturbance lasts for six months or longer

Adjustment Disorders are coded based on the subtype, which is selected according to the predominant symptoms. The specific stressor(s) can be specified on Axis IV.

309.0	**With Depressed Mood**
309.24	**With Anxiety**
309.28	**With Mixed Anxiety and Depressed Mood**
309.3	**With Disturbance of Conduct**
309.4	**With Mixed Disturbance of Emotions and Conduct**
309.9	**Unspecified**

increase their overall anxiety and focus their anxiety in one or more specific ways. Finally, the anxiety of these children can be maintained and intensified through operant conditioning and modeling (Muris & Merckelbach, 2001).

Of course anxiety disorders do not always develop in this way. As illustrated by the second vignette that began this chapter and by the creation of a specific phobia in Little Albert by John Watson, an anxiety disorder can develop in some children who do not have a genetic predisposition to anxiety. In addition, the temperaments of some children may be characterized by such intense fear that they develop an anxiety disorder even when their parents provide a home environment that helps them minimize their fears. However, it appears that most cases of anxiety disorder develop through the joint influences of temperament and experience.

Genetically Based Vulnerability to Anxiety
Genetic Influence on Anxiety

Family and twin studies suggest that genes account for about one-third of the variability in the levels of fear and anxiety experienced by children (Albano et al., 2003). Several studies of the relatives of children with anxiety disorders and of the children of parents with an anxiety disorder show that anxiety aggregates in families (*aggregate* is from the Latin *gregare,* "to herd"). This means that anxiety clumps together in families rather than being evenly distributed across families, suggesting the possibility of a genetic influence.

Many studies with twins show that there is a higher correlation between the levels of anxiety among MZ twins than DZ twins, which supports a genetic influence on anxiety (Eley, 2001). However, as with studies of the genetic influences on depression discussed in the previous chapter, higher correlations of anxiety symptoms in MZ twins occur when parents rate their children's anxiety symptoms than when the children rate their own symptoms. Although the reasons for this remain unclear, it may be that parents of MZ twins generalize their twins' anxiety levels to both twins more frequently than do parents of DZ twins (possibly because MZ twins look and act more alike) (Rowe & Jacobson, 1999). Consequently, the genetic influence on anxiety may be overestimated by twin studies that rely on parental reports of children's symptoms. However, even studies in which the children rate their own symptoms show a meaningful influence of genes on anxiety, so this influence does exist—although its strength remains in question.

An interesting finding from most studies of the genetic influence on anxiety is that anxiety symptoms are influenced to a greater degree by children's shared environment than occurs with other childhood disorders. That is, whereas many studies of depression, conduct disorder, or other disorders show that nonshared environmental influences are more important than shared environmental influences, studies of anxiety show a stronger influence of shared environment (Eley, 2001). This suggests that the shared components of the family environment play a greater role in the development of anxiety than other childhood disorders—a topic to which we will turn later in this section.

Most studies of the genetic influence on anxiety suggest that it influences a general predisposition toward anxiety rather than a predisposition to specific anxiety disorders (Albano et al., 2003). Thus genes do not appear to directly influence the development of separation anxiety disorder or social phobia, for example, but instead influence the development of high levels of anxiety in a child that later are directed toward particular issues or events by the child's experiences.

Two Temperaments and Their Influence on Anxiety

The genetic vulnerability to high levels of anxiety appears to be expressed through the temperament of anxious children. In this section we explore research programs that have identified two temperaments associated with higher levels of anxiety in children.

As discussed more thoroughly in other chapters, **temperament** consists of relatively consistent, basic dispositions inherent in a child. These dispositions are often apparent early in a child's life, and it is generally assumed that they are largely influenced by genes (Goldsmith et al., 1987). Both of the following theories about temperament and anxiety suggest that the temperaments of some children predispose them to feeling high levels of anxiety, particularly in situations that are novel or that they perceive as potentially dangerous.

Behavioral Inhibition   Probably the best-known temperament associated with anxiety was initially described by Jerome Kagan and his colleagues (Kagan, Reznick, & Gibbons, 1989; Kagan, Reznick, & Snidman, 1987; Kagan, Reznick, Snidman, & Gibbons, 1988). Through extensive longitudinal studies of toddlers and young children, Kagan found that about 15% of European–American children exhibited a temperament he labeled **behavioral inhibition.** These children showed physiological and behavioral differences from other children when in novel situations or meeting unfamiliar people. For example, the behaviorally inhibited children stayed closer to their mothers and expressed more distress when an unfamiliar adult was present, and they were more likely to remain with their mothers when they were free to play in a room with unfamiliar children. The behaviorally inhibited children also experienced increased heart rate and heart rate variability, pupillary dilation, **cortisol** secretion, and muscle tension when in novel situations, all of which are associated with higher levels of anxiety.

Although Kagan found that many children who were not behaviorally inhibited experienced some of these physiological and behavioral reactions when in novel situations, their reactions ended as they became familiar with their surroundings. However, the behaviorally inhibited children experienced these reactions for much longer periods, and some of them had no reduction in their reactions during the observations. Further, the reactions of the behaviorally inhibited children did not occur in familiar situations, suggesting that they were due to the children's response to the novel situations rather than basic physiological differences (Kagan, 1997).

Kagan's longitudinal research showed that most of the children in the behaviorally inhibited group remained in that group each time they were assessed through the seven years of the study, suggesting the stability of this temperament. Equally important, however, was the finding that some children moved from the behaviorally inhibited group to the noninhibited group during the seven years, suggesting that their behaviors and their physiological responses were being influenced by their socialization—an issue we will explore in a following section.

The connection between a behaviorally inhibited temperament and anxiety disorders can be seen in research showing that behaviorally inhibited children are more likely to develop anxiety disorders than are other children (Biederman et al., 1993). In addition, other research has shown that parents and siblings of behaviorally inhibited children have higher rates of anxiety disorders than do parents and siblings of other children (Rosenbaum, Biederman, Hirshfeld, & Bolduc, 1991). Thus a behaviorally inhibited temperament seems to provide the foundation for the development of an anxiety disorder for many children. However, only about one-third of behaviorally inhibited children develop an anxiety disorder (Kagan, 1997), suggesting that family and other experiences also play a role in the development of anxiety disorders in these children.

Tripartite Model   The **tripartite model** (see Figure 10.2) was developed partly to understand the similarities and differences between anxiety disorders and depressive disorders. As discussed in this chapter and the previous chapter about depressive disorders, anxiety and depressive disorders are often comorbid and share several features (Kovacs & Devlin, 1998). However, the behaviors and emotional experiences of children with an anxiety disorder and children with a depressive disorder differ. At issue, then, is how to understand characteristics that the disorders share and those that make them distinct.

Through an extensive review of studies of adults, Clark and Watson (1991) proposed three characteristics that linked and distinguished depression and anxiety: negative affect, positive affect, and physiological hyperarousal. Although it is not clear whether these characteristics are present from early in life and thus could be considered components of a temperament, some recent research has suggested that they are (Laurent & Ettelson, 2001). Consequently, it may be useful to think about them as part of a temperament that predisposes some children to either depression or anxiety.

The link between the depressive and anxiety disorders is that those with either type of disorder experience higher levels of negative affect than those with neither disorder. What distinguishes the two types of disorders is that those with depression have low levels of positive affect and normal levels of physiological arousal, whereas those with anxiety have normal levels of positive affect and high levels of physiological arousal. So people who are depressed seldom experience positive emotions, whereas people with anxiety experience positive emotions as frequently as those with neither disorder. Alternatively,

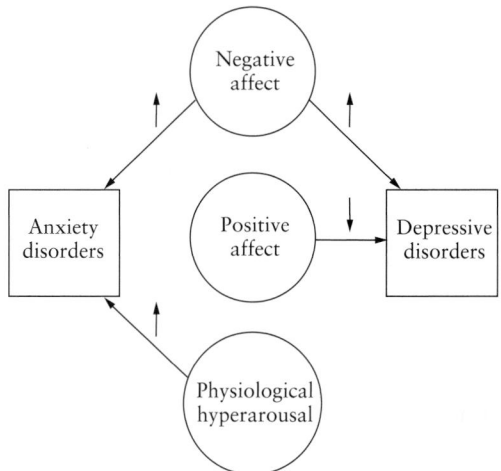

FIGURE 10.2   *The Tripartite Model*

those who are anxious often experience high levels of arousal, but this is not true for those who are depressed (Laurent & Ettelson, 2001).

Many children with high anxiety have a personality style characterized by negative affect and high levels of physiological arousal (Laurent & Ettelson, 2001). The negative affect puts them at risk for both anxiety and depressive disorders. High physiological arousal, a characteristic that may be genetically influenced, puts them at risk for anxiety disorders because their arousal increases the likelihood that they will experience anxiety in situations they consider dangerous. If they have learned that many situations are dangerous, they are likely to experience frequent anxiety, and this anxiety is likely to be more intense than that experienced by other children because of their high level of arousal. Over time, this frequent and intense anxiety can develop into an anxiety disorder.

A Brief Foray into Thinking about Risk Taking

Another way of thinking about children and adults who are highly anxious is to consider people who are just the opposite—those who seek novelty and danger. As discussed more fully in Haugaard (2001), these people are often described as engaging in risk taking or sensation seeking. In many ways these children and adults revel in experiences that would make most of us anxious. Considering their experiences will help us tie together the previous section's focus on temperamental influence on anxiety and the following section's focus on the influences of children's experiences on their anxiety.

An interesting discussion of those who like to live "on the dangerous edge of things" is found in Apter's (1992) book *The Dangerous Edge*. For example, he noted the following:

> From the moment the council of my hometown in Wales pronounced that the promenade along the seafront was in a dangerous condition, the crowds flocked not just to see it but to walk along it. The chance of the whole structure collapsing into the sea made it more popular than ever. Certainly the rope cordon intended to keep everyone out made not the slightest bit of difference. The young ducked under it, the old stepped over it, and those in wheelchairs—and even mothers pushing babies in prams—had it lifted for them. (p. 3)

How can we understand how some children and adults seek these dangerous situations while others do everything they can to avoid them? The answer involves both physiological arousal (which is biologically based) and a person's beliefs about what that arousal means (which is based on a person's experience).

Physiological Arousal

When we confront a novel or dangerous situation, the **sympathetic branch** of our autonomic nervous system is activated (Carlson, 1986). The purpose of the sympathetic branch is to arouse an organism and, if needed, to prepare it for "fight or flight."

The same behavior can be exciting for some children and anxiety-provoking for others.

Apter suggests the following model for conceptualizing this physiological arousal (see Figure 10.3). The safety zone represents an area where no risk exists—and consequently where there is no physiological arousal. Once a person enters the danger zone, physiological arousal begins because of the instinctual activation of the sympathetic nervous system. Arousal instinctively increases the closer the person comes to the dangerous edge. Just over the dangerous edge is the trauma zone, where some negative outcome occurs.

A straightforward example of this concept is how you respond when being at the top of a tall cliff. When you are back from the edge, you feel safe and so experience no arousal. As you approach the cliff's edge, physiological arousal begins. This arousal increases the closer you come to the edge of the cliff. The edge of the cliff is the dangerous edge, and just over the edge is the trauma zone, where a fall leads to injury or death. As another example, consider a child who experiences strong anxiety in social situations. When the child is far removed from a social situation, she

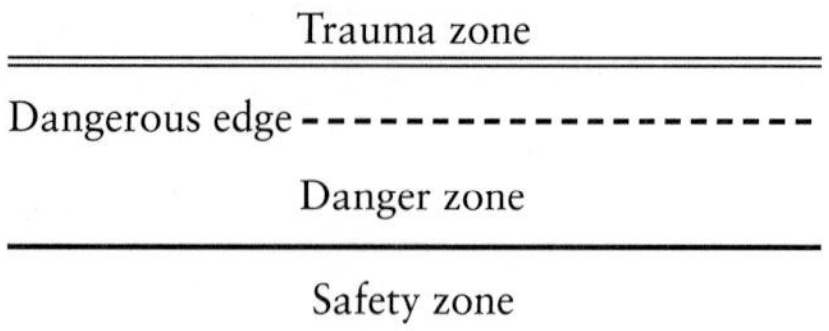

Trauma zone
_____
Dangerous edge -
Danger zone
_____
Safety zone

FIGURE 10.3 *Apter's Model*

experiences no arousal. As she enters the school cafeteria at lunchtime, she perceives it as dangerous and so experiences arousal. As she picks up her lunch tray and scans the room for a place to sit, her arousal increases; and as she goes to sit at the one open place at a table with several rambunctious children, her arousal increases even more. If she drops her tray and spills her food and the other children laugh at her, she has entered the trauma zone where damage to her fragile self-esteem occurs.

Cognitive Appraisal

Interestingly, the physiological arousal that occurs in dangerous situations can be experienced psychologically as either excitement or anxiety. In a series of famous experiments, Schachter and Singer (1962) showed that how a person thinks about a physiologically arousing event determines whether it is experienced as exciting or anxiety-provoking. What aspect of a person's thinking determines whether the arousal results in excitement or anxiety? Apter proposes that it involves beliefs about control. When a person is in the danger zone and feels enough control over the situation to avoid entering the trauma zone, the physiological arousal is experienced as excitement. Conversely, when the person is in the danger zone but feels no control, the physiological arousal is experienced as anxiety. When two friends ride on a roller-coaster, for example, one may scream with delight because she feels safe in the confines of her seat and so experiences her physiological arousal as excitement while her friend sitting next to her screams with terror because she does not feel safe and can envision the roller-coaster leaving the tracks.

As discussed in the previous section, the temperament of some children makes them more likely to experience high levels of physiological arousal when in novel situations or situations that they perceive as dangerous. What we will see in the next section is that the experiences of some of these children teach them both that they are in the danger zone frequently and that they have little control when in the danger zone. This combination of high biologically influenced arousal and their experiences with lack of control produces high and frequent levels of anxiety.

The Influence of Experience on the Development of Anxiety

Although temperamental styles may predispose some children to experiencing high levels of anxiety, what children learn through their experiences in life also significantly influences their level of anxiety and the specific focus of their anxiety (Albano et al., 2003). Because young children are so strongly influenced by the actions of parents and other caregivers, the experiences of young children in their families have a particularly powerful influence on the intensity and focus of their anxiety.

The Behavioral Inhibition System

To organize our discussion of ways in which children's experiences can influence anxiety, we will use the concept of the **behavioral inhibition system (BIS)**, originally proposed by Gray (1987) and applied to anxiety by several researchers including Chorpita (2001). Although there is not enough research to conclude decisively that the BIS exists or plays an essential role in anxiety, it is a useful concept for organizing our exploration of the literature.

Gray (1987) suggested that three independent but interrelated brain systems control behavior:

- The fight–flight system that responds to unexpected pain or punishment.
- The behavioral activation system that responds to stimuli that an organism has learned indicate the presence of reward or relief from punishment and that pushes the organism to act.
- The BIS, which responds to stimuli associated with innate fear and to stimuli that an organism has learned indicate the presence of punishment to produce cessation of behavior, increased nonspecific arousal, and focused attention on relevant stimuli.

A person's behavior in most situations is influenced by the balance between the behavioral activation system and the BIS. When the behavioral activation system is more active than the BIS, a person is engaged and involved. When the BIS is more active, a person is more withdrawn and aroused—two behaviors that are often associated with anxiety.

The relative activity of the behavioral activation system and the BIS is influenced by a subsystem that Gray and McNaughon (1996) called the **comparator.** As shown in Figure 10.4, when a person enters a situation or when the characteristics of a situation the person is in change, the comparator analyzes information from several sources to determine the person's response to the situation. The comparator analyzes information about the present (the state of the person and the situation the person is in), the past (learning from previous experiences), and the future (the person's goals and plans to meet those goals) (Chorpita, 2001). When the comparator determines that the possibility of reward is greater than the possibility of punishment, the behavioral activation system becomes more active than the BIS, and the person engages in whatever action he or she has learned is appropriate. If the possibility of reward is much greater than the possibility of punishment, the behavioral activation system becomes much more active, resulting in high levels of activity. If the possibility of reward is mixed with the possibility of punishment, the behavioral activation system becomes somewhat more active than the BIS, resulting in cautious activity.

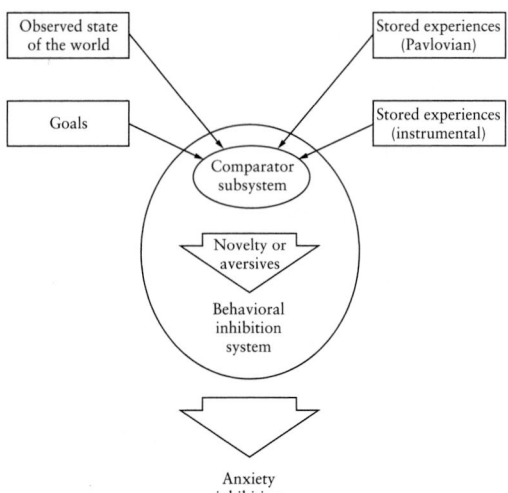

FIGURE 10.4 *Functioning of the Comparator*

On the other hand, when the comparator determines that the possibility of punishment or danger is greater than the possibility of reward, the BIS becomes more active. This causes reduced behavior, increased arousal, and a focus on stimuli considered relevant to the threatening situation. The intensity of these behaviors is influenced by the relative risk of punishment and reward. As an example of high activation of the BIS, consider how you are likely to act when you are sleeping alone in your apartment and you wake up hearing a noise coming from the area of the back door. You are likely to stop all movement; your physiological system becomes aroused (you may even feel your heart beat faster); and you focus all your senses on detecting what is happening by the back door.

Children, adolescents, and adults who engage in sensation seeking or risk taking have a comparator that frequently activates the behavioral activation system—they often engage in behaviors through which they receive reward in the form of excitement and thrills. Similarly, children, adolescents, and adults who are anxious have a comparator that activates the BIS often. In the next two sections we will explore how a child's experiences can influence the information available to the comparator and thus the extent to which the child's BIS is activated and anxiety occurs.

Classical Conditioning Influences on the Comparator

Learning that occurs through classical conditioning can teach a child that many aspects of life are threatening and dangerous. This learning influences the information available to the comparator about the state of the world (that it is often a dangerous place) and the child's goals (to avoid this danger).

Sometimes this learning may be similar to that described by Pavlov with his dogs and Watson with Little Albert. For example, a child could jump off a diving board, hit the water in a way that knocks the air out of his lungs, and have to be pulled from the pool. The pairing of the pain and the fear of drowning with jumping from a diving board may result in the child learning that diving into a pool is dangerous (or, more broadly, that being in a pool is dangerous). As another example, consider a toddler who has found a spider in his bedroom and is playing with it, and whose mother comes into the room, screams, pulls him away from the spider, and starts to cry. The pairing of his mother's frightened reaction and being near the spider may result in the toddler learning that spiders are dangerous.

Researchers since Pavlov have discovered that direct pairing of an unconditioned stimulus and a conditioned stimulus is not always required for classical conditioning to occur (Dadds, Davey, & Field, 2001). One alternative is for a child to be told about the pairing of two events. For example, consider a parent fussing and walking nervously by the side of a pool while her young son is splashing around. She might say, "Be careful or you'll drown; don't put your head under the water because you'll breathe in water and may drown." The hypothetical pairing between drowning and being in the pool that the mother suggests may be sufficient for her son to learn that being in a pool is dangerous, especially if this happens frequently. A second alternative is that a child can observe the pairing of an unconditioned stimulus and a conditioned stimulus. Kim, the girl in the second vignette at the beginning of this chapter, had this experience when she observed her brother's injury paired with being near a dog. Observing this pairing resulted in her learning that dogs are dangerous.

Cognitive Influences on the Comparator

As described in the chapter about basic psychological theories, a child's experiences help to establish various beliefs about the world, or **schemata**. A child's schemata provide important information to the comparator about the state of the world, thus influencing the degree to which the BIS is activated.

The leading model of the association between cognitions and anxiety was proposed by Aaron Beck (1976). From his work with anxious and depressed adults, Beck concluded that the thinking of anxious people is characterized by this pattern:

- Hypervigilance to the possibility of threat from the environment.
- Excessive attention given to cues that a threat may be present and insufficient attention given to cues that a threat is absent.
- Magnification of the importance of threat cues and of the severity of the threat they pose.
- Generalization of threat cues observed in one part of the environment to other parts of the environment.

A variety of laboratory studies have shown that anxious children have cognitions with these characteristics. One type of study involves reading short vignettes to children in which the actions of the characters are ambiguous and asking the children to describe what occurred in the vignettes. Anxious children are more likely than other children to provide threatening interpretations of the vignettes or to ascribe hostile or threatening intentions to the vignette characters (Barrett, Rapee, Dadds, & Ryan, 1996; Bell-Dolan, 1995).

The combination of a child's predisposition to anxiety (which may cause the child to see danger in situations that most children would not find dangerous) and his or her experiences is likely to create schemata that the world is a threatening and dangerous place (Beck, 1986). If the child's parents reinforce the potential danger of many situations through their comments or behaviors, the child's schemata are likely to be strengthened. In addition, the child's schemata will bias his or her perceptions, resulting in frequent perception of danger or threat even in situations where other children would not perceive danger or threat. These biased perceptions will further strengthen the child's schemata, resulting in a steady flow of information about the dangerousness of the world to the child's comparator.

Summary

Classical conditioning and a child's cognitive style can provide ongoing information to a child's comparator that the world is dangerous and threatening. As the comparator analyzes this information, the BIS is activated in many situations. This creates emotions and behaviors that are consistent with anxiety, resulting in a child experiencing high levels of anxiety in many situations.

Maintaining and Intensifying Anxiety

Once high levels of anxiety develop in a child, these levels can be maintained and intensified through avoidant behavior and operant conditioning, as we discuss in this section.

Avoidant Behavior

An important way in which parents can perpetuate and intensify childhood anxiety is by allowing or encouraging a child to avoid situations in which the child experiences anxiety (Ollendick, Vasey, & King, 2001). When parents do this, the child has no opportunity to learn that the situations are not as dangerous as the child fears or that the child can overcome his or her anxiety. For example, if the mother of a socially anxious boy lets him remain at home rather than engaging with friends or attending social events, he has no chance to experience the positive aspects of social interactions with friends, and he does not get the opportunity to learn that he can take actions to reduce his anxiety. Thus the information about the world that is available to the child's comparator remains focused on the dangerousness of many social situations, which will influence how the child continues to act in those situations.

Rather than letting children avoid anxiety-provoking situations, a more effective approach is for parents to gently encourage their children to be in situations that produce mild or moderate levels of anxiety and provide support when the children are in those situations (Kagan, 1997). For example, the mother of the boy who is socially anxious might arrange a time for her son to play with a neighbor's child and then accompany the son to the neighbor's house and chat with the parents while her son plays in the next room. The next day she might walk with her son to the neighbor's house and leave him to play on his own. Finally, she might encourage him to walk to the neighbor's house on his own. Because the child's anxiety is likely to dissipate during this supportive process, it allows him to recognize that the anxiety-provoking situation is not as bad as he had imagined and that he can overcome his anxiety.

Operant Conditioning

Another way in which a child's anxiety can be maintained or intensified is through reinforcement of anxious behaviors. Positive reinforcement from parents or other adults can increase a child's anxiety, although this is often done unintentionally. For example, if a child receives warmth and nurturing when he expresses anxiety about attending school, the reinforcement from the warmth and nurturing is likely to increase his expressions of anxiety (Ollendick et al., 2001). Similarly, if a child with social anxiety attends a slumber party but has to be picked up after being at the party for only one hour and then receives reassurance and nurturing when she returns home, her anxiety and her calling to have her parents pick her up from social events are likely to increase.

Negative reinforcement can also increase children's anxious behaviors. For example, if a child who is afraid of the dark is crying in bed and a parent responds by taking him into the parents' bed, the reduction of the child's anxiety negatively reinforces his crying behavior. (As you may have noticed, this scenario also positively reinforces his crying through the parent's nurturing; positive and negative reinforcement often occur together in this way.)

Another powerful mechanism for maintaining or increasing anxiety is **avoidance learning** (Ollendick et al., 2001), which occurs when a person is negatively reinforced for avoiding something that is anxiety-provoking. For example, consider an adolescent with social phobia who plans to attend a party. As he anticipates attending the party, his anxiety will build. If he then decides not to attend the party, his anxiety will end or be greatly reduced. The reduction of the anxiety negatively reinforces his behavior of deciding to avoid the social situation. As a result, his avoidant behavior is likely to increase, causing a steady decline in his social involvement. His declining attendance at social events is likely to impede the development of his social skills, thereby making him even more anxious about attending future social events (see Figure 10.5).

Key Concepts

- A child's genetically based predispositions to high levels of anxiety can interact with the learning that the child experiences in his or her family and social environment to cause the development of one or more anxiety disorders.
- About one-third of the influence on the development of high anxiety is genetic.

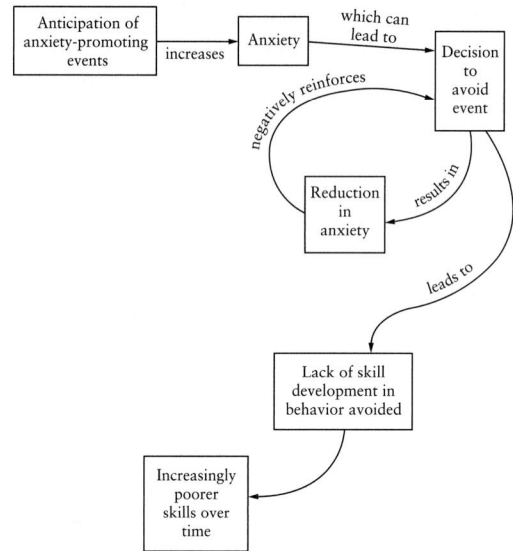

FIGURE 10.5 *Influence of Avoidance Learning*

- Shared environment plays a greater role in the development of anxiety disorders than most other childhood disorders.
- Children with a temperamental style described as *behavioral inhibition* show physiological and behavioral differences from other children in novel situations. These differences have many features of anxiety and are usually stable over childhood and adulthood.
- The tripartite model suggests that children high in anxiety or depression share the characteristic of high levels of negative affect. Children with anxiety problems have a high level of physiological hyperarousal, and those with depression have a low level of positive affect.
- Children and adults who are risk takers or sensation seekers experience the physiological arousal that comes from being in a dangerous situation as excitement, whereas many others experience it as anxiety. These different responses are related to cognitive appraisal of the dangerous situation and the sense of control that a person has in it.
- The BIS can help us understand the role of experience in anxiety. The comparator analyzes information about the past, present, and future when determining whether the behavioral activation system or the BIS should dominate in a specific situation. When the BIS dominates, a person can experience the symptoms of anxiety.
- Classical conditioning can influence the development of high levels of anxiety through a child's direct learning, observations of others, or suggestions from parents or others in the child's life.
- A child's experiences can create schemata that influence the development of anxiety through the functioning of the comparator.

- Operant conditioning can maintain or increase anxiety by reinforcing anxious behaviors.
- Avoidance learning, a form of operant conditioning, involves negative reinforcement of avoiding anxiety-provoking situations.

Prevention

A variety of programs have been used to prevent anxiety disorders and high levels of anxiety in children. Some prevention programs focus on children who are at risk for developing high levels of anxiety because they have experienced stressful events such as natural disasters or having a parent die. Other programs focus on children showing high levels of anxiety on self-report measures distributed to all the children in a grade or school; some include all children in a certain grade or school regardless of their level of anxiety (Spence, Sheffield, & Donovan, 2003).

Three basic strategies have been used in prevention programs: working with children to reduce their anxiety and increase their coping skills, working with parents to help them support their children and provide experiences that reduce their children's anxiety, and working with institutions to change procedures that increase children's anxiety (Foa et al., 2005).

Prevention programs for children usually have two primary goals: teaching them to cope with anxiety-provoking situations more effectively and changing problematic patterns of thinking (see Figure 10.5) (Donovan & Spence, 2000). One strategy for helping children cope with anxiety-provoking situations is to teach them relaxation skills. They can then relax before anxiety-provoking situations or as their anxiety starts to build, reducing the chance that their anxiety will reach debilitating levels. Another strategy for coping with anxiety is to help children identify specific situations that evoke anxiety and develop action plans for coping with those situations. For example, if a child experiences high anxiety in the school cafeteria, she can learn and practice skills that will help her act competently in the cafeteria (how to order her lunch, how to choose a place to sit, how to talk with other children). These skills will increase her success in the cafeteria, decrease her anxiety, and show her how active problem solving can reduce feelings of anxiety.

To ameliorate problematic patterns of thinking, most prevention programs help children identify their anxiety-provoking thought patterns and the situations in which they are most likely to arise. Strategies for modifying these patterns are then developed and practiced by the child (the procedures for this are described in the section about therapeutic interventions).

Evaluations of several prevention programs have shown that they reduce children's levels of anxiety and behavior problems, increase children's academic performance, and reduce the number of children receiving anxiety disorder diagnoses during follow-up assessments (Dadds et al., 1999; Hightower & Graden, 1991).

Because parenting style can influence children's anxiety (as just discussed in the section about etiology), some prevention programs are designed for parents rather than children (Spence et al., 2003). These programs help parents interact with their children in ways that help their children cope with fear and anxiety effectively (see Table 10.10). Parents may learn strategies for gently encouraging their children to engage in anxiety-provoking activities and reinforcing their participation in them. They may also learn how to avoid reinforcing their children's anxious behaviors. Some programs give parents the

TABLE 10.10

Prevention of Childhood Anxiety Disorders

Child-focused methods include
- Modeling of coping skills through successful handling of the stressful situation by peers or adults (live or videotaped).
- Direct instruction in the use of coping strategies such as cue-controlled relaxation, positive self-statements, breathing exercises, emotive imagery using models, and attention distraction.
- Behavioral rehearsal, role-play, and practice of coping skills for dealing with the stressful situation.
- Positive reinforcement of approach ("brave") behavior and use of coping skills.
- Providing information about feared situations so that children obtain a sense of control over the stressful event (verbally or filmed).
- Providing the child with as much control over the situation as possible.
- Nontraumatic preexposure prior to stressful situations (latent inhibition).
- Exposure to potentially stressful situations in the absence of feared consequences.
- Teaching children to gain access to social support; providing children with social support.

Parent-focused methods include
- Modeling of appropriate coping behavior.
- Encouragement and reinforcement of their child's use of coping skills.
- Reduction of their own anxious behaviors.
- Reduction of overprotective and critical child-rearing responses.
- Encouragement for children to expose themselves to appropriate situations.
- Ignoring and preventing avoidance of situations by their child (where avoidance is not an appropriate response).
- Avoiding focusing on, and communicating, the potentially threatening aspects of the child's environment.

Environmental restructuring methods include
- Reducing the risk involved in "high-risk" situations (e.g. reducing the inherent stressfulness of high school transition by reorganizing the school structure; Felner & Adan, 1988).
- Attempting to reduce the risk factor (e.g., prevention of divorce, car accidents, etc.).

opportunity to explore their own anxiety and how their anxiety may be influencing their parenting. They may learn to identify situations that evoke anxiety, understand their cognitive and behavioral responses to those situations, and identify how their behaviors may influence their children's anxiety.

Finally, some prevention efforts have focused on institutions, primarily schools. Rather than expecting children to make all the adjustments to cope with stressful institutional environments, the institutions are encouraged to change in ways that reduce the stress and anxiety experienced by some or many children in them. For example, Felner and Adan (1988) worked with high schools to create smaller homerooms for freshmen to reduce the anxiety that many adolescents experience as they move from smaller middle schools to larger high schools. Students participating in the program made an easier transition to high school and had higher academic performance than students in schools that did not participate in the program (Donovan & Spence, 2000).

Key Concepts

- Some prevention programs target children who are at risk for developing high anxiety; other programs are provided to all children in a certain class, grade, or school.
- Many prevention programs for children teach skills for coping with anxiety-provoking situations, encourage children to engage in active solutions to situations that cause them anxiety, and help children identify and modify anxiety-provoking thought patterns.
- Other prevention efforts focus on parents, helping them deal with anxiety they experience and helping them provide a supportive environment for their children.
- Still other programs work to modify institutional practices to reduce the likelihood that children in those institutions will experience high levels of anxiety.

Therapeutic Interventions

As one should expect from the discussion of the development of anxiety disorders, therapeutic interventions focus on children's behaviors and cognitions, as well as on family interactions. Some interventions focus on the child, such as systematic desensitization and cognitive–behavioral therapy; other interventions focus on parents to improve their parenting. In addition, medication has been used to treat some children.

Systematic Desensitization

Systematic desensitization was described in the chapter about basic psychological theories and thus will be described only briefly here. Wolpe developed systematic desensitization based on the principles of classical conditioning (Wolpe, 1958). It is often used to treat specific phobias but can be used with other anxiety disorders. Given the importance of classical conditioning in the development of anxiety, it is not surprising that systematic desensitization, which employs the techniques of classical conditioning, is an effective treatment for anxiety.

Systematic desensitization uses a process called *reciprocal inhibition,* which pairs a response that inhibits anxiety (typically relaxation) with the source of the anxiety. If the source of the anxiety can be paired with relaxation frequently enough, the connection will be diminished or broken between the source of the anxiety and feelings of anxiety. For example, if a child who experiences high levels of anxiety when taking tests in school can repeatedly experience test taking in a relaxed state, the connection between taking a test and anxiety will be weakened or eliminated. A therapist accomplishes this by helping the child learn to relax and then presenting a series of test-taking situations that the child finds increasingly anxiety-provoking while the child remains relaxed. By doing this, the therapist pairs relaxation with test taking; and because relaxation and anxiety cannot occur simultaneously, the feelings of anxiety while taking a test are diminished.

Cognitive–Behavioral Psychotherapy

Cognitive–behavioral therapy (CBT) is the most widely used form of therapy for children with an anxiety disorder, and it has the most empirical support (Kendall & Gosch, 1994). It combines several treatments into a strategy that influences various issues related to anxiety. It uses the concept of classical conditioning to gradually expose children to anxiety-provoking situations (as in systematic desensitization); it uses operant conditioning to reduce reinforcement of avoidance behaviors and increase reinforcement for behaviors that cope with anxiety effectively; and it uses cognitive therapy to teach children to identify and modify cognitions that support their anxiety.

Kendall and Gosch (1994) describe a 16-week individual therapy program for children with anxiety disorders. The first eight weekly sessions are primarily educational. Children are taught to recognize physical sensations indicating that they are beginning to feel anxious and to recognize the types of cognitions they have before and during these sensations. They are also taught relaxation skills and are asked to practice these skills when they are not feeling anxious and also when they first notice the physical sensations associated with anxiety. Employing relaxation skills encourages the children to act purposefully to reduce feelings of anxiety rather than remaining passive in the face of these feelings.

To change their cognitions, children are taught a process of "self-talk." This requires that they recognize when they are experiencing anxiety-provoking cognitions and then actively engage in a process of talking their way through them. Talking through cognitions involves examining them and replacing illogical cognitions with logical ones ("I know that I think that something terrible is going to happen to my mother when I'm at school, but I also know that she's safe and that nothing really is going to happen to her"). This is often done aloud with the therapist during the early stages of therapy, with the child gradually learning to do this silently in an anxiety-provoking situation. As with relaxation skills, self-talk helps a child cope with his or her cognitions actively rather than accepting them passively.

Next, children are taught strategies for changing the behaviors that result from their anxiety. For example, a child with social phobia might learn effective social skills and how to use them in various social situations. Similarly, a child with a checking compulsion might be taught strategies for checking the safety of something once and then refraining from rechecking it after that.

Finally, children are taught strategies for reinforcing their own effective behavior in anxiety-provoking situations. These reinforcements might include something tangible (like buying candy on the way home from school after answering a question in class) or intangible (perhaps taking some time to reflect on their performance and feel proud).

The second eight-week phase of the therapy program involves having the child and therapist actively engage in activities that the child finds anxiety-provoking, based on the concept of systematic desensitization. These tasks are approached gradually and always include coaching and support from the therapist, with reinforcement from the therapist if they are accomplished or analysis of reasons for failure. Successes in situations that are less anxiety-provoking are used to encourage engaging in situations that produce more anxiety. For example, over several weeks or months a child who is afraid of entering public places might go first to a small store with the therapist several times, next to a local library by himself several times, and eventually to a shopping mall. The goal of this phase of therapy is to help a child understand that he or she can engage in anxiety-provoking situations, that catastrophic consequences will not occur, and that he or she has begun to develop the skills to successfully cope with other anxiety-provoking situations.

Short- and long-term evaluations of such programs have shown their effectiveness. For example, Kendall and Southam-Gerow (1996) found that most children who had completed their treatment program remained free of anxiety disorders two to five years after the end of the program, and they continued to use the active strategies taught by the program when they were in situations that caused them anxiety.

Group treatments have also been used for children with a variety of anxiety disorders. Group treatment may be particularly useful because children can practice the skills they learn during the group sessions and because the cost of treating several children at one time is often similar to that of treating an individual (Bernstein, Layne, Egan, & Tennison, 2005; Labellarte & Ginsburg, 2002). One study compared a group intervention for children with social phobia to an attention comparison intervention that provided study skills (Beidel, Turner, & Morris, 2000). At the end of treatment, 67% of the children in the group intervention no longer met the diagnostic criteria for social phobia, compared with 5% of those in the study skills group. Interestingly, at a six-month follow-up assessment, 85% of the children in the group intervention no longer met the criteria for social phobia, suggesting that the value of the intervention continued to grow after it ended. Two studies that compared the effectiveness of group CBT to individual CBT for children with a variety of anxiety disorders found that both types of treatment were effective and that there was little difference in their effectiveness at the end of the study and at follow-up (Barrett, Healy Farrell, & March, 2004; Flannery Schroeder & Kendall, 2000). These studies suggest that group treatment can be as effective as individual treatment for anxious children.

Family Interventions

The goals of most family interventions are to help parents address their own anxiety and to give them skills to support their children's attempts to overcome anxiety. An example of a family intervention is provided by Barrett and colleagues (1996). They contrasted the effectiveness of two treatment strategies for children who had been diagnosed with an anxiety disorder: CBT for the children and a combination of CBT for the child and family treatment. The CBT for both groups was based on the program of Kendall and his colleagues that was just described. The family treatment consisted of

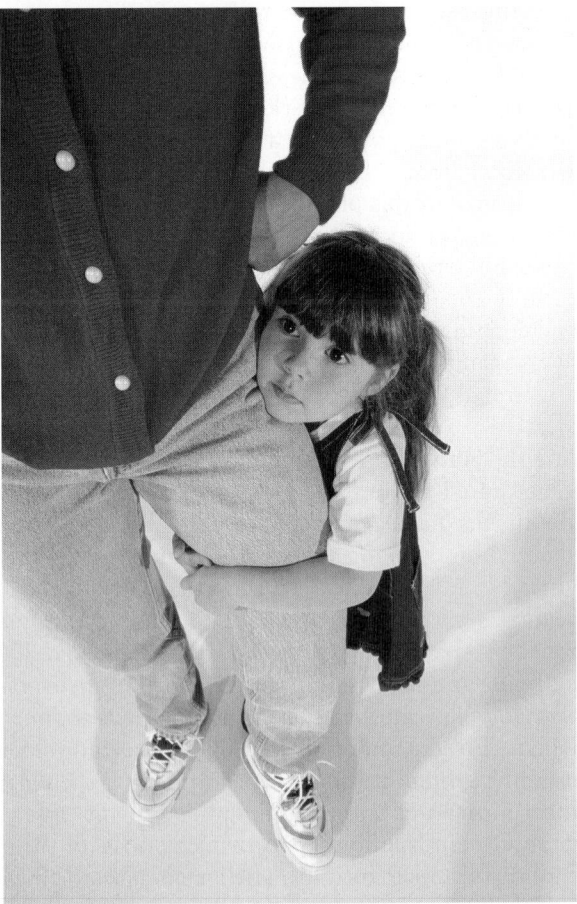

Many parents benefit from therapy that gives them the skills to help their anxious children.

several components: training parents how to ignore their children's anxious behavior and reinforce courageous behavior; exploring the parents' own anxiety and using cognitive and behavioral strategies to reduce their anxiety; and teaching parents to communicate with each other and work together to provide the appropriate responses to their children's anxious and nonanxious behaviors.

An evaluation of this intervention showed that, compared to children and families in a wait-list comparison group, children in both treatment groups improved during treatment and maintained their improvements at 6- and 12-month follow-up assessments. Children in the combined treatment group improved more than those receiving individual treatment only. For example, at the end of the treatment program, 57% of the children in individual treatment and 84% of those in the combined treatment group no longer met the diagnostic criteria for an anxiety disorder, compared with 26% in the wait-list comparison group. At the 12-month follow-up, 70% of the children receiving individual treatment and 95% of those in the combined therapy group did not meet the diagnostic criteria for an anxiety disorder. (Information was not available for those in the wait-list comparison group because they had been provided therapy after the initial outcome measures were completed.)

Treatment for parents appears particularly important when parents have significant problems with anxiety. For example, one study examined the relative effectiveness of CBT for children alone and a combination of CBT for children and anxiety management training for parents (Cobham, Dadds, & Spence, 1998). In families in which just the child had an anxiety disorder, CBT and the combined treatments were equally effective (80% and 82% of the children no longer had an anxiety disorder at the end of treatment). However, in families in which the parents also had an anxiety disorder, the combined treatment was more effective than CBT alone (77% and 39% of the children no longer had an anxiety disorder).

Medication

Selective serotonin reuptake inhibitors (SSRIs) and tricyclic antidepressants are the medications used most frequently to treat children with anxiety disorders (Foa et al., 2005; Labellarte & Ginsburg, 2002). In some studies medication has been used alone, but in most it is used with some type of psychotherapy (usually CBT).

As an example of the use of medication alone, one study found that 61% of children with a variety of anxiety disorders responded to treatment with an SSRI, compared with 35% of those taking a placebo (Birmaher et al., 2003). Children with separation anxiety disorder and generalized anxiety disorder responded particularly well to the medication, whereas there was little response in children with social phobia. In addition, children with less intense symptoms were more likely to respond to medication than those with more intense symptoms. This pattern of results was replicated in a separate study with another group of children (The Research Unit on Pediatric Psychopharmacology Anxiety Study Group, 2003).

Studies that have combined medication with CBT have also shown the effectiveness of treatment with medications. In a large study, the Research

Unit on Pediatric Psychopharmacology Anxiety Study Group (2001) provided CBT to all children with a variety of anxiety disorders and provided an SSRI to half of them, with the other half receiving a placebo. More of the children receiving the SSRI (76%) responded favorably than did the children receiving a placebo (29%).

SSRIs have been used for many years to treat obsessive–compulsive disorder in adults, and recent studies have explored their effectiveness in children. However, the response of children with obsessive–compulsive disorder to SSRI treatment has been modest (Geller & Spencer, 2003). Fewer children with obsessive–compulsive disorder appear to benefit from medication treatment than do adults. The reasons for this lower response remain unclear.

As with the use of medications for other disorders, children receiving medication for anxiety disorders experience a variety of side effects. The side effects are usually mild or moderate, and most children can tolerate them during treatment. Common side effects include restlessness, dry mouth, nausea and other gastrointestinal complaints, tiredness, and dizziness (Geller & Spencer, 2003).

Key Concepts

- Systematic desensitization is a process of gradually pairing relaxation with stimuli that produce anxiety. It is a common treatment for specific phobias and can be used for other anxiety disorders.
- CBT for anxiety disorders involves several components that focus on helping children relax in anxiety-producing situations, modify anxiety-provoking cognitions, learn strategies for active behavior in anxiety-provoking situations, and reinforce these active behaviors. It is the most widely used therapeutic strategy for children with anxiety disorders.
- Group interventions using CBT allow children to practice their developing skills with others who also experience anxiety.
- Family interventions include training parents to reinforce appropriate behavior in their children and avoid reinforcing anxious behavior; exploring the parents' own anxiety; and teaching parents skills to work together to provide the appropriate responses to their children's anxious behaviors. Family interventions are particularly effective in families where the parents experience problems with anxiety.
- Medication is used with some children who have anxiety disorders. It appears to be less effective with children than with adults, and less effective with children who have social phobia.

Chapter Glossary

Adjustment disorders is a category of disorders in the DSM characterized by short-term disturbances in mood or behavior related to difficulty adjusting to a specific stressor.

Agoraphobia is a fear of being in a place where, if a panic attack were to occur, escape would be impossible or difficult.

Anticipatory anxiety is anxiety experienced while considering something that may happen in the future.

Avoidance learning occurs when a person is negatively reinforced for avoiding something that is anxiety-provoking.

Behavioral inhibition is a temperament characterized by cautiousness and timidity in novel situations or situations involving unfamiliar people.

The **behavioral inhibition system** (BIS) is a theoretical system in the brain that responds to stimuli that an organism has learned indicate the presence of punishment or nonreward and that motivates the organism to stop acting, increase arousal, and focus attention on relevant stimuli.

Cognitive–behavioral therapy combines several types of cognitive and behavioral treatment strategies and is the most widely used form of therapy for children with anxiety disorders.

The **comparator** is a theoretical brain component that analyzes information from several sources and, based on this analysis, regulates the balance between the behavioral activation system and the BIS.

Compulsions are repeated behaviors over which a child feels little or no control. Common compulsions are washing, checking, and ordering.

Cortisol is a hormone secreted by the adrenal gland.

Displacement, as used in psychoanalytic theory, is an unconscious defense mechanism that shifts anxiety, anger, or another troubling emotion from a more threatening target onto a less threatening target (in the case of Little Hans, from his father to a horse).

The **general type** of social phobia is diagnosed when the child's anxiety occurs in many settings.

Obsessions are persistent thoughts that intrude into a person's mind and that cause the person marked anxiety.

A **schema** is a fundamental belief system about how we and the world function (the plural of *schema* is *schemata*).

Situationally bound (cued) panic attacks are diagnosed when an attack almost always occurs in a particular situation.

Situationally predisposed panic attacks are diagnosed when attacks are more likely to occur in a particular situation but do not occur invariably.

The **specific type** of social phobia is diagnosed when a child experiences high levels of anxiety in only one or two settings.

The **sympathetic branch** is the portion of the autonomic nervous system that primarily arouses an organism.

Systematic desensitization is a process of therapy, originally formulated by Wolpe, that gradually introduces a feared object or situation to a person in a relaxed state so that the classically conditioned connection between the object or event and the anxiety is gradually lessened.

Temperament is a construct representing basic dispositions inherent in a person that underlie and modulate the expression of activity, reactivity, emotionality, and sociability.

The **tripartite model** was developed to understand the similarities and differences between anxiety disorders and depressive disorders. Its key concepts are negative affect, positive affect, and physiological hyperarousal.

Unexpected (uncued) panic attacks occur apparently at random and for no apparent reason.

C H A P T E R   **11**

Mental Retardation

Many children with Down Syndrome are more social than are children with other forms of mental retardation.

Cognitive abilities, such as reasoning and remembering, are important in all modern human cultures, and they probably always have been (Sternberg, 2004). Cognitive abilities are highly prized in modern, industrialized human societies and, for the most part, are required among those who are considered successful in these societies. In this chapter we focus on children whose cognitive abilities are significantly below the average of most children. Many of these children are considered to have mental retardation.

Children with mental retardation can be at a significant disadvantage in our society (Baroff & Olley, 1999). They struggle not only with tasks that are primarily cognitive (like completing school assignments) but also with social relationships; and they are more likely than other children to be depressed, anxious, or angry. In the United States and many other industrialized countries, they live in a society where many people view them as fundamentally flawed and where their personal qualities and their contributions to society are often unappreciated (Zigler, 1999).

Children with mental retardation form a heterogeneous group. Most develop basic academic skills such as reading, writing, and arithmetic, although at a lower level than that of their peers. A few, however, have such profound mental retardation that they never develop language and need help with basic living skills throughout their lives. We need to keep the diversity of children with mental retardation in mind as we explore their experiences so that we do not fall into the trap of thinking about them as one homogeneous group.

Although those with mental retardation have lower levels of cognitive abilities, their levels of other characteristics, such as humor, pleasantness, drive to succeed, and generosity, are as varied as among those of us who do not have mental retardation. Cognitive abilities are important in our society, but so are many other abilities; we must be able to recognize and appreciate these abilities in all children and adults.

Chapter Plan

Because an understanding of intelligence is essential for understanding mental retardation, we start this chapter with an exploration of intelligence and how it is measured. This discussion is brief by necessity (entire books have been written about intelligence) but covers information that is essential for understanding how mental retardation is defined. Following this, we explore a brief history of the ways that people with mental retardation have been characterized and dealt with over the past century or two. This will provide a background for understanding services that are now provided for them and their families. We then examine the current definitions of mental retardation and discuss the characteristics and experiences of children with varying levels of mental retardation. The central part of this chapter examines the causes of the intellectual impairments that are at the foundation of mental retardation and how people with these impairments develop during childhood and adolescence. Our next focus is on the families of children with mental retardation—how they are affected by having children with mental retardation and how they contribute to the development of their children. We then explore strategies for preventing mental retardation. Our discussion about treatment for children with mental retardation largely addresses their education because schools provide most of these interventions; but we also look at interventions designed to support families.

Case Study: The Early Life of a Girl with Mild Mental Retardation

Julie was born to a single mother, age 22, who came from a large, rural family that lived in poverty. Julie's mother was one of eight children, most of whom had not completed high school. (Julie's mother had dropped out of high school during her first pregnancy, which had ended in a miscarriage.) Julie's mother did not know who Julie's father was; it could have been one of several men with whom she had short relationships. Julie's mother had been depressed since her earlier miscarriage, and she coped with her depression by drinking during her pregnancy with Julie. She received almost no prenatal care because she lived in a small mobile home many miles from the nearest city and did not have a car. In addition, Julie's mother had little money and was often undernourished during her pregnancy.

After she was born Julie saw a pediatrician rarely because of her mother's financial and transportation problems. Her mother's sense was that Julie was slow to learn to talk and walk but did not show any severe problems in these areas. Because her mother continued to experience periodic depressions, there were many times that Julie was left alone in her bed for most of the day as an infant, although she and her mother watched a lot of television. Julie was an active child once she began to walk, and she spent many hours each day playing by herself in the area surrounding their home. She never attended preschool but enjoyed coloring and cutting out figures from paper. Her mother described Julie as a happy girl, and Julie made friends easily with other children when she met them.

Julie was excited to begin school, and she enjoyed the 45-minute ride to school each day on the bus. She chatted with other children, and her smile made the bus driver and her teachers take an instant liking to her. She had a difficult time staying in her seat in kindergarten and the first grade, and she lagged behind the other students in learning the letters of the alphabet. She was still struggling with recognizing letters and numbers when the other children were beginning to read and do arithmetic. She often became frustrated at school and would pace around the room chatting with other students. Her behavior gradually became problematic, which resulted in her being punished many days by having to stay in from recess.

Julie continued to struggle academically during her first three years in school. By the third grade, she was struggling to read the first-grade reader; and although she could add, she did not seem to understand subtraction. Her third-grade teacher became increasingly concerned about Julie's lack of academic progress and referred her to the school psychologist.

The school psychologist assessed Julie's intelligence and academic skills after contacting Julie's mother and explaining the reason for doing this. The psychologist encouraged Julie's mother to contact her or Julie's teachers with questions, but she never did. The results of several tests suggested that Julie's IQ was approximately 60—considerably below the average for children her age. At a meeting with her teachers and others from her school, the psychologist, and Julie's mother (the school sent a car to transport Julie's mother to the meeting), it was determined that Julie qualified for special education services for children with mental retardation. Her individual educational plan specified that Julie would receive special education services in the school's resource room in math and reading and that she would remain with her class during the rest of the day.

Initially Julie enjoyed going to the resource room because the special education teacher could give her individualized help. Julie began to develop better skills in reading and math and was pleased with herself. However, after a few months she reported that the other children teased her during recess for being "a retard." She responded by withdrawing from the other children. She missed playing with her friends but hated being teased. Her mother had no suggestions for how to handle the teasing, and it appeared that her teachers did not notice it. Julie continued to progress in reading and math, but she fell progressively behind in her other subjects, primarily because she felt increasingly hostile to the other children and often sat quietly by herself in class. She was afraid to participate in class activities because of her concern that others would tease her if she made an error.

During the rest of her elementary school years, Julie became a more frequent target of taunting by her classmates. She continued to withdraw from them and was increasingly absent from school. Based on her request, she spent more time in the resource room with the special education teacher, whom Julie liked very much. She continued to struggle with academic subjects, although she made steady progress in them. She often felt a strong sense of pride when she learned a new skill or could take home a paper that had a good grade.

At home, Julie spent more and more time watching television with her mother, who continued to experience depression. As she came home from her last day at elementary school, her bus driver, who had known Julie since kindergarten, could not help but wonder what had happened to the happy, energetic girl he had met several years before.

Some Issues Worth Noting

- The possible low levels of intelligence in Julie's mother and extended family, and the influence this may have had on her development.

- The combination of prenatal and early life experiences that may have influenced Julie's intelligence.
- The extent to which the teasing Julie endured had a negative influence on her academic abilities and social skills.

Case Study: A Young Boy's Influence on His Family

Even before Sean was born, his family knew that he had Down syndrome. The news of Sean's condition was one more blow to a family that had experienced tragedy and confusion.

Sean's mother, Mary, was 40 when she unexpectedly became pregnant with Sean. Sean's parents and his siblings, Anne (age 14) and Patrick (age 17), were ambivalent about having a new baby in the family. Two months into Sean's pregnancy, his father was killed in a car accident. Soon after that, his mother learned that Sean had Down syndrome, based on the results of an amniocentesis done by her physician.

The death of Sean's father was a blow to each member of his family. Mary, who had always had a loving relationship with her husband, was grief-stricken, as were her children. Neighbors and extended family members brought food each day for several weeks and were emotionally supportive; but this seemed to have little influence on everyone's grief.

Near the end of the first trimester of her pregnancy, Mary's physician raised the issue of a possible abortion. He described the added challenges that a child with Down syndrome brings to families, and he wondered whether raising a child with Down syndrome might be too difficult for the family as they continued to struggle with their grief. Mary's initial reaction was that an abortion would be for the best. However, as she thought about the abortion and talked with her sister about it, she felt that her future child was the last "gift" she would receive from her husband; so she decided to keep the baby.

Mary's pregnancy was difficult. She had much less energy than she had 15 years before during her earlier pregnancies. She was often sick, but her physician assured her that the pregnancy was proceeding normally. Anne tried to help around the house, but Patrick, who wanted his mother to have an abortion, increasingly stayed away from home. Mary worried about losing her job as a warehouse supervisor because of the time she spent at home either tired or sick. The pregnancy, her grief, and her worries weighed on Mary, and she gradually became more withdrawn at home and at her job. Anne also became more withdrawn, spending most of her time in her bedroom at home, and Patrick continued to stay away from home most of the day. Mary's brother and sisters encouraged her and tried to keep in contact with Anne and Patrick, but they became increasingly concerned about what seemed to be a strong depression that had fallen over each member of the family.

When Sean was born, he had some facial features typical of children with Down syndrome. He was a happy baby and met most of the developmental milestones on time during his first year. Mary, Anne, and Patrick were pleased with his development and began to hope that he would develop normally and not show any of the impairments common to Down syndrome. Their spirits lifted, and the family seemed to be functioning with less depression. However, at about 1½ years, Sean's development regressed. The language that had started to develop stopped, and he no longer babbled or made noises. He stopped trying to crawl and would lie on his back for hours. Mary and her other children reacted negatively, and Sean's change in behavior appeared to make them all more depressed again.

One of Mary's sisters became increasingly alarmed at what she perceived to be the lack of care that Sean received. All of his basic needs were being met, but she worried that he was not getting the physical contact and cognitive stimulation he needed. She arranged a meeting with Mary and a friend of hers who had a 7-year-old girl, Lisa, with Down syndrome. Mary was reluctant to meet the other mother but did so at her sister's insistence. Mary was surprised to see that Lisa was a happy, energetic, social girl, who took Mary on a tour of her house and showed her all of her toys and the work she had brought home from school posted on all the walls of her bedroom. Lisa's mother described the many hours of work that she and the other members of her family put into raising their daughter, and she explained the variety of cognitive tasks they had used over the years to ensure that Lisa developed as fully as she could. Clearly she was proud of all that her daughter had accomplished. She gave Mary several boxes of materials they had used with their daughter when she was younger, and she encouraged Mary to join her at an informal support group that several parents of children with Down syndrome had formed in their community.

Meeting Lisa and her mother inspired and energized Mary. She began to organize activities for Sean and insisted that her other children help with these activities. Using the skills she had developed as a warehouse supervisor, she created a detailed schedule of tasks for Sean and the rest of her family. She read all that she could about Down syndrome, and through the support group she contacted some educational specialists who helped her modify her schedule of activities for Sean. Anne and Patrick seemed to catch their mother's enthusiasm, and they gradually became more interested in working with Sean. Their enthusiasm spilled over into the rest of their lives, and they began to be more engaged with friends and to focus more on their own schoolwork.

Over the next several years, Sean thrived with the ongoing attention he received from his family. His cognitive abilities were estimated to be in the moderate range of mental retardation, and it was difficult for him to learn new tasks. He seemed reluctant to speak, and Anne and Patrick spent many hours coaxing him to say the names of various objects.

Patrick came home from graduate school and Anne came home from her summer job at her college for Sean's fifth birthday—a month before he was to start kindergarten at their local public school. After a long day with family and friends, and after Sean had been put to bed, they sat and talked about the amazing transformation that had happened to all of them because of Sean. They wondered how their lives would have been different if Sean had been "normal." They felt that none of their lives would have been nearly as good.

Some Issues Worth Noting

- The issues Sean's mother faced while deciding whether to have an abortion.
- The value to Sean's mother of support from another mother who had a child with Down syndrome.
- The many ways that Sean enriched the life of his family.

Intelligence and Intelligence Testing

Because intelligence is a central issue in a discussion of mental retardation, we should explore intelligence and how it is measured. Most people have a sense of what intelligence is. When a large number of people in the United

States were asked to describe intelligence, many included three features: practical problem-solving ability, verbal ability, and social competence (Sternberg, 2000). The concept of intelligence appears in many cultures. Neisser (1979), for example, described a researcher in Africa who asked the elders of several tribes in Botswana to provide words in their language that seemed similar to the word *intelligence.* The word *bothale* seemed closest; when the elders were asked to point out children with high levels of *bothale,* these children showed better memory than other children for tribal stories.

Alfred Binet, one of the people credited with creating one of the first tests of intelligence, described **intelligence** as "judgment, otherwise called good sense, practical sense, initiative, the faculty of adapting one's self to circumstances. To judge well, to comprehend well, to reason well . . ." (Binet & Simon, 1905). David Wechsler, the developer of several widely used intelligence tests, described intelligence as "the overall capacity of an individual to understand and cope with the world around him" (Wechsler, 1974).

These and other definitions of intelligence are broad and perhaps even vague. What does it mean to "understand and cope with the world," for example? To understand more specifically what theorists and researchers mean by *intelligence,* it is helpful to examine the skills that are measured in trying to determine a person's level of intelligence. Before we do that, however, we must first explore the structure of intelligence. Is it one thing or is it a collection of skills and competencies?

Intelligence as One Trait or Many Traits

A *trait* is a characteristic that resides in an individual and is stable. A longstanding debate in the study of intelligence is whether it is best thought of as one trait that has a significant influence on all of a person's cognitive abilities or as a set of traits that are distinct but related (Sternberg, 2000). All theorists and researchers acknowledge that cognitive abilities are related. However, just because things are related does not mean that they are best thought of as components of a single trait. For example, height and weight are related. However, it is not clear whether we should consider height and weight as two aspects of one trait (what we might call *size*) or whether it would be more appropriate to consider height and weight as two distinct but related characteristics (Vandenberg & Volger, 1985). This same argument about intelligence has lasted for years.

Almost 80 years ago, Charles Spearman used the statistical technique of factor analysis to develop a hierarchical model of intelligence (Brody, 2000). Spearman argued that a person's ability on any cognitive task was composed of a **general factor** (**g,** sometimes called *little g*) that influences all cognitive tasks and a **specific factor** (*s*) that influences that particular cognitive task (Spearman, 1927). So a person's ability to solve a math problem, figure a way through a complex maze, and play the piano are all influenced by *g*, and each of these abilities is influenced by *s* for that ability (see Figure 11.1).

Spearman considered *g* to be intelligence and so was one of the first to argue that intelligence was a single trait. Spearman's model was very

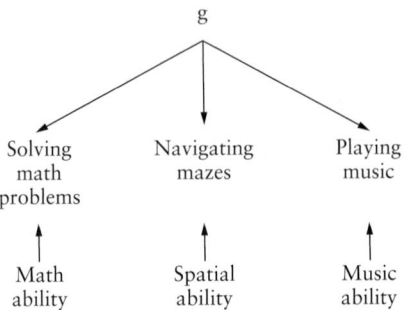

FIGURE 11.1   *A Model of the Influence of General Intelligence and Specific Intelligence on Three Cognitive Tasks*

influential; and although it contained both g and s, the search to understand the nature of g became paramount because it was seen as the fundamental characteristic that distinguished people's cognitive abilities.

Other theorists have argued that intelligence is best viewed as a collection of abilities. For example, a few years after Spearman described g, Louis Thurstone (1938) argued that there were nine *primary mental abilities,* including space (spatial or visual imagery), perceptual speed (noting visual details), verbal meaning (understanding meanings of words), memory (rote memory), and inductive reasoning (abstracting a rule common to a set of particulars) (Kamphaus, 2001).

In an influential program of research, Carroll (1993) completed a massive factor analysis on the results of 460 studies exploring the correlations between various cognitive abilities. He described a hierarchy of cognitive abilities composed of three strata. As shown in Figure 11.2, the top stratum (Stratum III) is general intelligence, similar to g, which represents the ability to handle complex cognitive tasks (Pennington & Bennetto, 1999). Stratum II consists of eight cognitive abilities that are influenced by general intelligence but have qualities distinct from general intelligence. Finally, Stratum I comprises specific abilities grouped by their relation to the eight cognitive abilities in the second stratum. The influence flows down through the strata. For example, general intelligence influences fluid intelligence, which influences quantitative reasoning ability. Similarly, the ability to maintain and judge rhythm is influenced by broad auditory perception, which is influenced by general intelligence.

Where do psychologists stand today on the issue of intelligence as one trait or a collection of related traits? Although there remains some disagreement, most researchers concur that something like Spearman's g exists and has an important influence on the collection of our cognitive abilities (Plomin, DeFries, McClearn, & McGuffin, 2001). Debate continues, however, because researchers and theorists can interpret data from studies of intelligence in different ways. Some psychologists look at the pattern of correlations of various cognitive abilities and believe that the size of the correlations indicates that general intelligence exists. Other psychologists look at the same correlations and argue that their pattern and size indicate that several

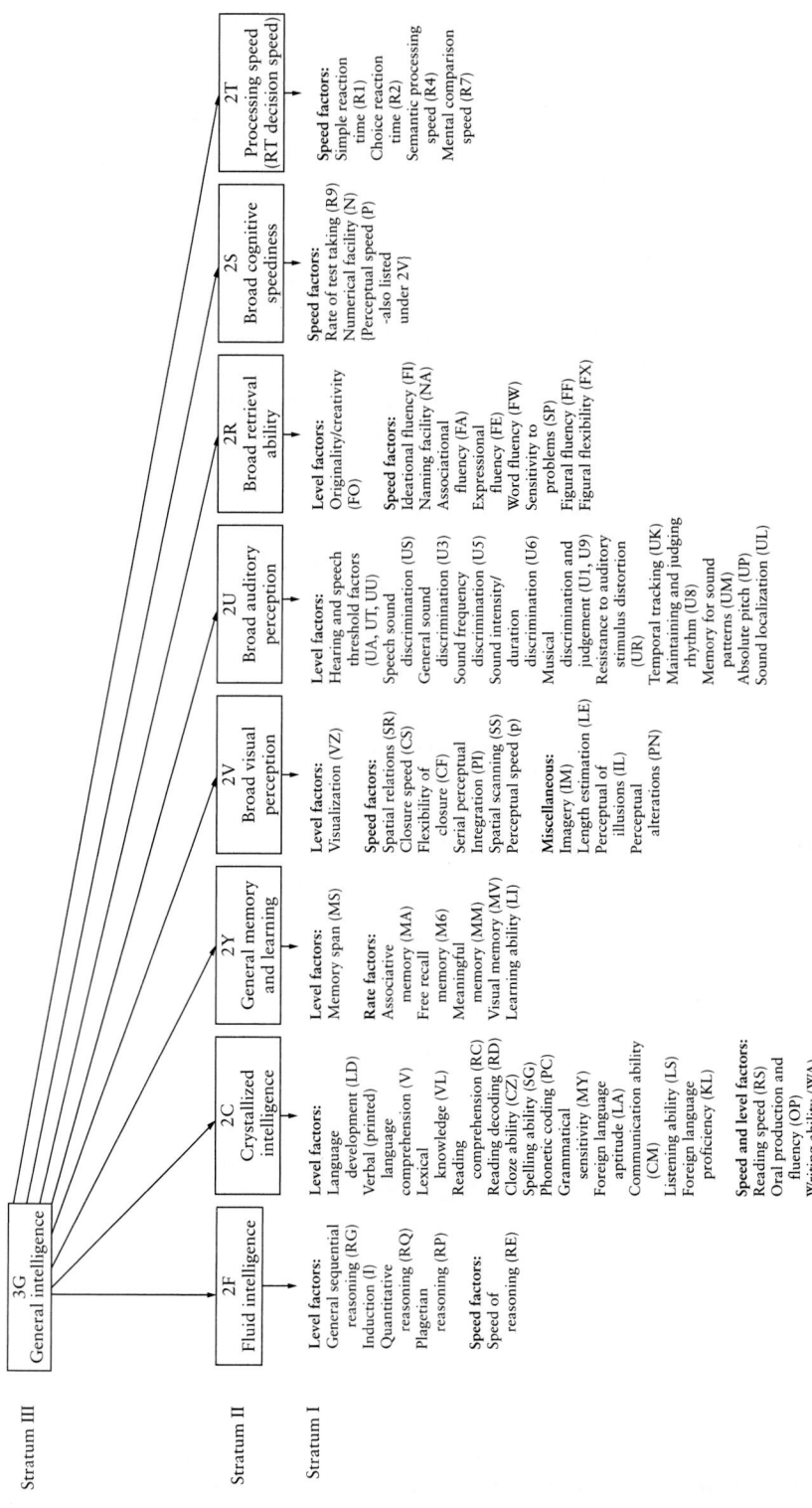

FIGURE 11.2 *Human Cognitive Abilities*

intelligences exist (Kamphaus, 2001). So the debate about intelligence as one trait or many traits has not been completely resolved. It is worth noting that many of those who construct tests to measure intelligence in school-age children, adolescents, and adults believe that general intelligence exists—as shown by the fact that each of these tests produces a single number that represents general intellectual ability.

Culture and Intelligence

An important and frequently debated issue is whether intelligence is the same across cultures and whether a test of intelligence can be used with children and adults in different cultures or only in the culture in which the test was developed. Sternberg (2004) asserts that these issues can be conceptualized in a 2 × 2 matrix (see Table 11.1). For example, Model I is that intelligence is the same across cultures and that a well-designed test can measure intelligence across cultures, whereas Model IV is that intelligence differs fundamentally across cultures and that, consequently, tests of intelligence can be used only in the culture in which they were developed.

Sternberg prefers Model III. He argues that the basic characteristics of intelligence are the same across cultures and include the ability to "(a) recognize the existence of problems, (b) define what the problems are, (c) mentally represent the problems, (d) formulate one or more strategies for solving the problems, (e) allocate resources to solving the problems, (f) monitor solution of the problems, and (g) evaluate problem solving after it is done" (Sternberg, 2004, p. 327). What differs across cultures, he argues, are the types of knowledge and skills used to recognize and handle problems.

Sternberg argues that because the knowledge and skills needed to perform mental activity may vary across cultures, tests of intelligence must reflect the knowledge and skills used by those in the culture where the tests are given. He provides two examples using mathematical ability. In the first, Brazilian street children who could do the mathematics needed to run their businesses on the streets were unable to perform the same types of mathematics when solving problems at school. Similarly, a study of homemakers in California showed that they could perform mathematics while deciding what to buy in

TABLE 11.1

Models of the Relationship of Culture to Intelligence

		Dimensions of Intelligence	
	Relation	Same	Different
Tests of Intelligence	Same	Model I	Model II
	Different	Model III	Model IV

a grocery store but could not do similar problems when they were presented in a more abstract way in a school setting. These examples, and many others like them, show that people who can perform mental tasks in one setting may not be able to perform them in another. A test of mathematics skills given to the Brazilian children or the California homemakers might show that they had poor skills if the test reflected the "school" culture, whereas another test reflecting the "everyday business" culture would show that they had good skills.

Sternberg's thought-provoking arguments help us understand the importance of measuring intelligence in ways that reflect a child's true abilities, and that the abilities of some children may be underestimated if they are tested in ways that do not reflect the types of knowledge and skills with which they are familiar. For example, an intelligence test given to two third graders at a U.S. school—one who spent much of his early life in a preschool setting and one who spent much of his early life exploring and working on a farm—might assign them quite different scores, even if their true intelligence was the same. If the test reflected the skills and knowledge employed in the culture of preschool, the child raised on the farm might appear to have much lower cognitive abilities than the child who attended preschool. In a broader context, an intelligence test that measures the skills and knowledge commonly employed in one culture may underestimate the intelligence of a person raised in another culture.

Measuring Intelligence

Several tests exist to measure a child's general intelligence. Alfred Binet and Theophilius Simon (1905) developed the first useful intelligence test, which was designed to determine which French children had the cognitive abilities to profit from public education. To create their test, they devised a variety of tasks and administered them to children that teachers rated as having normal intelligence and children that teachers considered to have mental retardation (Kamphaus, 2001). The tasks on which the children of normal intelligence consistently outperformed the children with mental retardation were combined into the test.

Lewis Terman produced the first English version of Binet's intelligence test, the Stanford–Binet, in 1916, which has since been revised four times (Kaufman, 2000). David Wechsler produced the first widely used intelligence test for adults in 1939: the Wechsler–Bellevue. In 1949 he published his first intelligence test for children, the Wechsler Intelligence Scale for Children (WISC), and later published a test for young children, the Wechsler Preschool and Primary Scale of Intelligence (WPPSI). The WISC has undergone several revisions; the most current test, the WISC-IV, was published in 2003.

All modern intelligence tests require that children complete a wide range of tasks, each of which is believed to assess a skill influenced by general intelligence. Each task includes items ranging from very easy to very difficult. The more items that a child answers or completes correctly, the higher the score the child receives on the task. The score for the child's general intelligence is obtained by combining the scores from all of the tasks.

The Intelligence Quotient

The Stanford–Binet was the first intelligence test to produce an **intelligence quotient (IQ),** which was a ratio calculated as $100 \times MA/CA$, where MA represented the child's **mental age** (which was determined by the number of items on the test that the child answered correctly) and CA represented the child's chronological age (Brody, 2000). Although the ratio IQ is no longer in use, the concept of mental age continues to be an important one in the field of mental retardation—as we will see later in this chapter.

Wechsler developed the **deviation IQ** that is now used in all IQ tests. The deviation IQ describes how far a particular child's score on an intelligence test deviates from the average scores of all children of that age. A mathematical formula was created to convert the scores that children received on an intelligence test so that the scores have a mean of 100 and a standard deviation of 15 (except the Stanford–Binet, which has a standard deviation of 16). An individual's score on an intelligence test can then be converted to an IQ score that describes how far from the mean it is. On the WISC-IV, for example, a child whose score is one standard deviation above the mean has an IQ of 115 (the mean of 100 plus one standard deviation of 15); those whose scores are one standard deviation below the mean have an IQ of 85.

It is important to note that all tests produce an estimate of a child's intelligence (Kamphaus, 2001). All tests have some error in their measurement. In a hypothetical situation that could never exist, if a child were to take the same intelligence test 20 times, under the same conditions and with no benefit from taking the test before, his score would not be the same every time. The scores would be similar, but they would differ by a few points. The child's **true intelligence** would be somewhere in the range of scores that he received on the tests. Statistical procedures produce a *confidence interval* for each intelligence test that describes the confidence we have that a child's true intelligence is within a certain interval around the score he or she received on the test. As an example, the 95% confidence interval for the WISC-IV is 6 points on either side of the score a child receives. If a child received a score of 105 on the WISC-IV, we could say with 95% confidence that the child's true intelligence lies somewhere between 99 and 111.

Intelligence Testing and Preschool Children   Measuring intelligence in young children continues to be problematic. Although intelligence is stable after about age 7 or 8 years, there is much less stability during the preschool years and between the preschool and school-age years (Kamphaus, 2001). The reasons for this lack of stability remain unclear.

The most widely used scales for preschool children, the Bayley Scales of Infant Development—II (developed by Nancy Bayley in 1969 and revised in 1993) and the McCarthy Scales of Children's Abilities (developed by Dorothea McCarthy in 1972), do not claim to measure intelligence. Instead they measure the developmental level of children: the extent to which a child's cognitive and motor development is similar to the development of other children his or her age (Kaufman & Kaufman, 1977). Although some tests continue to provide IQ scores for preschool children, the tendency among many who assess young children is to avoid the issue of intelligence and focus instead on the level of the child's cognitive and motor development.

Cultural Bias in Intelligence Testing

Considerable concern has been raised over the past several decades about possible biases in intelligence tests. These concerns have been raised because of the consistent differences between racial groups in the United States on tests of intelligence. Results from all the widely used intelligence tests show that the average for African–American children is lower than the average for Native American children, which is lower than the averages for European–American and Asian–American children (which are about the same) (Loehlin, 2000). (It is essential to note that these differences are between group means. Significant variability in scores exists in all racial groups. Consequently, there are many African–American children whose scores are higher than many European–American and Asian–American children, even though the mean for African–American children is lower.)

The reasons for the differences between African–American children and European–American children have been hotly debated for years (my apologies to those from other racial and cultural groups—the research has focused primarily on these two groups of children). Do the tests accurately show differences in group averages of intelligence? Does something in the tests cause children from one racial group to receive higher scores than those from another racial group when they have the same level of true intelligence? For example, if an intelligence test tested types of knowledge or skills that are more commonly found in one racial group than another, then racial group differences in test performance could be due to the relative familiarity that the children had with the task rather than differences in their intelligence (Sternberg, 2004).

This debate is not simply an intellectual exercise because, as we describe later in this chapter, IQ tests play an important role in determining which children are placed in special education classes for children with mental retardation. If children from a cultural or racial group are placed in these classes inappropriately because of biases in IQ tests, they will not be receiving an appropriate education. This is fundamentally unfair. Biased tests could also have broader influences. Consider, for example, how you and others in this class respond when you are told that you are in a cultural group with higher or lower intelligence scores than others. This could influence how you think about yourself and others, which can influence many of your thoughts, feelings, and behaviors about those in various racial or cultural groups.

ILLUSTRATING AN IMPORTANT RESEARCH ISSUE: DISTINGUISHING BETWEEN GROUP AVERAGES AND INDIVIDUAL BEHAVIORS

Most social science research involves comparing groups on one or more characteristics: Do Native Americans have more or less of a characteristic than Asian–Americans? Do girls have more or less of a characteristic than boys? When statistically significant group differences are found, the conclusion can be drawn that one group has more or less of some characteristic than the other group. The mistake that many of us make, however, is to translate that in our minds to "Everyone in one group has more or less of the characteristic than everyone in the other group." Great care must be taken not to do this because it will lead to inaccurate conclusions.

Examination of the IQ scores of large samples of people randomly chosen from the population will usually show that they are normally distributed. When two samples are compared, it may be found that one group has a mean that is higher than another. However, as shown in Figure 11.3, there is often a considerable overlap in the distributions of the two groups. In other words, many people in the group with the lower mean will have an IQ that is higher than many people in the group with the higher mean. It is important to keep these individual differences in mind.

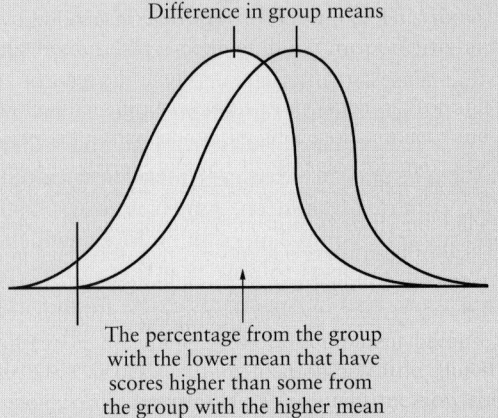

FIGURE 11.3   *Mean Group Differences Tell Us, Little about Specific Individual Scores*

The argument that bias exists in IQ tests is based primarily on the assumption that group differences in true intelligence do not exist, and therefore any test that produces group differences must be biased (Kamphaus, 2001). This argument has been persuasive in several settings. For example, in the case *Larry P. v. Riles* (1979), a federal judge ruled, in large part, that group differences in intelligence tests were evidence, by themselves, that bias existed in the tests.

However, extensive research in the 1970s and 1980s failed to identify any specific source of bias in the most commonly used tests. A few individual items on the tests were found to be answered correctly by one racial group more than another, but no consistent pattern in these differences emerged. (For example, African–American children answered some questions correctly more often than European–American children; European–American children answered other questions correctly more often than African–American children.) In addition, correlations between the various subtests showed that the construct of intelligence was the same for

African–American and European–American children (Kamphaus, 2001; Loehlin, 2000). Consequently, the research literature does not support the hypothesis that some systematic bias exists in intelligence tests. My sense from the literature today is that most psychologists and other researchers accept that racial group differences exist for reasons other than biases in intelligence tests. A host of other possible reasons for these group differences exist, including genetic differences, differences in prenatal environments, family and neighborhood environments, the emphasis in families on teaching school readiness skills, quality of child care, and quality of schools. The relative importance of these or other possible reasons for racial differences on IQ tests remains controversial and unresolved (Plomin et al., 2001).

Key Concepts

- *Intelligence* is usually defined as a person's general cognitive ability.
- Debate continues about whether intelligence is one trait or a series of distinct but related traits, although most researchers today believe that intelligence is best thought of as one trait.
- Binet and Simon created the first widely used test of intelligence to identify children with a higher likelihood of succeeding in public school.
- Intelligence tests for children include a variety of tasks, all of which are related to a child's general cognitive ability.
- The intelligence quotient (IQ) was initially derived by the formula of mental age/chronological age 3 100. This formula is no longer used. Rather, the deviation IQ now indicates how far a child's score on an intelligence test is from the average of other children the same age.
- The measurement of intelligence in preschool children continues to be problematic.
- All of the major intelligence tests used with children older than preschool age produce racial group differences in IQ when given to many children. The sources of these differences remain hotly debated, although claims that the tests are biased against children of some racial groups have not been supported by research to date.

History

Beirne Smith, Ittenbach, and Patton (2002) suggest that the history of societal attitudes and behaviors toward those with mental retardation can be divided roughly into five periods: antiquity (before 1700), emergence and disillusionment (1700–1890), facilities-based orientation (1890–1960), services-based orientation (1960–1985), and support-based orientation (1985–present).

Before 1700, cases of what we now characterize as mild mental retardation probably went unnoticed because few people needed sophisticated cognitive skills. Many of those with severe forms of mental retardation probably died as infants or children. Those who lived were sheltered, perhaps in monasteries; others were used in circuses or considered possessed by demons and killed.

Beginning in the 1700s and 1800s, some people with severe mental retardation became the focus of study and support. In Europe some physicians believed they could "cure" children or adults with severe mental retardation by providing extensive training in daily living and working skills. Pioneering advocates in the United States, such as Dorothea Dix and Samuel Howe, campaigned for humane treatment of those with mental retardation, saying that proper treatment would allow them to be reintegrated into society. However, despite the best efforts of many treatment programs, it became clear that severe mental retardation could not be "cured." This led to a sense of disillusionment regarding the treatment of mental retardation.

As attitudes toward those with mental retardation became more negative and pessimistic in the late 1800s, many communities began to focus on "protecting" themselves from those with mental retardation. Institutions were created where those with mental retardation could be housed and segregated from the rest of society. Most of these quickly became overwhelmed and degenerated into wretched institutions.

Eugenics, or the attempt to improve the human race through selective breeding, became a focal point of many efforts during this time. Central to the eugenics movement in the United States were laws in many states requiring the sterilization of adolescents and adults with mental retardation. These laws were upheld by the U.S. Supreme Court in the case of *Buck v. Bell* (1927) and this infamous opinion written by Justice Oliver Wendell Holmes, justifying forced sterilization:

> We have seen more than once that the public welfare may call upon the best citizens for their lives. It would be strange if it could not call upon those who already sap the strength of the State for these lesser sacrifices, often felt to be much by those concerned, in order to prevent our being swamped with incompetence. It is better for all the world, if instead of waiting to execute degenerate offspring for crime, or let them starve for their imbecility, society can prevent those who are manifestly unfit from continuing their kind. . . . Three generations of imbeciles are enough. (p. 207)

Changing attitudes in the mid-1900s about the responsibility of the federal government in helping individual citizens increased the role of the government with citizens who had mental retardation. In addition, the national Association of Parents and Friends of Retarded Children was founded in 1950, becoming a powerful force advocating for better services for those with mental retardation. Many states initiated or expanded educational programs for children with mental retardation. However, most of these programs required those with mental retardation to attend separate schools—often many miles from their families' homes (Patton, Polloway, & Smith, 2000).

During the early 1960s, President Kennedy's concern for those with mental retardation prompted the establishment of the President's Panel on Mental Retardation. The panel recommended increased research to understand the development of mental retardation and the creation of better educational programs for children with mental retardation (Mayo, 1962). A central goal urged by the panel was the integration of those with mental retardation into their communities by providing needed services in public schools and other community institutions. Judicial and legislative actions during this time also changed how children with mental retardation were educated. Actions in state courts resulted in several legal mandates for public schools to provide services for children with mental retardation in their home school districts (*Mills v. Board of Education of the District of Columbia*, 1972; *Pennsylvania Ass'n for Retarded Children v. Pennsylvania*, 1971). Perhaps the most important federal legislation for children with a wide range of disabilities was the Education for All Handicapped Children Act, known as Public Law (PL) 94-142 and enacted in 1975. PL 94-142 mandated free, appropriate public education for every child with a disability from age 3 years to 21 years in the least restrictive environment necessary. All disabled children were to receive services in their local communities and be educated in regular classrooms whenever possible. In many ways this was a major turning point in the treatment of children and adults with mental retardation. No longer were they to be sent off to facilities that educated them and "protected" society from them. Rather, they were to be considered members of their communities and our society.

Key Concepts

- Before 1700 cases of mild mental retardation probably went unnoticed, and most of those with severe forms of mental retardation died as infants or children.
- In the 1700s and early 1800s there was a sense that those with severe forms of mental retardation could be cured. When this proved to be incorrect, there was a sense of disillusionment about working with children and adults with mental retardation.
- Attitudes toward those with mental retardation became more negative in the late 1800s, when efforts to protect society from them and stop them from having children predominated.
- Attitudes about governments' roles in helping citizens began to change in the mid-1900s, resulting in more services for those with mental retardation. Most of these services were provided in separate facilities that were often removed from their clients' communities.
- Legislation and court rulings reshaped how children with mental retardation were educated in the 1960s and 1970s, requiring that they receive free and appropriate education, in the least restrictive environment, from age 3 to age 21, and that they be integrated into their communities.

Diagnosis and Assessment

Mental retardation is diagnosed today using two components: intelligence and adaptive functioning. Intelligence was discussed earlier in this chapter. **Adaptive functioning** refers to "the collection of conceptual, social, and practical skills that have been learned by people in order to function in their everyday lives" (American Association on Mental Retardation, 2002). For children, this means skills to function effectively in school (such as attending to the teacher and learning the material presented), in social situations (being able to play with peers), and at home (self-care, participating in family activities and responsibilities). For older adolescents and adults, *adaptive functioning* may also refer to skills needed to participate in the workforce and live independently. Several scales have been created to measure adaptive functioning, including the Vineland Adaptive Behavior Scales and the American Association on Mental Retardation Adaptive Behavior Scale. These scales are completed by a trained professional during a conversation with a child's parents or other caregivers. The Vineland Adaptive Behavior Scales also include a scale completed by a child's teachers (American Association on Mental Retardation, 2002).

Diagnostic Criteria

The DSM-IV-TR diagnostic criteria for mental retardation are shown in Table 11.2. As shown, the criteria require significant impairments in intellectual functioning and adaptive functioning. Deficits in adaptive functioning are typically indicated by scores on a scale of adaptive functioning that fall two standard deviations below the mean.

As shown in Table 11.2, the DSM-IV-TR divides those with mental retardation into several subcategories, reflecting the level of their intellectual impairment. Ranges of IQ are given for each level of retardation; ranges are used because determining the IQ of children with more severe forms of mental retardation can be difficult. Intelligence tests often require that a child physically manipulate test materials and provide verbal answers. As described in the following sections, children with more severe levels of retardation often have considerable problems with speech and physical dexterity. Consequently, when these children cannot complete a task, it can be unclear whether this reflects an intellectual limitation or a problem with speech or physical dexterity. Thus intelligence scores for those with more severe forms of mental retardation can at best be rough estimates.

Determining that an Individual Child Has Mental Retardation

The determination that a child has mental retardation can be a significant event in his or her life. As described in this chapter, if a child is determined to have mental retardation, he or she qualifies for a variety of special education services. These services may help a child with low levels of intelligence and adaptive functioning by providing a setting where he or she can learn more than would be possible in a regular classroom. However, a child diagnosed with mental retardation may be removed from a regular classroom for part or all of a day, which may harm his or her educational and social development, especially if the child's education is not enhanced by special

TABLE 11.2

Diagnostic Criteria for Mental Retardation

A. Significantly subaverage intellectual functioning: an IQ of approximately 70 or below on an individually administered IQ test (for infants, a clinical judgment of significantly subaverage intellectual functioning).

B. Concurrent deficits or impairments in present adaptive functioning (i.e., the person's effectiveness in meeting the standards expected for his or her age by his or her cultural group) in at least two of the following areas: communication, self-care, home living, social/interpersonal skills, use of community resources, self-direction, functional academic skills, work, leisure, health, and safety.

C. The onset is before age 18 years.

   Code based on degree of severity reflecting level of intellectual impairment:

   317   **Mild Mental Retardation:**   IQ level 50–55 to approximately 70
   318.0 **Moderate Mental Retardation:** IQ level 35–40 to 50–55
   318.1 **Severe Mental Retardation:**   IQ level 20–25 to 35–40
   318.2 **Profound Mental Retardation:** IQ level below 20 or 25
   319   **Mental Retardation, Severity Unspecified:** when there is strong presumption of Mental Retardation but the person's intelligence is untreatable by standard tests

classes. In addition, the changes in self-concept that the child may experience after being told that he or she has mental retardation, and the changes in the concept of the child that peers, family, teachers, and others can experience, may significantly influence the child's life. Consequently, determining whether a child has mental retardation must be done with great care.

Children with severe forms of mental retardation are often identified at a young age. Their significant lag in meeting developmental milestones may be obvious, and the causes of their mental retardation (such as Down syndrome) may have been identified early in life.

The determination for children with milder forms of mental retardation is most frequently done after the child enters school because children with mild cognitive impairments often do not appear much different from their peers until they begin to struggle with academic demands (Baroff & Olley, 1999). If a parent, teacher, counselor, or other school official is concerned that a child's intelligence and adaptive functioning may be too low for the child to succeed in a regular classroom, this person may ask for an assessment of the child's abilities. If an assessment is requested, a clearly defined, legally mandated process is put into motion (Kamphaus, 2001). An assessment involves a team of professionals, including a psychologist, an education expert, and possibly a social worker and nurse (American Association on Mental Retardation, 2002). The psychologist and the education expert administer a series of tests to a child, including tests of intelligence and academic ability. Measures of adaptive functioning are completed, based on conversations with parents, teachers, or others who know the child well. One or more team members may observe the child in class and on the playground, and the child's teachers may be asked to complete reports about the child's behaviors. Each professional writes a detailed report; these reports are shared among the professionals, with the child's parents, and with the teachers and administrators in the child's school. A meeting is then held with all these people: The child's abilities are discussed, and a determination is made regarding the child's educational classification. Parents have the right to appeal the determination if they disagree with it.

Some circumstances make assessing a child's intellectual abilities even more complex. Consider, for example, a child for whom English is not the first language. Low scores on an intelligence test might reflect a lack of English skills, significant cognitive limitations, or both. Alternatively, consider a child raised in a deprived environment. Perhaps a low score on an intelligence test during his first year or two in school reflects the consequences of the deprived environment (which might be overcome through schooling), significant cognitive limitations, or both.

When an assessment of a child's abilities is done well, these and other potential influences on the child's performance are considered by the professionals conducting the assessment. This is often done by observing differences in the child's performance on various tasks or in different settings. For example, a child for whom English is a second language may perform much better on nonverbal tasks than verbal tasks on an intelligence test, and this may suggest that her performance on the verbal tasks is inhibited by her knowledge of English. A child from a deprived environment who can learn new, nonacademic tasks as quickly as his peers may not have significant intellectual impairments even if his scores on an intelligence test are low.

Key Concepts

- Current definitions of *mental retardation* comprise two components: intelligence and adaptive functioning.
- *Adaptive functioning* refers to the conceptual, social, and practical skills that people learn and use in their everyday lives.
- Children whose intelligence and adaptive functioning are two standard deviations below the mean of those their age can be diagnosed with mental retardation.
- The DSM-IV-TR defines different degrees of mental retardation—mild, moderate, severe, and profound—based on a child's estimated IQ.
- Determining that a child has mental retardation is usually done once the child enters school following careful evaluation of the child by a team of professionals. Consideration must be given to language and cultural issues in this process, as well as any significant deprivation the child has experienced that may be temporarily influencing the scores on his or her intelligence tests.

Characteristics and Experiences of Children with Mental Retardation

As we turn from describing mental retardation to describing people who have mental retardation, it is important to emphasize two points. First, the cognitive impairments of a child with mental retardation do not make the child less of a person. Just as I am no less a person than one of my friends because she has better athletic ability than I do, another of my friends is no less a person than me because he has lower intelligence. Intellectual ability is just one component that makes each of us who we are. The abilities to be warm, caring, humorous, hard-working, and proud are all possible in those with mental retardation, although the forms of their warmth, care, humor, hard work, and pride may be influenced by their intellectual limitations (Zigler, 1999). Second, it is important to acknowledge that intellectual limitations have broad consequences for those living in complicated, industrialized societies. Lower intellectual abilities do not affect children only when they are in a classroom: They affect them on the playground, when shopping, and when riding public transportation. The challenges faced by those with mental retardation can be extensive—as can the challenges faced by their family members and others who care for them. We should not underestimate these challenges as we think about children with mental retardation and their families.

Cognitive Abilities

By definition, children with mental retardation have significant cognitive limitations. As shown in Figure 11.4, mental growth in children with mental retardation is slower than that in others and reaches a lower peak.

The cognitive abilities of children with mild mental retardation may not be distinguishable from those with average intelligence during the preschool years, and they develop language and other communication skills at about

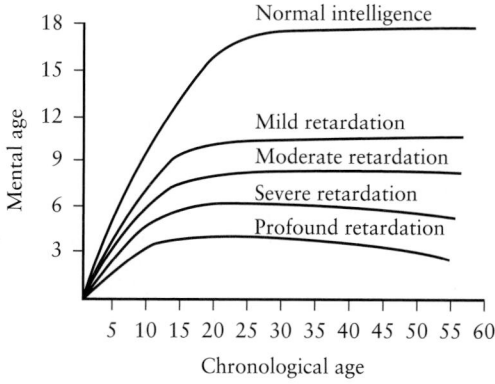

FIGURE 11.4 *Mental Growth in Children*

the same rate as other children. During their preschool and early school-age years, children with mild mental retardation may be slower than other children in developing reading and numbers skills, but most of them do learn these skills. As their schoolwork becomes more complex during their elementary school years, their cognitive limitations become more apparent (APA, 2000). Most achieve their highest level of cognitive ability, which is similar to that of most sixth-grade children, by mid-adolescence. Their thinking is usually concrete in nature, and they show particular problems in conceptual thinking and in planning (Baroff & Olley, 1999). Consequently, their accomplishments in subjects such as spelling are likely to be higher than those in writing, and they may be better at multiplication than they are at solving mathematical word problems.

Children with moderate levels of mental retardation can develop language and communication skills during their preschool years, but this development is often delayed by several years (for example, skills expected of a typically developing 24-month-old may not be apparent until 60 months). By adolescence, most attain the cognitive functioning of a second-grade child—meaning that they can read simple instructions and do rudimentary arithmetic.

Those with severe mental retardation tend not to develop language or other communication skills until their school-age years. They can usually identify letters and learn simple counting. They can learn a few simple "survival" words (*stop, hot*) but are unable to read beyond that. Finally, those with profound retardation often do not develop language, but some may recognize and respond to a few words (APA, 2000).

Self-Image

Although only a small amount of research on self-image in children with mental retardation has been conducted, it suggests that the self-image of children with mild mental retardation follows the same developmental pattern as that of other children (Evans, 1999). For example, on average, the self-image of most school-age children is inflated: They report that they are better in many areas of functioning than objective measures or the assessments of parents of teachers suggest they are. This pattern holds true for children who have mental retardation and other children of the same mental age. Similarly, the difference between adolescents' idealized selves and their views of who they are is larger than the difference found among school-age children, and adolescents have more accurate assessments of their abilities than do school-age children. Again, this pattern holds true for children who have mental retardation and those of the same mental age (Evans, 1999).

The content of the self-image of children with mental retardation, however, is often more negative than that of other children of the same mental or chronological age. This more negative self-image may be the result of (1) their interactions with others, in which they are likely to be much less successful and be the targets of insulting comments; (2) their struggles and relative lack of success as they deal with the complexities of school and of life; and often (3) their relegation to special education programs that are often located in separate areas of schools (Glick, 1999). In addition, adolescents who have mental retardation often have an ideal self-image that is much more negative than that of other adolescents (Zigler, Balla, & Watson, 1972). This may reduce their motivation to succeed, which can influence their success levels and further influence their self-image (Zigler, 1999).

Sociability and Peer Relationships

Positive relationships with other children and adults are important in the lives of all children. As is true with almost all children, children with mental retardation who have positive peer relationships are happier than are those with poor peer relationships (Wallander & Hubert, 1987).

However, the cognitive limitations of children with mental retardation can significantly influence their abilities to form and maintain friendships. Success in social situations requires several skills (Leffert, Siperstein, & Millikan, 2000). First, a person must recognize what is happening in a social situation by analyzing cues from others. For example, if you are bumped from behind and turn toward the person who bumped you, you must read a variety of cues to determine whether you were bumped accidentally, on purpose to anger you, or on purpose as a friendly gesture. Second, a person must choose an appropriate response by accessing memory for what responses are appropriate and then initiating one of them. For example, if you believe you were bumped by accident, you have to decide between actions such as smiling and saying "no problem" or pushing the person back and saying "don't ever do that again."

The cognitive limitations of children with mental retardation influence both skills. They have difficulty accurately assessing social situations. For example, they have more difficulty than other children in recognizing benign intent: They are more likely to attribute hostile intent to another person in ambiguous situations (Leffert et al., 2000). (Unfortunately, this bias may be related to their past experiences: If they have experienced other children mocking or hitting them, they may be more likely to believe that actions directed at them are hostile or insulting.) Children with mental retardation are also less able to consider more than one interpretation of a social situation and often rely on their initial impression when deciding how to respond (Leffert et al., 2000). So even if a classmate smiles and says "sorry" after bumping a child with mental retardation, the child's assessment of the social situation may not change from his initial assessment that he was bumped in a hostile way.

Because of their cognitive limitations, children with mental retardation exhibit less mature social skills in a variety of situations than other children of the same chronological or mental age (Kasari & Bauminger, 1999). For example, a 16-year-old with a mental age of 12 years may act in social situations as one would expect a 9- or 10-year-old to act. Consequently, other children often exclude children with mental retardation from games or other social activities because they find them immature or bothersome. Thus children with mental retardation spend much of their time alone while at school, even when they are included in regular classes much or all of the day (Heiman, 2000; Wallander & Hubert, 1987). After school hours, many children with mental retardation spend time by themselves at home, watching television or napping, and they report being lonely most of the time (Heiman, 2000).

In addition, many children with more severe forms of mental retardation engage in behaviors that can be distracting and annoying to other children, such as head rolling, rocking, teeth grinding, and inappropriate vocalizations (Drew, Logan, & Hardman, 1992). These behaviors can increase during times of stress, making it more difficult for other children to want to associate with children with severe mental retardation.

Health Problems

Several health problems are more common among children with severe forms of mental retardation than other children. They are more likely to have **cerebral palsy,** a neuromuscular disorder resulting from damage to the brain (Beirne-Smith et al., 2002). It affects a child's posture and how he or she can move, and it can also affect speech and perception. Consequently, cerebral palsy can severely restrict a child's ability to play with other children and engage in school activities. Children with severe forms of mental retardation are also more likely to have **seizure disorders:** uncontrolled electrical activity in the brain that can last for just a second or two or for minutes, resulting in muscle twitching and loss of consciousness.

Children with all levels of mental retardation are at greater risk for contracting the normal diseases of childhood (Beirne-Smith et al., 2002). This is due in part to issues related to family income. As we will discuss later, children with mild mental retardation are more likely to be from low-income families than more affluent families, and the poor housing and other conditions in which these low-income families must live contribute to the poorer health of the children in them. Nutrition in many low-income families is poorer than in more affluent families, which can also influence children's health. In addition, their cognitive limitations may place children with mental retardation at risk for poorer health. For example, they may be less able to remember to act in ways that promote good health, such as washing their hands after using the bathroom. Children with mental retardation are also at greater risk for accidents and injuries (Sherrard, Tonge, & Ozanne-Smith, 2002). Poorer physical coordination caused by cerebral palsy or other disorders put some of them at greater risk for accidents and injuries, as does their impaired ability to think through activities and identify risks they should avoid (like riding a bicycle too fast down a hill). Taunting or encouragement from other children may also put them at greater risk for attempting risky behaviors.

Comorbid Disorders

Estimates of the percentages of children who have mental retardation and who have another behavioral or emotional disorder vary widely, but there is general agreement that they have higher rates of disorders than do other children. Various studies have estimated that 30–70% of children with mild to moderate levels of mental retardation also experience another disorder (American Academy of Child and Adolescent Psychiatry, 1999).

The causes of this higher prevalence are not clear (Dekker, Koot, van der Ende, & Verhulst, 2002). For some children, the causes of their cognitive impairments may also cause other disorders. For example, as discussed in more detail in a following section, some children with mental retardation have Fragile X syndrome. Many children with Fragile X syndrome are highly anxious, and the genetic abnormalities that cause these children's cognitive impairments may also cause the hyperarousal believed to be at the foundation of their anxiety (Belser & Sudhalter, 2001). In other children, the consequences of their mental retardation can put them at an increased risk for developing another disorder. For example, the problematic social relationships that many children with mental retardation experience could increase their likelihood of developing depression. Similarly, the stress that many of them experience in academic and social situations may increase their risk for developing an anxiety disorder.

Key Concepts

- The cognitive abilities of children with mental retardation grow more slowly than those of other children and reach a lower peak.
- The cognitive abilities of children with mild mental retardation may be similar to those of other children during preschool years. Their cognitive abilities usually peak at about the abilities of an average sixth-grade child.
- Children with moderate mental retardation usually have significant delays in language development. Their cognitive abilities tend to peak at about the level of an average second grader.
- Most children with severe mental retardation do not develop language until their school-age years. Most of those with profound retardation do not develop language, but some may recognize and respond to a few words.
- The self-image of most children with mental retardation develops in the same way as that of other children; however, many children with mental retardation have a more negative self-image than do other children.
- The cognitive limitations of children with mental retardation inhibit their ability to assess social situations and respond in appropriate ways. As a result, many children with mental retardation are shunned by their peers, spend a considerable amount of time by themselves, and report feeling lonely much of the time.
- Some children with mental retardation have physical disorders linked to the cause of their mental retardation, such as cerebral palsy. Children with mental retardation have more physical health problems than other children, which may be related to the environments in which they live or their relative inability to avoid situations in which they might contract a disease or be injured.
- Children with mental retardation are more likely than other children to have another behavioral or emotional disorder.

Prevalence

Most large-scale studies of mental retardation report prevalence rates between 1.8% and 2% (Murphy, Boyle, Schendel, Decoufle, & Yeargin-Allsopp, 1998; Roeleveld, Zielhaus, & Gabreels, 1997). About 85% of people with mental retardation have IQs in the mild mental retardation range. Those with moderate levels of mental retardation comprise about 10% of those with mental retardation, while approximately 3–4% have severe mental retardation and about 1–2% have profound mental retardation (APA, 2000).

Notes from the Author: An Unconscious Bias?

Partway through my lectures about mental retardation each year, I ask my class, "If you had to guess, what percentage of Americans would you say have below-average intelligence?" This is a trick question. Because intelligence is assumed to be distributed normally, the mean and the median of intelligence are the same. So by definition, 50% of the people in America have below-average intelligence. Very rarely, however, do my students "guess" 50% right away. (I admit that my phrase "if you had to guess" is designed to make them think that a guess is required.) Usually several people guess a figure much lower (such as 25% or 30%) before someone figures out the trick and states that it is 50%. I think it is instructive that students' guesses about the percentage of those with below-average intelligence are so low. My sense is that because most of us in a college environment have lived primarily surrounded by people of about our intellectual ability, it is hard for us to recognize that there are so many people with below-average intelligence. Below-average intelligence is different from mental retardation—as we will see, only the lowest 5% of those with below-average intelligence have mental retardation—but I still believe it is useful to reflect on how we can be "intelli-centric," thinking that most people have the same level of intelligence that we do.

Sex and Race Differences

More boys than girls are diagnosed with mental retardation in the United States, and a higher percentage of African–American than European–American children are diagnosed with mental retardation. (Most research in this area has compared only African–American and European–American children.) Several explanations for these sex and racial differences exist, and it is interesting to observe their similarities. First, it is possible that the true prevalence of mental retardation is higher for boys and for African–American children. For example, X-linked chromosomal problems resulting in mental retardation (such as Fragile X syndrome, described later in this chapter) are more common in boys than girls; and there is some evidence that low birth weight and maternal smoking, two issues related to mental retardation, affect boys more than girls (Leonard & Wen, 2002). Similarly, African–American children are more likely to live in poverty than are European–American children, and some causes of mental retardation are more prevalent in families living in poverty—such as exposure to lead and other environmental toxins, poor nutrition, and inadequate prenatal care (Mendola, Selevan, Gutter, & Rice, 2002). (Remember: Families in all racial groups are found throughout the socioeconomic strata in our society. Because poverty is more prevalent in African–American families does not mean that all African–Americans are financially poor—despite this common stereotype.)

Alternatively, perhaps boys and African–American children are referred for testing in school more frequently than are girls and European–American children because of conscious or unconscious biases of teachers, counselors, or others who make the referrals. For example, more boys than girls are disruptive in class, which may bring them to the attention of their teachers more often than girls. If a disruptive boy is experiencing academic difficulty, a teacher may be more likely to refer him for testing than a withdrawn or quiet girl experiencing academic difficulty (Leonard & Wen, 2002; Murphy, Yeargin-Allsopp, Decoufle, & Drews, 1995).

It is worth noting that boys are classified as having severe mental retardation more frequently than are girls, and African–American children are classified as having severe mental retardation more often than are European–American children (Leonard & Wen, 2002). Because it seems unlikely that being classified as having severe mental retardation is simply an issue related to bias in referral or testing, there is some evidence that boys and African–American children more frequently have experiences that result in severe forms of mental retardation.

Key Concepts

- About 1.8–2% of children are diagnosed with mental retardation.
- About 85% of those who have mental retardation fall into the mild mental retardation range, with about 10% in the moderate range and the remaining 5% in the severe and profound ranges.
- Studies of racial differences have focused primarily on African–American and European–American children, finding a higher prevalence of mental retardation among African–American children.
- More boys than girls are diagnosed with mental retardation.

Families of Children with Mental Retardation

Almost all children with mental retardation live with their families. Exceptions might be children whose parents cannot give them needed care, whose impairments are so severe that they can do little for themselves, or whose behaviors are dangerous enough that they need continuous monitoring (Rimmerman & Duvdevani, 1996). Many of those with mental retardation live with their families well into their adulthood; consequently, their involvement with their families is often more intense than that of people who do not have mental retardation (Freedman & Boyer, 2000).

Most research in this area has been done with families in which there is a child with mental retardation of known organic cause. As described soon, these families usually have only one member with mental retardation, and the other family members' intelligence is almost always significantly above that of the child with mental retardation. Thus we know more about these families than we know about families in which several members may have low intelligence.

Parents

The influence on parents and other family members of having a child with mental retardation begins when they first learn that their child is likely to have significant cognitive impairments. Frequently this occurs during the pregnancy because tests to detect a variety of genetic and chromosomal abnormalities that cause cognitive impairments are widely available (Alexander, 1998). Most parents experience a sense of shock when they hear this news about their child. Their initial reactions often resemble those of bereavement as they mourn the loss of their "normal" child and begin to accept that they will have a child with significant cognitive impairments (Marvin & Pianta, 1996). Some parents can mobilize internal and external resources to prepare for the birth of their child, whereas others freeze and are unable to plan or cope effectively (Heiman, 2002). There does not appear to be any research on the characteristics of parents or their environments that predict how they respond to this circumstance. Perhaps the same factors known to positively influence how families facing a wide range of difficulties function increase the likelihood of successful coping by families that learn they will have a child with mental retardation: (1) open discussions within the nuclear and extended families, and consultation with friends and professionals; (2) a positive and supportive relationship between the parents; and (3) the use of ongoing educational and psychological support for the parents, siblings, and extended family members (Hawley & De Haan, 1996).

Tests for many genetic and chromosomal abnormalities can be done during the period in which a mother can choose to have an abortion rather than give birth (Alexander, 1998). Deciding whether to have an abortion or continue the pregnancy is likely to be fairly straightforward for some parents but extremely difficult for others.

After the child's birth, parents of children with mental retardation experience higher levels of stress than other parents; as one might expect, the level of their stress often increases with the severity of the mental retardation (Roach, Orsmond, & Barratt, 1999; Weinger, 1999). This stress can influence the parents' individual functioning and their ability to parent all of their children effectively. The sources of this stress can be divided into two broad categories: worry and coping with the child's behaviors and needs.

Most parents worry about their children, but the parents of children with mental retardation report many more worries than do other parents (Heiman, 2002; Roll-Pettersson, 2001). They worry about the extent to which their children's cognitive impairments will limit their occupational, social, and family goals, as well as about whether their other children will be affected by having a sibling with mental retardation. When their children are playing or socializing with friends, parents worry about whether their children's cognitive impairments will result in the children making wrong choices or getting caught up in situations from which they cannot untangle themselves. Many parents of children with mental retardation report worrying about their children's social lives. One mother noted that whenever she saw teenagers enjoying themselves in town, she worried about her daughter being alone at home (Roll-Pettersson, 2001). Parents often worry about their child's future: whether the child will need to continue living at home into the child's adulthood, and what will happen to their child after they are unable to care for him or her.

Parents must also cope with the stress associated with caring for a child with cognitive impairments. Many parents report chronic fatigue from having to monitor their child closely; from the social isolation that results from them staying home to care for their child; and from their lack of freedom to pursue work, volunteer, or social interests (Heiman, 2002). Many families feel financial pressure because one parent may be unable to work so that she (it is usually the mother) can stay home and care for the child. Coping with behavioral problems that a child with mental retardation may exhibit can be tiring; and many children with mental retardation do not sleep well and can be up and around the house during the night, which can dramatically reduce the sleep of one or both parents (Richdale, Francis, Gavidia-Payne, & Cotton, 2000).

Despite the stresses they experience, many parents of children with mental retardation love and cherish them and learn to appreciate their children for who they are (Heiman, 2002; Roll-Pettersson, 2001). Some parents report that having a child with mental retardation has had an overall positive influence on them and their family because they came together to address the many challenges that their child presented. For example, consider these comments by a parent of a boy with Down syndrome:

> For fourteen years, Adam has been turning my attention to the happiness available in almost any situation: the appreciation of a good hamburger, the hilarity of playing with our dog, the fabulous feel of clean sheets. Every day, his ready grin and easy gratitude teach me more about how to enjoy life than I learned during the twenty-plus years of my formal education. As Adam's younger sister put it one day when he was delightedly exploring the way his new electric toothbrush worked, "Well, Adam's overwhelmed by joy again." (Beck, 2002)

Siblings

Researchers exploring the experiences of siblings of children with mental retardation have reported contradictory findings. Some studies have found that siblings report more social isolation than children in other families and have fewer friends and participate in fewer extracurricular activities (Freeman & Alkin, 2000; Rossister & Sharpe, 2001). The sense of isolation

Some siblings of children with mental retardation benefit from their relationship.

may come from several experiences. Some siblings report being teased about having a sibling with mental retardation and being ostracized by peers. Many siblings report having more household tasks to complete than their peers, which can keep them at home and isolate them from peers. In addition, parents must often devote more attention to the child with mental retardation, which may make the other siblings feel isolated in their own families.

Several studies have found that siblings of children with mental retardation experience higher levels of anxiety and depression than their peers (Rossister & Sharpe, 2001). This anxiety and depression may be influenced by the social problems many of them experience at school and by their isolation from peers. The greater stress and worry that may pervade their families may also influence their depression and anxiety.

Other studies of siblings, however, have not found that they experience heightened levels of social or psychological problems (Bischoff & Tingstrom, 1991; Lynch, Fay, Funk, & Nagel, 1993). In addition, some studies have found that siblings of children with mental retardation were more empathic toward their peers—especially peers who were experiencing problems—a characteristic that might have been an outgrowth of the empathy and patience they learned while living with their sibling (Weinger, 1999). Many siblings of children with mental retardation report having more positive relationships with their sibling than do siblings of children without mental retardation (Roeyers & Mycke, 1995).

It is difficult to reconcile the differences in these studies because they used different measures and different samples. Perhaps the research points to what we know is often true: Some people respond positively to stressful situations such as having a sibling with mental retardation, and others respond negatively.

Key Concepts

- Most information about families comes from families with children who have a known organic cause of their mental retardation.
- Parents often must mourn the loss of their "normal" child when they first find out that their child is likely to have mental retardation. Some parents can overcome this loss and function well, whereas others have a difficult time accepting their child's cognitive limitations.
- Most parents of a child with mental retardation experience higher than usual levels of stress, caused by worry and the extra work associated with caring for and educating their child.
- Despite higher levels of stress, many parents of children with mental retardation love and cherish them and find that they bring many joys to them and their families.
- Research with siblings of children with mental retardation has reported conflicting findings. Some studies find higher levels of stress, anxiety, and depression in the siblings. Other studies report that siblings develop greater levels of empathy and patience and that they have close relationships with their siblings who have mental retardation.

Etiology

Two Groups of Children Who Have Mental Retardation

Years ago, Zigler (1967) hypothesized that those with mental retardation could be divided into two groups. This suggestion was based on prevalence data showing that there were higher numbers of those with severe forms of mental retardation than one would expect if cognitive abilities were distributed normally (see Figure 11.5). Zigler reasoned that, other than those at the lower end of the normal distribution of intelligence, there must be a second group of more severely affected individuals whose mental retardation was

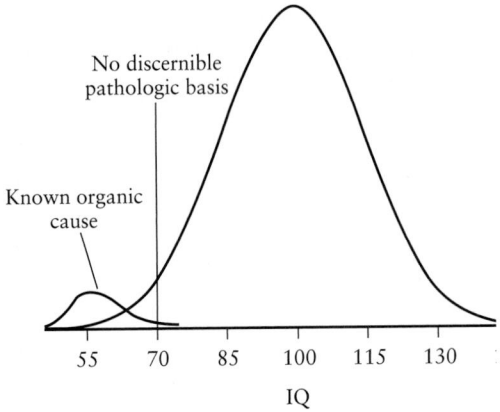

FIGURE 11.5   *Two Groups of Childern with Mental Retardation*

caused by other factors. Considerable evidence gathered since then has supported Zigler's hypothesis. The two groups are these:

- *People at the lower end of the normal distribution of intelligence:* These people represent about half the people with mental retardation, and most of them experience mild forms of mental retardation. Their development generally follows the same pattern as that seen in other people, but the development proceeds more slowly and attains a lower upper limit, as shown in Figure 11.4 (Glick, 1999). Most children in this group have an IQ that is similar to that of their other family members (Simonoff, Bolton, & Rutter, 1999).
- *People with identified, organically based causes of mental retardation:* The cognitive functioning of these people has its own normal distribution, as shown in Figure 11.5, with the mean being in the moderate to severe range. Almost all people with severe or profound mental retardation are in this group. Their development often follows a pattern that is different from others, and they often possess patterns of cognitive, emotional, and behavioral strengths and limitations that are specific to their organically based problems. They often come from families with no other members who have mental retardation, and they are often physically different from other family members (Baroff & Olley, 1999; Simonoff et al., 1999).

An ongoing issue has been the labels that should be used for these two groups. As one might expect, the second group has been labeled as those with *organic mental retardation* or *organically based mental retardation* or *known organic cause of mental retardation* or something similar. I prefer **mental retardation of known organic cause** because it suggests, accurately, that additional organically based causes of mental retardation may yet be discovered. The appropriate label for the first group has been more controversial. Zigler initially suggested *familial* because mental retardation of this type runs in families. The label was somewhat problematic, however, because it seemed to suggest that families might be the cause of mental retardation (just as the mental retardation of those in the second group is caused by organic factors). Terms such as *familial–cultural* or *cultural–familial* or *socio–familial* have been used to indicate that mental retardation of this type does run in families but that it is culturally defined and that the influences on this type of mental retardation come from both family and social sources. I have not liked any of these labels and believe that the label used by Murphy and colleagues (1998), **mental retardation with no discernible pathologic basis,** is better. This is a more complex phrase but is the most accurate and descriptive; so I will use it throughout the rest of this text.

Mental Retardation of Known Organic Cause

Some cases of mental retardation can be caused by identifiable biologically based problems, including chromosomal and genetic malformations, toxins from the environment, nutritional deficits in pregnant women and infants, and diseases that afflict pregnant women, infants, and children (Leonard & Wen, 2002).

Chromosome and Gene Abnormalities

Down Syndrome   Down syndrome is the most common chromosomal cause of mental retardation (Simonoff et al., 1999). Down syndrome is usually caused by a nondysjunction of the 21st chromosome from the mother. That is, the mother's 21st pair of chromosomes fails to separate during meiosis (cell division that occurs during the formation of reproductive cells). When this undivided pair is combined with the father's 21st chromosome, the child receives three copies of the 21st chromosome (thus the label **trisomy 21** that is also used to describe Down syndrome). In rare cases, Down syndrome is caused by the translocation of part of chromosome 21 onto chromosome 14 (Chapman & Hesketh, 2000). Either type of chromosomal damage has extensive influences on the developing brain of the fetus and infant, often resulting in a brain that is about 25% smaller than would be expected (Pennington & Bennetto, 1999).

Down syndrome occurs in about 1.5 of every 1,000 births. Because the chromosomal damage originates in the mother's egg cells in about four-fifths of all cases, the prevalence of Down syndrome is strongly related to maternal age (Simonoff et al., 1999). For example, estimates are that Down syndrome occurs in about 1 out of 1,000 births to mothers under the age of 33 and about 38 out of 1,000 births to mothers over the age of 44 (Trimble & Baiord, 1978).

Although infants with Down syndrome can develop normally during their first year, there is a progressive decline in their development after this, occasionally including the loss of previously developed skills (for example, a child who had started speaking single words may stop speaking altogether) (Chapman & Hesketh, 2000). A few children with Down syndrome develop average levels of intelligence, but most are in the mild to severe range of mental retardation, with an average IQ of about 50.

Children with Down syndrome exhibit particular impairments in **expressive language,** although they understand language (Nadel, 1999). Most of them show little interest in learning language, and those working with children who have Down syndrome must often struggle to get them to use language at all. Their speech usually consists of simple phrases, and they often have problems with articulation, making what little speech they have difficult to understand (Dodd & Thompson, 2001; Pennington & Bennetto, 1999). Their verbal short-term memory is also usually impaired, and it is often difficult for them even to repeat sentences they have just heard (Marcell & Weeks, 1988).

Children with Down syndrome are often described as very social, and as a group they present fewer behavioral problems than do children with other organically caused forms of mental retardation (Einfeld, Tonge, Turner, Parmenter, & Smith, 1999). They often focus their attention on people. For example, when given the opportunity to play with toys, they attend much more than other children to people who are near them than they do to the toys (Sigman, 1999). Many children with Down syndrome have better social skills than other children with mental retardation and make friends more easily (Walz & Benson, 2002).

Fragile X Syndrome   Fragile X syndrome is the most common cause of inherited mental retardation (Mazzocco, 2000). It is found in about 1 of 4,000 births in males and 1 in 8,000 births in females.

Fragile X syndrome is caused by a mutation on the long arm of the X chromosome (Mazzocco, 2000). This mutation is located in what is now called the **Fragile X mental retardation gene (FMR1)**. The FRM1 gene is composed partly of cytosine, thymine, and guanine sequences that are repeated in each gene between 6 and 54 times. The number of repeats is stable from one generation to the next. The mutation of this gene results in a greater number of repeats, and this number is unstable and can increase from one generation to the next. The greater number of repeats in the FMR1 gene appears to cause the outcomes associated with Fragile X syndrome, although the mechanism through which the gene produces the consequences is not understood (Simonoff et al., 1999).

When 55–200 repeats are present, rather than the normal 6–54 repeats, a gene is considered a **premutation.** When more than 200 repeats are present, the gene is considered to be fully mutated. Those with premutations experience no consequences from them. However, because the number of repeats in a premutation is unstable from one generation to the next, parents with premutations may give birth to a child with the full mutation. Children with the full mutation experience the negative consequences of Fragile X syndrome (Mazzocco, 2000).

The intensity of the consequences of Fragile X syndrome appears to be governed by the number of cells in a person's body that contain a fully mutated FMR1 gene. The number can vary substantially. Females are generally less affected than males because only one X chromosome is active in each cell. Because females have two X chromosomes, an X chromosome with a normal FRM1 gene is likely to be active in many cells that also contain an X chromosome with a fully mutated FRM1 gene, resulting in their having fewer affected cells. On the other hand, males have only one X chromosome, so all cells with an X chromosome with a fully mutated FRM1 gene will be affected (Mazzocco, 2000). Almost all males with Fragile X syndrome have cognitive impairments, and most of these are in the moderate to severe range. Only about half of females with the full mutation have mental retardation (Pennington & Bennetto, 1999).

Cognitive impairments are obvious in almost all affected boys by age 4 years. Their cognitive abilities plateau at about age 10 and then begin to decline. Consequently, after puberty many boys' cognitive impairments are more pronounced than they were before puberty. The reason for this decline is not well understood (Pennington & Bennetto, 1999). Girls show a more variable developmental path than do boys, although it is not clear why (Mazzocco, 2000).

Boys with Fragile X syndrome have particular impairments in expressive speech, although their verbal comprehension is as good as that of children with similar IQs (Belser & Sudhalter, 2001). They often speak very quickly, repeating themselves several times; and their speech is difficult to understand. Expressive language is somewhat less affected in girls (Mazzocco, 2000).

Children with Fragile X syndrome often exhibit behaviors suggesting high levels of social anxiety. This appears to be due to hyperarousal of the autonomic nervous system that causes much higher overall reactivity to social situations than other children experience (Belser & Sudhalter, 2001; Cohen, 1995). As a consequence, children with Fragile X syndrome are often socially withdrawn and can be difficult to engage in conversation or other social interactions (Bailey, Hatton, & Skinner, 1998).

Phenylketonuria   Phenylketonuria (PKU) is a disorder that results from a mutation of the phenylalanine hydroxylase (PAH) gene, which is found on the short arm of chromosome 12 (Dyer, 1999). The prevalence of PKU is estimated at 1 in 10,000 births among those of northern European ancestry, with a lower prevalence among those with other racial or ethnic ancestry (Simonoff et al., 1999).

The mutation of the PAH gene causes a lack of liver enzymes for metabolizing phenylalanine into tyrosine (**phenylalanine** is found in milk, cheese, eggs, and many other food proteins). The accumulating phenylalanine is instead metabolized into **phenylpyruvic acid** (DiLella & Woo, 1987). Phenylpyruvic acid interferes with the process of **myelination** of white matter in the central nervous system, and this interference causes the cognitive deficits in those with PKU (Dyer, 1999). PKU that is not treated usually results in severe mental retardation within several months of birth; and once the damage is done to the developing brain of an infant it is not reversible.

Fortunately, screening for PKU is possible soon after birth, and this is routinely done throughout the United States and many other countries (Alexander, 1998). Children with PKU must be placed on a phenylalanine-free diet to avoid the consequences of PKU. A phenylalanine-free diet requires avoiding many forms of protein. As is easy to imagine, this diet is often difficult to enforce once children reach the age where they can obtain food for themselves, and it is often seen as a considerable burden by children and their parents (Simonoff et al., 1999). (You may have wondered why some food labels, such as those on artificially sweetened soft drinks, include a statement that the food contains phenylalanine; this is done partly to warn those with PKU which foods to avoid.) The belief years ago was that after childhood brain development, the restricted diet could be relaxed. However, more recent evidence suggests that diets with phenylalanine can harm adults also, so current advice is that a person with PKU must remain on the restricted diet for life (Dyer, 1999).

Williams Syndrome   Williams syndrome is a disorder caused by genetic deletions on the 7th chromosome (Mervis & Klein-Tasman, 2000). Although its prevalence continues to be debated, a recent estimate puts it at 1 in 7,500 births (Stromme, Bjornstad, & Ramstad, 2002). The IQs of children with Williams syndrome range broadly, although about 75% are in the range of 50–70. Those with IQs in the average ranges often show significant learning disabilities (Mervis & Klein-Tasman, 2000). When compared with children of the same mental age, children with Williams syndrome show strengths in the areas of language and auditory memory; however, they exhibit particular delays in the areas of visual–spatial perception and construction. For example, Figure 11.6 shows a drawing of a bicycle by a child with Williams syndrome.

Notes from the Author: Difficulties with Visual–Spatial Skills

Those of us who do not have visual–spatial problems often find it difficult to comprehend the difficulties that those with significant problems face. It may seem unbelievable that a 9-year-old (or even a 4-year-old) would draw a picture of a bicycle that looks like the one in Figure 11.6. A test that I commonly give during psychological assessments of children is the Bender Visual–Motor Gestalt Test. In this test, children are asked to copy a variety of simple figures. For example, they might be asked to copy the top figure in Figure 11.7. Although most children can copy the figure accurately, some will produce a figure like the one shown at the bottom of Figure 11.7. I ask those who produce inaccurate figures if their drawings look like the figures I gave them. Some say that their drawings do not look like the figures; but even when I give them additional chances to draw the figures, they cannot make them look as they should. Others state (and appear to believe) that their inaccurate drawings do look like the figures I gave them. Imagine for a minute how difficult it must be for children with significant visual–spatial problems to function in our world—especially the world of school, where much of what we do involves looking at the figures we call *words*, which are really shapes put together, just like the figures they cannot copy.

Children with Williams syndrome are very social. They approach others, even strangers, more frequently than other children, and they are consistently outgoing and friendly (Gosch & Pankau, 1997). Despite this,

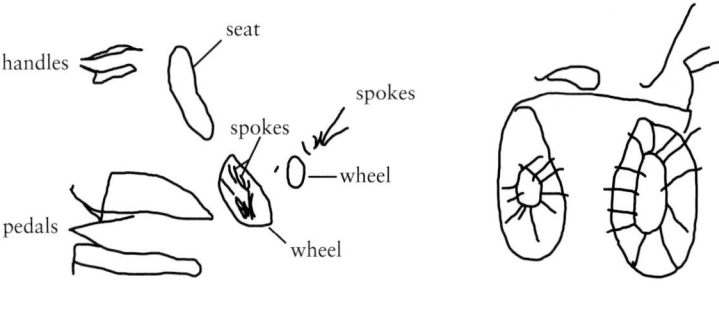

Age: 9 years 7 months   Age: 12 years 11 months

FIGURE 11.6   *Two Drawings of a Bicycle by the Same Girl with Williams Syndrome*

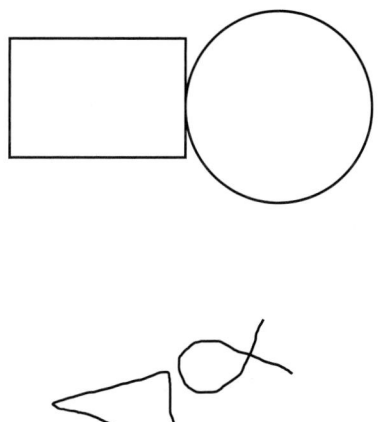

FIGURE 11.7   *An Item from the Bender Visual–Motor Gestalt Test*

they often have difficulty making friends. This may be related to their cognitive deficits or possibly to a level of outgoingness that other children find intrusive. It may also be due to their relatively high levels of hyperactivity, which other children may find annoying. Older children and adults with Williams syndrome often experience high levels of anxiety and say that they worry much of the time and have many fears (Gosch & Pankau, 1997).

Prader–Willi Syndrome   Prader–Willi syndrome is caused by abnormalities of the 15th chromosome. In about 65% of cases, this abnormality is due to several gene deletions from the paternal chromosome; in most remaining cases it is due to a person receiving both copies of chromosome 15 from the mother (Dimitropoulos et al., 2000). Prader–Willi syndrome affects about 1 in every 1,000 births (Murphy et al., 1998). Prader–Willi syndrome appears to depress cognitive functioning, although not all children with Prader–Willi syndrome have mental retardation. IQ generally ranges from low–average to the moderate levels of mental retardation. Children with Prader–Willi syndrome have particular deficits in visual organization.

The most striking feature of Prader–Willi syndrome is obesity. Children and adults with Prader–Willi syndrome are almost always hungry and are preoccupied with food. Eating problems are often evident by 2 years of age. Parents and other caregivers must expend considerable effort to limit the food consumed by children with Prader–Willi syndrome because their obesity can eventually become life-threatening (Dykens & Cassidy, 1996). In addition, children with Prader–Willi syndrome exhibit a variety of **compulsions,** many of which focus on obtaining and eating food. Skin picking is another common compulsion, which can result in frequent infections and permanent scarring. Children with Prader–Willi syndrome also exhibit many emotional problems. Many are described as emotionally labile, argumentative, stubborn, and irritable. They are quite sensitive and anxious, and they can cry and have their feelings hurt easily (Walz & Benson, 2002).

Angelman Syndrome   Angelman syndrome is caused by abnormalities in the same areas of the 15th chromosome as those causing Prader–Willi syndrome. In Angelman syndrome, however, the deletions come from the maternal chromosome (Murphy et al., 1998). Also similar to Prader–Willi syndrome, Angelman syndrome appears to affect about 1 in every 1,000 births. The cognitive impairments associated with Angelman syndrome are more severe than those associated with Prader–Willi syndrome, with most children experiencing mental retardation in the severe to profound range. Most children with Angelman syndrome are unable to speak, have somewhat atypical facial features, and are frequently described as having what appears to be a happy expression on their face (Oliver, Demetriades, & Hall, 2002). Most children with Angelman syndrome laugh excessively and in situations in which other children would not laugh.

Environmental Toxins

Several environmental toxins cause mental retardation. In high doses toxins can cause severe or profound mental retardation; in smaller doses they may have a negative but less noticeable influence on the child (such as a loss of 10 IQ points).

Lead   Lead poisoning occurs when a child ingests a large amount of lead during a relatively short time. The effects can be severe and permanent (see Figure 11.8). Lower levels of lead ingestion produce milder but still noticeable effects on cognitive functioning, such as lower IQ scores and reading problems (Needleman et al., 1979).

Lead has been used in many industrial applications for decades. Several decades ago lead was used as an additive in gasoline and paint, was present

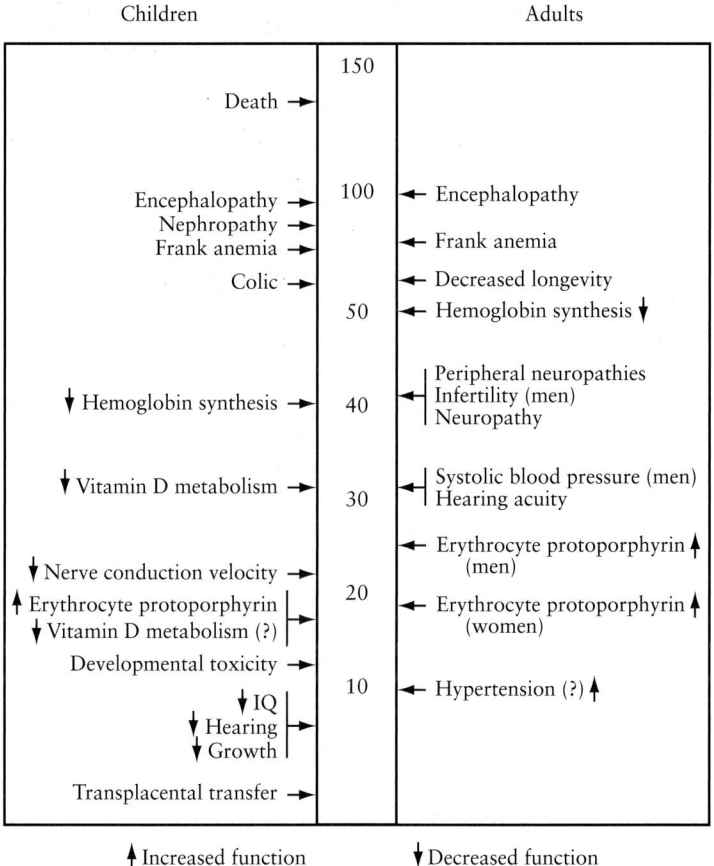

FIGURE 11.8   *Effects of Inorganic Lead (μPb/dl) in Children and Adults—*
Lowest Observable Adverse Effect Levels

in water pipes and the solder that held the pipes together, and was a component of food cans (Baroff & Olley, 1999). What is most significant about these uses of lead is that they resulted in small amounts of lead being expelled into the air, drinking water, and food, ensuring that many people of all ages regularly ingested small amounts of lead. Most of these sources of lead have been phased out of our environment. This has significantly cut the number of children with levels of lead in their bodies that have been associated with cognitive impairments—which, as determined by the Centers for Disease Control and Prevention (CDC), is 10 micrograms of lead in a decaliter of blood. Studies in the late 1970s found that 88% of children had blood lead levels higher than 10 micrograms/decaliter. The same type of studies in the late 1980s found 9% of children with this level and 4% in the mid-1990s (Centers for Disease Control and Prevention, 2001).

Notes from the Author: Yes, You Are Smarter than Your Parents

Children born in the 1950s and 1960s have, on average, higher concentrations of lead in their bodies than people born in the 1980s and 1990s. Consequently, it is probable that your parents experienced a more negative influence of lead on their cognitive abilities than you have. Many parents of teenagers and young adults complain that their children think they are smarter than their parents. But this is probably true—you *are* smarter than your parents. (To be more accurate, your generation experienced fewer negative cognitive consequences of lead exposure than your parents' generation did.) Be sure to let your parents know this at an opportune time.

Recent research has shown, however, that blood lead levels of less than 10 micrograms/decaliter can influence IQ and that the IQ decline for each 1-microgram increase of lead is higher at low levels than at high levels (an increase from 2 to 3 micrograms produces more IQ impairment than does an increase from 12 to 13 micrograms; Canfield et al., 2003). This suggests that the levels of lead about which we should be concerned are lower than the current CDC standards, and that any level above zero may impair a person's IQ.

Although lead is no longer present in most goods produced today, significant amounts of lead remain in the environment. The primary sources of this residual lead are dirt in urban areas (largely from the lead in gasoline exhaust that settled on the ground) and lead-based paint in homes that have not been repainted in many years. Consequently, children in low-income families, particularly those in inner cities, are at risk for lead exposure. The lead enters their bodies when they put contaminated dirt in their mouths, when they breathe dust from the dirt or the paint, or when they put their fingers in their mouths after crawling in areas where small bits of paint have flaked off the walls (Mendola et al., 2002).

Mercury   Mercury is ingested primarily through seafood (Mendola et al., 2002). Mercury is used in several industrial applications; if it is discharged into water it can accumulate in the tissue of predator fish as they eat smaller fish or organisms exposed to mercury in the water. When humans eat these fish, the mercury is absorbed through the digestive tract and settles in the brain and the central nervous system.

Several incidents of mercury poisoning from eating fish with high levels of mercury have been reported in Japan. Mothers who ate the fish gave birth to babies with profound mental retardation, blindness, deafness, and cerebral palsy (Mendola et al., 2002). The effects of low levels of mercury on cognitive function are less clear; but some studies have shown moderate effects on several measures of cognitive functioning, such as memory, attention, and information processing (National Research Council, 2000).

Alcohol   Alcohol ingested by a woman during pregnancy can have many effects on the developing fetus, but its effects on fetuses are quite varied even when their mothers ingest similar amounts of alcohol. Although the mechanisms through which alcohol affects a fetus are not well understood, one possibility is that alcohol impairs circulation through the umbilical cord, which can reduce the oxygen reaching the fetus, thus impeding brain development (Baroff & Olley, 1999).

Women who frequently drink large amounts of alcohol (often defined as 4 ounces of hard liquor or its equivalent per day) during pregnancy may give birth to children with **fetal alcohol syndrome.** Children with fetal alcohol syndrome experience a wide range of problems, including small size, small brain mass (which may account for their many cognitive problems), delayed motor and language development, and hyperactivity (Baroff & Olley, 1999). However, fetal alcohol syndrome is reported in only about 250 per 10,000 births of mothers who drink large amounts of alcohol, and it is unclear why some children experience fetal alcohol syndrome and others do not. Perhaps genetic vulnerability makes some fetuses more susceptible to the effects of alcohol.

The influences on the developing fetus of lower levels of alcohol consumption are less clear. Fetal vulnerability to alcohol is particularly high during the earliest stages of pregnancy—often before a woman realizes she is pregnant (Russell & Skinner, 1988). Frequent ingestion by the mother of 1.5 ounces of hard liquor or its equivalent during the earliest stage of

Maternal behaviors can significantly influence children's cognitive abilities.

pregnancy appears to put her fetus at risk for cognitive problems, although these problems occur in only a small percentage of children whose mothers drink this amount. It appears that occasional high levels of alcohol consumption are potentially more damaging to a fetus during the first and second trimester than is moderate, ongoing use (Baroff & Olley, 1999).

Nutritional Deficits

Prenatal malnutrition or malnutrition during the first few years of life can harm cognitive functioning, but apparently only when the malnutrition is severe—the type of malnutrition that is seldom seen in industrialized countries. The most sensitive times for malnutrition's influence on cognitive functioning are during the third trimester and the first six months of life, when important spurts in brain development occur (Baroff & Olley, 1999). Moderate levels of malnutrition can impair cognitive functioning, although this might be reversible if adequate nutrition is supplied afterward. In essence, the brain appears to be able to "catch up" in its development once nutrition becomes adequate.

Infectious Diseases

The two most common infections that cause significant cognitive impairments in children are **bacterial meningitis** and **bacterial encephalitis** (Baroff & Olley, 1999). Meningitis is a swelling of the membranes that line the brain, and encephalitis is a swelling of the brain itself. Significant fever and the pressure within the brain caused by the swelling cause permanent damage that can devastate motor and cognitive abilities. These infections can cause children with normal IQs to suddenly have severe or profound mental retardation.

A variety of infectious diseases that impair brain development and cognitive abilities can be transmitted from a mother to her fetus. These diseases often have their most devastating influences during the first trimester of pregnancy because the brain in its early development lacks the ability to repair tissue damage, remove abnormal cells, or compensate for damage (Baroff & Olley, 1999). Rubella and syphilis are two diseases that can be transferred easily from the mother to the fetus. Many infected fetuses do not survive, and many of those that do survive have several physical and cognitive problems (Baroff & Olley, 1999).

Injuries

Head injuries can permanently impair cognitive functioning. Falls, such as from bicycles, out of windows, or off trampolines, are the primary source of these injuries (Alexander, 1998).

Mental Retardation with No Discernible Pathologic Basis

As described by Zigler (1967) and others, children who have mental retardation with no discernible pathologic basis have not experienced any identifiable organic disease or problem; rather, their cognitive and adaptive abilities are at the low end of the normal distribution of abilities found

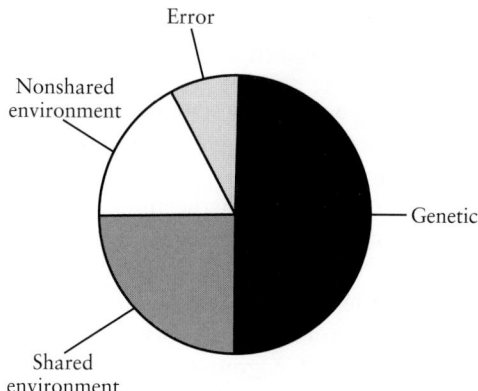

Error

Nonshared
environment

Genetic

Shared
environment

FIGURE 11.9   *Influences on Intelligence*

among children. It is generally acknowledged that genetic and environmental influences result in some children being at the low end of the distribution of intelligence, although the debate about the relative contributions of genes and the environment has been long and sometimes rancorous (Plomin et al., 2001).

As noted in the chapter about quantitative behavioral genetics, a variety of strategies exist for unraveling the relative influences of genes and environment on intelligence and other individual characteristics (see Figure 11.9). Based on the outcomes of family, twin, and adoption studies, most researchers today accept that about 50% of the influence on an individual's intelligence comes from his or her genes and about 40% comes from his or her environment; the remaining 10% is usually assigned to error of measurement (Plomin et al., 2001; Simonoff et al., 1999).

Current belief is that the genetic influence on intelligence is the sum of the influence of many different genes (Plomin et al., 2001). Genes can further influence children's IQ because they are related to the environments in which children are raised (this is a genotype–environment correlation). For example, parents who have lower levels of intelligence tend to have less income than those with higher levels of intelligence. Their income often restricts the environments in which they can raise their children: They may be able to afford housing only in neighborhoods that are problematic socially (high crime rates, for example) and physically (higher levels of lead and so on). Their children may spend considerable time in lower-quality child care during the day because the parents must work long hours; later these children may be educated in schools with fewer resources and more problems.

Although about 40% of a child's IQ is influenced by his or her environment, current estimates suggest that a meaningful amount of this influence comes from the child's prenatal environment—such as through the influences of the mother's nutrition and the intake of alcohol and other toxins (Plomin et al., 2001). Consequently, between genetic influences and prenatal environment influence, a substantial portion of the influences on a child's IQ are present at birth.

Although some may argue that the strong genetic influence on children's IQs means that those who have mental retardation are doomed to it by their genetic heritage, this is simply not true. Recall that a large percentage of children with mental retardation are in the mild mental retardation range. Therefore, the influences of postnatal environments, although not huge, may affect the extent to which many children have levels of intelligence in the low–average range or the mental retardation range.

Many environmental factors can influence a child's level of intelligence. Of particular importance is early cognitive stimulation (Drew et al., 1992). Stimulation early in a child's life can affect the number of neural connections in the brain, which can have a meaningful influence on cognitive abilities. Children who live in an environment with little cognitive stimulation, perhaps lying in a crib for much of the day or sitting quietly in a room, may eventually have lower cognitive abilities than they would have had if they experienced regular stimulation. Chronic poor nutrition and poor health care, issues that are usually associated with poverty, can also impede brain development and damage cognitive skills. Poor-quality preschool care and poor-quality schooling can influence a child's educational attainment, which can be reflected in poor scores on intelligence tests.

Key Concepts

- Two groups of children with mental retardation exist: those with mental retardation of known organic cause and those with mental retardation with no discernible pathologic basis.
- One category of known organic causes of mental retardation comprises genetic and chromosomal abnormalities. These disorders include Down syndrome, Fragile X syndrome, phenylketonuria (PKU), Williams syndrome, Praeder–Willi syndrome, and Angelman syndrome.
- Environmental toxins such as lead, mercury, and alcohol can cause severe mental retardation in high doses and appear to reduce cognitive abilities even at low doses.
- Extreme nutritional deficits in a pregnant woman or infant can impair the child's cognitive functioning, although the cognitive abilities of a child who receives adequate nutrition after this may improve.
- Infectious diseases contracted by a mother while pregnant can significantly affect her child's cognitive abilities. Bacterial meningitis and encephalitis can have devastating effects on the cognitive abilities of children who contract them.
- The etiology of mental retardation with no discernible pathologic basis is related to genes and environment. Current estimates are that about 50% of a child's cognitive abilities are due to genetic influences, with about 40% due to environmental influences (the other 10% is usually related to error of measurement).

Prevention

Prevention is particularly important in the field of mental retardation because it is usually not possible to reverse the cognitive impairments associated with mental retardation through treatment later in a child's life (Alexander, 1998). Prevention efforts with the two groups of children with mental retardation differ in important ways. Prevention of mental retardation of known organic cause is accomplished by avoiding the conditions that cause mental retardation; the outcomes of these prevention programs can be dramatic. Reducing the spread of bacterial meningitis, for example, can keep many children with normal levels of intelligence from suddenly having intelligence in the severely mentally retarded range. Preventing mental retardation of no discernible pathologic basis, however, involves different strategies and outcomes. Recall once again that IQ is a continuous variable, with most of those with an IQ below 70 considered to have mental retardation. Consequently, by intervening with a child in a way that raises his or her IQ from 67 to 75, a case of mental retardation is technically prevented. Although the benefit to a child of moderately increased intelligence can be noticeable, the benefit is not as dramatic as that seen when mental retardation due to a known organic cause is prevented. (I am not saying that efforts to help children who are at risk for mental retardation of no known pathologic basis are not appropriate—they are, and we should be doing more of this work because even moderate improvements in a child's cognitive abilities can improve his or her life.)

Mental Retardation of Known Organic Cause

Significant strides have been made in preventing many organically based causes of mental retardation. Some of these causes have been virtually eliminated in the United States and other industrialized countries. For example, required screening for PKU at birth and implementation of a phenylalanine-free diet for infants and young children have dramatically reduced the number of cases of mental retardation caused by PKU. In addition, vaccines to prevent rubella and medicines to cure syphilis have reduced mental retardation from these causes to just a few cases each year in the United States (Alexander, 1998).

Better understanding of the influences of maternal diet during pregnancy has also decreased cases of mental retardation. For example, the discovery of the importance of folic acid in the diets of pregnant women has led to fewer cases of birth defects and cognitive problems. Alexander (1998) notes that the value of dietary folic acid is highest during the early days of pregnancy—often before a woman realizes she is pregnant—and suggests that a bottle of vitamin tablets containing folic acid makes a wonderful wedding gift. In addition, clearer understanding of the negative consequences of moderate or heavy doses of alcohol on a developing fetus has influenced the behaviors of many pregnant women.

Changes in public policy have also reduced the number of children experiencing mental retardation. For example, legal prohibitions against lead in gasoline, paint, water pipes, and food cans have reduced the number of children with damaging levels of lead in their bodies from about 10 million in the 1970s to about 900,000 in 1996 (Alexander, 1998). Widespread use of bicycle helmets for children over the past few decades—often encouraged by local laws or school rules—has reduced the number of cases of mental retardation due to head injury.

Improved early prenatal diagnosis of many birth defects and chromosomal and genetic abnormalities through procedures such as ultrasound and amniocentesis has given many more families information that they can use to decide whether to end a pregnancy from which a child with significant cognitive impairments may emerge. Although these efforts are controversial because they may involve an abortion, they give families options they once did not have—including the option to prepare themselves for the birth of a child with cognitive impairments. Alexander (1998), for example, notes that when the ability to detect Down syndrome in fetuses first became available, there was a decline in the number of births of children with Down syndrome; but these births have been increasing lately because more older women are becoming pregnant and then deciding to give birth to children they know will have Down syndrome.

Mental Retardation of No Discernible Pathologic Basis

Strategies to prevent or reduce the cognitive impairments of children who are at risk for experiencing mental retardation of no discernible pathologic basis focus on giving them cognitive and social stimulation early in their lives. A variety of local, state, and national programs have been created to do this—the best known being the national Head Start program. Many of these programs demonstrate significant early gains in IQ among the children who participate in them; however, most of these gains disappear as the children mature toward school age (Guralnick, 1998). Critics of these programs use this information to suggest that they are not effective. Others argue that the lack of enduring influence of these programs is due to their seldom being pursued with enough intensity for a long enough period (Blair, 1999). More detailed information about these programs is given next.

Key Concepts

- Prevention of mental retardation is important because cognitive impairments usually cannot be reversed once they occur.
- Strategies to prevent mental retardation of known organic cause focus on preventing the conditions that cause cognitive impairments, such as preventing rubella or syphilis, treating PKU from birth, and reducing the ingestion of toxins by mothers and young children.
- Strategies to prevent mental retardation of no discernible pathologic basis focus on early interventions for children and their parents to increase the stimulation that the children experience.

Educational Interventions

Early Intervention

Early intervention comprises services to children and their families during the child's preschool years, generally from birth to 5 years. Whereas few early intervention programs existed 30 years ago, under federal and state laws they have grown dramatically in the past three decades. In 1997 about 750,000 children with a wide range of disabilities, or who were identified as being at risk for mental retardation or another developmental disability, were enrolled in publicly funded early intervention programs (Beirne-Smith et al., 2002).

Early intervention programs have been mandated by federal law since 1986, when Congress extended services that had previously been available to school-age children with disabilities to those ages 3–5 years (Beirne-Smith et al., 2002). Current federal law requires that all states provide services for 3- to 5-year-olds with an identified disability and mandates federal funding for states wishing to provide services to children from birth to age 2 who have an identified disability, have a condition associated with the development of a disability (like very low birth weight), or who are considered at substantial risk for a developmental delay because of social conditions (such as living in poverty). Through these programs, children learn basic cognitive skills, social skills, and self-care skills. The programs also provide cognitive stimulation, help children develop gross and fine motor skills, and teach school readiness skills (like sitting quietly and listening to a story) (Ramey & Ramey, 1999).

Federal law requires that all early intervention programs have strong family involvement, and this is particularly emphasized in programs for children from birth to 2 years. Each child aged from birth to 2 years enrolled in an early intervention program must have an **individual family service plan (IFSP)** (Beirne-Smith et al., 2002). IFSPs identify the needs and resources of individual families and specify how needed services for the families will be obtained. The direct involvement of parents is beneficial in many ways. It helps parents learn skills they can use with all their children; it impresses on parents that they are ultimately the ones responsible for raising their children; and it gives parents a sense of accomplishment that can bolster their self-efficacy and self-esteem, thereby enhancing their parenting.

Evaluations of early interventions have shown significant improvements in the children who participate (Ramey & Ramey, 1999). IQ scores of many children were higher at the end of the intervention than were the scores of the children receiving regular community services, although the IQ differences narrowed as the children progressed through school. Some studies have reported other benefits of early intervention programs: Children were referred for special education services less frequently, were retained less often, dropped out of school less often, and were arrested less often as adolescents and young adults. Consequently, these studies show that even without enduring influences on children's IQ, early intervention programs can have a meaningful influence on children's lives.

Elementary and High School Education

As noted earlier, before the 1970s many children with mental retardation or other disabilities were educated in separate schools or at home, or they received no education. The landmark **Education for All Handicapped Children Act (PL 94-142)**, passed in 1975, changed the entire process through which disabled children are educated. Although PL 94-142 has been amended and clarified over the years by additional federal laws and is now called the Individuals with Disabilities Education Act (IDEA), its fundamental components remain unchanged: Every child who is disabled has the right to education that is free (all services must be provided by school districts free of charge), appropriate (services are based on the needs of the individual child rather than on what the school district prefers to provide), and provided in the **least restrictive environment** (one that as much as possible resembles the environment provided to all children). In addition, this education must be provided from ages 3 years to 21 years—longer than the period mandated for children without disabilities. Imagine the changes that this law engendered. No longer were those with mental retardation and other disabilities to be provided *less* education by their public schools than nondisabled children—they were now to be provided *more* education. No longer were they to be hidden away—they were now to be educated in their communities and given the additional help they needed to succeed. Now and then Congress passes a law that has a major and enduring influence on our society, and PL 94-142 is one of those laws.

Vital components of PL 94-142 were its requirements that an **individual education plan (IEP)** be created by a team of educational and mental health experts for each disabled child; that parents have a right to be involved in the development and approval of the IEP; and that the IEP be updated regularly (Patton et al., 2000). The IEP specifies the educational, self-care, and social goals for each student and the setting in which the student will be educated. At regular intervals the student's progress toward these goals is reviewed, and the goals are modified if needed.

Several educational settings are available for students with disabilities. From the least to the most restrictive, these settings follow (Beirne-Smith et al., 2002):

- *Regular classes:* Students with disabilities can be enrolled in a regular class. Often a child in a regular class will receive special services to meet his or her needs. Special instructional materials can be provided, such as reading materials designed to interest students with limited reading skills. A special education teacher or consultant may spend part of the day in the regular classroom, working individually with the child on specific academic tasks or consulting with the classroom teacher on the best strategies for educating the child.
- *Resource room:* Students may spend part of each day in a regular classroom and part in a separate **resource room,** where they receive specialized instruction from special education teachers. For example, a

student with particular difficulties in reading or math may receive instruction in the resource room in these subjects, and then rejoin the regular classroom for other subjects.

- *Separate class:* Students who cannot participate in any regular classroom activities can be assigned to a special education class for the entire school day. Typically these classes have fewer students, allowing special education teachers to work individually with students.
- *Separate residential facilities:* Students whose disabilities are sufficiently severe, or who have behavioral or medical conditions that make it impossible for them to be cared for adequately at home, may live in a special residential facility where their medical, social, and educational needs can receive constant attention.

The primary focus of research in this area has been whether inclusion in regular classrooms benefits children with mental retardation. Research in this area has usually compared the academic and social achievements of children who have mental retardation and who are in separate classes or separate schools with those who spend all day or most of the day in regular classes. Overall, the research shows that (1) there is little difference between the academic achievement of children in separate classes and those integrated into regular classes and (2) the social skills and abilities of children integrated into regular classes are higher than the social skills and abilities of those in separate classes (Fisher & Meyer, 2002; Gottlieb, Alter, & Gottlieb, 1991; Villa & Thousand, 2002). In addition, it does not appear that having children with mental retardation in their class is detrimental to the education of children without mental retardation (Villa & Thousand, 2002).

Many advocates for children with mental retardation and other disabilities continue to press for greater inclusion of disabled children in regular classes. They assert that there is little evidence that separate classes provide superior education to children with disabilities and some evidence that their social abilities are enhanced in regular classes. They also point out that educating a child in a separate class or facility is more expensive than including a child in a regular class. Others argue that the pressures on regular classroom teachers are already high and that they often do not have enough time to spend on individual work with their current students. Adding children with mental retardation to the regular classroom, particularly those with moderate to severe retardation, would further stress teachers. This could hinder education for all, especially the children with mental retardation who are likely to need more individual attention than the other students (Gottlieb et al., 1991; Villa & Thousand, 2002).

Transition to Adulthood

For all of us, formal schooling ends at some point. Helping children with mental retardation make the transition from school to work or another activity is an important component of their educational program. Children with mild mental retardation may develop the skills for a variety of jobs after they leave school. Those with more severe forms of mental retardation may be able to hold some jobs, possibly with ongoing support, or may be employed in workshops specially designed for them.

Federal law now mandates that the IEP of children 14 years and older include information about their transition from school into work or another activity (Patton et al., 2000). The interests and skills of the students, and information from the students and their parents and other family members, are critical components in determining the goals of transition and how those transitions occur (Beirne-Smith et al., 2002).

Key Concepts

- Early interventions are mandated for disabled children aged 3 to 5, and states may provide services to those aged from birth to 2 years.
- Families must be a center of attention in all services for children from birth to 2 years, and each family must be given an individual family service plan.
- Evaluations of early intervention programs show that they can have lasting effects on children, even though the influence on their IQ appears to be short-lived.
- Elementary school children with disabilities may be educated in a regular classroom, receive resource room support, be educated in a separate class, or be educated in a separate facility. All children must be educated in the least restrictive environment that meets their educational needs.
- All children with disabilities must receive an individual education plan (IEP), which is updated regularly.
- The transition to life after school is an important component of the educational plan of each child with a disability.

Other Therapeutic Interventions

Psychopathology and Other Problem Behaviors
Psychopathology

As already noted, children with mental retardation experience other forms of psychopathology, such as depression and anxiety, more frequently than other children. Consequently, assessing and treating comorbid disorders is an important component of the overall services given to children with mental retardation (American Academy of Child and Adolescent Psychiatry, 1999).

Psychological treatment for children with mental retardation can take the same form as that provided to other children of the same mental age (American Academy of Child and Adolescent Psychiatry, 1999). School-age children or adolescents with mild mental retardation, for example, may benefit from the type of play therapy that would be appropriate for younger children. Play therapy may help a child express thoughts and feelings and can be the foundation for a therapist to modify irrational thoughts or help the child express feelings in appropriate ways.

Medication for comorbid disorders may be appropriate, and it appears that medication for disorders such as depression and anxiety are as effective with children who have mental retardation as they are for other children (American Academy of Child and Adolescent Psychiatry, 1999). Side effects of medication may be more pronounced in children with mental retardation, so special attention needs to be paid to them.

Other Problem Behaviors

Problem behaviors in children with mental retardation can develop for a variety of reasons, just as they do for other children. In addition, children with mental retardation may not have the cognitive skills to notice when their behavior has become problematic or may not be able to extricate themselves from difficult situations as easily as other children; so their problem behaviors may have greater consequences.

Most children with mild mental retardation can benefit from the same types of interventions for problem behaviors as other children (American Academy of Child and Adolescent Psychiatry, 1999). Counseling by parents, teachers, or mental health professionals can help them learn to express emotions and needs in ways other than through problem behavior. Behavioral interventions, such as providing positive reinforcement for socially appropriate behaviors, can help shift behaviors in more appropriate directions.

Behavioral interventions are the primary strategy for assisting children with severe forms of mental retardation, often using a strategy called **applied behavioral analysis** (Mace, Lalli, Lalli, & Shea, 1993; Pyles & Bailey, 1990). Applied behavioral analysis involves an initial assessment of the antecedents and consequences of the child's problem behavior. The assessment might show, for example, that the child engages in problem behavior when left alone, when required to attend physical education classes, or just after recess. The assessment might also show that certain behaviors of others reinforce the problem behavior; for example, a teacher or parent might provide more attention to a child when she acts out, or a child may be allowed to remain in the classroom if he acts out when told that he must go to the gym for physical education. The next step in applied behavioral analysis is to change the environmental conditions both before and after situations in which problem behaviors occur. A therapist may consult with a teacher or parents to create a new set of responses to the child's behavior that gradually shape the behavior to be more socially appropriate. For example, a teacher might spend individual time with a child while she is behaving and might ignore the child when she is misbehaving. The child who acts out before physical education might receive reinforcement each time he attends physical education without acting out and might be required to spend extra time in physical education when he acts out.

Self-Injurious Behavior

Self-injurious behavior (SIB) is among the most perplexing and serious behavior that mental health professionals treat because the reasons for its occurrence are often unclear and it can produce permanent physical damage and death in severe cases (Mace et al., 1993). In addition, children who exhibit serious levels of SIB are at risk for placement in an institution—isolating them from family and other members of their community (Thompson, Authier, & Ruma, 1994). SIB consists of a wide range of behaviors, including "head banging (with hands or against objects); self-biting; striking other parts of the body with hands or fists; self-scratching; gouging with fingernails in eyes, ears, mouth, throat, nose, or rectum; striking body parts with knees, shins, toes, heels or balls of feet against hard surfaces; and swallowing harmful substances" (Thompson et al., 1994, p. 80).

Children with mental retardation are at higher risk for SIB than are other children, and those with more severe forms of mental retardation are at the highest risk. For example, a large-scale study of people receiving services for mental retardation in California found that 4% of those with mild mental retardation, 7% of those with moderate retardation, 15% of those with severe retardation, and 25% of those with profound retardation engaged in frequent self-injury (Borthwick Duffy, 1994).

The causes of the initial development of SIB remain unclear. One possibility is that the genetic abnormalities that have caused some forms of mental retardation also cause SIB (MacLean, Stone, & Brown, 1994). Other explanations focus on learning: A child may engage in a variety of behaviors in a random way, and if reinforced for SIB engage in it more frequently.

Carr (1977) suggested three reasons for the maintenance and amplification of SIB once it has occurred: positive reinforcement, negative reinforcement, and sensory reinforcement. In the positive reinforcement model, the child receives something (often attention) when engaged in SIB, and this reinforces the SIB. For example, Pyles and Bailey (1990) described a case of a boy with profound mental retardation living in an institution who began injuring himself by falling out of his wheelchair. He received attention from the staff after he had fallen out of the wheelchair, but he was mostly left alone when he was sitting in the wheelchair appropriately; so his SIB increased. In the negative reinforcement model, a child learns that some aversive stimulus ends when he or she engages in SIB. For example, a child with mental retardation may engage in SIB during medical procedures until the procedures are stopped—thus escaping the procedures through SIB (Mace et al., 1993). In the sensory reinforcement model, the child experiences certain types of internal sensory reinforcement for his or her behavior. One theory, for example, is that the pain associated with SIB may release opiates in a child's brain, and this opiate release can reinforce SIB. Alternatively, a child who feels overwhelmed with sensory input may engage in SIB to focus his or her attention, thus feeling less overwhelmed.

Treating SIB is complicated because SIB has often been reinforced for a long time before attempts to correct it are made. In addition, because severe SIB can be life-threatening, rapid treatment is often important. The most common treatment involves applied behavioral analysis, which was described in the previous section.

Behavioral interventions for SIB can be conceptualized as involving extinction, positive reinforcement, or punishment (Pyles & Bailey, 1990). Extinction is based on the observation that behaviors that are not reinforced weaken over time. Thus one strategy is to stop caregivers from responding to SIB, with the lack of response causing extinction of the SIB. In cases of mild SIB or when the SIB has just begun, extinction can be a useful intervention. The problem with this approach is that the length of time required for extinction can be quite long, particularly when the SIB has been repeatedly reinforced in the past, and a child may do considerable harm to himself or herself before extinction occurs.

Interventions involving positive reinforcement involve two types:

- Reinforcing other behaviors so that a child does not need to engage in SIB to receive reinforcement, which is commonly called **differential reinforcement of other behaviors (DRO)**.
- Reinforcing behavior that is incompatible with the SIB, which is commonly called **differential reinforcement of incompatible behavior (DRI)**.

For example, in the example of the boy in the wheelchair, when the staff reinforced him for sitting in the wheelchair appropriately, they were providing DRI because sitting in the wheelchair is incompatible with falling out of it. Providing DRO or DRI is generally seen as a benevolent way of treating SIB; unfortunately, by themselves DRO and DRI are seldom effective (Pyles & Bailey, 1990). Children whose SIB has been reinforced for a long time are slow to change it, and children with mental retardation may be slower than others to recognize the new reinforcements and change their behaviors.

Punishment involves providing one of a variety of aversive consequences when a child engages in SIB. Mists of water in the face, aversive tastes such as lemon juice, aversive aromas such as ammonia, and mild electric shocks have all been used to reduce the occurrence of SIB. An advantage of using punishment is that it often reduces the frequency of the targeted SIB quickly, so the punishment can often end after a short period. However, SIB often returns or changes into other unwanted behavior after punishment ends, so punishment by itself seldom creates the permanent behavioral changes that are sought (Pyles & Bailey, 1990). Punishment is also very controversial. Ethical and moral questions arise when we punish children and adults who may not have the cognitive capacity to understand the motivations of their behaviors. Also, the short-term effectiveness of punishment can result in its overuse if care is not taken to prevent this. For example, if one SIB is stopped through punishment and another form of SIB starts a few days later, then that form of SIB might be stopped through punishment. If another form starts a few days later, punishment can be used for it. Soon a child's life may consist largely of punishment.

Medications have been used successfully in some cases of SIB. Medications seem most effective in cases where the sensory stimulation that a child is receiving from SIB maintains the SIB. For example, several drugs that block the effect of opiates in the brain have been used to treat cases of SIB. Without the reinforcing qualities of the opiate that is released by the SIB, the SIB is often extinguished (Thompson et al., 1994).

Most successful strategies for reducing SIB involve careful analysis of individual children's behaviors and a complex array of interventions. Punishment may be used to achieve an initial reduction in SIB, but this must almost always be followed by positive reinforcement to teach other behaviors (including DRO and DRI) and increased attention to the child's needs—some of which may have been expressed through the SIB. Medication may be useful in reducing the sensory reinforcement of SIB in some cases; but again, understanding and responding to the child's need for increased sensory input in some cases, or managing excessive sensory input in others, is an essential component of treating the child.

Family Training and Support

To parent any child effectively, a parent must have a sense of the child's capabilities at any age, the rate at which children of that age should be expected to learn, and the appropriate strategies for helping a child learn. Because children with mental retardation often learn in different ways and at a slower pace than other children, and because the capabilities of children with various disorders differ (for example, the capabilities of children with Down syndrome differ from those with Fragile X syndrome), parents often need special instruction to help them understand the capabilities of their children (Baroff & Olley, 1999). In addition, observing the slow development of their children can be frustrating and demoralizing for parents, which can impede their motivation to work closely with them. Understanding the rate at which their children can learn, and that their children are progressing at a rate that is expected, can provide comfort and encouragement to parents and other family members.

It often helps parents to receive specialized training on strategies for working with their children at home—teaching self-care skills such as toileting, brushing teeth, and bathing; helping their children develop or strengthen language skills; and reinforcing educational programs that the children receive in school (Harris, Alessandri, & Gill, 1991). Educators or specialists working through schools or other community agencies can provide this training. Parent education often includes instruction in basic behavioral interventions. They learn strategies for reinforcing appropriate behavior and extinguishing or punishing problem behavior. They may learn how to break a complex task into small steps and provide appropriate reinforcement as the child progresses through the steps. For example, learning to use the toilet requires a variety of steps: recognizing physical sensations indicating the need to use the toilet, going to the bathroom, opening the toilet lid or getting the seat in place, sitting on the seat appropriately, and so forth. A parent working with a child on this skill can learn to teach the child each step and reinforce the child each time he or she completes a step appropriately.

Notes from the Author: Teaching a New Task

Most children learn many self-care skills by observing and copying others. Many children with mental retardation have limited abilities to do this, so they need to be taught in a step-by-step way to perform many tasks that most of us complete without thinking. To get a sense of how challenging it can be to teach many self-care skills, try breaking down a behavior, such as brushing your teeth, into the specific steps that must be completed. List each of these steps, and then ask a friend to follow them exactly as written. You might leave out many steps if you are not careful. For example, if you write "Squeeze toothpaste onto the brush" without first writing "Remove cap from toothpaste," your friend will not be able to get any toothpaste on the brush. If you write "Remove cap from toothpaste" and then "Squeeze toothpaste tube to put toothpaste on brush," perhaps your friend will squeeze *lots* of toothpaste onto the brush, the basin, and everywhere else. Trying this with a few basic personal care skills can help you appreciate some of the challenges that many parents of children with mental retardation face.

Parent education often focuses on the mother because she is more likely to be available during the day for instruction (Harris et al., 1991). Although this can be more convenient for those providing the education, it is important to consider roles that the father or other caregivers can take, or they may become peripheral in the care of the child. Siblings can receive some training and can help teach their sibling skills. This can give them a sense of accomplishment and a sense of being helpful to their sibling and family. However, it is important that the siblings not feel overwhelmed by their responsibilities and that these responsibilities not interfere extensively with the siblings' own education and peer relationships.

Families that are functioning effectively provide better environments for all family members. Because families with a child who has mental retardation face stresses that can impair their functioning, it is important for them to develop strategies to help each family member cope effectively with stress (Heiman, 2002). Parents may need to develop strategies to attend to the needs of all siblings; and each spouse may need to develop sensitivity to whether the other spouse is experiencing excessive stress, as well as strategies for handling this stress.

Key Concepts

- Many children with mental retardation experience other forms of psychopathology, such as depression and anxiety. Therapeutic strategies that work with other children of the same mental age appear to be appropriate for children with mental retardation.
- Children with mental retardation may engage in problematic behaviors for several reasons, including expressing needs. Applied behavioral analysis can be used to understand these behaviors and design behavioral interventions to eliminate them.
- Self-injurious behavior is a particularly difficult behavior to treat. A combination of punishment and reinforcement (including DRO and DRI) can reduce the frequency of self-injurious behavior.
- Educating parents to help them work effectively with the strengths and limitations of their children is an important part of interventions for children with mental retardation and their families.
- Support is important for families to help them cope with the worry and stress often associated with having a child with mental retardation.

CHAPTER GLOSSARY

Adaptive functioning is "the collection of conceptual, social, and practical skills that have been learned by people in order to function in their everyday lives" (American Association on Mental Retardation, 2002). Adaptive functioning is a component of the definition of mental retardation.

Applied behavioral analysis is a strategy used by behavioral therapists to specify the antecedents and consequences of behaviors so that appropriate behavioral interventions can be introduced to change problem behaviors.

Bacterial encephalitis is an infection that results in swelling of the brain and high fever that can produce severe levels of mental retardation.

Bacterial meningitis is an infection that results in swelling of the membranes that line the brain (the meninges) and high fever that can produce severe levels of mental retardation.

Cerebral palsy is a neuromuscular disorder that affects a child's posture and how he or she can move; it may also affect speech and perception.

A **compulsion** is a repetitive, purposeful, ritualistic behavior that a person feels obliged to perform, such as arranging articles on a desk in a particular order.

Deviation IQ is an intelligence quotient score that indicates how far it deviates from the mean score of all children of that chronological age.

Differential reinforcement of incompatible behavior (DRI) is a behavioral intervention that provides reinforcement for a behavior that is incompatible with a problematic behavior.

Differential reinforcement of other behaviors (DRO) is a behavioral intervention that provides reinforcement for a variety of behaviors other than a problematic behavior so that a child does not have to engage in problematic behavior to receive reinforcement.

The **Education for All Handicapped Children Act (Public Law 94-142)** mandates that all disabled children between the ages of 3 and 21 have the right to a free, appropriate public education in the least restrictive environment.

Expressive language is the process of speaking or otherwise expressing oneself using language.

Fetal alcohol syndrome causes children to experience a wide range of problems, including small size, small brain mass, delayed motor and language development, and hyperactivity.

Fragile X mental retardation gene (FMR1) is the gene located on the long arm of the X chromosome that, when mutated, can result in Fragile X syndrome.

g (little *g*) is the symbol for the **general factor,** introduced by Spearman, that he argued influenced all cognitive abilities.

An **individual education plan (IEP)** is a required component of services provided to all children ages 3 to 21 years who receive services for disabled children. The IEP specifies the educational, self-care, and social goals for each student and the setting in which the student will be educated.

Individual family service plan (IFSP) is a required component of services provided to all children from birth to age 2 years who receive services for disabled children or children at risk for disability. Each plan highlights the needs and resources of a child's family and specifies how needed supports and services for the family will be obtained.

Intelligence is general cognitive ability and has been defined in a variety of ways. Wechsler, who devised several intelligence tests, described intelligence as the overall capacity of an individual to understand and cope with the world.

Intelligence quotient (IQ) is a score associated with early versions of intelligence tests, obtained by dividing mental age by chronological age and multiplying by 100.

Least restrictive environment is a concept found in the Education for All Handicapped Children Act, which mandates that the education of disabled children must be given in an environment that resembles the environment provided to all children, as much as possible, in keeping with the individual needs and abilities of a child.

Mental age is a concept used in early intelligence tests. It describes the age at which a particular child is functioning cognitively. A child with a mental age of 6, for example, has the cognitive ability of a typical 6-year-old.

Mental retardation of known organic cause is the term used in this text to describe mental retardation that can be traced to an identified, organically based problem.

Mental retardation with no discernible pathologic basis is the term used in this text to describe mental retardation that cannot be traced to an identified, organically based problem.

Myelin is a fatty substance that surrounds and insulates the axons of neurons.

Phenylalanine is an essential amino acid contained in many food proteins.

Phenylpyruvic acid is a metabolite of phenylalanine in those with PKU. Phenylpyruvic acid interferes with the process of myelination in the central nervous system, often resulting in severe forms of mental retardation.

Premutation is the term used to describe genetic abnormalities in Fragile X syndrome in which 55–200 repeats are present in the FRM1 gene (6–54 repeats are normal).

A **resource room** is a classroom where students with mental retardation or other disabilities may spend part of each day to receive specialized instruction from special education teachers.

A **seizure disorder** is a disorder involving uncontrolled electrical activity in the brain that can last for just a second or two or for minutes, resulting in muscle twitching and loss of consciousness. Epilepsy is a common seizure disorder.

Self-injurious behavior (SIB) is physically damaging behavior that a person does to himself or herself, such as head banging or striking parts of the body with hands or fists.

Specific factor was used by Spearman in his conceptualization of intelligence to denote a cognitive skill related to a particular task (such as solving a puzzle or playing a piece of music).

Trisomy 21 is a chromosomal abnormality in which a child has three copies of the 21st chromosome. It is the most frequent cause of Down syndrome.

True intelligence is a person's actual intelligence, which is estimated by results from an intelligence test.

Autism and Other Pervasive Developmental Disorders

Sudden, intense outbursts of emotion by children with autism can be frightening to them and their caregivers.

Autism is the most common of the pervasive developmental disorders—so named because the impairments associated with them pervade the development of a child. Although many disorders discussed in this text have extensive influences on the lives of children and their families, autism and the other pervasive developmental disorders are different in that they directly affect the normal development of many disparate characteristics of a child.

Autism is a baffling childhood disorder. It is baffling in part because it has such a strong disruptive influence on apparently unrelated elements of a child's development. Most children with autism never develop language, are unresponsive to people around them, engage in strange behaviors such as flapping their hands in front of their faces, and become very upset if small changes are made in their environment. What could have such a strong influence on all these different behaviors? Autism is also baffling because the deficits associated with it can be so specific. For example, children with autism who develop language have difficulty using personal pronouns. What type of disorder could impede a child's ability to communicate about people much more than his or her ability to communicate about toys? As we will see, the accumulating research is beginning to point to some core deficits that may be influencing the range of autistic symptoms; but our progress in understanding autism has been slow, and many questions about it and the other pervasive developmental disorders remain unanswered.

As with other severe disorders, such as childhood-onset schizophrenia, we are often prone to viewing those with autism as comprising one homogeneous group of severely affected people. However, as we will see, there is a wide range of functioning among children and adults who have autism. The functioning of some is so problematic that they need institutional care to ensure that they do not act in ways that threaten their health and lives. Others can live with their families and attend special education classes or work in sheltered workshops. A few people with autism are very successful in many aspects of their lives; for example, the vignette that follows is from a chapter written by a professor who has autism. We should keep this range of functioning in mind as we explore the experiences of those who have autism so that we can appreciate their diverse needs and talents.

Chapter Plan

After an intriguing description of what it is like to have autistic disorder, we will explore some early writings about two of the pervasive developmental disorders. Because so much more is known about autistic disorder and Asperger's disorder than the other pervasive developmental disorders, we will focus on them in the first part of the chapter. We start by reviewing their diagnostic criteria and discuss the controversy about whether they are distinct disorders or should be thought of as variants of a broader autism spectrum disorder. Next we focus on the characteristics and experiences of children who have been diagnosed with autism and Asperger's disorder. This will allow us to note some impairments that children with the two disorders have in common as well as the impairments that are specific to each disorder. We then examine the prevalence and developmental course of the two disorders, after which we discuss the families of children with a pervasive developmental disorder and how they are affected by these severe disorders. As with the other chapters, our primary focus will be on the etiology of the disorders. Unfortunately a clear picture of their etiology has yet to emerge. However, we will examine several theories about them and the neurological problems believed to be at their foundation. Short sections about Rett's disorder and childhood disintegrative disorder, two rare pervasive developmental disorders, will then be presented. Finally we will look at interventions for children with pervasive developmental disorders and their families, including some controversial interventions.

Case Study: Experiences of a High-Functioning Person with Autism

Several adolescents and adults with autism have written about their experiences. At the beginning of this chapter, I am going to share one of these insightful descriptions because the author's comments may help us better appreciate the struggles of many children and adults with autism. As we will see in this chapter, many children with autism never develop language, and the IQs of most of them are in the mentally retarded range. Consequently, the success of this author in meeting the demands of our society is unusual, and her success should not be viewed as something that many children or adults with autism could attain. The following material is a series of quotations from the chapter "An Inside View of Autism" by Temple Grandin (Grandin, 1992):

I am a 44-year-old autistic woman who has a successful international career designing livestock equipment. I completed my PhD in Animal Science at the University of Illinois in Urbana, and I am now an Assistant Professor of Animal Science at Colorado State University.

Not being able to speak (as a young child) was utter frustration. If adults spoke directly to me I could understand everything they said, but I could not get my words out. It was like a big stutter. . . . My speech therapist knew how to intrude into my world. She would hold me by my chin and make me look in her eyes and say *ball*. At age 3, *ball* came out "bah," said with great stress. If the therapist pushed too hard I threw a tantrum, and if she did not intrude far enough, no progress was made. My mother and teachers wondered why I screamed. Screaming was the only way I could communicate. Often I would logically think to myself, "I am going to scream now because I want to tell somebody I don't want to do something."

I still have many problems with rhythm. I can clap out a rhythm by myself, but I am unable to synchronize my rhythm with somebody else's rhythm. . . . People still accuse me of interrupting. Due to a faulty rhythm sense, it is difficult to determine when I should break into a conversation. Following the rhythmic ebb and rise of a conversation is difficult.

My hearing is like having a hearing aid with the volume control stuck on "super loud." It is like an open microphone that picks up everything. I have two choices: Turn the mike on and get deluged with sound, or shut it off. . . . Many autistics have problems with modulating sensory input. They either overreact or underreact. . . . I am unable to talk on the phone in a noisy office or airport. Everybody else can use the phones in a noisy environment, but I can't. If I try to screen out the background noise, I also screen out the phone. A friend of mine, a high-functioning autistic, is unable to hear a conversation in a relatively quiet hotel lobby. She has the same problem I have, only worse.

I often misbehaved in church because the petticoats itched and scratched. . . . My parents had no idea why I behaved so badly. A few simple changes in clothes would have improved my behavior. . . . Most people adapt to the feeling of different types of clothing in a few minutes. Even now, I avoid wearing new types of underwear. It takes me three to four days to fully adapt to new ones.

As a child I was hyperactive, but I did not feel "nervous" until I reached puberty. At puberty, my behavior took a bad turn for the worse. . . . Shortly after my first menstrual period, the anxiety attacks started. The feeling was like a constant feeling of stage fright all the time. . . . The "nerves" were almost like hypersensitivity rather than anxiety. It was like my brain was running at 200 miles an hour, instead of 60 miles an hour. . . . I was desperate for relief. At a carnival I discovered that riding on the Rotor ride provided temporary relief. Intense pressure and vestibular stimulation calmed my nerves.

While visiting my aunt's ranch, I observed that cattle being handled in a squeeze chute sometimes relaxed after the pressure was applied. A few days later, I tried the cattle squeeze chute, and it provided relief for several hours. At age 18, I built a squeezing machine. This device is completely lined with foam rubber, and the user has complete control over the duration and amount of pressure applied. The machine provides comforting pressure to large areas of the body. . . . The squeeze machine also had a calming effect on my nervous system.

All my thinking is visual. When I think about abstract concepts such as getting along with people I use visual images such as a sliding glass door. Relationships must be approached carefully otherwise the sliding door could be shattered. . . . I have an extremely poor long-term memory for things such as phone numbers unless I can convert them to visual images. For example, the number 65 is retirement age, and I imagine somebody in Sun City, Arizona. . . . Recently I was listening to a taped medical lecture while driving. To remember information such as the drug doses discussed on the tape I had to create a picture to stand for the dose. For example, 300 mg is a football field with shoes on it. The shoes remind me that the number is 300 feet, not yards.

There is, however, one area of visualization I am poor in. I often fail to recognize faces until I have known a person for a long time. This sometimes causes social problems because I sometimes don't respond to an acquaintance because I fail to recognize them.

I read in the medical library that antidepressant drugs such as Tofranil (imipramine) were effective for treating patients with endogenous anxiety and panic. . . . Fifty mg of Tofranil at bedtime worked like magic (for me). . . . During the eight years I have been taking antidepressants, there has been a steady improvement in my speech, sociability, and posture. My friend Billie Hart (tells) me that I am a completely different person. She said I used to walk and sit in a hunched-over position and now my posture is straight. Eye contact has improved, and I no longer shift around in my chair.

Today I have a successful career designing livestock equipment because my high school science teacher, Mr. Carlock, used my fixation on cattle chutes to motivate me to study psychology and science. He also taught me how to use the scientific indexes. This knowledge enabled me to find out about Tofranil. While the school psychologist wanted to take my squeeze machine away, Mr. Carlock encouraged me to read scientific journals so I could learn why the machine had a relaxing effect. Today I travel all over the world designing stockyards and chutes for major meat-packing firms. I am a recognized leader in my field and have written over 100 technical and scientific papers on livestock handling. If the psychologists had been successful in taking away my squeeze machine, maybe I would be sitting somewhere rotting in front of a TV instead of writing this chapter.

History

Several myths and legends suggest that people were aware of children with autistic symptoms centuries ago (Wing & Potter, 2002). For example, myths from many cultures describe "changeling children" who were left by elves after they had stolen someone's child. The descriptions of these children as beautiful, strange, and remote could be the descriptions of children with autism. Legend also describes a follower of St. Francis of Assisi who was gentle, naive, and stubborn and who lived his life in a very literal way. He once removed all his clothes in public and gave them to a stranger in need because it was important to help the poor. His description sounds like the description of someone with Asperger's disorder.

Modern research interest in children with autism began in the middle 20th century, when several physicians published case studies of children with "childhood psychosis"—so labeled because they displayed many behaviors that resembled the symptoms of adults who had schizophrenia (Wing, 1997). In the 1940s Leo Kanner from the United States and Hans Asperger from Austria wrote about groups of children with severe disorders and symptoms that were distinct from those found in adult schizophrenia and severe cases of mental retardation, thus bringing these children and their disorders (autism and Asperger's disorder) to the attention of the medical community (Klinger, Dawson, & Renner, 2003).

Autistic Disorder

Kanner described 11 children who had what he called **early infantile autism.** (*Autism* refers to a pathological preoccupation with the self to the exclusion of interest in the outside world. It comes from the Greek *autos,* "self," and *ismos,* "state or condition.") He described the three core symptoms of early infantile autism as an inability to relate to other people, language impairments, and an obsessive need for sameness (Kanner, 1943).

Kanner initially hypothesized that autism was a neurological disorder with a genetic foundation. However, in subsequent publications he noted the lack of evidence of neurological problems and suggested that the cause of early infantile autism might be parent–child relationships (Eisenberg & Kanner, 1955). He stated that the parents of most children with autism were high-achieving and distant from their children, noting "the dramatically evident detachment, obsessiveness, and coldness that is almost a universal feature of parents of autistic children" (Eisenberg & Kanner, 1955). The prevailing psychoanalytic thinking of this time reinforced this view and suggested that the parents of children with autism had consciously or unconsciously rejected their children and that the children, sensing this rejection, had withdrawn into themselves (Volkmar & Lord, 1998). This view was commonly held during much of the 1950s through the 1970s, leading to interventions designed to "coax" the children out of the protective shells into which they had retreated. Interventions were also aimed at parents to try to make them more receptive to their children.

Changes in thinking about the causes of autism were initially prompted by parents of children with autism in the United States and Great Britain who steadfastly refused to believe that they were the source of their children's autism. They formed support groups and advocated for methodologically sound research into the causes of autism (Wing & Potter, 2002). This research subsequently found no differences in the characteristics of the parents and families of children with autism and the parents and families of children who had no disorder, sending the search for the etiology of autism back in the direction initially suggested by Kanner (Klinger et al., 2003).

Asperger's Disorder

Asperger, writing at about the same time as Kanner but not known to him, described a group of children who had severely disturbed social relationships and problems with motor coordination, were inefficient in their use of language although they had normal language skills and cognitive abilities, and often became excessively preoccupied with one topic of interest (Asperger,

1991). Asperger's original writing received little notice until the 1980s, when it was translated into English (Wing & Potter, 2002). Considerable interest was then generated in this group of children who resembled children who had autistic disorder in some but not all ways.

Diagnostic Criteria in the DSM

The concepts of autism and pervasive developmental disorder have changed in the various editions of the DSM. In the DSM-II all children with severe, chronic symptoms were included in the category of *childhood schizophrenia* (Eggers & Bunk, 1997). Work by Kolvin in the late 1960s and Rutter in the 1970s suggested that autism should be considered a separate disorder because it began earlier in life, had a different pattern of symptoms, and had different long-term outcomes than what is now called *childhood-onset schizophrenia* (Kolvin, 1971; Rutter, 1972). Because of this work, autism first appeared as a distinct disorder in the DSM-III (APA, 1980).

The DSM-III included three disorders in the pervasive developmental disorder category: *infantile autism* (requiring an onset before 30 months of age), *childhood-onset pervasive developmental disorder* (with symptoms that are similar to the current diagnostic criteria for Asperger's disorder), and *atypical pervasive developmental disorder* for children experiencing significant disturbances in development who did not meet all the criteria for either of the other disorders. In the DSM-III-R (1987), the requirement of an age of onset before 30 months was dropped because of a lack of research support, and infantile autism and childhood-onset pervasive developmental disorder were combined into one diagnosis, *autistic disorder*, that could have either an early or late onset. It appears that children with what is now considered Asperger's disorder probably received the diagnosis of *pervasive developmental disorder not otherwise specified* in the DSM-III-R—a diagnosis similar to that of atypical pervasive developmental disorder in the DSM-III. The DSM-IV reversed the trend toward combining diagnoses by specifying five diagnoses, which are described in the next section. *Asperger's disorder* became a separate diagnosis; the age requirement for autistic disorder was reinstated (although changed to an onset before 36 months); and two new disorders, *Rett's disorder* and *childhood disintegrative disorder,* were included.

Key Concepts

- Myths and legends show that the special nature of children and adults with autism has been recognized for centuries.
- Leo Kanner and Hans Asperger were the first to write extensively about autistic disorder and Asperger's disorder. They described the ways in which children with these disorders had characteristics distinct from those with other severe disorders.
- The DSM-III was the first edition to include the pervasive developmental disorders. The diagnostic criteria for the pervasive developmental disorders have changed somewhat over time, and new pervasive developmental disorders have been added.

Diagnosis and Assessment

Diagnostic Criteria

Five pervasive developmental disorders are included in the DSM-IV-TR. Three of the disorders are described in this section. The other two—Rett's disorder and childhood disintegrative disorder—are described toward the end of this chapter. As discussed later in this section, controversy exists about whether these three disorders should be considered distinct disorders or whether they should be combined into one broader autism spectrum disorder (ASD).

As shown in Tables 12.1 and 12.2, the diagnostic criteria for autistic disorder and Asperger's disorder are similar to the descriptions initially given by Kanner and Asperger. The first two symptom categories of autistic disorder—significant deficits in social relationships and language development—are similar to Kanner's initial descriptions. The third category has been broadened to include restricted, stereotyped behaviors as well as a need for sameness. As is also shown, two criteria are shared between autistic disorder and Asperger's disorder: problems with social relationships and restricted, stereotyped behaviors. Asperger's disorder differs from autistic disorder in that language development follows a normal course and there is no significant delay in cognitive development.

Although not included in the diagnostic criteria for autistic disorder, most researchers and clinicians distinguish those with **high-functioning autism** from others with autism (some refer to the others as *low-functioning*, whereas others simply refer to them as having autism). The most common way of distinguishing these two groups is through **IQ**, with those whose IQ is above 70 (above the cutoff for mental retardation) included in the high-functioning group (Tanguay, 2000). Although IQ can be difficult to assess in children with autism, current estimates are that about one-third of them have an IQ above 70 and thus would be considered high-functioning (APA, 2000).

Finally, as with most disorder categories in the DSM, a diagnosis is included for children who meet many but not all of the criteria for one of the other pervasive developmental disorders: *pervasive developmental disorder not otherwise specified* (PDDNOS). For example, a child who meets the first two diagnostic criteria for autistic disorder, but not the third, could be given the diagnosis of PDDNOS, as could a child who has symptoms in each of the three diagnostic criteria, but whose symptoms are not severe enough to warrant a diagnosis of autistic disorder.

A Controversial and Unresolved Issue: Autism Spectrum Disorder

Several researchers and clinicians have argued that rather than conceptualizing autism, Asperger's disorder, and PDDNOS as distinct disorders, it would be better to consider them as components of a broader **autism spectrum disorder (ASD)** (Szatmari, 2000; Tanguay, 2000; Wing & Potter, 2002). Some

TABLE 12.1

Diagnostic Criteria for 299.00 Autistic Disorder

A. A total of six (or more) items from (1), (2), and (3), with at least two from (1) and one each from (2) and (3):

    (1) Qualitative impairment in social interaction, as manifested by at least two of the following:

        (a) Marked impairment in the use of multiple nonverbal behaviors such as eye-to-eye gaze, facial expression, body postures, and gestures to regulate social interaction.

        (b) Failure to develop peer relationships appropriate to developmental level.

        (c) A lack of spontaneous seeking to share enjoyment, interests, or achievements with other people (e.g., by a lack of showing, bringing, or pointing out objects of interest).

        (d) Lack of social or emotional reciprocity.

    (2) Qualitative impairments in communication as manifested by at least one of the following:

        (a) Delay in or total lack of, the development of spoken language (not accompanied by an attempt to compensate through alternative modes of communication such as gesture or mime).

        (b) In individuals with adequate speech, marked impairment in the ability to initiate or sustain a conversation with others.

        (c) Stereotyped and repetitive use of language or idiosyncratic language.

        (d) Lack of varied, spontaneous make-believe play or social imitative play appropriate to developmental level.

    (3) Restricted repetitive and stereotyped patterns of behavior, interests, and activities, as manifested by at least one of the following:

        (a) Encompassing preoccupation with one or more stereotyped and restricted patterns of interest that is abnormal either in intensity or focus.

        (b) Apparently inflexible adherence to specific, nonfunctional routines or rituals.

        (c) Stereotyped and repetitive motor mannerisms (e.g., hand or finger flapping or twisting, or complex whole-body movements).

        (d) Persistent preoccupation with parts of objects.

B. Delays or abnormal functioning in at least one of the following areas, with onset prior to age 3 years: (1) social interaction, (2) language as used in social communication, or (3) symbolic or imaginative play.

C. The disturbance is not better accounted for by Rett's Disorder or Childhood Disintegrative Disorder.

psychologists include Rett's disorder and childhood disintegrative disorder in ASD, but most do not (Bertrand et al., 2001). These researchers argue that autism, PDDNOS, and Asperger's disorder represent levels of severity of ASD, with autism the most severe, Asperger's disorder the least severe, and PDDNOS in the middle (Szatmari, 2000; see Figure 12.1 on page 462).

TABLE 12.2

Diagnostic Criteria for 299.80 Asperger's Disorder

A. Qualitative impairment in social interaction, as manifested by at least two of the following:
   (1) Marked impairment in the use of multiple nonverbal behaviors such as eye-to-eye gaze, facial expression, body postures, and gestures to regulate social interaction.
   (2) Failure to develop peer relationships appropriate to developmental level.
   (3) A lack of spontaneous seeking to share enjoyment, interests, or achievements with other people (e.g., by a lack of showing, bringing, or pointing out objects of interest to other people).
   (4) Lack of social or emotional reciprocity.
B. Restricted repetitive and stereotyped patterns of behavior, interests, and activities, as manifested by at least one of the following:
   (1) Encompassing preoccupation with one or more stereotyped and restricted patterns of interest that is abnormal in either intensity or focus.
   (2) Apparently inflexible adherence to specific, nonfunctional routines or rituals.
   (3) Stereotyped and repetitive motor mannerisms (e.g., hand or finger flapping or twisting, or complex whole-body movements).
   (4) Persistent preoccupation with parts of objects.
C. The disturbance causes clinically significant impairment in social, occupational, or other important areas of functioning.
D. There is no clinically significant general delay in language (e.g., single words used by age 2 years, communicative phrases used by age 3 years).
E. There is no clinically significant delay in cognitive development or in the development of age-appropriate self-help skills, adaptive behavior (other than in social interaction), and curiosity about the environment in childhood.
F. Criteria are not met for another specific Pervasive Developmental Disorder or Schizophrenia.

Support for an ASD comes from the experiences of clinicians and researchers who occasionally find it difficult to distinguish clearly between autism, PDDNOS, and Asperger's disorder when giving a diagnosis to an individual child. Although the correct diagnosis is obvious for some children, it is not clear for others because the diagnoses can meld into each other and the line between them can be ambiguous. For example, it can be difficult to determine whether the symptoms displayed by some children are severe enough to warrant a diagnosis of autistic disorder or whether they are "subthreshold," warranting a diagnosis of PDDNOS. Similarly, it can be difficult to determine whether a child with some delays in language development is displaying "clinically significant" delays (possibly warranting a diagnosis of autistic disorder) or delays that are not clinically significant (possibly warranting a diagnosis of Asperger's disorder).

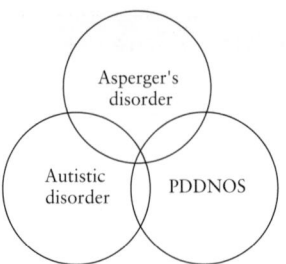

Model 1: Three distinct disorders that share some symptoms

Autistic spectrum disorder

Model 2: One disorder with three overlapping levels of severity

FIGURE 12.1   *Two Models of Three PDDs*

Some research supports the concept of an ASD. For example, one group of researchers assessed autistic symptoms in all the 7- to 9-year-old children in Bergen, Norway, and found that the distribution of scores was almost continuous, suggesting that the symptoms could best be described as being on a continuum rather than being in distinct groups (Posserud, Lundervold, & Gilberg, 2006). In addition, Miller and Ozonoff (2000) gave several neuropsychological tests to children with high-functioning autism and children with Asperger's disorder (for a description of neuropsychological tests, see the chapter about attention-deficit/hyperactivity disorder). They asserted that one would expect to see a pattern of differences on these tests if autistic disorder and Asperger's disorder were distinct. The group of children with Asperger's disorder had a higher average IQ than did the group with high-functioning autism, so the researchers controlled for IQ statistically in their analysis of the results. Once they did this, only 1 of the 12 tests showed group differences. The researchers concluded that children with Asperger's disorder and those with high-functioning autism differed only in IQ, which, they argued, is more indicative of Asperger's disorder being a less severe form of ASD than being a disorder distinct from high-functioning autism.

There are considerable differences in the long-term outcomes for those with autistic disorder, PDDNOS, and Asperger's disorder, which might suggest that they should remain distinct disorders (Klinger et al., 2003). However, differences in outcomes are not conclusive regarding whether the disorders are distinct. For example, those with milder symptoms of many physical disorders (such as cystic fibrosis or multiple sclerosis) have better long-term outcomes than those with more severe symptoms of the same disorders.

Ongoing research may provide additional information that will be useful in determining whether it is appropriate to continue to consider autism, Asperger's disorder, and PDDNOS as distinct disorders or whether they should be combined into one ASD. Research showing whether autism, PDDNOS, and Asperger's disorder have distinct etiologies would provide the most useful information; but as we will discuss later in this chapter, we still have much to learn about the etiology of all the pervasive developmental disorders.

Determining that an Individual Child Has a Pervasive Developmental Disorder

No biological markers exist for any of the pervasive developmental disorders (with the possible exception of Rett's disorder, which is discussed later). Consequently, diagnosis of a pervasive developmental disorder is made based on observations of a child's behaviors. These observations might be made by a clinician, reported to the clinician by a parent or teacher, or both. Several instruments are available to help clinicians make systematic observations of behaviors and rate the behaviors that are observed. The Childhood Autism Rating Scale (CARS) is the most commonly used scale with preschool children (Whitaker, 2002). Scores on the CARS, in conjunction with observations of whether the child's behaviors meet the diagnostic criteria set out by the DSM-IV-TR, can be used to determine whether the diagnosis of autism is appropriate for a child.

Early determination that a child has a pervasive developmental disorder is important because early, sustained treatment appears to result in better overall long-term functioning (Tanguay, 2000). However, it can be difficult to determine whether an infant's or toddler's behaviors indicate a pervasive developmental disorder because the variation in children's timing of development makes it difficult to determine whether an observed delay is just a delay or an indication of an underlying impairment. It is particularly difficult to distinguish the behaviors of young children with mental retardation from those with autism: Both can show marked delays in social functioning and language development (Gillberg, Nordin, & Ehlers, 1996). Consequently, the diagnosis of autism is often not made until age 3 or 4 years, when the normal development of social interactions and language has proceeded far enough that problems can be identified clearly (Whitaker, 2002). Even then, the diagnosis of autism is usually made on a preliminary basis, with a more confident final diagnosis made between 6 and 10 years of age (Gillberg et al., 1996).

Because of the importance of early intervention for those with autism, some behavior rating scales have been designed to be used early in life to screen infants or toddlers exhibiting behaviors that raise concerns about autism. Young children scoring in the problematic range on these instruments might be observed more closely over the next months and years to determine whether they have autism. (For examples from one screening instrument, see Table 12.3.)

Key Concepts

- Four specific disorders are included in the category of pervasive developmental disorders in the DSM-IV-TR: autistic disorder, Asperger's disorder, Rett's disorder, and childhood disintegrative

TABLE 12.3

Sample Items from the SAB-2, a Screening Instrument for Autism

Appears to be isolated from surroundings.
Doesn't smile when expected to.
Difficulties getting eye contact.
Doesn't try to attract adult's attention to own activity.
Difficulties imitating movements.
Doesn't play like other children.
There is (or has been) a suspicion of deafness.
Empty gaze.
Doesn't seem to react to cold.

disorder. An additional diagnosis, PDDNOS, is for children who show multiple developmental problems that do not meet the diagnostic criteria for any of the other four disorders.

- Although this is not specified in the DSM-IV-TR, many researchers and clinicians divide people with autistic disorder into those who are high-functioning (an IQ of 70 or more) and others.
- The diagnostic criteria for Asperger's disorder are similar to those for autistic disorder except for a lack of significant impairments in language and cognitive development.
- Many researchers and clinicians believe that autistic disorder, Asperger's disorder, and PDDNOS are better conceptualized as degrees of severity of a broader ASD rather than as distinct disorders.
- Individual children are diagnosed with a pervasive developmental disorder based on observations of their behaviors. Standardized measures of behaviors, such as the CARS, are also often used.

Characteristics and Experiences of Children with Autistic Disorder or Asperger's Disorder

Autistic Disorder: Core Features
Social Interaction

From early in their lives, children with autism show significant impairments in their social interactions. Whereas most infants mold themselves to the body of a parent when held, infants later diagnosed with autism are often stiff and unresponsive or passive and "floppy" (Prior & Ozonoff, 1998). They respond differently than other infants to touch and to attempts to comfort them when they are upset, showing either no response or an irritated or frightened response. Consequently, many parents find their interactions with an infant who is later diagnosed with autism to be unrewarding or unsatisfying.

Social impairments result in many children with autism having few interactions with peers or adults.

Toddlers and young children with autism do not initiate contact with others or respond when others try to get their attention. When entering a room, for example, they may interact with parents, siblings, or other familiar people as if they were furniture or other inanimate objects. This is very different from how other children—even those with mental retardation or other serious disorders—act around familiar people (Klinger et al., 2003). Whereas most young children are eager to show things they find interesting to others and to respond to parents' instructions ("Wave bye-bye"), young children with autism do not seem to comprehend the point of these social interactions (Prior & Ozonoff, 1998).

Children with autism show marked deficits in **reciprocal social interaction** (Prior & Ozonoff, 1998). They do not appear to understand the back-and-forth nature of most social interactions. Toddlers with autism, for example, do not engage in games requiring back-and-forth interactions (such as pat-a-cake), and older children do not engage in back-and-forth conversations. In addition, they often prefer to be by themselves and will shy away from contact with others.

Because of their social impairments, most children and adolescents with autism do not have friends and spend little or no time socializing with peers. High-functioning children with autism may have a friend, but the emotional closeness that characterizes the friendships of other children is usually absent in their friendships (Bauminger & Kasari, 2000). It appears as if they have a friend because they have learned that children should have a friend, rather than having a friend because they benefit from the closeness of the friendship.

Even high-functioning adults with autism do not seem to have the fundamental understanding of social interactions that the rest of us have. They may engage in social interactions, but their behaviors often seem wooden or contrived rather than natural. They may also engage in behaviors that, although correct, do not mesh with social expectations. For example, Kanner related this experience of a young adult who had been one of the original 11 children he described: "Attending a football rally of his junior college and called upon to speak, he shocked the assembly by stating that he thought that team was likely to lose—a prediction that was correct but unthinkable in the setting. The ensuing round of booing dismayed this young man, who was totally unable to comprehend why the truth should be unwelcome" (Eisenberg & Kanner, 1955).

Attachment

One area of social interaction that has received considerable research attention, and that is particularly important for parents of children with autism, is attachment (see the chapter about basic psychological theories for a description of attachment). Are children with autism capable of forming attachment bonds to their parents in the same way as other children? Because children with autism show so little interest in those around them, it seems reasonable to assume that attachments to parents would not form. However, several studies that have assessed attachment using the **Strange Situation** have found that children with autism do show many behaviors associated with an attachment to their primary caregiver, once adjustments are made for their stereotyped behaviors. In addition, the percentage of children with autism showing secure attachment behaviors is about the same as for other children (Capps, Sigman, & Mundy, 1994). Thus it appears that most children with autism recognize their parents and form attachments to them, even through the ways that they interact with them may differ from how most children interact with their parents.

Notes from the Author: Understanding the Social Difficulties of Those with Autism

Understanding the difficulties that those with autism have with social interactions can be difficult for most of us because we have an innate sense of social interactions and how to engage in them (at least when we are around familiar people). I have found that it can be useful to search for experiences in my life that might provide some hint of the difficulties that others experience when it is hard for me to understand them directly. Here is my example for understanding the social interactions of high-functioning people with autism: I have been trying to learn how to play golf for a few years. In some ways, it is amazing that anyone can hit a golf ball a long way straight down the fairway. As I have worked on my golf swing, it is clear that it is not "natural." Each time I swing I have to think about where my feet are, the position of my body, and what my arms and head are doing. I remind myself to keep my head still, rotate my shoulders, feel the swing with my left arm more than my right, keep my knees flexed, and so forth. I envy people who can step up to the ball and use a natural, smooth swing to hit it. Despite my many attempts, it never feels natural when I hit the ball. I think that this must be how people with high-functioning autism feel when they engage in social interactions with others. They can engage—but it never seems effortless, smooth, and natural. It would be very frustrating if I felt the same way each time I interacted with someone as I do when I try to hit a golf ball. As I think about this, I have a better sense of the struggles that those with autism must face as they negotiate their way through life. Perhaps you can think of something you do in your life that does not quite feel natural to you—which might give you a sense of the struggles of those with autism.

Developmental Impairments Leading to Problems with Social Interaction

Infants and toddlers who are later diagnosed with autism show a variety of impairments in behaviors that developmental psychologists believe form the foundation for the development of social interactions. Thus these early impairments are believed to cause the problems with social interactions that were just described. For example, as noted earlier, infants with autism do not orient their attention to social stimuli as do others of the same age. They seldom respond when their names are called and do not respond to other attempts to gain their attention (Osterling, Dawson, & Munson, 2002). Because orienting to social stimuli is the first step in most social interactions, an inability to orient to social stimuli significantly interferes with children's earliest social interactions, which can create subsequent problems.

A lack of ability to orient to social stimuli may influence another fundamental deficit of children with autism: **joint attention,** which is the ability of two people to attend to something together. Most infants look at an object when a caregiver places it in view and later will follow a caregiver's gaze or gesture to an object (Mundy & Sigman, 1989). Still later, infants gesture to an object to direct a caregiver's attention to it, showing that the infants have learned that they can gain the attention of another person. However, infants with autism do not engage in joint attention behaviors, and most preschoolers with autism continue to show difficulties with joint attention (Wimpory, Hobson, Williams, & Nash, 2000). Their inability to engage in this early form of interpersonal interaction is likely to inhibit the development of later interpersonal abilities.

Another fundamental social deficit of children with autism is imitation. The ability to imitate others begins early in life for most children. For example, most infants imitate others' body movements or activities with objects (such as shaking a rattle). The developing child can imitate increasingly complex behaviors (a toddler playing pat-a-cake with a parent, a 4-year-old raking leaves with a parent); and this ability to imitate others is an integral part of children's learning about things and the ways that social interactions occur. Infants, toddlers, and children with autism seldom imitate others.

Whether they do not attend to the actions of others, fail to understand that they can imitate the actions of another, or have difficulty coordinating their movements is unclear; but their lack of imitation can last a lifetime (Klinger et al., 2003).

An interesting and puzzling deficit of children with autism is their impaired ability to process the visual stimulation of seeing a face. For example, infants with autism do not prefer pictures of their mothers over those of strangers, and they do not prefer a picture of a face held straight up versus one held upside-down or sideways—preferences that other infants show. An fMRI (functional magnetic resonance imaging) study suggested a reason for this deficit by showing that individuals with autism process visual perceptions of faces in the part of the brain that those without autism use to process visual perceptions of objects (Dawson et al., 2002; Shultz, Scherman, & Marshall, 2000). This suggests the possibility that whereas most children recognize the features of a face and that it is part of a person, children with autism do not make this connection. Instead they perceive and then react to a face as another child may perceive and react to a truck or a flower.

Impairments in Language and Other Forms of Communication

Only about 50% of children with autism develop meaningful spoken language or other forms of communication (Klinger et al., 2003). Some children who do not develop language do acquire the ability to communicate through grunts or gestures, and a small percentage learn to use single words for some communication (Prior & Ozonoff, 1998). However, many cannot communicate directly with others. Most children who do not develop language by the age of 6 years remain thus impaired over their lifetime.

Children with autism who do acquire language exhibit problems in two areas: the use of deviant forms of language and marked difficulty with the pragmatics of language. (**Pragmatics** refers to the social use of language. For example, when you express disagreement or frustration to a professor, you may use different words, gestures, and emphasis than when you express disagreement or frustration to a friend or to a referee during a basketball game—which shows that you understand many pragmatic rules of language.)

Common deviant forms of language include echolalia, abnormal **prosody** (the volume, rhythm, and intonation of speech), and pronoun reversal or lack of pronoun use. When a child engages in **echolalia,** he or she repeats the last few words of the previous speaker. If I were to say to a child with autism, "What would you like for lunch, John?" and he responded, "Like for lunch, John," he would be engaging in echolalia. About 85% of children with autism who have acquired language engage in echolalia some of the time. The reasons for this are unclear, although Prizant and Rydell (1984) assert that many autistic people are trying to communicate when using echolalia, rather than simply repeating words they have just heard.

The prosody of children with autism is often odd. They may speak more loudly than others or with unusual rhythm or intonation (such as emphasizing words in a sentence that most children would not emphasize or creating markedly longer pauses between some words than others). Such difficulties with prosody can make it difficult to understand the conversation of a child with autism unless one pays close attention to it.

Children with autism have particular difficulty in using personal pronouns. Reversal of pronouns is common, with the child using "you" to refer to himself or herself and "I" to refer to a person being spoken to. Other children with autism do not use pronouns, referring to themselves and others by name or function (Lee, Hobson, & Chait, 1994).

Children and adults with autism have particular difficulty with the pragmatic aspects of language; that is, they have marked difficulty using language in a conversation to share information with others (Tager Flusberg, 2001). When they try to get a message across to another person, they often do not have the pragmatic skills to do so. This can make the other person have to guess the meaning of their speech (Landa, 2000). For example, a child who would like to go outside and play might say, "The sun is very bright. It is warm when the sun is bright." A listener who does not understand the intention of the statement may respond, "Yes, the sun is warm when it is bright," which may cause the child to experience frustration at not being understood— frustration that will not be understood by the listener.

In addition, children with autism often do not understand that the person to whom they are speaking does not have the same information that the child has, so they may speak as if the other person has this knowledge (Tager Flusberg, 2001). For example, consider a child whose shoes are causing significant pain. He may say "Take off shoes" rather than "These shoes hurt a lot, take them off" because he assumes that his parent knows, as he does, that his feet hurt. If the parent does not take the child's shoes off, he may conclude that his parent does not care about the pain he is experiencing, which can lead to an outburst of anger.

Children with autism also have difficulty with the back-and-forth aspects of conversation, which is probably related to their difficulties with reciprocal social interactions. After making a statement, for example, they may not attend to the response from the other person before making their next statement. As a result, it may appear that two separate conversations are taking place. Interestingly, many with autism will express a desire to have a two-way conversation with another person, but they simply do not seem to have the skills for such a conversation (Prior & Ozonoff, 1998).

Restricted, Repetitive, and Stereotyped Behaviors

Many behaviors are included in this category (Militerni, Bravaccio, Falco, Fico, & Palermo, 2002). *Repetitive behaviors* often relate to the child's need for sameness in his or her environment (this was a characteristic that Kanner first noticed distinguished children with autism from others). For example, a child may insist that items in her bedroom be arranged in the same way, and she may become very agitated if something is moved. Similarly, a child may demand that the same routine be followed each morning. Failure to follow this routine can result in high levels of agitation.

Restricted behaviors are those that focus intensely on one or a few things. They may be related to a need for sameness. For example, a child may have a restricted interest in parts of objects—being preoccupied with the ears on stuffed animals or on the wheels on toy cars (APA, 2000). This preoccupation can cause repetitive behaviors, such as flicking the ears on stuffed animals or spinning the wheels on toy cars for long periods. Restricted behaviors can also be associated with food, with some children being willing to eat only certain foods that have similar textures, such as mashed potatoes, creamed spinach, and pudding.

Stereotyped behaviors are repetitious, rhythmic behaviors that appear to have no function (Nijhof, Joha, & Pekelharing, 1998). Many stereotyped behaviors have a sensory component to them, such as a child moving his fingers repeatedly in front of his eyes, tapping his ears, flapping his hands, or rocking. Others can involve more complex motor patterns, such as repeatedly filling and emptying containers with sand or water, or gathering and dispersing items around a room (Militerni et al., 2002). Some patterns of stereotyped behaviors that involve self-injury, such as a child slapping or biting herself, can cause severe injuries if they are not interrupted. (A more thorough discussion of **self-injurious behavior** is found in the chapter about mental retardation.)

Notes from the Author: Stereotyped?

I have always wondered why the adjective *stereotyped* is used to describe the repetitive behaviors of those with autism and other disorders. My only experience with the word has been as a noun, meaning an oversimplified, usually negative view of a group of people. Looking through the *Dictionary of Psychology* (Colman, 2001), I found that the word *stereotype* was a term used in the printing trade to describe "a solid metallic printing plate containing a masthead or other stock image that was difficult to change once cast" (p. 706) (from the Greek *stereos*, "solid," and *typos*, "type"). So stereotyped behaviors are those that are difficult to change once they are in place—just as a stereotype of a group of people is often difficult to change once it is formed in a person's mind.

Militerni and colleagues (2002) found that younger children with autism and those whose IQs were in the severe or profound mentally retarded range were more likely to engage in stereotyped behaviors with a sensory component; older children and those with higher IQs were more likely to engage in complex motor patterns. They also found that behaviors with a sensory component were often exhibited in response to some type of external event that the child apparently found stressful (such as being moved from one area to another or not being allowed to do something he or she wanted to do). Conversely, complex motor patterns did not appear to follow any external event and seemed to occur without any reason.

Two broad functions of stereotyped behaviors have been suggested. First, they may help a child with autism influence the behaviors of those around him or her (Carr, 1977). For example, a child may learn that caregivers pay attention to him when he engages in stereotyped behaviors or that a caregiver ends some activity that the child finds stressful or bothersome when he engages in stereotyped behaviors. Second, stereotyped behaviors may either heighten an overall level of sensory stimulation when a child is feeling a lack of sensory stimulation or reduce sensory stimulation that the child finds overwhelming. For example, a child who is sitting alone and is bored may begin to rock or flick her fingers in front of her eyes to increase her sensory stimulation. Alternatively, a child who is feeling overwhelmed by sensory stimulation may begin to tap on his ears to focus his attention on the sensory stimulation from his ear tapping and thus reduce the overwhelming nature of the other stimulation (Guess & Carr, 1991).

Autistic Disorder: Associated Features
Intelligence and Academic Abilities

Current estimates are that about two-thirds of children with autism have IQs below 70; that is, they are in the mentally retarded range (APA, 2000). Of the third with IQs above 70, only a few have IQs above 80 (Gillberg & Coleman, 1996). Thus the intelligence range of most people with autism is quite limited, even for those with higher levels of intelligence.

Children with autism typically have strengths in academic tasks that are concrete and have more trouble with tasks that involve comprehension or seeing relationships between pieces of information (Prior & Ozonoff, 1998). For example, some children with autism can spell and read many words but cannot understand the meaning of a sentence or paragraph that they can read. Similarly, they may be able to add or subtract numbers, but they are less likely to be able to apply those skills to word problems.

Sensory Perception

Children with autism often exhibit disturbed patterns of sensory perception. They seem oversensitive to some sensory input that would not upset other children—perhaps finding the feel of certain clothes to be painful or refusing to eat certain foods because of their texture (APA, 2000). Conversely, they may seem impervious to sensory input that others would experience as painful—such as not reacting to self-injurious behavior. The patterns of these sensitivities vary between children, and there is no particular pattern of sensory perception disturbance that is common to many children with autism.

Splinter or "Savant" Skills

About 10–25% of children and adults with autism show a **splinter skill,** which is an ability that is considerably above what one would expect given the person's intelligence. For example, a child may have an ability in arithmetic, spelling, music, or drawing that is much above the abilities of others with his or her IQ (Prior & Ozonoff, 1998). **Savant abilities** (*savant* is from the French *savoir,* "to know") are abilities in certain areas that are far above what almost any other person has; these are found in a few children and adults with autism. For example, some people with savant skills can calculate large numbers in their heads or tell which day of the week a date will fall on many years in the future (Rimland, 1978). The source of these amazing abilities is not clear; however, Rimland (1978) suggests that they are related to some autistic individuals' ability to focus all their attention on small details. Unfortunately, splinter and savant abilities are almost never useful in the lives of children or adults with autism.

Other Forms of Psychopathology and Behavioral Problems

Many children with autism have behavioral problems that can be troubling to them and members of their families. For example, temper tantrums are frequent problems, and they often occur when a child's need for sameness is broken. In addition, problems associated with oversensitivity to sensory stimulation can cause temper tantrums that are often unpredictable. Aggression and self-injurious behaviors trouble some children and often escalate around the time of puberty (Nordin & Gillberg, 1998). Sleep problems are also common in young children with autism. They typically have difficulty falling asleep and may sleep for only a few hours a night (Richdale, 1999). This can create significant challenges for families because these children often need to be closely supervised when awake (Schall, 2000).

Children and adolescents with high-functioning autism are more likely to experience anxiety disorders and depression than are other children. Other children with autism may also experience these disorders, but their developmental impairments make it difficult or impossible to assess them (Kim, Szatmari, Bryson, Streiner, & Wilson, 2000). These disorders can impair the functioning of children with autism even further and appear to result in more conflicts with parents and teachers (Kim et al., 2000).

Asperger's Disorder

As noted earlier, the diagnostic criteria for Asperger's disorder resemble those for autistic disorder except that marked problems with language and cognitive development are not present. As we have already discussed, several researchers have investigated whether there is a clear distinction between Asperger's disorder and high-functioning autism; therefore, much of what we know about Asperger's disorder comes from comparisons of children with these two disorders.

Ozonoff, South, and Miller (2000) found that, by adolescence, there were no significant differences in the degree of social impairment between children with high-functioning autism and those with Asperger's disorder. Because we know, however, that IQ is correlated with severity of social impairments in those with autism (Klinger et al., 2003), it is probably safe to hypothesize that, as a group, those with Asperger's disorder have less severe social disturbance than those with lower-functioning autism, although no research directly addresses this issue.

Children with Asperger's disorder often exhibit strong, focused, idiosyncratic interests, which may have some relationship to repetitive behaviors (Volkmar & Klin, 2000). The topics of these strong interests are not unusual, but the attention given to them is often extreme. For example, a person with Asperger's disorder may have a strong interest in wildflowers, cats, or buttons and spend weeks and months gathering and reading extensive information about the topic of interest or collecting, cataloging, and displaying items. These strong interests can influence other aspects of the life of a child with Asperger's disorder. For example, the interest may be so intense that it is all the child is interested in communicating with others about, which can affect how much others want to associate with the child (as an example, see Table 12.4).

TABLE 12.4

A Letter from an Adult Son with Asperger's Disorder to His Mother

Dear Mom,

Have you heard about sunglasses that come in all styles? The solar shields are the big ones and come in all colors to suit the user's preference. All must claim to block 100% UV rays. Polycarbonate is plastic and not as good as Borosilicate glass at 1 cm. thick to block ultraviolet radiation. The tinted, hard, thick glass with gold particles (as in space suit) blocks UV and X rays. New picture tubes are that way also to reduce X-rays.

The color filter of sunglasses are grey, clear, neutral, which reduce all colors violet (reduces yellow), blue (reduces orange), green (reduces red, but still see traffic lights safely) yellow/amber (reduces violet) orange (reduces blue) red/pink (reduces green). All colors you see must combine to be white. The tint you see on white is the color of the sunglasses.

The "blue-blocks" filter sunglasses (amber colored) absorbs blue so effectively that you can hardly distinguish the blue. It makes blue light greenish. Fluorescent tubes yellow, incandescent bulbs orange, sun yellow, red still red.

Blue is more blurry and harder to see than yellow by over 400% on the naked eye. There is no blue traffic light.

The police car uses powerful blue flashers with the red flashers.

It's harder to see blue with cataracts. A professional treatment makes blue and violet easier to see. A new artificial lens inserted can make even Ultraviolet visible in a deep violet light.

The blue-white light comes from 3 basic ways. Daylight fluorescent tubes are bluish white with a lot of blue. A blue-white star far away also radiates bluish white light.

In a supernatural way, the Virgin Mary can also issue bluish white light in some ways. Blue is a lovely color which appears almost everywhere.

The sky is blue, on a clear day you can see far.

Source: Klin, Volkmar, & Sparrow (2000), p. 9.

Although children with Asperger's disorder can use language, most of them experience problems in communicating with others. Like those who have autism, their prosody is often impaired, giving their speech an odd quality that can impede others' ability to comprehend the purpose and meaning of their conversation (Klinger et al., 2003). In addition, many of them do not appear to comprehend the generally accepted rules through which conversations are structured (Landa, 2000). These rules of discourse include expectations about the back-and-forth nature of conversations, the situations in which verbal responses are appropriate, and the ways in which topics change. Children with Asperger's disorder are not able to discern these rules by observing how others interact or through their own conversational experience, so their conversations may seem immature or inappropriate. Landa (2000), for example, gives an example of a woman with Asperger's disorder who answered aloud the questions that a minister asked as part of a sermon. She seemed confused by the looks of disapproval that came from other members of the congregation, who clearly understood that verbal responses during the sermon were inappropriate. Another example of language problems can be seen in the letter in Table 12.4, which shows a letter from an adult son to his mother. The son moves through a string of related topics in a way that appears odd to most people. In addition, the letter shows the consequence of his strong, focused interests in light and sunglasses.

An initial observation by Asperger was that people with this disorder often exhibit physical clumsiness. Recent studies have shown more specifically that children with Asperger's disorder have more difficulty than other children with **gross motor and fine motor skills** (Smith, 2000). The exact source of this clumsiness is not well understood, but the assumption is that it has some neurological basis.

Key Concepts

- From early in their lives, children with autism show impairments in reciprocal social interactions. They do not respond to physical or verbal interactions initiated by others, and they usually treat other people as if they were objects.
- Specific impairments in face gazing, joint attention, and imitation are common in infants and young children with autism.
- Despite their social impairments, young children with autism do form attachment bonds to their primary caregivers.
- All children with autistic disorder have significant language impairments. About half remain mute throughout their lives. Those who develop language often exhibit unusual language and have significant problems with pragmatics.
- Language impairments include echolalia, problems with prosody, and difficulty in using personal pronouns.
- The restricted and stereotyped behaviors shown by children with autism often relate to their need for sameness in their environment and daily routines.

- The IQ of about two-thirds of children with autistic disorder is in the mentally retarded range, with very few having an IQ above 80.
- Many children with autistic disorder have unique patterns of sensitivity to sensory input.
- Some children with autism have splinter skills, and a few exhibit savant skills.
- Many children with autistic disorder have temper tantrums, aggressive behaviors, and self-injurious behaviors. Anxiety and depression are more common among children with autism than among other children.
- Children with Asperger's disorder experience social impairments that are similar to those of children with high-functioning autistic disorder.
- Many children with Asperger's disorder have strong, focused, idiosyncratic interests.
- Although children with Asperger's disorder have normal language development, most experience problems with prosody, pragmatics, and the rules of discourse.

Prevalence

Fombonne (2003) analyzed 32 studies of the prevalence of the pervasive developmental disorders and concluded that the best prevalence estimate for all the pervasive developmental disorders combined is about 30 children per 10,000. The best estimate for the prevalence of autistic disorders is about 15 children per 10,000. However, studies that have intensely searched for all children with a pervasive developmental disorder in small geographical areas have reported higher prevalence rates. For example, Bertrand and colleagues (2001) found 40 cases of autistic disorder and 67 cases of ASD per 10,000 children in a township in New Jersey; and Gillberg, Steffenburg, and Schaumann (1991) found 60 cases of ASD per 10,000 in a suburb of Göteborg, Sweden. It is unclear whether these higher prevalence estimates were due to the researchers' enhanced ability to locate all children with ASD in their small study area or whether some issue caused more ASD in those locations. However, these studies call into question whether ASD is as rare as it is generally believed to be.

Based on encountering increasing numbers of children diagnosed with autistic disorder, some clinicians and educators have expressed concern that its prevalence is rising. Some research supports this possibility. A study in Sweden found an increase in prevalence from 4 cases per 10,000 in 1980 to 7.6 cases in 1984 to 11.5 cases in 1988 (Gillberg & Wing, 1999). Croen, Grether, Hoogstrate, and Selvin (2002) found a prevalence of 5.8 cases of ASD per 10,000 among children born in California in 1987 and a prevalence of 14.9 cases per 10,000 among children born in 1994. Similarly, a study of all children registered in the United Kingdom general practice research database showed that 0.3 children per 10,000 born in 1988 were diagnosed with autistic disorder and that this increased to 2.1 children per 10,000 by 1999 (Kaye, de Mar Mellero-Montes, & Jick, 2001). Unfortunately, at this time we do not know whether these prevalence increases are due to more accurate identification of children with autism, relaxation of the criteria used to determine whether symptoms are severe enough to warrant a diagnosis of autism, or an actual increase in the prevalence of autism (Croen et al., 2002). Although it is hard to imagine what might cause a tripling of the prevalence of autism or ASD in a 7- to 10-year period, the possibility that the prevalence of this severe disorder is increasing should raise significant concern.

About three to four times as many boys are diagnosed with autistic disorder as girls (Klinger et al., 2003). As a group, however, girls with autism have more severe symptoms than boys do. In addition, girls with autism are less likely to have normal IQ levels and are more likely to be severely retarded than are boys with autism. Thus autism appears similar to several childhood disorders in which boys are more frequently affected but girls with the disorder have more severe symptoms (such as childhood-onset schizophrenia and attention-deficit/hyperactivity disorder).

Based on Kanner's initial observations, it was believed for many years that children from wealthier families were more likely to have autism than were children from lower-income families. However, systematic research over the past few decades has shown that this belief is inaccurate and was probably based on wealthier families' greater likelihood of pursuing services for their children. It is now believed that children from families across the economic spectrum are equally likely to have autistic disorder.

Little research on the prevalence of Asperger's disorder has been completed because it was so recently recognized as a separate disorder in the DSM-IV. Based on the ratio of cases of Asperger's disorder to autistic disorder found in a few studies, Fombonne (2003) estimated roughly that the prevalence of Asperger's disorder is 2.5 children per 10,000.

Key Concepts

- Although most broad-based studies suggest a prevalence of autistic disorder of 15 children per 10,000 and a prevalence of ASD of about 30 children per 10,000, studies in smaller geographic locations have found 40 cases of autistic disorder per 10,000 children and 60–67 cases of ASD per 10,000 children. The reasons for these differences remain unclear.
- Prevalence estimates for ASD have risen dramatically during the past few decades, although it is not clear whether this reflects an increased ability to diagnose ASD correctly, a relaxation of diagnostic criteria, or an actual increase in the prevalence of the disorder.
- The ratio of boys to girls with autistic disorder is 3–4:1. As a group, girls with autistic disorder show more severe symptoms than do boys.

Course

Initial Onset of Symptoms
Autistic Disorder and ASD

Although the diagnosis of autistic disorder is often not made until a child is 3 or 4 years old, many of these children display symptoms of autism as early as their first year of life. Much of this information comes from home movies or videotapes of infants who are later diagnosed with ASD. Researchers analyze these home movies and compare the behaviors of infants who are later diagnosed with ASD to the behaviors seen in home movies of infants later diagnosed with another disorder, such as mental retardation, or who develop typically (Adrien et al., 1993; Losche, 1990; Osterling et al., 2002; Werner, Dawson, Osterling, & Dinno, 2000). In these home movies, many infants later diagnosed with ASD show poor social attention, lack of social smiling, and failure to respond when their names are called. Failure to respond when their names were called was seen in children with ASD when they were as young as 8 months. The other differences did not occur frequently until about 1 year of age, which is when those skills have developed in most children (Werner et al., 2000). These studies suggest that for many children, ASD begins at birth or within several months of birth.

Not all children later diagnosed with ASD show symptoms during their first year. About one-quarter to one-third of them experience normal development of social and language skills during their first year, with a subsequent loss of these skills (Bertrand et al., 2001). For example, Osterling and colleagues (2002) observed home videotapes of infants later diagnosed with ASD and divided them into two groups: those whose parents recalled symptoms of autism within the first year and those who recalled normal development with a loss of skills after 12 months. They found that those with a loss of skills showed a higher frequency of orienting when their names were called, increased attention to objects held by others, and greater frequency of looking at other people than did the children with an early onset of symptoms. Thus it appears that some children who are diagnosed with ASD show normal development during part of their first year.

Children diagnosed with ASD who experience more normal development during their first year have a better long-term prognosis, are more likely to develop language, and are less likely to be mentally retarded than those who do not experience a period of normal development. This pattern of a later onset of symptoms being associated with better long-term functioning is also found in other severe disorders, such as childhood-onset schizophrenia (Volkmar & Cohen, 1989).

Asperger's Disorder

The onset age of Asperger's disorder is difficult to determine because its defining social impairments often do not become apparent before a child enters school (APA, 2000). Consequently, it is unclear whether the disorder begins early in life and becomes noticeable only later, or whether its initial onset is during the preschool years.

Development during Childhood and Adolescence

Autistic disorder and Asperger's disorder are chronic, and their symptoms occur throughout childhood and adolescence (APA, 2000). The intensity of some symptoms, such as repetitive, stereotyped behaviors, may fluctuate while the intensity of other symptoms, such as language and social impairments, are more constant.

IQ is an important predictor of the type and severity of symptoms that children with autistic disorder exhibit (Klinger et al., 2003). For example, repetitive, stereotyped behaviors are more common in children with low IQs than they are in those with IQs above 70. In addition, children with IQs higher than 70 are more likely to respond to intensive early interventions than are children with lower IQs (Piven, Harper, Palmer, & Arndt, 1996).

Significant changes occur during adolescence for many children with autistic disorder. About a third to half of them show a marked decline in functioning during early adolescence, with increased stereotyped behaviors, hyperactivity, and aggression. This decline in functioning has been associated with the onset of seizures in some but not all adolescents (Gillberg & Steffenburg, 1987; Kobayashi, Murata, & Yoshinaga, 1992). However, about 40% of adolescents show significantly improved functioning. The reasons why early adolescence is a time of significant improvement for some with autism and deterioration for others remain unclear.

Long-Term Prognosis

The long-term prognosis for most children with pervasive developmental disorder is poor. Even when they receive intensive interventions during their childhood, most adults with autism have difficulty caring for themselves and continue to show a variety of social and language deficits. Kobayashi and colleagues (1992), for example, found that only 27% of their sample of 197 people with autism who had received services during childhood were living independently, while the remaining 73% needed ongoing individual supervision. Higher IQ levels and the development of some language before age 5 are the best predictors of a better long-term outcome for those with autism (Klinger et al., 2003). However, even those with language and high IQs often experience ongoing difficulties in social relationships.

Children and adults with autism also have a higher rate of early death than others. Shavelle, Strauss, and Pickett (2001) found that among children born between 1983 and 1997 in California, those who had been diagnosed with autism were about 2½ times more likely to have died. Those with IQs in the normal or mild mental retardation range were about 1½ times more likely to have died, and those with moderate to profound mental retardation were 3 times more likely to have died. Seizures and respiratory problems were the most common medical conditions causing death, whereas drowning and suffocation were the most common accidents.

Key Concepts

- Pervasive developmental disorders are usually chronic.
- Although the diagnosis of autistic disorder is usually not made before age 3, home movies of infants who are later diagnosed with autistic disorder show that many exhibit symptoms of autism by their first birthdays.
- About a quarter to a third of children with autistic disorder appear to have normal development for the first months of their lives with a subsequent loss of skills.
- Early adolescence is a critical time for those with autistic disorder, with 33–50% showing a marked decline in functioning and about 40% showing marked improvement.
- About a quarter of those with autistic disorder can function somewhat independently as adults, although most need ongoing supervision.

Families of Children with a Pervasive Developmental Disorder

As one can imagine after reading about the characteristics of children with a pervasive developmental disorder, their families experience higher levels of stress than other families (Sivberg, 2002). This stress often starts soon after the parents suspect that something is wrong with their children. Many parents report that they cannot obtain useful information from their pediatricians or others with whom they consult, and this causes considerable frustration (Schall, 2000). Having a pervasive developmental disorder finally diagnosed provides relief to many parents because they can learn more about the situation they are confronting. However, the diagnosis also creates heartbreak, feelings of loss, and concern about how they will meet the needs of their children (Whitaker, 2002). Family stress increases if family members encounter health care or education professionals who appear distant or unconcerned or who do not know enough about a pervasive developmental disorder (Sivberg, 2002). Further, the family can experience financial stress because one parent may need to stay home to care for the child with ASD, which may reduce family income.

Coping with the child's behaviors can be exhausting. Schall (2000) describes it as having to cope with a child "who has the needs of 10 toddlers with no language or impulse control to keep him safe." One parent she interviewed described a son who had become increasingly uncontrollable: "Susie (his sister) and I would be just running around trying to hold onto this kid. And I'd be yelling and trying to just get him so he didn't just totally go through the house where he could hurt us, hurt himself. . . . He used to stick knives in the light sockets. I mean, it was like PANIC!" (p. 413).

Another parent noted, "I feel really bad about this, but we have to lock him in his room at night. It is the only way to keep him safe. Otherwise he might come downstairs and try to cook something, or start a fire in the fireplace, or worse leave the house and wander away" (p. 413).

Finding support can be difficult for parents of children with a pervasive developmental disorder. It is often difficult for them to interact with neighbors or friends who do not understand the struggles they experience. One mother noted, "I remember one time, and this was when Max was older, and I was finding cracker crumbs and pieces of food all over the house, stuffed in cushions and stuff and (my friend) said, 'Why don't you just make it a rule that you can only eat in the dining room?' And I remember thinking, 'NOW WHY DIDN'T I THINK OF THAT!' I remember just thinking, there is *no way* she could understand this; she has no conception, and I just distanced myself from her" (Schall, 2000).

Despite the challenges they present, the family members of many children with a pervasive developmental disorder love them and appreciate what they and their experiences bring to their families (Schall, 2000). Parents report feeling very close to their children and a sense that the children feel close to them, despite their difficulties with social relationships. Parents and siblings report that their families often feel closer than other families because of their need to work together, and that they take great pride in the accomplishments of the child with a pervasive developmental disorder and the role that the family has taken in helping the child with those accomplishments.

Studies of siblings provide mixed information about the effect of having a sibling with a pervasive developmental disorder (a pattern that is also true for studies of siblings of children with mental retardation, as discussed in that chapter). Some studies suggest that they experience higher levels of depression and anxiety and feel more isolated in their families than do other children (Kaminsky & Dewey, 2002; Rossister & Sharpe, 2001). Other studies, however, do not find increased problems in siblings. The reasons for these contradictory findings remain unclear. There is some evidence that siblings of children with a pervasive developmental disorder function better when there is more than one other sibling in the family, when the parents have higher levels of marital satisfaction, and when the parents are in a support group (Kaminsky & Dewey, 2002; Rivers & Stoneman, 2003). This may be due to the greater sense of support that these siblings receive—either through their relationships with their other siblings or through their relationships with parents who are functioning better.

Key Concepts

- Families with a child with a pervasive developmental disorder experience more stress than families of other children.
- Stress often starts with unanswered questions about an infant's or toddler's problem behaviors. A diagnosis of a pervasive developmental disorder helps parents understand what is happening with their child but also brings sadness and a sense of loss.

- Coping with a child who has a pervasive developmental disorder can be frustrating and exhausting.
- The evidence regarding the adjustment of the siblings of children with a pervasive developmental disorder is contradictory, although it appears that siblings who receive more support from other siblings or parents fare better.

Etiology

The search for the etiology of autism, Asperger's disorder, and PDDNOS is a complex process because it requires examining the causes of a wide range of apparently unrelated symptoms (Robbins, 1997). To date, this search has been largely unsuccessful. However, several theories regarding the development of ASD have been proposed, and these have guided the search for the etiology or etiologies of ASD. In addition, our improving ability to measure the brain and its functioning raises hopes that the neurological bases for ASD may begin to become clearer over the next few years.

Our strategy for exploring the etiology of ASD will be as follows: We will first focus on three theoretical perspectives regarding the fundamental deficit in ASD and how this fundamental deficit creates a cascade of symptoms as a child develops. Because all the current theories view these fundamental deficits as neurologically based, we will then discuss the research that has attempted to discover what neurological problems exist in children and adults with ASD. Finally, we will examine what may be causing these neurological problems by exploring genetic influences and then environmental influences occurring prenatally or very early in life.

Theoretical Perspectives on the Fundamental Deficits in ASD

Each of the three theoretical perspectives that we will discuss views ASD as a disorder that starts with one or two basic impairments that are present at birth or very early in life, with these impairments influencing an increasing number of issues as the infant and toddler develops. These issues then impair the subsequent development of the child and adolescent, as shown in Figures 12.2, 12.3, and 12.4. In addition, each of these theoretical perspectives assumes that the basic impairment is caused by a neurological problem, although our current understanding of the neurological problems associated with ASD does not allow further specification. The first two theories focus on the social and language problems of children and adults with ASD; the third incorporates issues related to the restricted, stereotyped behaviors of those with ASD.

Affective Impairments as the Foundation of ASD

Hobson (1989) and Mundy and Sigman (1989) have hypothesized that the fundamental deficit in autism is an affective deficit: Children with autism are unable to connect emotionally with other people. This is the same hypothesis suggested by Kanner (1943) in his initial article titled "Autistic Disturbances of Affective Contact."

Hobson (1989) asserts that most infants have an innate ability to sense and understand the affective states of other people, especially their caregivers. This ability lets them make emotional connections with other people and form bonds with them. These bonds provide the foundation for the infant's developing understanding of others as separate beings with their own feelings and beliefs.

Infants with ASD, however, do not have this innate capacity to form affective bonds with their caregivers. Without the ability to make affective connections, the connection between these infants and their caregivers is not much different from the connections between the infant and objects. Consequently, infants with ASD do not engage in interpersonal activities with caregivers. Mundy and Sigman (1989) suggest that joint attention is the first essential task of infancy disrupted by these children's inability to form emotional connections with caregivers.

As noted in Figure 12.2, because they have few meaningful interactions with caregivers, children with ASD do not have opportunities to develop an understanding of other people as unique and separate beings with different mental states. Because they lack this understanding, children with ASD develop patterns of interacting with others as if they were not distinct individuals. For example, their pragmatic language is of poor quality because they do not recognize that others do not have the same information as they do.

Cognitive Impairments as the Foundation of ASD

Baron-Cohen (1988), Happe and Frith (1995), and others have hypothesized that the fundamental deficit in ASD is cognitive: Infants and young children with ASD do not comprehend that others have feelings and thoughts that differ from their own.

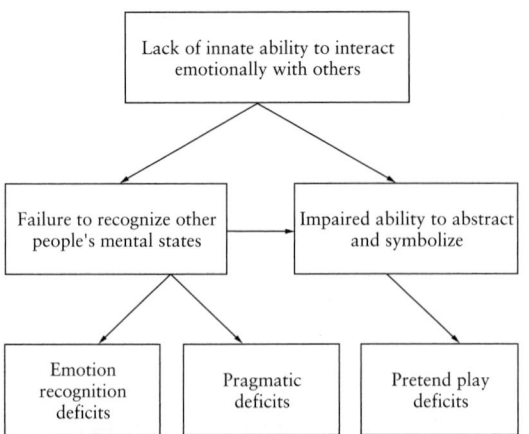

FIGURE 12.2 *The Affective Theory*

Each of us knows about our own feelings and beliefs. This knowledge can be considered a collection of representations. For example, I know that I believe hockey is more enjoyable to watch than soccer; I know that I feel the emotion of joy whenever I watch certain movie scenes. In addition to knowing about their own representations, most people have beliefs about others' representations. For example, I believe that my friends Steve and Martha have very liberal political views, and I believe that my friend Pat feels great satisfaction while fishing. These beliefs of mine are **meta-representations**—that is, representations about representations. My meta-representations help me to distinguish myself from my three friends: One of the reasons why I know that I am separate from Steve and Martha is because their political views are more liberal than mine; I know that I am separate from Pat because he gets much more enjoyment from fishing than I do.

It is argued that children with ASD do not have the innate ability of most humans for meta-representations. Without the ability to have meta-representations, children with ASD do not develop the understanding that other people have beliefs or feelings that are distinct from theirs; consequently, they do not develop the understanding that others have minds that are distinct from their minds (see Figure 12.3). The understanding that others have separate minds has been called a **theory of mind.** Except for some with the highest functioning, children with ASD do not possess theory of mind (Baron-Cohen, 2001).

Because of their lack of theory of mind, children with autism do not engage in a variety of social interactions in which other children innately engage. For example, they do not engage in joint attention because they do not understand that others can have attention on something other than what they have their attention on or that what another person is attending to might be interesting to them. Similarly, they do not have pragmatic language

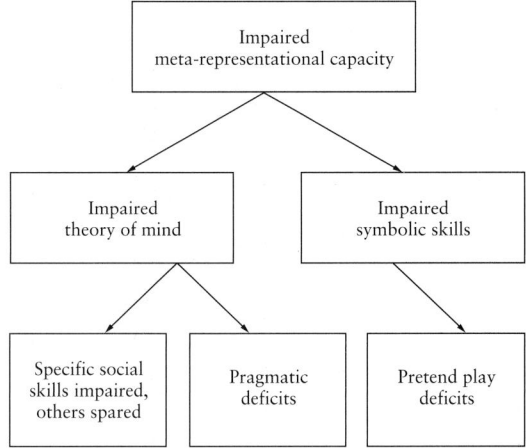

FIGURE 12.3 *The Cognitive Theory*

skills because these skills require that a person understand that another person needs to be given information that the speaker has.

Perceptual Impairments as the Foundation of ASD

Trepagnier (1996) and Smith and Bryson (1994) have proposed theories that, although different, both focus on perceptual impairments as the fundamental problem in autism. Both theories suggest that infants and children with ASD do not have the ability to perceive others and their actions in cohesive ways.

Trepagnier (1996) suggests that neurological problems associated with ASD cause most sensory perceptions to produce overstimulation that the infant finds stressful. She notes that all infants can at times become overstimulated by social contact, and when they do, a common strategy is to avert their gaze from others—a rudimentary form of self-regulation. She suggests that children with ASD may have perceptual systems that result in their being chronically overwhelmed by the sensory stimulation of social contact, so they withdraw from social contact as much as possible. The first indication of this, she argues, is failure to gaze into the faces of caregivers. This disrupts the pattern of social behaviors that develops naturally in other infants. For example, failing to gaze at others disrupts joint attention behaviors because the infant does not see that another person is attending to something; later this failure to gaze disrupts social imitation. Because it is through joint attention, imitation, and other social behaviors that the developing infant begins to understand the basic concept of "other" and that

Overwhelming perceptual experiences may be at the foundation of autistic symptoms in some children.

others have minds separate from the infant's, the child with ASD does not develop the sense that others have separate minds, which leads to a variety of social and language impairments (see Figure 12.4). Interestingly, Trepagnier also argues that the overstimulation experienced by infants and children with ASD leads directly to another group of symptoms—restricted and stereotyped behaviors—which, as discussed earlier, may be the child's attempt to focus perceptions and reduce their overwhelming nature (Guess & Carr, 1991).

Smith and Bryson (1994), building on the work of Dawson and Levy (1989), suggest that difficulty with integrating sensory input is the fundamental problem in ASD. One function of the brain is to integrate input from the various senses, produce an understanding of these perceptions, and then produce motor responses when needed. Smith and Bryson (1994) suggest that the relationship between the senses is unusual in children with ASD. This may interfere with their ability to comprehend what is being perceived and create a motor response to it. It is as if the sensory input comes in and is jumbled together into an experience that makes little or no sense instead of being merged into a meaningful perception upon which the child can act.

Smith and Bryson argue that this fundamental problem interferes with a child's ability to imitate others, which they view as a critical setback in the development of children with ASD. When interacting with another person, the sensory signals a child receives become muddled and thus make little sense to the child. This stops the child from being able to imitate an action

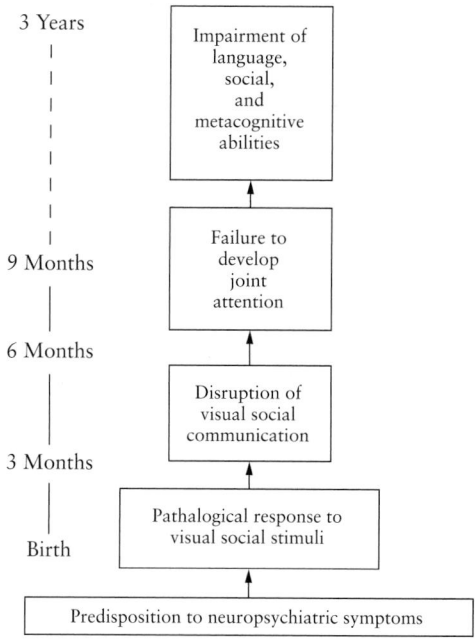

FIGURE 12.4   *Development of Social and Communicative Impairments of Autism*

because imitation requires a clear perception of an event that can be translated into an imitative motor response. This inability to imitate disrupts the development of the child's social interactions and fragments the child's social experiences. This can significantly damage the child's developing ability to be social with others, including using language in social contexts.

Analysis of the Theories

Each theory takes impairments in the development of children with ASD that are well documented by research and then speculates about events occurring before those impairments that are causing them—in essence reaching back in time and hypothesizing about the presence of some fundamental unseen problem. For example, infants and children with ASD clearly have disrupted abilities in joint attention, as suggested by the affective theories, in theory-of-mind abilities, as suggested by the cognitive theories, and in face gazing and imitation, as suggested by the perceptual theories. However, that the lack of joint attention is caused by a lack of affective connection, that the lack of theory of mind is caused by an inability to form meta-representations, and that the lack of face gazing and imitation is caused by perceptual problems remain hypotheses.

Each theory has weaknesses. For example, the affective theories have a difficult time explaining why children with autism develop attachment behaviors to their primary caregivers because these behaviors are based partly on an affective connection (Baron-Cohen, 1988). Mundy and Sigman (1989) suggest that one weakness of the cognitive theories is that joint attention skills appear to develop in all children before they develop meta-representational skills, so a lack of meta-representational skills cannot explain the problems with joint attention that are common to children with ASD. In addition, some high-functioning children with autism and some children with Asperger's disorder do have theory of mind. Perceptual theories that focus on imitation are also hard-pressed to explain problems with joint attention because the development of imitation follows the development of joint attention.

Despite their weaknesses, these theories suggest the unseen causes of the behaviors we can observe. In this way, each theory is valuable. At this time, however, we do not have enough information about the earliest development of children with ASD to know which theory or theories are most likely to be correct. Future research may help us with this task. At this point, it seems reasonable to appreciate each theory for the directions it provides for future research.

Neurological Bases for the Symptoms of ASD

Researchers now believe that one or more neurological problems are at the foundation of the fundamental deficits associated with ASD. Two areas of neurological functioning that have received the most attention are brain morphology (the structure of the brain) and neurotransmitter functioning.

Brain Morphology

Several basic conclusions about the influence of brain morphology on ASD can be drawn from years of studying the brains of children and adults with ASD, from studies of other animals in which autistic-like symptoms have been induced, and from the fact that the symptoms of autism are so varied:

- Problems in the structure and functioning of one or two areas of the brain are unlikely to be causing ASD. Many studies have looked for size differences in specific parts of the brain between those with ASD and others, or for differences in how specific parts of the brain function. Overall, these studies have either found no differences or found inconsistent results (Bauman & Kemper, 2005). In addition, it is unlikely that the range of symptoms of ASD would be caused by problems in one or two specific parts of the brain.

- Problems with connections between parts of the brain, and a consequent disruption in the organization of brain functions, may be causing ASD. We know far less about the complex ways in which parts of the brain interact with each other than we know about the functioning of the individual parts. Exploring problems with those connections may provide important insights into ASD (Robbins, 1997).

- Evidence suggests that abnormal developmental processes may cause impairments throughout the brains of those with ASD. It appears that these abnormal development processes occur during the prenatal period and early in life, which is when neurons proliferate, become interconnected, and then gradually decrease in size and number as some connections are used frequently and others become obsolete. These abnormal processes appear to lead to overdevelopment in some parts of the brain and underdevelopment in others (Klinger et al., 2003). Evidence for overdevelopment in parts of the brain comes from consistent findings that the brains of those with ASD are larger than those who do not have ASD, particularly in the parietal, temporal, and occipital lobes. In addition, higher densities of cells in various structures of the brain, such as the limbic system, have been found in the brains of those with ASD (Piven & O'Leary, 1997; Robbins, 1997). Evidence for underdevelopment in other parts of the brain comes from research documenting decreased size of several subcortical areas, particularly of the cerebellum (Courchesne, 1997). Evidence for imbalances in brain structures comes from Carper and Courchesne (2000), who found that the ratio of tissue in the frontal cortex to tissue in the cerebellum was larger for children with autistic disorder (more tissue in the frontal cortex, less in the cerebellum) than for children who did not have autism.

Carper and Courchesne (2000) discuss two possible mechanisms through which underdevelopment could occur in some parts of the brain and overdevelopment in others. The first is that some genetic or environmental problem could directly influence growth patterns in several parts of the brain. For example, a genetic influence could produce overdevelopment in the cortex and underdevelopment in the cerebellum. The second possibility is that genetic or environmental influences might produce underdevelopment in one part of the brain, and this underdeveloped area could cause overdevelopment in areas of the brain to which it has significant connections. As an example of this process, they note that abnormal neural signals from subcortical areas can produce enlargements of the cortex. They suggest that abnormal neural activity caused by problems in the development of the cerebellum in children with ASD could cause the type of overdevelopment in the cortex observed in many of them.

Carper and Courchesne's hypothesis could help to explain the pervasive nature of the impairments seen in children with autism. Whereas it might be difficult to imagine the type of genetic or environmental factors that could directly influence many regions of a developing brain, our current knowledge of brain functioning during development allows us to understand more easily how problems in one or two areas of a brain subsequently influence the development of other areas, thereby having an effect throughout the brain.

Neurotransmitter Abnormalities

Several neurotransmitters have been the focus of study because of their known relationship with some symptoms of autism. Serotonin, for example, has been linked to problems with sensory perception, motor function, and memory; dopamine has been linked to restricted and stereotyped behaviors; and norepinephrine has been linked to attention, arousal, memory, anxiety, and movement (Klinger et al., 2003). Overall, a substantial body of research shows no consistent pattern of differences in levels of dopamine or norepinephrine between children and adults with autism and other children and adults. About 40% of adults with autism have shown high concentrations of serotonin in their blood platelets (Poustka, 1998). However, the implications of these high levels of serotonin are not clear because investigations focused on serotonin in the cerebrospinal fluid have not found similar high levels. At this time, the role of neurotransmitters in the development or severity of autistic symptoms remains unclear.

Causes of the Yet-to-be-Understood Neurological Impairments

Genes, prenatal and postnatal injuries, and environmental toxins have all been explored as possible causes of the neurological impairments assumed to be at the foundation of ASD. As we will see, there is clear evidence of the role of genes, as well as clear evidence that injuries and environmental toxins play a rare or nonexistent role in the development of ASD.

Genetic Influences

The most compelling evidence for a genetic influence on autism comes from twin studies. As one can imagine, given the rarity of autism and the infrequency of twins, finding a large sample of twins in which one twin has ASD can be quite a challenge. However, a study in Great Britain found 25 MZ and 20 DZ twin pairs in which at least one twin had autistic disorder (Bailey et al., 1995). In 60% of the MZ twins, both twins had autistic disorder (that is, they were *concordant* for autism), and only one (5%) of the DZ pairs was concordant for autism. Further, when these researchers considered autistic-like symptoms that did not rise to the level warranting a diagnosis of autistic disorder (which may be synonymous with PDDNOS), 90% of the MZ twin pairs and 10% of the DZ twin pairs were concordant.

Family studies have also yielded important information about the genetic influences on autism. About 3% of the siblings of children with autism also met the criteria for autistic disorder in one large study in Great Britain—a prevalence much above that seen in the general population (Rutter, 2000). Another study found that about 12% of siblings of children with autism showed significant social or language impairments that did not rise to the level associated with autism (Bolton, MacDonald, & Pickles, 1994). In addition, parents of children with autism have higher rates of aloof, rigid, or anxious personality traits, an increased frequency of pragmatic language difficulties, and fewer friends than do parents of children who do not have autism (Piven, Palmer, Landa et al., 1997).

Rutter (2000) notes that the results of twin and family studies suggest several things. First, the heritability estimate for autistic disorder or ASD is about 90%. There are very few disorders for which heritability estimates are higher than 90%, indicating the strong genetic influence on autism and ASD. Second, the low concordance rate among DZ twins suggests that the genetic source of autistic disorder is not one gene but several genes interacting with each other. DZ twins share about 50% of the same genes, so one would expect a higher concordance rate than 5% or 10% if autism were largely influenced by one gene because any particular gene is likely to be shared by about· 50% of DZ twins. Third, the presence of milder forms of the symptoms of autistic disorder in a large percentage of MZ twin pairs that were not concordant for autism, and in the siblings and parents of children with autism, suggests that genetic influences play an important role in disturbances that resemble milder forms of autistic disorder. Finally, Rutter notes the wide range of the severity of the autistic symptoms seen within most of the MZ twin pairs who were concordant for autism in the Bailey study. Given that both members of each MZ pair had the same genes, and given the clear genetic influence on the disorder, Rutter found it noteworthy that the levels of their symptoms varied so extensively. Some process other than the genetic liability for the disorder apparently has a significant influence on the severity of the children's symptoms. To date, this process or the influences on this process have not been identified.

Notes from the Author: More than One Child with Autism

As we have seen throughout this chapter, the challenges to parents who are raising children with a pervasive developmental disorder, particularly autistic disorder, can be immense. In each of two studies of the genetic influences on autism (Bailey et al., 1995; Steffenburg et al., 1989), one set of triplets, all concordant for autism, was found. Imagine the challenges faced by those parents and all in their support network!

Studies conducted at the molecular level to find the genes that influence the etiology of autism have begun recently. There are few clues about which specific genes should be investigated, so work in this area is proceeding slowly. Areas of the X chromosome have been investigated because of the higher frequency of autism in boys and because of a suggested link between Fragile X syndrome and autism (**Fragile X syndrome** is discussed in the chapter about mental retardation). However, none of the genes investigated thus far on the X chromosome have been implicated in autism (Szatmari & Jones, 1998). Genome-wide studies have implicated all of the chromosomes as potential locations of genes related to autism. To date, work has focused on chromosomes 7 and 15, although no specific genes on these chromosomes have been found to be implicated in autism (Bespalova, Reichert, & Buxbaum, 2005).

Prenatal, Postnatal, and Perinatal Injuries

Because of the less than 100% concordance rate for autistic disorder among MZ twins, and because symptoms of autism have been found in young infants, many studies have explored whether prenatal, postnatal, or perinatal problems could influence the etiology of autism. Many of these studies have found one or two problems occurring more frequently in children with autism than in their siblings or other children, but no differences have been found consistently across studies (Klinger et al., 2003). This raises the possibility that a variety of problems during the prenatal to perinatal periods might influence the development of autism in some children; or perhaps researchers have been unable to identify the primary environmental influences on the development of autism.

Vaccines

Considerable concern was felt by many parents when Wakefield and colleagues (1998) proposed that the vaccine against measles, mumps, and rubella (MMR) commonly given to infants in the United States and many other industrialized countries might be causing late-onset autism in some cases. This claim was based on 12 cases of young children with late-onset symptoms of autism; the parents or physicians of 8 of the children linked the onset of their symptoms to the time of the MMR vaccine. Wakefield and colleagues (1998) suggested that the increase in the number of cases of autism during the past two decades might be partly caused by the MMR vaccine.

Two studies have refuted this claim by examining the number of reported cases of autism for several years and the use of the MMR vaccine during that time (Dales, Hammer, & Smith, 2001; Kaye et al., 2001). Both reports showed that the number of identified cases of autism had increased dramatically during the study years (children born in California from 1980 to 1994 for the Dales study; children born in Great Britain from 1988 to 1999 for the Kaye study) but that the percentage of children receiving the MMR vaccine remained constant over those years. Even stronger evidence comes from a study of all Japanese infants and young children in Yokohama. The use of the MMR vaccine decreased dramatically from 1988 through 1992; and from 1993 onward, virtually no infant received the MMR vaccine. However, the rate of autism increased dramatically during this time, particularly since 1993 (Honda, Shimizu, & Rutter, 2005). Although these studies do not address the issue of whether the MMR vaccine is associated with autism in some children, they do show clearly that the vaccine has not significantly influenced the increase in cases of autism seen over the past decade or two.

Key Concepts

- Although there is general agreement that the pervasive developmental disorders are neurological disorders, no specific neurological problems have been consistently implicated.
- Three theories describe how initial neurologically based problems lead to a cascade of problems as a child develops.
- A theory focused on affective connections suggests that a failure to connect emotionally to a caregiver inhibits the developing child from engaging in joint attention, which creates other problems and impedes understanding that others are distinct from the child and have their own thoughts and feelings.
- A cognitively based theory suggests that the developing child's inability to form meta-representations inhibits the child's ability to understand others as having distinct minds, which inhibits the child's ability to engage in joint attention, imitation, and a variety of social interactions.
- A theory based on problems with perceptions suggests that some infants experience sensory perceptions as overwhelming, which makes them withdraw into themselves and inhibits their ability to relate to others and understand that they are distinct. A second theory suggests that an infant's inability to integrate sensory perceptions obstructs his or her ability to imitate others, which fragments the child's social experiences and impedes social and language learning.
- Studies of the structure and function of the brains of children and adults with ASD have not revealed the neurological source of ASD but have suggested the following:
  - Problems in the structure and functioning of one or two areas of the brain are unlikely to be causing ASD.
  - Problems with connections between varying parts of the brain may be causing ASD.
  - Neurological problems may be caused by abnormal developmental processes during the prenatal and early postnatal periods, which cause overdevelopment in some parts of the brain and underdevelopment in others.
- Genes strongly influence the neurological problems assumed to cause ASD, although the specific genes that may be causing these problems have not been identified.

- ASD may be influenced by prenatal, postnatal, or perinatal problems, or by vaccines; but research to date has not identified problems associated with most cases of ASD.

In the next two sections, we explore the rarer pervasive developmental disorders: Rett's disorder and childhood disintegrative disorder. Afterward we examine therapeutic interventions for all the pervasive developmental disorders.

Rett's Disorder

In the 1960s Andreas Rett, an Austrian psychiatrist, was the first of several psychiatrists and other physicians to recognize a set of symptoms in a few girls whose development had proceeded normally during their early infancy and then had deteriorated (Hagberg, 2002). Conferences were organized to bring these physicians together, and it became clear that these girls had similar symptoms. An international conference in 1988 formalized a set of diagnostic criteria for what was labeled *Rett syndrome* (Volkmar & Lord, 1998).

The diagnostic criteria for Rett's disorder and childhood disintegrative disorder are similar, although there is more emphasis on problems with physical movement (particularly with hand movement) in Rett's disorder (see Table 12.5). Many symptoms of Rett's disorder are similar to those of autistic disorder, but the onset of symptoms follows a period of apparently normal development for at least five months.

TABLE 12.5

Diagnostic Criteria for 299.80 Rett's Disorder

A. All of the following:
    (1) Apparently normal prenatal and perinatal development.
    (2) Apparently normal psychomotor development through the first five months after birth.
    (3) Normal head circumference at birth.
B. Onset of all of the following after the period of normal development:
    (1) Deceleration of head growth between ages 5 and 48 months.
    (2) Loss of previously acquired purposeful hand skills between ages 5 and 30 months with the subsequent development of stereotyped hand movements (e.g., hand wringing or hand washing).
    (3) Loss of social engagement early in the course (although often social interaction develops later).
    (4) Appearance of poorly coordinated gait or trunk movements.
    (5) Severely impaired expressive and receptive language development with severe psychomotor retardation.

Characteristics and Experiences of Children with Rett's Disorder

Girls and women with Rett's disorder share a variety of characteristics with those who have autism, particularly low-functioning autism. They have marked impairments of language and social interaction and engage in stereotyped behaviors, although these behaviors are often limited to hand behaviors (Hagberg, 2002). The intelligence of those with Rett's disorder is almost always in the severe or profound range of mental retardation (APA, 2000).

Some characteristics distinguish those with Rett's disorder from those with other pervasive developmental disorders (Hagberg, 2002). Breathing is often affected; this includes episodes of hyperventilation and breath holding. Girls with Rett's disorder hold their breath frequently, sometimes for as long as a minute, which can be very disturbing to their caregivers. Many of them also swallow air, resulting in bloating of the stomach. Hagberg (2002) notes that in extreme cases enough air can be swallowed to make a girl appear as if she were in the later stages of a pregnancy. The reasons for these breathing problems are not known.

Two other behaviors that can be distressing to those around them are night laughter and screaming spells (Hagberg, 2002). **Night laughter** appears to occur mostly in younger girls. They wake in the middle of the night laughing loudly, and they continue laughing after waking, sometimes for hours. Some older girls experience spells of violent screaming that usually start for no apparent reason and can last for hours. The causes of this laughter and screaming remain unclear, although some parents and clinicians hypothesize that the screaming is in response to physical pain.

Another feature that distinguishes Rett's disorder from the other pervasive developmental disorders is gross motor problems that cause significant impediments to walking or other body movements (APA, 2000). Most girls with Rett's disorder have poor coordination and often walk with an awkward gait. Other physical problems magnify the impact of their coordination problems (Hagberg, 2002). Many girls experience a deceleration in foot growth so that they have much smaller feet than others their size. In addition, their feet and legs often become locked in rigid positions. Finally, back deformities are common, with a particularly problematic double curvature of the spine often developing throughout childhood and adolescence. In the best of circumstances, these problems make walking and standing more difficult. However, many of these girls are confined to wheelchairs, and the percentage of those with Rett's disorder who must use a wheelchair for mobility increases as they get older.

Prevalence and Developmental Course

The prevalence of Rett's disorder is much lower than that of autistic disorder or ASD. Tanguay (2000) estimates the prevalence of Rett's disorder at about 0.7 to 1 case per 10,000 children. Rett's disorder has been reported exclusively in females, apparently because the genetic mutation causing Rett's disorder is lethal to developing male fetuses (Tanguay, 2000).

Most children with Rett's disorder show typical development for the first several months of their lives; the first signs of significant loss of functioning usually appear only after about five months. However, retrospective reports from parents suggest that symptoms such as abnormal neck and hand movements and delayed language development occur in some children who are later diagnosed with Rett's disorder. These early symptoms are usually not of sufficient magnitude to raise concerns in the parents or the child's pediatricians, and their possible significance becomes apparent only after the other more obvious symptoms develop (Sandberg, Ehlers, Hagberg, & Gillberg, 2000).

The loss of previously developed skills occurs between 1 and 3 years of age for most children with Rett's disorder. The loss is very rapid in some children but may take as long as a year in others (Hagberg, 2002; Sandberg et al., 2000). During this time, early language development is lost, and children who once were saying words or sentences become mute. Social responding is lost, and many girls appear to have withdrawn into their own world. Most children with Rett's disorder lose the purposeful functioning of their hands during this time and begin stereotyped hand movements, such as hand wringing, twisting, or clapping. They also lose many of their gross motor skills, making walking and other large-body movements difficult. Breathing problems begin and increase in severity.

After this significant decline there is a plateau, usually between ages 3 and 10, with no further loss of physical function and a small to moderate improvement in social functioning. However, during this plateau, most children with Rett's disorder develop epilepsy, which is often severe. Beginning during adolescence and continuing into adulthood, most experience an ongoing decrease in gross motor skills to the point where many adults with Rett's disorder cannot walk (Hagberg, 2002; Sandberg et al., 2000).

Etiology

In the few incidents in which a twin has Rett's disorder, 100% of the MZ twin pairs have been concordant for Rett's disorder and no DZ twin pairs have been concordant (Tanguay, 2000). This suggests a strong genetic influence (or possibly an exclusively genetic influence—but the number of twin cases is small enough that such a strong conclusion is not warranted at this time). The search for the implicated gene or genes has focused on the X chromosome because all known cases involve girls, suggesting that male fetuses with the genetic problem do not survive the prenatal period and thus could be considered to have a more severe outcome of the disorder. (The X chromosome is indicated when males are more affected because the second X chromosome that all girls have may mollify the consequences to the girl of one damaged or mutated X chromosome, whereas boys, who have only one X chromosome, experience the full effect of a damaged or mutated X chromosome. A similar pattern is found in Fragile X disorder, which is described in the chapter about mental retardation.)

A mutation of one gene on the X chromosome, the MECP2 gene (methyl-CpG binding protein 2 gene), has been implicated in about 80% of the cases of Rett's disorder, as well as in other developmental disorders such as learning disabilities and Angelman syndrome (see the chapter about mental retardation for a description of Angelman syndrome) (Percy, 2002). Consequently, it appears that an important cause of Rett's disorder has been identified. Other genes may also be implicated through further research.

Key Concepts

- Children with Rett's disorder develop normally for the first several months of life and then experience the onset of symptoms.
- Children with Rett's disorder experience a loss of most acquired skills between 1 and 3 years, then a plateau where there may be some improvement in social functioning for about 10 years, and then a decline in motor functioning that can continue through adolescence and adulthood.
- Almost all children with Rett's disorder have an IQ in the severe or profound range of mental retardation. Few can speak, and all experience significant social impairments. Stereotyped hand movements, breathing abnormalities, night laughter, and screaming spells are common.
- Rett's disorder appears to be caused by a mutation in the MECP2 gene in most cases.

Childhood Disintegrative Disorder

The rarest of the pervasive developmental disorders, childhood disintegrative disorder, was first described by Theodore Heller in 1908, who used the term *dementia infantilis* (*dementia* is from the Latin *de,* "out or away from," and *mentis,* "the mind") to describe six children who developed normally for several years and then experienced an extreme loss of function. His writing does not seem to have been widely known until the 1970s, when other psychiatrists began to describe rare patients with similar symptoms. The diagnostic criteria for childhood disintegrative disorder are shown in Table 12.6.

Characteristics and Experiences of Children with Childhood Disintegrative Disorder

After the loss of abilities that characterizes the onset of childhood disintegrative disorder, children with this disorder appear similar to those with low-functioning autistic disorder (Zwaigenbaum et al., 2000). Assessments of the few children with childhood disintegrative disorder suggest that they have the lowest functioning of all children with a pervasive developmental disorder. Their IQ is most often in the severe or profound range of mental retardation, and most of them require institutional care to meet their daily needs (Volkmar & Lord, 1998).

TABLE 12.6

Diagnostic Criteria for 299.10 Childhood Disintegrative Disorder

A. Apparently normal development for at least the first two years after birth as manifested by the presence of age-appropriate verbal and nonverbal communication, social relationships, play, and adaptive behavior.

B. Clinically significant loss of previously acquired skills (before age 10 years) in at least two of the following areas:
   (1) Expressive or receptive language.
   (2) Social skills or adaptive behavior.
   (3) Bowel or bladder control.
   (4) Play.
   (5) Motor skills.

C. Abnormalities of functioning in at least two of the following areas:
   (1) Qualitative impairment in social interaction (e.g., impairment in nonverbal behaviors, failure to develop peer relationships, lack of social or emotional reciprocity).
   (2) Qualitative impairments in communication (e.g., delay or lack of spoken language, inability to initiate or sustain a conversation, stereotyped and repetitive use of language, lack of varied make-believe play).
   (3) Restricted, repetitive, and stereotyped patterns of behavior, interests, and activities, including motor stereotypies and mannerisms.

D. The disturbance is not better accounted for by another specific Pervasive Developmental Disorder or by Schizophrenia.

Prevalence and Developmental Course

Only 126 cases of childhood disintegrative disorder had been identified by 2002, indicating how rare this disorder is. The ratio of boys to girls with childhood disintegrative disorder appears to be 4–5:1 (Malhotra & Gupta, 2002).

Children with childhood disintegrative disorder, by definition, develop normally for at least two years (APA, 2000). One study found an onset of symptoms between 2½ and 7 years, with a mean of 3.8 years (Malhotra & Gupta, 2002). Because so few children with childhood disintegrative disorder have been identified and studied, it is unclear whether milder symptoms are present before the obvious disintegration occurs.

Little is known about the developmental course of children with childhood disintegrative disorder, although it is clear that their high levels of impairments remain throughout childhood and adolescence (APA, 2000).

Etiology

The causes of childhood disintegrative disorder remain a mystery. It is possible that childhood disintegrative disorder represents a specific form of ASD, with a later onset and more severe course than the others. In this case the etiology of childhood disintegrative disorder and the other autistic disorders would be linked. Perhaps some characteristic of a child protects him or her from the development of autistic symptoms early in life; but this characteristic then breaks down and the cause of the disorder begins to exert itself on the child's development, resulting in the late onset of the disorder. However, childhood disintegrative disorder could be distinct from ASD, with its own etiology. A significant impediment to learning much about childhood disintegrative disorder is the small number of cases that are available for study.

Key Concepts

- Children with childhood disintegrative disorder experience normal development for at least two years, with a sudden loss of acquired skills between ages 2 and 7.
- Children with childhood disintegrative disorder experience profound problems in social and language development and with restricted, stereotyped behaviors.
- The etiology of childhood disintegrative disorder remains a mystery.

Therapeutic Interventions

The puzzling nature of autism and the other pervasive developmental disorders, and the desperation of many parents to find some treatment that will help their children emerge from the clutches of these disorders, have led to the creation of a wide range of therapeutic interventions for children, adolescents, and adults. Some of these interventions have foundations in solid theory and have shown their effectiveness through well-designed research. Other interventions appear have no well-designed research to support their effectiveness. However, the parents of many children and adolescents with autism continue to pursue all sorts of interventions—often buoyed by anecdotal reports of the effectiveness of an intervention with some children.

In this section we discuss therapeutic interventions for those with a pervasive developmental disorder and their families. No legitimate interventions have a goal of "curing" autism or another pervasive developmental disorder. Rather, the goals of these interventions are to help individuals with pervasive developmental disorders live the most fulfilling lives they can and to help their families cope effectively with having children with pervasive developmental disorders. A two-pronged intervention, used in most cases, tries to reduce the symptoms of the pervasive developmental disorder and enhance the ability of those with a pervasive developmental disorder to learn skills that will provide a more fulfilling life.

The goals of each intervention depend on the functioning of the child. The focus may be on developing basic self-help and recreational skills for those who are low-functioning, whereas a goal for high-functioning children might be inclusion in a wide array of educational and social activities so that the developing person can participate as fully as possible in academic, social, and employment opportunities.

Early Interventions

Early interventions are considered an essential part of services to children with ASD and their families for several reasons (Erba, 2000). There is some indication that early interventions may influence the developing brains of young children with ASD, which can help redirect their brain development closer to the path that occurs with most children (Bristol et al., 1996). In addition, early interventions provide a foundation of social and cognitive skills that can be built on as the child develops. They can also enable parents to help the child gain control over problematic behaviors before these problems become ingrained. Finally, early interventions can help families feel involved in a positive way in the development of their children, which may enhance the lives of family members and reduce the intensity of family problems that arise because of the challenges posed by ASD.

The best-known early intervention was designed, implemented, and evaluated by Ivar Lovaas and his colleagues (Lovaas, 1987; Lovaas & Smith, 1989). Lovaas believed that the neurological systems of children with autism were not well suited for learning in the environment in which most children learn well. However, he believed that children with autism could learn in an environment adapted to their needs and that their learning followed the same basic principles of operant conditioning that influence the learning of others. (See the chapter about basic psychological theories for an explanation of operant conditioning.) The intervention designed by Lovaas is intensive, with a parent, college student, or professional working with a child 40 hours each week, 50 weeks a year, for two to three years. (Two thousand hours a year are devoted to each child, which is a tremendous amount of time. The time you spend on all your coursework in college each year is probably about two-thirds of this amount.)

The intervention starts with one-on-one work with the child and instructor. Behaviors that innately occur during the development of young children are taught by breaking those behaviors into smaller steps and reinforcing a child each time one of these smaller steps is completed. For example, consider a skill common to most young children: looking at a person who calls his or her name. An early task of a person working with a child with autism (I will call this person the teacher) is likely to be teaching the child to orient to an adult saying his or her name because looking at a teacher is essential for ongoing learning. A strategy for teaching this skill might be this:

- The teacher and the child sit close together in chairs facing each other.
- The teacher says the child's name every few seconds.
- When the child makes any movement of his head in response to his name, he receives some reinforcement (perhaps a small piece of food the child likes).
- If the child makes no response for a while, the teacher may gently hold his chin, move his head in the direction of the teacher, and then

provide reinforcement. This type of prompting is minimized, however, because the goal is to have the child initiate behaviors.

- After each reinforcement, the process begins again: The teacher says the child's name and reinforces head movements. This happens many times.
- When the child moves his head consistently in response to his name, the requirement for him to receive a reinforcement changes so that he must move his head farther toward the teacher to receive the reinforcement.
- After each reinforcement, the process is repeated until the child moves his head farther consistently.
- This process continues, with the teacher requiring that the child's head turn increasingly in the direction of looking at the teacher. The amount of increased head turning for each step is determined by the teacher, based on how the child is learning and other child characteristics.
- As the learning progresses, the child might need to look at the teacher's face and eventually might need to look at the teacher's eyes to receive the reinforcement.
- When the child can do this consistently, the skill of looking at the teacher when the child's name is called might be considered complete (this could take several weeks of work to accomplish).

Another typically developing skill might be taught next, such as a joint attention skill of looking toward an object that the teacher points to or imitating simple and then more complex actions of the teacher. Language skills are also taught in this fashion. The teacher might display an object and say its name—for example, "doll." When the child makes any sound, she is reinforced. Later the child will need to say a sound resembling "doll" to receive the reinforcement, and eventually the word "doll" will need to be said.

Reinforcements may be changed to maintain the child's attention or interest. An important goal of the intervention strategy is to have verbal praise, a smile, or a warm touch become important reinforcers for a child. This often takes a long period to accomplish and must be done in a way that is sensitive to the sensory perceptions of a child (touching a child on the cheek might be reinforcing for some children and frightening for others). The process of changing reinforcers may use classical conditioning—perhaps providing candy and saying "Good for you, Bobby" at the same time, and eventually providing only the verbal praise.

Once the child has learned a variety of basic skills using one-on-one instruction, the second phase of instruction begins, which involves activities with other children. Social and language skills with other children and adults are taught using the same principles from the one-on-one instruction. This second phase allows children to engage in activities with others in more normal settings, which is an important part of the intervention.

An assessment of this intervention has shown strong positive changes in children's behaviors that are maintained for many years. The initial evaluation of the program compared the skills of children with autism who were assigned to three groups: those receiving the intensive intervention, those receiving 10 hours a week of the same intervention, and those receiving no specific intervention but engaging in whatever other services in their communities the parents chose to use (a community-care control group). Of the 19 children in the intensive treatment group, nine (47%) developed the skills necessary to complete the first grade in a regular classroom and had IQ scores in the average or above-average range, and an addition eight (42%) completed first grade in a special education class for those with language or learning disabilities. The other two children were in special education classes for children with autism, and their IQs remained in the severely retarded range. Only one child from the other two groups completed first grade in a regular classroom, and 53% of these groups continued in special education classes for children with autism. A later follow-up showed that eight of the nine children in the intensive intervention group who had completed first grade in a regular classroom continued to succeed in regular classrooms and that one child who was in the special education class for language or learning disabled children had been moved to a regular classroom, for a sustained rate of 47% of the children continuing in regular education classes.

Other intensive early interventions (based on Lovaas's model) have been developed and implemented for home-based or school-based instruction (Birnbrauer & Leach, 1993; Smith, Groen, & Wynn, 2000). A review shows that most children involved in them show significant improvement in IQ, social skills, and language skills (Green, 1996). Problems such as stereotyped behaviors are reduced dramatically in most of these children. Children enrolled in the programs when they are younger (ages 2–4 years) make more improvements than those enrolled later, and children with higher initial levels of IQ make more improvements than those with lower levels. The intensity of the instruction also influences results. Those receiving 30–40 hours of instruction each week make more progress than those receiving 10–20 hours. In addition, the best results are obtained by children involved in the intensive interventions for two or more years.

Interventions during the School-Age Years

Interventions during their school-age years for children with more severe forms of pervasive developmental disorder are likely to focus on continuing their development of basic social, language, and self-care skills. The focus for many children with less severe forms of ASD is to enhance social skills and language and develop academic skills at rates appropriate for the children. With all children, there is effort to reduce problematic behaviors as needed or maintain low levels of problem behaviors.

Improving Social Interactions

Several strategies have been created to continue the development of social interactions of preschool and school-age children with ASD. Some try to improve social interactions between children and parents, teachers, or other caregivers (Dawson & Galpert, 1990; Tiegerman & Primavera, 1984). A limitation of many strategies for promoting adult–child interactions is that they usually do not result in the child with autism engaging in more peer interactions, which is an important goal for children with autism. Consequently, other efforts have focused on organizing interactions between children with ASD and peers who have received special training for interacting with them. These specially trained peers are brought together with a child who has ASD and either initiate interactions with the child or respond to the child when the child initiates an interaction after being prompted by an adult (Rogers, 2000). The peer is reinforced by an adult monitor for continuing the activity. The child with autism often engages with the peer at some point and is reinforced for doing so. As the interactions continue, the reinforcement from adults for the peers and the child with autism is gradually reduced (Strain, Kerr, & Ragland, 1979).

Peer interactions are useful for promoting social interactions with children who have ASD (Rogers, 2000). Play between the children often continues past the point where any reinforcement is offered by the adult, suggesting that the social interactions themselves become reinforcing for both children. The social interactions of the child with ASD often generalize to other children, especially if the child with autism has interacted with several trained peers in different settings. Strain and Danko (1995) found that parents could be taught to train the siblings of children with autism to interact with them, and this training increased interactions among the siblings in the home.

Reducing Problem Behaviors

Interventions to reduce the problematic behaviors of children with a pervasive developmental disorder may need to continue throughout childhood or may be used intermittently as new problem behaviors arise or old ones reemerge. As noted earlier, early adolescence is a time of increased problem behavior for many children with ASD, often requiring focused attention on these behaviors during those years (Gillberg & Steffenburg, 1987; Kobayashi et al., 1992).

Problem behaviors that are most frequently the targets of intervention are stereotyped behaviors, aggression, and self-injurious behaviors (a more thorough discussion of self-injurious behaviors is included in the chapter about mental retardation). These behaviors are often chosen for intervention because they can endanger the child's health and interfere with the child's ability to learn and form relationships with others (Matson, Benavidez, Compton, Paclawskyj, & Baglio, 1996).

Many interventions use positive reinforcement to encourage behaviors that reduce problem behaviors. **Differential reinforcement of other behaviors (DRO)** is a technique that reinforces behaviors that are socially acceptable and allows the child with a pervasive developmental disorder to obtain the same result that a problem behavior may have accomplished. For example, if a child has learned that she can stop a medical exam by beginning stereotyped behaviors, she could be reinforced for indicating that she would like to take a break (thus making the stereotyped behaviors unnecessary). Through **differential reinforcement of incompatible behavior (DRI)**, a child is reinforced for engaging in behaviors that do not allow a problem behavior to occur. For example, a child who has a stereotyped behavior of flapping his arms could be reinforced for keeping his arms at his side.

The use of punishment (an aversive technique) is also common in many interventions focused on problem behaviors, although aversive techniques are controversial. For example, a child who bites his fingers might receive a slight slap on his leg or a whiff of an ammonia capsule when he does this. Finally, extinction can be used. *Extinction* is based on the observation that many behaviors that receive no reinforcement stop occurring. Thus if a child who makes repetitive sounds is ignored by those around him, he may stop making those sounds (for a more extensive discussion of these techniques, see the chapter about mental retardation).

Level of Inclusion in Regular Classrooms

An ongoing controversy is the extent to which children with ASD should be included as students in regular classrooms or whether they should attend separate special education classes for children with disabilities. Because many children with ASD learn in ways that are quite different from other children and may be frightened or distracted by the sensory input that occurs in a regular classroom, they might make more progress in specialized classes with less sensory stimulation and learning strategies designed for their needs (Mesibov & Shea, 1996; Rotholz, 1987). However, high-functioning children with autism may be able to take advantage of education in regular classrooms, which may facilitate their inclusion in mainstream society. In addition, they are more likely to develop and maintain better social skills when they interact regularly with children who do not have autism (Smith, Lovaas, & Lovaas, 2002). Consequently, it may be to their advantage to spend all or most of the day in a regular classroom.

Children with ASD who have no language, who are unable to function well in a highly stimulating environment, or whose problem behaviors need frequent attention may be poor candidates for inclusion in a regular classroom; they may benefit more from the specialized services available in a separate special education classroom or program. However, other children with ASD may progress better academically and socially if they are in a regular classroom for part or all of the day, particularly if intensive early interventions have helped them develop the basic social and academic skills that can be built on in regular classrooms. Careful analysis of the strengths and limitations of each child, and a flexible system that allows changes in educational placement as his or her needs change, are likely to generate the best educational placement.

Medication

Occasionally over the past two decades, a report of a child or two who appeared to improve dramatically when given a particular medication or nutritional supplement has sparked the hope that this treatment might improve the lives of many children and adults who have autism. However, systematic studies of each of these medications or supplements have shown that none of them produce the types of widespread results hoped for (Steingard, Connor, & Au, 2005). Although a few children respond well to medications, most do not. Why a small percentage respond favorably remains a mystery.

Although no medication has been found to remediate the core symptoms of autism or the other pervasive developmental disorders, psychotropic medications are used frequently to alleviate other symptoms that a child or adult with autism may have. (**Psychotropic medications** are those that influence mental experience or behavior; the term comes from the Greek *psyche,* "mind," and *trapein,* "to turn"—turning the mind in a new direction.) Antidepressants are commonly used to relieve symptoms of depression. Stimulants have been used to reduce impulsivity and overactivity, and antipsychotic drugs are used to reduce overactivity, aggressiveness, and self-injurious behaviors (Tanguay, 2000).

The use of medication for children and adults with autism is increasing. For example, Langworthy-Lam, Aman, and Van Bourgondien (2002) found that 46% of children and adults with a pervasive developmental disorder in North Carolina were taking a psychotropic medication, and an additional 18% were taking another medication (such as antiseizure medication) or a nutritional supplement (most commonly large doses of vitamin B-6, which has been hypothesized to ameliorate autism). This represented a 50% increase from the percentage taking medication in their earlier study published in 1995.

Facilitated Communication

Facilitated communication was created by Rosemary Crossley in Australia, initially to help children with cerebral palsy whose limited gross and fine motor control impeded their communication with others. During **facilitated communication** a trained facilitator supports the hand of a child or adult and helps move the hand over a set of pictures or words, or over a computer keyboard, with the child or adult then pointing to pictures or words or typing letters to form words and sentences. This lets the person who has the cognitive ability to communicate, but not the motor ability to speak or write, communicate with others. Based on its success with children with cerebral palsy, Crossley used the technique with children who had autism and produced intelligible communication from them. The technique was introduced to the United States by Douglas Biklen (1990), who argued that, like those with cerebral palsy, many children and adults with autism have the cognitive ability to communicate but not the motor ability to do so. After exposure on national television, facilitated communication was seen as a major breakthrough in the treatment of children and adults with autism and was used by therapists across the country (Romanczyk, Arnstein, Soorya, & Gillis, 2003).

Concern was raised, however, about the extent to which the communication was being produced by the facilitators, rather than by the children and adults with autism, since the facilitators moved the children's or adults' hands over the keyboards or pictures. Several studies attempted to address this issue by presenting information to a child that the facilitator did not see and then asking the child to answer questions about it, or by presenting questions to the child but not the facilitator. Whenever the information or the question was presented only to the child, the facilitated response made sense (contained appropriately constructed phrases) but did not relate to the question (Mostert, 2001; Romanczyk et al., 2003). The facilitators stated emphatically that they were not directing the child's response, and there is no reason to believe that they were not being completely honest; but it became clear that in some way the facilitators were the ones creating the communication from the child.

Proponents of facilitated communication responded to these studies by saying that they were all carried out in contrived environments that were not familiar to the children with autism, and thus they did not accurately assess the value of facilitated communication. In response, Kerrin, Murdock, Sharpton, and Jones (1998) designed an intriguing experiment conducted with two children in their classroom. The speech pathologist who had used facilitated communication with the children often in the past, and so was familiar to the children, agreed to wear dark glasses whenever she interacted with the children for the week before the experiment. Once the experiment began, the teacher either was blind to the stimulus the children saw (the insides of her dark glasses were covered) or could see the stimulus (nothing impeded her ability to see through her dark glasses). When the teacher could not see the stimulus, the children's facilitated communication about it was seldom accurate and was much less accurate than when she could see the stimulus.

Most evidence suggests that facilitated communication does not result in a child with autism being able to communicate with others. It may allow communication when a child has the cognitive ability but not the motor ability to communicate; but these situations appear to be uncommon.

Interventions for Families

Interventions for families who have a child with a pervasive developmental disorder usually involve education about the child's disorder, instruction for implementing an early intervention program, and participation in support groups. A program in Great Britain designed to discover and meet the needs of parents with preschoolers with ASD found that receiving information about autism was very important. It helped the parents understand their children and their behaviors. Specific suggestions for how to manage behavior and facilitate language and social development were also important. In addition, the parents appreciated the opportunity to meet and talk regularly with other parents of children with ASD. One mother noted that in a setting with other parents experiencing the same struggles, "There's no need to explain," which was a great relief to her (Whitaker, 2002). As noted earlier, parents in support groups appear to experience less stress, and their children who do not have ASD appear to function better (Kaminsky & Dewey, 2002).

As noted in the section about early interventions, many parents choose to implement these interventions themselves. Williams and Wishart (2003) found both benefits and drawbacks from the parents implementing early intervention. The principal benefits were that the intervention made the family feel more positive about their interactions with the child with autism and increased interactions among family members. For example, one mother stated, "Every day we feel we are understanding life as well as our son. We are more open with each other . . . understanding our son's needs and joining him has made us all feel closer" (Williams & Wishart, 2003). The principal drawback was that the time it took to employ the intervention meant that the mother had much less time with other family members. One mother noted, "I certainly spend a lot more time with my son and little time with my daughter, whereas before I spent more time with her. She is very aware of this and extremely jealous. She also frequently comments that everyone comes to the house for my son and no one comes for her" (Williams & Wishart, 2003). Currently it is not clear which characteristics of families or their members are associated with positive or negative reactions to implementing an early intervention program.

Key Concepts

- Many interventions have reduced the impairments of ASD for children, although no intervention has been developed that "cures" the pervasive developmental disorders.
- Early interventions focus on teaching a child with ASD the skills that develop in other children naturally. Intensive early interventions have resulted in much better functioning in most children who participate in them.
- Some interventions with preschool and school-age children help them develop social skills by interacting with adults or specially trained peers.
- Interventions to reduce problem behaviors focus on reinforcing behaviors that inhibit the problem behaviors. In some cases, aversive techniques have been used to stop potentially harmful problem behaviors, although these techniques remain controversial.
- Some children with ASD have been successfully integrated into regular classrooms in their schools. Others appear to receive better education through separate special education classes.
- Interventions for families include information from professionals, instruction in implementing an early intervention program, and support groups.

Notes from the Author

At the end of our exploration of autism and other pervasive developmental disorders, I think that it is worth noting again some of the words in the opening vignette of the professor who discussed her experiences as a child and adult with autism: "My high school science teacher, Mr. Carlock, used my fixation on cattle chutes to motivate me to study psychology and science. . . . While the school psychologist wanted to take my squeeze machine away, Mr. Carlock encouraged me to read scientific journals so I could learn why the machine had a relaxing effect. . . . If the psychologists had been successful in taking away my squeeze machine, maybe I would be sitting somewhere rotting in front of a TV instead of writing this chapter" (Grandin, 1992).

It is often easy for psychologists and other professionals to think they know what is right for a child with a disorder and to ignore the individual strengths of the child that can direct an intervention in the most effective way. All children have strengths—even those with severely disabling disorders, although these strengths are often hidden by the children's impairments. However, effective professionals, like Mr. Carlock, will search for a child's strengths and use them to help move the child forward.

Chapter Glossary

Autism spectrum disorder (ASD) has been proposed by many researchers and clinicians as a better diagnosis for the range of children with autistic disorder, Asperger's disorder, and PDDNOS.

Differential reinforcement of incompatible behavior (DRI) is a behavioral intervention that provides reinforcement for a behavior that is incompatible with a problematic behavior.

Differential reinforcement of other behaviors (DRO) is a behavioral intervention that provides reinforcement for a variety of behaviors other than a problematic behavior so that a child does not have to engage in problematic behavior to receive reinforcement.

Echolalia is a deviant form of language in which a person repeats the last few words of the previous speaker.

Facilitated communication is a procedure to help children communicate with others despite their having severely limited gross and fine motor control.

Fine motor skills are physical skills (such as writing and speaking) that involve small muscles.

Fragile X syndrome is the most common known cause of inherited mental retardation, affecting boys more often and more severely than girls.

Gross motor skills are physical skills (such as running and lifting) that involve large muscles.

High-functioning autism is a term used by many researchers and clinicians to describe children with autistic disorder who have IQs of 70 or above (that is, who are not mentally retarded).

Infantile autism was the term used for autistic disorder in the DSM-III.

IQ is the acronym for *intelligence quotient,* a measure of a person's intelligence.

Joint attention is the ability to notice something to which another person is attending—a skill of almost all infants and one hypothesized to be a fundamental social skill upon which many other social skills are based.

Meta-representations refer to beliefs about others' beliefs. The ability to form meta-representations is essential to forming a theory of mind.

Night laughter is a behavior common to children with Rett's disorder in which they wake at night laughing and continue laughing for several hours.

Pragmatics refers to the social use of language. Children and adults with ASD who have language usually have impaired pragmatic skills.

Prosody refers to the volume, rhythm, and intonation of speech. Children and adults with ASD who have language usually have impaired prosody.

Psychotropic medications are medications that influence mental experience or behavior (such as antidepressants or antianxiety medications).

Receptive language is the process of understanding the speech and other forms of language from other people.

Reciprocal social interaction is social interaction between people in which they respond to the actions of others (such as in a conversation or in playing a game together). This social behavior is impaired in children with all pervasive developmental disorders.

Savant abilities are abilities that are far above what almost any other person has.

Self-injurious behavior is physically damaging behavior that a person does to himself or herself, such as head banging or striking parts of the body with hands or fists.

Splinter skills are skills that are considerably above what one would expect given a person's general level of intelligence.

Stereotyped behaviors are repetitious, rhythmic behaviors that appear to have no function.

The **Strange Situation** is a procedure to measure a young child's attachment to his or her primary caregiver.

Theory of mind is the understanding that others have minds that are distinct from one's own.

Childhood-Onset Schizophrenia

Positive symptoms can be frightening to children with schizophrenia and their family members.

Schizophrenia is a severe and usually chronic neurological disorder that is very debilitating to most who have it (American Academy of Child and Adolescent Psychiatry, 2000). During the acute phase of schizophrenia, children or adults can experience hallucinations, delusions, and grossly disturbed behaviors. They may stand in odd positions for hours, scream uncontrollably because they feel pins sticking into them, or kill themselves because they believe they have been commanded by aliens to do so. It is the disorder to which most people refer when they use the term *madness* (Gottesman, 1991).

The symptoms of schizophrenia usually first appear during late adolescence or early adulthood. However, a small percentage of people with schizophrenia experience the onset of symptoms during childhood or early adolescence, and we focus on them in this chapter (Volkmar, 1996). Whether schizophrenia that begins during childhood (childhood-onset schizophrenia) is the same as the form that begins later, and why schizophrenia develops during childhood in a small number of cases, remain unclear and continue to be the focus of research. As we will see throughout this chapter, our knowledge is limited about most issues related to childhood-onset schizophrenia, and we are just beginning to learn about its causes and about the experiences of children who live with it.

A considerable stigma continues to be attached to schizophrenia, and the strange behaviors of children and adults with schizophrenia can cause others to ridicule them and to think of them as less than human. We must be careful to avoid stigmatizing those with schizophrenia. They and their families must struggle with a debilitating and sometimes terrifying disorder, and the strength needed for this struggle can be considerable.

Chapter Plan

After two vignettes of children with schizophrenia, we briefly explore the history of schizophrenia and the recent focus on childhood-onset schizophrenia. We then examine the diagnostic criteria for schizophrenia and the characteristics and experiences of children who have schizophrenia. Next we look at the small amount of research on the prevalence of childhood-onset schizophrenia and the course that the disorder takes as it develops. We then struggle to understand the etiology of schizophrenia in general and childhood-onset schizophrenia in particular. We next examine some research on the experiences of the families of children with schizophrenia. Finally we look at some controversial strategies for preventing schizophrenia and at the current strategies for providing treatment for children with schizophrenia and their families.

Case Study: A Child with Many Risk Factors for Schizophrenia

Beth grew up in a very disorganized and dysfunctional home. Her mother was hospitalized for psychiatric problems several times during Beth's childhood. When at home, Beth's mother occasionally beat her in response to commands she experienced to "beat the devil out of her child." Beth's father, who was often unemployed, abused her sexually from the time she was 9 years old—initially fondling her and, by the time she was 10, having intercourse with her several times a week.

Beth was seldom allowed outside her family's apartment except when she went to school. Her mother feared that she would be harmed by the other children, and her father worried that she might tell the neighbors about the abuse she was experiencing. Consequently, Beth knew few children living in her neighborhood. At school, Beth was mostly withdrawn from the other children, who found her odd. Although some children teased her occasionally, they mostly ignored her and let her sit by herself during recess and lunch.

By the time Beth entered the fifth grade, the school nurse had been concerned about her for several years. Beth was often disheveled when she came to school. She wore odd clothes that often did not fit well, and the nurse was concerned that she did not bathe regularly. By the fourth grade, she often seemed tired when she arrived at school; and by the fifth grade, Beth was coming to the nurse's office to sleep two or three times a week because she could not stay awake in class. One day the nurse noticed some bruises on her legs and decided that she needed to report this to the local child protective services office.

An investigation by child protective services revealed the physical and sexual abuse that Beth was experiencing and the neglect of her basic needs that she had experienced for years. At age 11, Beth was removed from her parents and placed in foster care. Her foster parents had been foster parents for about 10 years and were known in their county as parents who could work with very troubled children. When Beth came to live with them, they had two other foster children who were younger than Beth.

Her foster parents reported that Beth was withdrawn and that her behavior was often strange, which they attributed to her lack of socialization while living with her parents. The other foster children in their home actively shunned Beth; and her foster parents reported that if they were to be honest, they did not like Beth as much as they liked their other foster children. She was often suspicious of the other children and got upset if she found them near her bedroom. She was very anxious when around her foster father and often refused to be in the same room with him. Her foster parents felt that this behavior was reasonable, given Beth's sexual abuse by her father. But although they did not like Beth much, her foster parents believed that she could overcome many of her problems with the support and guidance she was receiving from them.

Despite the efforts of her foster parents and her teachers, Beth became progressively withdrawn at home and school. She had increasing difficulty sleeping and was often up most of the night. Her speech seemed more confused, although it was assumed that this was due to her general tiredness. Beth often seemed frightened, although she would not tell her foster parents why. Occasionally her foster mother would find her huddled in the corner of her bedroom, slowly rocking. She found this very disturbing and would pick Beth up and have her sit on her lap. However, Beth would sit woodenly on her lap rather than snuggling into her as her other children had.

After being in the foster home for about six months, Beth began to lash out in anger at school and at home, and she was occasionally very aggressive. Because of her aggression and the concern that she would seriously hurt another child, she was referred to a residential treatment facility. Thirty girls lived at the facility, and Beth shared a cottage with five other girls. The psychiatrist who consulted with the staff of the residential treatment facility noted that her behavior included many "negative symptoms" of schizophrenia. Despite the supportive environment of the residential treatment facility, Beth's behavior became progressively more withdrawn and odd, with periodic incidents of aggression. Within three months of being admitted, Beth began to experience auditory hallucinations commanding her to kill herself. Partly because of the warning by the psychiatrist and the information she provided to the staff about schizophrenia, the presence of Beth's hallucinations was recognized quickly. The psychiatrist prescribed antipsychotic medication for Beth, and she was monitored closely by the staff. Within a few weeks her hallucinations had ended, and she seemed calmer. She was exhausted for the next two weeks and slept about 12 hours each day. Following this, she was more animated and engaged in more activities with the staff and other children at the facility. However, she remained more withdrawn than the other children, and her interactions with others always seemed a bit odd.

At a meeting with the staff of the residential treatment facility, her caseworker, and her foster parents, it was decided that Beth would remain in the residential center for at least six months so that any renewal of her hallucinations could be noticed quickly. After these six months passed, Beth returned to her foster parents' home. She remained on her medication, although she often resisted taking it and her foster parents found that it was a challenge to ensure that she took her medication each day. Beth returned to her school, but she struggled academically and had few interactions with other children.

Some Issues Worth Noting

- The possibility that Beth inherited a genetic tendency toward schizophrenia from one or both of her parents.
- The extent to which Beth's behavior before the onset of the acute symptoms of schizophrenia was odd and problematic.
- The ease with which Beth's behavior in her foster home could be attributed to her previous abuse and neglect rather than to the onset of schizophrenia or another disorder.
- The ongoing difficulties that Beth experienced even after returning to her foster home.

Case Study: Childhood-Onset Schizophrenia from "Out of the Blue"

Until age 9, Peter was a happy boy who developed normally, did well in school, was popular with his friends, and enjoyed being a big brother to his sister who was three years younger. His family functioned well and was free of major problems.

About three months after his ninth birthday, Peter's behavior began to change. He seemed less happy and was more moody. He played less with his friends and sister, although he would do so when prompted by his parents. The quality of his schoolwork began to decline. For example, his homework, which once had always been done neatly and on time, was now disorganized and often late.

When his parents talked with him about whether anything was wrong, he said that he often felt tired but that nothing else was wrong. Despite his parents' efforts to cheer him up by taking family trips to places he liked and by having meals that he enjoyed, he continued to appear sad and withdrawn. His parents consulted with Peter's pediatrician about what to do, and the pediatrician suggested some counseling sessions for Peter with a licensed clinical social worker who worked with the pediatrician. After several sessions with the social worker, she suggested that Peter was showing signs of depression, and she recommended ongoing therapy and the possibility of the pediatrician prescribing antidepressant medication for Peter. The parents reluctantly agreed to allow Peter to take the antidepressant medication and agreed to continue therapy for Peter. However, Peter did not respond to the medication or the therapy. Despite everyone's efforts, Peter's performance in school continued to decline, and he became more withdrawn. Everyone was baffled and frustrated.

About six months after he began therapy, Peter's mother found him in his bedroom one afternoon, huddled in the corner, crying and rocking fiercely. When she reached down to touch him, he looked at her and screamed. She thought he might be having a seizure, so she wrapped a blanket around him and rushed him to the hospital. Peter was very agitated in the hospital. None of the tests done by the emergency room physician revealed any medical problem that could be causing his behavior. Peter was given a sedative to relieve his agitation, and the hospital's child psychiatrist was called for a consultation. After two hours with Peter, the psychiatrist told his parents that it appeared Peter was experiencing psychotic symptoms. He said Peter had reported hearing voices for several days, and they had become increasingly loud and frightening. His parents were shocked and asked how this could be happening to their child, who, until about a year ago, was happy and normal. The psychiatrist said there were no answers to this question, but it was known that in rare cases children had these experiences. He gently raised the possibility that Peter might be showing signs of schizophrenia, which further shocked and dismayed his parents. They said that no one in their family had ever experienced anything like what Peter was experiencing, and asked again how it could be happening. The psychiatrist said he did not know why Peter was experiencing the symptoms.

Peter was transferred to a children's psychiatric hospital, where he stayed for about a month. His parents visited frequently. His psychiatrist prescribed a combination of two medications that reduced Peter's agitation and stopped the hallucinations.

Peter returned home and settled into his family. He returned to school but did not do as well as he had done before. His parents consulted with Peter's teachers and discussed his condition with them, although they worried that doing so would make his teachers leery of interacting with Peter. He renewed his friendships, although his friends seemed less eager to play with him than before.

Peter's parents hired a tutor to help him with his schoolwork, but Peter seemed to become upset when he had to focus so much energy on his studies. Their therapist encouraged them to stop the tutoring and to support Peter at school but not be demanding. Peter's parents worked hard to provide a safe and supportive environment for Peter at home. They were sad and confused about Peter's condition, and they often wondered whether they could have done something earlier to stop the schizophrenia from developing. They also worried about Peter's sister having the same disorder, so they watched her and her behaviors carefully.

Some Issues Worth Noting

- The sudden and unexpected onset of Peter's symptoms.
- The misdiagnosis of his behavioral problems as a more common childhood disorder.
- The lack of history of severe disorders in Peter's nuclear or extended family.
- The concern by his parents that they had done something wrong, thus causing Peter's schizophrenia.

History

People with the symptoms of schizophrenia have appeared in literature, religious documents, and medical texts for centuries. However, it was not until the late 1800s that Emil Kraepelin, a German psychiatrist, first described them as the symptoms of a mental disorder (Gottesman, 1991). Kraepelin used the term *dementia praecox* to describe a disorder that caused a gradual, complete loss of mental abilities beginning in adolescence or young adulthood (*dementia* is from Latin *de,* "out or away from," and *mentis,* "the mind"; *praecox* is from Latin meaning "precocious").

In 1911 Eugene Bleuler, a Swiss psychiatrist, wrote an influential monograph in which he agreed with most of Kraepelin's descriptions of the disorder but argued that it could begin in later adulthood and that not everyone who had the disorder lost all their mental abilities. Bleuler suggested the term *schizophrenia* (*schizo* from the Latin for "split" and *phren* from the Greek for "mind") because he believed that the various parts of the mind of a person with schizophrenia were split from each other and not integrated. Most of the symptoms of schizophrenia used throughout the various editions of the DSM are similar to those first proposed by Kraepelin and Bleuler.

Notes from the Author: Confusion of Names

Before I knew much about psychopathology, I shared the common belief that schizophrenia referred to someone with a "split personality."

This is a misinterpretation of the term "split mind" that Bleuler used. In some ways, a person with schizophrenia may seem to have a split personality. As we will see in this chapter, schizophrenia is a cyclic disorder: There are times when a person is actively psychotic—seeing and hearing things that are not there—and other times when the person is much more stable. Thus it may seem as if a person with schizophrenia has two personalities. However, the psychotic behaviors are not the manifestation of a second personality but instead are a disintegration of a person's personality. We now consider someone with two or more personalities to have *dissociative identity disorder* (formerly called *multiple personality disorder*)—which is the disorder that most people intend when they refer to someone as having a split personality.

It has long been known that a few children experience the same psychotic symptoms as adults with schizophrenia. However, because there were so few children with these symptoms, they received little research attention in the first half of the 1900s, despite considerable research on adults with schizophrenia. Until the 1970s, children who experienced a variety of severe, chronic symptoms all received the diagnosis of **childhood schizophrenia** in the DSM (Eggers & Bunk, 1997). Careful work by Kolvin in the late 1960s showed that the category of childhood schizophrenia included several disorders that could be distinguished from each other based on their patterns of symptoms and the timing of their onset (Kolvin, 1971). He argued, for example, that children with autism, who were then diagnosed as having childhood schizophrenia, had a unique disorder because it began earlier in life and had a unique pattern of symptoms.

The work by Kolvin and those who followed him encouraged the creation of several disorders from those that had previously been combined as childhood schizophrenia beginning in the DSM-III. For example, autism and other severe disorders that always begin in childhood were listed in a new *pervasive developmental disorders* category (APA, 1980). Children who met the diagnostic criteria for schizophrenia continued to be given that diagnosis.

Key Concepts

- In the late 1800s, Emil Kraepelin described a disorder, *dementia praecox,* which is similar to the disorder now known as schizophrenia. He believed that the disorder caused a gradual, complete loss of mental abilities.
- In 1911 Eugene Bleuler reconceptualized this disorder, labeled it *schizophrenia,* and argued that it resulted in a splitting of the various parts of a person's mind.
- Until the 1970s, the diagnosis of *childhood schizophrenia* was used for several severe, chronic disorders of childhood. The work of Kolvin and other researchers showed that the category included several disorders, including autism and what we now call childhood-onset schizophrenia.

Diagnosis and Assessment

Diagnostic Criteria

The symptoms of schizophrenia are the same for adults and children, although they may be exhibited in different ways by children (Nicolson, Lenane et al., 2000). These symptoms are divided into positive symptoms and negative symptoms (Volkmar & Tsatsanis, 2002). **Positive symptoms** are distortions of normal brain functioning and are considered psychotic symptoms. Hallucinations (seeing or hearing things that are not there) are examples of the distorted experiences that are considered positive symptoms. **Negative symptoms** refer to a loss of normal functions. Examples of negative symptoms are social withdrawal, a lack of emotional responding, and loss of motor control. (The positive and negative symptoms of childhood-onset schizophrenia are described in more detail in the following section.)

As shown in Table 13.1 (criterion A), a child does not have to experience positive and negative symptoms for the diagnosis of schizophrenia to be made. However, most children and adults with schizophrenia experience both types of symptoms (Volkmar & Tsatsanis, 2002). Different diagnoses are made based on the duration of the symptoms. A child must experience continuous signs of disturbance for at least six months, with at least one month of symptoms listed in criterion A, for the diagnosis of schizophrenia to be made. If symptoms are experienced for between one and six months, *schizophreniform disorder* is diagnosed. If the symptoms continue past six months, then the diagnosis is changed to schizophrenia. If a child experiences the positive symptoms of schizophrenia for one day to one month and then returns to a level of functioning that is the same as before the symptoms appeared, a diagnosis of *brief psychotic episode* can be given (APA, 2000).

Several types of schizophrenia are specified by the DSM-IV-TR, and each of these has been found in children and adults (information about these types comes from APA, 2000).

The principal symptoms of the **paranoid type** are delusions with persecutory and/or grandiose themes. For example, a child may believe that the other children in his neighborhood are plotting to kill him and his family, and he may hear voices telling him about the other children's latest meeting to plan the killings. Those with paranoid schizophrenia are at a higher risk for suicide because they may see suicide as the only way to escape their persecution. Similarly, they are at a higher risk for violence toward others because they may use violence to defend themselves from the perceived persecution.

The **disorganized type** is characterized by high levels of disorganized speech, thoughts, and behaviors. The disorganized behaviors may prevent a person from accomplishing even basic self-care, so many of those with the disorganized type must be supervised closely. Speech is usually incoherent and may seem like a jumble of unrelated words and phrases. (The term

TABLE 13.1

Diagnostic Criteria for Schizophrenia

A. *Characteristic symptoms:* Two (or more) of the following, each present for a significant portion of time during a one-month period (or less if successfully treated):

(1) Delusions.

(2) Hallucinations.

(3) Disorganized speech (e.g., frequent derailment or incoherence).

(4) Grossly disorganized or catatonic behavior.

(5) Negative symptoms, i.e., affective flattening, alogia, or avolition.

Note: Only one Criterion A symptom is required if delusions are bizarre or hallucinations consist of a voice keeping up a running commentary on the person's behavior or thoughts, or two or more voices conversing with each other.

B. *Social/occupational dysfunction:* For a significant portion of the time since the onset of the disturbance, one or more major areas of functioning such as work, interpersonal relations, or self-care are markedly below the level achieved prior to the onset (or when the onset is in childhood or adolescence, failure to achieve expected level of interpersonal, academic, or occupational achievement).

C. *Duration:* Continuous signs of the disturbance persist for at least six months. This six month period must include at least one month of symptoms (or less if successfully treated) that meet Criterion A (i.e., active-phase symptoms) and may include periods of prodromal or residual symptoms. During these prodromal or residual periods, the signs of the disturbance may be manifested by only negative symptoms or two or more symptoms listed in Criterion A present in an attenuated from (e.g., odd beliefs, unusual perceptual experiences).

D. *Schizoaffective and Mood Disorder exclusion:* Schizoaffective Disorder and Mood Disorder with Psychotic Features have been ruled out because either (1) no Major Depressive, Manic, or Mixed Episodes have occurred concurrently with the active-phase symptoms; or (2) if mood episodes have occurred during active-phase symptoms, their total duration has been brief relative to the duration of the active and residual periods.

E. *Substance/general medical condition exclusion:* The disturbance is not due to the direct physiological effects of a substance (e.g., a drug of abuse, a medication) or a general medical condition.

F. *Relationship to a Pervasive Developmental Disorder:* If there is a history of Autistic Disorder or another Pervasive Developmental Disorder, the additional diagnosis of Schizophrenia is made only if prominent delusions or hallucinations are also present for at least a month (or less if successfully treated).

word salad has been used to describe this type of speech—visualize many different words placed in a bowl and then tossed like a salad before being spoken.) Hallucinations and delusions are usually disorganized and have no coherent theme.

Marked psychomotor disturbance is the principal symptom of the **catatonic type**. The best known of these symptoms is lack of movement. Some individuals with this disorder stand or sit in odd positions for long periods, looking like a statue. Others exhibit excessive and apparently uncontrolled movement—for example, moving rapidly around a room while flailing their arms and legs. Those with the catatonic type may be in danger of hurting themselves through their excess movements or of experiencing circulation problems through lack of movement, and so may require careful supervision.

Undifferentiated type is diagnosed when a person meets the criteria for schizophrenia, but not for any of the other types, or when the criteria for two or three types are met. The diagnosis of **residual type** is made when a person has experienced at least one episode of the acute phase of schizophrenia but is currently not exhibiting any positive symptoms of schizophrenia and is experiencing one or more of the negative symptoms. These people are considered to be in *partial remission*.

Controversial Issue: Continuity between Childhood-Onset Schizophrenia and Adult-Onset Schizophrenia

Whether childhood-onset schizophrenia is the same disorder as adult-onset schizophrenia has been debated for many years. The prevailing theory through the 1970s was that neurological changes occurring during late adolescence "switched on" schizophrenia in some people who were genetically susceptible to it. This supported the view that childhood-onset schizophrenia and adult-onset schizophrenia were separate disorders because children had not experienced the neurological changes required for the onset of adult-onset schizophrenia (Weinberger, 1987). In addition, the fact that few cases of schizophrenia begin during childhood suggests that the disorder that starts in childhood may differ from the disorder that begins during adulthood.

However, two lines of research provide evidence that these are the same disorder. First, the psychiatric disorders that are more frequent in the parents of those with adult-onset schizophrenia (schizophrenia, schizotypal personality disorder, paranoid personality disorder, and avoidant personality disorder) are also more frequent in the parents of children with schizophrenia (Asarnow, Brown, & Strandburg, 1995; Nuechterlein et al., 2002). In addition, disorders that are not more frequent in the parents of those with adult-onset schizophrenia (borderline personality disorder and schizoid personality disorder) also are not more frequent in the parents of children with schizophrenia. If adult-onset schizophrenia and childhood-onset schizophrenia were different disorders, one would not expect to find so many similarities in disorders among the parents of those with the disorders.

The second line of research has shown that several neurobiological dysfunctions, such as difficulty with attention, working memory, and executive functions, are present in children and adults with schizophrenia (Nicolson & Rapoport, 2000). Likewise, similar differences in brain morphology, such as increased lateral ventricular volume and decreased cerebellar volume, have been found. These similarities suggest that the disorder causing them is the same in children and adults.

Cultural Issues When Diagnosing Childhood-Onset Schizophrenia

Attention to cultural issues is important when we diagnose any disorder in children or adults. This is particularly important when we diagnose schizophrenia because appropriate behaviors in one culture might be considered psychotic behaviors in another. For example, a person's belief that a sorcerer or witch has controlled his or her mind is not viewed as problematic in some cultures but could be considered a delusion in another. In addition, religious ceremonies in many cultures involve what those in other cultures might consider hallucinations (such as seeing the Virgin Mary or entering the body of another animal) (APA, 2000). Overall, experiences viewed by a culture as reasonable and that cause no distress or impairment for the person having them are not considered symptoms of schizophrenia or any other disorder.

Key Concepts

- The symptoms of schizophrenia are divided into positive symptoms and negative symptoms. Positive symptoms are distortions of normal functioning; negative symptoms represent a loss of normal functioning.
- The category of schizophrenia is divided into five types:
  1. The paranoid type is characterized by delusions with persecutory or grandiose themes.
  2. The disorganized type is characterized by high levels of disorganized speech, thoughts, and behaviors.
  3. The catatonic type is characterized by marked psychomotor disturbance—either lack of movement or excessive movement.
  4. The undifferentiated type is diagnosed when a person does not meet the criteria for any of the other types or meets the criteria for more than one type.
  5. The residual type is diagnosed when a person has experienced at least one episode of the acute phase of schizophrenia but currently is experiencing only negative symptoms.
- Schizophreniform disorder is diagnosed when the symptoms of schizophrenia have been present between one and six months.
- A brief psychotic episode is diagnosed if positive symptoms appear for one day to one month, with a subsequent return to previous levels of functioning.

- Family studies and studies of neurobiological functioning suggest that childhood-onset schizophrenia and adult-onset schizophrenia are the same disorder, although this issue remains unresolved.

Characteristics and Experiences of Children with Schizophrenia

As noted earlier, the symptoms of schizophrenia are often divided into two categories: positive symptoms and negative symptoms. We review these symptoms in this section and then note that they often appear as part of a cycle of symptoms that are experienced by most children and adults with schizophrenia.

Positive Symptoms
Hallucinations

Hallucinations are perceptual experiences that occur without any external stimuli (Volkmar & Tsatsanis, 2002). Hallucinations can involve any of the five senses. Visual hallucinations may include seeing colors, vague shapes, or specific things or people. Auditory hallucinations can involve hearing non-specific sounds such as ringing bells or thunder, or may involve one or more voices that speak directly to the child or have a conversation that the child can hear. **Command hallucinations** are auditory hallucinations in which a voice tells a child that he or she must engage in certain behaviors. Children experiencing tactile hallucinations can feel extreme heat or cold, or animals, people, or other things touching or crawling on them. Olfactory hallucinations involve vague or specific smells, and gustatory hallucinations involve vague or specific tastes.

Hallucinations are experienced as if they were actually occurring. Consider what it would be like if you were lying on a bed with spiders crawling on you, or if one of your parents stood behind you *all* the time telling you whether you are behaving properly. These can be the experiences of people having hallucinations—they really do feel or hear or see the events. Because they seem so real, hallucinations can be very disturbing and alarming.

Many children with schizophrenia experience hallucinations. Auditory hallucinations, the most common type, are reported in 75–80% of cases, with visual hallucinations reported in 20–30% of cases (Volkmar, 1996). Children's hallucinations are usually less organized than the hallucinations of adults, and they often involve things familiar to children such as animals and monsters (Volkmar & Tsatsanis, 2002).

Some preschool children experience transient visual or auditory hallucinations, particularly during times of high stress or anxiety, such as hearing their parents calling their names (Rothstein, 1981). These are accepted as developmentally appropriate and are not considered psychotic symptoms. Why these experiences occur in young children and then disappear as they age remains unclear.

Delusions

Delusions are false beliefs that a child holds onto persistently, despite evidence that they are not accurate (APA, 2000; Volkmar & Tsatsanis, 2002). Common types are **persecutory delusions,** in which a child believes that he or she is being tormented, followed, spied on, or ridiculed by others, and **referential delusions,** in which a child believes that certain information in the newspaper, comments on television, or passages in books are aimed specifically at him or her. Delusions are not suspicions about someone or something; they are clear, strong beliefs. If you suspect that a friend is spreading gossip about you and wonder why he is, you are not experiencing a delusion. However, if you are certain that your parents are planning to have you kidnapped, despite much evidence to the contrary, you may be experiencing a delusion. The problem, of course, is how to prove that someone is not doing or planning something. How can your parents prove to you that they are not planning to have you kidnapped?

Delusions are often based on misinterpretations of actual perceptions or experiences. Delusions are not created from hallucinations; rather, they are usually created and maintained by misinterpretations of actual events. For example, a child may believe that the teachers at her school plan to kidnap her and that they meet at lunch to plan the kidnapping. It is true that the teachers eat lunch together, but it is not true that they are discussing a kidnapping. Another child might believe that the characters on a television program are passing coded information to him through their dialogue. He can point out certain phrases that are spoken on each program but then misinterprets the characters' dialogue as being directed at him.

About half of children with schizophrenia experience delusions. Delusions in preschool and school-age children are less coherent than those in adolescents and adults. They may consist of a jumble of unrelated beliefs rather than a set of beliefs that all relate to a coherent theme (Caplan, 1994).

Disorganized Speech

Disorganized speech is a symptom of schizophrenia because it is used as an indication of disordered thinking. Although disordered thinking is considered by some as the hallmark of schizophrenia (APA, 2000), it is difficult to assess directly because one person does not have direct access to the thoughts of another. Consequently, disordered thinking is inferred from disorganized speech.

Disordered thinking refers to problems with the process of thinking, rather than problems with the content of thoughts (which are delusions) (Volkmar & Tsatsanis, 2002). Thoughts might jumble together in an incoherent pattern, or it might be difficult for a child to move logically from one thought to another. Several patterns of disorganized speech are believed to represent disordered thinking (the following examples are from Caplan, Guthrie, Fish, Tanguay, and David-Lando, 1989):

- *Illogical thinking* can be shown with statements that involve inappropriate reasoning: "I left my hat in her room because her name is Mary." "I don't like that story, but I liked it as a story."

- *Incoherence of thought* is inferred from scrambled syntax, in which words do not go together or follow from each other. Interviewer: "What happened next in the story?" Child: "The day no witches no day goes."
- *Loose associations* occur when a child's statements do not follow an expected sequence. Interviewer: "Why do you think that's a reason not to like Tim?" Child: "And I call my mom sweetie."
- *Poverty of thought content* can be shown by speech that has little substance: "I suppose . . . What? Maybe . . . Well yes, I see. I suppose that's all."

Disordered thinking is particularly difficult to assess in young children because their age-appropriate speech is periodically characterized by patterns that might suggest illogical thinking and loose associations. Consequently, it is often not until the school-age years that children's speech can be used as an indication of disordered thinking (Caplan, Guthrie, Tang, Komo, & Asarnow, 2000).

Grossly Disorganized Behavior

Grossly disorganized behavior is behavior that is obviously odd and inappropriate. For example, a child may appear very disheveled, insist on wearing several jackets and hats when the weather is warm, talk loudly to himself or herself, or pace frantically back and forth while flapping his or her arms (APA, 2000).

As is always true, it is important to keep a child's developmental level and life circumstances in mind when deciding whether his or her behaviors represent grossly disorganized behavior. For example, children who have been raised in chronically abusive or neglectful families may have developed behaviors that reflect their family environments (being disheveled) or their attempts to survive (eating unclean food with their hands). These behaviors can often be distinguished from psychotic behaviors because they occur only in specific circumstances and are likely to change if the children are placed in healthful environments.

Negative Symptoms

Negative symptoms represent a loss of normal functions. The three principal negative symptoms of schizophrenia are *flattened affect* (loss of emotion), *alogia* (loss of communication), and *avolition* (loss of purposeful behavior) (APA, 2000). Although positive symptoms are more obvious than negative symptoms and often demand more attention from others, negative symptoms are frequently more debilitating because they are usually chronic and unaffected by medications that reduce positive symptoms.

A child with **flattened affect** seems uninterested in his or her surroundings and seldom reacts to other people. The child's face often appears expressionless and does not change from one situation to another. When conversing with others, the child seldom makes eye contact, uses little or no body language, and usually speaks quietly and in a monotone.

Alogia (from the Greek *a,* "without," and *logia,* "words") is poverty of speech. Alogia is characterized by speech that is brief and often without meaningful content. A child may give only one- or two-word answers to questions, if he or she answers at all, and seldom initiates any conversation. In addition, a child's flattened affect usually makes what little speech is produced devoid of any emotion.

Avolition (from the Greek *a,* "without," and the Latin *volo,* "I will") is a lack of action or willful participation in activities. A child with avolition is withdrawn from others, does not initiate activities or interactions, and is reluctant to join others when asked to do so.

Negative symptoms cause emotional and social withdrawal from the world and those in it—a characteristic of most children and adults who have schizophrenia. For example, a child with schizophrenia might sit quietly on a chair for hours with a blank expression on her face, grunt or say only a word or two if others talk with her, and resist attempts from others to engage her in any activity.

Cycle of Symptoms

The symptoms of schizophrenia typically occur in a cycle. Even without treatment, the positive and negative symptoms of schizophrenia do not continue unabated once they emerge. Rather, they ebb and flow. The four phases of this cycle have been labeled *prodromal, acute, recovery,* and *residual* (APA, 2000).

The first phase in the cycle, the **prodromal phase,** involves a deterioration of functioning. Although, as discussed in the next section, children with schizophrenia usually experience many problems before the onset of the disorder, the prodromal phase is characterized by a deterioration of even this level of functioning. This deterioration may include marked social withdrawal, loss of concern about personal hygiene and appearance, heightened levels of disorganized thinking and behavior, and a significant decline in school performance. Some transient positive symptoms may occur.

The **acute phase** is characterized by positive and negative symptoms, as just described.

The **recovery phase** begins when the positive symptoms subside. The recovery phase is characterized by confusion, disorganization, and feelings of anxiety and discontent. It seems reasonable to conceptualize children in this phase as exhausted by, and trying to recover from, the acute phase. Just as someone with a severe bacterial infection may need days or weeks of rest to recover after the infection is no longer present, a child with schizophrenia appears to need time to recover from the trauma to his or her system caused by the acute phase.

The **residual phase** involves few obvious symptoms. However, children in this phase do not function as if they have no disorder. Most are withdrawn, and many experience negative symptoms that are less intense than those experienced during the acute phase. The child and parents may be concerned about when the next cycle may begin, and this concern is probably anxiety-provoking to the child and his or her parents and may have a substantial influence on their behaviors.

The negative symptoms of schizophrenia can result in severe withdrawal.

The "natural" course of this cycle is known mostly from information gathered from adults before the widespread use of antipsychotic medication: Once these medications became available, they were used to interrupt the acute phase. The extent to which a child responds positively to medication, and the skill with which the medication is prescribed and administered, have an important influence on the duration of each cycle and the intensity of the symptoms experienced during each cycle.

Key Concepts

- The symptoms of schizophrenia can be divided into positive symptoms and negative symptoms.
- Hallucinations are perceptual experiences with no external stimuli. They can involve any of the senses.
- Delusions are strongly held false beliefs. Common types are persecutory delusions and referential delusions.
- Disorganized speech can indicate disordered thinking, which refers to problems with the process of thinking.

- Grossly disorganized behavior is behavior that is obviously odd and inappropriate.
- Negative symptoms include flattened affect (loss of emotion), alogia (loss of communication), and avolition (loss of purposeful behavior).
- Most children with schizophrenia experience a cycle of symptoms with four phases: prodromal, acute, recovery, and residual.

Prevalence

The prevalence of childhood-onset schizophrenia is difficult to estimate, in part because it is rare and in part because most health care providers have little experience with childhood-onset schizophrenia and consequently have difficulty diagnosing it correctly (Kumra, 2000). The estimated prevalence of schizophrenia in the adult population is about 1% (Volkmar & Tsatsanis, 2002). In contrast, the prevalence of schizophrenia in children between the ages of 11 and 15 is about 1.4 in 10,000, and the prevalence in those under the age of 11 is about 1–5 children in 100,000 (Eggers & Bunk, 1997; Eggers, Bunk, & Krause, 2000). So childhood-onset schizophrenia in young children is very rare, with an increase in prevalence during the 11–15 year age range, and then a more substantial increase in prevalence beginning after age 15.

Course

Premorbid Functioning

Although a few children experience the symptoms of schizophrenia without having significant prior problems, most who eventually receive the diagnosis of childhood-onset schizophrenia show many premorbid problems before the positive and negative symptoms of schizophrenia appear. Werry described these children as "odd, anxious, and isolative" (1992). Two ongoing studies of children with schizophrenia provide examples of the premorbid problems they experience. A study of 46 children at the National Institute of Mental Health found that 48% of the children had exhibited social abnormalities such as isolation and odd interpersonal behaviors, 54% had motor abnormalities or had failed to meet developmental milestones for motor development, 48% had delays in language acquisition, and 50% had transient symptoms of autism. Many children had significant academic problems: 62% had either failed a grade or been placed in special education (Nicolson, Lenane et al., 2000; Nicolson & Rapoport, 2000). In the Colorado Childhood-Onset Schizophrenia Research Project, 17 children have been followed for several years (Schaeffer & Ross, 2002). The premorbid problems they displayed are described in Table 13.2. (The identification of hallucinations and delusions as premorbid problems is likely because they were transitory.)

TABLE 13.2

Premorbid Symptoms of 17 Children with COS

Symptom	Children with Symptom
Developmental delays/school problems/ learning disabilities	11 (65%)
Oppositional/violence/aggression/rages/ temper tantrums/fighting	6 (35%)
ADHD-type symptoms	5 (29%)
Delusions	3 (18%)
Social problems	3 (18%)
Low self-esteem/depression	2 (12%)
Auditory or visual hallucinations	2 (12%)
"Obsessive attachment"	1 (6%)
Severe mood swings	1 (6%)
Obsessive–compulsive behaviors	1 (6%)

Source: Schaeffer & Ross, 2002.

Most children who develop schizophrenia have premorbid problems that are more frequent and severe than those who develop schizophrenia as adults. In addition, children who have the earliest onset of symptoms are more likely to have severe premorbid problems than children whose symptoms first appear later in childhood (Alaghband Rad et al., 1995; Hollis, 2003). These age differences may be due to childhood-onset schizophrenia being a more severe disorder than schizophrenia that develops in late adolescence or adulthood—an issue to which we will turn in a subsequent section. Boys usually have more severe premorbid problems than do girls, although the reasons for this difference are not clear (Schaeffer & Ross, 2002).

Initial Onset of Symptoms

The onset of symptoms can follow one of three paths: (1) an acute onset, with few or no premorbid problems; (2) an insidious onset (onset that is slow and not easily apparent), with a sudden exacerbation of symptoms; and (3) an insidious onset with a gradual worsening of symptoms. Most children experience an insidious onset with a gradual worsening of symptoms—usually over two to three years (Asarnow et al., 1995; Vaughn, Wilson, & Dunlap, 2002). School-age children are more likely to experience an extended course of symptom exacerbation than are adolescents—a larger percentage of whom experience an insidious onset with a sudden exacerbation of symptoms (Eggers & Bunk, 1997).

The first obvious symptoms are usually positive symptoms. Hallucinations, particularly auditory hallucinations, are the first symptoms experienced by 80–90% of children with schizophrenia (Eggers et al., 2000; Russell,

1994). However, because it is more difficult to notice the onset of negative symptoms, in part because they can be difficult to distinguish from premorbid functioning problems, we may not be aware of the percentage of children who experience negative symptoms initially.

Among adults, males experience the initial onset of symptoms four to five years earlier than females (Schulz, Findling, Wise, Friedman, & Kenny, 1998). However, most studies of childhood-onset schizophrenia report no sex differences in the timing of the onset of symptoms (Eggers & Bunk, 1997; Schmidt, Blanz, Dippe, & Koppe, 1995). It is not clear why this age difference occurs in adults and not in children.

Long-Term Course

The long-term prognosis for those with childhood-onset or adolescent-onset schizophrenia is poor, and it is poorer than the prognosis for those with adult-onset schizophrenia (Jarbin, Ott, & von Knorring, 2003; McClellan & Werry, 1994). Those who experience the initial onset of symptoms during their school-age years are more likely to develop a chronic pattern of psychosis than are those with an initial onset during adolescence (Eggers & Bunk, 1997; Lay, Blanz, Hartmann, & Schmidt, 2000).

Several hypotheses have been suggested for the poorer prognosis among children. First, several types of schizophrenia may exist, and the types occurring in childhood may involve biochemical processes that are more severe. A second possibility is that a child's brain may be less capable of repairing the damage done by the disease process of schizophrenia, resulting in greater brain damage and a more severe disorder (DeLisi, 1997). Finally, because childhood-onset schizophrenia interferes with development early and continually during a child's life, those with childhood-onset schizophrenia will have had less opportunity to develop the social, cognitive, and educational skills needed to cope with their disorder than those with a later onset, resulting in a more severe disorder (Westermeyer, 1993).

Key Concepts

- The prevalence of childhood-onset schizophrenia is estimated at 1–5 children in 100,000 for those under 11 years, and 1.4 children in 10,000 for those between 11 and 15.
- Most children who develop schizophrenia show a high frequency of premorbid problems that include antisocial behaviors, expressive and receptive language deficits, gross motor impairments, learning and academic problems, and transient symptoms of autism.
- The onset of the symptoms of childhood-onset schizophrenia usually follows an insidious course, with a gradual increase in the number and intensity of symptoms over a two- to three-year period.
- Positive symptoms are often the first to appear, although negative symptoms may be present but more difficult to notice.
- The long-term prognosis for children with schizophrenia is poorer than the prognosis for people with adult-onset schizophrenia.

Families of Children with Schizophrenia

Little information is available about the families of children with schizophrenia. We do know, as described earlier, that there is a greater likelihood that relatives of a child with schizophrenia will also have schizophrenia or a related disorder. However, as Gottesman and Erlenmeyer Kimling (2001) point out, about 63% of all people with schizophrenia have no first-degree relatives with schizophrenia. Consequently, many children with schizophrenia may be the only ones in their families with such a severe disorder.

Schaeffer and Ross (2002) explored the experiences of 17 families who had a child with schizophrenia. Most of these parents believed that something was wrong with their child at an early age, and many parents took their child for psychological evaluations or psychotherapy. However, most found the assessments confusing and believed that psychotherapy was not helpful. Once the psychotic symptoms began, parents reported considerable frustration because the physicians or psychologists with whom they consulted could not clearly understand what was happening. This lack of clarity led to delays averaging two years before the appropriate diagnosis of childhood-onset schizophrenia was made. The parents reported trying a variety of treatments for their children, including child psychotherapy (generally viewed as unhelpful), family therapy (generally seen as useful in helping them cope with the stress they were experiencing), and a variety of medications (antidepressants and stimulants being the most common). This single brief glimpse into the lives of a few families suggests an atmosphere consisting at least partly of frustration, confusion, and concern, as well as many different attempts to discover and treat the roots of the problems that these children were experiencing.

Key Concepts

- Some children with schizophrenia live in families in which other members have schizophrenia or related disorders; however, most do not.
- Many parents of children with schizophrenia report believing that something was wrong with their children several years before the children were diagnosed with schizophrenia. They often feel frustrated with the inability of health care providers to determine the cause of their children's problems.

Etiology

In this section we discuss the etiology of childhood-onset schizophrenia. From the outset, we should note that a clear understanding of the etiology of schizophrenia remains elusive, despite decades of research. We know about how the brains, biological functioning, and experiences of some people who develop schizophrenia differ from most of those who do not; however, it is unclear how these differences influence the development of schizophrenia (Jacobsen & Rapoport, 1998a).

We will explore the etiology of childhood-onset schizophrenia in the following way. Our primary focus will be on the neurological functioning of children with schizophrenia because it is clear that problems with brain functioning are at the foundation of schizophrenia (Kirch, 1993). We first examine the research focused on the differences in neurological functioning between those with schizophrenia and others. Most researchers conceptualize these differences as indicating neurological dysfunctions in people with schizophrenia. We then address several possible causes of the neurological dysfunctions that many children with schizophrenia experience. Because many theories about the development of schizophrenia involve the role of stress in the onset of symptoms, we then focus on issues that can cause this stress. Next we review three theories about how the combination of neurological dysfunctions and stress can cause the development of schizophrenia. Finally, we explore why schizophrenia develops during childhood in a few cases.

Neurobiological Dysfunctions in Schizophrenia

Research on neurobiological dysfunctions in schizophrenia has focused primarily in three areas: **brain morphology** (the form and structure of the brain), brain functioning, and neurotransmission. Several characteristics of neurobiological functioning in these areas have been found to differ between those with schizophrenia and others. However, none of these characteristics has been found among all people who have schizophrenia, and some people who do not have schizophrenia have these same characteristics. In addition, the ways in which these characteristics may influence the development of schizophrenia remain unclear.

Brain Morphology

Research using brain-imaging techniques, such as magnetic resonance imaging (MRI), has found differences in the average brain size of children with schizophrenia and other children. The total brain volume and cerebellum volume are less for children with schizophrenia than for other children. [The cerebellum is a major structure of the brain that is located behind the brain stem and functions primarily to coordinate physical movement (Carlson, 1986).] In addition, the lateral ventricles in children with schizophrenia are larger than those of other children. [The lateral ventricles are interconnected chambers in the brain filled with cerebrospinal fluid (Alaghband Rad, Hamburger, Giedd, Frazier, & Rapoport, 1997; Frazier, Giedd, Hamburger, & Albus, 1996; Jacobsen et al., 1997).] Consequently, there is, on average, less mass to the brains of children with schizophrenia. In addition, the total cerebral volume and the volume of the cerebellum decrease more rapidly during adolescence in those with childhood-onset schizophrenia than they do in other adolescents (Keller et al., 2003). As a result, the average brain mass of children and adolescents with schizophrenia becomes progressively smaller, compared with other children and adolescents, as they develop.

Size differences in specific areas of the brain have also been identified, and many of these differences are in areas related to the symptoms of schizophrenia, such as movement, emotional regulation, and auditory comprehension (Frazier et al., 1996). The structures of the basal ganglia, which are primarily involved in coordinating voluntary movement, are larger in children with schizophrenia than in other children. The thalamus, which is part of the limbic system and plays an important role in emotional regulation and the coordination of thinking and emotion, is smaller in children with schizophrenia than in other children. The superior temporal gyrus, part of the temporal lobe associated with auditory perception and comprehension, is larger in children with schizophrenia than in other children.

Brain Functioning

Several researchers have used neuropsychological tests to explore for problems in brain functioning in children with schizophrenia. Neuropsychological tests involve tasks that people with known injuries to specific parts of their brains have difficulty completing. Consequently, these tests can suggest which parts of a person's brain are functioning poorly (see the chapter about attention-deficit/hyperactivity disorder for a fuller explanation).

Children with schizophrenia show deficits in three areas: attention, memory, and fine motor control (Asarnow et al., 1995). For example, children with schizophrenia have more difficulty than other children in tasks that require attending to auditory input, keeping that input in memory, and performing a fine motor activity such as reproducing progressively more complex rhythms by tapping on a table. In addition, most children with schizophrenia perform poorly on a test in which they put small metal pegs into rows of holes as quickly as they can—suggesting a deficit in fine motor control. Further, they perform more poorly with both their dominant and nondominant hands on fine motor tasks, which suggests that the problem with brain functioning is bilateral (Asarnow et al., 1995).

Neurotransmitter Activity

Early investigations of the influence of neurotransmitters on the development of schizophrenia focused on dopamine, particularly the role of dopamine in the limbic system (Weinberger, 1987). The **dopamine hypothesis** suggested that the symptoms of schizophrenia were caused by excessive levels of dopaminergic activity. Several studies supported this hypothesis. For example, medication that reduced the positive symptoms of schizophrenia was found to reduce dopaminergic activity by binding to dopamine receptor cells. In addition, the chronic use of amphetamines produced symptoms similar to those found in paranoid schizophrenia in some people, and it is known that amphetamines increase dopaminergic activity.

Recent work, however, has suggested that dopamine is not the only neurotransmitter involved in schizophrenia (Oltmanns & Emery, 1995). Some adults with schizophrenia do not respond to antipsychotic medications that focus on dopamine, but they do respond to medications that block serotonin receptors and have only a mild influence on dopamine receptors. Thus it appears that serotonin has an important influence on the symptoms of schizophrenia for some adults.

Two other complications associated with the dopamine hypothesis are worth noting. The first is that it does not explain why schizophrenia has its onset in late adolescence or early adulthood for most people (Weinberger, 1987). In addition, it does not explain why the positive symptoms of schizophrenia cycle over time. If dopamine levels are chronically high, we might expect chronic symptoms rather than cycling symptoms. Also, antipsychotic medication takes several days to have a noticeable influence on positive symptoms, although the blocking of dopamine receptors begins soon after the medication is given. Consequently, while dopamine, serotonin, and other neurotransmitters appear to play a role in schizophrenia, this role is not well understood.

Possible Causes of Neurobiological Dysfunction

At this point in our exploration of the etiology of schizophrenia, we have reviewed the neurobiological dysfunctions that are found in many adults and children with schizophrenia. We now turn to a discussion of the possible causes of these dysfunctions.

Genetic Influences

A long history of quantitative behavioral genetics research using family, twin, and adoption studies has shown a strong genetic influence on the development of schizophrenia. Current thinking is that several genes influence schizophrenia, rather than there being just one "schizophrenia" gene (Jacobsen & Rapoport, 1998b).

In a review of 40 family and twin studies, Gottesman (1991) showed the relative risk of developing schizophrenia for people with varying degrees of genetic relatedness to a person who has schizophrenia (see Figure 13.1). As you can see, there is about a 1% chance that a person with no relatives with schizophrenia will develop schizophrenia. This is considered the "general risk" for schizophrenia. The risk for those with a second-degree relative who has schizophrenia is higher than the general risk: about a 2–6% chance. The risk for those with a first-degree relative is even higher: between 6% and 17%. These data are consistent with a genetic influence on schizophrenia.

Also included in Figure 13.1 is information from twin studies. The significantly higher concordance rates between MZ than DZ twins also supports a genetic influence on schizophrenia. Twin studies also show the importance of environmental influences on the development of schizophrenia. Note that there is only a 48% risk for MZ twins, although they share all the same genes. Consequently, some environmental risks are clearly associated with the development of schizophrenia. Also note that DZ twins have a higher risk than do siblings, although they share the same percentage of genes. Perhaps DZ twins experience more shared environmental influences on the development of schizophrenia than do siblings born several years apart.

Adoption studies also show an important genetic influence on schizophrenia. In the first large adoption study, Heston (1966) examined two groups of adults who had been adopted as newborns. One group had been adopted from mothers who had schizophrenia, and the other group had been

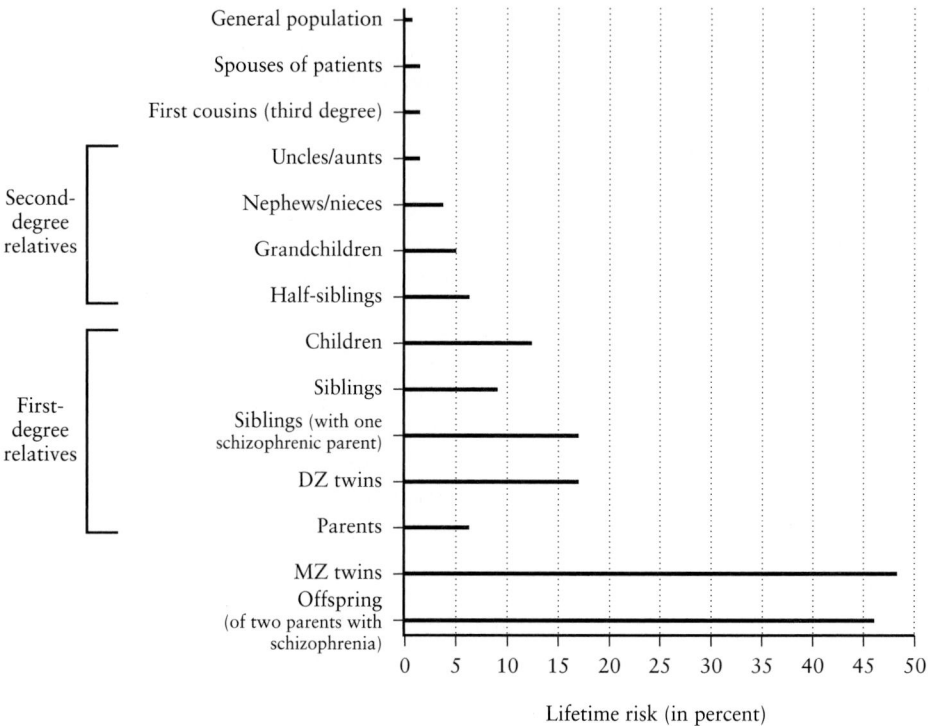

FIGURE 13.1 *Average Risk of Developing Schizophrenia*
Source: I. I. Gottesman, *Schizophrenia Genesis: The Origins of Madness* (New York: Freeman, 1991), p. 96.

adopted from mothers who did not have schizophrenia. None of those adopted from mothers who did not have schizophrenia developed schizophrenia. About 16% of those adopted from a mother who had schizophrenia developed schizophrenia, which is similar to the percentage who eventually develop schizophrenia after being born to and raised by a parent with schizophrenia (see Figure 13.1). Subsequent studies have shown similar results.

Viral Infections

Another possible cause of the neurobiological dysfunctions associated with schizophrenia is viral infection (Kirch, 1993). A virus could influence the development of schizophrenia in several ways. First, it could physically damage the brain. Second, it could interfere with the normal functioning of a person's brain, possibly by blocking one or more types of neurotransmitter receptors. Such a virus might be active periodically, which might explain the cyclic nature of schizophrenia. Finally, rather than a virus causing problems directly, a person's immune response to a viral infection could cause a neurobiological dysfunction.

Three intriguing lines of research point to the possibility of viral infections influencing schizophrenia, although all of this research has focused on adult-onset schizophrenia (Kirch, 1993). The first line of research explored differences in the prevalence of schizophrenia by geographical region and found different prevalence rates (Lewis, David, Andreasson, & Allbeck, 1992). This suggests that people living in certain areas are more susceptible to the type of viral infections that might be associated with schizophrenia. It is unclear, however, whether the observed differences in prevalence rates are due to different criteria for diagnosing schizophrenia or to actual differences in prevalence.

A finding that has received considerable attention is that people born during late winter and early spring months have a slightly higher chance of having schizophrenia than those born during other times of the year (Lewis, 1989). This pattern may be due to women being more susceptible to viral infections during certain months of the year, with this infection being transmitted to a fetus during a particularly sensitive time of neurological development. Finally, some studies have reported higher rates of schizophrenia after epidemics. One study followed children born after a large flu epidemic in Finland in 1957. Children who were exposed to the flu during the second trimester of their fetal development were more likely to develop schizophrenia than those exposed during their first or third trimesters, and it is during the second trimester that a significant amount of central nervous system (CNS) development takes place (Mednick, Machon, Huttunen, & Bonett, 1988).

Obstetric Complications

Complications during pregnancy or birth have been associated with an increased prevalence of schizophrenia in adults. The hypothesis has been that these complications cause brain injury that may have some influence on the development of schizophrenia. However, the single study with children did not find any association between obstetric complications and childhood-onset schizophrenia (Nicholson et al., 1999).

The Role of Stressful or Dysfunctional Family Environments

Several theories about the development of schizophrenia use a *diathesis–stress model* (a *diathesis* is a predisposition to a disorder). When applied to the etiology of schizophrenia, this model suggests that one or more problems with neurological functioning predispose a person to develop schizophrenia and that a physical or psychological stressor (an injury, a problem family environment) has a role in causing the disorder in some who are predisposed to it. Consequently, the role of stress in the onset of schizophrenia has been an important focus of research. Most of this research has focused on the role that family stress or dysfunction plays in the development of schizophrenia.

A particularly powerful research strategy for exploring the role of family environment in the development of behavioral or emotional disorders is *cross-fostering* research, which has been used in several studies of schizophrenia. These studies involve children of parents with schizophrenia and those of parents with no history of schizophrenia who are adopted into families that have significant mental health problems and those that do not. Consequently,

TABLE 13.3

Percentage of Severe Psychopathology in Children in Finnish Study

| | Birth Families | |
	Psychopathology	No Psychopathology
Adoptive Families — Psychopathology	62%	34%
Adoptive Families — No Psychopathology	3%	4%

Source: Tienari et al., 1994.

four groups of children are involved in the research. The results from a long-running cross-fostering study in Finland are displayed in Table 13.3 (Tienari et al., 1994). As shown, only a small percentage of children adopted into healthy adoptive families showed severe psychopathology, even if psychopathology existed in their birth families. This suggests that being raised in a healthy family environment protects those who might have a predisposition to schizophrenia. The high percentage of children adopted from birth families with histories of severe psychopathology and then raised in unhealthy adoptive families suggests that the combination of problematic genetic inheritance and problematic environment significantly raises the likelihood that a child will develop severe psychopathology.

Another family environment issue related to schizophrenia that has received research attention is **expressed emotion** (EE). Expressed emotion has been primarily investigated as a predictor of relapse in those who have schizophrenia, rather than as a causal influence on schizophrenia. Families that are high in EE are characterized by emotional overinvolvement among family members and interactions that are frequently hostile and critical. In a review of 25 studies of EE, Bebbington and Kuipers (1994) found an interesting interaction between the amount of contact in families with an adult member with schizophrenia, EE, and rate of relapse. As shown in Table 13.4, among families high in EE, the relapse rate was higher in families that had high contact and lower in families that low contact. The opposite was true in families with low EE: The

TABLE 13.4

Relapse Rate in Adults with Schizophrenia

| | Expressed Emotion | |
	High	Low
Contact — High	59%	18%
Contact — Low	42%	24%

relapse rate was higher in families with low contact and lower in families with high contact. Thus these studies suggest that frequent interactions among family members protect against relapse when those interactions are characterized by low EE and increase the chance of relapse when the interactions are characterized by high EE. Because high-EE interactions are likely to be stressful, this research suggests the role that stressful family interactions play in relapse.

Three Theories about the Development of Schizophrenia

Now that we have discussed the research on neurobiological functioning and family stress in children and adults with schizophrenia, we will focus on three theories about the development of schizophrenia. As we will see, two theories focus on a combination of neurobiological dysfunction and stress, and the third focuses solely on neurobiological dysfunction.

Two theorists have posed issues that need to be considered in a theory about the development of schizophrenia. Weinberger (1987) notes, "There are three inescapable clinical 'facts' about schizophrenia that should be taken into account by any effort to explain it: first, the very high probability that it will become clinically apparent in late adolescence or early adulthood; second, the role of 'stress' in onset and relapse; and third, the therapeutic efficacy of neuroleptic drugs" (p. 660). DeLisi (1997) asks, "What kind of process could lead to an illness characterized by subtle signs and symptoms for many years, leading to full-blown malfunctioning some time in early adulthood, with unpredictable recoveries and exacerbations and changeable predominance of clinical symptoms?" (p. 119). To these questions we should add this: What issues cause the onset of clinical symptoms in childhood for a small percentage of those who develop schizophrenia?

In 1962 Paul Meehl (1962) described a strategy for thinking about the etiology of schizophrenia that has been influential since. (Note that an address in 1962 was delivered before technology gave us more knowledge about brain functioning.) Meehl suggested that some people inherited a genetically based defect of the CNS, which he labeled as *schizotaxia*. Partly because of this CNS defect, most of those with schizotaxia developed a personality style during their childhood that Meehl labeled as a *schizotype*. This style was characterized by disordered thinking, interpersonal aversiveness, and **anhedonia** (an inability to experience pleasure).

Meehl argued that only a few people with a schizotype personality developed schizophrenia. He suggested that those who did not develop schizophrenia had also inherited one or more traits that protected them from schizophrenia, such as low anxiety, good physical health, or a resistance to stress. These people went on to be "well-compensated, 'normal' schizotypes" (p. 830). Others were pushed toward the development of schizophrenia by stressful experiences in their environments, in particular by stressful interactions with their mothers (recall that at that time fewer women worked outside the home, and the care of children, particularly young children, was primarily a maternal task). Meehl did not suggest that these mothers were uncaring or cruel. Rather, a significant influence on their stressful interactions with their children was the schizotypal personality that many of them had developed because of their own inherited schizotaxia.

Although some people might bristle at Meehl's suggestion that interactions with mothers can push some individuals toward schizophrenia, his basic concept of the interplay between a person's inherited characteristics and the environments in which he or she develops continues to influence our thinking about the development of schizophrenia and many other forms of child psychopathology.

The second theory we will explore was described by Daniel Weinberger (1987). Weinberger suggested that the symptoms of schizophrenia are caused by the interactions between a brain lesion and the normal course of brain development. Weinberger conceptualized the term *lesion* broadly, referring to some type of structural or functional problem of the brain. He speculated that this lesion is present early in life, perhaps even during fetal development, and that it likely has some influence on the limbic system (which could account for the positive symptoms of schizophrenia) and the prefrontal cortex (which could account for the negative symptoms).

Weinberger argued that this lesion can influence a child's functioning but does not cause the symptoms of schizophrenia during childhood because the areas in which this lesion is located do not have a significant role in children's functioning. He argued that the functioning of these areas becomes critical as the person begins to cope with the challenges of independent living during late adolescence and early adulthood. Consequently, the lesion has an important negative influence on the physiological and cognitive adaptations that are necessary during this developmental period. In addition, the influence of the lesion is magnified if the person experiences high levels of stress because the stress further inhibits the person from making necessary physiological and cognitive adaptations. The result of the presence of the lesion and high levels of stress can be many of the symptoms of schizophrenia: confused and delusional thinking that leads to social withdrawal, fear and agitation, and hallucinations.

Lynn DeLisi (1997) suggested a theory that differs from Weinberger's in two ways: It does not involve a brain lesion fixed early in life and does not involve the influence of stress. DeLisi argued that it is unlikely that a permanent lesion could cause the waxing and waning of symptoms that are typical in schizophrenia, and that it could not explain the recovery of some but not all people with schizophrenia.

DeLisi suggested that schizophrenia is a lifelong, progressive disorder, caused by a group of defective genes that influence the functioning of one or more neurotransmitters. She noted that neurotransmitters influence the brain differently throughout development, and these changes are influenced by certain genes becoming active or inactive during development. In addition, she noted that some neurotransmitters influence particular parts of the brain during some developmental periods but not others. Consequently, she asserted, the symptoms of schizophrenia may develop during late adolescence and early adulthood in most people because the neurotransmitters that have been affected by the defective genes play a particularly important role in brain functioning during this time.

DeLisi said some people experience only one or two episodes of schizophrenia because their brains can reverse the damage to neurotransmitter functioning that the defective genes have caused. She also suggested that antipsychotic medications may enhance the brain's ability to repair damage or prevent further damage, thus reversing the disease process or halting its progression. Further, she speculated that cases of childhood-onset schizophrenia are particularly severe because children's brains have had less opportunity to develop mechanisms to recover from the harm done by the defective genes.

Summary

All these theories suggest that the fundamental cause of schizophrenia is one or more neurobiological dysfunctions. Meehl is less clear about what this dysfunction might be (as one would expect from someone writing several decades ago), and Weinberger suggests a more fixed dysfunction than does DeLisi. The role of environmental stressors and other influences also differs between the theories. Meehl asserts that socialization in the family and other environmental influences that begin early in life can influence schizophrenia. Weinberger, on the other hand, suggests that the environmental influences are more focused in late adolescence and early adulthood. DeLisi appears to see less of a role for environmental influences than the other two theorists. Which of these theories is closest to describing the developmental process of schizophrenia remains to be seen—requiring future research. Of course, perhaps each theory is useful for describing the development of schizophrenia in some people but not others.

The Development of Schizophrenia during Childhood

If childhood-onset schizophrenia is the same disorder as adult-onset schizophrenia, a question that needs to be addressed is why such a small percentage of cases develop in childhood. Two possible answers have been suggested. The first possibility relates to the severity of the disorder: When the disorder is more severe the process through which it develops occurs more quickly, which results in a few cases developing in children. The second possibility is that an earlier onset is not due to characteristics of the disorder or the children who have it; rather, the age of onset can be represented by a normal distribution, with a few cases having an early onset, a few cases having a late onset, and most cases having an onset during late adolescence and early adulthood (Asarnow et al., 1995).

Three lines of research suggest that schizophrenia with childhood onset is more severe, although none shows this conclusively. We have already explored the first line of research, which is that the premorbid functioning of those who develop childhood-onset schizophrenia is more problematic than the premorbid functioning of those who develop schizophrenia in late adolescence or adulthood (Alaghband Rad et al., 1995; Hollis, 2003). More severe premorbid symptoms could indicate that the disorder is particularly virulent in those cases. The second line of research shows that more relatives of those with childhood-onset schizophrenia have schizophrenia or a related disorder than do relatives of those with adult-onset schizophrenia (Asarnow et al., 1995; Nicolson, Lenane et al., 2000). This increased prevalence suggests that a more severe form of the disorder may be present in these families. Finally, as discussed in a previous section, those with childhood-onset schizophrenia have poorer long-term outcomes than do those with adult-onset schizophrenia. This could also be due to childhood-onset schizophrenia being a more severe disorder. If, as this research suggests, childhood-onset schizophrenia is more severe than adult-onset schizophrenia, the first of the two possibilities receives more support than the second. If the onset was simply due to the normal distribution of onset timing, one would not expect more severe cases to appear. Consequently, current research points to the possibility that schizophrenia may develop in a few children because of its severity.

Key Concepts

- Three areas of neurobiological dysfunctions are associated with schizophrenia, although none of the identified dysfunctions appears in all cases of schizophrenia, and some people without schizophrenia also show these dysfunctions.
- As a group, children with schizophrenia have smaller cerebral volumes, smaller cerebellum volumes, larger lateral ventricles, larger structures in the basal ganglia, a larger superior temporal gyrus, and a smaller thalamus than do other children.
- Children with schizophrenia show deficits in three areas of brain functioning: attention, memory, and fine motor control.
- Dysfunctions in the dopaminergic system are associated with the positive symptoms of schizophrenia in many people. Recent studies have also implicated dysfunctions in the serotonergic system and in other neurotransmitter systems.
- Genes are involved in the etiology of schizophrenia, although which gene or genes remains unknown.
- Viral infections may play a part in the etiology of schizophrenia, either by causing CNS damage or by inhibiting CNS functioning. In addition, a person's immune response to a virus might cause CNS damage or dysfunction.
- Pregnancy and obstetric complications are associated with the development of adult-onset schizophrenia, but the same association has not been found in childhood-onset schizophrenia.
- A positive family environment may serve as a protective factor for those at risk for developing schizophrenia; a dysfunctional family environment may push those with a predilection toward schizophrenia to develop the disorder.
- Meehl's theory suggests that genetic heritage and social environment result in a schizotype personality, which can develop into schizophrenia after dysfunctional interactions with caregivers.

- Weinberger's theory suggests that a lesion in the brain causes the development of schizophrenia and that schizophrenia occurs as the damaged parts of the brain play a larger role in a person's functioning.
- DeLisi's theory suggests that schizophrenia is a lifelong, progressive disorder, caused by a defective gene or group of defective genes that have an ongoing influence on brain development.
- Current research suggests that schizophrenia develops in children when it is a more severe disorder.

Prevention

It is possible to identify some children who are at higher risk for developing schizophrenia based on other family occurrences of schizophrenia or patterns of neurobehavioral problems or other markers of vulnerability they exhibit. It may be possible to provide them or their families with some form of intervention, which may prevent the development of schizophrenia or reduce its severity.

Markers of Vulnerability

Several studies of children of mothers who have schizophrenia have shown that those who eventually receive a diagnosis of schizophrenia or a related disorder in adulthood exhibited one or more neurobehavioral dysfunctions when they were children. These dysfunctions are usually associated with verbal memory, attention, and gross motor skills (Erlenmeyer-Kimling, 2000). Some researchers have labeled these dysfunctions *markers of vulnerability*. In one study, 83% of children who eventually developed schizophrenia or a related disorder had verbal memory deficits, 75% had gross motor deficits, 58% had attention deficits, and 50% showed deficits in all three areas (Erlenmeyer-Kimling, 2000). Thus these deficits, particularly when occurring together, may indicate children who are at risk for developing schizophrenia as children or adults.

Another intriguing marker of vulnerability is **eye-tracking dysfunction.** Researchers have found that when some people are asked to follow visually the track of a pendulum or an oscillating light on a screen, their visual tracking does not follow smoothly but rather includes frequent rapid jittery movements. Adults and children with schizophrenia are more likely to exhibit this dysfunction than are those without schizophrenia (Kumra et al., 2001). In addition, eye-tracking dysfunction has been found more frequently in first-degree relatives of adults with schizophrenia than in others (Rosenberg et al., 1997). For example, Ross (2003) found that 94% of children with schizophrenia, 50% of children who had a first-degree relative with schizophrenia, and only 19% of other children exhibited eye-tracking dysfunction. This suggests that there is a genetic influence on the development of eye-tracking dysfunction and that the genes associated with the dysfunction may also be associated with the development of schizophrenia. Consequently, eye-tracking dysfunction may also indicate some children who are at risk for developing schizophrenia.

Possible Preventive Interventions

If children at a higher risk for schizophrenia can be identified, perhaps they could be given some type of intervention to reduce the chance that they will develop schizophrenia. One possibility is to provide low doses of medication used to treat schizophrenia, based on the hypothesis that these medications may protect the children's developing brains from the influence of the disease process of schizophrenia or may help their brains repair previous damage. Another possibility is to provide psychotherapy to those at risk for developing schizophrenia or their families. For example, therapies designed to improve parent–child interactions, reduce EE in families, or reduce the frequency or consequences of stress could generate an environment in which those with a genetic predisposition to schizophrenia are less likely to develop it.

Gottesman and Erlenmeyer-Kimling (2001), caution against too much enthusiasm for preventive efforts involving medication. They note that although we know which children are at higher risk for developing schizophrenia, our ability to predict which children will develop schizophrenia is "still an art in the process of becoming a science" (p. 96). For example, 89% of children who have a parent with schizophrenia and many children with one or more markers of vulnerability do *not* develop schizophrenia. They argue that if medications are given to children at risk for developing schizophrenia, many children who will never develop schizophrenia will risk side effects of the medication while receiving no benefit from it. However, they suggest that psychotherapy for these children and their families may be appropriate because psychotherapy that increases positive family interactions or children's ability to cope with stress may be valuable to all who receive it—even those who will never develop schizophrenia.

Key Concepts

- It is possible to identify some children who are at higher risk for schizophrenia through markers of vulnerability or because other family members have schizophrenia or a related disorder.
- Providing children at risk for developing schizophrenia with low doses of medication used to treat schizophrenia is possible. Concern has been raised that this would result in many children who will never develop schizophrenia receiving medication.
- Providing psychotherapy to reduce stress or improve family functioning may reduce a child's likelihood of developing schizophrenia.

Therapeutic Interventions

Because of the severe nature of childhood-onset schizophrenia, treatment for it usually involves a wide range of interventions provided by a multidisciplinary team of professionals, usually including a psychiatrist, a psychologist or other psychotherapist, a family social worker, and teachers or other education experts (American Academy of Child and Adolescent Psychiatry, 2000; Kumra, 2000).

Unfortunately little research has been done on the efficacy of the interventions that are commonly provided to children and their families; therefore much information about their usefulness comes from clinical experience rather than empirical evidence (Bryden, Carrey, & Kutcher, 2001; Pappadopulos et al., 2002).

Early detection and accurate diagnosis of childhood-onset schizophrenia are important. Starting antipsychotic medications soon after the initial onset of positive symptoms increases the likelihood of a better long-term outcome in adults, and the same may be true for children (Bryden et al., 2001). Unfortunately, as we saw in preceding sections, there are often delays in children being accurately diagnosed with schizophrenia, which may have significant long-term consequences for them.

Antipsychotic Medications

Antipsychotic medications are the foundation of therapy for most children with schizophrenia (Bryden et al., 2001). About 98% of them receive medication, and between 45% and 85% of them receive more than one medication (Pappadopulos et al., 2002). However, because so few children have schizophrenia, little research on the effectiveness of medications with them has been conducted (Dass, McNamara, & Findling, 2005).

Antipsychotic medications have been roughly divided into two groups: **typical** and **atypical**. Typical medications were the first effective medications developed and act primarily by blocking D2 dopamine receptors. Typical medications reduce or eliminate the positive symptoms in many adults and children; however, they have little or no influence on negative symptoms and usually produce significant side effects (Jensen et al., 1999; Weisz & Jensen, 1999). In response to the limitations of typical medications, the atypical medications were developed. These act primarily by blocking several types of dopamine and serotonin receptors and are effective in many people who do not respond to the typical medications. However, significant side effects have occurred in many children taking clozapine, one of the atypical medications commonly prescribed to adults; so it is used primarily when other medications are ineffective (Dass et al., 2005).

A higher percentage of children than adults do not respond to antipsychotic medication and experience significant side effects when on medication. Two issues may influence this (Bryden et al., 2001; Dass et al., 2005). First, as described earlier, childhood-onset schizophrenia may be a more severe form of schizophrenia, and medications may be less effective with severe cases. Second, the CNS of children is less mature and may react differently to medication, and the reactions of an individual child's CNS may change significantly as it develops. This may make it more difficult to identify an effective dose of a medication for children.

After medication has controlled the symptoms of childhood-onset schizophrenia, it is often continued at a lower dose for one to two years to reduce the chance of relapse (American Academy of Child and Adolescent Psychiatry, 2000). How long to continue medication is a clinical dilemma because the possibility of a relapse is always present, even if a child has been symptom-free for several years (Kumra, 2000). Children and their parents are often eager to end medication because of its side effects. However, psychiatrists may be less eager to end medication because of the increased probability of relapse.

Side Effects

All medications given for schizophrenia produce side effects in most children who take them. One study of an atypical medication, for example, showed side effects that were severe enough to warrant discontinuation of the medication for one-third of the children (Kumra et al., 1996).

The most common side effects occur in the **extrapyramidal system,** which is the system of neural pathways that connects the brain to the motor neurons in the spinal cord (McClellan & Werry, 1994). Side effects that commonly appear early in treatment include muscular rigidity, agitation, tremors, and involuntary muscle movements. These side effects can be very disturbing to a child and family, although they are not life-threatening and often end after several months. **Tardive dyskinesia** can develop after prolonged medication treatment. The most commonly reported dyskinesias are rhythmic, involuntary movements of the mouth, tongue, face, and jaw, although involuntary movements of the limbs and the trunk also occur (Bryden et al., 2001).

Sedation is another frequent side effect (Dass et al., 2005; McClellan & Werry, 1994). This can be particularly problematic in academic and social settings, where a child may not have sufficient energy to participate in school or engage in activities with peers. Additional side effects include dry mouth, constipation, and urinary hesitancy (Kumra, 2000). Weight gain is a common side effect of the atypical medications, which can particularly bother adolescents and can discourage them from continuing their medication. **Agranulocytosis,** a potentially lethal blood disorder, and **neuroleptic malignant syndrome,** a potentially life-threatening condition characterized by hyperthermia, muscular rigidity, and hypertension, have been reported in children but are rare (Campbell & Armenteros, 1996; Gerbino-Rosen et al., 2005).

Psychological Interventions

Psychological interventions focus on helping the child and family cope with the consequences of schizophrenia and reintegrating the child into his or her school and community if necessary (McClellan & Werry, 1994). A few studies with adolescents and several studies with adults have shown that combining psychological interventions with medication produces more positive outcomes than medication alone for those with schizophrenia (Sikich, 2005).

Psychoeducational interventions help the child and parents learn about the etiology of schizophrenia and its cycle of symptoms. They also learn about the importance of maintaining a healthful lifestyle, including consistent use of medication, proper diet, sufficient sleep, and healthy relationships (Sikich, 2005). Social skills training can be important because many children are withdrawn from others even before the initial onset of their symptoms and so may have developed few social skills. Studies with adults have shown that social skills training improves their interpersonal relationships, grooming and hygiene, and willingness to engage in activities (Dulmus & Smyth, 2000).

Finding an appropriate educational placement for a child with schizophrenia is important. Even after the symptoms of the acute phase are under control, the child may need a period of recovery before he or she can function in normal academic and social settings (Dulmus & Smyth, 2000). It may be appropriate for the child to be enrolled in a **partial hospitalization** program that provides academic, social, and therapeutic activities during the day, with the child returning home in the evening. Several types of academic placements are possible after a child is stable and ready to return to a more normal lifestyle, including a specialized school, special education services through a public school, or regular classes at a public school (Sikich, 2005).

Ensuring compliance with medication is an ongoing therapeutic issue with some children and their families, particularly for adolescents who must cope with conflicts between the needs for autonomy and the consistent use of medication. They may rebel against their parents, physicians, or therapists by refusing to take their medication or by taking it only periodically. In addition, as noted earlier, side effects such as weight gain can discourage adolescents from continuing their medication (Bryden et al., 2001).

Important therapeutic goals with families are increasing their understanding of schizophrenia, developing strategies to cope with their children's symptoms, and helping the parents become strong advocates for their children at their children's schools and in their communities. Parents may need help maintaining strong relationships with each other and with their other children, helping their other children cope with the issues they face because of the sibling with schizophrenia, and obtaining support to handle the stress associated with having a child with schizophrenia (Harle & McClellan, 2005; Kumra, 2000).

Key Concepts

- Early and appropriate intervention may result in a better prognosis for children with schizophrenia.
- Antipsychotic medications are the foundation of treatment with most children who have schizophrenia.
- Children experience more side effects, and more severe side effects, from antipsychotic medications than do adults. Common side effects include involuntary muscle movements, sedation, dry mouth, constipation, urinary hesitancy, and weight gain.
- After the acute phase ends, children are often maintained on a low dose of antipsychotic medication to reduce the chance of relapse.
- Psychological interventions focus on social skills training, medication compliance, educational placement, and family support.

CHAPTER GLOSSARY

The **acute phase** of schizophrenia is characterized by positive and negative symptoms.

Agranulocytosis is a potentially lethal blood disorder that is a side effect of antipsychotic medication.

Alogia, a negative symptom of schizophrenia, refers to a person producing minimal speech.

Anhedonia is an inability to experience pleasure.

Atypical antipsychotic medications are a second generation of antipsychotic medications that act primarily by blocking dopamine and serotonin receptors.

Avolition, a negative symptom of schizophrenia, refers to a person's lack of action or participation in activities.

Brain morphology refers to the form and structure of the brain.

The **catatonic type** of schizophrenia is characterized by psychomotor disturbance—either a lack of movement or excessive movement.

Childhood schizophrenia was a disorder that included a range of chronic, severe disorders of childhood, including what we now call childhood-onset schizophrenia and autism.

Command hallucinations occur when a person hears a voice telling him or her to behave in certain ways.

Delusions are false beliefs held persistently despite evidence to the contrary.

Dementia praecox is the term used by Kraepelin to describe the disorder we now call schizophrenia.

Disorganized speech is used to infer disordered thinking.

The **disorganized type** of schizophrenia is characterized by high levels of disorganized speech, thoughts, and behaviors.

The **dopamine hypothesis** suggests that the symptoms of schizophrenia are caused by problems with the dopamine neurotransmitter system.

Families in which high levels of **expressed emotion** occur are characterized by emotional overinvolvement and a high percentage of hostile and critical comments.

Extrapyramidal side effects of antipsychotic medications involve involuntary muscle movements or muscular rigidity.

Eye-tracking dysfunction is a possible marker of vulnerability for schizophrenia; it involves deficits in following a smooth visual stimulus such as a swinging pendulum.

Flattened affect, a negative symptom of schizophrenia, refers to a lack of emotion in a person's speech, facial expression, or action.

Grossly disorganized behavior, a positive symptom of schizophrenia, is behavior that is obviously odd and inappropriate.

Hallucinations are perceptions without corresponding external stimuli. They may involve any of the five senses.

Negative symptoms of schizophrenia represent a loss of normal functioning; they include flattened affect, alogia, and avolition.

Neuroleptic malignant syndrome is a potentially life-threatening side effect of antipsychotic medication, characterized by hyperthermia, muscular rigidity, parkinsonism, and hypertension.

The **paranoid type** of schizophrenia is characterized by delusions with persecutory and/or grandiose themes.

A **partial hospitalization** program provides treatment and support during the day, with the patient returning home in the evening.

Persecutory delusions are delusions in which a person believes that he or she is being threatened by others.

Positive symptoms of schizophrenia represent a distortion of normal functioning; they include hallucinations, delusions, disorganized speech, and grossly disorganized behavior.

Premorbid functioning refers to the functioning of a child before the onset of the symptoms of schizophrenia or other disorders.

The **prodromal phase** of schizophrenia is the phase before the acute phase. It is characterized by a substantial deterioration in functioning.

The **recovery phase** of schizophrenia occurs after the acute phase and is characterized by confusion, disorganization, and dysphoria.

Referential delusions are delusions in which a person believes that certain comments on television or passages in books are aimed specifically at him or her.

The **residual phase** of schizophrenia is the time between episodes. During this phase, most children are withdrawn and odd.

The **residual type** of schizophrenia is diagnosed when a person has experienced at least one episode of the acute phase of schizophrenia but is currently only experiencing negative symptoms.

Tardive dyskinesia is a side effect of antipsychotic medication that most commonly involves rhythmic, involuntary movements of the mouth, tongue, face, and jaw.

Typical antipsychotic medications were the first developed. They work primarily by blocking the D_2 dopamine receptors.

The **undifferentiated type** of schizophrenia is diagnosed when a person does not meet the criteria for any of the other types or meets the criteria for two or three types.

Word salad is a colloquial term used to describe speech in which words are jumbled and do not form coherent sentences.

Disorders Associated with Trauma or Maltreatment

The trauma experienced by children living in a war zone may lead to one or more serious disorders.

Many children experience one or more **traumatic events** at some point in their lives (Perrin, Smith, & Yule, 2000). A study of rural children, for example, showed that about 25% of them had experienced a trauma such as the death of a loved one, a serious illness or accident, a natural disaster, being the target of family violence, or being raped (Costello, Erkanli, Fairbank, & Angold, 2002). Trauma can cause one or more of many different outcomes for a child. Some children cope effectively with a traumatic event or even become stronger because of it. Other children experience behavioral or emotional problems as a result of the trauma. These problems can come in many forms: Some children may be depressed, others develop strong fears, and others engage in delinquent or other acting-out behaviors. Three disorders that are particularly associated with traumatic experiences are explored in this chapter. Posttraumatic stress disorder (PTSD) has been associated with a wide range of traumas, some that occur only once (such as being involved in a school shooting) and others that occur many times (such as being the repeated victim of child sexual abuse). The dissociative disorders and reactive attachment disorder are usually associated with severe, chronic child abuse or neglect. The type of stress a child experiences, the reactions of those around the child, and the child's genes may influence which, if any, of these disorders develops after a child experiences trauma.

Chapter Plan

In this chapter, as in the next one, we consider three types of disorders. First we focus on PTSD, then the dissociative disorders, and finally reactive attachment disorder. As with our exploration of the other disorders in this text, we consider the history, prevalence, and course of each disorder; the characteristics and experiences of the children who are diagnosed with the disorder; and the etiology of the disorder. We also examine preventive and therapeutic strategies for children experiencing each disorder and their families.

Posttraumatic Stress Disorder and Acute Stress Disorder

As just noted, many children experience a traumatic event. Although these events distress or overwhelm most children who experience them, many of them experience a reduction in their emotional and physical reactions to the trauma over time. However, some children seem to become "stuck" in their trauma. They continue to relive it through intrusive memories and dreams, they experience frequent and intense anxiety, and they are chronically "on edge" and concerned that another traumatic event will occur (van der Kolk, van der Hart, & Burbridge, 2002). These persistent memories and high levels of arousal form the core symptoms of *posttraumatic stress disorder (PTSD)* and *acute stress disorder.*

PTSD and acute stress disorder are included in the *anxiety disorders* category of the DSM-IV-TR because their primary symptoms are related to anxiety (APA, 2000). In this text, however, we consider them in this section about disorders related to trauma because it appears that their etiology differs from that of the other anxiety disorders. As discussed in the chapter about anxiety disorders, current hypotheses about their etiology involve a genetic predisposition to high levels of anxiety that is intensified and focused through learning. Acute stress disorder and PTSD, alternately, are believed to have their foundation in the physiological consequences of high stress levels, with these physiological consequences initiating a complex set of changes in brain functioning that cause the symptoms of the disorders (Stien & Kendall, 2004).

As we will see, acute stress disorder and PTSD share many diagnostic criteria. However, clinical and research literature focuses almost exclusively on PTSD. Consequently, PTSD will be our primary focus in this chapter. Future research will be needed to determine if acute stress disorder and PTSD are distinct, if they are different manifestations of the same disorder, or if acute stress disorder is an early form of PTSD.

Case Study: Living through a Tornado

When Maggie was 8 years old, her home was destroyed by a tornado that swept through part of a small town in Oklahoma where her family lived. All the adults and children in her town knew they lived in an area where tornadoes were likely, so they were prepared for them. Maggie's family had a "tornado drill" twice a year, during which the family pretended that a tornado was coming and went to the area of their basement that was the most protected. Maggie and her two brothers initially found these drills exciting, but they soon became commonplace and boring. One Saturday when Maggie and one of her brothers were at home with their father (her mother and other brother were at a shopping center about 30 miles away), the weather-alert monitor in their house activated—indicating that a tornado watch had been issued for their area. About 30 minutes later, a tornado warning was issued, indicating the possibility that a tornado would form somewhere in their area. Maggie's father turned on the television and tuned to the Weather Channel.

As a second thunderstorm approached, the Weather Channel announced that a tornado had touched down in their area; the siren in town used to warn people of an approaching tornado started to sound. Maggie, her brother, and her father went down to the "tornado area" in their basement. Soon the power went off. The sound of the storm continued to grow. They could hear their house groan as it was buffeted by the wind, and soon they began to hear things crashing against their house. As the noise grew louder, they could hear their house begin to crack and could hear windows breaking and their furniture being blown around inside the house. As the noise grew even louder, Maggie's father pushed her and her brother to the floor and lay on top of them. Suddenly the roof and walls of their house blew apart as the tornado passed close to them. Although some debris fell on Maggie's father, they were all safe and unharmed. After the tornado passed, they came out of the basement to see the complete destruction around them. They huddled together until rescue workers came by about an hour later. Soon Maggie's mother and brother arrived in their car, shocked at the destruction but happy that the whole family was safe. They gathered a few of their possessions and drove to a friend's house in a part of town that had not been affected by the tornado.

That night Maggie found it impossible to fall asleep. A rainstorm had begun, and the noise of the wind and rain made her feel as if she were back in the tornado. She finally crawled into bed with her mother and father and fell asleep. However, she woke up twice that night screaming from a nightmare in which she was in a tornado again. She continued to have nightmares over the next few days, which disturbed her sleep and the sleep of her other family members. She stayed close to her mother throughout the day and seemed to be frightened of her father and thus avoided him, which bothered him. When it came time to return to school several days later, Maggie was reluctant to leave her mother and demanded that she be allowed to stay home. When her parents insisted that she go to school, she did; but she cried throughout much of the day and was unable to do any of her schoolwork. This pattern continued for several days, and her teacher finally sat Maggie in the back of the classroom so she would not disturb the other children. At home, Maggie continued to have difficulty sleeping and had little appetite, even when her mother prepared some of her favorite foods. Her mother tried to get Maggie to talk about what was bothering her, but Maggie just cried and refused to talk about it.

About a week later, Maggie woke several times at night crying, saying she felt as if some huge weight was on top of her when she was lying in bed. Her parents arranged a way for her to sleep in more of a sitting position, but even then Maggie said that whenever she closed her eyes it felt as if a big weight was on top of her. Between her lack of sleep and her refusal to eat much, Maggie soon became listless during much of the day. Small noises startled her, and she was frightened whenever it rained or the wind blew loudly.

Although Maggie's parents had expected that their children would have high levels of anxiety after living through the tornado, they were increasingly concerned about Maggie. They talked with the psychologist at Maggie's school about what to do. He said that many children who had been traumatized by tornadoes or other natural disasters developed PTSD, and he recommended that Maggie be taken to a child psychologist in a nearby city. The child psychologist had been trained in a special program at the University of Oklahoma to help children with PTSD. Maggie's parents arranged for Maggie to see the psychologist, who asked that the whole family attend sessions with Maggie every other week and that Maggie attend sessions alone the rest of the time. Over the next few months of therapy, the psychologist talked with Maggie and her parents about reactions to traumatic events, taught them a relaxation technique that they all used each evening at home, and used cognitive–behavioral therapy with Maggie. Maggie's symptoms gradually diminished, and within six months her nightmares and other problems had ended.

Some Issues Worth Noting

- The differences in the responses of Maggie and her brother to their similar experience.
- Maggie's reluctance to talk about her fears and her avoidance of her father—which may have bothered her parents if they interpreted her avoidance as an indication of her feelings toward him.
- Maggie's experience of feeling as if a weight were on her when sleeping and its possible connection to her father lying on her to protect her from the storm.
- The conflicts that Maggie's mother may have had about sending her to school or allowing her to remain at home.

History

Most early attention to the symptoms of what is now called PTSD focused on soldiers' experiences in war, and historical accounts of these symptoms date as far back as Homer's *Iliad* (Lamprecht & Sack, 2002). Although soldiers in many wars experienced the symptoms of PTSD, little was known about the causes of these symptoms or why they occurred in some soldiers and not others. During World War I, many soldiers who showed the **hyper-vigilance,** intrusive memories, and nightmares that are symptoms of PTSD were diagnosed with *shell shock,* a term that was later changed to *combat fatigue* (Kardiner, 1941). Work with soldiers in World War II and the Korean war also showed that many of them experienced the symptoms of PTSD (Grinker & Spiegel, 1945; Noble, Roudebush, & Prince, 1952).

The studies of soldiers in war and other studies of concentration camp survivors led to the inclusion of *gross stress reaction* in the DSM-I (APA, 1952) and *transient situational disturbance* in the DSM-II (APA, 1968; Lamprecht & Sack, 2002). PTSD first appeared in the DSM-III and was included in the *anxiety disorder* category. The inclusion of diagnostic criteria for PTSD in the DSM-III led to a heightened research interest in the disorder (Perrin et al., 2000). The following editions of the DSM continued to use the diagnostic criteria from the DSM-III but expanded and refined them.

Despite the long-term interest in the effects of trauma on adults, it was not until the early 1980s that it was widely believed that children could experience prolonged reactions to traumatic events (Yule, 2001). Lenore Terr's ongoing clinical assessments of a group of 26 kidnapped school-age children were critical for bringing PTSD in children to the attention of clinicians and researchers (Terr, 1979, 1991). The children Terr interviewed had been kidnapped when their school bus in Chowchilla, California, was taken over by several adults who planned to hold the children for ransom. After taking over the bus, the kidnappers transferred the children to other vehicles and then buried the vehicles in a remote area to keep them from view. After 27 hours of being in these buried vehicles, the children escaped when the roof of one of them collapsed from the weight of the dirt on top of it. Terr interviewed 23 of the children several times over the next few years. Her initial interviews showed that the children experienced many symptoms of PTSD commonly seen in traumatized adults, and her ongoing interviews showed that these symptoms persisted for years in many of the children.

Additional interest in the effects of trauma on children came during the 1980s from studies of physically and sexually abused children (van der Kolk, McFarlane, & van der Hart, 1996). These studies showed that many children who had experienced repeated or severe abuse met the diagnostic criteria for PTSD. This realization led to the study of PTSD in children experiencing a variety of traumas, including automobile accidents, severe physical illness, family or neighborhood violence, and war. The results of these studies made it clear that children experience PTSD after many types of trauma and that children are even more likely than adults to experience PTSD after a trauma (Fletcher, 2003).

Key Concepts

- Early attention to symptoms of PTSD focused on soldiers in combat, and several names were used for these symptoms, including *shell shock* and *combat fatigue.*
- *Gross stress reaction* was included in the DSM-I; *transient situational disturbance* was included in the DSM-II; and PTSD was included in later editions of the DSM.
- During the 1980s, assessments of kidnapped children and children who had been physically or sexually abused showed that many of them experienced the symptoms of PTSD.

Diagnosis and Assessment

Diagnostic Criteria

As shown in Tables 14.1 and 14.2, acute stress disorder and PTSD share many features. Both require that a child experience one or more traumatic events involving actual or threatened death or severe injury, with this event evoking high levels of fear, helplessness, or horror. As such, PTSD and acute stress disorder are among the few diagnoses requiring that a child have a particular experience. Some traumatic events involve single incidents, such as being in a flood or being involved in a school shooting. Other traumatic events involve repeated incidents, such as being sexually abused many times or living in a war zone.

As can be seen, there are three clusters of symptoms for PTSD. First, a child must persistently reexperience the trauma. The reexperiencing of the trauma cannot simply involve painful memories of it—something that most or

TABLE 14.1

Diagnostic Criteria for 309.81 Posttraumatic Stress Disorder

A. The person has been exposed to a traumatic event in which both of the following were present:
   (1) The person experienced, witnessed, or was confronted with an event or events that involved actual or threatened death or serious injury, or a threat to the physical integrity of self or others.
   (2) The person's response involved intense fear, helplessness, or horror. **Note:** In children, this may be expressed instead by disorganized or agitated behavior.

B. The traumatic event is persistently reexperienced in one (or more) of the following ways:
   (1) Recurrent and intrusive distressing recollections of the event, including images, thoughts, or perceptions. **Note:** In young children, repetitive play may occur in which themes or aspects of the trauma are expressed.
   (2) Recurrent distressing dreams of the event. **Note:** In children, there may be frightening dreams without recognizable content.
   (3) Acting or feeling as if the traumatic event were recurring (includes a sense of reliving the experience, illusions, hallucinations, and dissociative flashback episodes, including those that occur on awakening or when intoxicated). **Note:** In young children, trauma-specific reenactment may occur.
   (4) Intense psychological distress at exposure to internal or external cues that symbolize or resemble an aspect of the traumatic event.
   (5) Physiological reactivity on exposure to internal or external cues that symbolize or resemble an aspect of the traumatic event.

C. Persistent avoidance of stimuli associated with the trauma and numbing of general responsiveness (not present before the trauma), as indicated by three (or more) of the following:
   (1) Efforts to avoid thoughts, feelings, or conversations associated with the trauma.
   (2) Efforts to avoid activities, places, or people that arouse recollections of the trauma.
   (3) Inability to recall an important aspect to the trauma.
   (4) Markedly diminished interest or participation in significant activities.
   (5) Feeling of detachment or estrangement from others.
   (6) Restricted range of affect (e.g., unable to have loving feelings).
   (7) Sense of a foreshortened future (e.g., does not expect to have a career, marriage, children, or a normal life span).

D. Persistent symptoms of increased arousal (not present before the trauma), as indicated by two (or more) of the following:
   (1) Difficulty falling or staying asleep.
   (2) Irritability or outbursts of anger.   *(continued)*

TABLE 14.1

Diagnostic Criteria for 309.81 Postraumatic Stress Disorder (*continued*)

	(3) Difficulty concentrating.
	(4) Hypervigilance.
	(5) Exaggerated startle response.
E.	Duration of the disturbance (symptoms in Criteria B, C, and D) is more than one month.
F.	The disturbance causes clinically significant distress or impairment in social, occupational, or other important areas of functioning.

Specify if:

   Acute: if duration of symptoms is less than three months

   Chronic: if duration of symptoms is three months or more

Specify if:

   With Delayed Onset: if onset of symptoms is at least six months after the stressor

---

all children will experience. Rather, the reexperiencing must have an intrusive quality to it, suggesting that it is outside the child's control. Second, a child must actively avoid stimuli that evoke memories of the traumatic event. Finally, a child must exhibit marked symptoms of increased arousal, such as difficulty sleeping or a heightened **startle response.** As with all disorders, a child must experience clinically significant distress or impairment because of the symptoms.

Compared with PTSD, acute stress disorder involves symptoms that are more severe, have a quicker onset, and last a shorter time (Harvey & Bryant, 2002). Acute stress disorder, and not PTSD, requires three or more dissociative symptoms (which are described in more detail later in this chapter). Thus acute stress disorder is often more intense than PTSD. Whereas the onset of PTSD can occur months or years after a traumatic event, the onset of acute stress disorder must occur within four weeks of a traumatic event. Finally, acute stress disorder can be diagnosed only for four weeks following the cessation of the traumatic event. If symptoms continue longer, the diagnosis can be changed to PTSD, which has no limit on the period that symptoms can be present.

As noted in Table 14.1, PTSD symptoms in children may differ from those of adults. One difference is that children may act out their intrusive recollections through their play or art rather than experiencing them as intrusive thoughts or memories (Rojas & Lee, 2004). A second difference is that the dreams of traumatized children often change from those involving the traumatic event to those with generally frightening themes (such as dreams in which they are attacked by monsters). A final difference is that some children may reenact the traumatic events and may engage others in their reenactments. For example, some sexually abused young children act sexually around adults or other children and may try to engage others in sexual activity (APA, 2000).

TABLE 14.2

Diagnostic Criteria for 308.3 Acute Stress Disorder

A. The person has been exposed to a traumatic event in which both of the following were present:
   (1) The person experienced, witnessed, or was confronted with an event or events that involved actual or threatened death or serious injury, or a threat to the physical integrity of self or others.
   (2) The person's response involved intense fear, helplessness, or horror.

B. Either while experiencing or after experiencing the distressing event, the individual has three (or more) of the following dissociative symptoms:
   (1) A subjective sense of numbing, detachment, or absence of emotional responsiveness.
   (2) A reduction in awareness of his or her surroundings (e.g., "being in a daze").
   (3) Derealization.
   (4) Depersonalization.
   (5) Dissociative amnesia (i.e., inability to recall an important aspect of the trauma).

C. The traumatic event is persistently reexperienced in at least one of the following ways: recurrent images, thoughts, dreams, illusions, flashback episodes, or a sense of reliving the experience; or distress on exposure to reminders of the traumatic event.

D. Marked avoidance of stimuli that arouse recollections of the trauma (e.g., thoughts, feelings, conversations, activities, places, people).

E. Marked symptoms of anxiety or increased arousal (e.g., difficulty sleeping, irritability, poor concentration, hypervigilance, exaggerated startle response, motor restlessness).

F. The disturbance causes clinically significant distress or impairment in social, occupational, or other important areas of functioning or impairs the individual's ability to pursue some necessary task, such as obtaining necessary assistance or mobilizing personal resources by telling family members about the traumatic experience.

G. The disturbance lasts for a minimum of two days and a maximum of four weeks and occurs within four weeks of the traumatic event.

H. The disturbance is not due to the direct physiological effects of a substance (e.g., a drug of abuse, a medication) or a general medical condition, is not better accounted for by Brief Psychotic Disorder, and is not merely an exacerbation of a preexisting Axis I or Axis II disorder.

Because acute stress disorder and PTSD are included in the anxiety disorder category of the DSM-IV-TR, children who experience many symptoms of either disorder, but who do not meet all the diagnostic criteria for them, can be given a diagnosis of **anxiety disorder not otherwise specified**. A fuller discussion of this diagnosis is in the chapter about anxiety disorders.

Controversial and Unresolved Issue: Different Diagnostic Criteria for Preschool Children

Scheeringa and his colleagues argue that different diagnostic criteria for PTSD should be used with preschool children than with older children or adults (Scheeringa, Peebles, Cook, & Zeanah, 2001). They note that the diagnostic criteria for PTSD were determined primarily through studies of adults. They raise concerns that some young children who are experiencing posttraumatic stress may not meet the adult-focused criteria for PTSD and thus may not be recognized as having a disorder that needs treatment.

To investigate their concerns, Scheeringa, Zeanah, Myers, and Putnam (2003) studied a group of 62 preschool children who had experienced a trauma. Using structured interviews, they found that none of them met all the diagnostic criteria for PTSD. They argued that this showed that the criteria were inappropriate for young children because no study of traumatized older children or adults had found a rate of 0% meeting the diagnostic criteria for PTSD. They then systematically altered the diagnostic criteria in several ways and noted the percentage of the preschool children who met each altered set of criteria. When they reduced the number of symptoms required in Cluster C from three to one, 26% of the preschool children met the altered diagnostic criteria for PTSD, which they believed was a reasonable percentage given the prevalence of PTSD observed in older traumatized children.

Of course, the basic assumption on which the conclusions of Scheeringa and his colleagues are based is that traumatized preschool children experience PTSD at about the same rate as traumatized older children. It is not clear that this is so, and additional research is needed to provide more information about whether the altered diagnostic criteria for preschool children are appropriate.

Determining that an Individual Child Has Acute Stress Disorder or PTSD

As with most disorders, the determination that a child meets the diagnostic criteria for acute stress disorder or PTSD is made by a clinician gathering information about the child's emotions and behaviors, in various ways and from various sources when possible. Unstructured and structured interviews often provide useful information about the child's experiences and can allow the child or parent to tell the story about the trauma in a way that is meaningful to them (Saigh, Brassard, & Peverely, 2004; Saigh, Yasik, Oberfield, Halamandaris, & McHugh, 2002).

The use of several informants is often essential when assessing traumatized children, especially young children, because describing their symptoms accurately is difficult for many of them (Lieberman & Van Horn, 2004; Newman, 2002). Parents can provide useful information about their children's behaviors that may indicate reexperiencing the trauma or avoiding stimuli associated with the trauma (Perrin et al., 2000). However, they may be less capable of describing the anxiety, other emotions, or increased physiological arousal that their children may be experiencing; the children may be the best informants about these issues.

Attention to Cultural Issues

Attending to cultural issues is important when assessing acute stress disorder and PTSD because the extent to which events are traumatic may be influenced by cultural expectations (Newman, 2002). For example, a girl from a culture in which sexual behavior before marriage is abhorrent may be traumatized by a relative touching her breasts, whereas the same experience may be painful but not traumatic to a girl from another culture. Consequently, clinicians must be careful not to assume whether an event is traumatic based on their own cultural values; rather, they must investigate the potentially traumatic nature of an event within the cultural context of the child who has experienced it.

Boys may be particularly loath to admit that an experience has been traumatic if they are raised in a culture where the ability to overcome any hardship is an indication of one's manhood. Consequently, clinicians and researchers need to be aware of the cultural and family values of the children they assess and form their questions about reactions to a potentially traumatic event in ways that allow a child or parent to describe the reactions without demeaning the child or his or her family (Lewis & Ippen, 2004).

Key Concepts

- Acute stress disorder and PTSD share many diagnostic criteria, including the occurrence of a traumatic event, reexperiencing the event, avoiding stimuli that remind the child of the traumatic event, and persistent symptoms of hyperarousal or anxiety.
- Acute stress disorder differs from PTSD in that its symptoms can be more severe, it must have an early onset, and its symptoms can last only four weeks following the cessation of the trauma.
- The symptoms of PTSD in children can differ from those in adults. Children often reexperience the trauma through their play or art; their dreams often develop into those that are generally frightening rather than those focused on the trauma; and they may behave in ways that draw others into a reenactment of the traumatic event.
- Using current diagnostic criteria with young traumatized children can result in few or none of them being diagnosed with PTSD. Reducing the number of symptoms required in Cluster C from three to one results in similar percentages of preschool and older traumatized children receiving a diagnosis of PTSD.
- Unstructured and structured interviews are often used to determine if a child meets the diagnostic criteria for PTSD. Reports from both the child and the child's parents are often essential in the assessment process.
- Cultural and family issues can influence how traumatized a child is by an event and can influence a child's or parent's willingness to acknowledge symptoms of PTSD.

Characteristics and Experiences of Children with PTSD

Core Features

As already described, children with PTSD have symptoms in three clusters. The first cluster represents the ways in which the memories of the trauma continue to intrude on the child's life; the second cluster represents the ways in which the child attempts to cope with these intrusive memories by avoiding situations that evoke them; and the third cluster represents symptoms of heightened physiological arousal.

Reexperiencing Trauma

Children with PTSD reexperience trauma in several ways. As shown in Table 14.3, the primary way in which a group of 56 children who were living in a shelter for battered women reexperienced trauma was through

TABLE 14.3

Number and Percentage of Children Endorsing Posttrauma Symptoms

Item	n^a	%
Reexperiencing of event		
1. Recurrent distressing thoughts	46	82
2. Recurrent distressing dreams	34	61
3. Acting or feeling as if event(s) recurring	2	4
Persistent avoidance and numbing		
1. Efforts to avoid thoughts, feelings etc.	55	98
2. Efforts to avoid activities, places, etc.	8	14
3. Inability to recall	2	4
4. Marked diminished interest/participation	6	11
5. Feelings of detachment	1	2
6. Restricted range of affect	21	38
7. Sense of foreshortened future	6	11
Persistent symptoms of increased arousal		
1. Difficulty falling or staying asleep	41	73
2. Irritability or outbursts of anger	38	68
3. Difficulty concentrating	34	61
4. Hypervigilance	47	84
5. Exaggerated startle response	30	54

[a]$N = 56$.

Source: Mertin & Mohr (2002).

intrusive, distressing thoughts. Although these thoughts can occur throughout a child's day, they are more likely to occur when a child's mind is not actively focused on other things—for example, when the child tries to fall asleep (Perrin et al., 2000).

Children also reexperience trauma in their play or art (APA, 2000). For example, a child who has been in an automobile accident may repeatedly recreate toy car crashes; or a child who has experienced a life-threatening illness may repeatedly draw pictures of children in a hospital. Although most children occasionally engage in play that has themes of trauma or disaster, two characteristics distinguish the play of children with PTSD. The first is the extent to which trauma themes dominate the play of children with PTSD. Much or most of their play is taken up with themes related to trauma. The second characteristic is the repetitive nature of the play of children with PTSD. Whereas other children experiment with changes to the play situations they create, most children with PTSD create the same traumatic scene time and time again. Thus children with PTSD use play not to explore new themes and issues but to relive old ones repeatedly (Stien & Kendall, 2004).

Many children reexperience trauma through recurrent dreams (De Bellis, 2001). As noted earlier, whereas the dreams of adults with PTSD tend to remain focused on the traumatic event, the dreams of many children change from a focus on the traumatic event to themes that are frightening but vague (APA, 2000).

Direct reexperiencing of a traumatic event through **flashbacks** occurs in many adults with PTSD, but this occurs infrequently in children (Fletcher, 2003). Flashbacks differ from intrusive memories in that a person feels as if the traumatic event is recurring during a flashback. Notable cases can be seen in the literature on combat veterans with PTSD, who may suddenly feel and act as if they are back on a battlefield. Children with flashbacks may suddenly feel as if they are back in a flooded house or that they are again being raped—and they reexperience many of the physical and emotional sensations they had during those events. Consequently, flashbacks can be very frightening to a child and can raise considerable concern for parents, teachers, or others around the child.

Avoiding Memories and General Numbing

The second cluster of symptoms of PTSD is characterized by efforts to avoid the memories of the traumatic event and a general **emotional numbing** of responsiveness to the environment (APA, 2000). These two symptoms are probably connected in most children: Their general numbing to the environment may be part of their attempt to reduce their intrusive memories by avoiding any stimuli that might encourage an intrusive memory. As shown in Table 14.3, the primary symptom of one group of traumatized children was deliberate attempts to avoid thoughts of the traumatic event, including efforts to avoid situations that reminded them of the event.

Amnesia for at least part of a traumatic event is reported frequently by adults. However, few children have amnesia for traumatic events either right after the event or several years later (Mertin & Mohr, 2002; Terr, 1985). The reasons for these differences in amnesia remain unclear.

Increased Arousal

Most children with PTSD experience heightened physiological arousal throughout the day and when they are asleep (APA, 2000; Mertin & Mohr, 2002). To get a sense of increased arousal, think about your level of arousal during a stressful event, such as an interview for a job or internship you would like to get. Your level of alertness is likely to be high, as are the psychological and physiological symptoms of anxiety, like excessive perspiration. In many ways your experience during the interview may be similar to what children with PTSD experience all the time.

This arousal has a quality that is similar to that experienced by children with other anxiety disorders. However, heightened arousal in children with most anxiety disorders occurs only when the events that they find frightening are likely to occur, whereas the arousal for children with PTSD is more chronic (American Academy of Child Adolescent Psychiatry, 1998). Heightened arousal can be seen in a variety of children's behaviors. For example, they often find it hard to concentrate on schoolwork or other activities, and they have a difficult time falling asleep at night. Another symptom of increased arousal is a heightened startle response to a wide range of events (APA, 2000). You may recall times when someone snuck up behind you and startled you by poking you or speaking loudly. Your experience on those rare occasions may be similar to that experienced often by children with an exaggerated startle response.

Weems, Saltzman, Reiss, and Carrion (2003) suggested that there may be a connection between hyperarousal and emotional numbing. Among a group of 42 children with symptoms of PTSD, they found that a high number of hyperarousal symptoms observed early in their study predicted the occurrence of emotional numbing a year later; however, symptoms of numbing early in the study did not predict hyperarousal later. They argued that hyperarousal creates "emotional exhaustion" for many children, which results in general numbing and withdrawal from those around them.

Associated Features

Problems with peer relationships occur for some children with PTSD. Peers and others often do not know how to respond to a child who has been traumatized and so may avoid talking with the child about his or her experience. This may cause peers to withdraw from a traumatized child. In addition, many traumatized children may avoid talking with others about their experiences to avoid traumatic memories, and so may deflect attempts by others to talk with them. This may encourage even greater withdrawal by peers. Some traumatized children interpret their peers' withdrawal as rejection, which can cause them to feel depressed or angry and to withdraw from their peers (Perrin et al., 2000; Yule, 2001).

Some children with PTSD experience academic difficulties (American Academy of Child Adolescent Psychiatry, 1998). This may be due, in part, to the difficulty with concentration that is brought on by their hyperarousal or intrusive memories. In addition, De Bellis, Baum, and colleagues (1999) argue that the biological changes that occur as the result of trauma (which are discussed in a following section) may result in a permanent loss of neurons or neural connections in the brain, thereby lowering a traumatized child's cognitive abilities.

Many children with PTSD experience symptoms of other disorders (American Academy of Child Adolescent Psychiatry, 1998; Saigh et al., 2002). Specific phobias related to the traumatic event develop in some children, and many show high levels of generalized anxiety (De Bellis, Baum et al., 1999). Depressive symptoms develop in many children with PTSD. Some longitudinal studies suggest that PTSD may predispose children to develop major depressive disorder later in their childhood or adolescence, possibly as a response to the trauma or to changes in peer and family relationships that occur after the trauma (Goenjian, Pynoos, & Steinberg, 1995; Mertin & Mohr, 2002). Finally, the hypervigilance and difficulty concentrating experienced by many children with PTSD may be mistaken as hyperactivity and inattention—two prominent symptoms of attention-deficit/hyperactivity disorder (ADHD). This may partly explain the frequent comorbidity of PTSD and ADHD, and it raises the possibility that some traumatized children who meet the diagnostic criteria for ADHD may instead be experiencing PTSD (American Academy of Child Adolescent Psychiatry, 1998; Fletcher, 2003).

A substantial association between PTSD and substance use disorders has been found among adolescents (American Academy of Child Adolescent Psychiatry, 1998; Giaconia et al., 2000). This association has raised questions about whether (1) PTSD puts adolescents at higher risk for substance abuse disorders because some of them may use drugs to cope with their PTSD symptoms or (2) drug use puts adolescents at higher risk for PTSD because it increases the chance that they will experience a trauma. The connection between PTSD and substance abuse problems was investigated by Giaconia and colleagues (2000) in their longitudinal study of a group of 384 high school seniors. They found that, among those who had a substance abuse disorder and had also experienced a significant trauma, the substance abuse disorder preceded the trauma in 55% of the cases, the onset of the substance abuse disorder was at about the same time as the trauma in about 20% of the cases, and the substance abuse disorder began after the trauma in about 25% of the cases. Thus their research suggests that there is no easy answer to the question of whether PTSD influences the development of a substance abuse problem or a substance abuse problem heightens one's chance of experiencing a traumatic event. Rather, the answer appears to be yes for both possibilities.

Key Concepts

- Reexperiencing trauma occurs through intrusive thoughts and dreams. In addition, many children with PTSD recreate their traumatic experiences through repetitive play.
- Flashbacks occur in a few children with PTSD.

- Children with PTSD try to avoid situations that evoke memories of the traumatic situation and may experience general numbing to their environment. This numbing may be in response to chronic heightened arousal.
- Heightened physiological arousal can result in difficulty concentrating, difficulty falling asleep, and an elevated startle response.
- Difficulties with conversations about the traumatic event can distance traumatized children from their peers, and some children interpret this as rejection by others.
- Some children with PTSD experience academic difficulties, partly because of their difficulty concentrating and possibly because of an influence of the trauma on their brain development.
- Depressive disorders, other anxiety disorders, and ADHD are often comorbid with PTSD in children.
- Many adolescents with PTSD also have a substance use disorder.

Prevalence

Studies of the prevalence of PTSD among large community samples of children have not been conducted in the United States; however, some smaller studies have been completed (Davis & Siegel, 2000). For example, Giaconia and colleagues (2000) found that 6.3% of their sample of 384 18-year-olds had experienced PTSD at one point in their lives based on their retrospective accounts. It is unclear, however, whether this percentage would be found among large community samples of children and adolescents.

Several studies have explored the prevalence of PTSD among children with traumatic experiences. For example, researchers followed 217 British schoolchildren for several years after a cruise ship they were on, the *Jupiter*, sank after being hit by an oil tanker. About five years after the incident, 52% had experienced PTSD, compared with 3% of a group of children who were friends of the survivors but had not been on the ship (Yule et al., 2000). A study of 26 children taken hostage at their school for two hours found that 81% showed an initial traumatic reaction, 27% developed PTSD at some point during the next 18 months, and 38% had "subclinical" PTSD that might qualify for a diagnosis of anxiety disorder not otherwise specified (Vila, Porche, & Mouren Simeoni, 1999).

Other studies have examined PTSD in children experiencing domestic violence or medical problems. For example, samples of children receiving clinical services for sexual abuse showed rates of PTSD ranging from 42% to 90% (De Bellis, 2001). Twenty percent of children who were living with their mothers in a shelter for battered women in Australia met the diagnostic criteria for PTSD (Mertin & Mohr, 2002). PTSD has also been found in 25% of children who had a spinal cord injury (Boyer, Knolls, Kafkalas, Tollen, & Swartz, 2000), 35% of adolescents with cancer (Pelcovitz et al., 1998), and 20% of children treated in a hospital emergency room for medical traumas (Gill, 2002).

Another set of studies has examined the intensity of PTSD symptoms in children exposed to war. One study found that 10% of children who had been exposed to war in Croatia had "severe" symptoms of PTSD (Kuterovac Jagodic, 2003); another found that 41% of children living in Sarajevo during wartime had "clinically significant" PTSD symptoms (Allwood, Bell Dolan, & Husain, 2002); and a study of children who had immigrated to the United States from a variety of war-torn areas found that 32% had PTSD symptoms in the clinical range (Jaycox et al., 2002).

Characteristics Distinguishing Children Who Do and Do Not Develop PTSD

As the prevalence studies show, somewhere between 25% and 50% of children exposed to either single or multiple traumatic events develop PTSD. An important issue is whether children with certain characteristics or experiences are more likely to develop PTSD after a traumatic experience. Understanding this issue may help us identify traumatized children who most need preventive or therapeutic interventions.

Child Characteristics

Whether boys or girls are more likely to develop PTSD remains unresolved. Studies have found that girls were more likely than boys to experience PTSD after a shipping accident (Udwin, Boyle, Yule, Bolton, & O'Ryan, 2000), exposure to a hurricane (Russoniello et al., 2002), living in a refugee camp (Rothe, 2005), and exposure to war (Jaycox et al., 2002). In addition, a study of approximately 3,000 school-age children in Oklahoma City seven weeks after the 1995 bombing of the Murrah Federal Building showed that girls scored higher than boys on a scale of PTSD symptoms (Pfefferbaum et al., 2003). However, studies of children taken hostage in their school (Vila et al., 1999) and children treated in an emergency room for accidents (Gill, 2002) showed no differences in the frequency or intensity of PTSD symptoms between boys and girls.

Only one study has examined the association between age and whether children develop PTSD. Rothe (2005) examined Cuban children living in a refugee camp after fleeing Cuba and found a linear relationship between age and severity of PTSD symptoms: More preschool children had severe symptoms than school-age children, and more school-age children had severe symptoms than adolescents.

Finally, traumatized children with preexisting behavioral or emotional problems are more likely to develop PTSD than are other traumatized children (Earls, Smith, Reich, & Jung, 1988; Udwin et al., 2000). Two possible reasons for this association are (1) the presence of another disorder reduces the likelihood of a child coping effectively with a trauma and (2) issues related to the development of another disorder may reduce a child's ability to cope with the trauma (for example, family circumstances that influence the development of depression may also reduce a child's coping ability).

Exposure to the Traumatic Event

Children with greater exposure to a traumatic event are more likely to develop PTSD than those who are more peripherally exposed. For example, children who were on a school playground when a sniper shot at those on the playground were more likely to develop PTSD than children who were inside the school building or who had left the school for the day (Pynoos et al., 1987). Children living in war zones or refugee camps were more likely to experience PTSD if they saw people being killed or if they were separated from parents (Jaycox et al., 2002; Kuterovac Jagodic, 2003; Rothe et al., 2002). Interestingly, the exposure to the trauma does not need to involve physical presence. Among schoolchildren in Oklahoma City after the bombing of the Murrah Federal Building, those who watched more television coverage of the bombing had more symptoms of PTSD than those who watched less television coverage (Pfefferbaum et al., 2003).

Greater exposure to a traumatic event may increase the severity of PTSD symptoms because the sensory experiences associated with the event are more likely to overwhelm a child than is knowledge about the event. Sensory experiences might also create memories that are more vivid or long-lasting and that therefore are more likely to intrude on a child's life.

Family Characteristics

Some family issues occurring after a trauma are related to increased risk for PTSD. When parents develop PTSD after a trauma, there is an increased risk that their children will also develop PTSD. This has been found among children sustaining a spinal cord injury (Boyer et al., 2000) and adolescents with cancer (Pelcovitz et al., 1998). In addition, children from families with high levels of parental conflict are more likely to develop PTSD after a trauma than are those from families with less conflict (Wasserstein & LaGreca, 1998). Perhaps parents who are experiencing PTSD themselves or who are in conflicted relationships are less available to help their children cope with a trauma.

Key Concepts

- Studies of children experiencing a variety of traumas suggest that between 25% and 50% of them develop PTSD.
- It is unclear whether girls or boys are more likely to develop PTSD.
- Children with preexisting disorders are more likely than other children to develop PTSD.

- Children with more intense exposure to a traumatic event are more likely than children with a more peripheral exposure to develop PTSD.
- Children whose parents have PTSD or who come from dysfunctional families are more likely than other children to develop PTSD.

Course

Not much research on the course of PTSD in children has been completed, and most of the relevant research has not taken into account whether a child with PTSD has received therapy or other clinical services (American Academy of Child Adolescent Psychiatry, 1998; Fletcher, 2003). Consequently, we are just beginning to understand the course of PTSD in children.

Initial Onset of Symptoms

Most children who develop PTSD after a single traumatic event do so soon after the event (De Bellis, 2001). For example, about 80% of the children who developed PTSD after the *Jupiter* shipping accident and 60% of children directly exposed to a school shooting developed significant symptoms within one month of their experience (Pynoos et al., 1987; Yule et al., 2000). However, the onset of symptoms is delayed in some children. Among those from the *Jupiter*, about 10% developed their first symptoms after 6 months, two developed symptoms between 6 and 12 months after the accident, and an additional four developed symptoms around its one-year anniversary. The reasons for the delay in the onset of symptoms in a small number of children remain unclear.

Unfortunately, no information is available about the initial onset of symptoms in children who have experienced repeated trauma, such as sexual abuse. It is not known, for example, whether they develop the symptoms of PTSD early during their abuse or only after the abuse has occurred for weeks or months (Fletcher, 2003).

Recovery from Symptoms

Follow-up evaluations of children with PTSD show that many "recover" from PTSD within several months (that is, they no longer meet the diagnostic criteria for PTSD) and that PTSD persists for years in other children. Among children with PTSD after the *Jupiter* accident, for example, about 25% recovered within one year, 50% recovered between one and five years, about 25% continued to have PTSD for more than five years (Yule et al., 2000). A similar pattern has occurred for children experiencing chronic trauma. Famularo, Fenton, and Kinscherff (1994) found that about two-thirds of children who had been diagnosed with PTSD after being removed from their homes because of sexual abuse had recovered within two years; and Kuterovac Jagodic (2003) found that the percentage of children with severe symptoms of PTSD after being exposed to war in Croatia declined from 25% to 10% during a three-year follow-up period.

Families of Children with PTSD

The families of children with PTSD have not been studied much, so we know little about them. However, a few studies have explored the functioning of parents who have experienced traumatic events along with their children, such as living through fires or floods or having a child contract a potentially fatal disease or get badly injured. In these situations, one or both parents may develop PTSD (Boyer et al., 2000). For example, one study of children who had a spinal cord injury found that more parents (41% of the mothers and 36% of the fathers) developed PTSD than the children who were injured (25%). These studies show that many children with PTSD live in a family where one or both of the parents also have PTSD or symptoms of PTSD.

Based on their clinical experience and a review of the research, Scheeringa and Zeanah (2001) suggest three patterns that are common in families in which both a parent and child experience PTSD. In the *withdrawn/unresponsive/unavailable pattern*, the parent is unavailable to provide support and guidance to the child. The parent may withdraw from all others because of the trauma or may withdraw from the child because he or she reminds the parent of the trauma. In the *overprotective/constricting pattern*, the parent becomes preoccupied with the belief that the child will be traumatized again and thus dramatically restricts the child's activities and the time that the child can be away from the parent. In the *reenacting/endangering/frightening pattern*, the parent tries to work through the consequences of the trauma by discussing it repeatedly with the child, which can force the child to reexperience the trauma, or may reenact the trauma by placing the child or other family members in situations like the trauma so that the fear associated with the trauma can be "conquered."

Of course not all families in which the child and parent experience PTSD will be characterized by one of these problematic patterns; in some families the parents can provide effective parenting to their children despite their own disorders. However, the occurrence of these problematic patterns suggests that therapeutic interventions for the parents of a traumatized child may be an essential part of the interventions provided for the child.

Key Concepts

- The initial onset of PTSD symptoms occurs soon after a traumatic event for most children but is delayed in a few.
- Many children recover from PTSD within several months of developing the disorder, although it persists in a sizable minority for many months and even years.
- PTSD may affect parents and their children when they experience traumatic events together or when the child experiences a trauma by himself or herself.

- Three problematic parenting styles in families experiencing PTSD have been identified: withdrawn/unresponsive/unavailable pattern, overprotective/constricting pattern, and reenacting/endangering/frightening pattern. However, it is not clear what percentage of families experiencing PTSD also experience a problematic parenting style.

Etiology

Two theories about the etiology of PTSD in children currently receive the most attention. The first focuses on biological changes that occur after a trauma, the effects of these changes on a child's brain development and functioning, and how this altered functioning produces the symptoms of PTSD. The second theory focuses on how traumatic events influence a child's cognitions and how these changed cognitions influence the development of PTSD symptoms.

Almost all of the research on the etiology of PTSD has been conducted with those who have experienced chronic trauma—in particular combat veterans, adults who experienced abuse as children, and sexually abused children. Consequently, although we know more about the prevalence and course of PTSD in children who have experienced a single trauma, we know more about the etiology of PTSD in children who have experienced chronic trauma. The extent to which the etiology of PTSD in chronically traumatized children is the same as the etiology of PTSD in children who have experienced one intense trauma is unknown. Some researchers have suggested that the ongoing reexperiencing of a single trauma through intrusive thoughts and dreams is similar to experiencing chronic trauma, and that repeatedly reexperiencing the trauma causes the same biological and psychological consequences caused by chronic trauma (van der Kolk et al., 2002). This may explain the similarity in symptoms among children who develop PTSD as the result of chronic trauma or one traumatic experience. However, future research will be required to determine whether the development of PTSD in these two groups of children is the same.

Influences of Trauma on Brain Development and Functioning

Humans have a well-tuned biological response to stressful situations involving danger, such as when we are accosted on a dark street, when our car suddenly enters a long skid on an icy hill, or when we find a fire engulfing the kitchen in our apartment (Bremner, 1999). This biological response consists of many neurotransmitter and hormonal actions that cause our brains to function differently during times of high stress—focusing our attention and giving us all the energy we can muster to avoid death or injury. Despite the value of these changes during stressful situations, they interfere with our ability to function effectively in nonstressful situations. Consequently, our brains must return to their prestress functioning after a stressful event for us to function well during the rest of our lives.

Researchers have discovered that chronic high levels of stress, such as those experienced by soldiers in combat or children who are frequently abused, result in changes in brain functioning that impede the brain from returning to the level of functioning that is appropriate for nonstressful situations. These changes are believed to underlie two symptom clusters of PTSD: reexperiencing the trauma and hyperarousal (Bremner, 1999). We will explore the influences of trauma on brain functioning first by reviewing two aspects of brain functioning related to PTSD—reaction to stress and the storage and recall of memories—and then by exploring how these functions can be impaired by chronic stress and how these impairments can produce PTSD symptoms.

The Brain's Reaction to Stress

Level of Arousal   As shown in Figure 14.1, the body's reaction to stress is initiated by the **amygdala,** which is part of the limbic system of the brain (the amygdala has an almond shape, and its name comes from the Latin *amygdala,* "almond"). The amygdala has many connections to the physical senses and is central to the recognition of many biologically relevant stimuli, such as the presence of danger (Carlson, 1986). When danger is recognized, the amygdala sends messages to a variety of brain systems, including (1) the **locus coeruleus,** which releases the neurotransmitter norepinephrine[1] that stimulates the body and narrows attention to the dangerous stimuli, and (2) the **hypothalamus,** which activates the sympathetic branch of the autonomic nervous system to focus on the source of danger and prepare to respond to it (Stien & Kendall, 2004). Both processes heighten awareness and prepare the body for "fight or flight."

At the same time, the amygdala stimulates the hypothalamic–pituitary–adrenal (HPA) axis. (The HPA axis is a self-regulating system that is part of the endocrine system. It has an important role in regulating basic functions such as hunger, sleep, mood, and sexual activity. We also explore its role in depression in the chapter about depressive disorders.) Through this activity, the hypothalamus (which has been stimulated by the amygdala) stimulates the pituitary gland through corticotropin-releasing factor (CRF), which stimulates the adrenal gland through adrenalcorticotrophic hormone (ACTH), which produces **cortisol** (Stien & Kendall, 2004). Cortisol then travels through the blood and binds to receptors in the brain, primarily in the hippocampus, amygdala, and frontal cortex (LeDoux, 1996). The **hippocampus** responds to this stimulation by sending messages to the amygdala and the hypothalamus to reduce the body's arousal. (The hippocampus is shaped like a sea horse, and its name comes from the Greek *hippos,* "horse," and *kampos,* "sea monster.") The release of cortisol and its effect on the hippocampus causes a reduction of the body's arousal. Thus two processes occur simultaneously: Certain parts of the brain increase the body's arousal while other parts reduce the body's arousal. In most of us

---

[1]*Norepinephrine* and *noradrenalin* are different names for the same neurotransmitter, just as *epinephrine* and *adrenalin* are different names for the same neurotransmitter. *Norepinephrine* and *epinephrine* are names commonly used in the United States, whereas *noradrenalin* and *adrenalin* are names commonly used in Great Britain and Europe (Colman, 2001). In this chapter I use the terms *norepinephrine* and *epinephrine.*

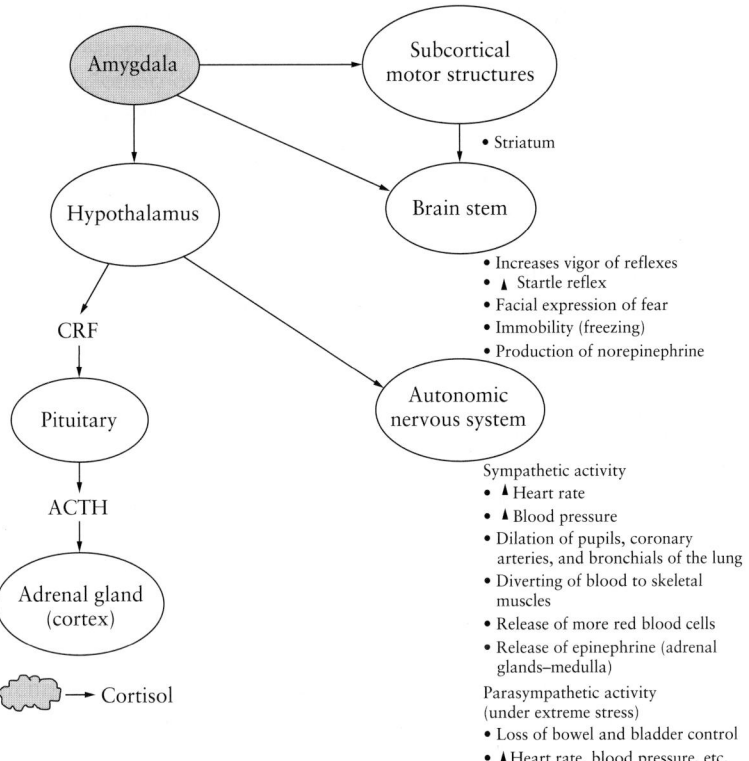

FIGURE 14.1   *The Fight-or-Flight Stress Response*

this "dance" between the arousal-increasing and arousal-decreasing functions continues until the level of our arousal is matched to the actual danger of the situation (LeDoux, 1996).

Memory   As they relate to our exploration of the etiology of PTSD, memories can be divided into two broad categories: declarative memories and implicit memories (Elzinga & Bremner, 2002; Squire & Zola-Morgan, 1991). **Declarative memories** are conscious memories related to events and facts. When you take an exam, you search your mind for declarative memories related to the material on the exam. **Implicit memories** are those that are emotional or those that are unconscious and relate to behaviors. For example, when you walk across campus to take an exam, your walking is controlled by your implicit memory—you do not have to think consciously about how to walk because your implicit memory for walking controls your behavior. Similarly, if a friend surprises you by poking you in the shoulder, you do not have to consciously think how to respond: Your implicit memory for what an unknown poke in the shoulder is likely to represent tells you how to react.

Norepinephrine and cortisol both have a role in memory as well as in stress reactions. Norepinephrine primarily influences implicit memories by making them more intense; cortisol inhibits the storage of declarative memories (Elzinga & Bremner, 2002).

Norepinephrine enhances emotionally laden memories through action on the amygdala (Elzinga & Bremner, 2002). The norepinephrine released during stressful or frightening events causes their memories to be more vivid and easily recalled than events without strong emotional components. From the perspective of ensuring our survival, this is helpful: We need to have quicker access to memories about situations that might be dangerous, and these memories need to be more vivid so that they are stronger than competing memories. A variety of studies have shown that higher levels of norepinephrine and epinephrine are associated with stronger implicit memories for frightening and other emotionally laden experiences while having little or no influence on declarative memories (Cahill, Babinsky, Markowitsch, & McGaugh, 1995; Cahill et al., 1996).

Cortisol influences memories through action on the hippocampus. The hippocampus is involved primarily in declarative memories, and these memories are initially stored in the hippocampus and then are organized with other memories and stored in other parts of the brain (Zola-Morgan & Squire, 1990). High levels of cortisol interfere with the ability of the hippocampus to store declarative memories and consequently can cause amnesia for stressful events (Elzinga & Bremner, 2002).

Taken together, the research on the influences of norepinephrine, epinephrine, and cortisol suggests that stressful events are likely to result in poorer declarative memories (which are conscious) and more vivid implicit memories (which are often unconscious). Thus a traumatized child may have conscious memory lapses for traumatic events yet be significantly influenced by implicit and unconscious memories of them (Elzinga & Bremner, 2002).

The Influence of Chronic Stress on Level of Arousal and Memory

Now that we have briefly reviewed the normal responses to stress and how two types of memories are stored, we can turn to the issue of how chronic levels of stress can influence these two systems, thereby producing symptoms of PTSD. Studies of the brains of humans and other animals have shown that several areas of brain development are affected by chronic stress, and we review these in this section as well as the implications of these effects for a child's functioning and the development of PTSD symptoms.

Brain Volume   De Bellis and his colleagues (De Bellis, Keshavan et al., 1999; De Bellis et al., 2002) studied the brains of maltreated children who had PTSD with brain-imaging techniques and found that, compared with a group of nonmaltreated children who had no disorder, the overall volume of their brains was smaller and their lateral **ventricles** were larger. Further, they found that children who were maltreated for longer periods and children whose maltreatment began earlier in their lives had smaller brain volumes than children who had been maltreated less or whose maltreatment began later in life. In addition, the number and intensity of the children's PTSD symptoms were negatively correlated with brain volume, showing that those with smaller volumes experienced more symptoms. Thus this work suggests links between frequency of abuse and the age at which it began, general damage to the developing brain, and subsequent intensity of PTSD symptoms.

Hippocampus   The frequent release of cortisol that occurs during chronic stress appears to damage the hippocampus (Bremner, 1999). Studies of animals other than humans have shown that high levels of cortisol cause a smaller hippocampus that has fewer neural connections. In addition, MRI studies of combat veterans with PTSD and adults with PTSD who experienced sexual abuse as children have shown that they have a smaller hippocampus and that the intensity of their PTSD symptoms is negatively correlated with the size of their hippocampus (Bremner et al., 1997; Stein, Koverola, Hanna, Torchia, & McClarty, 1997).

Because the hippocampus is involved in storing declarative memories, damage to the hippocampus may interfere with this storage. This may cause the amnesia that occurs in some cases of PTSD. As noted previously, amnesia is more common in adults with PTSD than in children with PTSD. This may be related to the finding that the hippocampus of traumatized children appears less damaged than the hippocampus of traumatized adults (Mertin & Mohr, 2002; Terr, 1985). De Bellis, Keshavan, and colleagues (1999) note that the hippocampus continues to develop during childhood and suggest that it may not be until after puberty that the negative influence of cortisol on the hippocampus becomes apparent. This degeneration after puberty may partly explain the greater frequency of amnesia in adults than in children with PTSD.

Damage to the hippocampus may also cause a stress response that is more intense and sustained. Recall that the hippocampus modulates stress-induced arousal (LeDoux, 1996). If the hippocampus is impaired because of repeated exposure to high levels of cortisol, it may not be able to modulate the stress response effectively. This can result in excessive arousal to mild stressors and a baseline level of arousal that is problematically high. The hyperarousal that is a frequent symptom of PTSD, and the heightened startle response to mild or moderate levels of stress that is another symptom, may thus be related to a compromised hippocampus.

Amygdala and Prefrontal Cortex   Although there is no direct evidence of damage from chronic stress to the amygdala and **prefrontal cortex,** several lines of research suggest that chronic stress may make the amygdala more sensitive to minor stressors and the prefrontal cortex less able to dampen the arousal from those stressors (Stien & Kendall, 2004). It also appears that heightened amygdala sensitivity causes quick and easy activation of emotionally charged implicit memories, such as those of trauma, which may result in the intrusive memories and dreams that are symptoms of PTSD (Elzinga & Bremner, 2002).

In addition, it appears that impairments of the prefrontal cortex and amygdala may inhibit the extinguishing of fear responses. Consider, for example, that you are in an automobile accident. Trauma from the accident may cause high levels of fear when you take future trips in an automobile. However, as you take more and more trips without further accidents, your fear gradually becomes extinguished; and within several months or years, your fear response when getting in a car is no higher than before your accident.

Many people with PTSD have an impaired ability to extinguish fear responses: They continue to experience high levels of fear in situations that are similar to the traumatic event, even if they have months or years of nontraumatic experiences in those situations. Experiments with rats have shown that those with lesions in specific parts of their prefrontal cortex cannot extinguish a learned fear response, whereas those without such lesions can extinguish the fear response (Morgan, Romaski, & LeDoux, 1993). In addition, neuroimaging studies of adults with PTSD show a deactivation of certain areas of their prefrontal cortex when they are given reminders of their traumatic experiences, and this deactivation may produce a consequence that is similar to that produced by lesions in the rats' brains (Bremner, 1999). This suggests that the functioning of the prefrontal cortex is impaired by chronic stress and that this impairment inhibits our ability to gradually recover from our fears.

HPA Axis   Finally, there is evidence that chronic trauma causes persistent heightened arousal in the HPA axis. Chronically maltreated children with PTSD show higher urine levels of the hormones associated with activation of the HPA axis than do nonmaltreated children who do not have PTSD, even years after their maltreatment has ended; and those with the highest levels of these hormones experience the greatest number of PTSD symptoms (De Bellis, Baum et al., 1999). The presence of these hormones suggests that the baseline functioning of their HPA axis is heightened. Because a function of the HPA axis is to modulate stress response, a chronically high level of HPA functioning suggests that the body is chronically experiencing a heightened stress response. One result of this chronically heightened stress response is symptoms of PTSD such as hypervigilance, increased startle response, and difficulty in concentrating.

Summary

In these past few pages we have explored how chronic stress can influence several brain systems. The changes to these systems can create two clusters of symptoms of PTSD: reexperiencing the trauma and increased arousal. In addition, we saw how influences of stress on the amygdala and prefrontal cortex may make it more difficult to extinguish the fear responses that are at the foundation of PTSD, which can make PTSD symptoms continue for many years after a trauma.

Cognitive Models of the Etiology of PTSD

Cognitive models of the etiology of PTSD focus on the extent to which traumatic memories do not fit into a child's schemata, or basic beliefs about the world (Foa, Steketee, & Rothbaum, 1989). In essence, memories of the traumatic event are so different from a child's view of the world that they cannot be integrated into this view, so they are kept separate—that is, they are dissociated from the rest of the child's memories. These memories are stored separately and may be more readily accessible because of the emotional salience attached to them by the amygdala.

Although some of these dissociated memories could best be classified as declarative (such as memories for how the traumatic event unfolded), others could best be classified as implicit (memories of emotional responses) (Brewin, Dalgleish, & Joseph, 1996). These implicit dissociated memories may be easily accessed when a child encounters stimuli or situations that are reminiscent of the traumatic event—for example, smelling smoke if once in a fire or hearing high winds if once in a tornado. The consequence of accessing these memories can be reexperiencing the trauma. Because implicit memories are mostly unconscious, the trauma may be reexperienced for no apparent reason and thus may be unpredictable and frightening.

A consequence of the dissociation of these memories is that they remain relatively unchanged over time (Foa et al., 1989). Consider, for example, that you are physically assaulted and robbed while walking alone one night. Although this will remain a frightening memory, if you can integrate the memory of this experience with your memories of many safe days and evenings, the emotional consequences of the memory of the assault become somewhat diluted as the memory is integrated with memories of your other experiences. If your memory for the assault remains dissociated, however, it cannot become diluted by your other memories; so the emotions attached to it remain strong. It is hypothesized that such failure to integrate traumatic memories results in their evoking high levels of emotional reactivity for many months and years.

Behavioral Responses to Emotionally Charged Memories

The cognitive consequences of reexperiencing traumatic memories can cause the avoidant behaviors that comprise Cluster C of the PTSD symptoms. Children who experience intrusive thoughts and dreams associated with a trauma may do whatever they can to reduce the frequency of these intrusions (van der Kolk et al., 2002). In some cases this may be relatively easy. For example, if they were injured while diving into a lake, they may be able to easily avoid being around lakes or other large bodies of water. However, avoiding stimuli related to traumas that occur in children's homes, schools, or other places they frequent may be impossible. As a result, they may withdraw emotionally and cognitively when in these places—essentially pulling into themselves to avoid interacting with people or places that remind them of the trauma. This may cause the emotional numbing that is one of the symptoms in Cluster C. Older children and adolescents may use alcohol or other drugs to numb their emotions and cognitions, which can result in the biological, emotional, and social changes that occur with frequent use of drugs (Haugaard, 2001).

Cognitions may also influence the strength of PTSD symptoms. For example, Feiring, Taska, and Chen (2002) found that sexually abused children who had stronger internal attributions for their abuse (that is, they felt a greater personal sense of responsibility for the abuse occurring) had higher levels of PTSD symptoms than did children with an external attribution for their abuse. In addition, the children who felt more shame over being abused had higher levels of PTSD symptoms than those who felt less shame.

Key Concepts

- Most research in this area has focused on children and adults experiencing chronic stress. Although there are reasons to believe that the etiology of PTSD after single incidents of trauma may be the same as for PTSD occurring after chronic trauma, additional research is needed to support this belief.
- Theories based on biological functioning focus on how the body's response to chronic stress can have lasting influences on brain functioning, which can produce symptoms of PTSD.
- During periods of stress, two brain systems interact. One system increases arousal and the other decreases arousal. In most cases these systems work together to create the correct level of arousal for a particular stressful situation.
- Memory can be divided into declarative and implicit memories. Actions by the amygdala increase the salience of implicit memories, and cortisol acts on the hippocampus to inhibit declarative memories.
- The brains of children with PTSD are smaller in volume than the brains of children without PTSD, suggesting a fundamental influence of chronic stress on brain development.
- The hippocampus is damaged by excessive cortisol. This can influence the storage of declarative memories, resulting in amnesia for traumatic events, and can reduce the ability of the hippocampus to modulate arousal during stressful situations.
- The ability of the prefrontal cortex and amygdala to extinguish fear responses is compromised in children with PTSD.
- The consequences of changes in brain functioning can result in chronic high levels of stress, as indicated by heightened activity in the HPA axis.
- The inability of children to integrate traumatic memories into their schemata may increase the availability of these memories and impede their association with less fearful memories—thereby keeping them strong for months or years.

Prevention

Programs to prevent PTSD and acute stress disorder would seem to be a logical extension of our knowledge about the development of PTSD and our ability to identify children who are at increased risk for developing it. Unfortunately, few programs to prevent PTSD have been created and tested. One possible reason for this is that programs to prevent PTSD after natural disasters or similar traumas would have to be created in advance and then held in abeyance waiting for the occurrence of a traumatic event that might never occur. Clinicians and researchers may be unenthusiastic about creating a prevention program that may never be needed. In addition, large-scale traumatic events, such as the destruction of the World Trade Towers on 9/11/01, create such pandemonium that the initiation of prevention programs for those affected by the trauma can be difficult (Litz, Gray, Bryant, & Adler, 2002).

Procedures to prevent disabling traumatic reactions have been used in the military for decades; they have primarily involved soldiers meeting individually or in groups with a trained counselor after battles to describe their experiences and to learn about the reactions to trauma that most people experience (Litz et al., 2002). Although these debriefings have theoretical support, the few randomized evaluations of them have shown that they do not reduce the frequency of the development of PTSD (Ruzek & Watson, 2001). It may be that the one or two sessions that are usually devoted to these programs do not provide sufficient time for participants to process the traumatic event.

Several short-term cognitive–behavioral prevention programs have been used with traumatized adults. These have mostly shown positive results, which may suggest their potential value for use with traumatized children (Ruzek & Watson, 2001). For example, a study of women who had been sexually assaulted showed that a four-session cognitive–behavioral intervention, in which they learned about common reactions to trauma, reexperienced their trauma through visualization, and changed dysfunctional cognitions, showed that those completing the prevention program had fewer symptoms of PTSD than a comparison group of sexually assaulted women who did not receive the program (Foa, Hearst Ikeda, & Perry, 1995).

Only one prevention program for traumatized children has been reported in the literature. It was designed for children who had recently immigrated to the United States from Central America or South America and who had witnessed or been the targets of community violence or war-related activity (Kataoka et al., 2003). During the eight-session program, children first learned about reactions to trauma, developed relaxation skills, and discussed circumstances that evoked high levels of fear. They then engaged in reexperiencing traumatic events through drawing, writing, and discussion. The children receiving the prevention program showed a significant reduction in PTSD symptoms when compared with children in a wait-list comparison group. This study, and the results of studies with adults, suggest that cognitive–behavioral prevention programs may be of value to children experiencing a wide range of traumatic events.

Key Concepts

- Psychological debriefing has been used with soldiers returning from combat, but the short duration of this intervention appears to limit its effectiveness.
- Short-term cognitive–behavioral preventive interventions have reduced PTSD symptoms in women who have been sexually assaulted.

- One cognitive–behavioral program to reduce PTSD symptoms in children who had been exposed to violence or war was effective in doing so.

Therapeutic Interventions

Interventions for the Child with PTSD

Interventions for children who have PTSD fall into two broad categories: medication to reduce reexperiencing the trauma and heightened arousal, and psychotherapy to help the child cope with the memories of the trauma and integrate them into his or her life. These interventions follow closely from what we know about the consequences of trauma: The use of medication is designed to dampen the biological consequences of the trauma, and psychotherapy is designed to help alleviate the cognitive and emotional consequences of the trauma.

Medication
Medication has been used with many adults who have PTSD to reduce their physiological reactivity, intrusive memories, and withdrawal. Medication (primarily the SSRIs) has also been used with children. However, few studies of the effectiveness of medication with children who have PTSD have been conducted (Foa et al., 2005). Consequently, most information about the usefulness of medication comes from studies of adults, and it remains unclear whether the medications that are useful for adults are also useful for children (American Academy of Child Adolescent Psychiatry, 1998; Cohen, Perel, DeBellis, Friedman, & Putnam, 2002; van der Kolk et al., 2002).

Psychotherapy
Cognitive–behavioral therapy is the type of therapy used most often with children who have PTSD (Foa et al., 2005). It is based on the cognitive model of the development of PTSD that focuses on how the unintegrated memories of trauma cause some of the symptoms of PTSD. Through cognitive–behavioral therapy, a child is helped to remember and talk about the traumatic experience in a supportive environment so that memories of it can be integrated into the child's view of the world.

Early stages of therapy with a child who has PTSD involve the therapist and child developing a close, supportive, and trusting relationship (Zoellner, Foa, & Fitzgibbons, 2002). Later in therapy, the clinician will be asking the child to do what the child fears doing—remembering the traumatic experience—so it is important for the child to feel that the clinician is supportive and can be trusted not to ask the child to do anything that he or she cannot handle. The clinician also spends time during the early part of therapy educating the child, and possibly his or her parents, about the biological, cognitive, and emotional consequences of traumatic experiences.

This helps the child understand the reasons for his or her symptoms and provides a foundation for the therapeutic work that follows.

Once a supportive relationship has been established between the child and clinician, most therapeutic strategies focus on having the child reexperience memories of the trauma in the supportive therapeutic environment (Deblinger & Heflin, 1996; van der Kolk et al., 2002). By having the child purposefully begin and end the process of remembering the trauma, the child learns that he or she has some control over the traumatic memories. This is critical for reducing the child's sense that he or she is a helpless victim of the trauma. In addition, this process helps the child begin to integrate the memories of the trauma into the fuller story of his or her life.

Several investigations of the value of reliving traumatic experiences in this way have shown that doing so reduces PTSD symptoms. For example, a study of a cognitive–behavioral treatment with sexually abused children showed that those in the treatment group had fewer symptoms of PTSD at the end of therapy and at a 12-week follow-up than a group of children in a wait-list comparison group (King et al., 2000).

Therapy to help a child gain mastery over his or her physiological responses to stress-producing situations also involves cognitive strategies (American Academy of Child Adolescent Psychiatry, 1998; Deblinger & Heflin, 1996). Children are taught to pay attention to the thoughts that occur when they begin to feel anxious, note how the thoughts influence their emotions, and analyze the thoughts objectively. For example, a child who developed PTSD after being in a tornado, and who begins to feel overwhelmed when listening to a strong wind, may find that he thinks, "I know that this is another tornado and that I'm going to die," and that he then experiences overwhelming fear. If he can learn to analyze his thoughts and decide whether they are logical, his fear may be decreased. For example, he may say, "I know that tornadoes are rare and that the wind often blows hard around my house, and that even a hard wind won't hurt the house or me." He may also learn to check the weather report to see if a tornado is in the area or to look outside to assess the strength of the wind. These behaviors help the child act purposefully to reduce his arousal rather than giving in to it passively.

Many children with PTSD are given relaxation training (Foa et al., 2005). They are encouraged to use relaxation techniques when they begin to feel fear, which can help reduce their arousal and give them a better chance to monitor and change dysfunctional cognitions. In addition, using relaxation techniques is another way that a child can act purposefully to cope with symptoms of PTSD, reinforcing the belief that the child can overcome the symptoms.

Finally, many children with PTSD are given social skills training as part of their therapy (King et al., 2003; van der Kolk et al., 2002). Social skills training can help children who have withdrawn from others reestablish positive peer relationships and can help them ignore or cope with unkind comments from others who may tease them about their anxiety. In addition, social skills training allows children to be more proactive in their relationships with others, reinforcing in another way that they can be proactive in their world.

Interventions for Family Members

The inclusion of parents in the treatment of children with PTSD is often an important component of therapeutic interventions. Interventions for parents usually include education about the types of reactions to trauma that are common among children (American Academy of Child Adolescent Psychiatry, 1998; King et al., 2003). Interventions may also focus on reducing the PTSD symptoms that the parents are experiencing. Recall from earlier sections in this chapter that many parents of traumatized children experience symptoms of PTSD and that traumatized children whose parents experience symptoms of PTSD are more likely to develop PTSD themselves (Boyer et al., 2000; Pelcovitz et al., 1998). Thus helping parents overcome their own reactions to the trauma may prevent the development of PTSD in their children or reduce the intensity of their children's symptoms.

Lieberman and Van Horn (2004) note that an important treatment issue in some families is healing a rift that may have formed between the child and parents because of the trauma. They note that most children, particularly young children, may expect to be protected from all hazards by their parents. They may view their traumatic experiences as a failure on the part of their parents to protect them, which can harm their relationships with their parents. Many young children may be unable or unwilling to express their feelings about the lack of protection they received from their parents, so they may need help to express and understand these feelings. Their parents may need help in accepting these feelings and understanding their foundation so that they do not react in an unhealthy way when these feelings arise.

Unfortunately, few studies have assessed the value of including parents in treatment programs for their traumatized children. One study found that including parents in treatment did not result in any greater reduction in children's symptoms than did providing treatment only to the traumatized children (King et al., 2000). The researchers suggested that the treatment the parents received, which focused on education about the consequences of trauma, may not have been sufficient. They noted that many parents were experiencing symptoms of PTSD themselves, but the intervention did not focus on helping the parents overcome these symptoms. They suggested that an intervention for parents that targeted their own reactions to their children's trauma may have been more effective, although ongoing research will be needed to explore whether this is so.

Key Concepts

- Medications have been used to treat adults with PTSD to reduce their physiological arousal and intrusive memories. However, the use of medication with children who have PTSD has been limited, and no research has addressed its effectiveness.

- Cognitive–behavioral therapy is the most common therapy provided to children with PTSD. After developing a supportive therapeutic environment, therapists help children describe their traumatic experiences so they can be integrated into the children's lives.
- Relaxation training gives children an active strategy with which they can cope with their fears.
- Social skills training is provided to many children to help them reconnect with peers and others.
- Treatment for parents focuses on education about trauma and on reducing symptoms of PTSD that they may be experiencing.

Dissociative Disorders

The dissociative disorders are characterized by a lack of an integrated "whole" to a child's psychological and behavioral self (APA, 2000). The perceptions, cognitions, emotions, behaviors, and memories of children with a dissociative disorder are split apart from each other—that is, dissociated—so that the children do not experience their lives as one ongoing process but rather as a series of unrelated bits and pieces. For example, a child with a dissociative disorder may have no memory of many events in her life because those memories are dissociated from her other memories. In severe cases of dissociative disorder, a child may appear to have multiple distinct personalities, with memories for events that occur when one personality is dominant not being available to the child when another personality is dominant. As you can imagine, this can be a very confusing life for a child.

You may have been introduced to dissociative disorders by reading *Three Faces of Eve* (Thigpen & Cleckley, 1957) or *Sybil* (Schreiber, 1973)—books that were clinical accounts of women with **multiple personality disorder** (multiple personality disorder, now called **dissociative identity disorder,** is considered the most severe form of dissociative disorder). The experiences of both women were as if several people, each with his or her own ways of perceiving and acting in the world, and each with his or her own set of memories, were living in the same physical body. That is, they experienced a high level of dissociation: Their lives when one "personality" was operating were dissociated from their lives when another personality was functioning. You may find it difficult to believe that a child or an adult can have several distinct personalities. You are not alone. Many people have been skeptical about the existence of dissociative disorders, in particular dissociative identity disorder, and we will discuss this skepticism later in this chapter (Spanos, 1994).

Almost all children and adults with a dissociative disorder have experienced severe and chronic physical or sexual abuse, usually beginning during their early childhood (Putnam, 1997). It is currently believed that most cases of dissociative disorder develop as the result of children's attempts to cope with the physical and emotional trauma they experience during repeated physical or sexual abuse. It is often difficult for those of us raised in reasonable environments to comprehend the abuse that some children suffer. Extreme cases of abuse or neglect are rare, for which we can be thankful; but they do occur. On average, for example, two to three children in the United States are beaten or starved to death by their parents every day (Advisory Board on Child Abuse and Neglect, 1995). Many other children experience severe and chronic abuse that is not fatal. Acknowledging that severe and chronic abuse does occur, and may be occurring in the community in which you live, is an important part of understanding the experiences of some children in our society.

Case Study: A Sexually Abused Boy

When Max was 6 years old, his father began sodomizing him at night. The abuse began while his mother was away visiting some relatives for two weeks and continued after she returned. His mother worked during the evenings, so Max and his father were always alone in their house during the abuse. There was little pattern to the abuse: Sometimes weeks would go by with no abuse, and other times Max was abused four or five times in a week. The only respite that Max had was on the weekends because his father never abused him when Max's mother was at home in the evening.

Max's father frequently threatened to kill Max if he ever revealed the abuse. When he was done abusing him the first time, Max's father grabbed him by the throat, said that choking him to death would be very easy, and said that this is what he would do if Max ever told anyone about the abuse. He also threatened to kill Max's mother if Max revealed the abuse.

After the abuse began, Max was always afraid of his father. He tried to avoid his father, but this was seldom possible because Max was alone with him most nights. Max often stayed by himself when at home, including when his mother was there, because he was afraid that he might inadvertently say something about the abuse to his mother. He often wondered why his mother did not put a stop to the abuse because he assumed that she must have known about it. As the abuse continued, he became increasingly angry with her and had fewer and fewer interactions with her.

While at school, Max was often withdrawn and his peers shied away from him. He was an easy target for bullying from bigger boys in his class. When the other children pushed him around or threatened him, he often seemed to "go blank" and just stared ahead. Occasionally he would get very angry and lash out at them—one time scratching another boy badly in the face. After that, the bigger boys tended to leave him alone.

At school, Max's behavior varied dramatically from day to day or from week to week. Some days he was calm, cooperative, and friendly; other days, however, his behavior was impulsive and he was unfriendly. His academic performance was also variable, although he seemed to be trying to work hard consistently. His teacher reported that some days it seemed as if he had simply forgotten everything he had learned the previous day. He was often lost in his thoughts. Max's erratic behavior confused those around him, although it did not appear to concern Max.

During the second grade, Max was referred to the school psychologist for testing to see if he might have attention-deficit/hyperactivity disorder (ADHD). The psychologist recommended that he have a physical exam as part of the evaluation process, and during this exam several injuries to his anal area were discovered. Max's pediatrician asked Max about the injuries, but Max responded that he did not know how they happened. Max's mother, who was present during the exam, was very upset and demanded that Max tell her what happened, but he simply looked blankly at her and said that he did not know. The pediatrician said that he would have to make a report to the state's child protective services and suggested that Max's mother talk with him more that evening. When they got home from the doctor's office, Max's mother told his father about what had occurred. Because she had to work that evening, she asked him to talk with Max and see if he could discover anything. About an hour after Max's mother had gone to work, Max's father locked him in a closet and then put most of his belongings in the family car and drove off. When Max's mother returned from work at midnight, she found the house empty and Max huddled in the closet.

Max's mother called the police and, while waiting for them to arrive, told Max that his father was gone and asked him what had happened. Max yelled at her in a tone she had never heard him use and said that it was all her fault—that she was busy working when she should have been home protecting him from his father. Max then described in detail all that had happened. His mother was horrified and told all this to the police when they arrived. A child protective services caseworker was called, and Max and his mother were taken to a shelter for the night. A preliminary investigation the next day suggested that Max's mother had nothing to do with the abuse, so Max was allowed to stay with her. She and Max went to stay at her sister's home in a nearby town.

A week later, Max's father was arrested. Eventually he pled guilty and was sent to prison with a long sentence. After his father's arrest, Max and his mother returned to their home. Both began seeing therapists, and a third therapist saw them together for family therapy. The therapists worked hard initially to help Max's mother create an environment in their home where Max felt safe and free from the threat of abuse. They helped Max understand that his father would not be released from prison for many years, although Max remained afraid for several months that his father would escape and kill him and his mother. Max's therapist helped him talk about his abuse and his physical and emotional responses to it, working to help Max see that the abuse was one terrible aspect of his life, rather than defining his life. As Max talked about the abuse, he often experienced intense emotions, and his behaviors at home and at school reflected the intensity of these emotions. However, the intensity of his emotions decreased and his behavior improved over time. The therapist working with Max's mother helped her express her anger at Max's father and the guilt that she felt about not knowing about the abuse. The therapist working with Max and his mother together helped them maintain an environment in their home that felt safe to both of them and helped Max's mother set appropriate limits on Max's behavior at home and at school in ways that did not feel harsh or abusive to Max.

Some Issues Worth Noting

- The possible emotional consequences to Max of not knowing, except on the weekends, whether he would be abused on any specific night.
- The variability in Max's behavior and his lack of memory for events at school.
- Max's belief that his mother must have known about the abuse, and the influence that this had on him and on his relationship with his mother.

History

Pierre Janet, a French psychiatrist, psychologist, and philosopher, was the first person to focus on dissociative experiences and coined the term *dissociation* in the 1890s (Kihlstrom, Glisky, & Anguilo, 1994). He asserted that some people were genetically predisposed to dissociate, and that part of their consciousness became separated, or dissociated, from the rest of their consciousness when they experienced high levels of stress. During the late 1800s and early 1900s a few case studies of dissociation appeared in the literature, including some involving late adolescents (Bowman, 1990). The cases were rare and mystified the clinicians who dealt with them.

Interest in dissociation diminished in the early 1900s, when many of those experiencing dissociative symptoms were considered to have schizophrenia (Rosenbaum, 1980). Although occasional case studies of dissociation in children and adults continued to appear in the literature, interest in dissociation languished until the 1980s when Kluft presented a series of case studies of children with dissociative symptoms that were distinct from the symptoms of schizophrenia (Kluft, 1984). Although Kluft's reports were met with skepticism, other psychiatrists and psychologists began reporting cases of children with similar symptoms (Fahey, 1988). At the same time, increased attention was being paid to the physical and sexual abuse of children (Finkelhor, 1979; Gelles, 1979), and it became clear that most children with dissociative symptoms had been chronically and severely abused. This increasing interest in dissociative disorders and in the consequences of physical and sexual abuse led clinicians and researchers to focus on the role that severe abuse could play in the development of dissociative disorders. The creation of several scales to measure dissociative symptoms allowed clinicians and researchers to detect them more reliably in children, which led to increasing numbers of children being diagnosed with a dissociative disorder (Putnam, 1997).

Dissociative disorders were included in the DSM-III (APA, 1980), and their diagnostic criteria have remained similar during each subsequent edition of the DSM. The names of most of the disorders have changed somewhat. For example, *psychogenic amnesia* and *psychogenic fugue* in the DSM-III are now called *dissociative amnesia* and *dissociative fugue*. As already noted, the name of *multiple personality disorder,* as it was called in the DSM-III and DSM-III-R, was changed to *dissociative identity disorder* in the DSM-IV.

Key Concepts

- Janet coined the term *dissociation* and described it as a splitting of one part of consciousness from another.
- Interest in dissociation declined during the late 1800s and early 1900s, possibly because of the belief that many people who had the symptoms of dissociation actually had schizophrenia.
- Clinical reports of dissociative symptoms in children in the 1970s and an increased focus on the consequences of child abuse led to heightened clinical and research interest in dissociation.
- The diagnostic criteria for the dissociative disorders have remained similar since the DSM-III, although the names of most of the disorders have changed.

Toward Understanding Dissociative Disorders: Common Dissociative Experiences

We all have dissociative experiences—that is, we all experience times when our perceptions, cognitions, emotions, and memories are not connected (Ross, Joshi, & Churrie, 1991). For example, think about a time that a friend was talking to you but you were not paying attention to her. Perhaps you found her story boring and so began thinking about a concert you were going to attend that evening. During this conversation, the auditory and visual perceptions of your friend were transmitted to your brain (your inner ear was stimulated by sound waves produced by your friend's speech and sent signals to your brain); but these perceptions went unnoticed by your consciousness. You may even have nodded occasionally as your friend spoke. But at the end of this conversation you would have had no memory of what your friend said. In essence, your thoughts and memories for the period of this conversation were dissociated from your perceptions and your behaviors.

The principal differences between the dissociative experiences of most of us and the dissociative experiences of those with a dissociative disorder are the control over the onset of dissociation and the degree to which the dissociative episode ends easily. With sufficient effort, you can pay attention to your friend's story even if your mind is occupied with other things. In essence, you can control the onset of your dissociation. In addition, when your mind is elsewhere, your friend can bring your attention back to her boring conversation if she touches your hand and asks, "Are you hearing what I'm saying?" Those with dissociative disorders, however, often have no control over the onset of their dissociative experiences and cannot end them when they want. We will explore why this occurs in the next sections of this chapter.

Normal Dissociation in Children

Certain forms of dissociation are common among young children and are considered developmentally appropriate. For example, many children engage in vivid daydreams in which they feel transported to another place or time. While daydreaming, the child's consciousness is focused on the daydream and not on events occurring around him or her—a dissociative experience. The child is in one place physically and in another place consciously. Think of a third grader sitting in a classroom at the end of the day daydreaming about a sleepover she will attend that evening, with her consciousness remaining on the sleepover despite the teacher calling her name several times and some of her classmates laughing at how she has "spaced out."

Dissociation can be a useful strategy for coping with difficult situations, and adults often encourage dissociation in children when it is to the child's benefit. A parent laughing and cajoling and yammering to a child who is about to get an injection in a physician's office is using dissociation: splitting the child's attention from the pain of the needle to something less anxiety-provoking. The same thing happens when a parent points out birds flying by to distract a toddler from the pain of a tumble he just took.

The patterns that normal dissociative experiences take across childhood and adolescence are not well established, and some disagreement about them exists. Putnam (1993) suggests that normative dissociative experiences peak around age 10 and then decline quickly. Wallach and Dollinger (1999) suggest that levels of normative dissociation increase gradually during childhood, peak during early adolescence, and then decline steadily. Despite the lack of clarity about the course of normal dissociation, it is clear that most children have experiences that have a dissociative quality to them. Knowing this is important for understanding the development of dissociative disorders because current theorizing about their etiology focuses on the ways in which normal dissociation becomes problematic when used frequently by traumatized children.

Key Concepts

- Most of us have dissociative experiences. Sometimes we may use dissociation intentionally; other times it may occur unintentionally.
- Common dissociative experiences differ from the experiences of those with dissociative disorders in control over the onset of the dissociation and the extent to which the dissociative experience ends easily.
- Dissociation is a normal experience for children.

Diagnosis and Assessment

Diagnostic Criteria

Five disorders are included in the dissociative disorders category of the DSM-IV-TR. Of these disorders, only two have received much attention related to children: *dissociative identity disorder* and *dissociative disorder not otherwise specified* (DDNOS). Consequently, we will focus on them in this section. Brief descriptions of the other three dissociative disorders are included to familiarize you with them.

Dissociative amnesia is diagnosed when a person has no memory for significant parts of his or her life that goes beyond normal forgetting (APA, 2000). Typically the events for which there is no memory are associated with a traumatic event. Most often the amnesia is for a short time. For example, a rape victim may have no memory of the evening during which she was raped, or a person involved in an automobile accident may have no memory of the drive during which the accident occurred. Longer amnesia is less common but may occur if traumatic experiences are chronic. For example, an adolescent who was repeatedly abused between the ages of 8 and 12 may have no memories of those years.

Dissociative fugue involves sudden travel for which the person has no memory (APA, 2000). The fugue often occurs during times of high stress and may continue for hours or, more rarely, for months or years. For example, a person may suddenly find himself sitting in a park several miles from his home and have no memory of how he got there or why he traveled there. In more protracted incidents, a person may travel to another area and take up life there, with no memory of his or her earlier life. The person may emerge from the fugue with no memory of starting this new life and no memory for what has happened since starting his or her travel. For example, a person may suddenly find herself a cook in a small restaurant in a town in Nebraska, with no memory of how she got to Nebraska from her home in Missouri, no memory of why she is in Nebraska, and no memory of her life there (and when in Nebraska she would have had no memory of her earlier life in Missouri).

Depersonalization disorder involves repeated episodes of feeling detached from oneself (APA, 2000). Depersonalization is often described as feeling as if one were observing oneself from afar rather than living one's life. The person often feels like a robot—as if he or she has little control over his or her behaviors, feelings, and thoughts.

Dissociative Identity Disorder and Dissociative Disorder Not Otherwise Specified

The diagnostic criteria for *dissociative identity disorder* are included in Table 14.4. As shown, dissociative identity disorder is diagnosed when a person has two or more distinct identities that emerge, individually, to direct the person's life.

One source of skepticism about dissociative identity disorder is the common view that it is a disorder in which 2 or 3 (or 10 or 12) separate individuals live in one body (Gleaves, 1996). This is a misconception. Dissociative identity disorder does not involve several individuals living in one

---

T A B L E   1 4 . 4

Diagnostic Criteria for 300.14 Dissociative Identity Disorder

A.   The presence of two or more distinct identities or personality states (each with its own relatively enduring pattern of perceiving, relating to, and thinking about the environment and self).

B.   At least two of these identities or personality states recurrently take control of the person's behavior.

C.   Inability to recall important personal information that is too extensive to be explained by ordinary forgetfulness.

D.   The disturbance is not due to the direct physiological effects of a substance (e.g., blackouts or chaotic behavior during Alcohol Intoxication) or a general medical condition (e.g., complex partial seizures). **Note:** In children, the symptoms are not attributable to imaginary playmates or other fantasy play.

body, each with their own personality. Instead it involves the fragmentation of a person's personality into several unintegrated pieces—**alternate personality identities** (Fraser, 1994). These fragments of a person's personality can appear to be distinct personalities.

Conceptualizing dissociative identity disorder in this way helps us understand it more clearly. Most of us exhibit different aspects of our personality at different times. For example, I can be shy at times, loud and boisterous at times, angry and hostile at times, and forgiving at times. Despite my different thoughts, feelings, and behaviors during each of these times, my sense of self remains intact throughout all of them, and I have an integrated set of memories that includes each of them. There is one "me" that can act, feel, and think in different ways. In contrast, the life of a person with dissociative identity disorder consists of a series of disjointed experiences, each directed by one of his or her alternate personality identities. For example, the person's shy "self" is split from the loud and boisterous "self." Consequently, the shy "self" has no connection to the loud and boisterous "self," and these are experienced as two distinct "selves" that emerge at different times, rather than as two components of one integrated "self."

Usually each alternate personality identity has a distinct name. Studies with adults suggest that the primary identity, which is the identity that is present most often and carries the given name of the person, is usually quiet, depressed, and withdrawn. The alternate personality identities often have aggressive or hostile characteristics (APA, 2000). These identities usually emerge in frightening or stressful situations and act in protective ways of which the primary identity seems incapable.

Dissociative disorder not otherwise specified (DDNOS) is the second dissociative disorder that has been studied in children (Putnam, 1997; Putnam, Hornstein, & Peterson, 1996). DDNOS is similar to the other disorders "not otherwise specified" in the DSM-IV-TR: It provides a diagnosis for children who have many symptoms of a dissociative disorder but who do not meet all the diagnostic criteria for any of them. Commonly, DDNOS is the diagnosis

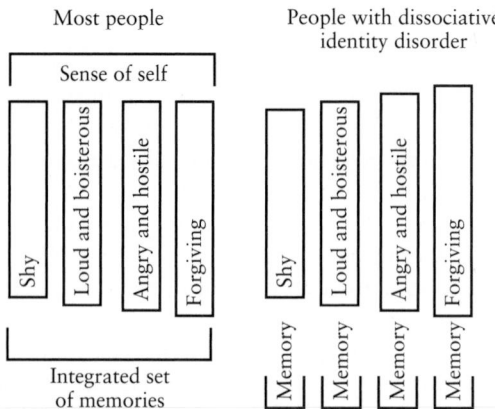

FIGURE 14.2 *Dissociative Identity Disorder*

given to children who have significant amnesia, experience trance states, and have significant and rapid shifts in interests or abilities, but who do not clearly exhibit two or more alternate personality identities (Hornstein & Putnam, 1992; Putnam et al., 1996).

At this time it is unclear whether DDNOS is a disorder separate from dissociative identity disorder, is a less severe form of dissociative identity disorder, or is an early form of dissociative identity disorder. Some evidence suggests that it may be a less severe form. Putnam and colleagues (1996) compared the symptoms of children who had received a diagnosis of disso-ciative identity disorder and those who had received a diagnosis of DDNOS. They found similar types of symptoms in the children in both groups but a greater frequency of symptoms among those with dissociative identity disor-der. However, this investigation also showed that older children were more likely to be diagnosed with dissociative identity disorder than DDNOS, which is consistent with DDNOS being an early form of dissociative identity disorder. Consequently, this issue remains unresolved; further study will be necessary before conclusions about any connections between dissociative identity disorder and DDNOS can be made.

Controversial Issue: Does Dissociative Identity Disorder Exist?

The controversy about multiple personalities began when the earliest cases were described in the late 1800s and reemerged when dissociative disorders became a focus of research and clinical work in the 1980s (Bowman, 1990; Putnam, 1997). The principal aspect of this controversy is whether the symptoms of dissociative identity disorder develop in a way that is outside a person's control or whether most people with these symptoms have created them purposefully because of (1) suggestions made to them by their therapist, (2) a desire to please their therapist, or (3) a desire to get attention from others (APA, 2000; Fahey, 1988; Spanos, 1994).

Several techniques used by therapists treating those diagnosed with dis-sociative identity disorder contribute to this controversy. From the earliest cases of dissociative identity disorder, some clinicians have used hypnosis to elicit and communicate with the alternate personality identities of their cli-ents—a technique that is still in use today. In addition, some clinicians may hypnotize a client who is suspected of having dissociative identity disorder to see if it is possible to communicate with an alternate personality iden-tity—thereby confirming that the client has dissociative identity disorder (Williams & Velazquez, 1996). Critics argue that rather than discovering existing alternate personality identities through hypnosis, it is more likely that alternate personality identities have been created through hypnotic sug-gestion from the therapist (Spanos, 1994). In addition, the alternate person-ality identities that emerge under hypnosis often report severe, chronic child abuse for which the primary identity has no memory. Skeptics argue that these abuse memories are likely to have been suggested to a client by a therapist who believes that they must have occurred. As this abuse is discussed repeatedly in therapy sessions when a client is not hypnotized, the client comes to believe that it occurred (Fahey, 1988).

Another concern is that the symptoms of dissociative identity disorder may be created and reinforced because of the special attention that those with the symptoms and their therapists receive. Spanos (1994), for example, points out that the number of cases of dissociative identity disorder increased dramatically after the publication of *Three Faces of Eve* and *Sybil*. He argues that due to the rare and intriguing nature of the dissociative disorders, therapists can be excited to find a client with one. Consequently, they may provide a client who shows some indications of having a dissociative disorder with special attention. If the therapist discusses the case with colleagues, the therapist may receive heightened attention from them. This increased attention may subtly push some therapists to see symptoms of a dissociative disorder that do not exist and may subtly push some clients to create and express these types of symptoms. Spanos (1994) also notes that most cases of dissociative identity disorder have been diagnosed by a few therapists and that most therapists have never had a client with dissociative identity disorder. He believes that this pattern supports his argument that the diagnoses made by some therapists are influenced, consciously or unconsciously, by the attention they receive when they have a client with a dissociative disorder.

Those who believe in the appropriateness of the diagnosis of dissociative identity disorder respond to these criticisms in several ways (Gleaves, 1996; Putnam, 1997). They argue that many people with dissociative symptoms emerge after well-publicized cases of dissociative identity disorder because they are finally willing to seek help for the confusing symptoms they have experienced for years after learning that others have the same symptoms. In addition, they point to the increasing number of clinicians identifying cases of dissociative identity disorder, asserting that many cases were not being identified earlier because most clinicians were not familiar with dissociative disorders and so were not asking clients about dissociative symptoms.

Further, they note that studies of the personalities of adults diagnosed with dissociative identity disorder show that most of them exhibit a pattern of withdrawal and avoidance, rather than a pattern of attention seeking. They argue that few of those with dissociative symptoms come forward to gain attention for themselves. Instead most of them have tried for years to avoid the attention that their odd behavior has created, and even when they seek therapeutic help they are reluctant to have others know about their symptoms (Fink & Golinkoff, 1990; Goff, Olin, Jenike, & Baer, 1992). Finally, they acknowledge that some cases of alternate personality identities may have emerged because of hypnotic suggestions made by therapists. However, they argue that the number of cases being identified by many different clinicians over the past decade show that it is unlikely that all or most of them are the result of suggestions from clinicians (Ross, 1996).

So where do we stand with this controversy? Most clinicians and researchers have accepted that dissociative disorders exist, including dissociative identity disorder; and dissociative disorders are a well-recognized category of disorders in the DSM-IV-TR. The concerns of those skeptical about the existence of dissociative identity disorder have been influential in clinical work and research, however. Clinicians and researchers now appear to take more care to avoid uncovering alternate personality identities that do not exist, suggesting to clients that they should exist, or providing increased attention if a client talks about alternate personality identities.

Determining that an Individual Child Has a Dissociative Disorder

The most common way of determining whether a child is experiencing a dissociative disorder is through interviews with the child and those who know the child well, as well as questionnaires completed by caregivers (Hornstein, R. T., 1996; Putnam, 1997). The clinician gathers information from the questionnaires and interviews and determines if the child is having dissociative symptoms that impair the child's functioning and differ significantly from what one would expect given the child's development. When appropriate, a diagnosis of a dissociative disorder is made.

Sample items from a commonly used questionnaire completed by a parent or other caregiver, the Child Dissociative Checklist, are shown in Table 14.5. As you can see, they focus on issues related to memory, experiencing trances, changes in preferences and abilities, and the possibility that the child experiences more than one "self."

Considering Culturally Sanctioned Behaviors

Whenever a child is assessed to see if he or she meets the diagnostic criteria for a disorder, the cultural values of the child and the child's family must be considered. As noted by the DSM-IV-TR,

> A cross-cultural perspective is particularly important in the evaluation of Dissociative Disorders because dissociative states are a common and accepted expression of cultural activities or religious experiences in many societies. In most such instances, the dissociative states are not pathological and do not lead to significant distress, impairment, or help-seeking behavior. (APA, 2000, p. 519)

For example, having a spirit speak during a religious ceremony through a child who later has no memory for the experience would not be considered a symptom of the child having an alternate personality identity—if the child's experience is seen as appropriate in his or her society and it causes no impairment or distress for the child. A clear understanding of the cultural background of a child who may be experiencing symptoms of dissociation is needed for an accurate assessment of the child's symptoms. Conversations with those who are familiar with the cultural values of the child and the

TABLE 14.5

Sample Items from the Child Dissociative Checklist, Version Three

Child does not remember or denies traumatic or painful experiences that are known to have occurred.

Child goes into a daze or trancelike state at times or often appears "spaced out." Teachers may report that he or she "daydreams" frequently in school.

Child has a very poor sense of time. He or she loses track of time, may think that it is morning when it is actually afternoon, gets confused about what day it is, or becomes confused about when something happened.

Child shows marked day-to-day or even hour-to-hour variations in his or her skills, knowledge, food preferences, athletic abilities (e.g., changes in handwriting, memory for previously learned information such as multiplication tables, spelling, use of tools, or artistic ability).

Child refers to himself or herself in the third person when talking about self, or at times insists on being called by a different name. He or she may also claim that things that he or she did actually happened to another person.

Child has a vivid imaginary companion or companions. Child may insist that the imaginary companion is responsible for things that he or she has done.

Source: Putnam, 1997.

child's family are usually essential for an accurate assessment of the child (Seeley, 2000).

Key Concepts

- Dissociative amnesia, dissociative fugue, and depersonalization disorder are dissociative disorders, but little mention of them is made in the literature about children and adolescents.
- Dissociative identity disorder is diagnosed when a child has two or more distinct alternate personality identities that emerge at separate times to direct the child's life.
- DDNOS is diagnosed when a child meets most of the criteria for a dissociative disorder but does not exhibit two or more alternate personality identities.
- It is not clear whether DDNOS is a less severe form of dissociative identity disorder, a precursor to dissociative identity disorder, or a distinct disorder.
- Controversy has occurred for many years about whether dissociative disorders exist. It is generally accepted at this time that they do exist.
- Interviews with children and their parents, and written measures completed by parents, are most commonly used when determining whether a child has a dissociative disorder.

Characteristics and Experiences of Children with Dissociative Disorders

Core Features
Memory Problems

Memory problems for short or long periods are a feature of all dissociative disorders, and memories for traumatic experiences are typically those that are lost (APA, 2000; Putnam, 1997). The loss of memories may be partly due to a child's active dissociation during the traumatic experiences. In some cases, a traumatic experience may have overwhelmed a child's memory system, resulting in no memory for the trauma being encoded (van der Kolk et al., 1996).

Children with dissociative identity disorder may experience extensive memory lapses because events occurring when one alternate personality identity is dominant are often not in the memories of other alternate personality identities (Dorahy, 2001; Eich, Macaulay, Loewenstein, & Dihle, 1997). Consequently, children with dissociative identity disorder may have many memory lapses even for events that are not traumatic. For example, a child may have no memory of lunch or his physical education class that day at school, a conversation with another student about meeting after school, or where he left his books or jacket. Typically the primary identity and any alternate identities with passive characteristics remember only events occurring when they are dominant. They have little or no memory of events that occur when the more hostile or aggressive alternate identities emerge. The hostile or aggressive identities, on the other hand, often have more thorough memories about a child's life and can describe events that occurred when the primary identity or passive alternate identities were present.

Memory loss can lead to problems with teachers and peers at school, as well as with parents and other caregivers at home. Parents and teachers may believe that a child is simply being obstinate when he insists that something never occurred or that he is trying to avoid responsibilities by saying that he has no memory of them. Peers may believe that a child is being rude when she agrees to meet them after school and then does not appear and argues the next day that they had never planned to meet.

Of course, memory loss can create considerable confusion for a child (Silberg, 2000). Imagine how confusing your life would be if once or twice a day you could not remember what happened during the previous hour, or once or twice a week you could not remember what happened the previous day. In addition, think about the strategies you would have to concoct to cope with your frequent memory losses.

Trance States

Observations of children with dissociative disorders show that they occasionally experience **trance states** in which they stare straight ahead and appear oblivious to what is going on around them. These trances have been observed during therapy sessions, psychological testing sessions, and school activities

(Putnam, 1996; Silberg, 1998). The function of these trance states is not clear. Some clinical reports suggest that they occur while one alternate personality identity is being replaced by another (Hornstein, R. T., 1996). Trances, however, are also observed in children with DDNOS. For these children, a trance may indicate an active dissociative state.

Changes in Preferences and Abilities

Many children with a dissociative disorder experience changes in preferences and abilities that are more intense than the changes experienced by other children. The changes may occur frequently, such as several times in a day, or infrequently, such as weekly or monthly (Macfie, Cicchetti, & Toth, 2001; Silberg, 2000; Wallach & Dollinger, 1999). Changes in preferences and abilities are hypothesized to indicate a lack of a single, coherent sense of self and, in some cases, to indicate the presence of two or more alternate personality identities, each of which has a different set of preferences and abilities.

Changes in abilities are often dramatic, and they usually create problems for a child. For example, a child may suddenly struggle with arithmetic problems that she answered easily a week before or may suddenly seem uncoordinated in dance class although she danced gracefully the previous month. Changes in preferences can also be dramatic. For example, a child may insist that he has always liked steak as he eats one, although he was an avowed vegetarian the week before.

Changes in preferences and abilities can be confusing to those around the child (Wallach & Dollinger, 1999). Peers and adults may believe that the child is purposefully changing patterns of preferences and activities for some nefarious reason, which can lead to conflicts. In addition, the child can experience considerable confusion as those around him or her respond with amazement or anger to changes in interests, friends, or activities. It would be as if suddenly everyone seemed amazed at who and what you liked, and you did not understand their amazement.

Associated Features

Clinical reports show that children with a dissociative disorder experience a wide range of mood and conduct disorder symptoms (Hornstein, N., 1996; Hornstein & Putnam, 1992; Putnam, 1996, 1997). Mood swings are common and can be as intense as those experienced by children with bipolar disorder. A high level of irritability, which is a common symptom of depression in children, is often present in children with a dissociative disorder and may cause aggression and other conduct problems.

Symptoms of anxiety and of posttraumatic stress disorder are also common in children with a dissociative disorder. Many such children experience high levels of generalized anxiety or anxiety about specific issues. This anxiety may occur primarily in settings in which their abuse occurred—for example, being very anxious around bedtime or when using the bathroom (Hornstein, N., 1996). Hypervigilance and intrusive memories—symptoms of posttraumatic stress disorder—are also often present.

Children with dissociative disorders make more suicide attempts than other children. Children with dissociative identity disorder make more attempts than do children with DDNOS, suggesting that these attempts are associated with the severity of the disorder (Putnam et al., 1996).

Prevalence and Course

The prevalence of dissociative disorders in children and adolescents is unknown because symptoms of dissociative disorders have not been included in large-scale studies of psychopathology in children (Silberg, 1998). From the number of children identified through clinical reports, dissociative disorders are rare.

Little is known about the course of dissociative disorders in children. Longitudinal studies of children with dissociative symptoms have not been completed, so it is not clear how their symptoms change during childhood, adolescence, and adulthood. Some relevant information comes from a cross-sectional study of children with dissociative identity disorder and DDNOS: Older children had more severe symptoms than younger ones (Hornstein & Putnam, 1992; Putnam et al., 1996). This suggests that symptoms may worsen over time without some type of intervention.

Key Concepts

- Amnesia and other memory problems occur in all dissociative disorders. The short- and long-term memory losses can disrupt children's lives.
- Trance states are common; they may indicate that a child is actively dissociating or that an alternate personality identity is emerging.
- Dramatic changes in preferences and abilities are common among children with dissociative disorders.
- Children with dissociative disorders experience a wide range of comorbid disorders, including anxiety and mood disorders; and their risk for conduct problems and suicide is heightened.
- No specific information is available about the prevalence of dissociative disorders in children, although they are probably rare.
- Little is known about the course of dissociative disorders.

Etiology

Current theorizing about the etiology of dissociative disorders is that it involves a process through which the use of dissociation by some abused children becomes so frequent and intense that it begins to dominate their lives. This process is hypothesized to occur in several steps:

1. Some children who experience severe abuse purposefully use dissociation to cope with the physical and emotional pain of the abuse.
2. If dissociation is effective in reducing the trauma of frequent abuse, some children begin to use it to cope with a wide range of stressful events.

3. As dissociation is used more frequently by these children, it begins to occur automatically when a child is faced with stress rather than being employed purposefully by the child.

4. Because of the increasing frequency with which it is used, at some point dissociation begins to dominate a child's life.

The development of alternate personality identities is believed to occur as an extension of this process. In this section we explore this process, first by exploring the development of the frequent use of dissociation and then by exploring the development of alternate personality identities in some children who dissociate frequently.

Development of Chronic Dissociation

It is believed that some children who experience repeated abuse begin to dissociate intentionally during abuse incidents: They deliberately send their minds elsewhere so that part of them can escape the abuse (Kluft, 1985; Putnam, 1997; Silberg, 2000). Dissociating can allow a child to escape the conscious experience of the physical pain of abuse, and this may be particularly beneficial if the child is expected to endure the abuse without fighting back, screaming, or crying. Dissociation can also allow the child to escape the psychological pain associated with memories of abuse by splitting those memories from consciousness.

To the extent that purposeful dissociation helps a child reduce the physical and emotional pain of abuse, he or she may use dissociation during each abuse experience. If those experiences happen frequently, the child may become more efficient at using dissociation to escape pain. In addition, repeated use of dissociation may strengthen the neural pathways used to dissociate, which can increase the efficiency of the child's dissociating and the likelihood that it will occur (Schore, 1996).

Chronically abused children may withdraw into a world of their own partially to avoid the pain of their abuse.

Because of the benefits of dissociation to a child, and possibly because of a neural sensitivity, a child who uses dissociation frequently to cope with abuse may begin to use it to cope with a wide variety of stressful social, academic, or family situations (Putnam, 1993). For example, a child may dissociate when being chastised by a parent for misbehaving or when being teased by children in her class. To the extent that this dissociation is effective in reducing the negative feelings associated with many stressful experiences, the child may dissociate more frequently.

It appears that the frequent use of dissociation by some children eventually results in their using it during stressful events without a conscious effort to do so. It is as if the child begins to lose purposeful control over the dissociation process; it becomes an automatic response to stress (Dell & Eisenhower, 1990). This can be thought of as the point at which the child's dissociation becomes disordered: He or she has little control over the dissociation, and consequently it can occur in situations that create an impairment for the child.

Frequent dissociation can impair a child's development because it separates a child mentally from the contexts in which development occurs. When a child dissociates during stressful academic tasks, he or she does not integrate what is learned; when a child dissociates during stressful social situations, he or she fails to learn and integrate social skills. Consequently, one result of frequent dissociation is that a child may fall behind academically and socially. As this occurs, he or she is likely to experience increased stress in academic and social settings, which may increase the use of dissociation. Thus a vicious cycle can be created in which dissociation that was once valuable to help a child escape from traumatic experiences begins to increase the stress in other parts of his or her life, which will increase the use of dissociation, which leads to more stress and a further increase in the use of dissociation.

Risk for Chronic Dissociation

Why some children engage in purposeful dissociation during abuse and others do not, and why this process becomes automatic for some children and not others, remain unclear. One group of researchers has found that a genetic influence on dissociative behaviors exists (Becker-Blease et al., 2004). This may suggest that there is some genetic risk for dissociation, and abused children with this risk may be more likely to use dissociation during stressful situations. However, much more research will need to be conducted before we begin to understand the characteristics or experiences of children that lead some to dissociate frequently and automatically.

Some researchers have argued that there is a *sensitive period* during which chronic abuse is likely to lead to problems with dissociation. For example, Putnam (1985) hypothesized that chronic abuse between the ages of 3 and 8 is more likely to cause the development of dissociation than abuse beginning after age 8. This hypothesis was based on clinical reports from children and adults diagnosed with dissociative identity disorder showing that their alternate personality identities began to emerge between ages 3 and

8. However, the hypothesis about this sensitive period needs further investigation before it can be accepted.

Development of Alternate Personality Identities

The processes through which alternate personality identities form remain unclear, but several researchers have hypothesized about them (Forrest, 2001; Pica, 1999; Putnam, 1997). We will review the most widely known of these hypotheses in this section. It is worth noting again that it is generally believed that alternate personality identities do not represent the development of new and different personalities within a child; instead they represent a lack of integration of fragments of a child's personality (Fraser, 1994). At issue, then, is how the fragments of some children's personalities do not become integrated.

Putnam bases his theorizing about the development of alternate personality identities on the concept of **discrete behavioral states.** A behavioral state is a "unique organization or structure of consciousness and behavior" (Putnam, 1997, p. 152). Discrete behavioral states have been studied in newborns and infants for years. For example, Wolff (1987) described five discrete behavioral states in newborns, each of which is characterized by distinct physiological functioning: State I, regular quiet, non–rapid-eye-movement (non-REM) sleep; State II, irregular or REM sleep; State III, alert with focused gaze and little movement; State IV, waking activity or precrying; and State V, crying. As the newborn develops, additional discrete behavioral states emerge, such as an active, focused state.

A primary task of infants and toddlers is learning to control these states and return to more pleasing states when in an unpleasant state (for example, stop crying and return to an active noncrying state). They can do this occasionally by self-soothing or self-stimulating, but most often they need the help of their parents in this process (such as when a parent holds and soothes a crying infant) (Schore, 1996). With the ongoing assistance of their parents and others, most children gradually develop the ability to cope with their states on their own. As they develop more control over these states, the states become integrated into what the child experiences as one "self."

However, young children who experience repeated trauma have great difficulty integrating their behavioral states. This is partly because of the difficulty of integrating the state experienced during trauma because it is so emotionally and physically intense, and partly because the parents of many abused young children are not available to help them learn to control their states (Putnam, 1997). Consequently, the behavioral states of chronically abused children are more likely to remain separate and unintegrated. In addition, if a child purposefully dissociates during traumatic experiences, he or she pushes the abusive state farther from the others—a process that is the opposite of the integration of states that is a goal of normal development. Thus rather than following the normal developmental path shown in Figure 14.3(a), some chronically abused children follow the path shown in

Figure 14.3(b). Because, as just noted, each discrete behavioral state has its own physiological, emotional, and cognitive activity, failure to integrate the states causes separation of the emotions, cognitions, and memories that occur during each state. Eventually these discrete states can become so separated that they begin to function as alternate personality identities, each with its own emotions, cognitions, and memories.

Putnam's model helps to explain why children who experience abuse early in life are more likely to develop dissociative identity disorder than those who first experience repeated abuse later. Those with a healthy early life have already proceeded through much of the developmental process of integrating their discrete behavioral states into one sense of self. Consequently, they are less likely to experience a lack of integration. Of course, children traumatized later in life may experience other disorders, such as posttraumatic stress disorder, depression, anxiety, or conduct disorders. However, they may be less likely to develop alternate personality identities and dissociative identity disorder (Putnam et al., 1996).

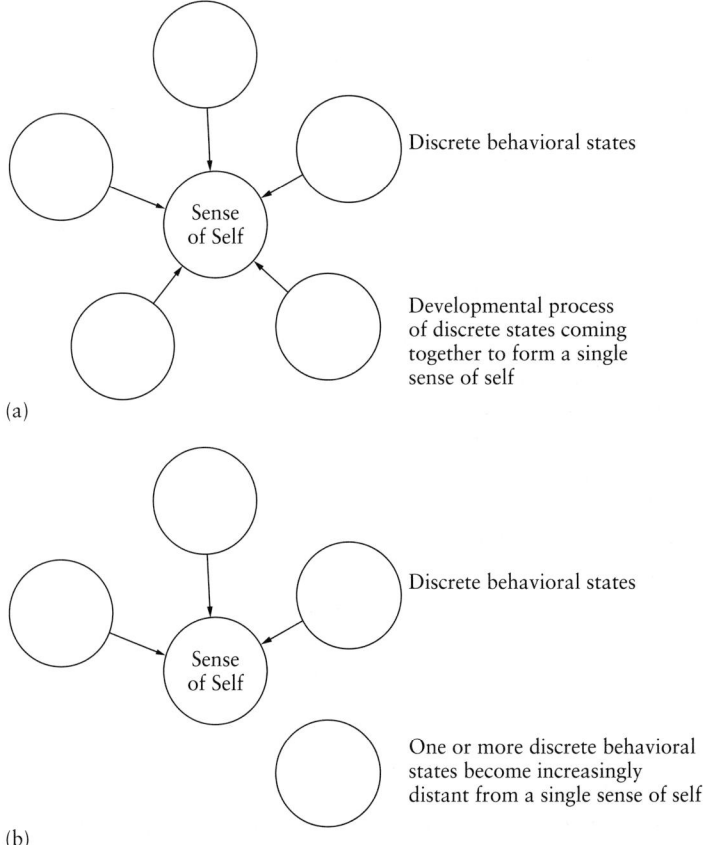

FIGURE 14.3   *Development of Alternate Personality Identities*

Key Concepts

- The frequent use of dissociation by some abused children may result in it becoming their strategy for coping with many types of stress.
- Frequent use of dissociation may increase neural sensitivity for dissociating, making it more likely to occur.
- Eventually the purposeful use of dissociation may become automatic in some children, which may cause it to occur during times that are stressful for them.
- Some children may have a genetically influenced predisposition toward dissociation.
- Some researchers have suggested that there is a sensitive period between the ages of 3 and 8 for the development of dissociative identity disorder.
- Putnam suggests that the discrete behavioral states that all infants experience fail to become integrated in a child who lives in an abusive family environment, which can eventually result in the development of two or more alternative personality identities.

Preventive and Therapeutic Interventions

Prevention

The literature contains no preventive interventions for children who may experience a dissociative disorder. To the extent that current beliefs about the etiology of dissociative disorders are correct, any efforts to prevent them must focus on early identification of children who are experiencing severe and chronic abuse and their removal from the abusive situations.

Because most chronically abused young children are abused by a family member or someone living with them, their abuse is usually first reported by someone outside their families—for example, teachers, physicians, or nurses (Reppucci & Haugaard, 1989). However, many severely abused children may be kept away from professionals who could identify them by their abusive parents. In addition, the developing alternate personality identities of some children who are experiencing severe abuse may make it more difficult to identify them. They may be quiet and withdrawn and have few interactions with adults outside their families. Ongoing vigilance of professionals who have contact with children may be the best chance for these children to be identified at a young age.

Therapeutic Interventions with the Child

Several clinicians have described their strategies for therapeutic interventions for children with dissociative problems and their families. It is important to note that no research has confirmed the effectiveness of these strategies or the relative effectiveness of one strategy over another. This is likely due to the rarity of dissociative disorders and the consequent difficulty of gathering a sufficient sample for research. As has happened in the past, we may eventually find that some strategies currently in use are effective and others are not; but that will require future research.

Focus on Dissociation

Therapeutic strategies for children with dissociative disorders are commonly described as having three components: providing a safe environment for the child; helping the child to remember and work through traumatic experiences; and for children experiencing dissociative identity disorder, integrating alternate personality identities into one cohesive personality (Kluft, 1996).

Ensuring a safe living environment for the child is essential before therapeutic work can begin (Wallach & Dollinger, 1999). Until the child is living in an environment that is free from abuse, he or she cannot be expected to give up the use of dissociation that has helped the child endure the abuse. In addition, the clinician must provide a therapeutic environment in which the child feels physically and emotionally safe. The therapeutic environment must be one in which the child does not feel forced to participate in therapy, which may recreate feelings that the child experienced when being abused; rather, the child must feel invited to engage in the needed therapeutic work at a pace that is comfortable (Hornstein, N., 1996).

Early stages of treatment often involve the clinician exploring with the child his or her use of dissociation (Wallach & Dollinger, 1999). It is helpful for the clinician to express understanding for the child's use of dissociation in abusive situations and to discuss the problems associated with the use of dissociation during other times in the child's life. In this way, the child and clinician can come to a common understanding of the child's use of dissociation and agree that it would be helpful to reduce its use in nonabusive situations. The clinician may suggest to the child that it would be helpful for the clinician to intervene when he or she observes the child using dissociation during therapy (Silberg, 2000). For example, the clinician may touch the child, say his or her name, or say, "I think that you are drifting away." In this way, the child and clinician can work together to reduce the child's use of dissociation and keep the child fully present during therapy sessions.

During the next phase of therapy, the child is encouraged, gently and gradually, to recall and describe the traumatic experiences that he or she experienced (Kluft, 1996; Shirar, 1996). As the child describes his or her traumatic experiences, the clinician can ask about the feelings and thoughts that the child had during them (Silberg, 2000). In this way, these feelings and thoughts are gradually brought back into the child's consciousness and become part of the child's memories.

Recollections of abuse may cause the emergence of alternate personality identities in children with dissociative identity disorder. Clinicians who work with children who have dissociative identity disorder write that when this happens, it is best to have conversations with these alternate personality identities—remembering that they represent components of the child's personality that have not been integrated (Hornstein, N., 1996; Putnam, 1997;

Silberg, 2000). These clinicians suggest that asking alternate personality identities about what makes them stay separate and why they feel that they cannot be a part of the child's integrated personality is a useful way of beginning to integrate the alternate personality identities into one personality.

Most clinical literature about children with dissociative identity disorder does not describe clearly the process through which the alternate personality identities can be integrated into one. However, the general process appears to be helping the child experience what each identity has to offer by having "group meetings" in which the child gradually can hear and appreciate the value of each of the separated parts of his or her identity (Waters & Silberg, 1996). In this way, the child can integrate the pieces that each of these alternate personality identities has to offer the child's personality. Although this process can sound fantastic, it involves a gradual process of breaking down the barriers between the distinct parts of the child's personality so that they can come together. Perhaps an analogue would be a mediator who works to bring several sides in a labor dispute together gradually, to the point where they can begin to agree on a common solution to their labor situation. With a child who has dissociative identity disorder, the therapist acts as the mediator who gradually brings the alternate personality identities together into a common personality (Shirar, 1996).

Focus on Family, Peer, and Social Issues

A child who has been dissociating for years may have poor social relationships—in part because of his or her tendency to withdraw from others, and in part because the dissociative behaviors are likely to be confusing to others, which may cause them to avoid the child. Considerable work may be needed to help the child develop needed social skills (Putnam, 1997). In particular, the child may need help to develop skills to deal with stressful events because these stressful situations may have caused the child to dissociate in the past.

The therapist may practice social skills with the child during therapy sessions and encourage the child to engage in them outside therapy (Waters & Silberg, 1996). The success of these interactions can be assessed in subsequent therapy sessions, with modification to the child's approach to these situations if necessary, and ongoing encouragement from the therapist to continue practicing the social skills. Stress reduction techniques, such as relaxation skills, may also be of benefit.

Interventions with Family Members and Other Caregivers

Parenting a child with a dissociative disorder can be confusing and unnerving to parents, foster parents, or other family members (Waters, 1996). Consequently, interventions focused on them are important. Interventions for caregivers can include (1) helping them understand dissociation and the reasons for its development and use by a child, (2) providing guidance in how to intervene with a child during dissociative episodes, and (3) minimizing the ways in which having a child with a dissociative disorder disrupts the family (Dell & Eisenhower, 1990; Silberg, 2004).

At some point during psychotherapy, the clinician will want to explore with the child the ways in which he or she dissociates outside therapy. The clinician may enlist the help of the child's family in identifying situations when the child dissociates and intervening to reduce the child's dissociation (Waters, 1996). For example, parents or other caregivers could form a partnership with the child to intervene gently when the child dissociates at home.

Key Concepts

- Prevention programs for dissociative disorders are not mentioned in the literature. The primary strategy for prevention is identification of children who are being severely abused and interventions to stop the abuse.
- Therapeutic strategies usually have three components: providing a safe environment for the child, helping the child work through traumatic experiences, and (for children experiencing dissociative identity disorder) integrating the alternate personality identities into one cohesive personality.
- Clinicians can help a child identify when he or she dissociates during therapy and provide strategies for interrupting the dissociative process.
- Helping a child remember and cope with traumatic experiences helps to integrate those experiences into the child's consciousness.
- Conversations with alternate personality identities help to integrate them into one cohesive identity.
- Strategies to promote social skills are often an important part of therapy for children with this disorder.
- Family members receive education about the dissociative process and may be brought into a partnership with the clinician and the child to help the child identify times outside therapy when the child dissociates.
- No interventions for children or families have been evaluated empirically.

Reactive Attachment Disorder

As discussed more fully in the chapter about basic psychological theories, human infants have an innate instinct to attach to one or two primary caregivers. Whatever the cultural setting or family structure into which they are born, whether they spend hours in day care each day or spend their early years at home, whether they are raised in a commune or by a single parent, all normal human infants form an attachment to one or two adult caregivers if given the opportunity to do so (Bowlby, 1969, 1973, 1980).

A few infants, sadly, do not form an attachment to a primary caregiver. Most of these infants have lived much or all of their lives in a very deprived environment. Some of them are raised by a parent or parents who do not respond to their signals of distress, seldom hold them, and do not consistently meet their needs for food or warmth. Others are raised in institutions where they lie in cribs for hours on end, receiving little human contact and only minimal attention to their basic physical needs. Some of these infants may be physically abused by their caregivers, particularly when they cry or show other normal signs of distress.

The experiences of these very deprived infants and their lack of an attachment to a primary caregiver make some of them incapable of forming meaningful relationships with others during their childhood, adolescence, and adulthood, and they may meet the diagnostic criteria for **reactive attachment disorder** (Haugaard & Hazan, 2003; Parker & Forrest, 1993). The inability of children with reactive attachment disorder to form meaningful relationships has a significant negative influence on many aspects of their lives, as we will explore in this section.

We are in the earliest stages of understanding reactive attachment disorder. Despite many years of research on attachment, only since the 1980s has reactive attachment disorder been a focus of research (Lyons-Ruth, Zeanah, & Benoit, 2003). Consequently, basic issues such as which behaviors are symptoms of reactive attachment disorder have yet to be agreed upon; and it remains a mystery why some severely deprived children develop reactive attachment disorder while other equally deprived children do not (Hanson & Spratt, 2000).

Several terms have been used to describe children who have attachment problems—such as *disordered attachment* and *severe attachment disorders* (Levy & Orlans, 2000). Although these terms are often only vaguely defined, they describe a group of children with a wider range of emotional and behavioral problems than those diagnosed with reactive attachment disorder. Consequently, although children with reactive attachment disorder would be included in the group of those with disordered attachment, some children with disordered attachment do not exhibit all the symptoms needed for a diagnosis of reactive attachment disorder. Therefore, we must be careful not to equate disordered attachment with reactive attachment disorder. In addition, it is important to note that an insecure attachment is different from reactive attachment disorder (Haugaard & Hazan, 2003). Children with an insecure attachment to a primary caregiver *have,* by definition, an attachment to that caregiver. Consequently, they are capable of forming attachments, although the quality of their attachments can be problematic. Children with reactive attachment disorder, on the other hand, *have not* formed an attachment to a primary caregiver and appear incapable of forming attachments.

Case Study: Researchers' Interactions with a Young Child

As the researchers approached the apartment of the next family on their interview list, they could hear a baby crying. They knocked, waited a few moments, knocked again, and waited some more. After almost five minutes, the door opened. Standing before them was a girl of about 3 or 4 years of age. The cries coming from a back room persisted. The researchers asked the girl her name (which was Sally) and if her mommy or daddy was at home. (An appointment to interview both parents had been made weeks beforehand and recently confirmed.) The girl ran down a hallway, and after several minutes returned tugging at the hand of her mother. Her mother appeared disheveled and somewhat dazed, and her speech was slightly slurred. She did not seem aware of the infant's cries, and she made no mention of them or her infant. The researchers noticed some drug paraphernalia on the cluttered coffee table. Despite her condition and the condition of the apartment, the mother insisted that the interview go on as scheduled and invited the researchers into her home. She asked if the researchers had brought the $15 that she had been promised for participating in the interview, and when they said that they had, she asked if she could be given the money before the interview began. The researchers gave her the $15, which she put on the coffee table.

By this time, the infant in the back room had stopped crying. One of the researchers cleared a space on the couch and sat next to the mother to conduct the interview, while the other found a spot on the floor from which to observe. Sally immediately walked over and climbed onto the lap of the researcher seated on the floor. She talked to him incessantly while exploring the contents of his pockets. She talked about toys she had in her bedroom and asked the researcher if he had any children. When he answered that he had a little girl, she asked if the little girl still wore diapers and said that she still wore diapers and stood so she could pull down her pants and show him her diapers. She then climbed back into his lap and began describing her toys again. Whenever the researcher listened to the mother's interview rather than attending to her, Sally would grasp his face in both hands and turn it toward her. Once when he smiled at her, she responded with a prolonged hug.

After about 15 minutes, Sally got up from the researcher's lap and began walking around the living room of the apartment, poking under seat cushions and pillows and pulling bits and pieces of things out and tossing them on the floor. Her mother paid no attention to her, and Sally apparently paid no attention to the adults in the room. The infant began to cry again, and cried for about 10 minutes and stopped. After a while, Sally returned to the researcher's lap and began to look through his pockets again. As the interview ended and the researchers got up to leave, Sally walked to the rear of the apartment without even a glance back at the researchers. As the researchers left the apartment, they could hear the infant begin to cry again.

Some Issues Worth Noting

- The extent to which Sally's "friendliness" seems out of place and thus may indicate a problem rather than good social skills.
- The lack of care provided to the unseen infant—care that may have been similar to that received by Sally when she was an infant.
- Whether, given their knowledge of appropriate parenting, the researchers would be required by most states to report the conditions in Sally's home to legal authorities.

History

The profound consequences of a very deprived environment during infancy have been known for many years. For example, Spitz (1945) and Bowlby (1951) both studied infants living in institutional nurseries during World

War II and described their highly anxious and withdrawn behaviors. These studies resulted in the concept of **anaclitic depression** described by Spitz (see the chapter about depressive disorders) and led Bowlby to develop **attachment theory** over the next few decades. Despite this interest in the consequences of early deprivation, it was not until the 1980s that much attention was devoted to specific disorders caused by this deprivation (Zeanah & Boris, 2000).

In 1980 the DSM-III included reactive attachment disorder in the category of Disorders Usually First Evident in Infancy, Childhood, or Adolescence. Over the next several editions, the diagnostic criteria for reactive attachment disorder changed significantly. Zeanah and Boris (2000) point out that the current diagnostic criteria for reactive attachment disorder were created without the benefit of research data. It was not until after the publication of the DSM-IV that the first article was published describing a series of case studies of children who met the diagnostic criteria for reactive attachment disorder (Richters & Volkmar, 1994). Consequently, the current diagnostic criteria were developed from individual reports of children's symptoms. Some researchers have argued that the current diagnostic criteria are incomplete—an issue we will explore next.

Diagnosis and Assessment

Diagnostic Criteria

As shown in Table 14.6, the diagnostic criteria for reactive attachment disorder require evidence of pathogenic care. **Pathogenic care** is care that is likely to result in some form of psychopathology. In the case of reactive attachment disorder, pathogenic care can involve the persistent disregard of a child's emotional and physical needs or changes in caregivers that are frequent enough to stop the child from attaching to a primary caregiver (such as a child moving between several foster homes during the first two years of life). Reactive attachment disorder is similar to posttraumatic stress disorder (PTSD) in that it requires that the child have specific problematic experiences, with these experiences believed to have the initial influence on the development of the disorder.

The core feature of reactive attachment disorder is that a child has not formed an age-appropriate attachment to a primary caregiver and appears incapable of forming attachments. This inability to form an attachment can be seen in two distinct types of behaviors, which are classified as the *inhibited type* and the *disinhibited type* of reactive attachment disorder. Children with the inhibited type show little inclination to engage with adults. In contrast, children with the disinhibited type approach many different people for comfort—even strangers who would be avoided by most children—instead of showing attachment to a primary caregiver.

TABLE 14.6

Diagnostic Criteria for 313.89 Reactive Attachment Disorder of Infancy or Early Childhood

A.   Markedly disturbed and developmentally inappropriate social relatedness in most contexts, beginning before age 5 years, as evidenced by either (1) or (2):

   (1)   Persistent failure to initiate or respond in a developmentally appropriate fashion to most social interactions, as manifest by excessively inhibited, hypervigilant, or highly ambivalent and contradictory responses (e.g., the child may respond to caregivers with a mixture of approach, avoidance, and resistance to comforting, or may exhibit frozen watchfulness).

   (2)   Diffuse attachments as manifest by indiscriminate sociability with marked inability to exhibit appropriate selective attachments (e.g., excessive familiarity with relative strangers or lack of selectivity in choice of attachment figures).

B.   The disturbance in Criterion A is not accounted for solely by developmental delay (as in Mental Retardation) and does not meet criteria for a Pervasive Developmental Disorder.

C.   Pathogenic care as evidenced by at least one of the following:

   (1)   Persistent disregard of the child's basic emotional needs for comfort, stimulation, and affection.

   (2)   Persistent disregard of the child's basic physical needs.

   (3)   Repeated changes of primary caregiver that prevent formation of stable attachments (e.g., frequent changes in foster care).

D.   There is a presumption that the care in Criterion C is responsible for the disturbed behavior in Criterion A (e.g., the disturbances in Criterion A began following the pathogenic care in Criterion C).

Specify type:

  Inhibited Type: if Criterion A1 predominates in the clinical presentation

  Disinhibited Type: if Criterion A2 predominates in the clinical presentation

Controversial and Unresolved Issues
Diagnostic Criteria

A variety of issues remain unresolved about the diagnostic criteria for reactive attachment disorder, probably because, as just described, the criteria were created without the benefit of empirical data. One issue is the criterion for the age of onset before age 5. No data show that age 5 is a better criterion than age 3 or 7 or another age in early childhood (Hanson & Spratt, 2000). The current age criterion may result in some children who develop the symptoms of reactive attachment disorder past the age of 5 not being diagnosed with the disorder. A second issue relates to the requirement that a history of pathogenic care be present. Some research since the DSM-IV was published suggests that pathogenic care may be an inappropriate criterion because some children who meet the other diagnostic criteria for reactive attachment disorder do not have a history of pathogenic care during their infancy (O'Connor, Marvin, Rutter, Olrick, & Britner, 2003). Pathogenic care may increase the likelihood of a child developing reactive attachment disorder, but it may not be necessary for the disorder to develop.

Is Reactive Attachment Disorder Being Overdiagnosed?

Hanson and Spratt (2000) raised concern that some children who have a history of maltreatment as infants are being diagnosed with reactive attachment disorder even though they do not meet all the diagnostic criteria, resulting in an overdiagnosis of reactive attachment disorder. The concern is that children exhibiting a wide range of behavior problems are being given the diagnosis of reactive attachment disorder because it is assumed by those providing the diagnosis that because they were maltreated as infants, their behaviors must reflect a primary problem with attachment. Hanson and Spratt worry that giving maltreated children who exhibit a wide range of behaviors a diagnosis of reactive attachment disorder will result in many of them receiving an inappropriate diagnosis and consequently the wrong type of treatment.

Hanson and Spratt's argument is similar to the one given by Hammen and Rudolf (2003) regarding the overdiagnosis of bipolar disorder in children (see the chapter about bipolar disorder). It is noteworthy that reactive attachment disorder and bipolar disorder have only recently begun to be diagnosed in children, and perhaps the lack of basic knowledge about these disorders provides an environment in which overdiagnosis is more likely to occur. Ongoing research may provide better diagnostic criteria for both disorders so they can be diagnosed more accurately.

Determining that an Individual Child Has Reactive Attachment Disorder

As with the other disorders discussed in this text, clinicians determine that a child meets the diagnostic criteria for reactive attachment disorder by observing the child's behaviors or by obtaining information about the child's behaviors from parents, teachers, or other adults who know the child well. In addition, the clinician must gather information about the child's early environment to determine if it was pathogenic.

Several issues complicate this process. First, information about the child's early environment may be difficult to obtain. For example, information about the early environments of children who have been removed to foster or adoptive homes may not be available (Richters & Volkmar, 1994). The birth parents may not be available to be interviewed or may be unwilling to provide accurate information about the child's early environment, particularly if they believe that doing so will impair their ability to be reunited with their child. If the child has continued to live with his or her birth parent, that parent may be reluctant to describe accurately the child's early environment, especially if the parent worries that doing so may result in the child being removed to foster care.

In addition, little information is available to help clinicians distinguish between an early environment that is problematic and one that is pathogenic (Hanson & Spratt, 2000). In some cases an infant's early environment may be clearly pathogenic, such as when an infant has been consistently confined to a dirty crib and her lack of physical growth shows that she has been chronically malnourished. In other cases, however, the nature of the child's early environment may be less clear. For example, it can be ambiguous whether an infant who has his basic physical needs met consistently but who receives little physical contact from a caregiver is experiencing a pathogenic environment.

Finally, there are no clear guidelines for distinguishing children with moderate attachment problems and those with attachment problems severe enough to warrant a diagnosis of reactive attachment disorder. As a result, if several clinicians were to assess a particular child, some might believe that his or her behavior warranted a diagnosis of reactive attachment disorders while others would disagree. Consequently, at this time there may be only moderate reliability with which children are diagnosed with reactive attachment disorder.

Key Concepts

- Although research with very deprived infants has occurred for decades, research interest in reactive attachment disorder developed only recently.
- The diagnostic criteria for reactive attachment disorder have changed in each edition of the DSM, although even the most current criteria were developed without a research base.
- Two subtypes of reactive attachment disorder have been identified: the inhibited type and the disinhibited type.
- It is not clear whether the criterion that symptoms of reactive attachment disorder are present before age 5 years is appropriate. It is also not clear whether pathogenic care must be present for the disorder to develop.
- Concerns have been raised that reactive attachment disorder is being overdiagnosed in maltreated children.
- Reactive attachment disorder is diagnosed after a clinician observes a child's behavior or receives reports from caregivers. Determining whether a child has received pathogenic care as an infant may be difficult in some cases.

Characteristics and Experiences of Children with Reactive Attachment Disorder

As already discussed, two types of reactive attachment disorder have been identified. Although reactive attachment disorder differs from insecure attachment, there are interesting connections between the two types of insecure attachment and the two subtypes of reactive attachment disorder (Haugaard & Hazan, 2003). The inhibited type of reactive attachment disorder has some connection to the avoidant type of insecure attachment in that both are characterized by a child's reluctance to initiate or respond to social contact. The disinhibited type has some connection to the anxious/resistant type of insecure attachment in terms of a child's frequent attempts to satisfy unmet needs for comfort and affection.

Core Features
Inhibited Type

Children with the inhibited type of reactive attachment disorder exhibit marked withdrawal from others (Zeanah & Boris, 2000). The characteristics of the inhibited type are most apparent when a child would be expected to turn to an adult for comfort or assistance, such as when needing a diaper changed as an infant or toddler, after falling and getting hurt as a young child, when struggling with homework as a school-age child, or after being sexually assaulted as an adolescent. Children with the inhibited type seldom seek the help of adults or peers, even when adults around them (such as caring foster parents or teachers) make it clear that they are available. It is as if the children have learned at some fundamental level that others in the world will not respond to their needs for comfort, so they have given up seeking comfort from them.

An inability to receive comfort from others may be at the foundation of the self-comforting behaviors observed in children and adolescents with reactive attachment disorder. **Stereotyped behaviors** (repetitious, rhythmic behaviors that appear to have no function, such as rocking; Nijhof, Joha, & Pekelharing, 1998) have been observed in many young children with reactive attachment disorder (Smyke, Dumitrescu, & Zeanah, 2002). Older children or adolescents may use alcohol or other drugs to soothe themselves.

An inability to turn to adults for help or comfort puts children with reactive attachment disorder at risk for physical disease (not seeking help when feeling sick), academic problems (not seeking help with schoolwork), poor peer relationships (not seeking the company of other children), or abuse (not seeking help when bullied) (Haugaard & Hazan, 2003). Consequently, children with the inhibited type of reactive attachment disorder can experience a wide range of physical, emotional, and social problems.

Disinhibited Type

Children with the disinhibited type of reactive attachment disorder may seem attached to others because they seek attention and comfort from adults (Zeanah & Boris, 2000). However, their behavior differs from that of most children in that they do not seek comfort or support from one or two primary caregivers but rather seem indiscriminate in their attempts to receive comfort and support.

Children with the disinhibited type may seek attention and comfort from strangers or people whom the child scarcely knows. Not only may this appear inappropriate to those from whom the child is seeking attention; it can place the child at risk for abuse or other problems. Young children with the disinhibited type do not obey the common rule of "do not talk with strangers" and thus put themselves at risk for interacting with adults who are interested in sexually or physically abusing them. School-age children or adolescents may seek attention from peers that is more like the attention that most children would seek from adults. Consequently, peers may experience them as pests and reject them. Other peers may abuse them because they may be willing to engage in a variety of risky behaviors to get attention (for example, a young adolescent may have sex with many older adolescents to get their attention).

Associated Features

High levels of physical aggression have been noted in some children with reactive attachment disorder. For example, when assessing a group of children with disordered attachment who had lived in orphanages in Romania, Smyke and colleagues (2002) found high levels of aggression in some toddlers and lower-than-normal levels of aggression in other toddlers in the same institution. The researchers hypothesized that some children had learned early in life that aggression resulted in obtaining more food or other necessities, and this learned behavior stayed with the children as they developed. The other children may have learned that aggression resulted in being hurt (perhaps they were not as strong or skilled at aggression as the others), so they developed a nonaggressive behavioral style.

Some authors have hypothesized that toddlers with reactive attachment disorder may develop into school-age children and adolescents who are highly aggressive (Levy & Orlans, 2000). They argue that their inability to form attachments to others results in their having none of the normal prohibitions against aggression against others, so they engage in high levels of aggression. However, it is not clear what percentage of children with reactive attachment disorder develop high levels of aggression, and further research will be needed to understand this issue more clearly.

Prevalence and Course

Almost no information exists about the prevalence of reactive attachment disorder. The most specific description in the DSM-IV-TR is a note that reactive attachment disorder "appears to be very uncommon" (APA, 2000, p. 129). Unfortunately, we also know little about the course of reactive attachment disorder (Lyons-Ruth et al., 2003). Research with children who have disordered attachment show that many of them exhibit an enduring pattern of aggression and other conduct problems during their school-age years and adolescence, suggesting that some negative consequences of disordered attachment may be long-lasting (Levy & Orlans, 1999). However, the percentage of children with disordered attachment who have enduring problems with aggression and those whose aggression and other problems may be more short-lived remains unclear.

Some information suggests that children with the inhibited type of reactive attachment disorder are more likely to recover than those with the disinhibited type. Evidence for this comes from studies of children adopted from Romanian orphanages into homes in Great Britain and Canada. Many of these adopted children exhibited symptoms of either the inhibited or disinhibited type while they were living in the orphanage before their adoption; but a few years after being adopted into nurturing homes, the percentage of children showing the inhibited type was reduced while the percentage showing the disinhibited type remained about the same (Chisholm, 1998; O'Connor, Bredenkamp, & Rutter, 1999). This suggests that placement in a nurturing environment may be particularly helpful to children with the inhibited type of reactive attachment disorder.

Notes from the Author: Child Rearing and Societal Violence

Are there consequences of societywide problems with attachment? In her intriguing history of life in the 1300s in France and England, Barbara Tuchman (1979) draws some interesting possible connections between the ways that infants and young children were raised and the level of societal violence. Regarding children, she notes, "Of all the characteristics in which the medieval age differs from the modern, none is so striking as the comparative absence of interest in children (p. 49). . . . Owing to the high infant mortality of the times, estimated at one or two in three, the investment of love in a young child may have been so unrewarding that by some ruse of nature, as when overcrowded rodents in captivity will not breed, it was suppressed. Perhaps also the frequent childbearing put less value on the product. A child was born and died and another took its place (p. 50). . . . On the whole, babies and young children appear to have been left to survive or die without great concern in the first five or six years. What psychological effect this may have had on character, and possibly on history, can only be conjectured. Possibly the relative emotional blankness of a medieval infancy may account for the casual attitude toward life and suffering of the medieval man" (p. 52).

Tuchman then describes the interest that many in medieval society had in the pain and suffering of others: "Violence was official as well as individual. The tortures and punishments of civil justice customarily cut off hands and ears, racked, burned, flayed, and pulled apart people's bodies. In everyday life passersby saw some criminal flogged with a knotted rope or chained upright in an iron collar. They passed corpses hanging on the gibbet and decapitated heads and quartered bodies impaled on stakes on the city walls. . . . In village games, players with hands tied behind them competed to kill a cat nailed to a post by battering it to death with their heads. . . . Accustomed in their own lives to physical hardship and injury, medieval men and women were not necessarily repelled by the spectacle of pain, but rather enjoyed it. . . . It may be that the untender medieval infancy produced adults who valued others no more than they had been valued in their own formative years" (p. 135).

Tuchman's analysis encourages us to think about the connection between a society's standards for raising children and the violence in that society. Could a society in which many children have the inability to attach to caregivers produce adults who are eager to inflict violence on others? Of course we cannot know for sure; but our knowledge about reactive attachment disorder makes speculating about this possibility interesting.

Key Concepts

- Children with the inhibited type of reactive attachment disorder exhibit general withdrawal from others. This withdrawal is most apparent when a child would normally seek the help of caregivers.
- Children with the disinhibited type seek comfort from many individuals rather than a primary caregiver, including strangers that most children would avoid.
- Physical aggression is exhibited by some children with reactive attachment disorder.
- Little information exists about the prevalence and course of reactive attachment disorder. Some information suggests that the disinhibited type may be more chronic than the inhibited type.

Etiology

Because reactive attachment disorder has been the focus of research for only a few years, we know little about its etiology. What we do know suggests that reactive attachment disorder usually has its foundation in environments in which an infant is deprived of the opportunity to develop an attachment to one or two primary caregivers. As described in this section, however, some children raised in very deprived environments do not show symptoms of reactive attachment disorder, and it is unclear whether certain characteristics of a child (such as temperament), the environment (level or duration of deprivation), or the caregivers (temperament or level of emotional problems) influence whether the child will develop reactive attachment disorder.

Current theorizing about the development of reactive attachment disorder comes from attachment theory (Bowlby, 1969, 1973, 1980). As described in more detail in the chapter about basic psychological theories, attachment theory states that children develop **internal working models** of relationships based on their attachment experiences in infancy. Their internal working models influence their emotions and behaviors in later relationships with caregivers, other adults, and peers. In essence, children learn about relationships from their initial attachment relationships, and their responses to future relationships are influenced by this early learning.

Some children raised in deprived environments develop a working model that includes beliefs that caregivers do not provide comfort or protection and that caregivers respond to attempts to receive comfort in a hostile, rejecting, or aggressive manner. This working model of relationships results in their avoiding

Infants who rarely have their basic needs met may not develop the ability to attach to an adult.

relationships and withdrawing from contact with others, and thus they display the symptoms associated with the inhibited type of reactive attachment disorder. Other children raised in deprived environments develop a working model that includes the belief that repeated and insistent attempts to receive comfort are met with neglect most times but are occasionally met with the comfort that is being sought. Their working model results in their frequently seeking comfort from many different people with the expectation that one or more of these people will eventually provide comfort; thus they display the symptoms associated with the disinhibited type of reactive attachment disorder.

These relationship styles have short-term benefits for a child living in a deprived environment because they can help the child survive in that environment (Haugaard & Hazan, 2003). For example, a toddler with the inhibited type of reactive attachment disorder may stop seeking comfort when hungry, lonely, or frightened because she has learned that her comfort-seeking behaviors achieve nothing and may result in angry or violent responses from caregivers. Similarly, a toddler with the disinhibited type may learn to seek comfort from any available adult because doing so increases the likelihood that he will occasionally receive it. Despite the short-term benefits of these behaviors, they create patterns of behavior that can be dysfunctional in the long term; these dysfunctional aspects of the child's style of relating to others are the symptoms of reactive attachment disorder.

It is important to note three issues before reviewing the limited research relevant to the etiology of reactive attachment disorder. First, this research has focused not on children with reactive attachment disorder but on children showing disturbances in their attachments (for example, see O'Connor et al., 2003). Consequently, the research tells us more about the development of problematic attachment than about reactive attachment disorder. Second, the two primary research programs in this area have focused on symptoms of a disinhibited attachment style, so we know more about it than the inhibited style. Finally, because most of the studies focus on children who have been raised in an institution during their infancy and then adopted by families in another country, it is not clear whether the attachment issues they face are the same as those faced by children raised by their birth parents in deprived conditions.

Studies of Children Raised in Deprived Institutions

Information about the development of attachment problems comes primarily from research with children adopted into homes in Great Britain and Canada from institutions in Romania. Soon after the fall of the Soviet Union, there was a sudden influx of infants and young children into orphanages in several countries in the former Soviet Union. Many children were placed there by destitute parents, and there was little money or staff to create a healthful environment in the institutions. Consequently, most of the children lived in very deprived conditions for months or years. Some of these children were later adopted into families in industrialized countries; and several groups of researchers followed the physical, emotional, and cognitive development of some of these children after their adoption.

The principal issue addressed to date is the association between the length of deprivation that children experience as infants and toddlers and the level of their attachment disturbance. For example, one set of studies assessed attachment disturbance in three groups of children adopted into families in Great Britain: (1) Romanian children adopted after spending 6 months or less in a Romanian orphanage; (2) Romanian children adopted after spending 7 to 24 months in a Romanian orphanage; and (3) children adopted from families in Great Britain who had not experienced severe deprivation. Two percent of the adopted children from Great Britain, 10% of the Romanians adopted before 6 months, and 21% of the Romanians adopted between 7 and 24 months showed moderate disturbance in their attachment when they were 4 years of age. Similar patterns were found during the assessment at 6 years, suggesting that the levels of disturbance were stable over this two-year period (O'Connor et al., 2003; O'Connor et al., 1999).

In another study with these same children, the security of their attachments was measured using a separation–reunion task similar to the **Strange Situation** developed by Ainsworth and her colleagues (see the chapter about basic psychological theories for a description of the Strange Situation). Approximately 55% of the children from Great Britain, 40% of the Romanian children adopted before 6 months, and 33% of the Romanian children adopted between 7 and 24 months showed secure attachments. A substantial portion of the Romanian children showed behavior patterns that were not classifiable using the Strange Situation (33% of those adopted before 6 months and 51% of those adopted between 7 and 24 months—compared to 16% of the children adopted from families in Great Britain). Thus many of the Romanian children exhibited behaviors that were uncharacteristic of attachment, and this percentage was higher among children adopted after spending more time in a deprived environment than among those spending less time in a deprived environment (O'Connor et al., 2003).

The second program of research has been following (1) 30 children who were in a Romanian orphanage for fewer than four months before adoption into a Canadian family; (2) 46 children who spent at least eight months in a Romanian orphanage before being adopted by a Canadian family; and (3) 46 nonadopted, never-institutionalized Canadian children. Attachment security and indiscriminate friendliness were assessed at about age 2 years (Chisholm, Carter, Ames, & Morison, 1995) and age 4½ years (Chisholm, 1998). At 2 years, the parents of the later-adopted Romanian children rated them significantly lower on security of attachment and significantly higher on indiscriminate friendliness than did the parents of the earlier-adopted or nonadopted children, and the scores of those in the latter two groups did not differ. At 4½ years there were no differences in security of attachment among the children in the three groups. However, differences did emerge on a separation–reunion task: 58% of the Canadian children had a secure attachment, compared with 65% of the earlier-adopted and 37% of the later-adopted children. In addition, 52% of the later-adopted children showed atypical patterns of attachment, compared with 17% of the Canadian children and 11% of the earlier-adopted children. The later-adopted children also continued to display more indiscriminate friendliness than the children in the two other groups.

Taken together, these studies show that children experiencing lengthier deprived institutional living are more likely to experience attachment disturbance than those living in an institution for shorter periods. Children living in an institution for shorter periods did not appear much different from adopted or nonadopted children who had not lived in a deprived environment. Thus it appears that a relatively short period of deprivation may not have an influence on the development of attachment problems.

Another important finding of one study was that a significant proportion of children living in a deprived environment for a long period showed no indications of attachment disruption: 38% of the Romanians adopted between 7 and 24 months showed no measurable disturbance (O'Connor et al., 2003; O'Connor et al., 1999). Thus living in a deprived environment as an infant and toddler does not appear to be sufficient to cause attachment disruption. Also of interest is the small percentage of children who had experienced no known significant deprivation yet showed symptoms of disturbed attachment. Perhaps some of these children experienced significant deprivation of which the researchers were unaware; or other childhood experiences may have influenced the development of their disturbed attachment. As already noted, it is not clear why some children develop problems with attachment and others do not, and future research will need to focus on this issue.

Key Concepts

- Children living for longer periods in a deprived environment as infants and toddlers are more likely to develop attachment problems than those living in a deprived environment for shorter periods.
- Some children who have not lived in a deprived environment exhibit signs of disordered attachment.

Preventive and Therapeutic Interventions

Prevention

Although prevention of reactive attachment disorder has received little attention in the clinical or research literature, two groups of studies provide some guidance about how reactive attachment disorder and other problems with attachment may be prevented. The first studies focused on infants at risk for developing attachment problems because their mothers had difficulty parenting them appropriately. These studies found that interventions to help the mother parent her child well, develop a closer emotional relationship with her child, and provide a healthful home environment resulted in higher levels of secure attachments than occurred in families that did not receive the intervention. Thus these studies suggest that helping mothers develop healthy relationships with their infants may reduce attachment problems (Toth, Maughan, Manly, Spagnola, & Cicchetti, 2002; Van den Boom, 1994).

The studies with adopted Romanian children also provide some guidance in this area. As just described, these studies showed that some infants and toddlers who have lived in deprived environments develop appropriate attachment relationships to adults once they are placed in nurturing families (Chisholm, 1998; O'Connor et al., 2003). In particular, those placed early in life, before attachment relationships developed completely, were the most likely to form normal attachment relationships with their adoptive parents. Although the percentage of children adopted after six months who formed appropriate attachment relationships with their adoptive parents was lower than those adopted before six months, many of them also formed secure attachments. Thus these studies suggest that placing deprived infants and toddlers in nurturing families may prevent the onset of disturbed attachment relationships in some children, even if placement occurs after the normal age of attachment to a primary caregiver. However, it remains unclear which children are most likely to benefit from placement in a nurturing home or what qualities of these nurturing homes are more likely to protect a child from developing reactive attachment disorder.

Therapeutic Interventions for Children and Families

To date, no therapeutic interventions based on attachment theory have been created to intervene directly with children to change their disturbed attachment patterns (Steele, 2003). However, several interventions for families of children with attachment problems have been created. Many of these have focused on foster and adoptive families into which maltreated children have been placed.

Most children placed into foster or adoptive homes have a history of severe maltreatment, and many of them experience multiple foster care placements even if they are eventually adopted into a permanent adoptive family (Goodman, Emery, & Haugaard, 1998). Consequently, the experience of most of these children is that adults mistreat and abandon them. It is reasonable but sad, therefore, that they are unwilling to form relationships with adults; and they may actively resist developing these relationships to shield themselves from further emotional turmoil. (You may have friends who have decided after several tumultuous romantic relationships that they will not become involved in another relationship; in many ways this is the same experience that some young children have in their relationships with adults.) Foster and adoptive parents may be troubled by the lack of a relationship between them and their children, and they may react in ways that perpetuate the children's difficulty with relationships. For example, an adoptive parent may stop trying to comfort a child who has difficulty accepting that comfort. This can reinforce the child's beliefs about adults being unavailable and strengthen the child's behavior.

Several therapeutic efforts have been designed to interrupt this pattern of parent–child interactions and help the parents create an environment in which their adoptive or foster children can gradually form relationships with them. Education about disordered attachment is a vital part of these therapeutic interventions (Sheperis, Renfro Michel, & Doggett, 2003). Parents of adopted and foster children are helped to understand that their children's behavior is reasonable given their history and are helped to understand the reasons for their children's resistance to developing relationships in their new families. In addition, parents are told that changing their children's difficulty with relationships will be a long process because the children will repeatedly test relationships to assess whether they are supportive and permanent.

As part of many interventions, parents are taught to be *sensitively relentless* in providing support and warmth to their foster or adoptive children even when the children seem to reject that support and warmth (Dozier, 2003). For example, if a parent attempts to pick up a young child who is crying and the child resists being picked up, the parent is encouraged to provide comfort that may be a bit more distant—such as talking in a comforting tone or touching the child on the shoulder—rather than leaving the child alone. Providing this type of comfort can be difficult for many parents, and they may need ongoing support and guidance from a therapist. In addition, the parents may be encouraged to actively seek support from others. Each member of a couple may provide support to the other, or the parents may seek support from other relatives or friends. Some parents of adopted or foster children have formed support groups with other adoptive or foster parents to provide mutual support.

Some interventions focus on the child with attachment problems, although these usually do not address attachment issues directly. For example, because many children with attachment problems have poor relationships with peers, working with them to understand the value of peer relationships and how to go about forming them can be important (Hanson & Spratt, 2000). Repeated work on peer relationships may be needed because the squabbles that are part of most peer relationships may be experienced as significant rejections by children with attachment problems.

A controversial therapy for attachment disorders is known as **holding therapy.** Its proponents describe holding therapy as a strategy for releasing a child's inner rage, thereby allowing him or her to attach successfully to his or her parents (Wilson, 2001). During holding therapy sessions, the child is restrained and is then provoked and aroused by the clinician yelling, poking the child, tickling the child, or pulling on her limbs (Hanson & Spratt, 2000). The child typically resists and becomes very angry but eventually breaks down and surrenders. At this point the child is placed in the arms of his or her parents with the goal of promoting attachment.

Holding therapy has increased in popularity, in part because of the frustration that adoptive and other parents have had in changing the behaviors of their children who have reactive attachment disorder. Holding therapy offers new hope for successfully treating children with reactive attachment disorder, and its proponents cite examples of children with whom it has been successful. However, it has been criticized because of the vulnerability of the children who are required to participate in the therapy—particularly children who have been severely physically or sexually abused; and it has been described by some as continuing the trauma that these children have experienced in other settings (Hanson & Spratt, 2000).

Key Concepts

- Interventions for mothers who are at risk for developing dysfunctional attachment relationships with their infants have increased the number of secure attachments.
- Placing severely deprived infants in nurturing adoptive homes has reduced the number experiencing attachment problems.
- Educational efforts to assist foster and adoptive parents in providing appropriate parenting to children with attachment problems may help the children gradually develop appropriate attachment relationships with these parents.
- Holding therapy is new and controversial. Proponents claim that holding therapy helps establish an attachment relationship between a child and parents; opponents claim that it continues the trauma faced by these children earlier in their lives.

Chapter Glossary

Alternate personality identities is the phrase used in this text for the unintegrated aspects of a child's personality that appear to be distinct personalities.

Amnesia is a loss of memory.

The **amygdala** is an almond-shaped structure in the limbic system associated with the experience of emotion and with motivation and aggression. It also plays a role in memory through its connections to the hippocampus.

Anaclitic depression is a state of severe withdrawal observed in infants raised in institutions where they received little human contact.

Anxiety disorder not otherwise specified is a disorder in the anxiety disorders category in the DSM-IV-TR. It can be diagnosed in children who show many symptoms of PTSD, acute stress disorder, or other anxiety disorders, but who do not meet all the diagnostic criteria for any anxiety disorder.

Attachment theory was developed by John Bowlby and describes an innate behavioral process through which infants become attached to a primary caregiver.

Cortisol is a hormone in the glucocorticoid group that is secreted by the adrenal gland and that helps prepare the body to face threats during stress.

Declarative memories are conscious memories related to events and facts.

Discrete behavioral states, commonly associated with infancy, are unique organizations of behavior and consciousness.

Emotional numbing is experienced by many children with PTSD and includes flat affect and withdrawal from the environment.

Flashbacks are memories of a traumatic event in which a child feels as if the traumatic event is recurring and reexperiences many of the same emotions and thoughts experienced during the trauma.

A **fugue** is a period of travel for which a person has no memory.

The **hippocampus** is part of the limbic system and is involved in emotion, motivation, and the consolidation of declarative memories.

Holding therapy is a controversial form of therapy for children with reactive attachment disorder that involves restraining and provoking the child, and then placing the child in the arms of his or her primary caregivers when the child surrenders to this provocation.

Hypervigilance refers to a state of heightened physiological arousal in which a person attends intensely to the environment for possible sources of physical or psychological threat.

The **hypothalamic–pituitary–adrenal (HPA) axis** is a self-regulating system that is part of the endocrine system. It has an important role in the regulation of basic functions such as hunger, sleep, mood, and sexual activity.

The **hypothalamus** is a small area of the brain below both sides of the thalamus in the limbic system that is involved in basic functions such as heart rate, hunger, sleep, aggression, and the fight-or-flight reaction.

Implicit memories are emotional memories or those that are unconscious and relate to behaviors.

Children develop an **internal working model** of relationships from their first attachment relationship; this model influences their future relationships and how they behave in them.

The **locus coeruleus** is an area in the brain near the pons that contains neurons that secrete norepinephrine and serotonin. It is involved in the experience of anxiety and fear.

Multiple personality disorder is the name for **dissociative identity disorder** used in the DSM-III and the DSM-III-R.

Pathogenic care is care that is likely to cause significant physical and psychological problems in a developing child.

The **prefrontal cortex** is the foremost part of the frontal cortex and is involved in behavioral planning, working memory, abstract thinking, and anxiety.

The **startle response** is the reaction a person has when surprised by something or someone.

Stereotyped behaviors are repetitious, rhythmic behaviors that appear to have no function, such as rocking.

The **Strange Situation** is an assessment of young children's attachment, developed by Mary Ainsworth and her colleagues, that observes how 18- to 24-month-old children react to separations and reunifications with their primary caregivers.

Trance states are believed to indicate that a child is actively engaging in dissociation or that one alternate personality identity is being replaced by another.

A **traumatic event**, as used in the diagnostic criteria for PTSD, requires that (1) a person experience or witness an event involving actual or threatened death, severe injury, or loss of physical integrity to self or others and (2) the person responds to this event with intense fear, helplessness, or horror.

Ventricles are cavities in the brain filled with cerebrospinal fluid (also cavities in the heart filled with blood).

Disorders Related to Physical Health and Functioning

Early eating habits can have long-lasting effects on a child's health.

In this chapter we explore several disorders and one problem, childhood obesity, that involve a clear connection between a psychological disorder and a medical condition. The understanding of disease in most Western cultures usually involves a distinction between medical conditions and psychological disorders (Campo & Garber, 1998). Physical symptoms are believed to be caused by an underlying medical condition, and the goal of physicians is to identify and treat the medical condition and thus end the symptoms. For example, a physician may conclude that a child with stomach pains and a fever has a bacterial infection in her digestive tract. The physician's goal is to treat the bacterial infection successfully, thereby eliminating the symptoms of pain and fever. In the same way, psychological symptoms are believed to be caused by an underlying psychological disorder; the goal of many mental health practitioners is to identify and treat the underlying psychological disorder, thereby ending the symptoms of the disorder. For example, a psychologist might conclude that a child's sadness, lethargy, and social withdrawal are caused by major depression. The psychologist's goal is to treat the major depression successfully, thereby eliminating the symptoms of sadness, lethargy, and social withdrawal.

As we have seen throughout this text, however, a clear-cut distinction between medical conditions and psychological disorders is often not appropriate. Many psychological disorders have physical symptoms, such as the heightened physiological arousal that is often present in anxiety disorders. Similarly, we have come to understand more clearly that psychological issues can influence the symptom severity of many medical conditions such as asthma or diabetes.

The disorders discussed in this chapter present an even stronger challenge to the clear-cut distinction between medical conditions and psychological disorders (Kirmayer & Young, 1998). One category of disorders we examine, somatoform disorders, have a psychological foundation but cause physical pain and suffering. Another category of disorders, elimination disorders, are usually caused by physical problems but can result in psychological pain and suffering.

Finally, eating disorders and childhood obesity, which are usually influenced by a mixture of physical and psychological issues, have consequences that can harm a person's physical and psychological health for months, years, or decades.

As discussed in all the chapters in this text, the preventive and therapeutic interventions used for each disorder are based on an understanding of the influences on the development of the disorder. We will also see this clearly in this chapter: The interventions for each disorder involve a mixture of medical and psychological treatments—showing that each of them develops through a blend of medical and psychological influences.

Chapter Plan

As with the chapter about disorders related to trauma, we follow a plan that is somewhat different from the plan of most other chapters in this text. This chapter is divided into four main sections: one about somatoform disorders, one about childhood obesity, one about the eating disorders anorexia nervosa and bulimia nervosa, and one about elimination disorders. In each section a vignette is presented to illustrate some of the challenges posed by these disorders. We then explore the diagnostic criteria, clinical presentation, prevalence, and course of each type of disorder. After exploring theories and research focused on the etiology of each disorder, we examine preventive and therapeutic interventions for them.

Somatoform Disorders and Somatization Problems

Somatization occurs when psychological distress such as anger, sadness, or stress is expressed through physical symptoms such as headaches, stomach pains, or blurred vision (*somatization* comes from the Greek *soma,* "body," and *izein,* "to become or resemble") (Campo & Fritsch, 1994; Campo & Garber, 1998). Children experiencing somatization have physical symptoms for which there is an insufficient medical explanation. In some cases no medical condition can be found that is causing the child's physical symptoms. For example, a child may have frequent stomachaches, and several examinations by a physician and extensive medical testing may not uncover any medical condition causing them. In other cases, a child's physical symptoms are more severe or chronic than would be expected from a medical condition that he or she has. For example, a child with occasional ear infections may experience pain that is more severe than would be expected from her infections.

When somatization symptoms are severe, chronic, or appear in a specific pattern, a child may be diagnosed with a *somatoform disorder.* These disorders are discussed in the first part of this chapter. However, children rarely experience the combination of symptoms required for the diagnosis of most somatoform disorders, and young children are particularly unlikely to experience the required symptoms (APA, 2000). Consequently, we also address the process of somatization more generally—exploring the types of somatization that are most common in children and current theories about their development and treatment.

Somatoform disorders, and somatization in general, are not diagnosed when a child is purposely faking an illness or making up symptoms. Children with somatization problems truly experience their physical symptoms: Their heads or stomachs ache, their hearing is impaired, or they have difficulty moving their legs (Campo & Garber, 1998). The diagnosis for a child or adult who is faking symptoms or purposely trying to appear sick is either **factitious disorder** or **malingering**. The difference between these two disorders is that malingering involves assuming a sick role to obtain some external incentives, such as a child trying to avoid having to participate in physical education classes. No external incentives need to be involved in factitious disorder (APA, 2000).

Somatization and somatoform disorders have been described as the "scourge" of many physicians and mental health providers (Mullins & Olson, 1990). Parents of children who have problems with somatization turn repeatedly to their pediatricians or family physicians to discover the medical causes of their children's symptoms, and the physicians cannot diagnose any such causes. This can lead to frustration for the parents, children, and physicians and can lead some physicians to doubt their competence. If a physician refers a child to a psychologist or other mental health professional, the child and parents may interpret this as an indication that the physician believes there is nothing wrong with the child physically and that the problem is "all in the child's head." This can create anger toward the physician and the psychologist to whom the child and family are referred. In addition, there can always be the suspicion that an unidentified medical condition is causing the child's symptoms, which can cause concern in all who are involved (Campo & Garber, 1998). Consequently, work with children who have problems with somatization and their families can be stressful and must be accomplished with sensitivity and tact.

Case Study: The Function of a Child's Injury in Her Family

Lauren and her brother, Sam, lived with their parents in an affluent suburb. Their mother was a lawyer and their father was an accountant. Both worked many hours each week, so Lauren and her brother were often cared for by babysitters. When Lauren was 7 and her brother 4, Lauren's parents began arguing with increasing frequency, primarily about how to parent Sam. Sam had been hyperactive as a preschooler, and when he entered kindergarten his hyperactivity had become more of a problem. Lauren's father believed that his wife should work fewer hours so she could monitor Sam's behavior at home and work with him at school if needed; but Lauren's mother had recently become a partner in her law firm and was not interested in curtailing her hours at work. Besides, she did not see the potential benefit to Sam if she were to be home more often. Lauren's parents also disagreed about how frequently to discipline Sam for his behavior and whether he should be placed on medication.

When Lauren was 9 and her brother 6, their father lost his job after a merger of his accounting firm with another. Although this created a financial burden on the family, between their savings and cutbacks on vacations and entertaining, Lauren's parents believed they would manage financially until Lauren's father found a new job. However, the arguing between Lauren's parents increased because her mother felt that her father was not pursuing a new job with sufficient intensity. Lauren's father, meanwhile, found that he liked being at home and caring for the children.

About two months after Lauren's father lost his job, Lauren fell out of a tree one Saturday and broke her right arm severely. Both parents were home at the time, and they rushed her to the hospital, where her arm was set and she was given pain medication. The physician recommended that Lauren stay home from school for a few days, saying that her pain should decrease over the next few days and then she could return to school.

However, Lauren continued to experience pain in her arm throughout the next week, and this pain gradually spread to her shoulder. She found it difficult to attend school because any movement of her arm was painful, so she stayed home a few days that week. X-rays of her arm and shoulder revealed no structural problems, but Lauren's pain persisted. Lauren began to miss school with greater frequency, but her father was home most days and could care for her easily. As her pain continued past one month, her parents consulted with two pediatric orthopedists, but neither could find an explanation for Lauren's pain. Both orthopedists encouraged Lauren to attend school even if her arm hurt, but Lauren's attendance continued to be sporadic.

Lauren's parents became increasingly concerned about her pain and began to search for other physicians who could discover its cause. Lauren's father took most of the responsibility for finding appropriate medical care for her. During this time, Lauren's parents' disagreement about Sam's hyperactive behavior diminished, and luckily, they thought, reports of his misbehavior at school decreased.

During a scheduled physical exam about six months after her injury, Lauren's pediatrician recommended that Lauren's parents consult with a child psychologist about her ongoing arm and shoulder pain. Her parents reacted angrily to the recommendation, saying that the problem was not in Lauren's head but in her arm and shoulder—a problem that none of the physicians had enough skill to find. The pediatrician persisted, however, and argued that until the source of Lauren's pain could be discovered, a psychologist could help Lauren and her family cope with the pain as effectively as possible. This seemed to satisfy Lauren's parents, and they set up an appointment with a psychologist the next week.

The psychologist commiserated with Lauren and her parents about the difficulty they faced coping with Lauren's pain. She talked with all of them about the ways in which Lauren's thinking and emotions could influence the intensity of her pain and about how her parents might be inadvertently influencing the intensity of Lauren's pain. She suggested several ways for Lauren's parents to change how they interacted with Lauren when her arm hurt, and she taught Lauren relaxation and other techniques for diverting her attention from the pain in her arm. After several weeks Lauren's pain had diminished, and she returned to school regularly. The psychologist encouraged Lauren's father to resume his search for a new job and encouraged her parents to continue to visit the psychologist every other week so they could discuss the best ways to work together parenting Lauren and her brother.

Some Issues Worth Noting

- The association between Lauren's ongoing pain and the reduction in Sam's behavior problems at school.
- The influence of Lauren's injury on her parents' behaviors.
- The strategy used by Lauren's pediatrician to get her parents to consult a psychologist.

Diagnosis and Assessment of Somatoform Disorders

As noted earlier, although many children experience somatization problems, most children's somatization is not extensive enough to meet the diagnostic criteria for a somatoform disorder (Campo & Fritsch, 1994; Garralda, 1999). This is primarily because the diagnostic criteria for somatoform disorders were developed from research and clinical observations with adults. Because few children meet the diagnostic criteria for a somatoform disorder, we focus on these criteria only briefly in this section.

Diagnostic Criteria for the Somatoform Disorders

All somatoform disorders involve the presence of physical symptoms that suggest a medical condition but that are not fully explained by a medical condition (APA, 2000). As noted earlier, in some cases symptoms will occur and no medical condition can be discovered that explain them; in other cases a medical condition is present but does not explain the severity of the symptoms. In addition, all the somatoform disorders require that either (1) medical treatment is sought repeatedly or (2) significant distress or impairment is caused by the physical symptoms (such as frequent pain or frequent absences from school). Information about the following disorders comes from APA (2000) and other sources, as noted.

Somatization disorder involves a pattern of multiple, recurring physical symptoms. Symptoms in each of four areas must be present—pain, gastrointestinal, sexual, and **pseudoneurological.** The symptoms must appear before age 30 and must occur over several years (although typically they fluctuate in intensity over the years). The requirement of an extensive combination of symptoms, and the requirement of a symptom of sexual functioning, make it unlikely that a child will be diagnosed with somatization disorder (Campo & Fritsch, 1994).

Undifferentiated somatoform disorder is diagnosed when one or more physical symptoms that cannot be fully explained by a medical condition are present for at least six months. Because of the requirement of only one physical symptom and the shorter period over which the symptom must be present, this is the somatoform disorder that is most commonly diagnosed with children (Dhossche, van der Steen, & Ferdinand, 2002).

Body dysmorphic disorder involves a preoccupation with an imagined or a slightly defective aspect of a child's physical appearance (a small bump on the nose, a discoloration of a small patch of skin). The issue is not that the slight or imagined defect is believed to be a symptom of a severe disease (which is hypochondriasis, described later), but that the defect is perceived as a significant deformity. Children with body dysmorphic disorder can spend hours each day worrying about their perceived deformity, and they may work hard to hide it from others. In many ways, body dysmorphic disorder has characteristics similar to those of **obsessive–compulsive disorder** (described in the chapter about anxiety disorders) in that a child thinks about the perceived physical problem often and frequently engages in behaviors such as checking the body part in a mirror. Interestingly, selective serotonin reuptake inhibitors (SSRIs)—medications that are effective in the treatment of obsessive–compulsive disorder—provide effective treatment for some children who have body dysmorphic disorder. This reinforces the belief that body dysmorphic disorder and obsessive–compulsive disorder may be related (Albertini & Phillips, 1999).

Albertini and Phillips (1999) studied 33 children diagnosed with body dysmorphic disorder. Thirty were female although, among adults, about equal numbers of men and women experience body dysmorphic disorder (APA, 2000). The average number of body areas that were of concern was five, and the areas of the body that were most often the source of concern were the skin (60% of cases), hair (55%), weight (48%), face (39%) teeth (30%), legs (27%), and nose (27%). The distress over the perceived problems was "severe" for 61% of the children and "extreme and disabling" for 11%, although the researchers could see nothing abnormal about any of the body areas that concerned the children. The most common impairment was social withdrawal. Most of the children avoided others because of embarrassment about their perceived physical unattractiveness.

Conversion disorder is diagnosed when one or more symptoms occur involving voluntary motor or sensory functions that suggest a neurological condition, such as a sudden inability to walk or sudden blindness. The initiation or exacerbation of the symptoms must be linked to specific psychological conflicts or stressors. For example, a child who suddenly cannot move her arms may have recently been in a fight with another child; or a child who suddenly cannot hear may have recently heard his parents arguing violently. Conversion disorder occurs in adolescents more frequently than school-age children, and it occurs rarely in young children (Beasley & DeMaso, 1997).

Spierings, Poels, Sijben, and Gabreels (1990) examined the case files of 84 children with conversion disorder. They found about twice the number of females as males among adolescents, but equal numbers of younger girls and boys. The most common symptoms involved pain (either heightened pain reactions or anesthesia) or seizures that often included the loss of consciousness. About 60% of the children had experienced a medical condition requiring hospitalization earlier in their lives, suggesting that experiencing a severe medical condition may play a role in the development of conversion disorder in some children. Although many adults with conversion disorder have the characteristic called *la belle indifference,* which is an apparent lack of concern about their symptoms (APA, 2000), few of the children studied by Spiering and colleagues experienced *la belle indifference;* most expressed concern about their sudden unexplained symptoms.

Pain disorder is diagnosed when the primary symptom is pain in one or more areas of the body. As with the other somatoform disorders, the pain does not have to be due entirely to psychological issues but may involve pain from a medical condition that is more severe than would be expected.

Hypochondriasis is diagnosed when a child is preoccupied with fears of having a serious disease, based on a misinterpretation of physical symptoms.

For example, a child may be preoccupied with fears that her occasional stomachaches indicate that she has stomach cancer or that a bump on her head indicates that she has a brain tumor. The fear or belief must be present for at least six months and must persist in spite of medical evidence that the serious disease is not present.

Determining that an Individual Child Has a Somatoform Disorder

Diagnosing a somatoform disorder is complicated by the fact that these disorders are diagnosed only when a physician cannot identify a medical condition that explains a child's physical symptoms (Campo & Garber, 1998). Determining that no medical condition is present is often more complicated than determining that one is present, which may result in a physician never being completely certain about the diagnosis of a somatoform disorder.

In addition to the complexity of diagnosing a somatoform disorder, several issues can delay the diagnosis for months or years. First, because missing a medical condition can have significant consequences for a child's health, physicians often feel pressured to do one more test or give one more examination to be sure no medical condition exists. Second, when a physician suggests that a child's symptoms may not be due to a medical condition, the child and parents may feel angry or insulted and may question the physician's competence (Kozlowska, 2003). This may delay the diagnosis of a somatoform disorder if the physician retreats from a discussion of the possible psychological influences on the child's symptoms and returns to exploring for a medical condition (Seltzer, 1985). Finally, indecisiveness by a physician may encourage a family to seek medical care from another physician, which can begin again the entire process of searching for the medical condition causing the child's symptoms.

Notes from the Author: Finding Rare Diseases

A paper written by one of my students recently brought to my attention the issue of medical and psychological influences on physical symptoms. In one of my courses, students have the option of analyzing one of their own problematic adolescent behaviors. One student wrote about what was considered a case of depression that she experienced for many years as a child and adolescent. She had many symptoms of depression: little energy or interest in activities, sleeping for long periods, lack of appetite, and withdrawal from others. After several years of being "depressed," she was finally discovered to have Lyme disease—a disease that is well known now but was not well known when she was a child. Medical treatment for her Lyme disease significantly reduced the symptoms that had been attributed to her depression, although unfortunately the undiagnosed Lyme disease had advanced to the point that it produced some permanent neurological problems.

It can be easy for us to fault physicians for not encouraging families to consider possible psychological issues related to physical symptoms when no medical condition is apparent. However, the example provided by my student shows that an undiagnosed rare disease may cause physical symptoms in a few cases. Knowing about these infrequent cases can prompt physicians to continue a search for a medical condition, although that search may frequently be futile. Missing a medical condition can have significant, permanent health consequences for children; thus many physicians will search long and hard to identify one that might be present.

At some point a physician may determine that psychological issues are playing an important role in a child's physical symptoms because of the inability to identify a medical condition causing them. If communicated to the child and parents effectively, this determination can help the child and family expand their thinking about the child's symptoms and involve a psychologist or other mental health professional in the child's treatment. If the interventions suggested by the psychologist reduce or eliminate the physical symptoms, the accuracy of the diagnosis of a somatoform disorder is strengthened (Garralda, 1999).

Considering Cultural Issues

The beliefs of people in some non-Western cultures, and the medical practices in some non-Western cultures, result in higher rates of somatization in those cultures (Kirmayer & Young, 1998). For example, there are higher rates of somatization among people in India, Turkey, and Vietnam than in most Western cultures (Campo & Garber, 1998; Kirmayer & Young, 1998). The reasons for these higher rates are varied. In some cultures, the expression of emotions such as sadness or anger is more acceptable through physical symptoms than psychological symptoms, resulting in more people expressing their emotions through physical symptoms. In addition, in many nonindustrialized countries there are few opportunities for people to receive psychotherapy, and the only access to treatment for any disorder is through a medical clinic. Consequently, emotional issues expressed through physical symptoms are more likely to receive some attention than those expressed through psychological symptoms.

Those working with children from diverse cultures must be aware of the meaning and acceptability of psychological and physical symptoms in those cultures, if interventions acceptable to the child and family are to be provided. Requiring that a child or family accept the sharp distinction between psychological and physical symptoms that is commonly accepted in Western cultures can impede the child and family from seeking care or responding favorably to psychological interventions. In addition, requiring that a child and family agree that a child's physical symptoms are caused by psychological issues as part of treatment may push children and families away from needed treatment. As discussed throughout this text, understanding how disorders are understood by children and families from different cultures is essential if good care is to be provided to them.

Key Concepts

- All somatoform disorders involve the presence of physical symptoms that suggest a medical condition but are not fully explained by a medical condition.
- Somatization disorder involves a pattern of multiple, recurring physical symptoms in each of four areas: pain, gastrointestinal, sexual, and pseudoneurological.
- Undifferentiated somatoform disorder is the most commonly diagnosed somatoform disorder in children; it is diagnosed when one or more symptoms are present for at least six months.
- Body dysmorphic disorder involves a preoccupation with an imagined or a slightly defective aspect of a child's body that is believed to represent a significant physical deformity.
- Conversion disorder is diagnosed when one or more symptoms involving voluntary motor or sensory functions occur and the symptoms can be linked to psychological conflicts or stressors.
- Pain disorder is diagnosed when the primary physical symptom is pain.
- Hypochondriasis involves a preoccupation with fears of having a serious disease, based on a misinterpretation of physical symptoms that persists despite medical evidence that the serious disease is not present.
- Diagnosing somatoform disorders is complicated because they are diagnosed only when no medical explanation for the child's symptoms can be found, and it may be difficult to determine that a rare or undiscovered medical condition is not causing the symptoms.
- Higher rates of somatoform disorders are found in some non-Western cultures, and this may be influenced by cultural values related to physical and psychological disorders and by access to health care.

Somatization Problems

Although only a small percentage of children meet the diagnostic criteria for a somatoform disorder, many children experience problems with somatization. In this section we explore the experiences of these children and the types of therapeutic interventions used to reduce their somatization problems.

Characteristics and Experiences of Children with Somatization Problems and Their Families

Little research on the characteristics of children with somatization problems has been completed, so we are just beginning to learn about them. Most such research has focused on the presence of comorbid disorders, and several studies have found that many children with somatization problems experience high levels of anxiety or anxiety disorders (Hyams, Burke, Davis, Rzepski, & Andrulonis, 1996; Walker, Garber, & Greene, 1993). Some children with somatization problems also experience high levels of depression (Hyams et al., 1996). What remains unclear from these few studies is (1) whether certain characteristics of the children or the children's experiences result in their having higher levels of both anxiety/depression and somatization problems, (2) whether their somatization problems create increased feelings of anxiety or depression, or (3) whether their heightened anxiety or depression is expressed through more frequent physical symptoms. Additional longitudinal research that compares the timing of anxiety/depression symptoms and somatization problems will be needed before the associations between these disorders can be better understood.

Clinical reports of children with somatization problems note that many of them are well-behaved, high-achieving children who are eager to please their parents, teachers, and other adults (Kozlowska, 2003). Interviews with these children suggest that they believe that they cannot express the occasional anger, frustration, or hostility they feel because of their desire to please adults. One hypothesis about the development of somatization problems in these children is that they express their anger, frustration, and hostility through somatic symptoms (Campo & Fritsch, 1994; Fritz, Fritsch, & Hagino, 1997). The extent to which this is true for many or most children with somatization problems awaits more systematic research; but these clinical observations suggest one way in which somatization symptoms can develop in children.

Many children with somatization problems have parents who experience physical symptoms, suggesting a connection between children's and parents' symptoms (Campo & Garber, 1998). For example, a clinical study found that 54% of children with conversion disorder had symptoms that mimicked a medical condition of one of their parents (Spierings et al., 1990). Similarly, Walker and colleagues (1993) found that abdominal pain symptoms increased in parents after their children were diagnosed with **recurrent abdominal pain.**

Two types of families have been described in clinical reports of children with somatization problems. The first type was described as chaotic and disorganized, with the parents experiencing many somatic symptoms (Goodyer & Taylor, 1985; Volkmar, Poll, & Lewis, 1984). The children experienced considerable stress because of their family situations, and it was hypothesized that they expressed this stress through somatization symptoms that were similar to those of their parents. The second type of family appeared to have no obvious problems and was characterized by high expectations for achievement, high anxiety, and high levels of concern about illness and loss (Kozlowska, 2003). As just noted, the high-achieving children who were commonly found in these families were believed to express their emotions through physical symptoms, resulting in the development of somatization symptoms. What is not known at this time is the percentage of families characterized by either of these patterns. Because the reports come from clinical samples, families with healthier functioning may not have been included in them. As is true with many issues discussed in this chapter, more systematic research will be required before we can more clearly understand how frequently either of these patterns exists in families that have children with problematic somatization.

Key Concepts

- Many children with somatization problems report high levels of anxiety, and some report symptoms of depression.
- Clinical reports from children with somatization problems show that some are well-behaved, high-achieving children who are eager to please adults.
- Many children with somatization problems have parents with physical symptoms, and their symptoms are often similar.
- Two types of families of children with somatization problems have been described in clinical reports: one that is chaotic and disorganized and one that has few obvious problems and has high expectations for achievement, high anxiety, and high levels of concern about illness and loss.

Prevalence and Course

Many studies have explored the prevalence of frequent physical symptoms among children. A shortcoming of these studies is that almost none have been comprehensive enough to assess whether the reported symptoms were due to a medical condition (Campo & Garber, 1998). Consequently, while we know something about the physical symptoms of children, we do not know what percentages of those symptoms are influenced significantly by psychological issues. The general assumption is that some of them are, but their percentages remain unknown.

Several physical complaints occur frequently among school-age children and adolescents. Across studies, 10–30% of school-age children report headaches that occur at least weekly, and 10–25% report recurring abdominal pain (Campo & Garber, 1998). A study of adolescents found that about 15% reported weekly abdominal pain and that 21% reported abdominal pain that was occasionally severe enough to curtail their activities (Hyams et al., 1996). Pains in limbs (commonly called "growing pains") have been reported in 5–20% of children and adolescents across several studies, and weekly chest pain has been reported by 7–15% (Campo & Garber, 1998). Fatigue is commonly reported by adolescents, with one study finding that 15% reported daily fatigue (Garber, Walker, & Zeman, 1991) and another that half the adolescents reported fatigue at least once a week (Larson, 1991).

There appears to be little or no difference in the frequency of somatic complaints between prepubertal girls and boys. However, more females than males report somatic complaints after puberty (Campo, Jansen McWilliams, Comer, & Kelleher, 1999; Egger, Costello, Erkanli, & Angold, 1999). There is some suggestion that this difference occurs because of a decrease in symptoms reported by males after puberty and little change in the frequency of symptoms reported by females, rather than an increase in females' physical symptoms (Garber et al., 1991).

Little is known about the course of physical symptoms in children and adolescents because few longitudinal studies in this area have been undertaken. Two studies suggest that, once begun, physical symptoms can be chronic in many children. One study found that six years after their diagnosis, children with recurrent abdominal pain experienced higher levels of abdominal pain than did a comparison group who had not experienced recurring abdominal pain as children (Walker, Garber, Van Slyke, & Greene, 1995). The second study found that the percentage of children experiencing one recurring physical symptom stays about the same throughout the school-age and adolescent years, but that the percentage experiencing two or more distinct physical symptoms increases during adolescence (Garrick, Ostrov, & Offer, 1988). This suggests that single physical complaints in some children become multiple physical complaints during adolescence without effective interventions.

Key Concepts

- Headaches, stomach pains, limb pains, chest pains, or fatigue occurring at least once a week have been reported by 10–25% of children.
- Few differences in the frequency of somatic complaints occur between prepubertal girls and boys; after puberty, more females than males report somatic complaints.
- The percentage of children experiencing more than one complaint increases during adolescence.

Etiology

It is developmentally appropriate for toddlers and preschool children to express some of their psychological distress through physical symptoms (Fritz et al., 1997). For example, young children who are anxious about attending preschool may express their anxiety through headaches or stomachaches that occur before leaving for preschool or while they are there (Garralda, 1999). As they get older, most children develop an increasing ability to express psychological distress verbally, which reduces the need to express it through physical symptoms. Consequently, there is a reduction in somatization for most children as they get older.

However, some children continue to express psychological distress through physical symptoms during their school-age years and adolescence, and others begin to express their distress in this way. Research to understand why this occurs has focused in three areas: biologically based vulnerability to disease or sensitivity to pain, high levels of stress, and learning. In addition, some family therapists have hypothesized that the function of a child's somatization problems in a family can prolong and intensify them.

Biologically Based Vulnerability

Some children with somatization problems have a greater susceptibility to disease than do other children. Their increased likelihood of experiencing frequent illnesses may predispose them to expressing psychological distress through physical symptoms (White, Alday, & Spirito, 2001). In addition, some children with somatization problems have an increased sensitivity to their internal states. For example, children with **irritable bowel syndrome** are more likely than other children to have heightened sensitivity in their rectum (Farthing, 1995). Perhaps children with greater physical sensitivity are more likely to experience physical symptoms. What is unclear at this time is whether this increased sensitivity is influenced primarily by physical issues (such as more nerve endings in an area) or by a cognitive style that focuses a child's attention on one or more specific areas (Garralda, 1996). Each explanation may apply to some children, and a combination of the two explanations may apply to others. (For example, more nerve endings in an area may make it more sensitive, which increases a child's cognitive focus on it, which intensifies the pain experienced from that area.)

Influences of Stress

Higher levels of stress are associated with increased levels of somatization problems (Robinson, Alverez, & Dodge, 1990; Torsheim & Wold, 2001). For example, higher overall levels of stress were associated with increased physical symptoms in a large sample of young adolescents (Reynolds, O'Koon, Papademetriou, Szczygiel, & Grant, 2001); and individual highly stressful events, such as the death of a family member, were associated with the onset of somatization symptoms in young and middle adolescents (Aro, Hanninen, & Paronen, 1989). The researchers hypothesized that because some children express psychological stress through physical symptoms, as their levels of stress increase, more children will experience physical symptoms.

Two studies that explored the relationships among stress, social support, and somatization problems found that children with low levels of social support were particularly vulnerable to the influence of stress on somatization problems (Torsheim & Wold, 2001; Walker, Garber, & Greene, 1994). The researchers hypothesized that peer support allowed stressed children to either ignore their stress or express it to their friends in ways that reduced their need to express it in other ways. Children who did not have this avenue for expressing their stress were more likely to express it through physical symptoms.

Learning through Reinforcement or Modeling

Although some children may be more likely to develop somatization problems because of a biological vulnerability, most researchers and clinicians believe that some form of learning, either through modeling or reinforcement, is needed for a child to develop intense or frequent somatization problems (Campo & Fritsch, 1994). Many researchers and clinicians refer to children with frequent somatization as those who have learned a **sick role**, arguing that this role often develops after a child has observed the benefits that others gain from this role (modeling) or after receiving benefits from it themselves (reinforcement).

The important role that modeling can have in the development of somatization problems is supported by the consistent finding that many children with somatization problems have parents with somatization problems (Craig, Cox, & Klein, 2002; Routh & Ernst, 1984; Walker, Garber, & Greene, 1991). Observing the advantages their parents experience by being in a sick role (increased attention, staying home more frequently) may encourage some children to develop a sick role to obtain the same advantages. Interestingly, one study found that fathers' somatization problems were associated with children's somatization problems more strongly than were mothers' somatization problems (Walker, Garber, & Greene, 1994). The researchers hypothesized that because somatization problems are less common in men than in women, they were particularly salient when they occurred in fathers.

Direct reinforcement of a child's sick-role behaviors can come from many sources. They can be positively reinforced by increased attention and caregiving by parents and others. This reinforcement may be particularly motivating for children who receive little attention otherwise. Some researchers have found that children are more likely to receive attention when they experience physical symptoms than when they experience distressing emotions such as depression or anxiety (Bennet-Osborne, Hatcher, & Richtsmeier, 1989; Walker et al., 1993). This may increase the frequency with which children express their distressing emotions through physical symptoms.

Negative reinforcement can prolong or intensify a child's sick-role behaviors. For example, sick-role behaviors such as taking medication and staying home in bed can be negatively reinforced if the child experiences a reduction of pain or discomfort after these behaviors (White et al., 2001).

Influences on the Family System

Family systems theorists and clinicians have proposed that a child's somatization can be maintained or strengthened over time if it plays an important role in the functioning of the child's family system (Mullins & Olson, 1990). For example, a child's ongoing physical symptoms may facilitate the functioning of the family by diverting attention from parental or parent–child conflict, by bringing parents together to deal with the child's symptoms, or by allowing the family to receive medical services and family support that they would not receive otherwise. Thus even if the child receives no direct benefit from being in a sick role, the benefit of the child's role to the family system can prolong or intensify the child's physical symptoms.

An Example of a Pathway to the Development of Somatization Problems

Our descriptions of the influences on the development of somatization problems provide a way to understand a pathway that some children may take in developing somatization problems. As with all disorders discussed in this text, children may follow many pathways in developing somatization problems; the pathway described in this section is just one of many that children may experience (Figure 15.1).

Initial physical symptoms may occur if a child experiences an injury or illness, if a child observes a family member cope with an injury or illness, or if a child exhibits the physical symptoms that are typical of young children facing emotional concerns. For some of these children, a heightened sensitivity to pain and other physical sensations may intensify their attention to their actual or imagined physical symptoms, and this attention may be particularly strong during times of stress. If the child is reinforced for exhibiting physical symptoms, the child's symptoms may increase. As the child's symptoms increase, many of his or her interactions with parents, teachers, and others may focus on physical symptoms. In addition, the child may receive little attention when not expressing physical symptoms if the parents or others use that time to focus on other siblings, children, or tasks. The attention a child receives while in a sick role and the lack of attention when he or she is not in a sick role can result in the child being in a sick role more frequently, to the point where the child's somatization becomes a prominent and disruptive part of his or her life.

Key Concepts

- Some children with somatization problems have a greater susceptibility to disease and an increased sensitivity to their internal states. It is not clear whether increased sensitivity is influenced by physical issues, cognitive style, or both.
- Higher levels of stress are associated with increased levels of somatization problems. Children with poor social support are particularly vulnerable to the influence of stress on somatization problems.
- Observing the advantages of parents being in a sick role can encourage some children to develop a sick role to obtain the same advantages.

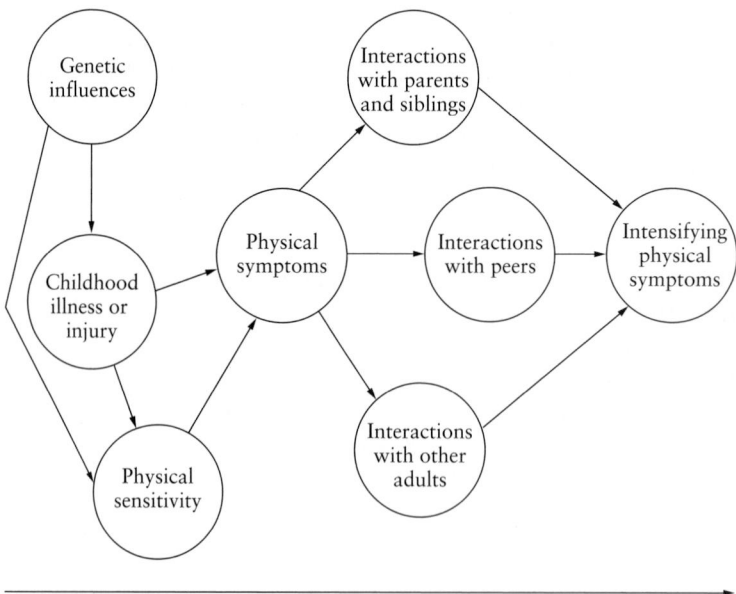

FIGURE 15.1 *One Model for the Development of Somatization Problems*

- Children's sick-role behaviors can be positively reinforced by attention received from parents and others, and this reinforcement may be particularly motivating for children who receive little attention otherwise.
- Negative reinforcement can prolong or intensify sick-role behaviors that decrease pain or discomfort (such as staying in bed).
- A child's somatization can be maintained over time if it plays an important function in the child's family.

Therapeutic Interventions for the Child and Family

The two primary strategies for therapeutic interventions follow from current theory and research about the development of somatization problems and somatoform disorders (Campo & Garber, 1998). Because many somatization problems have some foundation in a medical condition, the first strategy involves medical treatment to reduce any symptoms caused by the medical condition. The second strategy involves behavioral interventions to (1) reduce the intensity or frequency of physical symptoms so that they have a less important role in a child's life and (2) help the child cope effectively with the symptoms that remain. In addition to these strategies, family therapy may be used to change the functioning of a child's family so that the child's physical symptoms do not have an important role in that functioning.

Several authors suggest that it is most effective to have a physician as the primary person with whom the child and family interact during treatment, with a psychologist or other mental health professional acting as a consultant to the physician and family (Campo & Reich, 1999; Fritz et al., 1997; Garralda, 1999; Kager, Arndt, & Kenny, 1992). Having a physician as the primary provider acknowledges the child's and parents' perception that the symptoms involve a medical condition, so they are not forced to abandon their concerns about the medical nature of the child's symptoms. The inclusion of a mental health professional indicates that the child's symptoms are the result of a complex mix of physical and psychological influences and helps the parents and child broaden their understanding of the symptoms (Beasley & DeMaso, 1997; Garralda, 1999).

Another important component of treatment is to shift the child and family from being passive recipients of medical care to being active participants in the treatment process (Allen & Shriver, 1998). In the same way that a victim of an accident must understand that he is responsible for completing the physical therapy that will restore him to health, with the guidance of a physical therapist, a child with somatization problems and his family are helped to understand that they are responsible for restoring the child to health, with the guidance of their physician and psychologist.

Medical Interventions

Medically based treatment is needed to address any physical symptoms that have a medical foundation, even if the symptoms are exaggerated by the child. For example, many children with recurrent abdominal pain experience periodic or chronic constipation, and a high-fiber diet can be useful in reducing their abdominal pain (Edwards, Finney, & Bonner, 1991).

As noted earlier in this chapter, there is a compulsive nature to body dysmorphic disorder, and some children have been successfully treated with an SSRI, which has also been effective in the treatment of obsessive–compulsive disorder (Albertini & Phillips, 1999). Other than with this one somatoform disorder, however, the use of psychotropic medication occurs only rarely with children who have somatization problems.

Behavioral Interventions

Behavioral interventions usually focus on three areas: education, changes in reinforcement, and development of coping skills (Garralda, 1999). The interventions usually involve the child and his or her parents because it is important that they work together to reduce the child's somatization problems.

Education focuses on understanding the connections between the child's psychological and physical functioning (Wasserman, Whitington, & Rivara, 1988). The child and parents are helped to recognize the ways in which the child's cognitions and emotions can intensify physical symptoms and how the parents' reinforcement of the child's sick-role behaviors can prolong them. This helps them see that they can influence the frequency and intensity of the child's physical symptoms, gives them an increased sense of control over the symptoms, and prepares them for the changes in behaviors and cognitions that the therapist will suggest.

The therapist then describes how changes in reinforcement can increase the child's healthy behaviors and reduce complaints about symptoms (Campo & Fritsch, 1994; Campo & Reich, 1999). Based on the specific nature of the child's and parents' behaviors, the therapist can suggest several changes in how the parents respond to the child's healthy and sick-role behaviors:

- *Reinforcing the child for joining physical, educational, or social activities:* For example, the child may be reinforced for attending school every day for a week, attending physical education classes, or joining school activities. Early in treatment, these reinforcements may involve small gifts or later bedtimes on the weekend, with the goal of eventually having praise from parents replace them (Finney, Lemanek, Cataldo, & Katz, 1989).
- *Reinforcing the child for reducing complaints about symptoms:* For example, reinforcement might be given each day or each week that the child does not complain about physical symptoms.
- *Reducing reinforcement that the child receives for physical complaints:* For example, reinforcements such as watching television or staying in bed when the child complains of physical symptoms might be withdrawn. In addition, the parents may stop providing comfort to the child when he or she has physical complaints.
- *Reducing reinforcement that others receive when the child has physical complaints:* For example, a parent might no longer sit and talk with

the child when he or she is experiencing symptoms or might no longer stay home from work when the child has physical symptoms.

- *Encouraging the child and parents to engage in pleasant activities when the child is symptom-free:* This can reinforce healthy behaviors.

As you might imagine, many parents find it difficult to change the reinforcements they give their children and to maintain firmness in the face of a child's physical complaints (Campo & Reich, 1999). They may have provided warmth and caring in response to their child's physical symptoms for months or years, and they must change this pattern and be stern in the face of the child's symptoms. This may seem harsh to them and their child. In addition, the parents will have to act in ways that they and the child may perceive as unfair (like refusing to allow a child to engage in pleasurable evening activities if he has been sick during the day). Because of these difficulties, most parents need support and guidance from their psychologist and physician as their behaviors change.

Cognitive Interventions

Cognitive interventions can reduce the intensity and frequency of physical complaints and help children cope with those that remain. For example, relaxation techniques are often taught. Once the child learns relaxation techniques, he or she is encouraged to relax when physical symptoms first appear rather than reporting them to parents or other adults. Relaxation often reduces the intensity of the symptoms and helps the child cope successfully with them (Janicke & Finney, 1999).

Two other cognitive strategies can help children think differently or less frequently about their physical symptoms. **Cognitive restructuring** helps children and parents think differently about the child's symptoms, which may help the child ignore them (Garralda, 1996; Janicke & Finney, 1999). For example, when abdominal pain occurs, the child is helped to avoid exaggerating the importance of the pain by blocking irrational thoughts and substituting rational thoughts about it (for example, that it is normal and will pass soon). Another cognitive strategy is *refocusing,* through which a child learns to shift his or her attention when symptoms occur (Sanders, Shepard, Cleghorn, & Woolford, 1994). For example, a child might start a pleasant activity, watch television, listen to music, or talk with a parent when symptoms first appear to refocus her attention away from them.

Interventions for Parents and Families

In some cases it will be useful for a therapist to change the functioning of a family to reduce the role that a child's physical symptoms play in the family (Beasley & DeMaso, 1997; Mullins & Olson, 1990). Ministering to a sick child may have been a principal way that one or both parents felt close to the child or received warmth from the child. These parents will need to learn other ways of having positive and supportive interactions with their child. Some parents may have avoided less pleasant tasks (like working outside the home) by caring for their child; they will need to gain the strength to do these tasks regularly. Similarly, the child's symptoms may have reduced conflict between the parents and helped them work together. The parents will need to learn other ways of reducing their conflict and working together.

Therapeutic work with parents who have somatization problems can be an important component of the overall treatment for a child because convincing a child to end sick-role behaviors will be difficult if a parent is unwilling to do the same (Garralda, 1999). In addition, seeing a parent working to overcome somatization problems provides good modeling for the new behaviors expected from the child.

Key Concepts

- An important treatment component is to make the child and family active participants in the treatment rather than passive recipients of it.
- Medically based treatment focuses on reducing any physical symptoms that have a medical foundation, even if the child exaggerates those symptoms.
- SSRIs have been effective with some children who have body dysmorphic disorder.
- Behavioral interventions focus on three areas: education, changes in reinforcement, and development of coping skills.
- Education helps increase understanding of the connections between the child's psychological and physical functioning, the ways in which the child's cognitions and emotions can intensify physical symptoms, and the ways in which the parents' reinforcement of the child's sick-role behaviors can prolong them.
- Changes in reinforcement for the child focus on reducing reinforcement for sick-role behaviors and increasing reinforcement for healthy behaviors.
- Relaxation training, cognitive restructuring, and refocusing all help the child cope more effectively with physical symptoms.
- Interventions with parents involve providing support as they change the reinforcements they provide their child, addressing family system issues that may be supported by the child's somatization problems, and treating any of their somatization problems.

Childhood Obesity

Childhood obesity is a significant public health problem in many industrialized countries; it has been described by some researchers as a "pandemic of the new millennium" (Kim & Oberzanek, 2002; Mustillo et al., 2003). (The word *obese* comes from the Latin *obedere,* "to devour.") The percentage of children, adolescents, and adults who are overweight or obese has increased dramatically in the United States and other industrialized countries over the past four decades, putting increasing numbers at risk for weight-related illnesses such as cardiovascular diseases, gastrointestinal diseases, and type

2 **diabetes** (previously called adult-onset diabetes) (Surgeon General, 2004). In addition, some children who are obese or overweight experience social problems, such as being teased by their peers, which increase their risk for poor peer relationships, lowered self-esteem, and depression or anxiety.

The development of obesity in children occurs through a complex mixture of genetic, physiological, and environmental influences, and the relative importance of these influences changes throughout a person's life (Rosenbaum, Leibel, & Hirsch, 1997). Unfortunately the complexity of these influences is often not recognized, and many people view obesity as simply the result of an overindulgent lifestyle or lack of will. Views such as these can influence how we regard and interact with children who are obese or overweight and how they regard themselves (Rosenbaum et al., 1997). As we will see in this section, it is not simply poor self-control that leads to childhood obesity.

Case Study: A Girl's Ongoing Struggle with Weight

As she described her daughter's struggle with weight, Hannah's mother expressed both sadness that weight had been such a source of frustration for Hannah and her family over the years and a sense of relief that they were all finally comfortable with Hannah's weight. Hannah's mother recalled that, as an infant, Hannah was hungrier than her other children. Her mother had followed their pediatrician's instructions to feed Hannah when she wanted to be fed and not to worry about how much she was eating. Hannah was plump as an infant and remained plump as she grew during the first three years of her life—a pattern that differed from that followed by her older brother and older sister, who became more lean as they grew. When she entered kindergarten, Hannah was still plump, but her weight did not seem to interfere with her active lifestyle.

Hannah's parents became increasingly concerned about her weight during her preschool years. Although they and their other children were lean, Hannah's mother and father each had a sibling who had been overweight as a child and remained overweight as an adult. They recalled the teasing their siblings had endured and knew their siblings had become concerned about possible weight-related health problems as they got older. Hannah's mother encouraged Hannah to eat less, but Hannah resisted and often complained of being hungry.

During her school-age years, Hannah remained overweight. She was teased about her weight by some of the other children, which upset her. Her mother was unsure how to help Hannah. She knew that if Hannah lost some weight she would be teased less, but she did not want Hannah's weight to become a central issue in her life and a source of contention at home. After consulting with Hannah's pediatrician, her mother encouraged Hannah to continue to eat healthful meals and to reduce her snacking—deciding that it would be best to focus on eating in a healthful way rather than on losing weight. Hannah joined several activities at school, such as the orchestra and the art club; but she avoided sports, which were the favorite activities of her brother and sister.

Around the time of puberty, Hannah's weight increased more than is typical for children her age, and she became increasingly concerned about her size. Parties were occurring more frequently in her peer group, and several of her classmates had begun dating. Hannah worried that her weight would preclude her from these popular activities and decided to diet. Her parents insisted that she continue to eat healthful meals; but she took smaller helpings, skipped desserts, and did not eat between meals. She lost some weight initially and was delighted with the weight loss and the positive comments she received from her friends. One of her classmates asked her on a date with some of their friends, which she found exciting. After several weeks of dieting, however, her weight stopped declining. She decided to further reduce what she ate, and she quit the orchestra so she could exercise at home in the afternoon. Despite all her efforts, her weight declined slowly, which she found continually frustrating.

After several months on her diet, Hannah was hungry all the time and occasionally felt overwhelmed by her hunger. Sometimes when she was very hungry, Hannah ate large amounts of food—finishing whole bags of cookies and chips in an afternoon. Although this reduced her hunger, she felt terrible about what her eating was doing to her weight loss plans, so she exercised longer for the next several days to burn off the calories she had consumed.

Hannah felt continually frustrated with her inability to be as thin as she would like. She spent more time exercising and less time with friends and family. She began to dislike exercising but felt that she had to continue. As she exercised more and engaged in fewer of the activities she enjoyed, her mood gradually became more depressed. One day her mother found Hannah at home, sobbing uncontrollably. Hannah explained how frustrating her life was and that she did not see any way that it would become less frustrating. After discussing the problem with their family physician, Hannah's parents decided to have Hannah see a nutritionist to help her with her diet and a psychologist for some psychotherapy. Hannah protested loudly about having to see the psychologist, but her parents insisted. After several therapy sessions, Hannah found that psychotherapy was not as bad as she thought it would be; she found that it gave her a chance to talk about her frustrations with her weight and about her concerns that she would be left out of peer activities if she were not thin. The psychologist encouraged her to return to a more healthful lifestyle and encouraged her to rejoin the school orchestra and other activities that would put her in contact with peers rather than coming home each day to exercise.

Hannah returned to the orchestra, and several weeks later she became friends with a boy in the orchestra. He had once been on the football team, but he had been injured and so could not play any longer. Because he enjoyed music as well as athletics, he had joined the orchestra. As he and Hannah got to know each other better, they talked about their difficulties with weight. He had been trying for years to gain weight so he could be larger for football, but he had not been successful. Hannah found this amusing because, as she explained, gaining weight had never been a problem for her. As their friendship deepened, they began to date and soon were a couple. They often talked about how unfair it was that many people felt a strong need to be a different weight. Hannah found that she was becoming more comfortable with her weight, and she thought that it was her boyfriend's feelings toward her, whatever her weight, that helped her with this.

Some Issues Worth Noting

- The possible indirect genetic influence on Hannah's weight, observable through her increased appetite as an infant.
- The increasing role that weight played in Hannah's self-image as she became older.

- The struggles that Hannah's mother experienced in deciding how best to help Hannah.
- The important role that peers played in Hannah's initial frustration with her weight and in her eventual comfort with her weight.

Defining and Measuring Obesity

Although many people assume that obesity means that a person weighs too much and that it is assessed through a measurement of weight, neither assumption is accurate (Cole & Rolland-Cachera, 2002). Instead **obesity** refers to a person having excess fat tissue (**adipose tissue**). This distinguishes people who are heavy because of excess muscle from those who have excess fat. Consequently, the best way to assess obesity is through a measurement of body fat. This can be done in several ways; but the techniques that are most accurate are expensive and time-consuming (such as weighing underwater or use of magnetic resonance imaging), and those that are less expensive are less accurate (such as measuring the thickness of a skin fold in the triceps area or just under the shoulder blades) (Cole & Rolland-Cachera, 2002).

Because of the difficulty of measuring body fat accurately and inexpensively, a person's **body mass index** (BMI) is usually calculated and used as an estimate of his or her body fat. Body mass index is calculated by measuring a person's height and weight and then applying the formula $BMI = kg/m^2$ (weight in kilograms divided by the square of height in meters). For adults, a BMI of 19–24 is considered **healthy weight;** a BMI of 25–29 is considered **overweight;** and a BMI of 30 or greater is considered **obese.** These cutoffs represent those who are at or above the 85th percentile (overweight) or 95th percentile (obese) of weight in the adult population. The cutoffs have been determined from data showing greater health problems for those above these two percentiles. Thus the categories of *overweight* and *obese* in adults are based on evidence that they include those who have a higher risk for disease and early death (Cole & Rolland-Cachera, 2002).

However, it is not clear that the BMI cutoffs used with adults are appropriate for children because the health consequences of various BMI levels in children are less certain (Cole & Rolland-Cachera, 2002; Troiano & Flegal, 1998). As a result, some researchers categorize children with a BMI of 30 or greater as *overweight* and do not use the category of *obese* (National Center for Health Statistics, 2004). But not all researchers use this categorization, and many use the same cutoffs and categories for children and adults. This can lead to confusion when comparing studies because some researchers would classify a group of children as overweight and others would classify the same children as obese. To reduce this confusion, in this text I use the same terms and cutoffs used with adults in our discussion of children. This will allow us to compare studies more easily.

Notes from the Author: Calculating Your BMI

You can calculate your own BMI. Using measurements most familiar to those of us in the United States, BMI is calculated by BMI = (pounds/inches^2) × 703. For example, currently my weight is 205 and my height is 73 inches. So my BMI is (205/5,329) × 703 = 27 (BMI is usually rounded to the nearest whole number). This puts me in the overweight category (Surgeon General, 2004). To be at a healthy weight, I need to lose about 20 pounds. Based on recommzendations from my physician and my own common sense, I have started an exercise program and have started to moderate (somewhat, I must admit) my diet. I hope that this will help me lose some of my excess weight (although 185 pounds seems like a difficult goal to reach).

Key Concepts

- *Obesity* refers to a high percentage of body fat. Techniques to measure body fat can be cumbersome, so obesity is often assessed using BMI.
- It is not clear whether the BMI criteria used to define *overweight* and *obese* in adults are appropriate for children. Consequently, some researchers use the term *overweight* for all children above the 85th percentile for normal weight.

Prevalence and Course

Many children in the United States and other industrialized countries are overweight or obese, and the percentage of children who are overweight or obese has grown dramatically during the past few decades. As shown in Figure 15.2, data from an ongoing study of more than 5,000 children and adolescents shows that the percentage of children who are obese has grown from about 5% in the 1960s to about 16% today (National Center for Health Statistics, 2004). Information from this study also shows that the increase in the percentage of children who are obese is not due to all children becoming heavier; rather, heavy children are becoming even heavier while lighter children maintain their weight (Troiano & Flegal, 1998).

Rates of childhood obesity in the United States are similar to those found in other industrialized countries. For example, the percentages of children who are obese have been estimated at 15% in France, 11% in Italy, 13% in Singapore, and 12% in Japan (Guillaume & Lissau, 2002).

Most studies show no differences between the percentages of boys and girls who are obese or overweight (Mustillo et al., 2003). However, U.S. studies have found differences in obesity among racial and ethnic groups. African–American, Hispanic–American, and Native American children are at greater risk for obesity than are European–American or Asian–American children (Kim & Oberzanek, 2002; Salbe, Weyer, Lindsay, Ravussin, &

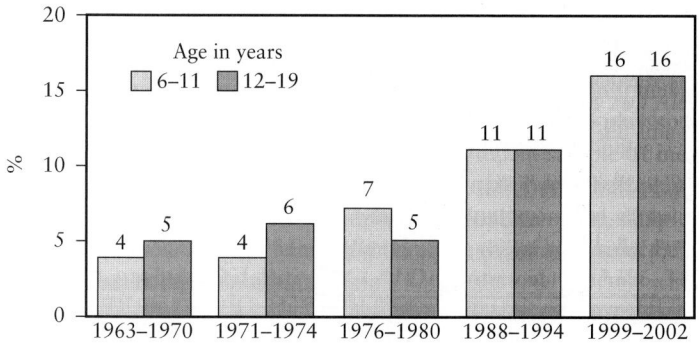

FIGURE 15.2   *Prevalence of Overweight among Children and Adolescents Ages 6–19 Years*

Note: Excludes pregnant women starting with 1971–1974. Pregnancy status not available for 1963–1965 and 1966–1970. Data for 1963–1965 are for children 6–11 years of age; data for 1966–1970 are for adolescents 12–17 years of age, not 12–19 years of age.

Source: CDC/NCHS, NHES and NHANES.

Tataranni, 2002; Vander Wal, 2004). For example, Kim and Oberzanek (2002) compared the weights of African–American and European–American girls at ages 9 and 19. They found that 31% of the African–American girls and 22% of the European–American girls were overweight at age 9, and that about half the African–American girls and one-third of the European–American girls were overweight by age 19. A study of American Indians in the Pima Tribe in Arizona, which has the highest percentage of people who are overweight or obese among American Indian tribes, found that 28% of the children were obese at age 5 and that 53% were obese by age 10 (Salbe, Weyer, Harper et al., 2002).

Most children who are obese continue to be obese through adolescence and adulthood (American Academy of Pediatrics Committee on Nutrition, 2003). Thus childhood obesity is a primary risk factor for adolescent and adulthood obesity. However, this general trend does not capture the complexity of the course of childhood obesity. As part of their longitudinal study of rural children in North Carolina, Mustillo and colleagues (2003) found four patterns of obesity from childhood through adolescence. The most common pattern was lack of obesity during either period (73% of children). The next most common was chronic obesity from ages 9 through 16 (15% of the children), then obesity beginning during adolescence (8%), and finally obesity during childhood that ended during adolescence (5%). As illustrated in Figure 15.3, age 12 was the most common time at which some children who were obese reduced their BMI (either by losing weight or growing in height while maintaining their weight); and some children who were not obese at that age began to increase their BMI. This finding provides important information to those designing prevention programs for obesity: Age 12 may be an important turning point in the weight of many children.

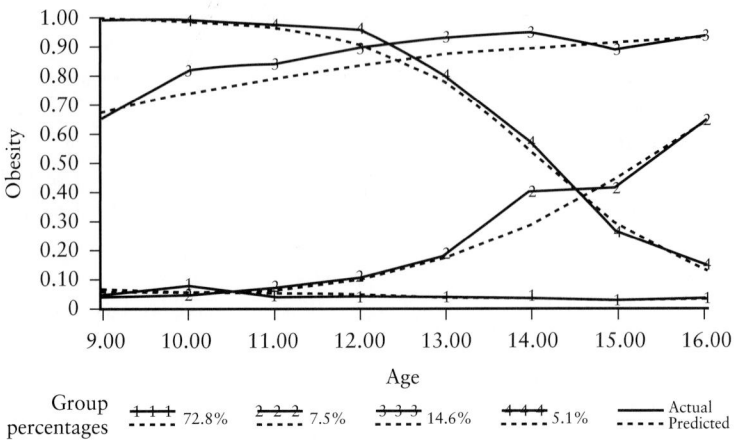

FIGURE 15.3 *Four Obesity Trajectories*

Source: Mustillo and colleagues (2003).

Key Concepts

- Approximately 16% of children in the United States are above the 95th percentile of their normal weight—an increase from about 5% in the 1960s. Similar percentages have been found in other industrialized countries.
- Approximately equal percentages of U.S. boys and girls are overweight or obese.
- African–American, Hispanic–American, and Native American children are more likely to be overweight or obese than are European–American or Asian–American children.
- Four patterns of the course of obesity have been identified in children. Although most children are never obese, some children remain obese throughout childhood and adolescence; others are obese as children and reduce their BMI during adolescence; and some become obese during adolescence.

Consequences of Childhood Obesity

Physical Health

Most children who are overweight or obese do not experience significant weight-related physical health problems. However, their childhood weight creates conditions that place them at higher risk for health problems during adolescence and adulthood (American Academy of Pediatrics Committee on Nutrition, 2003). For example, one study showed that children who are obese have higher levels than other children of **insulin**, triglycerides, and cholesterol, all of which are risk factors for coronary heart disease in adulthood (Freedman, 2004). This study also found that obese adults who were obese as children had many risk factors for coronary heart disease, although, interestingly, most healthy-weight adults who had been obese as children did not have these risk factors. This suggests that long-term obesity creates the most risk for coronary heart disease and that reducing obesity before children become adults has long-term health benefits.

Children who are obese are at risk for some medical problems during childhood. For example, they are at higher risk for developing type 2 diabetes (American Academy of Pediatrics Committee on Nutrition, 2003). The diagnosis of type 2 diabetes in children has increased dramatically during the past three decades, and its onset is largely attributed to weight and a sedentary lifestyle in those who have some genetic predisposition to the disease (Saenger, 2004). Children who are overweight or obese are also at greater risk for developing asthma and sleep apnea, which is a disorder in which breathing stops for at least 10 seconds while a child is asleep (Mullen & Shield, 2004).

Children who are obese are also at risk for musculoskeletal problems. Flat feet, which are characterized by a low arch at the bottom of the foot caused by the misalignment of bones in the feet, are found more frequently among children who are obese than others. Problems with knee and hip joints have also been reported (American Academy of Pediatrics Committee on Nutrition, 2003). One important consequence of these musculoskeletal problems is that they make physical activity more painful. This is likely to discourage children who are obese from engaging in physical activity, which increases their risk of remaining obese.

Psychological and Social Consequences

School-age children who are overweight or obese have lower self-esteem than other children about their physical appearance, but they do not experience lower global self-esteem (Strauss, 2000; Vander Wal, 2004). Nevertheless, as these children move into adolescence, their global self-esteem often decreases; thus the global self-esteem of obese adolescents is lower than that of their peers (Butor, 2004; Strauss, 2000). (Here I would like to remind readers, as I have occasionally done throughout this text, about the importance of understanding that mean differences between two groups on a measure do not indicate that everyone in one group has lower scores than everyone in the other group. Even though samples of obese adolescents have lower scores than other adolescents on measures of global self-esteem, we cannot conclude that all adolescents who are obese have low global self-esteem. An examination of the distribution of self-esteem in the two groups shows that some adolescents who are obese have global self-esteem that is higher than that of many nonobese adolescents.)

Whether being overweight is associated with disordered eating has also been investigated, with the main focus being on links between obesity and binge eating. Several studies have shown a pattern similar to the one found for global self-esteem: School-age children who are overweight or obese are not more likely than other children to binge-eat (Decaluwe & Braet, 2003; Vander Wal, 2004), although more adolescents who are overweight or obese binge-eat than do their healthy-weight peers (Berkowitz, Stunkard, & Stallings, 1993).

Many children experience social consequences of being overweight or obese (American Academy of Pediatrics Committee on Nutrition, 2003). They are more likely than other children to be ridiculed and are more often the targets of bullies (Butor, 2004). They are also viewed negatively by most of their peers and are frequently ranked by other children as being the least desirable as friends (Mullen & Shield, 2004). These factors increase their risk of experiencing anger, depression, or anxiety and can also lead to social withdrawal, which is likely to increase their sedentary behavior (American Academy of Pediatrics Committee on Nutrition, 2003).

Key Concepts

- Adults are more likely than children to experience health consequences from obesity; but children who are obese are more likely to have conditions that can eventually affect their health, such as high levels of cholesterol, insulin, and triglycerides.
- Children who are obese are at higher risk for developing type 2 diabetes, asthma, sleep apnea, and musculoskeletal problems.
- Global self-esteem among school-age children who are overweight or obese is about the same as their healthy-weight peers; adolescents who are obese or overweight have lower global self-esteem than their healthy-weight peers.
- Children who are overweight or obese are more likely than others to be the target of bullying and to be ridiculed by other children.

Etiology

In our exploration of the etiology of childhood obesity, we will first review briefly the physiology of the development of fat tissue. We also examine how genes, parental obesity, diet, and activity levels can influence how much fat tissue develops in a child and explore a model of how these influences can combine in the development of childhood obesity.

As noted earlier, *obesity* refers to excess fat. Fat (adipose) tissue is composed of fat cells (**adipocytes**). Adipocytes can be detected in a fetus beginning in the 15th week of gestation, and the percentage of body fat increases dramatically during the third trimester of fetal development (Rosenbaum et al., 1997; Wabitsch, 2002). During the first year after birth, the amount of adipose tissue increases in healthy infants, resulting in the common "chubby baby" look. This increase is due mostly to the enlargement of existing adipocytes rather than an increase in their number. During years 2 through 10, there is little increase in the size or number of adipocytes in most children. Because children are growing in height during this time, they become more lean than they were as infants. However, some children develop excessive adipose tissue during these years through a combination of an increase in the size of existing adipocytes and the development of new adipocytes.

Although the mechanism through which new adipocytes develop is not well understood, current thinking is that when existing adipocytes become enlarged to a certain point, the body creates new adipocytes (Wabitsch, 2002). Thus a combination of influences at the cellular level can create excessive fat in some children: The increasing size of adipocytes increases the volume of adipose tissue and triggers the development of new adipocytes that further increase the volume of adipose tissue.

The foundation of excessive adipose tissue in adults is a **positive energy balance** over time—that is, the intake of energy exceeds energy expenditures. The excess energy is stored as fat. Children, however, need a positive energy balance because they are growing (Surgeon General, 2004). Consequently, an *excessive* positive energy balance is at the foundation of excessive adipose tissue development in children. As noted in the introduction to this section, a complex web of factors influences the energy balance of children and consequently the development of excessive adipose tissue in some of them (Rosenbaum et al., 1997). A steadily increasing body of research shows that genes strongly influence this balance, while the behaviors of children and their parents, which may be influenced by their genes, also play an important role.

Many factors influence the amount of adipose tissue a child develops.

Genetic Influences

Genes play a strong role in the development of obesity for many children. Heritability estimates for obesity from family, twin, and adoption studies range from 50% to 90%, with some studies showing that the strength of the genetic influence on weight is similar to the strength of the genetic influence on height (Hebebrand, Wermter, & Hinney, 2004; Maffeis, 2000). How genes influence the development of adipose tissue is not clear, and the specific influences of genes are likely to vary from child to child. For example, genes may influence activity levels, how and where fat is stored, food preferences, and resting and active metabolism levels (Rosenbaum et al., 1997).

Genes can both directly and indirectly influence obesity (see Figure 15.4). For example, genes could directly influence the frequency of new adipocyte creation or the extent to which excess energy is stored as fat. As an example of an indirect effect, consider an infant who has a genetically influenced level of hunger that is more intense than that of most infants. It is likely that his parents will feed him more because of the soothing effect that eating has on him. The excess food he receives is the direct cause of fat development, but he receives this excess food partly because of his genetically influenced level of hunger. Consequently, his genes have an indirect influence on his weight through their influence on his level of hunger (Hebebrand et al., 2004).

Parental Obesity, Activity Levels, and Diet

The two most commonly reported factors associated with childhood obesity are having parents who are overweight or obese and having lower activity levels. Interestingly, the extent to which food intake is related to obesity remains unclear.

Many studies have reported an association between parental obesity and childhood obesity (Burke et al., 2005; Salbe, Weyer, Lindsay et al., 2002; Whitaker, 2004). As just noted, genetic influences could account for this association: Children may inherit their parents' genetic tendency toward obesity. In addition, parental modeling of certain behaviors such as eating high-calorie foods, eating large amounts of food, or engaging in sedentary activities may influence children's behaviors and consequently their weight (Burke et al., 2005).

Lower physical activity is consistently found among children who are overweight or obese, and this lower activity may start early in life. One study, for example, measured the physical activity of infants and found an association between lower levels of physical activity at 3 months and being overweight at 1 year (Roberts, Savage, & Coward, 1988).

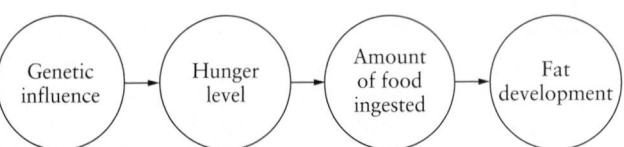

FIGURE 15.4 *An Indirect Genetic Influence on Fat Development*

Several studies of school-age children or adolescents show that physical activity is related to obesity. Children who are overweight watch more television, play more video games, and engage in physical activity less frequently than children who are not overweight (Janssen, Katzmarzyk, Boyce, King, & Pickett, 2004). In addition, longitudinal studies have found that children who watched more television and were less active had greater gains in BMI over a one-year period (Berkey et al., 2000), a two-year period (Burke et al., 2005), and a five-year period (Salbe, Weyer, Harper et al., 2002). Alternatively, children who engaged in increased physical activity over a one-year period had reduced BMI (Berkey, Rockett, Gillman, & Colditz, 2003). Hancox, Milne and Poulton (2004) found that the amount of television viewing between the ages of 5 and 15 was associated with obesity at age 26.

The role of diet in childhood obesity remains less clear than the role of physical activity. Some researchers have reported that children who are overweight eat more than their peers or have a higher level of fat in their diets (Berkey et al., 2000; Maffeis, 2000). However, other researchers have found no difference in the caloric intake of children who are overweight and those who are not (Janssen et al., 2004; Obarzanek, Schreiber, Crawford, & Goldman, 1994). One reason for the differing results may be the difficulty of accurately assessing caloric intake in children. This is usually done by asking parents or children to list the types and quantities of foods consumed during a day. There is some evidence that this strategy results in underreporting of caloric intake and that children who are overweight or obese may underreport caloric intake to a greater degree than their peers (Kim & Oberzanek, 2002; Maffeis, 2000). Consequently, until studies with strategies for assessing caloric intake more accurately are completed, the role of caloric intake in the development of childhood obesity will remain unclear.

A Model for the Development of Childhood Obesity

As with the other disorders discussed in this text, there are many different pathways through which children become obese and many different influences on these pathways. Genetic influences may push some children toward obesity despite efforts by their parents to provide healthful diets and encourage physical activity. Psychological or social influences may encourage other children to eat large amounts of food or engage in little physical activity, which can push them toward obesity even if they have no genetic predisposition for it. However, for many children genetic and environmental influences apparently combine to increase their risk for being overweight or obese (see Figure 15.5).

Genes may influence the number and size of children's adipocytes, food preferences, or energy expenditures. The children's parents may have similar genetically influenced characteristics as the children, which may affect the parents' attitudes about their children's weight, the food prepared for meals, or the extent to which the parents and children participate together in physical or sedentary activities. This combination of direct genetic influences and parenting behaviors can result in some young children being overweight. A young child who is overweight may be less likely to engage in physical

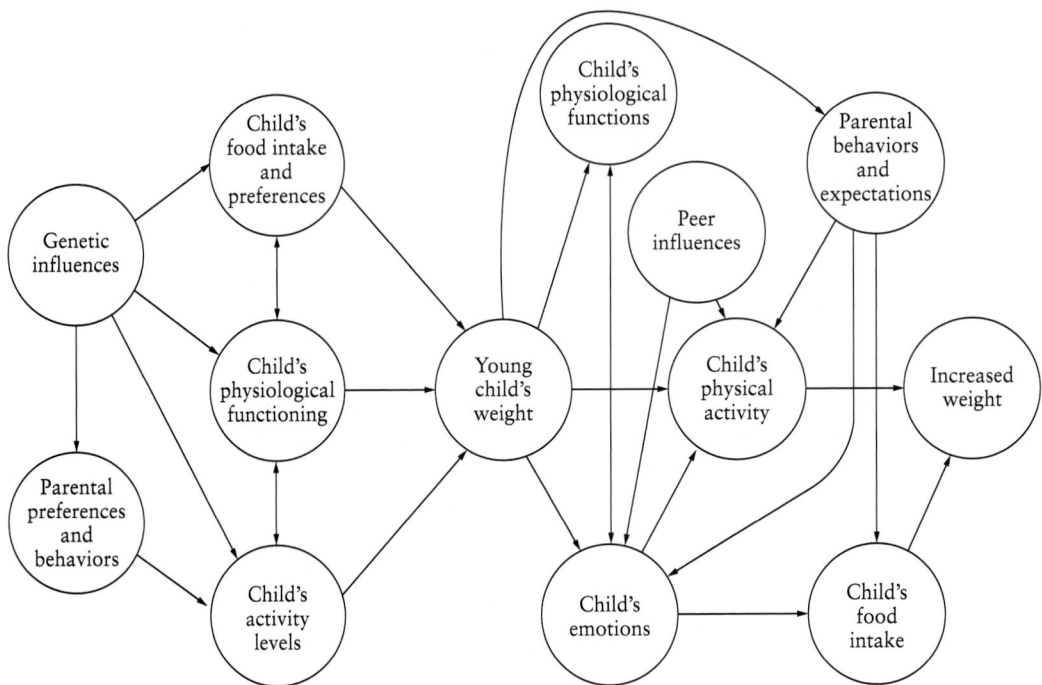

FIGURE 15.5   *One Model for the Development of Childhood Obesity*

activity because of the greater physical difficulty of doing so, a relative lack of physical coordination, withdrawal from peer activities because of teasing or bullying, or other reasons. The child may develop activities that are more sedentary (art, video games, reading). As the child's interest and expertise in sedentary activities increases, and he or she falls further behind in the skills related to active games and sports because of engaging in them infrequently, the child's sedentary activities are likely to increase. Because children are more likely to eat during sedentary than physical activities, the number of calories ingested may increase. As the overweight child becomes less and less engaged in peer and physical activities, his or her weight may increase, which may encourage further withdrawal from peers and physical activities and lead to even more weight gain.

Key Concepts

- Adipose tissue begins to grow during fetal development. During the first few years of a child's life, increased adipose tissue is due mostly to the enlargement of adipocytes. Enlarged adipocytes may trigger the creation of new adipocytes, further increasing the volume of adipose tissue.
- Genes play a strong role in the development of childhood obesity through their influence on adipocyte development, activity levels, how and where fat is stored, food preferences, and resting and active metabolism levels.

- Parental obesity is often associated with childhood obesity. This may indicate a similar genetic influence on the parents and children, the influence of parental modeling of excessive eating or engaging in sedentary activities, or both.
- Parents' attitudes about their own or their children's weight may influence their children's weight.
- Lower levels of physical activity are related to increased risk for obesity.
- The influence of food intake on childhood obesity remains unclear.

Prevention

As you might expect, prevention of obesity in children focuses on the two issues related to positive energy balance that can be influenced by people's behavior: reducing the consumption of high-calorie foods and increasing physical activity. Because a child's eating and activity patterns may develop early in life, encouraging behaviors that will reduce the risk of obesity early in a child's life is important (Surgeon General, 2004). In addition, prevention efforts are particularly important for children who are at a genetic risk for becoming overweight, and many of these children can be identified because their parents are overweight (American Academy of Pediatrics Committee on Nutrition, 2003).

At an individual level, the American Academy of Pediatrics Committee on Nutrition (2003) recommends that children's BMI be calculated each year, either by their physician or possibly through programs at preschools and

Regular exercise appears to be the most effective way to help children maintain a healthy weight.

schools, so that excessive weight gain can be identified early and efforts to increase physical activity or change the children's diet can be made. Educating parents about childhood obesity is also important. In particular, parents should be given information that will help them (1) understand the health consequences of obesity, (2) include healthful foods in their children's diets and limit foods with high sugar or fat content, and (3) increase their children's physical activity. In addition, parents should be encouraged to limit the time their children spend watching television or playing video games, and they should be encouraged to develop alternative activities for their children and engage in these activities with their children (Surgeon General, 2004).

Changes in public policy, particularly those focused on preschools and schools, can also prevent childhood obesity (Surgeon General, 2004):

- School curricula should emphasize the importance of a healthful diet and physical activity—with a focus on promoting good health rather than being concerned with weight or attractiveness.
- School breakfasts, lunches, and after-school snacks should consist of healthful foods; high-calorie, high-fat foods should be discouraged in school meals, and their availability in vending machines should be limited or prohibited.
- Children of all ages should be required to participate in daily physical education classes to increase their activity and give them skills in active games and sports. Not only will this increase their activity during school hours; it can also encourage them to participate in active games and sports in the afternoons and on the weekends.

Finally, the media could be involved in prevention efforts. For example, public service announcements on television or radio could describe the social and physical benefits of healthful eating. It may also be appropriate to limit or prohibit advertisements for high-calorie or high-fat foods aimed at young children (American Academy of Pediatrics Committee on Nutrition, 2003).

Key Concepts

- Educational efforts can help parents understand the potential consequences of obesity and the importance of a healthful diet and activity level for avoiding obesity.
- Public policy efforts can focus on educating children about obesity, providing healthful foods while children are at school, encouraging regular physical exercise at school, and possibly discouraging advertisements about high-calorie, high-fat foods aimed at young children.

Therapeutic Interventions

Interventions for children who are overweight or obese vary in their intensity and their content; but all have the basic goal of reducing a child's positive energy balance, usually through a combination of reduced calorie intake and increased activity. Children who are very heavy and whose weight poses near-term health risks may be involved in intensive interventions. These interventions involve low-calorie diets and increased exercise that create a negative energy balance and reduce a child's weight. Interventions for children who are moderately overweight may not involve dieting to create a negative energy balance because even a neutral energy balance allows moderately overweight children to "grow into" their weight over a period of months or years. However, these interventions may change diet content to reduce fats and sugars, as well as increasing physical activity (Mullen & Shield, 2004; Rosenbaum et al., 1997).

Many of the most successful interventions for children and their families have several characteristics in common:

- *Setting reasonable goals for a child:* The goal of returning to a healthy weight may be appropriate for many children, but a healthy weight may be an unreachable goal for some children who are obese. For these children, a reduction in BMI may be more appropriate because a meaningful reduction in BMI usually creates better health even if a child remains overweight (Poskitt, 2002).
- *Focusing on developing a permanent more healthful lifestyle:* This approach offers more long-term benefits than do short-term changes in diet or exercise to create immediate weight loss (Bauer & Maffeis, 2002).
- *Making gradual behavior changes that gradually reduce a child's BMI* (Bauer & Maffeis, 2002): Dramatic behavior changes (cutting out all snacks, running three miles each day) are often accepted initially but then resisted. Taking the long-term view and changing diets and activity patterns gradually over several months make each change more acceptable and easier to carry out. Poskitt (2002) even suggests gradually reducing the temperature in the family home during colder months by a degree every few months so that more energy must be expended to generate heat in a child's body.
- *Involving parents and families in the intervention* (Mullen & Shield, 2004; Poskitt, 2002): This makes the intervention a family effort rather than something that only the child must do. The content and frequency of family meals and snacks can be changed, and family activities can be altered to include more physical activity. Parents who are overweight or obese may be encouraged to model a more healthful lifestyle for their children and lose some weight along with them.
- *Encouraging the active participation and cooperation of the child in the development and application of the intervention:* Children are more likely to follow a new diet or exercise plan if they have some say in its creation and if they can veto any components they find unacceptable (Poskitt, 2002).

Intense interventions have resulted in significant weight loss for some children who are obese. For example, Braet, Tanghe, Decaluwe, Moens, and Rosseel (2004) evaluated a 10-month inpatient program in Belgium that focused on helping children develop more healthful lifestyles through diet changes, increased activity, and cognitive–behavioral therapy. During their treatment, the children lost almost 50% of their weight, and at a 14-month follow-up they continued to weigh 30% less than at the beginning of the program. Younger children lost more weight than older children. Although the program was successful, the cost of a 10-month inpatient program is very high and thus is unavailable to most children.

Comprehensive outpatient treatment programs have also been effective. Epstein and his colleagues (2004) have tested several interventions. For example, during a six-month intensive program, food intake was changed through the implementation of the Traffic Light Diet, with common foods classified as low in calories and fat (green foods), moderate in calories and fat (yellow foods), and high in calories and fat (red foods). Depending on the children's ages and sizes, daily intake targets of between 800 and 1,200 calories were established, with a weight loss goal of half a pound per week. To increase activity, three sedentary behaviors (watching television, playing video games, and using the computer for non–school-related activities) were limited to 15 hours a week. Parents who were overweight or obese were also encouraged to reduce their food consumption and sedentary behavior, so the intervention often became a family effort. Children were given positive reinforcement for meeting their 15-hour sedentary behavior limits and for attaining their weekly weight loss goals (Epstein, Paluch, Kilanowski, & Raynor, 2004).

At the end of the 6-month program and at a 12-month follow-up, the children exhibited significantly less consumption of high-fat foods, greater consumption of fruits and vegetables, and less sedentary behavior. There was also a significant decrease in the weight of the children and the parents. Children who substituted active behaviors for the targeted sedentary behaviors rather than engaging in other nonactive behaviors (such as reading) lost more weight at the 6-month and 12-month assessments. Those who ate fewer foods from the red group of foods lost more weight at the 6-month assessment but not at the 12-month assessment, suggesting that activity level changes were more important than food consumption changes for long-term weight control.

An interesting 12-week experiment made television viewing contingent on pedaling a stationary bicycle (Faith et al., 2001). Children in the experimental group could watch two minutes of television for every one minute during which they pedaled at or above a specific rate. Children in the control group also had a stationary bicycle and a television, but their television viewing was not contingent on pedaling. At the end of the intervention period, children in the experimental group watched television 5 hours a week compared with 21 hours a week for the control group. They also experienced a greater reduction in total body fat. Thus this intervention combined healthful physical activity (pedaling) with an activity the children enjoyed (watching television), showing that the two do not have to be mutually exclusive.

Bariatric surgery has become increasingly popular as a treatment for chronic and severe obesity in adults, and its use with adolescents and children has increased recently (Inge et al., 2004; Salvatoni, 2002). Two types of surgery are used: One decreases the size of the stomach, which reduces how much food can be consumed; the other bypasses much of the intestine, which diminishes the absorption of calories and nutrients from food. Both have caused significant weight reductions in adults. However, both create the possibility of significant medical complications, including cardiorespiratory impairment, infection, gastrointestinal leakage, ulcers, and malnutrition (Salvatoni, 2002). In addition, the potential negative consequences to a child's physical development of the dramatically reduced food consumption that occurs after the surgery are not well understood.

Several permanent lifestyle changes must occur after the surgery: Food intake must be closely regulated so that sufficient protein and nutrients are ingested, and liquids are significantly reduced to avoid flushing nutrients through the system. Because of these lifestyle changes and the potential medical complications, strict criteria are often established for adults or children undergoing bariatric surgery—including high levels of obesity (usually a BMI of at least 40), the failure of other methods for reducing obesity, and a psychological profile that suggests the ability to make major lifestyle changes (Inge et al., 2004; Salvatoni, 2002).

Key Concepts

- Interventions should involve reasonable weight loss goals for a child that can be met through gradual changes in behavior.
- Parents and children should be active participants in any intervention.
- Intense inpatient and outpatient interventions have been successful with many children who are obese.
- Bariatric surgery has become increasingly popular as a treatment for chronic and severe obesity in adults, but this procedure remains controversial for use with children and adolescents.

Anorexia Nervosa and Bulimia Nervosa

Over the past few decades, there has been a dramatic increase in concern about *anorexia nervosa* and *bulimia nervosa*. (*Anorexia nervosa* comes from the Greek *an*, "without," and *orexis*, "appetite," and Latin *nervus*, "a nerve"; *bulimia nervosa* comes from the Greek *bous*, "ox," and *limos*, "hunger," and Latin *nervus*, "nerve," or someone who is hungry enough to eat an ox—rather than someone who has an appetite like an ox, a species not known for eating voraciously; Colman, 2001.) Colman (2001) notes that the correct terms for the eating disorders found in the DSM-IV-TR require the word *nervosa* because *anorexia* (loss of appetite) and *bulimia* (voracious appetite) represent only one symptom of each disorder. Both disorders can cause severe medical consequences, and both can disrupt the lives of those who have them (Rome & Ammerman, 2003). As extreme examples, one study found that 6% of a group of adolescents diagnosed with anorexia nervosa died within 12 years of their diagnosis—about half from suicide and half from the physical consequences of anorexia nervosa (Neumarker, 1997); another study found a mortality rate of 3% among a group of adolescents and adults with bulimia nervosa (Patton, 1988).

Anorexia nervosa and bulimia nervosa are diagnosed primarily in middle to late adolescence and early adulthood, and they rarely occur in children. For example, a study of about 1,300 sixth- through ninth-grade girls found only six cases of bulimia nervosa over the three years of the study (McKnight Investigators, 2003). However, other research shows that some young girls and boys develop attitudes and behaviors that raise their risk of developing anorexia nervosa or bulimia nervosa as adolescents or young adults (Cattarin & Thompson, 1994). In addition, some children exhibit some symptoms of an eating disorder, raising concern about their psychological and physical health. The McKnight study just mentioned, for example, found that about 4% of the girls exhibited several symptoms of an eating disorder during the three years of the study (McKnight Investigators, 2003).

Because our primary focus in this text has been on children and younger adolescents, we will start our exploration of eating disorders by examining the attitudes (such as a desire to be thin) and behaviors (such as dieting) that are occurring with increasing frequency among school-age children and young adolescents. We will then discuss what is known about anorexia nervosa and bulimia nervosa, how the attitudes and behaviors of school-age children raise their risk of developing an eating disorder, and how these disorders develop during adolescence and young adulthood.

Prevalence of Body Dissatisfaction and Dieting among School-Age Children

Although it has been well known for years that many adolescents, particularly female adolescents, are dissatisfied with their bodies (Ricciardelli & McCabe, 2001), recent research has shown that this dissatisfaction is also found in younger children. Whether adolescents who are dissatisfied with their bodies have felt that way since they were children remains unclear; but it may be reasonable to assume that body dissatisfaction is experienced by some children and adolescents for years. A recent study of second to fifth graders, for example, showed that 61% of the girls and 36% of the boys wanted to lose weight (Phares, Steinberg, & Thompson, 2004). Similarly, a study of 12- to 16-year-olds found that only 12% of the girls and 17% of the boys were at their desired weight (Ricciardelli & McCabe, 2001). Most of the girls wanted to be thinner (77%), whereas a small percentage wanted to be heavier (11%). Among the boys, 30% wanted to be thinner and 54% wanted to be heavier. The results of this study remind us that not all children who are dissatisfied with their bodies want to be thinner, although it is clear that most girls do. Interestingly, most of the boys wanted to be larger, which is probably related to cultural values that boys should be large and powerful. Although their desire to be larger does not put boys at risk for developing an eating disorder, it may put them at risk for unhealthful eating to gain weight or the use of steroids or other drugs to achieve a larger body (Ricciardelli & McCabe, 2001).

Dieting in young children is of particular concern because excessive dieting can lead to irreversible growth retardation, failure to accumulate appropriate bone mass, and delayed onset of puberty (Rome & Ammerman, 2003; Steiner & Lock, 1998). In addition, elementary school students who diet are more likely to continue dieting during middle school and high school, which can put them at risk for developing eating disorders (Shisslak et al., 1998). Two studies have reported a high prevalence of dieting among school-age children and young adolescents. Shisslak and colleagues (1998) found that 50% of elementary school girls and 66% of middle school girls had engaged in one or more dieting behaviors within the previous year (see Table 15.1). Although it is not clear what percentage engaged in highly restrictive diets or excessive exercise, the percentages who engaged in behaviors such as using diet pills or laxatives, self-starvation, or vomiting are alarmingly high. A study of seventh-grade girls and boys showed that 37% of the girls and 15% of the boys had dieted at least once during their lives. Interestingly, when the parents of the children in the study were asked about their children's dieting, only 12% of the parents of girls and 5% of the parents of boys reported that their children had ever dieted, suggesting that many children kept their diets secret from their parents.

Development of Body Dissatisfaction and Dieting

Family, Peer, and Media Influences

In an influential paper, Stice (1998) drew on the work of Kandel (1982), who had studied influences on adolescent drug use, to suggest two primary influences on adolescents' beliefs about their bodies and the appropriateness of dieting: social reinforcement and modeling. *Social reinforcement* refers to a process through which a person internalizes certain attitudes or engages in certain behaviors because they are promoted by significant others. Social reinforcement can occur directly (such as being encouraged to diet or being teased about being overweight) or indirectly (seeing those in the media criticized or praised for their weight). *Modeling,* on the other hand, refers to imitation of another person's behavior without that person specifically encouraging the imitation. For example, a child whose parents diet may decide to diet, or a child who observes friends or television characters dieting may decide to diet. Although Stice focused on the influence of social reinforcement and modeling on adolescents' eating attitudes and behaviors, others have investigated the extent to which they are also influential with younger children.

Several studies have found a strong influence of parents' social reinforcement on children's eating attitudes and behaviors, with this influence affecting both girls and boys. Parents' comments about their children's weight and the importance of being thin, and pressure they put on their children to lose weight, strongly affect the children's body dissatisfaction and initiation of dieting (Attie & Brooks-Gunn, 1995; Levine, Smolak, & Hayden, 1994; Thelen & Cormier, 1995). Two studies that assessed both social reinforcement and modeling by parents found that social reinforcement had more influence on children's attitudes about their weight than did parental modeling of dieting (Smolak, Levine, & Schermer, 1999; Wertheim, Martin, Prior, Sanson, & Smart, 2002).

TABLE 15.1

Weight Control Behaviors in Elementary and Middle School Girls

Weight Loss Behaviors	Elementary School % (n)		Middle School % (n)	
	Sometimes	A Lot	Sometimes	A Lot
Eating less	22.8% (23)	16.8% (17)	36.2% (151)	25.2% (105)
Diet pills	2.9% (3)	1.9% (2)	3.9% (16)	1.2% (5)
Exercise	36.3% (37)	19.6% (20)	42.5% (177)	28.8% (120)
Laxatives	1.9% (2)	3.9% (4)	4.3% (18)	1.7% (7)
Skipping meals	15.7% (16)	7.8% (8)	27.9% (116)	14.4% (60)
Self-starvation	13.6% (14)	6.8% (7)	21.2% (88)	11.1% (46)
Eating fewer fats/sweets	36.0% (36)	17.0% (17)	43.1% (179)	26.7% (111)
Self-induced vomiting	3.9% (4)	2.9% (3)	6.7% (28)	1.4% (6)

Source: Shisslak et al. (1998).

Whether social reinforcement and modeling from parents or peers has more of an influence on children's body dissatisfaction and dieting remain unclear. One study found that parental encouragement to diet was more influential than peer encouragement for young adolescents' decisions to diet (Strong & Huon, 1998). However, a study of elementary and middle school girls reported that once the influence of weight-related pressure from peers on children's dieting behaviors was taken into account, pressure from parents to be thin had no additional influence (Shisslak et al., 1998).

The relative influences of the media, parents, and peers on eating attitudes and behaviors have been investigated by two studies. Although these studies investigated children of different ages and explored the development of different issues (attitudes in one, bulimic behaviors in the second), their results suggest hypotheses that could be investigated more fully in the future. One study of 10- to 13-year-old girls found that social reinforcement from the media, but not from parents or peers, influenced the girls' internalization of a thin ideal weight (Blowers, Loxton, Grady-Flesser, Occhibinti, & Dawe, 2003). In contrast, Stice (1988) measured the influence of the media, parents, and peers on undergraduates' bulimic behaviors and found that family and peer social reinforcement was associated with bulimic behaviors and that social reinforcement through the media was not.

So where are we in our understanding of the development of body dissatisfaction and dieting behaviors in children? Some evidence exists to support the influence of parents, peers, and the media on body dissatisfaction and dieting behaviors, and the evidence for social reinforcement is stronger than the evidence for modeling. The relative influence of parents, peers, and the media is less clear, however. Following a pattern that we have seen throughout this text, current research on this topic points to possibilities—but additional research is needed before we can be more certain about the influences of parents, peers, and the media on the development of body dissatisfaction and dieting in children.

Influences of Body Size and Timing of Puberty

As might be expected, girls with a higher BMI are more likely than other girls to be dissatisfied with their bodies and to diet (Shisslak et al., 1998; Wiseman, Peltzman, Halmi, & Sunday, 2004). The associations among the timing of puberty and body dissatisfaction and dieting are more complex. The timing of puberty is a potentially important issue because the physical changes associated with puberty, which include breast development and increases in subcutaneous fat, can be alarming for girls who feel pressure to be thin (Gross, 1984). Girls who experience this physical transition while they are making the social transition of moving from elementary school to junior high school—where dating, relationships, and physical attractiveness are suddenly more important—may be particularly alarmed (Attie & Brooks-Gunn, 1995). McCabe and Ricciardelli (2004) found that girls who experienced early onset of puberty were more likely than later-maturing girls to be dissatisfied with their bodies and to diet. However, a study of adolescents did not find an association between early onset of puberty and the development of anorexia nervosa or bulimia nervosa (Stice, Presnell, & Bearman, 2001). These two studies suggest, therefore, that early onset of puberty may increase the risk for body dissatisfaction and dieting, but not necessarily the development of an eating disorder. In the following section we will address some issues other than timing of puberty onset that may push some girls who are dieting to develop an eating disorder.

Key Concepts

- Most school-age girls and about a third of school-age boys express the desire to lose weight.
- The percentage of children unhappy with their weight increases during middle school, with only about 15% of children expressing satisfaction with their weight. Most girls want to be thinner; most boys want to be heavier.
- About 60% of middle school girls report that they have engaged in some dieting behaviors within the previous year.
- Pressure from parents, peers, and the media encourage body dissatisfaction and dieting in some school-age children and adolescents. The relative importance of the pressure from these three sources remains unclear.
- Girls with larger bodies are more likely to be dissatisfied with them and to diet.
- Girls with an early onset of puberty are more likely to be dissatisfied with their bodies and to diet, although they may not be at increased risk for the development of an eating disorder.

Diagnostic Criteria for Anorexia Nervosa and Bulimia Nervosa

The DSM-IV-TR diagnostic criteria for anorexia nervosa and bulimia nervosa are shown in Tables 15.2 and 15.3. In the DSM-III and the DSM-III-R, the

TABLE 15.2

Diagnostic Criteria for 307.1 Anorexia Nervosa

A. Refusal to maintain body weight at or above a minimally normal weight for age and height (e.g., weight loss leading to maintenance of body weight less than 85% of that expected; or failure to make expected weight gain during period of growth, leading to body weight less than 85% of that expected).

B. Intense fear of gaining weight or becoming fat, even though underweight.

C. Disturbance in the way in which one's body weight or shape is experienced, undue influence of body weight or shape on self-evaluation, or denial of the seriousness of the current low body weight.

D. In postmenarcheal females, amenorrhea, i.e., the absence of at least three consecutive menstrual cycles. (A woman is considered to have amenorrhea if her periods occur only following hormone, e.g., estrogen, administration.)

Specify type:

Restricting Type: during the current episode of Anorexia Nervosa, the person has not regularly engaged in binge-eating or purging behavior (i.e., self-induced vomiting or the misuse of laxatives, diuretics, or enemas).

Binge-Eating/Purging Type: during the current episode of Anorexia Nervosa, the person has regularly engaged in binge-eating or purging behavior (i.e., self-induced vomiting or the misuse of laxatives, diuretics, or enemas).

---

two disorders were included in the category of *disorders usually first evident in infancy, childhood, or adolescence*. In the DSM-IV, they were removed from this category and placed in a new *eating disorders* category. This category also includes *eating disorder not otherwise specified*, which can be diagnosed if a person has most but not all of the needed symptoms (for example, a girl meets all the criteria for anorexia nervosa except that she continues to have regular menstrual cycles).

Some changes have occurred in the diagnostic criteria for anorexia nervosa over the various editions of the DSM. In the DSM-III a person's weight had to be at least 25% below his or her normal body weight; this was changed to 15% in the DSM-III-R and remained at 15% in the DSM-IV. In addition, in the DSM-III and the DSM-III-R, a **disturbed body image** was required: The person had to believe that he or she was fat despite his or her low weight. This was broadened in the DSM-IV to include either an inappropriate belief that one is fat or an excessive influence of weight on one's self-image. This change was made because of research showing that some individuals who met all the other diagnostic criteria for anorexia nervosa did not believe that they were fatter than they were (Horne, Van Vactor, & Emerson, 1991; Probst, Vandereycken, Coppenole, & Pieters, 1998).

Changes have also occurred to the diagnostic criteria for bulimia nervosa, although the core feature of the disorder, binge eating followed by purging, has remained the same. Beginning in the DSM-III-R, two criteria

TABLE 15.3

Diagnostic Criteria for 307.51 Bulimia Nervosa

A. Recurrent episodes of binge eating. An episode of binge eating is characterized by both of the following:
   (1) Eating, in a discrete period of time (e.g., within any two-hour period), an amount of food that is definitely larger than most people would eat during a similar period of time and under similar circumstances.
   (2) A sense of lack of control over eating during the episode (e.g., a feeling that one cannot stop eating or control what or how much one is eating).
B. Recurrent inappropriate compensatory behavior in order to prevent weight gain, such as self-induced vomiting; misuse of laxatives, diuretics, enemas, or other medications; fasting; or excessive exercise.
C. The binge eating and inappropriate compensatory behaviors both occur, on average, at least twice a week for three months.
D. Self-evaluation is unduly influenced by body shape and weight.
E. The disturbance does not occur exclusively during episodes of Anorexia Nervosa.
   Specify type:
   Purging Type: during the current episode of Bulimia Nervosa, the person has regularly engaged in self-induced vomiting or the misuse of laxatives, diuretics, or enemas.
   Nonpurging Type: during the current episode of Bulimia Nervosa, the person has used other inappropriate compensatory behaviors, such as fasting or excessive exercise, but has not regularly engaged in self-induced vomiting or the misuse of laxatives, diuretics, or enemas.

were added: a frequency requirement for binge-eating episodes (at least twice a week for at least three months) and a requirement of persistent overconcern with body size and shape. These changes continued into the DSM-IV. Finally, in the DSM-IV, two subtypes of anorexia nervosa and bulimia nervosa were specified for the first time.

Prevalence and Course of Anorexia Nervosa and Bulimia Nervosa

The prevalence of bulimia nervosa has been estimated at between 1% and 3% for adolescent and young adult females, and the prevalence of anorexia nervosa is about 0.5% (APA, 2000). More females than males have eating disorders. The ratio of females to males with anorexia nervosa is about 10:1 and with bulimia nervosa is about 5:1 (Attie & Brooks-Gunn, 1995; Steiner & Lock, 1998). However, some researchers argue that there may be significant underreporting of eating disorders among males because of their greater unwillingness to acknowledge that they have an eating disorder or their rationalization of eating-disordered behavior ("I only eat this way during wrestling season") (Carlat & Camargo, 1991).

College students have higher rates of eating disorders than their peers who do not attend college. Surveys of college women have found rates of anorexia nervosa between 1% and 2% and rates of bulimia nervosa between 3% and 19% (Alexander, 1998). In addition, many college students engage in binge eating, purging, and restricted eating that have health consequences but do not meet all the diagnostic criteria for an eating disorder (Steiner & Lock, 1998). For example, one study found that 61% of college women reported problematic eating patterns that did not rise to the level of an eating disorder (Mintz & Betz, 1988).

Eating disorders often first appear in middle to late adolescence. Halmi, Casper, Eckert, Goldberg, and Davis (1979) found two peaks of onset age for anorexia nervosa: 14.5 years and 18 years (notably around the times of entry into high school and college). The course of eating disorders is variable, with some adolescents experiencing one short occurrence of an eating disorder and others struggling for years with one eating-disorder episode or fluctuating between periods of healthy eating and periods of disordered eating (Steiner & Lock, 1998). Patterns of disordered eating are often very resistant to change, with anorexia nervosa being even more resistant than bulimia nervosa. For example, Herzog and colleagues (1999) examined the recovery of females with anorexia nervosa and bulimia nervosa 7.5 years after diagnosis; these researchers found that only 33% of those with anorexia nervosa and 74% of those with bulimia nervosa had made a full recovery.

Key Concepts

- The prevalence among women is about 0.5% for anorexia nervosa and about 1–3% for bulimia nervosa.
- Both disorders are more common among women than men, and they are more common among women in college than among their peers not in college.

Development of Anorexia Nervosa and Bulimia Nervosa

In another textbook (Haugaard, 2001) I argued that the best way to describe the development of eating disorders is with a four-stage model (see Figure 15.6). Each stage has features that distinguish it from the others, although they often blend into each other so they are not completely distinct. The early stages of the model involve dieting. The biological and behavioral changes that occur during these early stages can lead to the development of an eating disorder during the later stages. Here are the four stages:

1. A child or adolescent decides to begin dieting, develops a strategy to lose weight, and puts it into action. (The decision to diet is primarily influenced by the social issues discussed earlier in this section; they will not be reexamined here.)

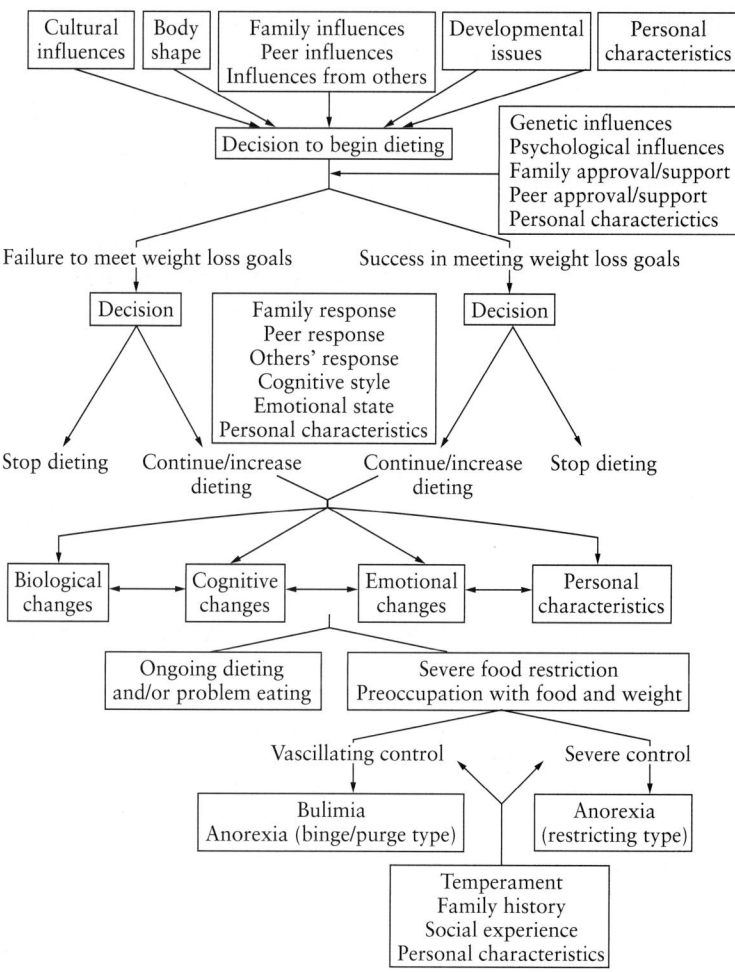

FIGURE 15.6   *A Model for the Development of Eating Disorders*

Source: Haugard (2001).

2. The dieting strategy leads to success or failure, and the child or adolescent decides to end the diet, continue it, or intensify it.

3. The physical and psychological changes caused by extended dieting lead to prolonged food restriction and a preoccupation with food and weight.

4. The physical and psychological changes associated with prolonged food restriction and preoccupation with food and weight cause severely disordered eating patterns that constitute an eating disorder. The level of control that the adolescent has over his or her eating determines whether the eating disorder involves binge eating and purging.

Dieting Success or Failure, and the Decision to Stop, Continue, or Intensify Dieting

Dieting Success or Failure   Dieting is difficult, as anyone who has been on a diet knows. However, the difficulty of dieting is not the same for everyone. Several biological, psychological, and social factors influence the extent to which a child's or adolescent's attempts to lose weight will be successful.

As discussed in the section about childhood obesity, genes have an important influence on body size and shape. Children and adolescents whose dieting goals involve weight levels that are difficult to reach because of their genetically influenced body size are less likely to successfully meet their weight loss goals (Attie & Brooks-Gunn, 1995).

Reinforcement and support from friends and family can encourage dieting success (Strong & Huon, 1998). Comments about noticeable weight loss or about control over eating when a person restricts meals or snacks can encourage continued efforts to meet weight loss goals. Conversely, lack of peer or family support for dieting, or failure of anyone to notice and comment on initial weight loss, may discourage dieting and thus the ability to meet weight loss goals.

The Decision to Stop, Continue, or Intensify Dieting   Those who have started dieting face the decision of when to stop. The decision may come at specific points, such as reaching a goal of losing 10 pounds, or may be an ongoing process occurring each day or perhaps at every meal. Those who meet their weight loss goals may decide to continue dieting toward a lower weight or stop dieting. Those who do not meet their goals may intensify their dieting or may consider themselves dieting failures and stop dieting.

The responses of many people can influence this decision. Adults or peers who discourage ongoing dieting may dissuade a person from continuing; however, ongoing negative comments about body size may influence continued dieting (Strong & Huon, 1998). Positive responses to a child's or adolescent's ability to restrict food intake may influence ongoing dieting because these responses would stop if he or she were to resume normal eating. Those who have failed to attain their weight loss goals may be encouraged to redouble their efforts ("I know you can do it if you just try harder"), which can encourage continued dieting. Children in families or social groups where perfection or high levels of success are expected may be particularly vulnerable to this argument (Tyrka, Waldron, Graber, & Brooks-Gunn, 2002).

Certain styles of thinking may influence some children or adolescents to continue dieting. **Dichotomous thinking,** in which issues are viewed as one or another extreme rather than throughout their range, may encourage ongoing dieting (Kales, 1989; Polivy & Herman, 1993). Those with a dichotomous thinking style believe they are either thin or fat. If they weigh even one pound over their desired weight, they believe they are fat. This cognitive style encourages ongoing dieting because the child or adolescent must remain at or below his or her weight goal to avoid believing that he or she is fat.

Individuals with a greater sense of self-worth are less likely to continue dieting (Strong & Huon, 1998). A stronger sense of self-worth may allow children or adolescents to focus on other more successful aspects of their lives whether or not they can reach their weight goal. Those who are perfectionistic are more likely to continue dieting, and this may be related to a lower sense of self-worth when they compare their own views of perfection to what they see in themselves (Tyrka et al., 2002).

Development of Prolonged Food Restriction and a Preoccupation with Food and Weight

In several controlled studies of restricted eating, researchers have taken healthy young adults, restricted their diets for several days to several months, and looked for changes in the participants' biological, cognitive, and emotional functioning (Fichter & Pirke, 1986; Keyes, Brozek, Henschel, Mickelsen, & Taylor, 1950; Schweiger et al., 1986). Because these changes occurred in healthy individuals after a period of food restriction, a strong argument can be made that the food restriction caused them.

Studies of complete food abstinence for three weeks (Fichter, 1992) and food restriction to 1,000 calories per day (Schweiger et al., 1986) showed several endocrine and neurotransmitter changes during food restriction. Many of these changes reduced the energy expended by the body and improved the efficiency with which calories were absorbed and used by the body (Rosenbaum & Leibel, 1998). In addition, changes in levels of luteinizing hormone, follicle-stimulating hormone, and growth hormone occurred during food restriction, and levels of the neurotransmitters serotonin and norepinephrine were reduced. What is noteworthy about these changes is that they are all considered biological markers of depression (Armitage et al, 2002). This suggests that the depressed mood that many people feel when dieting may directly result from the biological changes caused by reduced food intake.

Many emotional changes have been observed during food restriction (Keyes et al., 1950; Schweiger et al., 1986). The most notable emotional change is the increase in depression (Smoller, Wadden, & Stunkard, 1987). As noted in our chapter about depression, symptoms of this disorder include heightened irritability, which is also commonly found during food restriction. An increase in emotional lability has also been associated with ongoing dieting: Moods can change quickly, and levels of depression and elation are heightened. One consequence of increased mood lability is that small failures in dieting after a long time on a diet can evoke higher levels of emotion than would have been experienced earlier in the diet (Polivy & Herman, 1993).

Cognitive changes that can encourage ongoing dieting have also been found during extended food restriction. Dichotomous thinking may be exacerbated, with the adolescent monitoring his or her weight closely and seeing any small increase as an indication that the diet is a failure (Polivy & Herman, 1985). Thinking often becomes more constricted; and as a dieter's thinking becomes more constricted, he or she focuses more intently on food and the diet. Other aspects of his or her life can fade into the background, and his or her self-image can become increasingly based on weight and dieting. This can create a preoccupation with food and dieting.

Dieting also can alter a person's perception of the attractiveness of food overall or of certain types of food (Keyes et al., 1950). The enjoyment of the taste of food may be heightened, which further increases its desirability and can increase an adolescent's preoccupation with food. This can increase the likelihood that he or she will binge on these foods (Polivy & Herman, 1993).

Severe Food Restriction and the Development of an Eating Disorder

At this point in the sequential model, we have an adolescent whose ongoing dieting has caused a series of biological, cognitive, and emotional changes, as well as a preoccupation with food and dieting. This preoccupation produces a strong psychological desire to continue intense dieting. Opposing this psychological desire, however, is a strong biologically based urge to eat. Consequently, the adolescent is caught between two strong forces: a psychologically based desire to diet and a biologically based urge to eat. These forces can cause behaviors, biological functioning, and psychological functioning that constitute an eating disorder.

Most people with eating disorders develop a cycle of binge eating and purging (Heatherton, Herman, & Polivy, 1991). Research shows mainly that dieting leads to the development of binge eating, rather than binge eating leading to dieting (Lowe, 1993). The hypothesis for this developmental pattern is that after a period of food restriction, biological and psychological mechanisms create an irresistible urge to consume large amounts of food. Binge eating can be viewed as succumbing to this urge. In addition, binge eating often relieves the depression and anxiety that many extended dieters experience (Elmore & De Castro, 1990). Consequently, binge eating is negatively reinforced by reductions in distressing emotions and hunger, which increase the likelihood that the person will binge-eat in the future when facing strong hunger and depression. However, the positive consequences of binge eating are short-lived because most dieters experience distressing emotions (depression, anxiety, guilt), distressing cognitions ("I'll become hugely fat"), and sometimes uncomfortable physical sensations after eating a large amount of food (Elmore & De Castro, 1990). To reduce these unpleasant consequences, **purging** occurs. As with the binge-eating part of the cycle, purging is negatively reinforced by a reduction in distressing emotions and cognitions, increasing the likelihood that purging will occur after future incidents of binge eating. As the adolescent continues his or her intense dieting, the cycle is repeated: eating to dispel hunger and bothersome emotions, and then purging to get rid of the food just consumed and the bothersome sensations occurring after eating.

A minority of those with eating disorders do not binge and purge; rather, they restrict their food intake consistently. There is some indication that adolescents who have severely restricted their eating for a considerable time are less sensitive to feelings of hunger (Lowe, 1993). These adolescents may feel less urge to eat, which may reduce their likelihood of developing a **binge–purge cycle**. However, this relative lack of hunger does not develop quickly, and these adolescents may have endured many months of feeling a strong urge to eat.

The issues that influence whether an adolescent develops a binge–purge cycle or restricts food intake consistently have not been investigated extensively (Attie & Brooks-Gunn, 1995). An interesting avenue of inquiry focuses on the consistency of the adolescent's control over his or her eating. The strong biological urges to eat erode most adolescents' control. Their control vacillates, and they find themselves in a binge–purge cycle. The length of time between binges may indicate the consistency of their control. A small percentage of adolescents can maintain control over their eating consistently, despite their strong urges to eat, and they develop a consistently restrictive pattern of eating. Because most adolescents who have severely restricted their food intake are unable to maintain control over their eating in the face of biological urges to eat, more adolescents develop binge–purge cycles than consistently restrictive eating patterns. The specific personal, family, or social characteristics that influence whether an adolescent has vacillating or consistent control over his or her eating remain unknown.

Key Concepts

- The first stage of the development of an eating disorder, the decision to diet, is primarily influenced by social pressures from the media, parents, and peers. Children or adolescents with a genetically influenced larger body size may be more susceptible to these pressures.
- In the second stage, decisions are made about whether to continue dieting, intensify dieting, or end dieting. Reinforcement for dieting from parents or peers, dichotomous thinking, and low self-esteem or self-esteem based primarily on body size may encourage ongoing or intensified dieting.
- Those who keep dieting for prolonged periods experience several physiological, cognitive, and emotional changes that can create a preoccupation with food and weight.
- Those who continue dieting may experience extreme hunger that is satisfied through binge eating followed by purging. These people are likely to develop bulimia nervosa. Others can consistently restrict their eating, which may result in anorexia nervosa.

Prevention

Efforts to prevent unhealthful dieting and eating disorders usually involve educational programs about the composition of healthful and unhealthful diets; understanding the role of the media in establishing body shape standards that are impossible for most people to attain; learning about the variety of body shapes and the genetic influence on body shape; feeling more comfortable with one's body shape; and resisting urges to diet in unhealthful ways (Piran, 1998). Such interventions are typically provided to females and may be offered during health classes in elementary, junior high, or high school or to groups of women in college residence halls or sororities.

Unfortunately there is little evidence that these educational programs influence the attitudes or behaviors of most who participate in them (Ebeling et al., 2003). Some programs have a positive short-term influence, as measured by participants' attitudes at the end of the program; but this influence usually disappears within several weeks (Tilgner, Wertheim, & Paxton, 2004). In fact, concern has been raised that some prevention programs may be counterproductive. For example, a group of 13- to 14-year-old girls reduced their dieting behavior immediately after a prevention program, but at a six-month follow-up their dieting had increased to levels above those before the prevention program (Carter, Stewart, Dunn, and Fairburn, 1997). A program for undergraduates featuring several students who had recovered from eating disorders resulted in increases in dieting among program participants. These researchers suggested that efforts to destigmatize disordered eating, so that those with disordered eating would be more willing to seek help, may have inadvertently normalized the behavior (Mann et al., 1997). Clearly we need to reconsider how to prevent unhealthful dieting and how to use this knowledge to create effective prevention programs for children and adolescents.

Key Concept

- Eating disorder prevention programs focus on educational efforts to teach children and adolescents (mostly females) about the problems associated with dieting. However, most prevention programs have little positive influence on participants' dieting behaviors, and increased dieting has been observed after some prevention programs.

Individual and Family Treatment

Because of the many biological, psychological, and social issues that adolescents with anorexia nervosa or bulimia nervosa face, treatment for these disorders must be multifaceted (Steiner & Lock, 1998). Treatment may include strategies to increase weight and stabilize metabolic functioning, change eating patterns, reduce troubling emotions, change destructive patterns of thinking, and improve family and social relationships.

Hospitalization may be needed for some adolescents with anorexia nervosa and a few with bulimia nervosa (Robin, Gilroy, & Dennis, 1998). Ebeling and colleagues (2003) have suggested several criteria indicating that hospitalization is needed (see Table 15.4). The primary goals of hospitalization are to save the adolescent's life if biological functioning has become precarious and to begin the process of recovery that will continue after the adolescent leaves the hospital (Ebeling et al., 2003). Hospital interventions usually focus on helping the adolescent eat reasonable amounts of nutritious foods to begin the process of weight gain. Behavioral interventions are often employed in this process. For example, patients can earn visiting or television privileges by eating appropriately and may need to stay in bed, without visitors, when refusing to eat (Robin et al., 1998).

TABLE 15.4

Indications for Inpatient Treatment

Somatic Indications
- Body mass index <13kg/m^2 or <70% of relative weight corresponding to height or a rapid loss of weight (25% in three months)
- Severe disturbances of electrolyte or metabolic homeostasis
- Systolic blood pressure <70 mmHg or heart rate <40/min or aberrant ECG

Psychiatric Indications
- Psychotic symptoms
- Severe self-harm or tendency toward suicide
- Severe depression
- Severe problems within family

Failure of outpatient treatment

Source: Ebeling and colleagues (2003).

Several medications have been used with adults who have eating disorders, such as antianxiety medications to reduce anxiety about eating and antidepressant medications to reduce binge eating and purging. These medications have been effective in many cases (Ebeling et al., 2003). Little research has occurred with medication use among children and adolescents, however. One study explored the use of fluoxetine (a selective serotonin reuptake inhibitor, or SSRI) for eight weeks with thirteen 12- to 18-year-old females with bulimia nervosa. Before the eight-week medication trial, all participants received four weeks of psychotherapy. As shown in Figure 15.7, a significant decrease in binges and purges occurred during the eight weeks of medication. Although the mechanisms through which SSRIs influence binges and purges are not understood, this study suggests that further research using placebo control groups is appropriate and that SSRIs may be an important part of treatment for some adolescents who have bulimia nervosa.

Nutritional counseling, often provided by a dietitian, focuses on helping the adolescent create and follow a healthful eating plan (Steiner & Lock, 1998). The dietitian often defines a target weight for the adolescent and then monitors his or her weight and metabolic rate. For most females the initial target weight is 90% of their normal weight, which is the weight at which menstrual cycles often return (Ebeling et al., 2003).

Two styles of individual therapy are used most frequently with adolescents who have eating disorders: cognitive–behavioral therapy and psychodynamic therapy. Cognitive–behavioral therapy focuses on enhancing self-esteem and changing cognitions (such as "I must be thin to be liked") and thought patterns (such as dichotomous thinking) that can lead to severe dieting. Adolescents in treatment may be asked to keep detailed records of their food intake and to monitor and record their thoughts about themselves, their eating, and their social relationships. These thoughts are then explored with the therapist (Fairburn, Marcus, & Wilson, 1993; Peterson & Mitchell,

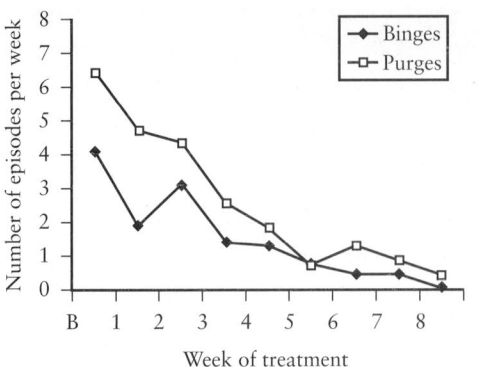

FIGURE 15.7 *Mean Weekly Binge and Purge Frequencies*
Source: Kotter et al. (2003).

1999). Therapy outcome studies have consistently shown the effectiveness of cognitive–behavioral therapy: About 75% of participants improve their eating patterns, and about 40% develop healthful eating patterns that continue for months or years after therapy (Peterson & Mitchell, 1999).

Psychodynamic therapy is less directive than cognitive–behavioral therapy. It focuses on helping the adolescent explore concerns about identity, interpersonal issues with family members and peers, and personal challenges (Robin et al., 1998). Therapists focus less on promoting changes in eating patterns and more on helping adolescents understand the role that food plays in their lives. A few assessments of psychodynamic individual therapy have shown it to be effective in many cases of anorexia nervosa; it has not been evaluated in the treatment of bulimia nervosa (Robin et al., 1998).

Family therapy is a common treatment for adolescents with eating disorders. It may be used as the only form of treatment or with individual therapy. The goals of various family therapy approaches vary; most have a primary focus of helping the family function in a way that will promote the adolescent's ongoing recovery from the eating disorder. Some family therapy approaches consider the eating disorder as resulting from problematic family functioning, and they work to change family functioning to eliminate the need for the eating disorder within the family (Minuchin et al., 1975). Others focus on establishing the family as a force to help the adolescent regain his or her health, with the issue of why the adolescent has an eating disorder receiving little or no attention (Dare & Szmukler, 1991). Work with parents to deal with any eating disorders or patterns of unhealthful eating is an important part of family therapy in some cases. Family therapy has been shown to be an effective treatment in cases of anorexia nervosa (Robin et al., 1998). Russell, Szmukler, Dare, and Eisler (1987) found that family therapy was more effective than individual therapy in cases where anorexia nervosa began before the age of 18 and where it had been of short duration, and that individual therapy was superior in cases with older clients.

Key Concepts

- Hospitalization may be needed for some adolescents with eating disorders. The primary goals of hospitalization are to save the adolescent's life if biological functioning has become precarious and begin the process of recovery that will continue after the adolescent leaves the hospital.
- Antianxiety medications can reduce anxiety about eating. SSRIs may be effective in reducing binge-eating episodes for some adolescents.
- Nutritional counseling helps establish reasonable and healthful diets.
- Cognitive–behavioral therapy focuses on reducing problematic cognitions about weight and self-esteem that may be at the foundation of dieting.
- Psychodynamic therapy focuses on understanding the roles that food and weight play in a person's life and in his or her self-evaluation.
- Family therapy focuses either on changing the functioning of the family so that the eating disorder no longer plays an important role in that functioning or in helping the family assist the adolescent in ending his or her eating-disordered behaviors.

Elimination Disorders

The DSM-IV-TR includes *enuresis* and *encopresis* in the elimination disorders section of the disorders usually first diagnosed in infancy, childhood, or adolescence category. Enuresis (from the Greek *ouresis*, "urination") is repeated urination in inappropriate places after a child is past the age at which most children have learned to urinate in a toilet. Encopresis (from the Greek *kopros*, "excrement") is the repeated passage of feces in inappropriate places after the age at which most children have learned to have bowel movements in a toilet.

Children with elimination disorders experience a variety· of negative consequences (Mikkelsen, 2001; Theunis, Van Hoecke, Paesbrugge, Hoebeke, & VandeWalle, 2002). Not only must they cope with the immediate consequences of wetting or soiling their beds or clothes; they must also cope with the emotional consequences of knowing that they have not developed the type of control over bodily functions that is often viewed as an important part of growing up. In addition, many of them must endure negative reactions from those around them. Other children may make fun of them and avoid them, which can harm their peer relationships. Parents and siblings may be embarrassed by them and may openly express hostility or disapproval, which can disrupt family relationships. Exasperation may cause parents to use harsh parenting practices and steadily increasing punishments for the children's "misbehavior." All these consequences can significantly affect a child's self-esteem, frustration, and anger, and may influence the development of anxiety disorders, depressive disorders, or conduct disorders (Ondersma, Ondersma, & Walker, 2001).

Elimination disorders provide an interesting example of how thinking can change about the relationships between psychological and physical symptoms. Early conceptualizations of enuresis and encopresis were that they were caused by psychological problems. Many of these conceptualizations were based on psychodynamic theory suggesting that a child's problems with urination or bowel movements were expressions of unconscious conflicts. More recent research, however, has shown that these conceptualizations were backward. We now know that most cases of enuresis and encopresis are caused by biological problems, and that the psychological problems seen in some children are consequences of enuresis or encopresis rather than their causes (Djurhuus, 2002; Moffatt, Kato, & Pless, 1987).

Case Study: Primary Enuresis

As Trudy was beginning the first grade, she and her parents had become increasingly concerned about her periodic bed-wetting. Her parents knew that their nieces and nephews had all stopped wetting their beds by age 4, and they could not understand why Trudy could not do this. At the suggestion of one of Trudy's uncles several months earlier, her parents had begun limiting the fluids that Trudy drank in the afternoon and evening and had begun waking her at about 11 p.m. to use the toilet. However, Trudy continued to wet her bed about twice each week. Neither Trudy nor her parents could understand why she wet the bed some nights and not others, and her parents began to question whether she was doing it on purpose. Trudy claimed that this was not true and insisted that she was never aware of wetting the bed until the next morning.

As the problem continued after Trudy's sixth birthday, her parents began to disagree about how they should handle her wetting incidents. Her father wanted to punish her each time one occurred; her mother argued that they should be patient and not punish Trudy. They were unable to resolve their disagreement, but they did agree to begin setting an alarm clock in Trudy's room to ring at 2 a.m., and Trudy was instructed to get out of bed when the alarm rang and use the bathroom. Although this strategy reduced Trudy's wetting incidents to about one a week, Trudy found that sometimes when she woke at 2 a.m. she had already wet the bed; other times when she woke and used the bathroom, she would wet the bed between 2 a.m. and when she woke again at about 7 a.m.

Trudy's bed-wetting continued at the same rate for two more years, and she and her parents became increasingly frustrated with it. Her parents finally decided to consult with Trudy's pediatrician. The physical exam done by the pediatrician could find no medical reason for Trudy's bed-wetting. During a conversation about the physical exam, the pediatrician asked Trudy's parents if anyone else in the family had experienced problems with bed-wetting. Trudy's mother reluctantly said that she had wet her bed until about age 9. Trudy and her father were amazed, and they asked why her mother had never said anything about it. Her mother replied that she had always been ashamed of wetting the bed, and she worried that telling Trudy about it might make Trudy feel that wetting the bed was not a problem. But hearing about her mother's bed-wetting made Trudy feel better about her own bed-wetting.

The pediatrician suggested that Trudy take a medication, desmopressin acetate, that had been shown to reduce bed-wetting. Trudy and her parents agreed. Within a week Trudy's bed-wetting had stopped—much to everyone's relief. After about five months of taking desmopressin acetate, her pediatrician recommended that Trudy stop taking it. Within a week Trudy's bed-wetting returned to the level it was at before she took the medication. This upset everyone very much, particularly Trudy. The pediatrician did not recommend using the medication again because it had not ended Trudy's bed-wetting. The pediatrician recommended ending all treatment, including waking Trudy at night, and suggested that Trudy simply be told to change her sheets every morning after a wetting incident.

Two weeks after her ninth birthday, Trudy's bed-wetting stopped for reasons that no one understood. Although she never wet the bed again, it was not until six months had passed that Trudy and her parents could believe that her bed-wetting problem had ended for good. All were delighted.

Some Issues Worth Noting

- The lack of effectiveness of any interventions attempted.
- Whether withdrawing all interventions influenced the cessation of Trudy's enuresis.
- The similarity in the timing of the cessation of Trudy's and her mother's enuresis.

Enuresis

For most of us, the ability to withhold urination until it can be done in a toilet or other appropriate place has become so automatic that it is easy to disregard the complex coordination of physical and cognitive abilities that this requires (Butler, 1998). First, a child's bladder must develop to a size that can hold a meaningful amount of urine; second, the child must develop voluntary control over the **external urinary sphincter,** which holds urine in the bladder; third, the child must develop the cognitive ability to recognize the physical sensations indicating that his or her bladder is full and the physical ability to inhibit contractions of the bladder until in an appropriate place for urination; and fourth, the child must be able to relax the external urinary sphincter while contracting the muscles around the bladder to expel the urine (Husmann, 1996). A problem with any of these abilities can cause enuresis.

Diagnostic Criteria

Table 15.5 shows the diagnostic criteria for enuresis in the DSM-IV-TR. As you can see, enuresis can be diagnosed if a child urinates in inappropriate places either intentionally or unintentionally. Most cases of enuresis involve unintentional urination; children who intentionally urinate improperly have not been the focus of research, so we know little about them.

A child must be 5 years old to be given the diagnosis of enuresis; this is the age at which most children have developed the ability to control their urination (children with mental retardation and other developmental disabilities must have reached a mental age of at least 5 years). In addition, a child must urinate inappropriately at least twice a week for three consecutive months or at a frequency that causes significant distress or impairment. Consequently, a child who wets her bed occasionally and is not overly concerned about this would not be given the diagnosis of enuresis; but a child who occasionally urinates in his clothes at school might experience enough distress or impairment to be given the diagnosis (Mikkelsen, 2001).

The DSM specifies three subtypes of enuresis: **nocturnal only** when the child has wetting incidents only when asleep in bed, **diurnal only** when the child has wetting incidents only during the day when awake, and **nocturnal and diurnal** when both occur. As we will see in the next section, *nocturnal only* is the most common type of enuresis (Mikkelsen, 2001). Enuresis can also be classified as **primary**, indicating that the child has never had a period of urinary continence, and **secondary**, indicating that the child has had a period of urinary continence and has returned to wetting incidents (the length of this period is not specified, but it must be long enough to show that the child has control over his or her urination) (APA, 2000).

Based on his review of research into the causes of enuresis, von Gontard (1998) suggested subtyping cases of enuresis into three groups based on their primary cause. The value of these three groups is that the most effective interventions for children in each group may be different. **Urge incontinence** occurs when a child cannot suppress bladder contractions while his or her bladder is filling with urine. The result is frequent, uncontrollable voiding of small amounts of urine. In a study of Swedish 7-year-olds, about 75% of the children with wetting problems showed symptoms of urge incontinence, suggesting that it is the most common type of enuresis (Olbing, 1993, cited in von Gontard, 1998). **Voiding postponement** occurs when a child purposely does not urinate for long periods. The reasons for not urinating are varied; they include fear of using the toilet, fear of using an unfamiliar bathroom, and a desire not to leave other activities. At a certain point a child can no longer hold the urine in his or her bladder, resulting in a sudden, uncontrollable voiding of large amounts of urine. Finally, in the **detrusor–sphincter dyscoordination** type, a child cannot relax the external urinary sphincter

---

TABLE 15.5

Diagnostic Criteria for 307.6 Enuresis

A. Repeated voiding of urine into bed or clothes (whether involuntary or intentional).

B. The behavior is clinically significant as manifested by either a frequency of twice a week for at least three consecutive months or the presence of clinically significant distress or impairment in social, academic (occupational), or other important areas of functioning.

C. Chronological age is at least 5 years (or equivalent developmental level).

D. The behavior is not due exclusively to the direct physiological effect of a substance (e.g., a diuretic) or a general medical condition (e.g., diabetes, spina bifida, a seizure disorder).

Specify type:
   Nocturnal Only
   Diurnal Only
   Nocturnal and Diurnal

while contracting the muscles around the bladder. This results in the child having to strain to urinate and usually voiding only small amounts of urine. Wetting incidents can occur if the child's bladder fills to the point where involuntary urination occurs.

Interestingly, the urge incontinence type appears related to the first and second skills needed for appropriate urination mentioned in the introduction to this section (development of sufficient bladder capacity and control over the external urinary sphincter); the detrusor–sphincter dyscoordination type appears related to the fourth skill (coordination of sphincter relaxation and bladder contractions). The voiding postponement type appears to be related primarily to psychological issues associated with a child's unwillingness to urinate at certain times or in certain places (von Gontard, 1998).

Key Concepts

- Enuresis can be diagnosed only after a child has reached the age of 5 years.
- A child must have wetting incidents at least twice a week for three consecutive months or at a frequency that causes significant distress or impairment.
- One researcher has suggested three types of enuresis based on their primary cause: urge incontinence, voiding postponement, and detrusor–sphincter dyscoordination.

Characteristics and Experiences of Children with Enuresis

The physiological and psychological functioning of children with enuresis has been investigated by many studies over the years. The focus of studies of physiological functioning has been to identify potential physical causes of enuresis; the focus of studies of psychological functioning has been to identify potential causes and consequences of enuresis. Research on the characteristics of children with enuresis has been done almost exclusively with children who have nocturnal enuresis.

Physiological Functioning

Bladder capacity, sleep patterns, and hormones influencing the production of urine have been the primary focus of physiological studies because of their obvious connection to nocturnal enuresis.

The issue that is most important in the assessment of bladder capacity is **functional bladder capacity,** which refers to the amount of urine the bladder can hold before a child experiences an urge to urinate. The functional capacity of the bladder is always less than its actual capacity, which is one reason we can avoid urinating even when we feel a strong urge to do so. Once the functional bladder capacity is reached, children with nocturnal enuresis may automatically void their bladders while asleep. Consequently, a smaller functional bladder capacity may result in frequent voiding during the night.

One study found no difference in the daytime functional bladder capacities of children who do and do not have nocturnal enuresis. However, the nighttime functional bladder capacities of children with nocturnal enuresis were smaller than those of other children. In addition, the nighttime functional bladder capacities of children with nocturnal enuresis were smaller than their daytime functional bladder capacities, whereas other children's daytime and nighttime functional bladder capacities were similar (Kawauchi et al., 2003). Perhaps their smaller nighttime functional bladder capacities caused nighttime wetting incidents in some children with nocturnal enuresis.

Information about children's sleep patterns and the timing of wetting incidents may be important for understanding enuresis. Because children are more difficult to wake during their early hours of sleep and during periods of deeper sleep, wetting incidents during primarily these times may indicate that they are being caused by a child's inability to wake when his or her functional bladder capacity has been reached (Neveus, Stenberg, Lackgren, Tuvemo, & Hetta, 1999). The research in this area has produced conflicting results. Early studies of the timing of wetting incidents showed that they occurred throughout the night and during all four stages of sleep [rapid eye movement sleep (**REM sleep**) and stages 2, 3, and 4 of non-REM, deeper sleep] (Mikkelsen & Rapoport, 1980). However, a more recent study found that although voiding occurred throughout the night in a sample of children with nocturnal enuresis, with the first incident happening 10 minutes after a child fell asleep and the last occurring almost 8 hours into sleep, none of the 37 wetting incidents occurred during a normal cycle of REM sleep (Neveus et al., 1999). The researchers also found that the children had longer periods of deep sleep (stages 3 and 4) during the nights that they wet their beds, and shorter periods of deep sleep during nights that they remained dry. Thus this more recent study suggests that deep sleep may be associated with wetting incidents, although further work is needed to resolve these contradictory findings.

The ease with which children who have enuresis can be roused from sleep has also been explored because children who are more difficult to rouse may not wake when their functional bladder capacities are reached, resulting in a wetting incident. Parents of children with enuresis report that their children are particularly difficult to rouse when asleep (Wille, 1994). In addition, one study found that 9% of children with enuresis and 40% of children who did not have enuresis woke when presented with 120 decibels of noise (Wolfish, Pivik, & Busby, 1997). Thus it appears that at least some children with enuresis have difficulty waking, and this may be a factor in their wetting incidents.

Another physiological characteristic of some children with nocturnal enuresis is a reduced secretion of the hormone **anginine vasopressin,** which is an antidiuretic—that is, it reduces the amount of urine produced by the body. Most people secrete more anginine vasopressin at night than during the day, which reduces urine production during the night (Devitt et al., 1999). This is one way that most of us can avoid urinating even if asleep for 8–10 hours, something that we cannot usually do during the day. Children who secrete less anginine vasopressin during the night produce more urine while they are asleep, which may increase the risk of nighttime wetting (Devitt et al., 1999). As we will discuss in the section about treatment, the antidiuretic medication **desmopressin acetate** produces a reduction in enuresis in many children, which reinforces the hypothesis that antidiuretics influence wetting incidents in some children.

Taken together, these studies suggest that some children with enuresis have physiological characteristics that influence the frequency of nighttime wetting. Some of them may be more difficult to wake, some may spend more time in deeper sleep, some may have a smaller functional bladder capacity at night, and some may secrete lower levels of anginine vasopressin. Each of these physiological characteristics, either individually or in combination, may be associated with the etiology of enuresis in some children.

Psychological Functioning

Clinical reports and empirical studies paint somewhat conflicting pictures of the psychological functioning of children with enuresis. Clinical reports suggest that children experience many negative consequences of their enuresis, and older children and those who have been treated unsuccessfully experience the most negative consequences (Theunis et al., 2002). Many are bothered by their inability to control their urination, causing lower self-esteem. Some with nocturnal enuresis are unwilling to spend the night at friends' homes or attend slumber parties, and this may make them seem unfriendly to those around them and hurt their peer relationships (Butler, 1998). Children with diurnal enuresis may be humiliated by their occasional wetting incidents, and other children may mock them or shun them.

Empirical studies show a more complicated picture. Some studies show no differences in levels of behavior problems between children who have enuresis and those who do not (Hirasing, van Leerdam, Bolk-Bennink, & Bosch, 1997), and some have found that the behavior of children with enuresis falls within normal ranges on scales of child behaviors (Wagner & Matthews, 1985). However, other studies have found the rate of behavior problems in children with enuresis to be three to four times higher than expected from behavioral norms (von Gontard, 1998).

How can we reconcile these different views of the psychological functioning of children with enuresis? A study of the perceived impact of enuresis may help (Foxman, Valdez, & Brook, 1986). When asked about their level of distress about their enuresis, about 25% of a sample of 5- to 13-year-olds said they experienced a great deal of distress, about 25% said they experienced some or a little distress, and about 50% experienced no distress. This shows the wide range of distress levels among children with enuresis. Because the parents of children experiencing higher levels of distress are more likely to seek treatment for their children, clinical reports are more likely to include children experiencing high distress. This may explain the higher levels of problems seen in clinical reports. Although we do not know for certain from empirical studies, some of them may include samples of children experiencing less distress, whereas others may include children experiencing more distress, which may explain the variability in their results.

It appears that the best conclusion at this point is that some children with enuresis experience significant psychological difficulties and others do not. Ongoing research will be needed to identify the characteristics of children, their families, or their circumstances associated with higher levels of psychological difficulties.

Key Concepts

- Some children with enuresis have a smaller nighttime functional bladder capacity than daytime functional bladder capacity—a pattern seen less often in children who do not have enuresis.
- Children have wetting incidents throughout the night, although there is some controversy about whether they have them solely during deeper periods of sleep or also have them during REM sleep.
- Some children with enuresis are harder to rouse from sleep than most children, suggesting that this may play a role in their nighttime wetting.
- Some children with enuresis secrete lower levels of the antidiuretic hormone anginine vasopressin, which increases their production of urine at night.
- Clinical case reports show that some children experience stress and embarrassment because of their enuresis and have higher levels of behavior disturbances.
- Some empirical studies show no difference in levels of behavioral problems between children with enuresis and children who do not have enuresis, whereas other studies show that children with enuresis have heightened levels of behavior problems. The varied levels of distress experienced by children with enuresis may explain these differences.

Prevalence and Course

The DSM-IV-TR estimates for the prevalence of enuresis are 5–10% at age 5, 3–5% at age 10, and 1% at age 15 (APA, 2000). Some research has explored the prevalence of wetting incidents that occur less frequently than is required for the diagnosis of enuresis. For example, a study of 5- to 12-year-olds in Australia found that 5% wet their beds at least once a week. This is similar to a study of 5- to 13-year-olds in the United States that found that 7% of boys and 6% of girls wet their beds at least once a week, and that 16% of boys and 12% of girls wet their beds at least once during a three-month period (Foxman et al., 1986).

Problems with bed-wetting are more prevalent among boys than girls, and nocturnal problems are more common than diurnal problems. However, more girls than boys experience the diurnal or combined types of enuresis (APA, 2000; Landgraf et al., 2004). This may be because of the role that bacterial infections play in the development of diurnal enuresis and because

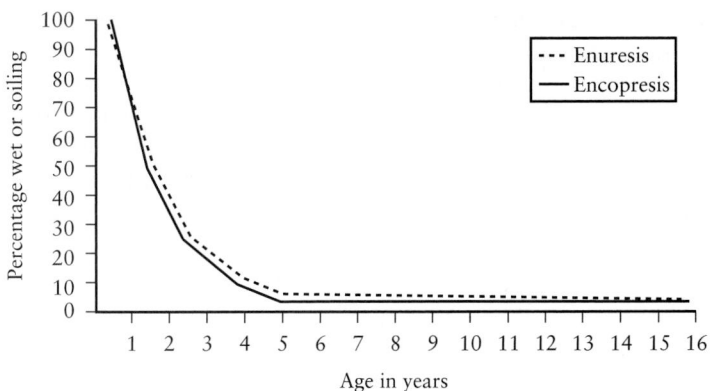

FIGURE 15.8   *Prevalence by Age of Enuresis and Encopresis*
Source: Murphy & Carr (2000).

these infections occur more frequently in girls; we will examine this topic in the section about etiology (Husmann, 1996).

Observing the prevalence of primary enuresis over time shows that about 15% of the children with primary enuresis at any single age will no longer meet the diagnostic criteria for enuresis when they are a year older (Norgaard & Djurhuus, 1993). Thus there is a more rapid decline in the percentage of children with primary enuresis during the early years of childhood and a more gradual decline during the later years (see Figure 15.8). This decline in prevalence occurs even among children who receive no treatment, suggesting that one important cause of enuresis is an immature system for controlling urination, and that this system reaches maturity slowly in some children (Forsythe & Redmond, 1974).

Research on secondary enuresis has reported rates in preschool and school-age children between 3% and 8% (Fergusson, Horwood, & Shannon, 1990; Wille, 1994). High levels of stress are often associated with the onset of secondary enuresis. Secondary enuresis shows the same 15% decline each year as primary enuresis.

Families of Children with Enuresis

Families with a child who has enuresis experience a wide range of responses to the child's disorder. One study found that 38% of parents of 5- to 13-year-olds with enuresis experienced little worry or distress about the enuresis, 46% worried some or a little, and 17% worried a great deal (Foxman et al., 1986). Unfortunately, no information has been published about the characteristics of families or children associated with levels of worry or distress.

After a review of the clinical literature, Butler (1994) suggested two patterns of parental behaviors in families that experienced stress and disruption because of their children's enuresis. The most frequent pattern was characterized as a "maintaining cycle" in which the parents felt a sense of helplessness regarding their children's enuresis. These parents believed that the enuresis was uncontrollable, and their principal interventions were to restrict fluids during the evening and take their half-asleep children to sit on the toilet during the night. As described in more detail in the next section, these strategies often prolong enuresis rather than reducing it. The second pattern was intolerance. These parents believed that their children's enuresis was due to the children's laziness or lack of concern, and they were often angry with the children. Their principal intervention was punishment for wetting incidents. Unfortunately, punishment often creates higher levels of stress for a child, which also can increase the frequency of wetting.

We know little about families that experience little stress over their children's enuresis. It may be that one or both parents in these families experienced enuresis during childhood and learned either that enuresis ends on its own eventually or that an angry attitude toward the child is not helpful. Another possibility is that the wetting incidents may be less frequent and occur only at night, resulting in little public exposure of the child's problem. Understanding how these families cope with their children's enuresis might point to parenting practices that are supportive of children who have enuresis, but we must await future research to learn about them.

Key Concepts

- The percentage of children meeting the diagnostic criteria for enuresis is about 5–10% at age 5, 3–5% at age 10, and 1% at age 15.
- In addition, about 5–7% of 5- to 13-year-old children have wetting incidents at least once a week, and about 14% having wetting incidents at least once in a three-month period.
- Nocturnal enuresis is more common than diurnal enuresis.
- Boys are more likely than girls to have nocturnal enuresis, and girls are more likely than boys to have diurnal enuresis.
- The percentage of children with primary or secondary enuresis declines by about 15% each year, even without treatment.
- Some families of children who have enuresis experience high levels of stress, whereas many families experience little or no stress.
- Two types of responses in families experiencing high stress have been documented: one in which parents feel helpless to intervene with their children and one in which the parents are angry with their children.

Etiology

The search for the etiology of enuresis is complicated by the many forms it can take and because issues that influence the etiology of one type of enuresis may have little influence on other types (Husmann, 1996). Consequently, most researchers believe that searching for the causes of each type of enuresis will be more productive than searching for one or more causes of enuresis overall. However, most research to date has focused on nocturnal, primary enuresis.

Exploring for the etiology of primary enuresis differs in one fundamental way from looking for the etiology of most other disorders discussed in this text. With other disorders we have focused our attention on issues that influence the initial and ongoing development of the symptoms of the disorder (such as how the symptoms of depression, PTSD, or a somatoform disorder begin and then develop over time). In contrast, our search for the etiology of primary enuresis focuses on issues that result in a child's normal behavior continuing past the age at which most children have ended this behavior. Because children do not have control over urination during their early years, the symptoms of enuresis do not emerge at one point in a child's life and then develop over time. Rather, a child is given the diagnosis of enuresis if he or she fails to end the lack of control over urination that all young children experience (i.e., fails to develop urinary continence). Thus our exploration of the etiology of primary enuresis will focus on issues that prolong urinary incontinence rather than issues that initiate it.

Genetic Influences

Most children with primary enuresis have one or two parents who had enuresis during childhood, suggesting that there is a genetic influence on the disorder (Mikkelsen, 2001). Several researchers have looked for the specific genes associated with enuresis by studying groups of families in which enuresis occurs across generations. They have found genes on chromosomes 12q (Arnell et al., 1997), 13q (Eiberg, Berendt, & Mohr, 1995), and 22 (Von Gontard, Eiberg, Hollmann, Rittig, & Lehmkuhl, 1999) that are associated with enuresis. However, the ways in which enuresis is affected by these genes remain unclear because each gene is associated with enuresis in some but not most cases and because many cases of enuresis running in families do not show any indication of being affected by these genes.

One way in which several different genes could be involved in enuresis is that each of them could influence one aspect of a child's ability to develop urinary continence (such as functional bladder capacity or production of anginine vasopressin), with any of these influences decreasing the likelihood of a child developing urinary continence. Alternatively, several different combinations of genes could impede the overall maturation of the system needed for urinary continence, increasing the risk for enuresis.

Infections

Bacterial infections of the urinary tract can interfere with the body's ability to store urine and discharge it voluntarily, thus increasing the likelihood of wetting incidents. Bacterial infections play a role mostly in diurnal enuresis and affect girls more than boys. For example, Husmann (1996) found that about 50% of girls and 5% of boys with diurnal enuresis had urinary tract infections.

The direct influence of bacterial infections on diurnal enuresis is supported by a study showing that 68% of a group of children with diurnal enuresis and a urinary tract infection ended their enuresis after successful antibiotic treatment of the infection. Bacterial infections seldom play a role in nocturnal enuresis. Even when a bacterial infection is present with nocturnal enuresis, curing the infection seldom reduces nighttime wetting (Husmann, 1996).

Psychologically Based and Learning-Based Influences

The use of certain strategies by parents for handling a young child's normal nighttime wetting can prolong it past the age at which it might normally stop or increase its frequency. Although the parents' intent is to end nighttime wetting by using strategies that seem logical, the strategies do just the opposite for reasons we will see.

A common error made by parents is to pick their young child up several hours after he or she has gone to bed and then hold the child on the toilet to urinate (Husmann, 1996). The parents believe that reducing the amount of urine in the child's bladder will decrease the likelihood of the child urinating in bed later that night. One problem with this strategy is that because the child is usually only half-awake when urinating, the child learns to urinate when half-awake. This creates a pattern in which a sleeping child wakes only partly when his or her functional bladder capacity is reached, urinates in bed, and then falls back asleep—the exact pattern that the parents are trying to eliminate. A second problem is that the child is urinating at a time other than when his or her functional bladder capacity has been reached, which can reduce the child's ability to identify the signal from his or her bladder that its functional capacity has been reached.

Another problematic parenting strategy is limiting the fluids given to a child during the evening or all day long (Butler, 1998). The parents believe that this strategy will reduce the child's urine output at night and thus reduce wetting incidents. However, its more likely outcome is to impede the development of functional bladder capacity because the child's bladder is not required to hold developmentally appropriate amounts of urine at night. This results in a child needing to urinate frequently even when only small amounts of urine are in the bladder. Consequently, the child is likely to continuing wetting the bed, although the amount of urine expelled may be reduced.

As noted earlier, some parents punish their children for wetting incidents. They may believe that punishment will reduce wetting incidents because it has been successful in reducing other problem behaviors in the past. However, if a child is not urinating in his or her bed voluntarily, punishment cannot directly affect nighttime wetting. In addition, the threat of punishment can increase a child's stress at bedtime, and because heightened stress increases the likelihood of a wetting incident, the threat of punishment may increase wetting incidents (Butler, 1998). Finally, punishment can create an environment in which a child and parent are not working together to solve the problem of nighttime wetting, and this may encourage some children to wet the bed voluntarily or resist efforts to develop urinary continence.

The search for psychological influences on the development of *secondary* enuresis has focused on stress. One study found an association between experiencing four or more stressful experiences in one year and the development of secondary enuresis (Fergusson et al., 1990) while another found that children with secondary enuresis had experienced parental divorce or other separations from parents more frequently than other children (Jarvelin, Moilanen, Vekevainen-Tervonen, & Huttunen, 1990). Fergusson and colleagues (1990) suggested that a possible connection between stress and secondary enuresis was that children with a delayed maturation of the urination system might be particularly susceptible to developing enuresis when facing high levels of stress, suggesting that the psychological issue of stress interacts with physiological maturation to create the symptoms of secondary enuresis in some children.

Key Concepts

- Genes on several chromosomes have a role in the development of enuresis in some children.
- In some cases, one gene may influence one component of a child's ability to develop urinary continence. In other cases, two or more genes may combine to impede the maturation of a child's system for urinary continence.
- Bacterial infections influence diurnal enuresis but have little affect on nocturnal enuresis.
- Parenting practices such as having a half-awake child urinate in a toilet, reducing fluid intake, and punishment can interfere with a child's ability to develop urinary continence.
- High levels of stress are associated with the development of secondary enuresis.

Prevention

Although prevention of enuresis receives little attention in the literature, our knowledge about the influence of parenting practices on the development of urinary continence provides information that can guide parents as they work with their children to develop urinary continence. Because parents who experienced enuresis as children are more likely than other parents to have children with enuresis, it may be particularly helpful for them to learn effective parenting practices (Mikkelsen, 2001).

Some children with diurnal enuresis purposely avoid urinating for long periods (von Gontard, 1998), so it may be helpful for parents to learn about this issue, possibly from their pediatricians or family physicians. If they notice a pattern of avoidance developing, they could work with their children to overcome whatever concerns or fears are causing their avoidance before the pattern becomes ingrained in the children's behavior.

Therapeutic Interventions

The two principal strategies used to treat enuresis over the past few decades have been medication and behavioral interventions. Most research on the treatment of enuresis has focused on nocturnal enuresis, so we know more about the effectiveness of treatment for nocturnal enuresis than diurnal enuresis.

Medication

The two medications most commonly prescribed for enuresis are **tricyclic antidepressants** and desmopressin acetate (Mikkelsen, 2001). Although the specific mechanisms through which antidepressants reduce enuresis are not clear, they are hypothesized to either (1) increase the tone of the bladder, thus reducing the need for nighttime urination, or (2) decrease the depth of a child's sleep, thus increasing the likelihood of the child waking to a full bladder (Husmann, 1996). As noted earlier, desmopressin acetate reduces the production of urine and thus reduces the likelihood of a child's bladder filling and the child urinating in bed. Both medications produce side effects in some children. Headaches and stomach problems are the most common side effects, although more serious medical conditions can occur infrequently (Thompson & Rey, 1995).

Both medications effectively reduced nighttime wetting in placebo-controlled and wait-list comparison studies, and older children were particularly likely to respond to either medication (Husmann, 1996; Mikkelsen, 2001). For example, Monda and Husmann (1995) found that, when given either a tricyclic antidepressant or desmopressin acetate for six months, 36% and 68% (respectively) of children with primary nocturnal enuresis had stopped wetting the bed, compared with only 6% of the children in a no-treatment comparison group.

However, neither medication is effective in the long term, and most children return to wetting incidents when the medications are ended (Mikkelsen, 2001; von Gontard, 1998). In the Monda and Husmann (1995) study, for example, only 16% of the children who had taken a tricyclic antidepressant and 10% of the children who had taken desmopressin acetate remained continent six months after the use of medication had ended, compared with 16% of the children in the no-treatment comparison group (see Figure 15.9).

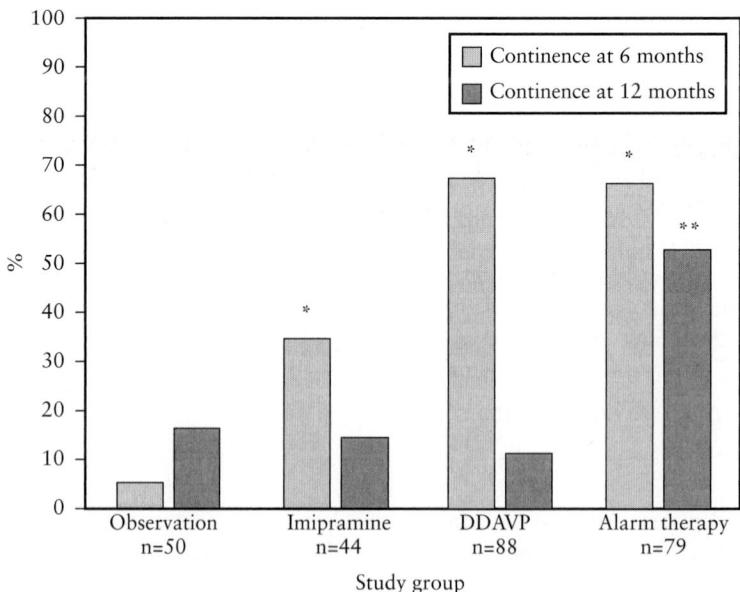

FIGURE 15.9 *Short-Term and Long-Term Effectiveness of Medication for Enuresis*

*p<0.001 compared to the observation study group at 6 months.

**p<0.001 compared to the observation, imipramine, and DDAVP study groups at 12 months.

Source: Monda & Husmann (1995).

The lack of long-term effectiveness of both medications suggests that they should not be used as the sole treatment for enuresis. However, they may have a role in treatment. Von Gontard (1998), for example, suggests that desmopressin acetate may be a useful component of treatment when it is used by children who need reassurance that they will not have a wetting incident on a particular night. For instance, a child might take desmopressin acetate on a night when she attends a sleepover party, decreasing the likelihood that she will have a wetting incident that night and giving her more confidence that she can engage in peer activities without embarrassment. In addition, Husmann (1996) found that combining desmopressin acetate with behavioral treatments was useful because desmopressin acetate often results in a quick reduction of wetting incidents, whereas behavioral treatments often require several weeks to be effective. He argued that parents and children are more likely to feel optimistic and continue behavioral treatments when a rapid reduction in wetting incidents occurs because of the medication.

Behavioral Interventions

The oldest and most effective intervention for enuresis is the **bell and pad** procedure (see Figure 15.10) (Butler, 1998; Mikkelsen, 2001). The equipment for the bell and pad procedure includes two layers of cloth with metallic fibers separated by a third layer of cloth with no metal. The metallic layers are connected to a bell. When a child wets the bed, the urine in the middle cloth layer connects the two metallic layers, and the bell rings. The bell wakes

ILLUSTRATING AN IMPORTANT RESEARCH ISSUE: THE IMPORTANCE OF FOLLOW-UP ASSESSMENTS

Several interesting pieces of information are available in Figure 15.9. One noteworthy point is the reduction of 16% in enuresis at the 12-month follow-up in the no-treatment group. This is close to the 15% yearly reduction in enuresis that occurs even without treatment, discussed in the section about prevalence and course. A second point is the dramatic difference in the 6-month and 12-month reductions in enuresis among children taking medication. Although the 6-month reduction was pronounced, the 12-month data show that enuresis returned for most children after they stopped taking the medication. Because the goal of most interventions is long-term effectiveness, the 12-month follow-up data make

it clear that medication alone is not an effective treatment for enuresis. Without this follow-up data, however, the effectiveness of medication could be overestimated.

Many intervention studies do not include long follow-up periods. In some cases, researchers may not believe that long-term follow-ups are important; in others, there may be no funds for long-term research. This is often unfortunate: Without long-term follow-ups it is not possible to tell whether an intervention has the desired ongoing influence on the lives of children. As we can see from the Monda and Hussman study, it cannot be assumed that interventions with short-term effectiveness will be effective in the long term.

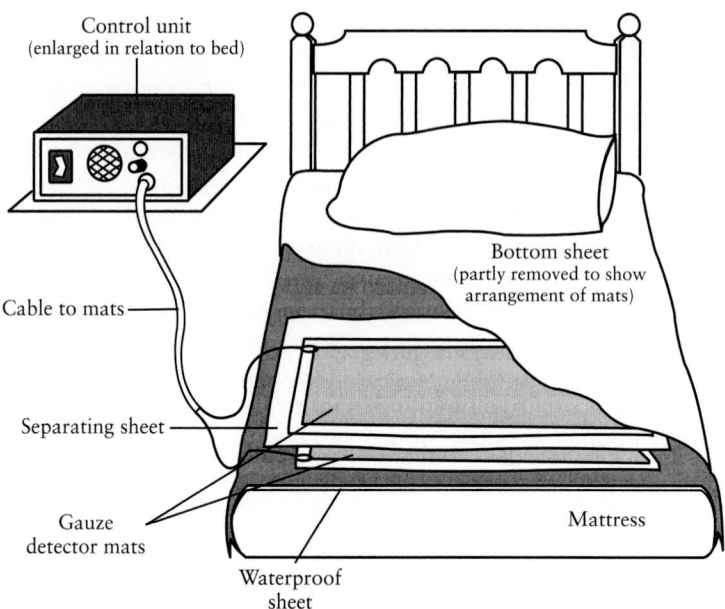

Control unit
(enlarged in relation to bed)

Cable to mats

Separating sheet

Gauze
detector mats

Waterproof
sheet

Bottom sheet
(partly removed to show
arrangement of mats)

Mattress

FIGURE 15.10   *A Bedwetting Alarm Showing the Arrangement of the Two
Detector Mats*

Source: Adapted from an illustration used by N. H. Eastwood & Son Ltd., with permission.

the child just as he or she begins to urinate. When this occurs, the child is instructed to stop urinating immediately, go to the bathroom, and finish urinating in the toilet.

Most studies show a short-term success rate using the bell and pad of about 60–70% (Mikkelsen, 2001), which is similar to the results shown by Monda and Husmann (1995; see Figure 15.9). Some children resume bed-wetting once the bell and pad procedure ends; but many of them will end their bed-wetting for good if they return to using the bell and pad for some additional time.

How the bell and pad reduce or eliminate nighttime wetting is not well understood. Some children begin to wake at night and use the bathroom to urinate, and perhaps the bell and pad help them identify and attend to the specific physical sensations indicating that their bladders have reached functional capacity (Ondersma et al., 2001). Other children begin to sleep through the night without urinating. Use of the bell and pad increases some children's functional bladder capacity, and this larger capacity may allow them to sleep through the night without having to urinate (Oredsson & Jorgensen, 1998).

One disadvantage of the bell and pad is that it often takes three weeks or longer of consistent use to be effective. Many families, particularly those with higher levels of conflict, stop using the bell and pad too soon or use it inconsistently, which dramatically reduces its effectiveness (Devlin & O'Cathain, 1990; Husmann, 1996). Thus ongoing support and encouragement are often needed for children and families to persist with the treatment until it succeeds. As noted previously, Husmann (1996) found that combining the bell and pad with desmopressin acetate more quickly reduced bed-wetting, resulting in more families being willing to continue the bell and pad procedure until bed-wetting ended permanently.

A technological innovation that may work the same way as the bell and pad involves an ultrasound monitor attached to a belt that a child wears to bed. The monitor assesses bladder capacity; when it reaches a certain point, an alarm wakes the child, who gets up to urinate in the toilet (Pretlow, 1999). Results similar to those from the use of the bell and pad were produced in one evaluation of this procedure, with approximately 60% of children attaining urinary continence. The functional bladder capacity of the children increased an average of about 70%, allowing many of them to sleep through the night without having to urinate (Pretlow, 1999).

Which Procedures Are Used Frequently

Despite the research showing poor long-term effectiveness of medication and better effectiveness of the bell and pad, physicians (to whom families typically turn for help with enuresis) are more likely to prescribe medication than the bell and pad or other behavioral treatments (Mikkelsen, 2001). For example, Foxman and colleagues (1986) recorded the treatment given to 92 children who had visited a physician for enuresis. Only 55% received any treatment, with about 60% of these children receiving only medication. The other children received one or more of several treatments, including psychotherapy, restricting water intake, and surgery. The bell and pad were prescribed for only three children.

The reasons for the frequent use of medication, despite its lack of long-term effectiveness, are unclear. Treatment with medication is certainly easier than behavioral interventions, and it may be less expensive. In addition, medications often produce a quick cessation of wetting incidents, whereas behavioral treatments for enuresis, like behavioral treatments for many disorders, take longer to work and require more effort (Husmann, 1996).

Key Concepts

- Prevention strategies include education that can help parents avoid actions that prolong the development of their children's urinary continence or help their children overcome fears that may lead to voiding postponement.
- Tricyclic antidepressants and desmopressin acetate are the medications most commonly prescribed for enuresis.
- Both medications are effective for reducing wetting incidents in the short term, but neither is effective in the long term.
- The bell and pad procedure is the most commonly used behavioral intervention, and a recent variant of this procedure, which monitors a child's bladder capacity with an ultrasound device, has been introduced.

- Most children whose parents consult a physician about enuresis are prescribed medications, and behavioral interventions are prescribed infrequently.

Encopresis

Less is known about encopresis than enuresis because it has been the focus of less research. For example, Mikkelsen (2001) searched for references to enuresis and encopresis in the *Medline* database for the two previous years and found 585 citations for enuresis and 127 citations for encopresis. Most research with children who have encopresis has been done with small samples of children or by reviewing the medical charts of children brought to clinics for treatment. Consequently, we still have much to learn about this disorder.

Diagnostic Criteria

As shown in Table 15.6, encopresis involves the voluntary or involuntary passage of feces into inappropriate places, such as in bed at night or in clothes during the day. (The word *feces* comes from the Latin *faeces*, "dregs or lees," and refers to any material expelled from the bowels.) The diagnostic criteria specify that a child must pass feces in an inappropriate place at least once a month for at least three months, so children who have rare incidents of this behavior would not meet the diagnostic criteria for encopresis. In addition, children must be at least 4 years of age to receive a diagnosis of encopresis; this is the age at which most children have learned to use the toilet for their bowel movements (children with developmental delays, such as those with mental retardation, must have reached a mental age of at least 4 years).

Two subtypes of encopresis are specified in the DSM-IV-TR. The first is **with constipation and overflow incontinence.** This is the most common form of encopresis; between 80% and 95% of children diagnosed with

---

TABLE 15.6

Diagnostic Criteria for Encopresis

A. Repeated passage of feces into inappropriate places (e.g., clothing or floor) whether involuntary or intentional.

B. At least one such event a month for at least three months.

C. Chronological age is at least 4 years (or equivalent developmental level).

D. The behavior is not due exclusively to the direct physiological effects of a substance (e.g., laxatives) or a general medical condition except through a mechanism involving constipation.

Code as follows:

787.6   With Constipation and Overflow Incontinence

307.7   Without Constipation and Overflow Incontinence

encopresis have this type (Brooks et al., 2000; Ondersma et al., 2001). The second type is **without constipation and overflow incontinence.**

Although not specified as subtypes of encopresis in the DSM, in clinical practice encopresis may also be classified as either *primary* or *secondary* or as *diurnal* or *nocturnal* (or both), using the same criteria as for enuresis (Mikkelsen, 2001). Ondersma and colleagues (2001) have suggested a different set of subtypes for encopresis based on their primary cause: *retentive* (which is similar to *with constipation and overflow incontinence*); *manipulative,* in which a child purposely expels a stool to achieve some goal (attention, expression of anger); and *stress-related,* in which encopresis occurs when the child experiences high levels of stress.

It is helpful to understand the process through which bowel movements occur to recognize the two types of encopresis (McGrath, Mellon, & Murphy, 2000). As food passes through the digestive system, the waste products (feces) are collected in the colon. One of the colon's functions is to remove moisture from the feces, which causes the feces to form into a relatively solid cylindrical **stool** (a person with diarrhea expels very loose feces because the feces have not remained in the colon long enough for the moisture to be extracted from them). As the stool accumulates, it moves into the rectum. This causes stretching of the rectum, and this stretching is recognized by a person as the need to have a bowel movement. The stretching of the rectum also results in (1) relaxation of the internal anal sphincter that allows the stool to move into the anal canal and (2) contraction of the external anal sphincter that keeps the stool within the anal canal until a person is seated on a toilet and purposely expels the stool.

When a person is constipated—that is, when he or she does not have regular bowel movements—the colon removes moisture from the feces for an extended period, creating a stool that is harder and more solid than normal. This can cause impaction of the stool within the colon, which makes it harder and more painful to expel. The result is a protracted, painful bowel movement. Consequently, children who have frequent constipation often resist having bowel movements because of the pain involved; and this, unfortunately, results in prolonged constipation and even harder stools.

If constipation occurs frequently, the accumulation of stool causes the colon to enlarge and lose its shape. The walls of the colon become flaccid, which can allow feces that have just entered the colon to move past the stool impacted in the colon. These watery feces can then flow through the rectum and anal canal without the child being able to stop them (much like diarrhea). This is what is considered **overflow incontinence** (see Figure 15.11). When these watery feces flow from the colon, it is called **soiling.**

Children with constipation and overflow incontinence experience periodic soiling, or the expulsion of a small amount of watery feces into their beds or clothes. This is different from the experience of children with the *without constipation and overflow incontinence* type, who are more likely to expel stools into their beds, clothes, or other inappropriate places.

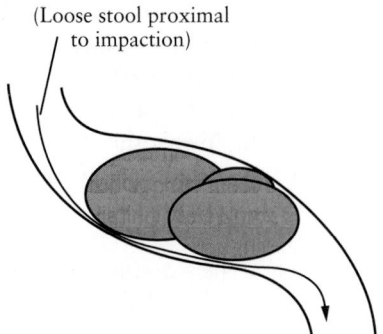

(Loose stool proximal
to impaction)

FIGURE 15.11   *Overflow Incontinence*

Source: Ondersma & colleagues (2001).

Key Concepts

- The two subtypes of encopresis are *with constipation and overflow incontinence* and *without constipation and overflow incontinence.*
- The type of *with constipation and overflow incontinence* is the most prevalent form of encopresis and results in soiling.
- As with enuresis, encopresis can also be classified as nocturnal or diurnal and primary or secondary.

Characteristics and Experiences of Children with Encopresis

The bowel movements of children with constipation and overflow incontinence usually follow a cycle in which feces are maintained in the colon for three or four days followed by a large, painful bowel movement (Mikkelsen, 2001). Children are usually aware that this large bowel movement is imminent, so they are usually able to have it in a toilet. It is during the last day or so of the accumulation of feces in the colon that overflow incontinence is most likely to occur. Consequently, the soiling that occurs with this type of encopresis may happen one or two days a week.

Most children who have encopresis without constipation and overflow incontinence have regular bowel movements (Ondersma et al., 2001). Some of them may be unaware that a bowel movement is imminent, possibly because the signal from their enlarging rectum is not being transmitted to their brain or because they have not learned to recognize the meaning of this signal. Others may be aware of the bowel movement but choose to have it in a place other than the toilet. As noted earlier, not much is known about these children or the reasons for their encopresis.

Little has been written about the experiences of children who have been diagnosed with encopresis, and much of what has been written comes from clinical case reports. These reports suggest that soiling occurs more frequently during the day than at night. Because the feces expelled during overflow incontinence are especially pungent, many children with encopresis give off a foul smell. Consequently, encopresis is often much more stigmatizing than enuresis. Many children with encopresis are described as wanting to stop soiling yet appearing to be indifferent to the problems caused by their soiling (Ondersma et al., 2001). What is unclear from these reports is whether the children truly are indifferent to their soiling or whether this apparent indifference is a defensive posture about events over which they feel no control.

In their review of the medical files of boys with encopresis, Foreman and Thambirajah (1996) found that many with primary encopresis also experienced other developmental delays, suggesting that their encopresis might be part of a larger picture of delayed physical, cognitive, and emotional development. They also found an association between conduct disorder and secondary encopresis, but not primary encopresis. Of course this correlational finding does not reveal whether the encopresis was part of a broader range of conduct problems in the boys or whether the other conduct problems were caused by the encopresis. (Perhaps some children who were ridiculed by others because of their soiling might have responded with aggression.)

Prevalence and Course

As shown in Figure 15.8, the percentage of children with encopresis drops dramatically during the preschool years. At age 4, when encopresis can first be diagnosed, about 10% of children could receive the diagnosis, and by age 5 the percentage drops to about 1% (APA, 2000). The percentage drops slightly during the following years, and by adolescence about 0.25–0.50% of children continue to experience encopresis. Although this is a small percentage, it still means that many children across the United States experience problems with encopresis through their childhood and into their adolescence.

Boys are more likely than girls to have encopresis, although the ratio of boys to girls with encopresis remains unclear. A study using the Child Behavior Checklist showed a ratio of boys to girls of about 2:1 having occasional or frequent problems with bowel movements in inappropriate places (Achenbach & Edelbrock, 1981). However, a medical chart review of children with encopresis treated in a child psychiatric clinic in England found 64 boys and only 2 girls (a ratio of 32:1), even though the ratio of boys to girls brought for treatment for all psychiatric problems was 2:1 (Foreman & Thambirajah, 1996). It is not clear whether this very high ratio of boys to girls is due to boys with encopresis being brought for treatment more frequently, or whether it suggests that the ratio of boys to girls is higher than the 2:1 found in community samples.

The small drop in the prevalence of encopresis each year after the age of 5 or 6 shows that it can continue for some children over many years. However, even for these children the problem is usually not chronic. Rather, it waxes and wanes; thus many of them are free of encopresis symptoms for months or years, with occasional exacerbations (APA, 2000). The reasons for these exacerbations are not completely clear, but they often occur during times of heightened stress.

Key Concepts

- Children with constipation and overflow incontinence have cycles of several days of constipation with soiling occurring during the last day or two of the cycle. This is usually followed by a large, painful bowel movement.
- Children with encopresis without constipation and overflow incontinence may not be aware of an imminent bowel movement because of a failure to notice the sensations from the stretching of their rectum; or they may be aware of the need to have a bowel movement but choose to have it in a place other than a toilet.
- Children who have problems with soiling often have a foul odor and so may experience significant stigmatization.
- Some studies have found associations between conduct problems and encopresis, although it is not clear whether the conduct problems are a child's response to stigmatization or whether the encopresis is one aspect of a wider conduct disorder problem.
- About 1% of 5-year-old children experience encopresis.
- Boys experience encopresis more often than do girls.
- Older children and adolescents with encopresis have periods of encopresis interspersed with months or years of no encopresis problems.

Etiology

Because most children with encopresis have the type with constipation and overflow incontinence, studies of the etiology of encopresis have focused on them. The underlying cause of encopresis in these children is chronic constipation; consequently, an exploration of the etiology of encopresis often involves the etiology of chronic constipation.

Genes appear to increase some children's risk for developing constipation. Ways in which genes may influence constipation include (1) reducing a child's awareness of a full colon and the need to have a bowel movement or (2) causing a child to have more difficulty with normal bowel movements (Stark et al., 1997). A low-fiber diet may cause infrequent bowel movements and thus may also lead to constipation (Issenman, Filmer, & Borski, 1999).

Brooks and colleagues (2000) note that children with stool-toilet refusal are also at risk for developing constipation. They define **stool-toilet refusal** as occurring when a child refuses to use the toilet for bowel movements for at least one month after he or she has learned to use the toilet consistently for urination. Children with stool-toilet refusal often withhold bowel movements as long as they can, and many of them refuse to have a bowel movement until they are given a diaper to wear. The causes of this refusal remain unclear and are probably varied. Some causes may be associated with the type of toilet training a child receives. For example, young children can have difficulty being trained on a regular toilet because they cannot get in a position to apply the needed pressure to expel feces, making the process of using the toilet lengthy and frustrating (Issenman et al., 1999). In addition, some children may have developed fears around toileting, including that they will fall in the toilet or be flushed down the toilet (Blum, Taubman, & Osborne, 1997).

Once the painful bowel movements associated with constipation begin, children may be increasingly reluctant to have bowel movements. They may purposely try to avoid having a bowel movement even when they feel the sensation indicating the need to have one. Some may refuse to attempt bowel movements even if required to sit on a toilet for hours. As noted earlier, withholding bowel movements increases the risk of stools becoming impacted in the colon, which can create constipation that is more intense and chronic. A vicious cycle can result as the pain of bowel movements causes a child to avoid them, which makes them more painful. The result can be stools that are frequently impacted and the soiling that can occur with impacted stools.

The etiology of encopresis in children who do not have chronic constipation, and who may use their encopresis in a manipulative way, is not clear. Some of these children may have bowel movements in inappropriate places to express anger at parents or others or to manipulate others to treat them in certain ways. Additional information about this small percentage of children is obviously needed.

Key Concepts

- Chronic constipation is at the foundation of most children's encopresis.
- Constipation may be caused by a genetic predisposition or by a diet that is low in fiber.
- Stool-toilet refusal, in which a child refuses to use the toilet for a bowel movement, can also cause constipation.
- Little is known about children with the other type of encopresis.

Prevention

Studies of the prevention of encopresis have focused on interventions to prevent chronic constipation in children who have stool-toilet refusal. The preventive interventions used in these studies were quite varied, yet most were effective. For example, Taubman (1997) assigned children to one of two treatments based on the severity of their stool-toilet refusal. Younger children and those who had occasional bowel movements when on a toilet were assigned to a no-treatment group, and 74% of these children were using the toilet for bowel movements regularly within six months. Older children and those with consistent stool-toilet refusal were assigned to a group where the use of diapers was reinstated and no other treatment was given. Of those, 89% were using the toilet regularly for bowel movements within six months. The success rate of the large percentage of children in both groups suggests that many of them may not have been physically or psychologically ready to use the toilet for bowel movements, and simply delaying this expectation by a few months helped them develop appropriate toileting skills.

In another study, Loening-Baucke (1993) found that returning children with stool-toilet refusal to diapers and introducing mild laxatives each day resulted in regular bowel movements, and that then having the children sit on the toilet for a specified period each day resulted in them having bowel movements in the toilet. After four months, about half of the 90 preschool children in the study were having regular bowel movements in the toilet.

Both studies found that most children could be helped to overcome stool-toilet refusal through interventions that involved no medical intervention or mild forms of medical intervention (the use of mild laxatives). What remains unclear is which children are more likely to benefit from these preventive interventions and which are more likely to experience chronic constipation despite the interventions.

Therapeutic Interventions

As with the literature about the etiology of encopresis, the literature about treatment of encopresis focuses almost exclusively on children with chronic constipation. Treatment is often twofold: medical interventions to eliminate chronic constipation and educational interventions to train parents in behavioral techniques that encourage their children to have regular bowel movements while seated on a toilet.

Medical intervention involves the use of enemas and laxatives to clear impacted stools, and then ongoing use of daily laxatives to promote the regular passage of feces through the child's system. The ongoing use of laxatives may continue for up to one year, which is the time that may be required for the colon to gradually regain its appropriate shape and strength. At the end of this period, the laxatives are gradually withdrawn, which allows the body to return to normal functioning (Mikkelsen, 2001).

Medical treatments also involve teaching a child the skills to have a voluntary bowel movement: tightening the stomach muscles to move the feces through the anal canal while relaxing the external anal sphincter to allow passage of the feces. (This simultaneous tightening of muscles and relaxing the external anal sphincter is not an easy task to learn. Those of us who have been defecating appropriately for years do it almost without thinking, so we may not appreciate the complexity of learning the maneuver.) Biofeedback has been used with some children, with sensors placed near the external anal sphincter that inform a child when he or she has successfully relaxed the sphincter (McGrath et al., 2000).

Educational interventions involve helping parents create an environment that encourages their children to have regular bowel movements in a toilet. One common strategy is to have the child sit on a toilet for a specified time each day when a bowel movement is most likely (Brooks et al., 2000; McGrath et al., 2000). Care is taken not to increase stress on the child during this time because the child must relax his or her external anal sphincter. Consequently, the parents are discouraged from sitting in the bathroom with their children. Rather, in as normal a way as possible, a child sits on the toilet, tightens his or her stomach muscles, relaxes the external anal sphincter, and waits for a bowel movement to occur. Some interventions use positive reinforcement when a child has a bowel movement in the toilet successfully.

In their reviews of several studies using different combinations of medical and educational interventions, McGrath and colleagues (2000) and Brooks and colleagues (2000) concluded that medical interventions by themselves and educational interventions by themselves were seldom effective—but their combination was often effective.

An interesting intervention used the Internet to provide information about defecation and encopresis through the U-CAN-POOP-TOO Web site (that is the real name!) (Ritterband et al., 2003). Families were randomly assigned to an experimental group that was given access to the Web site or a community-care comparison group that received normal care from their physicians. Eighty percent of those in the experimental group and 55% of those in the comparison group were experiencing one or fewer soiling incidents per week at the end of the intervention period. The researchers believed that having information available to children and their families on the Web allowed them to access it when they wanted and in the privacy of their homes, which resulted in their using the information more effectively.

Key Concepts

- Studies of children with stool-toilet refusal suggest that many of them may not be physically or psychologically ready to use a toilet for bowel movements.
- A combination of medical treatment (to remove impacted stools and help the colon return to its normal function) and educational interventions (to encourage regular use of the toilet) can be effective in treating many cases of encopresis.

Chapter Glossary

Adipose tissue is fat tissue. It consists of **adipocytes** (fat cells).

Anginine vasopressin is an antidiuretic hormone typically secreted more at night than during the day, which reduces nocturnal urine production.

Bariatric surgery involves procedures to either decrease the size of the stomach or bypass much of the intestine.

The **bell and pad** is the most commonly used behavioral intervention for enuresis.

Binge eating is defined in the DSM-IV-TR as an episode of eating a large amount of food in a discrete period, accompanied by a sense of lack of control over the amount eaten.

A **binge–purge cycle** is a diagnostic criterion for bulimia nervosa and involves a cycle of binge eating followed by purging.

Body mass index (BMI) is a measure of a person's body size. It is calculated with the formula $BMI = kg/m^2$ or $BMI = (pounds/inches^2) \times 703$.

Cognitive restructuring is a cognitive–behavioral therapy technique in which a child is encouraged to think differently about the meaning of an emotion, behavior, or physical symptom.

Desmopressin acetate is an antidiuretic medication that produces a short-term reduction in enuresis in many children but usually has little long-term effectiveness.

Detrusor–sphincter dyscoordination occurs when a child is unable to relax the external urinary sphincter while contractions of the bladder occur, which results in a child having to strain to expel even small amounts of urine.

Diabetes is a disease in which the body either does not produce insulin (type 1, sometimes called *childhood-onset* or *insulin-dependent diabetes*) or does not make or use insulin well (type 2, sometimes called *adult-onset* or *non–insulin-dependent diabetes*). Either type of diabetes causes an inability to metabolize carbohydrates and a consequent increase in blood and urine sugar levels.

Dichotomous thinking occurs when a person views issues as one extreme or another rather than throughout their range.

Disturbed body image involves a person's belief that he or she is fat despite having a low weight.

Diurnal enuresis or **encopresis** occurs only during the day when the child is awake.

Emotional lability involves intense swings of emotions.

Energy balance is the balance between energy taken in through food and energy expended. A **positive energy balance** means that more energy is being taken in than expended.

The **external urinary sphincter** is the muscle that holds urine in the bladder.

Factitious disorder is diagnosed when a person purposefully assumes a sick role.

Functional bladder capacity refers to the capacity of the bladder when a person experiences an urge to urinate.

Healthy weight is commonly defined as a BMI between 19 and 24.

Insulin is a hormone secreted by the pancreas that lowers the level of glucose in the blood.

Irritable bowel syndrome is a chronic condition of abdominal pain accompanied by constipation or diarrhea, in the absence of any apparent medical condition.

La belle indifference is an apparent lack of concern about physical symptoms associated with conversion disorder.

Malingering is diagnosed when a person purposefully assumes a sick role to obtain some external incentives.

Nocturnal enuresis or **encopresis** occurs only at night when a child is asleep.

Obese is commonly defined as a BMI of 30 or more in adults.

Obesity is having excess fat tissue.

Obsessive–compulsive disorder is diagnosed when a person experiences recurrent thoughts (obsessions) or behaviors (compulsions) that are time-consuming and create marked distress or impairment.

Overflow incontinence occurs when watery feces flow involuntary from the colon.

Overweight is commonly defined as a BMI of 25–29 in adults.

Primary enuresis or **encopresis** is diagnosed when a child has never had a period of continence.

Pseudoneurological symptoms are those that mimic neurological problems such as lack of balance, loss of sense of touch, blindness, or deafness.

Purging is the use of vomiting, laxatives, or other measures to rid the body of food before the nutrients can be extracted from the food.

Recurrent abdominal pain involves frequent or chronic gastrointestinal pain without any apparent medical explanation.

REM (rapid eye movement) sleep is a stage of sleep that occurs in progressively longer episodes throughout the night and is characterized by vivid dreams and rapid eye movements.

Secondary enuresis or **encopresis** is diagnosed when a child has had a significant period of continence followed by a return to wetting or soiling incidents.

Children who develop a **sick role** experience physical symptoms in the absence of a medical condition and often begin to develop a personal and behavioral style that emphasizes being sick.

Soiling refers to the involuntary expelling of a small amount of watery feces that have typically moved around an impacted stool in a child's colon.

A **stool** is feces that have formed into a relatively solid mass.

Stool-toilet refusal occurs when a child who has learned to use the toilet for urination refuses to use the toilet for bowel movements.

Tricyclic antidepressants are antidepressant medications that block the reuptake of norepinephrine and serotonin. Their name comes from three rings that occur in their molecular structure.

Urge incontinence is the frequent voiding of small amounts of urine caused by a child's bladder being unable to contain a sufficient amount of urine.

Voiding postponement occurs when a child purposefully withholds urination for long periods. It is characterized by the sudden discharge of a large amount of urine.

With constipation and overflow incontinence is the most common type of encopresis; it involves a child with frequent constipation who expels small amounts of watery feces every few days (soiling).

References

Abela, J. R. Z., Brozina, K., & Haigh, E. P. (2002). An examination of the response styles theory of depression in third- and seventh-grade children: A short-term longitudinal study. *Journal of Abnormal Child Psychology, 30,* 515–527.

Abramson, L., Seligman, M., & Teasdale, J. (1978). Learned helplessness in humans: Critique and reformulation. *Journal of Abnormal Psychology, 37,* 49–74.

Achenbach, T. M. (1990). What is "developmental" about developmental psychopathology? In J. Rolf, A. Masten, D. Cicchetti, K. Nuechterlein, & S. Weintraub (Eds.), *Risk and protective factors in the development of psychopathology* (pp. 29–48). New York: Cambridge University Press.

Achenbach, T. M., Conners, C. K., Quay, H. C., & Verhulst, F. C. (1989). Replication of empirically derived syndromes as a basis for taxonomy of child/adolescent psychopathology. *Journal of Abnormal Child Psychology, 17,* 299–323.

Achenbach, T. M., & Edelbrock, C. S. (1981). Behavioral problems and competencies reported by parents of normal and disturbed children aged four through sixteen. *Monographs of the Society for Research in Child Development, 46,* 1–82.

Adrien, J. L., Lenoir, P., Martineau, J., Perot, A., Hameury, L., Larmande, C., et al. (1993). Blind ratings of early symptoms of autism based upon family home movies. *Journal of the American Academy of Child and Adolescent Psychiatry, 33,* 617–625.

Advisory Board on Child Abuse and Neglect. (1995). *A nation's shame: Fatal child abuse and neglect in the United States.* Washington, DC: U.S. Department of Health and Human Services.

Aguilar, B., Sroufe, L. A., Egeland, B., & Carlson, E. (2000). Distinguishing the early-onset/persistent and adolescence-onset antisocial behavior types: From birth to 16 years. *Development and Psychopathology, 12,* 109–132.

Ainsworth, M. D. S., Blehar, M. C., Waters, E., & Wall, S. (1978). *Patterns of attachment: A psychological study of the Strange Situation.* Hillsdale, NJ: Erlbaum.

Akiskal, H. S., Downs, J., & Jordan, P. (1985). Affective disorders in referred children and younger siblings of manic-depressives: Mode of onset and prospective course. *Archives of General Psychiatry, 42.*

Alaghband Rad, J., Hamburger, S. D., Giedd, J. N., Frazier, J. A., & Rapoport, J. (1997). Childhood-onset schizophrenia: Biological markers in relation to clinical characteristics. *American Journal of Psychiatry, 154,* 64–68.

Alaghband Rad, J., McKenna, K., Gordon, C. T., Albus, K. E., Hamburger, S., Rumsey, J., et al. (1995). Childhood-onset schizophrenia: The severity of premorbid course. *Journal of the American Academy of Child and Adolescent Psychiatry, 34,* 1273–1283.

Albano, A. M., Chorpita, B. F., & Barlow, D. H. (2003). Childhood anxiety disorders. In E. J. Mash (Ed.), *Child psychopathology* (2nd ed., pp. 279–329). New York: Guilford Press.

Albertini, R., & Phillips, K. (1999). Thirty-three cases of body dysmorphic disorder in children and adolescents. *Journal of the American Academy of Child and Adolescent Psychiatry, 38,* 453–459.

Alexander, D. (1998). Prevention of mental retardation: Four decades of research. *Mental Retardation and Developmental Disabilities Research Reviews, 4,* 50–58.

Alexander, L. A. (1998). The prevalence of eating disorders and eating-disordered behaviors in sororities. *College Student Journal, 32,* 66–75.

Allen, K. D., & Shriver, M. D. (1998). Role of parent-mediated pain behavior management strategies in biofeedback treatment of childhood migraines. *Behavior Therapy, 29,* 477–490.

Allgood-Merten, B., Lewinsohn, P. M., & Hops, H. (1990). Sex differences and adolescent depression. *Journal of Abnormal Psychology, 99,* 55–63.

Allwood, M. A., Bell Dolan, D., & Husain, S. A. (2002). Children's trauma and adjustment reactions to violent and nonviolent war experiences. *Journal of the American Academy of Child and Adolescent Psychiatry, 41,* 450–457.

Alvarez, H. K., & Ollendick, T. H. (2003). Individual and psychosocial risk factors. In C. A. Essau (Ed.), *Conduct and oppositional defiant disorders: Epidemiology, risk factors, and treatment* (pp. 97–116). Mahwah, NJ: Erlbaum.

American Academy of Child and Adolescent Psychiatry. (1997). Practice parameters for the assessment and treatment of children and adolescents with bipolar disorder. *Journal of the American Academy of Child and Adolescent Psychiatry, 36,* 138–157.

American Academy of Child and Adolescent Psychiatry. (1998). Summary of the practice parameters for the assessment and treatment of children and adolescents with posttraumatic stress disorder. *Journal of the American Academy of Child and Adolescent Psychiatry, 37,* 997–1001.

American Academy of Child and Adolescent Psychiatry. (1999). Practice parameters for the assessment and treatment of children, adolescents, and adults with mental retardation and comorbid mental disorders. *Journal of the American Academy of Child and Adolescent Psychiatry, 38 (supplement),* 5S–31S.

American Academy of Child and Adolescent Psychiatry. (2000). Summary of the practice parameters for the assessment and treatment of children and adolescents with schizophrenia. *Journal of the American Academy of Child and Adolescent Psychiatry, 39,* 1580–1582.

American Academy of Pediatrics Committee on Nutrition. (2003). Prevention of pediatric overweight and obesity. *Pediatrics, 112,* 424–430.

American Association on Mental Retardation (AAMR). (2002). *Mental retardation: Definition, classification, and systems of supports.* Washington, DC: Author.

Andujo, E. (1988). Ethnic identity of transethnically adopted Hispanic adolescents. *Social Work, 33,* 531–535.

Angold, A., & Costello, E. J. (2001). The epidemiology of depression in children and adolescents. In I. Goodyer (Ed.), *The depressed child and adolescent: Developmental and clinical perspectives* (2nd ed., pp. 143–178). Cambridge, England: Cambridge University Press.

Angold, A., Costello, E., & Erkanli, A. (1999). Comorbidity. *Journal of Child Psychology and Psychiatry, 40,* 57–88.

Angold, A., Costello, E. J., Erkanli, A., & Worthman, C. (1999). Pubertal changes in hormone levels and depression in girls. *Psychological Medicine, 29,* 1043–1053.

Angold, A., Erkanli, A., Farmer, E. M. Z., Fairbank, J. A., Burns, B. J., Keeler, G., et al. (2002). Psychiatric disorder, impairment, and service use in rural African American and White youth. *Archives of General Psychiatry, 59,* 893–904.

Angold, A., & Rutter, M. (1992). Effects of age and pubertal status on depression in a large clinical sample. *Development and Psychopathology, 4,* 5–28.

APA. (1952). *Diagnostic and statistical manual for mental disorders.* Washington, DC: American Psychiatric Association.

APA. (1968). *Diagnostic and statistical manual of mental disorders (DSM-II)* (2nd ed.). Washington, DC: American Psychiatric Association.

APA. (1980). *Diagnostic and statistical manual of mental disorders (DSM-III)* (3rd ed.). Washington, DC: American Psychiatric Association.

APA. (1987). *Diagnostic and statistical manual of mental disorders (DSM-III-R)* (3rd revised ed.). Washington, DC: American Psychiatric Association.

APA. (1994). *Diagnostic and statistical manual of mental disorders (DSM-IV)* (4th ed.). Washington, DC: American Psychiatric Association.

APA. (2000). *Diagnostic and statistical manual of mental disorders (DSM-IV-TR)* (4th Text Revision ed.). Washington, DC: American Psychiatric Association.

APA. (2002). Ethical principles of psychologists and code of conduct. *American Psychologist, 57,* 1060–1073.

Applegate, B., Lahey, B. B., Hart, E. L., Waldman, I., Biederman, J., Hynd, G. W., et al. (1997). Validity of the age-of-onset criterion for ADHD: A report of the DSM-IV field trials. *Journal of the American Academy of Child and Adolescent Psychiatry, 36,* 1211–1221.

Apter, A., & Wasserman, D. (2003). Adolescent attempted suicide. In R. King & A. Apter (Eds.), *Suicide in children and adolescents* (pp. 63–85). Cambridge, England: Cambridge University Press.

Apter, M. J. (1992). *The dangerous edge: The psychology of excitement*. New York: Free Press.

Arlow, J. (1989). Psychoanalysis. In R. Corsini & D. Wedding (Eds.), *Current psychotherapies* (pp. 19–62). Itasca, IL: Peacock Publishing.

Armitage, R., Hoffmann, R. F., Emslie, G. J., Weinberg, W. A., Mayes, T. L., & Rush, A. J. (2002). Sleep microarchitecture as a predictor of recurrence in children and adolescents with depression. *International Journal of Neuropsychopharmacology, 5*, 217–228.

Arnell, H., Hjalmas, K., Jagervall, M., Lackgren, G., Stenberg, A., Bengtsson, B., et al. (1997). The genetics of primary nocturnal enuresis: Inheritance and suggestion of a second major gene on chromosome 12q. *Journal of Medical Genetics, 34*, 360–365.

Arnold, L. E., Stoff, D. M., Cook, E., Wright, C., Cohen, D. J., Kruesi, M., et al. (1996). Biologic procedures: Ethical issues in research with children and adolescents. In K. Hoagwood & P. S. Jensen (Eds.), *Ethical issues in mental health research with children and adolescents* (pp. 89–112). Hillsdale, NJ: Erlbaum.

Aro, H., Hanninen, V., & Paronen, O. (1989). Social support, life events, and psychosomatic symptoms among 14–16-year-old adolescents. *Social Science and Medicine, 29*, 1051–1056.

Asarnow, R. F., Brown, W., & Strandburg, R. (1995). Children with a schizophrenic disorder: Neurobehavioral studies. *European Archives of Psychiatry and Clinical Neuroscience, 245*, 70–79.

Asperger, H. (1991). Autistic psychopathy in childhood. In U. Frith (Ed.), *Autism and Asperger syndrome* (pp. 37–92). Cambridge, England: Cambridge University Press.

Attie, I., & Brooks-Gunn, J. (1995). The development of eating regulation across the life span. In D. Cicchetti & D. J. Cohen (Eds.), *Developmental psychopathology, vol. 2: Risk, disorder, and adaptation* (pp. 332–368). New York: John Wiley & Sons.

Axelson, D. A., & Birmaher, B. (2001). Relation between anxiety and depressive disorders in childhood and adolescence. *Depression and Anxiety, 14*, 67–78.

Bailey, A., LeCouteur, A., Gottesman, I., Bolton, P., Simonoff, E., Yuzda, F., et al. (1995). Autism as a strongly genetic disorder: Evidence from a British twin study. *Psychological Medicine, 25*, 63–77.

Bailey, D., Hatton, D., & Skinner, M. (1998). Early developmental trajectories of males with Fragile X syndrome. *American Journal of Mental Retardation, 1*, 29–39.

Banaschewski, T., Brandeis, D., Heinrich, H., Albrecht, B., Brunner, E., & Rothenberger, A. (2003). Association of ADHD and conduct disorder: Brain electrical evidence for the existence of a distinct subtype. *Journal of Child Psychology and Psychiatry, 44*, 356–376.

Barkley, R. (1990). *Attention deficit hyperactivity disorder: A handbook for diagnosis and treatment*. New York: Guilford.

Barkley, R., & Cunningham, C. (1979). The effects of methylphenidate on the mother–child interactions of hyperactive children. *Archives of General Psychiatry, 36*, 201–208.

Barkley, R., Shelton, R., Crosswait, C., Moorehouse, M., Fletcher, K., Barrett, S., et al. (2000). Multi-method psycho-educational intervention for preschool children with disruptive behaviors: Preliminary results at post-treatment. *Journal of Child Psychology and Psychiatry, 41*, 319–332.

Barkley, R. A. (2003). Attention-deficit/hyperactivity disorder. In E. J. Mash & R. Barkley (Eds.), *Child psychopathology* (2nd ed., pp. 75–143). New York: Guilford.

Barkley, R. A., Fischer, M., Smallish, L., & Fletcher, K. (2006). Young adult outcome of hyperactive children: Adaptive functioning in major life activities. *Journal of the American Academy of Child and Adolescent Psychiatry, 45*, 192–202.

Baroff, G. S., & Olley, J. G. (1999). *Mental retardation: Nature, cause, and management* (3rd ed.). Ann Arbor: Edwards Brothers.

Baron-Cohen, S. (1988). Social and pragmatic deficits in autism: Cognitive or affective? *Journal of Autism and Developmental Disorders, 18*, 379–402.

Baron-Cohen, S. (2001). Theory of mind and autism: A review. In L. M. Glidden (Ed.), *International review of research in mental retardation: Autism (vol. 23)* (pp. 169–184). San Diego, CA: Academic Press.

Barrett, P., Healy Farrell, L., & March, J. S. (2004). Cognitive–behavioral family treatment of childhood obsessive–compulsive disorder: A controlled trial. *Journal of the American Academy of Child and Adolescent Psychiatry, 43*, 46–62.

Barrett, P., Rapee, R., Dadds, M., & Ryan, S. (1996). Family enhancement of cognitive style in anxious and aggressive children. *Journal of Abnormal Child Psychology, 24*, 187–203.

Bates, J. E., Pettit, G. S., Dodge, K. A., & Ridge, B. (1998). Interaction of temperamental resistance to control and restrictive parenting in the development of externalizing behavior. *Developmental Psychology, 34*, 982–995.

Bauer, B., & Maffeis, C. (2002). Psychosocial interventions. In W. Burniat, T. J. Cole, I. Lissau, & E. Poskitt (Eds.), *Child and adolescent obesity* (pp. 361–376). Cambridge, England: Cambridge Press.

Bauman, M. L., & Kemper, T. L. (2005). Structural brain anatomy in autism: What is the evidence? In M. L. Bauman & T. L. Kemper (Eds.), *The neurobiology of autism* (2nd ed., pp. 121–135). Baltimore, MD: The Johns Hopkins Press.

Baumeister, R. F., Smart, L., & Boden, J. M. (1996). Relation of threatened egotism to violence and aggression: The dark side of high self-esteem. *Psychological Review, 103*, 5–33.

Baumgaertel, A., Wolraich, M. L., & Deitrich, M. (1995). Comparison of diagnostic criteria for attention deficit disorders in a German elementary school sample. *Journal of the American Academy of Child and Adolescent Psychiatry, 34*, 629–638.

Bauminger, N., & Kasari, C. (2000). Loneliness and friendship in high-functioning children with autism. *Child Development, 71*, 447–456.

Baylis, F., Downie, J., & Kenny, N. (1999). Children and decision making in health research. *IRB: A Review of Human Subjects Research, 21*, 5–10.

Beardslee, W., Wright, E., Salt, P., Drezner, K., Gladstone, T., Versage, E., et al. (1997). Examination of children's responses to two preventive intervention strategies over time. *Journal of the American Academy of Child and Adolescent Psychiatry, 36*, 196–204.

Beardslee, W. R., & Gladstone, T. R. G. (2001). Prevention of childhood depression: Recent findings and future prospects. *Biological Psychiatry, 49*, 1101–1110.

Beasley, P., & DeMaso, D. (1997). Conversion and somatoform disorders. In H. Steiner (Ed.), *Treating school-age children* (pp. 123–151). San Fransico: Jossey-Bass.

Bebbington, P., & Kuipers, L. (1994). The predictive utility of expressed emotion in schizophrenia: An aggregate analysis. *Psychological Medicine, 24*, 707–718.

Beck, A. (1967). *Depression: Clinical, experimental, and theoretical aspects.* New York: Harper & Row.

Beck, A., & Weishaar, M. (1989). Cognitive therapy. In R. Corsini & D. Wedding (Eds.), *Current psychotherapies* (pp. 285–320). Itasca, IL: Peacock Publishing.

Beck, A. T. (1976). *Cognitive therapy and the emotional disorders.* New York: International Universities Press.

Beck, A. T. (1986). Cognitive therapy: A sign of retrogression or progress. *Behavior Therapist, 9*, 2–3.

Beck, A. T. (1993). Cognitive therapy: Past, present, and future. *Journal of Consulting and Clinical Psychology, 61*, 194–198.

Beck, A. T. (1999). *Prisoners of hate: The cognitive basis of anger, hostility, and violence.* New York: Harper Collins Publishers.

Beck, A. T., Rush, A. H., Shaw, B. F., & Emery, G. (1979). *Cognitive therapy of depression.* New York: Guilford.

Beck, M. (2002). The gifts of Down syndrome: Some thoughts for new parents. In M. Cohen, L. Nadel, & M. Madnick (Eds.), *Down syndrome* (pp. 134–148). New York: Wiley-Liss.

Beck, S. J. (2000). Behavioral assessment. In M. Hersen & R. Ammerman (Eds.), *Advanced abnormal child psychology* (2nd ed., pp. 177–195). Mahwah, NJ: Erlbaum.

Becker-Blease, K. A., Deater-Deckard, K., Eley, T., Freyd, J. J., Stevenson, J., & Plomin, R. (2004). A genetic analysis of individual differences in dissociative behaviors in childhood and adolescence. *Journal of Child Psychology and Psychiatry, 45*, 522–532.

Beh, H. G. (2002). The role of institutional review boards in protecting human subjects: Are we really ready to fix a broken system? *Law and Psychology Review, 26*, 1–47.

Beidel, D. C., Turner, S. M., & Morris, T. L. (2000). Behavioral treatment of childhood social phobia. *Journal of Consulting and Clinical Psychology, 68*, 1072–1080.

Beirne-Smith, M., Ittenbach, R., & Patton, J. R. (2002). *Mental retardation* (6th ed.). Upper Saddle River, NJ: Merrill Prentice Hall.

Bell-Dolan, D. (1995). Social cue interpretation of anxious children. *Journal of Clinical Child Psychology, 24*, 1–10.

Bell-Dolan, D., & Brazeal, T. J. (1993). Separation anxiety disorder, overanxious disorder, and school refusal. *Child and Adolescent Psychiatric Clinics of North America, 2*, 563–580.

Belser, R. C., & Sudhalter, V. (2001). Conversational characteristics of children with Fragile X syndrome: Repetitive speech. *American Journal on Mental Retardation, 106*, 28–38.

Bennet-Osborne, R., Hatcher, J. W., & Richtsmeier, A. J. (1989). The role of social modeling in unexplained pediatric pain. *Journal of Pediatric Psychology, 14*, 43–61.

Berkey, C., Rockett, H., Field, A., Gillman, M., Frazier, A., Camargo, C., et al. (2000). Activity, dietary intake, and weight changes in a longitudinal study of preadolescent and adolescent boys and girls. *Pediatrics, 105*, 56–66.

Berkey, C., Rockett, H., Gillman, M., & Colditz, G. (2003). One-year changes in activity and in inactivity among 10- to 15-year-old boys and girls: Relationship to change in body mass index. *Pediatrics, 111*, 836–843.

Berkowitz, R., Stunkard, A. J., & Stallings, V. A. (1993). Binge-eating disorder in obese adolescent girls. *Annals of the New York Academy of Science, 699*, 200–206.

Bernstein, G., Layne, A., Egan, E., & Tennison, D. (2005). School-based interventions for anxious children. *Journal of the American Academy of Child and Adolescent Psychiatry, 44*, 1118–1127.

Bertelsen, A., Harvald, B., & Hauge, M. (1977). A Danish twin study of manic-depressive disorders. *British Journal of Psychiatry, 130*, 330–351.

Bertrand, J., Mars, A., Boyle, C., Bove, F., Yeargin-Allsopp, M., & Decoufle, P. (2001). Prevalence of autism in the United States population: The Brick Township, New Jersey, investigation. *Pediatrics, 108*, 1155–1161.

Bespalova, I. N., Reichert, J., & Buxbaum, J. D. (2005). Candidate susceptibility genes for autism. In M. L. Bauman & T. L. Kemper (Eds.), *The neurobiology of autism* (2nd ed., pp. 217–232). Baltimore, MD: The Johns Hopkins Press.

Biederman, J., Faraone, S., Keinan, K., Knee, D., & Tsuang, M. (1990). Family–genetic and psychosocial risk factors in DSM-III attention deficit disorder. *Journal of the American Academy of Child and Adolescent Psychiatry, 29*, 526–533.

Biederman, J., Faraone, S., Mick, E., & Lelon, E. (1995). Psychiatric comorbidity among referred juveniles with major depression: Fact or artifact? *Journal of the American Academy of Child and Adolescent Psychiatry, 34*, 579–590.

Biederman, J., Faraone, S., Mick, E., Wozniak, J., et al. (1996). Attention-deficit hyperactivity disorder and juvenile mania: An overlooked comorbidity? *Journal of the American Academy of Child and Adolescent Psychiatry, 35*, 997–1008.

Biederman, J., Faraone, S. V., Chu, M. P., & Wozniak, J. (1999). Further evidence of a bidirectional overlap between juvenile mania and conduct disorder in children. *Journal of the American Academy of Child and Adolescent Psychiatry, 38*, 468–476.

Biederman, J., Mick, E., & Faraone, S. (1998). Depression in attention deficit hyperactivity disorder (ADHD) children: "True" depression or demoralization? *Journal of Affective Disorders, 47*, 113–122.

Biederman, J., Mick, E., Faraone, S. V., Braaten, E., Doyle, A., Spencer, T., et al. (2002). Influence of gender on attention deficit hyperactivity disorder in children referred to a psychiatric clinic. *American Journal of Psychiatry, 159*, 36–42.

Biederman, J., Mick, E., Faraone, S. V., Spencer, T., Wilens, T. E., & Wozniak, J. (2000). Pediatric mania: A developmental subtype of bipolar disorder? *Biological Psychiatry, 48*, 458–466.

Biederman, J., Mick, E., Spencer, T. J., Wilens, T. E., & Faraone, S. V. (2000). Therapeutic dilemmas in the pharmacotherapy of bipolar depression in the young. *Journal of Child and Adolescent Psychopharmacology, 10*, 185–192.

Biederman, J., Rosenbaum, J., Bolduc-Murphy, E., Faraone, S., Chaloff, J., Hirshfeld, D., & Kagan, J. (1993). Behavioral inhibition as a temperamental risk factor for anxiety disorders. *Child and Adolescent Psychiatric Clinics of North America, 2*, 667–684.

Biklen, D. (1990). Communication unbound: Autism and praxis. *Harvard Educational Review, 60*, 291–314.

Binet, A., & Simon, T. (1905). New methods for the diagnosis of the intellectual level of subnormals. *L'Anne's Psychologique, 11*, 191–244.

Birmaher, B., Arbelaez, C., & Brent, D. (2002). Course and outcome of child and adolescent major depressive disorder. *Child and Adolescent Psychiatric Clinics of North America, 11*, 619–638.

Birmaher, B., Axelson, D. A., Monk, K., Kalas, C., Clark, D. B., Ehmann, M., et al. (2003). Fluoxetine for the treatment of childhood anxiety disorders. *Journal of the American Academy of Child and Adolescent Psychiatry, 42*, 415–423.

Birmaher, B., Ryan, N. D., Williamson, D. E., Brent, D. A., Kaufman, J., Dahl, R., et al. (1996). Childhood and adolescent depression: A review of the past 10 years, Part I. *Journal of the American Academy of Child and Adolescent Psychiatry, 35*, 1427–1439.

Birnbrauer, J., & Leach, D. (1993). The Murdoch early intervention program after 2 years. *Behaviour Change, 10*, 63–74.

Bischoff, L., & Tingstrom, D. H. (1991). Siblings of children with disabilities: Psychological and behavioral characteristics. *Counseling Psychology Quarterly, 4*, 311–321.

Blair, C. (1999). Science, policy and early intervention. *Intelligence, 27*, 93–110.

Bloomquist, M. L., August, G. J., Cohen, C., & Doyle, A. (1997). Social problem solving in hyperactive–aggressive children: How and what they think in conditions of automatic and controlled processing. *Journal of Clinical Child Psychology, 26*, 172–180.

Blowers, L., Loxton, N., Grady-Flesser, M., Occhibinti, S., & Dawe, S. (2003). The relationship between sociocultural pressure to be thin and body dissatisfaction in preadolescent girls. *Eating Behaviors, 4*, 229–244.

Blum, N. J., Taubman, B., & Osborne, M. L. (1997). Behavioral characteristics of children with stool-toileting refusal. *Pediatrics, 99*, 50–53.

Bolton, P., MacDonald, H., & Pickles, A. (1994). A case-control family history study of autism. *Journal of Child Psychology and Psychiatry, 35*, 877–900.

Borduin, C. M., Schaeffer, C. M., & Ronis, S. T. (2003). Multisystemic treatment of serious antisocial behavior in adolescents. In C. A. Essau (Ed.), *Conduct and oppositional defiant disorders: Epidemiology, risk factors, and treatment* (pp. 299–318). Mahwah, NJ: Erlbaum.

Borst, S. R., & Noam, G. G. (1993). Developmental psychopathology in suicidal and nonsuicidal adolescent girls. *Journal of the American Academy of Child and Adolescent Psychiatry, 32*, 501–508.

Borthwick Duffy, S. A. (1994). Epidemiology and prevalence of psychopathology in people with mental retardation. *Journal of Consulting and Clinical Psychology, 62*, 17–27.

Bouchard, T. (1994). Genes, environment, and personality. *Science, 264*, 1700–1701.

Bouchard, T., Lykken, D. T., McGue, M., Segal, N. L., & Tellegen, A. (1990). Sources of human psychological differences: The Minnesota Study of Twins Reared Apart. *Science, 250*, 223–228.

Bowlby, J. (1951). *Maternal care and mental health*. Geneva: World Health Organization.

Bowlby, J. (1969). *Attachment*. New York: Basic Books.

Bowlby, J. (1973). *Separation: Anxiety and anger*. New York: Basic Books.

Bowlby, J. (1980). *Loss: Sadness and depression*. New York: Basic Books.

Bowman, E. S. (1990). Adolescent MDP in the nineteenth and early twentieth centuries. *Dissociation, 3*, 179–187.

Bowring, M. A., & Kovacs, M. (1992). Difficulties in diagnosing manic disorders among children and adolescents. *Journal of the American Academy of Child and Adolescent Psychiatry, 31*, 611–614.

Boyer, B. A., Knolls, M. L., Kafkalas, C. M., Tollen, L. G., & Swartz, M. (2000). Prevalence and relationships of posttraumatic stress in families experiencing pediatric spinal cord injury. *Rehabilitation Psychology, 45*, 339–355.

Boyle, M. H., Offord, D. R., Racine, Y., & Sanford, M. (1993). Evaluation of the Diagnostic Interview for Children and Adolescents for use in general population samples. *Journal of Abnormal Child Psychology, 21*, 663–681.

Braaten, E. B., Biederman, J., DiMauro, A., Mick, E., Monuteaux, M. C., Muehl, K., et al. (2001). Methodological complexities in the diagnosis of major depression in youth: An analysis of mother and youth self-reports. *Journal of Child and Adolescent Psychopharmacology, 11*, 395–407.

Braet, C., Tanghe, A., Decaluwe, V., Moens, E., & Rosseel, Y. (2004). Inpatient treatment for children with obesity: Weight loss, psychological well-being, and eating behavior. *Journal of Pediatric Psychology, 29*, 519–529.

Breggin, P. R. (1999). Psychostimulus in the treatment of children diagnosed with ADHD: Part 1—Acute risks and psychological effects. *Ethical Human Sciences and Services, 1*, 13–33.

Bremner, J. D. (1999). Does stress damage the brain? *Biological Psychiatry, 45*, 797–805.

Bremner, J. D., Randall, P., Vermetten, E., Staib, L., Bronen, R., Mazure, C., et al. (1997). Magnetic resonance imaging–based measurement of hippocampal volume in posttraumatic stress disorder related to childhood physical and sexual abuse: A preliminary report. *Biological Society, 41*, 23–32.

Brent, D., & Mann, J. (2003). Familial factors in adolescent suicidal behavior. In R. King & A. Apter (Eds.), *Suicide in children and adolescents* (pp. 86–117). Cambridge, England: Cambridge University Press.

Brent, D. A., Kerr, M. M., Goldstein, C., Bozigar, J., Wartella, M., & Allan, M. J. (1989). An outbreak of suicide and suicidal behavior in a high school. *Journal of the American Academy of Child and Adolescent Psychiatry, 28*, 918–924.

Brewin, C. R., Dalgleish, T., & Joseph, S. (1996). A dual representation theory of posttraumatic stress disorder. *Psychological Review, 103*, 670–688.

Bristol, M., Cohen, D., Costello, E., Denckla, M., Eckberg, T., Kallen R., et al. (1996). State of the science in autism: Report to the National Institutes of Health. *Journal of Autism and Developmental Disorders, 26*, 121–154.

Brody, N. (2000). Theories and measurements of intelligence. In R. Sternberg (Ed.), *Handbook of Intelligence* (pp. 16–33). Cambridge, England: Cambridge University Press.

Bronfenbrenner, U. (1979). *The ecology of human development: Experiments by nature and design.* Cambridge, MA: Harvard University Press.

Brook, J. S., Whiteman, M., & Zheng, L. (2002). Intergenerational transmission of risks for problem behavior. *Journal of Abnormal Child Psychology, 30*, 65–76.

Brooks, R. C., Copen, R. M., Cox, D. J., Morris, J., Borowitz, S., & Sutphen, J. (2000). Review of the treatment literature for encopresis, functional constipation, and stool-toileting refusal. *Annals of Behavioral Medicine, 22*, 260–267.

Brooks-Gunn, J., Auth, J., Petersen, A., & Compas, B. (2001). The depressed child and adolescent. In I. Goodyer (Ed.), *The depressed child and adolescent* (2nd ed., pp. 79–118). Cambridge, England: Cambridge University Press.

Brooks-Gunn, J., & Warren, M. (1989). Biological contributions to affective expression in young adolescent girls. *Child Development, 60*, 372–385.

Brown, L. K., Overholser, J., Spirito, A., & Fritz, G. K. (1991). The correlates of planning in adolescent suicide attempts. *Journal of the American Academy of Child and Adolescent Psychiatry, 30*, 95–99.

Bruch, M. A., & Heimberg, R. G. (1994). Differences in perceptions of parental and personal characteristics between generalized and nongeneralized social phobics. *Journal of Anxiety Disorders, 8*, 155–168.

Bruch, M. A., Heimberg, R. G., Berger, P., & Collins, T. M. (1989). Social phobia and perceptions of early parental and personal characteristics. *Anxiety Research, 2*, 57–63.

Bryden, K. E., Carrey, N. J., & Kutcher, S. P. (2001). Update and recommendations for the use of antipsychotics in early-onset psychoses. *Journal of Child and Adolescent Psychopharmacology, 11*, 113–130.

Buck v. Bell, 274 U.S. 200 (1927).

Burke, V., Beilin, L., Simmer, K., Oddy, W., Blake, K., Doherty, D., et al. (2005). Predictors of body mass index and associations with cardiovascular risk factors in Australian children: A prospective cohort study. *International Journal of Obesity, 29*, 15–23.

Burt, S. A., Krueger, R. F., McGue, M., & Iacono, W. G. (2001). Sources of covariation among attention-deficit hyperactivity disorder, oppositional defiant disorder, and conduct disorder: The importance of shared environment. *Journal of Abnormal Psychology, 110*, 516–525.

Buss, A. H. (1986). A theory of shyness. In W. Jones, J. Cheek, & S. Briggs (Eds.), *Shyness: Perspectives on research and treatment* (pp. 39–46). New York: Plenum Press.

Butler, R. (1998). Annotation: Night wetting in children, psychological aspects. *Journal of Child Psychology and Psychiatry, 39*, 453–463.

Butler, R. J. (1994). *Enuresis: The child's experience*. Oxford: Butterworth Heinemann.

Butor, P. M. (2004). Some psychological viewpoints on obesity. In W. Kiess, C. Carcus, & M. Wabitsch (Eds.), *Obesity in childhood and adolescence* (pp. 124–136). Basel, Switzerland: Karger.

Cahill, L., Babinsky, R., Markowitsch, H., & McGaugh, J. L. (1995). The amygdala and emotional memory. *Nature, 377,* 295–296.

Cahill, L., Hurer, R. J., Fallon, J., Alhire, M. I., Tang, C., Keator, D., et al. (1996). Amygdala activity at encoding correlated with long-term free recall of emotional information. *Proceedings of the National Academy of Sciences, 23,* 8016–8031.

Campbell, D. T., & Stanley, J. C. (1963). *Experimental and quasi-experimental designs for research.* Chicago: Rand McNally.

Campbell, M., & Armenteros, J. L. (1996). Schizophrenia and other psychotic disorders. In J. M. Wiender (Ed.), *Diagnosis and psychopharmacology of childhood and adolescent disorders* (2nd ed., pp. 193–227). Oxford, England: John Wiley & Sons.

Campbell, S. B., Shaw, D. S., & Gilliom, M. (2000). Early externalizing behavior problems: Toddlers and preschoolers at risk for later maladjustment. *Development and Psychopathology, 12,* 467–488.

Campbell, S. M. (2000). Attention-deficit/hyperactivity disorder: A developmental view. In A. J. Sameroff & M. Lewis (Eds.), *Handbook of developmental psychopathology* (2nd ed., pp. 383–401). Dordrecht, Netherlands: Kluwer Academic Publishers.

Campo, J. V., & Fritsch, S. L. (1994). Somatization in children and adolescents. *Journal of the American Academy of Child and Adolescent Psychiatry, 33,* 1223–1235.

Campo, J. V., & Garber, J. (1998). Somatization. In R. T. Ammerman & J. V. Campo (Eds.), *Handbook of pediatric psychology and psychiatry: Psychological and psychiatric issues in the pediatric setting.* (Vol. 1, pp. 137–161). Needham Heights, MA: Allyn & Bacon.

Campo, J. V., Jansen McWilliams, L., Comer, D. M., & Kelleher, K. J. (1999). Somatization in pediatric primary care: Association with psychopathology, functional impairment, and use of services. *Journal of the American Academy of Child and Adolescent Psychiatry, 38,* 1093–1101.

Campo, J. V., & Reich, M. D. (1999). Somotofrom disorders. In S. D. Netherton, D. Holmes, & C. E. Walker (Eds.), *Child and adolescent psychological disorders* (pp. 321–343). Oxford: Oxford University Press.

Campos, J. J., Barrett, K., Lamb, M. E., Goldsmith, H. H., & Stenberg, C. (1983). Socioemotional development. In P. H. Mussen (Ed.), *Handbook of child psychology: Infancy and developmental psychobiology* (Vol. 2, pp. 783–915). New York: Wiley.

Canfield, R. L., Henderson, C. R., Cory Slechta, D. A., Cox, C., Jusko, T. A., & Lanphear, B. P. (2003). Intellectual impairment in children with blood lead concentrations below 10 mug per deciliter. *New England Journal of Medicine, 348,* 1517–1526.

Cantwell, D. P. (1996). Classification of child and adolescent psychopathology. *Journal of Child Psychology and Psychiatry and Allied Disciplines, 37,* 3–12.

Cantwell, D. P., & Baker, L. (1991). Manifestations of depressive affect in adolescence. *Journal of Youth and Adolescence, 20,* 121–133.

Caplan, R. (1994). Thought disorder in childhood. *Journal of the American Academy of Child and Adolescent Psychiatry, 33,* 605–615.

Caplan, R., Guthrie, D., Fish, B., Tanguay, P. E., & David-Lando, G. (1989). The Kiddie Formal Thought Disorder Rating Scale: Clinical assessment, reliability, and validity. *Journal of the American Academy of Child and Adolescent Psychiatry, 28,* 408–416.

Caplan, R., Guthrie, D., Tang, B., Komo, S., & Asarnow, R. F. (2000). Thought disorder in childhood schizophrenia: Replication and update of concept. *Journal of the American Academy of Child and Adolescent Psychiatry, 39,* 771–778.

Capps, L., Sigman, M., & Mundy, P. (1994). Attachment security in children with autism. *Development and Psychopathology, 6,* 249–261.

Carlat, D. J., & Camargo, C. A. (1991). Review of bulimia nervosa in males. *American Journal of Psychiatry, 148,* 831–843.

Carlson, C. L., & Mann, M. (2000). Attention-deficit/hyperactivity disorder, predominantly inattentive subtype. *Child and Adolescent Psychiatric Clinics of North America, 9,* 499–510.

Carlson, E. A., Jacobvitz, D., & Stroufe, L. A. (1995). A developmental investigation of inattentiveness and hyperactivity. *Child Development, 66,* 37–54.

Carlson, G. A. (1998). Mania and ADHD: Comorbidity or confusion. *Journal of Affective Disorders, 51,* 177–187.

Carlson, N. R. (1986). *Physiology of behavior* (3rd ed.). Needham Heights, MA: Allyn and Bacon.

Carper, R. A., & Courchesne, E. (2000). Inverse correlation between frontal lobe and cerebellum sizes in children with autism. *Brain, 123,* 836–844.

Carr, E. G. (1977). The motivation of self-injurious behavior: A review of some hypotheses. *Psychological Bulletin, 84,* 800–816.

Carroll, J. B. (1993). *Human cognitive abilities: A survey of factor-analytic studies.* New York: Cambridge University Press.

Carter, J. C., Stewart, D. A., Dunn, V. J., & Fairburn, C. G. (1997). Primary prevention of eating disorders: Might it do more harm than good? *International Journal of Eating Disorders, 22,* 167–172.

Casey, B., Trainor, R., Orendi, J., Schubert, A., Nyustrom, L., Giedd, J., et al. (1997). A developmental functional MRI study of prefrontal activation during performance of a go/no-go task. *Journal of Cognitive Neuroscience, 9,* 835–847.

Caspi, A., & Moffitt, T. E. (1995). The continuity of maladaptive behavior: From description to understanding in the study of antisocial behavior. In D. Cicchetti & D. J. Cohen (Eds.), *Developmental psychopathology: Risk, disorder, and adaptation* (pp. 472–511). Oxford, England: John Wiley & Sons.

Castellanos, F. X. (1997). Toward a pathophysiology of attention-deficit/hyperactivity disorder. *Clinical Pediatrics, 36,* 381–393.

Cattarin, J. A., & Thompson, J. K. (1994). A three-year longitudinal study of body image, eating disturbance, and general psychological functioning in adolescent females. *Eating Disorders: The Journal of Treatment and Prevention, 2,* 114–124.

Centers for Disease Control and Prevention. (2001). CDC lead factsheet. From http://www.cdc.gov/nnceh/lead/factsheets/leadfacts/htm.

Cerel, J., Roberts, T. A., & Nilsen, W. (2005). Peer suicidal behavior and adolescent risk behavior. *Journal of Nervous and Mental Disease, 193,* 237–243.

Chapman, R. S., & Hesketh, L. J. (2000). Behavioral phenotype of individuals with Down Syndrome. *Mental Retardation and Developmental Disabilities Research Reviews, 6,* 84–95.

Chisholm, K. (1998). A three year follow-up of attachment and indiscriminate friendliness in children adopted from Romanian orphanages. *Child Development, 69,* 1092–1106.

Chisholm, K., Carter, M. C., Ames, E. W., & Morison, S. J. (1995). Attachment security and indiscriminately friendly behavior in children adopted from Romanian orphanages. *Development and Psychopathology, 7,* 283–294.

Chorpita, B. F. (2001). Control and the development of negative emotion. In M. Vasey & M. Dadds (Eds.), *The developmental psychopathology of anxiety* (pp. 112–142). Oxford, England: Oxford University Press.

Christian, R., Frick, P., Hill, N., & Tyler, L. (1997). Psychopathy and conduct problems in children: II. Implications for subtyping children with conduct problems. *Journal of the American Academy of Child and Adolescent Psychiatry, 36,* 233–241.

Cicchetti, D. (1984). The emergence of developmental psychopathology. *Child Development, 55,* 1–7.

Cicchetti, D. (2002). How a child builds a brain: Insights from normality and psychopathology. In W. Hartup & R. A. Weinberg (Eds.), *Child psychology in retrospect and prospect* (pp. 23–71). Mahwah, NJ: Erlbaum.

Cicchetti, D., & Toth, S. L. (1998). The development of depression in children and adolescents. *American Psychologist, 53,* 221–241.

Clark, L. A., & Watson, D. (1991). Tripartite model of anxiety and depression: Psychometric evidence and taxonomic implications. *Journal of Abnormal Psychology, 100,* 316–336.

Clark, W. R., & Grunstein, M. (2000). *Are we hardwired? The role of genes in human behavior.* New York: Oxford University Press.

Cobham, V. E., Dadds, M. R., & Spence, S. H. (1998). The role of parental anxiety in the treatment of childhood anxiety. *Journal of Consulting and Clinical Psychology, 66,* 893–905.

Cohen, I. L. (1995). A theoretical analysis of the role of hyperarousal in the learning and behavior of Fragile X males. *Mental Retardation and Developmental Disabilities Research Reviews, 1,* 286–291.

Cohen, J. A., Perel, J. M., DeBellis, M. D., Friedman, M. J., & Putnam, F. W. (2002). Treating traumatized children: Clinical implications of the psychobiology of posttraumatic stress disorder. *Trauma Violence and Abuse, 3,* 91–108.

Coie, J. D., & Dodge, K. (1983). Continuities and changes in children's social status: A five-year longitudinal study. *Merrill-Palmer Quarterly, 29,* 261–282.

Coie, J. D., & Dodge, K. (1998). Aggression and antisocial behavior. In N. Eisenberg (Ed.), *Handbook of child psychology* (Vol. 3, pp. 779–862). New York: Wiley.

Cole, D. A., Tram, J. M., Martin, J. M., Hoffman, K. B., Ruiz, M. D., Jacquez, F. M., et al. (2002). Individual differences in the emergence of depressive symptoms in children and adolescents: A longitudinal investigation of parent and child reports. *Journal of Abnormal Psychology, 111,* 156–165.

Cole, T. J., & Rolland-Cachera, M. F. (2002). Measurement and definition. In W. Burniat, T. J. Cole, I. Lissau, & E. Poskitt (Eds.), *Child and adolescent obesity* (pp. 3–27). Cambridge, England: The Cambridge Press.

Colin, V. L. (1996). *Human attachment.* New York: McGraw-Hill, Inc.

Collishaw, S., Maughan, B., Goodman, R., & Pickles, A. (2004). Time trends in adolescent mental health. *Journal of Child Psychology and Psychiatry, 34,* 1350–1362.

Colman, A. (2001). *Dictionary of psychology.* New York: Oxford Press.

Connor, D. F. (2002). Preschool attention deficit hyperactivity disorder: A review of prevalence, diagnosis, neurobiology, and stimulant treatment. *Journal of Developmental and Behavioral Pediatrics, 23,* S1–S9.

Cook, E. H. (1999). Genetics of attention-deficit hyperactivity disorder. *Mental Retardation and Developmental Disabilities Research Reviews, 5,* 191–198.

Cooperative Group MTA. (1999). A 14-month randomized clinical trial of treatment strategies for attention-deficit/hyperactivity disorder. *Archives of General Psychiatry, 56,* 1073–1086.

Costello, E., Angold, A., Burns, B., Strangl, D., Tweed, D., Erkanli, A., et al. (1996). The Great Smoky Mountains Study of Youth: Goals, design, methods, and the prevalence of DSM-III-R disorders. *Archives of General Psychiatry, 53,* 1129–1136.

Costello, E., Egger, H., & Angold, A. (2005). 10-year research update review: The epidemiology of child and adolescent psychiatric disorders: Methods and public health burden. *Journal of the American Academy of Child and Adolescent Psychiatry, 44,* 972–986.

Costello, E. J., Erkanli, A., Fairbank, J. A., & Angold, A. (2002). The prevalence of potentially traumatic events in childhood and adolescence. *Journal of Traumatic Stress, 15,* 99–112.

Costello, E. J., Foley, D. L., & Angold, A. (2006). 10-year research update review: The epidemiology of child and adolescent psychiatric disorder: II: Developmental epidemiology. *Journal of the American Academy of Child and Adolescent Psychiatry, 45,* 8–25.

Courchesne, E. (1997). Brainstem, cerebellar, and limbic neuroanatomical abnormalities in autism. *Current Opinion in Neurobiology, 7,* 269–278.

Craig, T. K. J., Cox, A. D., & Klein, K. (2002). Intergenerational transmission of somatization behaviour: A study of chronic somatizers and their children. *Psychological Medicine, 32,* 805–816.

Crick, N., Ostrov, J., Appleyard, K., Jansen, E., & Casas, J. (2004). Relational aggression in early childhood: "You can't come to my birthday party unless . . ." In M. Putallaz & K. L. Bierman (Eds.), *Aggression, antisocial behavior, and violence among girls: A developmental perspective* (pp. 71–89). New York: Guilford.

Crick, N. R., & Dodge, K. A. (1994). A review and reformulation of social information-processing mechanisms in children's social adjustment. *Psychological Bulletin, 115,* 74–101.

Croen, L. A., Grether, J. K., Hoogstrate, J., & Selvin, S. (2002). The changing prevalence of autism in California. *Journal of Autism and Developmental Disorders, 32,* 207–215.

Curry, J. F. (2001). Specific psychotherapies for childhood and adolescent depression. *Biological Psychiatry, 49,* 1091–1100.

Dadds, M. R., Davey, G. C., & Field, A. P. (2001). Developmental aspects of conditioning processes in anxiety disorders. In M. Vasey & M. Dadds (Eds.), *The developmental psychopathology of anxiety* (pp. 205–230). London: Oxford University Press.

Dadds, M. R., & Fraser, J. A. (2003). Prevention programs. In C. A. Essau (Ed.), *Conduct and oppositional defiant disorders: Epidemiology, risk factors, and treatment* (pp. 193–222). Mahwah, NJ: Erlbaum.

Dadds, M. R., Holland, D. E., Laurens, K. R., Mullins, M., Barrett, P. M., & Spence, S. H. (1999). Early intervention and prevention of anxiety disorders in children: Results at 2-year follow-up. *Journal of Consulting and Clinical Psychology, 67*, 145–150.

Dales, L., Hammer, S., & Smith, N. (2001). Time trends in autism and in MMR immunization coverage in California. *Journal of the American Medical Association, 285*, 1183–1185.

Danforth, J. S., Barkley, R. A., & Stokes, T. F. (1991). Observations of parent–child interactions with hyperactive children: Research and clinical implications. *Clinical Psychology Review, 11*, 703–727.

Daniel, D. G., Zigun, J. R., & Weinberger, D. R. (1994). Brain imaging in neuropsychiatry. In S. Yudofsky & R. E. Hales (Eds.), *Synopsis of neuropsychiatry* (pp. 143–156). Washington, DC: American Psychiatric Association.

Dare, C., & Szmukler, G. (1991). The family therapy of short-history, early-onset anorexia nervosa. In D. B. Woodside & L. Skekter-Wolfson (Eds.), *Family approaches to eating disorders* (pp. 25–47). Washington, DC: American Psychiatric Press.

Dass, S., McNamara, N. K., & Findling, R. L. (2005). Pharmacological treatment. In R. L. Findling & S. C. Schultz (Eds.), *Juvenile-onset schizophrenia* (pp. 232–256). Baltimore, MD: Johns Hopkins University Press.

Davis, L., & Siegel, L. J. (2000). Posttraumatic stress disorder in children and adolescents: A review and analysis. *Clinical Child and Family Psychology Review, 3*, 135–154.

Dawson, G., Carver, L., Meltzoff, A., Panagiotides, H., McPartland, J., & Webb, S. (2002). Neural correlates of face recognition in young children with autism spectrum disorder, developmental delay, and typical development. *Child Development, 73*, 700–717.

Dawson, G., & Galpert, L. (1990). Mothers' uses of imitative play for facilitating social responsiveness and toy play in young autistic children. *Development and Psychopathology, 2*, 151–162.

Dawson, G., & Levy, A. (1989). Arousal, attention, and the socioemotional impairments of individual with autism. In G. Dawson (Ed.), *Autism: Nature, diagnosis, and treatment* (pp. 49–74). New York: Guilford.

Deater Deckard, K., Dodge, K. A., Bates, J. E., & Pettit, G. S. (1998). Multiple risk factors in the development of externalizing behavior problems: Group and individual differences. *Development and Psychopathology, 10*, 469–493.

De Bellis, M. D. (2001). Developmental traumatology: The psychobiological development of maltreated children and its implications for research, treatment, and policy. *Development and Psychopathology, 13*, 539–564.

De Bellis, M. D., Baum, A. S., Birmaher, B., Keshavan, M. S., Eccard, C. H., Boring, A. M., et al. (1999). Developmental traumatology: I. Biological stress systems. *Biological Psychiatry, 45*, 1259–1270.

De Bellis, M. D., Keshavan, M. S., Clark, D. B., Casey, B. J., Giedd, J. N., Boring, A. M., et al. (1999). Developmental traumatology: II. Brain development. *Biological Psychiatry, 45*, 1271–1284.

De Bellis, M. D., Keshavan, M. S., Shifflett, H., Iyengar, S., Beers, S. R., Hall, J., et al. (2002). Brain structures in pediatric maltreatment-related posttraumatic stress disorder: A sociodemographically matched study. *Biological Psychiatry, 52*, 1066–1078.

Deblinger, E., & Heflin, A. H. (1996). *Cognitive behavioral interventions for treating sexually abused children.* Thousand Oaks, CA: Sage.

Decaluwe, V., & Braet, C. (2003). Prevalence of binge-eating disorder in obese children and adolescents seeking weight-loss treatment. *International Journal of Obesity, 27*, 404–409.

Dekker, M. C., Koot, H. M., van der Ende, J., & Verhulst, F. C. (2002). Emotional and behavioral problems in children and adolescents with and without intellectual disability. *Journal of Child Psychology and Psychiatry and Allied Disciplines, 43*, 1087–1098.

DeLisi, L. E. (1997). Is schizophrenia a lifetime disorder of brain plasticity, growth and aging? *Schizophrenia Research, 23*, 119–129.

Dell, P. F., & Eisenhower, J. W. (1990). Adolescent multiple personality disorder: A preliminary study of eleven cases. *Journal of the American Academy of Child and Adolescent Psychiatry, 29,* 359–366.

Delligatti, N., Akin Little, A., & Little, S. G. (2003). Conduct disorder in girls: Diagnostic and intervention issues. *Psychology in the Schools, 40,* 183–192.

Devitt, H., Holland, P., Butler, R., Redfern, E., Hiley, E., & Roberts, G. (1999). Plasma vasopressin and response to treatment in primary nocturnal enuresis. *Archives of Disease in Childhood, 80,* 448–451.

Devlin, J. B., & O'Cathain, C. (1990). Predicting treatment outcome in nocturnal enuresis. *Archives of Diseases in Childhood, 65,* 1158–1161.

Dhossche, D., van der Steen, F., & Ferdinand, R. (2002). Somatoform disorders in children and adolescents: A comparison with other internalizing disorders. *Annals of Clinical Psychiatry, 14,* 23–31.

Diener, M. B., & Milich, R. (1997). Effects of positive feedback on the social interactions of boys with attention deficit hyperactivity disorder: A test of the self-protective hypothesis. *Journal of Clinical Child Psychology, 26,* 256–265.

DiLalla, L. F. (2002). Behavior genetics of aggression in children: Review and future directions. *Developmental Review, 22,* 593–622.

DiLella, A., & Woo, S. (1987). Molecular basis of phenylketonuria and its clinical implications. *Biology and Medicine, 4,* 183–192.

Dimitropoulos, A., Feurer, I. D., Roof, E., Stone, W., Butler, M. G., Sutcliffe, J., et al. (2000). Appetitive behavior, compulsivity, and neurochemistry in Prader–Willi syndrome. *Mental Retardation and Developmental Disabilities Research Reviews, 6,* 125–130.

Dishion, T. J., & Granic, I. (2004). Naturalistic observation of relationship processes. In S. Haynes & E. M. Heiby (Eds.), *Comprehensive handbook of psychological assessment: Behavioral assessment* (Vol. 3, pp. 143–161). Hoboken, NJ: John Wiley & Sons.

Dixon, J. F., & Ahrens, A. H. (1992). Stress and attributional style as predictors of self-reported depression in children. *Cognitive Therapy and Research, 16,* 623–635.

Djurhuus, J. C. (2002). Editorial comment. *European Urology, 41,* 667.

Dodd, B., & Thompson, L. (2001). Speech disorder in children with Down's syndrome. *Journal of Intellectual Disability Research, 45,* 308–316.

Dodge, K. A., & Frame, C. L. (1982). Social cognitive biases and deficits in aggressive boys. *Child Development, 53,* 629–635.

Dong, Q., Yang, B., & Ollendick, T. H. (1994). Fears in Chinese children and adolescents and their relations to anxiety and depression. *Journal of Child Psychology and Psychiatry, 35,* 351–363.

Donovan, C. L., & Spence, S. H. (2000). Prevention of childhood anxiety disorders. *Clinical Psychology Review, 20,* 509–531.

Dorahy, M. J. (2001). Dissociative identity disorder and memory dysfunction: The current state of experimental research and its future directions. *Clinical Psychology Review, 21,* 771–795.

Dozier, M. (2003). Attachment-based treatment for vulnerable children. *Attachment and Human Development, 5,* 253–257.

Drew, C. J., Logan, D. R., & Hardman, M. (1992). *Mental retardation: A life cycle approach* (5th ed.). New York: MacMillan.

Dubey, D., O'Leary, S., & Kaufman, K. (1983). Training parents of hyperactive children in child management: A comparative outcome study. *Journal of Abnormal Child Psychology, 11,* 229–246.

DuBois, D. L., Felner, R. D., Bartels, C. L., & Silverman, M. M. (1995). Stability of self-reported depressive symptoms in a community sample of children and adolescents. *Journal of Clinical Child Psychology, 24,* 386–396.

Dulmus, C. N., & Smyth, N. J. (2000). Early-onset schizophrenia: A literature review of empirically based interventions. *Child and Adolescent Social Work Journal, 17,* 55–69.

Dunne, M. P., Martin, N., Stratham, D., Slutske, W., Dinwiddie, S., & Ducholz, K. (1997). Genetic and environmental contributions to variance in age at first sexual intercourse. *Psychological Science, 8,* 211–216.

DuPaul, G. J., Barkley, R. A., & McMurray, M. B. (1991). Therapeutic effects of medication on ADHD: Implications for school psychologists. *School Psychology Review, 20,* 203–219.

DuPaul, G. J., McGoey, K. E., Eckert, T. L., & VanBrakle, J. (2001). Preschool children with attention-deficit/hyperactivity disorder: Impairments in behavioral, social, and school functioning. *Journal of the American Academy of Child and Adolescent Psychiatry, 40,* 508–515.

DuRant, R. H., Getts, A., Cadenhead, C., Emans, S., & Woods, E. R. (1995). Exposure to violence and victimization and depression, hopelessness, and purpose in life among adolescents living in and around public housing. *Developmental and Behavioral Pediatrics, 16,* 233–237.

Dyer, C. A. (1999). Pathophysiology of phenylketonuria. *Mental Retardation and Developmental Disabilities Research Reviews, 5,* 104–112.

Dykens, E. M., & Cassidy, S. B. (1996). Prader–Willi syndrome: Genetic, behavioral, and treatment issues. *Child and Adolescent Psychiatric Clinic of North America, 5,* 913–927.

Earls, F., Smith, E., Reich, W., & Jung, K. (1988). Investigating psychopathological consequences of a disaster in children. *Journal of the American Academy of Child and Adolescent Psychiatry, 27,* 90–95.

Eaves, L. J., Silberg, J. L., Maes, H. H., Simonoff, E., Pickles, A., Rutter, M., et al. (1997). Genetics and developmental psychopathology: 2. The main effects of genes and environment on behavioral problems in the Virginia Twin Study of Adolescent Behavioral Development. *Journal of Child Psychology and Psychiatry and Allied Disciplines, 38,* 965–980.

Ebeling, H., Tapanainen, P., Joutsenoju, A., Koskinen, M, Morin-Papunen, L., et al. (2003). A practice guideline for treatment of eating disorders in children and adolescents. *Annals of Medicine, 35,* 488–501.

Edens, J. F., Cavell, T. A., & Hughes, J. N. (1999). The self-systems of aggressive children: A cluster-analytic investigation. *Journal of Child Psychology and Psychiatry and Allied Disciplines, 40,* 441–453.

Edwards, M., Finney, J., & Bonner, M. (1991). Matching treatment with recurrent abdominal pain symptoms: An evaluation of dietary fiber and relaxation treatments. *Behavior Therapy, 22,* 257–267.

Egger, H., & Angold, A. (2006). Common emotional and behavioral disorders in preschool children: Presentation, nosology, and epidemiology. *Journal of Child Psychology and Psychiatry, 47,* 313–337.

Egger, H. L., Costello, E. J., Erkanli, A., & Angold, A. (1999). Somatic complaints and psychopathology in children and adolescents: Stomachaches, musculoskeletal pains, and headaches. *Journal of the American Academy of Child and Adolescent Psychiatry, 38,* 852–860.

Eggers, C., & Bunk, D. (1997). The long-term course of childhood-onset schizophrenia: A 42-year followup. *Schizophrenia Bulletin, 23,* 105–117.

Eggers, C., Bunk, D., & Krause, D. (2000). Schizophrenia with onset before the age of eleven: Clinical characteristics of onset and course. *Journal of Autism and Developmental Disorders, 30,* 29–38.

Ehringer, M., Rhee, S., Young, S., Corley, R., & Hewitt, J. (February 2006). Genetic and environmental contributions to common psychopathologies of childhood and adolescence: A study of twins and their siblings. *Journal of Abnormal Child Psychology, Online Publishing.*

Eiberg, H., Berendt, I., & Mohr, J. (1995). Assignment of dominant inherited nocturnal enuresis to chromosome 13q. *Nature and Genetics, 10,* 354–356.

Eich, E., Macaulay, D., Loewenstein, R. J., & Dihle, P. H. (1997). Memory, amnesia, and dissociative identity disorder. *Psychological Science, 8,* 417–422.

Einfeld, S., Tonge, B., Turner, G., Parmenter, T., & Smith, A. (1999). Longitudinal course of behavioural and emotional problems of young persons with Prader–Willi, Fragile X, Williams, and Down syndromes. *Journal of Intellectual and Developmental Disability, 24,* 349–354.

Eisenberg, L., & Kanner, L. (1955). Early infantile autism 1943–1955. In *Childhood schizophrenia* (pp. 556–566). Baltimore, Maryland: Children's Psychiatric Service.

Eley, T. (2001). Contributions of behavioral genetics research: Quantifying genetic, shared environmental and nonshared environmental influences. In M. Vasey & M. Dadds (Eds.), *The developmental psychopathology of anxiety* (pp. 49–59). Oxford, England: Oxford University Press.

Ellis, A. (1989). Rational–emotive therapy. In R. Corsini & D. Wedding (Eds.), *Current psychotherapies* (pp. 197–238). Itasca, IL: Peacock Publishing.

Ellis, A. (1993). Reflections on rational–emotive therapy. *Journal of Consulting and Clinical Psychology, 61,* 199–201.

Elmore, D. K., & De Castro, J. M. (1990). Self-rated moods and hunger in relation to spontaneous eating behavior in bulimics, recovered bulimics, and normals. *International Journal of Eating Disorders, 9*(2), 179–190.

Elzinga, B. M., & Bremner, J. D. (2002). Are the neural substrates of memory the final common pathway in posttraumatic stress disorder? *Journal of Affective Disorders, 70*, 1–17.

Emslie, G. J., Heiligenstein, J. H., Wagner, K. D., Hoog, S. L., Ernest, D. E., & Brown, E. (2002). Fluoxetine for acute treatment of depression in children and adolescents: A placebo-controlled, randomized clinical trial. *Journal of the American Academy of Child and Adolescent Psychiatry, 41*, 1205–1215.

Emslie, G. J., & Mayes, T. L. (2001). Mood disorders in children and adolescents: Psychopharmacological treatment. *Biological Psychiatry, 49*, 1082–1090.

Emslie, G. J., Rush, J., Weinberg, W. A., Kowatch, R. A., Hughes, C. W., Carmody, T., et al. (1997). A double-blind, randomized, placebo-controlled trial of fluoxetine in children and adolescents with depression. *Archives of General Psychiatry, 54*, 1031–1037.

Epstein, L., Paluch, R., Kilanowski, C., & Raynor, H. (2004). The effect of reinforcement or stimulus control to reduce sedentary behavior in the treatment of pediatric obesity. *Health Psychology, 23*, 371–380.

Erba, H. W. (2000). Early intervention programs for children with autism: Conceptual frameworks for implementation. *American Journal of Orthopsychiatry, 70*, 82–94.

Erlenmeyer-Kimling, L. (2000). Neurobehavioral deficits in offspring of schizophrenic parents: Liability indicators and predictors of illness. *American Journal of Medical Genetics, 97*, 65–71.

Espelage, D., Holt, M., & Henkel, R. (2003). Examination of peer group contextual effects on aggression during early adolescence. *Child Development, 74*, 205–220.

Essau, C. A. (2003). Epidemiology and comorbidity. In C. A. Essau (Ed.), *Conduct and oppositional defiant disorders: Epidemiology, risk factors, and treatment* (pp. 33–59). Mahwah, NJ: Erlbaum.

Evans, D. L., Beardslee, W., Biederman, J., Brent, D., Charney, D., & Coyle, J. (2005). Depression and bipolar disorder. In D. L. Evans, E. B. Foa, & R. E. Gur (Eds.), *Treating and preventing adolescent mental health disorders* (pp. 4–47). Oxford, England: Oxford University Press.

Evans, D. W. (1999). Development of the self-concept in children with mental retardation: Organismic and contextual factors. In J. A. Burack, R. M. Hodapp, & E. Zigler (Eds.), *Handbook of mental retardation and development* (pp. 462–480). Cambridge, England: Cambridge University Press.

Fagan, J. (1996). Gangs, drugs, and neighborhood change. In C. Huff (Ed.), *Gangs in America* (pp. 39–73). London: Sage.

Fahey, T. A. (1988). The diagnosis of multiple personality disorder: A clinical review. *British Journal of Psychiatry, 153*, 597–606.

Fairburn, C. G., Marcus, M. D., & Wilson, G. T. (1993). Cognitive–behavioral therapy for binge eating and bulimia nervosa: A comprehensive treatment manual. In C. G. Fairburn & G. T. Wilson (Eds.), *Binge eating: Nature, assessment, and treatment* (pp. 361–404). New York: Guilford Press.

Faith, M., Berman, N., Heo, M., Pietrobelli, A., Gallagher, D., Epstein, L., et al. (2001). Effects of contingent television on physical activity and television viewing in obese children. *Pediatrics, 106*, 1043–1048.

Famularo, R., Fenton, T., & Kinscherff, A. (1994). Maternal and child posttraumatic stress disorder in cases of maltreatment. *Child Abuse & Neglect, 18*, 27–36.

Farmer, E. M. Z., Compton, S. N., Burns, J. B., & Robertson, E. (2002). Review of the evidence base for treatment of childhood psychopathology: Externalizing disorders. *Journal of Consulting and Clinical Psychology, 70*, 1267–1302.

Farthing, M. J. (1995). Irritable bowel, irritable body, or irritable brain? *British Medical Journal, 310*, 171–175.

Feingold, B. F. (1975). *Why your child is hyperactive*. New York: Random House.

Feiring, C., Taska, L., & Chen, K. (2002). Trying to understand why horrible things happen: Attribution, shame, and symptom development following sexual abuse. *Child Maltreatment, 7*, 26–41.

Felner, R. D., & Adan, A. M. (1988). The School Transitional Environment Project: An ecological intervention and evaluation. In R. H. Price & E. L. Cowen (Eds.), *Fourteen ounces of prevention: A casebook for practitioners* (pp. 111–122). Washington, DC: American Psychological Association.

Fergusson, D. M., Horwood, L. T., & Shannon, F. T. (1990). Secondary enuresis in a birth cohort of New Zealand children. *Paediatric and Perinatal Epidemiology, 4,* 53–63.

Fergusson, D. M., & Lynskey, M. T. (1995). Childhood circumstances, adolescent adjustment, and suicide attempts in a New Zealand birth cohort. *Journal of the American Academy of Child and Adolescent Psychiatry, 34,* 612–622.

Fergusson, D. M., & Woodward, L. J. (2000). Educational, psychosocial, and sexual outcomes of girls with conduct problems in early adolescence. *Journal of Child Psychology and Psychiatry and Allied Disciplines, 41,* 779–792.

Fichter, M. M. (1992). Starvation-related endocrine changes. In K. A. Halmi (Ed.), *Psychobiology and treatment of anorexia nervosa and bulimia nervosa* (pp. 102–126). Washington, DC: American Psychiatric Press.

Fichter, M. M., & Pirke, K. M. (1986). Effect of experimental and pathological weight loss upon the hypothalamo–pituitary–adrenal axis. *Psychoneuroendocrinology, 11*(3), 295–305.

Findling, R. L., Feeny, N. C., Stansbrey, R. J., Delporto Bedoya, D., & Demeter, C. (2002). Somatic treatment for depressive illnesses in children and adolescents. *Child and Adolescent Psychiatric Clinics of North America, 11,* 555–578.

Findling, R. L., Gracious, B. L., McNamara, N. K., Youngstrom, E. A., Demeter, C. A., Branicky, L. A., et al. (2001). Rapid, continuous cycling and psychiatric comorbidity in pediatric bipolar I disorder. *Bipolar Disorders, 3,* 202–210.

Fink, D. L., & Golinkoff, M. (1990). MPD, borderline personality disorder and schizophrenia: A comparative study of clinical features. *Dissociation: Progress in the Dissociative Disorders, 3,* 127–134.

Finkelhor, D. (1979). *Sexually victimized children.* New York: Free Press.

Finney, J. W., Lemanek, K. L., Cataldo, M. F., & Katz, H. P. (1989). Pediatric psychology in primary health care: Brief targeted therapy for recurrent abdominal pain. *Behavior Therapy, 20,* 283–291.

Firestone, P., Musten, L. M., Pisterman, S., Mercer, J., & Bennett, S. (1998). Short-term side effects of stimulant medication are increased in preschool children with attention-deficit/hyperactivity disorder: A double-blind placebo-controlled study. *Journal of Child and Adolescent Psychopharmacology, 8,* 13–25.

Fisher, M., & Meyer, L. H. (2002). Development and social competence after two years for students enrolled in inclusive and self-contained educational programs. *Research and Practice for Persons with Severe Disabilities, 27,* 165–174.

Flannery Schroeder, E. C., & Kendall, P. C. (2000). Group and individual cognitive–behavioral treatments for youth with anxiety disorders: A randomized clinical trial. *Cognitive Therapy and Research, 24,* 251–278.

Fletcher, K. E. (2003). Childhood posttraumatic stress disorder. In E. Mash & R. Barkley (Eds.), *Child psychopathology* (2nd ed., pp. 330–371). New York: Guilford.

Foa, E. B., Costello, E. J., Franklin, M., Kagan, J., Kendall, P., & Klein, R. (2005). Anxiety disorders. In D. L. Evans, E. B. Foa, & R. E. Gur (Eds.), *Treating and preventing adolescent mental health disorders* (pp. 161–256). Oxford, England: Oxford University Press.

Foa, E. B., Hearst Ikeda, D., & Perry, K. J. (1995). Evaluation of a brief cognitive–behavioral program for the prevention of chronic PTSD in recent assault victims. *Journal of Consulting and Clinical Psychology, 63,* 948–955.

Foa, E. B., Steketee, G., & Rothbaum, B. O. (1989). Behavioral/cognitive conceptualization of post-traumatic stress disorder. *Behavioral Therapy, 20,* 155–176.

Fombonne, E. (2003). Epidemiological surveys of autism and other pervasive developmental disorders: An update. *Journal of Autism and Developmental Disorder, 33,* 365–377.

Fontaine, R. G., Salzer Burkes, V., & Dodge, K. A. (2002). Response decision processes and externalizing behavior problems in adolescents. *Development and Psychopathology, 14,* 107–122.

Foreman, D., & Thambirajah, M. (1996). Conduct disorder, enuresis and specific developmental delays in two types of encopresis: A case-note study of 63 boys. *European Journal of Child and Adolescent Psychiatry, 5,* 33–37.

Forrest, K. A. (2001). Toward an etiology of dissociative identity disorder: A neurodevelopmental approach. *Conciousness and Cognition, 10,* 259–293.

Forsythe, W. I., & Redmond, A. (1974). Enuresis and spontaneous cure rate. *Archives of Diseases of Children, 49,* 259–263.

Foxman, B., Valdez, R. B., & Brook, R. H. (1986). Childhood enuresis: Prevalence, perceived impact, and prescribed treatments. *Pediatrics, 77,* 482–487.

Francis, D., Caldji, C., Champagen, F., Plotsky, P., & Meaney, J. (1999). The role of corticotropin-releasing factor–norepinephrine systems in mediating the effects of early experiences on the development of behavioral and endocrine responses to stress. *Biological Psychiatry, 46,* 1153–1166.

Francis, S., & Chorpita, B. F. (2004). Behavioral assessment of children in outpatient settings. In S. Haynes & E. M. Heiby (Eds.), *Comprehensive handbook of psychological assessment: Behavioral assessment* (Vol. 3, pp. 291–319). Hoboken, NJ: John Wiley & Sons.

Fraser, G. (1994). Dissociative phenomena and disorders: Clinical presentations. In R. Klein & B. Doane (Eds.), *Psychological concepts and dissociative disorders* (pp. 131–151). Hillsdale, NJ: Lawrence Erlbaum.

Frazier, J. A., Giedd, J. N., Hamburger, S. D., & Albus, K. E. (1996). Brain anatomic magnetic resonance imaging in childhood-onset schizophrenia. *Archives of General Psychiatry, 53,* 617–624.

Freedman, D. S. (2004). Childhood obesity and coronary heart disease. In W. Kiess, C. Carcus, & M. Wabitsch (Eds.), *Obesity in childhood and adolescence* (pp. 160–169). Basel, Switzerland: Karger.

Freedman, R. I., & Boyer, N. C. (2000). The power to choose: Supports for families for individuals with developmental disabilities. *Health and Social Work, 25,* 59–68.

Freeman, S. F. N., & Alkin, M. C. (2000). Academic and social attainments of children with mental retardation in general education and special education settings. *Remedial and Special Education, 21,* 3–18.

Freud, S. (1909/1955). Analysis of a phobia in a five-year-old boy. In J. Strachey (Ed.), *The standard edition of the complete psychological works of Sigmund Freud.* London: Hogarth Press.

Frick, P. J., & Ellis, M. (1999). Callous–unemotional traits and subtypes of conduct disorder. *Clinical Child and Family Psychology Review, 2,* 149–168.

Frick, P. J., Lahey, B. B., Loeber, R., Tannenbaum, L., Van Horn, Y., Christ, M. A. G., et al. (1993). Oppositional defiant disorder and conduct disorder: A meta-analytic review of factor analyses and cross-validation in a clinic sample. *Clinical Psychology Review, 13,* 319–340.

Fristad, M. A., Goldberg Arnold, J. S., & Gavazzi, S. M. (2002). Multifamily psychoeducation groups (MFPG) for families of children with bipolar disorder. *Bipolar Disorders, 4,* 254–262.

Fritz, G., Fritsch, S., & Hagino, O. (1997). Somatoform disorders in children and adolescents: A review of the last 10 years. *Journal of the American Academy of Child and Adolescent Psychiatry, 36,* 1329–1339.

Garber, J. (1984). Classification of childhood psychopathology: A developmental perspective. *Child Development, 55,* 30–48.

Garber, J., Braafladt, N., & Weiss, B. (1995). The regulation of sad affect: An information-processing perspective. In J. Garber & K. Dodge (Eds.), *The development of emotional regulation and dysregulation* (pp. 208–242). Cambridge, England: Cambridge University Press.

Garber, J., & Kaminski, K. M. (2000). Laboratory and performance-based measures of depression in children and adolescents. *Journal of Clinical Child Psychology, 29,* 509–525.

Garber, J., Walker, L. S., & Zeman, J. (1991). Somatization symptoms in a community sample of children and adolescent: Further validation of the children's somatization inventory. *Psychological Assessment: A Journal of Consulting and Clinical Psychology, 3,* 588–595.

Garber, J., Weiss, B., & Shanley, N. (1993). Cognitions, depressive symptoms, and development in adolescents. *Journal of Abnormal Psychology, 102,* 47–57.

Garland, A. F., & Zigler, E. (1993). Adolescent suicide prevention: Current research and social policy implications. *American Psychologist, 48,* 169–182.

Garmezy, N. (1985). Stress-resistant children: The search for protective factors. In J. E. Stevenson (Ed.), *Recent research in developmental psychopathology: Journal of Child Psychology and Psychiatry Book Supplement #4* (pp. 213–233). Oxford, England: Pergamon Press.

Garmezy, N., & Rodnick, E. (1959). Premorbid adjustment and performance in schizophrenia: Implications for interpreting heterogeneity in schizophrenia. *Journal of Nervous and Mental Disease, 129,* 450–466.

Garmezy, N., & Rutter, M. (Eds.). (1983). *Stress, coping, and development in children.* New York: McGraw-Hill.

Garralda, M. E. (1996). Somatization in children. *Journal of Child Psychology and Psychiatry and Allied Disciplines, 37*, 13–33.

Garralda, M. E. (1999). Assessment and management of somatisation in childhood and adolescence: A practical perspective. *Journal of Child Psychology and Psychiatry and Allied Disciplines, 40*, 1159–1167.

Garrick, T., Ostrov, E., & Offer, D. (1988). Physical symptoms and self-image in a group of normal adolescents. *Psychosomatics, 29*, 73–80.

Gaub, M., & Carlson, C. L. (1997). Gender differences in ADHD: A meta-analysis and critical review. *Journal of the American Academy of Child and Adolescent Psychiatry, 36*, 1036–1045.

Ge, X., Conger, R. D., & Elder, G. H. (1996). Coming of age too early: Pubertal influences on girls' vulnerability to psychological distress. *Child Development, 67*, 3386–3400.

Ge, X., Conger, R. D., & Elder, G. H. (2001). Pubertal transition, stressful life events, and the emergence of gender differences in adolescent depressive symptoms. *Developmental Psychology, 37*, 404–417.

Ge, X., Kim, I. J., Brody, G. H., Conger, R. D., Simons, R. L., Gibbons, F. X., et al. (2003). It's about timing and change: Pubertal transition effects on symptoms of major depression among African American youths. *Developmental Psychology, 39*, 430–439.

Geller, B., Bolhofner, K., Craney, J. L., Williams, M., DelBello, M. P., & Gundersen, K. (2000). Psychosocial functioning in a prepubertal and early adolescent bipolar disorder phenotype. *Journal of the American Academy of Child and Adolescent Psychiatry, 39*, 1543–1548.

Geller, B., Cooper, T. B., Sun, K., Zimermann, B., Frazier, J., Williams, M., et al. (1998). Double-blind and placebo-controlled study of lithium for adolescent bipolar disorders with secondary substance dependency. *Journal of the American Academy of Child and Adolescent Psychiatry, 37*, 171–178.

Geller, B., Craney, J. L., Bolhofner, K., Nickelsburg, M. J., Williams, M., & Zimerman, B. (2002). Two-year prospective follow-up of children with a prepubertal and early adolescent bipolar disorder phenotype. *American Journal of Psychiatry, 159*, 927–933.

Geller, B., Zimerman, B., Williams, M., Bolhofner, K., Craney, J. L., Delbello, M. P., et al. (2000). Diagnostic characteristics of 93 cases of prepubertal and early adolescent bipolar disorder phenotype by gender, puberty, and comorbid attention deficit hyperactivity disorder. *Journal of Child and Adolescent Psychopharmacology, 10*, 157–164.

Geller, B., Zimerman, B., Williams, M., Del Bello, M. P., Bolhofner, K., Craney, J. L., et al. (2002a). DSM-IV mania symptoms in a prepubertal and early adolescent bipolar disorder phenotype compared to attention-deficit hyperactive and normal controls. *Journal of Child and Adolescent Psychopharmacology, 12*, 11–25.

Geller, B., Zimerman, B., Williams, M., DelBello, M. P., Frazier, J., & Beringer, L. (2002b). Phenomenology of prepubertal and early adolescent bipolar disorder: Examples of elated mood, grandiose behaviors, decreased need for sleep, racing thoughts and hypersexuality. *Journal of Child and Adolescent Psychopharmacology, 12*, 3–9.

Geller, D. A., & Spencer, T. (2003). Obsessive–compulsive disorder. In A. Martin, S. Scahill, D. Charney, & J. Leckman (Eds.), *Pediatric psychophamacology* (pp. 511–525). New York: Oxford University Press.

Gelles, R. (1979). *Family violence.* Beverly Hills: Sage.

Gerbino-Rosen, G., Roofeh, D., Tompkins, D., Feryo, D., Nusser, L., Kranzler, H., et al. (2005). Hematological adverse events in clozapine-treated children and adolescents. *Journal of the American Academy of Child and Adolescent Psychiatry, 44*, 1024–1031.

Giaconia, R. M., Reinherz, H. Z., Hauf, A. C., Paradis, A. D., Wasserman, M. S., & Langhammer, D. M. (2000). Comorbidity of substance use and post-traumatic stress disorders in a community sample of adolescents. *American Journal of Orthopsychiatry, 70*, 253–262.

Gill, A. C. (2002). Risk factors for pediatric posttraumatic stress disorder after traumatic injury. *Archives of Psychiatric Nursing, 16*, 168–175.

Gillberg, C., & Coleman, M. (1996). Autism and medical disorders: A review of the literature. *Developmental Medicine and Child Neurology, 38*, 191–202.

Gillberg, C., Nordin, V., & Ehlers, S. (1996). Early detection of autism: Diagnostic instruments for clinicians. *European Child and Adolescent Psychiatry, 5*, 67–74.

Gillberg, C., & Steffenburg, S. (1987). Outcome and prognostic factors in infantile autism and similar conditions: A population-based study of 46 cases followed through puberty. *Journal of Autism and Developmental Disorders, 17,* 273–287.

Gillberg, C., Steffenburg, S., & Schaumann, H. (1991). Is autism more common now than ten years ago? *British Journal of Psychiatry, 158,* 403–409.

Gillberg, C., & Wing, L. (1999). Autism: Not an extremely rare disorder. *Acta Psychiatrica Scandinavia, 99,* 399–406.

Gillham, J., & Reivich, K. (1999). Prevention of depressive symptoms in school children: A research update. *Psychological Science, 10,* 461–462.

Gillham, J. E., Reivich, K. J., Jaycox, L. H., & Seligman, M. E. P. (1995). Prevention of depressive symptoms in schoolchildren: Two-year follow-up. *Psychological Science, 6,* 343–351.

Gillis, J. J., Gilger, J. W., Pennington, B. F., & DeFries, J. C. (1992). Attention deficit disorder in reading-disabled twins: Evidence for a genetic etiology. *Journal of Abnormal Child Psychology, 20,* 303–315.

Gingerich, K. J., Turnock, P., Litfin, J. K., & Rosen, L. A. (1998). Diversity and attention deficit hyperactivity disorder. *Journal of Clinical Psychology, 54,* 415–426.

Gladstone, T. R. G., & Kaslow, N. J. (1995). Depression and attributions in children and adolescents: A meta-analytic review. *Journal of Abnormal Child Psychology, 23,* 597–606.

Glantz, L. H. (1996). Conducting research with children: Legal and ethical issues. *Journal of the American Academy of Child and Adolescent Psychiatry, 35,* 1283–1291.

Glaser, K. (1968). Masked depression in children and adolescents. *Annual Progress in Child Psychiatry and Child Development, 1,* 345–355.

Gleaves, D. H. (1996). The sociocognitive model of dissociative identity disorder: A reexamination of the evidence. *Psychological Bulletin, 120,* 42–59.

Glick, M. (1999). Developmental and experiential variables in the self-images of people with mild mental retardation. In E. Zigler & D. Bennett-Gates (Eds.), *Personality development in individuals with mental retardation* (pp. 47–69). Cambridge, England: Cambridge University Press.

Goenjian, A. K., Pynoos, R. S., & Steinberg, A. M. (1995). Psychiatric comorbidity in children after the 1988 earthquake in Armenia. *Journal of the American Academy of Child and Adolescent Psychiatry, 34,* 1174–1184.

Goff, D. C., Olin, J. A., Jenike, M. A., & Baer, L. (1992). Dissociative symptoms in patients with obsessive–compulsive disorder. *Journal of Nervous and Mental Disease, 180,* 332–337.

Goldsmith, H. H., Buss, A. H., Plomin, R., Rothbart, T. A., Chess, S., Hinde, R. A., et al. (1987). Round table: What is temperament? Four approaches. *Child Development, 58,* 505–529.

Goodman, G., Emery, R., & Haugaard, J. J. (1998). Developmental psychology and the law: Divorce, child maltreatment, foster care, and adoption. In I. Sigel & A. Renninger (Eds.), *Handbook of child psychology* (5th ed., Vol. 4: *Child psychology in practice,* pp. 775–876). New York: Wiley.

Goodman, S. H., Schwab Stone, M., Lahey, B. B., Shaffer, D., & Jensen, P. S. (2000). Major depression and dysthymia in children and adolescents: Discriminant validity and differential consequences in a community sample. *Journal of the American Academy of Child and Adolescent Psychiatry, 39,* 761–770.

Goodyer, I., & Taylor, D. (1985). Hysteria. *Archives of the Diseases of Children, 60,* 680–681.

Gosch, A., & Pankau, R. (1997). Personality characteristics and behaviour problems in individuals of different ages with Williams syndrome. *Developmental Medicine and Child Neurology, 39,* 327–333.

Gotlib, I. H., & Robinson, L. A. (1982). Responses to depressed individuals: Discrepancies between self-report and observer-rated behavior. *Journal of Abnormal Psychology, 91,* 231–240.

Gottesman, I. I. (1991). *Schizophrenia genesis: The origins of madness.* New York: Freeman.

Gottesman, I. I., & Erlenmeyer Kimling, L. (2001). Family and twin strategies as a head start in defining prodomes and endophenotypes for hypothetical early interventions in schizophrenia. *Schizophrenia Research, 51,* 93–102.

Gottlieb, J., Alter, M., & Gottlieb, B. W. (1991). Mainstreaming mentally retarded children. In J. Matson & J. Mulick (Eds.), *Handbook of mental retardation* (pp. 63–73). New York: Pergamon.

Gould, M., Greenberg, T., Velting, D., & Shaffer, D. (2003). Youth suicide risk and preventive interventions: A review of the past 10 years. *Journal of the American Academy of Child and Adolescent Psychiatry, 42,* 386–405.

Gould, M., Shaffer, D., & Greenberg, T. (2003). The epidemiology of youth suicide. In R. King & A. Apter (Eds.), *Suicide in children and adolescents* (pp. 1–40). Cambridge, England: Cambridge University Press.

Gould, M. S., Fisher, P., Parides, M., Flory, M., & Shaffer, D. (1996). Psychosocial risk factors of child and adolescent completed suicide. *Archives of General Psychiatry, 53,* 1155–1162.

Grandin, T. (1992). An inside view of autism. In E. Schopler & G. Mesibov (Eds.), *High-functioning individuals with autism* (pp. 105–126). New York: Plenum.

Gray, J. A. (1987). *The psychology of fear and stress.* New York: Cambridge University Press.

Gray, J. A., & McNaughon, N. (1996). The neuropsychology of anxiety: A reprise. In D. Hope (Ed.), *Nebraska symposium on motivation: Perspectives on anxiety* (pp. 61–134). Lincoln, NE: University of Nebraska Press.

Green, G. (1996). Early behavioral intervention for autism: What does research tell us? In C. Maurice & G. Green (Eds.), *Behavioral intervention for young children with autism: A manual for parents and professionals* (pp. 29–44). Austin, TX: PRO-ED, Inc.

Greene, R. W., & Doyle, A. E. (1999). Toward a transactional conceptualization of oppositional defiant disorder: Implications for assessment and treatment. *Clinical Child and Family Psychology Review, 2,* 129–148.

Grimes v. Kennedy Krieger Institute, 782 A.2d 807 (2001).

Grinker, R., & Spiegel, J. (1945). *Men under stress.* Philadelphia: Blakiston.

Gross, R. T. (1984). Patterns of maturation: Their effects on behavior and development. In M. Levine & P. Satz (Eds.), *Middle childhood: Development and dysfunction* (pp. 62–84). Baltimore: University Park Press.

Grossman, F. (1973). *Manual on terminology and classification in mental retardation.* Washington, DC: AAMD.

Guess, D., & Carr, E. (1991). Emergence and maintenance of stereotypy and self-injury. *American Journal of Mental Retardation, 96,* 299–319.

Guevremont, D., & Dumas, M. (1994). Peer relationship problems and disruptive behaviour disorders. *Journal of Emotional and Behavioural Disorders, 2,* 164–172.

Guillaume, M., & Lissau, I. (2002). Epidemiology. In W. Burniat, T. J. Cole, I. Lissau, & E. Poskitt (Eds.), *Child and adolescent obesity* (pp. 28–49). Cambridge, England: Cambridge University Press.

Guralnick, M. J. (1998). Effectiveness of early intervention for vulnerable children: A developmental perspective. *American Journal on Mental Retardation, 102,* 319–345.

Gurley, D., Cohen, P., Pine, D., & Brook, J. (1996). Discriminating depression and anxiety in youth: A role for diagnostic criteria. *Journal of Affective Disorders, 39,* 191–200.

Hagberg, B. (2002). Clinical manifestations and stages of Rett Syndrome. *Mental Retardation and Developmental Disabilities Research Reviews, 8,* 61–65.

Hagen, R. L. (1997). In praise of the null hypothesis statistical test. *American Psychologist, 52,* 15–24.

Hall, G. S. (1904). *Adolescence: Its psychology and its relations to physiology, anthropology, sociology, sex, crime, religion, and education.* Englewood Cliffs, NJ: Prentice-Hall.

Halmi, K. A., Casper, B., Eckert, J., Goldberg, J., & Davis, A. (1979). Pretreatment predictors of outcome in anorexia nervosa. *British Journal of Psychiatry, 134,* 71–78.

Hammen, C. (1992). Life events and depression: The plot thickens. *American Journal of Community Psychology, 20,* 179–193.

Hammen, C., & Rudolph, K. (2003). Childhood mood disorders. In E. Mash & R. Barkley (Eds.), *Child psychopathology* (2nd ed., pp. 233–278). New York: Guilford.

Hancox, R., Milne, B. J., & Poultron, R. (2004). Association between child and adolescent television viewing and adult health: A longitudinal birth cohort study. *Lancet, 364,* 257–262.

Hankin, C. S. (2001). ADHD and its impact on the family. *Drug Benefit Trends, 13,* 15–16.

Hanson, R. F., & Spratt, E. G. (2000). Reactive attachment disorder: What we know about the disorder and implications for treatment. *Child Maltreatment, 5,* 137–145.

Happe, F., & Frith, U. (1995). Theory of mind in autism. In E. Schopler & G. Mesibov (Eds.), *Learning and cognition in autism* (pp. 177–197). New York: Plenum.

Harle, J. M., & McClellan, J. M. (2005). Family and group psychosocial interventions for child- and adolescent-onset schizophrenia. In R. L. Findling & S. C. Schultz (Eds.), *Juvenile-onset schizophrenia* (pp. 288–301). Baltimore, MD: Johns Hopkins University Press.

Harris, S. L., Alessandri, M., & Gill, M. J. (1991). Training parents of developmentally disabled children. In J. Matson & J. Mulnick (Eds.), *Handbook of mental retardation* (pp. 373–381). New York: Pergamon.

Harvey, A. G., & Bryant, R. A. (2002). Acute stress disorder: A synthesis and critique. *Psychological Bulletin, 128*, 886–902.

Haugaard, J. J. (2001). *Problematic behaviors during adolescence*. Boston: McGraw-Hill.

Haugaard, J. J. (2006). Characteristics of child maltreatment definitions: The influence of professional and social values. In M. Feerick, J. Knutson, P. Trickett, & S. Flanzer (Eds.), *Child abuse and neglect: Definitions, classifications, and a framework for research* (pp. 49–68). Baltimore, MD: Brookes.

Haugaard, J. J., & Hazan, C. (2003). Adoption as a natural experiment. *Development and Psychopathology, 15*, 909–926.

Haugaard, J. J., & Reppucci, N. D. (1988). *The sexual abuse of children: A comprehensive guide to current knowledge and intervention strategies*. San Francisco: Jossey-Bass.

Hawley, D. R., & De Haan, L. (1996). Toward a definition of family resilience: Integrative life span and family perspectives. *Family Process, 35*, 283–298.

Hayward, C., Killen, J. D., Hammer, L. D., Litt, I. F., Wilson, D., Simmonds, B., et al. (1992). Pubertal stage and panic attack history in sixth- and seventh-grade girls. *American Journal of Psychiatry, 149*, 1239–1243.

Heath, P. A., & Camarena, P. M. (2002). Patterns of depressed affect during early adolescence. *Journal of Early Adolescence, 22*, 252–276.

Heatherton, T. F., Herman, C. P., & Polivy, J. (1991). Effects of physical threat and ego threat on eating behavior. *Journal of Personality and Social Psychology, 60*, 138–143.

Hebebrand, J., Wermter, A., & Hinney, A. (2004). Genetic aspects. In W. Kiess, C. Carcus, & M. Wabitsch (Eds.), *Obesity in childhood and adolescence* (pp. 80–90). Basel, Switzerland: Karger.

Hechtman, L. (1996). Families of children with attention deficit hyperactivity disorder: A review. *Canadian Journal of Psychiatry, 41*, 350–360.

Heim, C., & Nemeroff, C., B. (2001). The role of childhood trauma in the neurobiology of mood and anxiety disorders: Preclinical and clinical studies. *Society of Biological Psychiatry, 29*, 1023–1039.

Heiman, T. (2000). Friendship quality among children in three educational settings. *Journal of Intellectual and Developmental Disability, 25*, 1–12.

Heiman, T. (2002). Parents of children with disabilities: Resilience, coping, and future expectations. *Journal of Developmental and Physical Disabilities, 14*, 159–171.

Helms, J. E., & Cook, D. A. (1999). *Using race and culture in counseling and psychotherapy*. Boston: Allyn and Bacon.

Henggeler, S. W., & Borduin, C. M. (1990). *Family therapy and beyond: A multisystemic approach to treating the behavior problems of children and adolescents*. Pacific Grove, CA: Brooks/Cole.

Henggeler, S. W., Pickrel, S. G., & Brondino, M. J. (1999). Multisystemic treatment of substance abusing and dependent delinquents: Outcomes, treatment fidelity, and transportability. *Mental Health Services Research, 1*, 171–184.

Henkelman, J. J., & Everall, R. D. (2001). Informed consent with children: Ethical and practical implications. *Canadian Journal of Counseling, 35*, 109–121.

Herzog, D. B., Dorer, D. J., Keel, P. K., Selwyn, S. E., Ekeblad, E. R., Flores, A. T., et al. (1999). Recovery and relapse in anorexia and bulimia nervosa: A 7.5-year follow-up study. *Journal of the American Academy of Child and Adolescent Psychiatry, 38*, 829–837.

Heston, L. (1966). Psychiatric disorders in foster home reared children of schizophrenic mothers. *British Journal of Psychiatry, 112*, 819–825.

Hibbs, E. D., & Krener, P. (1996). Ethical issues in psychosocial treatment research with children and adolescents. In K. Hoagwood & P. S. Jensen (Eds.), *Ethical issues in mental health research with children and adolescents* (pp. 59–72). Hillsdale, NJ: Erlbaum.

Hightower, A., & Graden, J. (1991). Prevention. In T. Kratochwill & R. Morris (Eds.), *The practice of child therapy* (pp. 410–440). New York: Pergamon.

Hill, J. (2002). Biological, psychological, and social processes in the conduct disorders. *Journal of Child Psychology and Psychiatry and Allied Disciplines, 43*, 133–164.

Hinshaw, S. P., Klein, R. G., & Abikoff, H. B. (2002). Childhood attention-deficit hyperactivity disorder: Nonpharmacological treatments and their combination with medication. In P. E. Nathan & J. M. Gorman (Eds.), *A guide to treatments that work* (2nd ed., pp. 3–23). London: Oxford University Press.

Hinshaw, S. P., Lahey, B. B., & Hart, E. L. (1993). Issues of taxonomy and comorbidity in the development of conduct disorder. *Development and Psychopathology, 5,* 31–49.

Hinshaw, S. P., & Lee, S. S. (2003). Conduct and oppositional defiant disorders. In E. J. Mash & R. Barkley (Eds.), *Child psychopathology* (2nd ed., pp. 144–198). New York: Guilford.

Hirasing, R., van Leerdam, F., Bolk-Bennink, L., & Bosch, J. (1997). Bedwetting and behavioural and/or emotional problems. *Acta Paediatrica, 86,* 1131–1134.

Hobson, R. P. (1989). Beyond cognition: A theory of autism. In G. Dawson (Ed.), *Autism: New perspectives on diagnosis, nature, and treatment* (pp. 24–48). New York: Guilford.

Hodgens, J. B., Cole, J., & Boldizar, J. (2000). Peer-based differences among boys with ADHD. *Journal of Clinical Child Psychology, 29,* 443–452.

Hollis, C. (2003). Developmental precursors of child- and adolescent-onset schizophrenia and affective psychoses: Diagnostic specificity and continuity with symptom dimensions. *British Journal of Psychiatry, 182,* 37–44.

Honda, H., Shimizu, Y., & Rutter, M. (2005). No effect of MMR withdrawal on the incidence of autism: A total population study. *Journal of Child Psychology and Psychiatry, 46,* 572–579.

Hoover, D., & Milich, R. (1994). Effects of sugar ingestion expectancies on mother–child interactions. *Journal of Abnormal Child Psychology, 22,* 501–514.

Horne, L. R., Van Vactor, J. C., & Emerson, S. (1991). Disturbed body image in patients with eating disorders. *American Journal of Psychiatry, 148,* 211–215.

Hornstein, N. (1996). Dissociative disorders in children and adolescents. In L. Michelson & W. Ray (Eds.), *Handbook of dissociation: Theoretical, empirical, and clinical perspectives* (pp. 139–159). New York: Plenum Press.

Hornstein, N. L., & Putnam, F. W. (1992). Clinical phenomenology of child and adolescent dissociative disorders. *Journal of the American Academy of Child and Adolescent Psychiatry, 31,* 1077–1085.

Hornstein, R. T. (1996). An exploration of women's attitudes toward closeness in intimate relationships. *Dissertation Abstracts International: Section B: The Sciences and Engineering, 57,* 4089.

Humphries, T., Kinsborne, M., & Swanson, J. (1978). Stimulant effects on cooperation and social interaction between hyperactive children and their mothers. *Journal of Child Psychology and Psychiatry and Allied Disciplines, 19,* 13–22.

Husmann, D. (1996). Enuresis. *Urology, 48,* 184–193.

Hyams, J., Burke, G., Davis, P., Rzepski, B., & Andrulonis, P. (1996). Abdominal pain and irritable bowel syndrome in adolescents: A community-based study. *Journal of Pediatrics, 129,* 220–226.

Inge, T., Keiebs, N., Garcia, V., Skelton, J., Giuce, K., Strauss, R., et al. (2004). Biariatric surgery for severely overweight adolescents: Concerns and recommendations. *Pediatrics, 114,* 217–223.

Issenman, R., Filmer, R. B., & Borski, P. A. (1999). A review of bowel and bladder control development in children: How gastrointestinal and urologic conditions related to problems in toilet training. *Pediatrics, 103,* 1346–1352.

Jackson, D., & Weakland, J. (1959). Schizophrenic symptoms and family interaction. *Archives of General Psychiatry, 1,* 618–621.

Jacobsen, L. K., Giedd, J. N., Berquin, P., Krain, A., Hamburger, S., Kumra, S., et al. (1997). Quantitative morphology of the cerebellum and fourth ventricle in childhood-onset schizophrenia. *American Journal of Psychiatry, 154,* 1662–1669.

Jacobsen, L. K., & Rapoport, J. L. (1998a). Childhood-onset schizophrenia: Implications of clinical and neurobiological research. *Journal of Child Psychology and Psychiatry and Allied Disciplines, 39,* 101–113.

Jacobsen, L. K., & Rapoport, J. L. (1998b). Research update: Childhood-onset schizophrenia: Implications of clinical and neurobiological research. *Journal of Child Psychology and Psychiatry and Allied Disciplines, 39,* 101–113.

Jaffee, S., Caspi, A., Moffitt, T. E., Belsky, J., & Silva, P. (2001). Why are children born to teen mothers at risk for adverse outcomes in young adulthood? Results from a 20-year longitudinal study. *Development and Psychopathology, 13,* 377–397.

Jaffee, S. R., Moffitt, T. E., Caspi, A., Fombonne, E., Poulton, R., & Martin, J. (2002). Differences in early childhood risk factors for juvenile-onset and adult-onset depression. *Archives of General Psychiatry, 59,* 215–222.

Jain, A., Sherman, S., Chamberline, L., Carter, Y., Powers, S., & Whitaker, R. C. (2001). Why don't low-income mothers worry about their preschoolers being overweight? *Pediatrics, 107,* 1138–1146.

James, A. C. D., & Javaloyes, A. M. (2001). The treatment of bipolar disorder in children and adolescents. *Journal of Child Psychology and Psychiatry and Allied Disciplines, 42,* 439–449.

Jamison, K. R. (1995). *An unquiet mind.* New York: Vintage Press.

Janicke, D. M., & Finney, J. W. (1999). Empirically supported treatments in pediatric psychology: Recurrent abdominal pain. *Journal of Pediatric Psychology, 24,* 115–127.

Janssen, I., Katzmarzyk, P., Boyce, W., King, M., & Pickett, W. (2004). Overweight and obesity in Canadian adolescents and their associations with dietary habits and physical activity patterns. *Journal of Adolescent Health, 35,* 360–367.

Jarbin, H., Ott, Y., & von Knorring, A. L. (2003). Adult outcome of social function in adolescent-onset schizophrenia and affective psychosis. *Journal of the American Academy of Child and Adolescent Psychiatry, 42,* 176–183.

Jarvelin, M., Moilanen, I., Vekevainen-Tervonen, L., & Huttunen, N. (1990). Life changes and protective capacities in enuretic and non-enuretic children. *Journal of Child Psychology and Psychiatry, 31,* 763–774.

Jaycox, L. H., Stein, B. D., Kataoka, S. H., Wong, M., Fink, A., Escudero, P., et al. (2002). Violence exposure, posttraumatic stress disorder, and depressive symptoms among recent immigrant schoolchildren. *Journal of the American Academy of Child and Adolescent Psychiatry, 41,* 1104–1110.

Jenkins, S. R., Goodness, K., & Buhrmester, D. (2002). Gender differences in early adolescents' relationship qualities, self-efficacy, and depression symptoms. *Journal of Early Adolescence, 22,* 277–309.

Jensen, A. T. (1969). How much can we boost IQ and scholastic achievement? *Harvard Educational Review, 39,* 1–123.

Jensen, P. S., Bhatara, V. S., Vitiello, B., Hoagwood, K., Feil, M., & Burke, L. B. (1999). Psychoactive medication prescribing practices for U.S. children: Gaps between research and clinical practice. *Journal of the American Academy of Child and Adolescent Psychiatry, 38,* 557–565.

Jensen, P. S., Martin, D., & Cantwell, D. P. (1997a). Comorbidity in ADHD: Implications for research, practice, and DSM-V. *Journal of the American Academy of Child and Adolescent Psychiatry, 36,* 1065–1079.

Jensen, P. S., Mrazek, D., & Knapp, P. K. (1997b). Evolution and revolution in child psychiatry: ADHD as a disorder of adaptation. *Journal of the American Academy of Child and Adolescent Psychiatry, 36,* 1672–1681.

Johnson, B. (2000). Using video vignettes to evaluate children's personal safety knowledge: Methodological and ethical issues. *Child Abuse and Neglect, 24,* 811–827.

Johnston, C., & Mash, E. J. (2001). Families of children with attention-deficit/hyperactivity disorder: Review and recommendations for future research. *Clinical Child and Family Psychology Review, 4,* 183–207.

Johnston, C., Reynolds, S., Freeman, W., & Geller, J. (1998). Assessing parent attributions for child behavior using open-ended question. *Journal of Clinical Child Psychology, 27,* 87–97.

Jones, R. R., Reid, J. B., & Patterson, G. R. (1975). Naturalistic observation in clinical assessment. In P. McReynolds (Ed.), *Advances in psychological assessment* (Vol. 3). San Francisco: Jossey-Bass.

Jurich, A. P., & Collins, O. P. (1996). Adolescents, suicide, and death. In C. A. Corr & D. E. Balk (Eds.), *Handbook of adolescent death and bereavement* (pp. 65–84). New York: Springer.

Kagan, J. (1982). *Psychological research on the human infant: An evaluative summary.* New York: W. T. Grant Foundation.

Kagan, J. (1997). Temperament and the reactions to unfamiliarity. *Child Development, 68,* 139–143.

Kagan, J., Reznick, J. S., & Gibbons, J. (1989). Inhibited and uninhibited types of children. *Child Development, 60,* 838–845.

Kagan, J., Reznick, J. S., & Snidman, N. (1987). The physiology and psychology of behavioral inhibition. *Child Development, 58,* 1459–1473.

Kagan, J., Reznick, J. S., Snidman, N., & Gibbons, J. (1988). Childhood derivatives of inhibition and lack of inhibition to the unfamiliar. *Child Development, 59,* 1580–1589.

Kager, V., Arndt, E., & Kenny, T. (1992). Psychosomatic problems of children. In C. E. Walker & M. C. Roberts (Eds.), *Handbook of clinical child psychology* (pp. 303–317). New York: John Wiley & Sons.

Kahn, M. (2002). *Basic Freud: Psychoanalytic thought for the 21st century*. New York: Basic Books.

Kales, E. F. (1989). A laboratory study of cognitive factors in bulimia. *Annals of the New York Academy of Science, 575*, 535–537.

Kaminsky, L., & Dewey, D. (2002). Psychosocial adjustment in siblings of children with autism. *Journal of Child Psychology and Psychiatry and Allied Disciplines, 43*, 225–232.

Kamphaus, R. W. (2001). *Clinical assessment of child and adolescent intelligence* (2nd ed.). Boston: Allyn and Bacon.

Kandel, D. B. (1982). Epidemiological and psychosocial perspectives in adolescent drug use. *Journal of the American Academy of Child Psychiatry, 20*, 328–347.

Kanner, L. (1943). Autistic disturbances of affective contact. *Nervous Child, 2*, 217–250.

Kardiner, A. (1941). *The traumatic neuroses of war*. Washington, DC: National Research Council.

Kasari, C., & Bauminger, N. (1999). Social and emotional development in children with mental retardation. In J. A. Burack, R. M. Hodapp, & E. Zigler (Eds.), *Handbook of mental retardation and development* (pp. 411–433). Cambridge, England: Cambridge University Press.

Kaser-Boyd, N., Adelman, H. S., & Taylor, L. (1985). Minors' ability to identify risks and benefits of therapy. *Professional Psychology: Research and Practice, 16*, 411–417.

Kashani, J. H., & Orvaschel, H. (1988). Anxiety disorders in midadolescence: A community sample. *American Journal of Psychiatry, 145*, 960–964.

Kaslow, N. J., Brown, R. T., & Mee, L. L. (1994). Cognitive and behavioral correlates of childhood depression: A developmental perspective. In W. Reynolds & H. Johnston (Eds.), *Handbook of depression in children and adolescents* (pp. 97–121). New York: Plenum.

Kataoka, S. H., Stein, B. D., Jaycox, L. H., Wong, M., Escudero, P., Tu, W., et al. (2003). A school-based mental health program for traumatized Latino immigrant children. *Journal of the American Academy of Child and Adolescent Psychiatry, 42*, 311–318.

Kaufman, A. (2000). Tests of intelligence. In R. Sternberg (Ed.), *Handbook of intelligence* (pp. 445–476). Cambridge, England: Cambridge University Press.

Kaufman, A. S., & Kaufman, N. L. (1977). *Clinical evaluation of young children with the McCarthy scales*. New York: Grune and Stratton.

Kaufman, J., Birmaher, B., Perel, J., Dahl, R., Moreci, P., & Nelson, B. (1997). The corticotropin-releasing hormone challenge in depressed abused, depressed nonabused, and normal control children. *Biological Psychiatry, 42*, 669–679.

Kaufman, J., Martin, A., King, R. A., & Charney, D. (2001). Are child-, adolescent-, and adult-onset depression one and the same disorder? *Biological Psychiatry, 49*, 980–1001.

Kawauchi, A., Tanaka, Y., Naito, Y., Yamao, Y., Ukimura, O., Yoneda, K., et al. (2003). Bladder capacity at the time of enuresis. *Pediatric Urology, 61*, 1016–1018.

Kaye, J., de Mar Mellero-Montes, M., & Jick, H. (2001). Mumps, measles, and rubella vaccine and the incidence of autism recorded by general practitioners: A time trend analysis. *Boston Medical Journal, 322*, 460–463.

Kazdin, A. E. (2005). *Parent management training*. New York: Oxford University Press.

Kazdin, A. E., Siegel, T. C., & Bass, D. (1992). Cognitive problem-solving skills training and parent management training in the treatment of antisocial behavior in children. *Journal of Consulting and Clinical Psychology, 60*, 733–747.

Kazdin, A. E., & Whitley, M. K. (2003). Treatment of parental stress to enhance therapeutic change among children referred for aggressive and antisocial behavior. *Journal of Consulting and Clinical Psychology, 71*, 504–515.

Keenan, K., Loeber, R., & Green, S. (1999). Conduct disorder in girls: A review of the literature. *Clinical Child and Family Psychology Review, 2*, 3–19.

Keenan, K., & Shaw, D. S. (1997). Developmental and social influences on young girls' early problem behavior. *Psychological Bulletin, 121*, 95–113.

Keller, A., Castellanos, F. X., Vaituzis, A. C., Jeffries, N. O., Giedd, J. N., & Rapoport, J. L. (2003). Progressive loss of cerebellar volume in childhood-onset schizophrenia. *American Journal of Psychiatry, 160*, 128–133.

Kendall, P. C. (1993). Cognitive–behavioral therapies with young children: Guiding theory, current status, and emerging developments. *Journal of Consulting and Clinical Psychology, 61*, 235–247.

Kendall, P. C., & Gosch, E. (1994). Cognitive–behavioral interventions. In T. Ollendick, N. King, & W. Yule (Eds.), *International handbook of phobic and anxiety disorders in children and adolescents* (pp. 415–438). New York: Plenum.

Kendall, P. C., Kortlander, E., Chansky, T. E., & Brady, E. U. (1992). Comorbidity of anxiety and depression in youth: Treatment implications. *Journal of Consulting and Clinical Psychology, 60*, 869–880.

Kendall, P. C., & Southam-Gerow, M. A. (1996). Long-term follow-up of a cognitive–behavioral therapy for anxiety-disordered youth. *Journal of Consulting and Clinical Psychology, 64*, 724–730.

Kendler, K., & Eaves, L. (1986). Models for the joint effect of genotype and environment on liability to psychiatric illness. *American Journal of Psychiatry, 143*, 279–289.

Kennedy, R. L. (1924). The prognosis of sequelae of epidemic encephalitis in children. *American Journal of Diseases of Children, 28*, 158–172.

Kerrin, R. G., Murdock, J. Y., Sharpton, W. R., & Jones, N. (1998). Who's doing the pointing? Investigating facilitated communication in a classroom setting with students with autism. *Focus on Autism and Other Developmental Disabilities, 13*, 73–79.

Kessler, R. C., Avenevoli, S., & Merikangas, K. R. (2001). Mood disorders in children and adolescents: An epidemiologic perspective. *Biological Psychiatry, 49*, 1002–1014

Kessler, R. C., & Frank, R. G. (1997). The impact of psychiatric disorders on work loss days. *Psychological Medicine, 27*.

Kessler, R. C., & Walters, E. E. (1998). Epidemiology of DSM-III-R major depression and minor depression among adolescents and young adults in the National Comorbidity Survey. *Depression and Anxiety, 7*, 3–14.

Keyes, A., Brozek, J., Henschel, A., Mickelsen, O., & Taylor, H. (1950). *The biology of human starvation.* Minneapolis: University of Minnesota Press.

Kihlstrom, J. F., Glisky, M. L., & Anguilo, M. J. (1994). Dissociative tendencies and dissociative disorders. *Journal of Abnormal Psychology, 103*, 117–124.

Kim, J. A., Szatmari, P., Bryson, S. E., Streiner, D. L., & Wilson, F. J. (2000). The prevalence of anxiety and mood problems among children with autism and Asperger syndrome. *Autism, 4*, 117–132.

Kim, S., & Oberzanek, E. (2002). Childhood obesity: A new pandemic of the new millennium. *Pediactrics, 110*, 1003–1007.

King, N. J., Heyne, D., Tonge, B. J., Mullen, P., Myerson, N., Rollings, S., et al. (2003). Sexually abused children suffering from post-traumatic stress disorder: Assessment and treatment strategies. *Cognitive Behaviour Therapy, 32*, 2–12.

King, N. J., Tonge, B. J., Mullen, P., Myerson, N., Heyne, D., Rollings, S., et al. (2000). Treating sexually abused children with posttraumatic stress symptoms: A randomized clinical trial. *Journal of the American Academy of Child and Adolescent Psychiatry, 39*, 1347–1355.

King, N. M. P., & Churchill, L. R. (2000). Ethical principles guiding research on child and adolescent subjects. *Journal of Interpersonal Violence, 15*, 710–724.

Kirch, D. G. (1993). Infection and autoimmunity as etiologic factors in schizophrenia: A review and reappraisal. *Schizophrenia Bulletin, 19*, 355–370.

Kirmayer, L. J., & Young, A. (1998). Culture and somatization: Clinical, epidemiological, and ethnographic perspectives. *Psychosomatic Medicine, 60*, 420–430.

Klein, R., & Abikoff, H. (1997). Behavior therapy and methylphenidate in the treatment of children with ADHD. *Journal of Attention Disorders, 2*, 89–114.

Klinger, L., Dawson, G., & Renner, P. (2003). *Autistic disorder* (2nd ed.). New York: Guilford.

Kluft, R. P. (1984). Treatment of multiple personality disorder. *Psychiatric Clinics of North America, 7*, 9–29.

Kluft, R. P. (1985). Using hypnotic inquiry protocols to monitor treatment progress and stability in multiple personality disorder. *American Journal of Clinical Hypnosis, 28*, 63–75.

Kluft, R. P. (1996). Outpatient treatment of dissociative identity disorder and allied forms of dissociative disorder not otherwise specified in children and adolescents. *Child and Adolescent Psychiatric Clinics of North America, 5,* 471–494.

Kobayashi, R., Murata, T., & Yoshinaga, K. (1992). A follow-up study of 201 children with autism in Kyushu and Yamaguchi areas, Japan. *Journal of Autism and Developmental Disorders, 22,* 395–411.

Kolvin, I. (1971). Studies in the childhood psychoses: Diagnostic criteria and classification. *British Journal of Psychiatry, 118,* 381–384.

Koocher, G. P., & Keith-Spiegel, P. C. (1990). *Children, ethics, & the law: Professional issues and cases.* Lincoln: University of Nebraska Press.

Koss-Chioino, J. D., & Vargas, L. A. (1992). Through the cultural looking glass: A model for understanding culturally responsive psychotherapies. In L. A. Vargas & J. D. Koss-Chioino (Eds.), *Working with culture: Psychotherapeutic interventions with ethnic minority children and adolescents* (pp. 1–24). San Francisco: Jossey-Bass.

Kotch, J. B. (2000). Ethical issues in longitudinal child maltreatment research. *Journal of Interpersonal Violence, 15,* 696–709.

Kotler, L., Devlin, M., Davies, M., & Walsh, B. (2003). An open trial of fluoxetine for adolescents with bulimia nervosa. *Journal of Child and Adolescent Psychopharmacology, 13,*329–335.

Kovacs, M., Akiskal, H., Gatsonis, C., & Parrone, P. (1994). Childhood onset dysthymic disorder: Clinical features and prospective naturalistic outcome. *Archives of General Psychiatry, 51,* 365–374.

Kovacs, M., & Devlin, B. (1998). Internalizing disorders in childhood. *Journal of Child Psychology and Psychiatry and Allied Disciplines, 39,* 47–63.

Kovacs, M., & Goldston, D. (1991). Cognitive and social cognitive development of depressed children and adolescents. *Journal of the American Academy of Child and Adolescent Psychiatry, 30,* 388–392.

Kovacs, M., Obrosky, D. S., & Sherrill, J. (2003). Developmental changes in the phenomenology of depression in girls compared to boys from childhood onward. *Journal of Affective Disorders, 74,* 33–48.

Kovacs, M., Paulauskas, S., Gatsonis, C., & Richards, C. (1988). Depressive disorders in childhood: III. A longitudinal study of comorbidity with and risk for conduct disorders. *Journal of Affective Disorders, 15,* 205–217.

Kovacs, M., & Sherrill, J. (2001). The psychotherapeutic management of major depressive and dysthymic disorders in childhood and adolescence: Issues and prospects. In I. Goodyer (Ed.), *The depressed child and adolescent* (2nd ed., pp. 325–352). Cambridge, England: Cambridge University Press.

Kowatch, R. A., Suppes, T., Carmody, T. J., Bucci, J. P., Hume, J. H., Kromelis, M., et al. (2000). Effect size of lithium, divalproex sodium, and carbamazepine in children and adolescents with bipolar disorder. *Journal of the American Academy of Child and Adolescent Psychiatry, 39,* 713–720.

Kozlowska, K. (2003). Good children with conversion disorder: Breaking the silence. *Clinical Child Psychology and Psychiatry, 8,* 73–90.

Kumra, S. (2000). The diagnosis and treatment of children and adolescents with schizophrenia: "My mind is playing tricks on me." *Child and Adolescent Psychiatric Clinics of North America, 9,* 183–199.

Kumra, S., Frazier, J., Jacobsen, L., McKenna, K., Gordon, C., & Lenane, M. (1996). Childhood-onset schizophrenia: A double-blind clozapine-haloperidol comparison. *Archives of General Psychiatry, 53,* 1090–1097.

Kumra, S., Sporn, A., Hommer, D. W., Nicolson, R., Thaker, G., Israel, E., et al. (2001). Smooth pursuit eye-tracking impairment in childhood-onset psychotic disorders. *American Journal of Psychiatry, 158,* 1291–1298.

Kupersmidt, J. B., Coie, J. D., & Dodge, K. A. (1990). The role of poor peer relationships in the development of disorder. In S. R. Asher (Ed.), *Peer rejection in childhood* (pp. 274–305). New York: Cambridge University Press.

Kuterovac Jagodic, G. (2003). Posttraumatic stress symptoms in Croatian children exposed to war: A prospective study. *Journal of Clinical Psychology, 59,* 9–25.

Labellarte, M. J., & Ginsburg, G. S. (2002). Anxiety disorders. In A. Martin, S. Scahill, D. Charney, & J. Leckman (Eds.), *Pediatric psychopharmacology* (pp. 497–510). New York: Oxford University Press.

Ladd, G. W., & Burgess, K. B. (1999). Charting the relationship trajectories of aggressive, withdrawn, and aggressive/withdrawn children during early grade school. *Child Development, 70,* 910–929.

Laederach, J., Fischer, W., Bowen, P., & Ladame, F. (1999). Common risk factors in adolescent suicide attempters revisited. *Crisis, 20,* 15–22.

La Greca, A. M., & Lopez, N. (1998). Social anxiety among adolescents: Linkages with peer relations and friendships. *Journal of Abnormal Child Psychology, 26,* 83–94.

Lahey, B., Pehlam, W., Schaughency, E., Atkins, M., Murphy, H., Hynd, G., et al. (1988). Dimensions and types of attention deficit disorder with hyperactivity in children: A factor and cluster-analytic approach. *Journal of the American Academy of Child and Adolescent Psychiatry, 27,* 330–335.

Lahey, B. B., Gordon, R. A., Loeber, R., Stouthamer Loeber, M., & Farrington, D. P. (1999). Boys who join gangs: A prospective study of predictors of first gang entry. *Journal of Abnormal Child Psychology, 27,* 261–276.

Lahey, B. B., Loeber, R., Quay, H. C., Frick, P. J., & Grimm, J. (1997). Oppositional defiant disorder and conduct disorder. In T. A. Widiger, A. J. Frances, H. A. Pincus, R. Ross, M. B. First, & W. Davis (Eds.), *DSM-IV sourcebook* (Vol. 3, pp. 189–209). Washington, DC: American Psychiatric Press.

Lahey, B. B., Loeber, R., Stouthamer Loeber, M., & Christ, M. A. (1990). Comparison of DSM-III and DSM-III-R diagnoses for prepubertal children: Changes in prevalence and validity. *Journal of the American Academy of Child and Adolescent Psychiatry, 29,* 620–626.

Lahey, B. B., Waldman, I. D., & McBurnett, K. (1999). The development of antisocial behavior: An integrative causal model. *Journal of Child Psychology and Psychiatry and Allied Disciplines, 40,* 669–682.

Laird, R. D., Jordan, K. Y., Dodge, K. A., Pettit, G. S., & Bates, J. E. (2001). Peer rejection in childhood, involvement with antisocial peers in early adolescence, and the development of externalizing behavior problems. *Development and Psychopathology, 13,* 337–354.

Lamprecht, F., & Sack, M. (2002). Posttraumatic stress disorder revisited. *Psychosomatic Medicine, 64,* 222–237.

Landa, R. (2000). Social language use in Asperger syndrome and high-functioning autism. In A. Klin, F. Volkmar, & S. Sparrow (Eds.), *Asperger syndrome* (pp. 125–158). New York: Guilford.

Landgraf, J. M., Abidari, J., Cilento, B. G., Cooper, C., Schulman, S., & Ortenberg, J. (2004). Coping, commitment, and attitude: Quantifying the everyday burden of enuresis on children and their families. *Pediatrics, 113,* 334–344.

Langworthy Lam, K. S., Aman, M. G., & Van Bourgondien, M. E. (2002). Prevalence and patterns of use of psychoactive medicines in individuals with autism in the Autism Society of North Carolina. *Journal of Child and Adolescent Psychopharmacology, 12,* 311–321.

Larry P. v. Riles, 495 F. Supp. 926 (1979).

Larson, B. S. (1991). Somatic complaints and their relationship to depressive symptoms in Swedish adolescents. *Journal of Child Psychology and Psychiatry, 32,* 821–832.

Last, C. G., Hersen, M., Kazdin, A., Finkelstein, R., & Strauss, C. C. (1987). Comparison of DSM-III separation anxiety and overanxious disorders: Demographic characteristics and patterns of comorbidity. *Journal of the American Academy of Child and Adolescent Psychiatry, 26,* 527–531.

Last, C. G., & Strauss, C. C. (1989). Obsessive–compulsive disorder in childhood. *Journal of Anxiety Disorders, 3,* 295–302.

Laurent, J., & Ettelson, R. (2001). An examination of the tripartite model of anxiety and depression and its application to youth. *Clinical Child and Family Psychology Review, 4,* 209–230.

Lay, B., Blanz, B., Hartmann, M., & Schmidt, M. H. (2000). The psychosocial outcome of adolescent-onset schizophrenia: A 12-year followup. *Schizophrenia Bulletin, 26,* 801–816.

LeDoux, J. (1996). *The emotional brain.* New York: Simon and Schuster.

Lee, A., Hobson, R., & Chait, S. (1994). I, you, me, and autism: An experimental study. *Journal of Autism and Developmental Disorders, 24,* 155–176.

Leech, S. L., Larkby, C. A., Day, R., & Day, N. (2006). Predictors and correlates of high levels of depression and anxiety symptoms among children at age 10. *Journal of the American Academy of Child and Adolescent Psychiatry, 45,* 223–230.

Leenaars, A. A., & Lester, D. (1995). Assessment and prediction of suicide risk in adolescents. In J. Zimmerman & G. Asnis (Eds.), *Treatment approaches with suicidal adolescents* (pp. 47–70). New York: John Wiley & Sons.

Leffert, J. S., Siperstein, G. N., & Millikan, E. (2000). Understanding social adaptation in children with mental retardation: A social–cognitive perspective. *Exceptional Children, 66,* 530–545.

Leibenluft, E., Charney, D. S., Towbin, K. E., Bhangoo, R. K., & Pine, D. S. (2003). Defining clinical phenotypes of juvenile mania. *American Journal of Psychiatry, 160,* 430–437.

Leitenberg, H., Yost, L. W., & Carroll Wilson, M. (1986). Negative cognitive errors in children: Questionnaire development, normative data, and comparisons between children with and without self-reported symptoms of depression, low self-esteem, and evaluation anxiety. *Journal of Consulting and Clinical Psychology, 54,* 528–536.

Leonard, H., & Wen, X. (2002). The epidemiology of mental retardation: Challenges and opportunities in the new millennium. *Mental Retardation and Developmental Disabilities Research Reviews, 8,* 117–134.

Levine, M. P., Smolak, L., & Hayden, H. (1994). The relation of sociocultural factors to eating attitudes and behaviors among middle school girls. *Journal of Early Adolescence, 14,* 471–490.

Levy, T. M., & Orlans, M. (1999). Kids who kill: Attachment disorder, antisocial personality, and violence. *Forensic Examiner, 8,* 19–24.

Levy, T. M., & Orlans, M. (2000). Attachment disorder as an antecedent to violence and antisocial patterns in children. In T. M. Levy (Ed.), *Handbook of attachment interventions* (pp. 1–26). San Diego, CA: Academic Press.

Lewin, K. (1951). *Field theory in social science.* New York: Harper.

Lewinsohn, P. M., & Clarke, G. N. (1999). Psychosocial treatments for adolescent depression. *Clinical Psychology Review, 19,* 329–342.

Lewinsohn, P. M., Clarke, G. N., Seeley, J. R., & Rohde, P. (1994). Major depression in community adolescents: Age at onset, episode duration, and time to recurrence. *Journal of the American Academy of Child and Adolescent Psychiatry, 33,* 809–818.

Lewinsohn, P. M., Klein, D. N., & Seeley, J. R. (1995). Bipolar disorders in a community sample of older adolescents: Prevalence, phenomenology, comorbidity, and course. *Journal of the American Academy of Child and Adolescent Psychiatry, 34,* 454–463.

Lewinsohn, P. M., Rohde, P., & Seeley, J. R. (1996). Adolescent suicidal ideation and attempts: Prevalence, risk factors, and clinical implications. *Clinical Psychology: Science and Practice, 3,* 25–46.

Lewis, A. (2002). Accessing, through research interviews, the views of children with difficulties in learning. *Support for Learning, 17,* 110–116.

Lewis, G., David, A., Andreasson, S., & Allbeck, P. (1992). Schizophrenia and city life. *Lancet, 340,* 137–140.

Lewis, M. L., & Ippen, C. G. (2004). Rainbows of tears, souls full of hope: Cultural issues related to young children and trauma. In J. D. Osofsky (Ed.), *Young children and trauma: Intervention and treatment* (pp. 11–76). New York: Guilford.

Lewis, M. S. (1989). Age incidence and schizophrenia: Part I: The season of birth controversy. *Schizophrenia Bulletin, 15,* 59–73.

Lieberman, A. F., & Van Horn, P. (2004). Assessment and treatment of young children exposed to traumatic events. In J. D. Osofsky (Ed.), *Young children and trauma: Intervention and treatment* (pp. 111–138). New York: Guilford.

Linares, L. O., Heeren, T., Bronfman, E., Zuckerman, B., Augustyn, M., & Tronick, E. (2001). A mediational model for the impact of exposure to community violence on early child behavior problems. *Child Development, 72,* 639–652.

Litz, B., Gray, M., Bryant, R., & Adler, A. (2002). Early intervention for trauma: Current status and future directions. *Clinical Psychological Science and Practice, 9,* 112–134.

Loeber, R., Burke, J. D., Lahey, B. B., Winters, A., & Zera, M. (2000). Oppositional defiant and conduct disorder: A review of the past 10 years, Part I. *Journal of the American Academy of Child and Adolescent Psychiatry, 39,* 1468–1484.

Loeber, R., & Farrington, D. P. (2000). Young children who commit crime: Epidemiology, developmental origins, risk factors, early interventions, and policy implications. *Development and Psychopathology, 12,* 737–762.

Loeber, R., Green, S. M., Lahey, B. B., & Stouthamer Loeber, M. (1991). Differences and similarities between children, mothers, and teachers as informants on disruptive child behavior. *Journal of Abnormal Child Psychology, 19*, 75–95.

Loeber, R., & Hay, D. (1997). Key issues in the development of aggression and violence from childhood to early adulthood. *Annual Review of Psychology, 48*, 371–410.

Loeber, R., & Stouthamer Loeber, M. (1998). Development of juvenile aggression and violence: Some common misconceptions and controversies. *American Psychologist, 53*, 242–259.

Loehlin, J. C. (2000). Group differences in intelligence. In R. Sternberg (Ed.), *Handbook of Intelligence* (pp. 176–197). Cambridge, England: Cambridge University Press.

Loening-Baucke, V. (1993). Constipation in early childhood: Patient characteristics, treatment, and long-term follow-up. *Gut, 34*, 1400–1404.

Loney, B. R., & Lima, E. N. (2003). Classification and assessment. In C. A. Essau (Ed.), *Conduct and oppositional defiant disorders: Epidemiology, risk factors, and treatment* (pp. 3–31). Mahwah, NJ: Erlbaum.

Lonigan, C. J., & Phillips, B. M. (2001). Temperamental influences on the development of anxiety disorders. In M. Vasey & M. Dadds (Eds.), *The developmental psychopathology of anxiety* (pp. 60–91). New York: Oxford University Press.

Losche, G. (1990). Sensorimotor and action development in autistic children from infancy to early childhood. *Journal of Child Psychology and Psychiatry, 31*, 749–761.

Lovaas, O. I. (1987). Behavioral treatment and normal education and intellectual functioning in young autistic children. *Journal of Consulting and Clinical Psychology, 55*, 3–9.

Lovaas, O. I., & Smith, T. (1989). A comprehensive behavioral theory of autistic children: Paradigm for research and treatment. *Journal of Behavior Therapy and Experimental Psychiatry, 20*, 17–29.

Lowe, M. R. (1993). The effects of dieting on eating behavior: A three-factor model. *Psychological Bulletin, 114*, 100–121.

Luby, J., Sullivan, J., Belden, A., Stalets, M., Blankenship, S., & Spitznagel, E. (2006). An observational analysis of behavior in depressed preschoolers: Further validation of early-onset depression. *Journal of the American Academy of Child and Adolescent Psychiatry, 45*, 203–212.

Lynam, D., Moffitt, T. E., & Stouthamer Loeber, M. (1993). "Explaining the relation between IQ and delinquency: Class, race, test motivation, school failure, or self-control?" Correction. *Journal of Abnormal Psychology, 102*, 552.

Lynch, D., Fay, R., Funk, J., & Nagel, R. (1993). Siblings of children with mental retardation: Family characteristics and adjustment. *Journal of Child and Family Studies, 2*, 87–96.

Lyons-Ruth, K., Zeanah, C. H., & Benoit, D. (2003). Disorder and risk for disorder during infancy and toddlerhood. In E. Mash & R. Barkley (Eds.), *Child psychopathology* (2nd ed., pp. 589–631). New York: Guilford.

Lyoo, I. K., Lee, H. K., Jung, J. H., Noam, G. G., & Renshaw, P. F. (2002). White matter hyperintensities on magnetic resonance imaging of the brain in children with psychiatric disorders. *Comprehensive Psychiatry, 43*, 361–368.

Lyubomirsky, S., & Nolen-Hoeksema, S. (1993). Self-perpetuating properties of dysphoric rumination. *Journal of Personality and Social Psychology, 65*, 339–349.

Maccoby, E. E. (2000). Parenting and its effects on children: On reading and misreading behavior genetics. *Annual Review of Psychology, 51*, 1–27.

Maccoby, E. E. (2004). Aggression in the context of gender development. In M. Putallaz & K. L. Bierman (Eds.), *Aggression, antisocial behavior, and violence among girls: A developmental perspective* (pp. 3–22). New York: Guilford.

Mace, F. C., Lalli, J. S., Lalli, E. P., & Shea, M. C. (1993). Functional analysis and treatment of aberrant behavior. In R. Van Houten & S. Axelrod (Eds.), *Behavior analysis and treatment. Applied clinical psychology* (pp. 75–99). New York: Plenum.

Macfie, J., Cicchetti, D., & Toth, S. L. (2001). The development of dissociation in maltreated preschool-aged children. *Development and Psychopathology, 13*, 233–254.

MacLean, W., Stone, W., & Brown, W. (1994). Developmental psychopathology of destructive behavior. In T. Thompson & D. B. Gray (Eds.), *Destructive behavior in developmental disabilities: Diagnosis and treatment* (pp. 68–79). Thousand Oaks, CA: Sage.

Maedgen, J. W., & Carlson, C. L. (2000). Social functioning and emotional regulation in the attention deficit hyperactivity disorder subtypes. *Journal of Clinical Child Psychology, 29*, 30–42.

Maffeis, C. (2000). Etiology of overweight and obesity in children and adolescents. *European Journal of Pediatrics, 159*, S35–S44.

Main, M., Kaplan, N., & Cassidy, J. (1985). Security in infancy, childhood, and adulthood: A move to the level of representation. *Monographs of the Society for Research in Child Development, 50*, 66–104.

Malhotra, S., & Gupta, N. (2002). Childhood disintegrative disorder: Reexamination of the current concept. *European Child and Adolescent Psychiatry, 11*, 108–114.

Mann, E. M., Keda, Y., Mueller, C. W., Takahashi, A., Tao, K. T., Humris, E., et al. (1992). Cross-cultural differences in rating hyperactive–disruptive behaviors in children. *American Journal of Psychiatry, 149*, 1539–1542.

Mann, T., Nolen Hoeksema, S., Huang, K., Burgard, D., et al. (1997). Are two interventions worse than none? Joint primary and secondary prevention of eating disorders in college females. *Health Psychology, 16*, 215–225.

Mannuzza, S., & Klein, R. G. (2000). Long-term prognosis in attention-deficit/hyperactivity disorder. *Child and Adolescent Psychiatric Clinics of North America, 9*, 711–726.

Marcell, M., & Weeks, S. L. (1988). Short-term memory difficulties in Down's syndrome. *Journal of Mental Deficiency Research, 32*, 153–162.

Marlow, N., Wolke, D., Bracewell, M., & Samara, M. (2005). Neurologic and developmental disability at six years of age after extremely preterm birth. *New England Journal of Medicine, 352*, 9–19.

Marsh, D. T. (1997). Ethical issues in professional practice with families. In D. T. Marsh & R. D. Magee (Eds.), *Ethical and legal issues in professional practice with families* (pp. 3–26). New York: John Wiley & Sons.

Marton, P., Connolly, J., Kutcher, S., & Korenblum, M. (1993). Cognitive social skills and social self-appraisal in depressed adolescents. *Journal of the American Academy of Child and Adolescent Psychiatry, 32*, 739–744.

Marvin, R. S., & Pianta, R. C. (1996). Mothers' reactions to their child's diagnosis: Relations with security and attachment. *Journal of Clinical Child Psychology, 25*, 436–445.

Masten, A. S., & Coatsworth, J. D. (1998). The development of competence in favorable and unfavorable environments: Lessons from research on successful children. *American Psychologist, 53*, 205–220.

Masten, A. S., & Powell, J. L. (2003). A resilience framework for research, policy, and practice. In S. S. Luthar (Ed.), *Resilience and vulnerability: Adaption in the context of childhood adversities* (pp. 1–28). Cambridge, England: Cambridge University Press.

Matas, L., Arend, R. A., & Sroufe, L. A. (1978). Continuity of adaptation in the second year: The relationship between quality of attachment and later competence. *Child Development, 49*, 547–556.

Matson, J. L., Benavidez, D. A., Compton, L. S., Paclawskyj, T., & Baglio, C. (1996). Behavioral treatment of autistic persons: A review of research from 1980 to the present. *Research in Developmental Disabilities, 17*, 433–465.

Mayo, L. (1962). *A proposed program for national action to combat mental retardation.* Washington, DC: U.S. Government Printing Office.

Mazzocco, M. (2000). Advances in research on the Fragile X syndrome. *Mental Retardation and Developmental Disabilities Research Reviews, 6*, 96–106.

McCabe, M., & Ricciardelli, L. (2004). A longitudinal study of pubertal timing and extreme body change behaviors among adolescent boys and girls. *Adolescence, 39*, 145–166.

McCall, R. (1970). *Fundamental statistics for psychology.* New York: Harcourt, Brace & World.

McClellan, J., & Werry, J. (1994). Practice parameters for the assessment and treatment of children and adolescents with schizophrenia. *Journal of the American Academy of Child and Adolescent Psychiatry, 33*, 616–635.

McGee, R., Feehan, M., Williams, S., & Anderson, J. (1992). DSM-III disorders from age 11 to age 15 years. *Journal of the American Academy of Child and Adolescent Psychiatry, 31*, 50–59.

McGee, R., Feehan, M., Williams, S., Partridge, F., Silva, P. A., & Kelly, J. (1990). DSM-III disorders in a large sample of adolescents. *Journal of the American Academy of Child and Adolescent Psychiatry, 29,* 611–619.

McGrath, E. P., & Repetti, R. L. (2002). A longitudinal study of children's depressive symptoms, self-perceptions, and cognitive distortions about the self. *Journal of Abnormal Psychology, 111,* 77–87.

McGrath, M. L., Mellon, M. W., & Murphy, L. (2000). Empirically supported treatments in pediatric psychology: Constipation and encopresis. *Journal of Pediatric Psychology, 25,* 225–254.

McKnight Investigators (2003). Risk factors for the onset of eating disorders in adolescent girls: Results of the McKnight Longitudinal Risk Factor Study. *American Journal of Psychiatry, 160,* 248–254.

McRoy, R. G., Zurcher, L. A., Lauderdale, M. L., & Anderson, R. N. (1982). Self esteem and racial identity in transracial and inracial adoptees. *Social Work, 27,* 522–526.

Meaux, J. B., & Bell, P. L. (2001). Balancing recruitment and protection: Children as research subjects. *Issues in Comprehensive Pediatric Nursing, 24,* 241–251.

Mednick, S. A., Machon, R., Huttunen, M., & Bonett, D. (1988). Adult schizophrenia following prenatal exposure to an influence epidemic. *Archives of General Psychiatry, 45,* 189–192.

Meehl, P. (1962). Schizotaxia, schizotypy, schizophrenia. *American Psychologist, 17,* 827–838.

Melton, G. B., & Ehrenreich, N. S. (1992). Ethical and legal issues in mental health services for children. In C. E. Walker & M. C. Roberts (Eds.), *Handbook of clinical child psychology* (2nd ed., pp. 1035–1055). New York: John Wiley & Sons.

Mendola, P., Selevan, S. G., Gutter, S., & Rice, D. (2002). Environmental factors associated with a spectrum of neurodevelopmental deficits. *Mental Retardation and Developmental Disabilities Research Reviews, 8,* 188–197.

Mercugliano, M. (1995). Neurotransmitter alterations in attention-deficit/hyperactivity disorder. *Mental Retardation and Developmental Disabilities Research Reviews, 1,* 220–226.

Mertin, P., & Mohr, P. B. (2002). Incidence and correlates of posttrauma symptoms in children from backgrounds of domestic violence. *Violence and Victims, 17,* 555–567.

Mervis, C. B., & Klein-Tasman, B. P. (2000). Williams syndrome: Cognition, personality, and adaptive behavior. *Mental Retardation and Developmental Disabilities Research Reviews, 6,* 148–158.

Mesibov, G. B., & Shea, V. (1996). Full inclusion and students with autism. *Journal of Autism and Developmental Disorders, 26,* 337–346.

Mesman, J., & Koot, H. (2000a). Child-reported depression and anxiety in preadolescence: I. Associations with parent- and teacher-reported problems. *Journal of the American Academy of Child and Adolescent Psychiatry, 39,* 1371–1378.

Mesman, J., & Koot, H. M. (2000b). Child-reported depression and anxiety in preadolescence: II. preschool predictors. *Journal of the American Academy of Child and Adolescent Psychiatry, 39,* 1379–1386.

Messer, J., Goodman, R., Rowe, R., Meltzer, H., & Maughan, B. (2006). Preadolescent conduct problems in girls and boys. *Journal of the American Academy of Child and Adolescent Psychiatry, 45,* 184–191.

Meyer, J. M., Rutter, M., Silberg, J. L., Maes, H. H., Simonoff, E., Shillady, L. L., et al. (2000). Familial aggregation for conduct disorder symptomatology: The role of genes, marital discord and family adaptability. *Psychological Medicine, 30,* 759–774.

Mikkelsen, E. J. (2001). Enuresis and encopresis: Ten years of progress. *Journal of the American Academy of Child and Adolescent Psychiatry, 40,* 1146–1158.

Mikkelsen, E. J., & Rapoport, J. L. (1980). Enuresis: Psychopathology, sleep stage, and drug response. *Urology Clinics of North America, 7,* 361–377.

Milich, R., Balentine, A. C., & Lynam, D. R. (2001). ADHD combined type and ADHD predominantly inattentive type are distinct and unrelated disorders. *Clinical Psychology: Science and Practice, 8,* 463–488.

Militerni, R., Bravaccio, C., Falco, C., Fico, C., & Palermo, M. T. (2002). Repetitive behaviors in autistic disorder. *European Child and Adolescent Psychiatry, 11,* 210–218.

Miller, J. N., & Ozonoff, S. (2000). The external validity of Asperger disorder: Lack of evidence from the domain of neuropsychology. *Journal of Abnormal Psychology, 109,* 227–238.

Mills v. Board of Education of the District of Columbia, 348 F. Supp. 866 (1972).

Mintz, L. B., & Betz, N. E. (1988). Prevalence and correlates of eating disordered behaviors among undergraduate women. *Journal of Counseling Psychology, 35,* 463–471.

Minuchin, S. (1974). *Families and family therapy*. Cambridge, MA: Harvard University Press.

Minuchin, S., & Fishman, H. (1981). *Family therapy techniques*. Cambridge, MA: Harvard University Press.

Minuchin, S., Baker, L., Rosman, B., et al. (1975). A conceptual model of psychosomatic illness in children. *Archives of General psychiatry, 32*, 1031–1038.

Mitchell, M., & Jolley, J. (2001). *Research design explained* (4th ed.). Fort Worth, TX: Harcourt.

Moffatt, M., Kato, C., & Pless, I. (1987). Improvements in self-concept after treatment of nocturnal enuresis. *Journal of Pediatrics, 110*, 647–652.

Moffitt, T. E. (1993). Adolescence-limited and life-course-persistent antisocial behavior: A developmental taxonomy. *Psychological Review, 100*, 674–701.

Moffitt, T. E., & Caspi, A. (2001). Childhood predictors differentiate life-course persistent and adolescence-limited antisocial pathways among males and females. *Development and Psychopathology, 13*, 355–375.

Moffitt, T. E., Caspi, A., Dickson, N., Silva, P. A., & Stanton, W. (1996). Childhood-onset versus adolescent-onset antisocial conduct in males: Natural history from age 3 to 18. *Development and Psychopathology, 8*, 399–424.

Moffitt, T. E., Caspi, A., Harrington, H., & Milne, B. J. (2002). Males on the life-course-persistent and adolescence-limited antisocial pathways: Follow-up at age 26 years. *Development and Psychopathology, 14*, 179–207.

Monda, J. M., & Husmann, D. (1995). Primary nocturnal enuresis: A comparison among observation, imipramine, desmopressin acetate, and bed-wetting alarm systems. *Journal of Urology, 154*, 745–748.

Moos, R. H. (1974). *Family Environment Scale*. Palo Alto, CA: Consulting Psychologists Press.

Morales, A. T. (1992). Therapy with Latino gang members. In L. A. Vargas & J. D. Koss-Chioino (Eds.), *Working with culture: Psychotherapeutic interventions with ethnic minority children and adolescents* (pp. 129–156). San Francisco: Jossey-Bass.

Morgan, M. A., Romaski, L. M., & LeDoux, J. E. (1993). Extinction of emotional learning: Contribution of medial prefrontal cortex. *Neuroscience Letters, 163*, 109–113.

Mostert, M. P. (2001). Facilitated communication since 1995: A review of published studies. *Journal of Autism and Developmental Disorders, 31*, 287–313.

Mufson, L., Weissman, M. M., Moreau, D., & Garfinkel, R. (1999). Efficacy of interpersonal psychotherapy for depressed adolescents. *Archives of General Psychiatry, 56*, 573–579.

Mullen, M. C., & Shield, J. (2004). *Childhood and adolescent overweight: The health professional's guide to identification, treatment, and prevention*. Chicago: American Dietetic Association.

Mullins, L. L., & Olson, R. A. (1990). Familial factors in the etiology, maintenance, and treatment of somatoform disorder in children. *Family Systems Medicine, 8*, 159–175.

Mundy, P., & Sigman, M. (1989). The theoretical implications of joint-attention deficits in autism. *Development and Psychopathology, 1*, 173–184.

Munroe, R. L. (1955). *Schools of psychoanalytic thought: An exposition, critique, and attempt at integration*. Ft Worth, TX: Dryden Press.

Muris, P., Meesters, C., Merchelbach, H., Sermon, A., & Zwakhalen, S. (1998). Worries in normal children. *Journal of the American Academy of Child and Adolescent Psychiatry, 37*, 703–710.

Muris, P., & Merckelbach, H. (2001). The etiology of childhood specific phobia: A multifactorial model. In M. W. Vasey & M. R. Dadds (Eds.), *The developmental psychopathology of anxiety* (pp. 355–385). London: Oxford University Press.

Murphy, C. C., Boyle, C., Schendel, D., Decoufle, P., & Yeargin-Allsopp, M. (1998). Epidemiology of mental retardation in children. *Mental Retardation and Developmental Disabilities Research Reviews, 4*, 6–13.

Murphy, C. C., Yeargin-Allsopp, M., Decoufle, P., & Drews, C. D. (1995). The administrative prevalence of mental retardation in 10-year-old children in metropolitan Atlanta, 1985 through 1987. *American Journal of Public Health, 85*, 319–323.

Murphy, E., & Carr, A. (2000). Enuresis and encopresis. In A. Carr (Ed.), what works with children and adolescents? A critical review of psychological interventions with children, adolescents and their families (pp. 49–64). Florence, KY: Taylor & Frances Routledge.

Mustillo, S., Worthman, C., Erkanli, A., Keeler, G., Angold, A., & Costello, J. (2003). Obesity and psychiatric disorder: Develpmental trajectories. *Pediatrics, 111*, 851–859.

Nadel, L. (1999). Down syndrome in cognitive neuroscience perspective. In H. Tager-Flusberg (Ed.), *Neurodevelopmental disorders* (pp. 197–222). Cambridge, MA: MIT Press.

National Center for Health Statistics. (2004). Prevalence of overweight among children and adolescents: United States, 1999–2002. Retrieved January 10, 2005, from http://www.cdc.gov/nchs/products/pubs/pubd/hestats/overwgt99.htm.

National Center for Health Statistics. (2006). *Health, United States, 2006, with chartbook on trends in the health of Americans.* Hyattsville, MD: Centers for Disease Control and Prevention.

National Institute of Mental Health. (2001). National Institute of Mental Health research roundtable on prepubertal bipolar disorder. *Journal of the American Academy of Child and Adolescent Psychiatry, 40*, 871–878.

National Research Council. (2000). *Toxicological effects of methylmercury.* Washington, DC: National Academy Press.

Needleman, H. L., Gunnoe, D., Leviton, A., Reed, R., Peresie, H., Maher, C., et al. (1979). Deficits in psychologic and classroom performance of children with elevated dentine lead levels. *New England Journal of Medicine, 300*, 689–695.

Neisser, U. (1979). The concept of intelligence. *Intelligence, 3.*

Neumarker, K., Dudeck, U., Meyer, U., & Neumarker, U. (1997). Mortality and sudden death in anorexia nervosa. *International Journal of Eating Disorders, 21*, 205–212.

Neveus, T., Stenberg, A., Lackgren, G., Tuvemo, T., & Hetta, J. (1999). Sleep of children with enuresis: A polysomnographic study. *Pediatrics, 103*, 1193–1197.

Newcorn, J. H., & Halperin, J. M. (2000). Attention-deficit disorders with oppositionality and aggression. In T. E. Brown (Ed.), *Attention deficit disorders and comorbidities in children, adolescents, and adults* (pp. 171–207). Washington, DC: American Psychiatric Publishing.

Newman, D., Moffitt, T., Caspi, A., Magdol, L., Silva, P., & Stanton, W. (1996). Psychiatric disorders in a birth cohort of young adults: Prevalence, comorbidity, clinical significance, and new case incidence from ages 11 to 21. *Journal of Consulting and Clinical Psychology, 64*, 552–562.

Newman, E. (2002). Assessment of PTSD and trauma exposure in adolescents. *Journal of Aggression, Maltreatment and Trauma, 6*, 59–77.

Nichols, M. P., & Schwartz, R. C. (1998). *Family therapy: Concepts and methods* (4th ed.). Needham Heights, MA: Allyn & Bacon.

Nicholson, R., Malaspina, D., Giedd, J. N., Hamburger, S., Lenane, M., Bedwell, J. S., et al. (1999). Obstetrical complications and childhood-onset schizophrenia. *The American Journal of Psychiatry, 156*, 1650–1652.

Nicolson, R., Lenane, M., Hamburger, S. D., Fernandez, T., Bedwell, J., & Rapoport, J. L. (2000). Lessons from childhood-onset schizophrenia. *Brain Research Reviews, 31*, 147–156.

Nicolson, R., & Rapoport, J. L. (2000). Childhood-onset schizophrenia: What can it teach us? In J. L. Rapoport (Ed.), *Childhood onset of "adult" psychopathology* (pp. 167–192). Washington, DC: American Psychiatric Publishing.

Nigg, J. T. (2001). Is ADHD an inhibitory disorder? *Psychological Bulletin, 127*, 571–598.

Nijhof, G., Joha, D., & Pekelharing, H. (1998). Aspects of stereotypic behaviour among autistic persons: A study of the literature. *British Journal of Developmental Disabilities, 44*, 3–13.

Nixon, E. (2001). The social competence of children with attention deficit hyperactivity disorder: A review of the literature. *Child and Adolescent Mental Health, 6*, 172–180.

Noble, D., Roudebush, M., & Prince, D. (1952). Studies of Korean Ward calamities: Psychiatric manifestations in wounded men. *American Journal of Psychiatry, 108*, 495–499.

Nolen-Hoeksema, S. (1987). Sex differences in unipolar depression: Evidence and theory. *Psychological Bulletin, 101*, 259–282.

Nolen-Hoeksema, S., & Girgus, J. S. (1994). The emergence of gender differences in depression during adolescence. *Psychological Bulletin, 115*, 424–443.

Nolen-Hoeksema, S., Seligman, M., & Girgus, J. (1992). Predictors and consequences of childhood depressive symptoms: A 5-year longitudinal study. *Journal of Abnormal Child Psychology, 101*, 405–422.

Nordin, V., & Gillberg, C. (1998). The long-term course of autistic disorders: Update on follow-up studies. *Acta Psychiatrica Scandinavica, 97*, 99–108.

Norgaard, J. P., & Djurhuus, J. C. (1993). The pathophysiology of enuresis in children and young adults. *Clinical Pediatrics, 9*, 5–9.

Nuechterlein, K., Asarnow, R., Subotnik, K., Fogelson, D., Payne, D., Kender, K., et al. (2002). The structure of schizotypy: Relationships between neurocognitive and personality disorder features in relatives of schizophrenic patients in the UCLA Family Study. *Schizophrenia Research, 54*, 121–130.

Nurcombe, B. (1994). The validity of the diagnosis of major depression in childhood and adolescence. In W. M. Reynolds & H. F. Johnston (Eds.), *Handbook of depression in children and adolescents. Issues in clinical child psychology* (pp. 61–77). New York: Plenum.

Nye, R. (1979). *What is B.F. Skinner really saying?* Englewood Cliffs, NJ: Prentice-Hall.

Nye, R. (1986). *Three psychologies: Perspectives from Freud, Skinner and Rogers.* Monterey, CA: Brooks/Cole.

Obarzanek, E., Schreiber, G. B., Crawford, P. B., & Goldman, S. (1994). Energy intake and physical activity in relation to indices of body fat: The National Heart, Lung, and Blood Institute Growth and Health Study. *American Journal of Clinical Nutrition, 160*, 15–22.

O'Connor, T., Bredenkamp, D., & Rutter, M. (1999). Attachment disturbances and disorders in children exposed to early severe deprivation. *Infant Mental Health Journal, 20*, 10–29.

O'Connor, T., Marvin, R., Rutter, M., Olrick, J., & Britner, P. (2003). Child–parent attachment following early institutional deprivation. *Development and Psychopathology, 15*, 9–38.

O'Connor, T. G., Deater Deckard, K., Fulker, D., Rutter, M., & Plomin, R. (1998). Genotype–environment correlations in late childhood and early adolescence: Antisocial behavioral problems and coercive parenting. *Developmental Psychology, 34*, 970–981.

OHSR Information Sheet #10. (1993). Attachment 5-12. Details for determining level of risk and benefit to children. Office of Human Subjects Research, National Institutes of Health. http://www.nihtraining.com/ohsrsite/irb/Attachments/5-12_Children.doc (retrieved 4/18/07).

Olds, D., Henderson, C. R., Jr., Cole, R., Eckenrode, J., Kitzman, H., Luckey, D., et al. (1998). Long-term effects of nurse home visitation on children's criminal and antisocial behavior: 15-year follow-up of a randomized controlled trial. *Journal of the American Medical Association, 280*, 1238–1244.

Olds, D. L. (1989). The Prenatal/Early Infancy Project: A strategy for responding to the needs of high-risk mothers and their children. *Prevention in Human Services, 7*, 59–87.

Oliver, C., Demetriades, L., & Hall, S. (2002). Effects of environmental events on smiling and laughing behavior in Angelman syndrome. *American Journal on Mental Retardation, 107*, 194–200.

Ollendick, T. H., & Hirshfeld Becker, D. R. (2002). The developmental and psychopathology of social anxiety disorder. *Biological Psychiatry, 51*, 44–58.

Ollendick, T. H., Vasey, M. W., & King, N. J. (2001). Operant conditioning influences in childhood anxiety. In M. W. Vasey & M. R. Dadds (Eds.), *The developmental psychopathology of anxiety* (pp. 231–252). London: Oxford University Press.

Oltmanns, T. F., & Emery, R. E. (1995). *Abnormal psychology.* Upper Saddle River, NJ: Prentice-Hall.

Ondersma, M. L., Ondersma, S. J., & Walker, C. E. (2001). Enuresis/encopresis. In H. Orvaschel & J. Faust (Eds.), *Handbook of conceptualization and treatment of child psychopathology* (pp. 399–416). Amsterdam, Netherlands: Pergamon/Elsevier.

Oredsson, A. F., & Jorgensen, T. M. (1998). Changes in nocturnal bladder capacity during treatment with the bell and pad for monosymptomatic nocturnal enuresis. *Journal of Urology, 160*, 166–169.

Osterling, J. A., Dawson, G., & Munson, J. A. (2002). Early recognition of 1-year-old infants with autism spectrum disorder versus mental retardation. *Development and Psychopathology, 14*, 239–251.

Ozonoff, S., South, M., & Miller, J. N. (2000). DSM-IV-defined Asperger syndrome: Cognitive, behavioral, and early history differentiation from high-functioning autism. *Autism, 4*, 29–46.

Pappadopulos, E., Jensen, P. S., Schur, S. B., MacIntyre, J. C., Ketner, S., Van Orden, K., et al. (2002). "Real world" atypical antipsychotic prescribing practices in public child and adolescent inpatient settings. *Schizophrenia Bulletin, 28,* 111–122.

Parham v. J. R., 442 U.S. 584 (1979).

Parker, K. C., & Forrest, D. (1993). Attachment disorder: An emerging concern for school counselors. *Elementary School Guidance and Counseling, 27,* 209–215.

Parry-Jones, W. (1995). Historical aspects of mood and its disorders in young people. In I. Goodyer (Ed.), *The depressed child and adolescent: Developmental and clinical perspectives* (pp. 1–26). Cambridge, England: Cambridge University Press.

Paternite, C., Loney, J., & Roberts, M. (1996). A preliminary validation of subtypes of DSM-IV attention deficit/hyperactivity disorder. *Journal of Attention Disorders, 1,* 70–86.

Patterson, G. R. (1982). *Coercive family process.* Eugene, OR: Castalia.

Patterson, G. R., Forgatch, M. S., Yoerger, K. L., & Stoolmiller, M. (1998). Variables that initiate and maintain an early-onset trajectory for juvenile offending. *Development and Psychopathology, 10,* 531–547.

Patterson, G. R., Reid, J. B., & Dision, T. J. (1992). *Anti-social boys.* Eugene, OR: Castalia.

Patton, G. (1988). The spectrum of eating disorders in adolescence. *Journal of Psychosomatic Research, 32,* 579–584.

Patton, J. R., Polloway, E. A., & Smith, T. E. C. (2000). Educating students with mild mental retardation. *Focus on Autism and Other Developmental Disabilities, 15,* 80–89.

Pelcovitz, D., Libov, B., Mandel, F., Kaplan, S., Meinblatt, M., & Septimus, A. (1998). Posttraumatic stress disorder and family functioning in adolescent cancer. *Journal of Traumatic Stress, 11,* 205–221.

Pelham, W., Hoza, B., Kipp, H., & Gnagy, E. (1997). Effects of methylphenidate and expectancy of ADHD children's performance, self-evaluations, persistence, and attributions on a cognitive task. *Experimental and Clinical Psychopharmacology, 5,* 3–13.

Pelham, W. E., & Fabiano, G. A. (2000). Behavior modification. *Child and Adolescent Psychiatric Clinics of North America, 9,* 671–688.

Pennington, B. F., & Bennetto, L. (1999). Toward a neuropsychology of mental retardation. In J. A. Burack, R. M. Hodapp, & E. Zigler (Eds.), *Handbook of mental retardation and development* (pp. 80–114). New York: Cambridge University Press.

Pennington, B. F., & Ozonoff, S. (1996). Executive functions and developmental psychopathology. *Journal of Child Psychology and Psychiatry and Allied Disciplines, 37,* 51–87.

Pennsylvania Ass'n for Retarded Children v. Pennsylvania, 334 F. Supp. 1257 (1971).

Pepler, D. J., & Craig, W. M. (1995). A peek behind the fence: Naturalistic observations of aggressive children with remote audiovisual recording. *Developmental Psychology, 31,* 548–553.

Percy, A. K. (2002). Clinical trials and treatment prospects. *Mental Retardation and Developmental Disabilities Research Reviews, 8,* 106–111.

Perrin, S., Smith, P., & Yule, W. (2000). Practitioner review: The assessment and treatment of post-traumatic stress disorder in children and adolescents. *Journal of Child Psychology and Psychiatry and Allied Disciplines, 41,* 277–289.

Peterson, C. B., & Mitchell, J. E. (1999). Psychosocial and pharmacological treatment of eating disorders: A review of research findings. *Journal of Clinical Psychology, 55,* 685–697.

Pfefferbaum, B., Sconzo, G. M., Flynn, B. W., Kearns, L. J., Doughty, D. E., Gurwitch, R. H., et al. (2003). Case findings and mental health services for children in the aftermath of the Oklahoma City bombing. *Journal of Behavioral Health Services and Research, 30,* 215–227.

Pfiffner, L., & McBurnett, K. (1997). Social skills training with parent generalization: Treatment effects for children with attention deficit disorder. *Journal of Consulting and Clinical Psychology, 65,* 749–757.

Pfiffner, L. J., Calzada, E., & McBurnett, K. (2000). Interventions to enhance social competence. *Child and Adolescent Psychiatric Clinics of North America, 9,* 689–709.

Phares, V., Steinberg, A., & Thompson, J. (2004). Gender differences in peer and parental influences: Body image disturbance, self-worth, and psychological functioning in preadolescent children. *Journal of Youth and Adolescence, 33,* 421–429.

Pica, M. (1999). The evolution of alter personality states in dissociative identity disorder. *Psychotherapy, 36,* 404–415.

Pillai, J. J., Friedman, L., Stuve, T. A., Trinidad, S., Jesberger, J. A., Lewin, J. S., et al. (2002). Increased presence of white matter hyperintensities in adolescent patients with bipolar disorder. *Psychiatry Research: Neuroimaging, 114,* 51–56.

Piran, N. (1998). Prevention of eating disorders: The struggle to chart new territories. *Eating Disorders: The Journal of Treatment and Prevention, 6,* 365–371.

Pisterman, S., McGrath, P., Firestone, P., Goodman, J., Webster, I., & Mallory, R. (1989). Outcome of parent-mediated treatment of preschoolers with attention deficit disorder with hyperactivity. *Journal of Consulting and Clinical Psychology, 57,* 628–635.

Piven, J., Harper, J., Palmer, P., & Arndt, S. (1996). Course of behavioral change in autism: A retrospective study of high-IQ adolescents and adults. *Journal of the American Academy of Child and Adolescent Psychiatry, 35,* 523–529.

Piven, J., & O'Leary, D. (1997). Neuroimaging in autism. *Child and Adolescent Psychiatric Clinics of North America, 6,* 305–323.

Piven, J., Palmer, P., Landa, R., Santangelo, S., Jacobi, D., & Childress, D. (1997). Personality and language characteristics in parents from multiple-incidence autism families. *American Journal of Medical Genetics, 74,* 398–411.

Pliszka, S. R., Borcherding, S. H., Spratley, K., & Leon, S. (1997). Measuring inhibitory control in children. *Journal of Developmental and Behavioral Pediatrics, 18,* 254–259.

Plomin, R. (1990). *Nature and nurture: An introduction to human behavioral genetics.* Pacific Grove, CA: Brooks/Cole.

Plomin, R., DeFries, J. C., McClearn, G. E., & McGuffin, P. (2001). *Behavioral genetics.* New York: Worth.

Polivy, J., & Herman, C. P. (1985). Dieting and binging: A causal analysis. *American Psychologist, 40,* 193–201.

Polivy, J., & Herman, C. P. (1993). Etiology of binge eating: Psychological mechanisms. In C. G. Fairburn & G. T. Wilson (Eds.), *Binge eating: Nature, assessment, and treatment* (pp. 173–205). New York: Guilford Press.

Porter, J. (1996). Regulatory considerations in research involving children and adolescents with mental disorders. In K. Hoagwood, P. Jensen, & C. Fisher (Eds.), *Ethical issues in mental health research with children and adolescents* (pp. 15–28). Hillsdale, NJ: Lawrence Erlbaum.

Poskitt, E. (2002). Home-based management. In W. Burniat, T. J. Cole, I. Lissau, & E. Poskitt (Eds.), *Child and adolescent obesity* (pp. 50–68). Cambridge, England: Cambridge University Press.

Posserud, M., Lundervold, A. J., & Gillberg, C. (2006). Autistic features in a total population of 7–9-year-old children assessed by the ASSQ (Autism Spectrum Screening Questionnaire). *Journal of Child Psychology and Psychiatry, 47,* 167–175.

Post, R. M., Leverich, G. S., Xing, G., & Weiss, S. R. B. (2001). Developmental vulnerabilities to the onset and course of bipolar disorder. *Development and Psychopathology, 13,* 581–598.

Poustka, F. (1998). Neurobiology of autism. In F. R. Volkmar (Ed.), *Autism and pervasive developmental disorders* (pp. 130–168). Cambridge, England: Cambridge University Press.

Poznanski, E. O., & Mokros, H. B. (1994). Phenomenology and epidemiology of mood disorders in children and adolescents. In W. M. Reynolds & H. F. Johnston (Eds.), *Handbook of depression in children and adolescents* (pp. 19–39). New York: Plenum.

Pretlow, R. A. (1999). Treatment of nocturnal enuresis with an ultrasound bladder volume controlled alarm device. *Journal of Urology, 162,* 1224–1228.

Prinz, R. J., Blechman, E. A., & Dumas, J. E. (1994). An evaluation of peer coping-skills training for childhood aggression. *Journal of Clinical Child Psychology, 23,* 193–203.

Prinz, R. J., & Miller, G. E. (1994). Family-based treatment for childhood antisocial behavior: Experimental influences on dropout and engagement. *Journal of Consulting and Clinical Psychology, 62,* 645–650.

Prior, M., & Ozonoff, S. (1998). Psychological factors in autism. In F. R. Volkmar (Ed.), *Autism and pervasive developmental disorders* (pp. 64–108). Cambridge, England: Cambridge University Press.

Prizant, B., & Rydell, P. (1984). An analysis of the functions of delayed echolalia in autistic children. *Journal of Speech and Hearing Research, 27*, 183–192.

Probst, M., Vandereycken, W., Coppenolle, H. V., & Pieters, G. (1998). Body size estimation in anorexia nervosa patients: The significance of overestimation. *Journal of Psychosomatic Research, 44*, 451–456.

Putnam, F. W. (1985). Multiple personality disorder. *Medical Aspects of Human Sexuality, 19*, 59–74.

Putnam, F. W. (1993). Dissociative disorders in children: Behavioral profiles and problems. *Child Abuse and Neglect, 17*, 39–45.

Putnam, F. W. (1996). Child development and dissociation. *Child and Adolescent Psychiatric Clinics of North America, 5*, 285–301.

Putnam, F. W. (1997). *Dissociation in children and adolescents: A developmental perspective.* New York: Guilford.

Putnam, F. W., Hornstein, N., & Peterson, G. (1996). Clinical phenomenology of child and adolescent dissociative disorders: Gender and age effects. *Child and Adolescent Psychiatric Clinics of North America, 5*, 351–360.

Pyles, D. A. M., & Bailey, J. S. (1990). Diagnosing severe behavior problems. In A. C. Repp (Ed.), *Perspectives on the use of nonaversive and aversive interventions for persons with developmental disabilities* (pp. 381–401). Sycamore, IL: Sycamore Publishing.

Pynoos, R. S., Frederick, C., Nader, K., Arroyo, W., Steinberg, A., Eth, S., et al. (1987). Life threat and posttraumatic stress in school-age children. *Archives of General Psychiatry, 44*, 1057–1063.

Quay, H. (1997). Inhibition and attention deficit hyperactivity disorder. *Journal of Abnormal Child Psychology, 25*, 7–13.

Rae, W. A., & Fournier, C. J. (1999). Ethical and legal issues in the treatment of children and families. In S. W. Russ & T. H. Ollendick (Eds.), *Handbook of psychotherapies with children and families. Issues in clinical child psychology* (pp. 67–83). Dordrecht, Netherlands: Kluwer Academic Publishers.

Rafalovich, A. (2001). The conceptual history of attention deficit hyperactivity disorder: Idiocy, imbecility, encephalitis, and the child deviant, 1877–1929. *Deviant Behavior, 22*, 93–115.

Ramey, S. L., & Ramey, C. (1999). Early experience and early intervention for children "at risk" for developmental delay and mental retardation. *Mental Retardation and Developmental Disabilities Research Reviews, 5*, 1–10.

Rao, U., Ryan, N. D., Birmaher, B., Dahl, R. E., Williamson, D., Kaufman, J., et al. (1995). Unipolar depression in adolescents: Clinical outcome in adulthood. *Journal of the American Academy of Child and Adolescent Psychiatry, 34*, 566–578.

Rapoport, J. L., Inoff Germain, G., Weissman, M. M., Greenwald, S., Narrow, W. E., Jensen, P. S., et al. (2000). Childhood obsessive–compulsive disorder in the NIMH MECA Study: Parent versus child identification of cases. *Journal of Anxiety Disorders, 14*, 535–548.

Raskin, N., & Rogers, C. (1989). Person-centered therapy. In R. Corsini & D. Wedding (Eds.), *Current psychotherapies* (pp. 155–194). Itasca, IL: Peacock Publishing.

Reinherz, H. Z., Giaconia, R. M., Silverman, A. B., & Friedman, A. (1995). Early psychosocial risks for adolescent suicidal ideation and attempts. *Journal of the American Academy of Child and Adolescent Psychiatry, 34*, 599–611.

Reiss, D., & Neiderhiser, J. (2000). The interplay of genetic influences and social processes in developmental theory: Specific mechanisms are coming into view. *Development and Psychopathology, 12*, 357–374.

Reiss, D., Neiderhiser, J., Hetherington, M., & Plomin, R. (2000). *The relationship code: Deciphering genetic and social patterns in adolescent development.* Cambridge, MA: Harvard University Press.

Rekers, G. A., Bentler, P. M., Rosen, A. C., & Lovaas, O. I. (1977). Child gender disturbances: A clinical rationale for intervention. *Psychotherapy: Theory, Research and Practice, 14*, 2–11.

Rende, R. D., Plomin, R., Reiss, D., & Hetherington, E. M. (1993). Genetic and environmental influences on depressive symptomatology in adolescence: Individual differences and extreme scores. *Journal of Child Psychology and Psychiatry and Allied Disciplines, 34*, 1387–1398.

Reppucci, N. D., & Haugaard, J. J. (1989). Prevention of child sexual abuse: Myth or reality. *American Psychologist, 44*, 1266–1275.

Reyno, S. M., & McGrath, P. J. (2006). Predictors of parent training efficacy for child externalizing behavior problems: A meta-analytic review. *Journal of Child Psychology and Psychiatry, 47*, 99–111.

Reynolds, L., O'Koon, J., Papademetriou, E., Szczygiel, S., & Grant, K. (2001). Stress and somatic complaints in low-income urban adolescents. *Journal of Youth and Adolescence, 30*, 499–514.

Rhee, S. H., & Waldman, I. D. (2002). Genetic and environmental influences on antisocial behavior: A meta-analysis of twin and adoption studies. *Psychological Bulletin, 128*, 490–529.

Ricciardelli, L., & McCabe, M. (2001). Dietary restraint and negative affects as mediators of body dissatisfaction and bulimic behavior in adolescent girls and boys. *Behaviour Research and Therapy, 39*, 1317–1328.

Rice, F., Harold, G. T., & Thapar, A. (2002). Assessing the effects of age, sex, and shared environment on the genetic etiology of depression in childhood and adolescence. *Journal of Child Psychology and Psychiatry and Allied Disciplines, 43*, 1039–1051.

Richdale, A. (1999). Sleep problems in autism: Prevalence, cause, and intervention. *Developmental Medicine and Child Neurology, 41*, 60–66.

Richdale, A., Francis, A., Gavidia-Payne, S., & Cotton, S. (2000). Stress, behaviour, and sleep problems in children with an intellectual disability. *Journal of Intellectual and Developmental Disability, 25*, 147–161.

Richters, M. M., & Volkmar, F. R. (1994). Reactive attachment disorder of infancy or early childhood. *Journal of the American Academy of Child and Adolescent Psychiatry, 33*, 328–332.

Rimland, B. (1978, August). Inside the mind of the autistic savant. *Psychology Today*, 69–80.

Rimmerman, A., & Duvdevani, I. (1996). Parents of children and adolescents with severe mental retardation: Stress, family resources, normalization, and their application for out-of-home placement. *Research in Developmental Disabilities, 17*, 487–494.

Ritterband, L. M., Cox, D. J., Walker, L. S., Kovatchev, B., McKnight, L., Patel, K., et al. (2003). An Internet intervention as adjunctive therapy for pediatric encopresis. *Journal of Consulting and Clinical Psychology, 71*, 910–917.

Rivers, J., & Stoneman, Z. (2003). Sibling relationships when a child has autism: Marital stress and support coping. *Journal of Autism and Developmental Disorders, 33*, 383–394.

Roach, M. A., Orsmond, G. I., & Barratt, M. S. (1999). Mothers and fathers of children with Down syndrome: Parental stress and involvement in childcare. *American Journal on Mental Retardation, 104*, 422–436.

Robbins, T. W. (1997). Integrating the neurobiological and meuropsychologocal dimensions of autism. In J. Russell (Ed.), *Autism as an executive disorder* (pp. 21–53). London: Oxford University Press.

Roberts, S., Savage, J., & Coward, W. (1988). Energy expenditure and intake in infants born to lean and overweight mothers. *New England Journal of Medicine, 318*, 461–466.

Robin, A. L., Gilroy, M., & Dennis, A. B. (1998). Treatment of eating disorders in children and adolescents. *Clinical Psychology Review, 18*, 421–446.

Robins, C. J., & Hayes, A. M. (1993). An appraisal of cognitive therapy. *Journal of Consulting and Clinical Psychology, 61*, 205–214.

Robinson, J., Alverez, J., & Dodge, J. (1990). Life events and family history in children with recurrent abdominal pain. *Journal of Psychosomatic Research, 34*, 171–181.

Roeleveld, N., Zielhaus, G. A., & Gabreels, F. (1997). The prevalence of mental retardation: A critical review of recent literature. *Developmental Medicine and Child Neurology, 39*, 125–132.

Roeyers, H., & Mycke, K. (1995). Siblings of a child with autism, with mental retardation, and with a normal development. *Child: Care, Health, and Development, 21*, 305–319.

Rogers, C. R. (1992). The necessary and sufficient conditions of therapeutic personality change. *Journal of Consulting and Clinical Psychology, 60*, 827–832.

Rogers, S. J. (2000). Interventions that facilitate socialization in children with autism. *Journal of Autism and Developmental Disorders, 30*, 399–409.

Rogler, L. H. (1993). Culturally sensitizing psychiatric diagnosis. *Journal of Nervous and Mental Disease, 181*, 401–408.

Rojas, V. M., & Lee, T. N. (2004). Childhood vs. adult PTSD. In R. Silva (Ed.), *Posttraumatic stress disorders in children and adolescents* (pp. 237–256). New York: W. W. Norton.

Roll-Pettersson, L. (2001). Parents talk about how it feels to have a child with a cognitive disability. *European Journal of Special Needs Education, 16*, 1–14.

Romanczyk, R. G., Arnstein, L., Soorya, L. V., & Gillis, J. (2003). The myriad of controversial treatments for autism: A critical evaluation of efficacy. In S. O. Lilienfeld & S. J. Lynn (Eds.), *Science and pseudoscience in clinical psychology* (pp. 363–395). New York: Guilford.

Rome, E., & Ammerman, S. (2003). Medical complications of eating disorders: An update. *Journal of Adolescent Health, 33*, 418–426.

Rose, A. J. (2002). Co-rumination in the friendships of girls and boys. *Child Development, 73*, 1830–1843.

Rose, R., Dick, D., Viken, R., Pulkkinen, L., & Kaprio, J. (2001). Drinking or abstaining at age 14? A genetic epidemiological study. *Alcoholism: Clinical and Experimental Research, 25*, 1594–1604.

Rosenbaum, J., Biederman, J., Hirshfeld, D., & Bolduc, E. (1991). Behavioral inhibition in children: A possible precursor to panic disorder or social phobia. *Journal of Clinical Psychiatry, 52(Suppl)*, 5–9.

Rosenbaum, J. L. (1989). Family dysfunction and female delinquency. *Crime and Delinquency, 35*, 31–44.

Rosenbaum, M. (1980). The role of the term *schizophrenia* in the decline of diagnoses of multiple personality. *Archives of General Psychiatry, 37*, 1383–1385.

Rosenbaum, M., & Leibel, R. L. (1998). The physiology of body weight regulation: Relevance to the etiology of obesity in children. *Pediatrics, 107*, 525–538.

Rosenbaum, M., Leibel, R. L., & Hirsch, J. (1997). Medical progress: Obesity. *New England Journal of Medicine, 337*, 396–407.

Rosenberg, D., Sweeney, J., Squires-Wheller, E., Keshaven, M., Cornblatt, B., & Erlenmeyer-Kimling, L. (1997). Eye-tracking dysfunction in offspring from the New York High-Risk Project. *Psychiatry Research, 66*, 121–130.

Ross, C. A. (1996). Epidemiology of dissociation in children and adolescents: Extrapolations and speculations. *Child and Adolescent Psychiatric Clinics of North America, 5*, 273–284.

Ross, C. A., Joshi, S., & Churrie, R. (1991). Dissociative experiences in the general population: A factor analysis. *Hospital and Community Psychiatry, 42*, 297–301.

Ross, R. (2003). Early expression of a pathophysiological feature of schizophrenia: Saccadic intrusions into smooth-pursuit eye movements in school-age children vulnerable to schizophrenia. *Journal of the American Academy of Child and Adolescent Psychiatry, 42*, 468–476.

Rossister, L., & Sharpe, D. (2001). The siblings of individuals with mental retardation: A quantitative integration of the literature. *Journal of Child and Family Studies, 10*, 65–84.

Rothe, E. M. (2005). Posttraumatic stress symptoms in Cuban children and adolescents during and after refugee camp confinement. In T. Corales (Ed.), *Trends in posttraumatic stress disorder research* (pp. 101–128). Hauppauge, NY: Nova Science Publishers.

Rothe, E. M., Lewis, J., Castillo Matos, H., Martinez, O., Busquets, R., & Martinez, I. (2002). Posttraumatic stress disorder among Cuban children and adolescents after release from a refugee camp. *Psychiatric Services, 53*, 970–976.

Rotholz, D. A. (1987). Current considerations on the use of one-to-one instruction with autistic students: Review and recommendations. *Education and Treatment of Children, 10*, 271–278.

Rothstein, A. (1981). Hallucinatory phenomena in childhood: A critique of the literature. *Journal of the American Academy of Child Psychiatry, 20*, 623–635.

Rothstein, M. (1999). Behavioral genetic determinism: Its effects on culture and law. In R. A. Carson & M. A. Rothstein (Eds.), *Behavioral genetics: The clash of culture and biology* (pp. 89–115). Baltimore, MD: Johns Hopkins University Press.

Routh, D., & Ernst, A. (1984). Somatization disorder in relatives of children and adolescents with functional abdominal pain. *Journal of Pediatric Psychology, 9*, 427–437.

Rowe, D. C., & Jacobson, K. C. (1999). In the mainstream: Research in behavioral genetics. In R. Carson & M. Rothstein (Eds.), *Behavioral genetics: The clash of culture and biology* (pp. 12–34). Baltimore, MD: The Johns Hopkins University Press.

Rowe, R., Maughan, B., Pickles, A., Costello, E. J., & Angold, A. (2002). The relationship between DSM-IV oppositional defiant disorder and conduct disorder: Findings from the Great Smoky Mountains Study. *Journal of Child Psychology and Psychiatry and Allied Disciplines, 43*, 365–373.

Russell, A. T. (1994). The clinical presentation of childhood-onset schizophrenia. *Schizophrenia Bulletin, 20*, 631–646.

Russell, G. F., Szmukler, G. I., Dare, C., & Eisler, I. (1987). An evaluation of family therapy in anorexia nervosa and bulimia nervosa. *Archives of General Psychiatry, 44*, 1047–1056.

Russell, M., & Skinner, J. B. (1988). Early measures of maternal alcohol misuse as predictors of adverse pregnancy outcomes. *Alcoholism: Clinical and Experimental Research, 12*, 824–830.

Russoniello, C. V., Skalko, T. K., O'Brien, K., McGhee, S. A., Bingham Alexander, D., & Beatley, J. (2002). Childhood posttraumatic stress disorder and efforts to cope after Hurricane Floyd. *Behavioral Medicine, 28*, 61–70.

Rutter, M. (1972). Childhood schizophrenia reconsidered. *Journal of Autism and Childhood Schizophrenia, 2*, 315–338.

Rutter, M. (1981). Stress, coping and development: Some issues and some questions. *Journal of Child Psychology and Psychiatry, 22*, 323–356.

Rutter, M. (2000). Genetic studies of autism: From the 1970s into the millennium. *Journal of Abnormal Child Psychology, 28*, 3–14.

Rutter, M. (2005). Environmentally mediated risks for psychopathology: Research strategies and findings. *Journal of the American Academy of Child and Adolescent Psychiatry, 44*, 3–18.

Rutter, M., Moffitt, T., & Caspi, A. (2006). Gene–environment interplay and psychopathology: Multiple varieties but real effects. *Journal of Child Psychology and Psychiatry, 47*, 226–261.

Rutter, M., Silberg, J., Connor, T., & Simonoff, E. (1999). Genetics and child psychiatry: Advances in quantitative and molecular genetics. *Child Psychology and Psychiatry, 40*, 3–18.

Ruzek, J., & Watson, P. (2001). Early intervention to prevent PTSD and other trauma related problems. *PTSD Research Quarterly, 12.*

Sachs, G., & Lafer, B. (1998). Child and adolescent mania. In P. J. Goodnick (Ed.), *Mania: Clinical and research perspectives* (pp. 37–60). Washington, DC: American Psychiatric Press.

Saenger, P. (2004). Type 2 diabetes mellitus in children and adolescents: The new epidemic. In W. Kiess, C. Carcus, & M. Wabitsch (Eds.), *Obesity in childhood and adolescence* (pp. 181–193). Basel, Switzerland: Karger.

Safer, D. J., Zito, J. M., & Fine, M. (1996). Increased methylphenidate usage for attention deficit disorder in the 1990's. *Pediatrics, 98*, 1084–1088.

Sagrestano, L. M., Paikoff, R. L., Holmbeck, G. N., & Fendrich, M. (2003). A longitudinal examination of familial risk factors for depression among inner-city African American adolescents. *Journal of Family Psychology, 17*, 108–120.

Saigh, P. A., Brassard, M. R., & Peverely, S. T. (2004). Cognitive–behavioral interventions for children and adolescents with PTSD. In S. Taylor (Ed.), *Advances in the treatment of posttraumatic stress disorder: Cognitive–behavioral perspectives* (pp. 243–263). New York: Springer.

Saigh, P. A., Yasik, A. E., Oberfield, R. A., Halamandaris, P. V., & McHugh, M. (2002). An analysis of the internalizing and externalizing behaviors of traumatized urban youth with and without PTSD. *Journal of Abnormal Psychology, 111*, 462–470.

Salbe, A., Weyer, C., Harper, I., Lindsay, R., Ravussin, E., & Tataranni, A. (2002). Assessing risk factors for obesity between childhood and adolescence: II. Energy metabolism and physical activity. *Pediatrics, 110*, 307–314.

Salbe, A., Weyer, C., Lindsay, R., Ravussin, E., & Tataranni, A. (2002). Assessing risk factors for obesity between childhood and adolescence: I. Birth weight, childhood adiposity, parental obesity, insulin, and leptin. *Pediatrics, 110*, 299–306.

Salvatoni, A. (2002). Surgical treatment. In W. Burniat, T. J. Cole, I. Lissau, & E. Poskitt (Eds.), *Child and adolescent obesity* (pp. 355–360). Cambridge, England: Cambridge University Press.

Sandberg, A. D., Ehlers, S., Hagberg, B., & Gillberg, C. (2000). The Rett syndrome complex: Communicative functions in relation to developmental level and autistic features. *Autism, 4*, 249–267.

Sanders, M., Shepard, R., Cleghorn, G., & Woolford, H. (1994). The treatment of recurrent abdominal pain in children: A controlled comparison of cognitive–behavioral family intervention and standard pediatric care. *Journal of Consulting and Clinical Psychology, 306–314.*

Sandler, I., West, S., Baca, L., Pillow, D., Gersten, J., & Rogosch, F. (1992). Linking empirically based theory and evaluation: The Family Bereavement Program. *American Journal of Community Psychology, 20, 491–521.*

Santelli, J., & Rogers, A. S. (2002). Parental permission, passive consent, and "children" in research. *Journal of Adolescent Health, 31, 303–304.*

Sattler, J. M. (1998). *Clinical and forensic interviewing of children and families.* San Diego: Sattler, Inc.

Sattler, J. M. (2001). *Assessment of children: Cognitive applications* (4th ed.). La Mesa, CA: Jerome M. Sattler.

Saywitz, K., Mannarino, A. P., Berliner, L., & Cohen, J. A. (2000). Treatment for sexually abused children and adolescents. *American Psychologist, 55, 1040–1050.*

Scahill, L., & Schwab-Stone, M. (2000). Epidemiology of ADHD in school-age children. *Child and Adolescent Psychiatric Clinics of North America, 9, 541–555.*

Schachar, R., Tannock, R., Marriott, M., & Logan, G. (1995). Deficient inhibitory control in attention deficit hyperactivity disorder. *Journal of Abnormal Child Psychology, 23, 411–437.*

Schachter, S., & Singer, J. (1962). Cognitive, social, and physiological determinants of emotional state. *Psychological Review, 69, 379–399.*

Schaeffer, J. L., & Ross, R. G. (2002). Childhood-onset schizophrenia: Premorbid and prodromal diagnostic and treatment histories. *Journal of the American Academy of Child and Adolescent Psychiatry, 41, 538–545.*

Schall, C. (2000). Family perspectives on raising a child with autism. *Journal of Child and Family Studies, 9, 409–423.*

Scheeringa, M. S., Peebles, C. D., Cook, C. A., & Zeanah, C. (2001). Toward establishing procedural, criterion, and discriminant validity for PTSD in early childhood. *Journal of the American Academy of Child and Adolescent Psychiatry, 40, 52–60.*

Scheeringa, M. S., & Zeanah, C. H. (2001). A relational perspective on PTSD in early childhood. *Journal of Traumatic Stress, 14, 799–815.*

Scheeringa, M. S., Zeanah, C. H., Myers, L., & Putnam, F. W. (2003). New findings on alternative criteria for PTSD in preschool children. *Journal of the American Academy of Child and Adolescent Psychiatry, 42, 561–570.*

Schmidt, M., Blanz, B., Dippe, A., & Koppe, T. (1995). Course of patients diagnosed as having schizophrenia during first episode occurring under age 18 years. *European Archives of Psychiatry and Clinical Neuroscience, 245, 93–100.*

Schore, A. (2001). The effects of early relational trauma on right brain development, affect, regulation, and infant mental health. *Infant Mental Health Journal, 22, 201–269.*

Schore, A. N. (1996). The experience-dependent maturation of a regulatory system in the orbital prefrontal cortex and the origin of developmental psychopathology. *Development and Psychopathology, 8, 59–87.*

Schreiber, F. R. (1973). *Sybil.* Chicago: Regnery.

Schultz, E., & Remschmidt, H. (2001). Psychopharmacology of depressive states in childhood and adolescence. In I. Goodyer (Ed.), *The depressed child and adolescent* (2nd ed., pp. 292–324). Cambridge, England: Cambridge University Press.

Schultz, R., Gauthier, I., Klin, A., Fulbright, R., Anderson, A., Volkmar, F., et al. (2000). Abnormal ventral temporal cortical activity during face discrimination among individuals with autism and Asperger syndrome. *Archives of General Psychiatry, 57, 331–340.*

Schulz, S. C., Findling, R. L., Wise, A., Friedman, L., & Kenny, J. (1998). Child and adolescent schizophrenia. *Psychiatric Clinics of North America, 21, 43–56.*

Schweiger, U., Laessle, R., Kittl, S., Dickhaut, B., Schweiger, M., & Pirke, K. (1986). Macronutrient intake, plasma large neural amino acids, and mood during weight-reducing diets. *Journal of Neural Transmission, 67, 77–86.*

Scotti, J., & Morris, T. (2000). Diagnosis and classification. In M. Hersen & R. Ammerman (Eds.), *Advanced abnormal child psychology* (2nd ed., pp. 15–32). Mahwah, NJ: Lawrence Erlbaum.

Seeley, K. M. (2000). *Cultural psychotherapy*. Northvale, NJ: Jason Aronson.

Seltzer, W. J. (1985). Conversion disorder in childhood and adolescence: A familial/cultural approach. *Family Systems Medicine, 3*, 261–280.

Sergeant, J., & Van der Meere, J. (1990). Convergence of approaches in localizing the hyperactivity deficit. In B. Lahey & A. Kazdin (Eds.), *Advances in clinical child psychology* (pp. 207–246). New York: Plenum.

Shaffer, D., Fisher, P., Lucas, C. P., Dulcan, M. K., & Schwab-Stone, M. (2000). NIMH Diagnostic Interview Schedule for Children, Version IV: Description, differences from previous versions, and reliability of some common diagnoses. *Journal of the American Academy of Child and Adolescent Psychiatry, 39*, 28–38.

Shavelle, R. M., Strauss, D. J., & Pickett, J. (2001). Causes of death in autism. *Journal of Autism and Developmental Disorders, 31*, 569–576.

Shaw, D. S., Owens, E. B., Vondra, J. I., & Keenan, K. (1996). Early risk factors and pathways in the development of early disruptive behavior problems. *Development and Psychopathology, 8*, 679–699.

Shaw, J. A., & Campo Bowen, A. (1995). Aggression. In G. P. Sholevar (Ed.), *Conduct disorders in children and adolescents* (pp. 45–57). Washington, DC: American Psychiatric Press.

Sheeber, L., Allen, N., Davis, B., & Sorensen, E. (2000). Regulation of negative affect during mother–child problem-solving interactions: Adolescent depressive status and family processes. *Journal of Abnormal Child Psychology, 28*, 467–479.

Shelton, R., Barkley, R., Crosswait, C., Moorehouse, M., Fletcher, K., Barrett, S., et al. (2000). Multimethod psychoeducational intervention for preschool children with disruptive behavior: Two-year post-treatment follow-up. *Journal of Abnormal Child Psychology, 28*, 253–266.

Shepard, B. A., Carter, A. S., & Cohen, J. E. (2000). Attention-deficit/hyperactivity disorder and the preschool child. In T. E. Brown (Ed.), *Attention deficit disorders and comorbidities in children, adolescents, and adults* (pp. 407–436). Washington, DC:American Psychiatric Publishing.

Sheperis, C. J., Renfro Michel, E. L., & Doggett, R. A. (2003). In-home treatment of reactive attachment disorder in a therapeutic foster care system: A case example. *Journal of Mental Health Counseling, 25*, 76–88.

Sherman, D. K., Iacono, W. G., & McGue, M. K. (1997). Attention-deficit hyperactivity disorder dimensions: A twin study of inattention and impulsivity–hyperactivity. *Journal of the American Academy of Child and Adolescent Psychiatry, 36*, 745–753.

Sherrard, J., Tonge, B. J., & Ozanne-Smith, J. (2002). Injury risk in young people with intellectual disability. *Journal of Intellectual Disability Research, 46*, 6–16.

Shirar, L. (1996). *Dissociative children*. New York: W. W. Norton & Company.

Shisslak, C., Crago, M., McKnight, K, Estes, L., Gray, N., & Parnaby, O. (1998). Potential risk factors associated with weight control behaviors in elementary and middle school girls. *Journal of Psychosomatic Research, 44*, 301–313.

Shneidman, E. S. (1991). The commonalities of suicide across the life span. In A. A. Leenaars (Ed.), *Life span perspectives of suicide: Time lines in the suicide process* (pp. 39–52). New York: Plenum.

Short, E., Manos, M., Findling, R., & Schubel, E. (2004). A prospective study of stimulant response in preschool children: Insights from ROC analyses. *Journal of the American Academy of Child and Adolescent Psychiatry, 43*, 251–259.

Shultz, S. K., Scherman, A., & Marshall, L. J. (2000). Evaluation of a university-based date rape prevention program: Effect on attitudes and behavior related to rape. *Journal of College Student Development, 41*, 193–201.

Siegel, S. J., & Alloy, L. B. (1990). Interpersonal perceptions and consequences of depressive/significant other relationships: A naturalistic study of college roommates. *Journal of Abnormal Psychology, 99*, 361–373.

Sigman, M. (1999). Developmental deficits in children with Down syndrome. In H. Tager-Flusberg (Ed.), *Neurodevelopmental disorders* (pp. 179–196). Cambridge, MA: MIT Press.

Sikich, L. (2005). Psychotherapy and school interventions. In R. L. Findling & S. C. Schultz (Eds.), *Juvenile-onset schizophrenia* (pp. 257–287). Baltimore, MD: Johns Hopkins University Press.

Silberg, J. L. (1998). Dissociative symptomatology in children and adolescents as displayed on psychological testing. *Journal of Personality Assessment, 71*, 421–439.

Silberg, J. L. (2000). Fifteen years of dissociation in maltreated children: Where do we go from here? *Child Maltreatment, 5*, 119–136.

Silberg, J. L. (2004). The treatment of dissociation in sexually abused children from a family/attachment perspective. *Psychotherapy: Theory, Research, Practice, Training, 41*, 487–495.

Silove, D., & Manicavasagar, V. (2001). Early separation anxiety and its relationship to adult anxiety disorders. In M. Vasey & M. Dadds (Eds.), *The developmental psychopathology of anxiety* (pp. 459–480). Oxford, England: Oxford University Press.

Silverman, W. K., La Greca, A. M., & Wasserstein, S. (1995). What do children worry about? Worries and their relation to anxiety. *Child Development, 66*, 671–686.

Silverthorn, P., & Frick, P. J. (1999). Developmental pathways to antisocial behavior: The delayed-onset pathway in girls. *Development and Psychopathology, 11*, 101–126.

Simonoff, E., Bolton, P., & Rutter, M. (1999). Genetic perspectives on mental retardation. In J. A. Burack, R. M. Hodapp, & E. Zigler (Eds.), *Handbook of mental retardation and development* (pp. 41–79). Cambridge, England: Cambridge University Press.

Sivberg, B. (2002). Family system and coping behaviors: A comparison between parents of children with autistic spectrum disorders and parents with non-autistic children. *Autism, 6*, 397–409.

Skinner, B. F. (1953). *Science and human behavior*. New York: Macmillan.

Slutske, W. S., Cronk, N. J., & Nabors Oberg, R. E. (2003). Familial and genetic factors. In C. A. Essau (Ed.), *Conduct and oppositional defiant disorders: Epidemiology, risk factors, and treatment* (pp. 137–162). Mahwah, NJ: Erlbaum.

Smith, I. (2000). Motor functioning in Asperger syndrome. In A. Klin, F. Volkmar, & S. Sparrow (Eds.), *Asperger syndrome* (pp. 97–124). New York: Guilford.

Smith, I. M., & Bryson, S. E. (1994). Imitation and action in autism: A critical review. *Psychological Bulletin, 116*, 259–273.

Smith, T., Groen, A. D., & Wynn, J. W. (2000). Randomized trial of intensive early intervention for children with pervasive developmental disorder. *American Journal on Mental Retardation, 105*, 269–285.

Smith, T., Lovaas, N. W., & Lovaas, O. I. (2002). Behaviors of children with high-functioning autism when paired with typically developing versus delayed peers: A preliminary study. *Behavioral Interventions, 17*, 129–143.

Smolak, L., Levine, M., & Schermer, F. (1999). Parental input and weight concerns among elementary school children. *International Journal of Eating Disorders, 25*, 263–271.

Smoller, J. W., Wadden, T. A., & Stunkard, A. J. (1987). Dieting and depression: A critical review. *Journal of Psychosomatic Research, 31*, 429–440.

Smyke, A. T., Dumitrescu, A., & Zeanah, C. H. (2002). Attachment disturbances in young children. I: The continuum of caretaking casualty. *Journal of the American Academy of Child and Adolescent Psychiatry, 41*, 972–982.

Sokolov, S., & Kutcher, S. (2001). Adolescent depression: Neuroendocrine aspects. In I. M. Goodyer (Ed.), *The depressed child and adolescent (2nd ed.). Cambridge child and adolescent psychiatry* (pp. 233–266). New York: Cambridge University Press.

Sonuga-Barke, E. J. S., Lamparelli, M., Stevenson, J., & Thompson, M. (1994). Behaviour problems and pre-school intellectual attainment: The associations of hyperactivity and conduct problems. *Journal of Child Psychology and Psychiatry and Allied Disciplines, 35*, 949–960.

Southam-Gerow, M. A. (2003). Child-focused cognitive–behavioral therapies. In C. A. Essau (Ed.), *Conduct and oppositional defiant disorders: Epidemiology, risk factors, and treatment* (pp. 257–277). Mahwah, NJ: Erlbaum.

Spanos, N. P. (1994). Multiple identity enactments and multiple personality disorder: A sociocognitive perspective. *Psychological Bulletin, 116*, 143–165.

Spearman, C. (1927). *The nature of intelligence and the principles of cognition* (2nd ed.). Oxford, England: Macmillan.

Spence, S. H., Rapee, R., McDonald, C., & Ingram, M. (2001). The structure of anxiety symptoms among preschoolers. *Behaviour Research and Therapy, 39*, 1293–1316.

Spence, S. H., Sheffield, J. K., & Donovan, C. L. (2003). Preventing adolescent depression: An evaluation of the Problem Solving for Life program. *Journal of Consulting and Clinical Psychology, 71*, 3–13.

Spencer, T. J., Biederman, J., Wozniak, J., Faraone, S. V., Wilens, T. E., & Mick, E. (2001). Parsing pediatric bipolar disorder from its associated comorbidity with the disruptive behavior disorders. *Biological Psychiatry, 49*, 1062–1070.

Spierings, C., Poels, P. J., Sijben, N., & Gabreels, F. J. (1990). Conversion disorders in childhood: A retrospective follow-up study of 84 inpatients. *Developmental Medicine and Child Neurology, 32*, 865–871.

Spitz, R. (1945). Hospitalism: An inquiry into the genesis of psychiatric conditions in early childhood. *Psychoanalytic Study of the Child, 1*, 53–74.

Sprich, S., Biederman, J., Crawford, M. H., Mundy, E., & Faraone, S. V. (2000). Adoptive and biological families of children and adolescents with ADHD. *Journal of the American Academy of Child and Adolescent Psychiatry, 39*, 1432–1437.

Squire, L. R., & Zola-Morgan, S. (1991). The medial temporal lobe memory system. *Science, 253*, 1380–1386.

Sroufe, L., & Rutter, M. (1984). The domain of developmental psychopathology. *Child Development, 55*, 17–29.

Sroufe, L. A. (1983). Infant–caregiver attachment and patterns of adaptation in preschool: The roots of maladaptation and competence. In M. Perlmutter (Ed.), *Minnesota Symposium on Child Psychology* (Vol. 16, pp. 41–83). Hillsdale, NJ: Erlbaum.

Sroufe, L. A., & Waters, E. (1977). Attachment as an organizational construct. *Child Development, 48*, 1184–1199.

Stark, L. J., Opipari, L. C., Donaldson, D. L., Danovsky, M. B., Rasile, D. A., & DelSanto, A. F. (1997). Evaluation of a standard protocol for retentive encopresis: A replication. *Journal of Pediatric Psychology, 22*, 619–633.

Steele, H. (2003). Holding therapy is not attachment therapy. *Attachment and Human Development, 5*, 219–220.

Steffenburg, S., Gillberg, C., Hellgren, L., Andersson, I., Gillberg, I., Jacobsson, G., et al. (1989). A twin study of autism in Denmark, Finland, Iceland, Norway, and Sweden. *Journal of Child Psychology and Psychiatry, 40*, 405–416.

Stein, M. B., Koverola, C., Hanna, C., Torchia, M. G., & McClarty, B. (1997). Hippocampal volume in women victimized by childhood abuse. *Psychological Medicine, 37*, 951–959.

Steiner, H., & Lock, J. (1998). Anorexia nervosa and bulimia nervosa in children and adolescents: A review of the past 10 years. *Journal of the American Academy of Child and Adolescent Psychiatry, 37*, 352–359.

Steingard, R. J., Connor, D. F., & Au, T. (2005). Approaches to psychopharmacology. In M. L. Bauman & T. L. Kemper (Eds.), *The neurobiology of autism* (2nd ed., pp. 79–102). Baltimore, MD: The Johns Hopkins Press.

Sternberg, R. (2000). The concept of intelligence. In R. Sternberg (Ed.), *Handbook of intelligence* (pp. 3–15). Cambridge, England: Cambridge University Press.

Sternberg, R. J. (2004). Culture and intelligence. *American Psychologist, 59*, 325–338.

Stevens, G. (1981). Bias in the attribution of hyperkinetic behavior as a function of ethnic identification and socioeconomic status. *Psychology in the Schools, 18*, 99–106.

Stice, E. (1998). Modeling of eating pathology and social reinforcement of the thin-ideal predict onset of bulimic symptoms. *Behaviour Research and Therapy, 36*, 931–944.

Stice, E., Presnell, K., & Bearman, S. (2001). Relation of early menarch to depression, eating disorders, substance abuse, and comorbid psychopathology among adolescent girls. *Developmental Psychology, 37*, 608–619.

Stien, P., & Kendall, J. (2004). *Psychological trauma and the developing brain: Neurologically based interventions for troubled children*. New York: Haworth Press.

Still, G. F. (1902). The Coulston Lectures on some abnormal physical conditions in children. *Lancet, 1*, 1008–1012.

Stoolmiller, M. (2001). Synergistic interaction of child manageability problems and parent-discipline tactics in predicting future growth in externalizing behavior for boys. *Developmental Psychology, 37*, 814–825.

Stormont, M. (2001). Social outcomes of children with AD/HD: Contributing factors and implications for practice. *Psychology in the Schools, 38*, 521–531.

Strain, P., & Danko, C. (1995). Caregivers' encouragement of positive interaction between preschoolers with autism and their siblings. *Journal of Emotional and Behavioral Disorders, 3*, 2–12.

Strain, P., Kerr, M., & Ragland, E. (1979). Effects of peer-mediated social initiations and prompting/reinforcement procedures on the social behavior of autistic children. *Journal of Autism and Developmental Disorders, 9,* 41–54.

Strauss, R. (2000). Childhood obesity and self-esteem. *Pediatrics, 105,* e15.

Strober, M., Schmidt Lackner, S., Freeman, R., Bower, S., Lampert, C., & DeAntonia, M. (1995). Recovery and relapse in adolescents with bipolar affective illness: A five-year naturalistic, prospective follow-up. *Journal of the American Academy of Child and Adolescent Psychiatry, 34,* 724–731.

Stromme, P., Bjornstad, P. G., & Ramstad, K. (2002). Prevalence estimation of Williams syndrome. *Journal of Child Neurology, 17,* 269–271.

Strong, K. G., & Huon, G. F. (1998). An evaluation of a structural model for studies of the initiation of dieting among adolescent girls. *Journal of Psychosomatic Research, 44,* 315–326.

Stubbe, D. E. (2000). Attention-deficit/hyperactivity disorder overview: Historical perspective, current controversies, and future directions. *Child and Adolescent Psychiatric Clinics of North America, 9,* 469–479.

Sullivan, P., Neale, M., & Kendler, K. (2000). Genetic epidemiology of major depression: Review and meta-analysis. *American Journal of Psychiatry, 157,* 1152–1562.

Surgeon General. (2004). The facts about overweight and obesity. In M. Frugier (Ed.), *Childhood obesity in the United States* (pp. 123–138). New York: Novinka Books.

Susman, E., & Pajer, K. (2004). Biology–behavior integration and antisocial behavior in girls. In M. Putallaz & K. Bierman (Eds.), *Aggression, antisocial behavior, and violence among girls: A developmental perspective* (pp. 23–47). New York: Guilford

Swanson, J., Castellanos, F. X., Murias, M., LaHoste, G., & Kennedy, J. (1998). Cognitive neuroscience of attention deficit hyperactivity disorder and hyperkinetic disorder. *Current Opinion in Neurobiology, 8,* 263–271.

Swanson, J. M., Kraemer, H. C., Hinshaw, S. P., Arnold, L. E., Conners, C. K., Abikoff, H. B., et al. (2001). Clinical relevance of the primary findings of the MTA: Success rates based on severity of ADHD and ODD symptoms at the end of treatment. *Journal of the American Academy of Child and Adolescent Psychiatry, 40,* 168–179.

Sykes, D., Hoy, E., Bill, J., McClure, B., Halliday, H., & Reid, M. (1997). Behavioral adjustment in school of very low birthweight children. *Journal of Child Psychology and Psychiatry, 38,* 315–325.

Szatmari, P. (2000). The classification of autism, Asperger's syndrome, and pervasive developmental disorder. *Canadian Journal of Psychiatry, 45,* 731–738.

Szatmari, P., & Jones, M. (1998). Genetic epidemiology of autism and other pervasive developmental disorders. In F. R. Volkmar (Ed.), *Autism and pervasive developmental disorders* (pp. 109–129). Cambridge, England: Cambridge University Press.

Tager Flusberg, H. (2001). Understanding the language and communicative impairments in autism. In L. M. Glidden (Ed.), *International review of research in mental retardation: Autism* (pp. 185–205). San Diego, CA: Academic Press.

Tanguay, P. E. (2000). Pervasive developmental disorders: A 10-year review. *Journal of the American Academy of Child and Adolescent Psychiatry, 39,* 1079–1095.

Tannock, R. (1998). Attention deficit hyperactivity disorder: Advances in cognitive, neurobiological, and genetic research. *Journal of Child Psychology and Psychiatry, 39,* 65–100.

Taubman, B. (1997). Toilet training and toilet training refusal for stool only: A prospective study. *Pediatrics, 99,* 54–58.

Taylor, E., Chadwick, O., Heptinstall, E., & Danckaerts, M. (1996). Hyperactivity and conduct problems as risk factors for adolescent development. *Journal of the American Academy of Child and Adolescent Psychiatry, 35,* 1213–1226.

Taylor, T. K., Eddy, J. M., & Biglan, A. (1999). Interpersonal skills training to reduce aggressive and delinquent behavior: Limited evidence and the need for an evidence-based system of care. *Clinical Child and Family Psychology Review, 2,* 169–182.

Terr, L. (1979). Children of Chowchilla: A study of psychic trauma. *Psychoanalytic Study of the Child, 34,* 552–623.

Terr, L. (1985). Children traumatized in small groups. In S. Eth & R. Pynoos (Eds.), *Posttraumatic stress disorder in children* (pp. 45–70). Washington, DC: American Psychiatric Press.

Terr, L. (1991). Childhood traumas: An outline and overview. *American Journal of Psychiatry, 148,* 10–20.

Thapar, A. J. (1999). Genetic basis of attention deficit and hyperactivity. *British Journal of Psychiatry, 174,* 105–111.

Thelen, M. H., & Cormier, J. F. (1995). Desire to be thinner and weight control among children and their parents. *Behavior Therapy, 26,* 85–99.

The Research Units on Pediatric Psychopharmacology Anxiety Study Group. (2001). Fluvoxamine for the treatment of anxiety disorders in children and adolescents. *New England Journal of Medicine, 344,* 1279–1285.

The Research Units on Pediatric Psychopharmacology Anxiety Study Group. (2003). Searching for moderators and mediators of pharmacological treatment effects in children and adolescents with anxiety disorders. *Journal of the American Academy of Child and Adolescent Psychiatry, 42,* 13–21.

Theunis, M., Van Hoecke, E., Paesbrugge, S., Hoebeke, P., & VandeWalle, J. (2002). Self-image and performance in children with nocturnal enuresis. *European Urology, 41,* 660–667.

Thigpen, C., & Cleckley, H. (1957). *Three faces of Eve.* New York: McGraw-Hill.

Thompson, R. W., Authier, K., & Ruma, P. (1994). Behavior problems of sexually abused children in foster care: A preliminary study. *Journal of Child Sexual Abuse, 3,* 79–91.

Thompson, S., & Rey, J. M. (1995). Functional enuresis: Is desmopressin the answer? *Journal of the American Academy of Child and Adolescent Psychiatry, 34,* 266–271.

Thomsen, P. H., Moller, L. L., Dehlholm, B., & Brask, B. H. (1992). Manic-depressive psychosis in children younger than 15 years: A register-based investigation of 39 cases in Denmark. *Acta Psychiatrica Scandinavica, 85,* 401–406.

Thorne, B. (1992). *Carl Rogers.* London: Sage.

Thurstone, L. L. (1938). *Primary mental abilities.* Chicago: University of Chicago Press.

Tiegerman, E., & Primavera, L. (1984). Imitating the autistic child: Facilitating communicative gaze behavior. *Journal of Autism and Developmental Disorders, 14,* 27–38.

Tienari, P., Wynne, L. C., Moring, J., Lahti, I., Naarala, M., Sorri, A., et al. (1994). The Finnish Adoptive Family Study of Schizophrenia: Implications for family research. *British Journal of Psychiatry, 164,* 20–26.

Tilgner, L., Wertheim, E., & Paxton, S. (2004). Effect of social desirability on adolescent girls' responses to an eating disorders prevention program. *International Journal of Eating Disorders, 35,* 211–216.

Timimi, S. (2005). *Naughty boys: Anti-social behaviour, ADHD, and the role of culture.* New York: Palgrave MacMillian.

Toolan, J. M. (1962). Depression in children and adolescents. *American Journal of Orthopsychiatry, 32,* 404–415.

Torsheim, T., & Wold, B. (2001). School-related stress, school support, and somatic complaints: A general population study. *Journal of Adolescent Research, 16,* 293–303.

Toth, S., Maughan, A., Manly, J., Spagnola, M., & Cicchetti, D. (2002). The relative efficacy of two interventions in altering maltreated preschool children's representational models: Implications for attachment theory. *Development and Psychopathology, 14,* 877–980.

Trepagnier, C. (1996). A possible origin for the social and communicative deficits of autism. *Focus on Autism and Other Developmental Disabilities, 11,* 170–182.

Trimble, B. K. I., & Baiord, P. A. (1978). Maternal age and Down syndrome: Age-specific incidence rates by single year intervals. *Journal of Medical Genetics, 2,* 1.

Troiano, R., & Flegal, K. (1998). Overweight children and adolescents: Description, epidemiology and demographics. *Pediatrics, 101,* 497–504.

Tuchman, B. W. (1979). *A distant mirror: The calamitous 14th century.* New York: Ballantine Books.

Twenge, J. M., & Nolen Hoeksema, S. (2002). Age, gender, race, socioeconomic status, and birth cohort difference on the children's depression inventory: A meta-analysis. *Journal of Abnormal Psychology, 111,* 578–588.

Tyrka, A., Waldron, I., Graber, J., & Brooks-Gunn, J. (2002). Prospective predictors of the onset of anorexic and bulimic syndromes. *International Journal of Eating Disorders, 32,* 282–290.

Udwin, O., Boyle, S., Yule, W., Bolton, D., & O'Ryan, D. (2000). Risk factors for long-term psychological effects of a disaster experienced in adolescence: Predictors of posttraumatic stress disorder. *Journal of Child Psychology and Psychiatry and Allied Disciplines, 41,* 969–979.

U.S. Public Health Service. (2001). *Report of the Surgeon General's conference on children's mental health: A national action agenda.* Rockville, MD: Department of Health and Human Services.

Vaidaya, C., Austin, G., & Kirkorian, G. (1998). Selective effects of methylphenidate in attention deficit hyperactivity disorder: A functional magnetic resonance study. *Proceedings of the National Academy of Sciences, 95,* 14494–14499.

Vandenberg, S. G., & Volger, G. P. (1985). Genetic determinants of intelligence. In B. Wolman (Ed.), *Handbook of Intelligence* (pp. 3–57). New York: Wiley.

Van den Boom, D. (1990). Preventive intervention and the quality of mother–infant interaction and infant exploration in irritable infants. In W. Koops, H. J. G. Soppe, J. L. van der Linden, P. C. M. Molenaar, & J. J. F. Schroots (Eds.), *Developmental psychology behind the dikes: An outline of developmental psychology research in the Netherlands.* The Netherlands: Uitgeverij Eburon.

Van den Boom, D. C. (1994). The influence of temperament and mothering on attachment and exploration: An experimental manipulation of sensitive responsiveness among lower-class mothers with irritable infants. *Child Development, 65,* 1449–1469.

Van den Boom, D. C. (1995). Do first-year intervention effects endure? Follow-up during toddlerhood of a sample of Dutch irritable infants. *Child Development, 66,* 1798–1816.

Van der Kolk, B., van der Hart, O., & Burbridge, J. (2002). Approaches to the treatment of PTSD. In M. B. Williams & J. Sommer (Eds.), *Simple and complex post-traumatic stress disorder: Strategies for comprehensive treatment in clinical practice* (pp. 23–45). New York: Haworth

Van der Kolk, B. A., McFarlane, A. C., & van der Hart, O. (1996). A general approach to treatment of posttraumatic stress disorder. In B. A. van der Kolk, A. C. McFarlane, & L. Weisaeth (Eds.), *Traumatic stress* (pp. 417–440). New York: Guilford.

Van der Meere, J., Shalev, R., Burger, N., & Gross-Tsur, V. (1995). Sustained attention, activation, and MPH in ADHD. *Journal of Child Psychology and Psychiatry, 36,* 697–703.

Van der Meere, J. J. (1996). The role of attention. In S. Sandberg (Ed.), *Hyperactivity disorders of childhood* (pp. 111–148). Cambridge, England: Cambridge University Press.

Vander Wal, J. (2004). Eating and body image concerns among average-weight and obese African American and Hispanic girls. *Eating Behaviors, 5,* 181–187.

Vargas, L. A., & Koss-Chioino, J. D. (1992). *Working with culture: Psychotherapeutic interventions with ethnic minority children and adolescents.* San Francisco: Jossey-Bass.

Vaughn, B. J., Wilson, D., & Dunlap, G. (2002). Family-centered intervention to resolve problem behaviors in a fast-food restaurant. *Journal of Positive Behavior Interventions, 4,* 38–45.

Verma, S. K. (2000). Some popular misconceptions about inkblot techniques. *Journal of Projective Psychology and Mental Health, 7,* 79–81.

Vieweg, W. V., Linker, J. A., Anum, E., Turf, E., Pandurangi, A., Sood, B., et al. (2005). Child and adolescent suicides in Virginia: 1987–2003. *Journal of Child and Adolescent Psychopharmacology, 15,* 655–663.

Vila, G., Porche, L. M., & Mouren Simeoni, M. C. (1999). An 18-month longitudinal study of posttraumatic disorders in children who were taken hostage in their school. *Psychosomatic Medicine, 61,* 746–754.

Villa, R. A., & Thousand, J. (2002). Inclusion: Welcoming, valuing, and supporting the diverse learning needs of all students in shared general education environments. In W. I. Cohen & L. Nadel (Eds.), *Down syndrome: Visions for the 21st century* (pp. 339–356). New York: Wiley-Liss.

Vitiello, B., & Jensen, P. S. (1997). Medication development and testing in children and adolescents: Current problems, future directions. *Archives of General Psychiatry, 54,* 871–876.

Vitiello, B., Jensen, P. S., & Hoagwood, K. (1999). Integrating science and ethics in child and adolescent psychiatry research. *Biological Psychiatry, 46,* 1044–1049.

Vitiello, B., & Stoff, D. M. (1997). Subtypes of aggression and their relevance to child psychiatry. *Journal of the American Academy of Child and Adolescent Psychiatry, 36,* 307–315.

Volkmar, F., & Cohen, D. (1989). Disintegrative disorder in "late onset" autism. *Journal of Child Psychology and Psychiatry and Allied Disciplines, 30*, 717–724.

Volkmar, F., & Klin, A. (2000). Diagnostic issues in Asperger syndrome. In A. Klin, Volkmar, F., & Sparrow, S. (Ed.), *Asperger syndrome* (pp. 25–71). New York: Guilford Press.

Volkmar, F., & Lord, C. (1998). Diagnosis and definition of autism and other pervasive developmental disorder. In F. R. Volkmar (Ed.), *Autism and pervasive developmental disorders*. Cambridge, England: Cambridge University Press.

Volkmar, F. R. (1996). Childhood and adolescent psychosis: A review of the past 10 years. *Journal of the American Academy of Child and Adolescent Psychiatry, 35*, 843–851.

Volkmar, F. R., & Tsatsanis, K. (2002). Psychosis and psychotic conditions in childhood and adolescence. In D. T. Marsh (Ed.), *Handbook of serious emotional disturbance in children and adolescents* (pp. 266–283). New York: John Wiley & Sons.

Volkmar, R., Poll, J., & Lewis, M. (1984). Conversion reactions in childhood and adolescence. *Journal of the American Academy of Child and Adolescent Psychiatry, 23*, 424–430.

Von Gontard, A. (1998). Annotation: Day and night wetting in children: A pediatric and child psychiatric perspective. *Journal of Child Psychology and Psychiatry, 39*, 439–451.

Von Gontard, A., Eiberg, H., Hollmann, E., Rittig, S., & Lehmkuhl, G. (1999). Molecular genetics of nocturnal enuresis: Linkage to a locus on chromosome 22. *Scandinavian Journal of Urology and Nephrology, 202*, 76–80.

Wabitsch, M. (2002). Molecular and biological factors with emphasis on adipose tissue development. In W. Burniat, T. J. Cole, I. Lissau, & E. Poskitt (Eds.), *Child and adolescent obesity* (pp. 50–68). Cambridge, England: Cambridge University Press.

Wagner, W. G., & Matthews, R. (1985). The treatment of nocturnal enuresis. *Journal of Development and Behavioral Pediatrics, 6*, 22–26.

Wakefield, A., Murch, S., Anthony, A., Linnell, J., Casson, D., Malik, M., et al. (1998). Ileal–lymphoid–nodular hyperplasia, non-specific colitis, and pervasive developmental disorder in children. *Lancet, 351*, 637–641.

Waldman, I. D. (1996). Aggressive boys' hostile perceptual and response biases: The role of attention and impulsivity. *Child Development, 67*, 1015–1033.

Waldron, H. B. (1997). Adolescent substance abuse and family therapy outcome: A review of randomized trials. *Advances in Clinical Child Psychology, 19*, 199–234.

Walker, L., Garber, J., & Greene, J. (1993). Psychosocial correlates of recurrent childhood pain: A comparison of pediatric patients with recurrent abdominal pain, organic illness, and psychiatric disorders. *Journal of Abnormal Psychology, 102*, 248–258.

Walker, L. S., Garber, J., & Greene, J. W. (1991). Somatization symptoms in pediatric abdominal pain patients: Relation to chronicity of abdominal pain and parent somatization. *Journal of Abnormal Child Psychology, 19*, 379–394.

Walker, L. S., Garber, J., & Greene, J. W. (1994). Somatic complaints in pediatric patients: A prospective study of the role of negative life events, child social and academic competence, and parental somatic symptoms. *Journal of Consulting and Clinical Psychology, 62*, 1213–1221.

Walker, L. S., Garber, J., Van Slyke, D. A., & Greene, J. W. (1995). Long-term health outcomes in patients with recurrent abdominal pain. *Journal of Pediatric Psychology, 20*, 233–245.

Wallach, H. R., & Dollinger, S. J. (1999). Dissociative disorders in childhood and adolescence. In S. D. Netherton & D. Holmes (Eds.), *Child & adolescent psychological disorders: A comprehensive textbook* (pp. 344–366). New York: Oxford University Press.

Wallander, J. L., & Hubert, N. C. (1987). Peer social dysfunction in children with developmental disabilities: Empirical basis and a conceptual model. *Clinical Psychology Review, 7*, 205–221.

Walz, N. C., & Benson, B. A. (2002). Behavioral phenotypes in children with Down syndrome, Prader–Willi syndrome, or Angelman syndrome. *Journal of Developmental and Physical Disabilities, 14*, 307–321.

Wasserman, A. L., Whitington, P. F., & Rivara, F. P. (1988). Psychogenic basis for abdominal pain in children and adolescents. *Journal of the American Academy of Child and Adolescent Psychiatry, 27*, 179–184.

Wasserstein, S. B., & LaGreca, A. M. (1998). Hurricane Andrew: Parent conflict as a moderator of children's adjustment. *Hispanic Journal of Behavioral Sciences, 20,* 212–224.

Waters, F. S. (1996). Parents as partners in the treatment of dissociative children. In J. L. Silberg (Ed.), *The dissociative child: Diagnosis, treatment, and management.* Lutherville, Maryland: Sidran Press.

Waters, F. S., & Silberg, J. L. (1996). Therapeutic phases in the treatment of dissociative children. In J. L. Silberg (Ed.), *The dissociative child: Diagnosis, treatment, and management.* Lutherville, MD: Sidran Press.

Watson, J., & Rayner, P. (1920). Conditioned emotional reactions. *Journal of Experimental Psychology, 3,* 1–14.

Watson, J. B. (1924). *Behaviorism.* New York: Peoples Publishing Company.

Webster-Stratton, C., & Hammond, M. (1997). Treating children with early-onset conduct problems: A comparison of child and parent training interventions. *Journal of Consulting and Clinical Psychology, 65,* 93–109.

Webster Stratton, C., & Hammond, M. (1990). Predictors of treatment outcome in parent training for families with conduct problem children. *Behavior Therapy, 21,* 319–337.

Webster Stratton, C., & Taylor, T. (2001). Nipping early risk factors in the bud: Preventing substance abuse, delinquency, and violence in adolescence through interventions targeted at young children (0 to 8 years). *Prevention Science, 2,* 165–192.

Wechsler, D. (1974). *Manual for the Wechsler Intelligence Scale for Children—Revised.* New York: Psychological Corporation.

Weckerly, J. (2002). Pediatric bipolar mood disorder. *Journal of Developmental and Behavioral Pediatrics, 23,* 42–56.

Weems, C. F., Saltzman, K. M., Reiss, A. L., & Carrion, V. G. (2003). A prospective test of the association between hyperarousal and emotional numbing in youth with a history of traumatic stress. *Journal of Clinical Child and Adolescent Psychology, 32,* 166–171.

Weems, C. F., Silverman, W. K., & La Greca, A. M. (2000). What do youth referred for anxiety problems worry about? Worry and its relation to anxiety and anxiety disorders in children and adolescents. *Journal of Abnormal Child Psychology, 28,* 63–72.

Weinberger, D. R. (1987). Implications of normal brain development for the pathogenesis of schizophrenia. *Archives of General Psychiatry, 44,* 660–669.

Weinger, S. (1999). Views of the child with retardation: Relationship to family functioning. *Family Therapy, 26,* 63–79.

Weise, K. L., Smith, M. L., Maschke, K. J., & Copeland, H. L. (2002). National practices regarding payment to research subjects for participating in pediatric research. *Pediatrics, 110,* 577–582.

Weissman, M. M., Wolk, S., Goldstein, R. B., Moreau, D., Adams, P., Greenwald, S., et al. (1999). Depressed adolescents grown up. *Journal of the American Medical Association, 281,* 1707–1713.

Weisz, J. R., & Jensen, P. S. (1999). Efficacy and effectiveness of child and adolescent psychotherapy and pharmacotherapy. *Mental Health Services Research, 1,* 125–157.

Weisz, J. R., Thurber, C. A., Sweeney, L., Proffitt, V. D., & LeGagnoux, G. L. (1997). Brief treatment of mild-to-moderate child depression using primary and secondary control enhancement training. *Journal of Consulting and Clinical Psychology, 65,* 703–707.

Weller, E. B., Danielyan, A. K., & Weller, R. A. (2002). Somatic treatment of bipolar disorder in children and adolescents. *Child and Adolescent Psychiatric Clinics of North America, 11,* 595–618.

Weller, E. B., Weller, R. A., & Fristad, M. A. (1995). Bipolar disorder in children: Misdiagnosis, underdiagnosis, and future directions. *Journal of the American Academy of Child and Adolescent Psychiatry, 34,* 709–714.

Weller, E. B., Weller, R. A., Fristad, M. A., Rooney, M. T., & Schecter, J. (2000). Children's Interview for Psychiatric Syndromes. *Journal of the American Academy of Child and Adolescent Psychiatry, 39,* 76–84.

Werner, E., Dawson, G., Osterling, J., & Dinno, N. (2000). Brief report: Recognition of autism spectrum disorder before one year of age: A retrospective study based on home videotapes. *Journal of Autism and Developmental Disorders, 30,* 157–162.

Werry, J. S. (1992). Child and adolescent (early onset) schizophrenia: A review in light of DSM-III-R. *Journal of Autism and Developmental Disorders, 22*, 601–624.

Wertheim, E., Martin, G., Prior, M., Sanson, A., & Smart, D. (2002). Parent influences in the transmission of eating and weight-related values and behaviors. *Eating Disorders: The Journal of Treatment and Prevention, 10*, 321–334.

Westermeyer, J. F. (1993). Schizophrenia. In P. Tolan & B. Cohler (Eds.), *Handbook of clinical research and practice with adolescents* (pp. 359–386). New York: Wiley.

Westermeyer, J. F., & Dieperink, E. (2001). The cognitive socialization of stress and anxiety. In J. Schumaker & T. Ward (Eds.), *Cultural cognition and psychopathology* (pp. 67–80). Westport, CT: Praeger.

Whalen, C. K., Henker, B., & Dotemoto, S. (1980). Methylphenidate and hyperactivity: Effects on teacher behaviors. *Science, 208*, 1280–1282.

Whalen, C. K., & Kenker, B. (1985). The social worlds of hyperactive (ADHD) children. *Clinical Psychology Review, 5*, 447–478.

Whitaker, A., Johnson, J., Shaffer, D., Rapoport, J., Kalikow, K., Walsh, B., et al. (1990). Uncommon troubles in young people: Prevalence estimates of selected psychiatric disorders in a nonreferred adolescent population. *Archives of General Psychiatry, 47*, 487–496.

Whitaker, P. (2002). Supporting families of preschool children with autism. *Autism, 6*, 411–426.

Whitaker, R. C. (2004). Predicting preschooler obesity at birth: The role of maternal obesity in early pregnancy. *Pediatrics, 114*, 29–36.

White, K. S., Alday, C. S., & Spirito, A. (2001). Characteristics of children presenting to a behavioral treatment program for pediatric headache. *Journal of Clinical Psychology in Medical Settings, 8*, 109–117.

Widom, C. S. (1989). Does violence beget violence? A critical examination of the literature. *Psychological Bulletin, 106*, 3–28.

Wilkinson, R. B., & Walford, W. A. (1998). The measurement of adolescent psychological health: One or two dimensions? *Journal of Youth and Adolescence, 27*, 443–455.

Wille, S. (1994). Nocturnal enuresis: Sleep disturbance and behavioral patterns. *Acta Paediatrica, 83*, 772–774.

Williams, D. T., & Velazquez, L. (1996). The use of hypnosis in children with dissociative disorders. *Child and Adolescent Psychiatric Clinic of North America, 5*, 495–508.

Williams, K., & Wishart, J. (2003). The Son-Rise Program intervention for autism: An investigation into family experiences. *Journal of Intellectual Disability Research, 47*, 291–299.

Williams, P. G., Colder, C. R., Richards, M. H., & Scalzo, C. A. (2002). The role of self-assessed health in the relationship between gender and depressive symptoms among adolescents. *Journal of Pediatric Psychology, 27*, 509–517.

Wilson, G. T. (1989). Behavior therapy. In R. Corsini & D. Wedding (Eds.), *Current psychotherapies* (pp. 241–282). Itasca, IL: Peacock Publishing.

Wilson, S. L. (2001). Attachment disorders: Review and current status. *Journal of Psychology, 135*, 37–51.

Wimpory, D. C., Hobson, R. P., Williams, J. M. G., & Nash, S. (2000). Are infants with autism socially engaged? A study of recent retrospective parental reports. *Journal of Autism and Developmental Disorders, 30*, 525–536.

Winerman, L. (2005). Researchers are using neuroimaging techniques to delve into the neurobiological underpinnings of phobias, with a view to improving treatments. *Monitor on Psychology, 36*, 96–99.

Wing, L. (1997). The history of ideas on autism: Legends, myths, and reality. *Autism, 1*.

Wing, L., & Potter, D. (2002). The epidemiology of autistic spectrum disorders: Is prevalence rising? *Mental Retardation and Developmental Disabilities Research Reviews, 8*, 151–161.

Wiseman, C., Peltzman, B., Halmi, K., & Sunday, S. (2004). Risk factors for eating disorders: Surprising similarities between middle school boys and girls. *Eating Disorders: The Journal of Treatment and Prevention, 12*, 315–320.

Wittchen, H. U., Reed, V., & Kessler, R. C. (1998). The relationship of agoraphobia and panic in a community sample of adolescents and young adults. *Archives of General Psychiatry, 55*, 1017–1024.

Wolff, P. H. (1987). *The development of behavioral states and the expression of emotions in early infancy: New proposals for investigation*. Chicago, IL: University of Chicago Press.

Wolfish, N. M., Pivik, R., & Busby, K. A. (1997). Elevated sleep arousal thresholds in enuretic boys: Clinical implications. *Acta Paediatrica, 86,* 381–384.

Wolpe, J. (1958). *Psychotherapy by reciprocal inhibition.* Standford, CA: Stanford University Press.

Wolraich, M. L. (1999). Attention deficit hyperactivity disorder: The most studied and yet most controversial diagnosis. *Mental Retardation and Developmental Disabilities Research Reviews, 5,* 163–168.

Wood, J. M., Lilienfeld, S. O., Garb, H. N., & Nezworski, M. T. (2000). The Rorschach test in clinical diagnosis. *Journal of Clinical Psychology, 56,* 395–430.

Woodward, L., & Fergusson, D. (2001). Life course outcomes of young people with anxiety disorders in adolescence. *Journal of the American Academy of Child and Adolescent Psychiatry, 40,* 1086–1093.

Woodward, L., Fergusson, D., & Horwood, L. (2000). Driving outcomes of young people with attentional difficulties in adolescence. *Journal of the American Academy of Child and Adolescent Psychiatry, 39,* 627–634.

World Health Organization (WHO). (1992). *International classification of diseases* (10th ed.). Geneva, Switzerland: World Health Organization.

Wozniak, J., & Biederman, J. (1996). A pharmacological approach to the quagmire of comorbidity in juvenile mania. *Journal of the American Academy of Child and Adolescent Psychiatry, 35,* 826–828.

Wozniak, J., Biederman, J., Kiely, K., Ablon, J. S., Faraone, S. V., Mundy, E., et al. (1995). Mania-like symptoms suggestive of childhood-onset bipolar disorder in clinically referred children. *Journal of the American Academy of Child and Adolescent Psychiatry, 34,* 867–876.

Wozniak, J., Biederman, J., Monuteaux, M. C., Richards, J., & Faraone, S. V. (2002). Parsing the comorbidity between bipolar disorder and anxiety disorders: A familial risk analysis. *Journal of Child and Adolescent Psychopharmacology, 12,* 101–111.

Wu, P., Hoven, C., Liu, X., Cohen, P., Fuller, C., & Shaffer, D. (2004). Substance use, suicidal ideation, and attempts in children and adolescents. *Suicide and Life-Threatening Behavior, 34,* 408–420.

Yanagida, E. H. (1998). Ethical dilemmas in the clinical practice of child psychology. In R. M. Anderson & T. L. Needels (Eds.), *Avoiding ethical misconduct in psychology specialty areas* (pp. 47–77). Springfield: Charles C. Thomas.

Yates, T. M., Egeland, B., & Sroufe, A. (2003). Rethinking resilience: A developmental process perspective. In S. S. Luthar (Ed.), *Resilience and vulnerability: Adaption in the context of childhood adversities* (pp. 243–266). Cambridge, England: Cambridge University Press.

Young, L., Robaey, P., Karayanidis, F., Bourassa, M., Pelletier, G., & Geoffroy, G. (2000). ERPs and behavioral inhibition in a go/no-go task in child with attention-deficit hyperactivity disorder. *Brain and Cognition, 43,* 215–220.

Yule, W. (2001). Posttraumatic stress disorder in the general population and in children. *Journal of Clinical Psychiatry, 62,* 23–28.

Yule, W., Bolton, D., Udwin, O., Boyle, S., O'Ryan, D., & Nurrish, J. (2000). The long-term psychological effects of a disaster experienced in adolescence: I: The incidence and course of PTSD. *Journal of Child Psychology and Psychiatry and Allied Disciplines, 41,* 503–511.

Zahn-Waxler, C. (1993). Warriors and worriers: Gender and psychopathology. *Development and Psychopathology, 5,* 79–89.

Zeanah, C. H., Jr., & Boris, N. W. (2000). Disturbances and disorders of attachment in early childhood. In C. H. Zeanah (Ed.), *Handbook of infant mental health* (2nd ed., pp. 353–368). New York: Guilford.

Zhang, L., Xing, G., Levine, S., Post, R., & Smith, M. (1997). Maternal deprivation induces neuronal death. *Society for Neuroscience Abstracts, 23,* 1113.

Ziegler, D. J. (2002). Freud, Rogers, and Ellis: A comparative theoretical analysis. *Journal of Rational–Emotive & Cognitive–Behavior Therapy, 20,* 75–91.

Zigler, E. (1967). Familial mental retardation: A continuing dilemma. *Science, 155,* 292–298.

Zigler, E. (1999). The individual with mental retardation as a whole person. In E. Zigler & D. Bennett-Gates (Eds.), *Personality development in individuals with mental retardation* (pp. 1–16). Cambridge, England: Cambridge University Press.

Zigler, E., Balla, D., & Watson, N. (1972). Development and experiential determinants of self-image disparity in institutionalized and noninstitutionalized retarded and normal children. *Journal of Personality and Social Psychology, 23,* 81–87.

Zito, J., Safer, D., dosReis, S., Gardener, J., Boles, M., & Lynch, F. (2000). Trends in the prescribing of psychotropic medication to preschoolers. *Journal of the American Medical Association, 283,* 1024–1030.

Zoccolillo, M., Tremblay, R., & Vitaro, F. (1996). DSM-III-R and DSM-III criteria for conduct disorder in preadolescent girls: Specific but insensitive. *Journal of the American Academy of Child and Adolescent Psychiatry, 35,* 461–470.

Zoellner, L., Foa, E., & Fitzgibbons, L. (2002). Cognitive–behavioral treatment of PTSD. In M. B. Williams & J. Sommer (Eds.), *Simple and complex post-traumatic stress disorder: Strategies for comprehensive treatment in clinical practice* (pp. 75–97). New York: Haworth Press.

Zola-Morgan, S. M., & Squire, L. R. (1990). The primate hippocampal formation: Evidence for a time-limited role in memory storage. *Science, 250,* 288–290.

Zwaigenbaum, L., Szatmari, P., Mahoney, W., Bryson, S., Bartolucci, G., & MacLean, J. (2000). High-functioning autism and childhood disintegrative disorder in half brothers. *Journal of Autism and Developmental Disorders, 30,* 121–126.

Name Index

Abela, J. R. Z., 325, 327
Abikoff, H. B., 248, 250, 251, 253
Abramson, L., 327, 328
Achenbach, T. M., 13, 143, 175, 687
Adan, A. M., 388, 389
Adelman, H. S., 50
Adler, A., 571
Adrien, J. L., 477
Advisory Board on Child Abuse and Neglect, 576
Aguilar, B., 174, 181, 183, 189, 194, 205
Ahrens, A. H., 328, 330
Ainsworth, M. D. S., 88
Akin Little, A., 164
Akiskal, H. S., 262, 300
Alaghband Rad, J., 524, 527, 535
Albano, A. M., 344, 345, 351, 354, 355, 357, 360, 361, 363, 365, 366, 368, 370, 372, 375, 381
Albertini, R., 621, 632
Albus, K. E., 527
Alday, C. S., 627
Alessandri, M., 448
Alexander, D., 422, 429, 436, 439, 440, 658
Alkin, M. C., 423
Allbeck, P., 531
Allen, K. D., 631
Allen, N., 324
Allgood-Merten, B., 313
Alloy, L. B., 331
Allwood, M. A., 559
Alter, M., 443
Alvarez, H. K., 169, 170
Alverez, J., 628
Aman, M. G., 503
American Academy of Child and Adolescent Psychiatry, 244, 246, 247, 257, 266, 278, 284, 285, 286, 419, 444, 445, 508, 538, 539, 556, 557, 561, 572, 573, 574
American Academy of Pediatrics Committee on Nutrition, 639, 640, 641, 642, 647, 648
American Association on Mental Retardation, 412, 413, 450

American Psychiatric Association (APA), 7, 43, 49, 55, 122, 124, 129, 130, 131, 133, 157, 160, 211, 212, 258, 262, 265, 272, 275, 295, 304, 305, 307, 350, 352, 354, 356, 357, 358, 360, 361, 362, 363, 366, 367, 369, 370, 371, 372, 416, 420, 458, 470, 471, 478, 493, 496, 513, 514, 517, 519, 520, 521, 545, 547, 550, 555, 556, 575, 578, 580, 581, 582, 583, 585, 587, 605, 617, 618, 620, 621, 657, 670, 674, 687
Ames, E. W., 610
Ammerman, S., 651, 653
Anderson, J., 163
Anderson, R. N., 30
Andreasson, S., 531
Andrulonis, P., 624
Andujo, E., 30
Angold, A., 1, 129, 130, 162, 178, 225, 226, 298, 306, 307, 313, 354, 357, 369, 544, 626
Anguilo, M. J., 577
Applegate, B., 227
Appleyard, K., 164
Apter, A., 318, 319
Apter, M. J., 378
Arbelaez, C., 309
Arend, R. A., 90
Arlow, J., 66, 69
Armenteros, J. L., 540
Armitage, R., 2, 299, 661
Arndt, E., 631
Arndt, S., 478
Arnold, L. E., 50
Arnstein, L., 503
Aro, H., 628
Asarnow, R. F., 516, 520, 524, 528, 535, 536
Asperger, H., 457, 458
Attie, I., 653, 655, 657, 660, 663
Au, T., 503
August, G. J., 223
Austin, G., 235
Auth, J., 299

Authier, K., 446
Avenevoli, S., 271
Axelson, D. A., 298, 299, 338, 361, 368

Babinsky, R., 566
Baer, L., 584
Baglio, C., 501
Bailey, A., 489
Bailey, D., 429
Bailey, J. S., 445, 446, 447
Baiord, P. A., 427
Baker, L., 288
Balentine, A. C., 123, 215
Balla, D., 417
Banaschewski, T., 134, 172, 216, 217
Barkley, R., 123, 215, 220, 224, 225, 227, 228, 231, 233, 234, 239, 240, 246, 247, 248
Barkley, R. A., 144, 215, 230, 246
Barlow, D. H., 344
Baroff, G. S., 396, 413, 416, 426, 433, 435, 436, 448
Baron-Cohen, S., 482, 483, 486
Barratt, M. S., 422
Barrett, K., 90
Barrett, P., 384, 392
Bartels, C. L., 298
Bass, D., 202
Bates, J. E., 158, 171, 187, 191
Bauer, B., 649
Baum, A. S., 557, 568
Bauman, M. L., 487
Baumeister, R. F., 171
Baumgaertel, A., 227
Bauminger, N., 417, 465
Bayley, N., 406
Baylis, F., 51
Beardslee, W. R., 335
Bearman, S., 655
Beasley, P., 621, 631, 633
Bebbington, P., 532
Beck, A., 81, 82, 84, 85, 383, 384
Beck, A. T., 326
Beck, M., 423
Beck, S. J., 143
Becker-Blease, K. A., 591
Beh, H. G., 60, 61
Beidel, D. C., 391

Beirne-Smith, M., 248, 249, 409, 418, 441, 442, 444
Bell, P. L., 48, 51
Bell-Dolan, D., 368, 384, 559
Belser, R. C., 419, 429
Belsky, J., 183
Benavidez, D. A., 501
Bennet-Osborne, R., 629
Bennett, S., 247
Bennetto, L., 402, 427, 428, 429
Benoit, D., 598
Benson, B. A., 428, 432
Bentler, P. M., 54
Berendt, I., 677
Berger, P., 362
Berkey, C., 645
Berkowitz, R., 642
Berliner, L., 85
Bernstein, G., 391
Bertelsen, A., 281
Bertrand, J., 460, 475, 477
Bespalova, I. N., 490
Betz, N. E., 658
Bhangoo, R. K., 273
Biederman, J., 172, 226, 238, 258, 270, 271, 274, 276, 338, 376
Biglan, A., 202
Biklen, D., 503
Binet, A., 401, 405
Birmaher, B., 298, 299, 304, 305, 309, 334, 338, 361, 368, 393
Birnbrauer, J., 500
Bischoff, L., 424
Bjornstad, P. G., 430
Blair, C., 440
Blanz, B., 525
Blechman, E. A., 201
Blehar, M. C., 88
Bleuler, E., 512
Bloomquist, M. L., 223
Blowers, L., 654
Blum, N. J., 689
Boden, J. M., 171
Boldizar, J., 220
Bolduc, E., 376
Bolhofner, K., 276, 279, 280
Bolk, -Bennink, L., 673
Bolton, D., 559
Bolton, P., 426, 489
Bonett, D., 531
Bonner, M., 632
Borcherding, S. H., 236
Borduin, C. M., 203, 204
Boris, N. W., 600, 604

Borski, P. A., 688
Borst, S. R., 318
Borthwick Duffy, S. A., 446
Bosch, J., 673
Bouchard, T., 105, 110
Bowen, P., 317
Bowlby, J., 87, 293, 324, 597, 599, 607, 614
Bowman, E. S., 578
Bowring, M. A., 266, 267, 271
Boyce, W., 645
Boyer, B. A., 421, 558, 560, 562, 574
Boyle, C., 420
Boyle, M. H., 168
Boyle, S., 559
Braafladt, N., 325
Braaten, E. B., 302
Bracewell, M., 112
Braet, C., 641, 649
Brask, B. H., 278
Brassard, M. R., 552
Bravaccio, C., 469
Brazeal, T. J., 368
Bredenkamp, D., 606
Breggin, P. R., 244, 245, 247
Bremner, J. D., 563, 564, 565, 566, 567, 568
Brent, D., 309, 317
Brent, D. A., 320
Brewin, C. R., 569
Bristol, M., 498
Britner, P., 602
Brody, N., 401, 406
Brondino, M. J., 203
Bronfenbrenner, U., 6, 137
Brook, J., 299
Brook, J. S., 189
Brook, R. H., 673
Brooks, R. C., 685, 688, 690, 691
Brooks-Gunn, J., 299, 313, 321, 653, 655, 657, 660, 663
Brown, L. K., 318, 319
Brown, R. T., 305
Brown, W., 446, 516
Brozek, J., 661
Brozina, K., 325
Bruch, M. A., 362
Bryant, R., 571
Bryant, R. A., 550
Bryden, K. E., 539, 540, 541
Bryson, S. E., 472, 484, 485
Buhrmester, D., 314
Bunk, D., 458, 513, 523, 524, 525
Burbridge, J., 545

Burger, N., 221
Burgess, K. B., 181
Burke, G., 624
Burke, J. D., 158, 163, 165, 166, 178
Burke, V., 644, 645
Burns, J. B., 246
Burt, S. A., 186, 196
Busby, K. A., 672
Buss, A. H., 362
Butler, R., 669, 673, 675, 678, 681
Butor, P. M., 641, 642
Buxbaum, J. D., 490

Cadenhead, C., 329
Cahill, L., 566
Caldji, C., 282, 324
Calzada, E., 246
Camarena, P. M., 310, 329, 333
Camargo, C. A., 658
Campbell, D. T., 37
Campbell, M., 540
Campbell, S. B., 162, 179, 182, 183, 184, 191, 194, 232, 233
Campo, J. V., 123, 616, 617, 618, 620, 622, 623, 625, 626, 628, 631, 632, 633
Campo Bowen, A., 177
Campos, J. J., 90
Canfield, R. L., 434
Cantwell, D. P., 227, 268, 288
Caplan, R., 519, 520
Capps, L., 466
Carlat, D. J., 658
Carlson, C. L., 2, 215, 220, 223, 227, 228
Carlson, E., 174, 224, 246
Carlson, E. A., 240
Carlson, G. A., 266, 267
Carlson, N. R., 281, 321, 329, 378, 527, 564
Carper, R. A., 487
Carr, E. G., 446, 470, 471, 485
Carrey, N. J., 539
Carrion, V. G., 556
Carroll, J. B., 402
Carroll Wilson, M., 326
Carter, A. S., 218
Carter, J. C., 664
Carter, M. C., 610
Casas, J., 164
Casey, B., 234
Casper, B., 658
Caspi, A., 104, 152, 163, 169, 180, 181, 183, 184, 186, 196, 197

Cassidy, J., 91, 340
Cassidy, S. B., 432
Castellanos, F. X., 239, 244
Cataldo, M. F., 632
Cattarin, J. A., 652
Cavell, T. A., 171
Centers for Disease Control and Prevention, 433
Cerel, J., 320
Chadwick, O., 223
Chait, S., 469
Champagen, F., 282, 324
Chapman, R. S., 427
Charney, D. S., 272, 288
Chen, K., 569
Chisholm, K., 606, 610, 611
Chorpita, B. F., 143, 344, 381
Christ, M. A., 157
Christian, R., 170, 171
Chu, M. P., 258
Churchill, L. R., 49, 53
Churrie, R., 579
Cicchetti, D., 12, 15, 308, 309, 320, 324, 325, 329, 332, 588, 611
Clark, L. A., 377
Clark, W. R., 104, 109, 118
Clarke, G. N., 325
Cleckley, H., 575
Cleghorn, G., 633
Coatsworth, J. D., 16
Cobham, V. E., 393
Cohen, C., 223
Cohen, D., 477
Cohen, I. L., 429
Cohen, J., 136
Cohen, J. A., 85, 572
Cohen, J. E., 218
Cohen, P., 299
Coie, J. D., 11, 160, 161, 163, 171, 176, 177, 193, 194, 223
Colder, C. R., 314
Colditz, G., 645
Cole, D. A., 302, 310
Cole, J., 220
Cole, T. J., 637
Coleman, M., 471
Colin, V. L., 88
Collins, O. P., 318
Collins, T. M., 362
Collishaw, S., 178
Colman, A., 275, 470, 564, 651
Comer, D. M., 626
Compas, B., 299
Compton, L. S., 501

Compton, S. N., 246
Conger, R. D., 190, 314
Conners, C. K., 175
Connolly, J., 298
Connor, D. F., 206, 218, 246, 247, 503
Connor, T., 116
Cook, C. A., 552
Cook, D. A., 162, 199
Cook, E. H., 239
Cooperative Group MTA, 244, 252
Copeland, H. L., 50
Coppenole, H. V., 656
Corley, R., 354
Cormier, J. F., 653
Costello, E., 1, 162, 178, 225, 298, 306, 307, 313, 544, 626
Cotton, S., 423
Courchesne, E., 487
Coward, W., 644
Cox, A. D., 628
Craig, T. K. J., 628
Craig, W. M., 163
Craney, J. L., 276, 279, 280
Crawford, M. H., 238
Crawford, P. B., 645
Crick, N., 164
Crick, N. R., 169, 191, 193
Croen, L. A., 475
Cronk, N. J., 186
Crossley, R., 503
Cunningham, C., 231, 246
Curry, J. F., 335, 339

Dadds, M. R., 199, 200, 383, 384, 387, 393
Dales, L., 490
Dalgleish, T., 569
Danckaerts, M., 223
Danforth, J. S., 144, 230, 242, 248
Daniel, D. G., 148
Danielyan, A. K., 271
Danko, C., 501
Dare, C., 666
Darwin, C., 103
Dass, S., 539, 540
Davey, G. C., 383
David, A., 531
David-Lando, G., 519
Davis, A., 658
Davis, B., 324
Davis, L., 558
Davis, P., 624
Dawe, S., 654

Dawson, G., 148, 457, 467, 468, 477, 501
Day, N., 320
Day, R., 320
Deater Deckard, K., 190, 191, 194
De Bellis, M. D., 555, 557, 558, 561, 566, 567, 568, 572
Deblinger, E., 573
Decaluwe, V., 641, 649
De Castro, J. M., 662
Decoufle, P., 420, 421
DeFries, J. C., 9, 102, 238, 402
De Haan, L., 422
Dehlholm, B., 278
Deitrich, M., 227
Dekker, M. C., 419
DeLisi, L., 525, 533, 534
Dell, P. F., 591, 596
Delligatti, N., 164, 178
Delporto Bedoya, D., 338
De Mar Mellero-Montes, M., 476
DeMaso, D., 621, 631, 633
Demeter, C., 338
Demetriades, L., 432
Dennis, A. B., 664
Devitt, H., 672, 673
Devlin, B., 298, 338, 377
Devlin, J. B., 682
Dewey, D., 480, 504
Dhossche, D., 620
Dick, D., 112
Dickson, N., 180
Diener, M. B., 223
Dieperink, E., 344, 351, 352
Dihle, P. H., 587
DiLalla, L. F., 109, 111, 117
DiLella, A., 118, 429
Dimitropoulos, A., 9, 432
Dinno, N., 477
Dippe, A., 525
Dishion, T. J., 143
Dision, T. J., 187
Dix, D., 410
Dixon, J. F., 328, 330
Djurhuus, J. C., 668, 675
Dodd, B., 428
Dodge, J., 628
Dodge, K. A., 11, 158, 160, 161, 163, 169, 170, 171, 176, 177, 187, 191, 193, 194, 223
Doggett, R. A., 612
Dollinger, S. J., 580, 588, 595
Dong, Q., 361
Donovan, C. L., 335, 387, 389

Dorahy, M. J., 587
Dotemoto, S., 246
Douglas, V., 211
Downie, J., 51
Downs, J., 262
Doyle, A., 223
Doyle, A. E., 162
Dozier, M., 612
Drew, C. J., 418, 438
Drews, C. D., 421
Dubey, D., 248
DuBois, D. L., 298, 307, 334
Dulcan, M. K., 140
Dulmus, C. N., 541
Dumas, J. E., 201
Dumas, M., 223, 241
Dumitrescu, A., 604
Dunlap, G., 524
Dunn, V. J., 664
Dunne, M. P., 112
DuPaul, G. J., 144, 215, 230, 241, 242, 246, 253
DuRant, R. H., 329
Duvdevani, I., 421
Dyer, C. A., 429, 430
Dykens, E. M., 432

Earls, F., 559
Eaves, L., 117
Eaves, L. J., 186
Ebeling, H., 664, 665
Eckert, J., 658
Eckert, T. L., 144
Eddy, J. M., 202
Edelbrock, C. S., 143, 687
Edens, J. F., 171
Edwards, M., 632
Egan, E., 391
Egeland, B., 16, 174
Egger, H., 1, 129, 130, 178, 226, 306, 354, 357, 369, 626
Eggers, C., 458, 513, 523, 524, 525
Ehlers, S., 463, 494
Ehrenreich, N. S., 49, 50, 52, 57, 58
Ehringer, M., 354, 369
Eiberg, H., 677
Eich, E., 587
Einfeld, S., 428
Eisenberg, L., 457, 466
Eisenhower, J. W., 591, 596
Eisler, I., 666
Elder, G. H., 190, 314
Eley, T., 375
Ellis, A., 82, 83, 84, 85

Ellis, M., 151, 157, 171, 177
Elmore, D. K., 662
Elzinga, B. M., 565, 566, 567
Emans, S., 329
Emerson, S., 656
Emery, G., 326
Emery, R., 110, 612
Emery, R. E., 528
Emslie, G. J., 257, 300, 338
Endicott, J., 136
Epstein, L., 650
Erba, H. W., 498
Erkanli, A., 225, 313, 544, 626
Erlenmeyer-Kimling, L., 526, 537, 538
Ernst, A., 628
Espelage, D., 171
Essau, C. A., 4, 172, 178
Ettelson, R., 350, 377, 378
Evans, D. L., 267, 278, 283, 284, 293, 307, 313, 316, 321, 322, 338
Evans, D. W., 416
Everall, R. D., 49, 51

Fabiano, G. A., 246, 250, 253
Fagan, J., 156
Fahey, T. A., 578, 583, 584
Fairbank, J. A., 544
Fairburn, C. G., 664, 665
Faith, M., 650
Falco, C., 469
Famularo, R., 561
Faraone, S. V., 172, 226, 238, 258, 270, 276, 338
Farmer, E. M. Z., 246
Farrington, D. P., 115, 189, 194
Farthing, M. J., 628
Fay, R., 424
Feehan, M., 163
Feeny, N. C., 338
Feingold, B. F., 240
Feiring, C., 569
Felner, R. D., 298, 388, 389
Fendrich, M., 329
Fenton, T., 561
Ferdinand, R., 620
Fergusson, D., 344
Fergusson, D. M., 180, 220, 319, 329, 675, 678
Fichter, M. M., 661
Fico, C., 469
Field, A. P., 383
Filmer, R. B., 688
Findling, R., 246

Findling, R. L., 262, 271, 279, 280, 281, 338, 525, 539
Fink, D. L., 584
Finkelhor, D., 578
Finkelstein, R., 354
Finney, J., 632
Finney, J. W., 632, 633
Firestone, P., 247, 249
Fischer, M., 228
Fischer, W., 317
Fish, B., 519
Fisher, M., 443
Fisher, P., 140, 317
Fishman, H., 94, 96
Fitzgibbons, L., 572
Flannery Schroeder, E. C., 392
Flegal, K., 637, 638
Fleiss, J. L., 136
Fletcher, K., 228
Fletcher, K. E., 548, 555, 557, 561
Flory, M., 317
Foa, E. B., 345, 351, 387, 393, 568, 569, 571, 572, 573
Foley, D. L., 178
Fombonne, E., 475, 476
Fontaine, R. G., 170, 193
Foreman, D., 687
Forgatch, M. S., 174
Forrest, D., 598
Forrest, K. A., 592
Forsythe, W. I., 675
Fournier, C. J., 49, 50, 52, 55, 57, 58
Foxman, B., 673, 674, 683
Frame, C. L., 170
Francis, A., 423
Francis, D., 282, 324
Francis, S., 143
Frank, R. G., 361
Fraser, G., 582, 592
Fraser, J. A., 199, 200
Frazier, J. A., 527, 528
Freedman, D. S., 640
Freedman, R. I., 421
Freeman, S. F. N., 423
Freeman, W., 230
Freud, S., 65–70, 343, 349
Frick, P. J., 151, 157, 163, 170, 171, 176, 177, 178, 181, 183, 184
Friedman, A., 318
Friedman, L., 525
Friedman, M. J., 572
Fristad, M. A., 140, 262, 286
Frith, U., 482

Fritsch, S. L., 617, 620, 625, 628, 632
Fritz, G. K., 318, 625, 627, 631
Fulker, D., 190
Funk, J., 424

Gabreels, F. J., 420, 621
Galpert, L., 501
Galton, F., 103
Gannert, A., 75
Garb, H. N., 147
Garber, J., 123, 262, 301, 307, 325, 616, 617, 618, 622, 623, 624, 625, 626, 627, 628, 629, 631
Garfinkel, R., 339
Garland, A. F., 318
Garmezy, N., 15, 16
Garralda, M. E., 620, 623, 627, 628, 631, 632, 633, 634
Garrick, T., 627
Gatsonis, C., 10, 172, 300
Gaub, M., 2, 227, 228
Gavazzi, S. M., 286
Gavidia-Payne, S., 423
Ge, X., 190, 310, 313, 314, 329, 333
Geller, B., 257, 267, 270, 272, 275, 276, 279, 280, 284, 286
Geller, D. A., 394
Geller, J., 230
Gelles, R., 578
Gerbino-Rosen, G., 540
Getts, A., 329
Giaconia, R. M., 317, 557, 558
Gibbons, J., 376
Giedd, J. N., 527
Gilger, J. W., 238
Gill, A. C., 558, 559
Gill, M. J., 448
Gillberg, C., 463, 471, 472, 475, 478, 494, 501
Gilles, J., 503
Gillham, J. E., 335
Gilliom, M., 162
Gillis, J. J., 238
Gillman, M., 645
Gilroy, M., 664
Gingerich, K. J., 228
Ginsburg, G. S., 391, 393
Girgus, J. S., 313, 314, 332
Gladstone, T. R. G., 298, 327, 335
Glantz, L. H., 48, 50
Glaser, K., 293
Gleaves, D. H., 581, 584
Glick, M., 417, 426

Glisky, M. L., 577
Gnagy, E., 247
Goenjian, A. K., 557
Goff, D. C., 584
Goldberg, J., 658
Goldberg Arnold, J. S., 286
Goldman, S., 645
Goldsmith, H. H., 90, 186, 376
Goldston, D., 306
Golinkoff, M., 584
Goodman, G., 110, 612
Goodman, R., 178
Goodman, S. H., 301
Goodness, K., 314
Goodyer, I., 625
Gordon, R. A., 189
Gosch, A., 430, 431
Gosch, E., 390
Gotlib, I. H., 331
Gottesman, I. I., 108, 508, 512, 526, 529, 530, 538
Gottlieb, B. W., 443
Gottlieb, J., 443
Gould, M., 316, 317, 318, 319
Gould, M. S., 317
Graber, J., 660
Graden, J., 387
Grady-Flesser, M., 654
Grandin, T., 454, 506
Granic, I., 143
Grant, K., 628
Gray, J. A., 236, 381
Gray, M., 571
Green, G., 500
Green, S., 152
Green, S. M., 166
Greenberg, T., 316, 317, 318
Greene, J. W., 624, 627, 628, 629
Greene, R. W., 162
Grether, J. K., 475
Grimm, J., 162
Grinker, R., 547
Groen, A. D., 500
Gross, R. T., 655
Gross-Tsur, V., 221
Grunstein, M., 104, 109, 118
Guess, D., 471, 485
Guevremont, D., 223, 241
Guillaume, M., 638
Gupta, N., 496
Guralnick, M. J., 440
Gurley, D., 299
Guthrie, D., 519, 520
Gutter, S., 240, 421

Hagberg, B., 492, 493, 494
Hagen, R. L., 40
Hagino, O., 625
Haigh, E. P., 325
Halamandaris, P. V., 552
Hall, G. S., 156
Hall, S., 432
Halmi, K. A., 655, 658
Halperin, J. M., 216
Hamburger, S. D., 527
Hammen, C., 262, 272, 280, 301, 307, 308, 322, 325, 329, 330, 602
Hammer, S., 490
Hammond, M., 200, 201, 202
Hankin, C. S., 229
Hanna, C., 567
Hanninen, V., 628
Hanson, R. S., 598, 601, 602, 603, 613
Happe, F., 482
Hardman, M., 418
Harle, J. M., 541
Harold, G. T., 109, 323
Harper, I., 639, 645
Harper, J., 478
Harrington, H., 180
Harris, S. L., 448, 449
Hart, E. L., 172
Hartmann, M., 525
Harvald, B., 281
Harvey, A. G., 550
Hatcher, J. W., 629
Hatton, D., 429
Haugaard, J. J., 110, 128, 314, 378, 569, 594, 598, 604, 608, 612, 658, 659
Hauge, M., 281
Hawley, D. R., 422
Hay, D., 17, 170, 186
Hayden, H., 653
Hayes, A. M., 81, 84
Hayward, C., 373
Hazan, C., 598, 604, 608
Healy Farrell, L., 392
Hearst Ikeda, D., 571
Heath, P. A., 310, 329, 333
Heatherton, T. F., 662
Hebebrand, J., 644
Hechtman, L., 228, 238
Heflin, A. H., 573
Heim, C., 324
Heiman, T., 418, 422, 423, 449
Heimberg, R. G., 362
Heller, T., 495

Helms, J. E., 162, 199
Henggeler, S. W., 203
Henkel, R., 171
Henkelman, J. J., 49, 51
Henker, B., 246
Henschel, A., 661
Heptinstall, E., 223
Herman, C. P., 660, 661, 662
Hersen, M., 354
Herzog, D. B., 658
Hesketh, L. J., 427
Heston, L., 529
Hetherington, E. M., 323
Hetherington, M., 102
Hetta, J., 672
Hewitt, J., 354
Hibbs, E. D., 57
Hightower, A., 387
Hill, J., 151, 152, 174, 177
Hill, N., 170, 171
Hinney, A., 644
Hinshaw, S. P., 156, 157, 162, 171, 172, 178, 185, 248, 250, 253
Hirasing, R., 673
Hirsch, J., 635
Hirshfeld, D., 376
Hirshfeld Becker, D. R., 358, 360, 361
Hoagwood, K., 55
Hobson, R., 469
Hobson, R. P., 467, 481, 482
Hodgens, J. B., 220, 223
Hoebeke, P., 667
Hoffman, H., 211
Hollis, C., 524, 535
Hollmann, E., 677
Holmbeck, G. N., 329
Holmes, O. W., 410
Holt, M., 171
Honda, H., 491
Hoogstrate, J., 475
Hoover, D., 249
Hops, H., 313
Horne, L. R., 656
Hornstein, N. L., 582, 583, 589
Hornstein, R. T., 585, 588, 595
Horwood, L., 220
Horwood, L. T., 675
Howe, S., 410
Hoza, B., 247
Hubert, N. C., 417, 418
Hughes, J. N., 171
Humphries, T., 231, 246
Huon, G. F., 654, 660
Husain, S. A., 559

Husmann, D., 669, 675, 676, 677, 678, 680, 681, 682, 683
Huttunen, M., 531
Huttunen, N., 678
Hyams, J., 624, 626

Iacono, W. G., 186, 238
Inge, T., 650, 651
Ingram, M., 344
Ippen, C. G., 553
Issenman, R., 688
Ittenbach, R., 248, 409

Jackson, D., 92
Jacobsen, L. K., 526, 529
Jacobson, K. C., 104, 109, 110, 114, 115, 116, 117, 118, 323, 375
Jaffee, S., 183, 323
James, A. C. D., 276, 283, 285
Jamison, K. R., 274
Janicke, D. M., 633
Jansen, E., 164
Jansen McWilliams, L., 626
Janssen, I., 645
Jarbin, H., 525
Jarvelin, M., 678
Javaloyes, A. M., 276, 283, 285
Jaycox, L. H., 335, 559, 560
Jenike, M. A., 584
Jenkins, S. R., 314
Jensen, A. T., 104
Jensen, P. S., 53, 54, 55, 227, 228, 301, 539
Jick, H., 476
Joha, D., 470, 604
Johnson, B., 230
Johnston, C., 229, 230
Jolley, J., 27, 29
Jones, M., 490
Jones, N., 504
Jones, R. R., 145
Jordan, K. Y., 158, 171
Jordan, P., 262
Jorgensen, T. M., 682
Joseph, S., 569
Joshi, S., 579
Jung, J. H., 269
Jung, K., 559
Jurich, A. P., 318

Kafkalas, C. M., 558
Kagan, J., 88, 376, 377, 384
Kager, V., 631
Kahn, M., 69, 70, 71

Kales, E. F., 660
Kaminski, K. M., 301
Kaminsky, L., 480, 504
Kamphaus, R. W., 402, 404, 405, 406, 408, 409, 413
Kandel, D. B., 653
Kanner, L., 457, 466, 482
Kaplan, N., 91, 340
Kaprio, J., 112
Kardiner, A., 547
Kasari, C., 417, 465
Kaser-Boyd, N., 50
Kashani, J. H., 369
Kaslow, N. J., 298, 305, 320, 326, 327
Kataoka, S. H., 571
Kato, C., 668
Katz, H. P., 632
Katzmarzyk, P., 645
Kaufman, A., 405
Kaufman, A. S., 407
Kaufman, J., 288, 294, 299, 300, 324
Kaufman, K., 248
Kaufman, N. L., 407
Kawauchi, A., 672
Kaye, J., 476, 490
Kazdin, A. E., 200, 201, 202, 203, 354
Keenan, K., 152, 163, 178, 194
Keinan, K., 238
Keith-Spiegel, P. C., 43, 49, 53, 54, 55, 58, 59
Kelleher, K. J., 626
Keller, A., 527
Kemper, T. L., 487
Kendall, J., 545, 555, 564, 567
Kendall, P. C., 85, 99, 338, 340, 390, 391, 392
Kendler, K., 117, 322
Kenker, B., 223
Kennedy, J., 239
Kennedy, J. F., 410
Kennedy, R. L., 211
Kenny, J., 525
Kenny, N., 51
Kenny, T., 631
Kerr, M., 501
Kerrin, R. G., 504
Keshavan, M. S., 566, 567
Kessler, R. C., 271, 279, 281, 307, 361, 373
Keyes, A., 661, 662
Kihlstrom, J. F., 577
Kilanowski, C., 650
Kim, J. A., 472
Kim, S., 42, 634, 638, 639, 645
King, M., 645

King, N. J., 384, 574
King, N. M. P., 49, 53, 573
King, R. A., 288
Kinsborne, M., 231
Kinscherff, A., 561
Kipp, H., 247
Kirch, D. G., 527, 530
Kirkorian, G., 235
Kirmayer, L. J., 123, 616, 623
Klein, D. N., 276
Klein, K., 628
Klein, R. G., 206, 228, 248, 250, 251, 253
Klein-Tasman, B. P., 430
Klin, A., 473
Klinger, L., 457, 462, 465, 468, 472, 474, 476, 478, 487, 488, 490
Kluft, R. P., 578, 590, 595
Knapp, P. K., 228
Knee, D., 238
Knolls, M. L., 558
Kobayashi, R., 478, 501
Kolvin, I., 125, 458, 513
Komo, S., 520
Koocher, G. P., 43, 49, 53, 54, 55, 58, 59
Koot, H. M., 3, 302, 308, 419
Koppe, T., 525
Korenblum, M., 298
Koss-Chioino, J. D., 42, 198, 303, 341
Kotch, J. B., 57, 58
Kovacs, M., 9, 10, 172, 266, 267, 271, 298, 300, 306, 309, 320, 338, 339, 340, 377
Koverola, C., 567
Kowatch, R. A., 284
Kozlowska, K., 622, 625
Kraepelin, E., 512
Krause, D., 523
Krener, P., 57
Krueger, R. F., 186
Kuipers, L., 532
Kumra, S., 523, 537, 538, 540, 541
Kupersmidt, J. B., 171
Kutcher, S., 298
Kutcher, S. P., 322, 539
Kuterovac Jagodic, G., 559, 560, 561

Labellarte, M. J., 391, 393
Lackgren, G., 673
Ladame, F., 317
Ladd, G. W., 181
Laederach, J., 317
Lafer, B., 268
La Greca, A. M., 360, 366, 560
Lahey, B., 212

Lahey, B. B., 157, 158, 162, 163, 165, 166, 172, 178, 187, 189, 301
LaHoste, G., 239
Laird, R. D., 158, 171, 180, 194, 195
Lalli, E. P., 445
Lalli, J. S., 445
Lamb, M. E., 90
Lamparelli, M., 169
Lamprecht, F., 547
Landa, R., 469, 474, 489
Landgraf, J. M., 674
Langworthy Lam, K. S., 503
Larkby, C. A., 320
Larson, B. S., 626
Last, C. G., 351, 354, 355, 365
Lauderdale, M. L., 30
Laurent, J., 350, 377, 378
Lay, B., 525
Layne, A., 391
Leach, D., 500
LeDoux, J., 564, 565, 567, 568
Lee, A., 469
Lee, H. K., 269
Lee, S. S., 156, 157, 162, 171, 178, 185
Lee, T. N., 550
Leech, S. L., 320, 325
Leenaars, A. A., 319
Leffert, J. S., 417
LeGagnoux, G. L., 339
Lehmkuhl, G., 677
Leibel, R. L., 635, 661
Leibenluft, E., 272
Leitenberg, H., 326
Lelon, E., 172
Lemanek, K. L., 632
Lenane, M., 514, 523, 536
Leon, S., 236
Leonard, H., 420, 421, 427
Lester, D., 319
Leverich, G. S., 280
Levine, M., 653
Levine, M. P., 653
Levine, S., 282
Levy, T. M., 598, 605
Lewin, K., 92
Lewinsohn, P. M., 276, 278, 279, 308, 313, 315, 325
Lewis, A., 52
Lewis, G., 531
Lewis, J., 104
Lewis, M., 625
Lewis, M. L., 553
Lewis, M. S., 531
Lieberman, A. F., 552, 574
Lilienfeld, S. O., 147

Lima, E. N., 165
Linares, L. O., 189, 192
Lindsay, R., 42, 638, 644
Lissau, I., 638
Litfin, J. K., 228
Little, S. G., 164
Litz, B., 571
Lock, J., 653, 657, 658, 664, 665
Loeber, R., 17, 115, 152, 157, 158, 162, 163, 165, 166, 170, 175, 176, 178, 181, 184, 186, 189, 190, 194, 196
Loehlin, J. C., 407, 409
Loening-Baucke, V., 689
Loewenstein, R. J., 587
Logan, D. R., 418
Logan, G., 236
Loney, B. R., 165
Loney, J., 229
Lopez, N., 360
Lord, C., 457, 492, 495
Losche, G., 477
Lovaas, N. W., 502
Lovaas, O. I., 54, 498, 502
Lowe, M. R., 662
Loxton, N., 654
Luborsky, L., 136
Luby, J., 172, 305
Lucas, C. P., 140
Lundervold, A. J., 462
Lykken, D. T., 105
Lynam, D., 169
Lynam, D. R., 123, 215
Lynch, D., 424
Lynskey, M. T., 319, 329
Lyons-Ruth, K., 598, 605
Lyoo, I. K., 269, 281
Lyubomirsky, S., 314

M., F. E., 245
Macaulay, D., 587
Maccoby, E. E., 109, 114, 152
MacDonald, H., 489
Mace, F. C., 445, 446
Macfie, J., 588
Machon, R., 531
MacLean, W., 446
Maedgen, J. W., 215, 220, 223
Maffeis, C., 644, 645, 649
Main, M., 91, 340
Malhotra, S., 496
Manicavasagar, V., 352, 354, 355
Mann, E. M., 219
Mann, J., 317
Mann, M., 224, 246

Mann, T., 664
Mannarino, A. P., 85
Mannuzza, S., 206, 228
Manos, M., 246
Marcell, M., 428
March, J. S., 392
Marcus, M. D., 665
Markowitsch, H., 566
Marlow, N., 112
Marriott, M., 236
Marsh, D. T., 49
Martin, A., 288
Martin, D., 227
Martin, G., 653
Marton, P., 298
Marvin, R. S., 422, 602
Maschke, K. J., 50
Mash, E. J., 229, 230
Masten, A. S., 16, 17
Matas, L., 90
Matson, J. L., 501
Matthews, R., 673
Maughan, B., 162, 178, 611
Mayes, T. L., 257
Mayo, L., 411
Mazzocco, M., 428, 429
McBurnett, K., 187, 246, 250
McCabe, M., 652, 655
McCall, R., 41
McCarthy, D., 407
McClarty, B., 567
McClearn, G. E., 9, 102, 402
McClellan, J. M., 525, 540, 541
McDonald, C., 344
McFarlane, A. C., 548
McGaugh, J. L., 566
McGee, R., 163, 361, 369
McGoey, K. E., 144
McGrath, E. P., 288
McGrath, M. L., 685, 690, 691
McGrath, P. J., 200, 201
McGue, M., 105, 186
McGue, M. K., 238
McGuffin, P., 9, 102, 402
McHugh, M., 552
McKnight Investigators, 652
McMurray, M. B., 215, 246
McNamara, N. K., 539
McNaughon, N., 381
McRoy, R. G., 30
Meaney, J., 282, 324
Meaux, J. B., 48, 51
Mednick, S. A., 531
Mee, L. L., 305
Meehl, P., 533

Meesters, C., 369
Mellon, M. W., 685
Melton, G. B., 49, 50, 52, 57, 58
Meltzer, H., 178
Mendola, P., 240, 421, 434
Mercer, J., 247
Merchelbach, H., 369
Merckelbach, H., 357, 358, 369, 374
Mercugliano, M., 239
Merikangas, K. R., 271
Mertin, P., 554, 556, 557, 558, 567
Mervis, C. B., 430
Mesibov, G. B., 502
Mesman, J., 3, 302, 308
Messer, J., 178
Meyer, J. M., 186
Meyer, L. H., 443
Mick, E., 172, 226, 258, 276, 338
Mickelsen, O., 661
Mikkelsen, E. J., 667, 669, 670, 672,
    677, 679, 680, 681, 682, 683, 684,
    685, 686, 690
Milich, R., 123, 215, 223, 249
Militerni, R., 469, 470
Miller, G. E., 201
Miller, J. N., 462, 472
Milne, B. J., 180
Mintz, L. B., 658
Minuchin, S., 94, 95, 96, 666
Mitchell, J. E., 665, 666
Mitchell, M., 27, 29
Moens, E., 649
Moffatt, M., 668
Moffitt, T. E., 104, 152, 163, 169, 174,
    179, 180, 181, 183, 184, 186, 193,
    194, 196, 197, 205
Mohr, J., 677
Mohr, P. B., 554, 556, 557, 558, 567
Moilanen, I., 678
Mokros, H. B., 298
Moller, L. L., 278
Monda, J. M., 680, 682
Monuteaux, M. C., 270
Moos, R. H., 146
Morales, A. T., 168
Moreau, D., 339
Morgan, M. A., 568
Morison, S. J., 610
Morris, T., 124
Morris, T. L., 391
Mostert, M. P., 504
Mouren Simeoni, M. C., 558
Mrazek, D., 228
Mufson, L., 339
Mullen, M. C., 641, 642, 649

Mullins, L. L., 618, 629, 633
Mundy, E., 238
Mundy, P., 466, 467, 481, 482, 486
Munroe, R. L., 293
Munson, J. A., 467
Murata, T., 478
Murdock, J. Y., 504
Murias, M., 239
Muris, P., 357, 358, 369, 374
Murphy, C. C., 420, 421, 427, 432
Murphy, L., 685
Musten, L. M., 247
Mustillo, S., 634, 638, 639
Mycke, K., 425
Myers, L., 552

Nabors Oberg, R. E., 186
Nadel, L., 427
Nagel, R., 424
Nash, S., 467
National Center for Health Statistics,
    316, 637, 638
National Institute of Mental Health,
    257, 271
National Research Council, 434
Neale, M., 322
Needleman, H. L., 432
Neiderhiser, J., 102, 112
Neisser, U., 401
Nemeroff, C., 324
Neumarker, K., 651
Neveus, T., 672
Newcorn, J. H., 216
Newman, D., 307
Newman, E., 552, 553
Nezworski, M. T., 147
Nichols, M. P., 92, 93, 95, 96, 97
Nicholson, R., 531
Nicolson, R., 514, 517, 523, 536
Nigg, J. T., 233, 234, 235
Nijhof, G., 470, 604
Nilsen, W., 320
Nixon, R., 223
Noam, G. G., 269, 318
Noble, D., 547
Nolen-Hoeksema, S., 307, 310, 313,
    314, 332
Nordin, V., 463, 472
Norgaard, J. P., 675
Nuechterlein, K., 516
Nurcombe, B., 288, 298
Nye, R., 68, 74, 76, 77

Obarzanek, E., 645
Oberfield, R. A., 552

Oberzanek, E., 42, 634, 638, 639, 645
Obrosky, D. S., 9
O'Cathain, C., 682
Occhibinti, S., 654
O'Connor, T., 190, 602, 606, 609, 610, 611
Offer, D., 627
Offord, D. R., 168
O'Koon, J., 628
Olds, D., 17, 199, 200
O'Leary, D., 487
O'Leary, S., 248
Olin, J. A., 584
Oliver, C., 432
Ollendick, T. H., 169, 170, 358, 360, 361, 384, 385
Olley, J. G., 396, 413, 416, 426, 433, 435, 436, 448
Olrick, J., 602
Olson, R. A., 618, 629, 633
Oltmanns, T. F., 528
Ondersma, M. L., 667, 682, 685, 686, 687
Ondersma, S. J., 667
Oredsson, A. F., 682
Orlans, M., 598, 605
Orsmond, G. I., 422
Orvaschel, H., 369
O'Ryan, D., 559
Osborne, M. L., 689
Osterling, J. A., 467, 477
Ostrov, E., 627
Ostrov, J., 164
Ott, Y., 525
Overholser, J., 318
Owens, E. B., 194
Ozanne-Smith, J., 418
Ozonoff, S., 234, 459, 462, 464, 465, 468, 469, 471, 472

Paclawskyj, T., 501
Paesbrugge, S., 667
Paikoff, R. L., 329
Palermo, M. T., 469
Palmer, P., 478, 489
Paluch, R., 650
Pankau, R., 430, 431
Papademetriou, E., 628
Pappadopulos, E., 539
Parides, M., 317
Parker, K. C., 598
Parmenter, T., 428
Paronen, O., 628
Parrone, P., 300

Parry-Jones, W., 293
Paternite, C., 229
Patterson, G. R., 145, 174, 180, 181, 187, 194, 200
Patton, G., 651
Patton, J. R., 248, 409, 410, 444
Paulauskas, S., 10, 172
Pavlov, I., 73
Paxton, S., 664
Peebles, C. D., 552
Pekelharing, H., 470, 604
Pelcovitz, D., 558, 560, 574
Pelham, W. E., 246, 247, 250, 253
Peltzman, B., 655
Pennington, B. F., 234, 238, 402, 427, 428, 429
Pepler, D. J., 163
Percy, A. K., 495
Perel, J. M., 572
Perrin, S., 544, 547, 552, 555, 556
Perry, K. J., 571
Petersen, A., 299
Peterson, C. B., 665, 666
Peterson, J., 582
Pettit, G. S., 158, 171, 187, 191
Peverely, S. T., 552
Pfefferbaum, B., 559, 560
Pfiffner, L. J., 246, 250
Phares, V., 652
Phillips, K., 621, 632
Pianta, R. C., 422
Pica, M., 592
Pickett, J., 478
Pickett, W., 645
Pickles, A., 162, 178, 489
Pickrel, S. G., 203
Pieters, G., 656
Pillai, J. J., 280, 281
Pine, D. S., 272, 299
Piran, N., 663
Pirke, K. M., 661
Pisterman, S., 247, 248
Piven, J., 478, 487, 489
Pivik, R., 672
Pless, I., 668
Pliszka, S. R., 236
Plomin, R., 9, 102, 103, 104, 105, 109, 111, 112, 113, 114, 116, 117, 119, 190, 323, 402, 409, 437
Plotsky, P., 282, 324
Poels, P. J., 621
Polivy, J., 660, 661, 662
Poll, J., 625
Polloway, E. A., 410

Porche, L. M., 558
Porter, J., 54
Poskitt, E., 649
Posserud, M., 462
Post, R. M., 280, 281, 282, 283, 284
Potter, D., 456, 457, 458, 459
Poustka, F., 488
Powell, J. L., 16, 17
Poznanski, E. O., 298
Presnell, K., 655
Pretlow, R. A., 683
Primavera, L., 501
Prince, D., 547
Prinz, R. J., 201
Prior, M., 459, 464, 465, 468, 469, 471, 472, 653
Prizant, B., 468
Probst, M., 656
Proffitt, V. D., 339
Pulkkinen, L., 112
Putnam, F. W., 552, 572, 575, 578, 580, 582, 583, 584, 585, 586, 587, 588, 589, 590, 591, 592, 593, 595, 596
Pyles, D. A. M., 445, 446, 447
Pynoos, R. S., 557, 560, 561

Quay, H., 162, 175, 236

Racine, Y., 168
Rae, W. A., 49, 50, 52, 55, 57, 58
Rafalovich, A., 211
Ragland, E., 501
Ramey, C., 441
Ramey, S. L., 441
Ramstad, K., 430
Rao, U., 309
Rapee, R., 344, 384
Rapoport, J. L., 351, 365, 517, 523, 526, 527, 529, 672
Raskin, N., 68
Ravussin, E., 42, 638
Rayner, P., 349
Raynor, H., 650
Redmond, A., 675
Reed, V., 373
Reich, M. D., 631, 632, 633
Reich, W., 559
Reichert, J., 490
Reid, J. B., 145, 187
Reinherz, H. Z., 317
Reiss, A. L., 556
Reiss, D., 102, 112, 323
Reivich, K. J., 335
Rekers, G. A., 54

Remschmidt, H., 337, 338
Rende, R. D., 323
Renfro Michel, E. L., 612
Renner, P., 457
Renshaw, P. F., 269
Repetti, R. L., 288
Reppucci, N. D., 314, 594
Research Units on Pediatric
    Psychopharmacology Anxiety
    Study Group, 393, 394
Rey, J. M., 680
Reyno, S. M., 200, 201
Reynolds, L., 628
Reynolds, S., 230
Reznick, J. S., 376
Rhee, S. H., 186, 354
Ricciardelli, L., 652, 655
Rice, D., 109, 240, 323, 421
Richards, C., 10, 172
Richards, J., 270
Richards, M. H., 314
Richdale, A., 423, 472
Richters, M. M., 600, 602
Richtsmeier, A. J., 629
Ridge, B., 187
Rimland, B., 472
Rimmerman, A., 421
Ritterband, L. M., 691
Rittig, S., 677
Rivara, F. P., 632
Rivers, J., 480
Roach, M. A., 422
Robbins, T. W., 481, 487
Roberts, M., 229
Roberts, S., 644
Roberts, T. A., 320
Robertson, E., 246
Robin, A. L., 664, 666
Robins, C. J., 81, 84
Robinson, J., 628
Robinson, L. A., 331
Rockett, H., 645
Rodnick, E., 15
Roeleveld, N., 420
Roeyers, H., 425
Rogers, A. S., 51
Rogers, C., 65, 68, 69, 71
Rogers, S. J., 501
Rogler, L. H., 352
Rohde, P., 315
Rojas, V. M., 550
Rolland-Cachera, M. F., 637
Roll-Pettersson, L., 422, 423
Romanczyk, R. G., 503, 504
Romaski, L. M., 568

Rome, E., 651, 653
Ronis, S. T., 203
Rooney, M. T., 140
Rose, A. J., 314, 327
Rose, R., 112
Rosen, A. C., 54
Rosen, L. A., 228
Rosenbaum, J., 376
Rosenbaum, J. L., 183
Rosenbaum, M., 578, 635, 642, 643,
    644, 649, 661
Rosenberg, D., 537
Ross, C. A., 579, 584
Ross, R. G., 523, 524, 526, 537
Rosseel, Y., 649
Rossister, L., 423, 424, 480
Rothbaum, B. O., 568
Rothe, E. M., 559, 560
Rotholz, D. A., 502
Rothstein, A., 518
Rothstein, M., 103, 104
Roudebush, M., 547
Routh, D., 628
Rowe, D. C., 104, 109, 110, 114,
    115, 116, 117, 118, 323, 375
Rowe, R., 162, 178
Rudolph, K., 262, 272, 280, 301,
    307, 308, 322, 325, 329, 602
Ruma, P., 446
Rush, A. H., 326
Russell, A. T., 524
Russell, G. F., 666
Russell, M., 435
Russoniello, C. V., 559
Rutter, M., 13, 16, 102, 104, 112,
    116, 117, 118, 186, 190, 313,
    426, 458, 489, 491, 602, 606
Ruzek, J., 571
Ryan, S., 384
Rydell, P., 468
Rzepski, B., 624

Sachs, G., 268
Sack, M., 547
Saenger, P., 641
Safer, D. J., 245
Sagrestano, L. M., 329
Saigh, P. A., 552, 557
Salbe, A., 42, 638, 639, 644, 645
Saltzman, K. M., 556
Salvatoni, A., 650, 651
Salzer Burks, V., 170, 193
Samara, M., 112
Sandberg, A. D., 494
Sanders, M., 633

Sandler, I., 335
Sanford, M., 168
Sanson, A., 653
Santelli, J., 51
Sattler, J. M., 131, 139, 147
Savage, J., 644
Saywitz, K., 85
Scahill, L., 206, 217, 226
Scalzo, C. A., 314
Schachar, R., 236
Schachter, S., 380
Schaeffer, C. M., 203
Schaeffer, J. L., 523, 524, 526
Schall, C., 472, 479, 480
Schaumann, H., 476
Schecter, J., 140
Scheeringa, M. S., 552, 562
Schendel, D., 420
Schermer, F., 653
Schmidt, M. H., 525
Schore, A. N., 324, 590, 592
Schreiber, F. R., 575
Schreiber, G. B., 645
Schubel, E., 246
Schultz, E., 337, 338
Schultz, R., 148
Schulz, S. C., 525
Schwab-Stone, M., 140, 206,
    217, 226, 301
Schwartz, R. C., 92, 93, 95,
    96, 97
Schweiger, U., 661
Scotti, J., 124
Seeley, J. R., 276, 315
Seeley, K. M., 341, 352, 586
Segal, N. L., 105
Selevan, S. G., 240, 421
Seligman, M., 327
Seligman, M. E. P., 332, 335
Seltzer, W. J., 622
Selvin, S., 475
Sergeant, J., 237
Sermon, A., 369
Shaffer, D., 140, 301, 316, 317, 319
Shalev, R., 221
Shannon, F. T., 675
Sharpe, D., 423, 424, 480
Sharpton, W. R., 504
Shavelle, R. M., 478
Shaw, B. F., 326
Shaw, D. S., 162, 163, 178, 194
Shaw, J. A., 177
Shea, M. C., 445
Shea, V., 502
Sheeber, L., 324, 330

Sheffield, J. K., 335, 387
Shelton, R., 248
Shepard, B. A., 218
Shepard, R., 633
Sheperis, C. J., 612
Sherman, D. K., 238
Sherrard, J., 418
Sherrill, J., 9, 320, 339, 340
Shield, J., 641, 642, 649
Shimizu, Y., 491
Shirar, L., 595, 596
Shisslak, C., 653, 654, 655
Shneidman, E. S., 317, 318
Short, E., 246, 247
Shriver, M. D., 631
Siegel, L. J., 558
Siegel, S. J., 331
Siegel, T. C., 202
Sigman, M., 428, 466, 467,
    481, 482, 486
Sijben, N., 621
Sikich, L., 540, 541
Silberg, J. L., 116, 587, 588,
    589, 590, 595, 596
Silove, D., 352, 354, 355
Silva, P. A., 180, 183
Silverman, A. B., 317
Silverman, M. M., 298
Silverman, W. K., 366
Silverthorn, P., 152, 163, 178,
    181, 183, 184
Simon, T., 401, 405
Simonoff, E., 116, 426, 427,
    428, 429, 430, 437
Singer, J., 380
Sivberg, B., 479
Skinner, B. F., 73, 74
Skinner, J. B., 435
Skinner, M., 429
Slutske, W. S., 186
Smallish, L., 228
Smart, D., 653
Smart, L., 171
Smith, A., 428
Smith, E., 559
Smith, I., 474
Smith, I. M., 484, 485
Smith, M., 282
Smith, M. L., 50
Smith, N., 490
Smith, P., 544
Smith, T., 498, 502
Smith, T. E. C., 410, 500
Smolak, L., 653
Smoller, J. W., 661

Smyke, A. T., 604, 605
Smyth, N. J., 541
Snidman, N., 376
Sokolov, S., 322
Sonuga-Barke, E. J. S., 169
Soorya, L. V., 503
Sorensen, E., 324
South, M., 472
Southam-Gerow, M. A., 203, 391
Spagnola, M., 611
Spanos, N. P., 575, 583, 584
Sparrow, S., 473
Spearman, C., 401
Spence, S. H., 335, 336, 344, 345,
    358, 360, 387, 388, 389, 393
Spencer, T., 394
Spencer, T. J., 270, 276, 338
Spiegel, J., 547
Spierings, C., 621, 625
Spirito, A., 318, 627
Spitz, R., 293, 599
Spitzer, R. L., 136
Spratley, K., 236
Spratt, E. G., 598, 601, 602, 603, 613
Sprich, S., 238
Springer, J., 104
Squire, L. R., 565, 566
Sroufe, A., 16
Sroufe, L. A., 13, 88, 90, 174, 324
Stallings, V. A., 642
Stanley, J. C., 37
Stansbrey, R. J., 338
Stanton, W., 180
Stark, L. J., 688
Steele, H., 90, 612
Steffenburg, S., 475, 478, 489, 501
Stein, M. B., 567
Steinberg, A., 652
Steinberg, A. M., 557
Steiner, H., 653, 657, 658, 664, 665
Steingard, R. J., 503
Steketee, G., 568
Stenberg, A., 672
Stenberg, C., 90
Sternberg, R. J., 396, 401, 404, 407
Stevens, G., 219
Stevenson, J., 169
Stewart, D. A., 664
Stice, E., 653, 654, 655
Stien, P., 545, 555, 564, 567
Still, G., 211
Stoff, D. M., 177
Stokes, T. F., 144, 230
Stone, W., 446
Stoneman, Z., 480

Stoolmiller, M., 174, 187
Stormont, M., 223, 224, 241, 242
Stouthamer Loeber, M., 157, 166,
    169, 175, 176, 181, 184, 186,
    189, 190, 196
Strain, P., 501
Strandburg, R., 516
Strauss, C. C., 351, 354, 355, 365
Strauss, D. J., 478
Strauss, R., 641
Streiner, D. L., 472
Strober, M., 285
Stromme, P., 430
Strong, K. G., 654, 660
Stubbe, D. E., 211, 250
Stunkard, A. J., 642, 661
Sudhalter, V., 419, 429
Sullivan, P., 322
Sunday, S., 655
Surgeon General, 635, 638,
    643, 647, 648
Swanson, J., 231, 239, 244
Swanson, J. M., 253
Swartz, M., 558
Sweeney, L., 339
Sykes, D., 240
Szatmari, P., 459, 460, 472, 490
Szczygiel, S., 628
Szmukler, G. I., 666

Tager Flusberg, H., 469
Tang, B., 520
Tanghe, A., 649
Tanguay, P. E., 131, 459, 463,
    493, 494, 503, 519
Tannock, R., 212, 235, 236
Taska, L., 569
Tataranni, A., 42, 639
Taubman, B., 689
Taylor, D., 625
Taylor, E., 223
Taylor, H., 661
Taylor, L., 50
Taylor, T. K., 199, 202
Teasdale, J., 327
Tellegen, A., 105
Tennison, D., 391
Terr, L., 547, 556, 567
Thambirajah, M., 687
Thapar, A., 109, 323
Thapar, A. J., 239
Thelen, M. H., 653
Theunis, M., 667, 673
Thigpen, C., 575
Thompson, J., 652

Thompson, J. K., 446, 448, 652
Thompson, L., 428
Thompson, M., 169
Thompson, S., 680
Thomsen, P. H., 278
Thorne, B., 68, 71
Thousand, J., 443
Thurber, C. A., 339
Thurstone, L., 402
Tiegerman, E., 501
Tienari, P., 532
Tilgner, L., 664
Timimi, S., 162, 168
Tingstrom, D. H., 424
Tollen, L. G., 558
Tonge, B. J., 418, 428
Toolan, J. M., 293
Torchia, M. G., 567
Torsheim, T., 628
Toth, S., 17, 611
Toth, S. L., 308, 309, 320,
    324, 325, 329, 332, 588
Towbin, K. E., 272
Tremblay, R., 164
Trepagnier, C., 484
Trimble, B. K. I., 427
Troiano, R., 637, 638
Tsatsanis, K., 514, 518, 519, 523
Tsuang, M., 238
Tuchman, B., 606
Turner, G., 428
Turner, S. M., 391
Turnock, P., 228
Tuvemo, T., 672
Twenge, J. M., 307, 310
Tyler, L., 170, 171
Tyrka, A., 660, 661

Udwin, O., 559
U. S. Public Health Service, 4

Vaidaya, C., 235
Valdez, R. B., 673
Van Bourgondien, M. E., 503
VanBrakle, J., 144
Vandenberg, S. G., 401
Van den Boom, D., 90, 340, 611
Van der Ende, J., 419
Vandereycken, W., 656
Van der Hart, O., 545, 548
Van der Kolk, B. A., 545, 548, 563,
    569, 572, 573, 587
Van der Meere, J., 221, 222, 237
Van der Steen, F., 620
Vander Wal, J., 42, 639, 641

Vande Walle, J., 667
Van Hoecke, E., 667
Van Horn, P., 552, 574
Van Leerdam, F., 673
Van Slyke, D. A., 627
Van Vactor, J. C., 656
Vargas, L. A., 42, 198, 303, 341
Vasey, M. W., 384
Vaughn, B. J., 524
Vekevainen-Tervonen, L., 678
Velazquez, L., 583
Velting, D., 316
Verhulst, F. C., 175, 419
Verma, S. K., 147
Vieweg, W. V., 316
Viken, R., 112
Vila, G., 558, 559
Villa, R. A., 443
Vitaro, F., 164
Vitiello, B., 53, 54, 55, 177
Volger, G. P., 401
Volkmar, F. R., 457, 473, 477, 492,
    495, 508, 514, 518, 519,
    523, 600, 602
Volkmar, R., 625
Vondra, J. I., 194
Von Gontard, A., 670, 671,
    673, 677, 679, 680, 681
Von Knorring, A. L., 525

Wabitsch, M., 642, 643
Wadden, T. A., 661
Wagner, W. G., 673
Wakefield, A., 490
Waldman, I. D., 169, 186, 187, 191
Waldron, H. B., 99
Waldron, I., 660
Walford, W. A., 298
Walker, C. E., 667
Walker, L., 624, 625
Walker, L. S., 626, 627, 628, 629
Wall, S., 88
Wallach, H. R., 580, 588, 595
Wallander, J. L., 417, 418
Walters, E. E., 307
Walz, N. C., 428, 432
Warren, M., 313
Wasserman, A. L., 632
Wasserman, D., 318, 319
Wasserstein, S., 366
Wasserstein, S. B., 560
Waters, E., 88, 324
Waters, F. S., 596, 597
Watson, D., 378
Watson, J., 73, 349

Watson, N., 417
Watson, P., 571
Weakland, J., 92
Webster-Stratton, C., 199, 200,
    201, 202
Wechsler, D., 401, 405, 406
Weckerly, J., 262, 271, 272
Weeks, S. L., 428
Weems, C. F., 366, 369, 556
Weinberger, D., 516, 528, 529,
    533, 534
Weinberger, D. R., 148
Weinger, S., 422, 425
Weise, K. L., 50, 55
Weishaar, M., 81, 84
Weiss, B., 325
Weiss, S. R. B., 280
Weissman, M. M., 309, 339
Weisz, J. R., 339, 539
Weller, E. B., 140, 262, 271, 285
Weller, R. A., 140, 262, 271
Wen, X., 420, 421, 427
Wermter, A., 644
Werner, E., 477
Werry, J., 523, 525, 540
Wertheim, E., 653, 664
Westermeyer, J. F., 344, 351,
    352, 525
Weyer, C., 42, 638, 639, 644, 645
Whalen, C. K., 223, 246
Whitaker, A., 365, 373
Whitaker, P., 463, 479, 504
Whitaker, R. C., 644
White, K. S., 627, 629
Whiteman, M., 189
Whitington, P. F., 632
Whitley, M. K., 201
Widom, C. S., 183
Wilens, T. E., 338
Wilkinson, R. B., 298
Wille, S., 672, 675
Williams, D. T., 583
Williams, J. M. G., 467
Williams, K., 505
Williams, M., 257, 267, 270, 272,
    275, 276, 279, 286
Williams, P. G., 314
Williams, S., 163
Wilson, D., 524
Wilson, F. J., 472
Wilson, G. T., 73, 75, 665
Wilson, S. L., 613
Wimpory, D. C., 467
Winerman, L., 78
Wing, L., 456, 457, 458, 459, 475

Winters, A., 158, 163, 165, 166, 178
Wise, A., 525
Wiseman, C., 655
Wishart, J., 505
Wittchen, H. U., 373
Wold, B., 628
Wolff, P. H., 592
Wolfish, N. M., 672
Wolke, D., 112
Wolpe, J., 73, 76, 389
Wolraich, M. L., 206, 211, 217, 218, 227, 244, 245, 247
Woo, S., 118, 429
Wood, J. M., 147
Woods, E. R., 329
Woodward, L., 344
Woodward, L. J., 180, 220
Woolford, H., 633
Worthman, C., 313
Wozniak, J., 258, 270, 274, 276

Wu, P., 317
Wynn, J. W., 500

Xing, G., 280, 282

Yanagida, E. H., 50
Yang, B., 361
Yasik, A. E., 552
Yates, T. M., 16
Yeargin-Allsopp, M., 420, 421
Yoerger, K. L., 174
Yoshinaga, K., 478
Yost, L. W., 326
Young, A., 123, 616, 623
Young, L., 234
Young, S., 354
Yule, W., 544, 547, 556, 558, 559, 561

Zahn-Waxler, C., 164
Zeanah, C. H., 552, 562, 598, 604

Zeanah, C. H., Jr., 600, 604
Zeman, J., 626
Zera, M., 158, 163, 165, 166, 178
Zhang, L., 282
Zhen, L., 189
Ziegler, D. J., 65, 68, 69
Zielhaus, G. A., 420
Zigler, E., 318, 396, 415, 417, 425, 436
Zigun, J. R., 148
Zimerman, B., 257, 267, 270, 272, 275, 276, 279, 286
Zito, J. M., 245
Zoccolillo, M., 164
Zoellner, L., 572
Zola-Morgan, S. M., 565, 566
Zurcher, L. A., 30
Zwaigenbaum, L., 495
Zwakhalen, S., 369

Subject Index

ABC model of behavior, 83
Academic achievement
  ADHD, 224–225
  autism, 471
  depression, 305–306
  PTSD, 557
Active genotype-environment
    correlations, 120
Activity levels, and childhood obesity,
    644–645
Actualizing tendency, 68, 100
Acute phase, 521, 542
Acute stress disorder, 545; *see also*
    Posttraumatic stress disorder
  diagnostic criteria, 550, 551t
Adaptive functioning, 411–412, 450
ADHA; *see* Attention-deficit/
    hyperactivity disorder
Adipocytes, 642
Adipose tissue, 637, 691
Adjustment disorders
  with anxiety, 373
  definition, 341, 394
  with depressed mood (ADDM),
    295, 298
  diagnostic criteria, 295, 374t
Adolescent-limited behaviors,
    174, 205
Adolescent onset, 158, 205
Adolescent-onset conduct problems
  case study, 154–156
  classification, 174
  definition, 205
  developmental course,
    181–182
  etiology, 196–197
Adolescent-onset depression,
    333–334
Adolescents
  autism, 478
  depression and gender, 313–315
  therapeutic interventions, 203–204
Adoption studies, 110–111, 120
Affective aggression, 177
Affective impairments
  autism, 481–482, 482f
  schizophrenia, 520
Affect regulation, depression and,
    324–325

African-Americans
  anxiety, 351
  intelligence testing, 407
Aggression
  ADHD and, 223
  affective, 177
  disruptive behavior and, 191,
    193–194
  Freudian theory, 66
  instrumental, 177
  predatory, 177
  reactive, 177
  reactive attachment disorder, 605
  relational, 164
  suicide and, 319
  young children, 184
Agoraphobia, 371–372, 372t, 394
Agranulocytosis, 540, 542
Alcohol, and mental retardation,
    434–436
Alleles, 102, 120
Alogia, 521, 542
Alternate personality identities, 582,
    592–593, 593f, 595–596, 614
American Association on Mental
    Retardation Adaptive
    Behavior Scale, 412
American Psychiatric Association, 122
American Psychological Association
    (APA), 43, 48
Amnesia, 556, 614
Amygdala, 564, 567–568, 614
Anaclitic depression, 293, 341, 600, 614
Angelman syndrome, 432
Anger, and suicide, 318, 319
Anginine vasopressin, 672–673, 691
Anhedonia, 304, 341, 533, 542
Anorexia nervosa; *see* Eating disorders
Anticipatory anxiety, 395
Antipsychotic medications, 539–540
Anxiety
  cultural factors, 351–352
  meanings of, 351
  role of, 344, 345f
Anxiety disorders, 344–394; *see also*
    Posttraumatic stress disorder
  ADHD and, 225–226
  adjustment disorder with
    anxiety, 373

autism and, 472
bipolar disorders and, 276
case studies, 44–46, 345–348
causes, 77t
childhood-specific, 350, 351
depression and, 377
etiology, 373–387
  behavioral influences, 382–385
  cognitive influences, 383–384
  experiential influences, 380–384
  genetic influences, 375–378
    maintenance and intensification,
      384–385
  generalized anxiety disorder,
    366–369
  history, 349–350
  medication, 393–394
  not otherwise specified, 373,
    551, 614
  obsessive-compulsive disorder,
    362–366
  panic disorder, 369–373
  prevention, 387–389, 388t
  separation anxiety disorder,
    345–347, 352–355
  social phobia, 358–362
  specific phobias, 347–348, 355–358
  therapeutic interventions, 389–394
    cognitive-behavioral
      psychotherapy, 390–392
    family issues, 392–393
    medication, 393–394
    systematic desensitization,
      389–390
Anxious/resistant attachment,
    89, 100
Applied behavioral analysis, 76–77,
    100, 445, 450
Arousal, 237, 377–380, 556,
    564–565
ASD; *see* Autism spectrum disorder
Asperger's disorder; *see also* Autism
    spectrum disorder; Pervasive
    developmental disorders
  autism spectrum disorder, 459–463
  course
    childhood/adolescence, 478
    long-term, 478–479
    onset, 477–478

diagnostic criteria, 458–459, 461i
features, 472–474
high-functioning autism and, 472
history, 456–458
language/communication
    impairments, 474
motor skills, 474
personal interests, 473
prevalence, 476
Assent, 51, 61
Assessment; *see* Clinical assessment
Association of Parents and Friends of
    Retarded Children, 410
Attachment, autism and, 466–467
Attachment behavioral system,
    87, 100
Attachment disorder; *see* Reactive
    attachment disorder
Attachment theory, 86–92
    affect regulation, 324–325
    basis, 87–88
    child psychopathology
        applications, 91
    definition, 341–342, 614
    development of attachment, 87
    importance of attachment, 88–89
    internal working model, 90
    origins, 600
    patterns of attachment, 89–90
    therapeutic process, 91
Attention
    focused, 222
    sustained, 222
Attention comparison group, 61
Attention control group, 35
Attention deficit disorder, 211, 254
Attention-deficit hyperactivity disorder,
    211–212, 254
Attention-deficit/hyperactivity disorder
    (ADHD), 206–254
    academic achievement, 224–225
    age of onset, 215
    anxiety and, 225–226
    assessment, 217–219
    associated features, 223–226
    bipolar disorders and, 270–271
    case studies, 207–210
    central deficit, 233–237
    combined treatments, 250–253
    combined type, 212, 255
    conduct disorder and, 172, 216–217
    core features, 220–222
        hyperactivity/impulsivity,
            220–221
        inattention, 221–222

course, 227–229
depression and, 225–226
developmental model, 241–242
diagnostic criteria, 212,
    213–214t, 214
educational interventions, 248–249
etiology, 232–243
    behavioral inhibition, 234–236
    birth/pregnancy complications,
        239–240
    environmental influences, 240–241
    family influences, 240–241
    food ingredients, 240
    genetic influences, 238–239, 238f
    neurological issues, 237–240
    optimum arousal, 237
    toxins, 240
family issues, 229–232, 240–241
gender, 227, 228
history, 211–212
informants' reports, 217–218
issues, 214–217
medication, 244–248, 250–253
motor skills, 225
name, 212, 254
neurological problems, 237–240
oppositional defiant disorder and,
    216–217
parenting interventions, 248
peer issues, 223
predominantly hyperactive-impulsive
    type, 212, 255
predominantly inattentive type, 212,
    215, 256
prevalence, 226–227
prevention, 243
PTSD and, 557
study of, 219–220
therapeutic interventions, 243–254
    combined treatments, 250–253
    educational interventions, 248–249
    medication, 244–248, 250–253
    outstanding issues, 253
    parenting interventions, 248
    psychosocial interventions,
        249–250
Attributional style/theory,
    327–329, 342
Atypical antipsychotic medications,
    539, 542
Autism spectrum disorder (ASD),
    459–463, 462f, 506
Autistic disorder; *see also* Autism
    spectrum disorder; Pervasive
    developmental disorders

anxiety disorders and, 472
assessment, 463, 464t
associated features, 471–472
    intelligence/academic
        abilities, 471
    sensory perception, 471
    splinter/savant skills, 471–472
baffling nature of, 453
case study, 454–456
core features, 464–471
    attachment, 466–467
    developmental impairments,
        467–468
    language/communication
        impairments, 468–469
    restricted/repetitive/stereotyped
        behaviors, 469–471
    social interaction, 464–468,
        500–501
course
    childhood/adolescence, 478
    long-term, 478–479
    onset, 477
depression and, 472
diagnostic criteria, 458–459, 460t
etiology, 481–492
    affective impairments,
        481–482, 482f
    cognitive impairments,
        482–484, 483f
    genetic influences, 488–490
    injuries, 490
    neurological issues, 486–488
    perceptual impairments,
        484–486
    vaccines, 490–491
family issues, 457, 476, 504–505
fundamental deficits, 481–486
gender, 476
high-functioning, 459
history, 456–458
medication, 502–503
prevalence, 475–476
spectrum of, 453–454
therapeutic interventions, 497–505
    early, 498–500
    facilitated communication,
        503–504
    family issues, 504–505
    medication, 502–503
    school-age children, 500–502
Automatic thoughts, 84, 100
Autonomy, 49–53
    definition, 49, 61
    informed consent, 49–50

Autonomy (*Cont.*)
    research participation, 50–52
    therapy participation, 50–52
Avoidance learning, 385, 386f, 395
Avoidant attachment, 89, 100
Avoidant behavior, 384–385
Avolition, 521, 542

Bacterial encephalitis, 436, 450
Bacterial meningitis, 436, 450
Bariatric surgery, 650–651, 691
Bayley Scales of Infant
        Development–II, 406
Behavior
    autism, 472, 501–502
    cognitive influences on, 82–84
    direct versus indirect influences, 192
    family systems theory, 94–95
    grossly disorganized, in
        schizophrenia, 520
    observations, 141, 143–145
    response to emotionally charged
        memories, 569–570
    suicide and, 319
Behavioral activation system, 236, 254
Behavioral assessments, 143–145
    behavior observations, 143–145
    behavior rating scales, 143
    definition, 149
    limitations, 145
Behavioral genetics; *see* Quantitative
        behavioral genetics
Behavioral inhibition, 234–236, 376–377
Behavioral inhibition system (BIS),
        236, 254, 381–382, 395
Behavioral interventions
    cognitive-behavioral psychotherapy,
        390–392
    depression, 340
    enuresis, 681–683
    mental retardation, 445–447
    somatization problems, 632–633
Behavioral or emotional disorders,
        continuum of, 10
    co-occurrence of, 9–10
    definition, 3n, 123
    development of, 5
    medical conditions and, 616
Behavioral theories, 72–80
    anxiety, 349
    behavioral focus, 73
    child psychopathology applications,
        79–80
    environmental factors, 74–75
    origins, 73

present focus, 73–74
    therapeutic process, 76–79
Behavior observations, 143–145, 149
Behavior rating scales, 143, 149
Bell and pad procedure, 681–683,
        682f, 691
Belle indifference, 621, 692
Bender Visual-Motor Gestalt Test,
        430, 431f
Beneficence, 53–56, 61
    definition, 53
    research, 53
    therapy, 53–55
Between-group research designs,
        34–36, 61
Binge eating, 666f, 691
    bulimia nervosa, 656–657
    childhood obesity, 641–642
    eating disorders, 662–663
Binge-purge cycle, 662–663, 691
Biological influences
    depressive disorders, 321–324, 661
    eating disorders, 661
    somatization problems, 627–628
Bipolar disorder not otherwise specified
        (BPDNOS), 262, 266
Bipolar disorders, 257–286
    ADHD and, 270–271
    anxiety and, 276
    assessment, 266–267
    associated features, 276
    case studies, 258–261
    childhood-onset versus adult-onset,
        271–272, 273–274t, 283
    conduct disorder and, 276
    core features, 272, 273–274t,
        274–276
        dangerous behaviors, 275–276
        grandiosity, 274–275
        hyperactivity, 274–275
        irritability, 274
    course, 278–279
    diagnostic criteria, 262–266, 263t,
        264t, 265t
    etiology, 280–283
        diathesis-stress model, 282–283
        environmental influences, 282
        genetic influences, 281–282
        neurological issues, 281
    family issues, 279–280
    genetic influences, 280
    history, 262
    medication, 284–285
    as mood disorder, 342
    peer issues, 276

prepubertal children, 268–272
    prevalence, 278
    prevention, 283
    substance abuse, 276
    suicide, 276
    therapeutic interventions, 284–286
        medication, 284–285
        psychosocial interventions,
            285–286
Bipolar I disorder, 262–263, 265, 265f
Bipolar II disorder, 262–263, 265f, 266
Birth complications; *see* Childbirth
        complications
Body dissatisfaction, 652–656
Body dysmorphic disorder, 620–621
Body mass index (BMI), 637–638, 691
Bowel movements, 685; *see also*
        Encopresis
Boys; *see also* Gender
    puberty, 314
    stress, 314
Brain
    autism, 487–488
    functioning, 528, 563–568
    lesions, 534
    morphology, 487–488,
        527–528, 542
    PTSD, 563–568
    schizophrenia, 527–528,
        534–535
    stress reaction, 564–566
    volume, 566–567
Breathing, Rett's disorder and, 493
Brief psychotic episode, 514
Buck v. Bell (1927), 410
Bulimia nervosa; *see* Eating disorders

Callous-unemotional personality trait,
        171, 205
Capacity, attention, 222, 254
Carbamazepine, 284, 287
Case studies
    ADHD, 207–210
    autism, 454–456
    bipolar disorders, 258–261
    childhood obesity, 635–637
    childhood-onset schizophrenia,
        509–512
    conduct problems, adolescent-onset,
        154–156
    conduct problems, early-onset,
        153–154
    depression, 289–293
    dissociative disorders, 576–577
    enuresis, 668–669

family system and child's disorder, 618–619

medication, 46–47, 207–210

mental retardation, 397–400

parental expectations, 44–46

PTSD, 545–547

researchers' interactions with young child, 598–599

separation anxiety, 345–347

sexual abuse, 576–577

somatization problems, 618–619

specific phobia, 347–348

Catastrophizing, 83

Catatonic type of schizophrenia, 516, 542

Categorical classification, 129–131, 149

Causation, 32, 95

Central nervous system (CNS), 321

Cerebral palsy, 418, 450

Certificate of confidentiality, 57, 61

Child Behavior Checklist (CBCL), 143, 166

Childbirth complications
 ADHD, 239–240
 schizophrenia, 531

Child Depression Inventory, 301

Child development, influences on, 5–11

Child Dissociative Checklist, 585, 586t

Childhood Autism Rating Scale (CARS), 463

Childhood disintegrative disorder, 458, 495–497
 course, 496
 diagnostic criteria, 496t
 etiology, 496–497
 features, 495
 prevalence, 496

Childhood obesity, 634–651
 case study, 635–637
 consequences, 640–642
 course, 639, 640f
 defining and measuring, 637–638
 etiology, 642–647
  activity levels, 644–645
  diet, 645
  fat tissue development, 642–643
  genetic influences, 644, 644f
  model of, 645–646, 646f
  parental obesity, 644
 prevalence, 638–639
 prevention, 647–648
 therapeutic interventions, 648–651

Childhood onset, 158, 205; see also Early-onset

bipolar disorders, 271–272, 273–274t, 283

depressive disorders, 299–300

Childhood-onset schizophrenia, 508–541
 adult-onset versus, 516–517
 autism and, 458
 case studies, 509–512
 course
  initial onset, 524–525
  long-term, 525
  premorbid functioning, 523–524, 524t
 cultural factors, 517
 diagnostic criteria, 514, 515t, 516
 etiology, 526–537
  birth/pregnancy complications, 531
  developmental theories, 533–535
  genetic influences, 529–530
  neurobiological dysfunctions, 527–529
  peculiar features, 535–536
  stress, 531–533
  viral infections, 530–531
 family issues, 526, 531–533, 541
 history, 512–513
 medication, 539–540
 negative symptoms, 514, 520–521
  alogia, 521
  avolition, 521
  flattened affect, 520
 positive symptoms, 514, 518–520
  delusions, 519
  disorganized speech, 519–520
  grossly disorganized behavior, 520
  hallucinations, 518
 prevalence, 523
 prevention, 537–538
 symptoms
  cycle of, 521–522
  negative, 514, 520–521
  positive, 514, 518–520
 therapeutic interventions, 538–541
  medication, 539–540
  psychological, 540–541

Childhood schizophrenia, 513, 542

Child psychopathology; see also Developmental psychopathology
 children as focus of, 11
 principles of, 5–12
 professions utilizing, 3–4
 research on, 1–2, 2f

Child rearing, and societal violence, 606–607

Children, as informants, 166, 301–302

Children's Depression Inventory, 146

Chromosomal abnormalities
 mental retardation, 427–432
 Rett's disorder, 494–495

Classical conditioning, 73, 76–78, 100, 382–383

Classification
 advantages, 125–126
 categorical, 129–131
 dimensional, 129–131
 disadvantages, 126–127
 DSM system, 132–137
 "not otherwise specified," 131
 reliability, 131–132
 systems, 128
 validity, 132

Classification system, 128, 149

Clinical assessment, 137–149; see also Information gathering
 ADHD, 217–219
 autism, 463, 464t
 behavioral assessment, 143–145
 bipolar disorders, 266–267
 cultural factors, 168
 definition, 149
 depressive disorders, 301–303
 disruptive behavior, 165–168
 dissociative disorders, 585–586
 family factors, 168
 follow-up, 681
 information gathering, 137–139
 interviews, 139–142
 limitations, 142, 145, 147, 148
 mental retardation, 412–414
 neuroimaging, 147–148
 pervasive developmental disorders, 463
 psychological tests, 145–147
 PTSD, 552–553
 reactive attachment disorder, 602–603
 somatoform disorders, 622–623

Clinical interviews, 139–142
 behavioral observations, 141
 definition, 149
 developmental history, 140–141
 limitations, 142
 structured versus unstructured, 139–140

Cognitive abilities; see Intelligence

Cognitive-behavioral psychotherapy (CBT)

Cognitive-behavioral (*Cont.*)
  anxiety disorders, 390–394
  definition, 395
  eating disorders, 665–666
  PTSD, 572–574
Cognitive distortions, 82
Cognitive factors
  anxiety disorders, 383–384
  autism, 482–484, 483*f*
  depression, 325–329
  disruptive behavior, 192, 193–194
  eating disorders, 661
  mental retardation, 415–416
  PTSD, 568–570
  somatization problems, 633
  suicide, 318–319
Cognitive restructuring, 633, 691
Cognitive theories, 80–86
  attributional style, 327–329
  belief systems, 80–82
  child psychopathology
    applications, 86
  emotions/behaviors influenced by
    cognitions, 82–84
  negative thinking, 326
  therapeutic process, 84–86, 339
Cohort, 36, 61
Cohort effects, 36, 61
Colon, 685
Combat fatigue, 547
Combined type (ADHD), 212, 254
Command hallucinations, 518, 542
Communication; *see also* Language
  Asperger's disorder, 474
  autism, 468–469, 485*f*, 503–504
  facilitated, 503–504
  schizophrenia, 514, 516, 519–520
Community-care control group, 35,
  61, 252, 254
Comorbid disorders
  ADHD, 216–217
  anxiety disorders, 377
  bipolar disorders, 270
  definition, 149, 342
  depression, 298–299, 302, 309
  disruptive behavior, 172
  mental retardation, 418–419,
    444–445
  multiaxial system, 133
  overview, 9–10
  PTSD, 557
  somatization problems, 624–625
Comparator
  classical conditioning influences,
    382–383

cognitive influences, 383–384
  definition, 395
  function, 381–382, 382*f*
Completed suicides, 316, 342
Compliance, medication, 541
Compulsions, 363, 395, 432, 450
Computerized tomographic (CT)
  scanning, 148, 149
Concordance, 113, 120
Concurrent validity, 132, 149
Conduct disorder; *see also* Disruptive
  behavior
  ADHD and, 172, 216–217
  age of onset, 174
  behavior patterns, 175–177,
    175*f*, 176*t*
  bipolar disorders and, 276
  depression and, 9–10
  diagnostic criteria, 158, 159*t*, 160
  family issues, 171–172, 182–183
  girls, 163–164
  intelligence, 169
  mood disorders and, 172
  motivation, 177
  oppositional defiant disorder versus,
    162–163
  peer issues, 171
  personality issues, 170–171
  prevalence, 178–179
  social cognition, 169–170
  social costs, 151–152
  subtypes, 173–178
Confidence interval, 406
Confidentiality, 56–60
  definition, 62
  research, 57–59
  therapy, 56–58
Constipation, 685
Constriction, 318–319, 342
Constructs, 28, 62
Construct validity, 28–30, 62
Content validity, 29, 62
Continuous performance test, 235, 255
Control groups, 35
Convergent validity, 29, 62
Conversion disorder, 621*f*
Correlation, 113, 120
Correlational research, 31–32, 62
Corticotrophin-releasing hormone
  (CRH), 322, 324, 342
Cortisol, 299, 322, 342, 376, 395,
  564–567, 614
Co-rumination, 314, 327, 342
Counselors, 3
Covariation, 106–107, 106n, 120

Covert disruptive behavior,
  175–177, 205
Cross-fostering research, 531–532
Cross-sectional designs, 36, 62
Cultural factors
  ADHD, 219
  anxiety, 351–352
  childhood-onset schizophrenia, 517
  depression, 302–303, 341
  disruptive behavior, 168
  dissociative disorders, 585–586
  ethics, 43–44
  intelligence, 404–405, 404*t*
  intelligence testing, 407–409
  PTSD, 553
  social phobia, 361
  somatization, 623
  therapeutic/preventive interventions,
    198–199, 341
Cyclothymia, 262, 265*f*, 266

Dangerous behaviors, 275–276
Death instinct, 66
Declarative memories, 565, 569, 614
Defiant disruptive behavior, 175, 205
Delinquent behavior; *see* Disruptive
  behavior
Delusions, 519, 542
Dementia praecox, 512, 542
Dependent variable, 31, 62
Depersonalization disorder, 581
Depression, meanings of, 288–289
Depressive disorders, 288–341
  academic achievement, 305–306
  ADHD and, 225–226
  adolescent-onset, 333–334
  anxiety and, 377
  assessment, 301–303
  associated features, 305–306
  autism and, 472
  case studies, 289–293
  childhood-onset versus adult-onset,
    299–300
  comorbidity, 298–299, 302, 309
  continuum of, 10
  core features, 304–305
  course, 308–313
    depressive disorders, 308–309
    depressive symptoms, 309–311
  cultural factors, 302–303
  diagnostic criteria, 294–295, 296*t*,
    297*t*, 298
  early-onset, 331–333
  eating disorders and, 9, 309, 661
  etiology, 320–334

adolescent-onset, 333–334
affect regulation, 324–325
biological influences, 321–324
cognitive influences,
    325–329, 328f
early-onset, 331–333
environmental influences,
    323–324
genetic influences, 322–323
interpersonal factors,
    330–331
life stress, 329–330
family issues, 302–303, 320,
    340–341
gender, 307, 310–311, 311f, 311t,
    313–315
history, 293–294
impact of, 288
major depression versus dysthymia,
    300–301
medication, 321, 337–338
not otherwise specified
    (DDNOS), 298
outstanding issues, 298–301
prevalence, 306–308
prevention, 334–337
PTSD and, 557
suicide, 315–320
terminology, 288–289
therapeutic interventions, 337–341
    family issues, 340–341
    medication, 337–338
    psychosocial interventions,
        338–340
Descriptive statistics, 40
Desensitization, systematic; see
    Systematic desensitization
Desipramine, 244
Desmopressin acetate, 673,
    680–681, 691
Detrusor-sphincter dyscoordination,
    670–671, 692
Developmental history, 140–141, 149
Developmental psychopathology; see
    also Child psychopathology
concepts in, 14–17
field of, 12–14, 13f
Deviation IQ, 406, 450
Dexamethasone suppression test,
    299, 342
Dextroamphetamine, 244
Diabetes, 641, 692
Diagnosis
    advantages, 125–126
    disadvantages, 126–127

Diagnostic and Statistical Manual of
    Mental Disorders (DSM); see
    also Diagnostic criteria
classification system, 122, 129,
    132–137
definition, 149
Diagnostic criteria
    acute stress disorder, 550, 551t
    ADHD, 212, 213–214t, 214
    agoraphobia, 372t
    anorexia nervosa, 656t
    Asperger's disorder, 458–459, 461t
    autism, 458–459, 460t
    bipolar disorders, 262–266, 263t,
        264t, 265t
    bulimia nervosa, 657t
    childhood disintegrative
        disorder, 496t
    childhood-onset schizophrenia, 514,
        515t, 516
    conduct disorder, 158, 159t, 160
    depressive disorders, 294–295, 298
    disruptive behavior, 157–158
    disruptive behavior not otherwise
        specified, 161
    dissociative disorders, 580–583
    dissociative identity disorder,
        581–582, 581t
    dysthymic episode, 297t
    eating disorders, 655–657, 656t, 657t
    encopresis, 684–686, 684t
    enuresis, 669–671, 670t
    generalized anxiety disorder,
        366–368, 367t
    major depressive episode, 296t
    mental retardation, 411–412, 413t
    obsessive-compulsive disorder, 363,
        364t, 365
    oppositional defiant disorder,
        160, 161t
    panic attack, 370t
    panic disorder, 370–372, 371t
    pervasive developmental disorders,
        458–459
    PTSD, 548, 549–550t, 550, 552
    reactive attachment disorder,
        600–602, 601t
    Rett's disorder, 492t
    separation anxiety disorder,
        352–353, 353t
    somatoform disorders, 620–622
    specific phobias, 356–357, 356t,
        359–360, 359t
Diagnostic Interview Schedule for
    Children (DISC), 166

Diathesis, 282, 287
Diathesis-stress model, 282–283, 287,
    329–330, 342, 531
Dichotomous thinking, 660, 692
Diet
    ADHD, 240
    childhood obesity, 645, 650
    eating disorders, 652–655,
        660–663
Differential reinforcement of
    incompatible behavior (DRI),
    447, 450, 502, 506
Differential reinforcement of other
    behaviors (DRO), 447, 450,
    501, 506
Dimensional classification,
    129–131, 149
Direct influences on behavior, 192
Discrete behavioral states, 592, 614
Discriminant validity, 29, 62
Discussion, of research results, 42
Disease, Western concept of, 616
Disordered attachment, 598
Disorders
    concept of, 124–127
    definition, 123–124, 149–150
    determination of, 268–269, 268f
    not otherwise specified, 131
Disorganized speech, 519–520, 542
Disorganized type of schizophrenia,
    514, 516, 542
Displacement, 349, 395
Disruptive behavior; see also Conduct
        disorder; Oppositional
        defiant disorder
    assessment, 165–168
    case study of adolescent-onset,
        154–156
    case study of early-onset, 153–154
    course, 179–182
    cultural factors, 168
    diagnostic criteria, 157–158
    etiology, 184–198
        adolescent onset, 196–197
        cognitive influences, 191,
            193–194
        early onset, 184–191, 193–196
        genetic influences, 185–187
        parenting influences, 187–190
        peer influences, 194
    family issues, 168
    gender, 163–164, 178
    history, 156–158
    informants' reports, 167t
    not otherwise specified, 161

Disruptive behavior (*Cont.*)
  prevalence, 178–179
  prevention, 198–200
  social costs, 151–152
  study of, 152
  therapeutic interventions, 198
    adolescents and families, 203–204
    early, 200–202
    school-age children, 202–203
  violence and, 189*f*
Dissociation
  historical diagnosis of, 577–578
  normal, 579–580
  therapeutic interventions, 595–596
Dissociative amnesia, 578, 580
Dissociative disorders, 575–597; *see also*
    Dissociative identity disorder
  assessment, 585–586
  associated features, 588–589
  case study, 576–577
  chronic, 590–592
  core features
    changes in preferences/abilities, 588
    memory problems, 587
    trance states, 587–588
  course, 589
  cultural factors, 585–586
  diagnostic criteria, 580–583
  etiology, 589–594
    alternate personality identities,
      592–593
    chronic dissociation, 590–592
  family issues, 596–597
  history, 577–578
  normal dissociation, 579–580
  not otherwise specified, 582–583
  prevalence, 589
  prevention, 594
  therapeutic interventions, 594–597
    child-centered, 594–596
    family-centered, 596–597
Dissociative fugue, 578, 580–581
Dissociative identity disorder
  concept of, 575, 578
  controversies over, 583–585
  diagnostic criteria, 581–582, 581*t*
  memory, 587
  model of, 582*f*
  split personality, 513, 575
  therapeutic interventions,
    595–596
Distractibility, 222, 255
Disturbed body image, 656, 692
Diurnal only enuresis, 670, 692
Divalproex sodium, 284, 287

Dizygotic (DZ) twins, 108–109, 120
Dopamine
  ADHD, 239, 244
  schizophrenia, 528–529
Dopamine hypothesis, 528–529, 542
Down syndrome, 427–428
DSM; *see Diagnostic and Statistical
    Manual of Mental Disorders*
Dysthymic disorder, 295, 297*t*,
    300–301, 309

Early infantile autism, 457
Early-onset conduct problems
  case study, 153–154
  classification, 174
  consequences, 194
  initial development, 184–190, 185*f*
    genetic influences, 185–187
    parenting influences, 187–190
  limited duration
    developmental course, 180–181
    etiology, 194–196
  persistent
    cognitive influences, 191, 193–194
    definition, 205
    developmental course, 179–180
    etiology, 190–194, 191*f*
    peer influences, 194
    risk factors, 195*t*
Early-onset depression, 331–333
Eating disorders, 651–667
  biological changes, 661
  body dissatisfaction, 652–656
  cognitive changes, 661
  course, 658
  depression and, 9, 309, 661
  developmental model, 658–663, 659*f*
  diagnostic criteria, 655–657,
    656*t*, 657*t*
  dieting, 652–655, 660–663
  emotional changes, 661
  family issues, 653, 666
  gender, 657–658
  medication, 665
  not otherwise specified, 656
  Prader-Willi syndrome, 432
  prevalence, 657–658
  prevention, 663–664
  therapeutic interventions, 664–667
    cognitive-behavioral
      psychotherapy, 665–666
    hospitalization, 664, 665*t*
    medication, 665
    nutritional counseling, 665
  weight control behaviors, 654*t*

Echolalia, 468, 506
Educational interventions; *see also*
    Teachers
  ADHD, 248–249
  autism
    early, 498–500
    elementary/high school,
      500–502
  childhood obesity, 648
  childhood-onset schizophrenia,
    540–541
  eating disorders, 663–664
  encopresis, 690–691
  mental retardation
    early, 441
    elementary/high school, 442–443
    transition to adulthood, 443–444
  Education for All Handicapped
    Children Act, 411, 442, 451
  Educators, 3
  Ego, 66–67, 100
  Electroencephalograph (EEG),
    234, 255
  Elimination disorders; *see Encopresis;*
    Enuresis
  Emotional disorders; *see Behavioral or
    emotional disorders*
  Emotional lability, 661, 692
  Emotional numbing, 555, 614
  Emotions
    cognitive influences, 82–84
    eating disorders, 661
    expressed emotion, 532–533
    suicide, 318
  Encephalitis lethargica, 211, 255
  Encopresis, 667–668, 684–691
    consequences, 667
    with constipation and overflow
      incontinence, 684–685, 693
    without constipation and overflow
      incontinence, 684–685
    course, 687
    diagnostic criteria, 684–686, 684*t*
    etiology, 688–689
      revision of theory, 667–668
    features, 686–687
    gender, 687
    prevalence, 687
    prevention, 689–690
    therapeutic interventions, 690–691
      educational, 690–691
      medical, 690
  Encounter group movement, 92
  Energy balance, 643, 692
  Enuresis, 667–684

case study, 668–669
consequences, 667
diagnostic criteria, 669–671, 670t
etiology, 676–679
    genetic influences, 677
    infections, 677
    learning, 678–679
    psychological basis, 678–679
    revision of theory, 667–668
family issues, 675–676
gender, 674–675
medication, 679–681, 680f, 683
physiological functioning, 671–673
prevalence, 674–675, 675t
prevention, 679
psychological functioning, 673–674
therapeutic interventions, 679–684
    behavioral, 681–683
    medication, 679–681, 680f, 683
Environmental influences; see also
    Family context
ADHD, 240–241
behavioral theories, 74–75
bipolar disorders, 282
depression, 323–324
genes and, 102, 117–120
mental retardation, 432–438
nonshared, 116–117
shared, 114–116
Equifinality, 15, 18
Error, 27
Error of measurement, 116–117, 120
Ethical behavior, 43
Ethical standards, 43
Ethics, 43–61
    between-groups intervention
        research, 35
    case studies, 44–47
    cultural differences, 43–44
    definition, 43, 62
    guidelines, 43, 48
    institutional review boards, 60–61
    laws, 48
    principles, 49–60
    therapist-client relations, 43
Ethics code, 43, 62
Eugenics, 104, 410
Event-related potentials, 217, 255
Evocative genotype-environment
    correlations, 120
Executive functions, 234, 255
Exosystem, of child development, 6
Experience, and anxiety disorders,
    380–384
Experimental research, 31, 62

Expressed emotion, 532–533, 542
Expressive language, 427–428, 451
Externalizing disorders, 258
External urinary sphincter, 669, 692
External validity, 38–39, 62
Extinction, 446–448, 502
Extinguishing of behaviors, 74, 100
Extrapyramidal side effects, 542
Extrapyramidal system, 540
Eye-tracking dysfunction, 537, 542

Face recognition, 468
Facilitated communication,
    503–504, 506
Factitious disorder, 618, 692
Family context; see also Environmental
    influences; Genetic
    influences; Parents and
    parenting; Siblings
ADHD, 229–232, 240–241
anxiety disorders, 392–393
autism, 457, 476, 504–505
bipolar disorders, 279–280
case study, 618–619
childhood-onset schizophrenia, 526,
    531–533, 541
depression, 302–303, 320,
    340–341
disruptive behavior, 168, 171–172,
    182–183, 203–204
dissociative disorders, 596–597
eating disorders, 666
enuresis, 675–676
mental retardation, 421–425,
    448–449
pervasive developmental disorders,
    479–480
PTSD, 560, 562, 574
reactive attachment disorder,
    612–613
separation anxiety disorder, 355
somatization problems, 618–619,
    625, 633–634
therapeutic interventions, 203–204,
    340–341, 392–393, 448–449,
    504–505, 574, 596–597,
    612–613, 666
Family Environment Scale, 146
Family Interaction Coding System, 145
Family studies, 108, 120–121
Family systems theories, 92–98
    behavior in family context, 94–95
    child psychopathology applications,
        97–98
    circular causation, 96

family as unit of analysis, 93–94
homeostasis, 95
origins, 92–93
somatization problems,
    618–619, 629
therapeutic process, 96–97
Feces, 684
Feingold Diet, 240
Felt security, 324
Females; see Girls
Fetal alcohol syndrome, 435, 451
Fine motor skills, 474, 506
Flashbacks, 555, 614
Flattened affect, 520, 542
Flight-or-fight stress response, 565f
Focused attention, 222, 255
Fragile X mental retardation gene
    (FMR1), 428, 451
Fragile X syndrome, 428–429,
    490, 506
Free association, 70
Freud's psychodynamic theory, 66–68
Fugue, 614
Functional behavioral assessment,
    143, 150
Functional bladder capacity, 671, 692
Functional magnetic resonance imaging
    (fMRI), 148, 150, 234, 255
Functional studies, 234, 255

g (cognitive ability), 401–402, 451
Gender; see also Girls, Boys
ADHD, 227, 228
autism, 476
body dissatisfaction, 652
depression, 307, 310–311, 311f,
    311t, 313–315
disruptive behavior, 163–164, 178
eating disorders, 657–658
encopresis, 687
enuresis, 674–675
Fragile X syndrome, 428–429
mental retardation, 420–421
PTSD, 559
somatization problems, 626
Gender identity disorder, 54, 62
Gene, 102–103, 121
General factor (g) (cognitive ability),
    401–402, 451
Generalized anxiety disorder,
    366–369
course, 369
diagnostic criteria, 366–368, 367t
features, 368
prevalence, 369

Genetic influences
    ADHD, 238–239
    anxiety disorders, 375–378
    autism, 488–490
    bipolar disorders, 280, 281–282
    childhood obesity, 644, 644f
    depression, 322–323
    disruptive behavior, 185–187
    enuresis, 677
    mental retardation, 427–432,
        436–438
    neurological functioning, 238–239
    Rett's disorder, 494–495
    schizophrenia, 529–530
    suicide, 317
Genome, 103, 121
Genotype, 103, 121
Genotype-environment correlations,
    9, 118–120
    active, 120
    definition, 121
    evocative, 120
    passive, 119–120
Genotype-environment interactions,
    117, 121
Genotype-environment relationships,
    117–120
Girls; see also Gender
    conduct disorder, 163–164
    depression, 313–315
    puberty, 313–315
    Rett's disorder, 492–495
    stress, 313–315
Global assessment of functioning, 134,
    135–136t, 150
Go/no-go test, 235, 255
Grandiosity, 274–275, 287
Grossly disorganized behavior,
    520, 542
Gross motor skills, 474, 506
Gross stress reaction, 547
Group treatment, for anxiety
    disorders, 391–392

Hallucinations, 518, 542
Health
    childhood obesity, 634–651
    eating disorders, 651–667
    elimination disorders, 667–691
    mental retardation, 418
    somatization problems, 617–634
Healthy weight, 637, 692
Helplessness; see Learned helplessness
Heritability, 112–114, 121
High-functioning autism, 459, 506

Hippocampus, 564, 566, 567, 614
Holding therapy, 613, 614
Homeostasis, 94, 100
Hopelessness, 319
Hospitalization
    bipolar disorders, 284
    childhood-onset schizophrenia, 541
    eating disorders, 664, 665t
Hyperactivity
    ADHD, 220–221
    bipolar disorders, 275
Hyperkinetic conduct disorder, 216
Hyperkinetic impulse disorder,
    211, 255
Hypersexuality, 275–276
Hypersomnia, 304, 342
Hypervigilance, 547, 614
Hypnosis, 583
Hypochondriasis, 621–622
Hypomanic episode, 263–264,
    264t, 287
Hypothalamic-pituitary-adrenal
    (HPA) axis, 322, 342,
    564, 568, 614
Hypothalamus, 564, 614

Id, 66, 100
Imipramine, 244
Imitation, 467–468, 485–486
Implicit memories, 565, 569, 614
Impulsivity, 170, 220–221
Inattention, 221–222
Inclusive classrooms, 442, 502
Independent variable, 31, 62
Indirect influences on behavior, 192
Individual education plan (IEP), 442,
    444, 451
Individual family service plan (IFSP),
    441, 451
Individuals with Disabilities Education
    Act (IDEA), 442
Infantile autism, 458, 506
Infections, and enuresis, 677
Infectious diseases, mental retardation
    resulting from, 436
Inferential statistics, 23, 40, 62
Influences on child development
    Bronfenbrenner's model of,
        6–7, 6f
    combinations of, 7–8
    interactions of, 9–11
    values as, 10–11
    variability of, 8
Informants, 166, 168, 217–218,
    301–302, 552–553

Information gathering
    in clinical assessment, 137–139
    informants, 166, 168, 217–218
    methods, 165–166
Informed consent, 49–50, 62
Injuries
    autism resulting from, 490
    mental retardation resulting
        from, 436
Insecure attachment, 89–90, 598,
    603–604
Instincts, 65–69, 100
Institutional review boards (IRBs),
    60–61, 62
Instrumental aggression, 177, 205
Insulin, 640, 692
Intelligence, 400–409
    autism, 471
    concept of, 401
    cultural factors, 404–405, 404t
    definition, 451
    development, 415f
    disruptive behavior, 169
    distribution, 420
    influences, 437f
    measurement, 405–409
    single versus multiple traits,
        401–402, 403f, 404
    true, 406, 452
Intelligence quotient (IQ), 406–407,
    451, 459, 506
Intelligence testing, 405–409
    cultural bias, 407–409
    IQ, 406–407
    origins, 405
Interest, lack of, 304
Internal consistency, 29, 62
Internalizing disorders, 258
Internal validity, 37–38, 62
Internal working model, 90, 101,
    607, 614
International Classification of Diseases
    (ICD), 216, 255
Interpersonal factors, depression and,
    330–331
Interrater reliability, 28, 62, 132, 150
Intervention research, 35–36
Interviews; see Clinical interviews
Introjection, 67
IQ; see Intelligence quotient
Irritability, 274, 304
Irritable bowel syndrome, 627–628, 692

Japanese men, and anxiety, 351
Joint attention, 467, 506

Language; *see also* Communication
  Asperger's disorder, 474
  autism, 468–469, 485*f*
  expressive, 427–428, 451
  pragmatics, 468–469, 507
  receptive, 507
Larry P. v. Riles (1979), 408
Lead poisoning, 240, 432–434, 433*f*
Learned behavior
  enuresis, 678–679
  somatization, 628–629
Learned helplessness, 327–328, 342
Least restrictive environment, 249,
  442, 451, 502
Legal professionals, 4
Life-course-persistent behaviors, 174,
  179–180, 205
Life instinct, 66
Life stress, 329–330
Lifetime prevalence, 307, 342
Lithium carbonate, 284, 287
Locus coeruleus, 564, 614
Longitudinal designs, 36, 63

Macrosystem, of child development, 7
Magnetic resonance imaging (MRI),
  148, 150
Major depressive disorder, 295,
  300–301, 308–309
Major depressive episode, 265, 287,
  295, 296*t*
Malingering, 618, 692
Mania, 257, 272, 273–274*t*,
  274–276, 287
Manic episode, 263, 263*t*, 287
Markers of vulnerability, 537–538
Masked depression, 293–294, 342
McCarthy Scales of Children's
  Abilities, 406
Mean, 310
Media, and body dissatisfaction, 654
Median, 310
Medically significant suicide attempt,
  315–316, 342
Medical professionals, 3
Medication
  ADHD, 206, 207–210, 244–248,
    250–253
  anxiety disorders, 393–394
  autism, 502–503
  bipolar disorders, 284–285
  case studies, 46–47, 207–210
  childhood-onset schizophrenia,
    539–540
  compliance, 541

  depression, 321, 337–338
  eating disorders, 665
  enuresis, 679–681, 680*f*, 683
  PTSD, 572
  self-injurious behavior, 448
  side effects, 247–248, 285, 338, 394,
    540, 680
Melancholia, 293, 342
Memory
  cognitive factors, 568–570
  declarative versus implicit,
    565, 569
  dissociative disorders, 587
  neurological basis, 565–567
  PTSD, 565–570
Mental age, 406, 451
Mental disorders; *see* Behavioral or
  emotional disorders
Mental retardation, 396–450
  assessment, 412–414
  case studies, 397–400
  challenges for individuals with,
    396, 415
  cognitive abilities, 415–416
  comorbidity, 418–419, 444–445
  diagnostic criteria, 411–412, 413*t*
  diverse forms of, 396
  etiology, 425–438
    known organic cause, 426–436
    no discernible pathologic basis,
      426–427, 436–438
    two groups, 426*f*
  family issues, 421–425, 448–449
  gender, 420–421
  health problems, 418
  history, 409–411
  intelligence, 400–409
  medication, 448
  peer issues, 417–418
  prevalence, 420–421
  prevention, 439–440
  race, 420–421
  self-image, 416–417
  sociability, 417–418
  therapeutic interventions, 441–450
    educational interventions,
      441–444
    family issues, 448–449
    medication, 448
    problem behaviors, 445–446
    psychopathology, 444–445
    self-injurious behavior,
      446–448
Mental retardation of known
  organic cause

  chromosome/gene abnormalities,
    427–432
    Angelman syndrome, 432
    Down syndrome, 427–428
    Fragile X syndrome, 428–429
    phenylketonuria (PKU), 429–430
    Prader-Willi syndrome, 431–432
    Williams syndrome, 430–431
  concept of, 426–427
  definition, 451
  environmental toxins, 432–436
    alcohol, 434–436
    lead, 432–434
    mercury, 434
  infectious diseases, 436
  injuries, 436
  nutritional deficits, 436
  prevention, 439–440
Mental retardation with no discernible
  pathologic basis
  concept of, 426–427
  definition, 451
  gene-environment relationships,
    436–438
  prevention, 440
Mercury, 434
Mesosystem, of child development, 6
Meta-representations, 483, 506
Methods, 23–40
  measures, 26–30
  participants, 23–26
  procedures, 30–39
  significance of, 20–21, 23
Methylphenidate (MPH), 206, 244–248,
  245*f*, 250–253, 255
Microsystem, of child development, 6
Minimal risk, 54, 55, 63
Minnesota Study of Twins Reared
  Apart, 105
Mixed episode, 264–265, 265*t*, 287,
  295, 343
Mode, 310
Modeling
  body dissatisfaction and
    dieting, 653
  somatization, 628–629
Molecular behavioral genetics, 102, 121
Monoamine hypothesis, 321, 343
Monoamine neurotransmitters, 321
Monoamines, 343
Monozygotic (MZ) twins, 108–110, 121
Mood disorders
  bipolar and depressive disorders as,
    294, 342
  conduct disorder and, 172

Mothers
  depression etiology, 325, 330
  schizophrenia etiology, 533–534
Motivation, for disruptive behavior, 177
Motor skills
  ADHD, 225
  Asperger's disorder, 474
  Rett's disorder, 493
  schizophrenia, 528
MPH; see Methylphenidate
Multiaxial system of classification,
  133–136, 134t
Multifinality, 18
Multiple personality disorder, 575,
  578, 615
Multisystemic therapy, 203–204
Must-urbation, 83–84, 101
Mutifinality, 14–15
Myelin, 451
Myelination, 429

Nature–nurture controversy, 102, 121
Negative affect, 377–378
Negative reinforcement, 74, 187–188,
  188f, 205, 629
Negative symptoms, of schizophrenia,
  514, 520–521, 542
Negative thinking, 326
Neurobiological dysfunctions in
  schizophrenia
  brain morphology, 527–528
  causes
    genetic influences, 529–530
    viral infections, 530–531
Neuroimaging, 147–148
Neuroleptic malignant syndrome,
  540, 542
Neurological issues
  ADHD, 237–240
  birth/pregnancy complications,
    239–240
  etiology
    ADHD, 237–240
    autism, 486–488
    bipolar disorders, 281
  food ingredients, 240
  genetic influences, 238–239
  memory, 565–567
  toxins, 240
Neuropsychological tests, 147, 150,
  235, 255
Neurotransmitters
  autism, 488
  schizophrenia, 528–529, 534–535
Night laughter, 493, 507

Nocturnal and diurnal enuresis, 670
Nocturnal only enuresis, 670, 692
Nonmaleficence, 53–56, 63
Nonshared environmental influences,
  115–116, 121
Noradrenalin, 564n
Norepinephrine, 564n, 565–566
Norms, test, 145–146
Not otherwise specified disorders,
  131, 150
  anxiety, 373, 551
  disruptive behavior, 161
  dissociation, 582–583
  eating disorders, 656
Nuremberg Trials, 48
Nutrition, and mental retardation,
  436; see also Diet

Obese, 637, 692
Obesity, definition of, 692; see also
  Childhood obesity
Objective psychological tests, 146, 150
Obsessions, 362–363, 395
Obsessive-compulsive disorder,
  362–366
  assessment, 365
  body dysmorphic disorder and,
    620–621
  course, 365–366
  definition, 692
  diagnostic criteria, 363, 364t, 365
  features, 365
  prevalence, 365
Operant conditioning, 74, 76–77,
  101, 385
Oppositional defiant disorder; see also
  Disruptive behavior
  ADHD and, 216–217
  conduct disorder versus, 162–163
  diagnostic criteria, 160, 161t
  diagnostic issues, 161–162
  family issues, 171–172
  intelligence, 169
  peer issues, 171
  personality issues, 170–171
  prevalence, 178–179
  social cognition, 169–170
  social costs, 151–152
Organismic valuing, 68, 101
Orientation and reorientation, of
  attention, 222, 255
Overflow incontinence, 685, 686f, 692
Overprotective/constricting pattern, 562
Overt disruptive behavior, 175–177, 205
Overweight, 637, 639f, 692

Pain disorder, 621
Pairwise concordance, 113
Panic attacks, 370–371, 370t
Panic disorder, 369–373
  diagnostic criteria, 370–372, 371t
  prevalence, 372–373
Paranoid type of schizophrenia, 514, 542
Parent management training, 200–201
Parents and parenting; see also Family
  context; Genetic influences
  ADHD, 230–232, 248
  anxiety disorders, 387–389
  autism, 457
  bipolar disorders, 285–286
  case study on expectations of, 44–46
  childhood obesity, 644
  child psychopathology knowledge
    of, 4
  child's temperament, 189–190
  confidentiality, 57–59
  contextual influences, 189
  disruptive behavior, 187–190
  early intervention programs,
    200–201
  eating disorders, 653
  ineffective, 188–190
  as informants, 166, 217–218
  mental retardation, 422–423
  mothers and depression, 325, 330
  permission for child participation in
    research/therapy, 50–56
  social phobia, 361–362
  somatization problems, 628–629
Partial hospitalization, 541, 542
Passive genotype-environment
  correlations, 119–120, 121
Pathogenic care, 600, 615
PDD; see Pervasive developmental
  disorders
PDDNOS; see Pervasive developmental
  disorder not otherwise
  specified
Peers
  ADHD, 223
  autism, 501
  bipolar disorders, 276
  disruptive behavior, 171, 194
  mental retardation, 417–418
Perceptual impairments, autism and,
  484–486
Perfectionism, 368
Permoline, 244
Persecutory delusions, 519, 542
Personality, 170–171
Person-centered therapy, 71

Pervasive developmental disorder not otherwise specified (PDDNOS)
  autism spectrum disorder, 459–463
  diagnostic criteria, 459
Pervasive developmental disorders, 453–506; *see also* Asperger's disorder; Autism; Autism spectrum disorder
  assessment, 463
  diagnostic criteria, 458–459
  family issues, 479–480
  history, 456–458
  prevalence, 475–476
  two models, 462*f*
Phenotype, 103, 121
Phenylalanine, 429, 451
Phenylketonuria (PKU), 429–430
Phenylpyruvic acid, 429, 451
Physiological arousal, 377–380
PL 94-142, 411, 442, 451
Placebos, 34, 63, 249, 255
Population, 23–24, 63
Positive affect, 377
Positive behaviors, rewarding, 231, 330, 447
Positive energy balance, 643, 692
Positive reinforcement, 74, 629
Positive symptoms, of schizophrenia, 514, 518–520, 543
Positron emission tomography (PET), 148, 150
Posttraumatic stress disorder (PTSD), 545–575
  ADHD and, 557
  assessment, 552–553
  associated features, 556–557
  case study, 545–547
  characteristics of sufferers versus non-sufferers, 559–560
  core features, 554*t*
    avoidance/numbing, 555–556
    increased arousal, 556
    reexperiencing trauma, 554–555
  course, 561–562
  cultural factors, 553
  depression and, 557
  diagnostic criteria, 548, 549–550*t*, 550, 552
  etiology, 563–670
    brain development/functioning, 563–568
    cognitive influences, 568–570
  family issues, 560, 562, 574
  gender, 559

history, 547–548
medication, 572
prevalence, 558–559
prevention, 570–571
specific phobias and, 557
substance abuse and, 557
therapeutic interventions, 572–574
  cognitive-behavioral psychotherapy, 572–574
  family issues, 574
  medication, 572
Prader-Willi syndrome, 9, 431–432
Pragmatics, of language, 468–469, 507
Predatory aggression, 177
Predictive validity, 132, 150
Predominantly hyperactive-impulsive type, 212, 255
Predominantly inattentive type, 212, 256
Prefrontal cortex, 234, 256, 567–568, 615
Pregnancy
  ADHD and complications in, 239–240
  alcohol consumption, 434–436
  maternal diet, 439
  schizophrenia and complications in, 531
  tests for genetic/chromosomal abnormalities, 422, 440
Premorbid functioning, 523–524, 524*t*, 543
Premutation, 428, 451
Prepotent, 233, 256
Preschool children
  autism, 498–500
  early intervention programs, 441–442
  intelligence testing, 406–407
  PTSD, 552
President's Panel on Mental Retardation, 410
Presumption, 49–50, 63
Prevention
  ADHD, 243
  anxiety disorders, 387–389, 388*t*
  bipolar disorders, 283
  childhood obesity, 647–648
  childhood-onset schizophrenia, 537–538
  cultural factors, 198–199
  depression, 334–337
  disruptive behavior, 198, 199–200
  dissociative disorders, 594
  eating disorders, 663–664
  encopresis, 689–690

enuresis, 679
mental retardation, 439–440
protective factors utilized, 17
PTSD, 570–571
reactive attachment disorder, 611–612
research, 35–36
risk factors utilized, 17
Primary enuresis, 670, 676–677, 692
  case study, 668–669
Probability, 40–41
Probandwise concordance, 113
Prodromal phase, 521, 543
Project Competence, 15–16
Projective psychological tests, 146–147, 150
Pronoun use, autism and, 469
Prosody, 468–469, 507
Prospective research, 33–34, 63
Protective factors
  community-level, 16
  concept of, 15–17
  definition, 18
  family-level, 16
  individual-level, 16
  predictive value of, 17
  preventive/therapeutic interventions using, 17
Pseudoneurological, 620, 692
Psychiatric disorders; *see* Behavioral or emotional disorders
Psychoanalytic theory, 293, 343, 349
Psychodynamic theories, 65–72
  childhood experiences, 70
  child psychopathology applications, 71–72
  instincts versus societal expectations, 65–69
  therapeutic process, 70–71
  unconscious, 69–70
Psychodynamic therapy, for eating disorders, 666
Psychogenic amnesia, 578
Psychogenic fugue, 578
Psychological disorders; *see* Behavioral or emotional disorders
Psychological tests, 145–147
  definition, 150
  limitations, 147
  neuropsychological, 147, 235
  objective, 146
  projective, 146–147
Psychological theories
  attachment theory, 87–92
  behavioral theories, 72–80

Psychological theories (*Cont.*)
  choosing among, 99–100
  cognitive theories, 80–86
  common features, 98–99
  family systems theories, 92–98
  psychodynamic theories, 65–72
  value of, 64
Psychologists, 3
Psychosocial interventions
  ADHD, 249–250
  bipolar disorders, 285–286
  depression, 338–340
Psychotherapists, 3
Psychotherapy
  anxiety, 390–392
  cognitive-behavioral, 390–394,
    572–574
  PTSD, 572–574
Psychotropic medications, 503, 507
PTSD; *see* Posttraumatic stress disorder
Puberty
  body dissatisfaction and dieting, 655
  depression and gender, 313–315
Public Health Service Act, 57
Public Law (PL) 94–142, 411, 442, 451
Public policy, 4
Punishment, 74, 447–448, 502, 676, 678
Purging, 662–663, 666*f*, 692
p value, 40–41

Quantitative behavioral genetics,
    102–120
  adoption studies, 110–111
  basic research strategy, 105–107
  family studies, 108
  gene-environment relationships,
    117–120
  heritability, 112–114
  history, 103–105
  nonshared environmental influences,
    116–117
  shared environmental influences,
    114–116
  terminology, 102–103
  twin studies, 108–110

Race
  childhood obesity, 638–639
  intelligence testing, 407–409
  mental retardation, 420–421
Random assignment, 31, 63
Random selection, 25, 63
Rapid-eye-movement (REM) sleep; *see*
    REM (rapid-eye-movement) sleep
Rational emotive therapy (RET), 85–86

Reactive aggression, 177, 205
Reactive attachment disorder, 597–613
  assessment, 602–603
  associated features, 605
  controversies over, 601–602
  core features, 604–605
  course, 605–606
  diagnostic criteria, 600–602, 601*t*
  etiology, 607–611
  family issues, 612–613
  history, 599–600
  inhibited versus disinhibited type,
    600, 604–605, 607–609
  prevalence, 605
  prevention, 611–612
  therapeutic interventions, 612–613
Receptive language, 507
Reciprocal inhibition, 76, 101, 390
Reciprocal social interaction, 465, 507
Recovery phase, 521, 543
Recurrent abdominal pain, 625, 692
Reenacting/endangering/frightening
    pattern, 562
Referential delusions, 519, 543
Refocusing, 633
Regression to the mean, 37, 336,
    337*f*, 343
Reinforcement, 74, 632–633; *see also*
    Negative reinforcement;
    Positive reinforcement
Relational aggression, 164, 205
Relaxation, 573, 633
Reliability, 27–28, 63, 131–132
REM (rapid-eye-movement) sleep, 299,
    343, 672, 692
Repetition compulsion, 69–70, 101
Repetitive behaviors, 469
Repression, 67, 101
Research; *see* Methods; *terms beginning
    with* Research
Research designs, 31–37
  between-group, 34–36
  correlational, 31–32
  cross-sectional, 36
  experimental, 31
  longitudinal, 36
  prospective, 33–34
  retrospective, 33
  single-case, 34
Research issues
  direct/indirect influences on
    behavior, 192
  follow-up assessments, 681
  group averages and individual
    behaviors, 408

mean, median, and mode, 310
  placebos, 249
  regression to the mean, 336, 337*f*
Research participation
  confidentiality, 57–59, 58–59
  ethical issues, 50–52, 55–56, 56*t*,
    58–59
  parental permission, 50–52, 55–56
Research presentation
  discussion section, 42
  introduction section, 21–23
  methods section, 23–40
  results section, 40–41
Reserpine, 321, 343
Residual phase, 521, 543
Residual type of schizophrenia,
    516, 543
Resource rooms, 442, 452
Response rate, 25–26, 63
Restricted behaviors, 470
Results
  discussion of, 42
  presentation of, 40–41
Retrospective research, 33, 63
Rett's disorder, 458, 492–495
  course, 494
  diagnostic criteria, 492*t*
  etiology, 494–495
  features, 493
  prevalence, 493
Reuptake, 239, 256
Risk factors
  child delinquency and juvenile
    offending, 195*t*
  concept of, 15–17
  definition, 18
  predictive value of, 17
  preventive/therapeutic interventions
    using, 17
Risk taking, 378–380
Ritalin; *see* Methylphenidate
Rogers's psychodynamic theory,
    68–69
Romanian children, deprivation and
    attachment disturbances of,
    609–611
Rorschach Inkblot Test, 146
Rumination, 326–327, 343

Sadness, 304
Sample
  definition, 63
  representativeness, 23–24
  response rate, 25–26
  selection, 25

Savant abilities, 472, 507
Schedule for Affective Disorders and Schizophrenia for School-Aged Children (K-SADS), 301
Schemata, 80–82, 101, 383, 395
Schizophrenia; see also Childhood-onset schizophrenia
  definition, 287
  family systems theory, 93
  risk of developing, 530f
  and split personality, 512–513
Schizophreniform disorder, 514
Schizotaxia, 533
Schizotype, 533
Secondary enuresis, 670, 693
Secure attachment, 89, 101
Seizure disorders, 418, 452
Selective serotonin reuptake inhibitors (SSRIs), 338, 343, 393–394, 572, 621, 665
Self-actualization, 68, 101
Self-esteem
  childhood obesity, 641
  disruptive behavior, 170–171
Self-image
  body dissatisfaction, 652–656
  mental retardation, 416–417
Self-injurious behavior (SIB), 446–448, 452, 470, 507
Self-talk, 390–391
Sensory perception, autism and, 471
Separation anxiety disorder, 352–355
  case study, 345–347
  course, 354–355
  diagnostic criteria, 352–353, 353t
  family issues, 355
  features, 354
  prevalence, 354
Serotonin, 488; see also Selective serotonin reuptake inhibitors
Severe attachment disorders, 598
Sexual abuse, case study, 576–577
Sexuality
  Freudian theory, 66
  mania, 275–276
Shared environmental influences, 114–116, 121
Shell shock, 547
Siblings
  mental retardation, 423–425
  pervasive developmental disorders, 480
Sick role, 628–629, 693

Side effects of medication, 247–248, 285, 338, 394, 540, 680
Significance, statistical, 40
Single-case research designs, 34, 63
Situationally bound (cued) panic attacks, 370, 395
Situationally predisposed panic attacks, 370, 395
Sleep; see also REM (rapid-eye-movement) sleep
  autism, 472
  depression, 299, 304
  enuresis, 672
Social cognition
  definition, 205
  disruptive behavior, 169–170
Social interaction, autism and, 464–468, 500–501
Socialized delinquent children, 156, 205
Social phobia, 358–362
  course, 361
  cultural factors, 361
  features, 360
  general type, 360, 395
  parenting, 361–362
  specific type, 360, 395
Social reinforcement, 653–654
Social skills training
  ADHD, 250
  childhood-onset schizophrenia, 540–541
  depression, 339–340
  disruptive behavior, 202–203
  dissociative disorders, 596
  PTSD, 573–574
Social workers, 3
Soiling, 685, 693
Somatization disorder, 620
Somatization problems, 617–618, 624–634
  case study, 618–619
  comorbidity, 624–625
  course, 626–627
  cultural factors, 623
  etiology, 627–631
    biological influences, 627–628
    learning, 628–629
    model of, 630f
    stress, 628
  family issues, 618–619, 625, 633–634
  gender, 626
  prevalence, 626

therapeutic interventions, 631–634
  behavioral, 632–633
  cognitive influences, 633
  family issues, 633–634
  medical, 631–632
Somatoform disorders, 617–624
  assessment, 622–623
  diagnostic criteria, 620–622
Special education, ADHD and, 248–249
Specific factor (cognitive ability), 401–402, 452
Specific phobias, 355–358
  case study, 347–348
  course, 358
  diagnostic criteria, 356–357, 356t, 359–360, 359t
  features, 357
  prevalence, 357
  PTSD and, 557
Splinter skills, 471, 507
Split personality, 512–513; see also Dissociative identity disorder
SSRIs; see Selective serotonin reuptake inhibitors
Standardized tests, 145, 150
Stanford-Binet test, 405
Startle response, 550, 615
State arousal, 237
Statistics
  descriptive, 40
  inferential, 23, 40, 62
  significance measure, 40
Stereotyped behaviors, 470–471, 507, 604, 615
Sterilization, of mentally retarded individuals, 410
Stool, 685, 693
Stool-toilet refusal, 688–689, 693
Stop signal test, 235, 256
Strange Situation, 89–90, 101, 466, 507, 610, 615
Stress; see also Acute stress disorder; Posttraumatic stress disorder
  adolescent females, 313–315
  bipolar disorders, 282–283
  brain reaction, 564–566
  chronic, 566–568
  depression, 313–315, 329–330
  diathesis-stress model, 282
  enuresis, 678–679
  families of PDD individuals, 479
  parents of mentally retarded individuals, 422–423

Stress (*Cont.*)
  schizophrenia, 531–533
  somatization problems, 628
  suicide, 317–318
Substance abuse disorders
  bipolar disorders, 276
  PTSD and, 557
  suicide and, 317
Substance-induced mood disorder, 263, 287
Substance use disorders, and depression, 295, 309
Subtraction/proportion method, 270, 287
Suicide, 315–320
  attempts, 319–320
  bipolar disorders, 276
  characteristics and experiences of suicidal children, 317
  conduct disorder, 317
  depression, 309, 317
  dissociative disorders, 588–589
  etiology
    behavioral influences, 319
    cognitive influences, 318–319
    emotional influences, 318
    stress, 317–318
  genetic influences, 317
  prevalence, 316
  substance abuse disorders, 317
  terminology, 315–316
Suicide attempt, 315–316, 319–320, 343
Suicide contagion, 319–320, 343
Suicide ideation, 315, 343
Summer camps, ADHD interventions at, 250
Superego, 67, 101
Sustained attention, 222, 256
Sybil (Schreiber), 575, 584
Sympathetic branch of autonomic nervous system, 378, 395
Syndrome, 124, 150
Systematic desensitization, 77–79, 389–390, 395

Tardive dyskinesia, 540, 543
Teachers, as informants, 166, 218; *see also* Educational interventions
Temperament
  anxiety disorders, 376–378
  definition, 205, 395
  disruptive behavior, 185–187
  parenting influenced by child's, 189–190
Test–retest reliability, 27–28, 63

T-group movement, 92
Thematic Apperception Test, 146
Theory of mind, 483, 507
Therapeutic interventions
  ADHD, 243–253
  anxiety disorders, 389–394
  attachment theory, 91
  autism, 497–505
  behavioral theories, 76–79
  bipolar disorders, 284–286
  childhood obesity, 648–651
  childhood-onset schizophrenia, 538–541
  cognitive theories, 84–86, 339
  confidentiality, 56–58
  cultural factors, 198–199
  depression, 337–341
  disruptive behavior, 198, 200–204
  dissociative disorders, 594–597
  eating disorders, 664–667
  encopresis, 690–691
  enuresis, 679–684
  ethical issues, 52–55, 54–55, 57–58
  family systems theories, 96–97
  group, 391–392
  mental retardation, 441–450
  parental decision-making, 52–55
  protective factors utilized, 17
  psychodynamic theories, 70–71
  PTSD, 572–574
  reactive attachment disorder, 612–613
  research, 35–36
  risk factors utilized, 17
  somatization problems, 631–634
Three Faces of Eve (Thigpen and Cleckley), 575, 584
Toilet training, 688–689
Traffic Light Diet, 650
Trait, 401
Trait arousal, 237
Trance states, 587–588, 615
Transference, 70, 101
Transient situational disturbance, 547
Traumatic events, 544, 615
Tricyclic antidepressants, 321, 343, 393, 679–680, 693
Tripartite model, 377–378, 377*f*, 395
Trisomy 21, 427, 452
True intelligence, 406, 452
t-test, 41
Tunneling, 319, 343

Twin studies, 104–105, 108–110, 121
Typical antipsychotic medications, 539, 543

U-CAN-POOP-TOO Web site, 691
Unconditional positive regard, 68, 101
Unconscious, 68–69, 101
Undersocialized delinquent children, 156, 205
Undifferentiated somatoform disorder, 620
Undifferentiated type of schizophrenia, 516, 543
Unexpected (uncued) panic attacks, 370, 395
Urge incontinence, 670–671, 693
Urination, control of, 669; *see also* Enuresis
U.S. Department of Health and Human Services, 48
U.S. Department of Health, Education, and Welfare, 48

Vaccines, and autism, 490–491
Validity
  classification system, 132, 150
  concurrent, 132
  construct, 28–30
  definition, 63
  external, 38–39
  internal, 37–38
  predictive, 132
Values, 10–11
Ventricles, 566, 615
Vineland Adaptive Behavior Scales, 412
Violence
  disruptive behavior, 190*f*
  societal, child rearing and, 606–607
Viral infections, schizophrenia and, 530–531
Visual-spatial ability, 430
Voiding postponement, 670–671, 693
Voluntary organizations, 4

Wait-list control group, 35, 63
Wechsler Intelligence Scale for Children (WISC), 405
White matter, 281, 287
Williams syndrome, 430–431, 431*f*
Withdrawal, suicide and, 319
Withdrawn/unresponsive/unavailable pattern, 562
Word salad, 516, 543